Agile Automation and Unified Functional Testing

Agile Automation and Unified Functional Testing

Rajeev Gupta

Pearson

Editor—Acquisitions: Neha Goomer
Editor—Production: Vipin Kumar

ISBN 978-93-325-7365-9

First Impression

Published by Pearson India Education Services Pvt. Ltd, CIN: U72200TN2005PTC057128, formerly known as TutorVista Global Pvt. Ltd, licensee of Pearson Education in South Asia.

Head Office: A-8(A), 7th Floor, Knowledge Boulevard, Sector 62, Noida 201 309, U.P., India.

Registered Office: 4th floor, Software Block, Elnet Software City, TS 140 Block 2 & 9,
Rajiv Gandhi Salai, Taramani, Chennai 600 113, Tamil Nadu, India.
Fax: 080-30461003, Phone: 080-30461060, www.pearson.co.in,
Email: companysecretary.india@pearson.com

Compositor: D Book Media
Printed in India by Shree Maitrey Printech Pvt. Ltd., Noida

Brief Contents

	Synopsis	*xxi*
	About the Author	*xxiii*
	Acknowledgement	*xxiv*
	About the Book	*xxv*
	Section 1 Test Automation	**1**
1.	Introduction	3
2.	Test Automation Life Cycle	14
3.	Test Automation Approach	22
4.	Test Automation Framework	36
5.	Test Automation Metrics	47
6.	Test Automation Process	58
	Section 2 Agile Test Automation	**83**
7.	Agile Methodology	85
8.	Agile Automation	111
9.	Agile Automation Framework	121
	Section 3 VBScript	**163**
10.	VBScript	165
11.	Dictionary	190
12.	Regular Expressions	198
	Section 4 Basic UFT	**209**
13.	Introduction to UFT	211
14.	UFT Installation	233
15.	UFT Configuration	240
16.	Test Script Development	258
17.	Environment Variables	268
18.	Library	279
	Section 5 GUI Testing	**287**
19.	Solution, Test and Action	289
20.	Canvas	320
21.	Objects	327
22.	Test Object Learning Mechanism	342

23. Object Repository 358
24. Object Repository Design 389
25. Datatables 398
26. Working with Web Application Objects 410
27. Descriptive Programming 451
28. Synchronization 478
29. Checkpoints 484
30. Debugging 517
31. Recovery Scenario and Error Handler 525
32. Test Results 541

Section 6 API Testing 555

33. API Testing: Introduction 557
34. Automated Web Service Testing 562

Section 7 Object Identification 579

35. Object Identification Mechanism 581
36. Object Identification Using Source Index and Automatic Xpath 585
37. Object Identification Using XPath 590
38. Object Identification Using CSS Selectors 616
39. Object Identification Using Visual Relation Identifiers 636
40. Smart Identification 646
41. Object Identification Using Ordinal Identifiers 651
42. Image-based Identification (Insight) 654

Section 8 Advanced VBScript 663

43. Windows Scripting 665
44. Working with Notepad 680
45. Working with Microsoft Excel 687
46. Working with Database 710
47. Working with XML 724
48. Working with Microsoft Word 739
49. Working with An E-Mail Client 747

Section 9 Advanced UFT 765

50. Working with Object Native Properties 767
51. HTML DOM 776
52. Object Repository Automation 788
53. UFT Automation Object Model 791

Section 10 Business Process Testing 823

54. Integrating UFT with ALM 825
55. Business Process Testing 845

Appendices 875

Index 885

Contents

Synopsis *xxi*
About the Author *xxiii*
Acknowledgement *xxiv*
About the Book *xxv*

Section 1 Test Automation **1**

1. Introduction **3**

Test Automation—3
SWOT Analysis—9
Test Automation Guidelines—11
Test Automation: Myths and Realities—11

2. Test Automation Life Cycle **14**

Feasibility Analysis Phase—14
Framework Design—18
Business Knowledge Gathering—19
Script Design—19
Test Execution and Test Result Analysis—20
Maintenance—20
Quick Tips 21
Practical Questions 21

3. Test Automation Approach **22**

Test Automation Approach—22
Test Automation Scope—23
Test Automation Development Model—23
Test Automation—Testing Types to Be Covered—31
Test Automation Project Infrastructure—33
Test Automation—Team Dynamics—34
Quick Tips 35
Practical Questions 35

4. Test Automation Framework 36

Framework Components—36
Framework Types—37
Quick Tips 46

5. Test Automation Metrics 47

Technical/Functional Interchanges and Walk-through—47
Configuration Management—48
Test Automation Metrics—49
Quick Tips 57
Practical Questions 57

6. Test Automation Process 58

Need Analysis Process Flow—59
ROI Analysis Process Flow—60
Tool Analysis Process Flow—62
Proof of Concept—63
Framework Design Process Flow—64
Business Knowledge Gathering Process Flow—66
Script Design Process Flow—69
Script Execution Process Flow—71
Test Results Analysis Process Flow—72
Maintenance Process Flow—75
Building One-Point Maintenance—76
Version Control Strategy—77
Communication Model—78
Test Automation Documents—79
Quick Tips 81
Practical Questions 81

Section 2 Agile Test Automation 83

7. Agile Methodology 85

Agile Values—85
Agile Principles—86
Why Agile?—86
Agile Methodologies and Practices—86
Agile Team Dynamics—89
Scrum—91
How Scrum Works?—93
Scrum Workflow—94
Scrum of Scrums—101
Kanban—102
Feature-driven Development (FDD)—104

Extreme Programming (XP)—105
Test-Driven Development (TDD)—105
Devops—109

8. Agile Automation 111

Why Agile Automation—112
Agile Automation values—114
Agile Automation Principles—114
Agile Automation Challenges—115
Agile Automation Team Composition—116
Agile Automation Practices—118

9. Agile Automation Framework 121

Framework Components—122
Screen Components—123
Business Components—124
Framework Structure—137
Quick Tips 140
Practical Questions 140

Section 3 VBScript 163

10. VBScript 165

VBScript Editors—165
Data Types—166
VBScript Variables—166
VBScript Operators—168
VBScript Conditional Statements—169
VBscript Looping statements—170
VBScript Functions—172
Option Explicit—181
Error Handling—181
Examples—182
Quick Tips 188
Practical Questions 188

11. Dictionary 190

Methods—190
Properties—192
Creating Dictionary Object—193
Creating Dictionary of Dictionary Object—194
Quick Tips 197
Practical Questions 197

12. Regular Expressions 198

How to Create a Regular Expression Object—198
Meta Characters—200
How to Use VBScript Regular Expression Object—201
Parsing Dates—205
E-mail Matching—205
Replacing String Using Regular Expression—206
Quick Tips 208
Practical Questions 208

Section 4 Basic UFT 209

13. Introduction to UFT 211

UFT Main Window Overview—212
Toolbars and Menus—213
PANES—213
FEATURES—218
AUTOMATING COMPLEX AND CUSTOM GUI OBJECTS—221
UFT TEST AUTOMATION PROCESS—227
USING UFT HELP—229
Quick Tips 232
Practical Questions 232

14. UFT Installation 233

Recommended System Requirements—233
Access Permissions—233
Access Permissions for BPT—234
Installing UFT—234
Installing UFT Licenses—238

15. UFT Configuration 240

UFT Global Options—240
UFT Test Settings—246
Object Identification Configuration—252
Object Identification Dialog Box—254

16. Test Script Development 258

Business Scenario Identification—258
Business Knowledge Gathering—258
Planning Script Development—258

Scripting Methods—261
Scripting Guidelines—266
Quick Tips 267
Practical Questions 267

17. Environment Variables 268

When to Use Environment Variables—268
How to Define Environment Variables—269
Quick Tips 277
Practical Questions 277

18. Library 279

Creating a New Library File—279
Associating a Library file to a Test Script—280
Designing Custom Library (DLL) Files—282
Calling MS windows DLL functions from QTP—284
Quick Tips 285
Practical Questions 286

Section 5 GUI Testing 287

19. Solution, Test and Action 289

Solution —289
GUI Test—290
Action—295
Quick Tips 319
Practical Questions 319

20. Canvas 320

Canvas Features—321

21. Objects 327

UFT Object Class—327
Object Descriptions—328
Which Descriptions to Choose to Describe an Object—337

22. Test Object Learning Mechanism 342

How UFT Learns Object Definition?—342
Which Object Definitions UFT Learns?—343
What is Source Index?—343
What is Automatic XPath?—343

What are Description Properties?—344
What are Ordinal Identifiers?—346
Does UFT Learns all Object Definitions?—346
How UFT Decides it has Captured Sufficient Information to Uniquely Describe an Object?—346
SOURCE Index Learning Mechanism—346
Automatic XPath Learning Mechanism—347
Description Properties Learning Mechanism—347
Configuring Mandatory/Assistive Properties—354
Configure Ordinal Identifiers—355
Why to Configure Object Identification Properties?—355
Points to Consider for Configuring Object Identification Settings—356
Quick Tips *356*
Practical Questions *357*

23. Object Repository 358

Types of Object Repositories—358
Adding New Objects to Shared OR—361
Adding New Objects to Local OR—364
How to Avoid Object Duplication in Object Repository—364
Add/Remove Object Properties—364
Modify Object Property Values–Regular Expression—366
Associating a Shared Object Repository to a Test Script—372
Update Object Properties From Application—374
Highlight Test Object in Application GUI—374
Highlight Application Object in Object Repository—375
Define New Test Object—375
Object Spy—375
Identification and Native Properties—377
Test and Run-Time Objects—378
Comparing Shared Object Repositories—380
Analyzing Comparison Results—380
Merging Shared Object Repositories—383
The Repositories Collection Object—386
Quick Tips *388*
Practical Questions *388*

24. Object Repository Design 389

Object Repository Design—390

25. Datatables 398

Working with Global and Action Sheets—398
Parameterize Action with Local Datatable—402
Parameterize Action with Global Datatable—402

Add/Update Data to Datatable—402
Design and Run-time Datatable—402
Datatable Methods—403
How to Read all Data of Global Datasheet—407
Local Datatable Settings—407
Global Datatable Settings—408
Quick Tips 409
Practical Questions 409

26. Working with Web Application Objects 410

Working with Browser—410
Launch Internet Explorer and Web Application—414
Working with Page—416
Working with WebEdit—420
Working with Web Button—421
Working with WebCheckBox—422
Working with WebList—423
Working with Link—424
Working with Web RadioGroup—426
Working with Web Table—427
Function to Find Cell Ordinates of a Keyword Present in Webtable—430
Exporting WebTable values to DataTable—432
Exporting Web Table values to dictionary object—433
Some Useful Methods—438
Some Useful Utility Objects—442
Some Useful Examples—446
Quick Tips 450
Practical Questions 450

27. Descriptive Programming 451

When to Use Descriptive Programming—451
Descriptive Programming Syntax—453
Regular Expressions—455
Child Objects—458
Converting an OR-Based Test Script to a DP-Based Test Script—459
Using DP-Based Object Repository—459
Function to Close all Opened Browsers Except the One Which was Opened First—473
Advantages of Descriptive Programming—474
Disadvantages of Descriptive Programming—474
Comparison of OR and DP Approaches—476
Quick Tips 477
Practical Questions 477

28. Synchronization 478

Synchronization Methods—479
Browser Native Synchronization Methods—481
Defining Default Timeout Time—482
Quick Tips 482
Practical Questions 483

29. Checkpoints 484

Checkpoint—484
Standard Checkpoint—487
Table Checkpoint—494
Page Checkpoint—496
Image Checkpoint—498
Bitmap Checkpoint—500
Text Checkpoint—502
Text Area Checkpoint—504
Database Checkpoint—506
Accessibility Checkpoint—508
Xml Checkpoint—509
Quick Tips 515
Practical Questions 516

30. Debugging 517

Breakpoints—518
Step Commands—519
Debug Viewer Pane—519
Quick Tips 524
Practical Questions 524

31. Recovery Scenario and Error Handler 525

Modifying UFT Test Settings—526
Recovery Scenarios—527
Recovery Scenario Design—528
Recovery Scenario Object—537
Adding Recovery Scenario to Scripts at Run-time—538
Scenarios where Recovery Scenario Fails—538
Vbscript Error Handlers—539
Quick Tips 540
Practical Questions 540

32. Test Results 541

UFT Run Result ViewerPanes—542
Test Result Filters—545
Reporter Object—547
Customizing Test Results—547
Screen Recorder Tab—550
Setting Test Run Options—550
Exporting Captured Movie Files—552
System Monitor Tab—552
Exporting System Monitor Tab Results—553
How to Jump to a Step In UFT—553
Quick Tips 554
Practical Questions 554

Section 6 API Testing 555

33. API Testing: Introduction 557

Web service Communication Process—557
API Testing—559
Why to automate API testing—560
UFT API Testing—561

34. Automated Web Service Testing 562

Testing Web Services Manually—562
Manual Testing Using HTTP POST Request—565
Testing Web Services Using UFT—565
Testing Web Services Programmatically—573

Section 7 Object Identification 579

35. Object Identification Mechanism 581

Object Identification Methods—582
UFT Test Object Identification Mechanism—582
Insight Identification Mechanism—584

36. Object Identification Using Source Index and Automatic Xpath 585

Source Index—585
Automatic XPath—588
Quick Tips 588
Practical Questions 589

37. Object Identification Using XPath 590

How to find XPath of a GUI Object?—590
Object Identification using XPath—593
XPath based Object Identification Mechanism—594
Why to Build Custom Relative XPath of an Object—594
XPath Query Language Features—597
How to Build Custom XPath Expression?—599
How to Verify that Custom XPath Works?—613
Defining Description Properties including XPath in Object Repository—613
Quick Tips 615
Practical Questions 615

38. Object Identification Using CSS Selectors 616

How to Find CSS Styles of an Element?—618
How to Locate Elements Using CSS Attributes?—618
Difference Between CSS and Sizzle—620
Object Identification Using CSS Selectors—620
Css Selector Methods—621
Building CSS Locator Paths—623
Quick Tips 634
Practical Questions 635

39. Object Identification Using Visual Relation Identifiers 636

How Visual Relation Identifiers Work—636
VRI based Object Identification Mechanism—637
How to Define Visual Relation Identifiers in OR—638
Creating Visual Relation Identifiers using Code—643
Practical Questions 645
Quick Tips 645

40. Smart Identification 646

SI Mechanism—646
Configuring SI—649
When to Use Smart Identification?—649
Quick Tips 650
Practical Questions 650

41. Object Identification Using Ordinal Identifiers 651

Quick Tipw 653
Practical Questions 653

42. Image-based Identification (Insight) 654

Insight Identification Mechanism—654
Insight Test Object Descriptions—654
Adding Insight Objects to OR—655
Developing Code using Insight Test Objects—659
Configuring Insight Learning/Identification Mechanism—660
Quick Tips 662
Interview Questions 662

Section 8 Advanced VBScript 663

43. Windows Scripting 665

Managing Files—665
Accessing File Properties—667
Managing Folders—667
Accessing Folder Properties—669
Enumerating Files and Folders—669
Connecting to Network Computers—672
Windows Script Host (WSH)—675
Windows API (Application Programming Interface)—677
Quick Tips 678
Practical Questions 678

44. Working with Notepad 680

Methods—680
Properties—682
Creating a New Notepad File—683
Open an Existing Notepad File—683
Append Data to an Existing Notepad File—683
Quick Tips 686
Practical Question 686

45. Working with Microsoft Excel 687

Excel Object Model—687
Excel Object Browser—698
Excel as Database—698
Quick Tips 709
Practical Questions 709

46. Working with Database 710

Connection Object—710
Recordset Object—712

Connection to a Database—713
Connecting to MS Excel Database—716
Connecting to MS Access Database—717
Connecting to MS SQL Server Database—718
Connecting to Oracle Database—719
Function to Execute Query on Oracle DB—720
Quick Tips 723
Practical Questions 723

47. Working with XML **724**

XML Structure—724
XML DOM—725
QTP XML Objects—727
Locating XML Elements XPath Query—729
Quick Tips 737
Practical Questions 738

48. Working with Microsoft Word **739**

Word Automation Object Model—739
Quick Tips 746
Practical Questions 746

49. Working with An E-Mail Client **747**

Microsoft Outlook—747
IBM Lotus Notes—756
Quick Tips 763
Practical Questions 763

Section 9 Advanced UFT **765**

50. Working with Object Native Properties **767**

Finding Object Native Properties—767
Retrieving Object Native Properties—768
Using attribute/* Notation to Read native Properties—770
Object Identification using Object Native properties—771
Viewing Custom Attributes in Object Spy Tool—774

51. HTML DOM **776**

HTML DOM—776
HTML DOM Objects—777
Quick Tips 786
Practical Questions 787

52. Object Repository Automation 788

TOCollection Object—790

53. UFT Automation Object Model 791

Automating UFT—792
Launching UFT—792
Launching UFT on Remote Machine—793
UFT Object Model—795
ObjectRepositories Collection Object—798
TestLibraries Collection Object—801
Recovery Object—804
Recovery Scenario Object—807
RunSettings Object—809
RunOptions Object—811
Test Object—815
Quick Tips 822
Practical Questions 822

Section 10 Business Process Testing 823

54. Integrating UFT with ALM 825

Integrating QTP with QC—825
Quick Tips 844
Practical Questions 844

55. Business Process Testing 845

Life Cycle of BPT—847
Creating Business Components—852
Defining Component Details—853
Adding Snapshot—854
Defining Business Component Parameters—855
Adding Design Steps—857
Converting Manual Component to Automated Component—858
Opening Automated Component in QuickTest—859
Creating Business Process Tests—859
Debugging Business Process Tests—865
Creating Test Set—867
Executing Test Set—868
Developing Business Components—873
Creating Application Area—873

Appendices 875

Appendix A—Test Script Template—877
Appendix B—Scripting Guidelines—878
Appendix C—VBScript Naming Conventions—879
Appendix D—Script Review Checklist—880
Appendix E—Test Tool Evaluation CHART—882
Appendix F—Object Identification Standards for a Typical Web Application—883

Index *885*

Online Chapters

Working with PuTTY

Working with UFT XML OR

Reserved Objects

Synopsis

PREFACE

Test automation is the use of software to develop code that when executed replicates the manual tasks performed by a user on the application screen. Test automation essentially involves setting of test preconditions, execution of tests, comparison of expected results with actual results, and reporting test execution status. Generally, test automation is done as a manual process that is already in place with formalized testing procedures.

Unified Functional Testing (UFT) Professional tool was first launched by Mercury Interactive, an Israel-based company, in 2001. The first version of UFT Pro was 5.5. In 2006, Hewlett Packard (HP) acquired the company. Since then, a number of features and add-ins have been added to UFT Professional package. The latest version UFT 12.01 was launched in July 2014.

HP UFT Functional Testing is a test automation software designed to automate various software applications and environments. The automated test scripts are used for carrying out GUI and API testing. UFT works by identifying objects in application user interface and performing desired actions on it, such as, mouse click or keyboard events. It captures the properties of user interface objects, such as, name and html tag and uses these properties to identify the objects in GUI applications. HP UFT supports VBScript as scripting language. Although HP UFT is usually used for automating user-interface-based test cases, it can also automate non-user-interface-based test cases, such as, API testing, database testing and file system operations to a certain extent.

It is a myth about test automation that it is a testing project and UFT is a testing tool makes people think that they do not need development skills for UFT. However, to create an effective test automation framework and design test scripts that require minimum maintenance, one needs to view test automation as a development project and UFT as a development tool. As record-and-playback method of scripting has lots of disadvantages, we will not discuss record-and-playback features of UFT throughout this book. Instead, we stress on using UFT as coding environment.

It is written with a purpose to help the beginners learn the basics of test automation and UFT tool. The objective of this book is to help readers learn and master the most advanced concepts and features of test automation. The book is replete with practical life problems faced in automation testing and their possible solutions to enable the reader quickly master the skills of test automation. It has been designed in a way that readers can learn and employ the best automation techniques in their work areas on their own. It starts with test automation basics and subsequently moves to its advanced concepts such as test automation life cycle, test automation approach, and framework design. The book assumes that the reader has little or no knowledge of programming environment. A separate section on VBScript is devoted to help the readers learn VBScript language. Here too, we start with the very basic of VBScript language, such as, variable declaration and control loops. In subsequent chapters, the advanced features of VBScript that are useful in UFT environment, have been described. We understand that our readers are serious programmers who aspire to be test automation and UFT experts. To fulfill this need, we have designed a separate section on advanced UFT concepts. In UFT automation object model, we learn how to execute UFT and set the UFT execution environment settings using code. Later, we discuss how to access external files, such as, MS Word, MS Excel, and Notepad; databases, such as, Oracle and My SQL from UFT environment. We also learn how to integrate UFT with ALM and Quality Centre.

Who This Book is For?

If you are quality assurance/testing professional, automation consultant, automation architect, automation engineer, software developer engineer in test or software developer looking to create automation test scripts, this is the perfect guide for you! This book attempts to provide easily consumable information on all major aspects of developing UFT tests. This book has been designed to suffice learning needs of both novice users as well as expert users. By efficient reading of this book, you will have acquired expert level knowledge in developing UFT automated tests.

This book also meets the needs of aspiring candidates who want to make sure they are ready for their next interview. It is also a great resource for interviewers as well.

Questions and Feedback Related to This Book

Thanks to the readers for their valuable comments and suggestions. This has helped to make this edition of the book as per your aspirations and needs. Further feedback from our readers is welcome. Let me know your thoughts about this edition of the book—what you liked or may have disliked or the enhancements that you seek. Your feedback is important for me to develop this content in a more efficient way that meets your requirements.

We Heard You

Thanks to all of you for providing your valuable suggestions and feedbacks on the book '*Test Automation and QTP*'. We must say that most of the suggestion are worthwhile and we ensure to incorporate all of those.

Many of you have mentioned the need of a book that covers the latest version of HP UFT. So, here we are with a new edition of the book that covers the latest features of UFT tool.

Most of the readers expressed their desire to know more about how object recognition works. In this book, we have dedicated a separate section for 'Object Identification' with eight chapters. This sections explains in detail all the aspects of object reconginition mechanism.

A lot of readers suggested the need to explain VBScript in further detail. New chapters such as 'Connecting to Network Computers' and 'Windows API' have been included to meet the current day job requirements skillsets.

Based on your feedbacks, we have worked on to develop this book as one stop guide for all your knowledge required on UFT. I hope you will enjoy reading this book and this new edition inspires you to bring your best every day. We wish you good luck as you move on to address different challenges of test automation. Though these challenges may be intimidating at first, but we are confident that this book will provide you the skills to solve any problem! Wish you all a great success in your career!

When writing a book, errors and inaccuracies are inevitable. I would very much like to hear about them. Readers can contact me at and also follow me at rajeevszone@twitter. com.

Rajeev Gupta

About the Author

Rajeev Gupta is a recognized Test Automation Consultant and QTP/UFT/Selenium – Solution Expert. He is the author of '*Test Automation and QTP*' and '*Selenium WebDriver*' widely read automation book. He has the expertise in Test Automation using various technologies such as Java, JavaScript, VB, VBScript, C#, Macros, etc. He has an extensive experience in setting up automation projects for Web applications, Java applications, POS application, SAP application, Power Builder application, Mobile web application, etc. Rajeev Gupta is one of the few automation experts who has worked to develop enterprise level automation frameworks that best meets the customer requirements and helps achieve high ROI. He is the designer and developer of widely used '*Agile Automation Framework*', first object-oriented automation framework that helps to effectively carry out test automation within agile environment.

He is also a corporate trainer for Agile Test Automation, QTP, UFT and Selenium WebDriver courses. He has been instrumental in setting up and guiding many core automation projects for many MNC companies.

Acknowledgements

I would like to express my gratitude to all those who provided extensive support in all the aspect of forming, offering, and design the content of the book. A special thanks to the readers for providing valuable suggestions for making this book more informative. I would like to thank my colleagues and friends for the inspiration, knowledge and learning opportunities provided by them. And finally, I want to thank my parents and rest of the family, who supported and encouraged me in spite of all the time it took me away from them.

Rajeev Gupta

About the Book

The book contains real-life test automation examples, so that it is easy for readers to understand and interpret this book. The book is divided into ten sections:

- Test Automation
- Agile Test Automation
- VBScript
- Basic UFT
- GUI Testing
- API Testing
- Object Identification
- Advanced VBScript
- Advanced UFT, and
- Business Process Testing

Test Automation section covers introduction to test automation, test automation life cycle, approaches to test automation, and framework design.

Agile Test Automation section explains in detail about the agile methodologies in use in most of the organizations round the globe. This section also explains why traditional test automation approach and frameworks are found to fail in an agile team.

VBScript section helps readers to learn how to code in VBScript language.

Basic UFT section introduces the readers to the UFT tool and guides them through the installation and configuration process. This section discusses how to develop test automation bed in UFT.

GUI Testing section helps readers learn how to write effective GUI test scripts in UFT. It introduces readers to the three forms of scripting—record/playback, object repository approach, and descriptive programming approach. This section provides the detail knowledge of best scripting procedures and techniques for automating a web application. This section also discusses how UFT learns AUT objects.

API Testing section introduces readers to application programming interfaces concept and how APIs are tested. Thereafter, it discusses in detail UFT API testing features. This section also explains programmatic way of automating API tests.

Object Identification section discusses the object identification mechanism of UFT. It explains in detail various UFT object identification mechanisms such as xpath, css selector, visual relation identifier, insight, smart identification, ordinal identification etc.This section also discusses various criteria that can be used to select the right mix of object identification mechanisms.

Advanced VBScript section realizes the need of readers to become expert level automation programmers. This section provides a comprehensive guide on working with external files and databases such as Notepad, MS Word, MS Excel, XML, Email clients, etc. using UFT.

Advanced UFT section deals with advanced UFT features, where it satisfies the knowledge need of advanced level UFT users. This section describes the UFT APIs which can be used to control UFT from outside UFT environment.

Business Process Testing section explains how to integrate UFT with ALM using UFT. It also explains how to use connect to ALM using ALM APIs. This section describes in detail how to carry out Business Process Testing.

Chapter Organization

Chapter 1 gives an overview of test automation. It explains the criteria for automating a test case, advantages, and disadvantages of test automation and test automation guidelines.

Chapter 2 discusses about the complete life cycle of test automation. In this chapter, we introduce our readers to feasibility study of test automation, automation return on investment, test tool analysis, test automation framework, test script development, execution, and maintenance.

Chapter 3 explains the various approaches to implement test automation and test automation team dynamics.

Chapter 4 introduces the test automation framework concept. It explains the various types of frameworks and the ways to design them. The chapter guides the readers in designing the best suitable framework for the application under test.

Chapter 5 discusses the various test automation metrics that can be used to monitor and measure the health of the automation project.

Chapter 6 explains the various standard processes that need to be implemented in a test automation project. The chapter focuses on standardizing the automation processes so that test automation projects are successful even in the toughest real-time conditions.

Chapter 7 introduces readers to agile software development methodology concept. It explains briefly all the agile methodologies that are mostly used in today's world.

Chapter 8 introduces to the readers a new concept—agile automation. It explains why traditional methods of test automation are bound to fail in an agile team. It also discusses how to setup an agile automation project. This section discusses the challenges to agile test automation and how to resolve them.

Chapter 9 introduces to the readers an Agile Automation Framework. This chapter explains in detail the "in and out" of this framework—framework components, framework components structure, framework architecture, and design and development of this framework. The chapter is supported with a case study to help users understand how to design, develop, and use this framework in the real-world conditions.

Chapter 10 explains how to code in VBScript language. It first explains how to declare variables and use conditional and control loop statement in VBScript. Thereafter, it discusses the VBScript functions viz. date/time functions, string functions, array functions, and conversion functions. Finally, we learn how to handle VBScript errors during run-time.

In Chapter 11, we learn how to use dictionary and dictionary of dictionary object. Dictionary object capture values in the form of key, value pairs.

Chapter 12 introduces the concept of regular expressions and its practical uses in automation environment.

Chapter 13 gives an overview of UFT tool and ways to use its help feature.

Chapter 14 guides the readers through UFT installation process.

Chapter 15 helps the users in configuring UFT for test development conditions.

Chapter 16 explains the procedure of writing test scripts. This chapter acts as a guide to the readers toward the best scripting technique and provide them a list of scripting guidelines.

Chapter 17 discusses various ways of declaring global variables and arrays in UFT. Here, we explain what are environment variables, the various types of environment variables in UFT, and how to use them.

Chapter 18 describes various ways to write functions and use them in UFT environment. Here, we discuss both the internal and external library files.

Chapter 19 introduces users to the UFt concept of solution, test and actions. It explains test script layout and how to write test scripts in UFT environment. It discusses about test script and action and input and output parameters of the same. We show the readers the ways to call actions and use them to create meaningful tests.

Chapter 20 introduces readers to the 'Canvas' concept of UFT. It explains how canvas for tests work and how it can be used to creating a meaningful test flow for top-down test development.

Chapter 21 explains the concept of UFT test objects. It also discusses how to look for an object definition in AUT.

Chapter 22 discusses how UFT learns AUT object identification attributes and stores them in UFT.

Chapter 23 starts with discussion on object repository and its types. We show the readers the ways to add, update, and delete objects from object repository. In this chapter, the readers will understand how to use regular expressions in property value of objects. Finally, we show the readers the use of object spy in identifying object properties and difference between test object and run-time object.

Chapter 24 explains how to organize test objects in object repository that results in maximum reusability and minimum maintenance.

Chapter 25 explains how to use data tables to parameterize test scripts. We explain local and global data tables and design time and run-time data table. In this chapter, the readers will learn various methods to insert and retrieve values from data tables.

Chapter 26 discusses in detail about the web application objects and ways to automate a web-based application. In this chapter, the readers will learn the ways to work on various web-based objects such as Webedit and Webcheckbox. They will also get to know various UFT methods available to work on web-application objects.

In Chapter 27, we show the readers the ways to write test scripts without using object repository. This is called descriptive programming. In this chapter, the readers will learn ways how to write test scripts using descriptive programming and when to use it.

Chapter 28 explains the ways to keep the UFT code in synchronization with the application under test.

Chapter 29 explains the various checkpoints available in UFT environment and how to use them. We also show the readers how to write coded checkpoints instead of using UFT checkpoints that are based on record/playback technique.

Chapter 30 discusses about the debugging features of UFT and how to use them to debug and correct code. Step over, step into, and step out are used for debugging test script step by step. Debug window is used to see and modify variable values. Debug window can be used to execute single-line UFT statement code as well.

Chapter 31 explains how to handle run-time errors using recovery scenarios and error handlers. We show the readers the exceptions for which recovery scenarios to be used and exceptions for which error handlers are to be used.

Chapter 32 explains how to analyze and interpret UFT test run reports. We show the readers the ways to write custom statements and attachments in test reports. The readers will also learn how to export test reports in HTML format.

Chapter 33 introduces readers to API testing concepts and UFT API testing features.

Chapter 34 discusses the steps to writing API tests in UFT. It also explains the programmatic way of automating API tests.

Chapter 35 discusses in detail UFT object identification mechanism. It explains the the identification flow UFT uses for identifying objects using various object identification mechanisms. The chapter also explains in detail how to configure UFT tool for various web applications to achieve maximum ROI.

Chapter 36 explains the object identification object attributes—source index and automatic xpath. It also discusses how and when to use it for identifying objects.

Chapter 37 explains in detail how to design meaning xpath description of an AUT object and use it for identifying objects.

Chapter 38 explains in detail how to design meaning CSS Selector description of an AUT object and use it for identifying objects.

Chapter 39 introduces users to visual relation identifier concept of UFT. This chapter discusses in detail on how and when to use this object identification mechanism.

Chapter 40 explains how Smart Identification mechanism works and when and how to use it.

Chapter 41 explains what ordinal identifiers are and when to use it for object identification.

Chapter 42 explains to readers UFT Insight mechanism of identifying object in UFT. This chapter also explains how image-based identification mechanism works and how and when to use it.

Chapter 43 explains in detail the ways to work with Windows files and folders, establishing connection with remote machine, executing commands on remote machine, and using windows dynamic link library files.

Chapter 44 explains how to read, write, and append data to Notepad. In this chapter, the readers will understand the various methods available to work with Notepad.

Chapter 45 explains in detail the ways to use MS Excel as test data file. Excel can be accessed in two ways—either as worksheet or as database. This chapter discusses both techniques in detail and finally explains the advantages of using Excel as database in test automation.

Chapter 46 discusses how to connect to various databases. We learn how to extract desired data from database as well as update records in database.

Chapter 47 explains on how to work with XML files. We will learn the various methods available to create, access, and update XML files in UFT environment. The readers will also learn how to convert text files to XML files and XML files to Excel files.

Chapter 48 explains how to read, write, and append data to MS Word. In this chapter, we will learn the various MS Word API methods and their usage to work with Word file.

Chapter 49 shows how to send mails and attachments using Lotus Notes and Microsoft Outlook mail clients from UFT environment using code.

Chapter 50 explains to readers on how to use native properties of AUT objects to create a unique identification description of the object.

Chapter 51 explains in detail the data object model of HTML. We learn how to use HTML DOM to access run-time object properties in UFT environment.

Chapter 52 discusses in detail on how to work on object repositories using VBScript code from outside UFT environment.

Chapter 53 discusses in detail the advanced UFT concepts. The readers will learn about the UFT automation object model. UFT AOM can be used to launch UFT from a remote machine. Using UFT AOM, we can write a code that can execute specified test scripts with specified UFT settings and desired test settings in a remote UFT machine.

Chapter 54 explains how to connect UFT with ALM/Quality Centre. This chapter introduces Quality Centre Open Test Architecture (OTA) to the readers. The QC OTA is used to automate QC process activities from UFT, namely, downloading/uploading files from QC, identifying input/output parameters of a test script or a BPT script, and updating test results from UFT to QC.

Chapter 55 describes the HP Business Process Testing package, which helps in structured testing of an application by enabling nontechnical subject-matter experts to collaborate effectively with automation engineers and by automating the creation of test-plan documentation.

Section 1 Test Automation

- Introduction – Test Automation
- Test Automation Life Cycle
- Test Automation Approach
- Test Automation Framework
- Test Automation Metrics
- Test Automation Process

Chapter 1

Introduction

TEST AUTOMATION

Software testing is an essential part of Software Development Life Cycle (SDLC). In current-world scenario, there is an increasing demand to reduce time to delivery of the software product and at the same time, maintain the highest standards of quality. Automation can play an important role in SDLC by speeding up the testing process and increasing the test coverage as well. Automation is the use of strategies, tools, and artifacts that augment or reduce the need of human interaction. Test automation is process of developing and executing test scripts that can run unattended, compare the actual to expected results and log test execution status. One very important reason for the implementation of test automation is to ensure that business is executed smoothly, even after continuous defect fixes. Test automation tries to increase test coverage to ensure no critical functionality of the application is breaking in case of defect fix. Test automation motive is to help clients run their business, unimpacted and unharmed, with no business losses because of continuous ongoing changes in business application. There are various tools available in the market for carrying out test automation viz. QuickTest Pro (QTP), Rational Functional Tester (RFT), Rational Robot, Selenium, SilkTest, Test Complete, etc.

History

Long ago, in the late 1940s, dedicated or professional testers were almost unknown. Software was tested by the programmers themselves. Throughout the 1960s, papers about testing, such as proceedings of the International Federation of Information Processing Societies (IFIPS) conference almost always assumed that programmers tested the software they built. There was no distinguished difference between code debugging and testing. In the 1970s, with more complex systems in place, the idea of dedicated testers came into existence. In 1972, at Chapter Hill, the first conference on software testing was held. With the software systems getting more complex, thereby, increasing the testing effort; the need to automate the manual procedures was felt.

In the mid-1980s, automated testing tools emerged with a motive to automate manual testing procedures to improve the quality and efficiency of the target application. It was now being anticipated that automation tools can execute more tests of a program than a human do manually and that too with more reliability. The initial automation tools were primitive in nature without any scripting language facilities. Tests were created by recording the manually performed tasks and the inputs and outputs were captured in background. During subsequent playback, the script repeated the same manual sequential procedure. Captured results were compared with actual responses to find the test results. Any difference observed was reported as error. All the Graphical User Interface (GUI) objects such as edit boxes and buttons were stored in scripts. This resulted in hard-coded data in scripts. This approach offered limited flexibility to change scripts in case anything changed in application. The maintenance cost of the scripts was huge and unacceptable. Moreover, the scripts were unreliable as scripts had no error handlers to handle run-time issues such as the occurrence of unexpected pop-up window. In addition, if the tester made any error while entering data, the scripts had to be rerecorded.

In the early 1990s, there was realization to redefine the testing process to improve software quality. There was general acceptance that software quality can be improved only by doing good testing that again can be achieved through managed process. With a growing realization and importance of testing came the more advanced capture/playback automation tools that offered rich scripting languages and reporting facilities. Now, the scripts developed were programs. Scripting languages offered the much-needed error handlers to handle run-time errors. With the automation tools getting more advanced, there came the need of specialized technical programmers (automation developers), who could write effective and easy maintainable codes.

In the time being, performance tools to test application performance also came into picture. Since now, programmers were handling test automation; they started redefining the automation process to improve the effectiveness of automation testing. Automation framework came into picture with *data-driven* testing where the input test data was removed from test scripts and kept in a separate file. This helped to reuse the same test script for a variety of test data inputs. However, with the increase in the test scripts being automated, maintenance effort and cost soon became a bottle-neck for test automation. To minimize the number of test scripts came the concept of *keyword-driven* framework. In keyword-driven framework, first of all keywords were defined. Thereafter, procedures and utility scripts were written to take desired action on screen for each specific keyword. Test cases were automated by defining the sequential flow of keywords in step tables. Test input data was defined in the step-table itself against the specific keyword. The basic disadvantage of this framework was a new step-table had to be designed, in case test input data changed/varied. To overcome this, test data was removed from step-tables and placed in separate data sheets. The framework so designed was called *hybrid* framework.

Objective

The objective of test automation is to perform testing in better, faster, and cheaper ways.

- ***Better***: Automated testing is more reliable than manual testing, as tasks performed by manual testers are prone to human error. Test coverage can be improved manifold using test automation.
- ***Faster***: The test execution speed of automation tools is higher than that of manual testers.
- ***Cheaper***: Test automation helps in testing large area of business application in minimum time that otherwise will require large number of manual testers, thereby increasing the testing cost.

In the project start-up phase, there are lesser modules to test and hence test coverage is high and as well cost to deliver is low. As the time proceeds, new functionalities are added to the business

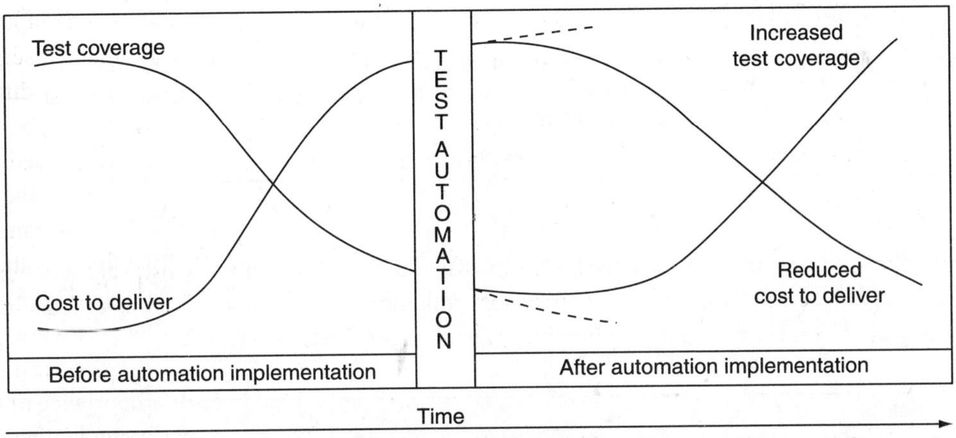

Figure 1.1 *Test coverage: Before and after test automation implementation*

application. The project gets complex with continuous ongoing change requests, bug fixtures, patches, etc. The focus of testing shifts to the testing of new added features. With the limited time and team available for testing, test coverage starts to fall, thereby, exposing the already developed modules. Defect accumulation and defect masking leads to defect multiplication, thereby, increasing the cost to find and fix defects. Test automation, if implemented properly, can help reverse this negative trend. As shown in Fig. 1.1, test automation can help test larger area of software. Test scripts execute at a much faster pace than that of manual testers. Test scripts execute in an unattended mode, thereby, saving the test case execution cost. In addition, test scripts are not prone to human errors. Test results obtained using test automation is accurate and more reliable. Deviations are easy to catch through test reports. These help to increase test coverage and as well ensure product quality. Reduced test execution cost, reduces cost to delivery. These benefits of test automation are realized over multiple test execution cycles.

Test Automation Key Factors

The key factors that are required for successful implementation and execution of a test automation project include:

- Committed management
- Budgeted cost
- Process
- Dedicated resources
- Realistic expectations

Committed Management

Management need to see test automation as necessary and critical. Project plans and test plans are to be designed keeping automation in mind. The higher management as well as the automation team should be completely committed to test automation. Test automation priority is to be assigned and targets need to be set.

Factors	Description
Plan approval	• Necessary steps to be taken to make the stakeholders, management, and the customer understand the importance of this one-time investment • Scheduled time-plan approval
Commitment on priority	• Commitment from the management on the priority assigned to this activity

Budgeted Process

Project budget estimates are to be planned keeping test automation cost in mind. Costs such as automation tool cost, hardware and software costs, resource cost, training cost, test automation implementation cost, and maintenance cost are to be included in the project budget sheet.

Factors	Description
Dedicated budget	Dedicated budget to be allocated, which includes test tool cost, software and hardware costs, implementation cost, development cost, deployment cost, maintenance cost, resource cost, and training cost

Process

Standardized process is one of the keys to successful execution of an automation project. Processes are to be defined for each stage of test automation life cycle. Quality control procedures to be defined to check and control the quality of test automation project and its deliverables. Test automation metrics are to be defined to measure the quality, effectiveness, and profitability of the automation project.

Factors	Description
Well-defined standard testing process	• Quality control procedures • Test design and execution standards • No *ad-hoc* testing • Define the tests • Define the test coverage and traceability matrix • Define test criteria at each stage
Well-defined standard test automation process	• Automation standards and guidelines • Scripting standards and guidelines • Well-defined standard test automation architecture and framework • Automation coverage and traceability matrix • Automation documents, training documents, and user manuals

Dedicated Resources

Skilled automation resources are to be allocated to test automation team. The use of manual testers as automation developers is to be avoided. Automation consultants are to be used to do automation project effort and cost estimation. Automation architects are to be assigned the task of feasibility analysis and framework design. Automation developers are to be used for test script development.

Factors	Description
Dedicated resources	A dedicated well-qualified test automation team is needed for effective test automation. Nondedicated team with lesser experience on test automation can lead to: • *Ad-hoc* automation • Focus on wrong area of application • Least maintainable and reusable code • Frequent failures of test scripts • Failure to execute regression runs • Huge maintenance cost • No information exchange between automation team members

Realistic Expectations

Management and test automation project team should have realistic achievable expectations from test automation project. Before starting automation project, a map table needs to be created, which maps management and testing expectations to the automation deliverables. Expectations that cannot be met by test automation need to be filtered out at this stage only. Expectations such as 100% automation and immediate payback are an unrealistic goal. 100% automation is not feasible, as there will always be test cases that cannot be automated such as reading specific data from PDF files. In addition, 100% automation will lead to huge set of test scripts. Maintenance cost associated with the test scripts will be huge. This leaves the test automation ineffective when there is need to do regression testing after a change in application. Again, record/playback hypothesis leads to low-quality use and throw scripts. The benefits of test automation are reaped in test execution phase over multiple test execution cycles.

Factors	Description
Expectations	• Achieving 100% automation is an unreachable goal • All business scenarios/test cases cannot be automated • Initial cost of investment and implementation cost is high • No immediate payback from investment • Benefits from test automation are achieved only after several cycles of test execution • Ramp up time will be required for tool selection and framework creation • No single automation tool supports all applications and GUI objects • Record/playback technique of automation hardly yields positive results • Testers cannot write effective test scripts. The availability of specialized resources (test automation consultant, test automation architect, and test automation developer) is must

What to Automate

Test automation is to support the manual testing process and not replace it. Achieving automation with 100% functionality coverage is rare. There are many instances where automation developers need to decide whether to automate a test case or not.

Business context analysis—Analysis to identify business scenarios (Fig. 1.2) that are available and complete. It implies business scenarios on which change request is not expected.

Prioritization analysis—Analysis to define priority of automation of the identified business scenarios.

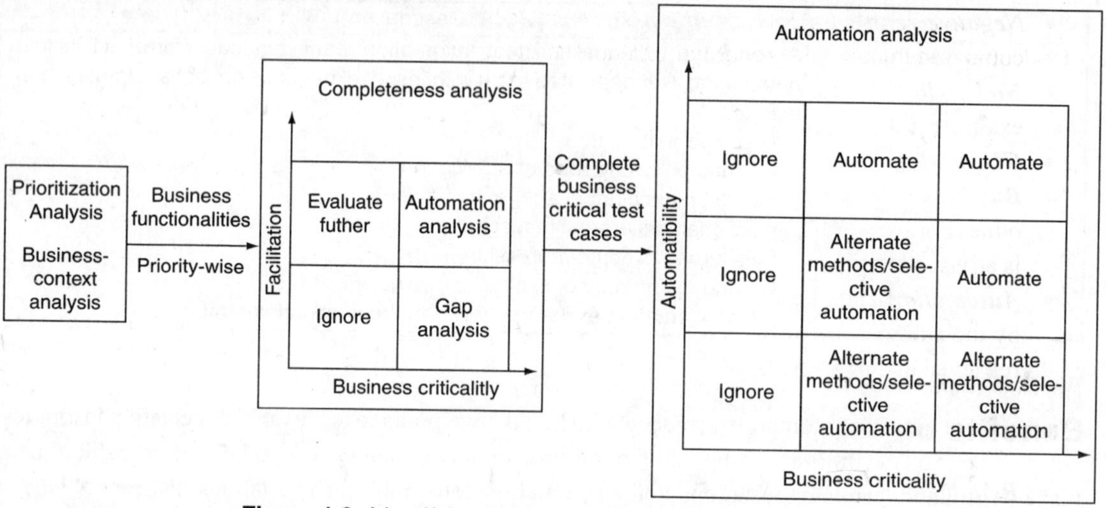

Figure 1.2 *Identifying business scenarios for automation*

Facilitation Analysis—Analysis to identify business scenarios whose all test cases have been written and test case review is done. If any gap is found, then gap analysis is carried out to identify if gaps can be closed. If the gap can be closed, then, it is evaluated further for gap closure. Business scenarios that are found incomplete or nonautomatable are ignored for automation.

Business criticality analysis—Analysis of business scenarios as per their exposure to business criticality.

Completeness analysis—Completeness analysis is done to identify business scenarios that are ready for automation.

Automatability analysis—Analysis to identify business scenarios/test cases that can be automated. Attempt is made to even partially automate a business scenario if complete automation is not feasible.

Following are few parameters based on which decision to automate a test case can be made:

- ***Business criticality:*** Test scenarios critical to business. For example, test scenarios whose failure even once in a while can result in huge monetary loss to the organization.
- ***Repeatability:*** Test scenarios that need to be executed again and again. For example, regression test scenarios.
- ***Reusability:*** Test scenario that needs to be executed over a wide range of input data variations. For example, testing the login screen with different set of input data.
- ***Robust:*** Test scenarios that are prone to human errors. For example, comparing data of two excel files.
- ***Execution time:*** Test scenarios that are time consuming. For example, transferring funds from the same account more than 100 times.

What not to Automate

It is equally important to decide which scenarios are not suitable for automation. Following arc fcw parameters based on that decision to reject a scenario for automation can be made:

- ***Negative return on investment (ROI):*** Test scenarios whose automated ROI is negative as compared to manual testing. For example, test scenarios that are executed once in a while.
- ***No baseline:*** Test scenarios for which accurate input data or expected output is not known. For example, format of PDF reports.
- ***GUI testing:*** Test scenarios that test the look, feel, color, etc. of GUI.
- ***Business complexity:*** Complex test scenarios that involve multiple steps unrelated to each other. For example, GUI test scenarios that interact with disintegrated independent systems. It is advised to automate such scenarios using API testing.
- ***Automation complexity:*** Test scenarios that involve GUI objects that cannot be recognized by the automation tool. It may also include test scenarios where actual output data cannot be retrieved accurately.

Benefits of Test Automation

- ***Reliable:*** Tests perform the same operations each time they are executed, thereby eliminating human error.
- ***Reusable:*** Same tests could be used to test AUT on different environment settings.
- ***Repeatable:*** Same tests could be executed repeatedly to test the AUT response to multiple execution of same operation.
- ***Fast:*** Test automation tools execute tests at much a faster pace than that of human users.
- ***Comprehensive:*** Test suite can be made that tests every feature of the AUT.
- ***Cost reduction:*** Tests can run in unattended mode 24/7 thereby reducing the human effort and cost.
- ***Programmable:*** Complex business scenarios can be automated to pull out the hidden information from the AUT.

SWOT ANALYSIS

Strength	Weakness
• Reduces testing cost and effort • Increases test coverage • Fast • Reliable • Programmable • Ensure product quality	• High initial cost of investment • No immediate payback • Maintenance cost • No usebility testing
Threats	**Opportunity**
• Unrealistic expections • Record/Playback hypothesis • Unskilled resoures • No human insight • Bad metrics	• Open soure test automation tools • Reduces time to delivery to market • Frees tester from mundane tasks

Strength

- **Reduces testing cost and effort**—Test automation reduces overall testing cost and effort. Unattended execution of data creation and regression test cases test scripts saves time and effort. Test automation test results help to concentrate on problematic areas of AUT only.
- **Increases test coverage**—Test automation helps to increase test coverage by executing more test cases during regression runs.
- **Fast**—Test automation tools execute at a pace much faster than a human can.
- **Reliable**—Test automation is not prone to human errors, as it is in manual testing. The code will perform the same action in all iterations.
- **Programmable**—Test automation provides programming environment to code actions on GUI.
- **Ensure product quality**—Increased test coverage ensures that delivered product is of good quality.

Weakness

- **High initial cost of investment**—Test automation implementation demands high initial investment in test automation tool and framework design.
- **No immediate payback**—There are no immediate paybacks from test automation. ROI can be achieved only after multiple regression cycles.
- **Maintenance cost**—Scripts developed need to be continuously updated/modified as per changes in business application.
- **No usability testing**—Test automation cannot be used to test the look and feel of application—color, objects orientation, GUI user friendliness, etc.

Opportunities

- **Open source test automation tools**—The market is buzzing with open source tools such as Watir, Selenium and FIT. The use of open source tools saves license cost.
- **Reduces time to delivery to market**—Test automation helps stabilizing the product earlier. The software application can be delivered to the market earlier than the other similar competitive products.
- **Frees tester time**—Test automation tool frees tester time from repetitive and mundane tasks. Tester can use freed up time on complex problems and innovative solutions.

Threats

- **Unrealistic expectations**—Unrealistic management expectations such as replacing manual testers, codeless test automation frameworks, and the use of manual testers for automation add to the automation woes resulting in failure of the automation project.
- **Record/playback hypothesis**—Experience shows 'record once and play anytime' expectation from test automation is one of the major reasons for failed automation projects. Record/playback technique results in least reusable code with very high maintenance effort. This

almost renders scripts ineffective in case of GUI changes. Test automation team fails to execute regression run after changes to application.

- **Unskilled resources**—Assumption that test automation is very easy and any manual tester can do it brings bad name to test automation. The use of unskilled resources results in poor test automation approach, bad framework design, and poor scripts with least reusability.
- **No human insight**—Test automation tools have no intelligence. They perform as coded. Therefore, even if a defect is present on a screen (suppose button is disabled, which can be seen by a tester), on which some action is being performed by the test script, the test automation tool will not be able to catch the defect unless it is coded for the same.
- **Bad metrics**—The use of bad metrics gives a bad impression of test automation tools. For example, metric to measure test automation performance from the number of defect caught by the automation tool may give a wrong picture of test automation. The number of defects found can be used to measure the effectiveness of the test cases (which have been automated) and not the test automation tool performance.

TEST AUTOMATION GUIDELINES

Automation developers must follow the following guidelines to get the benefits of automation:

- ***Concise:*** Test scripts should be concise and simple.
- ***Repeatable:*** Test script can be run many times in a row without human intervention.
- ***Robust:*** Test script should produce the same results always. Test script results are not to be affected by changes in the external environment.
- ***Sufficient:*** Test scripts should verify all the requirements of the test scenario being tested.
- ***Coverage:*** Test scripts should cover all the critical business scenarios of application as far as possible.
- ***Clear:*** Every statement is easy to understand.
- ***Efficient:*** Test scripts to execute in a reasonable amount of time.
- ***Independent:*** Each test script can be run by itself or in a suite with an arbitrary set of other test script in any order. Interdependency of one test case script on other should be avoided.
- ***Recovery scenario:*** Recovery scenarios (error handlers) to be designed to handle the script execution in case of the occurrence of unexpected errors during script execution.
- ***Test reports:*** Test reports should convey the exact status of test case executed.
- ***Custom comments:*** In case test script fails, test results should also have comments that can exactly point to the cause of failure. Screen shots of AUT to be attached, if necessary.
- ***Maintainable:*** Test script should be easy to understand and modify and extend.
- ***Traceable:*** Test case scripts should be traceable to manual test cases, requirement documents, and defects.

TEST AUTOMATION: MYTHS AND REALITIES

Test automation is not to replace testers. It is to help them carry out testing in a more effective manner by freeing up their time from repetitive and mundane tasks. Test automation cannot reproduce the thinking that testers do when they conceive of tests, control tests, modify tests, and observe and evaluate the product. Therefore, automation of testing does not mean automation of the service provided by the software tester.

- *Myth*: The automation tool is going to replace the testers.
  Reality: Test automation tools are to support and help the testers to do their job in a much better manner. They cannot replace them. Automation tools relieve the testers from performing repetitive, mundane, and boring tasks and free up their time, so that they can concentrate on the tasks involving human intelligence.
- *Myth*: 100% automation is possible.
  Reality: 100% automation is an unreachable goal. There will always be test cases such as analyzing PDF reports that are out of scope of automation. Moreover, 100% automation requires lot of development effort and with continuous ongoing changes to the application, test scripts need to be modified regularly. Huge script repository implies more maintenance. High maintenance effort and cost not only impacts ROI, but also leaves little time for test execution, thereby, defeating the basic purpose of test automation.
- *Myth*: Test automation will find more bugs.
  Reality: The process of test automation involves automation of existing manual test cases. From test cases to test scripts, automation does not add anything in the process to find more bugs. It is the test cases that find bugs (or do not find bugs), not the test scripts. The objective of test automation is to increase the test coverage to ensure the business is not impacted because of continuous ongoing changes in application.
- *Myth*: Training cost and effort involved in training the manual testers to use the tool is high.
  Reality: With proper training methodology, training cost can be reduced to a large extent.
- *Myth*: The tool will be too difficult for testers to use.
  Reality: With adequate training, the testers can easily learn any new testing tool.
- *Myth*: A single tester can easily perform a dual role of manual and automation.
  Reality: This rarely works and usually is one of the reasons for failure of an automation project. For any test automation project to succeed, it is imperative to have a dedicated team of automation developers comprising of test automation and tool experts.
- *Myth*: Test automation is very easy. Just record the scripts at any given point of time and replay them whenever you want to.
  Reality: Record and playback method of automation has very high maintenance effort and cost associated with it. High maintenance cost may result in negative ROI and is one of the reasons why an automation project fails to give desired results. Test automation is a script development project and requires a lot of planning, preparation, and skilled resources.
- *Myth*: Automation developers have better business knowledge than application developers and lesser than manual testers.
  Reality: Automation developers are technical experts and not functional experts. For example, suppose that there are eight modules in a business application. A tester may be working on the same module for more than a year; therefore, he or she has a lot of in-depth knowledge about that module. Same is the case with application developers. A Java developer may be developing code for the same module for more than a year. Therefore, again, he or she must have

gained more business knowledge of the same module. However, in case of test automation developers, they are expected to work on all the modules. Since, test automation developer task is not specific to any module; they do not have in-depth knowledge of any business module. Moreover, once test script development is over, scripts are executed in an unattended mode. This results in little time spent by the test automation developers with AUT, resulting in little business knowledge. One advantage of test script is the business knowledge that is coded in test scripts never gets lost. Automation developers can always rely on test script to know the exact business flow.

Disadvantages of Automation Testing

- ***High initial cost:*** Initial cost to start an automation project is high.
- ***Maintenance cost:*** Scripts need to be regularly updated as per the application changes.
- ***No human insight:*** Test automation tools cannot be used to test the GUI layout, readability of GUI, color appeal, etc.
- ***No usability testing:*** Test automation tools cannot be used to rate and analyze the usability of an application.

Chapter 2

Test Automation Life Cycle

Test Automation Life Cycle (TALC) is a conceptual model used to implement, execute, and maintain an automation project (Fig. 2.1). It describes the stages involved in a test automation project from an initial feasibility study through maintenance of the complete automation project. It consists of the following phases: feasibility analysis phase, framework design and development phase, identification of business scenarios and business knowledge-gathering phase, test script design and development phase, test script execution and test result analysis phase, and maintenance phase.

FEASIBILITY ANALYSIS PHASE

Feasibility analysis phase is comprised of four stages: need analysis, Return On Investment (ROI) analysis, tool analysis, and proof of concept.

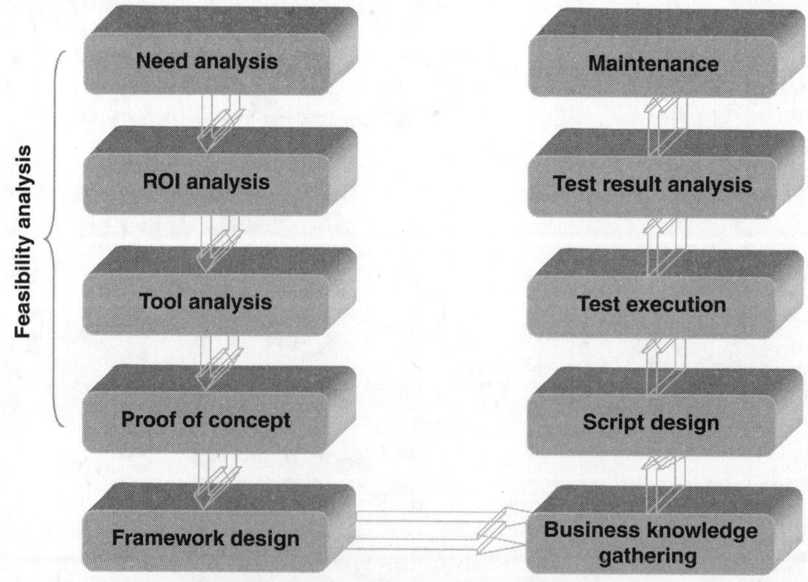

Figure 2.1 *Test automation life cycle*

Need Analysis

The first step before starting any automation project is to compare and analyze the expectations and the actual deliverables from the automation project. Project managers or automation consultants need to first list down the project requirements, management goals, expectations, etc. It needs to be analyzed that to what extent an automation project addresses these listed points. A map table is to be created that maps expectation from test automation to test automation deliverables. Expectations that are out of scope of automation are to be filtered out. Test automation project can be started once it is for sure that it will have a positive impact on the project. The following lists describe a few points that can be used for analyzing whether to implement an automation project or not.

Management goals/expectations

- Reduce testing cost
- Reduce time to delivery to market
- Increase reliability of software product/patch delivered

Manual testing problems

- High frequency of regression cycles
- Shorter regression testing time frames
- Executing regression run on short notice
- Time-consuming test data setup
- Low test coverage
- High defect leak rate

Need analysis phase should also include parameters such as testing life span and application stability.

Testing Life Span

Life span of testing is an important factor for deciding test automation project implementation. Projects with short testing life span or limited testing life span left are not good candidates for test automation. Short testing life span leaves little time for test script execution, thereby leaving little or no time to reap automation benefits. ROI analysis is to be done to find out whether with the testing life span left, automation will be beneficial or not.

Application Stability

Application to be tested should not be too stable or too unstable. Stable applications do not require continuous ongoing regression testing, thereby limiting the use of test automation. On the other hand, if application to be tested is too unstable, then, it will demand frequent changes to the application code. A change in the application code often requires a subsequent change in the impacted test scripts. Because of this test scripts cannot be executed during the subsequent regression runs.

Application stability is considered in the need analysis phase to analyze the maintenance cost of the project. Stability definition in automation differs than what is assumed from manual testing viewpoint. The stability of an application in test automation is analyzed from two perspectives:

1. **Business changes:** Business changes that impact the business flow or validation are accounted for defining application stability in test automation. For example, suppose that in a project,

business changes are expected to impact 30% of the application. Since the impacted area is less, stability factor is in favor of automation. Moreover, business changes that impact the business flow but do not impact graphical user interface (GUI) or business flow are not accounted while calculating stability factor. For example, business changes that demand the creation of new tables in database. This scenario does not impact the test scripts. Any business change that does not impact the test scripts are not accounted while calculating application stability.

2. **Object changes:** Objects in application such as edit boxes, buttons, etc. undergo continuous changes. These changes could be the addition/deletion of objects in GUI or manipulation of object properties. Object changes may occur because of change requests or code standardization; for example, updating "html id" property of all buttons and links in GUI. Any changes to the objects that are not part of test automation need not be considered while calculating application stability. For example, the addition of new button on GUI does not impact existing scripts. It may require automation of new test scripts as per the added business functionality.

ROI Analysis

ROI analysis is used for evaluating the financial consequence of implementing an automation project. It compares the magnitude and timing of investment gains that are obtained from test automation directly with the magnitude and timing of investment costs (Fig. 2.2). Timing of investment in test automation is an important factor. Test automation is beneficial if it is implemented from the very start of Software Development Life Cycle (SDLC). The implementation of test automation in the last phases of SDLC provides limited or negative ROI. Negative returns impact project balance sheet. A high ROI means that the implementation of test automation project is in the best benefits of financial health of the project.

The implementation of test automation project demands high initial investment leading to negative cash flow. The benefits of test automation are realized only after multiple test execution cycles. The point at which manual test execution cost is equal to test automation cost is called *break-even point*. ROI is an important factor while deciding the implementation of test automation. Automation ROI is positive after break-even point. ROI from test automation over testing life span of the project is to be calculated and analyzed. The factors that need to be considered while calculating ROI include manual test execution

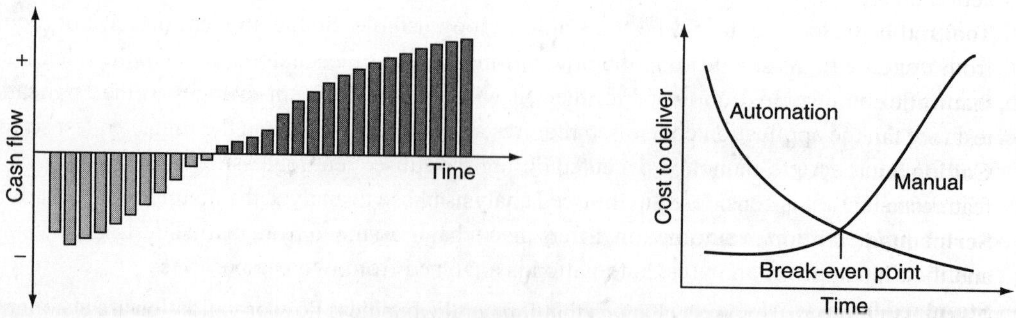

Figure 2.2 *ROI analysis*

cost, manual test maintenance cost, automation implementation cost, automation test development cost, automation test execution cost, automation maintenance cost, and hardware and software costs.

ROI analysis needs to be done and estimated ROI to be calculated before starting an automation project. A simple way to calculate ROI is:

ROI = total manual test execution cost – total automation cost

Suppose that 100 test cases need to be executed for 12 regression cycles with an average of one regression cycle/week, then,

total manual cost = manual cost to execute 100 test cases * 12

total automation cost = SDC + SMC + (SEC * 12),

where

SDC = script development cost,

SMC = script maintenance cost, and

SEC = script execution cost + test result analysis cost.

A more complex analysis should also include the costs of hardware and software, the cost of training staff, benefits gained from avoiding human errors, improving software quality and customer's faith, business value gained by reducing time to delivery to market, and client satisfaction.

Tool Analysis

Tool analysis is done to select the tool for carrying out test automation. The automation tool that best suits the testing requirements and Application Under Test (AUT) needs to be selected. The automation tool should support AUT user interface. The tool should have features such as scripting facility, error handlers, test script modularization, test script calls, function libraries, environment configuration, batch execution, external file support, and various standard frameworks. The cost of the automation tool is to be within project budget. Skilled resources are to be easily available. Tool support is to be easily available from parent company and elsewhere. Following factors can be considered while selecting tool for test automation:

- **AUT support:** Automation should support the user interface or GUI of the AUT. For example, if the application GUI is built on Java platform, then, tool should be able to recognize and take action on the application objects, viz., executing a click on Java button.
- **Tool stability:** Automation tool should be stable. It should not crash often. The results obtained from test tool should be reliable, accurate, and repeatable. For example, it should not happen that while coding objects in GUI are being recognized by the tool but during iterative execution, test tool fails to recognize the same object.
- **Coding language:** Automation tool should support scripting in some language. Coding language features to be available to code the business logic of the test case to be automated.
- **Script modularization:** Automation tool should support the creation of multiple test scripts and their integration. The tool should also support data-driving of test scripts.
- **Standard frameworks:** Tool should support easy integration with all of the standard automation frameworks.

- **Error handlers:** Tool should have error-handling features to control script execution during run-time.
- **Checkpoints:** Tool should have features to support various checkpoints, such as page checkpoint and text checkpoint. Feature to compare expected results with the actual outcomes need to be available with the test tool.
- **External file support:** Tool should support interaction with external files, such as text files, excel files, and word files.
- **Batch execution:** Tool should support to execute a batch of test scripts in one run.
- **Test results:** Tool should have features to capture and publish test execution results. Test results need to be easy to read and interpret. Features to be available to generate custom test reports.
- **Test environment support:** Automation tool should support test environment—operating system, internet explorer, database, etc.
- **Unattended execution:** Test automation benefits are reaped by reducing the manual test execution cost. Test tool should support unattended execution of test scripts.
- **Project budget:** The cost of the test automation tool has to be within project budget.

It is obvious that no tool may satisfy all the requirements; therefore, the tool that meets most of the evaluation criteria needs to be selected after discussion with stakeholders. A tool analysis table needs to be designed. Testing and application requirements can be split into mandatory and desirable requirements. The features of the automation tool can be mapped to these requirements to find the tool that best supports the project requirements. Appendix E provides a tool analysis chart that can be used to select the best suited automation tool.

Proof of Concept

Proof of concept is done to practically test the automation tool against the project requirements. It is done to find out whether the selected tool supports the application GUI objects or not, the average cost of developing scripts, the gaps in technical competencies of resources, etc. If the selected tool fails to meet the project requirements, then POC on next best suited tool needs to be done. Test scenarios for POC should be selected in a way that they test most of the application objects and few common features of the software product. The test scenarios should give the confidence that test automation with the selected tool will be a success. It is sufficient to use evaluation version of automation tools for POC.

FRAMEWORK DESIGN

Automation architects need to decide the automation approach and automation framework after discussion with the stakeholders. Automation approach refers to the set of assumptions, concepts, and standards and guidelines based on that the automation activities that will be carried out. They include:

- **Basis of selection of test cases for automation**—use-case diagrams, test plan documents, or simple interaction with functional team.
- Team structure.

- **Automation documents**—script and test case development layouts, standards and guidelines, etc.
- Automation project maintenance approach, standards and guidelines, etc.

A test automation framework is a hierarchical directory that encapsulates shared resources, such as dynamic shared library, image files, scripts, drivers, object repositories, localized strings, header files, and reference documentation, in a single package. Test automation framework needs to be designed in a way that best suits the AUT and project requirements. The framework design should support easy configuration of test settings, dynamic variable initialization, selective and exhaustive test scenario executions, unattended test script execution, easy-to-understand test result format, etc. In addition, the framework should support easy packaging and installation of automation project.

BUSINESS KNOWLEDGE GATHERING

Script development process starts with the requirement gathering phase. Automation developers need to gather the business knowledge of the business case identified for automation. Automation developers can gather business knowledge by using use-case diagrams and test plan documents or by directly interacting with the functional team depending on the feasibility and the automation approach decided. Functional team always has a lot to tell about the business case. It is the responsibility of the automation developers to gather only those information and data that are relevant to automation. An automation developer needs to extract the information that is sufficient to automate and maintain the business case and not the complete business knowledge, as it is time consuming and increases the cost and time of script development. For example, suppose after filling of form, form data are updated in various tables and a success message is shown on the web page. If GUI validation is sufficient, then automation developer need not gather information about various fields of table where data are updated. Listed in the following are few points that need to be kept in mind while gathering business knowledge for automation.

- **Test scenarios**—What is the number of test scenarios
- **Test cases**—What is the number of test cases
- **Test input and output data**—What is the input data for test execution? What is the expected output data after test execution?
- **Screen flow**—What is the flow of GUI pages for implementing the business logic.
- **Business logic flow**—What is the flow of business logic of the test scenario/case.
- **Application stability**—Are there change requests that can impact the existing business/screen flow? Are there any pending changes that can change the properties of the existing objects in the gui. If yes, then to what extent?
- **Validation points**—What are the types of the checkpoints required—Database or GUI. At what points in the test script these validation points are required?

SCRIPT DESIGN

After gathering requirements, automation developer needs to decide the components to be automated—business components, test scripts, test data sheet, functions, validation points, type of checkpoints, environment variables, recovery scenario, etc. Business scenario needs to be split into smaller reusable business functionalities that can be integrated sequentially later to implement various test cases of the business case. These reusable business functionalities are called as business components. In addition, automation developers need to design a layout of how the automated components to be integrated to implement the business case. Thereafter, code can be written to automate the components. Scripts should be coded in a way that no user intervention is required during script execution.

TEST EXECUTION AND TEST RESULT ANALYSIS

Test Execution

During test execution phase, the automated test scripts are executed as per the project requirements. A test suite comprising of test cases to be executed is formed and put to execution. Test cases should be robust enough to successfully execute in an unattended mode. Framework needs to be designed in such a way that it supports scheduling of test execution, setting test execution environment parameters, and auto-generating and auto-submitting reports.

Test Results Analysis

Once test execution is complete, the automation developers or functional team can analyze the test results to find out the defects, if any, that are present in the application. Test results should be easy to apprehend and understand. Pass/fail status should be marked against each test case. In case of occurrence of any deviations or error during script execution, test results should contain short and clear messages that points exactly toward the error reason. In addition, there should be a clear distinction between run-time script errors and result deviations (mismatch of expected and actual results). Test results need to also contain screenshots of application at the point when error occurred. Test result should also contain a unique identifier that can be used to debug and verify the executed test case. For example, transaction ID in case of funds transfer or ticket number in case of railway booking.

MAINTENANCE

During maintenance phase, automated scripts are modified as per the change in AUT. Generally, we observe that test automation maintenance becomes a bottleneck for an automation project. Change identification and implementation become time consuming, human resource intensive, and costly. To minimize the maintenance cost, the framework architecture should be designed in way that it supports centralized one-point maintenance. Change requests impacting business logic and flow is common phenomena of SDLC. The automation framework should be well designed to allow easy modification. *Driver* scripts should be designed to have one-point test execution control. *Business component* scripts can be easily added, deleted, and/or modified. The flow/logic of test execution can easily be changed in driver scripts by changing the flow of call to business component scripts. Moreover, documentation should be properly maintained, so that the change identification is easier and fast.

QUICK TIPS

- ✓ Irrespective of which methodology is being implemented, the essential thing is preparation.
- ✓ A good test environment should exist for the test automation team. Preferably, it should be a replica of the production environment.
- ✓ A good hardware setup is equally important in any test automation project. It is essential to have dedicated machines for script execution.
- ✓ The expected data against which the checks are to be performed should be a known baseline.
- ✓ Skilled and experienced resources should be hired.
- ✓ Test cases to be automated should be comprehensive and up to date.

PRACTICAL QUESTIONS

1. What is test automation life cycle?
2. What are the various stages of feasibility analysis?
3. What are the factors to be considered for deciding the implementation of a test automation in a project?
4. What are the considerations to be taken into account for analyzing application stability for test automation?
5. What is break-even point?

Chapter 3

Test Automation Approach

Simply installing an automated testing tool and recording scripts may jump-start the initial automated testing effort, but soon the automation project becomes too difficult and expensive to maintain. Success of an automation projects depends on a well-thought architected solution. A well-planned test automation approach needs to be handy when implementing the automation project. The test automation approach decides the automation scope, test automation development model, type of automation testing, automatability criteria, and team dynamics. This chapter explains the prior requirements for implementing an automation project. This chapter also discusses the factors and real-time conditions that the project managers need to take into account while deciding the test automation approach.

TEST AUTOMATION APPROACH

Test automation approach is a set of assumptions, concepts, standards, guidelines, and tools that support automation testing. It refers to the way an automation project is to be implemented. Automation approach needs to be decided before designing automation architecture and automation framework. Typically, test automation approach defines the following:

- Test automation scope
- Test automation development model
- Test automation basis
- Test Automation—testing types to be covered
- Test automation project infrastructure
- Test automation—team dynamics

Test automation scope defines the percentage of the application that will be automated. Test automation development model defines the development model that will be followed to develop and deliver test scripts. Test automation basis decides the basis of automation—use-case diagrams, business scenarios, test plans, test cases, or random automation based on functional expert's experience. One or more testing types can be covered in test automation, namely GUI testing, functional testing, DB testing, boundary value testing, equivalence partition testing, positive testing, and negative testing. To execute a test automation project, the infrastructure available to the automation team needs to be decided. This includes automation software, hardware configuration, number of licenses and system architecture. Finally, based on the above points, the dynamics of the automation team can be decided.

TEST AUTOMATION SCOPE

Before starting any automation project, it is essential to define the scope of test automation. *Test automation scope* defines the objectives, coverage, and expectations from the test automation project. It helps in determining which part and what percentage of the application is to be automated. Test automation scope helps to understand what to expect from the test automation project and what not. Based on these results, the objectives or goals of the test automation project can be set. Depending on the requirement of the project, test automation scope includes one or more of the following points:

1. What part of the application is to be automated?
2. What percentage of the application is to be automated?
3. Which modules and submodules are to be covered?
4. What percentages of the modules are to be automated?
5. What will be the priority of automation of various modules?
6. What will be the criteria to select/reject a test case for automation?
7. What types of testing will be covered by automation?
8. What will be the basis of automation?
9. What will be the automation development model?
10. What deliverables are to be from the test automation project?
11. What will be the frequency of automation deliverables?
12. What percent of the application is to be GUI tested or API tested?

TEST AUTOMATION DEVELOPMENT MODEL

The three types of test automation development models that are widely being used as of today are waterfall development model, W-model, and agile development model. In waterfall model, automation team waits till the application becomes stable before actually starting the automation. However, in agile model, automation of test scripts is started as soon as GUI end is ready or even before that. Hence, in waterfall model, minimum changes are required in the test scripts once they are developed, while in agile model, frequent changes/upgrades to the test scripts is obvious. This happens because in agile automation, script development is going along with application development. In agile model, the test automation architecture and framework need to be flexible enough to support rapid changes to the test scripts. Program managers or automation architects need to choose one of the test automation development models depending on the project requirements and resources available.

Waterfall Development Model

The waterfall model is a sequential design process where test automation starts once the application environment is stable. Generally, automation begins when the manual testing team has certified the build. The characteristics of waterfall development model are as follows:

- Automation starts after the application has become stable.
- A large part of application functionality is set to be automated in one go.
- Automation delivery is made once in several weeks/months after all the scripts have been developed.

Waterfall development model is a resource-intensive method of developing test scripts. Since a large chunk of application is taken for automation in one go, more resources are required to complete the script development process in a speedy way. Automation team first picks up the functionalities to automate and then the automation continues for weeks/months before final delivery of the automated scripts is made. Most of the time, automation team is busy developing new test scripts with little time left for script maintenance and enhancement. This results in older scripts becoming obsolete and failing during regression runs.

In waterfall model (see Fig. 3.1), the entry of the automation team in the software development process is delayed. This results in limited utilization of the test automation resources, sometimes even leading to negative automation ROI. It takes several weeks/months for the automation scripts to get ready even after the build is certified by the testing team or moved to production. Regression runs of newly implemented functionalities need to be carried out manually, till the test scripts are being developed. Functional testing is completely carried out by the manual testers. If the application development model is also waterfall, then it would take a long time for the automation team to start automating. In certain cases, it would take months after which real automation execution will kick-start.

In the waterfall model, need of manual testing team for executing regression runs is never ruled out, and test automation resources are never utilized to its full potential. The number of defects caught by the automation team is less, as the application tested by them is already a stable one. Here, the main role of test automation team is to ensure that the application does not break because of the newly applied code or code fix.

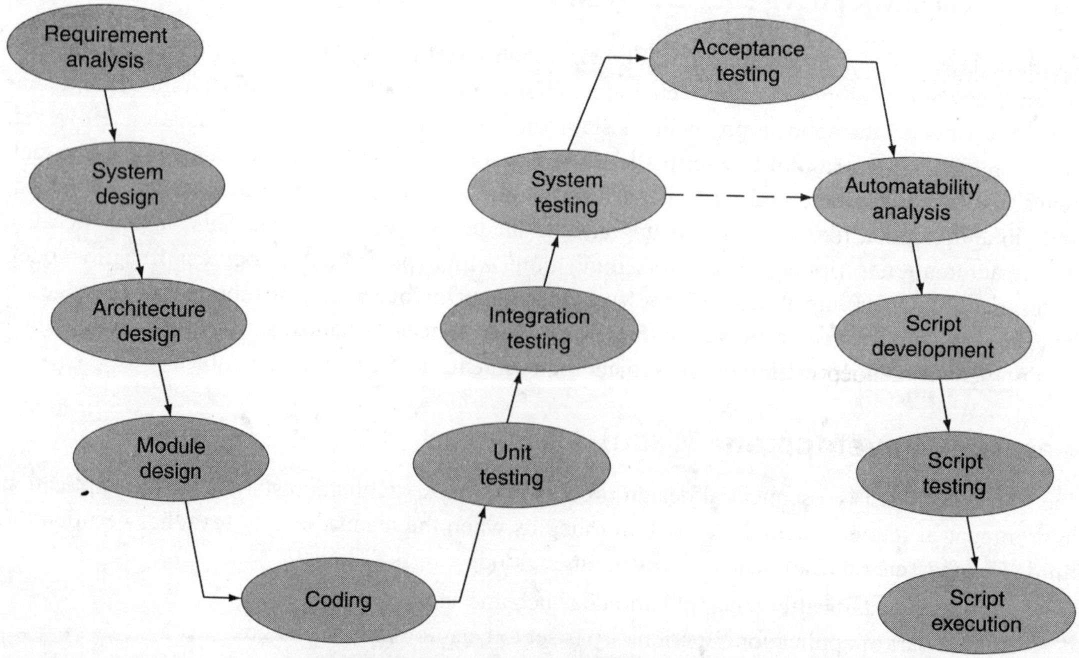

Figure 3.1 *Waterfall development model*

Figure 3.1 shows the waterfall development model of test automation when the application development model is also waterfall. Test automation waterfall development model can be used even if the application development model is other than waterfall model, namely V-model, iterative model, and agile model.

W-Model

W-model is an extension of waterfall model. In W-model, test automation process gets started as soon as the testing phase sets in. The automation processes are executed in parallel to the testing processes. The characteristics of W-development model are as follows:

- Automation planning is started when the test cases are being written.
- Automation development is started after the build is verified by the test team.
- A large part of application functionality is set to be automated in one go.
- Automation delivery is made once in several weeks/months after all the scripts have been developed.

Similar to waterfall model, W-model is also resource intensive, as huge chunk of application is selected for automation in one go. The main advantage of W-model is that the automation processes get started early in the software development life cycle (SDLC). The automation activities are carried out in parallel to the testing activities. Planning for automation starts parallel to the test case design phase. Automation environment is set up, while the manual testers are testing the application. As soon as the software/build is certified by the testing team, automation development

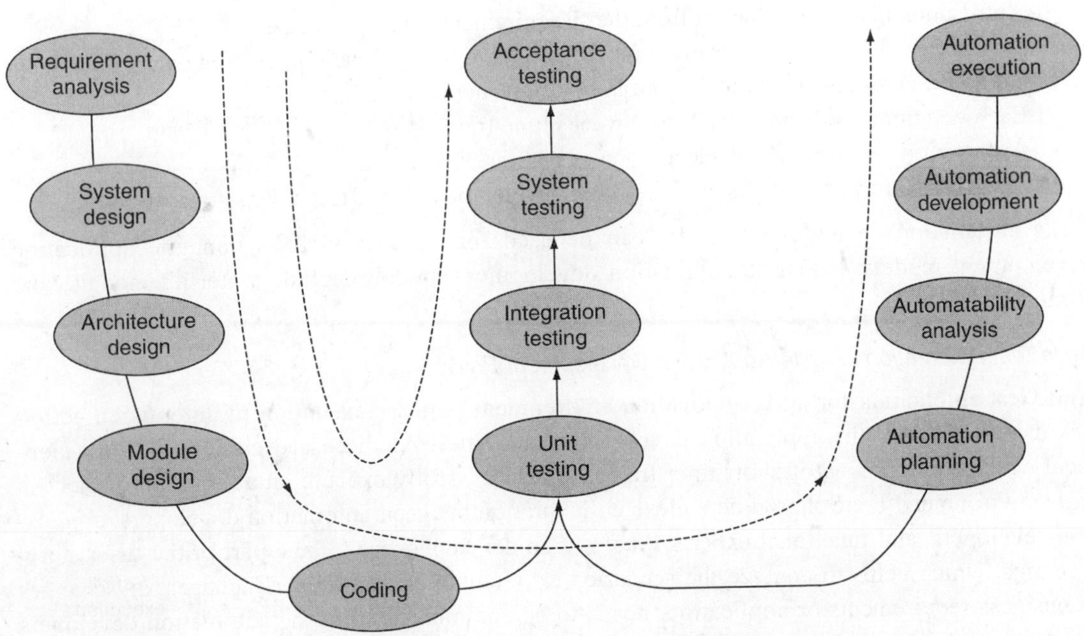

Figure 3.2 *W-development model*

starts. This results in automated scripts being available for regression runs earlier. This saves a lot of effort and cost which is otherwise required for executing manual regression runs for newly implemented features.

Figure 3.2 shows the W-development model of test automation when the application development model is also waterfall. Similar to test automation waterfall development model, test automation W-development model can also be used even if the application development model is other than waterfall model, namely V-model, iterative model, and agile model.

Agile Development Model

Agile development model refers to a software development approach based on iterative development. In agile model, test automation tasks are split into smaller iterations or parts. Long-term automation plans are split into short-term achievable goals or milestones. The test automation project scope and requirements are clearly laid down at the beginning of the development process. Plans regarding the number of iterations, the duration, and the scope of each iteration are clearly defined in advance.

Each iteration is a short time 'frame,' which typically lasts for 2 to 4 weeks. The division of the entire project into smaller parts helps to reduce the project cost. The automated scripts are delivered at short time intervals. In case application development environment is also agile, test scripts are ready by the time build is moved to production. This implies test scripts can be used for regression runs right from the day one regression cycle. This saves a lot of manual effort, which was earlier required for executing manual regression runs. The characteristics of agile development model are as follows:

- Automation planning is started from the 'Requirement Analysis' phase.
- Automation development is carried out in parallel to the application development.
- Complete automation activity is split into various iterations.
- Each iteration can range from 2- to 4-weeks time frame.
- Automation deliveries are made as soon as tests are developed.
- Agile development model is used for rapid development of the test scripts.

Agile automation development model can be used for agile as well as nonagile application development models. Nonagile application development models include waterfall models, and V-model.

Agile Test Automation in Agile Application Development Environment

Agile test automation for agile application environment requires execution of automation activities in parallel with the application development activities. As discussed earlier, agile development occurs in iterations of short time frames. To successfully execute an automation project in agile environment, there should be a close collaboration between automation developers, application developers, and functional experts. Automation developers are to be a part of the 'user story' meetings, which helps to analyze the scenarios to be automated at an early phase. Any changes in business requirements or application, needs to be communicated to the automation developers immediately. This will ensure that the corrective actions are taken in time. Script development in agile environment brings in lot more challenges than compared to nonagile environments, few of them are listed below:

- Object properties of objects may change multiple times as developers are still developing them.
- Automation to be carried out without the availability of GUI screen/objects wherever possible.
- Depending on the application changes, test scripts may need to be modified even after development.
- Automation development needs to be carried out in the same environment where application development is going on.
- Regularly, some pages may stop to respond as developers push code into it.
- Occasional shutdown of the application servers by the developers.
- Poor maintenance of database by the application developers.
- GUI screens being developed till the last day of the iteration cycle.

To address the challenges of the agile automation in an effective way, following techniques can be employed:

- GUI objects are to be captured in shared object repository. Automation developers to use the object information gathered from developers to create test objects.
- Self-defined test objects are to be created if GUI object is not available. The properties of these objects can be defined after discussion with the application developers.
- Automation developers need not wait for the GUI to get ready for each and every test case. Wherever possible, attempt is to be made to automate script components without GUI support. It may always happen that few parts of the screen are available and few are being coded. In this case, automation developers can proceed with the automation of script components, whose GUI is available. These components can be integrated later to implement a test case.
- Script components are to be designed in such a way that it supports easy upgradation and modification. Regular changes to script components are evitable in agile environment.
- Script components reusability is to be maximized in agile environment to reduce development cost. Attempt is to be made to upgrade the existing script components instead of developing new ones.
- All application objects are to be captured when the application pages are responding. Thereafter, business logic can be coded. This will ensure little or no impact because of problems arising of frequent code push to the development environment by the application developers. Also, automation developers can work on some other application pages, until the major deployment on the pages is not complete.
- It should be ensured that application database is in good condition that can support automation. Test data should be easily available in the database. Also, corrupt test data should be reduced to acceptable levels.
- Test cases for which business functionality is not clear or is pending for further information can be automated at the end of the iteration cycle.
- In exceptional scenarios, agile iteration cycle can be allowed to lag by one time frame to allow those scripts to be developed, for which GUI is ready in the last day of the iteration cycle.

Suppose, in agile environment the project is split into n iterations. Every iteration is of 3-week duration. Each iteration is further split into three time frames and each time frame is of one week duration (Fig. 3.3). In this case, the automation project can be lagged by one time frame to allow the time for automation of script components, whose GUI has been developed during the last days of the iteration cycle.

Iteration Cycle	Iteration 1			Iteration 2			Iteration 3
Application	Frame 1	Frame 2	Frame 3	Frame 1	Frame 2	Frame 3	Frame 1
Automation		Frame 1	Frame 2	Frame 3	Frame 1	Frame 2	Frame 3

Figure 3.3 *Agile automation in agile environment*

To execute an automation project in agile environment, the test automation architecture and framework are to be designed in such a way that it supports easy test script development, modification, and upgradation. The test automation architecture should support one-point maintenance. The test automation frameworks that best supports test automation in agile environment are:

- Agile Automation Framework
- BPT Framework
- Business model driven Framework

Test Automation Basis

Before starting the test script development process, the basis for automating an application is to be decided, that is, should the automation developers refer the use-case diagrams, test plans, or test cases for automation, or should the application be automated randomly as per the instructions of the functional experts. Program managers can choose one or more approaches for test automation, depending on the project requirements. Predominantly, test automation basis is of two types, namely test case-driven automation and business scenario-driven automation.

Test Case-driven Automation

In test case-driven automation, manual test cases form the basis of automation. Each test case is treated independent of the other. The number of test scripts is directly proportional to the number of test cases. There exists one-to-one mapping between the test cases and the test scripts. For example, for 500 test cases in Quality Centre (QC), 500 test scripts will exist in the automation project.

Business Scenario-driven Automation

Business scenario-driven test automation is the latest technique of test automation designed by the author 'Rajeev Gupta.' This technique not only reduces the number of automated test scripts but also increases the test coverage as well. This method has been developed to bring down the cost to test automation. In this type of automation, automation developers directly refer the use-case diagrams or test plans. In situations where only manual test cases are available, the test cases with similar workflow are clubbed together to form a business scenario. Automation of a business scenario is carried out as a single individual unit. One business scenario can automate many test scenarios and test cases in one go. For example, suppose there is a business scenario of 'Real-time Payment of e-bay product

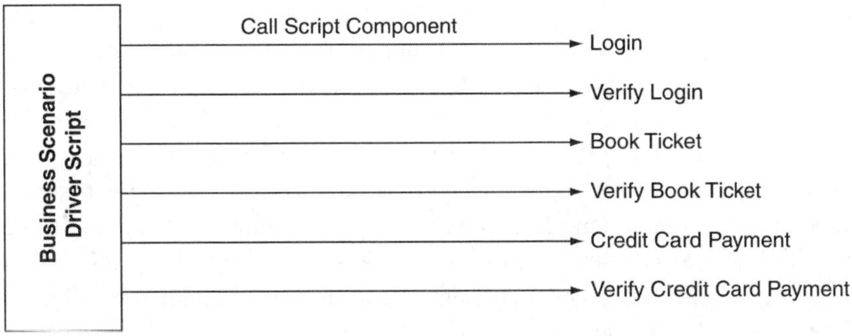

Figure 3.4 *Script layout—business scenario–driven approach*

using Credit Card.' There can be many test scenarios and test cases, such as payment through various card types, verification of payment amount and payment tax, invalid card number, valid CVV number, and invalid card dates. Suppose some of the test cases are as follows:

1. Login → Book Ticket → Credit Card Payment → Verify Product
2. Login → Book Ticket → Credit Card Payment → Verify Amount
3. Login → Book Ticket → Credit Card Payment → Verify Tax
4. Login → Book Ticket → Credit Card Payment → Verify Credit Card
5. Login → Book Ticket → Credit Card Payment → Verify Cancel Purchase
6. Login → Book Ticket → Credit Card Payment → Verify Edit Product

Assume all the above credit card verifications exist in one page, that is, 'Review Payment' page. In test case-driven automation approach, each and every test case is automated individually. Six test scripts will exist for six test cases. It can be observed that first few steps of the business scenario are similar for all test cases. This results in a lot of redundancy in the automated scripts. In addition, repeating the automation of same steps results in higher development effort and cost. Again, more test scripts imply high maintenance effort. These problems can easily be overcome by business scenario-driven approach of test automation. In this approach, first, all the test cases are clubbed together to form a business scenario. Then, flow of the business scenario is designed, which is as shown below:

Login → Verify Login → Book Ticket → Verify Book Ticket → Credit-Card Payment → Verify Credit-Card Payment

Script component 'Verify Credit Card Payment' verifies each and every field of 'Review Payment' page, including verification of Product, Amount, Tax, Order Dates, Shipping Dates, Credit Card Details, Order Cancel Option, and Order Edit Option as shown in Fig. 3.5. In the 'Review Payment' page itself, it is observed that this technique not only automates the above-mentioned six test cases, but also test cases related to Shipping Dates, Order Dates, etc. In addition, after each test step, there exists one verification script to verify that test step. Eventually,

Figure 3.5 *Script component—verify credit card payment*

in addition to the above-mentioned six test cases, a lot more test cases are also automated within one single driver test script by using this method. This technique is not only automating the test cases related to 'Real-time Payment' but also test cases related to 'Login' and 'Book Ticket.' Thus, using this technique not only the number of test script are reduced, but at the same time test coverage is also increased.

In business scenario-driven approach, the business scenario driver test script is implemented by sequentially calling various script components, such as Login and Verify Login as shown in Fig. 3.4. Here, no separate verification is done for test cases. In this method, 'Verification Code' exists as a separate entity either in the same test script or in a different test script. For example, 'Verify Login' code can exist in the same script component 'Login' or it can exist individually. In business scenario-driven approach, each and every business action is verified fully before moving to the next step. This helps in extensive testing of the application.

Moreover, it takes lesser time to execute regression runs using business scenario-driven approach as compared to the test case-driven approach. Suppose for test case-driven approach, each test case is executed against 10 sets of test data. Then, 10 executions of each test case will be required to complete the regression run. Therefore, the total numbers of executions are 60 for 6 test cases. Assuming, each execution takes 3 min; total time required for execution is 180 min (6 * 10 * 3). Now, let us assume that in the business scenario-driven approach the driver script execution takes 4 min. Then, the execution time for 20 test data sets will be 80 min (1 * 20 * 4). Thus, we observe that by using this technique, each and every test case is executed against 20 sets of data as against only 10 sets of data of the test case-driven approach. Again, it not only tests the 'Review Payment' page but also test 'Login' and 'Book Ticket' scenarios as well. Hence, using this technique, not only the coverage of testing has been increased but also the regression run execution time has been reduced. In projects that implement separate 'lab machines' for test execution, this technique of automation is very useful in reducing the number of UFT licenses and eventually the test automation project cost.

Again, let us assume that after some time new functionality of 'Real-time Online Payment' is implemented in the application. Suppose the following test cases are designed for this purpose:

1. Login → Book Ticket → Online Payment → Verify Product.
2. Login → Book Ticket → Online Payment → Verify Amount.
3. Login → Book Ticket → Online Payment → Verify Tax
4. Login → Book Ticket → Online Payment → Verify Account Number
5. Login → Book Ticket → Online Payment → Verify Account PIN

In test case-driven approach, six more test cases will be automated. For business scenario-driven approach, only the script components 'Credit Card Payment' and 'Verify Credit Card Payment' will be upgraded. Logic for automating 'Online Payment' scenario will be coded in the script 'Credit Card Payment' itself. Similarly, logic for verifying the online payment will be coded in the 'Verify Credit Card Payment' script itself. The business scenario driver script is not modified. Now the question arises how the driver script will know which logic code to run—Credit Card Payment or Online Payment. This is again achieved by passing suitable test data from test data sheets (MS Excel) to the driver script. This test data will control the logical flow of the code to execute various test scenarios. Thus, by updating few script components, new business scenario is automated using this approach. Thus, this technique not only reduces the number of test scripts but also reduces the automation development effort. Moreover, in test scenario-driven approach, again a different test data set is to be defined. While, in the business scenario-driven approach, the same old test data set can be used. Alternatively, if required more test data sets can be included. The advantage here is that not only the 'Online Payment' test cases, but also the test cases related to 'Login' and 'Book Ticket,' will get executed against this new test data set. Thus, the automation suite always remains updated.

Hence, it is concluded that 'business scenario-driven approach' not only reduces the number of test scripts but also reduces the test development, maintenance, and execution cost as well. As per my experience, in one of my projects, I was able to reduce the number of test scripts from 1800 to 450. The reduced automation suite offered more test coverage as well as reduced automation costs. Moreover, the new functionalities can be easily automated by just updating few script components. There are only two frameworks that best support business scenario-driven approach of test automation—Business model Driven Framework and Agile Automation Framework. Both the frameworks have been designed and developed by the author, Rajeev Gupta, and have been discussed in detail in the chapters 5 and 6.

In test case-driven approach, there is no end to script development. As long as the new functionalities are added to the application, new test scripts need to be automated. While, in business scenario-driven approach, during maintenance phase, test automation development either stops or reduces to minimum. depending on business changes. If the business changes are small, then just by updating few scripts, automation can be achieved. However, if the business change is major involving development of new pages, then new script components may need to be written. These script components can either be integrated with existing driver script or a new one can be written. In either case, the test development effort will be much less than as compared to the test case-driven approach. Figure 3.6 compares the effort and cost involved using both the techniques during different phases of test automation.

TEST AUTOMATION—TESTING TYPES TO BE COVERED

There are various types of testing that can be done using automated testing. These include:

- **GUI Testing**—GUI testing involves analyzing the behavior of various GUI objects, such as edit boxes and radio buttons. It involves test cases which check whether GUI object behavior is up to the expectation or not. For example, it can include test cases that verifies whether the
    - User is able to click on the button objects
    - User is able to enter text of various combination on edit boxes
    - User is able to enter text of maximum length in text boxes
    - User is able to select item(s) from list box or combo box
    - User is able to select radio buttons
    - User is able to select multiple checkboxes
    - GUI objects are enabled or disabled
    - Proper error messages are getting displayed on the screen
    - There are any broken links
    - Font is of various objects or texts on the page/screen is correct or not.

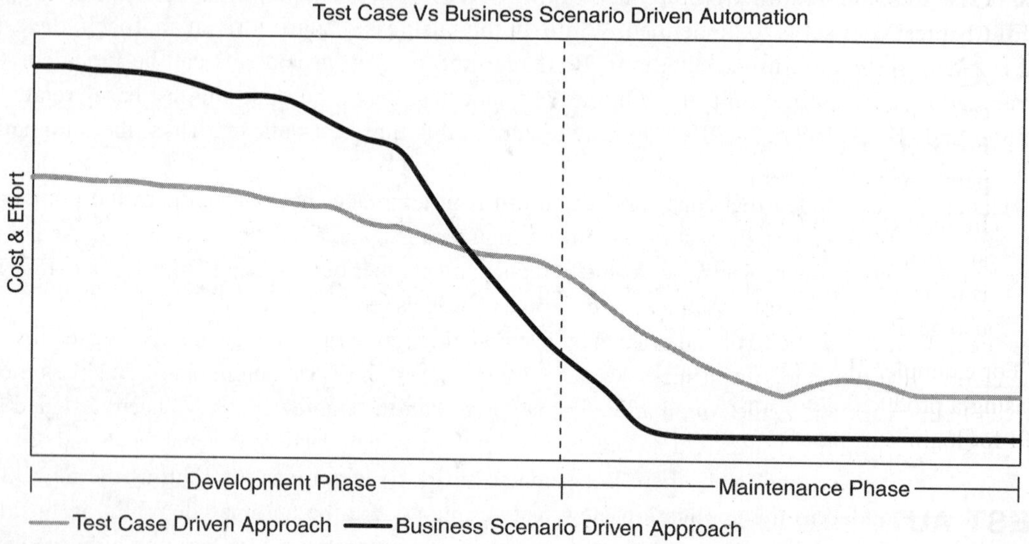

Figure 3.6 *Automation effort comparison analysis : Test case driven approach vs Business scenario driven approach*

GUI testing also includes testing the look and feel of GUI. However, QTP can not be used to test how appealing GUI is to the user.

- **Functional testing:** Functional testing involves testing the business functionality of the application. QTP provides wide range of inbuilt methods and properties to successfully test an application.
- **Database testing:** Database testing involves testing the database for data validity, data integrity, database performance, and testing database procedures, triggers, and functions. In data validity, front-end data is validated against the back-end data. In data integrity, referential integrity and different constants of the database is tested. In database performance testing, performance of the database is measured under various load conditions. This is generally done by performance tools. QTP can be used to successfully test the data validity of the database. After executing a test, the data visible on the GUI screen or the input data to the GUI screen can be validated against the database data. For example, after submitting user form, validating the user form data against the data updated in the database. Another example can be to verify the data visible of 'Review Payment' page with the data present in the database.
- **Positive testing:** Positive testing involves test cases that are designed for 'pass' criteria. These involve test cases aimed at showing that the application works.
- **Negative testing:** Negative testing involves test cases that aim at showing software does not crashes under error conditions. These involve test cases that check proper error messages are displayed on the screen in case of any unexpected or wrong user behavior, such as invalid text input.
- **Performance testing:** Limited performance testing is supported by QTP. QTP users can measure the page navigation time or response time of the application while executing a test.

QTP 10.0 and onward provide the flexibility to monitor system performance. For details refer Chapter 26.

- **API testing:** API testing involves testing the application APIs (webservices). Application APIs can also be used to speed by test execution. APIs execution is much faster than GUI execution. For a typical test case where GUI execution may take a minute or two; same execution can be performed using API in 1-3 seconds.

  In agile development world, API testing holds an important place. Attempts is to be made to automate maximum tests using APIs while GUI tests is to be kept to a minimum. GUI test suite is to be designed in a way that it covers all the UI pages. The rest of the tests is to be automated using APIs. Wherever possible, both GUI and API code is to be used.

For example, in a test suite of eCommerce site, most of the test cases involve logging in for purchasing a product. Here, we can automate one GUI test for login while the rest of the tests is to use API for login.

TEST AUTOMATION PROJECT INFRASTRUCTURE

The project managers need to decide the test automation project infrastructure as per the project requirement and available budget. Project infrastructure includes one or more of the following:

- Number of hardware systems
- Hardware configuration
- Software configuration
- Number of UFT licenses
- UFT add-ins
- Project server machine
- Requirement of 'Test Lab' machines
- Project tools—coverage analysis, effectiveness analysis, progress analysis, etc.
- Requirement of external tools—SQL Developer, Regular Expression developer, PuTTY, etc.
- System architecture

Typically, Pentium 4 processors or above with 2GB of RAM is sufficient for successfully working with UFT tool. UFT supports most of the windows operating system (both 32 bit and 64 bit)—Win 2000, Win XP, Win 2003, Vista, Windows 7 and Windows 7 and 8.

Figure 3.7 shows the system architecture of a typical automation project. Automation developers use the 'Test Automation Development' machines to develop the automated scripts. The automated components are saved on the 'Automation Project Server' machine. This machine acts as the central shared repository of the automation project. Business analysts and manual testers execute the developed automated test scripts to test the application. UFT is not installed on these 'Automation Execution Initiation Machines.' In fact, the run request raised by the business analysts/manual testers is first sent to the automation project server. The server receives these requests and executes these requests on automation lab machines which have UFT installed on them. Once test execution is over, lab machines update the test status back to the server. Thereafter, the testers can log-in to the server to analyze the test results.

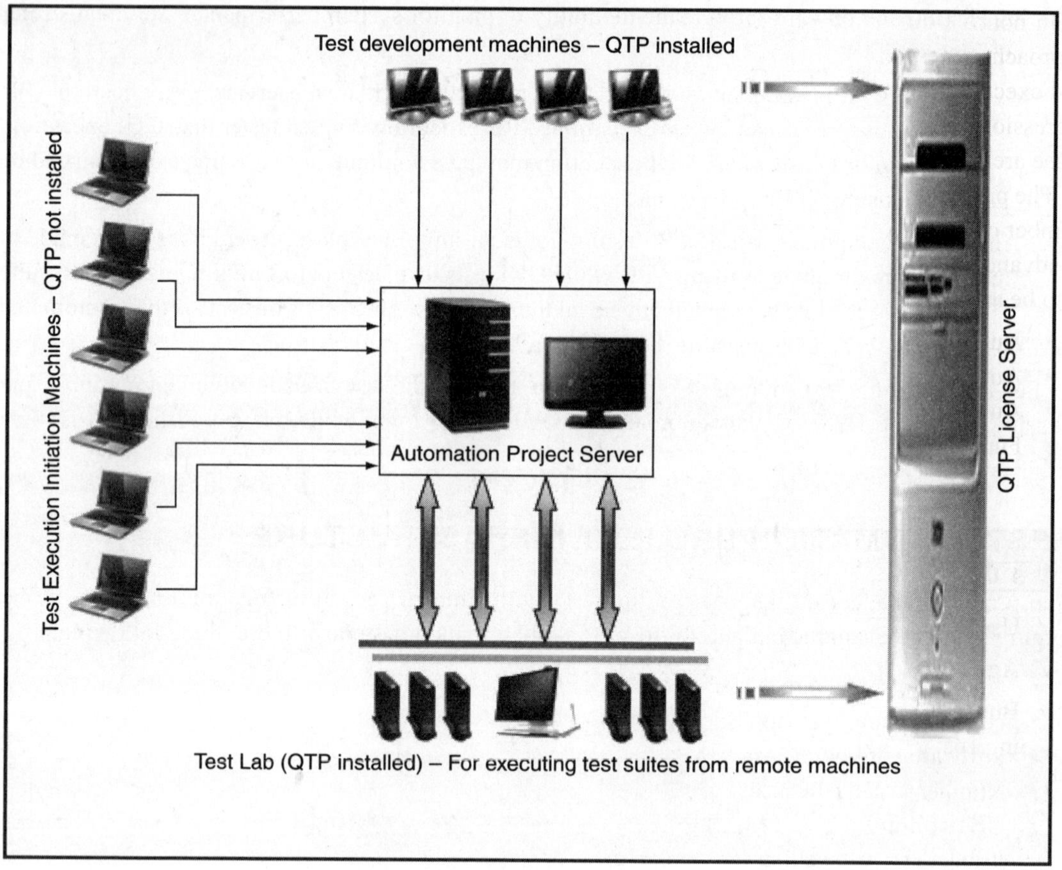

Figure 3.7 *System architecture*

TEST AUTOMATION—TEAM DYNAMICS

The program managers need to decide the dynamics of the automation team depending on the project requirements, automation development model, system architecture, and available resources. Team dynamics refer to the team formation and contexts that influences the team.

The program managers need to decide whether the project requires a role-driven or a nonrole-driven approach of test automation. In role-driven approach, each and every stage of test automation is handled by the respective experts. Business analysts identify which business components need to be automated. These business components are, then, sent to the automation developers for automation. Once automated, the automated components are sent to the manual testers. The manual testers use these business components to design a test case. The task of the automation experts here is limited to the development and maintenance of the business components. The execution of automated components is done by the manual testers. The only framework that best supports this team dynamics is Business Process Testing (BPT) framework.

In nonrole-driven framework, the program managers have to decide the team formation. In this approach, generally, functional experts identify the test cases for automation. Thereafter, automation and execution of the automated components is the responsibility of the automation developer. After regression runs, the test reports are analyzed by the automation team. If any deviations found, then those are sent to the functional experts for further analysis and defect logging.

The program managers also need to decide the size as well as the proficiency level of the team. The number of automation architects and automation developers required for the project is to be analyzed in advance. In addition, the effort, which the functional experts need to put in to support automation, is to be analyzed. Typically, the team dynamics will include the following:

- Automation team lead
- Automation architects
- Automation developers
- Functional experts

QUICK TIPS

✓ Use an automation approach that best suits the project requirements.

✓ Agile development model provides the best automation results.

✓ Business scenario-driven automation helps in increasing test coverage and as well as reducing cost to test automation.

PRACTICAL QUESTIONS

1. What are the various test automation–development models?
2. What are the benefits of the agile development model?
3. What is business scenario-driven approach?
4. What are the advantages of business scenario-driven approach?
5. What are the factors that have to be taken into account while deciding test automation team dynamics?

Chapter 4

Test Automation Framework

During the early years, record/playback method of test automation was widely used. All the data was hard-coded within the test scripts. Even a small change in application impacted hundreds of the test scripts. Maintenance cost associated with these impacted scripts was very high. Maintenance of these test scripts consumed much of the time of the automation developers. Most of the time scripts were not ready for regression run execution as they need to be modified as per the business functionality or application code change. This left the test automation team ineffective when they were required the most. As the test automation industry matured, came the concept of test automation framework. Test automation framework provided a standardized way of implementing a test automation project. Automation frameworks defined the way of developing and maintaining an automation project.

A test automation framework is a hierarchical directory that encapsulates shared resources, such as dynamic-shared library, image files, scripts, drivers, object repositories, localized strings, header files, and reference documentation in a single package. The main advantages of a test automation framework are the reusability of existing test scripts and low automation project maintenance cost and effort. It is much easier to maintain a test automation project built on standard framework as compared to an automation project with no standard frameworks. Automation framework helps in making change identification and implementation tasks easier.

FRAMEWORK COMPONENTS

Test automation frameworks segregated the automation project into various components to remove hard coding from the scripts. Test automation architects modified and remodified the existing frameworks to make it easier to reuse the same test scripts repeatedly to automate the various test cases. Test input data was removed from the test scripts and put in separate test data files. This helped to execute the same test script for varying test input data. Separate function libraries were designed to reduce code redundancy. With time, also, came the need to execute the same test scripts across various builds and environments. Separate environment configuration files were designed and scripts were parameterized to receive data from these files. As the automation industry matured, it became evident that centralized single-point maintenance is essential to minimize the maintenance costs of test automation. To achieve this goal, the complete test automation project was divided into various parts that can be maintained separately but in a way that change at one point automatically propagates to the complete automation project. Each of these parts was called *framework component* (Fig. 4.1).

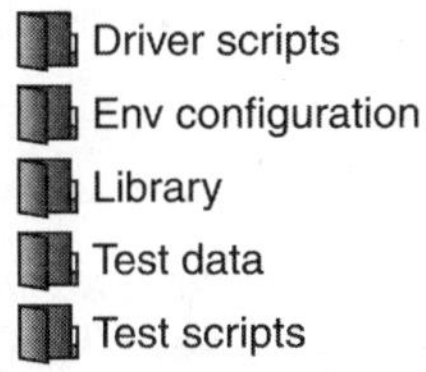

Figure 4.1 *Framework components*

A standardized automation project started to be comprised of following major framework components—test data files, function library files, environment configuration files, test scripts, and test driver scripts. Test scripts used the test data files and library files to automate a test case. Driver scripts integrated all the framework components to execute a set of test cases. First, driver scripts set the test execution environment settings using the environment configuration files and thereafter called test scripts one after another to execute multiple test cases.

FRAMEWORK TYPES

There are various types of frameworks available as of today:

- Modular-driven framework,
- Data-driven framework,
- Keyword-driven framework,
- Hybrid framework,
- Business model driven framework, and
- Agile automation framework.

Modular-driven Framework

Modular-driven framework requires creation of small, reusable, and independent scripts that represent a particular function of the application under test. These small scripts are then integrated in a hierarchical fashion to implement a test case. This framework applies the principle of abstraction to improve the maintainability and scalability of the automated test scripts.

Let us consider that we have www.irctc.com site as the application under test. Suppose we need to automate the following business scenarios:

1. Login → Book Ticket → Logout
2. Login → Cancel Ticket → Logout

Now, let us see how we can automate these scenarios using modular-driven framework. The first task is to split the business scenario into smaller reusable business functionalities.

Business functionalities—Login; Book Ticket—Plan Travel; Make Payment; Logout

Here, we observe that the specified business scenario has been split into four reusable business functionalities.

The next step is to design a driver that can sequentially call these reusable business functionalities to implement the business scenario.

```
'Start execution
Browser("Login").Page("Login").Sync
Browser("Login").Page("Login").WebEdit("Username").Set "User1"
Browser("Login").Page("Login").WebEdit("Password").Set "Pass1"
Browser("Login").Page("Login").WebButton("Login").Click
'---- validation ----
If Browser("PlanTrvl").Page("PlanTrvl").Exist(0.5) Then
    Reporter.ReportEvent micPass,"Login","Successful"
```

Figure 4.2 *Login business component*

Driver Scripts—Book Ticket, Cancel Ticket

Figure 4.2 shows the 'IRCTC_Login' test script, which automates the 'Login' business functionality. The login credentials are specified in the test script itself. If the 'Login' functionality needs to be tested against a different login credentials, then a copy of this test script needs to be created and then the login credentials need to be changed.

The major drawback of this framework is test input data-like login credentials, plan travel details, and payment details are hard-coded into the test scripts. This makes it impossible to execute the same test scripts against various sets of data. To achieve the same in this framework, automation developers had to create a copy of the existing test scripts and replace the hard-coded data with desired data set.

Advantages

- *Learning curve*: The framework is very easy to learn.
- *Implementation cost*: The framework does not require major setup and is easy to implement.

Disadvantages

- *Limited script reusability*: Test input data exists within the scripts. This results in the creation of multiple duplicate scripts in situation where same script needs to be executed for different sets of data.
- *High development cost*: Duplication of script requires extra effort, thereby increasing the script-development cost.
- *High maintenance cost*: A change in AUT may require same changes to be done in multiple scripts that have been duplicated. With number of scripts being huge, change identification and implementation become costly.

Data-driven Framework

The disadvantages of modular-driven framework gave rise to the need of removing the hard-coded data from the test scripts and putting them in separate test data files. The test scripts were parameterized to

```
'declaration
Dim sUsrNm, sPasswd
'test data
sUsrNm = GetDataFromExcel("UserName","Login")
sPasswd = GetDataFromExcel("Password","Login")
'Start execution
Browser("Login").Page("Login").Sync
Browser("Login").Page("Login").WebEdit("Username").Set sUsrNm
Browser("Login").Page("Login").WebEdit("Password").Set sPasswd
Browser("Login").Page("Login").WebButton("Login").Click
```

	A	B	C	D
1	SeqNo	TestCaseID	UserName	Password
2	1	T101	User1	Pass1
3	2	T102	User2	Pass2
4	3	T103	User3	Pass3

Login

Figure 4.3 *Login business functionality and its test data file*

receive the test data input from the test data files. The framework so developed was called data-driven framework.

Data-driven framework is a framework where test scripts interact with the data files for test input data and expected output data. Test data files could be Excel sheets or any other databases. Variables are used for both input values and expected output values. Test scripts are parameterized to receive and update to test data sheets.

Let us consider the IRCTC book ticket and cancel ticket scenarios once again. In this framework, the hard-coded test input data in test scripts is replaced by variables and test input data is kept in test data files (Excel sheets). This allows testing the same business scenario with a variety of test data set without changing the test scripts.

Business functionalities—Login, Book Ticket—Plan Travel, Make Payment, Logout

Test data files—Login Credentials, Plan Travel Details, Payment Details

Function library—Retrieve Data Set from Excel

Driver scripts—Book Ticket, Cancel Ticket

Figure 4.3 shows the test script 'IRCTC_Login,' which automates the 'Login' business functionality. The test script has been parameterized to receive the 'username' and 'password' from the test data files. The test data file contains a set of 'username' and 'password' data. The 'IRCTC_Login' test script can be executed sequentially against all the test data sets. This helps in testing the 'Login' screen against various permutations of valid and invalid data input.

Advantages

- *Reduced Code Redundancy*: Parameterization of the test script removes the need of script duplication.
- *Improved Test Script Maintainability*: Parameterization helps improving the test script maintainability.

Disadvantages

- *Skilled Resource*: Proficient automation developers are required.
- *Maintenance Cost*: Multiple test data files to be maintained for each test case.

Keyword-driven Framework

Keyword-driven framework is a framework where keywords are used to write test scripts step-wise in the form of table. This framework requires the development of data tables and keywords, which are independent of the test automation tool used. Every keyword has its own controller code, which specifies which steps will be executed when the specified keyword procedure is called. Test case steps are written in step table for which a separate processor code is designed. In this framework, the entire test case is data driven including the test data. Since users cannot use logical loops in Excel sheets, this framework requires a new test script design (step table) for any logic change. In addition, in case of executing the same test script with different sets of data, step table needs to be duplicated. This results in huge repository of Excel sheets, whose maintenance again becomes very difficult.

Let us take an example of login to IRCTC site. For keyword-driven framework, the first task is to identify all the actions that can be performed by a user on the GUI end. Next step is to assign a 'keyword' for all these actions. Once all the 'keywords' have been identified a 'keyword map' table is to be created.

Keyword map defines all the keywords available for the test automation project. Table 4.1 shows an example of keyword map table.

Table 4.1 Keyword map

Keyword	Description
LaunchApp	Launch AUT
VerifyLogin	Check if login is successful
EditBox	Enter text into EditBox
Button	Click on button

Once all the 'keywords' has been identified, The next task is to write a code for each keyword. The code so developed is called 'Keyword Controller Code'.

Each keyword represents an action. Users define keywords one after another in a table(MS Excel or a database) to automate a test case. The table so formed is called 'step table'. Code is written to read all the keywords from the step table and call the appropriate keyword processor code. This code so developed is called 'Step table processor' code.

Once step table processor code is developed, users can start automating the test case by writing the test case steps in *step table* as shown in Table 4.2. Next, component property map table needs to be designed. *Component property map* table defines the properties of the application objects. Automation tool uses these properties to identify the specified objects during run-time (Table 4.3).

Table 4.2 Step table for login

Object	Component	Action	Data
LaunchApp			
EditBox	UserName	EnterText	TestUser1
EditBox	Password	EnterText	TestPass1
Button	Login	Click	SingleLeftClick
VerifyLogin			

Table 4.3 Component property map

Component	Identification Property
UserName	name:=userName
Password	name:=password
Login	name:=Login, html id:=Button1

Framework Pseudocode

Step Table Processor

Find current step object, component, action, and data.
Call current object controller procedure.

Controller Procedures

EditBox

Verify EditBox with specified property exists.
Enter specified text into EditBox.

Button

Verify button with specified property exists.
Execute specified type of click on object.

LaunchApp

Launch application under test.
Verify whether the application is opened or not.

VerifyLogin

Verify whether the login is successful or not.

Advantages

- Reduces maintenance cost, as test cases are written in the form of table and not test scripts.
- After training, even testers can automate test cases.

Disadvantages

- *Framework design cost*: Initial cost of framework design is very high and is time consuming.
- *Dynamic objects*: Limited support for working with dynamic objects.
- *Logical conditions*: It is not possible to use logical conditions in step tables.
- *Logical loops*: Step tables do not support logical-looping statements.
- *Skilled resource*: Expert automation developers are required to develop and maintain the scripts.
- *Automation development cost*: New test case Excel sheet needs to be designed if test case involves logical flow change or test data change. This ultimately results in the duplication of Excel sheets in parts or whole, thereby increasing the development cost.
- *Maintenance cost*: Change identification and modification is time consuming as there is huge repository of Excel sheets.
- *Training cost*: Testers need to learn the 'keywords' and specialized formats before they can start automating.

Hybrid Framework

Hybrid framework is a combination of above frameworks, using their strengths and avoiding their weaknesses. Generally, 'data-driven framework' and 'keyword-driven framework' are combined to develop a hybrid keyword data-driven framework. This framework separates the test input data from step tables. A separate test data file is maintained and is associated with the step table during run-time. Thus, this framework avoids duplication of test cases (step tables) in case of variations of test input data.

Advantages

- Reduces maintenance cost, as test cases are written in the form of table and not test scripts.
- Avoids duplication of test cases design (Excel sheets).
- After training, even testers can automate test cases.

Disadvantages

- *Framework design cost*: Initial cost of framework design is high and is time consuming.
- *Dynamic objects*: Limited support for working with dynamic objects.
- *Logical conditions*: It is not possible to use logical conditions in step tables.
- *Logical loops*: Step tables do not support logical-looping statements.
- *Skilled resource*: Expert automation developers are required to develop and maintain the scripts.
- *Automation development cost*: New test case Excel sheet needs to be designed if test case involves logical flow change. This ultimately results in duplication of Excel sheets in parts, thereby increasing the development cost.
- *Maintenance cost*: Change identification and modification is time consuming as there is a huge repository of Excel sheets.
- *Multiple excel sheets*: Test data files need to be mapped to test case Excel sheets. Users need to check and keep in mind the test case before changing any data in test data files.
- *Training cost*: Testers need to learn the 'keywords' and specialized formats before they can start automating.

NOTES

'Keyword-driven' and 'hybrid' frameworks have very high development and maintenance costs; though there is some misconception that these frameworks reduce the development and maintenance costs of test automation. Under the light of some real-time practical scenarios, the reverse seems to be true. In the absence of logical conditioning and logical loops in the step tables, the step tables keep on repeatedly multiplying and ultimately reaching a point where no maintenance is possible. Moreover, most of the step tables contain similar test steps resulting in huge redundancy.

Let us analyze the development and maintenance efforts associated with the 'keyword-driven' and 'hybrid' frameworks.

Framework Setup Effort

The framework setup time of, any framework other than 'keyword-driven' or 'hybrid' framework, is minimal. However, 'keyword' or 'hybrid' framework requires huge framework setup effort in the form of development of 'keywords.'

Automation Development Effort

A test case may require execution over single or multiple set of data. If the test case contains decision points for execution on multiple sets of data, then a new step table needs to be designed for the same. For example, consider the test case below.

Login—Book Ticket—Make Payment—Verify Payment

Repeat the steps for one, two, three, four, and five passengers. Click on 'Add' button to add new passenger details.

In data-driven framework, 'if' condition can be used to check if data corresponding to the passenger details exists in the data table or not. If exists, then click on 'Add' button and 'input' data to screen. However, in step tables, it is difficult to use the same step table to input data for one passenger as well as multiple passengers. This is because a decision has to be made first whether the ticket needs to be booked for one passenger or more than one passenger. Since decision logic cannot be coded in step tables, a separate step table needs to be designed for each decision point. Therefore, for 'keyword' or 'hybrid' approach, a new step table needs to be designed for each 'passenger' variation. This test case can be automated using one test script in data-driven framework. However, for keyword-driven framework, five step tables need to be developed. Definitely, effort required to automate a step table is less than a test script. However, is the effort required to automate and test five step tables not greater than one test script? Similarly, the number of step tables can multiply if the test case has multiple exit points based on certain criteria. Moreover, all the step tables duplicate the first few steps of the test cases. This results in huge redundancy in step tables.

Let us assume that there are 500 test cases for automation. Consider the table below for estimating the effort required to automate these test cases using 'data driven' and 'hybrid' frameworks.

Test Cases #	Test Data Variation #	Data Driven (Scripts #)	Hybrid (Step Table #)
150	0	150	100
100	1	100	200
100	2	100	200
50	4	50	200
50	5	50	250
50	6	50	300
	Total	*500*	*1,250*

Suppose, it requires 2 h to automate one test script, then the time required to automate 500 test scripts is

$$T_d = 500 \times 2 \text{ h} = 1{,}000 \text{ h}$$

Suppose, it requires 1 h to automate one step table, then the time required to automate 1,250 step tables is

$$T_h = 1{,}250 \times 1 \text{ h} = 1{,}250 \text{ h}$$

It definitely requires less time to automate a step table than as compared to the time required to automate a test script. However, if the time required to automate a business scenario or business application is compared, then in most of the cases, hybrid framework will require more development effort.

Maintenance Effort

Now let us analyze the maintenance effort for data-driven and hybrid frameworks. For comparison analysis, let us consider the following business scenario:

For IRCTC application, presently, to book a ticket, a user enters the details of his or her credit card and submits it. Thereafter, real-time authentication of credit card takes place. The transaction is executed only if the credit card is valid. In future, an extra level of 'User Password Validation' is to be implemented to make the transaction of credit card secure. This validation will take place after the user submits the credit card data and before the real-time authentication of credit card.

Suppose there are 300 test cases that test the test case until card authentication phase. Now, in case of modular- or data-driven framework, just the test script that implements the business functionality of real-time authentication needs to be modified to test the new functionality. Let us assume that it takes 2 h to upgrade this test script. The change will automatically propagate to all automated test cases that use this test script.

Time required to upgrade 300 test scripts

$$T_{\text{Md}} = 1 \times 2\ \text{h} = 2\ \text{h}$$

Now, let us analyze the maintenance effort required to implement the same for 'keyword' or 'hybrid' framework. Consider the pseudocode for a step table is as follows:

1. Login
2. Book ticket
3. Make payment using credit card
4. Verify payment

For 300 test cases, minimum 300 step tables would exist. Now, a 'User Validation Step' needs to be inserted between step 3 and step 4, to test the new functionality. Suppose it takes 20 min to implement the same in 1 step table, then time required to upgrade all step tables will be as shown below.

Time required to upgrade 300 step tables

$$T_{\text{Mh}} = 300 \times 1/3 = 100\ \text{h}$$

It requires only 2 h to upgrade the test scripts to test new functionality in data-driven framework, while it takes 100 h in 'keyword-driven' or 'hybrid' framework. Instead of decreasing the testing cost, the testing cost will increase manifold. In addition, if this effort is not put in, then all 300 step tables will go obsolete in one go. This will leave the automation team handicapped and will defeat the main objective of test automation.

Let us consider one more example, where a new functionality needs to be implemented in the application.

In IRCTC application, presently, all payment is done through credit cards. As per the new business case, users are to be provided with the flexibility to make payment from 'Online Banking' as well.

Suppose, 20 new test cases have been designed to test this new functionality. To test the same, in data-driven framework, it may not require creation of new automated test cases. Instead, the new functionality can be automated separately and then this automated business functionality can be called in already automated test cases. 'Decision logic can be coded in the automated test cases to make payment either by credit card or by online banking payment depending on the data available in the data sheets. Suppose, it takes 2 h to automate the business functionality and 10 min to code the decision logic in the automated test cases, then the total effort to create scripts to test the new functionality is

Total effort to create scripts to test new functionality

$$T_{\text{Dd}} = 1 \times 2\text{ h} + 20 \times 1/6\text{ h} = 5.33\text{ h}$$

Now, let us analyze the effort required for the same in 'keyword' or 'hybrid' framework. Since the business case has decision logic (either through credit card or online banking), the step tables cannot be updated to test the new functionality. Creation of new step tables is must in 'hybrid' framework for this case. Assuming it takes 1 h to automate a test case using step table, the total effort to create 20 step tables is

Total effort to create 20 step tables to test new functionality

$$T_{\text{Dd}} = 20 \times 1\text{ h} = 20\text{ h}$$

Therefore, it takes 5.33 h to automate the functionality in data-driven framework while it takes 20 h in 'hybrid' framework. This effort goes on increasing with increase in the number of test cases.

As evident from the above examples, 'keyword' and 'hybrid' frameworks are not always cost effective. Most of the times, the automation cost with these frameworks can be much higher than as compared to other frameworks.

Business Model-driven Framework

Business model driven framework is a dynamic framework which supports dynamic creation of automated test cases by defining few 'keywords' in the test data tables. This framework has been designed and developed by the author, Rajeev Gupta. Test cases can be automated in Excel sheets by selecting few reserved business flow 'keywords' and defining their test data. This is a framework, where test cases and test data are present in the test data files themselves. The complete business scenario is split into reusable business functionalities. Each business functionality is automated as a reusable component. Driver scripts are designed, which call the reusable components one after another to automate a business scenario. Thus, the driver scripts automate almost all the test cases of the respective business scenario in one go, thereby saving the script development time. The test case to execute at run-time is decided by the keyword specified in the test data sheet. Since the number of scripts are less but coverage is much high, this framework reduces the cost to test the automation by a great margin.

Agile Automation Framework

Agile automation framework is a dynamic framework designed to achieve rapid automation. This framework has been designed and developed by the author, Rajeev Gupta. This framework minimizes the automation development and maintenance effort. The framework setup cost of agile automation framework is also very low. This framework enables the users to dynamically automate the test cases from Excel sheet. Just few 'keywords' and test data need to be defined in the Excel sheet. This saves a lot of time and effort. The framework offers the flexibility to the users to dynamically design the regression suite. Users can dynamically design the automation suite to do any of the testing types—selective testing, comprehensive testing, life-cycle testing, positive testing, negative testing, smoke testing, etc. Agile automation framework can be implemented to achieve low-cost rapid scale automation. It is not necessary for the application development model to be agile to use this framework. This automation framework supports all types of application development models and has special features to easily support agile application development model.

The life-cycle stages of the agile automation framework are so chosen that it best fits into the agile development environment. The automation developers can carry out the task of test automation in parallel with the application development. Automation developers engage themselves in knowledge gathering and component tables (test cases) design while the application under test is getting developed. Once the application is developed, automation developers quickly start developing test scripts by automating one screen at a time. All the functionalities of the screen are coded in the respective script itself. This requires extensive programing skills. This framework is steps ahead of all the existing frameworks.

QUICK TIPS

- ✓ Framework design is an important part of test automation. Framework should be designed in a way that suits the AUT.
- ✓ Framework designed should result in minimum development and maintenance cost and effort.
- ✓ Framework should support maximum reusability and should avoid code redundancy.
- ✓ Any form of hard coding in scripts should be avoided.
- ✓ Framework should support easy and rapid test script maintenance.
- ✓ Framework should support one-point maintenance.

Chapter 5

Test Automation Metrics

Test automation project monitoring and tracking is an important process of test automation life cycle (TALC). Most of us must have worked on or heard about at least one automation project that failed in spite of the best-laid plans. Most of the times, a single reason cannot be the cause of failure. Processes, people, targets, schedules, technical complexities, and budgets can all contribute. Based on such past experiences, I have learnt that to successfully implement a test automation project, it is required that people with right skills are hired; right automation tool is selected, appropriate automation architecture and framework are designed, and clear goals and strategies are defined and implemented. In addition to these steps, procedures and guidelines are put in place to continuously track, measure, and fine-tune automation processes, as needed, to accomplish the defined goals. In this chapter, we will discuss the importance and ways of tracking test automation project progress and effectiveness.

Test automation metrics help gauge the effectiveness and progress of automation project. In case of any issues, proper root-cause analysis is to be done and mitigation tasks laid down. For example, if a functionality in an application has too many high severity defects, then more resources are to be allocated to that module or the delivery date of the product could be deferred. In addition, root-cause analysis is to be done to identify the actual reason for such failures in application. If, suppose, the reason is business–knowledge gap, then proper actions need to be taken to fill this gap. At the same time, mitigation tasks have to be drafted and laid down to prevent reoccurrence of such failures.

TECHNICAL/FUNCTIONAL INTERCHANGES AND WALK-THROUGH

Peer reviews, walk-through and technical/functional interchanges with the client, and the test automation team are some of the techniques to measure the progress and quality of automation deliverables – Peer review and walk-through of automation artifacts will help in identifing test automation issues in advance. Issues such as business–knowledge gap, nonadherence to automation framework and guidelines, and missing deadlines could be identified in time. Interchanges with client help in aligning client expectation with automation deliverables. Reviews and inspections are the most effective ways to prevent miscommunications or communication gaps and meet customer expectations.

Internal Inspections

Internal inspections of test automation deliverables will help to identify gaps in client expectations and test automation deliverables. It helps in implementing best automation practices, reducing efforts and costs, minimizing defect leaks, and improving product quality. It ensures that standard product is delivered to the customer.

Risk Analysis and Risk Mitigation Strategies

Risk analysis procedures allow iterative risk assessment of the automation project and the automation processes. Risk analysis procedures should be 'lightweight' and it should not become an overhead for the project. Risk analysis helps in determining the risk/problem areas within the automation project. Once a risk is identified, appropriate risk mitigation strategies are to be defined and actions are to be taken as per the risk mitigation plan. For example, how to mitigate the risk of budget overrun? There are numerous possible answers: implement advanced frameworks that have low development and maintenance costs; use open source tools, reduce coverage; reduce automation team size, etc. Risk mitigation strategies should be thoughtfully designed, so that it does not impact the automation performance.

CONFIGURATION MANAGEMENT

Configuration management is an important aspect of test automation. Version control of object repository and test scripts is required to execute the test scripts on various development builds and releases. It is important to have version synchronization between test scripts and object repository, so that test execution on application release versions can be carried out smoothly.

A separate test environment needs to be created for test automation. The test environment should be under configuration management.

The use of configuration management tool to baseline the automation project helps in safeguarding the integrity of the automation testing process. All test automation framework components—business components, driver scripts, library files, configuration files, test data files, recovery scenarios, and other automation artifacts—should be under configuration management.

Configuration management tool ensures complete test automation framework with all automation artifacts being well-maintained and are under version control. In test automation, we must have observed that sometimes some of the files are corrupted/deleted due to one reason or other. Such file corruption results in huge loss of work. The destruction of library or configuration files may result in irreparable loss to test automation. Since test scripts are dependent on configuration and library files for successful execution, it is not possible to execute test scripts unless these files are created again with same environment variables and functions as was present in previous files. Moreover, it becomes difficult to identify which environment variables were defined in configuration files. Similarly, it becomes difficult to identify which functions were written in function library and for what purpose. Configuration management tool helps in recovering last updated version of the lost files, thereby, saving test automation from suffering huge losses.

Schedule and Cost Tracking

Automation deliverable schedules and automation cost need to be decided based on past experience and current environment, resource availability, and resource types. Defining automation schedules merely based on marketing-department deadlines is not good for test automation. Factors such as past experiences, estimates obtained from various stakeholders, resource availability, resource skill set, and project environment should be accounted before calculating the automation effort. Additionally, schedule dependencies and expected challenges should also be considered while deciding automation deadlines. During TALC, automation project should be continuously tracked and fine-tuned, if necessary, to meet customer expectations. Test automation schedules and deliverables should be well communicated among the stakeholders.

For example, in situations where test automation schedule is overloaded and tight, the prioritization of deliverables needs to be done. Only those deliverables are to be made part of schedule delivery whose priority is high and can be delivered within schedule. Low-priority deliverables can be planned for future scheduled deliveries. Approvals should be obtained from the client before proceeding ahead with the redefined automation schedules.

Test automation schedules are to be continuously evaluated and monitored. Test automation deliverables and deadlines are to be presented to customer for monitoring during walk-throughs and technical/functional interchanges. Potential schedule risks should be communicated in advance. Risk mitigation strategies to be explored and implemented for the identified risks. Any schedule slips need to be communicated to the client in advance.

ROI analysis needs to be done to keep a check on automation costs. Budget overrun needs to be predicted in advance and appropriate step to be taken.

Actions, Issues, and Defect Tracking

Procedures should be in place to track actions to completion. Appropriate templates must be used to track daily tasks and their progress. For any issues identified, alternative solutions are to be explored, implemented, and documented. Defect life cycle is to be followed for tracking defects.

TEST AUTOMATION METRICS

Metric is a standard measure to access the performance of a particular area. It is a set of quantitative methods to analyze the performance of existing projects, processes, and systems. Metrics can be used to measure and compare past and present performance and predict future performance.

Test automation metrics are the metrics used to measure test automation project and process performance. The metrics not only provide the past and present performance of the automation project but also provide the future trend. Test automation metrics can be divided into four categories.

1. **Coverage:** Coverage measures provide tools to measure the actual scope of test automation and risks associated with it. Scope could be further divided into two types; they are (i) total test scope coverage and (ii) functional test scope coverage. Risk factor is calculated for the test cases that are out of scope of automation.

2. **Progress:** Progress measures provide tools to measure the pace of test script automation, script maintenance, and regression run. Progress measures provide the information such as when the automation of the specified scenarios will be complete and whether the automation team is going to meet the deadlines. Measuring progress of regression run provides information such as when the regression run will be complete, whether the regression run be complete in time, and what will be the expected number of defects into the system. Proper root-cause analysis needs to be done to find the exact cause of problems in automation project.
3. **Quality:** Quality measures provide tools to measure the effectiveness of the test automation project. It includes the tools such as defect leak rate, defect removal efficiency defect trend analysis, etc. defect trend analysis help in predicting quality state of software being tested.
4. **Process:** Process measures provide tools to measure the efficiency of automation processes being followed in the automation project.

NOTES

For the examples in the following sections, we assume business scenarios can comprise of *n* sub-business scenarios; sub-business scenarios can comprise of *n* test scenarios; and test scenarios can contain *n* test cases.

Coverage

Test automation coverage measure tools identify the scope of automation. Coverage can be analyzed in two ways to find the actual scope of automation and the business risk areas; they are (i) percentage automatability (total) and (ii) percentage automatability (functional). Total test coverage measures the total number of test cases that are automated including the test data variation test cases. Functional test coverage measures the functionality of the application automated against the total functionality of the application. Functional test coverage scope is important to analyze how much area of the application is being tested and how much nontested area is prone to business risk. It may happen that automated test suite may be covering huge set of manual test cases that have large variation of test input data. In this case, though total test coverage is high the functional test coverage is low.

Percentage automatability (Total): Percentage automatability (total) is defined as the percentage of the total available test cases that are automatable. It refers to the percentage total area of the application automated.

$$PA_t = ATC/TC * 100,$$

where PA_t = percentage automatability (total), ATC = the total number of automatable test cases, and TC = total test cases.

Percentage automatability (Functional): Percentage automatability (functional) is defined as the percentage functionality coverage of the application under test in test automation. It is the ratio of automatable test scenarios to total available test scenarios. It refers to the percentage total functionality of the application automated.

$$PA_f = ATS/TS * 100,$$

where PA_f = percentage automatability (functional), ATS = the total number of automatable test scenarios, and TS = the total number of test scenarios.

If the application under test comprises of smaller business modules, then percentage automatability (total) and percentage automatability (functional) can be calculated separately for each module

(Table 5.1). Figures 5.1 and 5.2 show the percentage coverage variation of a hypothetical application that has four modules.

Note: If the automation suite is large, then it is available to dynamically form the regression set. A dynamic regression set lays more emphasis on testing the impacted area of the application. A dynamic regression set consists of a static regression suite and a dynamic regression suite. Static regression suite contains automated tests that test the basic and critical areas of the application, while dynamic regression suite is created dynamically before every regression. The automated tests for dynamic regression suite is selected in such a way that it tests the impacted areas of the application. The static regression suite needs to be verified and approved by the respective functional experts or client as applicable. Once a regression set is formed, its total and functional coverage can be calculated to identify the coverage scope.

Table 5.1 Automatability analysis

Business Modules	Test Cases		Percentage Automatability (Total)	Test Scenarios		Percentage Automatability (Functional)
	Total #	Automated #		Total #	Automated #	
A	100	50	50	10	4	40
B	200	80	40	20	10	50
C	50	15	30	20	9	45
D	100	85	85	40	32	80

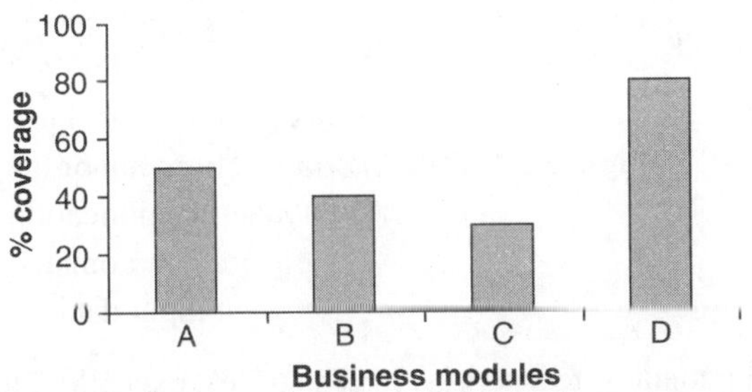

Figure 5.1 *Percentage automatability (total)*

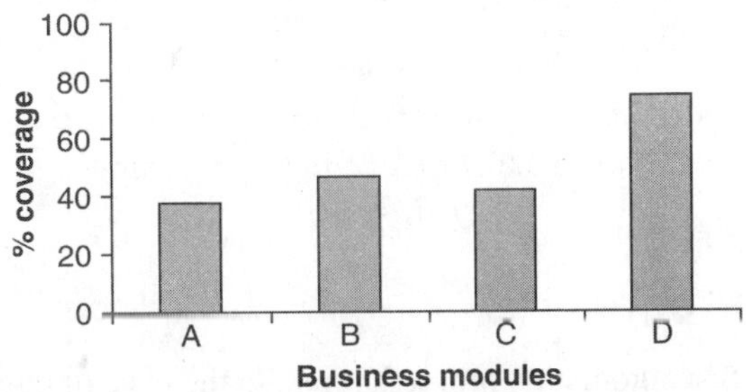

Figure 5.2 *Percentage automatability (functional)*

Test execution coverage (Total): Percentage test execution coverage (total) is defined as the percentage of the total test cases that are executed to total available manual test cases. It refers to the percentage total area of the application covered for test execution.

$$TEC_t = TCE/TC * 100,$$

where TEC_t = percentage test execution coverage (manual), TCE = the number of test cases that are executed, and TC = total test cases available.

Test execution coverage (Functional): Percentage test execution coverage (functional) is defined as the percentage of the total test scenarios that are executed to total available manual test scenarios. It refers to the percentage total functionality of the application covered for test execution.

$$TEC_f = TSE/TS * 100,$$

where TEC_f = percentage test execution coverage (functional), TSE = the number of test scenarios that are executed, and TS = the total number of test scenarios.

Let us suppose there are four modules (M1, M2, M3, and M4) in a business application. Table 5.2 shows analytical way of measuring coverage analysis.

Table 5.2 Coverage analysis

Business Module	Re-gression Suite	Data Creation Suite	Coverage Analysis				% Test Cover-age	% Regression Cover-age
			Automated Test Cases (#)	Static Regression Suite (#)	Manual Test Cases (#)	Manual Regression Test Cases (#)		
M1	✓	k	110	90	187	100	59	90
M2	✓	k	60	50	170	120	35	42
M3	✓	k	267	150	360	200	74	75
M4	✓	✓	100	90	1344	600	7	15

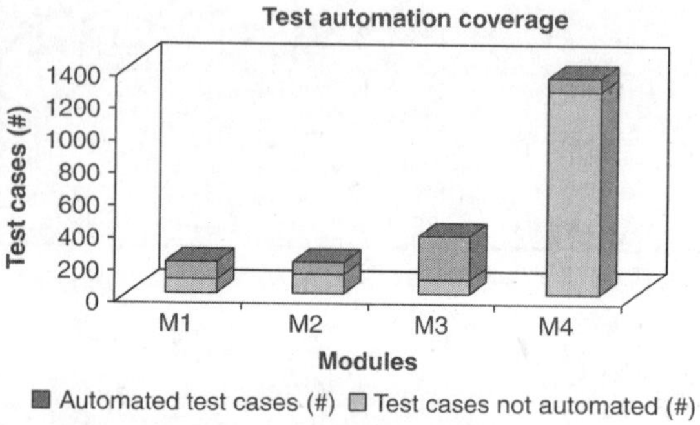

Figure 5.3 *Test automation coverage analysis*

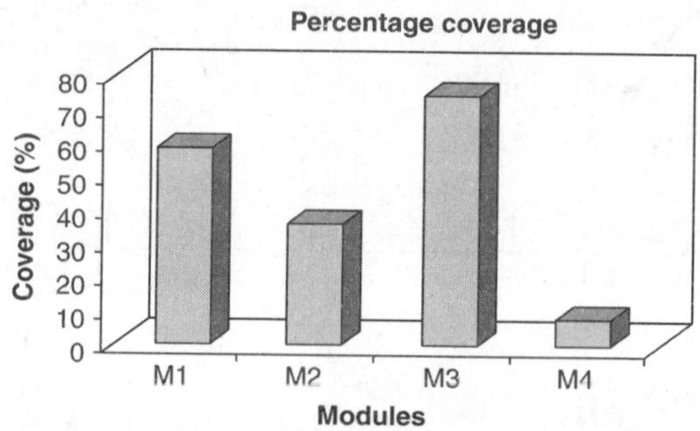

Figure 5.4 *Percentage test automation coverage analysis*

Progress

Test automation progress refers to the pace of development of test scripts. In case of test execution, it refers to the pace of execution of test suite. It is used to decide whether the automation team is going to meet the deadlines or not. Test automation progress metrics help in analyzing and identifying the efficiency of test automation teams. It helps in identifying bottlenecks and addresses them in time. Script development progress can be measured in two ways; they are (i) test automation progress (total) and (ii) test automation progress (functional).

Test automation progress (Total): Test automation progress (total) is defined as the percentage of total test cases automated to total available automatable test cases.

$$TAP_t = TCA/ATC * 100,$$

where TAP_t = percentage test automation progress (total), TCA = the number of test cases that are already automated, and ATC = the total number of test cases that are automatable.

Test automation progress (Functional): Test automation progress (functional) is defined as the percentage of total test scenarios automated to total available automatable test scenarios.

$$TAP_f = TSA/ATS * 100$$

where TAP_f = percentage test automation progress (functional), TSA = the number of test scenarios that are already automated, and ATS = the total number of test scenarios that are automatable.

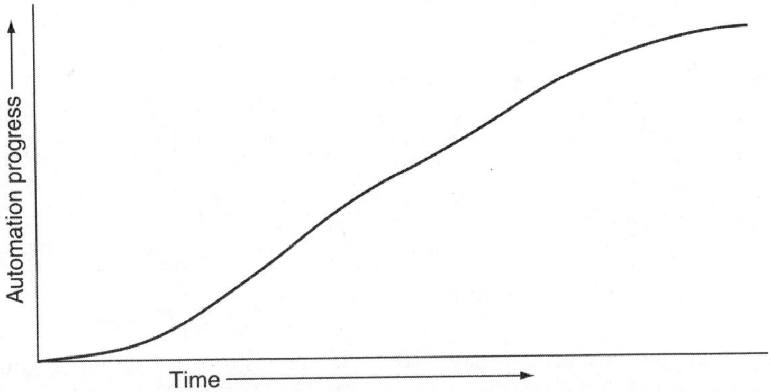

Figure 5.5 *Automation progress analysis*

Test execution progress: Test execution progress is defined as the percentage of the total test cases successfully executed to the total number of test cases present in test suite for execution.

$$TEP = TTE/TTS * 100,$$

where TEP = the percentage of test execution progress, TTE = the total number of test cases successfully executed, and TTS = the total number of test cases in test suite.

Quality

Test automation quality metrics measures the quality of the AUT. Defect density, defect trend analysis, and defect removal efficiency are few metrics used for measuring software quality.

Defect density: Defect density metric is used to find the areas/functionalities of software products that have higher concentration of defects. More the number of defects in a particular business functionality of business application is, higher would be the defect density. Business areas with higher defect density demand more retesting effort; therefore, they are perfect choices for test automation. Defect density helps in identifying the business risk areas, so that suitable mitigation plans can be drafted. Defect density graph helps in focusing in right areas of business application that needs attention. If a business application comprises of different business modules, then defect density of each module can be found and compared.

$$DD = DC/SS,$$

where DD = the defect density of a particular module, DC = the number of defects found in a particular module, and SS = the size of the particular module (software entity).

While interpreting defect density, defect severity should also be kept in mind. Business areas with defect density of 0.3 but comprising of high severity defects need more attention than business area with defect density 0.4 comprising of low severity defects.

Suppose there are four modules M1, M2, M3, and M4. Let us assume defects found in these modules that are depicted in Figure 5.6.

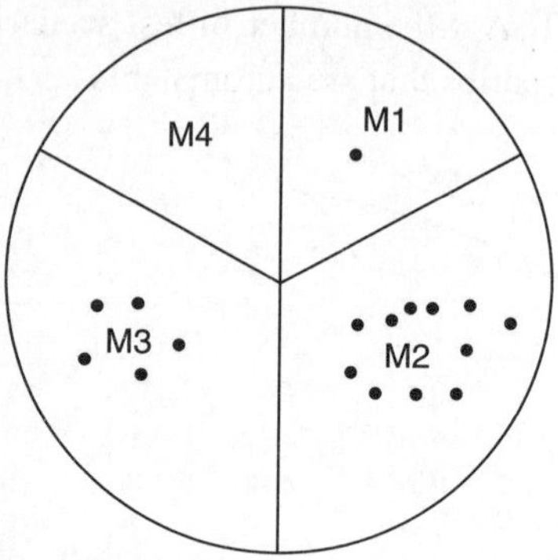

Module	M1	M2	M3	M4
Defect Count	1	10	5	0
Software Relative Size	1	2	2	1
Defect Density	1	5	2.5	0
Defect Area	17%	33%	33%	17%

Figure 5.6 *Defect density*

From Figure 5.6, it can be interpreted that module M2 needs more attention because of high defect density. In addition, modules M2 and M3 are more prone to defects. Therefore, 66% of the software area is prone to defects. Now, it may happen that severity of defects in module M3 is higher than that of defects of module M2. This will demand a change from our previous decision of giving more focus to module M2. Since module M3 defects are of high severity than that of module M2, the first focus would be to stabilize module M3. Table 5.3 analyzes the defect density of various modules based on defect severity.

Table 5.3 Calculating defect density for various application modules

Module	M1			M2			M3			M4		
Defect Severity	Low	Medium	High	Low	Medium	High	Low	Medium	High	Low	Medium	High
Defect Count	0	1	0	8	2	0	0	0	5	0	0	0
Software Relative Size	1			2			2			1		
Defect Density	0	1	0	4	1	0	0	0	2.5	0	0	0

Average defect catching rate: Average defect catching rate is defined as the average number of defects found in each regression cycle (Figure 5.7). It is the ratio of total number of defects found in *n* regression cycles to number (*n*) of regression cycles.

$$ADCR = TDF(n)/n,$$

where ADCR = average defect catching rate, TDF(n) = total defects found in n regression cycles, and n = the number of regression cycles.

Defect leak rate: Defect leak rate is defined as the ratio of number of defects leaked in production environment to the total number of regression defects found in the system. Defect leak rate helps in determining the effectiveness of the automation regression suite. It helps in identifying the gaps in the automation test suite. The reasons for the defect leak need to be identified. If certain scenarios are not part of regression suite, then a more effective regression suite should be formed. On the other hand, if

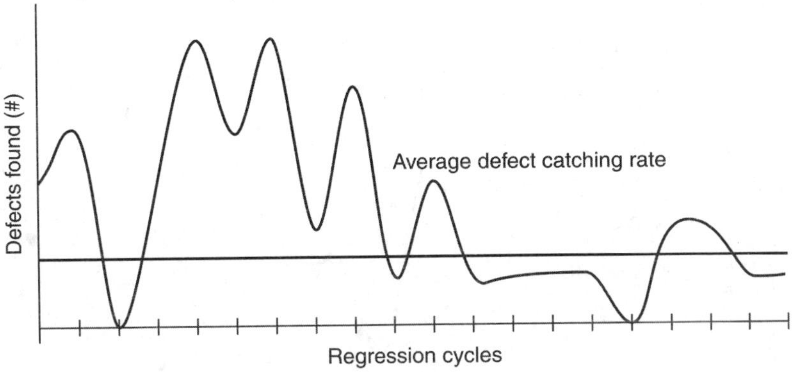

Figure 5.7 *Average defect catching rate*

defect leak occurred because of scenarios missing from testy automation, then those scenarios need to be identified and automated, if possible. Proper risk analysis should be done and risk mitigation steps should be prepared, in case, test scenarios are not automatable.

$$DLR = NDD/(NDR + NDD),$$

where DLR = defect leak rate, NDR = the number of defect found in regression (test automation), and NDD = the number of defect found after delivery.

Defect removal efficiency: Defect removal efficiency is defined as the ratio of defects found through test automation during regression run to the total defects found in application. It is used to measure the effectiveness of regression suite. Higher the defect removal efficiency is, more effective is the regression suite. If defect removal efficiency is low, then defect leak rate can be high and vice versa. It is always advisable to keep the regression suite dynamic to make it more effective. A dynamic regression suite is one which comprises of a static test suite and dynamic test suite. Static test suite comprises of test cases that tests basic and critical functionalities of the application. While dynamic test suite comprises of test cases that test the local area of defect fix. Therefore, depending on defect types (impacting business areas) from one regression to another, the test cases in dynamic suite will also vary.

$$DRR = NDR/(NDR + NDD),$$

where DRR = defect removal efficiency, NDR = the number of defect found in regression (test automation), and NDD = the number of defect found after delivery.

Defect trend analysis: Defect trend analysis helps in determining the trend of defects found over time. Defect trend analysis helps in analyzing and predicting the application stability. Is the defect trend improving with testing phase phasing out or is the defect trend static or is it worsening? In other words, defect trend analysis shows the health of the application. Defect trend analysis can be calculated over defined intervals of time. Figure 5.8 shows defects found in the application in each regression cycle. Figure 5.9 shows the number of defects found in the application in various months. We observe that using Figure 5.1, it is difficult to predict whether the application is stabilizing or not, as number of defects found keep on varying. If we observe Figure 5.9, it gives a clear picture of defect trend. It helps to determine and predict health of the application. Therefore, Figure 5.9, can be used for defect trend analysis. This is the simplest way for analyzing defect trend.

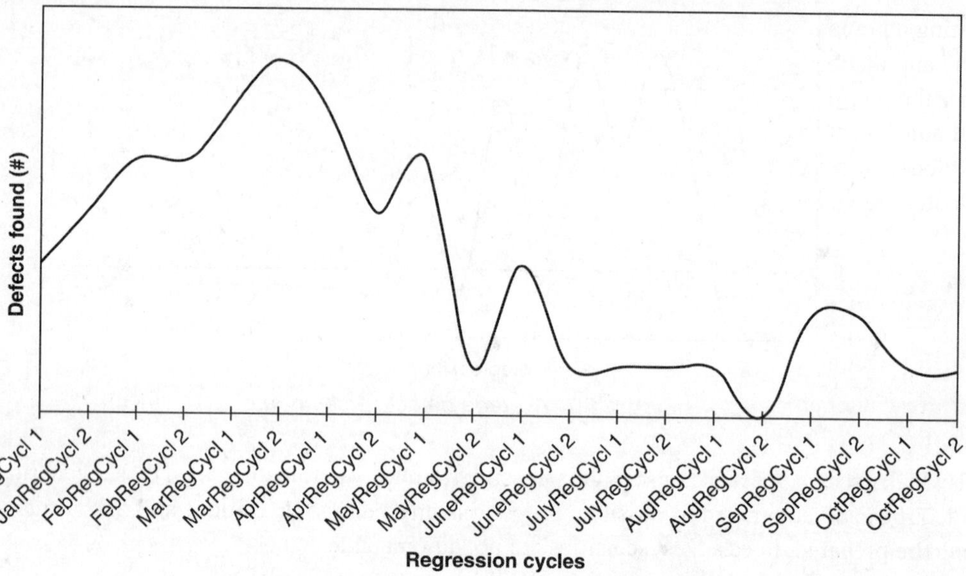

Figure 5.8 *Defects found per regression cycle*

Process

Process metrics are quantitative measures that enable to gain insight into the efficacy of the software process. Basic quality and productivity data are collected. These data are then analyzed, compared against past averages, and assessed to determine whether quality and productivity improvements have occurred. Metrics are also used to pinpoint problem areas so that remedies can be developed and the software process can be improved. The problem areas in the existing automation process can also be identified through inspections, walkthroughs or open-table discussions. The bottlenecks of the

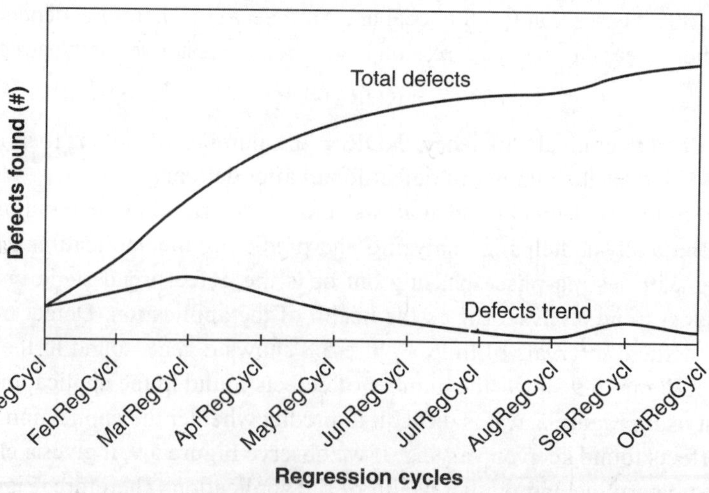

Figure 5.9 *Defect trend*

existing automation process can be replaced with a more efficient automation process. For example, if the automation team spends a lot of time say 3hrs for generating reports of regression runs; then either the report generation process be automated or it be made simple. Another classic example can be if automation team loses a lot of time because of the unavailability of the functional experts, then a protocol be defined that the functional experts are available for a time enough to at least kick-start the automation development.

QUICK TIPS

✓ It is essential to continuously monitor the health of the test automation project.

✓ Test automation metrics help in proving the contributions and importance of the test automation in reducing the cost to test automation.

✓ Metrics based on the total manual test cases do not reflect the true test automation coverage. This is because a part of the application can have more test cases based on test data variations. Metrics based on total functionality of the application automated to be calculated to find the total business functionality covered in test automation.

✓ Total business functionality covered helps in analyzing the business gap and risk areas that are not covered in test automation.

✓ Defect trend analysis helps in analyzing the health of the software application.

PRACTICAL QUESTIONS

1. What is the use of test automation metric?
2. How to do configuration management in test automation?
3. How schedule and cost tracking of a test automation project are done?
4. What are the various categories of test automation metrics?
5. A software application project has lot of manual test cases on test data variations. Which metric is to be used to find the actual business functionality coverage of the application?
6. Suppose that a client wants to know the actual productivity of the test automation team in the application development cycle. Which test automation metric is to be used for the same?
7. Which test automation metric is to be used to calculate the total savings achieved because of the test automation project?
8. A software application has an irregular pattern of defects in the various areas of the application. Which metric is to be used to identify the business area that needs more aggressive automation testing?
9. The client wants to know the time required to automate 30% business functionality of the application. Which test automation metric is to be used for the same?
10. Which test automation metric is to be used to predict the future health of the software application?

Chapter 6

Test Automation Process

The software industry, today, faces the challenge of developing and delivering quality software products within an ever-shrinking schedule and with minimal resources. This results in the demand to test major part of the software in the minimum time to ensure both quality and delivery deadline. To accomplish this goal, organizations are turning to automated testing. Though automation testing sounds simple with an understanding that test automation is all about record and playback, the experience shows that when it comes to success or failure of an automation project, the lack of standardized test automation processes and record/playback hypothesis are among the most common reasons for failure of an automation project. Automation project is a development project that has its own development cycle. Test automation life cycle (TALC) is a conceptual model used to implement, execute, and maintain an automation project (Figure 6.1). In this chapter, we will discuss the various automation processes within TALC that can make an automation project a success (Figure 6.2).

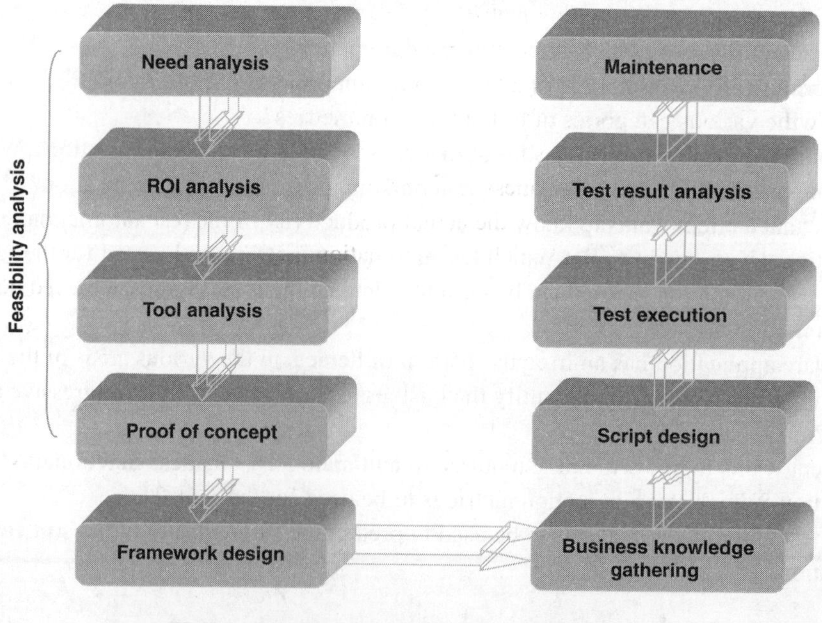

Figure 6.1 *Test automation life cycle (TALC)*

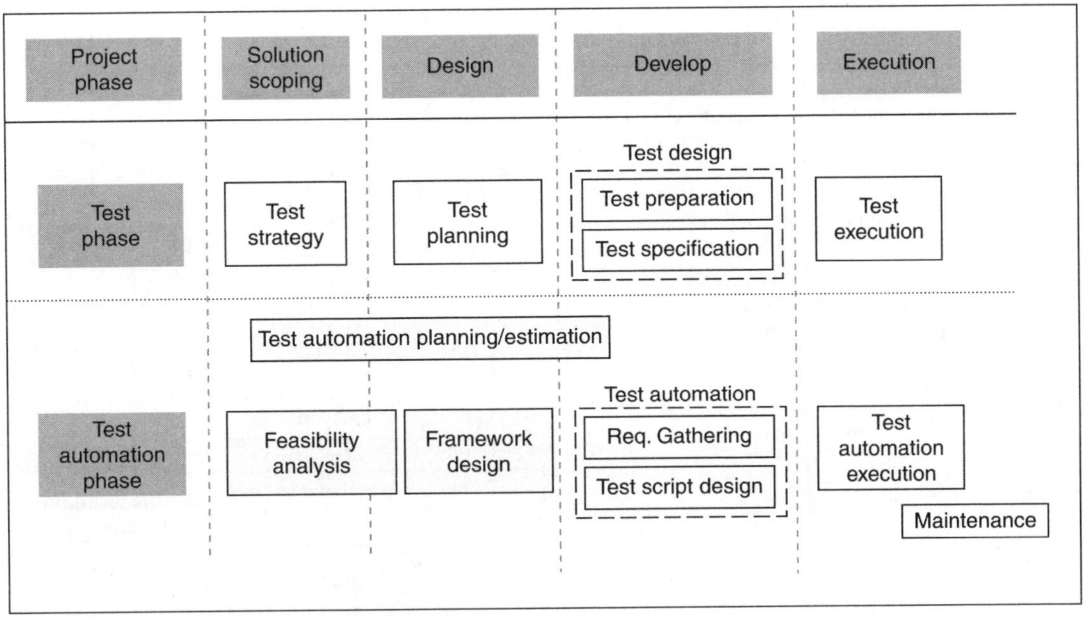

Figure 6.2 *Test automation process*

NEED ANALYSIS PROCESS FLOW

The decision to automate test is the first phase of TALC. This phase covers the entire process that goes into the decision to start an automation project. During this phase, it is extremely important to list down the expectations from the automation project, existing manual testing problems, automation testing benefits and limitations, etc. A reality checklist should be prepared, which should give a clear picture of what is expected from the test automation and what it can deliver. The misconceptions and over expectations from test automation need to be filtered out at this stage itself. Finally, a document needs to be prepared, which should clearly specify the need analysis of an automation project and expectations from the same. Figure 6.3 shows the process flow diagram of the need analysis of an automation project.

Objective

- Starting an automation project
- Defining the scope of automation

ETVX Model

Entry Criteria	• Strategic information (testing lifespan, upcoming programs/projects, testing requirements, management expectations, etc.) is available
Tasks	• Need analysis of test automation
Verification and Validation	• Expectations properly mapped to test automation deliverables • Expectations that cannot be met by test automation are filtered out
Exit Criteria	• Need analysis document is approved • Automation scope is approved

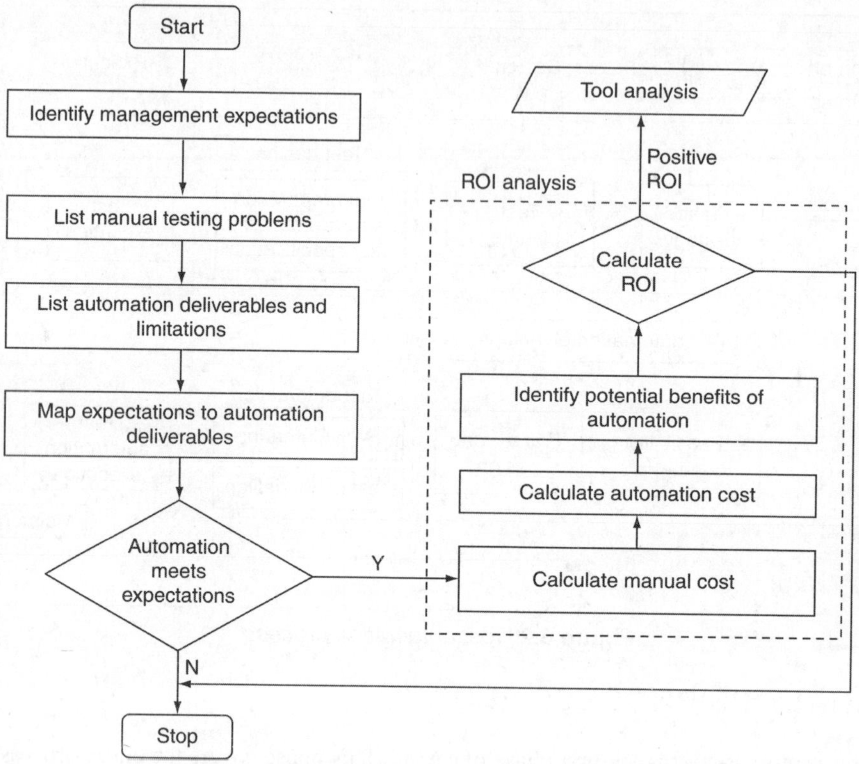

Figure 6.3 *Need analysis and ROI calculation process*

ROI ANALYSIS PROCESS FLOW

Return on Investment (ROI) is a major factor that decides the implementation of an automation project. Simple calculation based on the effort required to automate is not always sufficient. Factors impacting test automation, such as business functionality capture cost, maintenance cost, test script execution cost, test result analysis cost, software and hardware costs, and training cost need to be accounted while calculating total automation effort and cost. Figure 6.3 shows the process flow diagram of ROI analysis.

Test automation costs can also be divided into fixed and recurring costs. Fixed costs are one-time costs such as purchase of hardware/software. Recurring costs are those costs that a project has to bear throughout TALC such as human resource cost, script execution cost, and automation project maintenance cost. Recurring costs can vary from time to time such as variation in team size.

Fixed Automation Costs	Recurring/Variable Automation Costs
• Hardware • Testware software licenses • Testware software support • Automation environment design and implementation	• Test case design for automation • Test maintenance • Test case execution

Fixed Automation Costs	Recurring/Variable Automation Costs
• Automation environment maintenance • Scripting tools • Tool and environment licenses • Tool training • Tool introduction and ramp up	• Test results analysis • Defect reporting • Test results reporting • Test execution savings • Business knowledge capture cost

Total Common Development/Maintenance Cost (TCC)

It refers to the costs that are common to both manual and test automations, viz., manual test case creation.

$$TCC = CT_d$$

NOTES: Manual test case creation effort is accounted as common cost because for the traditional automation frameworks, test cases need to be ready for test automation. For agile automation framework, this cost can be ruled out.

Total Manual Cost (TMC)

It refers to the total cost involved for quality assurance in the Software Development Life Cycle (SDLC) cycle in the absence of the test automation project. These costs are in addition to the total common costs.

$$TMC = (MT_m * MN_1 + MT_e * MN_2) * N + P(TH) + P(TS)$$

where $MN_2 = MN_1 + n$ and $MN_2 > MN_1$; MT_m = average time to maintain a test case; MT_e = average time to execute a test case; MN_1 = the number of test cases to be maintained; MN_2 = the number of test cases to be executed; n = the number of test cases in static regression suite; N = the number of regression cycles; P(TH) = the price of test hardware; and P(TS) = the price of test software.

Total Automation Cost (TAC)

It refers to the total automation cost involved in implementing an automation project.

$$TAC = AT_{ias} + AT_b + AT_d + (AT_m * AN_1) + (AT_e * AN_2) + (AT_a) + P(AH) + P(AS)$$

where $AN_2 = AN_1 + n$ and $AN_2 > AN_1$; AT_{ias} = Time to initial automation setup (framework design); AT_b = time to capture business functionality to automate; AT_d = time to develop test scripts; AT_m = average time to maintain a test script; AT_e = average time to execute test scripts; AT_a = time to analyze test results; AN_1 = the number of test scripts to be maintained; AN_2 = the number of test cases to be executed; n = the number of test cases in static regression suite; N = the number of regression cycles; P(AH) = the price of automation hardware; and P(AS) = the price of automation software.

Return on Investment

$$ROI = (TMC - TAC)/TAC$$

Factors such as deadline constraints, organization commitments, delivery time constraints, and quality constraints should also be taken into account while calculating ROI. Business factors such as benefits gained by reducing time to delivery to the market by using test automation need also be accounted. Subjective analysis of estimated loss to the project for not implementing test automation should also be done.

Objective

- Finding ROI of the automation project
- Calculating estimated loss to project if test automation is not implemented

ETVX Model

Entry Criteria	• Need analysis of test automation is complete • Testing life span is known • Testing cycles and effort documents are available • Automation cost (hardware, software, scripting, maintenance, etc.) documents are available • Automation effort calculation formula is known
Tasks	• Calculate regression testing and data creation effort • Calculate test automation development and execution effort • Calculate profits gained/losses incurred for implementing test automation
Verification and Validation	• Formula of calculating manual testing effort is apt • Formula of calculating test automation effort is apt • External factors such as delivery deadlines, organization's reputation, and benefits gained from reducing time to delivery to the market have been accounted for calculating ROI
Exit Criteria	• ROI analysis is approved

TOOL ANALYSIS PROCESS FLOW

The next phase is tool analysis. Tool analysis is done to select the automation tool that best suits the testing as well as application under test (AUT) requirements. It includes steps and procedures that investigate the various tool features and map them to the AUT and testing requirements. In tool analysis phase, the process is to first identify a set of tools available in the market. The next step is to list down AUT and testing requirements. Finally, automation tool features are mapped to various requirements and a rank is assigned to them. It is obvious that no tool may satisfy all the requirements, so the tool that meets most of the evaluation criteria needs to be selected after discussion with stakeholders. Testing and application requirements can be split into mandatory and desirable requirements. The features of the automation tool can be mapped to these requirements to find the tool that best supports the project requirements. Appendix E provides a tool analysis chart that can be used to select the best-suited automation tool. Figure 6.4 shows the process flow diagram of Tool Analysis.

Objective

- Selecting best-fit tool for automation

ETVX Model

Entry Criteria	• ROI analysis is complete • List of test automation tools is available • Testing requirements are known • AUT requirements (coding language, architecture model, objects, screens, add-ins, etc.) are known • Automation tool features (ease of use, supported environments, support, etc.) documents are available • Automation tools license cost is known
Tasks	• Map AUT requirements to tool features • Map project/testing requirements to tool deliverables • Compare tool features and award ratings
Verification and Validation	• Automation tool documents are standard documents authorized by tool vendors • Rank allocation to tool features is correct
Exit Criteria	• Rank-wise list of automation tools that can be used for test automation • Tool analysis is approved

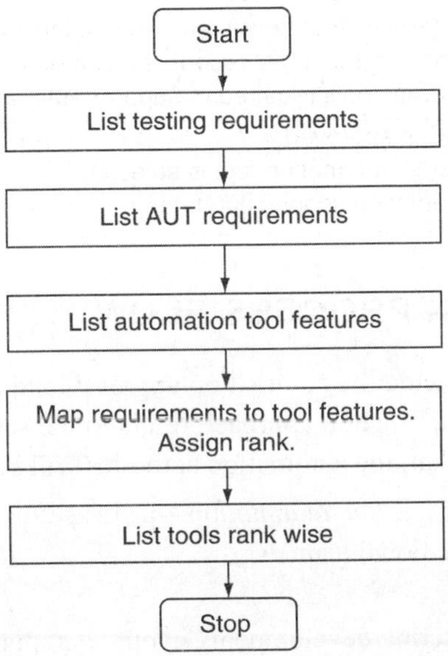

Figure 6.4 *Flow diagram of tool analysis*

PROOF OF CONCEPT

Proof of Concept (POC) is done to practically test the automation tool against the project requirements. It is done to find out whether the selected tool supports the application GUI objects or not, the average cost of developing scripts, the gaps in technical competencies of resources, etc. If the selected tool fails to meet the project requirements, then POC on next best-suited tool needs to be done. Test scenarios for POC should be selected in a way that they test most of the application objects and few common features of software product. The test scenarios should give the confidence that automation with the selected tool will be a success. It is sufficient to use evaluation version of automation tools for POC.

Objective

- Selecting best-fit tool for automation
- Calculating average cost of developing and maintaining scripts

ETVX Model

Entry Criteria	• Rank list of automation tools and AUT are available • Test automation tools and AUT are available • Test scenarios/cases available for automation
Tasks	• Select best-fit automation tool • Calculate average cost of developing and maintaining scripts • Identify competency gaps, if any • Identify the need of external tools, if any • Document tool issues and its workaround solutions • Define automation scope
Verification and Validation	• Selected tool evaluation criteria • Automation scope document • Average cost of developing and maintaining scripts • Checklist (trainings, resources, competencies, etc.) • External tools required to support automation
Exit Criteria	• POC is approved • Best-fit automation tool is selected • Automation scope is updated

FRAMEWORK DESIGN PROCESS FLOW

Automation architects need to decide the automation approach and automation framework after discussion with the stakeholders. Automation approach refers to the set of assumptions, concepts, standards, and guidelines; based on that, the automation activities will be carried out. It includes:

- *Basis of selection of test cases for automation*—use case diagrams, test plan documents, or simple interaction with functional team.
- Team structure.
- *Automation documents*—script development layout, automation standards and guidelines, training documents, user manuals layout, etc.
- Automation project maintenance approach, standards and guidelines, etc.

A test automation framework is a hierarchical directory that encapsulates shared resources, such as dynamic shared library, image files, scripts, drivers, object repositories, localized strings, header files, and reference documentation in a single package. Test automation framework needs to be designed in a way that best suits the AUT and project requirements. The framework design should support easy configuration of test settings, dynamic variable initialization, selective and exhaustive test scenario executions, unattended test script execution, easy-to-understand test result format, etc. Moreover, the framework should support easy packaging and installation of automation project. Figure 6.5 shows the process flow diagram of Framework Design.

Objective

- Initiating automation setup
- Deciding automation approach

ETVX Model

Entry Criteria	• Feasibility analysis is approved • Project/testing requirement documents are ready • Test automation deliverable documents are ready
Tasks	• Initial automation setup • Decide automation approach • Design best-suited framework • Configure automation tool as per AUT requirements
Verification and Validation	• Approach to select scenarios for automation • Framework design, structure, and layout • Automation documents—induction manual, design documents, training manuals, object standards, initial tool configuration parameters, etc. • Team structure • Automation task tracker
Exit Criteria	• Automation approach and framework approved • Test automation documents approved • Team size finalized

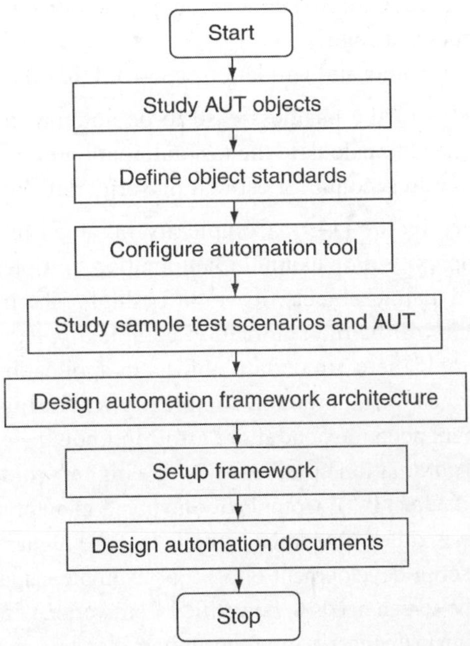

Figure 6.5 *Flow diagram of framework design*

BUSINESS KNOWLEDGE GATHERING PROCESS FLOW

Script development process starts with the business knowledge transition phase. Test managers/functional team first need to identify the business scenarios that needs to be automated. Automation developers, then, need to gather the business knowledge of the business case identified for automation. Automation developers can gather business knowledge from use case diagrams, test plan documents, or by directly interacting with the functional team depending on the feasibility and the automation approach decided. Functional team always has lot to share on the knowledge of the business case. It is the responsibility of the test automation developer to gather only those information and data that is specific to automation. Automation developer needs to extract the information that is sufficient to automate and maintain the business case and not the complete business knowledge, as it is time consuming and increases the cost and time of script development. For example, suppose after filling of form, form data is updated in various tables and a message appears on screen. If GUI validation is sufficient, then automation developer need not gather information about various fields of table where data is updated. Figure 6.6 shows the process flow diagram of Business Knowledge Gathering.

Listed below are few points that need to be kept in mind while gathering business knowledge for automation:

- Number of test scenarios.
- Number of test cases and their variations.
- Test input, expected output data, and expected test result.
- Screen flow.
- Business logic flow and stability—is business logic going to be changed?
- Objects involved, object recognition, static and dynamic objects, object stability—are object properties under continuous change?
- Validation points or checkpoints and validation type—GUI or database?

  Once business knowledge of the business case to be automated is sufficiently gathered, test automation developers need to calculate the test automation effort for the same. The following parameters can be taken into account for estimating script development effort:

- **Automation complexity factor (1–9):** Complexity involved in automating AUT objects is called automation complexity. For example, automation complexity for static AUT objects will be low, while for dynamic objects, it would be high. The more the dynamic objects in application is, the higher will be the automation complexity, and hence the more will be the automation effort. Again, if there are certain objects in application, which are not recognized by the automation tool, then the automation complexity will be high. This is for the reason that the automation developers need to spend more effort in finding a work-around solution for the same. The higher is the automation complexity is, the higher would be the factor value.
- **Functional complexity factor (1–9):** Complexity involved in automating the business case, business flow, or screen flow is called functional complexity. The higher the functional complexity is, the more would be the script development effort. For example, suppose that after execution of a test case, the results on the screen needs to be verified from various fields of around 10 tables in the database. SQL query design in this case is time consuming, thereby increasing the development effort.

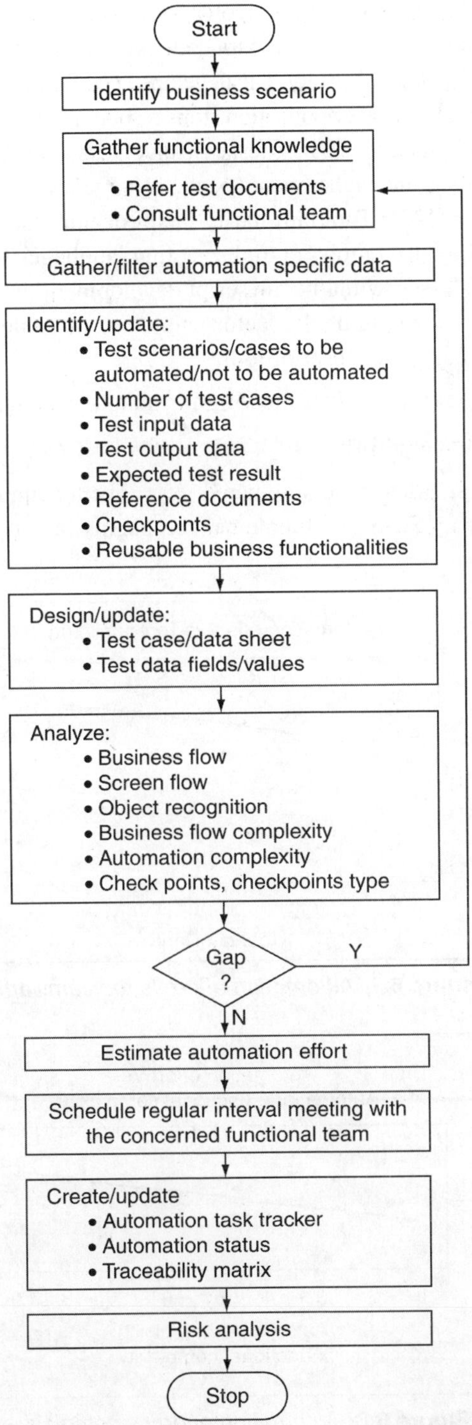

Figure 6.6 *Flow diagram of business knowledge gathering*

Consider again a scenario where a test case involves navigating through more than 10 screens. In this case, automation developers need to write extra code (sync points and checkpoints) on each screen to ensure that script executes successfully. The developed code should work fine even in case of high application response time or in case application stops responding while navigating. Functional complexity can also be high in situations where test case involves working with external files. The higher the functional complexity is, the higher would be the factor value.

- **Tool familiarity factor (1–5):** Tool familiarity factor decides how familiar the automation developer is with the automation tool and tool scripting language. The more the familiarity with the tool features is, the lesser would be the script development time. The greater the familiarity with the tool is, the lower would be the factor value. Factor value of 1 implies tool expert and factor value 5 implies basic level user of tool.

Test automation developers can use the following formula to calculate script development effort:

$$\text{Script development effort} = [0.1 * N_t * N_{ts}] * [1 + (a + f)/30 + \text{Log}_{10}(t)] \text{ Hrs}$$

where N_t = the number of test cases to be automated; N_{ts} = average number of test steps in each test case; a = automation complexity factor; f = functional complexity factor; and t = tool familiarity factor.

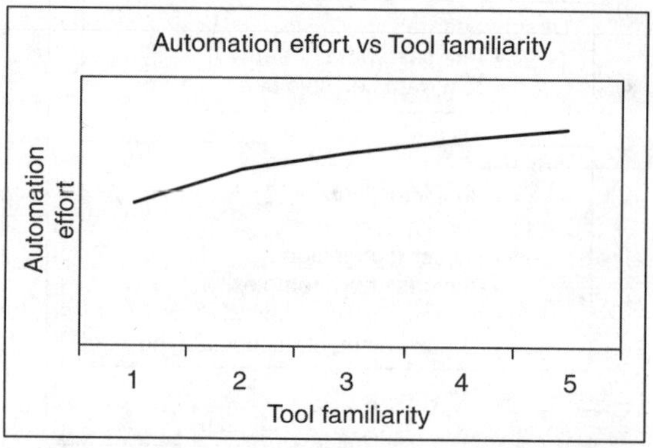

Figure 6.7 *Automation effort vs tool familiarity*

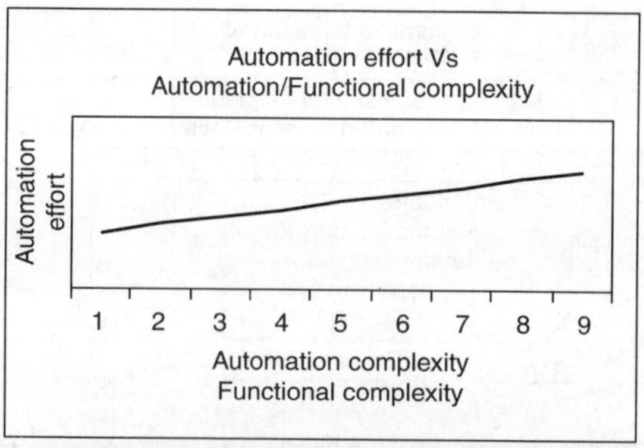

Figure 6.8 *Automation effort vs complexity*

In the above formula,

- Script development effort includes both script development and script debugging efforts.
- Script development effort includes the effort involved in developing business components and driver scripts.
- One-test step refers to a single action on an object. For example, click on a button.

Once business knowledge gathering is complete, automation developers should prepare a list of 'what to automate' and 'what not to automate'. Specific reasons for not automating a particular business case needs to be documented. Moreover, *risk analysis* should be done with the help of functional team. Risk analysis should be able to expose the risk on business for not automating particular business cases. The risk analysis needs to be shared with the higher management and functional team, so that appropriate action can be taken on it.

Objective

- Identifying 'what to automate' and 'how to automate'
- Calculating the estimation of test script development effort

ETVX Model

Entry Criteria	• Test documents are ready • Initial automation setup is done • Test automation environment is ready • Test documents—requirement documents, test plans, use cases, etc.
Tasks	• Identify 'what to automate' and 'how to automate' • Knowledge transition of business scenario to be automated • Estimate script development effort
Verification and Validation	• Selection criteria for automation • Scope of knowledge transition • Risk analysis documents • Traceability matrix
Exit Criteria	• Scenarios selected for automation approved • Script development effort approved

SCRIPT DESIGN PROCESS FLOW

After gathering requirements, automation developer needs to decide the components to be automated—business components, test scripts, test data sheet, functions, validation points, type of checkpoints, environment variables, recovery scenario, etc. Business scenario needs to be split into smaller reusable business functionalities that can be integrated sequentially later to implement various test cases of the business case. These reusable business functionalities are called as business components. Automation developers need also to design a layout of how the automated components are to be integrated to implement the business case. Thereafter, code can be written to automate the components. Scripts should be coded in a way that no user intervention is required during script execution. If any business knowledge gap is found during script development, then automation developers should interact with the concerned functional team to know the exact business case. Stress should be laid that automation developers fills all his business knowledge gaps during the regular interval meetings (decided during requirement gathering phase) with the concerned functional team. Figure 6.9 shows the process flow diagram of Script Design.

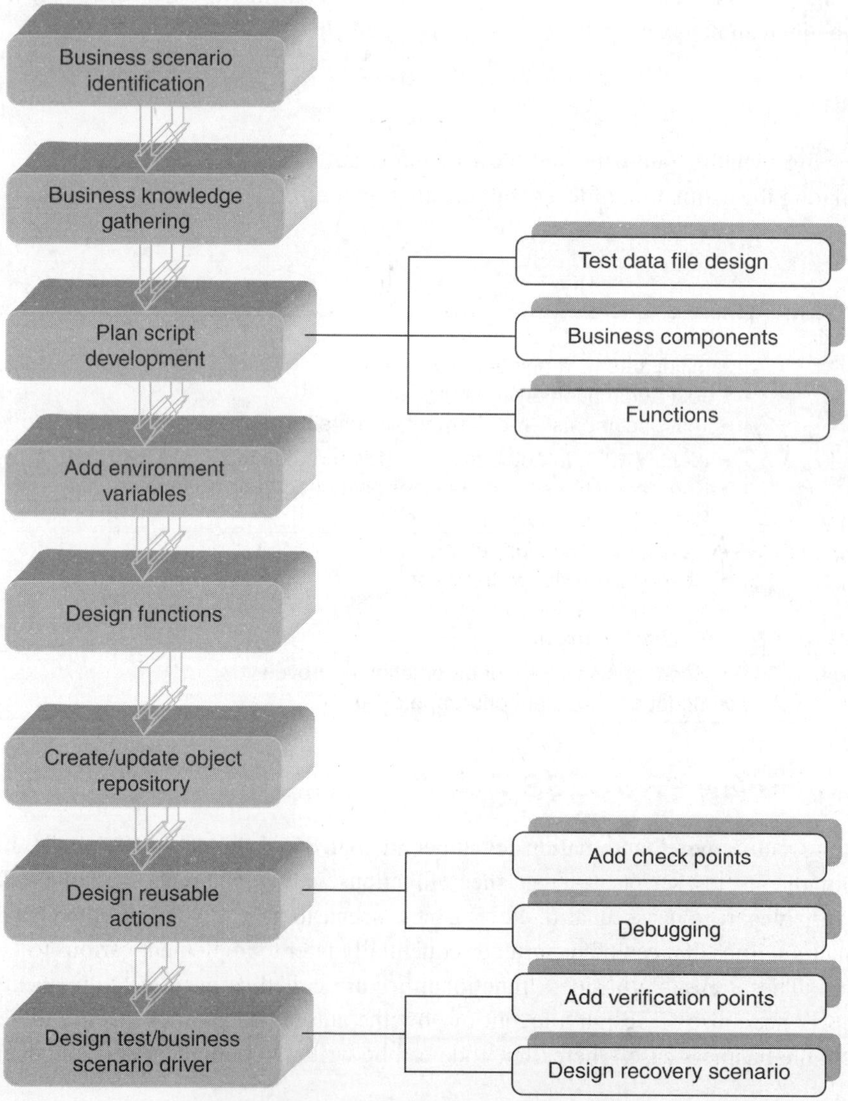

Figure 6.9 *Flow diagram of script design*

Objective

Automating business cases

ETVX Model

Entry Criteria	• Test scenarios/cases for automation identified • Business knowledge gathered with no identified gap
Task	• Design test scripts • Design user manual documents
Verification and Validation	• Automated scripts • Scripts adhere to selected automation approach and framework • Updated traceability matrix
Exit Criteria	• Automated test scripts are approved

SCRIPT EXECUTION PROCESS FLOW

During test execution phase, automated test scripts are executed as per the project requirements. To ease the test execution process, *master driver script* should be designed to have a single-point execution

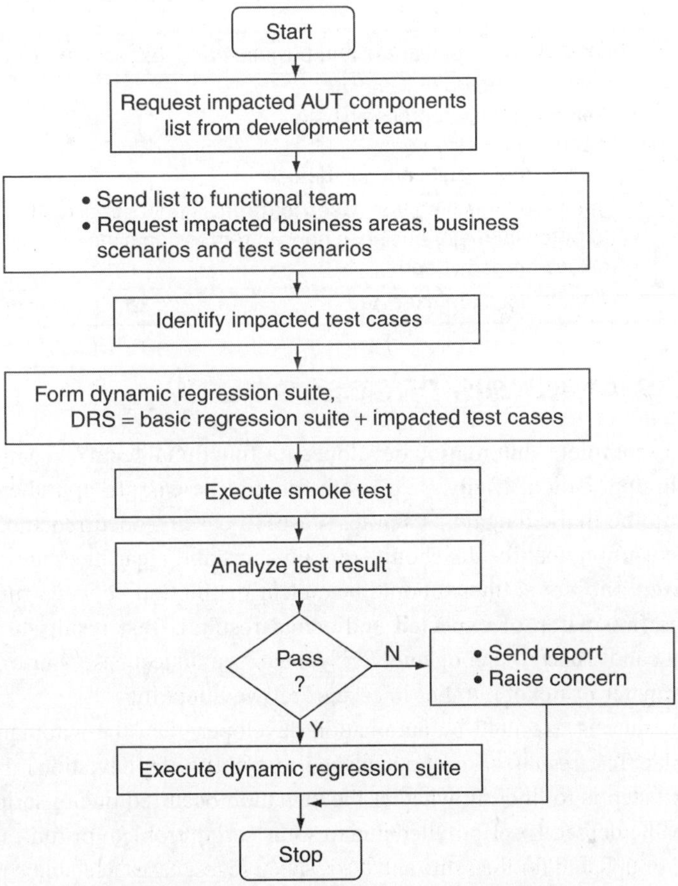

Figure 6.10 *Flow diagram of script execution*

control. A *test suite* comprising of test cases to be executed is formed and put to execution. Test cases should be robust enough to execute successfully in an unattended mode. In case, test suite size is large, a smaller but effective regression suite is to be formed. The basic *regression suite* should have test cases that test both the basic and critical functionalities of the business application. Before executing the test suite, impact analysis should be done to identify the impacted business areas. On the basis of impacted business areas, impacted business scenarios and test scenarios need to be identified. Once impacted test scenarios have been identified, automation developers need to identify the test cases for regression. A dynamic regression suite comprising of these test cases and basic regression suite need to be formed and executed. In addition to regression suite, a small *smoke test* suite should also be created. The smoke test suite should comprise of test cases, which tests whether the application is ready enough to be tested or not. Automation–regression suite should be put to run only if smoke test passes. Figure 6.10 shows the process flow diagram of Script Execution.

Objective

- Executing regression run in unattended mode

ETVX Model

Entry Criteria	• Impacted business areas and business and test scenarios are known
Tasks	• Identify impacted test cases • Create dynamic regression suite • Execute regression run • Analyze test results and log defects
Verification and Validation	• Criteria for selecting test cases for regression testing is apt • No potential major business gaps in regression suite • Test coverage is good
Exit Criteria	• All test cases are executed

TEST RESULTS ANALYSIS PROCESS FLOW

Once test execution is complete, automation developers or functional team can analyze the test results to find out defects in application, if any. Test results should be easy to apprehend and understand. Pass–fail status should be marked against each test case. In case of occurrence of any deviations or error during script execution, test results should contain short and clear messages that points exactly toward the error reason. Moreover, there should be a clear distinction between run-time script errors and result deviations (mismatch of expected and actual results). Test result should also contain a unique identifier that can be used to debug and verify the executed test case. For example, transaction id in case of funds transfer or ticket number in case of railway booking.

In case regression suite is executed by automation developer, then the automation developer may analyze the test results. Test results are to be analyzed to identify the deviations that occurred during script execution. Next step is to find out whether the deviation occurred due to script problem (or run-time issue) or a probable defect. If script failed due to some script problem or run-time issue, test script needs to be corrected or updated for the same and the respective test cases need to be re-run. If deviations seem to be probable defect in application, then the automation developer should request the concerned functional team for further analysis and defect logging. If functional team suggests that deviations are not defects, then test scripts need to be identified for potential business functionality gap and corrected for the same. The corrected or updated test scripts need to be re-run. However, if functional team confirms deviations to be defects, then defects needs to be logged in defect tracker by functional team. Automation team should have access to defect tracker to track defects. Finally, a test-run report needs to be prepared by the automation lead and shared with the concerned team members and higher management. The purpose of preventing automation team from logging defects is because of the fact that automation developers being more of technical experts, generally, cannot provide the application developers exact reason of failure, which is needed to fix the defect. Automation developers know the exact deviation that occurred but they cannot analyze the exact point/cause of failure from business viewpoint. For example, suppose that because of some user-level setup defect issue, a user is not able to transfer funds. An automation developer can explain the deviation that funds transfer is not taking place but he or she cannot explain the reason of the same. Moreover, the point of defect is in setup screen and not on the funds transfer screen. It is the functional team, who has better functional understanding of the application, can analyze and verify the same. Conveying of half or wrong information can result in unnecessary delays in defect fix. Moreover, functional impact analysis of the defect fix cannot be done by the automation developer. Therefore, if possible, it is better to avoid it. Figure 6.11 shows the process flow diagram of Test Results Analysis.

Test automation lead needs to prepare a test-run report, once test-run result analysis is over. Test-run report summarizes the test-run results. The test-run report should be sent to the concerned stakeholders. Test automation report can consist of two parts:

1. test results and
2. test result analysis.

Test Results

Test results contain the actual results of test run. It may include:

Summary

- Regression run on s/w release—xyz
- Regression run date
- Business areas covered
- Business scenarios covered
- Test scenarios covered, if required
- Number of test cases executed
- Number of defects found, defect severity, and priority
- Expected defect fix delivery date

Details

- Test cases executed (attach sheet, if required)
- Pass–fail status of each test case with proper comments
- Location of detailed/archived test results and screenshots (if required)

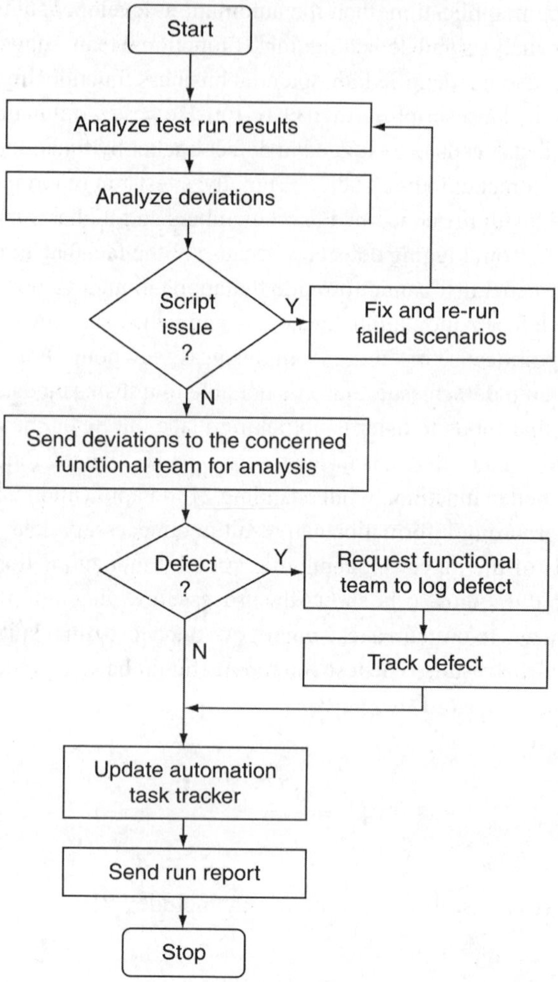

Figure 6.11 *Flow diagram of test results analysis*

Test Result Analysis

Test result analysis contains analysis of obtained test-run results to predict application stability, impacted business modules, impact severity, and defect trend. It can include:

Graph of:

- Comparison of defects found in last two regression cycles (module-wise)
- Comparison of defects found in various regression cycles
- Comparison of defects found in various regression months
- Average defect catching rate
- Test coverage—module-wise

A separate test report should also be prepared detailing the activities being carried out within automation team. This is called *test automation activity report*. This report may consist of:

- Business modules and business scenarios under automation
- Expected coverage of business scenarios being automated
- Expected date of completion of automation (business scenario-wise)
- Current completion status of each business scenario
- Data creation activity details (if any)
- Regression run summary report

The complete details of the test automation activity can be maintained in one file called *Automation task tracker.* This file should contain the complete details about the activities being carried out within test automation team and current status of the same. It may include:

- Business modules and business scenarios already automated/under automation
- Coverage of business modules already automated/under automation
- Expected date of completion of automation (business scenario-wise)
- Current individual completion status of each business scenario
- Details of test cases automated/not automated
- Reasons for not automating certain business cases
- Task allocation (team member-wise) including deadlines
- Daily activity report
- Regression run details
- Data creation details

Objective

- Test-run report
- Logging of defect logged in defect tracker
- Analyzing application stability, impacted business areas, impact severity, and defect trend

ETVX Model

Entry Criteria	• Test-run execution is complete • Availability of functional resources for clarification • Defect management and defect lifecycle is defined
Tasks	• Analyze test-run report • Log defects • Update traceability matrix
Verification and Validation	• Logged defects are valid defects • Analysis of test results is as per standards and guidelines
Exit Criteria	• All defects logged in defect tracker • Test-run report approved

MAINTENANCE PROCESS FLOW

During maintenance phase, automated scripts are modified as per the change in AUT. Generally, we observe that test automation maintenance becomes a bottleneck for an automation project. Change identification and implementation becomes time consuming, human resource intensive, and costly. It is a general observation that automation team reports that they cannot execute regression run because AUT objects or business flow has changed and scripts need to be updated for the same before test run can be executed. This raises serious questions on the automation team's reliability for executing regression runs and makes the automation team of little use when they are needed the most. Maintenance is an important phase of TALC. Test automation architecture and framework should be designed in a way that it makes change identification and implementation easy. Test scripts need to be coded with proper comments to support minimal modification effort. Test automation project should support centralized one-point maintenance to minimize maintenance costs. One-point maintenance helps in propagating changes to other part of the test scripts by just modifying at one single point. This saves a lot of effort, which otherwise would have been spent on identifying change and implementing it in various places in various scripts. Shared object repository needs to be maintained to have one-point control on AUT objects. Driver scripts are to be written to have single-point control on test execution flow logic. Master driver scripts to be designed to have one-point execution control. Separate test data sheets to be maintained for single-point control on test data variation. Moreover, documentation should be properly maintained, so that change identification is easier and fast.

Objective

- Maintaining automation project
- Automating new test scripts, if required

ETVX Model

Tasks	• Modified/updated test scripts • Automate new scripts
Verification and Validation	• Business change (change requests) • Functional team input • Gap analysis criteria
Exit Criteria	• Updated/modified test scripts approved • Updated traceability matrix
Entry Criteria	• Automation for the particular business scenario is complete • Gap analysis is complete

BUILDING ONE-POINT MAINTENANCE

Minimizing maintenance cost of a test automation project is an important aspect of test automation. Test automation architecture and framework should be designed in such a way that maintenance does not become a bottle-neck for automation team. This can be achieved if test automation architecture and framework support single-point maintenance. Following points need to be followed to implement single-point maintenance of the test automation project:

- *Shared object repository*–Shared object repository to be maintained for one-point control on AUT objects.
- *Business components* – Reusable business components to be designed, so that change in one business component is propagated to all driver scripts where it is called.

- *Driver*—Driver scripts to be designed for one-point access to business flow logic. Business flow logic of test case can easily be changed by changing the order in which business components have been called.
- *Master driver*—Master driver script that calls all driver scripts at run-time is to be designed for one-point test execution control.
- *Test data sheets*—Separate test data sheets to be designed to have single-point control on test data variations. Moreover, test data sheets should be designed in such a way that it supports both selective and exhaustive testings.
- *Configuration files*—Separate configuration file to be designed for one-point control on test execution environment settings. Configuration file can contain information such as DB settings, application URL, location of automation project, application username, password, global variables, and arrays.
- *Library*—Library file is a central repository for functions. Care should be taken to avoid multiple existences of library files. In case of multiple library files, it should be limited to 2–3. Moreover, the duplicity of functions in same or different library files should be avoided.
- *Recovery scenario*—Recovery scenario are to be created and maintained in separate central location, so that changes in one file automatically propagates to all driver scripts, wherever it is associated.
- *Utility*—Centralized location for all external executable files (.exe, .dll, .vbs, etc.) is required to be maintained for the automation project. Utility folder can contain executable files such as PuTTY.exe, WinZip.exe, and WinSCP.exe. It can also include .vbs files that prevent system automatic lock. The purpose of accessing these files in central location is that in case older files are updated with latest version, no code change is required, as the path of the file remains unchanged. Moreover, if .vbs file is updated, the change automatically propagates to all scripts, wherever it is used.
- *ErrScreenshots*—All the screenshots captured during test execution need to be kept in a central location, so that it can easily be accessed whenever required. A link of the same should exist in the test data sheets. Moreover, screenshots should have a standard naming convention that contains information such as location path of screenshot, date and time, test script in which error occurred, object name and type on which error occurred, and line number of code where error occurred.
- *ResultLog*—All the test execution results should be archived in a central location for easy reference. Scripts need to be designed in such a way that it supports automatic archiving of test results after test execution. Moreover, archived test results should also have a standard naming convention that contains information such as date and time, regression on s/w release, business scenario and test scenario names, and other relevant information.

VERSION CONTROL STRATEGY

Version control tools such as VSS are to be used to control the version of test scripts. It will also help in maintaining backup of test scripts. Regular backup of test automation project should be planned to prevent loss of effort. Version control and test automation project backup are important because:

- Loss of most recent version of scripts could lead to hampering the automation execution process.
- Multiple releases contain multiple versions of the scripts needed to be stored in version control.
- Onsite–offshore model requires proper backup to be taken of the code.

COMMUNICATION MODEL

Communication model refers to the mode and path of flow of information between automation team and other teams. A predefined communication model is necessary to avoid delays arising out of ownership issues. Verbal mode of information transfer is to be avoided and be replaced by some authentic mode such as e-mails. Information transfer should be well supported by proper documents/proofs, wherever required. Figure 6.12 shows a simple communication model diagram for automating new business scenario and executing regression runs. However, more elaborate communication model is required to establish the exact ownership and link between automation team and other teams—testing, functional, development, database, and configuration management team and higher management.

Communication Model for New Automation

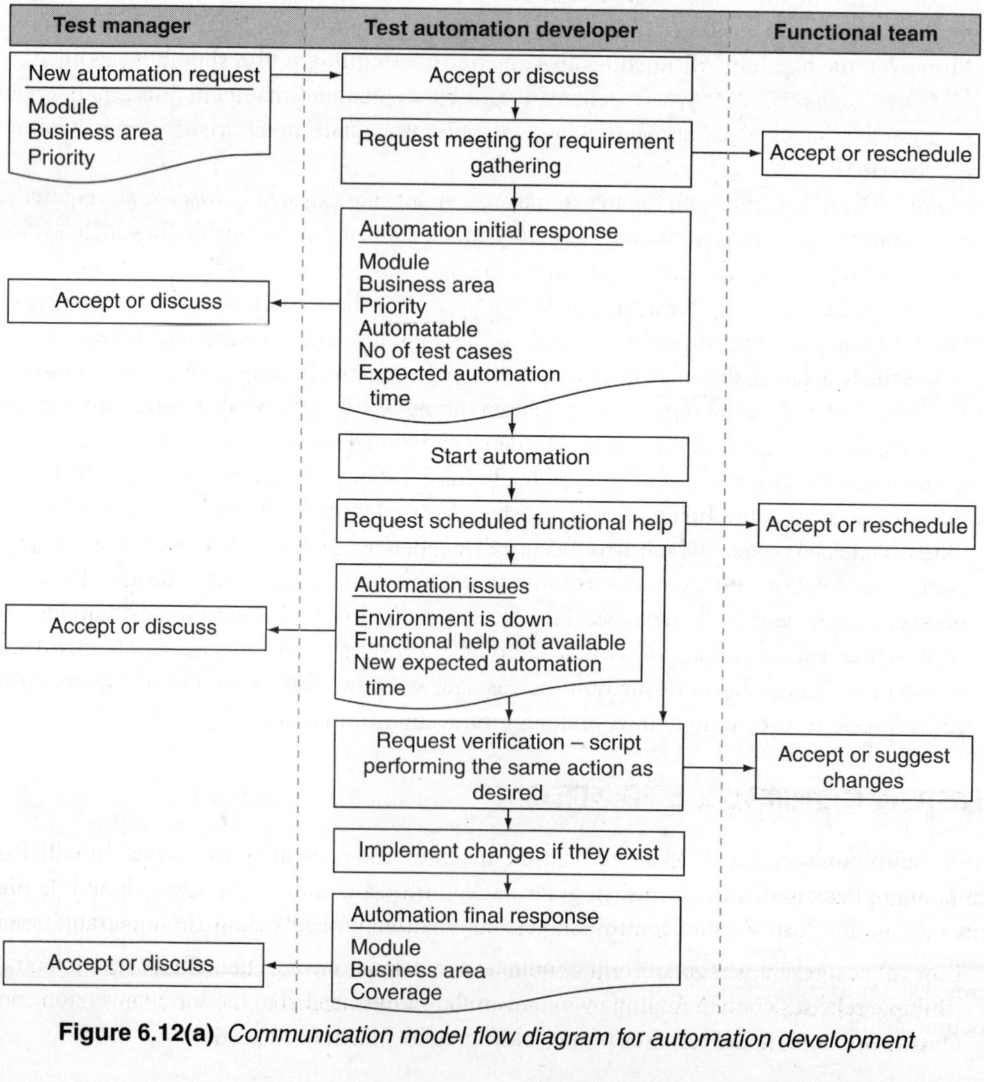

Figure 6.12(a) *Communication model flow diagram for automation development*

Communication Model for Regression Run

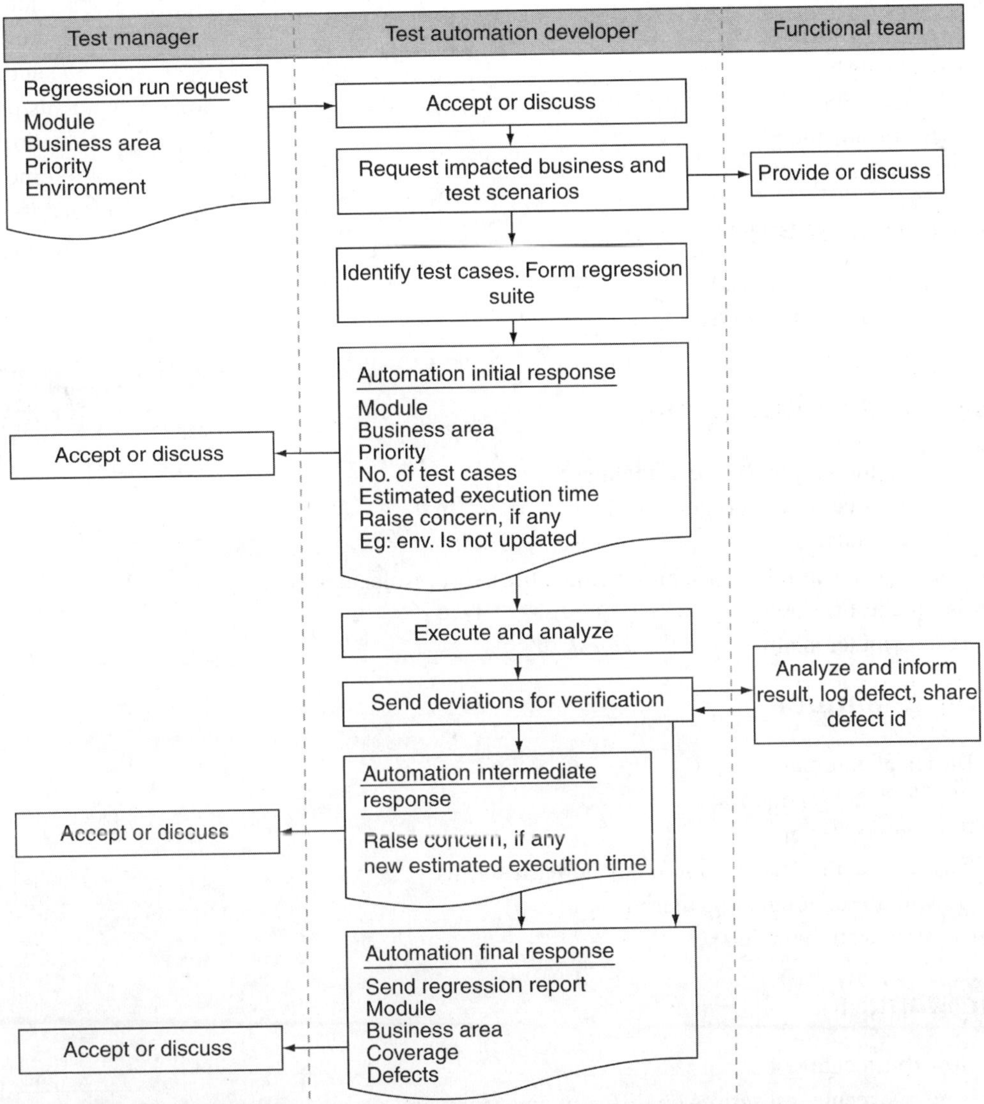

Figure 6.12(b) *Communication model flow diagram for regression run execution*

TEST AUTOMATION DOCUMENTS

Automation documents should be maintained by automation team for all automation activities and procedures. Documents help in executing automation activities smoothly in a cost-effective manner. Lists of documents that should be maintained with automation team are listed in the following sections.

Technical Documents

Feasibility analysis

- Requirement analysis
- ROI analysis
- Tool analysis
- POC documents
- Automation targets

Framework Design

- Framework architecture
- Framework components
- Framework layout

Standard and Guidelines

- Automation standards and guidelines
- Scripting standards and guidelines
- Object standards
- Naming convention—variables, scripts, files, test results, data sheets, etc.
- Sample test script
- Test script template

Training Manual

- Basics of automation
- Standard and guidelines
- Framework design
- How to use automation tool to develop test scripts
- How to do requirement gathering
- Communication model

User Manual

- How to execute test scripts
- How to execute test scripts on different environments
- How to analyze test results
- How to execute regression run

Automation Task Tracker

- Automation targets and deadlines
- Current automation activities/status—development, execution, maintenance, and data creation
- Task allocation

- Test automation suite coverage
- Planned regression run schedule
- Regression run summary reports (all past records)
- Project backup plan
- Automation issues

QUICK TIPS

✓ Automation project need analysis report should explicitly define and map the expectations from test automation to the limitations and deliverables of the automation project.

✓ The ROI analysis should also include factors such as customer confidence and early software release market benefits before accepting/rejecting implementation of test automation for a project.

✓ The tool analysis factors should also include resource availability, tool stability, script development/maintenance cost with the tool, etc. apart from tool cost to select the best-fit tool for test automation.

✓ The POC phase to include automation of those test cases after automation of which it can be safely assumed that test automation can be successfully implemented for the project.

✓ The automation framework should be designed in a way that it minimizes the cost to test automation and offers easy script development and maintenance.

✓ The automation framework should have one-point maintenance control.

✓ During business knowledge gathering phase, automation developers to focus on gathering only that much knowledge that is sufficient for developing/maintaining the automation scripts.

✓ The customized test execution results should be easy to read and understand. It needs to be designed in a way that it can also serve as test automation reports.

✓ All the automation documents are to be maintained in a separate location.

PRACTICAL QUESTIONS

1. What is TALC?
2. What are the various phases of TALC?
3. What are the inputs required for need analysis phase?
4. What are the various factors that need to be taken into consideration for selecting the best-fit tool for automation?
5. A software project has six months of testing lifespan left. The automation effort for 30% coverage is two months. Should test automation be implemented in this project?

6. A software project under development requires review of the 40% of the developed business functionality. The complete software is unstable and the object properties are being changed continuously by the developers. Is this project a good candidate for implementing test automation?
7. Why is one-point maintenance essential for test automation project?
8. Why is version control of the automation project important?

Section 2 Agile Test Automation

- Agile Methodology
- Agile Automation
- Agile Automation Framework

Chapter 7

Agile Methodology

Agile methodology is a software development method based on iterative and incremental development, where requirements and solutions evolve through collaboration between self-organizing, cross-functional teams and customer feedback. It promotes adaptive planning and evolution development and delivery. Delivery is based on time-boxed iterative approach. It encourages rapid and flexible response to change with minimum change impact. It requires very frequent and tight interactions with all the stakeholders throughout the development cycle.

In agile methodology, complete software is developed in small iterative and incremental development. It lays emphasis on compacting the software development life cycle rather than changing it as shown in Fig. 7.1.

AGILE VALUES

Agile development term was derived from the Agile Manifesto, which was written in 2001 by a group that included the creators of Scrum, Extreme Programming (XP), etc. The agile values as listed in the manifesto are as follows:

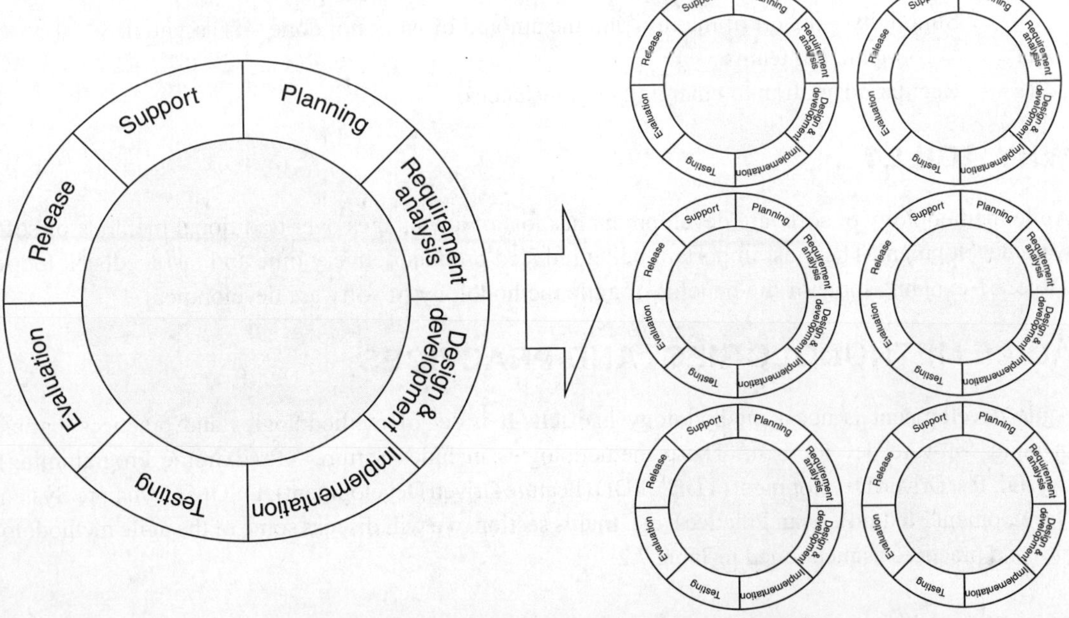

Figure 7.1 *Do not change the life cycle, compact it*

- **Individuals and interactions over processes and tools:** Agile software development methodology lays emphasis on self-organization, motivation and interactions such as co-location and pair programming as compared to any process or tool.
- **Working software over comprehensive document:** Working software is valued more useful than presentation documents in client meetings. Self-explanatory code is valued more than hundreds of pages of documents.
- **Customer collaboration over contract negotiation:** Agile methodology accepts the fact that with the ever-changing world change to software development requirements is a continuous process and all requirements cannot be fully collected at the beginning of the project. Therefore, continuous customer and stakeholder interaction is must at short periodic intervals.
- **Responding to change over following a plan:** Agile development focusses on quick response to change to minimize delivery to customer time.

AGILE PRINCIPLES

Agile manifesto is based on the following 12 principles:

1. Customer satisfaction by rapid delivery of useful software.
2. Welcome changing requirements, even late in development.
3. Working software is delivered frequently (weeks rather than months).
4. Working software is the principal measure of progress.
5. Sustainable development, able to maintain a constant pace.
6. Close, daily cooperation between business people and developers.
7. Face-to-face conversation is the best form of communication (co-location).
8. Projects are built around motivated individuals, who should be trusted.
9. Continuous attention to technical excellence and good design.
10. Simplicity—the art of maximizing the amount of work not done—is essential.
11. Self-organizing teams.
12. Regular adaptation to changing circumstances.

WHY AGILE?

Agile methodology of software development has lots of advantages over traditional methods of software development. The most important being reduced product delivery time and fast feedback loops. Table 7.1 explains some of the benefits of agile methodology of software development.

AGILE METHODOLOGIES AND PRACTICES

Agile development is not a methodology in itself. It is set of methodologies and practices that aid in rapid software development. These methodologies include: Scrum, XP (Extreme Programming), Crystal, Test Driven Development (TDD), FDD (Feature Driven Development), DSDM (Dynamic System Development Method), Lean Practices, etc. In this section, we will discuss some of the agile methodologies and practices as mentioned in Table 7.2.

Table 7.1 Benefits of agile methodology

Benefits		Description
	Revenue	Agile methodology delivers the features incrementally, thereby, helping some of the revenues to be gained early while the product is still under development.
	Risk Management	Continuous small deliveries help to identify the blocking issues early and quick adaptability to a change.
	Speed to Market	Continuous incremental deployments helps to release some of the product features early to the market.
	Quick Resolution	Agile methodology lays emphasis on quick small discussions based on practical ground realities to solve issues rather than holding meetings based on big specs. Developing specs, helping stakeholders understand them and holding discussion on it consumes time and money.
	Agility	Agile methodology accepts change as an integral part of software development process. In agile development, timescale is fixed while requirements emerge and evolve as product is developed. Acceptance of change among active stakeholders helps to make necessary trade-off decisions faster.
	Faster Customer Feedback	Early release of some product features helps to receive customer inputs while the product is still getting developed. This helps to tweak the product feature as per customer expectations as per budget overruns.
	Quality	Agile methodology integrates testing to the SDLC to the very beginning stage of software development. This helps to catch software issues early in SDLC. Since, feature gets developed in small chunks it is easier to fix the bugs. This helps product stability quickly.
	Customer Satisfaction	Continuous change to the product features as per customer feedbacks helps to achieve customer satisfaction.
	Visibility	Agile methodology lays stress on involving business owners and stakeholders throughout the development cycle. This helps to effectively manage stakeholders' expectations.
	More Enjoyable	Agile methodology replaces big specs and large group meetings with smaller workshop discussions based on practical facts. This results in active involvement and cooperation within agile team which makes it a fun place to work.

Table 7.2 Some of the agile methodologies/practices

Agile methodology/Practice		Objectives
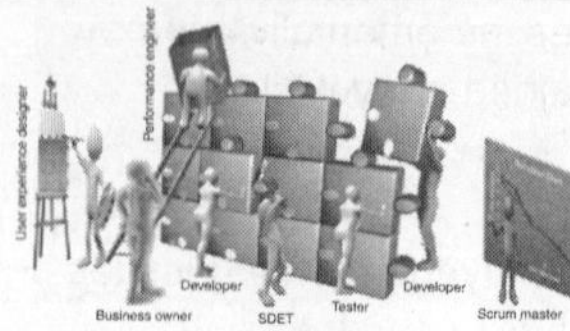	Agile team dynamics	Explains team formation
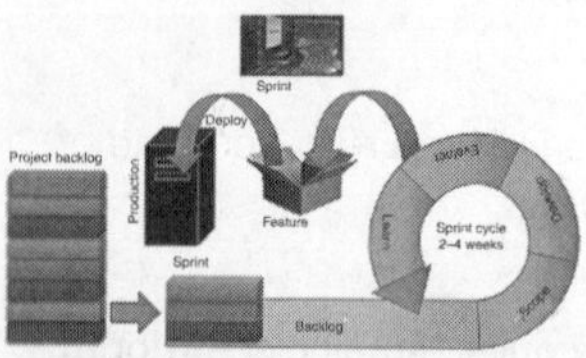	Scrum	Describes development methodology details
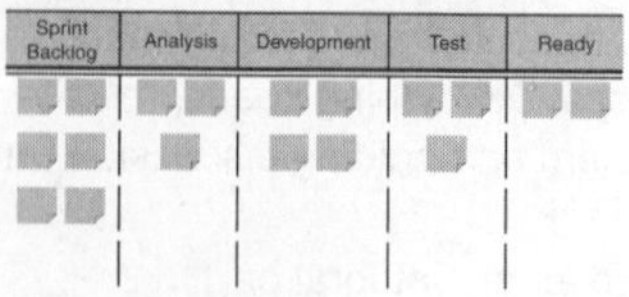	Kanban	Describes how to manage the development work
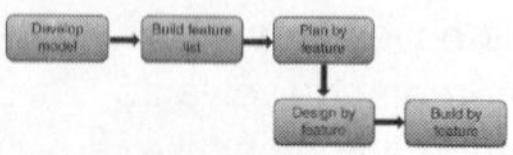	Feature Driven Development (FDD)	Development framework based on featured based development
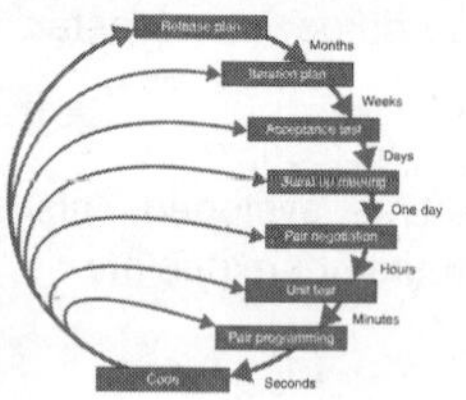	Extreme Programming (XP)	Development framework describing programming practice to follow
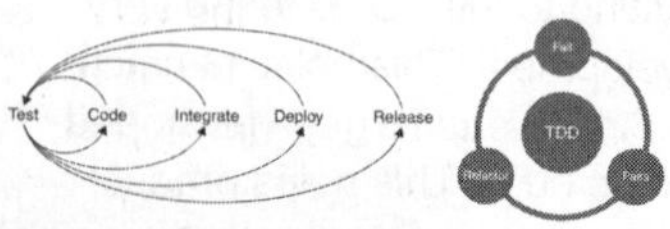	Test Driven Development (TDD)	Development framework that integrates testing practice within development practice
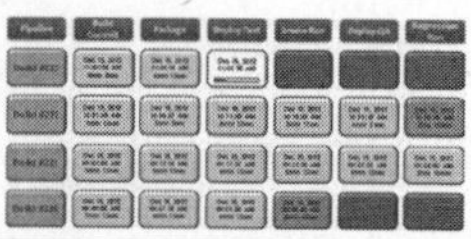	Continuous Integration (CI)	Practice that describes how to automate build deployment process

In this section, we will discuss how various agile methodologies and practices can be utilized to develop a true agile software development process for a project. We will *first* discuss how to form an agile team and define the role and responsibilities of the team members. Second, we will discuss the development methodology (Scrum) to be implemented for development. *Third,* we will discuss how the requirements to be chosen for development (FDD). Fourth, we will discuss the programming practices (XP) to be followed for development. *Fifth*, we will discuss how to integrate the testing practices within development to ensure a high quality defect-free deployment build (TDD). *Finally*, we will discuss how we can automate the complete build deployment process to ensure the complete agile process works smoothly (CI).

> The first step before implementing any agile project is to form the agile teams, set its goals and define the role and responsibilities of the team members. Following section 'Agile Team Dynamics' explains in detail the formation of an agile team.

AGILE TEAM DYNAMICS

Agile team dynamics defines the structure of the agile team and roles and responsibilities of the various team members. Generally, the team size of the agile team needs to be small, around seven team members. Agile teams generally comprises of business owners, scrum masters, developers, functional testers and SDETs (software developer engineers in test).

- **Business owner** carries out customer surveys and converts the customer requirements into meaningful themes on which agile teams can work on. They guide the team to develop the theme that meets the customer expectations.
- **User experience designers** design the user experience which is friendly to users.

They sometimes, also, take this design back to customers for their feedback.

- **Developers** write the code to develop the feature.
- **Functional testers** test the functionality of the code while SDETs using tools to speed up testing.
- **Performance engineers** test the performance of the code.

Figure 7.2 shows an agile team with their team members performing their tasks.

User Experience Designer

The role of user experience designer in agile team is to:

- Carry out customer surveys to identify the best user experience
- Design graphical user experience that is user-friendly and best meets the customer expectations

Developer

The role of a developer in agile team is to:

- Develop the application code.
- Deploy the code to testing environments (build manager).
- Fix bugs.
- Develop/execute unit/integration tests.

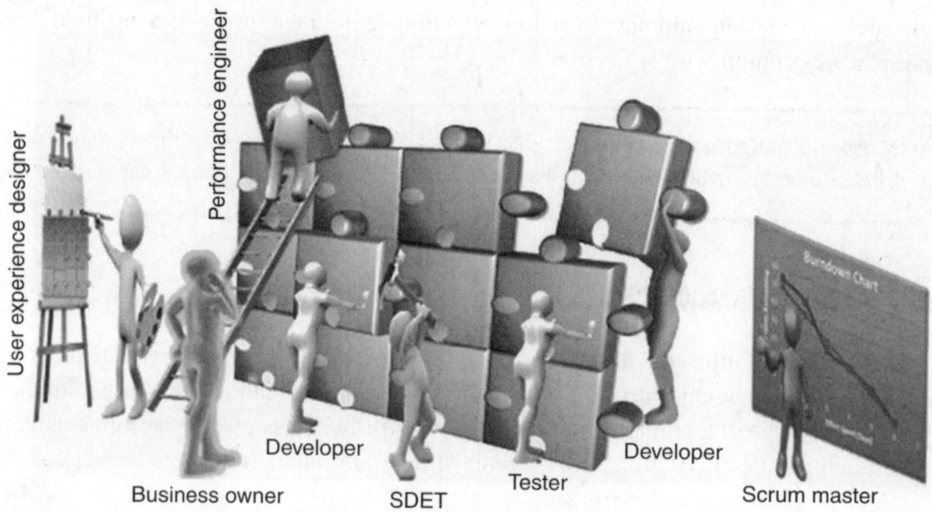

Figure 7.2 *Agile team dynamics*

Functional Tester

The role of a functional tester in agile team is to:

- Design traceability matrix.
- Develop manual tests.
- Test the feature under development.
- Targeted testing for the developed feature.
- Suggest user design experience improvizations.

Software Developer Engineer in Test (SDET)

The role of SDET (software developer engineer in test) in agile team is to:

- Develop/automate unit/integration/functional/regression/security/cross-platform/... tests.
- Execute automated tests.
- Test the application under development.
- Suggest technical (code) improvizations.

Performance Engineer

The role of a performance engineer in agile team is to:

- Develop/execute the performance tests.
- Suggest performance improvizations.

Business Owner

The role of a business owner (product owner) in an agile team is to:

- Carry out customer surveys and record customer requirements and expectations as user themes.
- Build the product backlog and prioritize it.

- Evaluate if developed components meets customer expectations or not.
- Guide the team to develop application as per customer expectations.

Scrum Master

The role of a scrum master in an agile team is to:

- Build and prioritize the sprint backlog.
- Co-ordinate to resolve blocking issues.
- Motivate the team, evaluate progress and publish Burndown charts.
- Synchronize business owner/management expectations and teams capabilities.

Once agile teams have been formed and their goals set; next step is to define the development framework for the agile team. In agile methodology, each agile team is free to decide the development framework it will follow. Among all the development frameworks Scrum is very popular. It best describes the process right from selecting requirements to work on to production ready requirements. Following section describes in detail Scrum development framework and how to implement it.

SCRUM

Scrum is an iterative and incremental agile software development framework for managing software projects. It promotes a flexible product development strategy where the agile team works as a unit to achieve a common goal. It enables teams to self-organize by encouraging physical co-location of all team members and daily face to face communication among all team members and disciplines in the project.

Scrum framework accepts the fact that in this dynamic and ever-changing world continuous change to requirements is obvious and hence, requirements can never be frozen. It also accepts that all requirements cannot be gathered in the initial phase of the project. Hence, scrum framework lays emphasis on working on smallest possible deliverable units first.

Customers and stakeholders are encouraged to suggest their feedbacks and changes. The suggestions are then implemented during the future sprint cycles. Scrum emphasizes on production ready work being delivered by the end of the sprint.

Sprint

A sprint (or iteration) is the basic unit of scrum development framework. The sprint is 'time-boxed', i.e., it is restricted to specific time duration. This duration is fixed in advance by the agile team and may vary from 2 to 4 weeks. Each sprint starts with sprint planning meeting where the team identifies the themes for implementation and creates tasks (or sub-stories) for the same. Sprint ends with sprint review-and-retrospective meeting where the progress is reviewed and lessons for the next sprint is identified. Figure 7.3 shows sprint cycles (iteration cycles) followed by different agile teams for a typical project. Agile team I has 2 week sprint cycle; agile team II has 4 week sprint cycle and agile team III has 1 week sprint cycle.

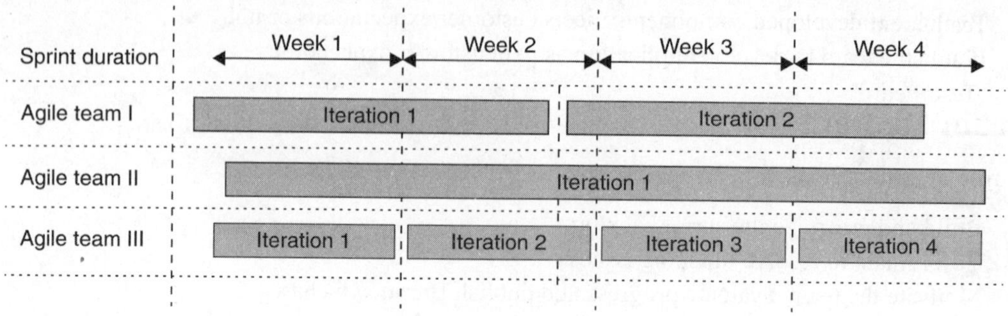

Figure 7.3 *Sprint cycles*

Sprint Meetings

Scrum advices few meetings to ensure smooth functioning of the team.

Backlog Grooming Meeting

Backlog Grooming Meeting is organized by the *product owner* (*business owner*) of the team. Product owners walkthrough the team on the various themes available in backlog for development. The team can ask questions and clarify their doubts regarding the 'ask' from the theme or functionality to be implemented as per the theme. Backlog grooming meeting generally lasts for 2–4 hrs.

The team then uses this information to estimate the implementation feasibility of stories and effort required for the same.

Sprint Planning Meeting

Sprint planning meeting is organized by the *scrum master* of the team. The objective of this meeting is to identify the set of prioritized stories that the team is comfortable delivering for the current sprint. This set of stories form the spring backlog. Also, tasks are created for each story and each task is assigned an owner. Sprint planning meeting generally lasts for 4–6 hrs.

For example, for a specific story, the generalized tasks would be analysis, UI design, development and testing.

Daily Scrum Meeting (Daily Stand-up Meeting)

Daily scrum meeting is organized by the scrum master. This meeting is scheduled to occur first thing in the morning every day during the sprint. This meeting has some specific guidelines:

- The meeting duration is time-boxed to 15 minutes.
- All members of the team to come prepared to the meeting.
- The meeting starts precisely on the same time and same location every day, even if some team members fail to make it on time.
- All team members are to give a summary update on below points:
  - What have you done since yesterday?
  - What have you planned to do today?
  - Do you face or foresee any impediments or stumbling blocks?

- Team members are to move the tasks on sprint board while providing the update. For example, if a task is done by a developer and now requires testing, he is expected to move the task to 'Test' board. (For details on tasks movement on sprint board refer section 'Kanban').

> NOTES
> Scrum master to publish the *burndown chart or velocity chart* on the basis of task completed. The objective of burndown chart or velocity chart is to help the team understand that with current development pace will the team be able to accomplish all the goals of the sprint. If not, then how much they can cover. Based on this, team can hold separate discussions to resolve the bottlenecks. If team foresees, it has more bandwidth left, then they can decide to add more themes to sprint backlog from product backlog.

- Scrum master to document the identified impediments and work outside this meeting to resolve them.
- No detailed discussion is to happen in this meeting.

Sprint Retrospective Meeting

Sprint review-and-retrospective meeting is organized by the scrum master at the end of the sprint. During this meeting, the team discusses to identify:

- What went well?
- What did not go well?
- What are the lessons learnt?
- What are the areas of improvement?

Sprint Demo Meeting

Sprint demo meeting is organized by the customer at the end of the sprint or as per a predefined schedule. All agile teams, stakeholders and customers are to be part of this meeting. In this meeting, agile team gives a demo of the working feature developed or in progress. The work done is reviewed by the stakeholders and customers. For precisely this reason, this meeting is also called *review meeting*.

> NOTES
> Some agile teams may also choose to hold the retrospective and demo meeting together. This is called sprint review-and-retrospective meeting. This meeting is attended by the respective agile team, concerned business owners of other teams, concerned stakeholders and customer. Whatever, be the strategy for a given project, all agile teams are to follow the same process. That is, all agile teams of a project are to hold a sprint review-retrospective meeting or spring retrospective and sprint review meeting.

HOW SCRUM WORKS?

In this ever-changing dynamic world where the technology and requirements change very fast, application design and development is getting more and more complex with every second day. Scrum provides a framework that allows agile teams to successfully work on complex projects. Section 'Agile Team Dynamics' explains in detail how the various members of the agile team work to deliver a successful product.

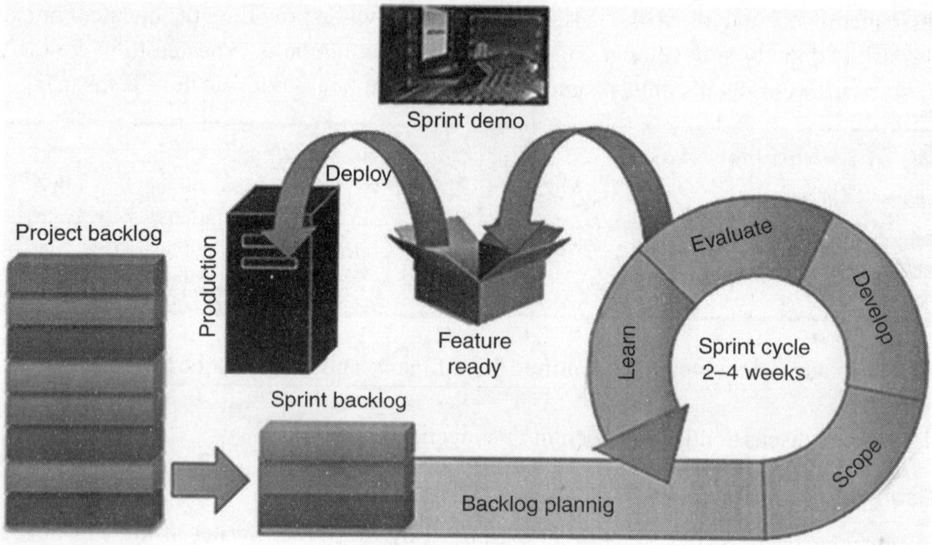

Figure 7.4 *Scrum*

SCRUM WORKFLOW

Figure 7.4 describes the work flow of scrum framework.

Product Backlog

The product backlog is a prioritized features list, containing short descriptions of all functionality or features desired in the product.

- Product backlog exists in the form of user themes
- Each user theme is a short and simple description of the desired functionality from the perspective of the user

Backlog Planning

Beginning of every sprint cycle, business owner organizes a *Backlog Grooming Meeting*.

- Objective of this meeting is to groom the team on the prioritized list of user themes that can be taken up for development in the current sprint.
- On the basis of team feedback, the business owner creates a list of user themes which is to be developed for the current sprint. This list is called *Sprint Backlog*.

Scope

After the backlog grooming meeting, the scrum master organizes a *Sprint Planning Meeting*.

- Objective of this meeting is identify the effort required to develop the sprint backlog themes
- Each team member submits his effort estimation for each and every theme

- On the basis of the teams' feedback, the scrum master refines the sprint backlog list to a list of themes that the team is comfortable developing for the current sprint.

How Scrum Team Estimates Effort?

Team members rate effort on a scale of 1 to 5, with 1 being simplest and 5 being toughest and most time and effort consuming. Teams may also choose this scale to be different say 1–10. This scale is called points. At the beginning of this meeting, the team decides how many total points the team can accommodate. Suppose, the team chooses to cover 50 points for a specific sprint (iteration). Following steps describe how effort is estimated for a theme:

- The scrum master pulls out the prioritized themes from the sprint backlog and asks team members to rate the effort on a pre-defined chosen scale, say 1–5.
- Suppose the UI designer rates the theme at 3 points; developer rates it at 3 and tester rates it at 4.
- The scrum master is to capture the maximum quoted point value out of all the team members. In this case, the maximum point quoted is 4. Thus, the theme is assigned 4 points.
- Similarly, other prioritized themes are also assigned points.
- The scrum master keeps track of the sum of points of all themes that are decided to be worked upon.
- The scrum master stops pulling themes from sprint backlog as soon as total points equal 50.
- If the themes in sprint backlog are over and still total points does not equals 50, then team can ask the product owner to move some more prioritized themes to the sprint backlog. However, as a general practice, business owners are encouraged to pull sufficient themes to sprint backlog during backlog planning phase itself.
- If the total number of points has reached 50 and still there are some themes in the sprint backlog then the scrum master updates the business owner of the themes that cannot be accommodated. The business owner then pulls these themes back to the project backlog.
- Once the sprint planning meeting is over, all team members are expected to identify (create) their tasks for each theme and update the scrum master.
- The scrum master then updates the scrum task board with list of all stories in spring backlog and all identified tasks for each theme. This is discussed in detail in the following section 'Scrum Task Board'
- The scrum master also publishes the Burndown chart and Velocity chart on a daily basis to update the team on its current progress and current pace of achieving sprint goals. This is discussed in detail in the following section 'BurnDown chart' and 'Velocity chart'.

The team members are expected to quote points to a theme on the basis of the knowledge they gathered during backlog grooming meeting and their experience. The team members quote the points more on their gut-feeling. This is accepted in scrum as at this phase no team member has a clear perception of what actually needs to be developed and tested. However, if during later stages it turns out that the effort required is more, then themes or sub-themes are to be created and assigned points accordingly. Once cre ated, these can again be prioritized by the business owner with feedback from the team. These stories can then be pulled in Sprint backlog or can be pushed to Project backlog as team deems fit.

Scrum is a continuous evolving process. Hence, no hard bound rules are drafted for Scrum. Scrum methodology provides the full flexibility to the team to choose how they can add maximum value to the business.

Develop

After sprint planning meeting, the team starts to develop the user themes. Table 7.3 shows the list of tasks performed by different team members of the agile team.

Table 7.3 List of tasks performed by different team members of the agile team

	User design	Developer	QA	Scrum Master	Business owner
Agile tasks	Designs the user experience design as small recursive components	Develops the business logic code Develps the GUI components for which user experience design is ready Fixes bugs	Builds test and automation strategy Tests the developed components of code Deveops the automated tests Identifies areas/scope of improvement	Co-ordinates inter and intra team meetings Publishes burn-down chart Analyses impact of blocking issues and coordinates to mitigate them	Evaluates developed components on the grounds of customer expeclations Provides feedback and improvements

Test

Once the components have been developed, the components are merged with the regression environment. In the regression environment, further testing takes place such as regression testing, multi-browser testing, performance testing, security testing, etc.

Evaluate

Once a user theme is fully developed, the business owner analyses the developed theme to check whether it meets the customer expectations.

- If yes, then the user story is marked 'Ready' for deployment to production.
- If no, then the team is required to work on the suggested improvements.

Learn

At the end of the sprint, the scrum master organizes a *retrospective meeting*. In this meeting, the team discusses on

- What the team did well?
- What went wrong?
- Areas of improvement

Feature Ready

A list of features ready for go-live is collected by the *build deployment manager*. The build deployment manager syncs up with various agile teams to collect dependencies for various features going live. Next, go-live steps for various features are drafted. This is to ensure minimum impact to go-live and no undesirable impact to production environment.

The go-live schedule could be daily, weekly or sprint end. Agile teams are free to choose the go-live schedule. However, all agile teams are encouraged to for a daily go-live so that features can be delivered early to the customers. In scenarios wherein feature is partially developed or feature developed has dependency on code being developed by other teams, a toggle switch is developed for the feature. Code as developed is pushed to production with toggle switch switched off, so that essentially the features do not go-live though code is already live in production.

NOTES: Only that code is marked ready which has been successfully tested and marked ready for go-live.

Sprint Demo

At the end of the sprint (or as per the demo schedule), all agile teams give a demo to all the stakeholders on:

- The features that have been deployed to production or are ready for production deployment
- The features which are under development
    - Development progress of the features under development
    - Expected production-ready date of the features under development

NOTES: For sprint demo, agile teams are encouraged to walk through the stakeholders through the working or the developed feature of the actual application. Presentations or any sort of documented presentation is discouraged for sprint demo meetings.

Scrum Task Board

Scrum task board provides an effective way to track the various tasks of the sprint as well as the impediments. Scrum task board is designed in a way that it is visible in both plan mode and work mode. That is, the scrum board helps the team plan out the various tasks for the sprint as well as to track progress. Figure 7.5 shows a typical scrum task board.

Once all the themes and its tasks have been identified, the scrum master prepares sticky notes. For every story, there exists one sticky note as shown in Fig. 7.6 and multiple task notes as shown in Fig. 7.7.

Story note provides details on: Theme number, theme points and theme short description. It also contains status checkboxes for different phases of story development. The respective owner of that phase is required to check the checkbox when they have completed their respective phases.

Story task note provides details on theme number, task number and task short description. It also specifies the owner who owns this task.

Once the scrum master has prepared all the sticky notes, next step is to paste these notes on the white board appropriately. This needs to be done right after the sprint planning meeting. Following steps describe a typical organization of tasks in task board:

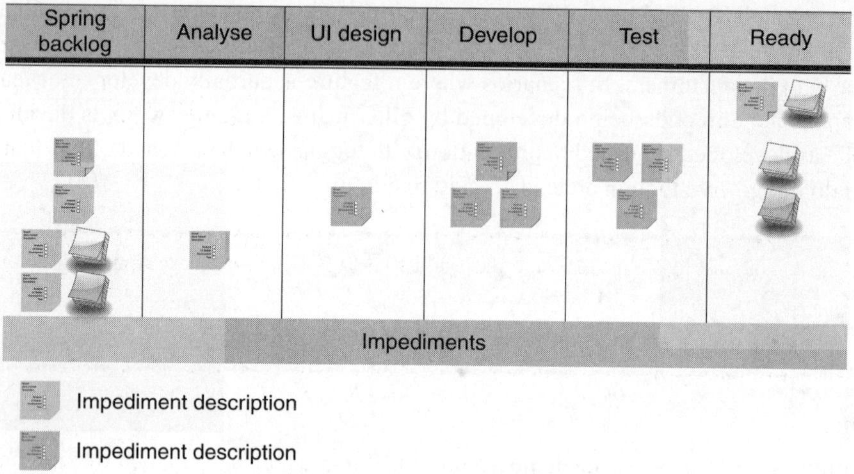

Figure 7.5 *Scrum task board*

- Reserve a row for each theme.
- Paste the theme note and task notes against column 'Sprint Backlog'. Task notes are to be stacked upon one another and placed next to story note as shown in Figure 7.5.

During the daily scrum meetings, respective owners of task update the scrum task board by moving the tasks around the board. Team member need to:

- Move the theme task note around the board appropriately
    - For example, if a developer team member is ready to pick new task then he is to move that task from column 'Spring Backlog' to column 'Develop'.
    - Or, If a developer team member has completed a specific task, then he is to move the specific task from column 'Develop' to column 'Ready'.
- Update the story note
    - For example, if a developer team member has completed all the development tasks of a story, he is to check the 'Develop' task of the story note.

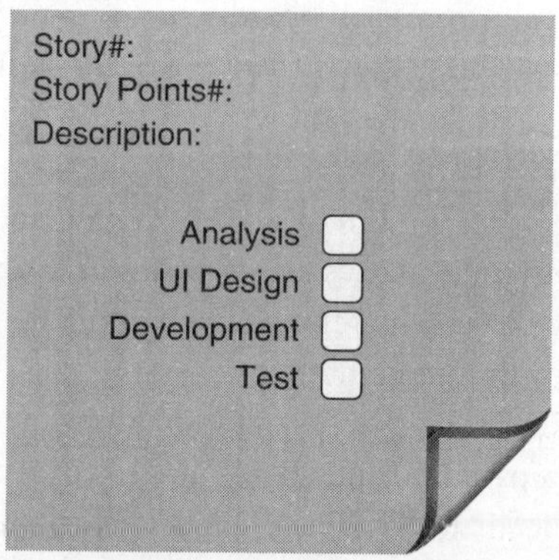

Figure 7.6 *Story note*

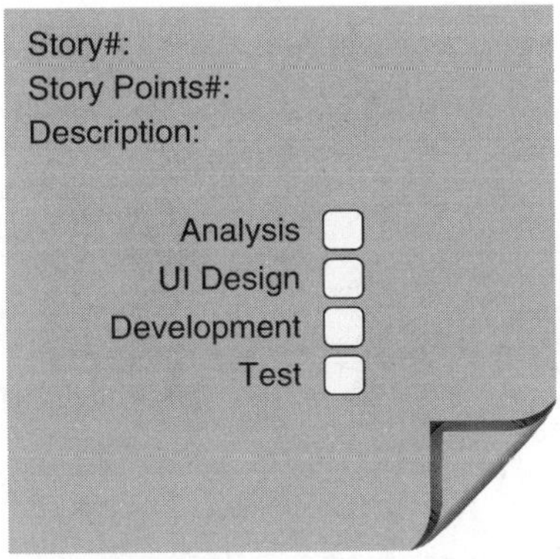

Figure 7.7 *Story task note*

Also, when a scrum master observes that all the tasks for a specific theme is complete or the other words theme has been successfully been implemented, then he is to move the specific tasks from column 'Spring Backlog' to column 'Ready'.

If any impediments are found for a theme, then the respective theme and all its tasks are to be moved to the 'Impediment' section of the board. Also, a short description of the impediment is to be written.

Burndown Chart

A *Burndown Chart* is a graphical representation of work left to do versus time.It measures whether with the current pace of development, team will be able to complete all spring tasks or not. The horizontal axis shows the time while the vertical axis shows the outstanding work (or backlog). Outstanding work can be in terms of themes or tasks or points.

Suppose, for a sprint cycle scrum team has chosen 10 themes for development. These themes have total of 45 tasks and the total points is 50.

Figure 7.8 shows a sample Burndown chart of a typical sprint cycle of 2 weeks. The vertical axis shows outstanding tasks while horizontal axis shows sprint days (time). Teams are to make an attempt

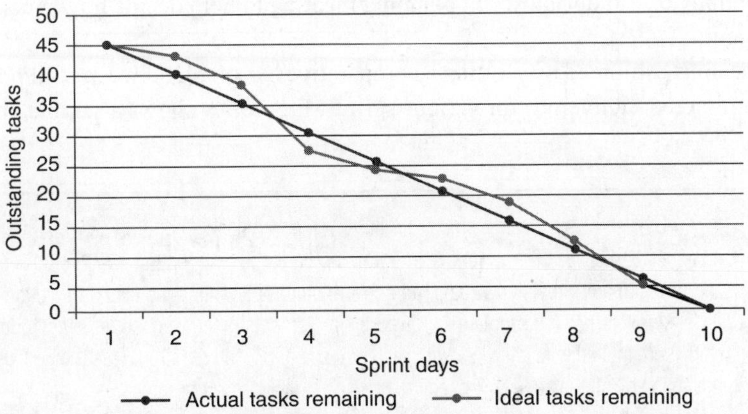

Figure 7.8 *Burndown chart*

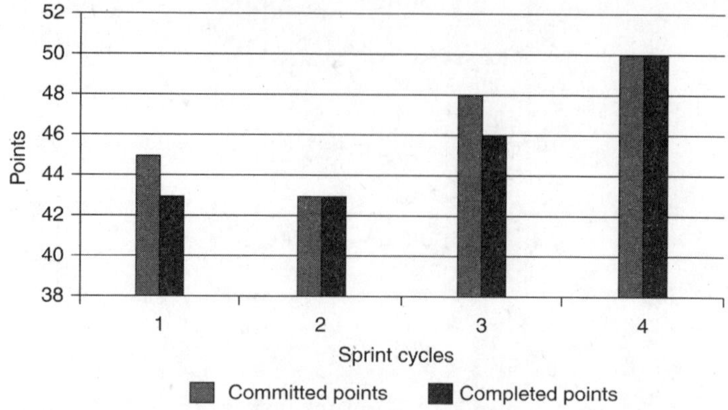

Figure 7.9 *Velocity chart*

to ensure that the current outstanding task line graph is close to ideal task remaining line graph. Ideal tasks remaining line graph is always a straight line with maximum outstanding tasks on day 1 and zero task on final sprint day which in this case is 10. This line is drawn as a reference line to show that the development pace is to match this line.

The scrum master is to publish this chart to team daily. This chart helps team to:

- Understand the current pace of development
- Understand whether team is on the track to achieve its sprint goals or not
- Warn if team may miss its sprint goals
- Show the impact of decisions

Velocity Chart

The *velocity chart* measures the amount of value delivered by each sprint as compared to the committed value. This enables agile teams to estimate how much work the team can get done in future sprints. It is essentially useful during sprint planning meeting to help decide how much work the team is feasible to commit.

Velocity of a team is estimated by plotting a comparative bar graph between total points committed Vs total points completed (delivered) for various sprints. Figure 7.9 shows a sample velocity chart for the last 5 sprints.

> Scrum method holds good for smaller projects which can be developed independently by separate agile teams. Bigger projects require strong cohesion between the various teams working on it and also require a way to track project progress. Scrum method does not provide any provision for a strong co-ordination between agile teams or to track the cumulative progress made by all the agile teams. This problem is solved by implementing scrum of scrums methodology. This technique extends scrum to ensure that agile teams work with each other as and when required. This method also helps to track the cumulative progress made by all the agile teams, and hence helps track project progress.

SCRUM OF SCRUMS

Scrum of Scrums is a technique to scale scrum for bigger projects that involve large development groups. This methodology allows clusters of scrum teams to discuss their work, focusing especially on areas of overlap and integration.

How Does Scrum of Scrum Works?

In scrum of scrums method, each scrum team works as normal but from each team one person is nominated as ambassador of the team (generally scrum masters or business owners). The responsibility of ambassador is to update higher management and enterprise architects on team progress, current impediments and issues faced. This update occurs in a meeting which is attended by all ambassadors and the stakeholders. This meeting is analogous to scrum meeting and is called *scrum of scrums meeting*. This meeting may occur daily or on alternate days. Figure 7.10 shows an illustration of scrum of scrums meeting.

The agenda of scrum of scrums meeting is analogous to daily scrum meeting and includes the following:

- What has your team done since we last met?
- What will your team do before we meet again?
- Is anything slowing your team down or getting in their way?
- Are you about to put something in another team's way?

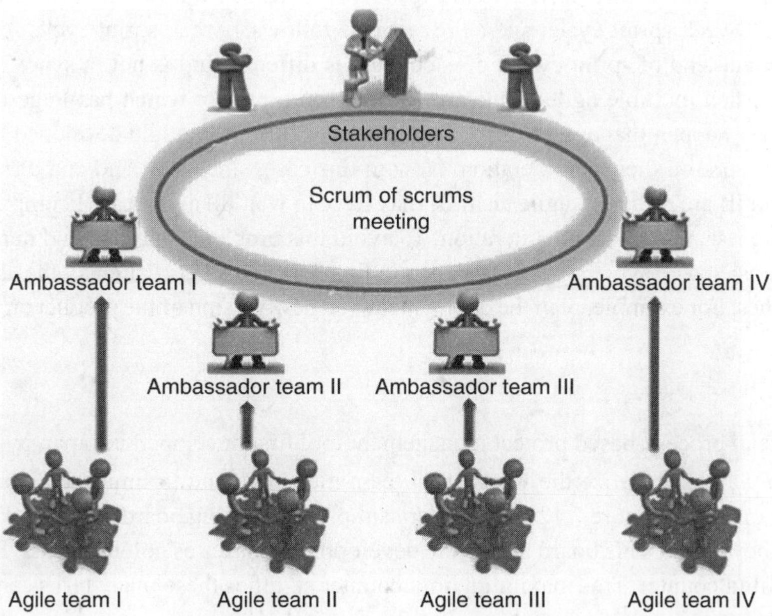

Figure 7.10 *Scrum of scrums meeting*

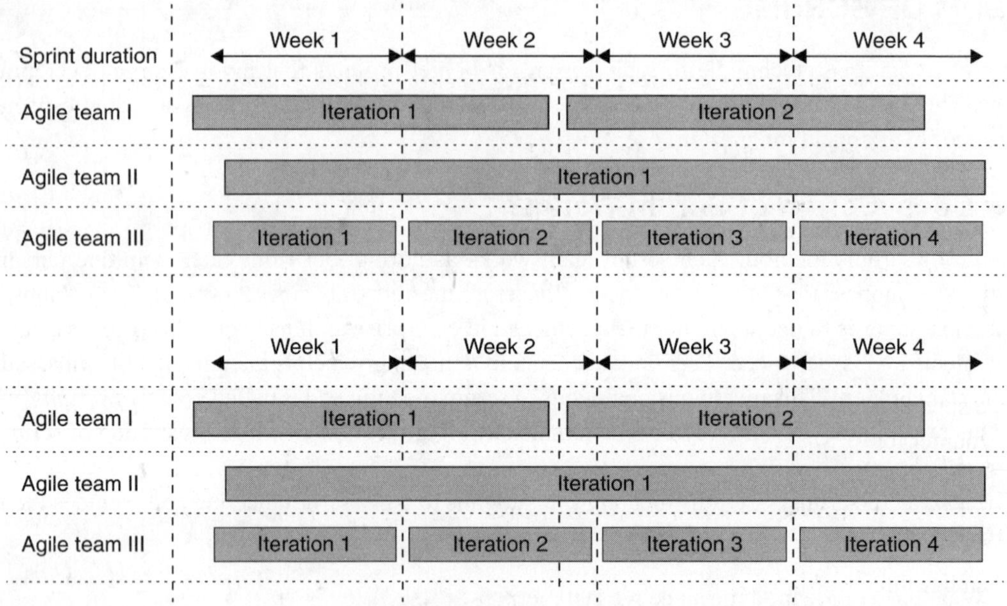

Figure 7.11 *Aligned sprint cycles*

Another technique that makes easier management of large projects using scrum of scrums is the alignment of iterations. Agile teams work on different project sizes, and also each agile team has a specific velocity, production capacity and learning curve. This results is different sprint duration (sizes) followed by different agile teams. As visible in Fig. 7.3, agile team I follows 2 week sprint cycle; agile team II follows 4 week sprint cycle; and agile team III follows 1 week sprint cycle. As evident from this figure, start and end of sprint cycles of each team is different and is not in sync. This could be a major problem when multiple agile teams are working on a project which has huge dependency on each other. It may happen that agile team 3 may have to wait for a module developed by agile team I before they can work on their next iteration. Now in this case, since start and end of sprint cycles of agile teams I and III are different, agile team III may have to wait till agile team I completes their iteration cycle before it can begin its next iteration. To avoid this problem, start and end iteration cycles of all the agile teams is to be synchronized as shown in Fig. 7.11. This helps align all the agile teams with project milestones. For example, plan the deployment of a new version of the product on a specific date.

KANBAN

Kanban is a visual process-based project management tool first developed in Japan by Toyota.

Kanban is a way to visualize the work of all team members, and to limit the amount of work in progress at any one time. Figure 7.12 shows a very simple Kanban big board. It consists of all the tasks and the status they are in. This board shows the development phases as column items. Each phase has the maximum limit counter. This maximum limit counter signifies these many tasks can be completed

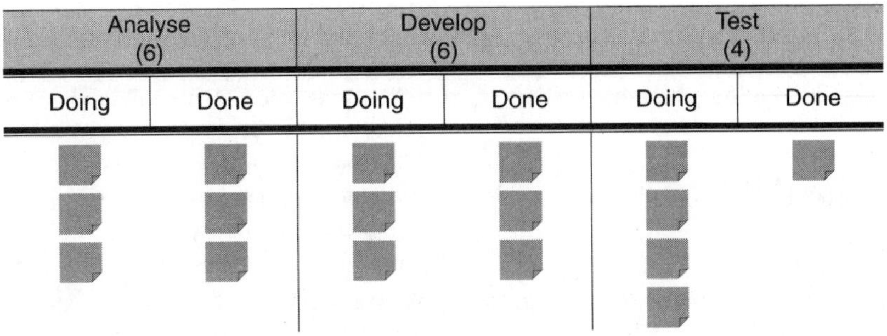

Figure 7.12 *Simple kanban board*

for the specific development phase in the given time period. If the task count exceeds the maximum limit counter for the specific phase, then a red flag is raised. Figure 7.12 shows maximum counter limit as 6 for Analysis phase 6 for development phase, and 4 for testing phase.

Kanban Principles

Kanban has three following core principles:

1. **Visualize what you have now:** Visualizing all the items in context of each other can be very informative
2. **Limit the amount of work in progress (WIP):**This helps to balance the flow-based approach so that teams do not overcommit.
3. **Enhance flow:** Continuously improving the way you work makes you more effective and happier.

Kanban promotes continuous collaboration and encourages active, ongoing learning and improving by letting the team define the best possible team workflow. Decisions in Kanban are made based on the scientific method instead of 'gut' feeling. Kanban discourages the idea of multi-tasking. This is because though multi-tasking gives an impression that lot is being done but in reality lot of time is lost when switching between works.

Why Kanban?

Kanban board is very effective in finding bottlenecks in the agile software development process. As in the case of Fig. 7.7, analysts can analyse maximum of 6 themes, developers can develop 5 themes and testers can test 4 theme. On any given day, it is observed that testers have 5 themes to test which 2 themes greater than what testers can handle. Though developers can deliver 6 themes but only 4 can be production ready as testers do not have bandwidth to test the remaining two. That is, here testers are bottleneck in the system.

If the team is not aware of this bottleneck, then with each development cycle backlog of work will begin to pile up in front of the testers. Work sitting in the pipeline ties down investment, creates distance from the market and drops in value as time goes by. To keep up, testers may start to cut corners. This will further result in bugs getting leaked to production.

Table 7.4 Differences between Kanban and scrum

Kanban	Scrum
No specific prescribed roles of team members	Prescribes roles of scrum master, Product owner and team member
Continuous delivery	Time-boxed delivery
Work is pulled from backlog one by one	Work is pulled from backlog in batches at the start of the sprint
Cycle time	Velocity
More appropriate in operational environments with a high degree of variability in priority	More appropriate in situations where work can be prioritized in batches that can be left alone

On the other hand, if the team is made aware of the bottleneck in time, then they could have redeployed resources to help relive the test team. For example, analysts could have helped testing while developers could have helped develop automated tests.

How is Kanban different from Scrum? Kanban and scrum both focus on releasing software early and often. Both require highly-collaborative and self-managed agile teams. Table 7.4, however, lists the few differences between their approaches.

FEATURE-DRIVEN DEVELOPMENT (FDD)

Feature-driven Development (FDD) is a client-centric and architecture-centric agile software development methodology. Here client refers to stakeholders/customers. As the name suggests, features are an important aspect of FDD. In FDD, *feature* is defined as small client deliverable functionality. For example, 'Password rest', 'Authorize a transaction', 'Validate password strength', etc.

FDD consists of five main activities as shown in Fig. 7.13. These include:

1. **Develop overall model:** The project starts with a high-level walkthrough of the system and its scope. Next detailed walk throughs are held for each module area with the help of small groups. Each group prepares a model after appropriate peer reviews and discussions. Finally, the model is integrated to come up with a high-level model of the system.

2. **Build feature list:** The overall model is used to decompose the complete functionality into small deliverable features.

3. **Plan by feature:** Next, ownership for development of various features is assigned to chief programmers.

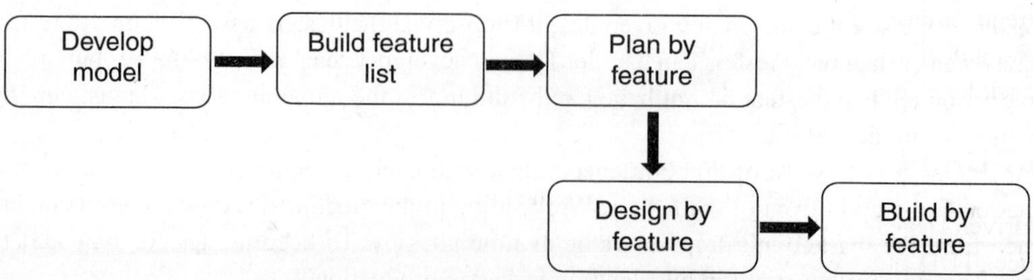

Figure 7.13 *Feature-driven development*

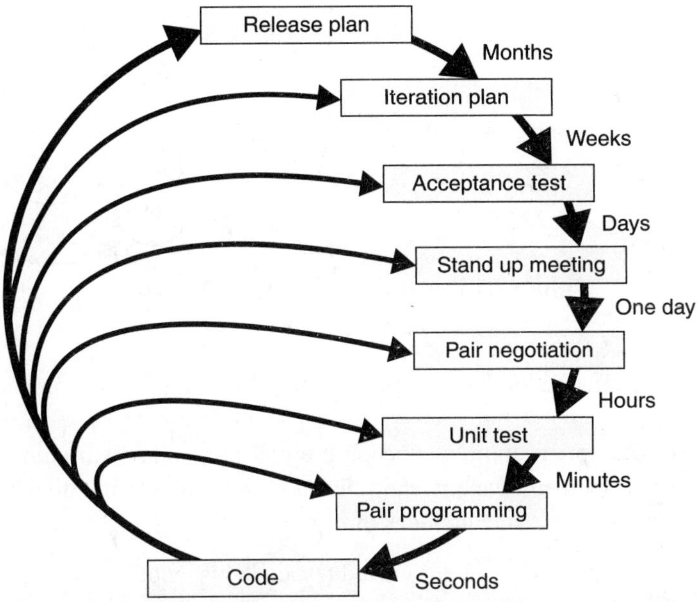

Figure 7.14 *Planning/Feedback loops of eXtreme programming*

4. Design by feature: Chief programmers select the list of features which can be developed in two week iteration. The team works out a detailed sequence diagram for each feature and refines the overall model. Next, the team writes class and method prologues and finally a design inspection is held.

5. Build by feature: After a successful design inspection, team works to develop the complete client-valued function (feature).

There are six primary roles for an FDD project: project manager, chief architect, development manager, chief programmer, class owner and domain expert.

EXTREME PROGRAMMING (XP)

Extreme Programming (XP) is an agile software development methodology which advocates frequent releases to production and improved programmers responsiveness to changing customer requirements. Extreme programming lays emphasis on pair programming, simplicity and clarity in code and frequent interaction code developers with customers. Pair programming involves extensive code reviews and continuous unit and integration testing of all code. Figure 7.14 shows the panning and feedback loops of XP methodology.

TEST-DRIVEN DEVELOPMENT (TDD)

Test-driven Development (TDD) is an agile practice that interweaves testing within the development practice. TDD promotes on very short development cycles with each cycle followed by a testing phase. As shown in Fig. 7.15 tests are executed after each phase of development—coding, integrating,

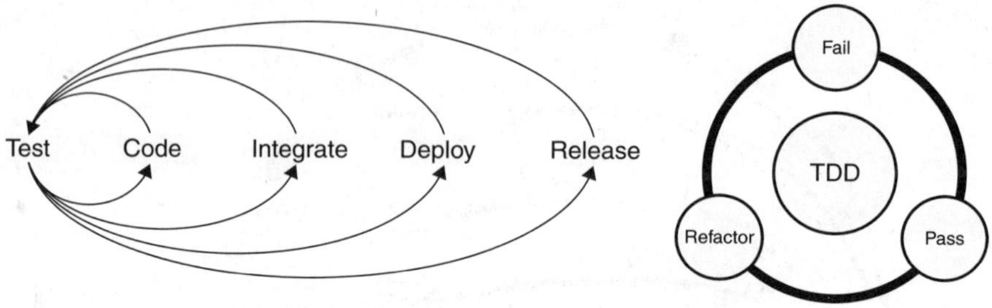

Figure 7.15 *Test-driven development (TDD)*

deploying and releasing. The developed code is rejected if either of development code or test code fails.

TDD advocates test-first programming concept. It emphasizes on repetition of a very short development cycle. Since development cycle is short, TDD relies heavily on automated tests to execute tests quickly. TDD development cycle includes three phases: fail, pass and refactor.

1. **Fail:** First the developer writes an automated test code just enough that it fails.
2. **Pass:** Next, writes the minimum code required to make the test pass.
3. **Refactor:** Finally, refactor the code to acceptable standards.

Test-driven Development Life Cycle

There are six steps for a typical TDD life cycle:

1. Add test: In test-driven development, development of each new feature begins with writing a test. This test must inevitably fail because it has been written before the actual feature has been implemented. To write a test, the developer must clearly understand the feature's specification and requirements. Developer can also modify an existing test, if that deems fit. This is the essential difference between test-driven development and unit tests (which are written after code is developed). This makes the developer focus on the requirements *before* writing the code.

2. Run all tests and verify if the new tests fail: Next step is to execute the complete test suite including the newly developed tests. Once execution is complete, verify the new tests that have failed. This ensures that test harness is working correctly and new tests do not give a false pass.

3. Write code: Next step is to write some code that causes the test to pass. At this stage, code is not expected to adhere to the project coding standards, so anything that just works fine (passes) is acceptable.

4. Run tests: Run all the tests to ensure all tests pass and meets all the testing requirements.

5. Refactor code: Next step is to clean up the code and move it to appropriate place in the test automation framework. Also, refactor code so that it adheres to the test automation framework standards. Any duplicate code needs to be removed at this stage.

6. Repeat: The size of changes made to code should always be restricted to small, say 1 to 10, edits between each test run. The code increments including external library file increments should always be small with each increment followed by the complete life cycle as discussed earlier.

CONTINUOUS INTEGRATION (CI)

Continuous Integration (CI) is a development practice that requires developers to merge their code into a centralized shared repository several times a day. Each check-in is verified by an automated build. This allows teams to detect problems early. Also, since build size is small, it makes it easier to track down the buggy code in case the code has defects. Moreover, since code commits are less it is easier to track the person whose code commit caused this bug. In short, bug detection, bug fix ownership assignment and buggy code detection becomes a lot faster and easier with continuous integration.

CI Principles

CI emphasizes on the practice of frequent integration on one's code with the existing code repository. This should happen frequently enough that no intervening window remains between commit and build. Any error in code check-in or build creation should create an alarm and should be addressed with no loss of time. The reason being a failed build or commit may block the continuous integration pipeline defeating the main objective on continuous integration of frequent deployment and frequent testing. CI hugely relies on complete automation of build creation and deployment and builds certification process. Following are some of the principles and practices of CI.

- Maintain a code repository
- Automate the build
- Make the build self-testing
- Everyone commits to the baseline every day
- Every commitment should build on integration machine
- Keep the build fast
- Test in a clone of the production environment
- Make it easy to get the latest executables
- Everyone can see the complete build pipeline and what is happening in there including the results of the builds
- Automate deployment

How CI Works?

In CI, multiple builds are committed in a day with each build on an eligible candidate of go-live build. If the build successfully passes the complete cycle then this build is deployed to production servers. Else if the build fails at any stage, then this build is rejected for go-live and next incoming build is considered. This loop continuously goes repeating.

Figure 7.16 shows a typical CI cycle. In CI cycle, developers commit code to the centralized repository multiple times in a day. As soon as the code is committed, the code is packaged as a build and

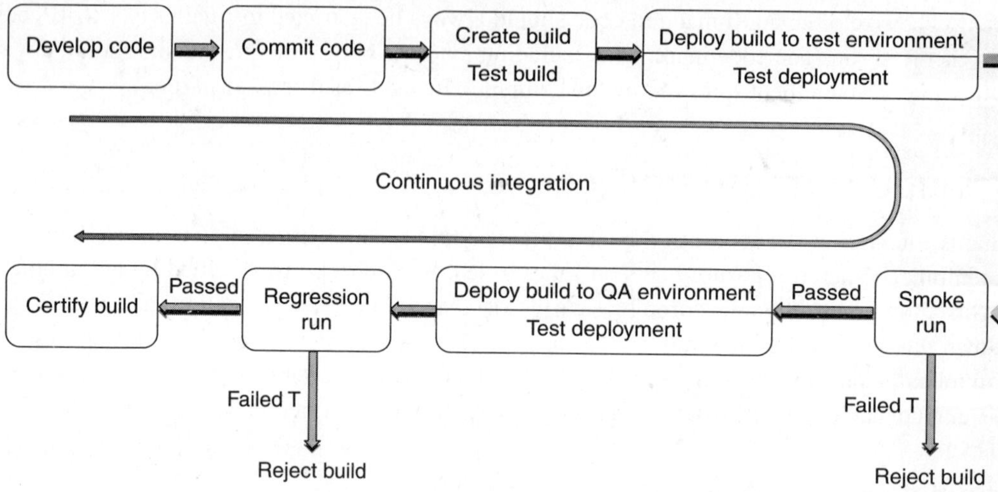

Figure 7.16 *Continuous integration cycle*

a build test is run to ensure build is fine. Next, the build is deployed to test servers where smoke run is executed. The smoke run can comprise of API tests, unit tests, integration tests, GUI tests, security tests, performance tests, etc. If smoke run fails, then the build is rejected and further steps of life cycle are not executed. Else, if smoke run passes, the build is deployed to QA servers and tests are executed to test that deployment has happened successfully. After deployment regression run is executed. Regression run can comprise of API tests, integration tests, GUI tests, security tests, performance tests, cross-platform tests, etc. If regression run passes, then the build is considered certified for production deployment.

One of the tools to easily achieve complete automation of CI cycle is Jenkins. An important feature of CI is both the application code and the test code flows in the same pipeline. So say if some new application code has been developed then the test code to test this application should also be checked in with the same build. This ensures any new code or changed code is tested. This is very essential as in CI every build is an eligible candidate of go-live. Figure 7.17 shows a typical CI pipeline of Jenkins. As the figure shows there is continuous code commits (8:40 am, 9:03 am, 10:01 am and 11:37 am). Each code commit is built and assigned a build number (or pipeline number). If the build fails at any stage during the pipeline, then that build is rejected (as candidate of go-live build) and the pipeline waits for the next build. Any failure in this pipeline generates an alarm. Whenever there is an alarm, developers or SDETs need to quickly develop a fix and commit it. For example, Build #220 in the figure failed at 'Smoke Run' stage. Hence, this build was rejected (as candidate of go-live build) and further stages of the pipeline were never executed. Build #221 in the pipeline passes all the stages and hence the build is certified for go-live. Again, Build #222 failed at 'Regression Run' stage. In this case, the agile team needs to analyse the failures for the root cause. If the failure is because of a problem in the test then the test needs to be fixed quickly and committed. If the failure is because of a bug, then the severity and priority of the bug is to be discussed with the business owner. If the team feels that the bug is of low severity and a fix for the same can be deployed within next few builds,

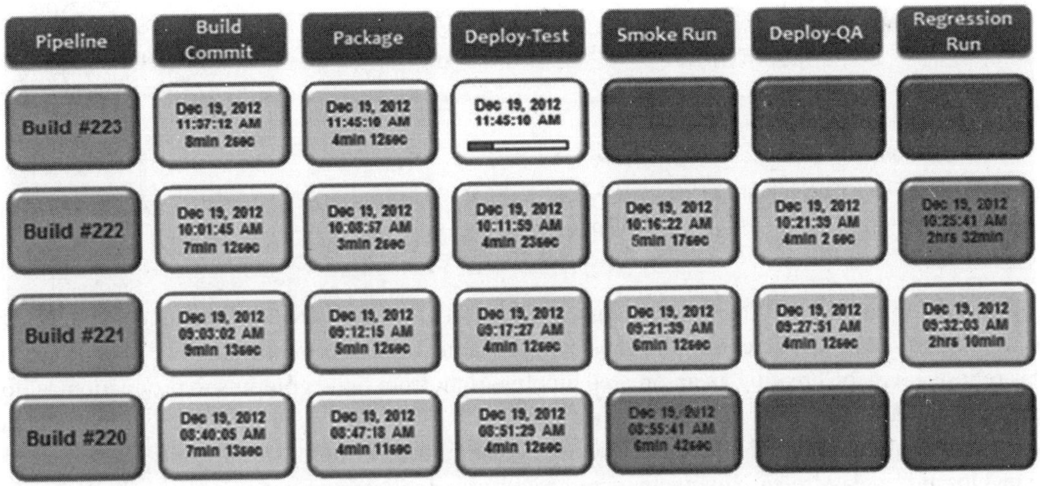

Figure 7.17 *Continuous integration pipeline*

then this build can be certified for go-live. In case bug severity is high, this build is again rejected (as candidate of go-live build). Build #223 pipeline shows that this build has successfully been packaged, and deployment of the build to TEST servers is in progress.

DEVOPS

DevOps is a software development method that emphasizes communication, collaboration and integration between development and IT operations team. DevOps is a response to the growing awareness that there is a disconnect between what is traditionally considered development activity and what is traditionally considered operations activity.

Development-centric folks embrace change. They come with a mindset that they are paid to accomplish change. Business depends on them to respond to the changing market needs. Hence, developers are encouraged to change as much as possible.

Operation folks embrace stability. They come with a mindset that they are paid to accomplish stability. Business depends on them to keep the applications stable as current business money is being generated from it only. Operations team is motivated to resist change that undermines stability and reliability.

The different goals of these two teams leads to a disconnect and confusion between the developers and the operations. Two classical examples of the same disconnect are:

1. Operations team saying that the release cannot be built as it is missing some components while developer team saying that it is getting built perfectly on their local machine.
2. Operations team saying that the release has bugs while the developer team saying that the bug is not reproducible on their local machine.

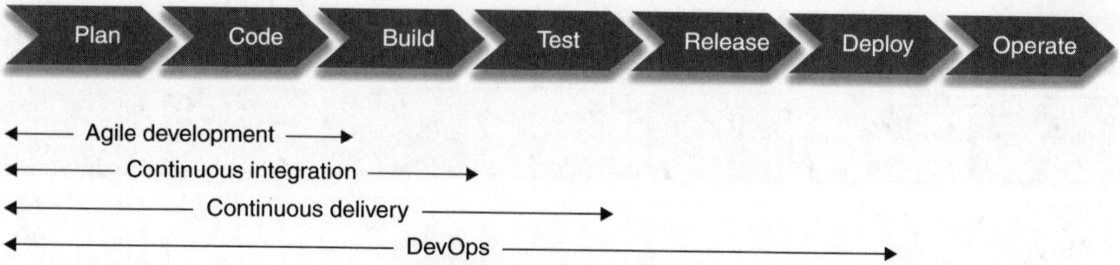

Figure 7.18 *DevOps*

To bridge the gap between these two teams, a new practice of software development called DevOps was developed. DevOps overcomes the gaps by automating both development and IT operations. DevOps relies heavily on creating an automated pipeline right from build commits to production deployment. This pipeline is similar to 'Continuous Integration' pipeline discussed earlier with production deployment phase also included in this pipeline. Figure 7.18 describes a DevOps pipeline.

DevOps aids in easy release management of a software application by standardizing both development as well as operations environments. In recent times, DevOps has evolved an enterprise standard for continuous software delivery that enables organizations to respond to market opportunities and customer feedbacks rapidly, and balance speed, cost, quality and risk. It has evolved as a practice that fully automates processes of development, technology operations and QA to achieve an end-to-end automated release management cycle. Figure 7.19 shows DevOps as intersection of development, quality assurance and technology operations.

By implementing DevOps, enterprises can:

- Automate continuous delivery and DevOps processes.
- Facilitate real-time collaboration between teams.
- Establish common standards and protocols for all teams.
- Avoid problems arising because of communication gaps between different teams.
- Reduce lifecycle costs.

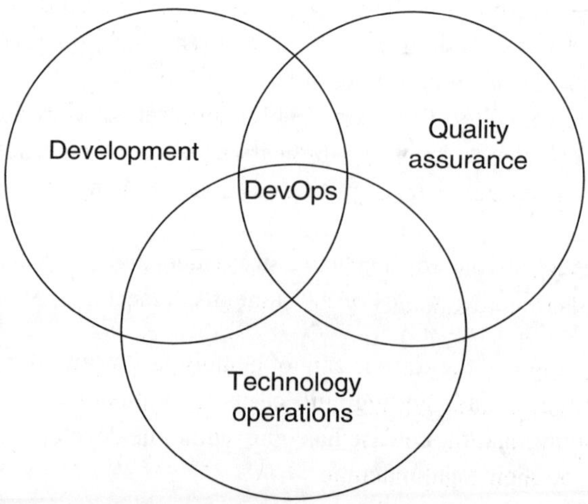

Figure 7.19 *DevOps as intersection of development, QA and technology operations*

Chapter 8

Agile Automation

Over the last decade, agile methodology has emerged from obscurity to most widely used software development methodology. Traditional approach of automation was designed to meet traditional development approach expectations. It no longer meets the expectations set by agile development approach. In traditional automation approach, automation activities started after application reached a specific state of stability; while in agile development methodology, automation is expected to start in parallel to the application development. That is, the automation activities should start even before application GUI is ready. Previously, test automation scope was limited to regression runs. In agile methodology, there are daily or weekly deployments to production. This creates a requirement to do functional testing, performance testing, and regression testing etc. on daily basis. With testing time squeezed out, test automation is expected to play a bigger role in testing. Test automation is expected to increase its horizon to all aspects of GUI and API testing. Previously first-hand testing using test automation was considered out of scope. But now with reduced testing time, this has become a necessity. Test automation team is expected to jump in and start testing the application as soon the application code is deployed in testing environment.

In agile automation, agile automation development iteration cycle is to be in sync with application development iteration cycle. Figure 8.1 shows a 3 week sprint (iteration cycle). As shown in the Figure 8.1 both application development and automation development iteration cycles are in sync. This implies application code and automation code that tests the application code are both delivered simultaneously. This is essentially important in agile methodology because the latest deployed application code is rejected for go-live if either the application code or the automation code that tests it fails.

In this chapter, we will discuss why agile automation is need of the hour and how to implement it.

Iteration Cycles	Sprint 1			Sprint 2			Sprint 3	
	week 1	week 2	week 3	week 1	week 2	week 3	week 1	w
Application Development								
Automation Development								

Figure 8.1 *Agile development iteration cycle*

WHY AGILE AUTOMATION

Today, organizations round the globe are embracing agile methodology of software development. Agile method with its core principle of frequent deploys to production has set stringent testing targets. Manual testing team with its limited capabilities can't alone meet the testing expectations set by agile methodology. In todays' world, Test team relies heavily on Test Automation to match agile methodology testing expectations. Traditional automation approaches with long cycles of test development fails to keep pace with these new expectations. This puts in place a requirement to develop a new test automation development methodology that best meets the agile software development expectations. This test automation methodology is called Agile Automation.

Continuously Changing Requirements

Agile methodology accepts the fact that changes to business requirements is obvious. Frequent changes in application code require frequent changes to test automation code as well. Traditional automation practices assume code maintenance to be costly and time consuming. It believes in developing and executing tests in relatively stable environment so that changes to automation code is minimal. This is not a realistic expectation for agile development. The test automation practices are to be agile enough to accept frequent changes as obvious. Test automation approach and framework should be agile enough to support easy, quick and frequent updates to the test automation code.

Frequent Code Deployments to Test/Automation Environment

In agile method of software development, code gets frequently deployed to test environment (or test automation development/testing environment). In most cases, there is a code deployment to test environment every hour or so. Traditional automation approach requires application to be stable for any automation activity to start, which means no frequent code deploys. This is an unrealistic expectation in agile. Hence, this requires replacing the traditional automation approach with a new agile automation approach that is dynamic enough to support test development in such a dynamic test environment.

Limited Time for Test Development

Agile methodology advocates automated testing of the code as soon as it is developed. This reduces test development time. Tradition automation approach which believes in starting automation activities once applicable is stable is no position to meet this agile development requirement. Hence, a new approach of agile automation is developed.

Test Development in Parallel to Application Development

As discussed above, agile methodology sets an expectation that code developed is to be automation tested as soon as it is deployed in Test environment. This requires that test automation code is ready as soon as application is ready. This is only achievable only if test automation development starts as soon as code development starts and test automation activities are carried in parallel to application environment. Traditional automation approach is not equipped with tools to carry out automation in parallel to application development. Hence, agile automation is the need of the hour.

Increased Test Automation Scope

Agile methodology advocates frequent deployment to production either daily or weekly and if possible multiple times in a way. This is because in agile methodology every checked in code is a candidate of go-live. This reduces the time available for testing time to few days or few hours (as per production deployment plan). Manual testing team cannot achieve the set testing expectations within this reduced time frame and hence, is heavily depended on test automation to speed up testing activities. This has increased the expectations and testing scope for test automation. Previously, test automation scope has mostly limited to regression testing. But now it has increased to all forms of GUI and API testing, including first-hand functional testing. Traditional approaches of automation are not equipped to effectively manage rapid GUI and API testing. Hence, it requires an automation approach which supports agility in true spirits.

Limited Time for Test Execution

Agile method advocates minimum time lag between code deployment to test environment and code deployment to production. This time lag, generally, is to be in hours. Such a short time span requires rapid test execution and quick analysis of failed results. This requires test automation framework to be competent enough to achieve quick testing and reliable to the point reports. Also, it requires that failures be notified to team as soon as they occur. Precious time is lost while waiting for automated runs to complete before failed tests analysis can begin. It requires a framework that supports agility in true spirits. Hence arises the need of agile automation framework.

Increased Test Execution Frequency

As discussed, in agile methodology each and every checked in code is an eligible candidate of go-live. This requires that every checked-in code goes through all types of testing. Since, developers checks in code multiple times a day. Hence, it is required that automated tests are also executed multiple times. This requires that test executes quickly within an hour or so. If automated test take more time for execution, then essentially it will block code deployment. This is because deploying code to test environment when automation tests are running is not advisable. Testing in such a way may result in defect migration to production. It may happen that after specific test were passed by automation new code deployment broke that functionality. This will give a wrong impression that application is working fine though it is not.

To let development code flow smoothly to build pipeline and get frequently deployed to test environment, it becomes imperative that the test automation framework supports rapid testing. The actual automated test execution time should not be more than 1–2 hours.

> **NOTES** It is strongly advised to block any code deployment to test environment when test execution is in progress.

AGILE AUTOMATION VALUES

Agile automation advocates similar values as advocated by agile manifesto. They include:

Individuals and Interactions Over Processes and Tools

Agile automation advocates resolving query and issues through quick meaningful discussions.

Working Test Code Over Documentation

Agile automation advocates developing self-readable code. Automation developers should spend time in developing code rather than developing documentation that helps develop code. Working test code is valued over any documents.

Responding To a Change Over Following a Plan

Agile automation advocates agility in test automation. It promotes quick adaptability of automation development and execution plan to changing business needs. New automation requirements which have high business criticality are to be prioritized over existing automation plans or activities. Agile automation framework is be flexible enough to accept frequent changes to both automation framework API code as well as test code.

Continuous Incremental Bundled Value Over Periodic Bundled Value

Traditional automation approaches believed in picking up functionality and delivering automated test code for the complete functionality at a time. Generally, it took weeks and months for automation code to get delivered. Periodic delivery of tests is to be avoided. Agile automation advocates continuous delivery of tests to production (test run execution). Automated tests are to be delivered (formed part of regression suite) as soon as they are developed. In a day, multiple automated tests should get added to the automation test suite.

In agile methodology basic features are developed first and then it is enhanced over further development cycles. Similarly, in agile automation basic code is developed and delivered first and then the developed code is enhanced in further development cycles as per application test requirements. This agile automation supports continuous incremental bundled value.

AGILE AUTOMATION PRINCIPLES

Agile automation is based on the following principles:

1. Customer satisfaction by rapid delivery of automation code and automated execution.
2. Welcome changes to automation test code, even late in test code development phase.
3. Working automation code is developed frequently, preferably, multiple times a day.
4. Working automated tests is the principle measure of progress.
5. Sustainable automation development with ability to maintain a constant pace.
6. Close daily co-operation between automation developers, agile team, toolsmiths and automation architects.

7. Face-to-face conversation is the best form of communication.
8. Automation team built around motivated individuals, who should be trusted.
9. Continuous attention to technical excellence and good framework design.
10. Automation developers are essentially part of agile teams.
11. Agile teams' test automation priorities supersede other automation activities.
12. Regular adaptation to changing requirements.

AGILE AUTOMATION CHALLENGES

The major assumptions of traditional approach of automation are:

- Application should be stable.
- Necessary documentation (or test cases) should be available.

These two assumptions of traditional approach are major challenges to agile automation. When agile automation starts neither application is ready not any documentation exists. No you may ask – How automation can be carried out when the know-how of the application as well as application itself is missing.

In this section, we will discuss how to address these challenges to successfully carry out automation within agile team. Figure 8.2 describes the various challenges while carrying automation within agile teams.

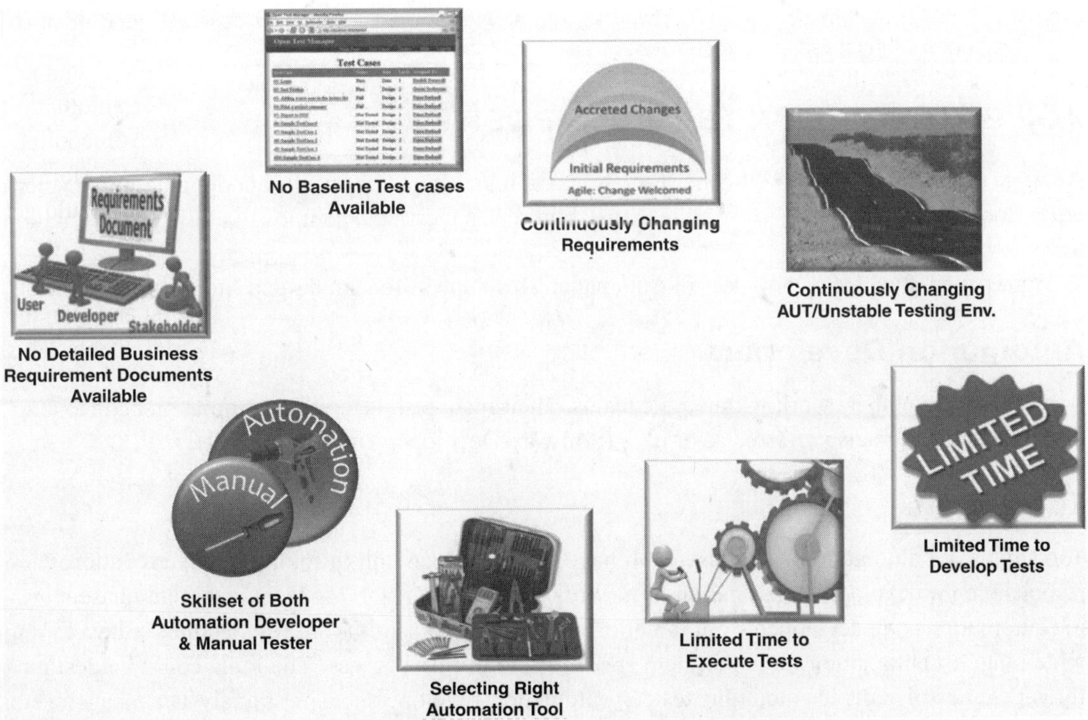

Figure 8.2 *Agile automation challenges*

Agile Automation Challenges	Solutions
• No Detailed Business Requirement Documents Available	Communicate with the business owner and stakeholders to gather business knowledge.
• No Baseline Test cases Available	Communicate with the testers, developers and other stakeholders to gather business knowledge.
• Continuously Changing Requirements	Develop re-usable code and framework APIs. APIs should implement smallest reusable functionalities so that changes to test code could be quick and easy.
• Continuously Changing AUT/Unstable Testing Env.	Develop one point maintenance framework and automation code versioning. Sync with developers, identify the changes and implement the changes in automation code. Both automation test code and application code should flow through the same build-pipeline. This will keep automation code in sync with application code. Such sync would ensure, application is always stable for any test run.
• Limited Time to Develop Tests	Develop automation code as incremental bundled value, i.e., develop basic code first and then enhance the code incrementally.
• Limited Time to Execute Tests	Use lab machines to reduce automation suite execution time. Avoid unnecessary use of wait statements in code. Prioritize tests on basis business criticality. Execute tests on the basis on business criticality and application code change impact.
• Selecting Right Automation Tool	Select automation tools that helps develop robust tests in less time.
• Skillset of Both Automation Developer & Manual Tester	Hire resources with skillset of both automation developer and manual tester.

AGILE AUTOMATION TEAM COMPOSITION

An agile automation team could consist of automation architect, toolsmiths and automation developers co-located with and supporting agile teams. Figure 8.3 shows the composition of agile automation team.

Agile Automation team comprises of Automation Developers, Toolsmiths and Automation Architects.

Automation Developers

Automation developers work within agile teams. Their main task is to write automation code to automate tests. They are also referred as SDETs (Software Developer Engineer in Test).

Toolsmiths

Toolsmiths are automation specialists who have experience coding in multiple languages. They are responsible for developing automation framework APIs, tools, resolving technical issues and reviewing automation code developed by automation developers. Toolsmiths are responsible for developing wide range of automation tools that help speed up the testing process. The tools could be designed for wide range of audience including testers, automation developers, business analysts, managers, etc. For example, developing tool that automatically compares the inventory levels of products in various

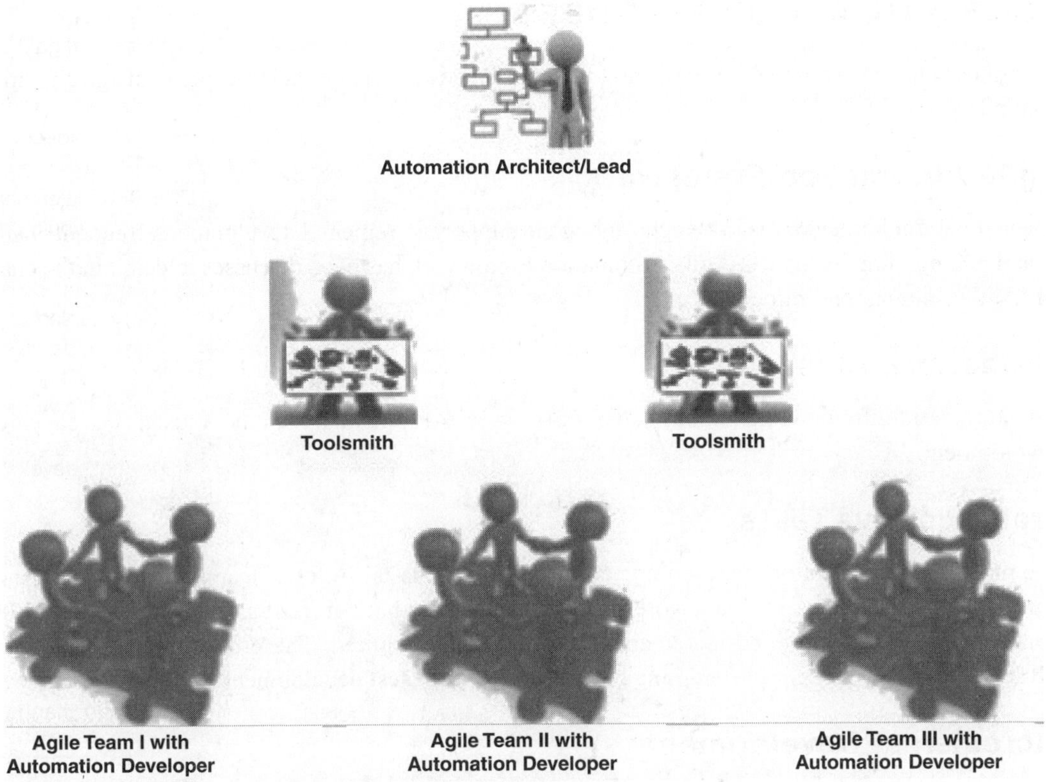

Figure 8.3 *Agile automation team composition*

databases or tools that help decide taxes applied are correct or tool that automatically extracts the test execution progress and sends it to a pre-defined audience. Automation developers may also substitute as toolsmiths depending on their expertise. It is advisable to train all the automation developers to be toolsmiths as well.

Automation Architects

Automation architects design and develop the automation architecture and framework for various test automation projects. They maintain the complete automation infrastructure. They are responsible for implementing innovative automated solutions within the team. They may also act as toolsmiths depending on project requirements.

In agile automation team composition, automation work to the automation developers is not assigned by the toolsmiths or automation architects. In agile methodology, automation developer decides the automation activities he would work on depending on the development activities picked up the team for the sprint. The decision regarding the automation activities that will worked upon is taken by the automation developer in collaboration with the team. It's Scrum Master who manages all the work being done by the agile team members.

AGILE AUTOMATION PRACTICES

Describes below are some of the agile automation practices which will helps implement agile automation in true spirits.

Agile Automation Framework

The automation framework is to be agile enough to support incremental development, frequent changes and one-point maintenance. Agile Automation Framework has been discusses in detail in the chapter 'Agile Automation Framework'.

Framework APIs

The automation framework should have framework APIs which can be reused for easy test development.

Framework vs Tests

The most important part of the test automation solution is 'tests'. A lot of teams spend most of their time and effort developing a framework with lots of features but bereft of any meaningful tests. The framework is to be developed incrementally as and when required. The proposition of creating an advanced framework is always tempting but at the same time test development should not be ignored.

Incremental Development

The process for creating automation code is to be same as agile development process. As in agile, basic features are developed first and then those features are enhanced during further iteration cycles. Similarly, basic automation code is to be developed first and then enhanced as application gets enhanced.

Use Checkpoints

A lot of teams end up automating test without any verification points or checkpoints. Absence of verification points in the test can make the test useless. In absence of verification points the test may show pass though there could be a bug. For example, if suppose test code is written to verify placing an order on a e-Commerce site without any verification, then it may happen that order number may not get generated on order confirmation page or amount does not gets deducted from customer account or it may happen that the taxes were applied incorrectly.

Same Build Pipeline

Both development code and automation code that tests it should flow through the same build pipeline. Automation developers can access the local machines of developers to understand the look and feel and business flow. Also, the same can be used to develop tests. As soon as the developer checks-in his code, automation developers can also check-in their code. If it is not possible to check-in both development code and test code for the same build, then attempt is to be made so that time lag between these two check-ins is minimal.

Test Code Versioning

Both development code and automation test code should follow the same version sequence number. This is essentially useful to ensure a specific build has successfully been tested using right test code version.

Get Tests Out of Local Machines

The automated tests should be checked-out to server and made part of regression suite as soon as it is successfully created. Keeping tests idle on local machines is of no use. Automation test code is to be delivered as soon as it is developed and not at periodic intervals.

Lab Machine Execution

It is of no use to execute automated tests on local machines. This is because local machines may not simulate the exact customer environment. Local machine may have special privileges for which application may work fine but may fail for customer environment. All the automated tests should execute on automation lab machines against test environment or build certification environment.

Execution Time Matters

The testing time is limited in agile methodology ranging from few hours to maximum a day. Because of this Test suite execution time is a critical concern. Any unnecessary wait time or long wait time should be avoided in tests. Also, the framework should be capable to quickly handle unexpected exceptions.

Keep It Green

All the test in the test suite should be kept 'green', i.e., running successfully. However, if because of certain reasons tests are failing, then the tests is to be appropriately tagged to ignore executing the tests or ignore analysis of the tests. For example:

- Use @Ignore to instruct framework not to execute those tests.
- Use @DefectID= to instruct automation developers that the test will be failing because of a defect.
- Use @Maintenance to instruct framework that the test is under maintenance and hence, should not be executed.
- Use @Unstable to instruct automation developers that the test is flaky and may fail for unknown reasons. The analysis of the test flakiness is in progress.
- Use @Retired to instruct framework not to execute these tests as they have been retired.

In Java automation environment say Selenium, above can be implemented using annotations. While in UFT environment, above can be implemented using ALM test suite custom definitions.

NOTES

There should be specific SLA's for fixing every failed and ignored test. For example, no test should remain in failed (automation failure) or ignored state for more than two days or 10 consecutive runs.

Create Meaningful Tests

The most important part of the test automation solution is 'tests'. Automation developers are not to automate everything. Only those tests that add value should be automated. Also instead of creating multiple tests attempt is to be made to consolidate tests and automate them as one test. This saves lot of test development as well as execution time.

Precise Reporting

Framework is to be support automatic generation and sharing of test execution reports within automation developers and concerned stakeholders. Test errors and failures are to be reported in clear and concise manner so that people who are investigating them need not spend too much time figuring out what went wrong and where. Reports should be as simple and as visual as possible.

Create Test Automation Backlog

A test automation backlog is to be maintained that provides all needed information on various automation tasks. The test automation backlog could be categorized into various types such as:

- Tool creation/maintenance backlog
- Framework APIs creation/maintenance backlog
- Generic framework enhancement backlog

All automation developers and toolsmiths are to be encouraged to pick up tasks from this backlog as per their time availability.

NOTES

There is no category for test creation/maintenance backlog because this needs to be handled by the automation developer within the agile team (that is agile team backlog).

Make it Visible

Framework should support automatic generation and sharing of summary of all test run results with the concerned stakeholders. The test execution history and trends is to be available online and if possible hooked to quality analysis tool like Sonar.

Chapter 9

Agile Automation Framework

In agile environment, by the time the GUI is ready there is very little time left for automation. Moreover, if the test cases are not ready, then automation cannot be started. This makes test automation very difficult in agile environment. Most of the existing frameworks fail to support agile test automation. This happens because of the high script development effort associated with them. The test automation team lags behind the agile iteration cycle. Most of the time reasons are that GUI was ready during the last iterations of the agile cycle, test cases were developed too late, environment is not stable, and test script development takes time. Automation in agile environment requires an automation technique that supports fast and reliable script development method, minimum dependency of script development on GUI, and no dependency on the manual test cases. In short, it requires an agile test automation framework.

Agile automation framework is a dynamic framework designed to achieve rapid automation. This framework has been designed and developed by the author, Rajeev Gupta. This framework minimizes the automation development and maintenance effort. The framework setup cost of Agile Automation Framework is also very low. Within few hours, the complete framework can be setup and the test automation activity can be started. This framework enables the users to dynamically automate the test cases from MS Excel sheet. Just few 'keywords' and test data need to be defined in the MS Excel sheet. This saves a lot of time and effort. The framework offers the flexibility to the users to dynamically design the regression suite. Users can dynamically design the automation suite to do any of the testing types—selective testing, comprehensive testing, life-cycle testing, positive testing, negative testing, smoke testing, etc. Agile Automation framework can be implemented to achieve low-cost rapid scale automation. It is not necessary for the application development model to be agile to use this framework. This automation framework supports all types of application development models and has special features to easily support agile application development model.

The life cycle stages of the agile automation framework are so chosen that they best fit into the agile development environment. The automation developers can carry out the task of test automation in parallel with the application development. Automation developers engage themselves in knowledge gathering and component tables (test cases) design while the GUI is getting developed. Once the application is developed, automation developers quickly start developing test scripts by automating one screen at a time. All the functionalities of the screen are coded in the respective script itself. This requires extensive programming skills. This framework is steps ahead of all the existing frameworks.

Previous to data-driven framework, record/playback method of script design was used. With data-driven framework came the concept of scripting methods of script design. Keyword-driven method brought out the concept of complex scripting to make test automation easier with a compromise on the automation cost. Agile automation framework brings in the concept of 'programming' or 'coding' to develop test automation scripts. The concept of programming reduces the cost of test automation by an extensive margin. Agile automation framework greatly reduces the framework setup cost, test development cost, and test maintenance cost. Agile automation framework achieves this by implementing the concepts of object-oriented programming—abstraction, inheritance, polymorphism, and encapsulation.

Agile automation framework uses the business-scenario-driven approach to increase the test coverage and as well reduce the test development effort. In agile automation framework, automation developer is expected to have the business knowledge of the functionality under implementation. The automation developer is responsible for identifying the test scenarios and test cases for automation. In this framework, first of all, a rough model of the business scenario is developed. This model helps in identifying the screen components, business components, and the decision logic 'keywords.' Decision logic keywords control the execution logic of both the screen component and the business component. In this framework, for every screen there exists an automated script called *Screen Component.* All the permutation and combination of the screen functionality is coded in the screen components using logical statements. The decision to execute the specific functionality is decided at run-time by the decision logic keywords. *Business Components* make a call to various screen components to automate the smallest reusable business functionality. Each and every screen component and business component have verification logic coded within them. It helps to check whether the respective script has executed successfully or not. It helps to identify the exact reason and point of error in case of script failure.

The specialized architecture of agile automation framework helps in maximizing reusability of the test scripts. Since all the functionality of the screen is coded in the screen component, it can easily be reused for automating any other business scenario that uses this screen. The decision logic to execute the specific functionality of the screen components or the business components is controlled by the keywords defined in the MS Excel sheet. These keywords form the decision logic inside the screen components and the business components. The driver sheet reads the data sheet and executes the test case as specified by the 'keyword' combination. The combination of these keywords can be varied to dynamically automate more and more test cases of the same business scenario. The MS Excel sheets are designed in a way that allows the users to dynamically decide which test cases to execute and which not. It even offers to perform negative testing easily by defining negative data in the data sheets. The driver script automatically captures the error reason along with the application screenshot and writes them to the data sheet. In this framework, data sheets also act as test reports. All pass/fail status along with fail reason and error screen shots are updated in the data sheet itself. It helps in quick analysis of test results.

FRAMEWORK COMPONENTS

The agile automation framework segregates the automation activities into several independent units called framework components. Each framework component refers to a specific test automation activity. These framework components are loosely coupled to each other and offer a centralized maintenance

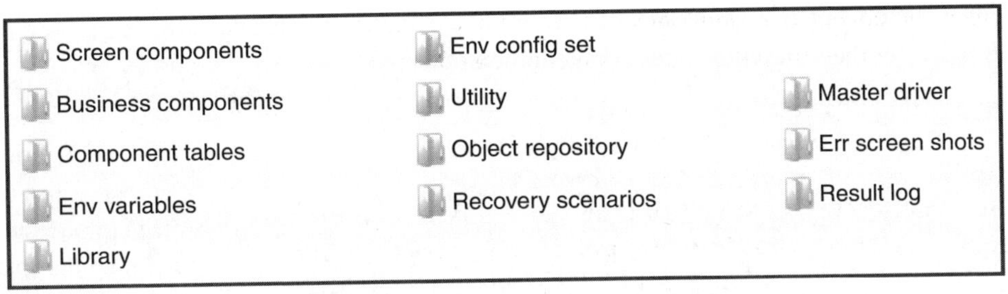

Figure 9.1 *Framework components*

control. All the framework components are designed to be independently managed. Figure 9.1 shows the framework components of the automation framework. It includes the following components:

SCREEN COMPONENTS

These are reusable test scripts (or actions). Screen components are the only components that are allowed to interact with GUI end in this framework. For each screen (or web page) in AUT, there exists one screen component. All the functionalities of the screen are implemented in these scripts. A screen of an application may implement various application functionalities. Scripts are coded to implement all the functionalities of the screen. Decision logic is used to decide which functionality to execute during run-time. A decision is made based on 'keywords' present in the component table. For every screen component, there exits one screen component table (SCT). All the keywords and data required to execute a screen component is defined in these tables. The keywords and test data are passed to the screen components using input parameters of an action. The test output data including pass/fail status and error reason is sent back to the calling script using output parameters. It is always advisable to keep all the screen components (actions) of the same business scenario in the same test. The SCT can be designed in the QTP data tables or MS Excel. Using MS Excel as component table has specific advantages over QTP data tables. For details, refer the chapter 'Working with MS Excel.' Screen components can receive the test input data either as value or as keyword. The various combinations that are allowed include:

AUTO: Screen component should itself select or extract the test input data that is required to execute the specific screen component. Screen components can execute SQL queries on AUT database to extract the valid test input data. It is always advisable to retrieve the valid test input data from the AUT database. This helps to:

- Reduce the chances of error while defining test input data in the component tables.
- Saves time as user need not specify the test input data.

NULL or "": Keyword 'NULL' or en empty value ("") in test input data implies that the screen component should not take any action on the object whose test input data is specified as 'NULL.'

RESET: Keyword 'RESET' in test input data implies that the screen component should reset the value of the object.

<value>: Any other values, other than the above-mentioned values, imply that the screen component should set the value of the object as specified in the input parameter.

In the screen component, decision logic is to be built to decide what value needs to be set for the object. For example, refer the following code for an edit box object.

```
    'Test input data
    iUserName = Parameter("UserName")
    iPassword = Parameter("Password")
'If test data 'User Name' value is neither NULL nor RESET,
'           then write the specified value to the object
    If iUserName <> "NULL" And iUserName <> "RESET" And iUserName<>""Then
       Browser("QTP").Page("QTP").WebEdit("UserName").Set iUserName
    'If the value is 'RESET' then reset the value of the object
    ElseIf iUserName = "RESET" Then
       Browser("QTP").Page("QTP").WebEdit("UserName").Set ""
    End If
```

It can be observed from the above code that no action will be taken on the object if the value of the test data is 'NULL.' The same code logic can be built for all the GUI objects including radio buttons, list box, check box, edit box, buttons, etc.

BUSINESS COMPONENTS

These are reusable test scripts (actions) that implement an end-to-end business functionality by calling the various screen components. Business components are coded to be flexible enough to implement most of the test scenarios of the business functionality. Business components are automated in a way to dynamically execute specific test case as per the data defined in the business component table (BCT) and Screen Component Table (SCT). Business components refer the respective BCT to identify the test cases to execute and the test data for the same. A BCT specifies the test cases and the SCT contains the test data for the same. Business components extract the test input data from the respective SCTs. This data is passed on the respective screen component scripts when they are called. Screen component updates back the business component with the execution pass/fail status and fail reason, if any. Screen components also pass on the specific transaction information such as booked ticket number to the business components. Business components update this data back to the BCT. The BCT is marked pass/fail and error reason, if any is updated. Business components also use the pass/fail status returned by the screen components to decide whether to stop the execution of the current test case or not. As mentioned earlier, business components call script components sequentially to automate business functionality. Suppose that business component calls three script components A, B, and C sequentially. If script component 'B' fails, then there is no point executing script component 'C.' In this case, a business component skips the execution of the current test case and starts executing the execution of the next test case in queue.

Component Tables

There are two component tables in the agile automation framework—SCT and BCT. SCT defines the test scenarios and test input data of the corresponding screen. 'Keywords' can be used to refer both the test scenarios and test input data, as required. BCT specifies the business functionality and the test input data for the same. The test input data is specified in the form of keyword that is a reference to a specific data of the script component table. The combination of these keywords can be varied to automate various test cases. Business components scripts automatically execute the test case as specified in the component tables. Both business component and script component may or may not exist in the same MS Excel file. SCT and BCT together offer the platform to dynamically automate the test cases. This makes the agile automation framework a dynamic framework.

Screen Component Tables

These are the MS Excel sheets containing the test scenarios and the input data. There exists an SCT for each screen component script. The test scenarios and test sub-scenarios exist in the form of 'keywords.' These keywords form the decision logic of the screen components. The screen components use these keywords to decide which test sub-scenario (code logic) to execute during run-time. The test input data can exist in the form of 'keyword' or the exact data value. Screen components table define data for both positive and negative testing. Figure 9.2 shows a template layout of the SCT.

SeqNo	TestDescription	Comments	TestType	TestScnro	TestSubScnro1	TestSubScnro2

iInputParam 1	iInputParam 2	iInputParam...n

iExpMsgOnPageLoad	iContinue	iSubmitPage	iExpMsgOnPageSubmit	iPageSubmitMsgLoc

Figure 9.2 *Screen component table design layout*

In Agile Automation Framework, the component table is treated as database. SQL queries are used to retrieve and update data in the component tables. Figure 9.2 shows a typical layout of the component table. The fields marked '*' are mandatory fields. The name of these fields should remain as it is across all the component tables. The various fields of the component table are:

SeqNo: Unique sequence identifier for the component table. It can take values 1, 2, 3, and so on.

TestDescription*: Description of the test data.

Comments*: This field can contain any other useful information apart from the data description.

TestType*: Indicates the type of testing that can be done using this data. It can take two values—Positive and Negative.

TestScnro: Indicates the test scenario that the specified test data can implement. Screen components use this 'keyword' to decide which test scenario (code logic) to execute during run-time. The keywords in this column provide information about the test scenarios that this screen component implements. All the keywords should be present in the form of list, so that users can easily select them.

TestSubScnro: Indicates the test sub-scenario that the specified test data can implement. This field contains a keyword that decides the test sub-scenario to execute during run-time. A combination of the keywords of the 'TestScnro' and 'TestSubScnro' field provides information about the test scenarios that have been automated. If there are more than one test sub-scenarios, then more fields can be added in the MS Excel sheet with name *TestSubScnro1, TestSubScnro2,..., TestSubScnron*. All the keywords should be present in the form of list, so that users can easily select them.

iInputParam: Indicates the test input data such as login username and password. The name of this field should be named after the GUI object to which data is inputted. The name could be so chosen that it easily helps to identify the data type and data purpose. For example, if the input parameter is for inputting data to the 'UserName' edit box, then name of this field could be 'iUserName.' 'i' in 'iUserName' stands for test input data. Similarly, if the test input parameter is for inputting data to the 'Country' list box for specifying the country name, then this field should be written as 'iCountry.' All the input parameters can be specified one after another in sequence. The various acceptable values that can be specified for this field include:

<value>: Actual value that needs to be inputted to the screen. For example, for 'UserName' edit box, the value can be 'Alex.' Similarly, for list box 'Country,' the value can be 'India.'

AUTO: Keyword 'AUTO' implies that test scripts should itself extract or select the valid test data. For example, suppose that the test case is to search and see if a transaction ID can be searched in the GUI. In this case, test script can directly connect to the AUT database and retrieve a valid transaction ID number. The same can be used as test input data for executing the test case. This relieves the user from manually searching the data in AUT and then specifying the same in the component table. This saves lot of time and effort.

NULL or " ": Keyword 'NULL' or an empty value ("") implies that the screen component should not take any action on the object for which this data is specified.

RESET: Keyword 'RESET' implies that the screen component should reset the value of the object for which this data is specified.

All the test input data may not have all the options as mentioned above. Either a list of acceptable values is to be created or a comment is to be added for the MS Excel cell defining the valid values that the column can accept as shown in Fig. 9.3.

SeqNo		iTranID
1		AUTO
2		AUTO
3		908990
4		AUTO

Acceptable values:

1. <value>
2. AUTO

Figure 9.3 *Specifying valid acceptable values for a field as cell comment*

Generally, after submitting a transaction on a page, a confirmation message appears on the screen. This message can either appear on the same page, on a pop-up window, or on the next page that loads. For example, after click the 'Login' button on login page, the message 'login successful' appears on the next page (say Enter Itinerary page) that loads. Since screen components automate one page at a time, it is not possible to verify the message 'login successful' in the login page screen component. As this message appears in the 'enter itinerary' page, it needs to be verified in the 'enter itinerary' screen component only. Again, enter itinerary page can also have messages on the screen when this page is submitted. Therefore, 'Enter Itinerary' page can contain two types of messages—one when the page loads and the other when the page is submitted. To implement the same, the component table contains two fields—*iExpMsgOnPageLoad* and *iExpMsgOnPageSubmit*. The first one specifies the messages of the page when the page loads and the other specify the messages of the page when the page is submitted. If this field is left 'blank,' then it implies that the screen component needs not verify the messages appearing on the screen when the page loads. Again, if it is required to validate the messages on the screen, there can be multiple conditions. Listed below are the various conditions that can occur at runtime.

Test Condition 1

Verify screen message when the page loads
Do not take action on page objects
Do not submit page
Do not verify screen message on page submit

Test Condition 2

Do not verify screen message when the page loads
Take action on page objects
Do not submit page
Do not verify screen message on page submit

Test Condition 3

Do not verify screen message when the page loads
Take action on page objects
Submit page
Verify screen message on page submit

Test Condition 4

Verify screen message when the page loads
Take action on page objects
Submit page
Do not verify screen message on page submit

Test Condition 5

Verify screen message when the page loads
Take action on page objects
Submit page
Verify screen message on page submit

To implement these test conditions, two more fields are defined in the component table—*iContinue* and *iSubmitPage*.

iExpMsgOnPageLoad*: It specifies the message to validate from the screen when the page loads. If screen message need not be verified on page load, then this field is left blank.

iContinue*: It indicates whether the screen component will exit after validating the screen message on page load or not. It can accept two values—'Yes' or 'No.' 'Yes' implies that the screen component should continue execution after validating the screen message that appears on page load. 'No' implies that the screen component should exit execution after validating the screen message.

iSubmitPage*: This field specifies whether the screen component should submit the page or not. It can take two values—'Yes' or 'No.' 'Yes' implies that the screen component should submit the page. 'No' implies that the screen component should not submit the page. It is not always required to submit the page after taking action on page objects. Moreover, during automation maintenance phase, it may be required to add more functionality to the screen component before submitting it. There are two ways of doing this—adding additional lines of code in the script component or writing another script component that can be called after the existing screen component. However, the second method requires that the page should not be submitted. To achieve the same, this field has been specified. If the value of this field is changed to 'No,' then automatically the script component will not submit this page.

iExpMsgOnPageSubmit*: It specifies that the message to validate from the screen when the page is submitted. If screen message on page submit need not be validated then this field is left blank.

iPageSubmitMsgLoc*: It specifies that the location where the message can be expected after page submit. Generally, when the page is submitted, the screen message can either appear on the same page, next page, or pop-up window. This field specifies where to look for the message on the screen. It can take three values—CurrentPage, Pop-up, or NextPage. *CurrentPage* implies that the expected message will appear on the same submit page. *Pop-up* implies that the screen message appears on the pop-up window. *NextPage* implies that the screen message appears on the next page that loads. 'NextPage' value has no significance for the screen components script as screen components can only automate one screen at a time. It is just specified to make the component tables more user-friendly and readable. Any such verification needs to be validated in the screen component of the next page by specifying the 'iExpMsgOnPageLoad' field.

Business Component Table

BCT are MS Excel sheets that define the test cases and test input data for the same. It also contains test case description and the type of testing (positive or negative) that can be performed with the specified data set. First of all, the business scenarios that are to be automated are decided. Business scenario, here, refers an end-to-end business functionality. Each and every business scenario and business sub-scenario is assigned a 'keyword.' For each business scenario 'keyword,' there exists a business component. The business component script makes a call to the various screen components to automate the business functionality. In addition, the test data required to execute the business scenarios is present in the form of 'keywords.' Each keyword is a reference to a specific data of a specific SCT. Users are allowed to select/define appropriate keywords to automate a test case. The business components read the data from the business components table. Depending on the 'keywords' defined, it automatically decides which test case (screen components) to execute at run-time. The permutation and combination of these keywords can be varied to automate hundreds of test cases in one go. This makes the agile automation framework a dynamic framework that allows dynamic automation of test cases by just defining few keywords in the component tables.

The BCT also provides the flexibility to both define the test data and analyze the test results from the same window. To achieve the same, pass/fail status field, fail reason, and error screenshots field are defined in the BCT itself. This helps in easy and fast analysis of the test results. The component table of various runs can be used to compare two or more regression run results. In addition, these component tables can be directly used for preparing *Regression Run Report.* Figure 9.4 shows the layout of the BCT.

SeqNo	TestCaseID	TestDescription	ExpectedResults	RunTest	Status	FailReason

Comments	ScenarioType	BusnScnro	BusnSubScnro	iTestInputRef1	iTestInputRef..n

iOutputParam 1	iOutputParam 2	iOutputParam...n

ErrScreenshotsPath

Figure 9.4 *Business component table design layout*

SeqNo: Unique sequence identifier for the component table. It can take values 1, 2, 3, and so on.

TestCaseID: Test case ID of the test case.

TestDescription: Description of the test case.

ExpectedResults: The expected results of the test case.

RunTest: This field specifies whether to execute this test case or not. It can accept three values—RUN, NORUN, and COMPLETE. 'RUN' implies that the specified test case needs to be executed. 'NORUN' implies that specified test is not being executed.

Once execution is over and test cases passes, the status of this field is updated to 'COMPLETE' by the business component.

Status: Indicates Pass/Fail status of the test case. This field is updated by the driver script at run-time. It can take four values:

Pass: The test case has passed.

Fail: The test case has failed. In this case, 'FailReason' field contains the fail reason.

Error: The test case failed due to a run-time error while script execution. In this case, 'Comment' field contains the fail reason.

NotComplete: The test case is not tested fully by the test script. It implies that after execution of the test script, there are few steps that need to be executed manually. Theses steps can be manually specified in the 'TestDescription' field or the test script can be coded to write those test steps in the 'FailReason' field. This is generally done when we are executing test cases involving reports such as PDF or MS Word reports. Since it is difficult to automate reports, remaining test steps need to be executed manually.

FailReason: This field specifies the reason why the test case has not passed. This field is updated only in case the status of the test case is not 'Passed.'

Comments: This field is manually updated by the user after test result analysis, if required. In certain situations, test scripts may fail but the test case is still 'Pass.' Since it is not always possible to fix scripts during regression, the test case can be assumed passed with appropriate comments in the comments column.

ScenarioType: It specifies the type of the test case—positive or negative. It can accept two values—Positive or Negative.

BusnScnro: It specifies the business scenario or the business functionality that can be executed. For each unique 'keyword' defined, there exists one business component.

BusnSubScnro: It specifies the business sub-scenario or the business functionality that can be executed. The 'keyword' defined in this field controls the decision logic of the business component script.

iInputTestData: It refers the location from where the test data can be fetched. There exists a column of input parameter for each and every screen component called in the business component. The naming convention of this field is:

```
<Workbook name>_<Worksheet name>_<Sequence number>
```

For example, if second sequence number data needs to be extracted from the 'Login' sheet of the 'BookTicket' MS Excel file, then the keyword will be:

```
BookTicket_Login_2
```

The purpose of specifying workbook name is to create a unique identifier for the test data. Agile automation framework also supports logical path definition. It implies that only the path of the framework components is to be specified. During test execution, automation framework automatically looks for the specified file inside the framework folders. This is achieved by using windows COM methods, which is discussed in detail in the chapter 'Windows Scripting.'

oOutputParam: It indicates the test output data such as booked ticket number and transaction ID. This field is updated by the driver script. The name of this field should be named after the GUI object from which data is extracted. The name should be so chosen that it easily helps to identify the data type and data purpose. For example, if the output parameter is for specifying booked ticket number, then the field name can be 'oTicketNbr.' The letter 'o' in 'oTicketNbr' stands for output test data. Similarly, if the output parameter is of a transaction ID generated after executing a bank transaction, then the name can be 'oTranID.' All the output parameters can be specified one after another in sequence.

ErrScreenshotsPath: It indicates the complete path where the application screenshot is saved. This field is updated by the driver script in case a run-time error occurs during script execution. In agile automation framework, recovery scenarios are designed in a way that in case a recovery scenario gets activated, it will first take a screenshot of the application and then save it to the specified location. The name of the screenshot file is dynamically generated. The name of the screenshot should include the following details—name of the test, name of the action, test object name for which error occurred, test object type, and date–time stamp. It should be like:

```
<Test Name>_<Action Name>_<Object Name>_<Object Type>_<Error Reason>_
<Date-TimeStamp>
```

Example:

```
Test1_Action2_UserName_EditBox_Object Not
Found_10June2010111159AM.png
```

> **NOTES** In agile environment, there is no need to develop detailed test cases as the test detailed knowledge is already coded in the test script. This saves a lot of manual testing time and effort that otherwise goes wasted in developing detailed manual test cases.

> **NOTES** The MS Excel sheet should be formatted as 'text' before designing it. This is a mandatory step, as it helps to easily use MS Excel as database. Converting MS Excel type to text implies that the MS Excel database can have only 'text' type values. This helps in easily executing SQL queries in MS Excel without the need to know the data type present in the MS Excel sheet. In case of MS Access, all the column fields' type should be defined as 'String' type. However, for agile automation framework and Business model driven framework, MS Excel is to be preferred as it has many advantages over MS Access such as creations of list, easy data fill features, and normal and advanced search filters. The MS Excel sheet data can be sorted and arranged as per the requirement. These features help in easily defining the test data as well as easy analysis of the test results. For further advantages of use of MS Excel as database over use of MS Excel as datasheet, refer chapter 'Working with MS Excel.' Moreover, MS Excel has specific advantages over MS Access or other databases such as easy creation, maintenance, packaging, and installation. Refer the following steps to change the format of MS Excel sheet to 'text.'
>
> 1. Open new MS Excel workbook.
> 2. Open the desired worksheet (component table).
> 3. Rename the worksheet to *ScreenComponent* name, of which this component table is.
> 4. Select complete worksheet.
> 5. Navigate *Format* → *Cells...* *Format* Cells dialog box opens.
> 6. Click on tab Number.
> 7. Select *Category* 'Text.'
> 8. Click button OK.

EnvVariables

These are VBScript or XML files containing global variables, global constant variables and global static and dynamic arrays. The environment variables are accessible to all the test scripts throughout the run session. Changes made by one test script or function to the environment variable are accessible to the other test scripts. Only those variables need to be defined in the environment variable whose scope is global. Following are the good candidates of the environment variable:

- Variables that need to be accessed by various test scripts such as variables or arrays that store the data retrieved from the AUT database.

- Variables that define the application settings such as application parameters, username, and password.
- Variables that define the test automation bed such as application URL and application database details.
- Variables that define the framework settings such as framework location and framework components path.
- Variables that define the QTP settings such as QTP execution mode (fast or slow) and associated recovery scenarios.
- Variables that help in executing the same test script across multiple browsers, various test environments, data bases, etc.

Environment variables help in achieving one-point control for executing the same test script across multiple test environments. Just the environment variable values need to be changed and the script will be ready to execute in different test environment settings. Refer Appendix C for the naming convention of the variables. Figure 9.5 shows an example environment variables file.

NOTES

It is advisable to use VBScript files as environment variables, as it allows declaring global arrays and global constant variables too. Fur further advantages of the VBScript environment files over XML environment files, refer the chapter 'Environment Variables.'

Library

Library file is a collection of reusable functions. It can be a .vbs, .txt, or .qfl file. Functions are written inside library files to maximize code reusability. These functions are available to all the test scripts.

EnvConfigSet

EnvConfigSet framework component is a collection of .vbs or .bat file that contains test environment and QTP configuration settings. Test environment configuration files can include scripts that disable tabbed browsing, delete cookies, create specific result folders, or pre-set the AUT to a specific configuration. QTP configuration file can include scripts that loads specific QuickTest dll files, sets QTP run mode, loads recovery scenario files, loads library files, loads environment files, etc. QTP configuration file can also include scripts that configure the object identification settings of QuickTest for various application objects such Web, Web Services, SAP, Terminal Emulator, etc. These scripts may also contain information about the 'Run' settings of the QTP for the project.

Utility

Utility framework component is a collection of custom library or executable files that are required to support the test automation project. It can include dynamic link library (DLL) files, VBScript files, .bat files, or executable files. For example, there could be

- Custom DLL files for automating the Windows application.
- VBScript files to prevent the QTP system from auto locking.

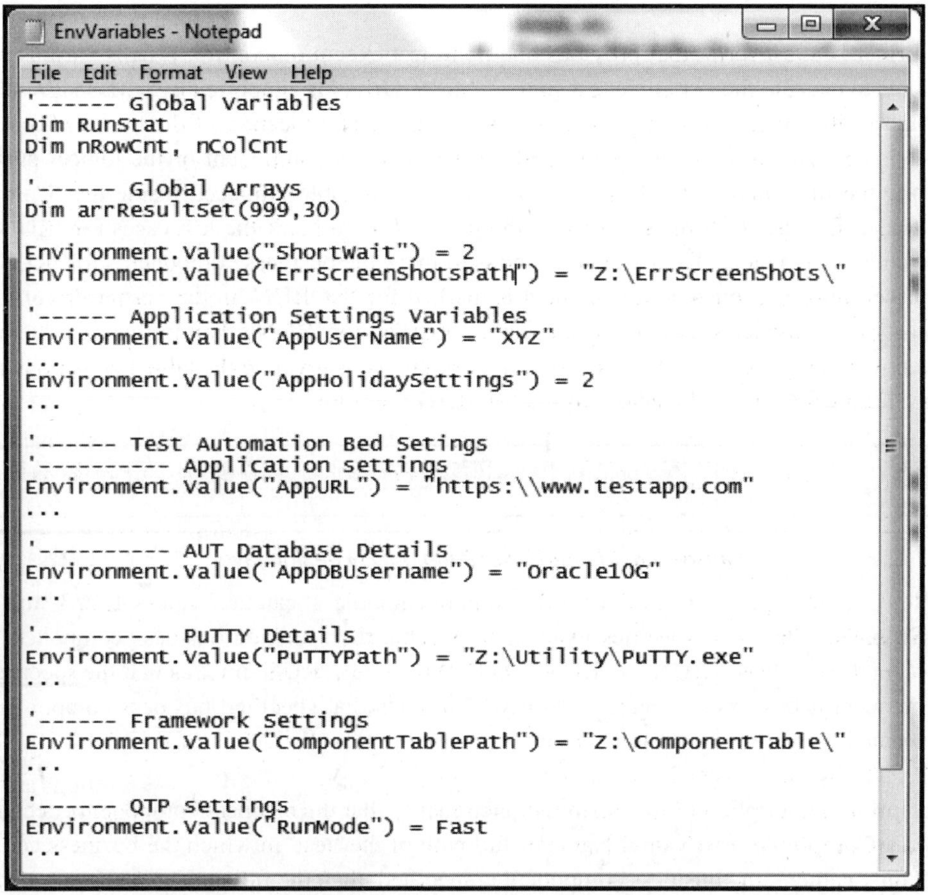

```
EnvVariables - Notepad
File Edit Format View Help
'------ Global Variables
Dim RunStat
Dim nRowCnt, nColCnt

'------ Global Arrays
Dim arrResultSet(999,30)

Environment.Value("ShortWait") = 2
Environment.Value("ErrScreenShotsPath") = "Z:\ErrScreenShots\"

'------ Application Settings Variables
Environment.Value("AppUserName") = "XYZ"
...
Environment.Value("AppHolidaySettings") = 2
...

'------ Test Automation Bed Setings
'---------- Application settings
Environment.Value("AppURL") = "https:\\www.testapp.com"
...

'---------- AUT Database Details
Environment.Value("AppDBUsername") = "Oracle10G"
...

'---------- PuTTY Details
Environment.Value("PuTTYPath") = "Z:\Utility\PuTTY.exe"
...

'------ Framework Settings
Environment.Value("ComponentTablePath") = "Z:\ComponentTable\"
...

'------ QTP settings
Environment.Value("RunMode") = Fast
...
```

Figure 9.5 *Environment variables file*

- .exe files such as PuTTY, WinScp, and Pfstp.
- .bat files for periodically taking the backup of the automation project.

Object Repository

This framework component consists of all the shared object repositories of the automation project. Object repository is a collection of GUI objects. It is always advisable to avoid multiple object repositories of the same application objects. For example, if in a project test automation is going for Web, SAP, and AS400 applications, then a single 'shared object repository' is to be maintained for all the three applications.

Recovery Scenarios

This component contains all the QuickTest Recovery Scenario (.qrs) files. These files are designed to ensure smooth execution of the automation suite in an unattended mode. These files are coded to handle the run-time exceptions, so that the exceptions do not stop or fail the automation suite.

Master Driver

Master Driver is a test script that provides one-point test execution control. It calls various business components to execute the complete test suite. A MasterDriver is supported by a *MasterDriverTable*. This table specifies which business components to execute and location of the business component. The table is designed to contain the full path of the business component or the logical path of the framework and the name of the business component. This table is placed inside the 'Component-Tables' folder. In order to form a test suite, the first task is to mark the test cases for 'RUN' in the business components table. Then, the next step is to mark the business components for 'RUN' in the master driver table. If a business component is marked for 'NORUN' in the master driver table but in the business components table the test cases are marked for 'RUN,' then in this case the business component will not get executed. This is because preference is given to the table that is highest in the hierarchy. Figure 9.6 shows the layout of the 'MasterDriverTable.'

SeqNo	RunScenario	Description	BusinessComponentTestName	BusinessComponentName

Figure 9.6 *MasterDriverTable (MDT) design layout*

SeqNo: Unique sequence identifier for the component table. It can take values 1, 2, 3, and so on.

RunScenario: This field specifies whether to execute the specified business component or not. It can accept three values—RUN, NORUN, and COMPLETE. 'RUN' implies that the specified business component needs to be executed. 'NORUN' implies that specified business component is not to be executed. Once execution is over and test cases passes, the status of this field is updated to 'COMPLETE' by the 'MasterDriver' script.

Description: Description of the business functionality that the business component executes.

BusinessComponentTestName: Name or full path of the 'test' in which the business component exists. If only name of the business component is specified, then the full path of the framework needs to be specified in the 'EnvVariables' file. A code also needs to be written that automatically searches the specified 'test' inside the framework folders in case only the logical path of the framework is specified in the environment variable file.

BusinessComponentName: Name of the business component.

NOTES

If the script development environment is not QTP, then all the business components can be treated as separate test scripts. In this case, the full path of the business component is to be provided in the 'Business-ComponentTestName' field while 'BusinessComponentName' field can be left blank or deleted.

ResultLog

This folder contains all the previous and current test run results. As we discussed earlier, in agile automation framework, the test results are updated in the component tables only. After the test execution is over, the master driver script exports all business components table, master driver table, and the QTP results to newly created folder in the 'ResultLog' component folder. The naming convention of the folder is shown as below.

```
   <RegressionRunName>_<Date>_<Time>
For example,
   Sprint32Regression_11-Dec-2009_11-12-59PM
```

Architecture

Agile automation framework is designed to achieve rapid automation. This framework has been developed to reduce cost to test automation. The architecture of this framework is robust and agile enough to support both positive and negative testing and as well offer an easy script development and maintenance environment. This framework offers centralized development, maintenance, and execution control. 'Environment Configuration Settings' file contains code that prepares the QTP machine for test development and execution. It includes settings that define QTP tool environment settings, loads system dll and custom dll files, presets the test environment, and defines the application configuration settings. In short, the purpose of this file is to prepare the *Test Automation Bed.* These files can either be scheduled for execution whenever the QTP machine restarts or can be called by the '*MasterDriver*' script. The master driver script refers to the 'MasterDriverTable' to identify the business components to execute. The master driver is a driver script that provides one-point execution control. It makes a call to the various business components specified in the master driver table to execute various business scenarios.

Business components are test scripts that calls various screen components to automate an end-to-end business functionality. However, at runtime, only specific test cases are executed at a time. The test case to execute depends on the test data specified in the BCTs. Business components refer the BCT and SCTs to identify the test cases that need to be executed and test data for the same.

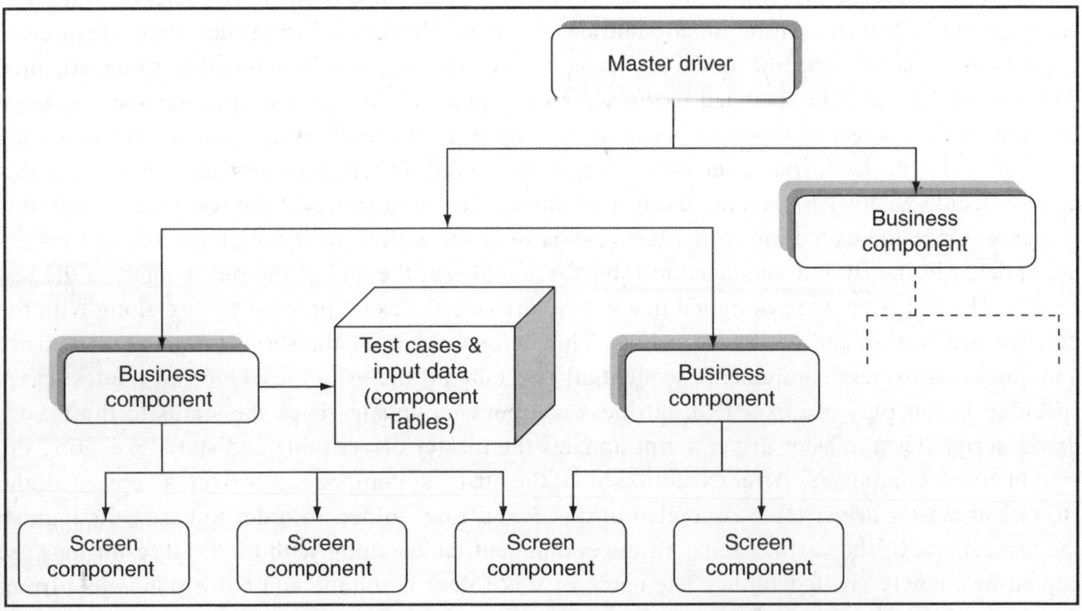

Figure 9.7 *Layout—agile automation framework*

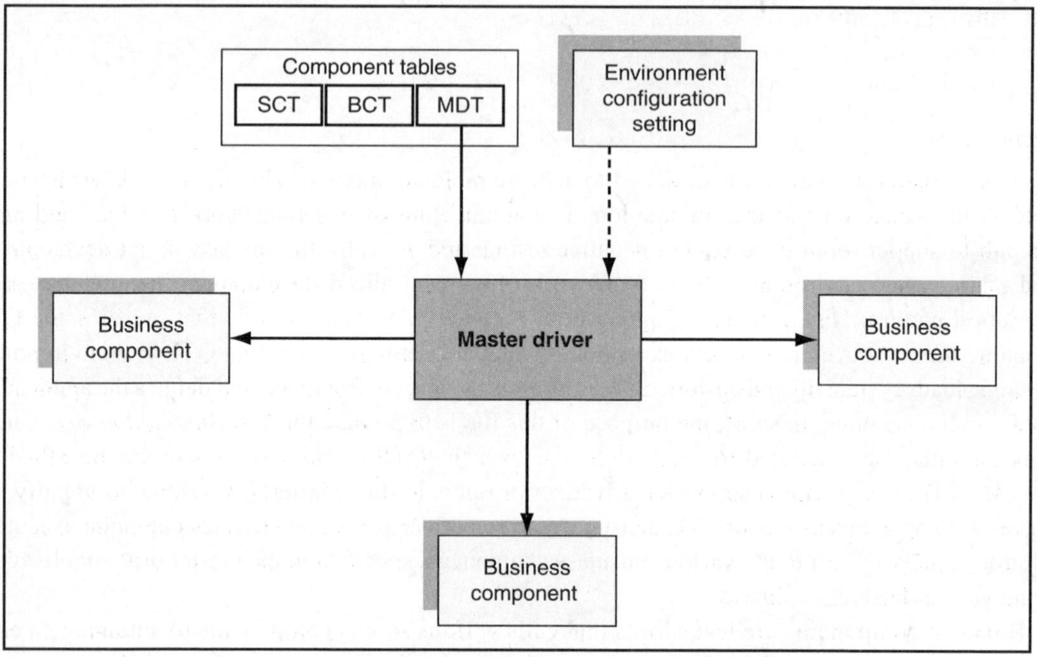

Figure 9.8 *Architecture: Master driver*

Thereafter, it calls various screen components sequentially and pass on the test data to them. Screen components are the test scripts that interact with the application GUI. A screen component is designed to automate all the functionalities of a page. However, during run-time, screen components execute only specific functionality at a time. The business functionality to be executed depends on the test data provided to the screen components through its input parameters. Once execution of the screen component is complete, it updates the business component script with the pass/fail status of the current execution along with the fail reason. Business components use this data to decide whether to execute the rest of the screen components of the test case or skip this test case. Once the execution of the test case is over (pass, fail, or incomplete), the test results are updated in the BCT. Users need to refer these tables at the end of the run to analyze the test results. The test scripts are designed in a way to provide the exact point of failure along with the detailed description and AUT screenshots. This helps to identify the script failure reason easily and quickly. Business components sequentially execute all the test cases. Once all the test cases specified in the BCT are executed, business components updates back the status to the master driver script. Then, master driver script updates the master driver table and starts executing the next business component. After execution of all the business components is over, a copy of all the BCTs and master driver table is created in the 'ResultLog' folder. In order to easily distinguish the test reports of the various runs, all the component tables along with the QTP result logs are copied in a newly created folder. The name of this folder is unique and corresponds to current data and time.

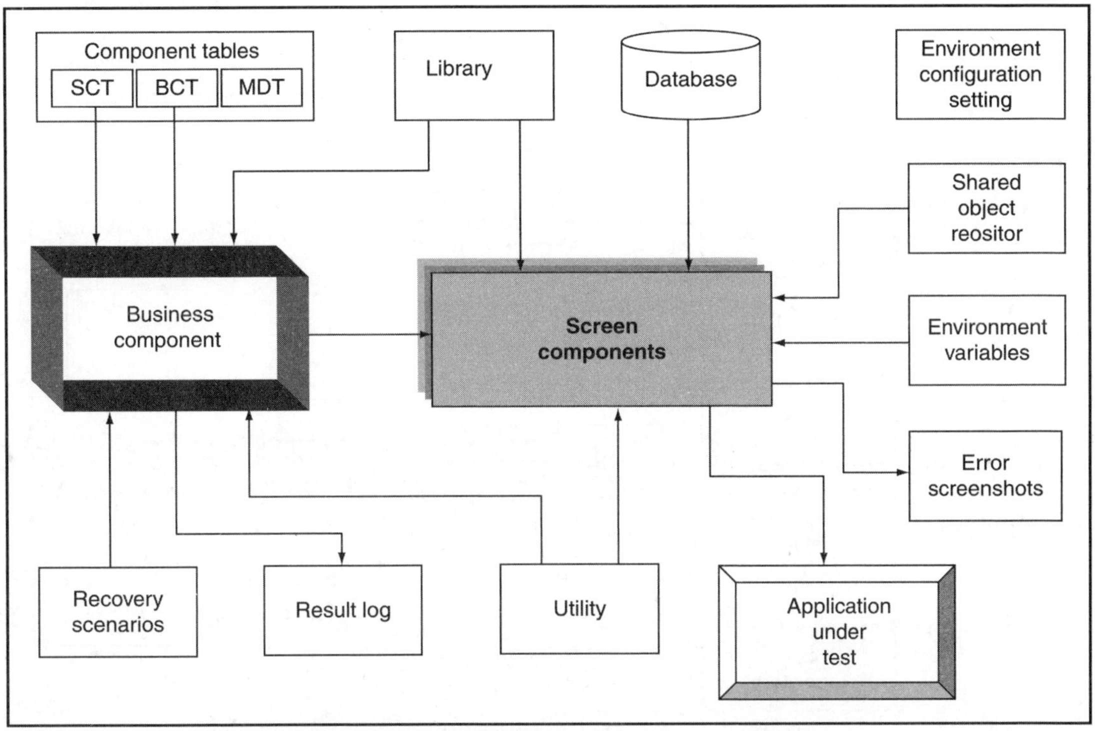

Figure 9.9 *Architecture: agile automation framework*

> **NOTES** It is much easier to analyze the test results from the BCTs than as compared to the QTP test results. This is because these tables point to the exact reason of script failure. The error reason is explained within few lines of text than as compared to the hundreds of lines of text as present in QTP result logs. For user convenience, QTP result logs are also saved. Users can refer these result logs whenever required.

FRAMEWORK STRUCTURE

Figure 9.10 shows the framework structure of the agile automation framework.

Apart from the above-mentioned components, there are other components such as task tracker and scripting guidelines that are part of the agile automation framework. These include:

- technical documents,
- standard and guidelines,
- training manual,
- user manual,
- task allocation tracker, and
- regression status tracker.

These components are to be created in a separate folder named 'Test Automation Documents.'

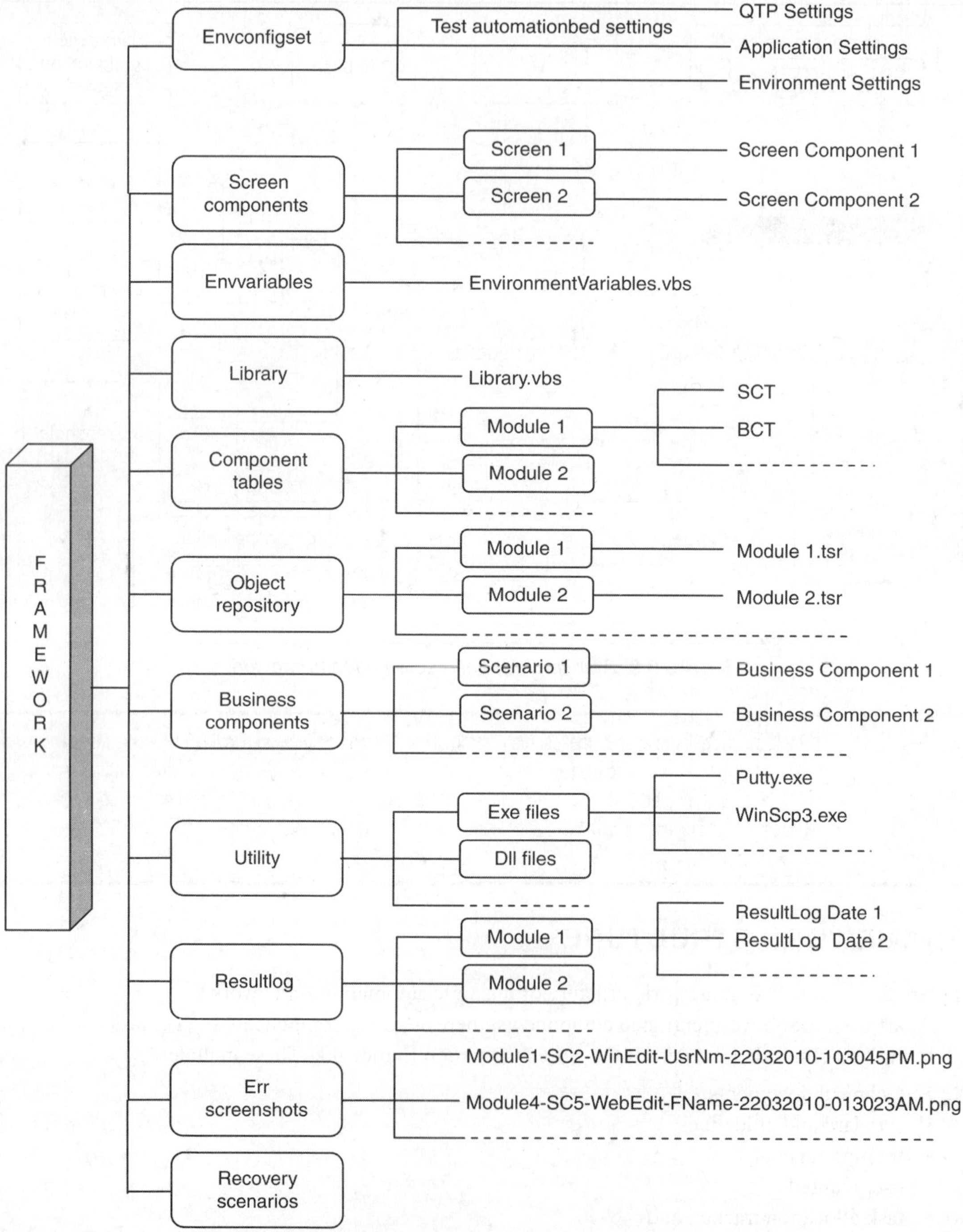

Figure 9.10 *Framework structure of agile automation framework*

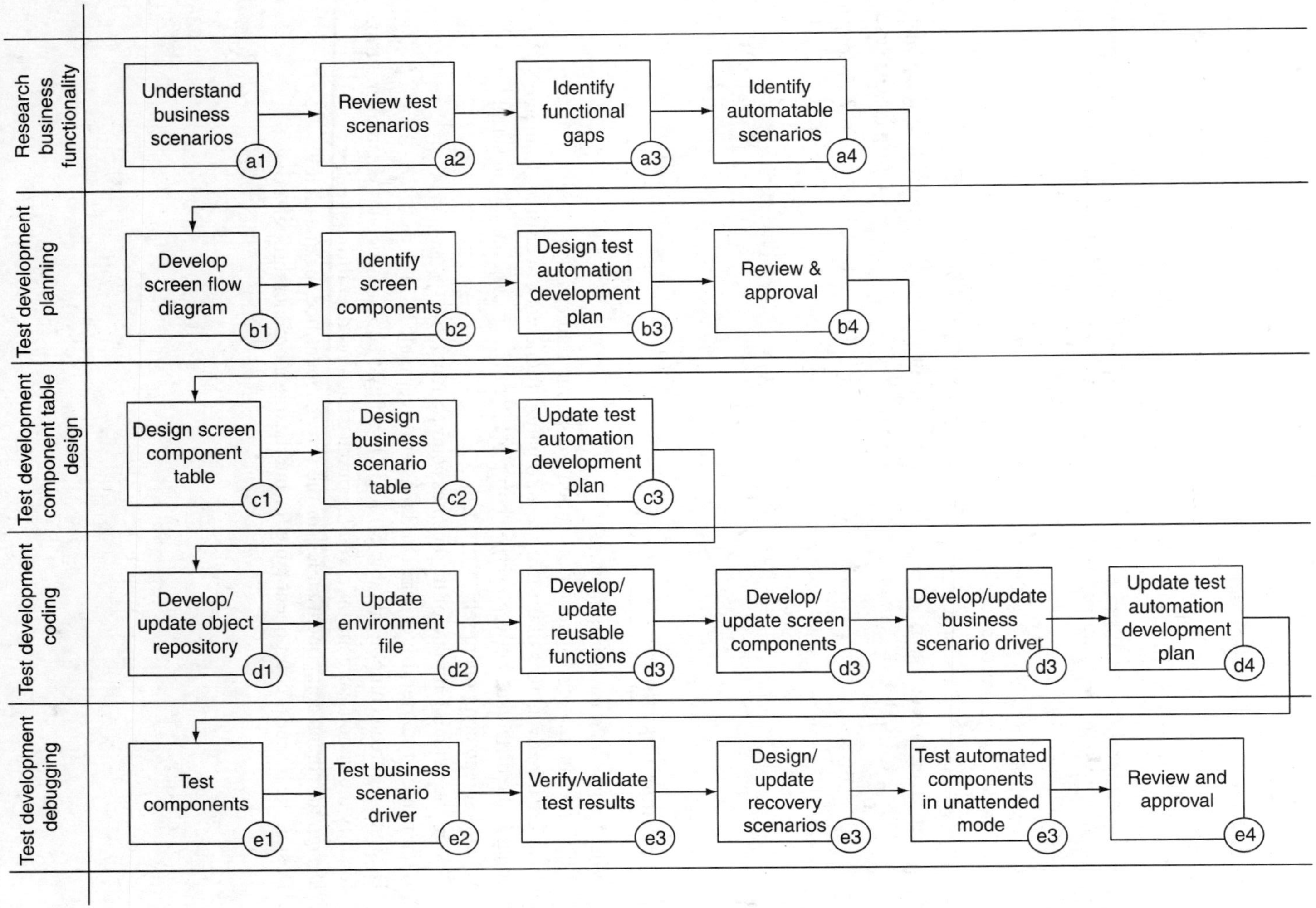

Figure 9.11 *Test automation process flow diagram of agile automation framework*

QUICK TIPS

- ✓ Use MS Excel as test data files.
- ✓ SQL queries to be used to retrieve/update data to MS Excel files.
- ✓ One-screen component should automate one screen at a time.
- ✓ Screen components to be designed in a way that in case of script failure, test execution control is transferred back to the business components along with proper execution status flags and error messages.
- ✓ Business components are to be designed in a way that current test script execution should exit in case of test case failure.
- ✓ Business component scripts are to be designed in a way that complete test suite is executed even if an error occurs during test execution. In case of an error, the current test case execution is to be exited and the business component script should start executing the next test case.
- ✓ Appropriate recovery scenarios are to be designed to ensure complete test suite is execute even in the worst case conditions (script failures).

PRACTICAL QUESTIONS

1. What is agile automation framework?
2. Why agile automation framework is called a dynamic framework?
3. What are the advantages of using agile automation framework over other frameworks?
4. What is the difference between screen component and business component script?
5. What is screen component table?
6. Design the default template of the business component table.
7. What is use of master driver script and master driver table?
8. Design the screen component table for login to a flight booking account viz. makemytrip.com.
9. Identify the various screens involved for purchasing a product through eBay.
10. Design the screen component tables for the screens identified for question 9.
11. Design the business component table for purchasing a product through eBay.

CASE STUDY
Automating a Business Scenario Using Agile Automation Framework

Now, let us see how we can automate a business scenario using agile automation framework. Let us assume that the scenarios for automation are to book a rail ticket. Figure C2.2 to C2.9 shows the various application pages involved while booking a ticket.

Framework Setup

Framework setup is one-time activity and needs to be done at the very start of the automation project. It is very simple and easy to setup the agile automation framework environment. First of all, a shared location drive needs to be created. Thereafter, all the framework folders or components, as shown in Fig. 9.1, need to be created. Next task is to develop the code for test automation bed settings. These include application settings, test environment settings, and QTP settings. Moreover, the basic library files, DLL files, and environment variable files are to be created at this stage only. Basic functions such as connection to MS Excel database, connection to application database, and creation of customized test results need to be made ready before starting the script development process. The executable files required by the project such as PuTTY.exe and psftp.exe are to be kept in the 'Utility' folder. In addition, a code needs to be developed that automatically takes the backup of the complete automation project at regular intervals. The rest of the framework sub-folders or sub-components such as business modules and sub-modules can be created now or at a later stage depending on the available information.

Apart from these, a separate framework component named 'Test Automation Documents' should be created. This component will contains all the test automation related files and documents. The various components of the 'Test Automation Documents' may include:

- Functional Docs
  - Documents (or document locations) related to various business scenarios
- SLA Docs
  - Service Level Agreement documents
  - SLA tracker and monitoring sheet
- Framework Design Docs
  - Automation project layout
  - Framework components
  - Framework architecture
- Training Manuals
  - Basics of test automation
  - Test script design as per tool and framework
  - Test automation requirement gathering procedure
  - Communication model etc.
  - Automation project backup plan
  - Automatability criteria

- Scripting and Guidelines
  - Test automation standards and guidelines
  - Coding standards and guidelines
  - Object identification standards
  - Naming conventions
  - Sample test scripts etc.
- Task Allocation Tracker
  - Test automation sprint cycle objectives and targets
  - Test automation task allocation sheet
  - Test automation development progress tracker etc.
- Regression Status Tracker
  - Regression execution schedule
  - Regression suite coverage
  - Regression suite effectiveness
  - Regression results tracker
  - Test automation metrics and graphs to analyze and interpret regression results etc.

The complete agile automation framework can be set up in 2–3 person days. This effort is far less when compared to the 'keyword'-driven framework where the effort is almost in months. Moreover, even after that, it cannot be considered fully complete. Agile automation framework is not only about creating an environment where test scripts can be developed. This framework is designed and developed in away to offer centralized one-point control over the complete automation environment. The framework has been split into various framework components to maximize framework reusability. The framework setup design helps to reduce both the development and maintenance costs of the test scripts. Moreover, it offers an environment where the test scripts can be programmed, a step above the previous frameworks where the method of automation was scripting. Most of the advanced coding features are implemented to make the test scripts reliable and robust. This framework best implements the principles of abstraction and encapsulation. Each screen is automated separately with appropriate input–output parameters to implement abstraction. A business components layer is developed above the script component layer to implement encapsulation. This layer hides the complexity that lies inside the script components. Automation developers are free to use most advanced programming logic and code inside the script components.

Test Automation Development

Test development can be started once the framework setup is complete. Figure C2.1 shows the agile automation test development cycle. The first step toward test development is to identify and prioritize the business scenarios to be automated. Automation developers are required to gather the business knowledge of the identified business scenarios. The technique for knowledge gathering can be either direct interaction with the functional experts or referring the requirement and functional documents or both. Based on the knowledge gathered, the automatable test scenarios are to be filtered out.

The next step for the automation developers is to familiarize themselves with the business flow, screen flow, and the various screens of the business scenario. Based on this knowledge, a rough screen

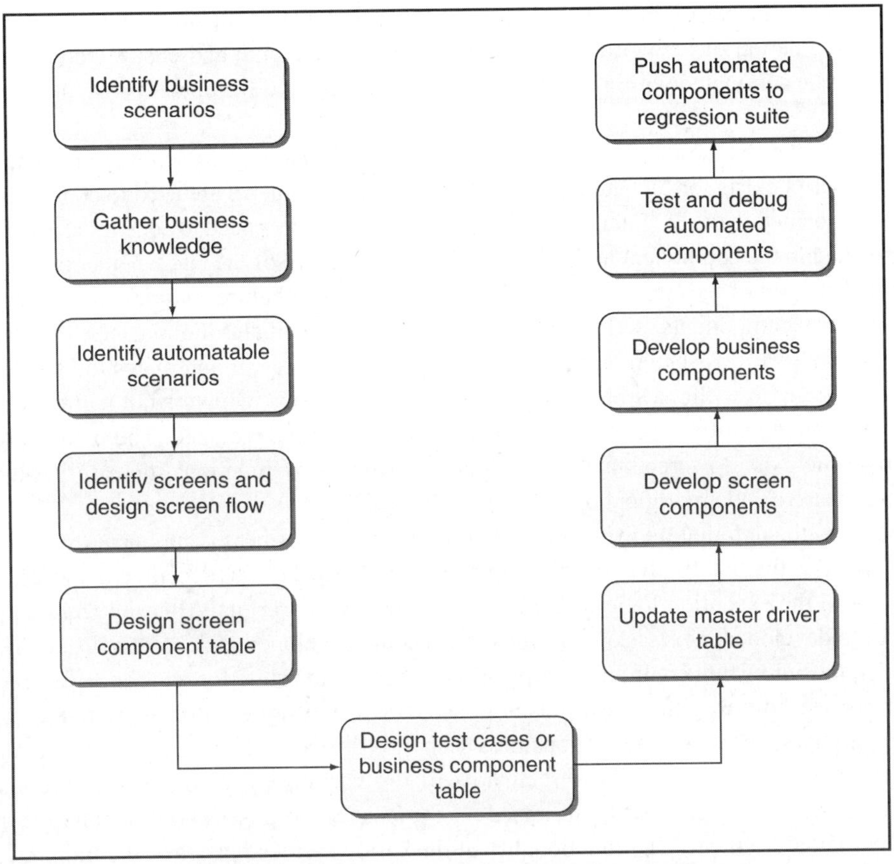

Figure C2.1 *Agile automation test development cycle*

flow diagram of the business scenario to be automated needs to be designed as shown in Fig. C2.10. The purpose of this diagram is to help understand the functionality of the various screens involved and their actual flow. This becomes very essential in situations where the application screens or pages are still under development.

Once the functionality of the various screens is fully understood, a SCT needs to be developed for each and every screen. The SCT contains information about the test sub-scenarios that the screen implements and the test data required for the same. The test sub-scenarios are specified as 'keywords' in the SCT. The test data can either be specified as value or as keyword as applicable. Users can vary the combination of the keywords and the test data to dynamically automate multiple test sub-scenarios. SCT implements all the functionalities of the screen irrespective of the fact whether the functionalities are going to be automated in the current agile cycle or not. The idea behind the same is to make future automation task easier. If the functionalities are already present in the component tables, then the scripts can easily be upgraded to automate new functionalities within hours.

The next step is to design the test cases in the BCT. BCT contains information about the test cases and the test data required to execute the same. The test cases are designed by varying the combination of multiple set of 'keywords' present in the table. The business scenarios, business sub-scenarios, and the test data exist as 'keyword' in the BCT. The flexibility to dynamically automate test cases by just varying the combination of keywords makes this framework dynamic and cost-effective. Hundreds of test cases can be automated within no time. This reduces the test development cost involved in this framework.

Once the BCT is ready, the automation developers can start developing the screen component scripts. A separate test script exists for each and every screen. Logical statements are used to control execution as per the data specified in the SCT at run-time. Automation developers need to code for all the functionalities as specified in the component tables. This is done irrespective of the fact whether the functionalities automated are part of the current agile cycle or not. This makes future automation task very easy.

Next, business components scripts are developed that automate the business scenarios by sequentially calling various screen components. A business component automates the test scenarios of the business scenario within a single script. For the test scenarios, which is not part of the current cycle or whose functionality is not clear; a template logic code is developed. The template helps to easily upgrade the existing scree/business components when new functionalities are implemented. This avoids excessive code modification.

It also reduces the automation effort of further automation. Business components scripts use the keywords defined in the BCT to dynamically execute specific test cases as specified in the BCT. These keywords control the execution logic of the business components scripts. After the required components have been developed, next task is to debug and test the developed code to remove all the coding errors. Finally, the automated components are pushed to regression suite for regression run execution.

Now, let us see how to automate a business scenario using agile automation framework. For explanation purposes, let us assume that business scenario to be automated is booking of a rail ticket through a train reservation site. The screenshots of the various pages of the site are shown in Figs. C2.2 to C2.9. The screenshots are just used for explanation purposes and is not an exact replication of any particular Web site. The functionality of the various screens/pages of the train reservation application is described below:

Login Screen—Login screen of AUT.
Enter Itinerary Screen—Screen to enter trip details and search for trains.
Check Schedule Screen—Screen to check arrival, departure, and train timings schedule of various trains.
Select Train Schedule—Screen to search and select appropriate train.
Summary Screen—Screen to display selected itinerary details.

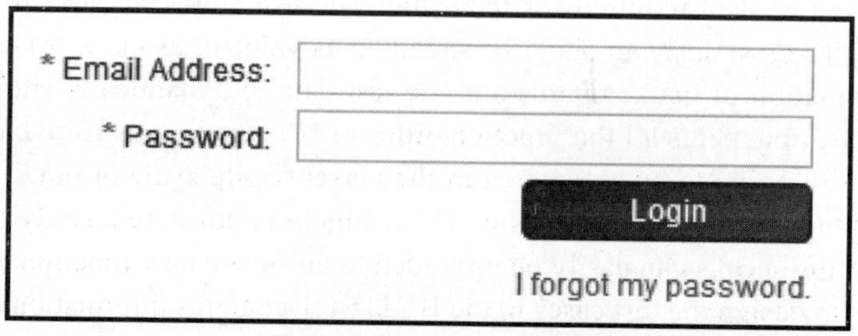

Figure C2.2 *Login Page*

Figure C2.3 *Enter itinerary page*

Figure C2.4 *Check schedule page*

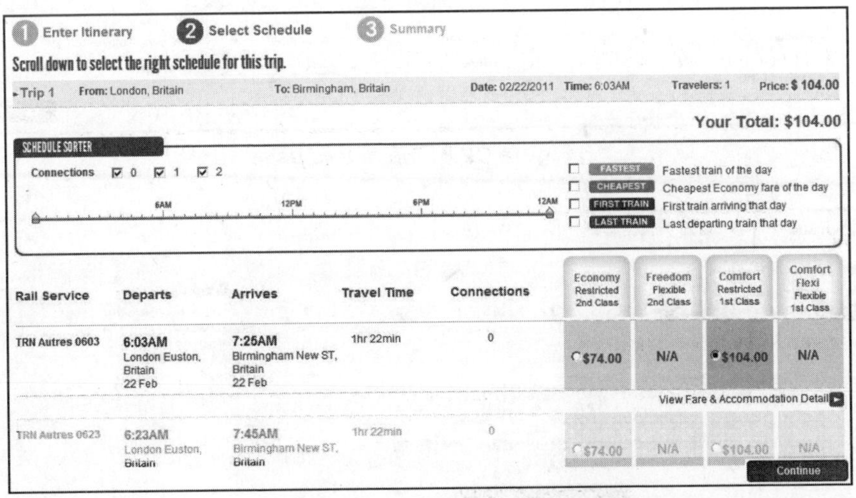

Figure C2.5 *Select schedule page*

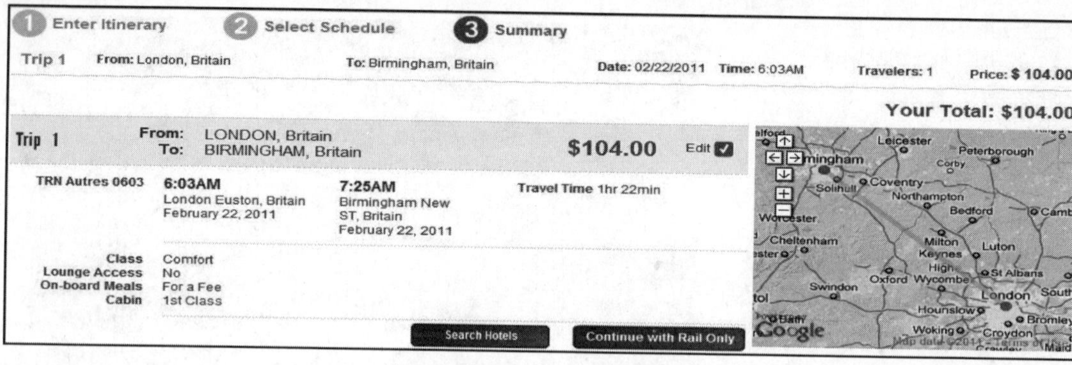

Figure C2.6 *Summary page*

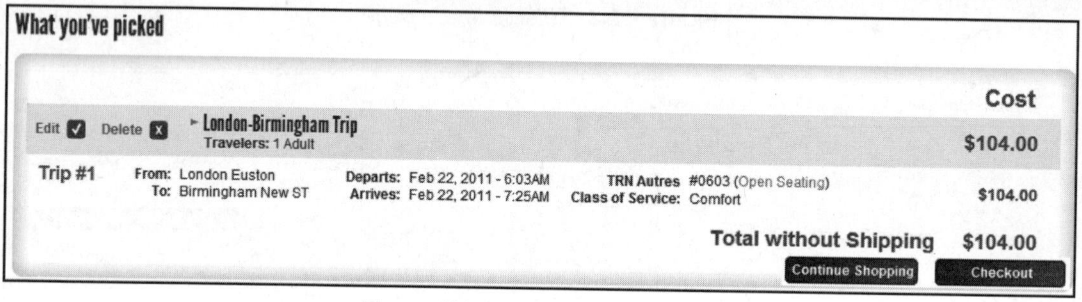

Figure C2.7 *Review itinerary page*

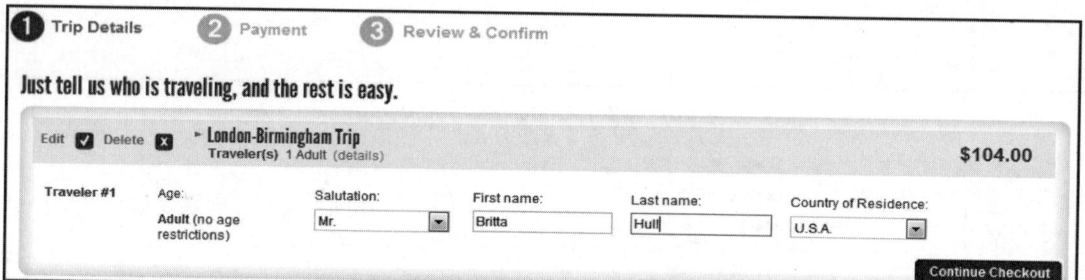

Figure C2.8 *Trip details page*

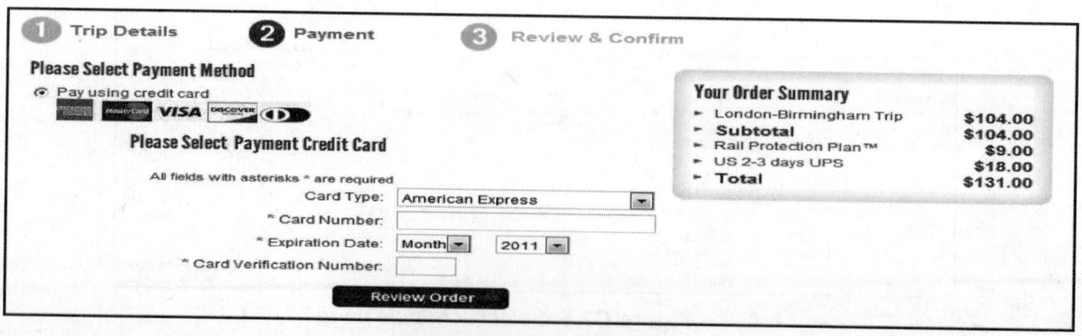

Figure C2.9 *Payment page*

Review Itinerary Screen—Screen to edit, delete, or select the itinerary.
Trip Details Screen—Screen to enter passenger details.
Payment Screen—Screen to make credit card payment.
Order Confirmation Screen—Screen to confirm ticket booking or edit or delete ticket itinerary.
Reservation Confirmation Screen—Screen to display the booked ticket details.

Once, the automation developers have gathered the requisite business knowledge, the next task is to prepare a rough screen flow diagram of the business scenario. For the train reservation application, the screen flow diagram will look like the one shown in Fig. C2.10.

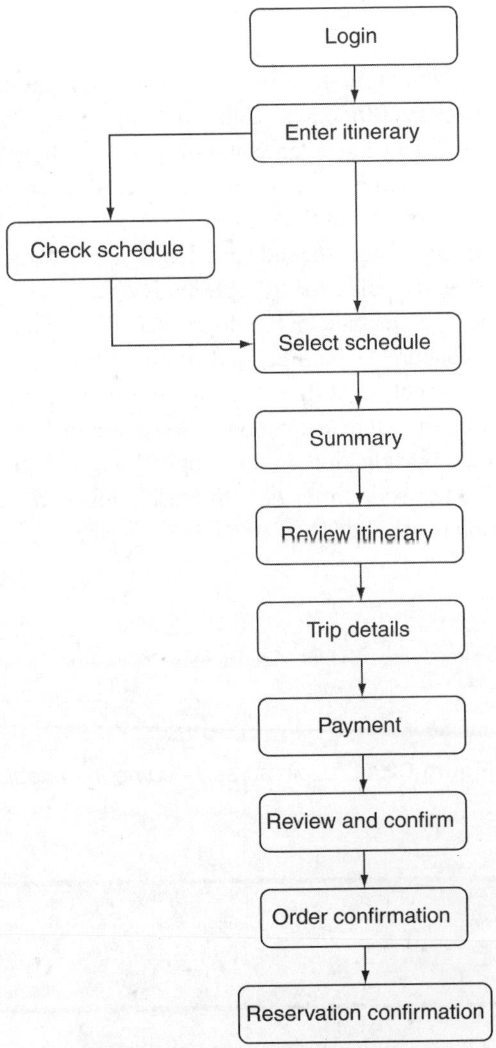

Figure C2.10 *Screen flow diagram*

Designing SCTs

Login Component Table

Figure C2.11 shows the 'Login Component Table' (Refer BookTicket.xls file available on the CD that has come with this book).In the table, 'SC" stands for the SCT and 'BC' stands for the BCT. It is not mandatory for the BCT to be in the same workbook as the SCTs. 'SC_Login' refers to the 'Login' SCT. The login screen implements one application functionality of 'logging-in to the application.' The keyword used for this functionality inside the component table is 'Login.' The 'TestType' field defines whether the test scenario is a positive test scenario or a negative test scenario. For positive test scenario, keyword 'Positive' is used while for negative scenario, keyword 'Negative' is used. 'iUsername' and 'iPassword' stand for login username and password. 'iExpMsgOnPageLoad' specifies the expected message on the screen when the page loads. Since mo message is expected on the screen, this field is left blank. 'iExpMsgOnPageSubmit' specifies expected message on the screen when the 'login' page is submitted. Here, there can be two cases—valid login message and invalid login message. In case of correct login, the current page will navigate to 'Enter Itinerary' page and on that page 'Login Successful' message will appear. Therefore, in this case, the value of 'iPageSubmitMsgLoc' will be 'NextPage.' This value is just to improve user readability has no significance for the test scripts as screen components only automate one page at a time. The validation of 'Login Successful' messages can be done in 'Enter Itinerary' page using option 'iExpMsgOnPageLoad.' The second case can be invalid login, where the error messages appear on the same screen. Here, the value for 'iPageSubmitMsgLoc' will be 'CurrentPage.' This field instructs the test script to verify the message on the 'login' screen after clicking the 'login' button. Next two fields in the component table are 'iContinue' and 'iSubmitPage.' 'iContinue' instructs the screen component to continue or exit execution of the test script after validating the message that appears on page load. 'iSubmitPage' instructs the screen component to submit or to not to submit the page. For this screen, the page can be submitted by clicking on the 'Login' button. If this option is turned 'NO,' then the screen component exits the test script after inputting username and password. It does not click on the 'Login' button. If this option is specified 'Yes,' then the screen component clicks on the login button.

	A	B	C	D	E	F	G	H	I	J	K	L
1	SeqNo	Description	Comments	TestType	TestScnro	iUserName	iPassword	iExpMsgOnPageLoad	iExpMsgOnPageSubmit	iPageSubmitMsgLoc	iContinue	iSubmitPage
2	1			Positive	Login	Alex	Durick		Login successful	NextPage	Yes	Yes
3	2			Positive	Login	Aryan	Silver@32		Login successful	NextPage	Yes	Yes
4	3			Negative	Login	!@#DF#$4	dewrty		Login failed	CurrentPage	Yes	Yes
5	4			Negative	Login	Jeff$#^&	skonjski		Login failed	CurrentPage	Yes	Yes

BC_BookTicket | SC_Login | SC_EnterItinerary | SC_SelectSchedules | SC_Summary | SC_ReviewItinerary | SC_TripDetails | SC_Payment | SC_ReviewAndConfirm

Figure C2.11 *Login screen—component table*

NOTES

Different font colors can be used to easily differentiate the positive and the negative scenarios and the test data.

EnterItinerary Component Table

'Enter Itinerary' page implements six application functionalities—Check Schedule, Check Fare, Find Rail Pass, Book Reservation for Your Pass, Reserve Hotel, and Find Activities. In other words, it is the initiation point for these functionalities. Each functionality is a test scenario. While designing the component table for this screen, a keyword is assigned for the each test scenario or application functionalities that it implements. As shown in Fig. C2.11 (Refer BookTicket.xls file available on the CD that has come with this book), the keywords for this screen are: CheckSchedule, CheckFares, FindRailPass, BookReservationForYourPass, ReserveHotel, and FindActivities. The test input data for these test scenarios are type of journey, departure–arrival date and location, and passenger travel details. Here, 'iJourneyType' can be considered as test sub-scenario of the scenarios—CheckSchedule and CheckFares. 'iExpMsgOnPageLoad' field specifies the message to validate on the enter itinerary page when this page loads. If 'iContinue' value is 'Yes,' the 'EnterItinerary' script component continues executing the rest of the script. If the value of 'iContinue' field is 'No,' then the screen component exits the script execution after validating the screen message. 'iExpMsgOnPageSubmit' specifies the message to validate when the page is submitted. This field is validated by the screen component only when the value of the 'iPageSubmitMsgLocation' is either 'CurrentPage' or 'Pop-up.' If the value is 'CurrentPage,' then it implies that the message will appear on the enter itinerary page. If the value is 'pop-up,' then it implies that the message appears on a pop-up dialog box. The screen component validates the message from the appropriate screen as specified by this field. In case the value of this field is 'NextPage,' then the 'EnterItinerary' screen component ignores this field. This is done to ensure that one screen component automates only one page at a time as mandated by the framework design. 'iSubmitPage' instructs the screen component to submit the page or not. A submit point of a page is an object on the page on which if an action is executed, the page navigates to a different page (URL). This page has multiple submit points. These include CheckSchedule, CheckFares, FindRailPass, BookReservationForYourPass, ReserveHotel, and FindActivities. A 'click' action on any of these objects (buttons) will force the current page to navigate to a different page (for positive happy path test scenarios). A condition logic is built to dynamically decide the page-submit point. For example, for this screen, field 'TestSubScenario' can be used to decide the page-submit point. If the field 'TestSubScnro' has value 'CheckFares,' then it implies that 'Check Fares' button is the page-submit point during run-time. Again, if the field 'TestSubScnro' has value 'FindRailPass,' then it implies that 'Find Rail Pass' button is the page-submit point during run-time.

Se	escripti	Comments	TestType	TestScnro	TestSubScnro	iJourneyTyp	iFrom	iTo	iDepartureDate	iReturnDate	iAdults	iYouth	iChildren	iSeniors	iExpMsgOnPag	iExpMsgOnPageSub	iPageSubmitMsg	iContinue	iSubmitPage
1			Positive	EnterItinerary	CheckScedules	OneWay	London	Birmingh	12-Jan-2011		1				Login Successful	Check Schedule	NextPage	Yes	Yes
2			Positive	EnterItinerary	CheckScedules	RoundTrip	London	Paris	AUTO	AUTO	1	1				Check Schedule	NextPage	Yes	Yes
3			Positive	EnterItinerary	CheckFares	OneWay	London	Paris	AUTO	AUTO	1	1	1					Yes	Yes
4			Positive	EnterItinerary	CheckFares	OneWay	London	Paris	AUTO	AUTO	1	1	1	1				Yes	Yes
5			Positive	EnterItinerary	CheckFares	OneWay	London	Paris	AUTO	AUTO		2						Yes	Yes
6			Positive	EnterItinerary	CheckFares	OneWay	London	Paris	AUTO	AUTO	1		2					Yes	Yes
7			Positive	EnterItinerary	CheckFares	OneWay	London	Paris	AUTO	AUTO				1				Yes	Yes
8			Positive	EnterItinerary	CheckFares	OneWay	London	Paris	TODAY	AUTO			2	1				Yes	Yes
9			Positive	EnterItinerary	CheckFares	OneWay	London	Paris	TODAY + 2	AUTO	1	1	1	1				Yes	Yes
10			Positive	EnterItinerary	CheckFares	OneWay	London	Paris	TODAY + 10	AUTO	1	1	1	1				Yes	Yes
11			Positive	EnterItinerary	CheckFares	OneWay	London	Paris	AUTO	AUTO	1	1	1	1				Yes	Yes
12			Positive	EnterItinerary	CheckFares	RoundTrip	London	Birmingh	12-Jan-2011		1							Yes	Yes
13			Positive	EnterItinerary	CheckFares	MultiCity												Yes	Yes
14			Positive	EnterItinerary	FindRailPass													Yes	Yes
15			Positive	EnterItinerary	BookReservationForYourPass													Yes	Yes
16			Positive	EnterItinerary	ReserveHotel													Yes	Yes
17			Positive	EnterItinerary	FindActivities													Yes	Yes
18	Blank 'From' field.		Negative	EnterItinerary	CheckFares	OneWay		Paris	14-Jan-2011	14-Feb-2011	1	1			Login Successful	Enter source station	Pop-up	Yes	Yes
19	Blank 'To' field.		Negative	EnterItinerary	CheckFares	OneWay	London		14-Jan-2011	14-Feb-2011	1	1				Enter destination station	Pop-up	Yes	Yes
20	Blank 'Departure Dat		Negative	EnterItinerary	CheckFares	OneWay	London	Paris		14-Feb-2011	1	1				Enter departure date	Pop-up	Yes	Yes
21	Blank 'Return' field fr		Negative	EnterItinerary	CheckFares	RoundTrip	London	Paris	14-Jan-2011		1	1				Enter return date	Pop-up	Yes	Yes
22	Blank passenger field		Negative	EnterItinerary	CheckFares	RoundTrip	London	Paris	14-Jan-2011	14-Feb-2011						Enter passenger details	Pop-up	Yes	Yes

BC_BookTicket / SC_Login / SC_EnterItinerary / SC_SelectSchedules / SC_Summary / SC_ReviewItinerary / SC_TripDetails / SC_Payment / SC_ReviewAndConfirm

Figure C2.12 *Enter itinerary screen—component table*

> **NOTES:** The field for which the specified test input field is not valid is grayed out for better user understanding. For example, for test scenario 'Find Rail Pass,' test data fields such as 'iJourneyType' and 'iFrom' do not hold any meaning. Therefore, these fields are grayed out for all the rows that implement this test scenario.

> **NOTES:** 'Check Schedule' page does not requires any test input data. This is the reason why no component table is created for this screen. However, definitely, screen component script is automated for this screen too.

SelectSchedules Component Table

'Select Schedule' screen has implements three functionalities. First, search of the desired train for travel. Second, view accommodation and fare details of the desired train. Third, select the train of travel among the searched list. Figure C2.13 shows the SCT of the 'Select Schedule' screen. For the three test scenarios identified for the screen, three keywords are selected—ScheduleSorter, ViewFareAndAccomodationDetails, and SelectTrain.

'Schedule Sorter' instructs the component script to search for the specific trains as per the test data specified in the component table. 'ViewFareAndAccomodationDetails' instructs screen component to validate the fare and accommodation details of a specific train. 'SelectTrain' specifies that a train is to be selected as per the test data provided in the component table to book a ticket. Test data 'iConnections,' 'iTrainType,' 'iTrainTime,' and 'iSeatType' arc used for searching specific trains. 'iExpMsgOnPageLoad' validates the message that appears on the screen when the 'Select Schedule' page loads. 'iContinue' field specifies whether to continue execution of the component script after validating the screen message on page load or not. 'iExpMsgOnPageSubmit' validates the message that appears on the screen after submitting the page. This page has only one submit point—'Continue' button as shown is Fig. C2.5. 'iSubmitPage' value specifies whether the screen component script should submit the page or not.

Summary Component Table

The 'Summary' page as shown in Fig. C2.6 provides the current travel itinerary details. This screen provides the flexibility to the user to edit the current itinerary, if required. In addition, a user can ei-

SeqNo	Description	Comments	TestType	TestScnro	TestSubScnro	iConnections	iTrainType	iTrainTime	iSeatType	iExpMsgOnPageLoad	iExpMsgOnPageSubmit	iPageSubmitMsgLoc	iContinue	iSubmitPage
1	Sort trains		Positive	SelectSchedule	ScheduleSorter		Fastest						Yes	No
2	Sort trains		Positive	SelectSchedule	ScheduleSorter		Cheapest						Yes	No
3	Sort trains		Positive	SelectSchedule	ScheduleSorter		FirstTrain						Yes	No
4	Sort trains		Positive	SelectSchedule	ScheduleSorter		LastTrain						Yes	No
5	Sort trains		Positive	SelectSchedule	ScheduleSorter	0							Yes	No
6	Sort trains		Positive	SelectSchedule	ScheduleSorter	1							Yes	No
[illegible]	Sort trains		Positive	SelectSchedule	ScheduleSorter	2							Yes	No
[illegible]	Sort trains		Positive	SelectSchedule	ScheduleSorter	01							Yes	No
17	Sort and select train		Positive	SelectSchedule	SelectTrain				Comfort				Yes	Yes
18	Sort and select train		Positive	SelectSchedule	SelectTrain	01			Freedom				Yes	Yes
19	Sort and select train		Positive	SelectSchedule	SelectTrain		Cheapest		Economy				Yes	Yes
20	Sort and select train		Positive	SelectSchedule	SelectTrain		Fastest	6:00AM	ComfortFlexi				Yes	Yes
21	Sort and select train		Positive	SelectSchedule	SelectTrain	0		1:00PM	Comfort				Yes	Yes
22	Sort and select train		Positive	SelectSchedule	SelectTrain	2	Fastest	6:00PM	Freedom				Yes	Yes
55	Blank 'Seat Type' field		Negative	SelectSchedule	ViewFareAndAccomodationDetail		LastTrain	AUTO			Specify seat type		Yes	Yes
56	Blank 'Seat Type' field		Negative	SelectSchedule	ViewFareAndAccomodationDetail						Specify seat type		Yes	Yes
60	Blank 'Seat Type' field		Negative	SelectSchedule	SelectTrain			9:30AM			Specify seat type		Yes	Yes

BC_BookTicket / SC_Login / SC_EnterItinerary / SC_SelectSchedules / SC_Summary / SC_ReviewItinerary / SC_TripDetails / SC_Payment / SC_ReviewAndConfirm

Figure C2.13 *Select schedules screen—component table*

SeqNo	Description	Comments	TestType	TestScnro	TestSubScnro	iExpMsgOnPageLoad	iExpMsgOnPageSubmit	iPageSubmitMsgLoc	iContinue	iSubmitPage
1			Positive	Summary	Edit				Yes	Yes
2			Positive	Summary	SearchHotels				Yes	Yes
3			Positive	Summary	ContinueWithRailOnly				Yes	Yes

BC_BookTicket / SC_Login / SC_EnterItinerary / SC_SelectSchedules / **SC_Summary** / SC_ReviewItinerary / SC_TripDetails / SC_Payment / SC_ReviewAndConfirm

Figure C2.14 *Summary screen—screen component table*

ther proceed ahead with the travel booking or can also book a hotel along with the train ticket booking. Figure C2.14 shows the SCT for the 'Summary' screen. For the three functionalities that this screen implements, three keywords are defined—Edit, SearchHotel, and ContinueWithRailOnly. Since this screen does not require test input data, the component table has no fields for the same. This page has multiple page-submit points. The 'Summary' page will navigate to a different page by clicking on any of the objects—'Edit' link, 'Book Hotel' button, or 'Continue with Rail Only' button. The page-submit point at run-time is decided by the value of the 'TestSubScnro' field at run-time. For example, for Seqno=2, at runtime the value test sub-scenario field will be 'SearchHotels.' It implies that 'Search Hotels' button is the page-submit point for the particular run session. If the value of the field 'iSubmitPage' is 'Yes,' then the script component will click on this button or else not.

ReviewItinerary Component Table

'Review Itinerary' page helps the user to review (edit, delete, or continue) the planned itinerary before making the payment. The users can either edit or delete one or more itineraries as shown in Fig. C2.7. If more itineraries (ticket booking) need to be planned, then the user can choose to click on the button 'Continue Shopping.' If the user feels that the current set of planned itineraries is final, then he or she can click the 'Checkout' button to enter the passenger details. As is visible on the screen, there is no test data input to the screen, but still one input parameter 'iTripNbr' is specified in the component table as shown in Fig. C2.15. This input parameter has been added to allow edit or delete of a specific itinerary out of the several planned itineraries as visible on the review itinerary page.

SeqNo	Description	Comments	TestType	TestScnro	TestSubScnro	iTripNbr	iExpMsgOnPageLoad	iExpMsgOnPageSubmit	iPageSubmitMsgLoc	iContinue	iSubmitPage
1			Positive	ReviewItinerary	Edit	1				Yes	Yes
2			Positive	ReviewItinerary	Delete	2				Yes	Yes
3			Positive	ReviewItinerary	ContinueShopping					Yes	Yes
4			Positive	ReviewItinerary	Checkout					Yes	Yes

BC_BookTicket / SC_Login / SC_EnterItinerary / SC_SelectSchedules / SC_Summary / **SC_ReviewItinerary** / SC_TripDetails / SC_Payment / SC_ReviewAndConfirm

Figure C2.15 *Review itinerary screen—component table*

TripDetails Component Table

'Trip Details' page is used for entering the passenger details such as name, age, and sex that are required for booking a rail ticket. This page also offers the feasibility to the user to edit or delete the planned itinerary as shown in Fig. C2.8. In other words, this page implements three functionalities—entering passenger details, edit an itinerary, and delete an itinerary. Figure C2.16 shows the component table for this page. For the identified three functionalities, three unique keywords have been selected for the field 'TestSubScnro.' These include Edit, Delete, or Continue Checkouts. 'Edit' keyword instructs the 'TripDetails' component script to edit an itinerary. Similarly, 'Delete' keyword instructs the component script to delete an itinerary. 'ContinueCheckout' implies that the screen component should proceed with the ticket booking after filling the required passenger details. The input parameter for edit or delete of an itinerary is the itinerary number. For 'ContinueCheckout' scenario, passenger details are specified as test data in the component table.

SeqNo	Description	Comments	TestType	TestScnro	TestSubScnro	iTripNbr	iSalutation	iFirstName	iLastName	Country	iExpMsgOnPageLoad	iExpMsgOnPageSubmit	iPageSubmitMsgLoc	iContinue	iSubmitPage
1			Positive	TripDetails	Edit	1								Yes	Yes
2			Positive	TripDetails	Delete	1								Yes	Yes
3			Positive	TripDetails	ContinueCheckout		Mr.	Alex	Durick	USA				Yes	Yes
4			Positive	TripDetails	ContinueCheckout		Ms.	Britta	Simpson	USA				Yes	Yes
5			Positive	TripDetails	ContinueCheckout		Ms.	Pratima	Singh	USA				Yes	Yes
6			Positive	TripDetails	ContinueCheckout		Ms.	Becky	Hudson	USA				Yes	Yes
7			Positive	TripDetails	ContinueCheckout		Mr.	Jhon	Carter	USA				Yes	Yes
8	Blank 'First Name' field.		Negative	TripDetails	ContinueCheckout		Ms.		Simpson	USA				Yes	Yes
9	Blank 'Last Name' field.		Negative	TripDetails	ContinueCheckout		Ms.	Preshika		USA				Yes	Yes
10	Blank 'Salutation' field.		Negative	TripDetails	ContinueCheckout			Deepika	Sinha	USA				Yes	Yes
11	Blank 'Country' field.		Negative	TripDetails	ContinueCheckout		Mr.	Trevor	Domingo					Yes	Yes

BC_BookTicket / SC_Login / SC_EnterItinerary / SC_SelectSchedules / SC_Summary / SC_ReviewItinerary / **SC_TripDetails** / SC_Payment / SC_ReviewAndConfirm /

Figure C2.16 *Trip details screen—component table*

> **NOTES**
> The fields that are not applicable to a particular scenario are grayed out. This is done to improve readability and usability of the component tables.

Payment Component Table

The 'Payment' page as shown in Fig. C2.9 implements only one application functionality of 'entering the credit card details.' Here, it can be observed that there can also be a test case that validates the total ticket amount as displayed in this page. As we discussed earlier, this framework does not separately validates different fields (Fig. C2.17). The validation of each page is inbuilt into the respective screen components. As soon as this page loads, the screen component validates all the amount fields of this page. This helps to merge multiple test scenarios within one screen component itself.

SeqNo	Description	Comments	TestType	TestScnro	iCardTyp	iCardNbr	iExpirationDate	iCVVNbr	iExpMsgOnPageLoad	iPageSubmitMsgLoc	iContinue	iSubmitPage
1			Positive	Payment	American Express	1111111111111111	Jan-2014	1231			Yes	Yes
2			Positive	Payment	American Express	1111111111111111	Mar-2016	1232			Yes	Yes
3			Positive	Payment	VISA	1111111111111111	AUTO	123			Yes	Yes
4			Positive	Payment	MasterCard	1111111111111111	AUTO	132			Yes	Yes
5			Positive	Payment	Discover	1111111111111111	Dec-2018	143			Yes	Yes
6	Blank 'Card Number' field		Negative	Payment	MasterCard		Jan-2013	134			Yes	Yes
7	Blank 'Expiration Date'		Negative	Payment	Discover	1212121212121212		112			Yes	Yes
8	Blank 'CVV Nbr'		Negative	Payment	BLANK	1111222233334444	Feb-2018				Yes	Yes
9	Invalid 'Card Number' field		Negative	Payment	MasterCard	0101010101010101	Jan-2013	134			Yes	Yes
10	Invalid 'Expiration Date'		Negative	Payment	Discover	1212121212121212	Dec-2008	112			Yes	Yes
11	Invalid 'CVV Nbr'		Negative	Payment	MasterCard	1111222233334444	Feb-2018	21			Yes	Yes

BC_BookTicket / SC_Login / SC_EnterItinerary / SC_SelectSchedules / SC_Summary / SC_ReviewItinerary / SC_TripDetails / **SC_Payment** / SC_ReviewAndCon

Figure C2.17 *Payment screen—component table*

ReviewAndConfirm Component Table

'Review and Confirm' page allows users to review the planned itinerary, ticket details, and the booking amount details. Users can also edit the planned itinerary or ticket details as required. Therefore, this screen implements three functionalities–edit itinerary, edit trip details, and confirm booking. We can observe that no mention has been made of the test cases pertaining to verify the itinerary, ticket, and amount details displayed on the screen. As discussed earlier, all such validations are always coded in the component scripts; no matter whether it is mandated by the manual test case or not. Since, agile automation framework follows a business-scenario-driven approach, the complete business scenario is tested exhaustively end-to-end. This helps to do the exhaustive testing of all scenarios leaving little room for defect leaks. This also helps to do maximum testing in minimum time.

Designing BCTs

BCT contains information about the test cases and the test data for the same. It is also used for analyzing the test results. The tests to be executed are defined by in these tables by selecting value 'RUN' in field 'RunTest.' The test data is defined by explicitly defining the workbook, worksheet, and the 'SeqNo' field of the worksheet where the test data exists. This helps the business components to select the specific test data as required for the test execution. Pass/fail status is updated by the business component scripts in the 'Status' field. The reason for test failure is updated in the 'FailReason' field during test run. Thus, business component table provides a one-point control over test execution and test result analysis.

Test cases can be designed in the BCT by selecting appropriate combination of business scenario and test data keywords. Most of the keywords exist in the form of 'drop-down list' to make test cases design easy and as well to avoid invalid test data input. Users can vary the combination of these keywords to dynamically automate hundreds of test cases in just few minutes. Business component scripts are programmed to execute all the valid scenarios or test cases. As we can observe in Fig. C2.18, 93 test cases have been automated using just eight script components and one business component. Moreover, these test cases do not include test cases that involve test data variations. Test cases related to the test data variations can easily be automated by creating a new row in the table and defining the appropriate business scenario keyword, business sub-scenario keyword, and test input data keyword for the same. This operation will take even less than a minute and the test case will be ready to execute. This feature of the agile automation framework reduces the script development effort by manifold. No other automation framework offers such huge savings in the test development effort as this framework does. The flexibility to dynamically automate test cases by defining few keywords makes the agile automation framework a dynamic framework.

The first task, while designing the BCT is to identify the business scenarios and the business sub-scenarios that are to be automated or that can be automated using the existing screen components. For example, 'railway ticket booking' scenario, the various business scenarios can be book a ticket, edit a ticket, find ticket fare, find train schedule, book hotel along with train ticket, etc. The various

SeqNo	TestCaseID	TestDescription	ExpectedResults	RunTest	Status	FailReason	Comments	ScenarioType	BusnScnro	BusnSubScnro
1		EnterItinerary -> CheckSchedule -> SelectSched		RUN				Positive	BookTicket	
2		EnterItinerary -> CheckFare -> SelectSchedule -		RUN				Positive	BookTicket	
27		Edit ticket from summary screen		RUN				Positive	EditTicket	SummaryScreen
28		Edit ticket from review itinerary screen		RUN				Positive	EditTicket	ReviewItineraryScreen
41		Delete ticket from ReviewItinerary screen		RUN				Positive	DeleteTicket	ReviewItineraryScreen
42		Delete ticket from TripDetails screen		RUN				Positive	DeleteTicket	TripDetailsScreen
49		Check schedule for 1 way travel		RUN				Positive	CheckTrainSche	CheckScheduleScreen
50		Check schedule for return travel		RUN				Positive	CheckTrainSche	CheckScheduleScreen
51		Sort trains by connection 0		RUN				Positive	CheckScheduleS	SelectScheduleScreen
52		Sort trains by connection 1		RUN				Positive	CheckScheduleS	SelectScheduleScreen
66		Check train fare & accomodation for return way t		RUN				Positive	CheckViewFareA	SelectScheduleScreen
67		Check train fare & accomodation for return travel		RUN				Positive	CheckViewFareA	SelectScheduleScreen
73		Enter Itinerary with blank From field		RUN				Negative	BookTicket	
74		Enter Itinerary with blank Departure Date field		RUN				Negative	BookTicket	
88		Marked for future automation		RUN				Positive	ContinueShopping	
93		Marked for future automation		RUN				Positive	FindActivities	

BC_BookTicket / SC_Login / SC_EnterItinerary / SC_SelectSchedules / SC_Summary / SC_ReviewItinerary / SC_TripDetails / SC_Payment / Sheet1 / SC_ReviewAndConfirm

Figure C2.18a *Business component table—book ticket*

iLogin	iEnterItinerary	iSelectSchedules	iSummary	iReviewItinerary	iTripDetails	iPayment
BookTicket_Login_1	BookTicket_EnterItinerary_1	BookTicket_SelectSchedule_17	BookTicket_Summary_3	BookTicket_ReviewItinerary_4	BookTicket_TripDetails_3	BookTicket_Payment_2
BookTicket_Login_1	BookTicket_EnterItinerary_3	BookTicket_SelectSchedule_18	BookTicket_Summary_3	BookTicket_ReviewItinerary_4	BookTicket_TripDetails_3	BookTicket_Payment_2
BookTicket_Login_1	BookTicket_EnterItinerary_1	BookTicket_SelectSchedule_22	BookTicket_Summary_1	BookTicket_ReviewItinerary_4	BookTicket_TripDetails_3	BookTicket_Payment_2
BookTicket_Login_1	BookTicket_EnterItinerary_2	BookTicket_SelectSchedule_22	BookTicket_Summary_3	BookTicket_ReviewItinerary_1	BookTicket_TripDetails_3	BookTicket_Payment_2
BookTicket_Login_1	BookTicket_EnterItinerary_3	BookTicket_SelectSchedule_22	BookTicket_Summary_3	BookTicket_ReviewItinerary_2		
BookTicket_Login_1	BookTicket_EnterItinerary_4	BookTicket_SelectSchedule_22	BookTicket_Summary_3	BookTicket_ReviewItinerary_4	BookTicket_TripDetails_3	
BookTicket_Login_1	BookTicket_EnterItinerary_1	BookTicket_SelectSchedule_22	BookTicket_Summary_3	BookTicket_ReviewItinerary_4	BookTicket_TripDetails_3	BookTicket_Payment_2
BookTicket_Login_1	BookTicket_EnterItinerary_2	BookTicket_SelectSchedule_22	BookTicket_Summary_3	BookTicket_ReviewItinerary_4	BookTicket_TripDetails_3	BookTicket_Payment_2
BookTicket_Login_1	BookTicket_EnterItinerary_1	BookTicket_SelectSchedule_5				
BookTicket_Login_1	BookTicket_EnterItinerary_2	BookTicket_SelectSchedule_6				
BookTicket_Login_1	BookTicket_EnterItinerary_2	BookTicket_SelectSchedule_23				
BookTicket_Login_1	BookTicket_EnterItinerary_2	BookTicket_SelectSchedule_23				
BookTicket_Login_1	BookTicket_EnterItinerary_18	BookTicket_SelectSchedule_23	BookTicket_Summary_3	BookTicket_ReviewItinerary_4	BookTicket_TripDetails_3	BookTicket_Payment_2
BookTicket_Login_1	BookTicket_EnterItinerary_20	BookTicket_SelectSchedule_23	BookTicket_Summary_3	BookTicket_ReviewItinerary_4	BookTicket_TripDetails_3	BookTicket_Payment_2

BC_BookTicket / SC_Login / SC_EnterItinerary / SC_SelectSchedules / SC_Summary / SC_ReviewItinerary / SC_TripDetails / SC_Payment / Sheet1 / SC_ReviewAndConfirm

Figure C2.18b *Business component table—book ticket*

iReviewAndConfirm	oTicketNbr	oRailService	oBookingAmt	ErrScreenshotsPath

BC_BookTicket / SC_Login / SC_EnterItinerary / SC_SelectSchedules / SC_Summary / SC_Revie

Figure C2.18c *Business component table—book ticket*

business sub-scenarios can be edit ticket from summary page, edit ticket from review itinerary page, edit ticket from review and confirm page, delete ticket from review itinerary page, check fare from enter itinerary page, check train schedule from enter itinerary page, book hotel from enter itinerary page, book hotel from review itinerary page, etc. Once the scenarios to be automated have been identified, the next step is to assign a unique 'keyword' for both business scenarios and business sub-scenarios. The 'keywords' are to be chosen in a way that it allows the users to design multiple test cases by varying the combination of these keywords. Moreover, none of these keywords should duplicate the scenarios already designed in the SCTs.

After identifying the business scenario identifier 'keywords,' the next task is to determine the various test input fields. All test input fields required by various test scenarios is to be created in the BCT. The various test input fields for the 'railway ticket booking' scenario are sequence number, test case ID, test description, expected test results, execute test, test execution result, script reason failure, comments, test scenario type, business scenario, business sub-scenario, login page test data, enter itinerary page data, select schedule page data, summary page test data, review itinerary page test data, trip details page test data, payment page test data, and review and confirm page test data. Next, the test data for the various scenarios is to be defined. Since test data is already defined in the SCTs, the requirement here is to create a keyword that points to a specific test data of the SCT. To achieve the same, following naming convention is used for defining the test data:

<Workbook Name>_<Worksheet Name>_<SeqNo>

For example, to select "SeqNo=2' test data of 'EnterItinerary' sheet, the keyword will be BookTicket_EnterItinerary_2

The next step is to identify the unique common identifiers for each test case execution. For example, in case of booking a ticket, the unique identifier can be 'ticket number.' Unique identifiers are chosen in a way that it helps to track or verify the test case (or transaction) executed by the test script. For example, 'ticket number' can be used to track the complete booked ticket details. It helps in easy test result analysis. In addition, other important information such as train number or rail service and booking amount can also be made part of the BCT. All these identifiers are collectively referred as output parameters of the test case and their naming convention starts with the letter 'o.' Apart from this, there is one more field 'ErrScreenshotsPath' in the BCT. This field is updated with the exact path of the screenshot that is taken by the test script if an unexpected error occurs during runtime.

Developing Screen Component Scripts

Once component tables have been developed, the automation developers can start developing the code of the screen components. The first step to develop a screen component is to decide the input and output parameters of the screen component. In QTP, an action can represent a screen component. The input parameters of the screen component are almost similar to the test input data fields of the respective SCT. Listed below are the various input–output parameters of the various screen components.

Login Screen Component

The various input–output parameters of the SCT are:
Input Parameters—TestType, TestScnro, iUserName, iPassword, iExpMsgOnPageLoad, iPageSubmitMsgLoc, iContinue, iSubmitPage.
Output Parameters—oRunStatus, oRtrnMsg.

> **NOTES**
>
> Output parameter 'RunStatus' can accept two value —0, –1 or –2. '0' implies that screen component has passed '–1' implies that screen component has failed. '–2' implies screen component has failed because of script run-time failure. The value of 'RunStatus' is changed to '–2' by the exception handlers (recovery scenarios), if any unexpected error occurs during script execution.
>
> Ouput parameter 'RtrnMsg' can accept any string value. The message type stored in the parameter 'RtrnMsg' depends on the value of the parameter 'RunStatus'
>
> oRunStatus = Pass Message, if RunStatus=0
>
> oRunStatus = Fail Message, if RunStatus=–1
>
> oRunStatus = Error Message, if RunStatus=–2. In this case, recovery scenarios also take a screenshot of the application and update the path of the screenshot in the environment variable 'ErrScreenshotsPath.'

Pseudo Code of the 'Login' Screen Component

```
'Read input parameters
    Identify test scenario and test input data
```

```
'Validate screen message, if required
   If iExpMsgOnPageLoad <>"" Then
      Validate message on the screen

'Store pass/status with proper message in the output parameters
      If TestCaseFailed Then
            RunStatus = -1
            RtrnMsg = FailMsg
      End If
   End If
'Exit test execution, if required
If iContinue = NO then
   Exit Test
End If
'Login to user screen
   Execute test steps for login
   If iSubmit=YES Then
      Execute click method on the login button
   End IF
'Validate screen message, if required
   If iExpMsgOnPageSubmit <> "" And iPageSubmitMsgLoc <> NextPage Then
      Select iPageSubmitMsgLoc
            Case CurrentPage
                  Validate message
                  'Store pass/status with proper message in the output
                  parameters
                  If TestCaseFailed Then
                        RunStatus = -1
                        RtrnMsg = FailMsg
                  End If
            Case PopUp
                  Validate message
                  'Store pass/status with proper message in the output
                  parameters
                  If TestCaseFailed Then
                        RunStatus = -1
                        RtrnMsg = FailMsg
                  End If
      End Select
   End If
'Return screen component pass/fail status along with proper message to
the calling script
'If script has not failed while executing the above steps then it has passed
If RunStatus <> "-1" Then
   RunStatus = "0"
   RtrnMsg = PassMsg
End If
```

Enter Itinerary Screen Component

The various input–output parameters of the SCT are:

Input Parameters—TestType, TestScnro, TestSubScnro, iJourneyType, iFrom, iTo, iDepartureDate, iReturnDate, iAdults, iYouths, iChildren, iSeniors iExpMsgOnPageLoad, iPageSubmitMsgLoc, iContinue, iSubmitPage.

Output Parameters—oRunStatus, oRtrnMsg.

Pseudo Code of the 'Login' Screen Component

```
'Read input parameters
   Identify test scenario and test input data
'Validate screen message, if required
   If iExpMsgOnPageLoad <> "" Then
      Validate message on the screen

'Store pass/status with proper message in the output parameters
      If TestCaseFailed Then
            RunStatus = -1
            RtrnMsg = FailMsg
      End If
   End If
'Exit test execution, if required
If iContinue = NO then
   Exit Test
End If
'Execute test sub scenario
Select TestSubScnro
   Case CheckSchedules
      Execute test steps
   Case CheckFares
      Execute test steps
   Case BookReservationForYourPass
      Execute test steps
   Case ReserveHotel
      Execute test steps
   Case FindActivities
      Execute test steps
End Select
'Validate screen message, if required
   If iExpMsgOnPageSubmit <> "" And iPageSubmitMsgLoc <>NextPage Then
      Select iPageSubmitMsgLoc
            Case CurrentPage
                  Validate message
```

```
                    'Store pass/status with proper message in the output
                    parameters
                    If TestCaseFailed Then
                          RunStatus = -1
                          RtrnMsg = FailMsg
                    End If
              Case PopUp
                    Validate message
                    'Store pass/status with proper message in the output
                    parameters
                    If TestCaseFailed Then
                          RunStatus = -1
                          RtrnMsg = FailMsg
                    End If
        End Select
   End If
'Return screen component pass/fail status along with proper message to
the calling script
'If script has not failed while executing the above steps then it has passed
If RunStatus <> "-1" Then
   RunStatus = "0"
   RtrnMsg = PassMsg
End If
```

Similarly, code can be developed for all the screen components

Developing Business Component Scripts

Automation developers can start developing the business components after all the requisite screen components have been developed and tested. As discussed, business components automate a complete end-to-end business scenario. The test case to be executed is decided dynamically depending on the combination of keywords specified in the BCT. Code development of the business component scripts requires better coding skills. Business components do not have any input or output parameter.

Pseudo code of the 'BookTicket' BCT

```
   'Load test automation bed settings
    Load QTP settings
    Load AUT settings
    Load environment files
    Load library files
    Load shared object repositories
    Load recovery scenarios, etc.

'Read specific business component table
   'Identify test cases to execute
   Identify all the test cases that need to be executed (marked RUN)
```

```
    'Identify test data of all test cases
    Identify business scenario keywords
    Identify test data keywords
'Extract test data
    Connect to specific screen component tables
    Extract specific sequence number (SeqNo) test data from the screen
component tables
    Extract test data from AUT database, if required
    Store business scenario keywords and test data in an array
'Execute business scenario
    Launch application
'Execute all test cases
For nBusnScnroCnt=1 To TotBusnScnroForExec
    Do
    'Reset input-output variable values such as sSeqNo, sUsername, sPass-
word, sRunStatus, sRtrnMsg, etc.
        sSeqNo = ""
        sUserName = ""

    'Store test data values in variables from arrays - This is done to
improve code readability.
        sSeqNo = arrArrayName(nBusnScnroCnt,1)
        sUserName = arrArrayName(nBusnScnroCnt,2)
        ….
    'Identify business scenario to be executed and implement its execution
        Login to the application
        Select BusnScnro
                Case BookTicket:
                        Run SC_EnterItinerary screen component and pass its
                        test data to it
                        'Validate screen component pass/fail status
                                Validate whether screen component  passed or
                                failed.
                                Update  status to business component table (to
                                specific 'SeqNo')
                                'If failed, skip current test execution and
                                start executing the next test case of the busi-
                                ness component table
                                Exit Do

                        Run SC_SelectScedules screen component and pass its
                        test data to it
                        'Validate screen component pass/fail status
                                Validate whether screen component passed or
                                failed.
```

```
                    Update status to business component table (to
                    specific 'SeqNo')
                    'If failed, skip current test execution and
                    start executing the next test case of the busi-
                    ness component table
                    Exit Do
'Alternatively, a function can also be written that validates the screen
component status and updates the business component table
                'Run SC_Summary screen component and pass its test
                data to it
                RunAction SC_Summary, TestScnro, iTestInp1, iT-
                estInp2, oTestOut1. oTestOut2, RunStatus, RtrnMsg
                Call ValidateScreenComponent(Parameter(sSeqNo, oTes-
                tOut1. oTestOut2, RunStatus, RtrnMsg)
                'If failed, skip current test execution and start ex-
                ecuting the next test case of the business component
                table
                Exit Do
                Similarly, call all the screen components sequen-
                tially to implement the business sub scenario

            Case EditTicket:
                Select BusnSubScnro
                    Case SummaryScreen:
                        'Write code to implement the business
                        sub scenario
                    Case ReviewItineraryScreen:
                    Case TripDetailsScreen:
                End Select
            Case DeleteTicket:
                Select BusnSubScnro
                    Case ReviewItineraryScreen:
                    Case TripDetailsScreen:
                End Select
            Case CheckTrainSchedule:
            Case ChekScheduleSorter:
            Case ViewFareAndAccomodationDetails:
            Case ContinueShopping:
            Case FindActivities:
        End Select
    Exit Do: Loop
Next
'Export test results to archive folder
Export business component table to 'ResultLog' folder
```

Developing Master Driver

Master driver scripts are used to execute various business scenarios from one centrally managed script. Master driver script dynamically makes a call to the various business components depending on the business component specified in the 'MasterDriver' table. If a new business scenario (business component script) is automated then, the details of the same needs to be specified in the master driver table. Here, there is no need to update or modify 'MasterDriver' code. Figure C2.19 shows a template 'MasterDriver' table.

SeqNo	RunTest	Description	Module	SubModule	BusinessComponentTestPath	BusinessComponentName
1	RUN		RailReservation	BookTicket	Z:\BusinessComponents\BookTicket	BookTicket
2	RUN		HotelReservation	Book	Z:\BusinessComponents\BookHotel	BookHotel
3	NORUN		RentCar	Rent	Z:\BusinessComponents\RentCar	RentCar
4	COMPLETE		PurchaseMembership	Rail	Z:\BusinessComponents\PurchaseMembership	Rail
5	COMPLETE		PurchaseMembership	Shopping	Z:\BusinessComponents\PurchaseMembership	Shopping

MasterDriver

Figure C2.19 *Master driver table*

The master driver reads the master driver table to identify all the business components to execute. Only those business components are executed that are marked 'RUN.' Thereafter, it calls all the business components one by one. Once a business component is executed, the value of 'RunTest' fields is updated as 'COMPLETE.' This helps the user to continuously keep track of the business scenarios under execution.

Pseudo Code for Master Driver Script

```
    'Load test automation bed settings
       Load QTP settings
       Load AUT settings
       Load environment files
       Load library files
       Load recovery scenarios, etc.
   'Identify business scenarios to execute
    Read master driver table
    Identify all business scenarios marked for run

   'Execute all business components
       For iCnt=1 To nBusinessScenarioCnt
               LoadAndRunAction BusinessComponentTestPath,
BusinessComponentName
      'Update master driver table
      Mark the business scenario as COMPLETE
  Next
```

Section 3 VBScript

- VBScript
- Dictionary
- Regular Expressions

Chapter 10

VBScript

VBScript is a light version of Microsoft's programming language that is modeled on Visual Basic. It is an active script language with a fast interpreter for use in a wide variety of Microsoft environments, including active scripting in Web client scripting in Microsoft Internet Explorer, and Web server scripting in Microsoft Internet Information Service. VBScript has been installed by default in every desktop release of Microsoft Windows since Windows 98. It is used as scripting language in QTP.

VBSCRIPT EDITORS

VBscript code can be written using VBScript editors such as EditPlus, Adobe Dreamweaver, HTML kit etc. Though, it is not necessary to have a VBscript editor to write and execute a VBscript code. VBScript code can be written in normal text editors. The text file is saved with an extension .vbs.

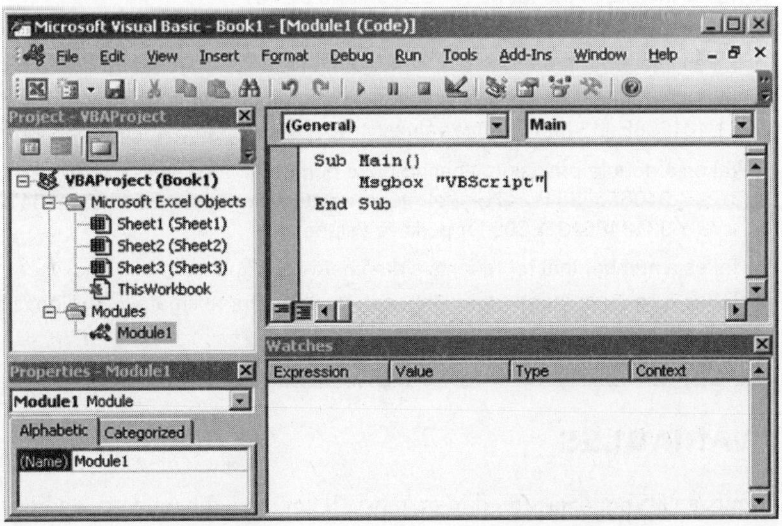

Figure 10.1 *Microsoft visual basic editor*

MS Office provides the flexibility to write and execute a VBScript code within the MS Office environment. Example below shows how to write a VBScript code in MS Excel environment.

1. Open Microsoft Excel.
2. Press ALT+F11. Microsoft Visual Basic Editor Window will open.
3. Right Click on VBAProject and select *Insert → Module.*
4. Microsoft VB Editor Window will open. Here, we can write, execute, and debug the VBScript code.

DATA TYPES

VBScript supports only one data type called 'Variant.' A 'Variant' can contain various types of data, namely numeric, floating-point number, or a string, depending on its usage. It behaves as a number when it is used in a numeric context and as a string when used in a string context. It is the default data type returned by all functions in VBScript.

Variant Datatypes

The various types of data that a variant can contain are called subtypes. The following table shows the subtypes of data that a variant can contain.

Subtype	Description
Empty	Variant is uninitialized. Variant value is zero-length string ("") for string variables and 0 for numeric variables
Null	Contains no valid data
Boolean	Takes true or false values
Byte	Takes integer in the range of 0–255
Integer	Takes integer in the range of –32,768 and 32,767
Currency	Takes number in the range of –922,337,203,685,477.5808–922,337,203,685,477.5807
Long	Takes integer in the range of –2,147,483,648 to 2,147,483,647
Single	Takes a single-precision, floating-point number in the range –3.402823E38 to –1.401298E–45 for negative values; 1.401298E–45 to 3.402823E38 for positive values
Double	Takes a double-precision, floating-point number in the range –1.79769313486232E308 to –4.94065645841247E–324 for negative values; 4.94065645841247E–324 to 1.79769313486232E308 for positive values
Date (Time)	Takes a number that represents a date between January 1, 100 and December 31, 9999
String	Takes a variable-length string that can be up to approximately 2 billion characters long
Object	Takes a object
Error	Takes an error number

VBSCRIPT VARIABLES

A variable represents a varying data stored in memory. It contains the memory address that stores the specific data.

Variable Declaration

Dim: Variables are declared in VBScript using Dim statement.

Example:

```
Dim sText
sText = "Variable Declaration"
```

Variable declaration and value assignment can also be done in the same statement.

```
Dim sText : sText = "Variable Declaration"
```

Example below shows how to declare static array in VBScript. A static array is one whose array dimensions are fixed.

```
Dim arrTemp(20)
Dim arrBooks(10,10)
```

ReDim: Reallocates storage space for dynamic array variable.

The following example shows how *ReDim* statement is used to declare dynamic arrays. The dimensions of the dynamic array can be changed as per the requirement..

Example:

```
Redim arrBooks(2) 'Declaring dynamic arrays
arrBooks(1) = "QTP"
arrBooks(2) = "VBScript"
'Increasing dimension of the dynamic array
Redim arrBooks(3)
Msgbox arrBooks(1)                'Output : Empty
Msgbox arrBooks(2)                'Output : Empty
```

Here, we observe that after redefining array upper boundary limits, existing values of the array are lost. ‘Preserve’ keyword is used to preserve the existing values of an array as shown below.

```
arrBooks(1) = "QTP"
arrBooks(2) = "VBScript"
arrBooks(3) = "Test Automation"
Redim Preserve arrBooks(10)
Msgbox arrBooks(1)                'Output : QTP
Msgbox arrBooks(2)                'Output : VBScript
Msgbox arrBooks(3)                'Output : Test Automation
arrBooks(4) = "Complete"
```

How to declare array boundary limit using a variable?

Suppose that we need to transfer values from a static array to a dynamic array.

```
'static variable of upper boundary 5
Dim arrStatic(5)
```

> **NOTES** Appendix C defines the standard naming convention that can be used to declare VBScript variables.

```
    arrStatic(1) = "Master"
    arrStatic(2) = "Test"
    arrStatic(3) = "Automation"
    arrStatic(4) = "&"
    arrStatic(5) = "QTP"
'Upper boundary limit of static array
nArrUBound = UBound(arrStatic)

    'Declaring dynamic array boundary limit with a variable
    ReDim arrDynamic(nArrUBound)
'Copying values from static array to dynamic array
arrDynamic = arrStatic
```

Variable Scope and Lifetime

The part of the code over which variable name can be referenced is defined as the scope of the variable. If procedures are not being used in the code, then variable scope is from the statement where it is defined to the last state of the code. If procedures are defined within the code, then variable scope gets more complex. The following are some basic rules to follow:

1. *Global:* If a variable is defined in the main code, then its scope is from the line it is defined to the last line of the main code. Global variables are accessible to procedures that are part of the main code.
2. *Local:* If a variable is defined inside a procedure, then its scope is from the line it is defined to the last line of the code in the procedure. Local variables cannot be accessed by the main code.
3. *Collision:* If a variable is defined with the same name in main as well as procedure codes, then the variable in the main code is not accessible in the procedure code. Similarly, variable in the procedure code is not accessible inside the main code.

Constant Variables

A constant variable is a one whose value cannot be changed within the scope of the variable. A constant variable can be declared using 'Const' statement.

Example: Const nEmployeeNbr = 18776512

VBSCRIPT OPERATORS

An operator is a symbol, which operates on one or more arguments to produce a result. VBScript provides wide range of operators, including arithmetic operators, comparison operators, concatenation operators, and logical operators. When several operators are used in an expression, the operation on operators is performed based on predefined *operator precedence*. Parentheses are used to override the order precedence and to force some parts of an expression to be evaluated before other parts.

Arithmetic Operators

Symbol	Description
=	Is equal to
<>	Is not equal to
<	Is less than
>	Is greater than
≤	Is less than or equal to
≥	Is greater than or equal to
Is	Is object

Comparison Operator

Symbol	Description
^	Exponentiation
-	Unary negation
*	Multiplication
/	Division
\	Integer division
Mod	Modulus
+	Addition
–	Subtraction
&	String concatenation

Logical Operators

Symbol	**Description**
Not	Logical negation
And	Logical conjunction
Or	Logical disconjunction
Xor	Logical exclusion
Eqv	Logical equivalence

VBSCRIPT CONDITIONAL STATEMENTS

In VBScript, we have four conditional statements:

- **If statement**: executes a set of code when a specified condition is true
- **If...Then...Else statement**: selects one of two sets of lines to be executed
- **If...Then...ElseIf statement**: selects one of many sets of lines to be executed
- **Select Case statement**: selects one of many sets of lines to be executed

If... Statement

If a number ,

```
n=5 , Then output "Outstanding Performance"
n=4 , Then output "Gud Performance"
```

```
    n<4  and n>=1, Then output "need to improve"
Dim nGrade
nGrade = 3
If   nGrade =5 Then
   Msgbox "Outstanding Performance"
ElseIf nGrade =4 Then
   Msgbox "Gud Performance"
ElseIf nGrade <4 And nNbr>=1 Then
   Msgbox "Need to Improve"
Else
   Msgbox "Invalid Grade"
End If
```

Select Case ... Statement

```
Dim nGrade : nGrade = 3
Select Case nGrade
   Case 5
      Msgbox "Outstanding Performance"
   Case 4
      Msgbox "Gud Performance"
   Case 3
      Msgbox "Need to Improve"
   Case 2
      Msgbox "Need to Improve"
   Case 1
      Msgbox "Need to Improve"
   Case Else
      Msgbox "Invalid Grade"
End Select
```

VBSCRIPT LOOPING STATEMENTS

In VBScript, we have four looping statements:

- **For ... Next statement**: runs a block of code a specified number of times
- **For Each ... Next statement**: runs a block of code for each item in a collection or for each element of an array
- **Do ... Loop statement**: loops a block of code while or until a Boolean condition is true
- **While ... Wend statement**: do not use it–use the Do...Loop statement instead

For Next

Runs a block of code a specified number of times
The code below print numbers from 1 to 10.

```
For iCnt=1 To 20 Step 1
   If iCnt >10 Then
```

```
      Exit For
   End If
      Msgbox "Counter : "& iCnt
End If
   'Output
   'Counter : 1
   'Counter : 2 and so on…
```

For Each

Repeats a block of code for each item in a collection, or for each element of an array

```
   Dim arrMonth(3)
   arrMonth(0) = "Jan"
   arrMonth(1) = "Feb"
   arrMonth(2) = "Mar"
   arrMonth(3) = "Apr"
   For Each Element in arrMonth
      Msgbox "Month : " & Element
   Next
   'Output
   'Month : Jan
   'Month : Feb and so on
```

Do

Repeat code while a condition is true

```
   Do While iCnt >10
      Msgbox  "Counter : "& iCnt
      iCnt = iCnt - 1
   Loop
   The code above will never be executed if iCnt value is ≤10
   Do
      Msgbox  "Counter : " & iCnt
      iCnt = iCnt - 1
   Loop While iCnt>10
   The code above will be executed at least once, even if value of iCnt
  is <11
```

While

Repeat code until a condition becomes true

```
   Do Until i=10c
      Msgbox  "Counter : " & iCnt
      iCnt = iCnt - 1
   Loop
   If iCnt=10, then code above will never get executed.
```

```
Do
   Msgbox  "Counter : " & iCnt
   iCnt = iCnt - 1
Loop Until iCnt = 10
```

The code inside this loop will be executed at least once, even if iCnt= 10.

Examples

Exit a do statement

```
Do Until iCnt = 10
   If  iCnt < 5 Then Exit Do
         Msgbox  "Counter : " & iCnt
   iCnt = iCnt - 1
Loop
   'Output if iCnt=7   'Output if iCnt=12
    Counter : 7        Counter : 12
    Counter : 6        Counter : 11
```

How to Skip Code and Continue Executing a For Loop from Beginning?

There could be scenarios where if a test case fails in between we need to skip the remaining part of code and move on to the execution of next test scenario.

The code below skips execution of line 5 and onward if value of iCnt = 5.

```
1. For iCnt=1 To 10 Step 1
2. Do
3.     If iCnt =5 Then
4.    Exit Do
5.     End If
6.     Msgbox iCnt
7. Exit Do : Loop
8. Next
   'Output  : 1 2 3 4 6 7 8 9 10
```

VBSCRIPT FUNCTIONS

Date–Time Functions (Table 10.1)

Date: Returns the current system date

```
Syntax : dtCurrDate = Date
```

Time: Returns the current system time

```
Syntax : dtCurrTm = Time
```

Now: Returns current system date and time

```
Syntax : dtmCurrDtm = Now
```

Hour: Returns a number that represents hour of the day (0–23)

```
Syntax : tmCurrTm = Hour(time)
```

Minute: Returns a number that represents minute of the hour (0–59)

```
Syntax : tmCurrTm = Minute(time)
```

Seconds: Returns a number that represents second of the minute (0–59)

```
Syntax : tmCurrTm = Second(time)
```

Day: Returns a number that represents day of the month (1–31)

```
Syntax : nDay = Day(date)
```

Month: Returns a number that represents month of the year (1–12)

```
Syntax : nMnth = Month(date)
```

MonthName: Returns the month name of the specified month

```
Syntax : nMnthNm = MonthName(integer)
```

Year: Returns a number that represents year

```
Syntax : nYr = Year(date)
```

WeekDay: Retuns a number that represents day of the week (1–7)

```
Syntax : nWeekday = WeekDay(date)
```

WeekDayName: Returns the weekday name of the specified day of the week

```
Syntax : nWeekdayNm = WeekDayName(integer)
```

DateAdd: Returns a date with specified added time interval

```
Syntax : DateAdd(interval, number, date)
```

DateDiff: Returns number of intervals between two dates

```
Syntax : DateDiff(interval, date1, date2)
```

FormatDateTime: Returns a date formatted as date or time

```
Syntax : FormatDateTime(date, format)
```

IsDate: Returns a Boolean value. It indicates whether the specified expression is date type or not

```
Syntax : IsDate(expression)
```

Table 10.1 Date–time functions

Action	Statement	Output
Calculate system date	`Date`	4/3/2010
Calculate system time	`Time`	4:25:33 PM
System date and time	`Now`	4/3/2010 4:25:33 PM
Adds 3 years	`DateAdd ("yyyy" , 3 , Date)`	4/3/2013
Adds 2 days	`DateAdd ("d" , 2 , "03-Apr-2010")`	4/5/2010
Adds 2 months	`DateAdd ("m" , 2 , "04/03/2010")`	6/3/2010
Adds 3 h	`DateAdd ("h" ,3,"3-Apr-2010 04:16:54 PM")`	4/3/2010 7:16:54 PM

(*Continued*)

Table 10.1 (*Continued*)

Action	Statement	Output
Adds 3 min	`DateAdd ("n", 3 , "3-Apr-2010 04:16:54 PM")`	4/3/2010 4:19:54 PM
Adds 3 s	`DateAdd ('s' , 3 , "3-Apr-2010 16:16:54")`	4/3/2010 4:16:57 PM
Year difference	`DateDiff ("yyyy" , "3-Apr-2006 ", "3-Apr-2010")`	4
Day difference	`DateDiff ("d" , "3-Apr-2006 ", "3-Apr-2010")`	1,461
Month difference	`DateDiff ("m" , "3-Apr-2006 ", "3-Apr-2010")`	48
Hour difference	`DateDiff ("h" , "3-Apr-2010 16:14:16", "3-Apr-2010 18:18:18")`	2
Minute difference	`DateDiff ("n" , "3-Apr-2010 16:14:16", "3-Apr-2010 18:18:18")`	124
Second difference	`DateDiff ("s" , "3-Apr-2010 16:14:16", "3-Apr-2010 18:18:18")`	7,442
Calculate system hour	`Hour (Now)`	16
Hour of date	`Hour ("4/3/2010 04:14:16 PM")`	16
Minute of date	`Minute ("4/3/2010 16:14:16")`	14
Second of date	`Second ("4/3/2010 16:14:16")`	16
Day of date	`Day ("4/3/2010")`	3
Month of date	`Month ("03-Apr-2010")`	4
Month name	`MonthName (Month ("04/03/2010") , True )`	Apr
Year of date	`Year ("03-Apr-2010")`	2010
Week day of date	`WeekDay ("03-Apr-2010")`	7
Week day name	`WeekDayName (WeekDay ("03-Apr-2010") , True)`	Sat
Is expression date type	`IsDate ("03-Apr-2010")`	True
Is expression date type	`IsDate ("32-Apr-2010")`	False
Is expression date type	`IsDate("abc")`	False

Date–time functions

Comments	Statement	Output
mm/dd/yyyy	`FormatDateTime ("03-Apr-2010")`	"4/3/2010"
Weekday, month name, year	`FormatDateTime ("03-Apr-2010" , 1)`	"Saturday, April 03, 2010"
mm/dd/yyyy	`FormatDateTime ("03-Apr-2010 10:23:24 PM" , 2)`	"4/3/2010"
hh:mm:ss AM/PM	`FormatDateTime ("03-Apr-2010 22:23:24" , 3)`	"10:23:24 AM"
hh:mm	`FormatDateTime ("03-Apr-2010 10:23:24 PM" , 4)`	"10:23"

String Functions (Table 10.2)

InStr: Returns the position of first occurrence of a specified expression in a string. Returns 0 if the specified expression is not found in the specified string

```
Syntax : InStr([start,]string1, string2 [, compare])
```

InStrRev: Returns the position of first occurrence of a specified expression in a string. The search begins at last character of the string

```
Syntax : InStrRev(string1, string2[, start[, compare]])
```

LCase: Converts specified string to lowercase

```
Syntax : LCase(string)
```

UCase: Converts the specified string to uppercase

```
Syntax : UCase(string)
```

Trim: Removes white spaces at the beginning and end of string

```
Syntax : Trim(string)
```

Left: Returns the specified number of characters from left side of the specified string

```
Syntax : Left(string, length)
```

Right: Returns the specified number of characters from right side of the specified string

```
Syntax : Right(string, length)
```

Mid: Returns the specified number of characters within a string

```
Syntax : (string, start, length)
```

Len: Returns the number of characters in a string

```
Syntax : Len(string)
```

StrComp: Compares two strings. Returns 0 if the specified strings match

```
Syntax : StrComp(string1, string2[, compare])
```

StrReverse: Reverses a string

```
Syntax : StrReverse(string)
```

Replace: Replaces a specified part of the string with another specified string

```
Syntax : Replace(string,find,replacewith[,start[,count[,compare]]])
```

Table 10.2 String functions

Action	Statement	Output
Textual comparison starting at position 1	`Instr (1 , "Find String" , "ring" , 1)`	8
Textual comparison starting at position 1	`Instr (1 , "Find String" , "STRING" , 1)`	6
Binary comparison starting at position 1	`Instr (1 , "Find String" , "ring" , 0)`	8
Binary comparison starting at position 1	`Instr (1 , "Find String" , "STRING" , 0)`	0

(*Continued*)

Table 10.2 (*Continued*)

Action	Statement	Output
Textual comparison starting at position 4	Instr (4 , "Find String" , "STRING" , 1)	6
Textual comparison starting at position 4	Instr (4 , "Find String" , "Find" , 1)	0
Textual comparison starting at position 1	Instr (1 , "Find String" , "QTP" , 1)	0
Textual comparison starting at position 1	Instr ("Data\M1\abc.xls" , "\")	5
Reverse textual comparison	InstrRev ("Data\M1\abc.xls" , "\")	8
Convert to lowercase	LCase ("Convert To LOWERcase")	convert to lowercase
Convert to uppercase	UCase ("Convert To LOWERcase")	CONVERT TO LOWERCASE
Trim white spaces	Trim ("QTP Code")	QTP Code
Retrieve characters from left of a string	Left ("VBScript Code" , 5)	VBScr
Retrieve characters from right of a string	Right ("VBScript Code" , 5)	Code
Retrieve characters from within a string	Mid ("VBScript Code" , 3 , 8)	Script C
Length of string	Len ("VBScript Code")	13
Textual comparison of two strings	StrComp ("VBScript" , "VBScript" , 1)	0
Textual comparison of two strings	StrComp ("VBScript" , "vbscript" , 1)	0
Binary comparison of two strings	StrComp ("VBScript" , "vbscript" , 0)	-1
Textual comparison of two strings	StrComp ("VBScript" , "Code" , 1)	1
Reverse a string	StrReverse ("VBScript Code")	edoC tpircSBV
Find and replace string contents	Replace ("3/4/2010 11:47:14 AM" , "/" , "-")	3 - 4 - 2 0 1 0 11:47:14 AM
Find and replace string contents	Replace ("3/4/2010 11:47:14 AM" , "/" , "")	3 - 4 - 2 0 1 0 11:47:14 AM

Conversion Functions (Table 10.3)

CInt: Converts an expression to a variant of subtype Integer

```
Syntax : CInt(expression)
```

CLng: Converts an expression to a variant of subtype Long

```
Syntax : CLng(expression)
```

CDbl: Converts an expression to a variant of subtype Double

```
Syntax : CDbl(expression)
```

CStr: Converts an expression to a variant of subtype String

```
Syntax : CStr(expression)
```

CDate: Converts an expression to a variant of subtype Date

```
Syntax : CDate(date)
```

CCur: Converts an expression to a variant of subtype Currency

```
Syntax : CCur(expression)
```

Asc: Returns ANSI code of the first character of the string

```
Syntax : Asc(string)
```

Chr: Returns character expression of the specified ANSI code

```
Syntax : Chr(ANSICode)
```

Table 10.3 Conversion functions

Action	Statement	Output
Convert a string to Integer	CInt ("36")	36
Convert a double to Integer	CInt (36.5)	36
Convert a double to Integer	CInt (36.51)	37
Convert a string to Integer	CInt ("-56")	-56
Convert a string to Integer	CInt("55555")	Error : Overflow
Convert to Long	CLng ("55555")	55555
Convert to Long	CLng ("55555.55")	55556
Convert to Double	CDbl ("55555.55")	55555.55
Convert to String	CStr (5555.55)	5555.55
Convert to String	CStr (#01-Jan-2010#)	1/1/2010
Convert to Date	CDate ("20 Mar, 2010")	3/20/2010
Convert to Date	CDate (#3/20/2010#)	3/20/2010
Convert to Date	CDate ("22:02:59")	10:02:59 PM
Find ASCI code	Asc ("R")	82
Find ASCI code	Asc ("g")	103
Find ASCI code	Asc (" ")	32
Find character expression	Chr (32)	(white space)
Find character expression	Chr (82)	R

Array Functions

Array: Returns a variant containing an array.

```
Syntax : Array(argument List)
```

Example:

```
arrTemp = Array(2,4,6,8,10)
Msgbox arrTemp(2)                  'Output = 6
For each Element in arrTemp
   Msgbox Element              'Output = 2 4 6 8 10
Next
```

LBound: Returns the lower boundary of an array. It is always 0.

```
Syntax : LBound(arrayname[,dimension])
```

Example:

```
Msgbox LBound(arrTemp)        'Output : 0
Dim arrBooks(4,3)        'Two dimensional array with dimensions 4 and 3
arrBooks(0,0) = "Book Category"
arrBooks(0,1) = "Book Name"
arrBooks(0,2) = "Author"
arrBooks(0,3) = "Publisher"
arrBooks(1,0) = "QTP"
arrBooks(1,1) = "Master Test Automation & QTP"
arrBooks(1,2) = "Rajeev Gupta"
arrBooks(2,0) = "VBScript"
arrBooks(2,1) = "Learn VBScript"
Msgbox LBound(arrBooks)       'Output : 0
Msgbox LBound(arrBooks,0)     'Output : 0
Msgbox LBound(arrBooks,1)     'Output : 0
Msgbox LBound(arrBooks,2)     'Output : 0
```

UBound: Returns the upper boundary of an array.

```
Syntax : UBound(arrayname[,dimension])
```

Example:

```
Msgbox UBound(arrTemp)        'Output : 4
Msgbox UBound(arrBooks)       'Output : 4

Msgbox UBound(arrBooks, 1 )   'Output : 4
Msgbox UBound(arrBooks, 2 )   'Output : 3
```

IsArray: Returns a Boolean value that indicates whether the specified variable is an array.

```
Syntax : IsArray(variable)
```

Example:

```
Msgbox IsArray(arrBooks)      'Output : True
Dim sVar : sVar = "String Text"
Msgbox IsArray(arrBooks)      'Output : False
```

Filter: Returns an array of the filtered contents from another array.

```
Syntax : Filter(inputstrings,value[,include[,compare]])
```

Example:

```
   arrFilterText = Array("Jan", "Feb", "Mar", "Apr", "May")
   arrFltrdTxt = Filter(arrFilterText, "M")
                              'Output arrFltrdTxt(0) = "Mar"
                                arrFltrdTxt(1) = "May"
   arrFltrdTxt = Filter(arrFilterText, "a")
                              'Output arrFltrdTxt(0) = "Jan"
                                arrFltrdTxt(1) = "Mar"
                                      arrFltrdTxt(2) = "May"
```

Split: Returns an array after splitting the string as specified.

```
Syntax : Split(expression[,delimiter[,count[,compare]]])
```

Example:

```
sText = "File Sequence Number is : 2234567"
arrText = Split(sText, " ", -1, 1)
                          'Output arrText(0) = "File"
                                  arrText(1) = "Sequence"
                                  arrText(2) = "Number"
                                  arrText(3) = "is"
                                  arrText(4) = ":"
                                  arrText(5) = "2234567"
arrTxt2 = Split(sText, ":", -1, 1)
              'Output arrTxt2 = "File Sequence Number is "
                      arrTxt2 = " 2234567"
```

Join: Returns a string that is obtained after joining the contents of an array.

```
Syntax : Join(list[,delimiter])
```

Example:

```
sJoinedString = Join(arrText, "_")
      'Output : File_Sequence_Number_is_:_2234567
```

Miscellaneous

CreateObject: Creates an object of a specified type.

```
Syntax : CreateObject(servername.typename[,location])
```

Example: Create a new excel file.

```
Set objExcel = CreateObject("Excel.Application")
objExcel.Visible = True   'Make excel visible
objExcel.WorkBooks.Add    'Add new excel
'Write to excel cells
objExcel.Cells(1,1).Value = "Testing"
objExcel.Cells(1,2).Value = "Testing Complete"
```

GetObject: Returns a reference to an automation object.

```
Syntax : GetObject([pathname][,class])
```

Example: Read a already opened excel file

```
Set objExcel = GetObject(,"Excel.Application")
objExcel.Visible = True'Make excel visible
'Bring Excel to front
objExcel.ActiveWorkbook.Activate
'Find complete path along with the excel file name
Msgbox objExcel.ActiveWorkbook.FullName
```

Round: Returns an Integer after it rounds a number to its specified number of decimal places.

```
Syntax : Round(expression[,numdecimalplaces])
```

Example:
```
Round(24.5)                          'Output : 24
Round(25.6)                          'Output : 25
Round(24.556, 2)                     'Output : 24.56
```

IsNumeric: Returns a Boolean value that indicates whether the specified expression is a number or not.

```
SynTax : IsNumeric(expression)
```

Example:
```
Dim nNbr
nNbr = 1
Msgbox IsNumeric(nNbr)               'Output : True
nNbr = "1"
Msgbox IsNumeric(nNbr)               'Output : True
nNbr = "1 Number"
Msgbox IsNumeric(nNbr)               'Output : False
nNbr = Empty
Msgbox IsNumeric(nNbr)               'Output : True
nNbr = Nulll
Msgbox IsNumeric(nNbr)               'Output : False
```

IsNull: Returns a Boolean value that indicates whether or not the specified expression contains no valid data.

```
Syntax : IsNull(expression)
```

Example:
```
Dim sVar
Msgbox IsNull(sVar)                  'Output : False
sVar = "1"
Msgbox IsNull(sVar)                  'Output : False
sVar = Empty
Msgbox IsNull(sVar)                  'Output : False
sVar = Null
Msgbox IsNull(sVar)                  'Output : True
```

IsEmpty: Returns a Boolean value that indicates whether the specified variable has been initialized or not.

```
Syntax : IsEmpty(expression)
```

Example:
```
Dim sVar
Msgbox IsNull(sVar)                  'Output : True
sVar = "1"
Msgbox IsNull(sVar)                  'Output : False
sVar = Empty
Msgbox IsNull(sVar)                  'Output : True
sVar = Null
Msgbox IsNull(sVar)                  'Output : False
```

RGB: Returns a number that represents an RGB color value

```
Syntax : RGB(red,green,blue)
```

Example: `Msgbox RGB(255,0,255)` 'Output : 16711935

MsgBox: Displays a msgbox, waits for user to click a button, and returns a value indicating which button was clicked.

```
Syntax :
```

Example:
```
nVal = MsgBox("Hello everyone!",65,"Information...")
    'Output on Clicking Ok button : 1
    'Output on Clicking Cancel button : 2
```

OPTION EXPLICIT

We observe that in VBScript there is no need to declare a variable before assigning a value to it, which otherwise throws error in other languages. In order to force programmers to declare a variable before using it, Option Explicit is written at the very top of the code. However, we cannot enforce Option Explicit in individual library files.

ERROR HANDLING

VBScript provides three ways to handle an error during runtime as follows:

On Error GoTo 0

This method indicates that when runtime error occurs, Visual Basic for Applications (VBA) should display its standard runtime error message box, allowing user to enter the code in debug mode or to terminate the VBA program. When On Error GoTo 0 is in effect, it is the same as having no enabled error handler. Any error will cause VBA to display its standard error message box. This method should be avoided while scripting because any runtime error will not allow the scripts to run in an unattended mode.

On Error GoTo <label>

This method is not supported by QTP. It tells VBA to transfer execution to the line following the specified line label.

Example:

```
On Error Goto ErrorHandler:
nNbr = 1/0
sVar = "Testing"
......... Code ......
......... Code ......
Exit Sub
ErrorHandler:
    'error handling code
    'MsgBox err.Number & "::" & err.Description
    End Sub
```

On Error Resume Next

This method instructs VBA to essentially ignore the error and resume execution on the next line of code. It is very important to remember that On Error Resume Next does not in any way "fix" the error. It simply instructs VBA to continue execution as if no error occurred.

Err.Number and Err.Description

Err.Number is used to retrieve or set the value that relates to a specific runtime error. This value is automatically generated when an error occurs and can be reset to zero (no error) by using the *Err. Clear* method. *Err.Description* specifies the description of the error.

Example :

```
On Error Resume Next
Dim nNbr, sVar
sVar = "Start"
nNbr =20/0
sVar = "End"
If Err.Number <>0  Then
     Msgbox Err.Number & "::" & Err.Description & "::" & sVar
End If
    'Output : 11::Division by zero::End
```

NOTES

1. Error handling codes ensures in catching the exact point of deviation
2. Error handling codes ensure proper execution of regression test suites in an unattended mode

EXAMPLES

Pass an Array to a Function

Example below shows how to pass an array to a function by reference. The changes made to the array inside in the function are reflected back outside the function code.

```
Dim arrBooks(3)
For iCnt=LBound(arrBooks) To UBound(arrBooks) Step 1
  arrBooks(iCnt) = iCnt
Next
Call fnTestEnvVarArrPass(arrBooks)
Msgbox arrBooks(UBound(arrBooks))                'Output : Done

Function fnTestEnvVarArrPass(arrVar)
  Msgbox arrVar(UBound(arrVar))                  'Output : 3
  arrVar(UBound(arrVar)) = "Done"
End Function
```

Function to Sort Numbers

Example below shows how to sort numbers given in string format.

Method 1

Function 'fnSortNbrs' sorts any string of numbers separated by a comma in ascending order. It takes the string of numbers and output string variable as input parameter. After sorting, the sorted string is saved in the output string variable.

Input parameters

```
sNbrToSort - string of numbers to sort
sSortedNbr - Variable to store sorted string
```

Output parameter

```
Returns '0' if the string is successfully sorted, else returns '-1.'
```

Usage

```
Dim sSortedNbr
Call fnSortNbrs("6,4,7,3,8,9", sSortedNbr)
Msgbox sSortedNbr                                  'Output : 3,4,6,7,8,9
Function fnSortNbrs(ByVal sNbrToSort, ByRef sSortedNbr)
On Error Resume Next
sSortedNbr = ""
arrNbr = Split(sNbrToSort,",",-1,1)
  For iCnt=0 To UBound(arrNbr) Step 1
        For jCnt=iCnt+1 To UBound(arrNbr) Step 1
              If arrNbr(iCnt) >arrNbr(jCnt) Then
                    nTemp = arrNbr(iCnt)
                    arrNbr(iCnt) = arrNbr(jCnt)
                    arrNbr(jCnt) = nTemp
              End If
        Next
  Next
  For iCnt=UBound(arrNbr) To 0  Step -1
        sSortedNbr = arrNbr(iCnt) & "," & sSortedNbr
  Next
```

> ByVal – Pass by Value
> ByRef – Pass by Reference
>
> VBScript passes value by reference by default. If a variable or an array is passed by value, then changes made to the variable/array value is local to the function code and not accessible outside the function code. In order to make the changes accessible outside the function code, the variable/array is to be passed by reference. If neither 'ByVal' nor 'ByRef' is defined before the function parameter, then by default the variable/array is passed by reference.

```
   If Err.Number <>0  Then
         fnSortNbrs = "-1"
         sSortedNbr = Err.Description
   End If
   sSortedNbr = Left(sSortedNbr,Len(sSortedNbr)-1)
   fnSortNbrs = "0"
End Function
```

Method 2

'fnSortArray' sorts an array contents in ascending order. It takes an array to sort as input parameter and returns the sorted array in the same input array.

Input parameters

```
   arrSortThisArray—array to sort
```

Usage

```
Dim arrSortThisArray(5)
arrSortThisArray(1) = 6
arrSortThisArray(2) = 5
arrSortThisArray(3) = 8
arrSortThisArray(4) = 9
arrSortThisArray(5) = 2
Call fnSortArray(arrSortThisArray)
      'Output: value of the array - 2, 5, 6, 8, 9

Function fnSortArray(arrSortThisArray)
   'Create an arraylist object
   Set oArrayList = CreateObject("System.Collections.ArrayList")

   For iElement = 0 To UBound(arrSortThisArray)
         oArrayList.Add arrSortThisArray (iElement)
   Next

   'Sort array list oArrayList.Sort

   'Save sorted array list
   Set arrSortThisArray = oArrayList
   Set oArrayList = Nothing
End Function
```

Function to Format Date

When inputting date to the application screen, different applications require date to be in different formats. Example below shows how to format the date to a desired format type. 'fnFormatDate' formats the specified date to a specified date format.

Input parameters

```
dtDate—Input date
sFormat—Expected date format
```

Output parameter

It returns the date in the specified format if date format conversion is successful, else returns a string with flag '-1' and error description.

Usage

```
dtDate = "04-Mar-2010"    'Or dtDate = Date
dtFormattedDate = fnFormatDate(dtDate, "ddmmyy")    'Output : 040310
dtFormattedDate = fnFormatDate(dtDate, "dmyyyy")    'Output : 432010
dtFormattedDate = fnFormatDate(dtDate, "mmddyyyy") 'Output : 04032010
dtFormattedDate = fnFormatDate(dtDate, "dd-mmm-yyyy")'Output : 04-Mar-2010
dtFormattedDate = fnFormatDate(dtDate, "dd/mm/yy") 'Output : 04/03/10
dtFormattedDate = fnFormatDate(dtDate, "m/d/yyyy") 'Output : 3/4/2010
```

```
Function fnFormatDate(dtDate, sFormat)
   On Error Resume Next
   Dim nDayLen, nMonLen, nYrLen, sSeparator, sExpDtFrmt, dtFrmtdDt
   nDayLen = nMonLen = nYrLen = 0
   sFormat = Trim(sFormat)

   '---- Find expected date format
   For iCnt = 1 To Len(sFormat) Step 1
        If Mid(sFormat, iCnt, 1) = "d" Then
              nDayLen = nDayLen + 1
              If Instr(1,sExpDtFrmt,"d",1)=0 Then
                    sExpDtFrmt = sExpDtFrmt & "d"
              End If
        ElseIf Mid(sFormat, iCnt, 1) = "m" Then
              nMonLen = nMonLen + 1
              If Instr(1,sExpDtFrmt,"m",1)=0 Then
                    sExpDtFrmt = sExpDtFrmt & "m"
              End If
        ElseIf Mid(sFormat, iCnt, 1) = "y" Then
              nYrLen = nYrLen + 1
              If Instr(1,sExpDtFrmt,"y",1)=0 Then
                    sExpDtFrmt = sExpDtFrmt & "y"
              End If
        Else
              sSeparator = Mid(sFormat,iCnt,1) 'Separator
        End If
    Next
   '---- Format day
   If nDayLen = "1" Then
        nDay = Day(dtDate)
   ElseIf nDayLen = "2" Then
        nDay = Day(dtDate)
        If Len(nDay) = "1" Then
```

```
            nDay = "0" & nDay
        End If
    End If
    '---- Format month
    If nMonLen = "1" Then
        nMonth = Month(dtDate)
    ElseIf nMonLen = "2" Then
        nMonth = Month(dtDate)
        If Len(nMonth) = "1" Then
            nMonth = "0" & nMonth
        End If
    ElseIf nMonLen = "3" Then
        nMonth = MonthName(Month(dtDate), True)
    End If

    '---- Format year
    If nYrLen = "2" Then
        nYr = Right(Year(dtDate), 2)
    Else
        nYr = Year(dtDate)
    End If

     '-----Format date
    Select Case sExpDtFrmt
        Case "dmy"
     dtFrmtdDt = nDay & sSeparator & nMonth & sSeparator & nYr
     Case "dym"
     dtFrmtdDt = nDay & sSeparator & nYr & sSeparator & nMonth
     Case "mdy"
     dtFrmtdDt = nMonth & sSeparator & nDay & sSeparator & nYr
     Case "myd"
     dtFrmtdDt = nMonth & sSeparator & nYr & sSeparator & nDay
     Case "ydm"
     dtFrmtdDt = nYr & sSeparator & nDay & sSeparator & nMonth
     Case "ymd"
     dtFrmtdDt = nYr & sSeparator & nMonth & sSeparator & nDay
    End Select
    If Err.Number <>0 Then
        fnFormatDate = "-1" & ":" & Err.Description
        Exit Function
    End If
    fnFormatDate = dtFrmtdDt
End Function
```

Function to Compare Two Strings

Example below shows how to compare two strings ignoring all types of white spaces.

```
sText1 = "Vehicles" & vbTab & "Cars" & vbTab & "Bikes" & vbCrLf &_
                 "1." & vbTab & "Car1" & vbTab & "Bike1"MsgBox sText
MsgBox sText1                    'Output :    Vehicles     Cars   Bikes
                                              1.           Car1   Bike1
Call fnRmvWhiteSpaces(sText1)
MsgBox sText1                    'Output : VehiclesCarsBikes1.Car1Bike1
sText2 = "Vehicles" & vbCrLf & "Cars" & vbCrLf & "Bikes " & vbCrLf &_
                 "1. " & vbCr & "Car1" & vbCr & "Bike1"
Call fnRmvWhiteSpaces(sText2)
Msgbox sText2                    'Output : VehiclesCarsBikes1.Car1Bike1
nStrCmprFlg = StrComp(sText1,
sText2,1)                        'Output : 0
Public Function fnRmvWhiteSpaces(sString)
   sString = Replace(sString, vbCrLf, "")
   sString = Replace(sString, vbCr, "")
   sString = Replace(sString, vbTab, "")
   sString = Replace(sString, vbVerticalTab, "")
   sString = Replace(sString, Chr(32), "")
End Function
```

Function to Pad Zeros

The current system date retrieved using VBScript command does not contain a zero padded to the day or month value (if the day or month value is a single digit number). While inputting date to the application screen, most of the time it is required for the date to be padded with zero if the length of date or month is a single digit number. Example below shows how to pad a zero to the day or month of a date.

'fnPadZeros' increases the length of an expression to a defined length by adding leading zeros to it.

Input parameters

dt = Day or month in numeric format
totalDigits = Expected length of day or month.
If the value of this variable is 2 and value of 'dt' variable is '9,' then the function pads an extra '0' to '9' to make its length 2 ('09').

Output parameter

Returns the formatted date if format conversion is successful else returns the error description with an error flag '-1' concatenated to it.

Usage

```
Syntax
sFrmtdTxt =  fnFormatDate(expression, desired length of expression)
```

fnFormatDate can be used to get always two digit day and month value.

```
dtCurrDt = fnFormatDate(Day(Date),2) & "/" & fnFormatDate(Month(Date),2)
```

Example:

```
sFrmtdTxt =  fnFormatDate(4,2)                    'Output : 04
sFrmtdTxt =  fnFormatDate(24,2)                   'Output : 24

Function fnPadZeros (dt, totalDigits)
    On Error Resume Next
    If totalDigits > len(dt) Then
                  'Pad required number of zeros
        fnFormatDate = String(totalDigits-len(dt),"0")&dt
    else
        fnFormatDate = dt
    end if
        If Err.Number <> 0 Then
                   fnFormatDate= "-1:" & Err.Description
   End If
End Function
```

QUICK TIPS

- ✓ As far as possible, VBScript functions should be used instead of designing new functions
- ✓ Error handling codes should be used wherever necessary to avoid QTP error pop-up window.

PRACTICAL QUESTIONS

1. Suppose variable,

   ```
   sVar  = "1,a;2,b;3,c;4,d;5,e"
   ```

   Write code to store numbers of variable 'sVar' in one array and alphabets in another array.
2. Suppose variable 'sVar' contains employee details in the format – Id, Name, Age

   ```
   sVar  = "11,Sam,24;12,Donna,28;18,Simpson,30;15,Taylor,32"
   ```

   Write code to store the employee details of variable 'sVar' in a two-dimensional array.
3. Suppose array

   ```
   arrMonths = Array("Jan", "Feb", "Mar", "Apr", "May")
   ```

   Write code to store the month names starting with 'M' in a separate array.
4. Suppose

   ```
   sVar1 = "This is to test VBScript functions."
   sVar2 = "TEST"
   ```

   (a) Write code to find whether text in variable 'sVar2' is present in variable 'sVar1' or not.
   (b) Write code to compare and find whether 'sVar1' contents are equal to 'sVar2' or not.
   (c) Write code to extract word 'VBScript' from variable 'sVar1.'

(d) Write code to remove all white spaces and special characters from the variable 'sVar1.'
(e) Write code to join the contents of the variables 'sVar1' and 'sVar2.'

5. Suppose

```
sVar1 = "1, 2, 6, 78, 65, 34"
```

(a) Write code to find the max value of variable 'sVar1.'
(b) Write code to find the average of all the numbers of the variable 'sVar1.'

6. Suppose

```
sVar1 = "24-Mar-2010 10:00:59AM"
sVar2 = "26-Mar-2011 06:18:00PM"
```

(a) Write code to find which date is greater: 'sVar1' or 'sVar2.'
(b) Write code to add 2 weeks to date of variable 'sVar1.'
(c) Write code to find the difference in days between dates 'sVar1' and 'sVar2.'
(d) Write code to find the hour value of the variable 'sVar1.'
(e) Write code to add the dates of variable 'sVar1' and 'sVar2.'

7. What is the difference between 'Pass By Value' and 'Pass By Reference'?

Chapter 11

Dictionary

Test scripts often retrieve information from outside source such as AUT screen and excel files and store them in a variable or array. Alternatively, the data can also be stored in a dictionary object. The dictionary object functions like an associative array and stores value in key-item pairs. Every *key* has a unique *item* and no two keys can be same. In case of an array, array data is stored and retrieved using array index; however, in case of dictionary, the value of an item is retrieved using its key. Therefore, in situations where data need to be accessed using a unique name identifier, dictionary object can be used. A dictionary object can contain any data including objects and dictionary objects. *For Each* construct can be used to loop through all key-value pairs of the dictionary object.

Employee ID	Employee Name
765865	Britta
987678	Sam
456345	Gabriel
324345	Sam
789765	Glenn
980980	Sam

Dictionary is COM object; therefore, it must be instantiated in the same fashion as any other COM object. Code shown below creates an instance of dictionary object 'dicObjectName.'

```
Syntax : Set dicObjectName = CreateObject("Scripting.Dictionary")
```

Example: `Set dicEmpDetails = CreateObject("Scripting.Dictionary")`

METHODS

Listed below are the various methods of the dictionary object:

Add: To add key/value pairs to a dictionary object.

After an instance of dictionary object has been created, *Add* method can be used to add key-item pairs to the dictionary object.

```
Syntax : dicObjectName.Add keyvalue, itemvalue
```

Example:

```
dicEmpDetails.Add "765865", "Britta"  'Key value is string type
dicEmpDetails.Add 789765, "Glenn"     'Key value is integer type
dicEmpDetails.Add 123, 789            'Both key and item value are int-
                                       eger type
```

Dictionary keys must be unique. For example, code below will throw run-time error when executed. The error occurs as key 'Sam' is already added to the dictionary object and no two keys can be same.

```
dicEmpDetails.Add "Sam", "765865"
dicEmpDetails.Add "Sam", "980980"              'run-time error
```

Exist: To check whether a key exists in the dictionary object or not.

The *Exist* method verifies whether the specified key is present in the dictionary object or not. Returns 'True' if the specified key exists in the dictionary object or else returns 'False.'

```
Syntax : dicObjectName.Exists(keyvalue)
```

Example:

```
bExist = dicEmpDetails.Exists("765865")       'Output : True
bExist = dicEmpDetails.Exists("111111")       'Output : False
```

Items: To retrieve all items stored in the dictionary object.

The *Items* method returns an array containing all the item values of the specified dictionary object.

```
Syntax : dicObjectName.Items
```

Example:

```
arrItemVal = dicEmpDetails.Items  'Output : arrItemVal(0) = "Britta"
                                            arrItemVal(1) = "Glenn"
                                            arrItemVal(2) = 789
```

Keys: To retrieve all the keys stored in the dictionary object.

The *Items* method returns an array containing all the key values of the specified dictionary object.

```
Syntax : dicObjectName.Keys
```

Example:

```
arrKeyVal = dicEmpDetails.Keys  'Output : arrKeyVal (0) = "765865"
                                          arrKeyVal (1) = 789765
                                          arrKeyVal (2) = 123
```

Remove: To remove a single key/item pair from the dictionary object.

The *Remove* method removes the specified key and its associated item from the dictionary object.

```
Syntax : dicObjectName.Remove (keyvalue)
```

Example:

```
dicEmpDetails.Remove(123)
arrKeyVal = dicEmpDetails.Keys  'Output : arrKeyVal (0) = "765865"
                                          arrKeyVal (1) = 789765
```

> **NOTES** If the key does not exist, then run-time error, "Element Not Found" occurs.

RemoveAll: To remove all the key/item pairs from dictionary.

The *RemoveAll* method resets the dictionary object. In other words, this method deletes all the keys and the items associated with it from the dictionary.

`Syntax : dicObjectName.RemoveAll`

Example: `dicEmpDetails.RemoveAll`

PROPERTIES

Listed below are the various properties of the dictionary object:

Count: To retrieve count of key, value pairs stored in the dictionary object.

The *Count* property returns the number of the key-item pairs stored in the dictionary object.

`Syntax : dicObjectName.Count`

Example: `nCnt = dicEmpDetails.Count`

Item: To retrieve item corresponding to a key.

The *Item* property retrieves the item value associated with the specified key.

`Syntax : dicObjectName.Item (keyvalue)`

Example: `sItemVal = dicEmpDetails ("765865")  'Output: "Britta"`

If an attempt is made to retrieve item value of a nonexistent key, then the key is added to the dictionary. The item value corresponding to the key is set as blank item.

> **NOTES** If the item to be retrieved or stored in a dictionary is an object then *Set* statement must be used.

Key: To replace an existing key value with another key value.

The *key* property replaces an existing key value with the specified key value.

`Syntax : dicObjectName.Key(key) = newkey`

Example:
```
dicEmpDetails.Key("765865") = "999999"
sVal = dicEmpDetails.Key("999999") = "Britta"
```

CompareMode: To set or return the comparison mode for comparing string keys of the dictionary object.

The *CompareMode* property is used to configure the dictionary object. It helps in determining which keys can be added to the dictionary object and which cannot. It can take two values 0 or 1.

0 – Sets the mode to binary. This is the default value.

1 – Sets the mode to text.

By default, dictionary object is created in binary mode. A dictionary object created in binary mode is case sensitive, i.e., it will treat "Key1" and "KEY1" as two different keys. If dictionary object is configured for text mode, then, it will throw an error on addition of "KEY1," if "Key1" is already added to the dictionary object. In other words, "Key1" and "KEY1" are treated as same key in text mode.

Syntax : `dicObjectName.CompareMode = [CompareMode]`

Example: `dicEmpDetails.CompareMode = 1`

> **NOTES** The *CompareMode* property of the dictionary object cannot be changed if it contains any key-item pairs.

CREATING DICTIONARY OBJECT

Figure 11.1 shows a table of list of trains. The code below creates a dictionary 'dicTrainList,' adds key/value pairs and retrieves value of a pair using its key. Here, train number has been used as key and train name as value.

List of Trains

Please Select A Train From The List

SN	Select	Train no	Train Name	Departure	Arrival	Runs on
1	○	2472	SWARAJ EXPRESS	21:50	17:21	– T W – F S –
2	○	2618	MNGLA LKSDP EXP	09:20	08:30	M T W TH F S SU
3	○	2904	GOLDN TEMPLE ML	07:45	05:40	M T W TH F S SU
4	○	2920	PASCHIM EXPRESS	16:55	14:18	M T W TH F S SU

Figure 11.1 *Table of list of trains*

```
'---- Declaration
Dim nTrainNo, arrTrainNo, arrTrainNm
'---- Create an object of type dictionary
Set dicTrainList = CreateObject("Scripting.Dictionary")
'---- Add key/value pairs
dicTrainList.Add "2472", "SWARAJ EXPRESS"
dicTrainList.Add "2618", "MNGLA LKSDP EXP"
dicTrainList.Add "2904", "GOLDN TEMPLE ML"
'---- Retrieve train name corresponding to train number 2618
nTrainNo = dicTrainList.Item("2618")
'---- Retrieve all keys - train numbers
arrTrainNo = dicTrainList.Keys

'---- Retrieve all items - train names
arrTrainNm = dicTrainList.Items
```

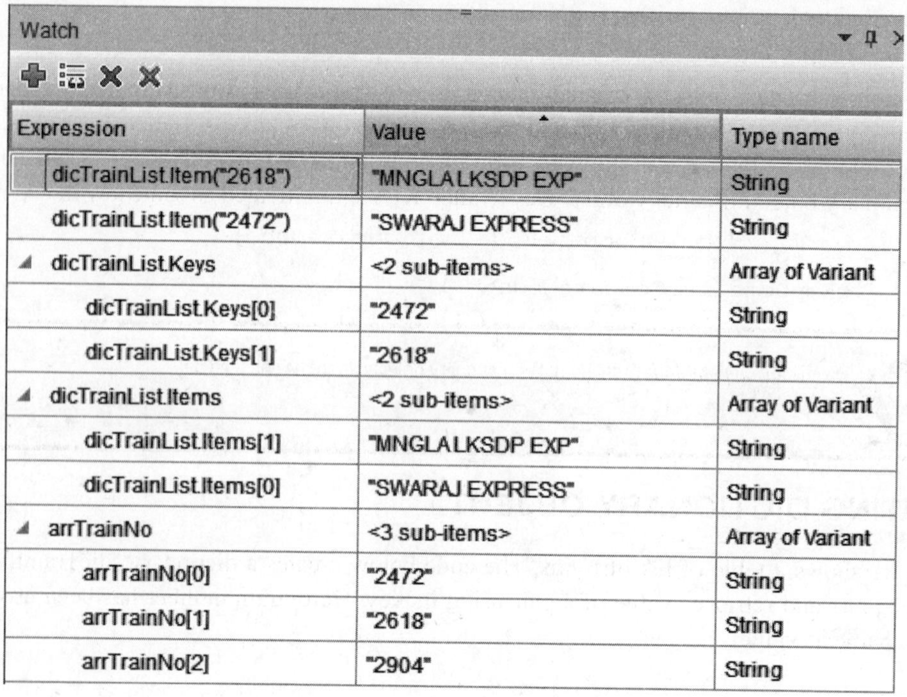

Figure 11.2 *Results of dictionary object*

```
'---- Removing a data associated with train number 2904 from dictionary
dicTrainList.Remove("2904")

'---- Removing all contents from dictionary
dicTrainList.RemoveAll
```

Results: Figure 11.2 shows dictionary object values as seen in QTP debugger window.

CREATING DICTIONARY OF DICTIONARY OBJECT

Now, suppose that we also need to extract departure and arrival details in dictionary, then the following statement will fail as a value is already associated with key '2472.'

```
dicTrainList.Add "2472", "21:50"   'will throw error at runtime
```

This occurs because one *key* can have only one *item* value and one *item* can have only one *key* value. Such problems can be solved by creating dictionary of dictionary object. In dictionary of dictionary object, *primary key* and *secondary key-item* pairs are defined. Corresponding to one primary key, there could be '*n*' secondary key-item pairs.

```
Syntax :
dicObjectName.add primarykey, CreateObject ("Scripting.Dictionary")
dicObjectName (primarykey).Add secondarykey,itemvalue
```

Table 11.1 Dictionary object

Key	Value
2472	SWARAJ EXPRESS
2618	MNGLA LKSDP EXP
2904	GOLDN TEMPLE ML

Table 11.2 Dictionary of dictionary object

Primary Key	Secondary Key	Secondary Item
2472	TrainName	SWARAJ EXPRESS
	TrainDepart	21:50
	TrainArrival	17:21
2618	TrainName	MNGLA LKSDP EXP
	TrainDepart	09:20
	TrainArrival	08:30

The *Count* property is used to retrieve count of key-item pairs stored in the secondary dictionary object.

```
dicObjectName (primarykey).Count
```

For example, in the code given below, *Train No.* has been used as primary key. There are three secondary key-item pairs corresponding to the primary key, viz. *TrainName—Name of Train*, *Train-Departure—Departure Time* and *TrainArrival—Arrival Time* (Table 11.1).

```
Set dicTrainList = CreateObject("Scripting.Dictionary")

'---- Creating dictionary of dictionary—Using train number as
primary key
dicTrainList.add "2472", CreateObject("Scripting.Dictionary")

'---- Adding train number, arrival, departure details to dictionary
'-- TrainName, TrainDepart and TrainArrival are secondary keys
dicTrainList("2472").Add "TrainName", "SWARAJ EXPRESS"
dicTrainList("2472").Add "TrainDepart", "21:50"
dicTrainList("2472").Add "TrainArrival", "17:21"

dicTrainList.add "2618", CreateObject("Scripting.Dictionary")
dicTrainList("2618").Add "TrainName", "MNGLA LKSDP EXP"
dicTrainList("2618").Add "TrainDepart", "09:20"
dicTrainList("2618").Add "TrainArrival", "08:30"

'---- Retrieving item value from dictionary
sTrainNm1 = dicTrainList("2472").Item("TrainName")
sTrainDepart1 = dicTrainList("2472").Item("TrainDepart")
sTrainNm2 = dicTrainList("2618").Item("TrainName")
sTrainArr2 = dicTrainList("2618").Item("TrainArrival")

'---- Retrieving primary keys
arrTrainNo = dicTrainList.Keys

'---- Retrieving all secondary keys corresponding to primary keys
arrSecondaryKeys = dicTrainList("2472").Keys
'---- Retrieving all items corresponding to a primary key
arrItems2472 = dicTrainList("2472).Items
```

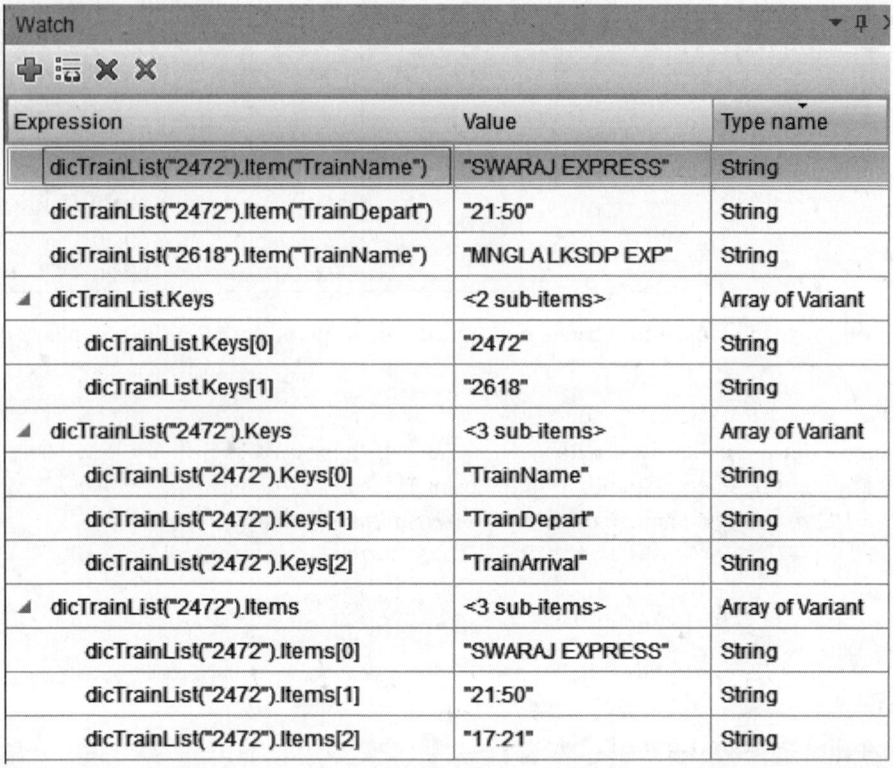

Expression	Value	Type name
dicTrainList("2472").Item("TrainName")	"SWARAJ EXPRESS"	String
dicTrainList("2472").Item("TrainDepart")	"21:50"	String
dicTrainList("2618").Item("TrainName")	"MNGLA LKSDP EXP"	String
dicTrainList.Keys	<2 sub-items>	Array of Variant
dicTrainList.Keys[0]	"2472"	String
dicTrainList.Keys[1]	"2618"	String
dicTrainList("2472").Keys	<3 sub-items>	Array of Variant
dicTrainList("2472").Keys[0]	"TrainName"	String
dicTrainList("2472").Keys[1]	"TrainDepart"	String
dicTrainList("2472").Keys[2]	"TrainArrival"	String
dicTrainList("2472").Items	<3 sub-items>	Array of Variant
dicTrainList("2472").Items[0]	"SWARAJ EXPRESS"	String
dicTrainList("2472").Items[1]	"21:50"	String
dicTrainList("2472").Items[2]	"17:21"	String

Figure 11.3 *Results of dictionary of dictionary object*

Results: Figure 11.3 shows the dictionary of dictionary object values as seen in QTP debugger window.
Example: Write a program to sort item values stored in the dictionary object

```
Set oDictionary = CreateObject("Scripting.Dictionary")

'Add key-item pairs
oDictionary.Add "Z1", "Z2"
oDictionary.Add "Z3", "Z4"
oDictionary.Add "A1", "A2"
oDictionary.Add "P1", "P2"
oDictionary.Add "B1", "B2"

'Retrieve all items
arrOrigItems = oDictionary.Items  'Output : "Z2", "Z4", "A2", "P2", "B2"

'Sort Items
Call fnSortDicItems(oDictionary)

'Retrieve all items
```

```
arrSortedItems = oDictionary.Items    'Output : "A2", "B2", "P2", "Z2",
                                               "Z4"

Function fnSortDicItems(oDictionary)
     Dim sTmp1, sKey1, sKey2

    'Sort item values of the dictionary object
    For Each sKey1 In oDictionary
       For Each sKey2 In oDictionary
              'If second item is greater then first item, then swap
               If  (oDictionary.Item(sKey1)  <=  oDictionary.Item(sKey2))
               Then
                    'Swap item values
                    sTmp1= oDictionary.Item(sKey1)
                    oDictionary.Item(sKey1) = oDictionary.Item(sKey2)
                    oDictionary.Item(sKey2) = sTmp1
              End If
       Next
    Next
End Function
```

QUICK TIPS

- ✓ Use dictionary object instead of arrays when value to be extracted is present in the form of key-value pair.
- ✓ Use dictionary of dictionary object to store data retrieved from a SQL query.

PRACTICAL QUESTIONS

1. What is the difference between a dictionary and an array?
2. Write a function to store the value of a table, say Table 11.2 in a dictionary object.
3. When dictionary of dictionary object is to be used?

Chapter 12

Regular Expressions

Regular expressions are a pattern matching standard for string parsing and replacement. The pattern describes one or more strings to match when searching a body of text. The regular expression serves as a template for matching a character pattern to the string being searched.

In its simplest form, a regular expression is a string of symbols to match "as is."

RegEx	Matches
abc	**Abc**abcabc
234	1**234**5

Here, we can see that regular expressions match the first case found, once, anywhere in the input string. Therefore, what if we want to match several characters? We need to use a quantifier or meta character. The most important quantifiers are *?+.

* matches any number of what is before it, from zero to infinity. ? matches zero or one. + matches one or more.

Regex	Matches
23*4	1**24**5, 1**234**5, 1**2334**5
23?4	1**24**5, 1**234**5
23+4	1**234**5, 1**2334**5
2*	1**2222**3

HOW TO CREATE A REGULAR EXPRESSION OBJECT

Code below shows how to create a regular expression object.

```
Set oRegExp = New RegExp
```

Properties

Described below are some of the properties of the regular expression object.

Global: Specifies whether regular expression search should match all occurrences within the specified string or match just the first string.

```
Syntax : Object.Global [ = True | False ]
```

Example 1: Find all the strings that match the regular expression

```
oRegExp.Global = True
```

Example 2: Find the first matched string that matches the regular expression

```
oRegExp.Global = True
```

Example 3: Find whether the regular expression search match is global or not

```
bGlobalFlg = oRegExp.Global
```

IgnoreCase: Specifies whether the regular expression search is case sensitive or not.

```
Syntax : Object.IgnoreCase [= True | False]
```

Example 1: Execute a case-sensitive regular expression search

```
oRegExp.IgnoreCase = False
```

Example 2: Execute a case-insensitive regular expression search

```
oRegExp. IgnoreCase = True
```

Example 3: Find whether the regular expression search match is case sensitive or not

```
bGlobalFlg = oRegExp.IgnoreCase
```

Pattern: Specifies the regular expression search string.

```
Syntax : Object.Pattern [= SearchPattern]
```

Example 1: Create a regular expression search pattern

```
oRegExp.Pattern = "QTP*"
```

Example 2: Find the regular expression search pattern

```
sSearchString = oRegExp.Pattern
```

Methods

Described below are some of the methods of the regular expression object.

Execute: Executes a search of specific string pattern against the specified string.

```
Syntax : Object.Execute (SearchString)
```

*Example: Find all instances of regular expression "Te*t" in string "Book on Test Automation"*

```
oRegExp.Pattern = "Te*t"
oRegExp.Execute("Book on Test Automation")
```

Replace: Replaces the matched text found with the specified string.

```
Syntax : Object.Replace (SearchString, ReplacementString)
```

*Example: Find and replace all occurrences of regular expression "Auto*n" with expression "Automation & QTP 11.0" in the string "Book on Test Automation"*

```
'Regular expression search pattern
oRegExp.Pattern = "Auto*n"
```

```
'String with which text found will be replaced
sReplacementString = "Automation & QTP 11.0"

'String against which find and replace will be executed
sSearchString = "Book on Test Automation"

'Replace the matched text with the specified text
oRegExp.Replace(sSearchString, sReplacementString)
```

Test: Specifies whether the searched regular expression was found in the searched text or not. Returns "True" if a match is found else returns "False."

Syntax : *Object*.Test (*SearchString*)

Example: Find whether or not regular expression string "QTP" exists in the text "Automation & QTP 11.0"*

```
'Regular expression search pattern
oRegExp.Pattern = "QTP*"

'Find whether a match is found or not
bMatchFnd = oRegExp.Test("Automation&QTP 11.0")
```

META CHARACTERS

Table 12.1 lists down some of the useful meta characters.

Table 12.1 Regular expression characters

Character	Description	RegExp	String	Matches
.	Matches any single character	Q.P	Book on QTP10.0	QTP
?	Matches zero or one character	Q?P	Book on QTP10.0	P (QTP)
+	Matches the preceding expression one or more times	Bo+k	Book on QTP10.0	Book
*	Matches the preceding expression zero or more times	Bo*k	Bk on QTP10.0, Book on QTP10.0	Bk, Book
\	Marks the next special character a literal	10\.0	Book on QTP10.0	10.0
^	Matches the beginning of a string	^Book	Book on QTP10.0	Book
$	Matches the end of a string	10\.0$	Book on QTP10.0	10.0
\n	Matches a newline character	\n	"Book on QTP10.0" & vbCrLf	(newline character)

(Continued)

Table 12.1 (Continued)

<table>
<tr><th>Character</th><th>Description</th><th>RegExp</th><th>String</th><th>Matches</th></tr>
<tr><td>\t</td><td>Matches a tab character</td><td>\t</td><td>“Book on QTP10.0”
& vbTab</td><td>(tab character)</td></tr>
<tr><td>\d</td><td>Matches a digit character</td><td>\d{2}</td><td>Book on QTP10.0</td><td>10</td></tr>
<tr><td>\D</td><td>Matches a non-digit character</td><td>\D{4}</td><td>Book on QTP10.0</td><td>Book, (space)
on(space)</td></tr>
<tr><td>\w</td><td>Matches an alphanumeric character</td><td>\w</td><td>Book on QTP10.0</td><td>B,o,o,k,o,n,Q,T,P,1,0,0</td></tr>
<tr><td>\W</td><td>Matches a non-alphanumeric character</td><td>\W</td><td>Book on QTP10.0</td><td>(white space), (white space), . (dot)</td></tr>
<tr><td>\s</td><td>Matches a whitespace character</td><td>\s</td><td>Book on QTP10.0</td><td>(white space), (white space)</td></tr>
<tr><td>\S</td><td>Matches a non-whitespace character</td><td>\S</td><td>Book on QTP10.0</td><td>B,o,o,k,o,n,Q,T,P,1,0,.,0</td></tr>
<tr><td>x|y</td><td>Matches either x or y</td><td>9\.2|10
(9\.2|10.0)
ver</td><td>9.2 or 10.0ver</td><td>9.2,10
10.0ver</td></tr>
<tr><td>[xyz]</td><td>Matches any one of the enclosed characters</td><td>[B10]</td><td>Book on QTP10.0</td><td>B,1,0,0</td></tr>
<tr><td>[^xyz]</td><td>Matches any character not enclosed</td><td>[^B10]</td><td>Book on QTP10.0</td><td>o,o,k, ,o,n, ,Q,T,P,.</td></tr>
<tr><td>[a-z]</td><td>Matches any character in the specified range</td><td>[a-n]</td><td>Book on QTP10.0</td><td>B,k,n</td></tr>
<tr><td>[^a-z]</td><td>Matches any character not in the specified range</td><td>[^a-n]</td><td>Book on QTP10.0</td><td>o,o, ,o,Q,T,P,1,0,.,0</td></tr>
<tr><td>{P}</td><td>Matches multiple occurrences of a pattern</td><td>o{1}
o{2}</td><td>Book on QTP10.0</td><td>o,o,o
oo</td></tr>
<tr><td>{P,}</td><td>Matches P or more occurrences of a pattern</td><td>o{1,}
o{2,}</td><td>Book on QTP10.0</td><td>oo,o
oo</td></tr>
<tr><td>{P,N}</td><td>Matches at least P and at most N times occurrences of a pattern</td><td>o{1,1}
o{1,2}
o{2,2}</td><td>Book on QTP10.0</td><td>o,o,o
oo,o
oo</td></tr>
</table>

HOW TO USE VBSCRIPT REGULAR EXPRESSION OBJECT

We can use regular expression in VBScript by creating one or more instances of the *RegExp* object. This object allows finding regular expression matches in strings and replacing regular expression matches in strings with other strings.

```
'Create regular expression
Set oRegExp = New RegExp
```

```
'Ignore case
oRegExp.IgnoreCase = True

'Match complete string
oRegExp.Global = True

'Pattern to look for
oRegExp.Pattern = "Q.P"

'Search String
sString = "Book on QTP11.0"

Set oMatches = oRegExp.Execute(sString)
For Each oMatch in oMatches
Msgbox oMatch.Value, 0, "Found Match"       'Matches; Output : QTP
Next
```

Match Any Single Character (.)

The "." character matches any single character.

For example,

```
"Q.P" will match "Q1P," "QDP," "Q&P," etc.
"B..k" will match "B12k," "BD%k," "B&fk," etc.
```

Match Zero or More Character (?)

The "?" character matches zero or one character.

For example,

```
"Q?P" will match "QP," "Q&fk90P," etc.
```

Match Single Preceding Expression (+)

The "+" character matches the preceding expression one or more times.

For example,

```
"Bo+k" will match  "Bok," "Book," "Booooooook," etc.
"[QTP][6-9]*" will match "Q6," "P7," "Q67," "T98"...
```

Match Zero or More Preceding Expression (*)

The "*" character matches the preceding expression zero or more times.

For example,

```
"Bo*k" will match  "Bk," "Bok," "Book," "Booooooook," etc.
"[QTP][6-9]*" will match "Q," "T," "P," "Q6," "P7," "Q67," "T98"...
```

Using Escape Character (\)

Backward slash (\) allows the next character to be treated as literal character instead of special character or as a special character instead of literal character.

For example,

```
"10.0" will match "10A0," "10$0," "10.0," "10c0," etc.
"10\.0" will match only "10.0"
"n" will match "n"
"\n" will match new line character
```

Match Beginning of a String (^)

The "^" character matches the beginning of a string.

For example,

```
"^Book" matches any line starting with "Book"
```

Match End of a String ($)

The "$" character matches the end of a string.

For example,

```
"10\.0$" matches any line ending with "10.0"
```

Match Digit Character (\d)

The "\d" character matches a digit character.

For example,

```
"\d{2}" will match any two digit number "01," "99," "50," "78," etc.
```

Match Non-digit Character (\D)

The "\D" character matches a non-digit character.

For example,

```
"\D{3}" will match any two non-digit number "Boo," "ok," "o," etc.
```

Match Alphanumeric Character (\w)

The "\w" matches an alphanumeric character. This is equivalent to using the regular expression [A-Za-z0-9].

For example,

```
"\w\w" will match "B_," "B1," etc.
```

Match Non-alphanumeric Character (\w)

The "\W" matches a non-alphanumeric character. This is equivalent to using the regular expression [^A-Za-z0-9].

For example,

```
"\W" will match "&," "$," "@," etc.
```

Match One of Several Regular Expressions (|)

The "|" character acts as logical OR operation between two regular expressions.

For example,

```
"9\.2|10" implies match "9.2" or "10"
QTP(9\.2|10)ver implies match QTP9.2ver or QTP10ver
```

Match Any Single Character in a List [xyz]

Matches any of the characters enclosed by square brackets.

For example,

```
"[QTP][10]" will match "Q1," "T1," "P1," "Q0," "T0," and "P0"
```

Match Any Single Character Not in a List [xyz]

Matches any character not enclosed by square brackets.

For example,

```
"[^Q][10]" will not match "Q1," "T1," "P1," "Q0," "T0," and "P0"
But will match "99," "78," "P1," etc.
```

Match Any Single Character within a Range [a-z]

Matches any single character in the specified range.

For example,

```
"[abcdefgh][12345]" can be written as "[a-f][1-5]"
"[a-f][1-5]" will match "a1," "s4," "d2," "f5," etc.
```

Match Any Single Character Not within a Range [^a-z]

Matches any single character not in the specified range.

For example,

```
"[^a-f][1-5]" will match "T1," "U5," "z1," "y5," etc.
```

Match Multiple Occurrences of a Pattern {}

The "{}" allows matching multiple occurrences of a pattern.
(refer Table 12.1).

PARSING DATES

Date strings are difficult to parse because there are so many variations. In some of the application, the name of the calendar object is current day, month, and year. Since date value changes every day and so the name of calendar object. We can use regular expressions for the name property of the calendar object.

Suppose that the name property of calendar object has date pattern dd-mmm-yyyy

The regular expression can be

```
^\d\d-[A-Z][a-z][a-z]-(\d\d\d\d)$

^\d\d              : Match two digit day of date
-                  : Match separator "-"
[A-Z][a-z][a-z]    : Match three-letter month. The first letter to be in
                     upper case
\d\d\d\d$          : Match four digits that make up the year
```

If the name property matches then, we can be sure that calendar object can be identified during run-time. However, a regular expression will not be able to verify that it is a real date. For example, it could be 92-Abc-9876. To make the regular expression match to the exact date type, we have to write a more limiting expression:

```
^(0[1-9]|[1-2][0-9]|3[01])- (Jan|Feb|Mar|Apr|May|Jun|Jul|Aug|Sep|Oct|
Nov|Dec)-(20\d\d)$
```

```
^(0[1-9]|[1-2][0-9]|3[01]) : Match two digits that make up the day. This
accepts numbers from 01 to 09, 10 to 29, and 30 to 31. What if the user
gives 2003-Feb-31? There are limitations to what regexes can do. If you
want to validate the string further, you need to use other techniques
than regexes.
-   : Match the separator '-'
(Jan|Feb|Mar|Apr|May|Jun|Jul|Aug|Sep|Oct|Nov|Dec) : Match the month
20\d\d  : Match year between 2000 and 2099
```

E-MAIL MATCHING

It is often necessary to check if a string is an e-mail address or not. Here is one way to do it.

```
^[A-Za-z0-9_\.-]+@[A-Za-z0-9_\.-]+[A-Za-z0-9_][A-Za-z0-9_]$
^[A-Za-z0-9_\.-]+  : Match a positive number of acceptable characters at
                     the start of the string
```

```
@                       : Match the "@" sign
[A-Za-z0-9_\.-]+        : Match any domain name, including a dot
[A-Za-z0-9_][A-Za-z0-9_]$ : Match two acceptable characters but not a
                            dot. This ensures that the e-mail address
                            ends with .xx, .xxx, .xxxx, etc.
```

REPLACING STRING USING REGULAR EXPRESSION

Regular expression can be used to find a pattern within a string and replace it with desired characters, words, or strings.

```
sText = "Book on QTP9.2"
sPatrn = "QTP9\.2"
sReplStr = "Test Automation & QTP10.0"
sNewText = fnReplaceText(sText, sPatrn, sReplStr)

Public Function fnReplaceText(sText, sPatrn, sReplStr)
 Set oRegEx = New RegExp        'Create regular expression
 oRegEx.Pattern = sPatrn        'Set pattern
 oRegEx.IgnoreCase = True       'Make case insensitive
 fnReplaceText = oRegEx.Replace(sText, sReplStr) 'Make replacement
 Set oRegEx = Nothing
End Function

Output : sNewText = "Book on Test Automation & QTP10.0"
```

Searching Notepad File for a Regular Expression String

```
Const nForReading = 1

Set oRegEx = CreateObject("VBScript.RegExp")
oRegEx.Pattern = "Function [a-z]"

Set oFSO = CreateObject("Scripting.FileSystemObject")
Set oFile = oFSO.OpenTextFile("C:\Temp\Test.txt," nForReading)

Do Until objFile.AtEndOfStream
   strSearchString = objFile.ReadLine
   Set colMatches = objRegEx.Execute(strSearchString)
   If colMatches.Count >0 Then
       For Each strMatch In colMatches
           MsgBox strSearchString
       Next
   End If
Loop

oFile.Close
```

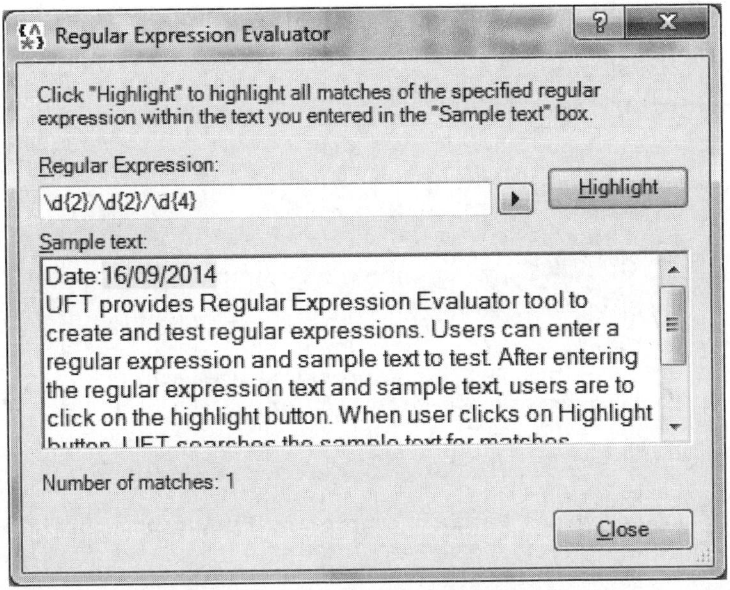

Figure 12.1 *UFT regular expression evaluator*

UFT Regular Expression Evaluator

UFT provides Regular Expression Evaluator tool to create and test regular expressions. Users can enter a regular expression and sample text to test. After entering the regular expression text and sample text, users are to click on the highlight button. When user clicks on Highlight button, UFT searches the sample text for matches, highlights these matches, and displays the number of matches as shown in the Fig. 12.1.

Firefox Add-on Regular Expression Tester

If for certain reasons, UFT regular expression evaluator is not accessible then Firefox add-on 'Regular Expression Tester' can be used to design and test regular expressions, Regular Expression Tester add-on can be downloaded from site–https://addons.mozilla.org/en-US/firefox/addon/rext/. Figure 12.2 shows regular expression tester dialog box.

Alternatively, there are many websites which provides regular expression design feature. For example, RegExr (www.regexr.com) is an online tool to build and test Regular Expressions.

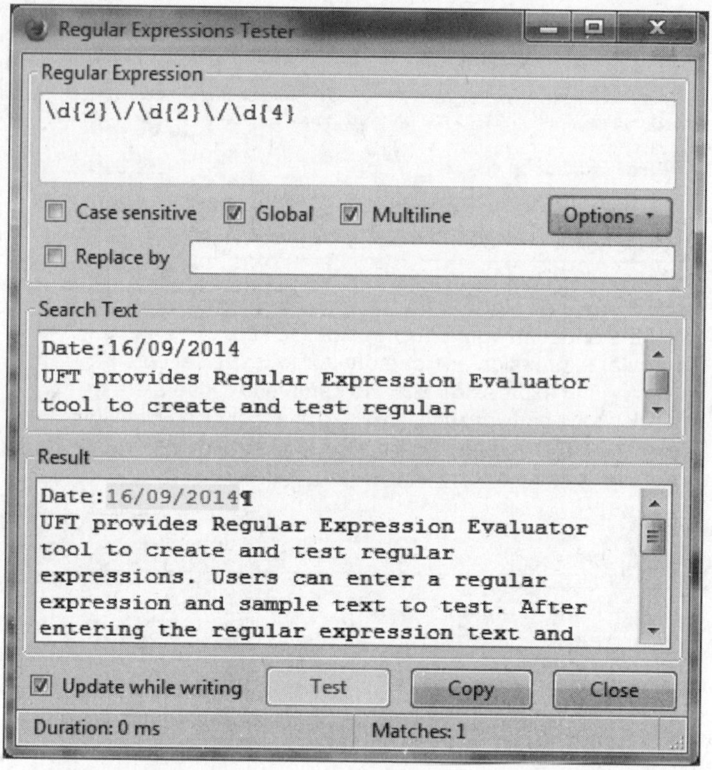

Figure 12.2 *Firefox add-on Regular Expression Tester*

QUICK TIPS

✓ Regular expressions are used to identify dynamically changing text pattern.

✓ Regular expressions are used to identify dynamic application objects during run-time.

PRACTICAL QUESTIONS

1. What is the use of regular expressions in test automation?
2. Write a regular expression for identifying date type data.
3. Write a regular expression for identifying e-mail address.
4. Write a function to identify all instances of dates in a notepad file.
5. Write a function to extract all e-mail addresses from a notepad file.

Section 4 Basic UFT

- Introduction to UFT
- UFT Installation
- UFT Configuration
- Test Script Development
- Environment Variables
- Library

Chapter 13

Introduction to UFT

Unified Functional Testing (UFT) is an automated Graphical User Interface (GUI) testing tool developed by the HP. It is designed for testing Web-based applications, Windows-based applications and Application Programming Interfaces (API). It is primarily used for functional and regression test automation. Like other test automation tools, it works by identifying the objects in the application User Interface (UI) or a web page and performing the desired operations on them such as mouse clicks or keyboard events. It can also be used to capture object properties such as *name* or *html id*. Apart from UI-based automation, it can also automate non-UI-based scenarios such as API testing (Web Services), File data validation testing, Database testing, etc. To perform these actions, UFT uses a scripting language built on top of VBScript to specify the test procedure and test script control flow. VBScript coding language is used to control, recognize, and manipulate the AUT objects. Table 13.1 shows the various UFT versions and the year in which they were released.

Table 13.1 UFT release dates

UFT Version	Release Date (Year)
HP UFT 12.5	2015
HP UFT 12	2014
HP UFT 11.5	2013
HP UFT 11.0	2010
HP UFT 10.0	2009
HP Mercury QuickTest Pro 9.5	2008
HP Mercury QuickTest Pro 9.2	2007
QuickTest Pro 9.0	2006
QuickTest Pro 8.2	2005
QuickTest Pro 8.0	2004
QuickTest Pro 6.5	2002
Astra QuickTest 5.0	2001
Astra QuickTest 4.0	2000

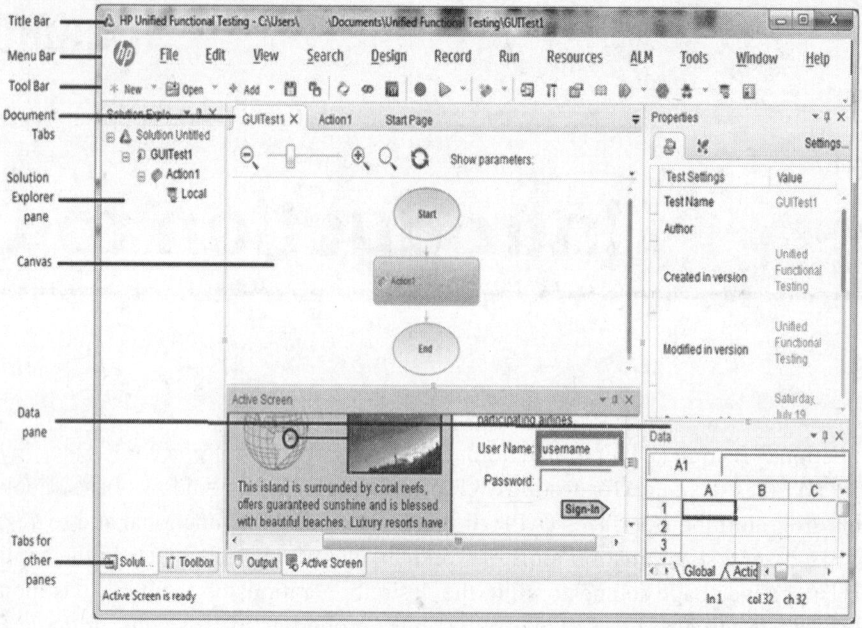

Figure 13.1 *UFT window*

UFT generally come with a 30-day demo license. UFT comes with both node- locked seat license and floating or concurrent license. UFT provides various add-ins to test a wide range of applications including Java, SAP, .Net, Power Builder, and Web Services. HP UFT comes with two installation packages:

- Full Unified Testing Package
- Unified Functional Testing Package for the Web

Full Unified Testing Package contains UFT and all its related products. While Unified Functional Testing Package for the Web is a compressed package containing UFT and add-ins for basic Web support.

UFT provides an integrated environment for following:

- UFT GUI Testing
- UFT API Testing
- UFT Business Process Testing (BPT)

UFT offers two code development environments – Keyword View and Editor. *Keyword View* can be used by novice users or non-technical staff to develop/maintain UFT tests. *Editor* view is to be used by UFT experts to develop complex code and automation framework APIs. Figure 13.1 shows the UFT window.

UFT MAIN WINDOW OVERVIEW

The main window of UFT provides multiple areas to design, edit, run and debug test documents. The section below briefly describes the key elements of the UFT window.

Start Page

This window welcomes users to UFT. It provides shortcut buttons and links to open new and existing documents.

TOOLBARS AND MENUS

- ***Title bar:*** Displays the path of current test or solution.
- ***Menu bar:*** Displays UFT Menu commands.
- ***UFT Toolbar:*** Displays commonly used buttons to assist in developing tests.

PANES

Described below are some of the UFT panes:

- ***Solution Explorer***—Displays the resources associated with the current tests and allows managing them. To display, either click on the *Solution Explorer* button in the toolbar or select *View → Solution Explorer*.
- ***Toolbox***—Displays library functions, test objects and test objects flow of current test. This pane also enables users to drag and drop objects, or calls to functions, from the Toolbox pane into the current test. To display, either click on the *Toolbox* button in the toolbar or select *View → Toolbox*.
- ***Document Pane***—Displays all open documents as separate tabs. To display, open or create a new document.
- ***Properties***—Displays all properties for the selected test, action, component, or application area. To display, either click on the *Properties* button in the toolbar or select *View → Properties*.
- ***Data***—Displays Data Table which enables users to parameterize tests. To display, either click on the *Data* button in the toolbar or select *View → Data*.
- ***Output***—Displays information updated during run session using *Print* utility. To display, select *View → Output*.
- ***Errors***—Displays a list of syntax errors found in the test or function library. Also, provides the list of missing resources (resources that are referenced in the test but cannot be found at the specified path). To display, select *View → Errors*.
- ***Debug pane***—Assists users in debugging test. The Debug panes include the *Breakpoints*, *Call Stack*, *Local Variables*, *Console*, and *Watch* panes. To display, either click on the *Debug* button in the toolbar or select *View → Debug*.
- ***Tasks***—Allows users to view and manage the tasks defined for the current test. It also displays the TODO comments. To display, select *View → Tasks*.
- ***Search Results***—Displays all occurrences of the search criteria that user define in the Find dialog box or using other Search menu items. To display, select *View → Search Results*.
- ***Bookmarks***—Displays the location of bookmarks in the current action, scripted component, or function library. It also enables user to navigate to these bookmarks. To display, select *View → Bookmarks*.

Solution Explorer Pane

The Solution Explorer pane displays all the resources associated with a test or a test component. It enables users to combine multiple types of tests, test components, application areas, function libraries and user code files into a single solution. To view Solution Explorer pane, select *View → Solution Explorer*. Fig. 13.2 shows an example Solution Explorer pane for a GUI test.

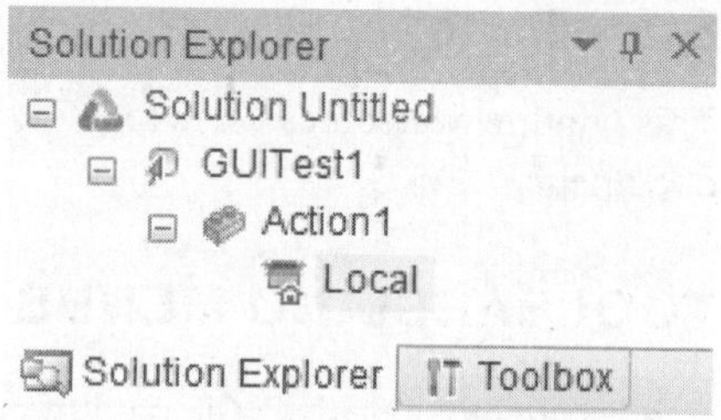

Figure 13.2 *Solution explorer pane for GUI test*

Toolbox Pane

For GUI testing, the Toolbox pane displays Library functions, Local functions and Test Objects as tree hierarchy of test flow.

For API testing, the Toolbox displays all the activities and flow control that can be used to create a API test.

For BPT in UFT, the Toolbox pane displays all the components and flows available to the business process test or flow. To view Toolbox pane, select *View → Toolbox*. Fig. 13.3 shows an example Toolbox pane for a GUI test.

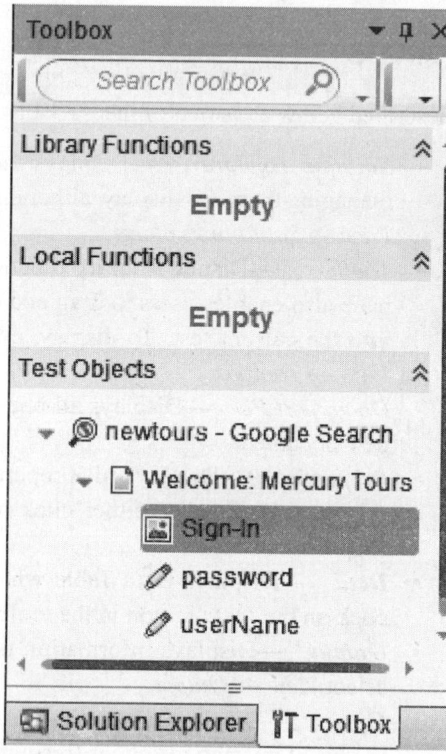

Figure 13.3 *Tool box pane for GUI test*

Document Pane

Document pane allows users to design and edit test documents.

- ***Canvas***: Canvas displays the test flow for GUI and API tests. Test flow is displayed as a series of actions for GUI tests and as steps for API tests. Figure 13.4 shows UFT *canvas* window.
- ***Editor***: Editor allows user to view, edit and write automation test code for GUI, API and BPT tests. It allows users to:
  - Create Actions with VBScript code
  - Create Function Libraries with VBScript code
  - Create API user code using C# code

Figure 13.4 shows Editor pane.

- ***Keyword View:*** Keyword view displays each test step code as icon-based tree hierarchy table. It enables users to automate tests using keyword methodology. Keyword View is only applicable for GUI tests. Figure 13.5 shows keyword view window.

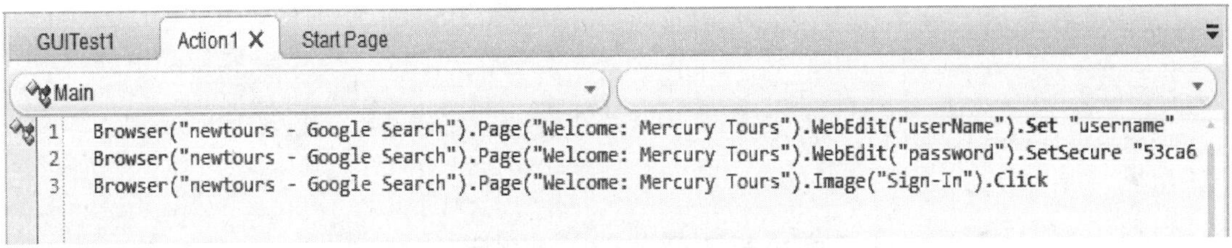

Figure 13.4 *UFT editor pane*

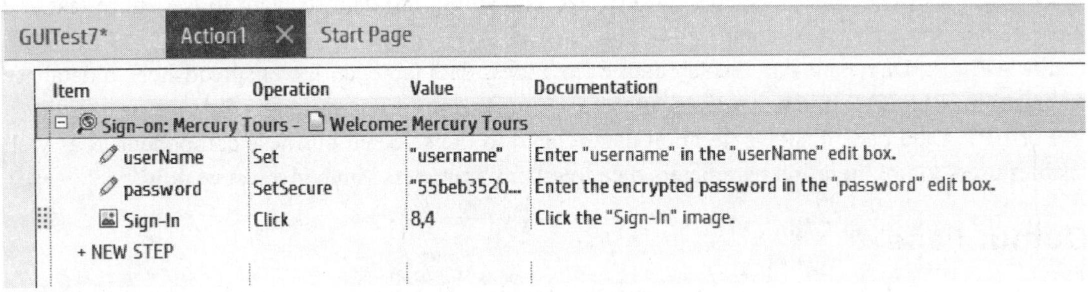

Figure 13.5 *UFT keyword view pane*

Properties Pane

The properties pane displays properties, parameters and test which use the specific selected test, action, component, function library or application area. The information displayed on this pane depends on the type of document open. To view Properties pane, select *View → Properties* Fig. 13.6 shows the properties pane of a GUI test.

Data Pane

The data pane displays the tets data information for the specific selected test, test component or business component. To view Data pane, select *View → Data*.

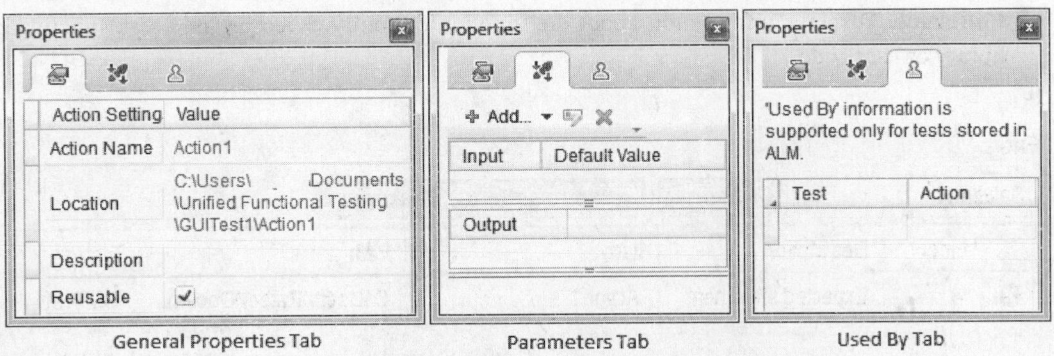

Figure 13.6 *Properties pane for a GUI test*

Figure 13.7 *Output pane for GUI test*

For GUI test, Data pane displays 'Global' tab containing the data relevant to the entire test and separate tabs for each action contained within the test.

For API test, Data pane can display data from a local data table, an Excel spreadsheet, a database connection, or an XML file.

For BPT, Data pane displays iteration data related to the selected business component. It as well enables users to link iteration parameters data to other parameters value in a test or flow.

Output Pane

For GUI tests, Output pane displays information that is sent using the Print Utility statement during the run session.

For API tests, Output pane displays output log for the compilation and test run.

To view the Output pane, select *View → Output*. Figure 13.7 shows output pane for a GUI test.

Errors Pane

The Error pane displays the list of missing resources and coding syntax errors of the test. This pane automatically opens up when an error is detected. Figure 13.8 shows error pane for a GUI test.

Debug Pane

Debug pane helps users to debug the automation code. It provides following options:

- ***Breakpoints***: Displays information about breakpoints inserted into tests, function libraries or user code files.
- ***Call stack:*** Displays information about the function currently executing in a test, functional library or user code.

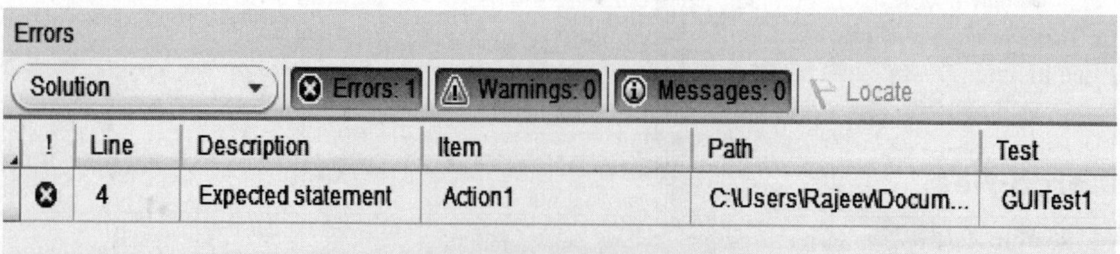

Figure 13.8 *Error pane*

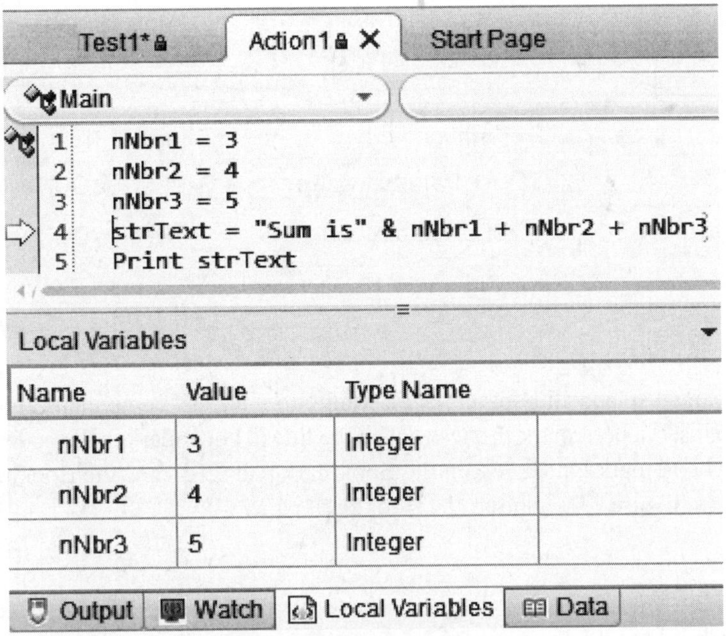

Figure 13.9 *Debug pane*

- ***Loaded modules (API test only):*** Displays information on the .dll files associated with the currently running test.
- ***Threads (API test only):*** Displays information about all the threads running in the context of current executing test.
- ***Local variables:*** Displays values of all the variables that were recognized up the current step. Users are allowed to set or modify values of the variables that are displayed.
- ***Console:*** Enables users to run lines of script to set or modify the value of a variable, code object, property, method, or function library or function call in the test.
- ***Watch:*** Enables users to view the value of any variable or expression by adding it to the watch pane.

To view the Debug pane, select *View → Debug*. Figure 13.9 shows debug pane.

Tasks Pane

The Tasks pane enables users to create, view, and manage TODO tasks (tasks to be done). TODO tasks can be inserted by adding a TODO comment in the test code. To view the Debug pane, select *View → Debug*. Figure 13.10 shows the Tasks pane.

Search Results Pane

The Search Results pane displays the results of searches performed using the *Search* menu. This pane allows users to browse the results of the search. To view the Search Results pane, select *View → Search Results*. Figure 13.11 shows the Search Results pane

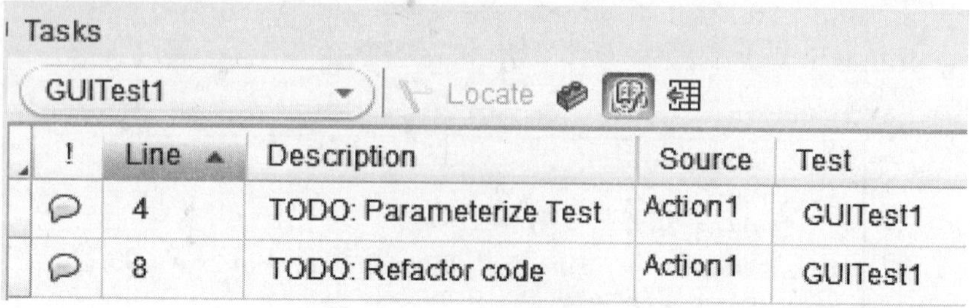

Figure 13.10 *Tasks pane*

Bookmarks Pane

The Bookmarks pane displays all bookmarks inserted into the tests, component, function libraries or user code files. To insert a bookmark in a test, select the line to book mark in the code and then click on the insert/remove book mark button on the Bookmark pane. To view the Bookmarks pane, select *View → Bookmarks*. Figure 13.12 shows the Bookmark pane.

FEATURES

Record/Playback

UFT is a record/playback tool. In record mode, UFT creates a script of all the actions user performs on the AUT screen. During playback, it executes the script against the application to replicate the user behavior. UFT provides various methods viz. checkpoints to verify the expected application response against the actual behavior.

In real-world scenarios, simply recording and playing-back actions fail to deliver the expected results. The use of UFT as a programming tool to code actions on GUI/API objects and analyze the application response helps to reduce testing cost and effort.

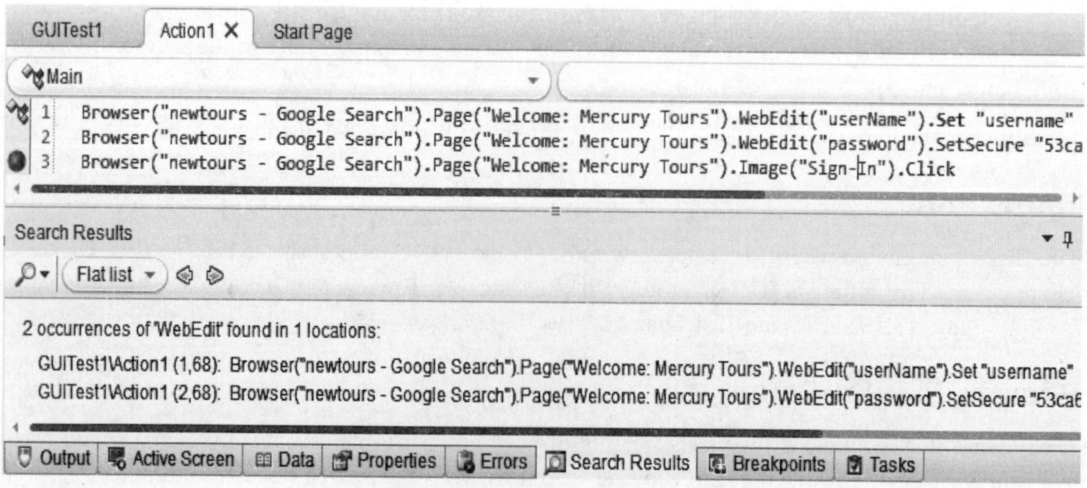

Figure 13.11 *Search results pane*

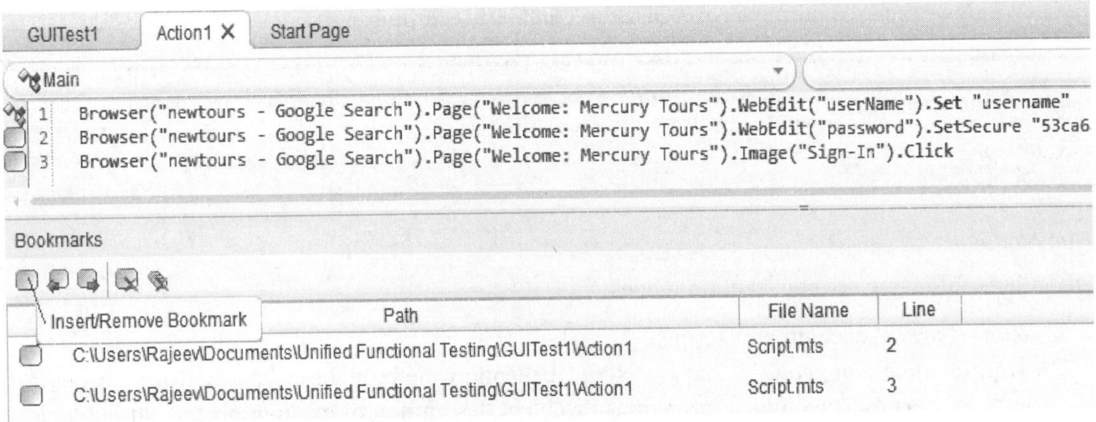

Figure 13.12 *Bookmarks pane*

UFT has three modes to view or edit a test script – Canvas, Keyword View and Editor. Canvas displays the test flow. Keyword View displays the test script in the form of keywords arranged in a tree format. Editor view displays the VBScript code of the particular keyword action. Canvas provides a visual representation of the GUI or API test flow. Keyword View is for basic-level UFT users who have little or no programming knowledge. Editor view is used by test automation developers to handle complex test automation scenarios and deliver reliable solutions.

Recording Modes

UFT offers five types of recording modes.

1. ***Normal recording***—This recording mode records the objects in the application and the operations performed on them. This method is the default mode of recording in UFT.
2. ***Anulog recording*** This recording method is used when user needs to capture exact mouse and keyboard operations in relation to either the screen or the application window. In this recording mode, UFT records and tracks every movement of the mouse as user drag the mouse around a screen or window. This mode is useful for recording operations that cannot be recorded at the level of an object; for example, recording a signature produced by dragging the mouse. User cannot edit *Analog Recording* steps from within UFT.
3. ***Low-level recording***—This mode of recording captures the exact coordinates of the object. It records at the object level and records all run-time objects as Window or WinObject test objects. Low-level recording is useful when UFT fails to recognize an object. Low-level recording needs to be avoided if coordinates of objects can change from time to time.
4. ***Insight recording***—In this mode, UFT recognizes objects based on their appearance and not on their native properties. This mode of recording captures the image of the object. During test execution, UFT identifies the GUI objects by matching them to the images saved with each of the Insight test objects.
5. ***Standard Windows Recording (SAP)***—This recording mode is to be used only when recording against SAP GUI for Windows applications. This mode helps user to record steps on standard

Windows controls during a SAP GUI for Windows recording session.

> NOTES
> Users should switch to *Standard Windows* Recording mode prior to performing steps on these controls, else both UFT and SAP may become unresponsive.

Run Modes

UFT offers following script execution modes.

1. ***Run***—Normal execution of scripts.
2. ***Maintenance run mode***—This test script execution mode to be used when user needs to add objects or change object properties or object description of existing objects during script execution.
3. ***Update run mode***—This execution mode is used when user has changed object identification properties—*mandatory* and *associative*—and same change needs to be propagated to all the objects present in object repository. Only the object identification properties of those objects will be changed that have been used in the action/test script.

Integrated GUI and API Testing

UFT provides an integrated environment to perform both GUI and API testing within a single test. This helps to test functionality across front-end GUI layer and backend service layer from the same test. Also, the integrated BPT features help both technical and non-technical users to develop automated tests.

Data-driven Testing

UFT supports data-driven testing. DataTables can be used to data to provide test input data to test scripts. The test output data can be saved as well in data tables. UFT also supports use of Microsoft Excel files as test data files. UFT provides methods to import an Excel sheet (or workbook) in datatable and to export datatable to an Excel workbook.

Verification

Checkpoints are a feature provided by UFT to verify the expected application behavior against the actual behavior. One can use a checkpoint to check whether a particular object, text, or a bitmap is present on the application screen or not. Checkpoints can also be used to control the code logic flow.

Object Repository

Object repository acts as a central storehouse for storing application GUI objects. For record/play-back, UFT automatically saves the GUI objects in the local object repository. UFT also allows the users to add specific objects to object repository. UFT also allows editing or modifying object properties.

Library

UFT allows users to create their custom functions and store them in a library file. Functions help to reduce code redundancy and increase code modularity.

Exception Handling

UFT supports exception handling through recovery scenarios. The purpose of exception handling to execute the complete test suite successfully even if unexpected errors (such as file not found error) occurs during execution of certain test scripts. Recovery scenarios are also used to handle expected errors (such as pop-up window) to continue test script execution.

> NOTES: A test suite comprises of various automated test cases (test scripts). In a test suite, it is advisable that no two test scripts (automated test cases) are depen- dent on each other.

AUTOMATING COMPLEX AND CUSTOM GUI OBJECTS

UFT provides rich set of methods to automate complex GUI objects and complex conditional and logical loops. UFT supports normal object identification, image based object identification, smart identification, and ordinal identification to ensure even minimally defined GUI object are recognized during run-time. Regular expressions support recognition of dynamic objects during run-time. Virtual object feature of UFT help to create identification definition for custom objects of applica- tion such as interface objects.

Results

UFT generates an easily readable test report at the end of run session. The test report is in the form of XML tree and provides information such as pass/fail of the test script, pass/fail of each test step, exact point of script failure, and script execution time. The test reports can also be configured to capture screenshot or movie of complete run session or of error steps only. From UFT 10.0 onwards, UFT also provides features to track and analyze AUT performance during script execution.

Add-in Extensibility

UFT provides a rich set of add-ins to automate a wide range of applications including Web, .Net, Java, PowerBuilder, PeopleSoft, SAP and Mainframes Terminal Emulator. For complete list of add-ins refer Appendix A.

Application Life Cycle Management (ALM) Integration

UFT can easily be integrated with Application Lifecycle Management (ALM). ALM helps managing the complete automation project. It also supports scheduled test script execution on remote UFT machines. The test results are automatically saved in ALM.

New Features and Enhancements in UFT 12.0

HP Unified Functional Testing (UFT) is one of the market leading tools used for automation testing. Listed below some of the advance featured introduced in UFT 12.0.

Faster, Smaller and More Secure Installation Package

UFT 12.00 provides a new installation package, enabling users to install UFT more quickly and with greater security:

- The size of the installation package is significantly smaller (1.5 GB) as compared to previous versions, thereby speeding up the installation time.
- Users can choose to install the UFT Add-in for ALM and the Run Results Viewer as part of the UFT installation.
- The installation process includes all of the configurations needed to run UFT. Users no longer have to run additional post-installation programs.
- The installation is more secure, enabling users to install UFT without needing to temporarily disable the User Account Control (UAC) for the computer.
- Users can now install UFT in any supported language without the need to install a separate language pack in addition to the UFT product installation.
- Users can now perform a single silent installation without the need to run additional installations and configurations.

Run GUI Tests on A Remote Mac Computer

UFT now supports running GUI tests against Safari browser of a remote Mac machine.

Conditionally Upload Run Results to ALM After A Run Session

ALM site administrator can now set a site parameter that instructs UFT to conditionally upload run results from a run session to ALM.

Enhancements

Listed below are some of the UFT 12.0 enhancements.

Connect to ALM Using External Authentication (e.g. CAC)

UFT can now use external authentication to connect to an ALM 12.00 server and project, instead of using the traditional model of entering the user name and password in the ALM Connection dialog box. This enables users to use their installed external authentication certificates or single sign-on mechanisms.

Enable or Disable Test Runs to Stop at Breakpoints during an ALM or Automation Run

A new RunDebug method is available in the UFT Automation Object Model (AOM). This method instructs UFT to stop at breakpoints when running a test using automation.

New Features and Enhancements of UFT 11.5

HP Unified Functional Testing (UFT) is one stop shop for GUI, API and Business Process testing. It offers an integrated environment to fully validate the functionality of both GUI layer and the business

(API/Web Services) layer of the application within a single test. This enables QA teams to start testing earlier by starting to test the API and Web Service layer of application while GUI layer is getting developed. Figure 13.13 shows the new Integrated Development Environment (IDE) of UFT.

UFT can display Canvas for both GUI and API tests. Canvas can be used to manage actions (for GUI tests) and test steps (for API tests) and change their order, run or debug from a selected action or up to a selected action, and manage testing parameters.

UFT provides the feature to open and work with multiple documents within the same solution, including GUI or API tests, individual actions, business components, function libraries, and code files.

New UFT Look and Feel for BPT

UFT now provides Business Process Testing from within UFT, using the native UFT user interface. This enables users to create, maintain, debug, and run BPT tests together with GUI and API tests. Thus, providing a single, one-stop-shop product for seamless functional testing.

Users can now use BPT in UFT to:

- Add components and flows to tests and flows by dragging them from the Toolbox pane to the test or flow opened in the document pane.
- Manage component iterations in the Data pane.
- Link and promote parameters in the Component Parameters tab of the Properties pane. Properties pane tabs to be used to view and modify various test, flow, component, or group details, such as descriptions, fields, and comments.
- Set parameter promotion options in the BPT Testing tab of the Options dialog box.

GUI Testing Features

Image Based Object Recognition (Insight)

UFT provides new way of identifying objects called *Insight*. In this method, UFT identifies the object by the look like by the object. This enables UFT to perform basic actions such as clicking, dragging, and dropping controls in applications that could not previously be tested. Image based object identification can also be used to test applications that run remotely on non-windows operating systems.

File Contents Checkpoints

UFT has introduced new checkpoint feature of verifying file contents. The new file content checkpoint compares the textual content of a file that is generated during run session with the textual content of baseline file. For example, this checkpoint can be used to verify whether the PDF bill (say Mobile Bill) file generated at run time contains the specific contact details such as contact number and address of store.

Enhanced Bit Map Checkpoint

The enhanced bitmap checkpoint now allows users to specify multiple areas to compare or ignore within the bitmap that is to be checked. It also supports verifying whether a specific image appears anywhere within the runtime bitmap. This image can be a segment of the bitmap that UFT captures when the checkpoint is created, or a externally loaded bitmap file.

Support for MSAA-Based (Microsoft Office and Plug-in) Controls

UFT has extended support to identify windowless objects that are developed using MSAA (Microsoft Active Accessibility) API. For example, the controls within the Microsoft Office ribbons are identified as independent objects. These controls are recognized by UFT as Standard Windows objects.

Generate Automated GUI Tests from Sprinter Exploratory Tests

Sprinter is HP's manual testing solution to perform exploratory tests using an enhanced set of capture and annotation tools. UFT provides the feature to export the captured user actions, test objects, and comments, to an XML file. This XML file can then be imported into UFT. UFT converts the imported file to a GUI test with a local object repository. Each step in the newly created test represents an operation as mentioned in Sprinter exploratory test.

This feature helps to create a more seamless workflow between manual testers and automation experts. Also, this helps to expedite the porting of manual tests to automated tests.

New GUI Testing Support for Qt and Adobe Flex Applications

UFT now includes support for automating Flex and Qt GUI applications. After compiling Flex application with the UFT Flex pre-compiled agent, users can use the Flex add-in to test Flex applications. Qt application can be tested by loading Qt add-in.

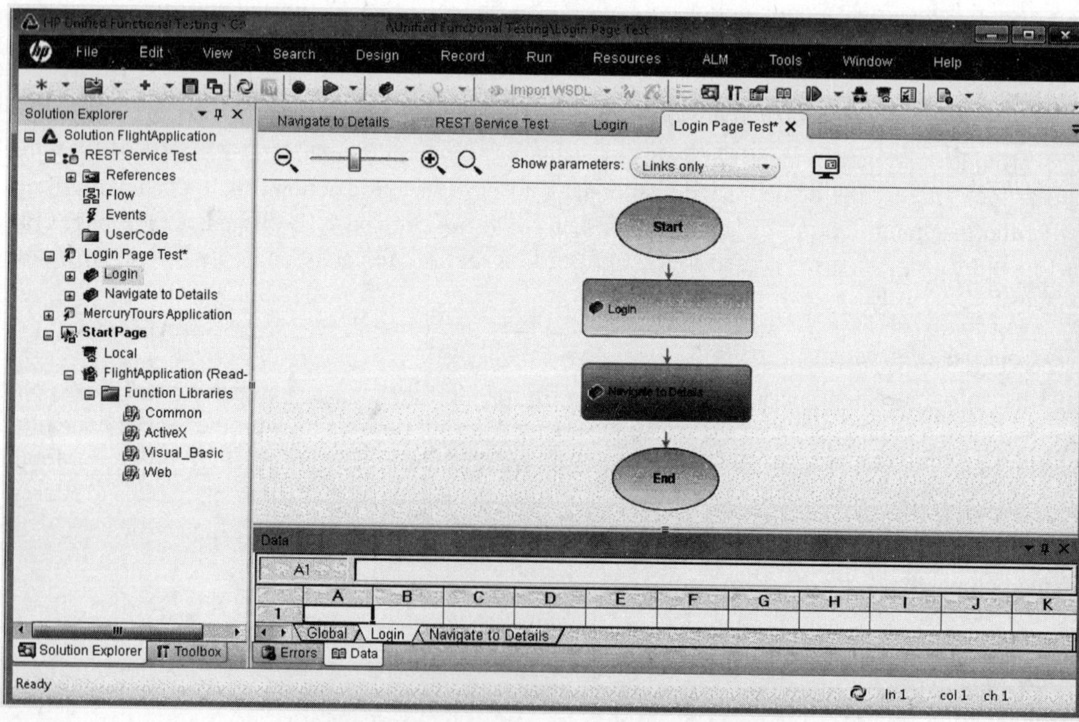

Figure 13.13 *UFT IDE (Reference: UFT Help)*

API Testing Features

SAP IDoc and RFC Imports

UFT now supports testing against an SAP server by importing IDocs and RFC definitions from SAP systems. This integration also lets users send IDocs to SAP systems, issue RFC calls, and create checkpoints on the responses.

JSON Document Testing

UFT provides an intuitive user-interface to test JSON-based REST APIs by generating JSON payloads and performing checkpoints on JSON responses.

Test Batch Runner

UFT test batch runner now supports executing both GUI and API tests as one test suite.

HP Service Virtualization Integration

HP Service Virtualization (SEV) helps create simulation projects that contain information about the virtualized services that simulate actual services. This is especially useful when the service is unavailable or broken. It is also valuable when running the service incurs a cost, such as credit card processing, gift card processing, etc.

UFT now can run GUI tests as well as API tests that use a virtualized service. This enables to run tests of the AUT using a service that would otherwise be inaccessible for test runs.

> **NOTES**
>
> UFT provides Service Virtualization to design a virtualized service. The virtualized service then can be deployed on a Service Virtualization server. When the test runs, the application accesses the virtual service instead of the real service

SoapUI Tests in UFT

UFT offers the feature to convert SoapUI test to UFT API test.

Compare API Testing Assets

HP ALM Asset Comparison Tool and Asset Viewer now allows users to view API tests as well as GUI assets. These tools enable users to:

- View any version of an asset using Asset Viewer
- Compare two versions of a selected asset using the Asset Comparison Tool
- View or compare versions of test resources such as the test source data

Other Enhancements

Listed below are some of the other enhancements.

ALM Application Parameters for Test Runs

HP ALM application under test (AUT) parameters can now be used to perform server-side execution in ALM. While working with server-side execution using ALM Lab Management, users can now take advantage of this option to link the parameters of the GUI test to ALM AUT Environment parameters. The AUT Environment parameters are then used when tests are run using server-side execution.

> **NOTES** In server-side execution, automated tests are run against remote host machines at predefined times or on an ad-hoc basis, not requiring anyone to be logged in to the host to initiate and control the test runs.

Test Editing Enhancements

- Users can specify a database using an OleDB or ODBC connection, and use it as the data source for a test.
- In API tests, users can create advanced array checkpoints to verify that an element exists in an array, or that every element of the array contains a specific value.
- For fixed-size arrays, users can assign each element of an array to any column in a data table.
- The Database Connection Builder lets users to add and encrypt a password when building a connection string.
- Users now have the option of selecting the transfer mode for Web Service and SOAP Request calls: HTTP or JMS.
- Users now have the option of selecting the transfer mode for FTP calls: Binary or ASCII.

Use the Run Results Deletion Tool Directly from the Run Results Viewer

The Run Results Deletion tool is now incorporated into the Run Results Viewer. This enables users to delete test results from tests and business process tests stored on ALM without needing to independently connect the Run Results Deletion tool to ALM.

Stop Run Session Using a Shortcut Key

UFT allows to define a shortcut key or key combination that would stop the current recording session (for GUI tests only) or text execution, even if UFT is not in focus or is in hidden mode.

> **NOTES** Shortcut key can be set in the Run Sessions pane in the Options dialog box. Navigate Tools → Options → General pane → Run Sessions and then click in the Stop command shortcut key field and then press the required key or key combination on the keyboard.
> The default key combination is CTRL+ALT+F5.

Continue Running GUI Tests on a Remote Computer After Disconnecting

When working with an RDP connection, UFT can continue running GUI tests or business process tests (GUI based) on a remote computer even after the local computer disconnect.

Additional Support for HTML5 Objects

The UFT Web Add-in now supports the additional objects for HTML5 object recognition. It includes – WebAudio, WebVideo, WebNumber, and WebRange

Create 64-Bit COM Object References

Standard VBScript provides the CreateObject function, which enables creating 32-bit COM object references. UFT now has added the CreateObject64 statement to create 64-bit COM object references.

Full Support for .XLSX Format Excel Files

UFT now fully supports the .xlsx format of MS Excel files for importing data to the Data Table or when specifying an Excel file for use with ALM configurations.

Web Add-in Enhancements

The new Style/* notation can be used to access the values of HTML5 CSS properties of Web-based objects.

UFT TEST AUTOMATION PROCESS

Basic Test Script Structure

- A test script comprises of calls to various actions. Actions help to divide the test script into logical units, such as Login → Search Ticket → Check Availability → Book Ticket → Logout. These logical units are designed in a way so that they can be reused to automate various test cases. More logical units (actions) help make test scripts more modular and efficient. With UFT 11.5 users can now combine API and GUI test components in one test. For example, users can login to AUT, search ticket and check availability using API calls and finally validate the book ticket scenario from GUI end.
- Every action comprises of test steps. These steps can be viewed as keywords in Keyword View and as VBScript statements in Editor View.
- During the test script execution, UFT executes all the test steps one by one. After the run session, a test report is generated. The test report contains the pass/fail status of each test step.

> NOTES: API testing saves a lot of execution time. For example, a ticket booking scenario may take around 30 seconds from GUI end while the same scenario may take less than 2 seconds when tested using APIs. A right approach would be to migrate the reusable GUI tasks to API calls. This saves lot of development as well as execution time and effort. Migrating even 30% of the GUI tests to API calls can reduce execution time by more than 70%.

UFT Automation Testing Workflow

In UFT, the following steps are followed to automate and execute a manual test case.

Analyze AUT

The first step to start an automation project is analyzing the AUT and determining the testing needs. One needs to:

- Determine the AUT development environment—Java, Power Builder, Web-based, SAP, or .Net.
- Based on application development environment, the type of add-ins to load can be decided.

- Determine the functionality to be tested. Effort should be made to replicate the end-user behavior.
- Determine how to break the business workflow into small reusable modular actions.

Preparing the Test Infrastructure

Test infrastructure is part of the test automation planning process. Test infrastructure includes test automation architecture, framework components, UFT server machines and local machines, test automation project, etc. Framework components can comprise of shared object repository, library files, configuration and environment files, etc. Test infrastructure must be properly planned and well set up.

UFT needs to be configured as per application needs at this step only. UFT configuration settings include object identification properties, global testing preferences, run session preferences, any test specific preferences, etc. Effort should be made to create a UFT configuration file that is automatically loaded when UFT machine starts up. This will avoid the need to configure all UFT machines separately.

Test automation framework should be well planned and designed to minimize not only the development effort but also the maintenance effort. Test automation framework should support maximum reusability as well as centralized maintenance and execution.

Creating Reusable Actions

The next step is to create reusable actions automating the smallest reusable business functionality. Functions are to be written to avoid code redundancy. Suitable environment variables can be declared in environment file. Test steps can be written in UFT in three ways – (i) record/playback approach, (ii) adding keywords and input data in Keyword View pane, and (iii) writing a VBScript code in the Editor view pane (iv) writing API tests. Record/playback approach automatically generates a VBScript code of the actions performed by the user on the application screen. Other two approaches require objects to be first added to object repository before any application specific code can be written. Writing API tests approach enables quick development of tests of high reliability and usability.

> **NOTES** API tests are more reliable and stable than as compared to GUI tests. Also API tests execution time is less than 5% of the execution time of GUI tests. Automation Architects to give priority to test business logic of AUT using API tests while screen validations are to be done by GUI tests.

Enhancing Test Scripts

Hard-coded data needs to be removed from the test script and needs to be migrated to test data files or data tables. Hard-coded data may include test input/output data, expected data, global environment data such as application username/password, etc.

Proper logical and conditional loops are to be used, so that the same action can be used in wide range of test conditions.

Dry Run, Script Debugging, and Code Fix

- ***Dry run:*** Once test script enhancement is complete, automation developers should analyze and review the code for any scripting mistakes and errors. Dry run is done to identify and remove hard-coding from the test scripts, resolve logical or conditional looping errors, fix error handling errors, etc. Effort should be made to resolve as many coding mistakes and errors as possible at this stage only.

- ***Debugging:*** Once scripting mistakes have been corrected in Dry Run phase, one can execute the test script to identify any hidden or run-time errors. Resolving coding errors at debugging stage consumes a lot of time as most of the times only few errors are caught per execution. Most of the times multiple test executions are required to fix all coding errors. For UFT beginners, the number of test executions required to properly fix a test script from errors is always higher. The proper use of UFT debugging features such as breakpoints, watch window, command window, and step execution helps resolving more errors in single execution only.

Analyzing Run Results and Reporting

The automated tests are executed as per the testing requirements. UFT develops a test execution report for every test script that is executed. The test report comprises of summary as well as step-by- step detailed report. The summary report contains the test pass/fail status, test script name, executions details, iterations, etc. The detailed report contains the execution status of each step along with pass/ fail status. The detailed test reports help finding the exact cause of test script failure. Once defects have been identified, a test automation report can be prepared and submitted to concerned persons. If ALM is integrated with UFT, then auto-defect logging into WC can also be done.

USING UFT HELP

UFT has inbuilt intellisense feature to help coding easier in UFT environment. UFT's intel- lisense automatically suggests the next step of code that can be written. This feature is very useful for beginners and helps in making their learning curve sharper. Apart from this UFT also comes with UFT tutorials and help files. UFT tutorials provide useful information such as introduction to UFT environment, UFT features and specification, and UFT learning tutorials. UFT help files are used for searching any sort of specific information on VBScript or UFT. UFT help consists of two types of Help documents:

- HP Unified Functional Testing Help as shown in Fig. 13.14.
- HP UFT GUI Testing Advanced References as shown in Fig. 13.15.

Contents Tab

Contents tab provides information topic-wise. This helps the user to navigate directly to the desired topic. The information topics are arranged in tree view. The pane next to the tree view shows the detailed description of the selected topic. The information present in this tab depends on the add-ins installed. As each add-in is installed, its help guide and object model reference also are added to the help file. Contents tab provides the following information:

- ***How to use document library:*** This section provides information on how the help file is organized and how to use it effectively.
- ***What is new in UFT:*** This section contains information about the UFT features, which has been newly added/updated to the current version.

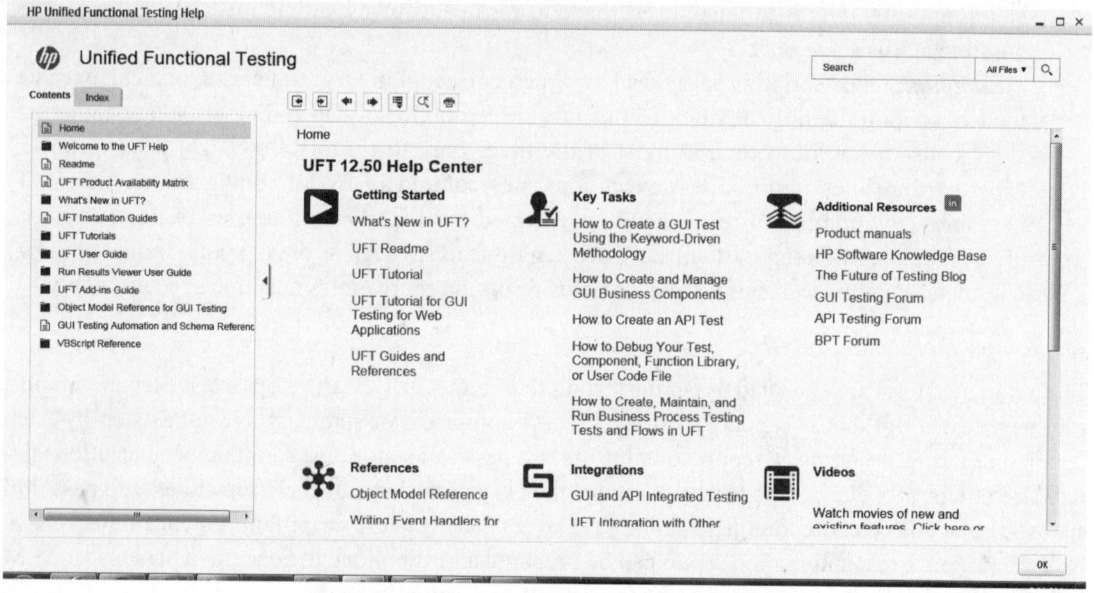

Figure 13.14 *HP UFT testing help window*

- ***User guide:*** This section provides information on how to use UFT to write test scripts in normal scripting as well as business process testing environment.
- ***Add-ins guide:*** This section contains help materials of the UFT add-ins.
- ***Object model reference:*** This section describes object model of UFT and its associated add-ins.

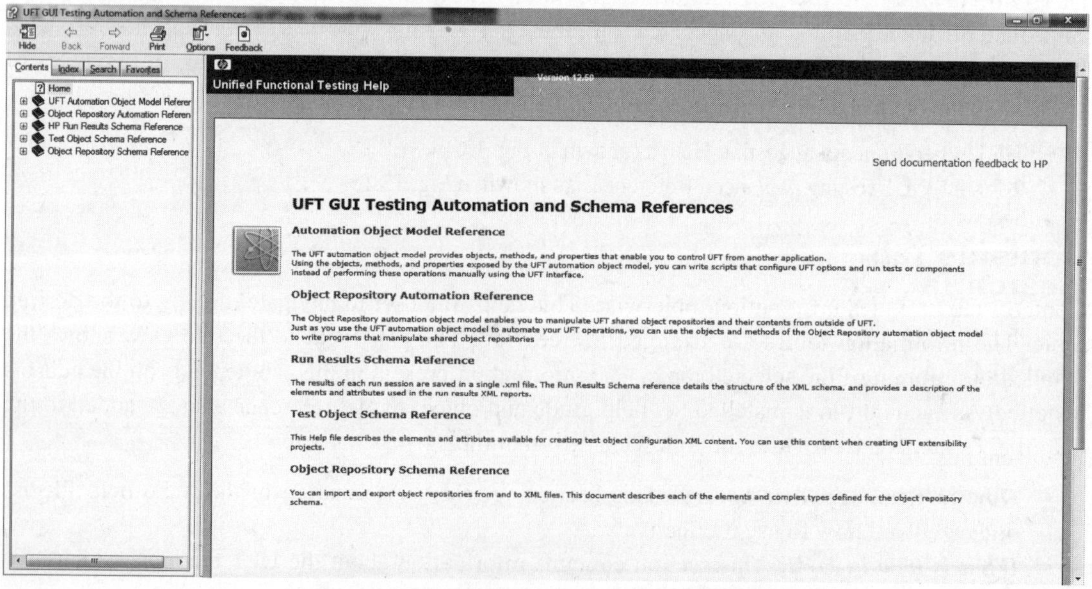

Figure 13.15 *Unified functional testing help*

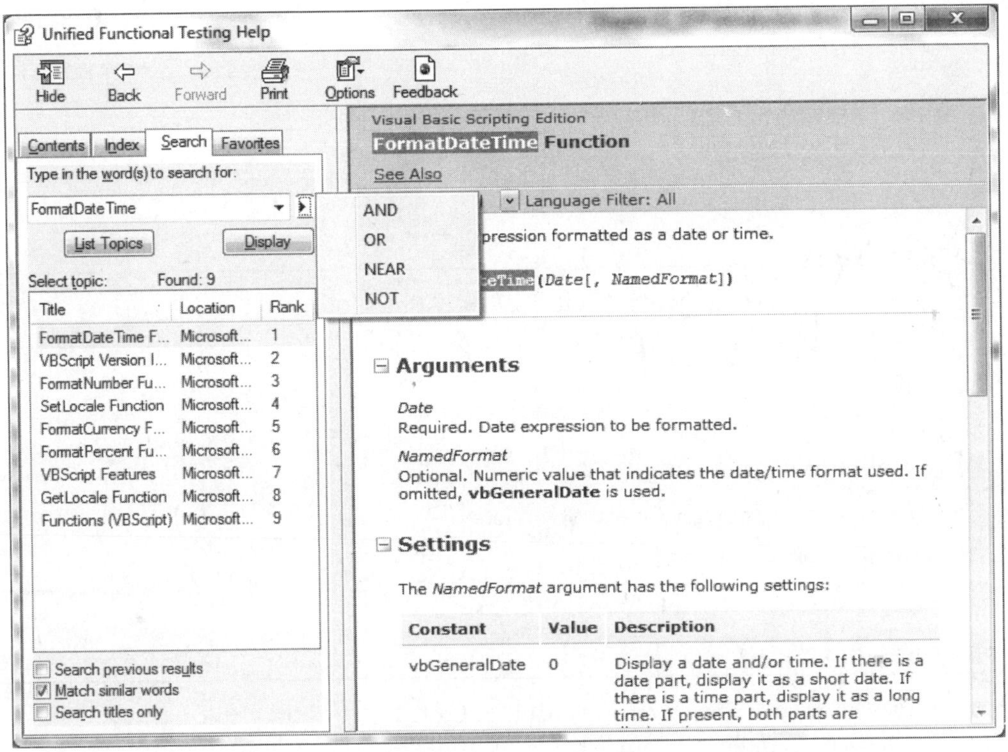

Figure 13.16 *Index tab*

- ***VBScript reference:*** This section provides reference tutorial for VBScript language as usable in UFT environment.

Index Tab

In index tab, information is organized alphabetically. A search field is also available to do specific search. Double-click on an index entry displays the corresponding page. Figure 13.16 shows the results obtained while doing a search in index tab.

Search Tab

Search tab enables users to search for specific topics or keywords. Search results are ranked in order. Search tab provides flexibility to filter search using the following options:

- *AND, OR, NEAR and NOT* logical operators. These options are available from the arrow present next to the search box.
- *Search previous results*. This option can be enabled by checking the checkbox available at the bottom of the *Search* tab.
- *Match similar words.* This option can be enabled by checking the checkbox available at the bottom of the *Search* tab.

- *Search titles only.* This option can be enabled by checking the checkbox available at the bottom of the *Search Tab* (Fig. 13.16).

Favorites Tab

This tab provides the flexibility to the user to bookmark specific help pages for quick reference.

QUICK TIPS

✓ UFT provides a single platform for both GUI and API testing.

✓ Scripting language of UFT is VBScript.

✓ Scripting language of API user code is C#.

✓ UFT has three modes to view/edit a test script—Canvas, Keyword View and Editor.

✓ UFT supports five recording modes and three playback modes.

✓ UFT supports Safari browser for test execution

✓ ALM supports single sign-on

PRACTICAL QUESTIONS

1. Explain the various recording modes available in UFT.
2. Describe the various run modes of UFT.
3. What is intellisense?
4. List the various operating systems and browsers supported by UFT 11.0.
5. What is a UFT add-in?
6. How can a user identify which UFT add-in is required for the application under test?
7. What are the advantages of API testing over GUI testing?

Chapter 14

UFT Installation

HP Unified Functional Testing the advanced keyword-driven testing solution for functional test and regression test automation. In this chapter, we will discuss step-by-step instructions on how to install and set up UFT on a standalone computer.

RECOMMENDED SYSTEM REQUIREMENTS

Before installing UFT, we need to ensure that the system meets the below requirements.

Computer Processor:	3 Ghz or higher
Operating System:	Windows 7 Service Pack 1 (32-bit or 64-bit)
Memory:	4 GB of RAM
Hard Disk Drive:	7200 RPM
Color Settings:	High Color (16 bit)
Graphics Card:	Graphics card with 64 MB video memory
Free Hard Disk Space:	25 GB of free disk space for application files and folders
Browser:	UFT supported browser versions

ACCESS PERMISSIONS

Below set of access permissions needs to be set to successfully install and run UFT.

Access Permission for UFT

Full read and write permissions to the:

- *Temp* folder.
- *<Program Files>\Common Files\Mercury Interactive* folder
- *<Program Data>\HP* folder
- User Profile folders
- *<Windows> \mercury.ini* file
- Following AppData folders and subfolders:

  - %userprofile%\AppData\Local\HP
  - *%appdata%\Hewlett-Packard\UFT*
  - *%appdata%\HP\API Testing*
- Following registry keys :
  - HKEY_CURRENT_USER\Software\Mercury Interactive or [HKEY_LOCAL_MACHINE\SOFTWARE\Wow6432Node\Hewlett-Packard]
  - HKEY_CURRENT_USER\SOFTWARE\Hewlett Packard
  - HKEY_LOCAL_MACHINE and HKEY_CLASSES_ROOT

> NOTES: User to be granted read/write to all the keys under the above registry key

- Folder and its subfolders where UFT tests or run results are to be saved

Read permissions to the

- Windows folder and to the System folder

Access Permissions for BPT

- Full read and write permissions to the ALM cache folder
- Full read and write permissions to the *<Program Data>\HP* folder
- Full read and write permissions to the UFT Add-in for ALM installation folder
- Administrative permissions for the first connection to ALM

INSTALLING UFT

UFT setup comes in a DVD. It can also be downloaded from HP site UFT comes with two installation packages:

- Compressed package that contains UFT only for web application automation.
- Full UFT package.

In this chapter, we will discuss installation steps for full UFT package.

Prerequisites

- UFT setup DVD or downloaded UFT software.
- Administration privileges over the machine where UFT is to be installed.

> NOTES: For UFT upgrade, in case web service tests was created using Service Test or earlier versions of UFT, the .NET Framework 3.5, WSE 2.0sp3 package, and WSE 3.0 package needs to be installed on the computer from below location of setup package:
>
> - NET 3.5 Framework: *<setup package>/prerequisites/dotnet35_1/donetfx35_sp1.exe*
> - WSE 2.0 sp3: *<setup package>/prerequisites/wse20sp3/MicrosoftWSE2.0SP3Runtime.msi*
> - WSE 3.0: *<setup package>/prerequisites/wse30/MicrosoftWSE3.0Runtime.msi*

Installation

1. Logon to the machine with administrator privileges.
2. Double-click on the setup.exe (setup) file. UFT setup window opens as shown in the Fig. 14.1.
3. Click on the link *Unified Functional Testing Setup*. A setup window, as shown in Fig. 14.2 opens to install the software programs that are required to run UFT.

> NOTES: This setup window identifies the missing programs and installs them.

4. Once installation is complete, the machine will automatically restart.
5. Logon with administration privileges of step 1.
6. Run the setup file as mentioned in step 2 and 3. HP UFT Setup Wizard window opens as shown in Fig. 14.3.

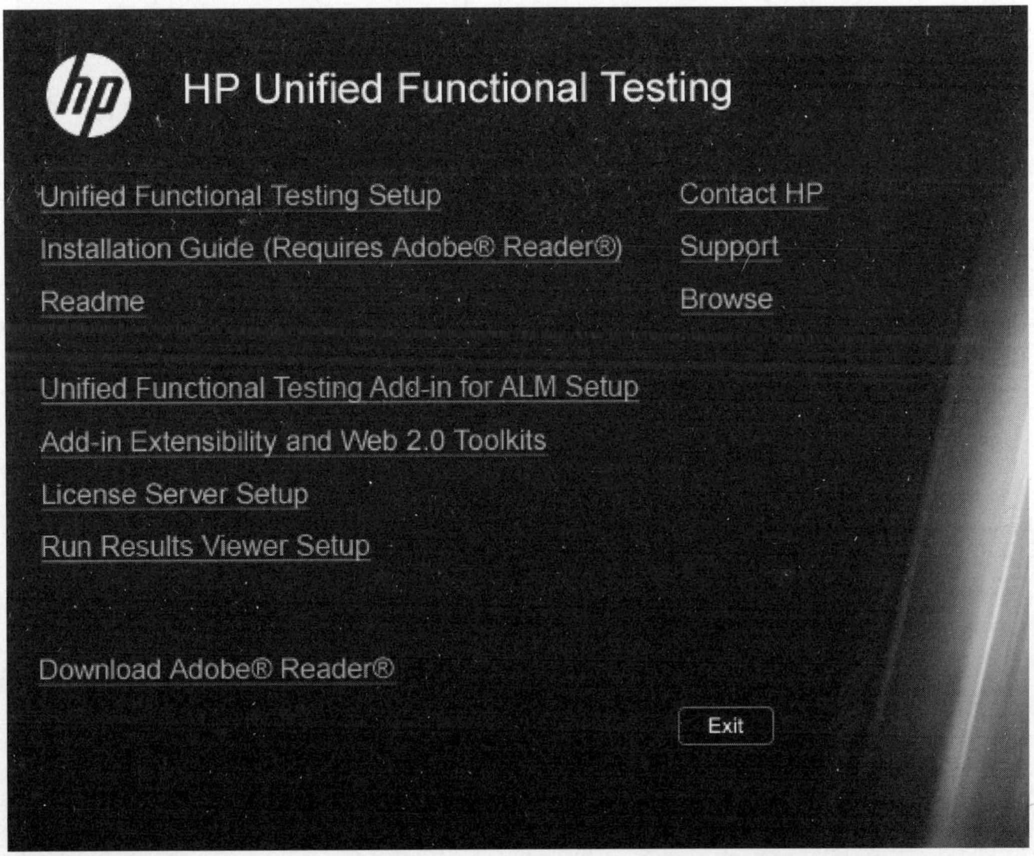

Figure 14.1 *HP UFT setup*

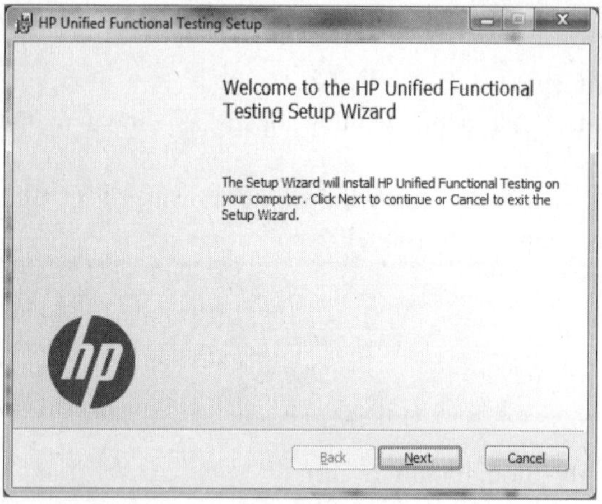

Figure 14.2 *UFT installation prerequisite programs*

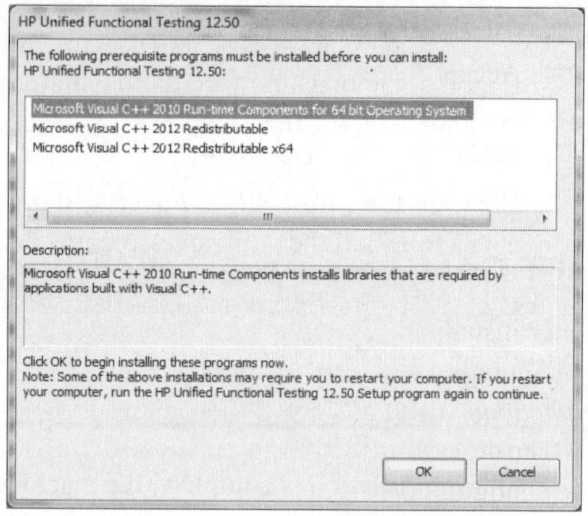

Figure 14.3 *HP UFT setup wizard*

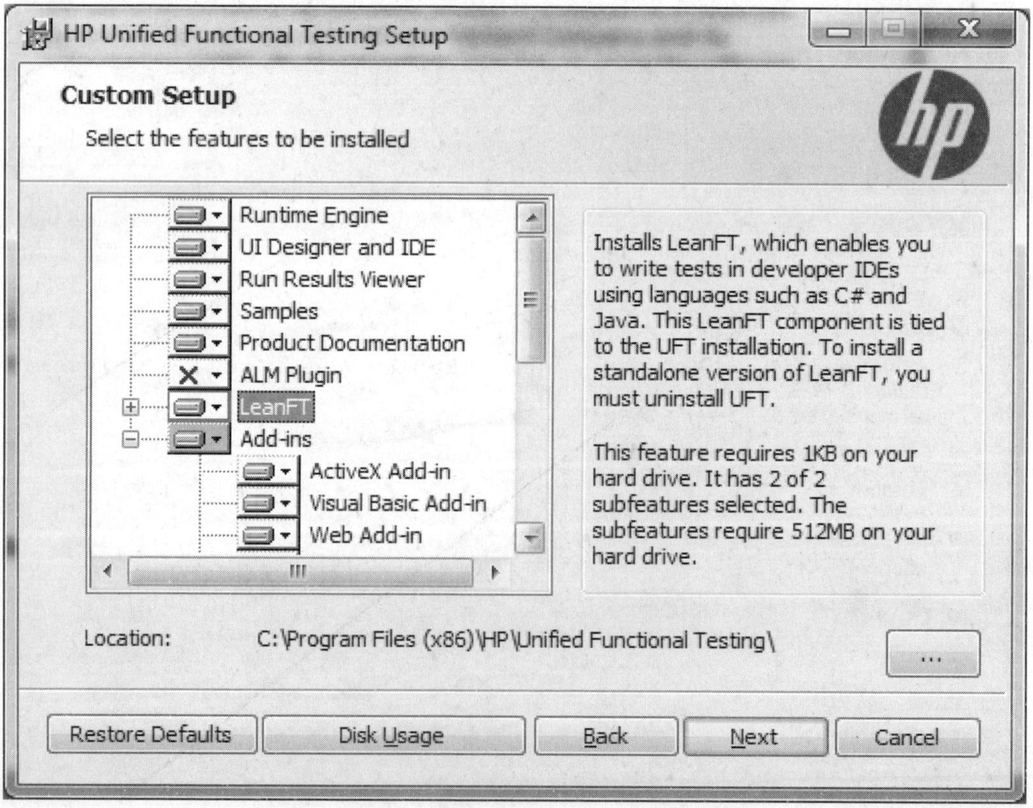

Figure 14.4 *Custom setup to select addins*

7. Click on *Next* button. *End-User License Agreement* window opens.
8. Accept the license agreement terms and click *Next* button. *Custom Setup window* opens as shown in Fig. 14.4.
9. Select the required add-ins to be installed and click *Next* button.
10. Hereafter, follow the instructions of UFT setup window to complete installation.

UFT Configuration

After installation is complete, UFT configuration window opens up as shown in the Fig 14.5. UFT configuration window can also be opened from *Start → All Programs → HP Software → HP Unified Functional Testing → Tools → Additional Installation Requirements*.

The description of various configurations is shown in figure below. Users are to select the appropriate configurations for setup. Also, option to install *Microsoft Script Debugger* will not be displayed if it is already installed on the machine.

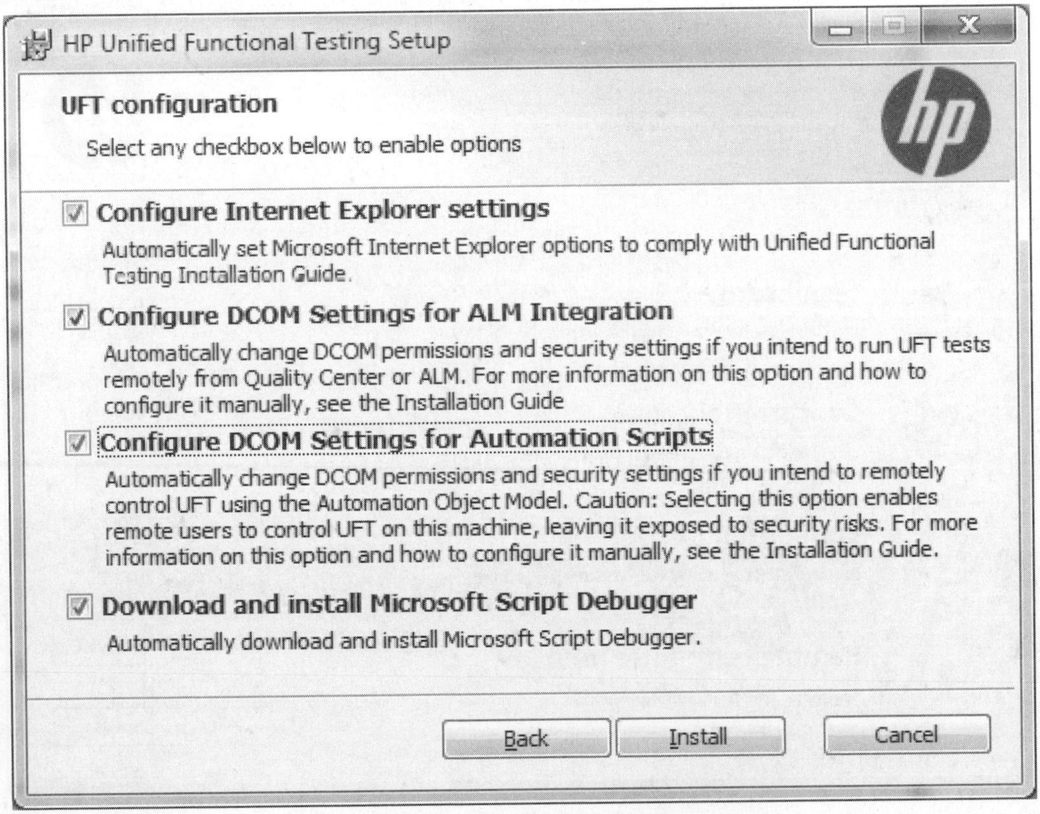

Figure 14.5 *UFT configuration*

> Internet Explorer settings can also be configured manually before running UFT. To configure, in Internet Explorer, select Tools → Internet Options → Advanced. Then select Disable script debugging and Enable third-party browser extensions.

INSTALLING UFT LICENSES

Once installation is complete, next step is to install the licenses. UFT licenses can be installed using *License Validation Utility as shown in Fig. 14.6*. This utility can be accessed from *Start → All Programs → HP Software → HP Unified Functional Testing → Tools → Functional Testing License Wizard.*

HP UFT comes with four types of licenses – Seat license, Concurrent License, Commuter License and Remote Commuter license. Seat license is specific to a machine while Concurrent license can be accessed by any UFT machine. In Seat license, license is installed on the specific UFT machine. While in Concurrent license, the license is installed on the server and any one of the UFT machines can use this license to run UFT.

The license keys are provided by HP to its HP UFT customers. Once licenses are installed HP UFT is ready for use in case of seat license. In case of concurrent license, users need to define the server address against license key field of Fig. 14.6 to access the UFT licenses from server.

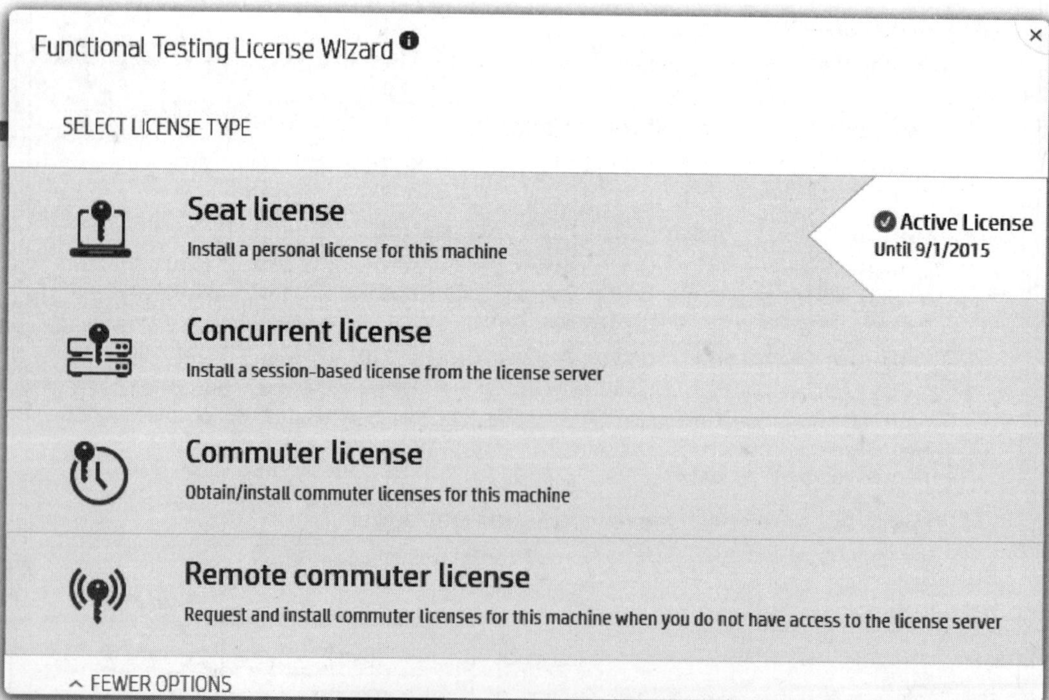

Figure 14.6 *HP UFT license installation*

Apart from Seat and Concurrent license, HP also provides Commuter and Remote Commuter license to (only) Concurrent license users. Commuter license allows users to checkout UFT license from a license server machine to a UFT machine. While remote commuter license allows users to install commuter licenses for a UFT machine when he cannot access license server. Commuter license is useful when a user cannot access the license server for any reason. For example, suppose a user needs to travel on a business trip with his laptop computer and wants to use UFT while he is away. He can check out a UFT license from the concurrent license server to use for the duration of his trip, and then checkin the license back in upon his return. Remote commuter license is useful when a user does not have access to license server, he can checkout a license with the assistance of another user with a connection to the license server. Remote Commuter licenses can be checkedout for 180 days.

Chapter 15

UFT Configuration

HP Unified Functional Testing provides various options to configure UFT for project specific requirements. It allows users to configure GUI, API and BPT testing features of UFT. UFT also provides the option to configure the UFT object properties capture and run-time object identification mechanism. In this chapter we will discuss in detail how to configure UFT.

UFT GLOBAL OPTIONS

UFT provides *Options* dialog box to configure the settings of UFT. Options dialog box can be launched by selecting *Tools → Options*. Figure 15.1 below shows Options dialog box.

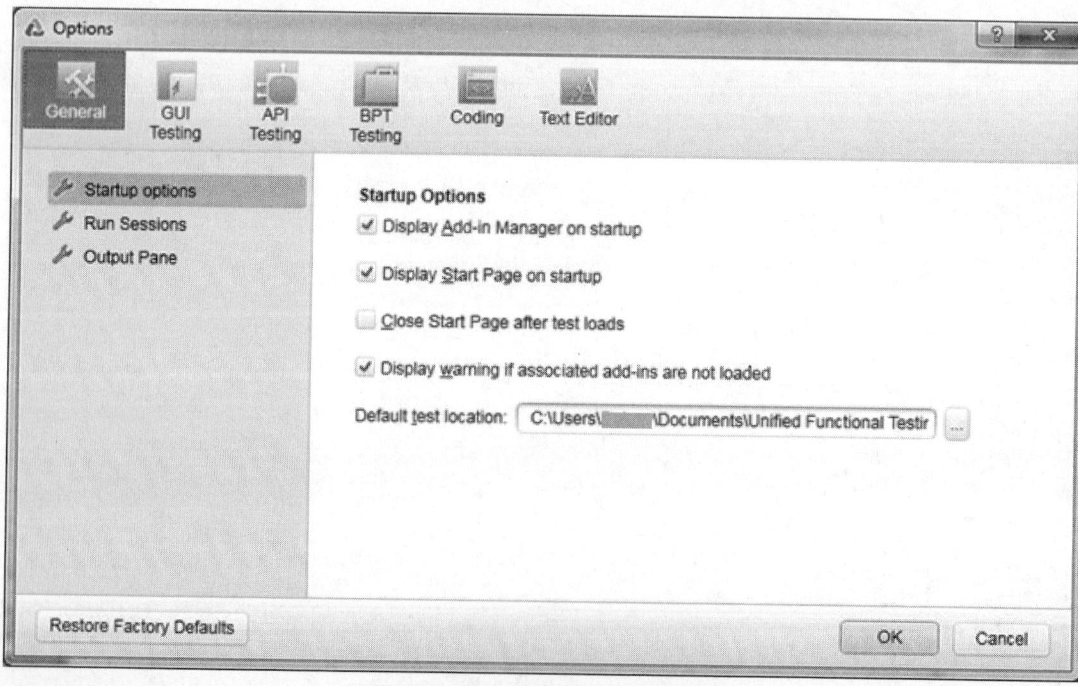

Figure 15.1 Options *dialog box*

Options dialog box contains six tabs. They are:

- General tab (Relevant for GUI tests and components and API testing)
- GUI Testing tab (Relevant for GUI tests and components)
- API Testing tab (Relevant for API testing)
- BPT Testing tab (Relevant for Business Process Tests and Flows)
- Coding tab (Relevant for GUI testing and API testing)
- Text Editor tab (Relevant for GUI testing and API testing)

> **NOTES** The *Restore Factory Defaults* button (Restore Factory Defaults)of Options dialog box resets all Options dialog box options to their defaults.

General Tab (Relevant for GUI Tests and Components and API Testing)

General tab allows users to define general options of UFT. Figure 15.1 shows the General tab. It has three panes – *Startup Options*, *Run Sessions* and *Output Pane*.

Panes	Description
Startup Options	This pane enables users to select what UFT displays when UFT opens.
Run Sessions	This pane enables users to determine global UFT run settings that are applicable to both GUI testing and API testing.
Output Pane	This pane enables users to define display options for the Output pane.

GUI Testing Tab (Relevant for GUI Tests and Components)

This tab enables users to modify global testing options for GUI tests and components. It has panes for general options and as well as panes for various UFT add-ins. Figure 15.2 below shows the GUI Testing tab.

> **NOTES** The *Generate Script...* button (Generate Script...) generates a UFT script containing most of the current global testing options.

In this section, we will discuss the panes – *General, Test Runs, Text Recognition, Folders, Active Screen, Screen Capture* and *Insight*.

Panes	Description
General	This pane provides general options for working with GUI tests and components.
Test Runs	This pane enables users to determine how UFT runs GUI tests and components. It enables users to: Select Normal (displays execution with a marker) or Fast execution mode. Select to automatically submit a defect in ALM for each failed step. Select the option ☐ Allow other HP products to run tests and components to allow triggering test execution from remote machine.

Text Recognition	This pane enables users to configure how UFT identifies text in the application under test. Users are to use this pane to modify the default text capture mechanism, OCR (optical character recognition) mechanism mode, and the language dictionaries the OCR mechanism uses to identify text.
Folders	This pane enables users to define the folders (search paths) in which UFT searches for UFT artifacts such as tests, components, actions, or resource files that are specified as relative paths in dialog boxes and steps.
Active Screen	This pane allows users to specify which information UFT saves and displays in the Active Screen while recording and running tests.
Screen Capture	This pane allows users to control how UFT captures images and movies of the application being tested.
Insight	This pane allows users to set options that customize how UFT handles Insight test objects when creating test object, and during record and run sessions. Insight based recognition is discussed in detail in section 'Objection Identification'.

API Testing Tab (Relevant for API Testing)

API Testing tab enables users to customize UFT work environment when working with API UFT tests or components. Figure 15.3 below shows API testing tab.

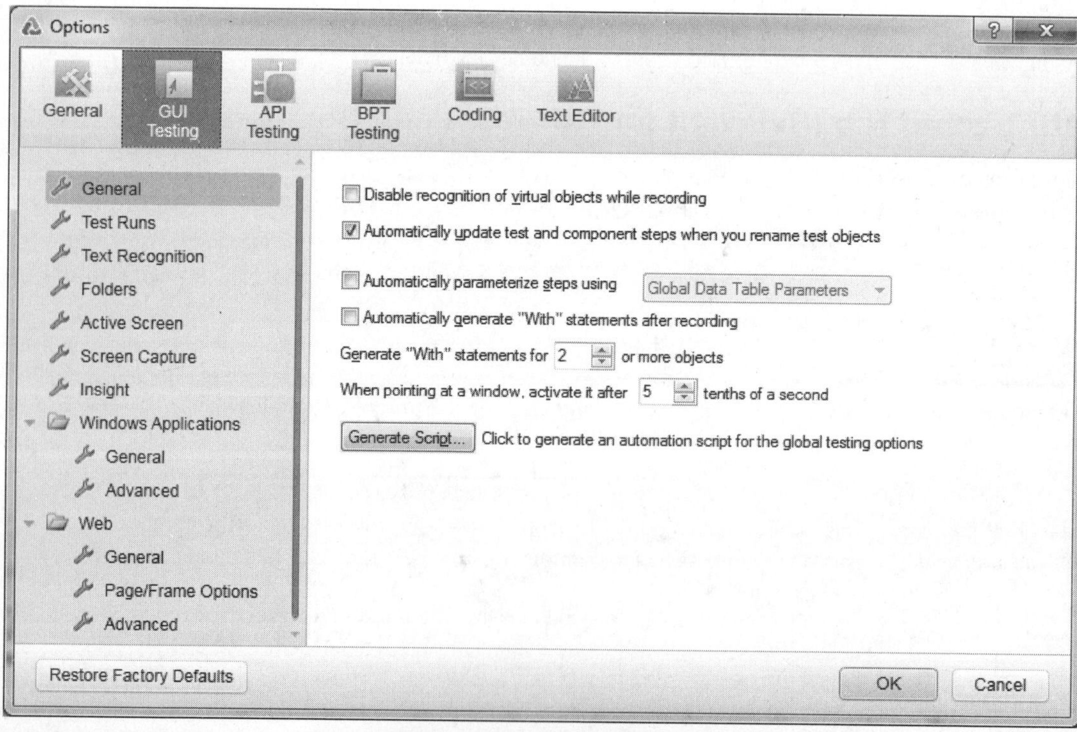

Figure 15.2 *GUI testing tab*

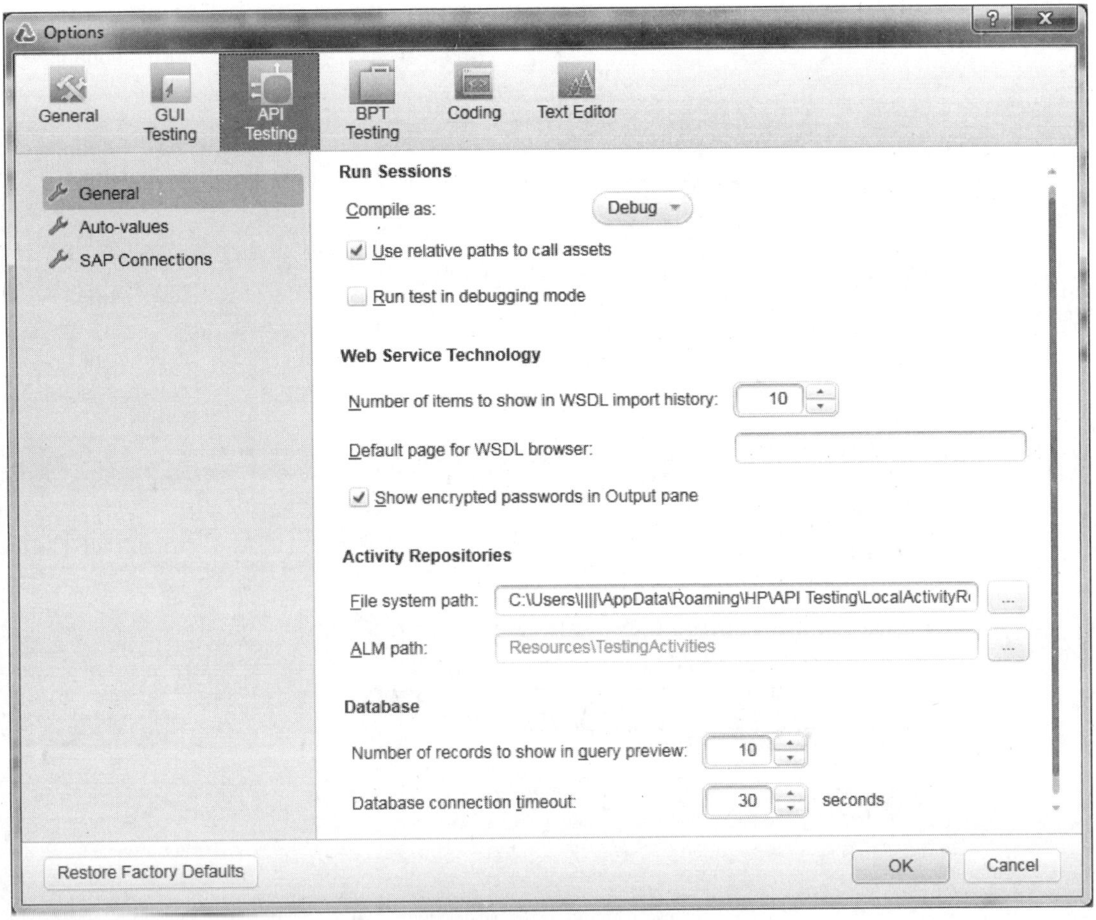

Figure 15.3 *API testing*

API Testing tab has three panes—*General, Auto-values,* and *SAP Connections.*

Panes	Description
General	This pane enables users to define the test execution mode, the default location for importing WSDL files, and the repository locations for activity sharing.
Auto-values	This pane enables users to provide default values to use various types of properties such as string, date/time, integer, etc.
SAP Connections	This pane enables users to add and remove SAP connections, add authentication information, and check the connection

BPT Testing Tab (Relevant for API Testing)

This tab allows users to set options for parameter use of a BPT test and its components in UFT. Figure 15.4 shows BPT Testing tab.

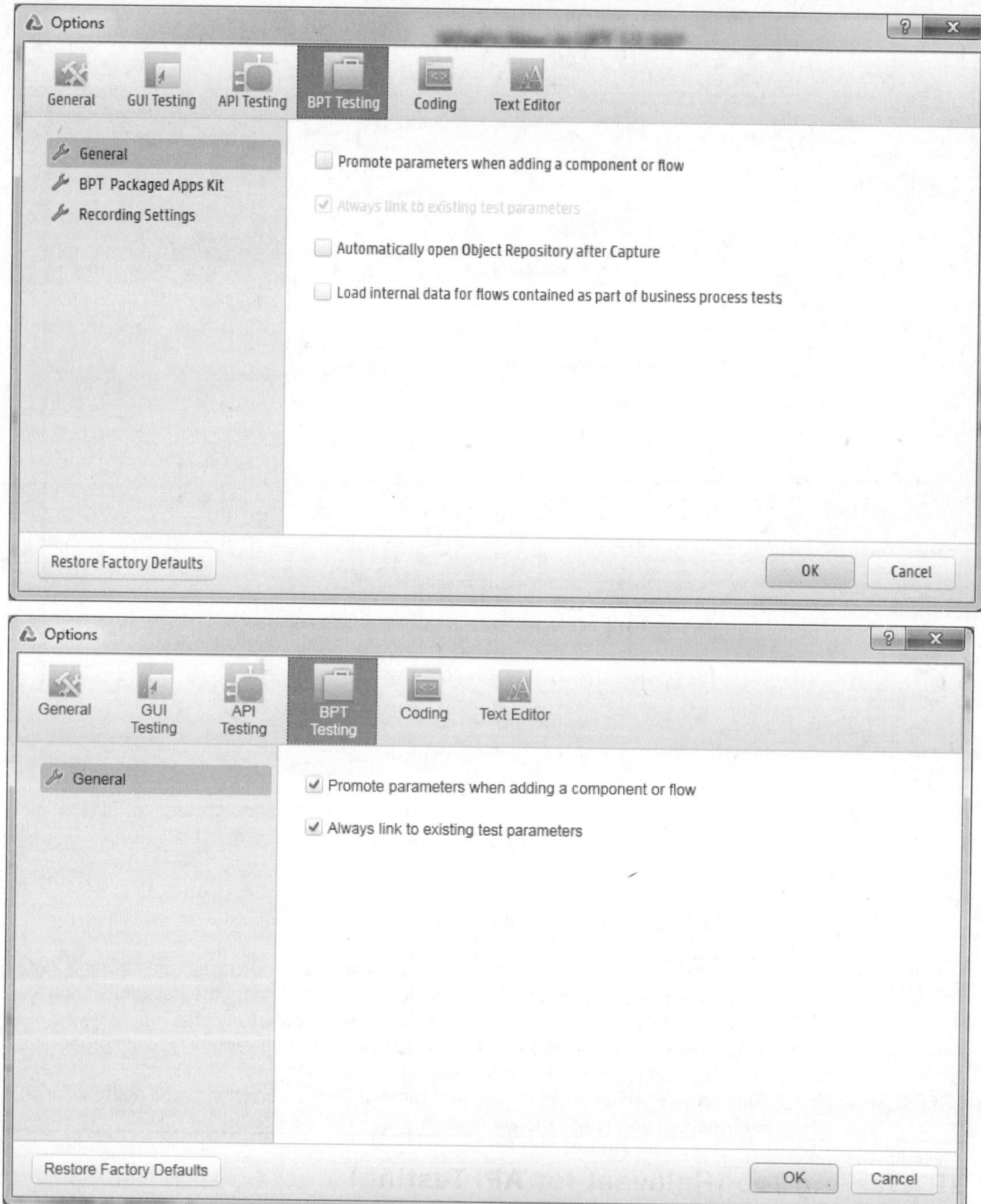

Figure 15.4 *BPT testing tab*

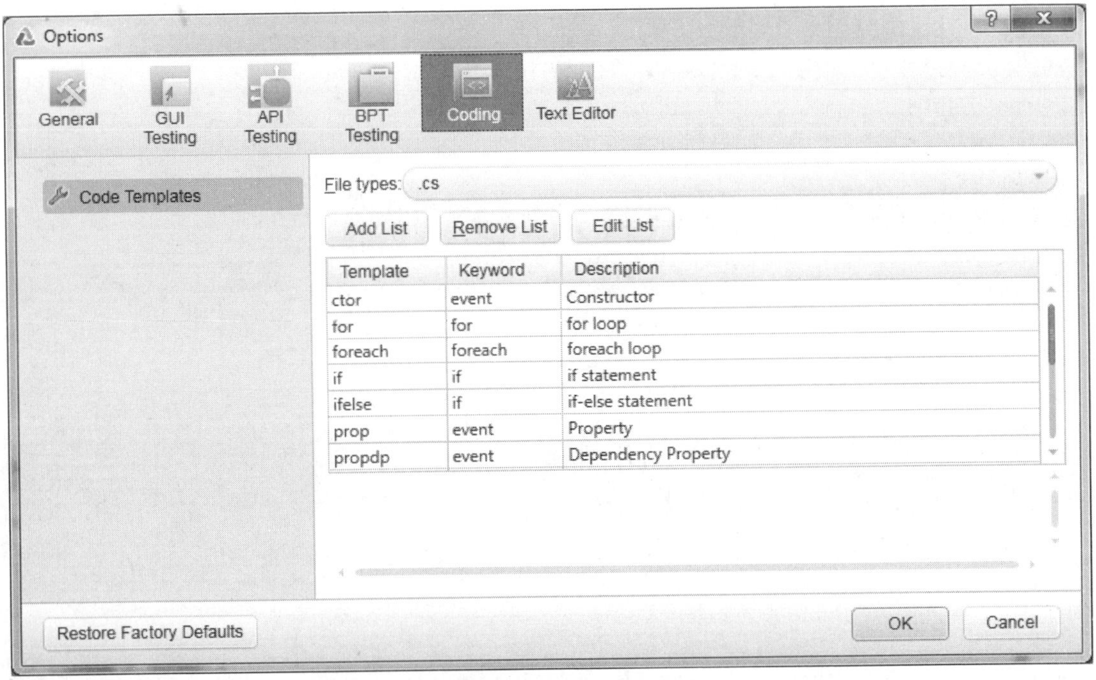

Figure 15.5 *Coding tab*

BPT Testing tab has one pane—*General*.

Panes	Description
General	This pane: Determines whether UFT automatically promotes parameters to the flow or test level. Determines whether UFT uses an existing test parameter during promotion or creates an additional test parameter, in scenarios where a parameter with the same name already exists in the test or flow.

Coding Tab (Relevant for GUI Testing and API Testing)

This tab enables users to set options that facilitate in developing code. Figure 15.5 shows Coding tab.

BPT Testing tab has one pane—*Coding Templates*.

Panes	Description
General	This pane enables users to create and edit templates of pre-designed code snippets or blocks of text used for automatic code completion.

Text Editor Tab (Relevant for GUI Testing and API Testing)

This tab allows users to set general preferences for editing code and text files and color coding of code. Figure 15.6 below shows Text Editor tab.

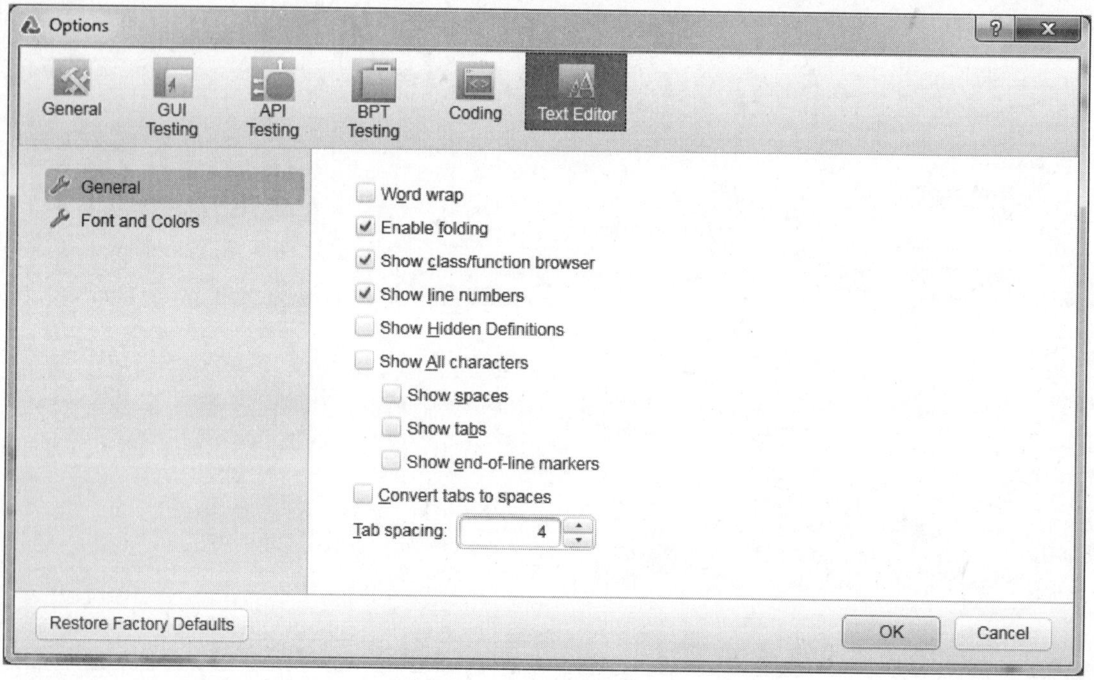

Figure 15.6 *Text editor tab*

Text Editor tab has two panes—*General* and *Font and Colors*.

Panes	Description
General	This pane enables users to set general preferences for editing code and text files.
Font and Colors	This pane enables users to specify color preferences for the code. Users can set unique coloring rules for each code element.

UFT TEST SETTINGS

UFT provides various options to configure UFT for specific test and business component requirements. It also provides additional settings pane to configure application area settings for specific group of business components. Listed below are the major setting options provided by UFT:

Settings Dialog Boxes	Description
Test Settings	Test Settings dialog box sets the testing options for a specific test. For example, test parameter settings of a parameterized test can be set to run the test against certain lines of test data of datatable.
Business Component Settings	Business components automatically inherit the settings defined from the Application Area Settings to which they are associated. Business Component Settings dialog box displays the inherited settings in read-only format. This dialog box also provides additional options to define business component-specific settings such as input/output parameters, component development status, component snapshot etc.
Application Area Settings	Application Area Settings dialog box defines the settings and resources needed for a business component. .

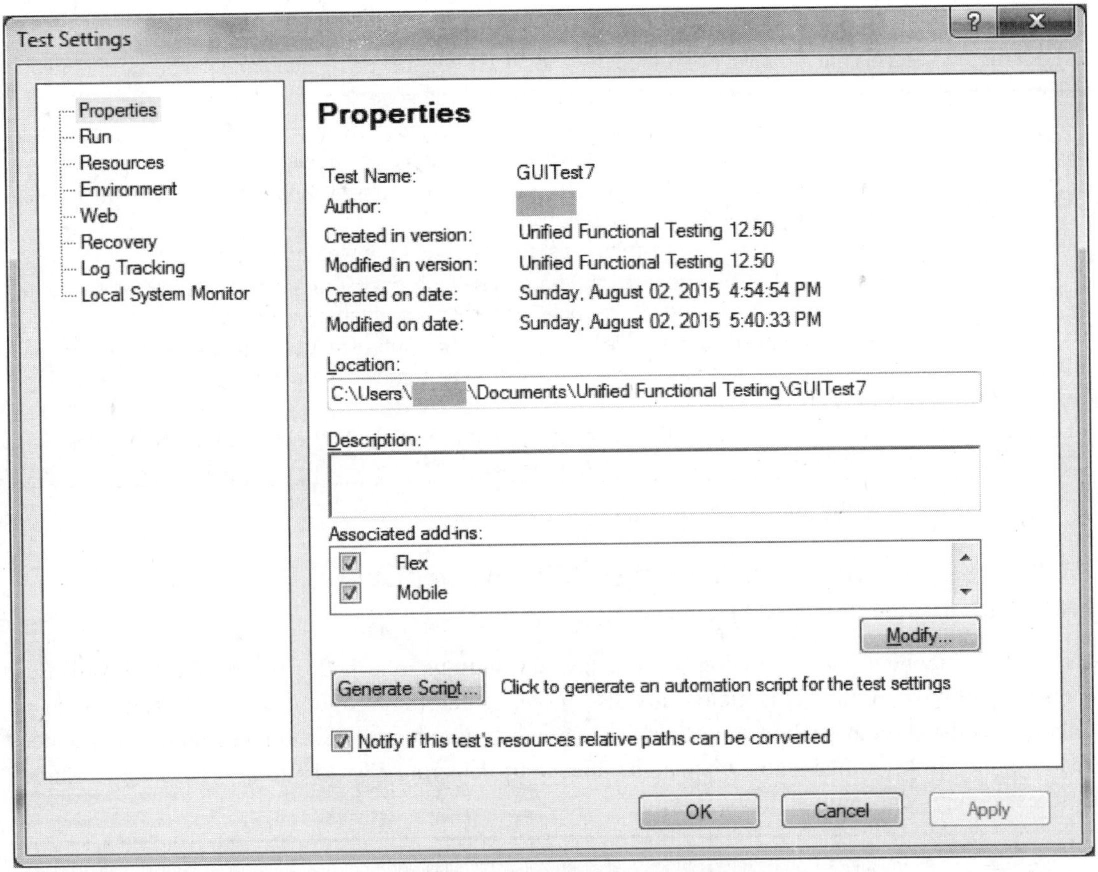

Figure 15.7 *Test settings dialog box*

Test Settings (Relevant for a Test or Action)

Test Settings dialog box defines the various settings of a test. Test Settings dialog box can be opened by selecting *File → Settings*. Figure 15.7 show test settings dialog box.

> **NOTES** Test Settings dialog box also displays additional panes for each add-in like Java, Terminal Emulator, etc. These panes are only displayed if the respective add-in is installed or loaded.

Test Settings dialog box offers various panes to configures different settings of a given test or action. It includes – Properties, Run, Resources, Environment, Web, Recovery, Log Tracking, and Local System Monitor.

Panes	Description
Properties	This pane displays test attributes, test location, test description and associated add-ins.
Run	This pane enables users to specify test execution settings.
Resources	This pane enables users to specify the resources associated with the test such as function libraries, shared object repositories, and data tables.
Environment	This pane displays built-in and user-defined environment variables. It also allows user to add and modify environment variables.
Web	This pane allows user to define test run settings for a web application.
Recovery	This pane allows users to associate recovery scenarios to a test. It also allows users to specify the trigger condition for activating recovery scenarios.
Log Tracking	This pane enables users to define options for activating and setting run-time preferences for tracking log messages generated by the log framework that monitors events occurring in the application under test.
Local System Monitor	This pane enables users to define options for activating and setting preferences for tracking system counters during a run session.

We will discuss all the above panes in detail in this book.

Business Component Settings (Relevant for a Business Component)

Business Component Settings dialog box displays the settings inherited from Application Area Settings in read-only format. This dialog box also provides additional options to define business component-specific settings such as input/output parameters, component development status, component snapshot etc. Test Settings dialog box can be opened by selecting *File → Settings*. Figure 15.8 shows business component settings dialog box.

> NOTES: Business Component Settings dialog box also displays additional panes for each add-in like Java, Terminal Emulator, etc. These panes are only displayed if the respective add-in is installed or loaded.

Test Settings dialog box offers various panes to configures different settings of a given test or action. It includes – *Properties, Snapshot, Applications, Resources, Parameters, Environment, Java, Web, Recovery,* and *Log Tracking*.

Panes	Description
Properties	This pane displays test attributes, test location, test description and associated add-ins.
Snapshot	This pane allows users to capture or load a snapshot image to be saved with the component for display in ALM
Applications	This pane displays the windows-based applications against which the business component can record and run.
Resources	This pane enables users to specify the resources associated with the test such as function libraries, shared object repositories, and data tables.
Parameters	This pane enables users to define the input and output parameters of a component.
Environment	This pane displays built-in and user-defined environment variables. It also allows user to add and modify environment variables.
Web	This pane allows user to define test run settings for a web application.

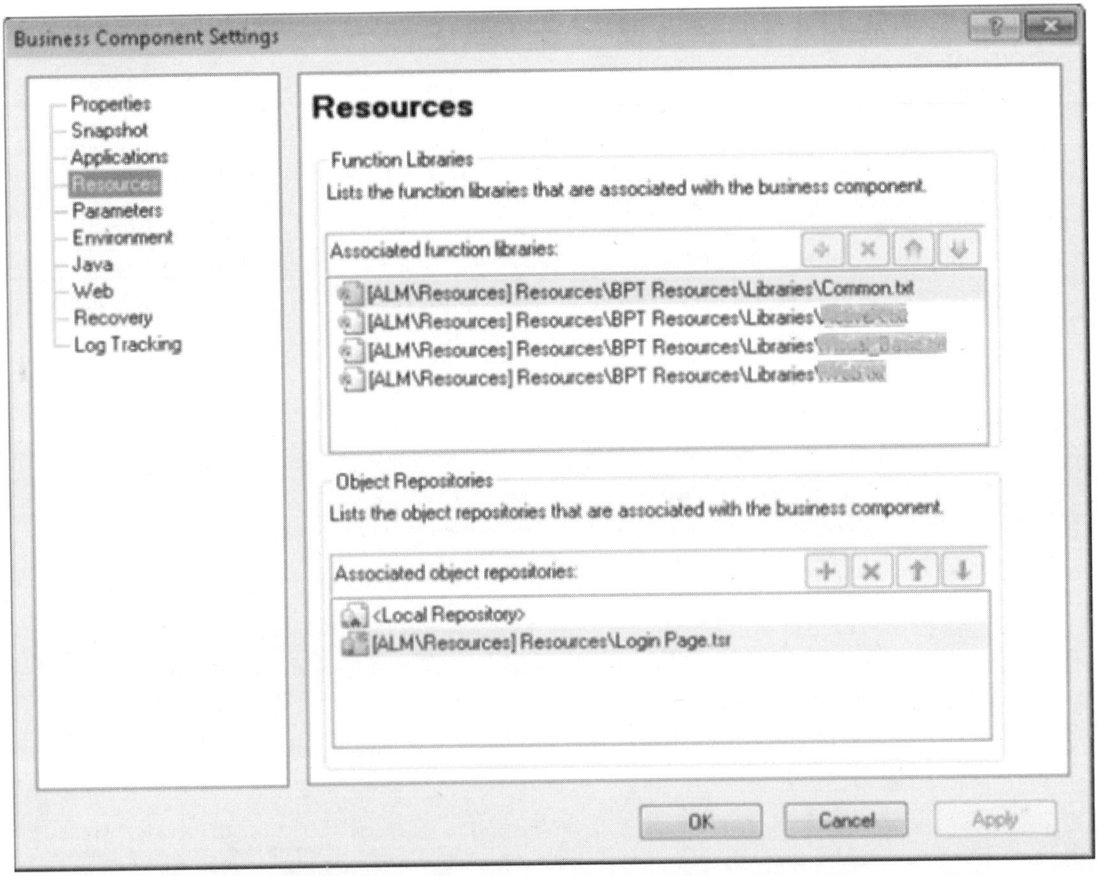

Figure 15.8 *Business component settings dialog box*

Recovery	This pane allows users to associate recovery scenarios to a test. It also allows users to specify the trigger condition for activating recovery scenarios.
Log Tracking	This pane enables users to define options for activating and setting run-time preferences for tracking log messages generated by the log framework that monitors events occurring in the application under test.

We will discuss all the above panes in detail in chapter 'Business Process Testing'.

Application Area Settings (Relevant for a Business Component) (Figure 15.9 & 15.10)

TODO: FIND UFT 12 APPLICATION SETTINGS WINDOW GUI

Record and Run Settings (Relevant for a GUI Tests)

Record and Run Settings enables users to set record and run options before recording or running any test. Record and Run Settings configuration window can be accessed by opening any test or

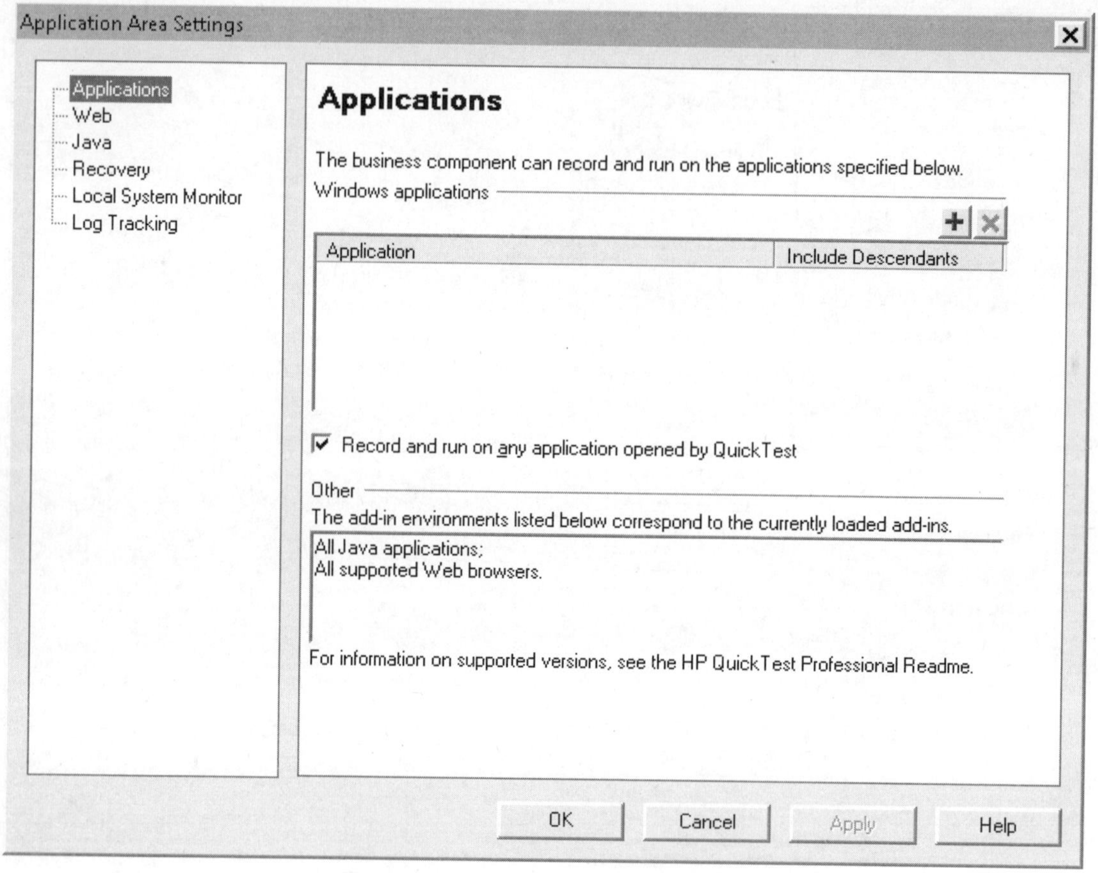

Figure 15.9 *Application area settings*

component and then selecting *Record → Record and Run Settings*. Figure 15.11 shows Record and Run Settings dialog box.

Web Event Recording Configuration (Relevant for a GUI Tests)

Web Event Recording Configuration dialog box enables users to select a predefined configuration level for recording user action against GUI events. Figure 15.12 shows the default web event recoding configuration. This default configuration can modified through *Custom Web Event Recording Configuration* dialog box as shown in Fig. 15.13. This dialog box can be opened by clicking on *Custom Settings...* button of the Web Event Recording Configuration dialog box.

Web Event Recording Configuration dialog box has three predefined recording levels – *Basic*, *Medium* and *High*.

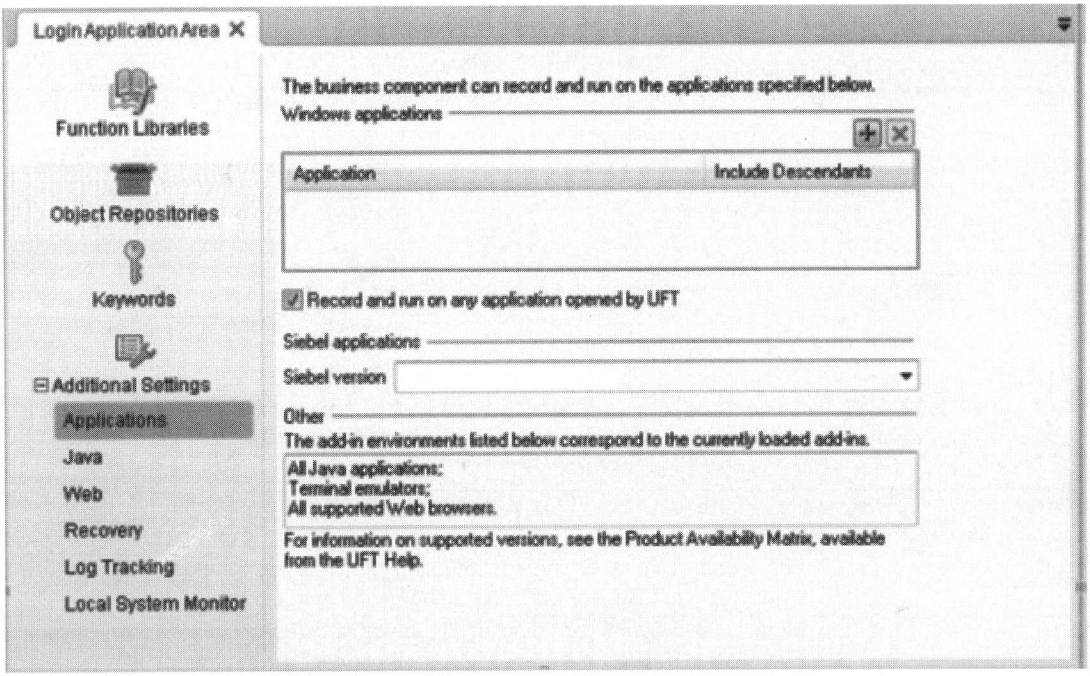

Figure 15.10 *Additional application area settings*

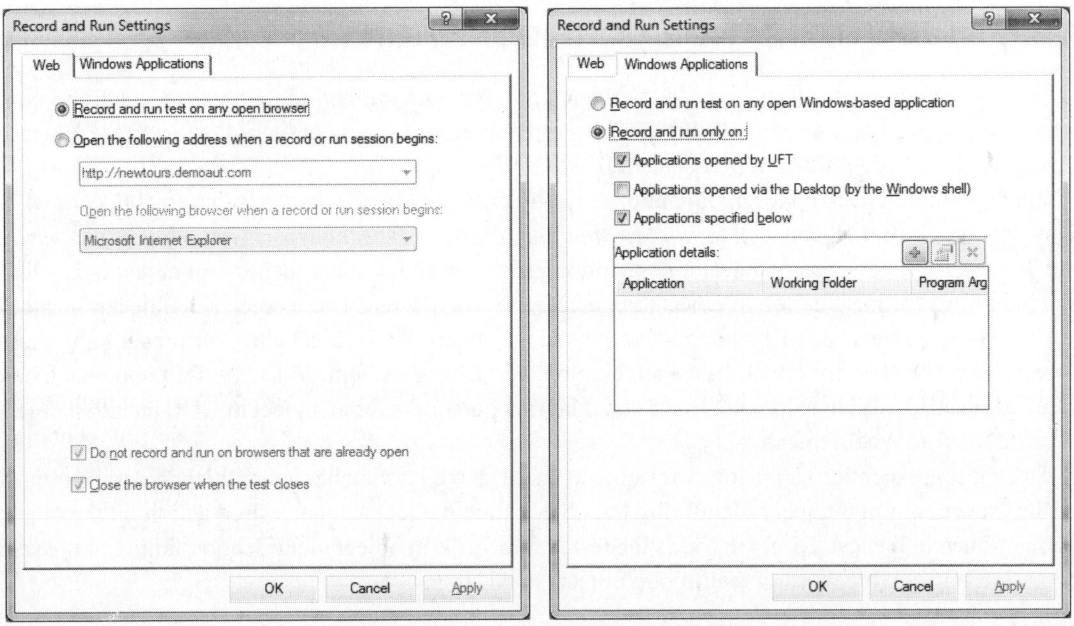

Figure 15.11 *Record and run settings*

Figure 15.12 *Web event recording configuration*

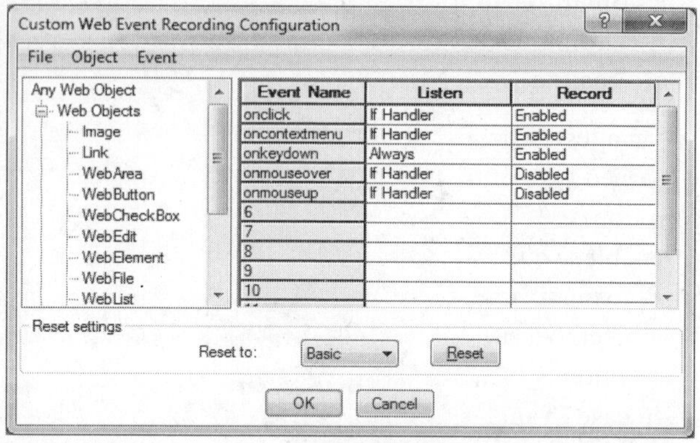

Figure 15.13 *Custom settings for web event recording configuration*

Web Event Recording Configurations	Description
Basic	Basic web event recording configuration records click events on all standard objects and mouseover events on images and image maps.
Medium	Medium web event recording configuration records click events on several additional HTML tag objects apart from those recorded in the standard level.
High	High web event recording configuration records all click, mouseover, mousedown and double-click events on standard objects with handlers or behaviors attached.

OBJECT IDENTIFICATION CONFIGURATION

(This is discussed in detail in Chapter '*Configuring Object Identification Mechanism*'. Why to configure UFT Object Identification Mechanism? How to decide object configuration settings?When to configure Object Identification Mechanism?)

All text boxes, check boxes, radio buttons, and other GUI objects are referred as an ***Object*** in UFT. The attributes of the object such as *html id, html tag, clas*s etc. are referred as ***description properties*** in UFT. UFT uses object attributes or description properties to uniquely identify an object in AUT.

UFT stores the information of objects in object repository (OR) . These objects in object repository are called *Test Objects*. UFT maps these objects to a standard UFT object class for recognizing these objects. For example, for a web-based application, text box is recognized as WebEdit and check box as WebCheckBox. If UFT does not find a standard mapping class for an object in GUI, then that object is recognized as WebElement.

During test execution, UFT looks for objects in AUT which matches Test Object's description. If UFT is successful in uniquely identifying the object, then it executes the desired action on the object as mentioned in the test. Else, UFT fails the test and records an object identification failure at the said point. UFT offers five ways of identifying objects in AUT:

- Object Description based object identification
- Visual Relation Identifier based object identification

- Smart Identification
- Ordinal Identifier based object identification
- Image based object identification (Insight)

When a test or component is executed, UFT searches for the object in UI that matches the description it learned (*test object*) without the ordinal identifier. If it cannot find any object that matches the description, or if more than one object matches the description, UFT uses the Visual Relation Identifier (if enabled) mechanism to uniquely locate the object. If UFT is not able to uniquely locate the Object in UI using this method, then it uses Smart Identification mechanism (if enabled) to uniquely identify the object. In case, Smart Identification mechanism also fails to identify the object, then the test object description is used together with the ordinal identifier only to uniquely locate the object.

In case Insight (image based recognition) has been used, then UFT looks for the Object that matches the image in UI.

When an object is added to OR, UFT captures the definition of the object. This definition of the object contains object properties that helps UFT uniquely identify the object in AUT at runtime. Figure 15.14 shows the 'Google Search Edit box' object details as captured by UFT.

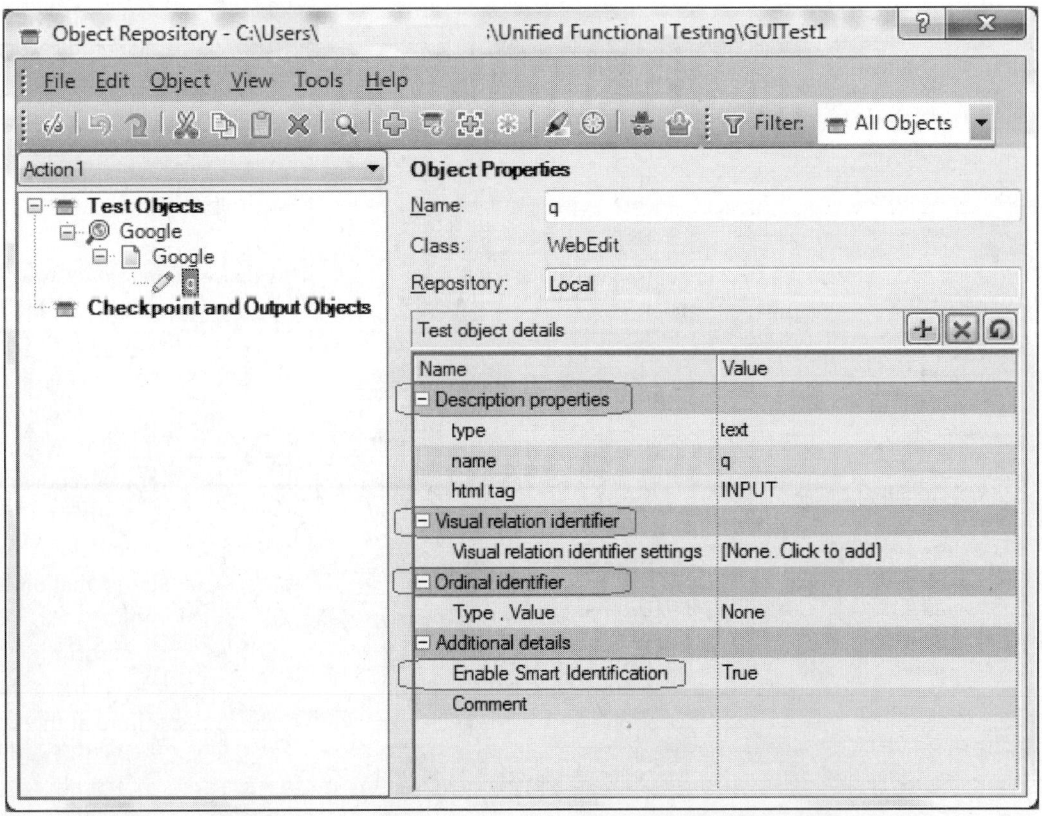

Figure 15.14 *Edit box object details as captured by UFT*

OBJECT IDENTIFICATION DIALOG BOX

When an object is added to OR, UFT captures the definition of the object. This definition of the object contains object properties that helps UFT uniquely identify the object in AUT at runtime. These include—object description properties and ordinal identifier. UFT also allows users to define visual relation identifier and image snapshot (Insight) of the object in OR.

UFT classifies the description properties (or object attributes) of the object as: Mandatory properties and Assistive properties.

Mandatory properties: are properties that UFT always learns for a particular test object class.

Assistive properties: are properties that UFT learns only if the mandatory properties that UFT learns for a particular object are not sufficient to uniquely locate the object. If several assistive properties are defined for an object class, then UFT learns one assistive property at a time and stops as soon as it creates a unique description for the object.

Ordinal identifier: is the index value or location value of the object. If the combination of all defined mandatory and assistive properties is not sufficient to uniquely locate an object in UI, then UFT also learns the value for the selected ordinal identifier.

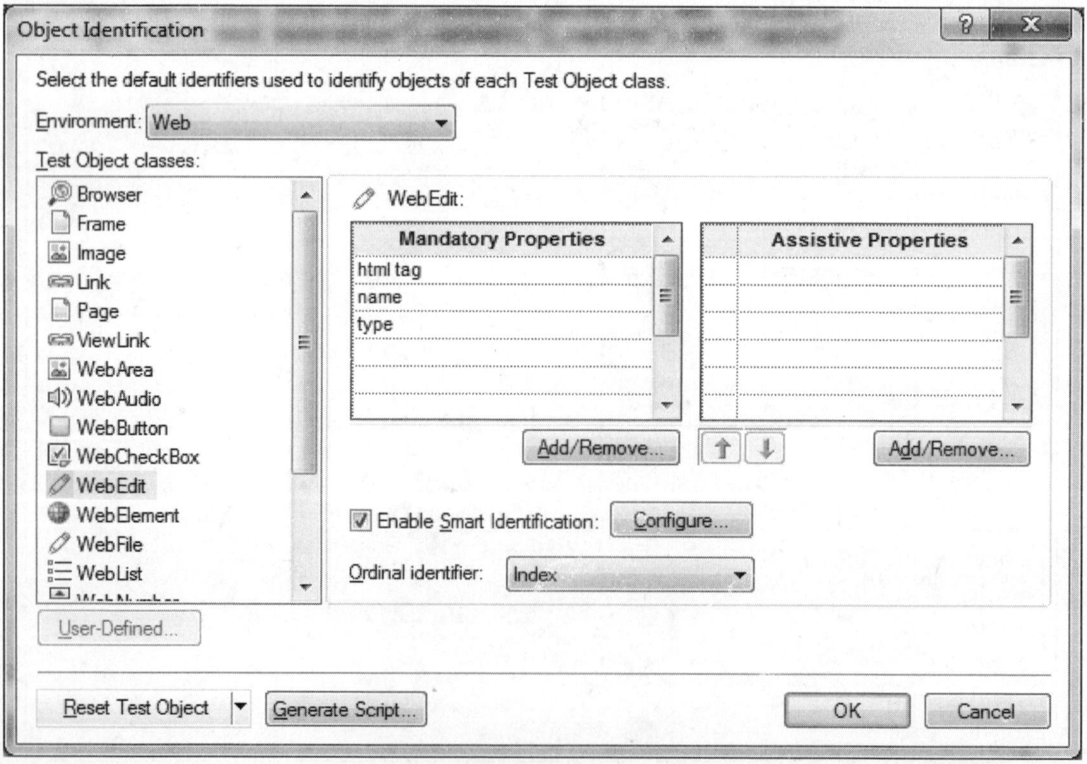

Figure 15.15 *Object identification dialog box*

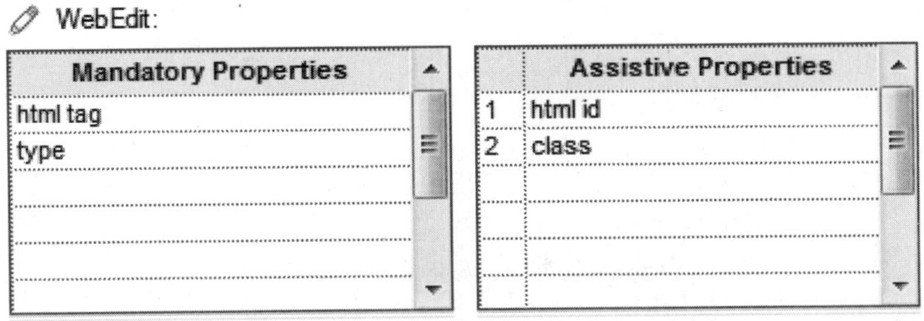

Figure 15.16 *Customized definition of mandatory and assistive properties of WebEdit test object*

An important question is how UFT decides:

- Which attributes of the object are to be treated as Mandatory properties?
- Which attributes of the object are to be treated as Assistive properties?
- Which ordinal identifier to capture – index or location?

UFT defines the above settings in *Object Identification* dialog box. This dialog box can be opened by selecting *Tools → Object Identification*. Figure 15.15 shows the object identification dialog box.

Object Identification dialog box defines the default identifier settings of all objects of different applications such as Web, Java, SAP, etc. Described below are the various features of this dialog box.

Environment dropdown Environment: Web : Users can view the default identifier settings of a specific add-in by selecting the add-in type from the Environment drop-down.

Test object classes frame: It displays all the test object classes of the selected Environment.

Mandatory properties and assistive properties frame: These show the default mandatory and assistive attributes of the selected object. When capturing an object to OR, UFT captures these attributes only to OR. In Fig. 15.15, the default mandatory properties specified for a WebEdit test class object are – html tag, name and type. When a web edit object is captured to object repository, UFT captures these attributes to OR.

How UFT Learns Object Description Properties

Assume mandatory and assistive properties for *WebEdit* test class object is defined as shown in the Fig. 15.16.

Here, *html tag* and *type* object attributes are defined as mandatory properties and *html id* and *class* are defined as assistive properties.

Now let's see, how UFT learns object identification information of a text box using the above setting. Figure 15.17 shows the identification attributes captured by UFT for search text box of Google Search page.

Here, UFT first captures all the mandatory properties of the object viz. *html tag* and *type* attribute of the object. Next, UFT checks if the captured attributes uniquely describe the object or in other words sufficient to uniquely locate the object in GUI. If the captured attributes are sufficient

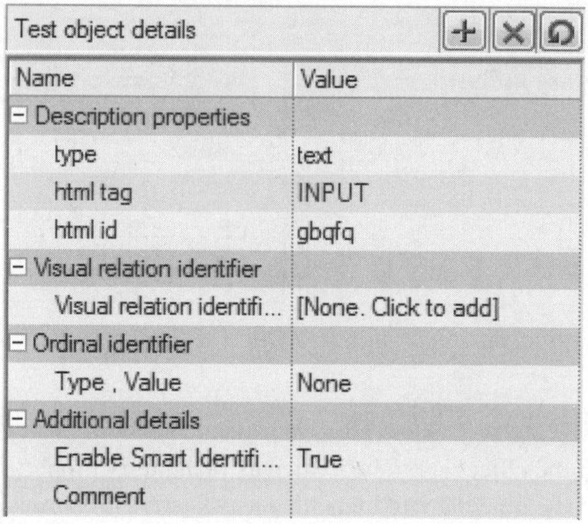

Figure 15.17 *Edit box object details as captured by UFT*

to uniquely describe (locate) the object, then UFT does not captures assistive properties and ordinal identifiers. Since, here the mandatory attributes are not sufficient to uniquely describe (locate) the object, UFT next captures the first assistive property of the element – *html id.* Now, UFT checks whether the captured mandatory properties (*html tag* and *type*) and assistive property (*html id*) uniquely describe the element. Here, since these three attributes *html tag, type* and *html id* uniquely describe the object, UFT does not capture rest of the assistive properties and ordinal identifiers. However, if the captured properties still does not uniquely describe the object, then UFT captures the next assistive property (*class*) of the object. Again UFT checks whether the currently captured mandatory and assistive properties (*html tag*, *type*, *html id* and *class*) uniquely describe the object. If not, then UFT again captures the next assistive property of the object. This process repeats till the captured object attributes are sufficient to uniquely describe the object or UFT has captured all the object attributes as defined in the *Object* Identification dialog box. In case, UFT has captured all the assistive attributes (as defined in *Object Identification* dialog box) and still is not able to uniquely describe the object, then UFT captures the ordinal identifiers of the object.

Add/Remove button (Add/Remove... ***)*** provides the flexibility to the user to configure mandatory and assistive properties. We will discuss in detail how to configure these properties in section 'Configuring Description Based Identification Mechanism' below.

Enable smart identification checkbox ☑ Enable Smart Identification: enables Smart Identification mechanism. Chapter 'Smart Identification' explains in detail how smart identification works.

Configure smart identification button Configure... enables users to configure smart identification mechanism of UFT. Section 'Configuring Smart Identification Mechanism' discusses in detail how to configure UFT Smart Identification mechanism.

Ordinal identifier dropdown Ordinal identifier: Index enables users to configure ordinal identifier object identification mechanism. Section 'Configuring Ordinal Identifier Identification Mechanism' discusses in detail how to configure UFT ordinal identifier mechanism.

Reset test object dropdown Reset Test Object enables user to rest the modified object identification settings to its default identification settings. It has three options – *Reset Test Object, Reset Environment* and *Reset All.*

Reset Option	Description
Reset Test Object	This option resets object identification settings of the selected test object to UFT defaults.
Reset Environment	This option resets object identification settings of the all the test objects of the selected Environment (UFT addin) to UFT defaults.
Reset All	This option resets object identification settings of the all the test objects of all the Environments (UFT addins) to UFT defaults..

Generate Script button Generate Script... enables users to generate an automation script (.vbs) that sets the current object identification settings. This code can be used to set the object identification settings programmatically using code. This feature is very useful to set the same object identification settings on multiple UFT computers.

> NOTES
>
> If Web object identifiers such as XPath and CSS properties are defined for the test objects, then they are used before the description properties. If one or more objects are found, UFT continues to identify the object using the description properties. For details, see the section on Web Object Identifiers (described in the HP Unified Functional Testing Add-ins Guide). Additional UFT-generated properties, such as source index or automatic XPath, may also affect the object identification process. You enable these properties in the Advanced Web Options tab of the Options dialog box (described in the HP Unified Functional Testing Addins Guide) (*Tools* → *Options* → *GUI Testing tab* → *Web* → *Advanced* node).

Chapter 16

Test Script Development

BUSINESS SCENARIO IDENTIFICATION

The automation developers need to interact with the business analysts, developers and testers to identify the business scenarios that need to be automated.

BUSINESS KNOWLEDGE GATHERING

Automation developers should gather the business knowledge required for automation. For business knowledge gathering, an automation developer should lay stress on:

1. How many test scenarios and test cases exist for the identified business scenario?
2. Graphical User Interface (GUI) screen workflow.
3. Test input data and expected data.
4. Verification points, including the method of verification of expected results – GUI verification or database verification.

Framework components or framework APIs (Application Programming Interfaces) are to be written first before writing the actual test. Framework APIs are to be used as building blocks to develop reusable business components. These reusable business components should then be used to develop tests. Business components are to be designed in a way that it implements the smallest reusable business functionality of the business scenario.

PLANNING SCRIPT DEVELOPMENT

In this step, automation developer should design the test data excel file. In addition, a checklist needs to be prepared, which should contain a list of:

1. Framework APIs that needs to be developed
2. Business components (actions) required to implement the business scenario and input and output parameters of the same.
3. Test scripts to be automated.
4. Functions to be designed or modified.

Adding Environment Variables

If some new environment or global variable is required for automation of the business scenario, it needs to be added to EnvVariable.vbs file.

Developing Framework APIs/ Designing Functions

Framework APIs and Functions listed down at planning stage need to designed/developed or modified as applicable at this step.

Creating/Updating Object Repository

New shared Object Repository (OR) to be created and objects related to the business scenario screens be added to the OR. If OR of this business module already exists, then only those objects to be added to OR that are not present in OR. Duplication of objects should be avoided.

Designing Reusable Actions

Each business component should be automated as an individual reusable action. Actions can have two parameters – input and output. Input parameter refers to the test input data that will be passed to the reusable actions by its calling action. Output parameters refer to the test output data such as actual data, pass/fail status, transaction id, and error messages that the reusable action sends back to its calling action. A test script can contain one or many actions (Fig. 16.1). Business components with similar input and output parameters need to be automated in the same test script itself. This will prevent unnecessary multiplication of test scripts. Lesser number of test scripts will make change identification an easier and quicker job.

Every reusable action should have verification points (checkpoints) to verify the business functionality. In addition, proper error-handling code should be written to handle the expected as well as unexpected exceptions. In no case, QTP should throw a pop error window. In case of an error, action script execution should stop and short and clear error messages should be sent to the calling action through output parameters. Once reusable actions have been developed, automation developers should carry out dry run and normal run in debug mode.

Dry run—Walkthrough or code review to identify compilation issues, spelling mistakes, variable declaration, code logic, logic flow defects, etc.

Debugging—Actions to be executed in debug mode with breakpoints and code errors need to be noted down. Once execution is over or the automation developer reaches a point where he or she cannot continue execution without script modification, script execution to be stopped and scripts be modified.

Designing Business Scenario Driver

Once business components have been automated, the automation developers can proceed with the development of business scenario driver script. Business scenario driver script needs to call various actions and functions sequentially to implement the identified business scenario.

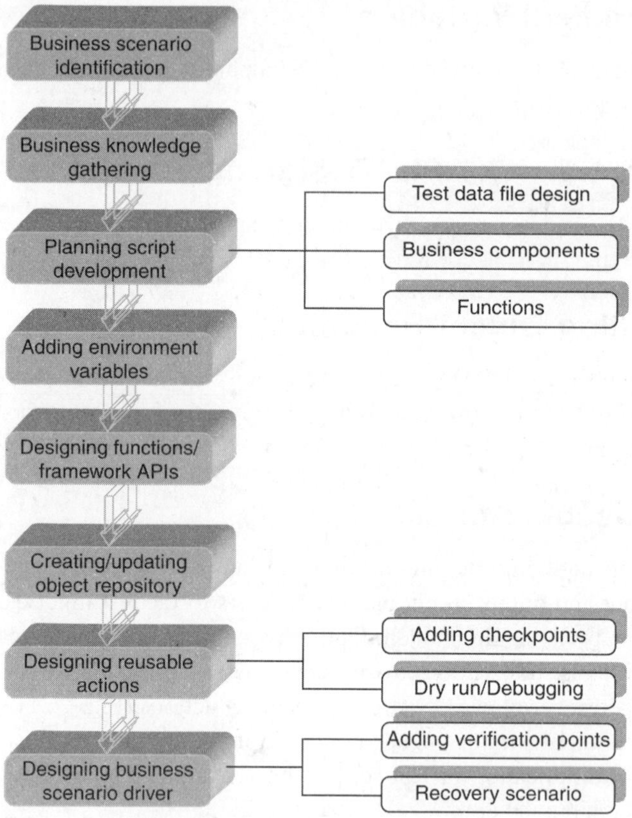

Figure 16.1 *Test script development*

Layout

1. Retrieve the test data from test data excel files.
2. Call various actions and functions sequentially to implement the business case.
3. Validation points for every action and function to identify the exact point and cause of failure.
4. Result log along with screenshots.
5. Recovery scenario to be associated with driver scripts, so that the driver script can be executed in unattended mode.

NOTES

1. In requirement gathering step, focus should not be on the in-depth business knowledge transfer. Automation developers should focus on gathering only those business aspects and data that are relevant to automation.
3. Duplication of objects on OR should be avoided.
4. Every reusable action and driver script should have proper verification points.
5. Recovery scenario to be designed in such a way that it handles both expected exceptions and unexpected run-time errors.

SCRIPTING METHODS

QTP provides following ways to write test scripts:

1. Record & Playback method
2. Object Repository (OR) method
3. Descriptive programming (DP) method
4. Hybrid method

Record and Playback Method

In *Record & Playback* method, QTP automatically generates a code and captures objects involved for all the activities we perform on application GUI. The captured objects are saved in local OR. The script needs to be customized as per requirement after recording is over.

Advantages

1. Automatic code generation.
2. Automatic capture of objects.

Disadvantages

1. *Least maintainable and reusable code*—Code is not user friendly and cannot be reused, as it contains hard-coded data.
2. *Bulky OR*—Most of the times, same object is captured again and again, which increases the size of OR unnecessarily.
3. *Code customization needed*—Code needs to be customized once recording is over to remove hard coding and to add comments.
4. *High maintenance cost*—High maintenance cost involved.

Figure 16.2 shows *Plan Travel* page of a train journey planner application. This page allows users to search for trains, check reservation availability status and book the ticket. When user clicks on 'Find Trains' button, the application refreshes the page and displays list of trains with option to book the ticket, get train fare, show train route and show train availability status. Figure 16.3 shows the code generated after recording activities on the application shown in the Fig. 16.2. We observe in Fig. 16.3 that Page object :: IRCTC :: - Plan My Plan Travel_2 has been captured twice in OR, though the properties of the object remain the same.

> **NOTES** It is always advised not to use *Record & Playback* method of any automation tool to develop scripts. Generally, this method results in least maintainable and reusable code with high maintenance cost involved.

In addition, in line 26, WebElements are captured, which will make it difficult to parameterize the 'station from' WebList.

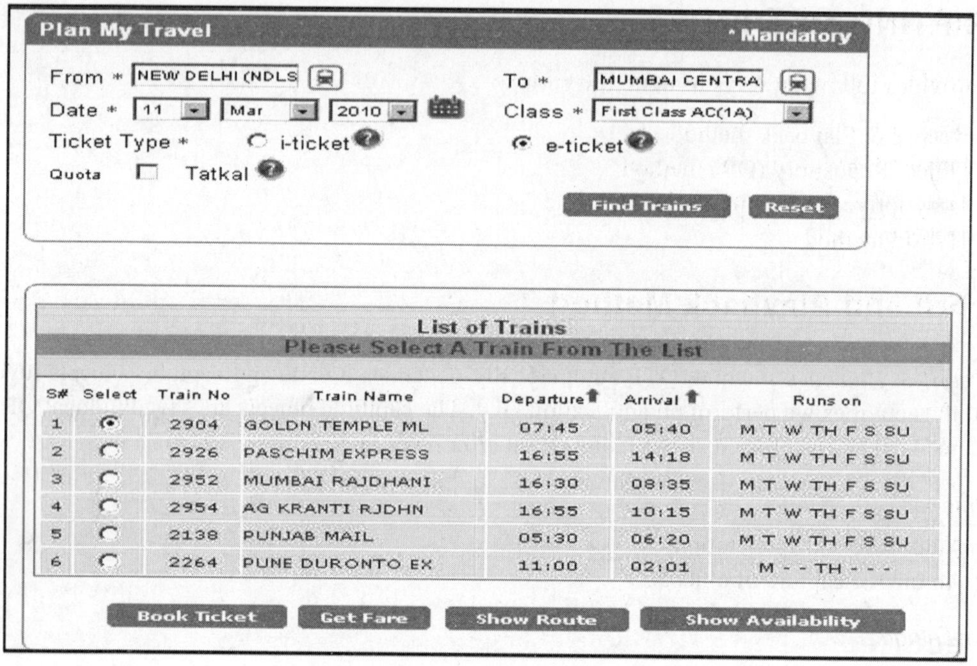

Figure 16.2 *Application under test*

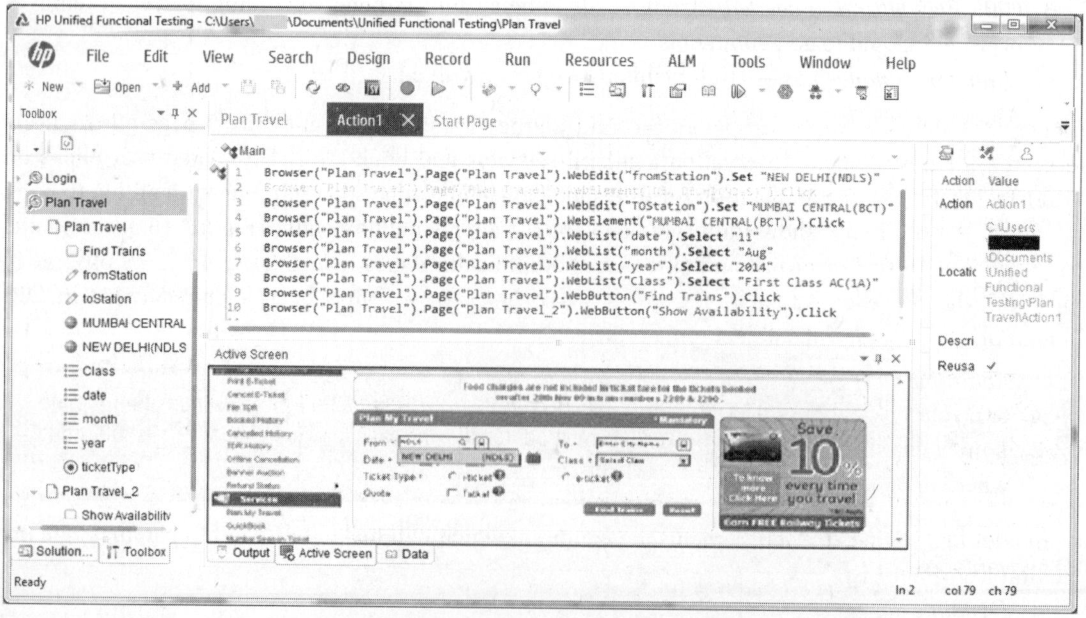

Figure 16.3 *Record & Playback method*

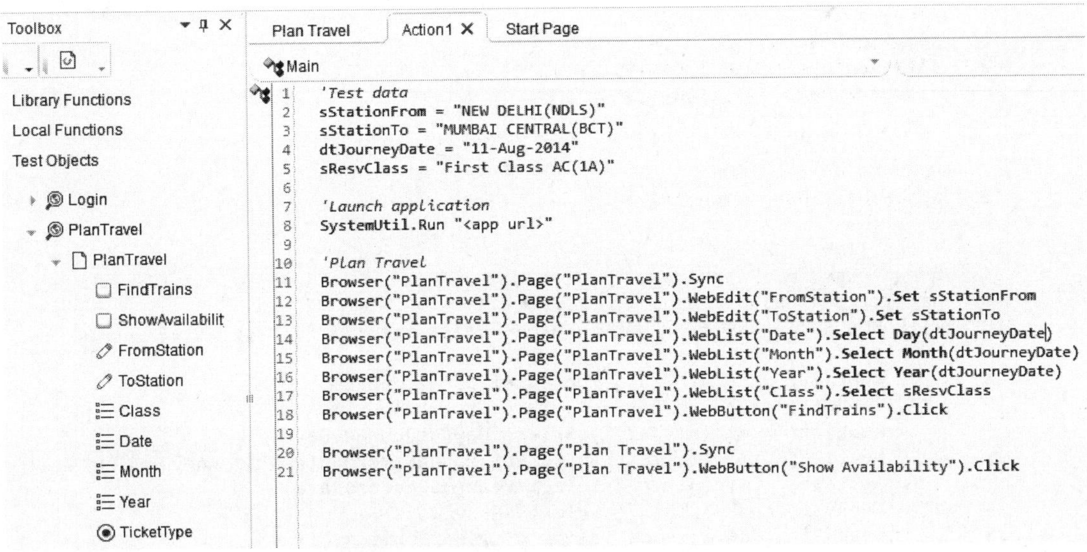

Figure 16.4 *Object Repository method*

Object Repositoy (OR) Method

In *OR* method, GUI objects are first captured in OR. Thereafter, we start writing the code to interact with GUI. Code quality is of high standards, as programmers are involved in writing of the code. Figure 16.4 shows the code written using OR method for application shown in Fig. 16.2.

Scripting Process

1. Turn off Smart Identification from test script.
2. Create a shared OR.
3. Capture required objects in shared OR.
4. Change logical name of objects, if required.
5. Change/modify object properties, if required.
6. Associate OR to test script.
7. Write code using OR to develop the framework APIs/functions and business components.
8. Write driver scripts to call various business components to implement a business scenario.

Advantages

1. *Re-usable code*—Since code is handwritten, programmers can write pieces of code with minimum or no hard coding that can be reused to automate different business scenarios.
2. *Low maintenance cost*—Changes made to objects in shared OR is reflected in all the scripts where that shared OR is used.
3. *Readable code*—Code is readable and easy to understand.

Disadvantages

1. *Dynamic objects*—Dynamic objects are those objects whose properties keep on changing. Sometimes, by using OR approach, sometimes it is difficuls.to uniquely locate a test object or a set of test objects.

```
'Test data
sStationFrom = "NEW DELHI(NDLS)"
sStationTo = "MUMBAI CENTRAL(BCT)"
dtJourneyDate = "11-Aug-2014"
sResvClass = "First Class AC(1A)"

'Launch application
SystemUtil.Run "<app url>"

'Plan Travel
browserName = "Plan Travel"
pageTitle = "Plan Travel"
With Browser("name:=" & browserName).Page("title:=" & pageTitle)
    .Sync
    .WebEdit("name:=fromStation").Set sStationFrom
    .WebEdit("name:=toStation").Set sStationTo
    .WebList("html id:=date").Select Day(dtJourneyDate)
    .WebList("html id:=month").Select MonthName(Month(dtJourneyDate))
    .WebList("html id:=yr").Select Year(dtJourneyDate)
    .WebList("name:=Class").Select sResvClass
    .WebButton("name:=Find Trains","type=Submit").Click

    .Sync
    .WebButton("name:=Show Availability").Click
End With
```

Figure 16.5 *DP code for login to IRCTC*

> To turn-off Smart Identification, navigate *File → Settings...* 'Test Settings' dialog box will open up. Select tab Run. Select the checkbox 'Disable Smart Identifica- tion during the run session.

Descriptive Programming

In DP method of scripting, QTP programmers code both the object properties and action to be taken on these objects (Fig. 16.5). OR is not used in DP method of script development. Figure 16.5 shows the descriptive code written using DP method for application shown in Fig. 16.2.

Advantages

1. Script development can be started even if AUT GUI is not ready.
2. Provides more flexibility to handle Dynamic objeced.

Disadvantages

1. *High maintenance cost*—Since all object properties are specified using code, if object property of some object changes, it would become a cumbersome task to identify test scripts and modify them. Using DP only in test script bears all the disadvantages that are otherwise associated with local OR.

Booked Ticket History

S#	Transaction ID	PNR Number	From	To	Resv Amount
1	T15664098	P22659593678	NDLS	HYD	976.0
2	T15664001	P28764988097	SCB	PUNE	889.0
3	T15234578	P75890589095	MUM	CHE	989.0

Cancelled Ticket History

S#	Transaction ID	PNR Number	From	To	Refund Amount
1	T15676589	P22659579878	HYD	MAS	976.0
2	T15664551	P67849880973	HRY	PUNE	889.0
3	T15234898	P75856890954	CHE	NDLS	989.0

Figure 16.6 *WebTable*

> NOTES: Descriptive method of scripting to be used only in scenarios where OR method fails to uniquely identize the object or the set of objects. Using completely descriptive method of scripting results iy high code maintenance effort.

Hybrid Method

Hybrid method of scripting uses both OR and DP methods to develop scripts. Shared OR is created and associated with the test scripts. DP method is used in scenarios where GUI objects cannot be automated using OR method, viz. dynamic objects).

Suppose, in a web application, the booked ticket history page displays details of booked and cancelled tickets as shown in the Fig. 16.6. The page displays list of last 10 booked and last 10 cancelled tickets in last 30 days. However, if in last 30 days a user has booked, say, only 3 tickets, then only three ticket details will be displayed. It implies that the number of transaction ids displayed on the page is dynamic in nature and would vary from one run to another. Assume, the requirement is to identify all *transaction id* links displayed on the page for booked tickets.,

Below are the two reasons why this scenario is not feasible to automate using OR approach only:

- Number of 'Transaction ID' links displayed on the page varies from time to time. Suppose at test design time only two links exist which were added to OR, But at run-time there are three links. This means the test code (based on OR approach only) will never know that third link exists. In this case, it is never possible to know at test design time how many links will exist at run-time. So, it is not possible to automate this scenario using OR approach only.
- The 'Transaction ID' links refer to the actual booked ticket 'transaction ids'. Suppose at design time there were 15 tickets booked which got added to OR. Assume during the time gap between test design and test run time, 20 more tickets got booked. Now during test run, the application will display last 10 booked tickets transaction ids. Since, these link objects were never added to OR and the ones added are not displayed on GUI, UFT tests will fail with 'object not found;' error. Since, these links are dynamic objects, it is not possible to automate this scenario by adding these link objects to OR.

```
'Open ticket history page
Browser("PlanTravel").Page("PlanTravel").Link("TicketHistory").Click

'Locate transaction ids of all booked tickets
Set oDescTranIds = Description.Create
oDescTranIds("micclass").Value = "Link"
oDescTranIds("name").value = "T.*"

Set oTable = Browser("PlanTravel").Page("PlanTravel").WebTable("BookedTicketHistory")
Set colTranIds = oTable.ChildObjects(oDescTranIds)
For iterator = 0 To colTranIds.count-1 Step 1
    Print colTranIds(iterator).getROProperty("name")
Next
```

Figure 16.7 *QTP code developed using hybrid method*

Now let's see how this scenario can be automated using DP approach. DP allows to locate all the transaction id links during run-time. Using DP, a test code can be written that dynamically looks for all 'transaction id' link objects of booked ticket history table.

Figure 16.7 shows the DP code to locate these dynamic elements.

Figure 16.8 shows the output of the code of Fig. 16.7.

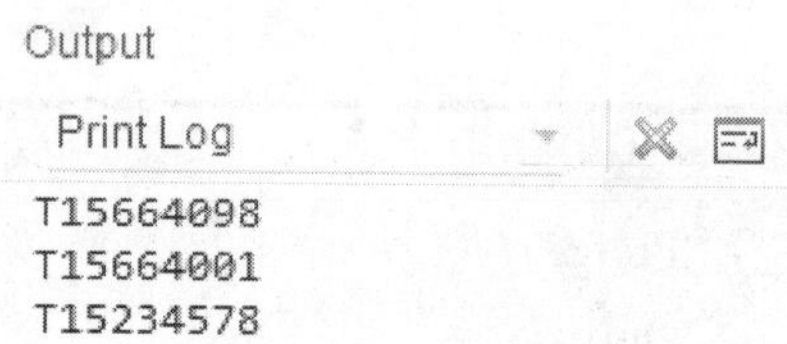

Figure 16.8 *Output of fig 16.7 coe*

SCRIPTING GUIDELINES

1. Script should not contain any message boxes, input boxes, or anything that requires manual intervention from the user.
2. Proper error-handling and recovery scenarios should be used in all scripts.
3. All test case prerequisites should be taken care of in the script.
4. Script command failure should be eliminated.
5. Only one instance of AUT should be opened at a time while playing back the script.
6. Very clear status messages should be used, which let the user know whether a particular step in the test cases has passed or failed.
7. All requisite transaction id, pass/fail statuses, error messages, etc. should be provided in the result log, which makes debugging easier in case of script failure.
8. Checking of business scenario workflow and exit conditions is required at the appropriate places.
9. Unnecessary verification points should be removed (to minimize the playback time). However, verification points should be included when required for a business scenario.
10. While picking up clipboard values from putty, ensure putty is maximized and the screen is cleared before picking up any value.
11. There should not be any hard coding in the scripts. For example, while inputting values to text fields.
12. Functions should be made use of wherever possible.

13. Ensure unique search criteria are specified as far as possible.
14. Ensure minimal or no use of WebElements in scripts.
15. Sync should be used whenever there is a change in page properties.
16. Appropriate delays should be built into the script to provide for differences in response times across environments.
17. All transaction flow status should be verified and handled appropriately.
18. Focused window should always be maximized.
19. Entry and exit points of an action (script) should be same.
20. Turn off Smart Identification while scripting.
21. Object Identification settings must not be changed frequently.
22. Proper indentation and comments should be placed in scripts.
23. Particular script layout should be followed (refer Appendix A).

QUICK TIPS

- ✓ Prefer *Hybrid* method of scripting.
- ✓ Only one instance of AUT should be opened at a time.
- ✓ Completely descriptive code to be avoided.
- ✓ No message boxes to be used in scripts.
- ✓ Turn off Smart Identification whle developing scripnt.

PRACTICAL QUESTIONS

1. Explain the test script development process.
2. What are the various methods of scripting in QTP?
3. Why is it necessary to avoid descriptive code completely?
4. Which method of scripting is to be preferred and why?
5. Explain two scenarios where descriptive code is to be used.

Chapter 17

Environment Variables

Environment variables in UFT are similar to global variables in other programming languages. These variables are used to define AUT login details, application URL, database connectivity details, etc. These variables can be accessed across any test script. The values of these variables remain unchanged unless it is modified programmatically.

WHEN TO USE ENVIRONMENT VARIABLES

The purpose of using environment variables is to ensure that the test script can be executed against multiple environments without any code change. For example, if the same test script needs to be run against different databases then only the database environment variable values need to be changed. In addition, if it is required to test the application with different sets of users, then only the environment variable values related to AUT login credentials needs to be changed. Environment variables can also be used when a global constant variable value needs to be accessed across different actions or across different test scripts, For example, updating of execution status (pass/fail) by a called action to its calling action.

The value of user-defined environment variable can be set as follows:

```
Syntax : Environment(VariableName) = NewValue
```

Example:

```
Declare an environment variable "AppUsrNm" and assign it value
"DefaultUsr."
        Environment.Value("AppUsrNm")  = "DefaultUsr"
Or,     Environment("AppUsrNm")   = "DefaultUsr"
```

The value of environment variable can be retrieved as follows:

```
Syntax : CurrentValue  = Environment(VariableName)
```

Example:
```
Retrieve the value of environment variable "AppUsrNm"
sEnvVarValue = Environment("AppUsrNm")
```

HOW TO DEFINE ENVIRONMENT VARIABLES

UFT offers three ways of defining environment variables:

1. Built-in
2. User-defined internal
3. User-defined external
    (a) .xml environment variable file
    (b) .vbs environment variable file

1. **Built-in:** Built-in variables are those environment variables that are provided by UFT by default. These variables are read only and represent information about the test script, action, and the computer environment on which the test script is run. These variables provide valuable information such as the path of the folder where test script is located, the path of the results folder, and the name of the action, action iteration, or the OS version.

    The complete list of built-in environment variables can be seen in the test settings window. To view built-in environment variables, navigate *File → Settings ... → Environment* (Fig. 17.1).

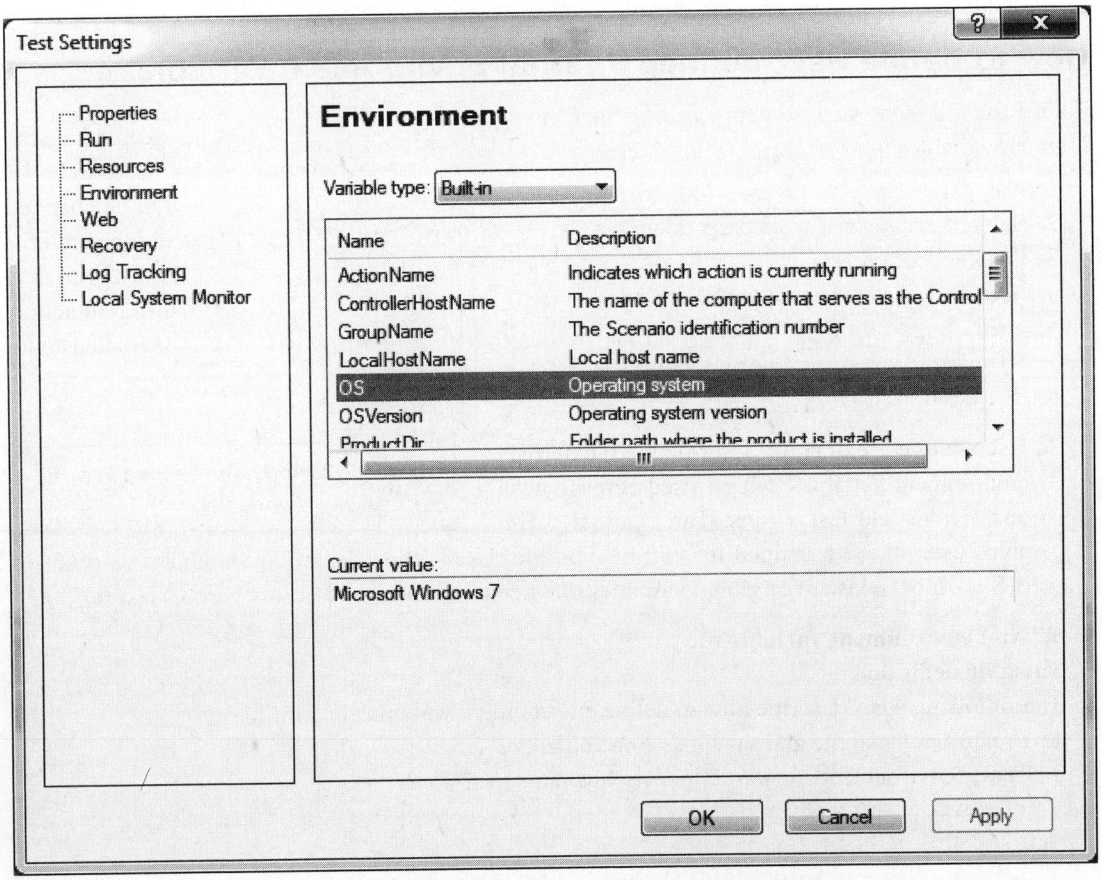

Figure 17.1 *Built-in environment variables*

The "Name" column specifies the environment variable and the "Description" column describes the variable. "Current Value" field displays the value of the variable (if it is not a run-time variable). Few of the in-built environment variables are explained in the following list.

- ***ActionIteration***: Indicates which action iteration is currently executing.
- ***ActionName***: Name of the action currently executing.
- ***ResultDir***: Folder path where current test reports are saved.
- ***TestDir***: Folder path where the test script in execution is located.
- ***TestIteration***: Indicates which test iteration is currently executing.
- ***TestName***: Name of the test script in execution.
- ***UserName***: Windows login user name.

2. **User-defined internal:** UFT provides the flexibility to define new environment variables as per test automation requirements. The scope of these variables is limited to the test script in which they are defined. We can design our own environment variables in the Environment tab of the test settings window. To define or view user-defined environment variables navigate *File → Settings ... → Environment* and then select *User-defined* from the drop-down list. The purpose of user-defined variable is to parameterize test script or action-specific variables such as the number of iterations of execution and test output data.

How to Define User-defined Internal Environment Variables

Follow the following steps to define user-defined environment variables in a test script (Fig. 17.2):

1. Navigate *File → Settings ... → Environment.*
2. Select *User-defined* from drop-down list.
3. Click on button [+].
4. *Add New Environment Parameter* window will open.
5. Specify the variable name and value.
6. Click button [OK].

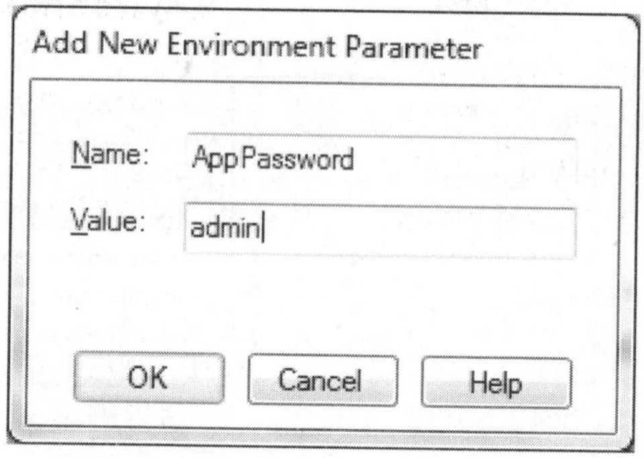

Figure 17.2 *Add user-defined internal variables*

3. **User-defined external:** User-defined external environment variables can be used across various actions and test scripts. The external variables can either be defined in .xml or .vbs file. User-defined external variables are used to define global constant or global variables that need to be accessed across various test scripts.

a. **.xml environment variable file**

Variable definition

The following steps describe how to define environment variables in .xml file

1. Create a notepad file and save it as *FileName*.xml
2. Create environment and variable tag-value pairs as follows.

```
<Environment>
        <Variable>
                <Name>DbSIDName</Name>
```

```
            <Value>ORA10G</Value>
        </Variable>
        <Variable>
            <Name>DbUserName</Name>
            <Value>Admin</Value>
        </Variable>
<Environment>
```

3. To add a new environment variable, insert the following code in between <Environment> … </Environment>

```
<Variable>
        <Name>Name_of_variable</Name>
        <Value>Value_of_variable</Value>
</Variable>
```

4. Save the file and close it.

Loading .xml environment file in a test script

Follow the following steps to load an .xml file in a test script (Fig. 17.3):

1. Navigate *File → Settings … → Environment.*
2. Select *User-defined* from drop-down list.
3. Select the load variable checkbox.
4. Specify the file path of .xml file
5. Click button *Apply*

User-defined internal variables appear in black color while user-defined external variables appear in blue color.

Alternatively, .xml file can also be loaded programmatically.

```
Syntax : Environment.LoadFromFile FileNamewithFilePath
```

Example: `Environment.LoadFromFile  "Z:\Config\EnvVar.xml"`

There is one limitation to XML environment files. Only one XML file can be loaded at a time. If another XML file is loaded at runtime then the previous one is lost.

b. .vbs environment variable file

Variable definition

The following steps describe how to define environment variables in a .vbs file:

1. Create a notepad file and save it as *FileName*.vbs
2. Create environment variable and assign value to it as follows.

```
Syntax : Environment.Value(VarName) = VarValue
       : Environment(VarName) = VarValue
```

Example:

```
Environment.Value("DbSID")      = "ORA10G"
Environment.Value("DbUserNm") = "admin_user"
```

3. Save the file and close it.

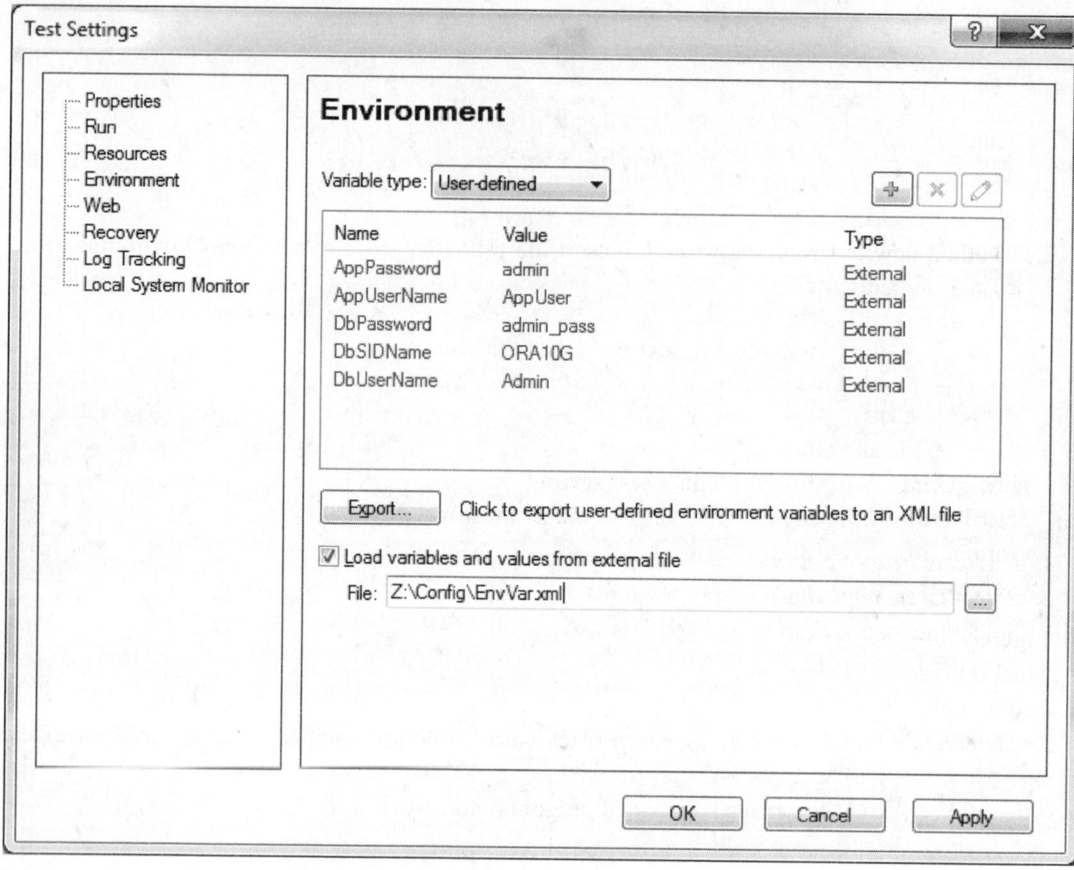

Figure 17.3 *External environment variables*

Advantage:

- **Load multiple environment files:** Multiple .vbs files can be associated to a test script. In case of XML file, only one XML file can be loaded.
- **Global variable and arrays:** In a .vbs file, global arrays and global constant variables can also be defined. These variables can be used across all test scripts and actions.

  Suppose that we need to execute an SQL (standard query language) query on AUT database to compare the actual and expected results. We can design a function that will receive the SQL query as input parameter and will output the query results. The problem here is function can return only one value. To overcome these situations, we can use global array. This array will be available to the function as well as to the test script. When function will write any values in this array, test script can easily read these values. VBS file provides the flexibility to declare static as well as dynamic arrays. In .xml file, global constant variables or global arrays cannot be defined.
- **High readability and low maintainability:** VBS environment variables are more readable as compared to .xml environment variable. Both variable name and its value are declared in one

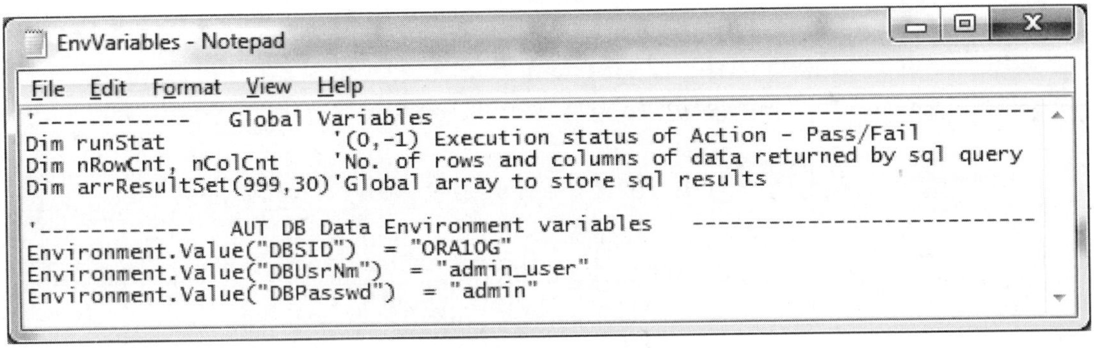

Figure 17.4 *EnvVariable.vbs*

line. XML environment variables exist in tag-value pairs. It requires four lines of code to declare one environment variable in XML format while the same can be done in one line in VBS format. Improved readability and lesser lines of code make it easier to modify environment values as and when required.

Figure 17.4 shows how to define environment and global variables in a .vbs file. “arResultSet” is a global array used to store SQL query results. “nRowCnt” and “nColCnt” store the number of rows and columns of data returned by SQL query.

Declaring global constant variables

```
Const AppUrl = "<application url>"
```

Loading .vbs environment file in a test script

Described below are the steps to associate a .vbs file to UFT test scripts (Fig. 17.5):

1. Navigate *File → Settings … → Resources.*
2. Click on button [+].
3. Specify the complete path of .vbs file.
4. Click button *Apply*

Alternatively, .vbs file can also be loaded programmatically.

```
Syntax : ExecuteFile FileName_with_FilePath
```

Example: `ExecuteFile "Z:\Config\EnvVariables.vbs"`

Let us assume that,

```
EnvVariable1.vbs
   Environment.Value("DBSID") = "ORA10G"
```

> **NOTES** In case two different environment files have the same environment variable name (or global variable name), the one nearer to the top will be used. For example, suppose that we have two actions named “Driver” and “BusinessComponent” with environment files EnvVariable1.vbs and EnvVariable2.vbs respectively. Let us say Environment.Value(“DBSID”) is used in both environment files.

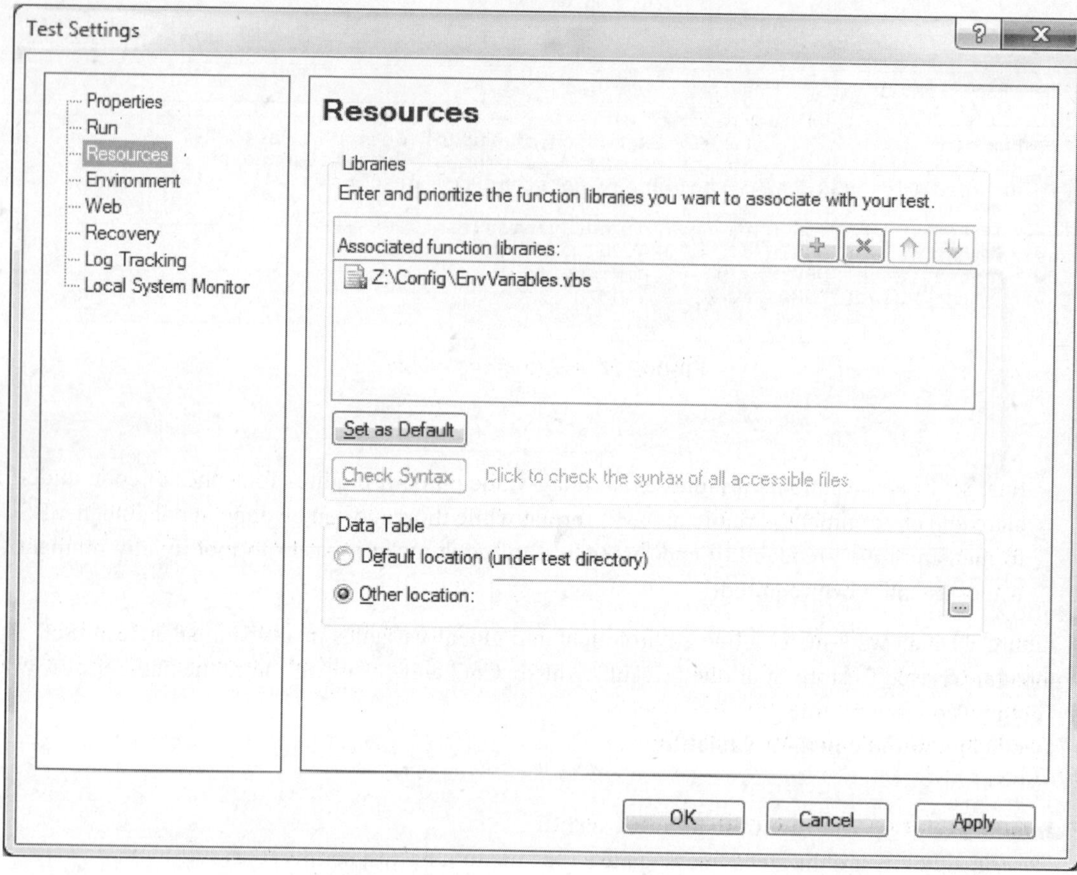

Figure 17.5 *Loading environment variable file to a test script*

```
EnvVariable2.vbs
   Environment.Value("DBSID") = "ORA11i"
```

Now, suppose that action "Driver" calls the action "BusinessComponent." Then in this case since EnvVariable1.vbs is at the top in hierarchy, value of Environment.Value("DBSID") will be "ORA10G." This value will be valid for both "Driver" and "BusinessComponent" action.

Clear Value of an Environment Variable

Value of an environment variable can be reset by using *Empty* or *Nothing*.

```
'Declare environment variable
Environment("BookTitle") = "Master Test Automation & UFT"

'Check the existence of environment variable
If IsEnvExist(Environment("BookTitle")) Then  'Returns True
   Environment("BookTitle") = Nothing
End If
```

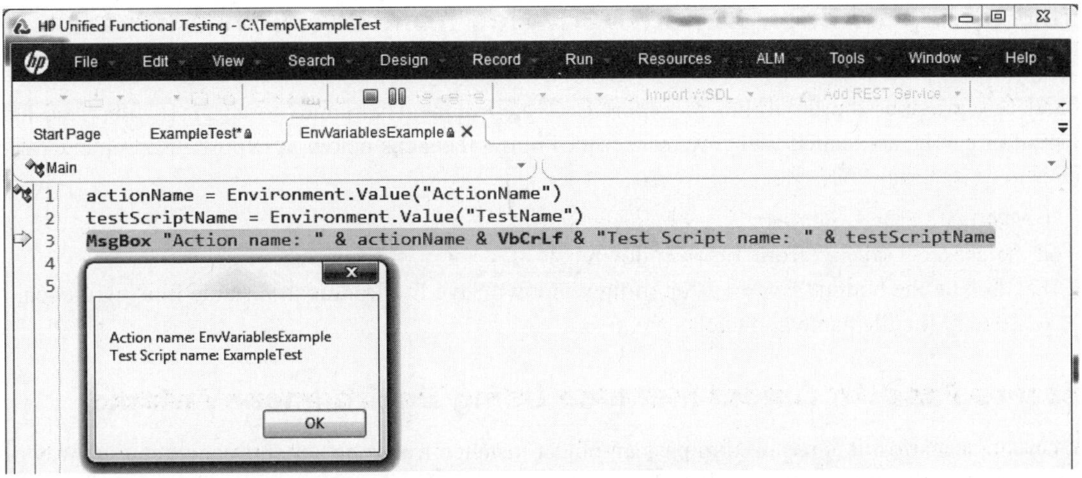

Figure 17.6 *Code to access environment variables during run-time*

```
'Check the existence of environment variable
Msgbox  IsEnvExist(Environment("BookTitle"))  'Output: False
```

How to Access Environment Variables in Test Scripts (Fig. 17.6)

Syntax : Environment.Value(*environment_variable_name*)

Example:

```
sActionName = Environment.Value("ActionName")
sAppUserName = Environment.Value("AppUserName")
sDbSID = Environment("DbSID")
```

How to Load XML Environment File during Run-Time

The following example uses the *ExternalFileName* property of *Environment* object to check whether an XML environment file is loaded or not. If not, then it loads a specific XML file and displays the name of the environment file and one of its environment variables.

```
'Check if external XML environment file is loaded or not. If not load it.
sEnvFileNm = Environment.ExternalFileName
If sEnvFileNm = "" Then
   Environment.LoadFromFile("Z:\Environment\Environment.xml")
End
'Display the environment file name
Print Environment.ExternalFileName
'Display the environment variable value
Print Environment("VariableName")
```

How to Export Environment Variables from UFT Environment Tab to An External XML File

QuickTest provides the flexibility to export UFT environment variables to an XML file. This file thereafter can be associated with any test script. Follow the steps below to export environment variables to an external XML file.

1. Navigate *File → Settings ... → Environment.*
2. Select *User-defined* from the drop-down list.
3. Click on the button "Export." A pop-up window "Save Environment Variable File" will open.
4. Specify the file name and click save.

How to Pass An Object Instance Using Environment Variable

In certain scenarios, it is required to pass an object instance from one action to another. One way of doing is to use environment variables for storing the object instance as string. This way the object reference will be available to all actions within for the same run-session.

```
'Save object reference in an environment variable
Environment("oBrowser") = Browser("creationtime:=0")
Set oBrowser = Environment("oBrowser")
oBrowser.Sync
```

How to Store Arrays in Environment Variable

As we have discussed earlier, global arrays cannot be declared in XML files. Suppose that we have designed a function that extracts value from a webtable and stores it in an array. One option is to pass an array as input parameter to the function. Another option of implementing the same is use of environment variable for storing arrays. As environment variable can be accessed from any action throughout its life, values of the array can be accessed easily from any of the actions. This will prevent the need of explicitly passing an array. QuickTest throws a run-time error if an attempt is made to store a static array in an environment variable. The solution is to save the array reference in another variable and then pass this array reference to the environment variable.

```
'Create a static array of fixed length
Dim arrStatic(4)

'Assign values to array
arrStatic(1) = 1
arrStatic(2) = "Two"
arrStatic(3) = "This is an array"

'Assign array reference to another variable
arrDynamic = arrStatic

'Assign the dynamic variable to the environment variable
```

```
Environment("DynamicArray") = arrDynamic

'Print array values
Print Environment("DynamicArray")(3) 'Output: "This is an array"

'Assign the array from environment variable to another variable
arrPrevious = Environment("DynamicArray")

'Print array values
Print arrPrevious(3)                 'Output: "This is an array"
```

QUICK TIPS

- ✓ Avoid using multiple environment files as this will make the maintenance of environment files costly and difficult.
- ✓ Avoid duplication of the environment variables.
- ✓ Use only one environment file. Vary the values of environment variable to execute in different environments. A copy of this environment file could be created for temporary use in scenarios where two different driver scripts need to be executed in two different environments.
- ✓ Use VBScript file to define environment variables and arrays.

PRACTICAL QUESTIONS

1. What are the various ways in which environment variables can be defined in UFT?
2. What is the difference between internal and external environment variables?
3. What are the disadvantages of using XML environment file?
4. Why VBScript environment file is to be preferred over XML environment file? What are the advantages of using .vbs environment file?
5. How is a .vbs file associated to a test script?
6. How does one access the environment variables inside the test script?
7. Suppose that there are two environment files loaded in a test script with "EnvVariable1.vbs" higher in hierarchy than "EnvVariable2.vbs." The environment variables are as follows:

   ```
   EnvVariable1.vbs
      Environment("DbName") = "Oracle9i"
   EnvVariable2.vbs
      Environment("DbName") = "Oracle10G"
   ```

   What will be the value of the above environment variable inside the test script during run-time?
8. Suppose that there are two test scripts: Test1 and Test2. Test1 calls Test2. Environment files "EnvVariable1.vbs" is associated with Test1 and "EnvVariable2.vbs" is associated with Test2. The environment variables of the two files are as follows:

   ```
   EnvVariable1.vbs
      Environment("DbName") = "Oracle9i"
   ```

```
EnvVariable2.vbs
    Environment("DbName") = "Oracle10G"
```

What will be the value of the above environment variable inside the test script during run-time?

8. Suppose that there are two test scripts: Test1 and Test2. Test1 calls Test2. Environment files "EnvVariable1.vbs" is associated with Test1 and "EnvVariable2.vbs" is associated with Test2. The environment variables of the two files are as follows:

```
EnvVariable1.vbs
    Environment("DbName") = "Oracle9i"
EnvVariable2.vbs
    Environment("DbName") = "Oracle10G"
```

   a. What will be the value of the above environment variable when Test1 is executed without any call to Test2?
   b. What will be the value of the above environment variable when Test2 is executed separately?
   c. What will be the value of the above environment variable in Test1 before and after the call to test script Test2?
   d. What will be the value of the above environment variable in Test2 when Test2 is called from Test1?

Chapter 18

Library

Library is a collection of functions, classes, variables, etc. It contains VBScript code and data that provide services to various QuickTest actions. Library files allow one-point sharing and changing of code and data across all test scripts in a modular fashion. Changes made to variables value or function definition is automatically passed on to all the test scripts that access it. During run-time too, changes made to global variable values by one part of the code can be accessed and used by other part of the code. Designing of function helps reducing code redundancy and maximizing code reusability. Library files in UFT can be designed in three ways:

1. .qfl file (UFT function library),
2. .vbs file (visual basic script), and
3. .txt file (text).

CREATING A NEW LIBRARY FILE

Functions are written in library file. A library file can be created in QTP by following the steps.

1. Navigate File → New → Function Library.
2. New library file will open; here, we can write our functions.
3. Click Save button.
4. Save the file as .vbs, .qfl, or .txt as desired.

Figure 18.1 shows an example of library file containing two functions – fnA and fnB. Functions designed in VBScript can receive multiple input values but can return only one value. The parameters can be passed to functions either by value or by reference. If either of 'ByVal' or 'ByRef' is not specified while declaring input parameters of the function, then by default the variable is passed by reference. When a variable is passed as 'ByVal,' then inside function, the value of the variable will be copied in another local variable and all operations will be performed on the copy of that variable only. When the function exits, the original value of the variable is restored. If a variable is passed by reference, then all operations inside the function are performed on the original variable. When the function exits, the modified value of the variable is reflected in the test script.

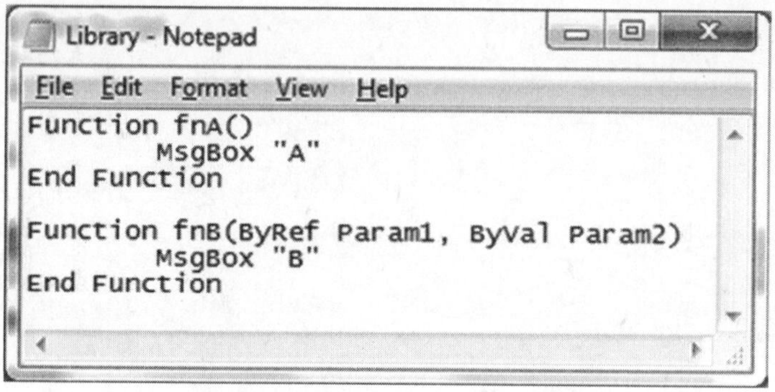

Figure 18.1 *Function library file*

ASSOCIATING A LIBRARY FILE TO A TEST SCRIPT

UFT provides two ways of loading functions to an action or test – Static functional load and Dynamic function load. In static function load, the sail function library file is associated with the action or test as resource. In dynamic function call, the said function library is loaded at run-time when the code to dynamically load the function library runs.

Static Load of Function Library

Functions of library file are accessible to the test script only when the library file is associated it or to one of the test scripts above its hierarchy (Fig. 18.2). The following steps show how to associate a library file to a test script.

1. Navigate Test → Settings …
2. Test Settings window opens up. Click on tab Resources.
3. Click on button +.
4. Specify the complete path of .vbs, .qfl, or .txt file.
5. Click button *Apply*.

Alternatively, *Library* files can also be loaded programmatically.

```
Syntax : ExecuteFile FileName_With_FilePath
```

Example: `ExecuteFile "Z:\Library\library.vbs"`

> **NOTES** If two or more functions with same name are present in two or more library files, then the function of that library file will be valid, which is top most in the hierarchy. Suppose that two library file 'LibraryA' and 'LibraryB' have a function with name 'fnPrintMessage.'

```
LibraryA
   Function fnPrintMessage()
      MsgBox "Hierarchy Position : A"
   End Function
```

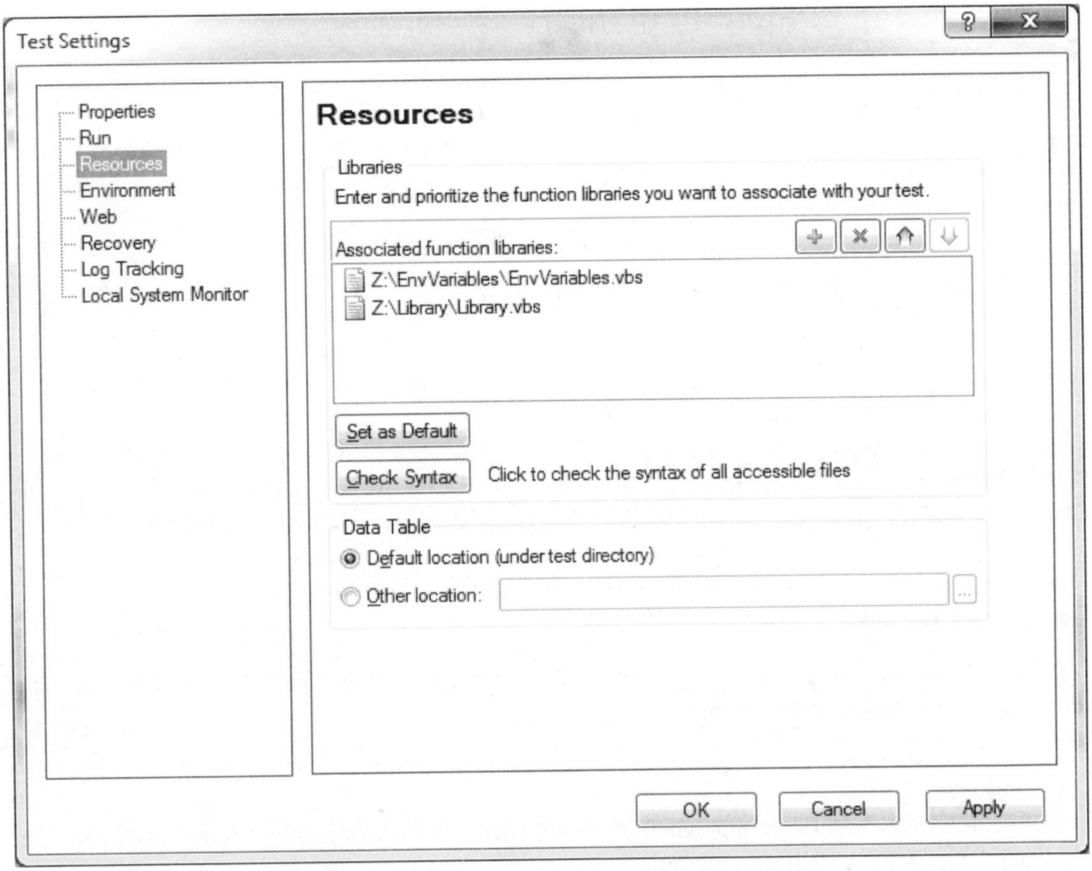

Figure 18.2 *Associating a library file to a test script*

```
LibraryB
   Function fnPrintMessage()
      MsgBox "Hierarchy Position : B"
   End Function
```

Suppose that 'LibraryB' is at the top of the hierarchy. Now, when 'fnPrintMessage' will be called in any test script, then the output will be 'Hierarchy Position: B.'

Similarly, suppose that there are two actions 'ActionA' and 'ActionB.' 'LibraryA' is associated with 'ActionA' and 'LibraryB' is associated with 'ActionB.' Let us assume that 'ActionA' makes a call to 'ActionB.' 'ActionB' calls function 'fnPrintMessage.' The output at run-time in this case will be 'Hierarchy Position: A' (Fig. 18.3). This happens because 'LibraryA' is at the top in the hierarchy; therefore, the function defined in 'LibraryA' is used.

Figure 18.3 *Library files association hierarchy*

Dynamic Load of Function Library

UFT offers the flexibility to dynamically load the function libraries during run-time. UFT provides *ExecuteFile and LoadFunctionLibrary* statements to load the specified function library when the test code is running. *ExecuteFile and LoadFunctionLibrary* executes the VBScript statements in the specified file. After the function library is loaded, the definitions in the library (functions, classes, subroutines etc,) are available.

Syntax:

ExecuteFile(*Path*)
Where,

Path is the absolute file path or relative path of the library file.

LoadFunctionLibrary(Path)
Where,

Path is the absolute file path, relative path or ALM path of the library file. In case, multiple library files are to be loaded, the paths of various files is to be separated using comma delimiter.

Difference Between LoadFunctionLibrary and ExecuteFile Statement

LoadFunctionLibrary statement provides functionality similar to the ExecuteFile statement. The difference between these two statements is:

- LoadFunctionLibrary enables users to debug the functions in the function library during run-time.
- For tests, the definitions in a function library loaded by LoadFunctionLibrary statement are available globally until the end of the run session. Whereas the definitions in a function library run by ExecuteFile statement are available only within the scope of the action that called the statement.

For business components, in both cases the definitions of the function are available in the scope of the component that called the statement.

DESIGNING CUSTOM LIBRARY (DLL) FILES

Sometimes, automation of the AUT requires designing of dynamic-link library (DLL) files and calling them from QTP environment. The following section explains how to design a custom library file using Visual Basic and then use this file in UFT environment.

Designing DLL Files Using Visual Basic

1. Open Visual Basic.
2. Create a new ActiveX DLL project (Fig. 18.4).
3. Specify project name, say *QTPLibrary* (Fig. 18.5).

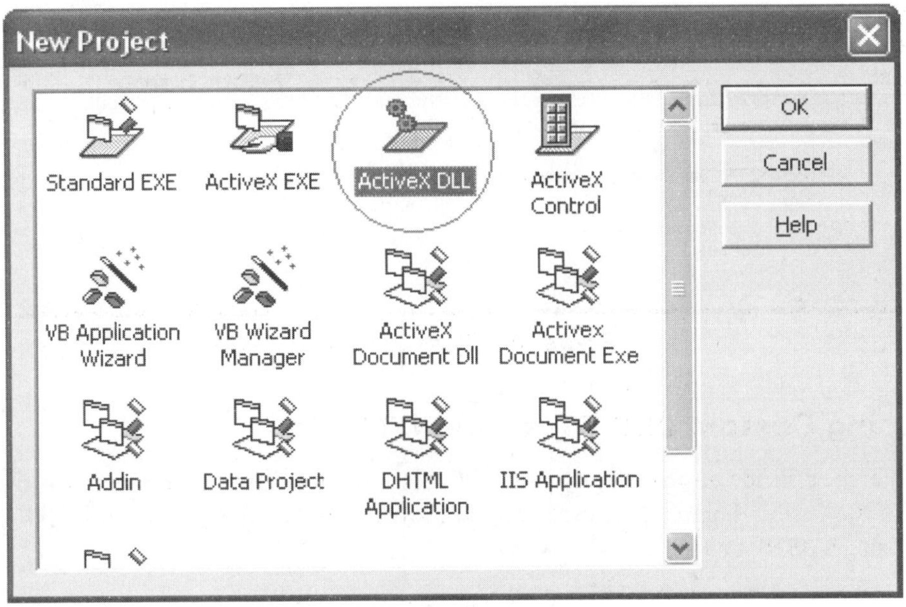

Figure 18.4 *Creating a new ActiveX DLL*

4. Specify Class library name, say *ClassLibrary* (Fig. 18.6).
5. Add a function to the specified class library 'ClassLibrary' as shownin Fig. 18.7.
6. Select *File → Make QTPLibrary.dll.* A DLL of this class library will be created.
7. Register the DLL file to OS as mentioned below.

NOTES

- The created DLL class library file can be executed and debugged in VB environment.
- The DLL needs to be registered to operating system (OS) environment before it can be accessed. To register the DLL on any machine, simply drag and drop the file onto the file "RegSvr32.exe." This file can be found in "Windows/System32" folder.
- For registering the DLL to 64-bit OS, use file regsvr32 located inside 'Windows/SysWOW64' folder.
- The DLL file can also be registered from command prompt using command: regsvr32 <dll file name>. For example, "cd \windows\syswow64\regsvr32 c:\temp\filename.dll".

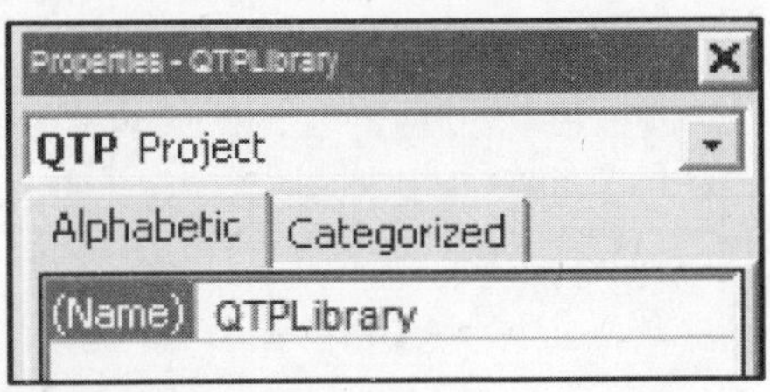

Figure 18.5 *Specifying project name*

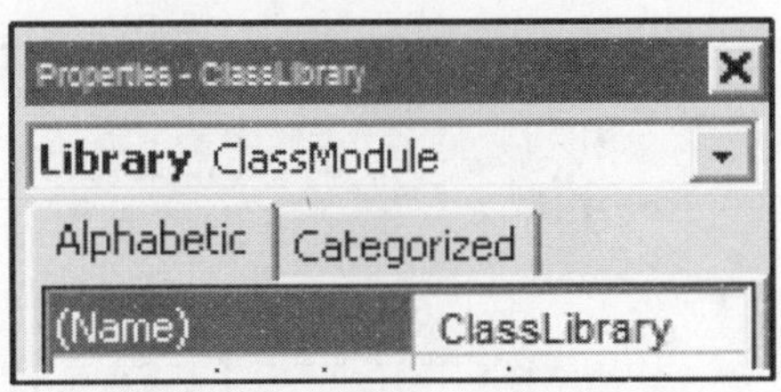

Figure 18.6 *Specify library name*

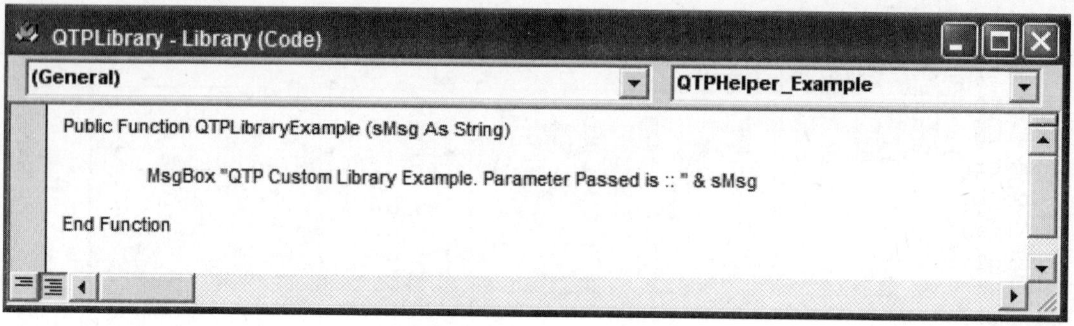

Figure 18.7 *Defining function*

Accessing Custom DLL Files from QTP

Functions created inside custom library files can be accessed in QTP environment by creating an instance of the custom library (Fig. 18.8). The following code shows how to call a custom library function using VBScript code.

```
'Create an instance of QTPLibrary
Set oCustomDLL = CreateObject("QTPLibrary.Library")
'Call the function from the custom library
oCustomDLL.QTPLibraryExample "Custom Library Function"
'Destroy the object
Set oCustomDLL = Nothing
```

CALLING MS WINDOWS DLL FUNCTIONS FROM QTP

Dynamic-linked library is an MS implementation of shared library concept in Windows environment. Dynamic-linked library files are loaded into an application at run-time, rather than being linked in at compile time. DLL files remain as separate files on disk.

Extern Object

QTP provides an *Extern* object that can be used declare DLL files and access DLL functions. The *Declare* method of *Extern* object can be used to declare DLL files.

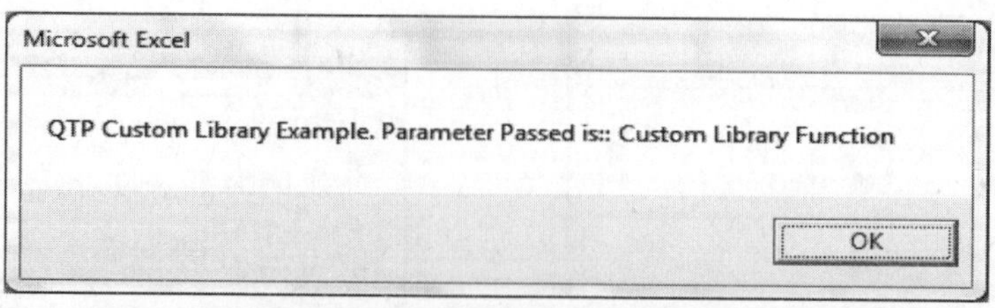

Figure 18.8 *Accessing custom DLL functions from QTP*

```
Syntax : Extern.Declare (RetType, MethodName, LibName, Alias [,ArgType(s)])
    RetType - Return type of the function
    MethodName - Name of the function
    LibName - Library file name where the function exists. In situations
    where custom library files are being used, then complete file path is
    to be specified.
    Alias - Alias name of the method. This parameter can be left blank ("").
    ArgType(s) - Arguments that need to be passed to the calling function
```

Example: The following example declares a call to a function called GetForegroundWindow, located in user32.dll.

```
Extern.Declare (micLong, "GetForegroundWindow", "user32.dll", ""
```

Example 1: Retrieve the value of windows environment variables (viz. Temp, Path, OS).

Windows environment variable values can be retrieved by using *GetEnvironmentVariable* method of *Kernel32.dll* library file.

```
'Declare the API GetEnvironmentVariable
Extern.Declare micLong, "GetEnvironmentVariable", "kernel32.dll",_
          "GetEnvironmentVariableA", micString, micString+micByRef,
          micLong

'Get the environment variable TEMP value
Extern.GetEnvironmentVariable "TEMP", sEnvVal, 255

MsgBox sEnvVal          'Output: C:\Users\Admin\AppData\Local\Temp
```

NOTES

Option Explicit

We observe that in VBScript, there is no need to declare a variable before assigning a value to it, which otherwise throws error in other languages. In order to force programmers to declare a variable before using it, Option Explicit is written at the very top of the code. However, we cannot enforce Option Explicit in individual library files.

QUICK TIPS

- ✓ Avoid using multiple library files, as this will make maintenance of library files costly and difficult.
- ✓ Avoid duplication of functions.

PRACTICAL QUESTIONS

1. What are the various library file formats supported by QTP?
2. What is the use of library file in test automation?
3. How to load a library file in an action?
4. Write the VBScript code to load a library file in an action?
5. Explain how a DLL can be created?
6. How custom DLL files can be accessed from QTP?
7. Suppose that there are two library files 'LibraryA' and 'LibraryB' that are associated with an action 'ActionA.' LibraryB is in higher in hierarchy than LibraryA.

```
LibraryA
    Function fnPrintMsg()
        MsgBox "A"
    End Function

LibraryB
    Function fnPrintMsg ()
        MsgBox "B"
    End Function
```

   What will be the output if 'fnPrintMsg' is called inside 'ActionA'?

8. Suppose that there are two library files. 'LibraryA' and 'LibraryB' are associated with action 'ActionA' and 'ActionB,' respectively.

```
LibraryA
    Function fnPrintMsg()
        MsgBox "A"
    End Function

LibraryB
    Function fnPrintMsg ()
        MsgBox "B"
    End Function
```

   a. What will be the output if function 'fnPrintMsg' is called in 'ActionA'?
   b. What will be the output if function 'fnPrintMsg' is called in 'ActionB'?
   c. What will be the output if 'ActionA' calls 'ActionB' and a call to the function 'fnPrintMsg' is made inside 'ActionA'?
   d. What will be the output if 'ActionA' calls 'ActionB' and a call to the function 'fnPrintMsg' is made inside 'ActionB'?
   e. What will be the output if 'ActionB' calls 'ActionA' and a call to the function 'fnPrintMsg' is made inside 'ActionA'?

Section 5 GUI Testing

- Solution, Test and Action
- Canvas
- Objects
- Test Object Learning Mechanism
- Object Repository
- Object Repository Design
- Datatables
- Working with Web Application Objects
- Descriptive Programming
- Synchronization
- Checkpoints
- Debugging
- Recovery Scenario and Error Handler
- Test Results

Chapter 19

Solution, Test and Action

An action is the place where all UFT scripts are written. It consists of UFT and VBScript statements. Actions are used to divide the test script into logical units or sections. Each action is to automate specific reusable business functionality. An automated test is created by calling the already developed reusable actions.

A test is comprised of calls to actions. When a new test is created, it contains a call to a single action. By creating tests that call multiple actions, users can design tests that are more modular and efficient. In UFT, every *Action* is contained within a *Test* and every *Test* is contained within a *Solution*.

SOLUTION

Solution defines the type of automated solution. A *Solution* can contain one or more *Tests, Business Components* or *Application Areas*.

Creating New Solution

Steps below describe how to create a new *Solution*:

1. From Menu Bar, select *File* → *New* → *New Solution*. '*Create Solution*' dialog box opens.
2. Select the location where *Solution* object is to be created and Specify name of the *Solution* say *Amazon_UserAccount_ScreenComponent*.
3. A new *Solution* will be created as shown in the Fig. 19.1 below.

Solution Properties Pane

The *Properties* pane displays the attributes of the *Solution* when specific *Solution* is selected in the *Solution Explorer* pane. Figure 19.2 above shows the *properties* pane for the solution of Fig. 19.1.

When to Create a New Solution

Solution feature of UFT can be used to categorize the tests and actions developed. It can also be used to categorize actions and tests developed for various applications. For example, a specific Solution can be created for each application automated. All actions and tests of the application can be devel-

Figure 19.1 *Solution*

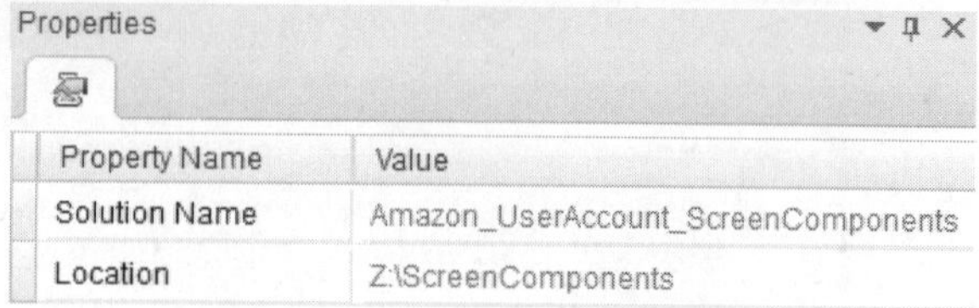

Figure 19.2 *Properties pane for solution*

oped under the same Solution. For example WebApp, SAPApp, SterlingApp etc. However, if the application is big enough, it would be advisable to develop a new Solution for every application module. For UserAccount, ProductSearch, ProductPage, Checkout, Payment, OrderHistory, etc. Another good way of using Solution feature is to categorize tests as per framework components. For example ScreenComponents, BusinessComponents etc. It is recommended to define *Solutions* in a way that helps to easily categorize the actions and tests from three perspective—application type, application module type, and framework component type. For instance naming *Solutions* as <WebApp name>_<App module name>_<ScreenComponents or BusinessComponents>.

Example: Amazon_UserAccount_ScreenComponents, Amazon_UserAccount_BusinessComponents, etc.

A *Solution* can contain one or more *Tests, Business Components, Application Area or Function Library*. Either new test components can be created for a Solution or existing test components can be added to a Solution. Figure 19.3 below shows how to add new or existing *Test*, *Business Component, Application Area* or *Function Library* to a Solution.

GUI TEST

A *Test* is contained within a Solution and can comprise of one or more than one *Actions*.

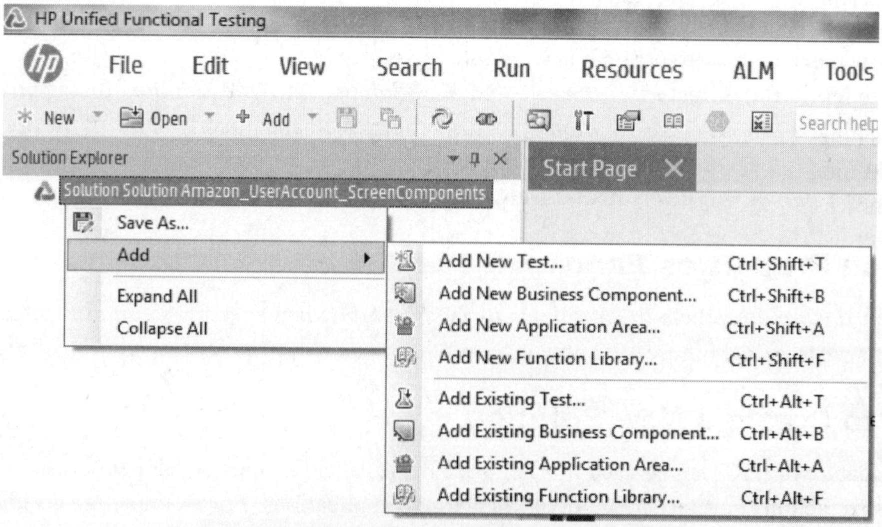

Figure 19.3 *Adding test components to solution*

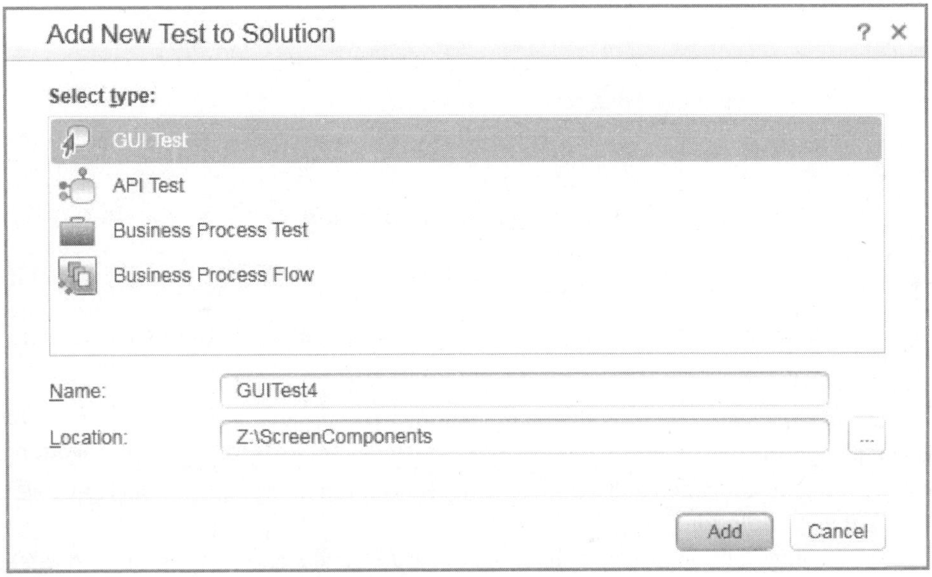

Figure 19.4 *Add new test to solution*

Creating/Adding New GUI Test to a Solution

Steps below describe how to create a new *Test*:

1. Open *Solution Explorer* pane and Open the specific *Solution*.
    - If the specific *Solution* to which test is to be added is not open, the specific *Solution* can be opened from Menu bar. To open the specific solution, select *File → Open → Solution*. '*Open Solution*' dialog box opens. Specify the path and name of the solution and click '*Open*' button. The specific *Solution* will be displayed in *Solution Explorer* pane.
    - If the specific *Solution* is already open but hidden, then Solution Explorer pane can be brought in view by clicking on the Solution Explorer button or by pressing keys CTRL+ALT+L.
2. Select the *Solution* to which new or existing test is to be added.
3. Right mouse click and select *Add → Add New Test*. '*Add New Test to Solution*' window opens as shown in the Fig. 19.4 below.
4. Select the location where *Test* object is to be created and Specify name of the *Test* say *Login-Page*.
5. A new *Test* and *Action* will be created as shown in Fig. 19.5 below.

> **NOTES** Whenever a new *Test* is created, a new *action* 'Action1' and new local object repository 'Local' is created by default as shown in the Fig. 19.3.

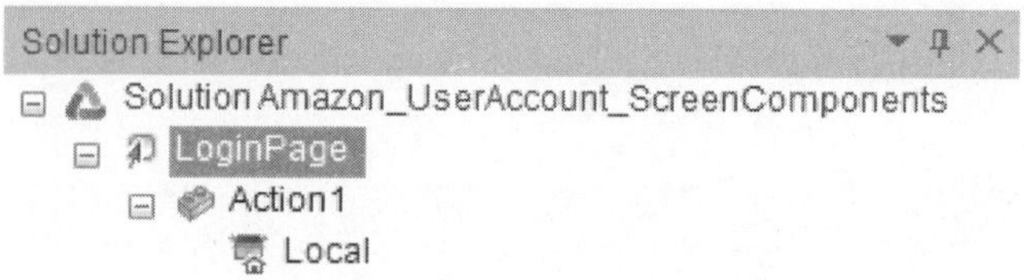

Figure 19.5 *Test **LoginPage***

New tests can also be created from *Menu Bar*. To create tests from *Menu* Bar follow the below steps:

- From Menu Bar, select *File → New → Test* as shown in the Fig. 19.6.
- Dialog box *'New Test'* opens as shown in the Fig. 19.7 below.
- Select test type as *GUI Test*.
- Specify test name, location and solution name. If no solution name is provided a test is created under a default Solution.
- Click on '*Create*' button to create the test. A new *Test* and *Action* will be created as shown in Fig. 19.5.

GUI Test Flow View (Canvas)

Test flow of any test can be viewed in *Canvas*. *Canvas* provides a visual representation of the test flow for GUI and API tests. Test flow is displayed as a series of actions for GUI tests and as steps for API tests. Figure 19.8 shows the *canvas* pane for test *LoginPage*.

> **NOTES** Business process tests and flows are displayed only in a grid view, and are not shown in the canvas at all.

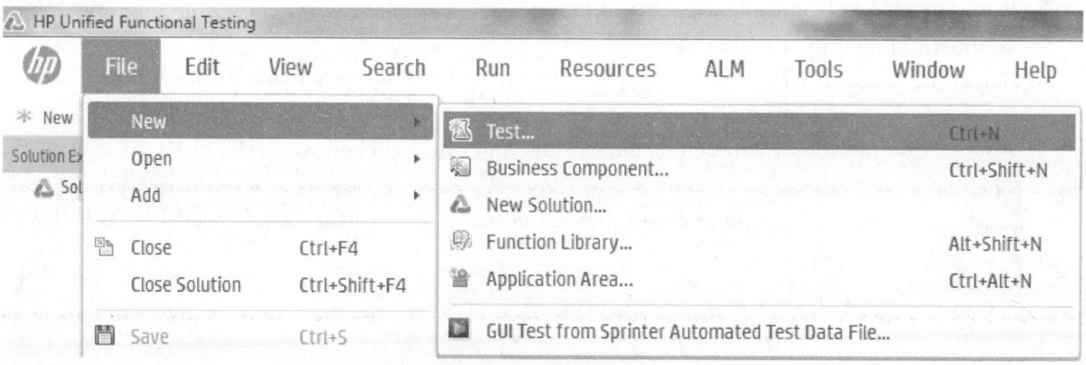

Figure 19.6 *Creating new test from menu bar*

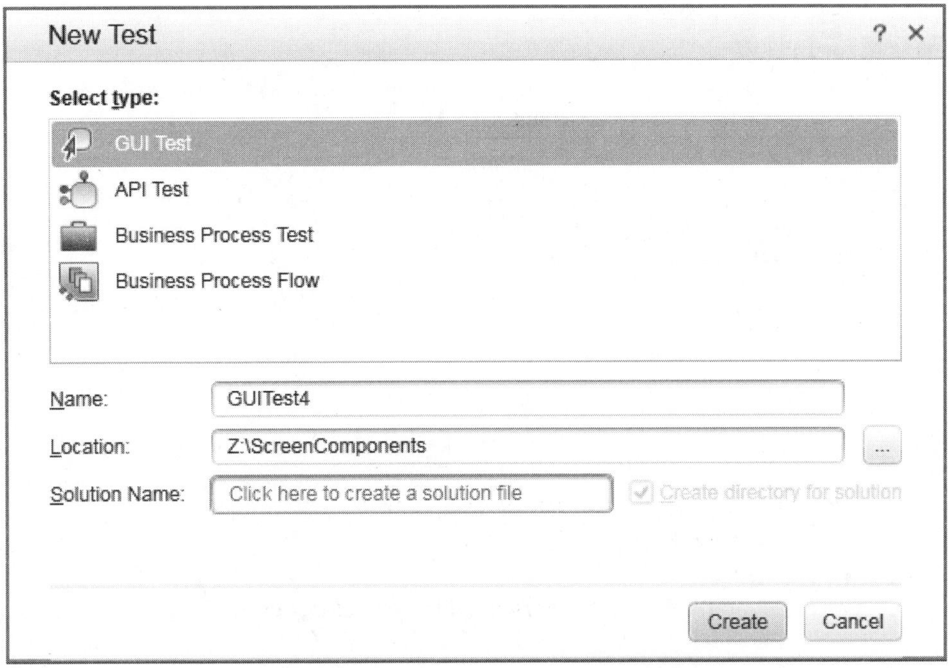

Figure 19.7 *New test creation dialog box*

GUI Test Properties Pane

Details of the test such as name, description, author, creation date, modification date, etc. are displayed in the *properties* pane. Figure 19.9 shows the *Properties* pane for the test '*LoginPage*'.

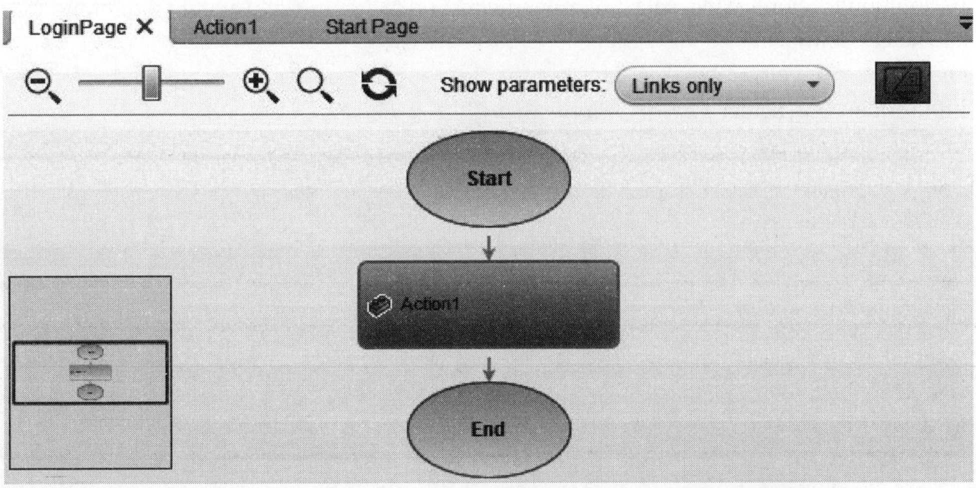

Figure 19.8 *Canvas (Test flow view) view of test* ***LoginPage***

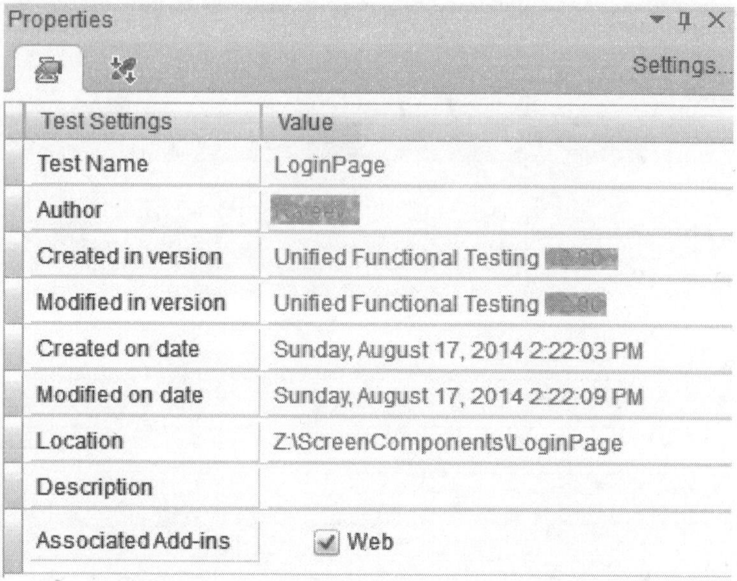

Figure 19.9 *Properties pane of test* ***LoginPage***

GUI Test Settings

UFT allows applying specific settings or preferences for a test. Figure 19.10 shows the *Test Settings* window for the test *LoginPage*.

Test Settings window can be opened by:

- Clicking on the 'Settings…' link of the properties pane as shown in the Fig. 19.6.
- Or,
- In Solution Explorer pane, select the specific test (here *LoginPage*) and do a right mouse click and select Settings.
- Or,
- From Menu Bar, select *File → Settings…*

> **NOTES:** Either action or test must be selected in Solution Explorer pane, for *File → Settings…* link to be enabled.

> **NOTES:** Test Settings pane is discussed in detail in various chapters of this book.

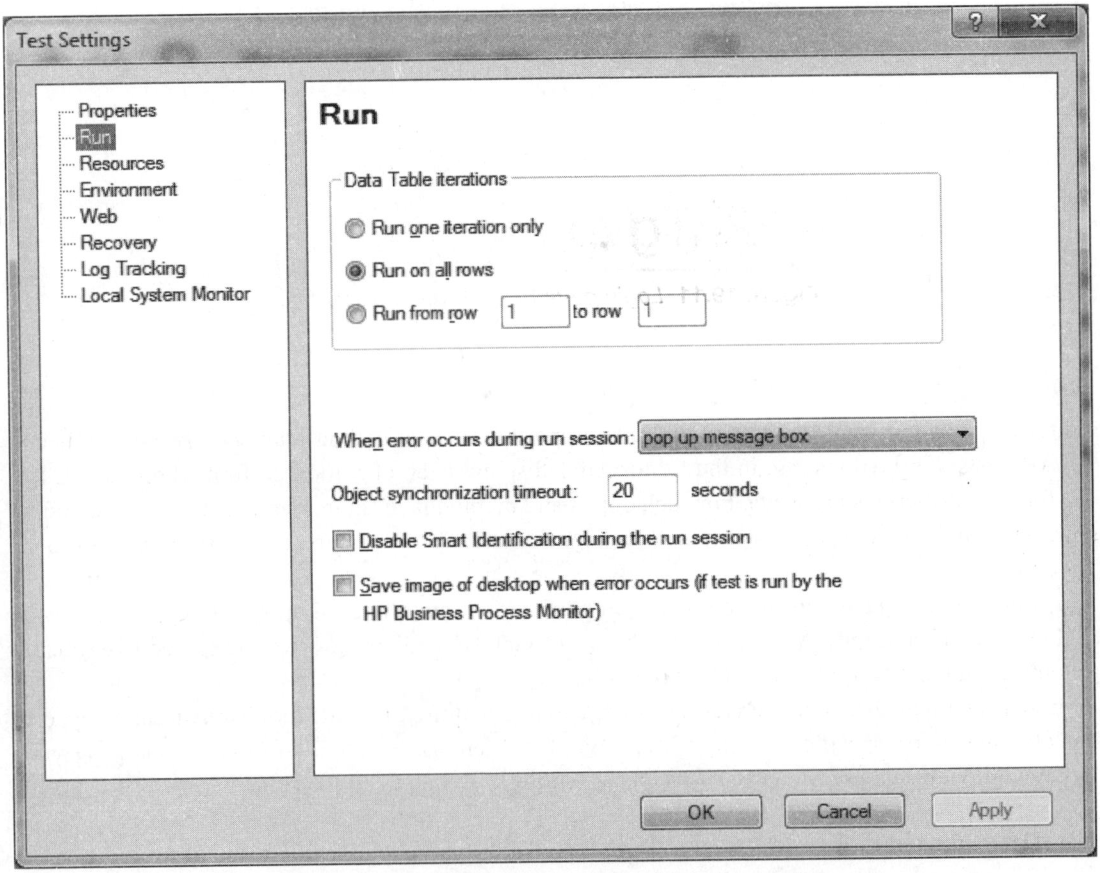

Figure 19.10 Test settings *window for test* LoginPage

ACTION

An action consists of test code, any objects in its local object repository, any associated shared object repositories, any input/output parameters, and any associated recovery scenarios. Action is created by default whenever a new *GUI Test* is created. Figure 19.5 shows the default action 'Action 1' which is automatically created while creating GUI Test *LoginPage*.

Action Views

Action has two views—Keyword View and Editor View.

Keyword View

Keyword View enables users to create and view the steps of the GUI test or component in a keyword-driven, modular, table format. The Keyword View is a table-like view, in which each step is a separate row in the table, and each column represents different parts of the steps.

Figure 19.11 *Login page of application under test*

Editor

Editor displays test steps as lines of code. It supports VBScript coding language for GUI tests and C# API tests. For GUI testing, in the Editor, UFT displays each operation performed on the AUT in the form of VBScript statements. For each object and method in an Editor statement, a corresponding row exists in the Keyword View. For API testing, Editor enables users to write customized user code for API tests.

Assume Fig. 19.11 shows the login page of a train reservation IRCTC application.

Figure 19.12 and Fig. 19.13 shows the keyword view and editor view for the test code written to automate the login feature of IRCTC application.

Users can toggle between the views using the toggle button of the tool bar. Alternatively, user can also switch to a specific view from Menu Bar. Use Menu Bar → *View* → *Keyword View* to switch to keyword view and use Menu Bar → *View* → *Editor* to switch to editor view.

Writing Action Code

In this section, we will briefly discuss how to write GUI test code in an Action. The first step to automate GUI is adding the required objects to object repository. Thereafter, test code can be written in *Editor* or *Keyword* View.

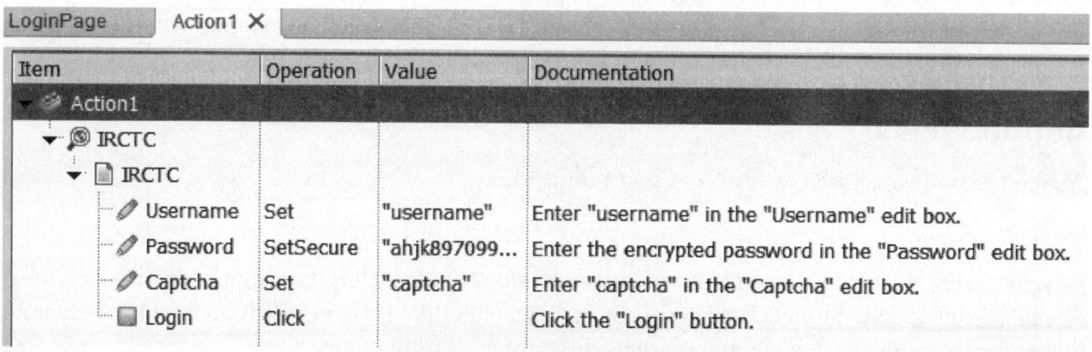

LoginPage | Action1

Item	Operation	Value	Documentation
Action1			
IRCTC			
IRCTC			
Username	Set	"username"	Enter "username" in the "Username" edit box.
Password	SetSecure	"ahjk897099...	Enter the encrypted password in the "Password" edit box.
Captcha	Set	"captcha"	Enter "captcha" in the "Captcha" edit box.
Login	Click		Click the "Login" button.

Figure 19.12 *Keyword view*

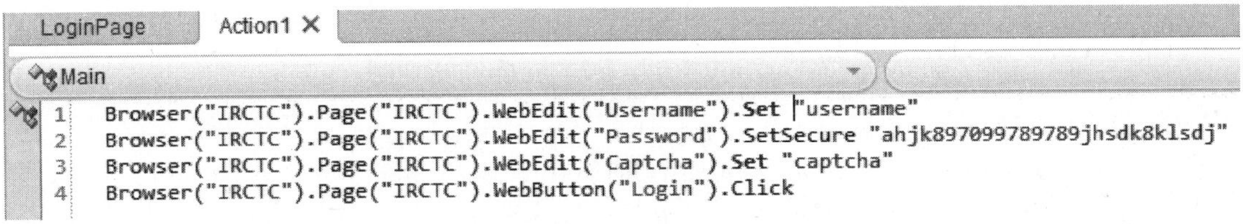

Figure 19.13 *Editor view*

Local Object Repository (OR)

Every Action has a local object repository associated with it. Local Object Repository window can be launched by clicking on the object repository button on the tool bar. Alternatively, Local Object Repository can also be launched from Menu Bar as *Resources → Object Repository* or by pressing keys CTRL+R. Fig. 19.14 below shows Local Object Repository window.

GUI objects can be added to Local OR using button 'Add Objects to Local' of Local object repository window. On user click on this button, a hand tool appears. This hand tool when pointed

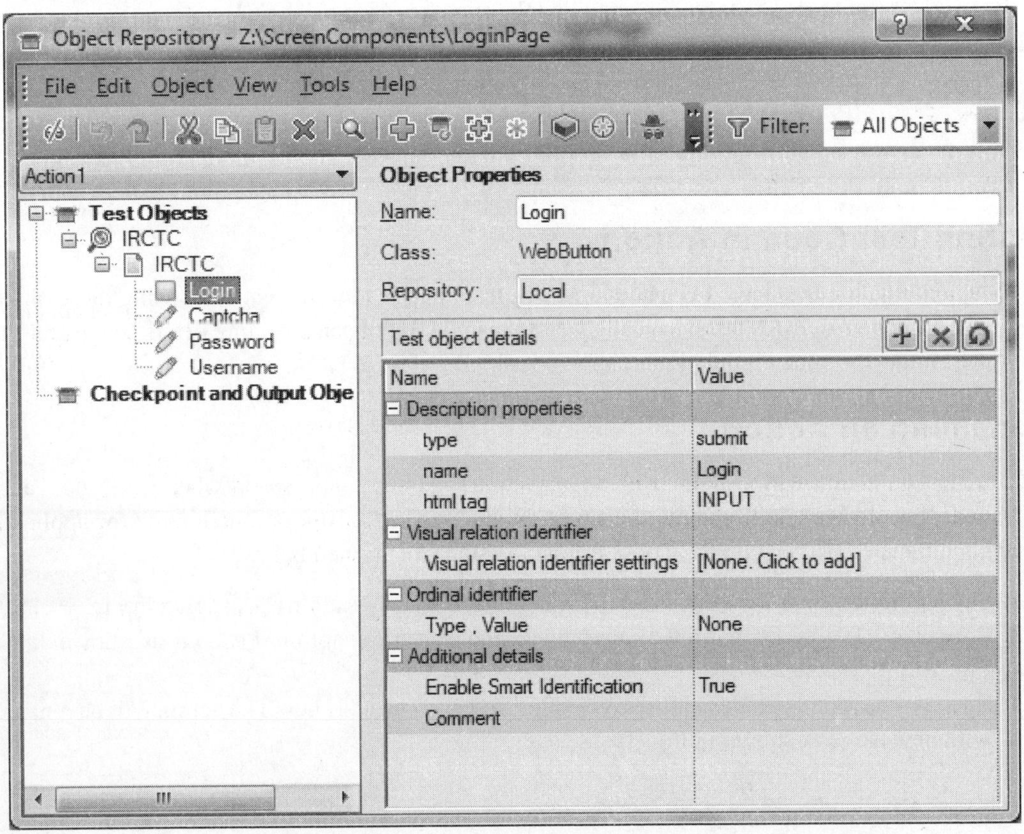

Figure 19.14 *Local object repository window*

and clicked on the GUI object captures the identification attributes of the object and adds the same to Local OR as shown in Fig. 19.14.

> NOTES: UFT provides two Object Repository options—Local Object Repository and Shared Object Repository. Users are advised to use Shared OR for storing all GUI objects. Object Repository is discussed in detail in the chapter 'Object Repository'.

Object Spy

GUI objects can also be added to OR from Object Spy window. Object Spy window can be launched by clicking on the Object Spy button located on Tool bar of UFT window or located on tool bar of Local Object Repository window. Figure 19.15 below shows Object Spy window.

GUI objects can be added to OR using button hand tool button of Object Spy window. On user click on this button, a hand tool appears. This hand tool when pointed and clicked on the GUI object captures the identification attributes of the object as shown in Fig. 19.15. The objects captured in object spy window can be added to OR using 'Add Object to Repository' button. Users to select the specific object from Object Spy window (say WebEdit or Page object of Fig. 19.15) and then click on the ;Add Object to Repository' button to add the specific object to the OR.

> NOTES: Object Spy is discussed in detail in the chapter 'Object Repository'.

Writing Test Code in Action

Once the required objects have been added to OR, next step is to write test code using these objects. UFT offers the *intellisense* feature to easily write test code. Intellisense feature offers suggestions and facilitates automatic code completion as shown in the Fig. 19.16.

Renaming an Action

UFT creates an action with a default name as Action1, Action2, and so on whenever a new action is created. It is always good to name the action on the basis of business functionality or application screen it automates. To rename an action, follow the steps mentioned below:

1. Open Solution Explorer and select the specific action say 'Action1' as shown in Fig. 19.17.
2. Press key 'F2' or do a right mouse click and selection option *Rename* as shown in the Fig. 19.17.
3. Specify a new name to the action say 'Login' and press 'Enter' key. The action will be renamed with new name as shown in Fig. 19.18.

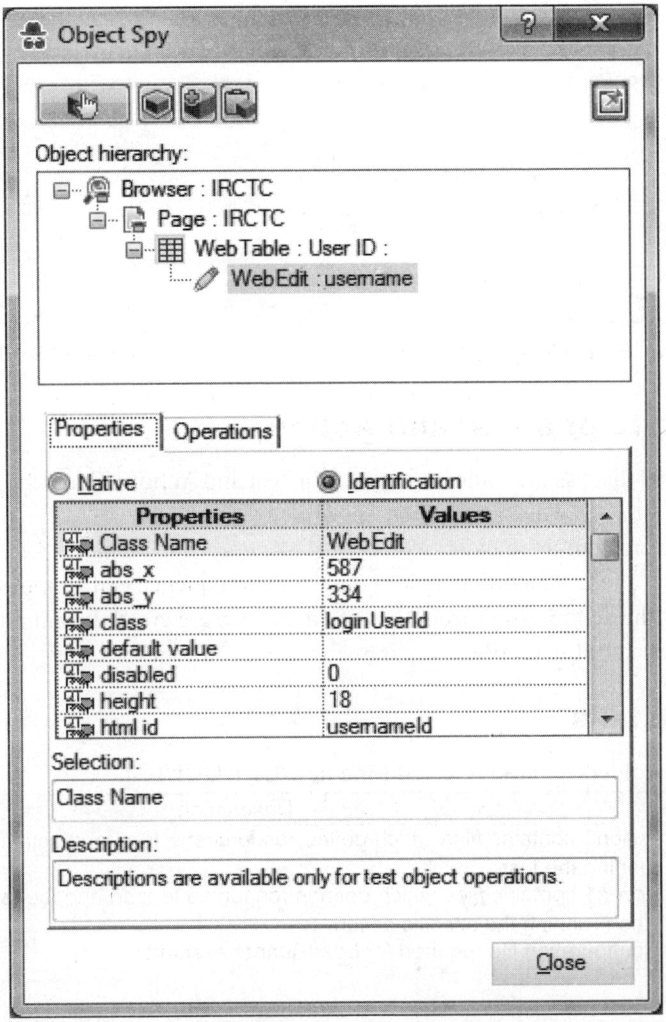

Figure 19.15 *Object spy*

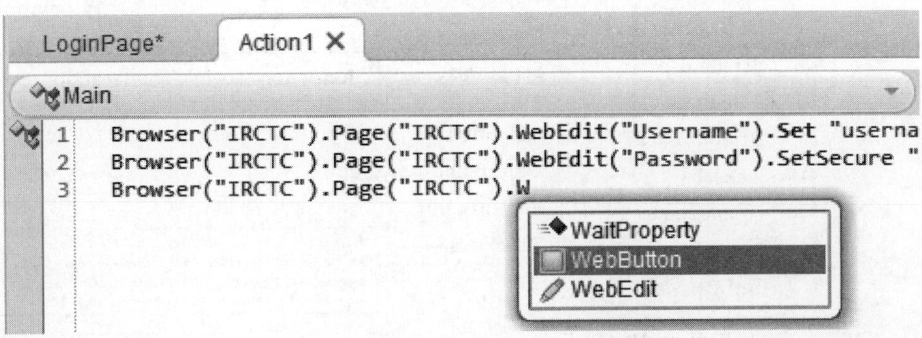

Figure 19.16 *UFT intellisense feature*

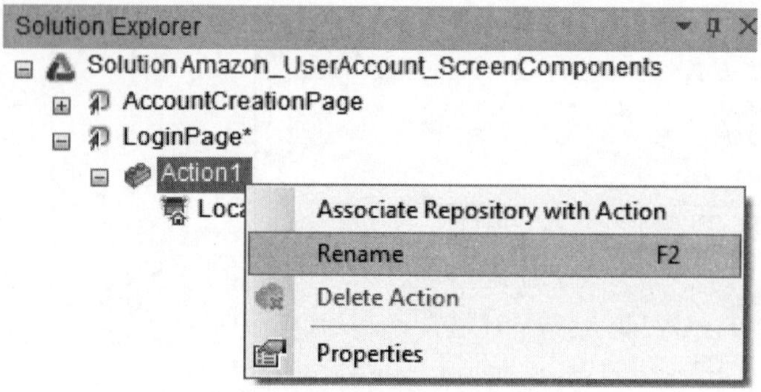

Figure 19.17 *Renaming an action*

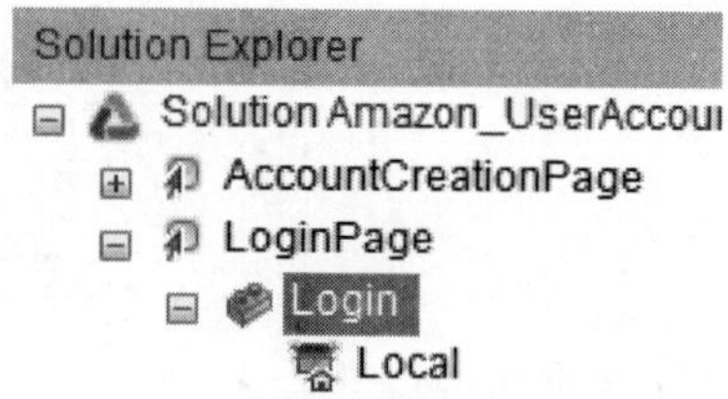

Figure 19.18 *Renamed action*

Folder Structure of a Test and Action

In this section, we will discuss the folder structure of a Test and Action. Figure 19.19 below shows the folder structure of Test *LoginPage* and Action *Login*.

For any new *Test* created, there exist two actions—*Action0* and *Action1*. Action0 folder contains the script settings to load the supportive actions and actions sequence call scripts. Action1 folder contains the test code of the action. Apart from these folders, also are created configuration file, run logic file, test data files, test script main file, test parameters file, and user lock files.

Test Folder Details

Described below are folders and files created for a new UFT GUI Test.

Test Folder/Files	Description
Action0	Action0 contains files which define resources to load and actions to execute when running the test.
Action1	Action1 contains files which defines resources to load and the test code to execute when running the specific action.
default.cfg	Configuration file required for LoadRunner execution.

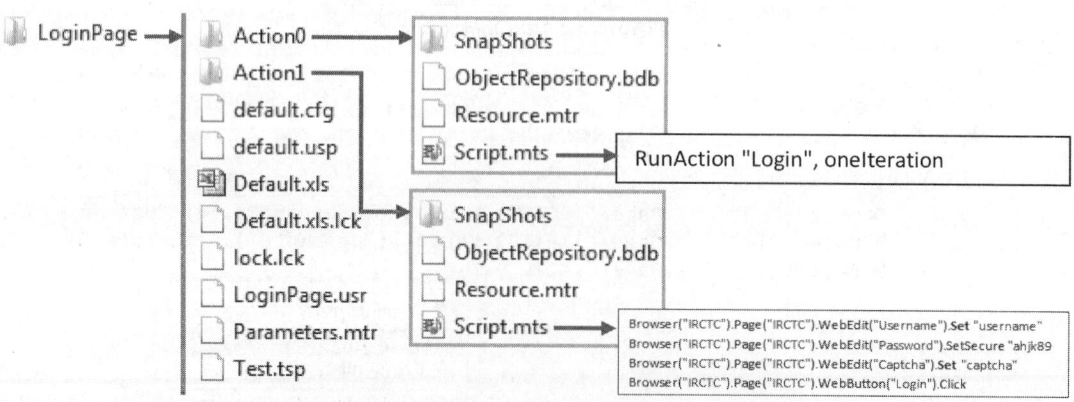

Figure 19.19 *Folder structure of a test and action*

default.usp	Contains additional runtime configuration information for LoadRunner execution.
Default.xls	Contains DataTables test data information in MS Excel file format. For any Test, there exists a 'Global' sheet which defines data global to all actions and a local sheet which contains data specific to an action. Figure 19.20 below shows default.xls file. Example 1: If a Test say LoginPage contains one action say Login, then there will be two excel sheets within Default.xls – Global and Login. Example 2: If a Test say LoginPage contains three actions say Login, ForgotPassword, and ResetPassword; then there will be four excel sheets within Default.xls – Global, Login, ForgotPassword and ResetPassword.
Default.xls.lck	Binary file which specifies this file (DataTable) is locked for editing in UFT. This file is automatically created when the DataTable of the specific test is opened in UFT for editing. Once the DataTable is closed, this file is automatically deleted. This file prevents multiple users from editing the DataTable data simultaneously.
lock.lck	Binary file which specifies that this Test is locked for editing in UFT. This file is automatically created when the specific test is opened in UFT for editing. Once the test is closed, this file is automatically deleted. This file prevents multiple users from editing the test script actions simultaneously.
LoginPage.usr	Defines the location of all the files of the test LoginPage such as Action0\Script.mts, default.cfg, etc. Name of this file is always same as name of the test.
Parameters.mtr	Binary file which contains test input/output parameters information.
Test.usp	Binary file which contains test settings information of the Test.

NOTES

For any UFT Test, there exists an Action folder for every action created in UFT. For example, suppose a test *BookTicket* contains five actions – *Login, SearchItinerary, SelectItinerary, MakePayment, Verify-BookedTicket.* For this scenario, the test will contain one folder, namely, 'Action0' for test definition and five folders for definition of five actions. 'Action0' contains information related to test settings, test resources, test actions, etc. Five action folders, namely, Action1, Action2, Action3, Action4, and Action5 contains information related to the specific actions such as action associated resources, action parameters, action test code, etc.

The test script file (Script.mts) of this Action0 folder will contain calls to the five actions in sequence as:

```
RunAction "Login", oneIteration
RunAction "SearchItinerary", oneIteration
RunAction "SelectItinerary", oneIteration
RunAction "MakePayment", oneIteration
RunAction "VerifyBookedTicket", oneIteration
```

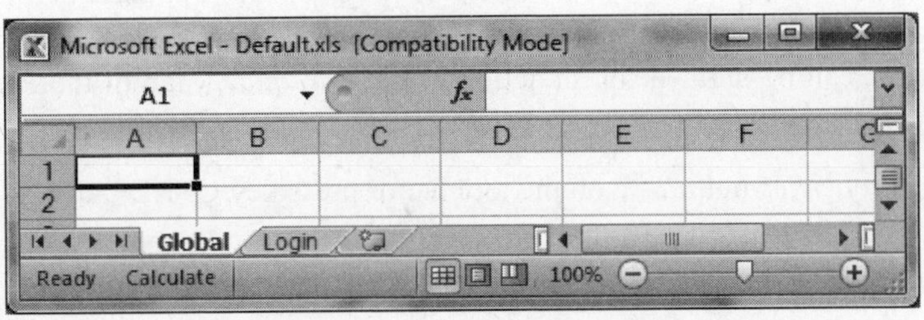

Figure 19.20 *Default.xls file of* ***Test*** *folder*

Action1, Action2, Action3, Action4, and Action5 folders contain information related to the specific actions. Script.mts file of the specific actions contains the test code of the specific action.

As new actions are created in the UFT *Test*, new actions folders are created with the same numbering sequence.

Action Folder Details

Described below are the files created for an action.

Action Folder/Files	Description
Snapshot	This folder contains the UFT Active Screen snapshots. These snapshots are taken by UFT during recording. It contains HTML, XML & PNG files.
ObjectRepository.bdb	(Berkeley Data base, an oracle product) This is the local object repository of the action.
Resource.mtr	Binary file which contains information related to the resources associated with the action such as function library, recovery, shared object repository, action input/output parameters, etc.
Script.mts	For Action0, this file defines the actions to execute for the test, their execution sequence and the execution iterations for each action. For Action1,Action2, ..., this file contains the test code for the specific action.

Action Parameterization

Action parameterization means replacing the hard-coded data such as application URL, username, and password from the action with variables. The hard-coded data (test data) is then defined in test data files. In this way, the same action can be executed with various sets of test data. This helps maximize script reusability and reduce code redundancy. There are three ways to parameterize an action—action data tables, external data files, and action input/output parameters. Action parameterization using a data table is discussed in detail in the chapter 'DataTables.' In addition, action parameterization using external files are described in the chapter 'Working with Excel.' In the section below, we discuss how to parameterize or data-drive actions using action input/output parameters

> **NOTES** It is a good practice to parameterize Action using Action parameters while the test parameters data is to be defined in MS Excel file or CSV file. The *Test* that calls the action is to retrieve the test data from the test data files and pass it on to the action through action parameters.

An Action can have two types of parameters—input and output. The input parameter is used for passing test data to the action. The output parameters are used to store the test output data such as the booked ticket number. Action passes the test output data to its calling action using output parameters.

Action parameters can be defined for an action in the *Parameters* tab of the *Properties* pane. To open parameters tab:

1. Click on the *Properties* button on the tool bar or press key CTRL+ALT+P. *Properties* pane opens.
2. On the *Properties* pane, select the *Parameters* tab. *Parameters* tab opens as shown in the Fig. 19.21.

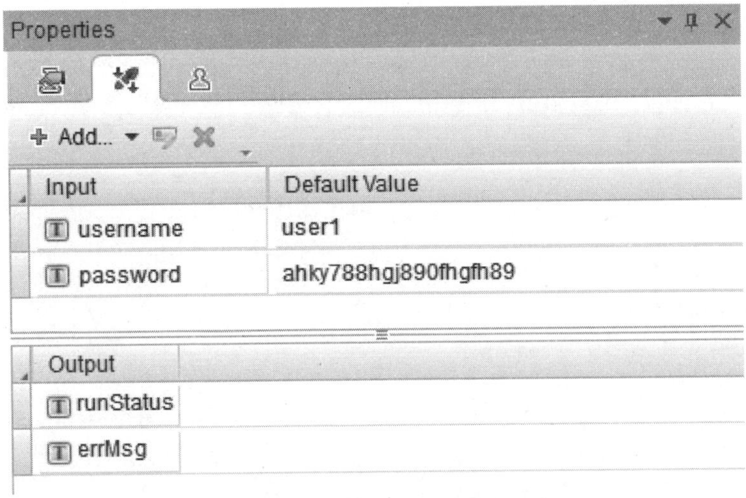

Figure 19.21 *Parameters tab*

The defined parameters for an action can also be viewed in canvas pane as shown in the Fig. 19.22.

Also, canvas pane provides options to edit the action parameters from *Action Properties* dialog box. Follow the steps below to open action properties dialog box:

1. Open canvas pane of the test.
2. Right click on the action and select *Action Properties*. Action properties window opens as shown in the Fig. 19.23.
3. Select the tab *Parameters* to view, add, edit or delete input or output parameters.

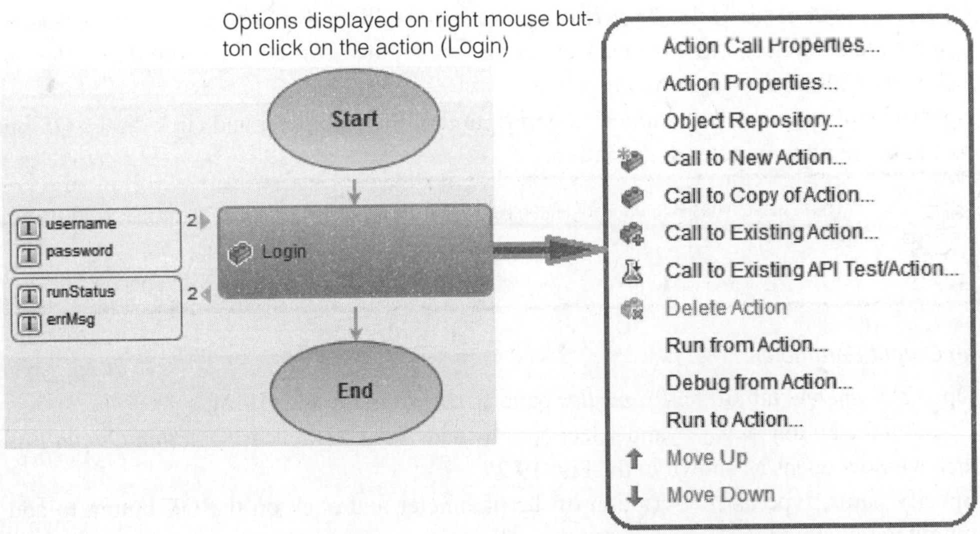

Figure 19.22 *Canvas display of test* LoginPage

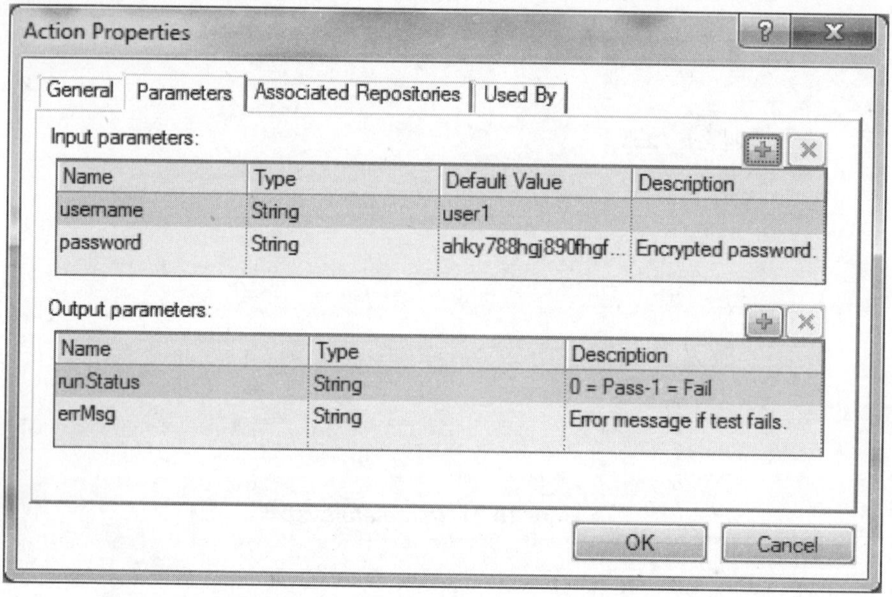

Figure 19.23 *Parameters tab of the action properties dialog box*

Defining Input and Output Parameters of an Action

As discussed above action input and output parameters can be defined either from *Properties* pane or *Action Properties* window. Steps below describe how to define action parameters using *Properties* pane (refer Fig. 19.21).

Defining Input Parameter

1. Open *Parameters* tab of the *Properties* pane as shown in the Fig. 19.21.
2. Click on the button Add... and select option Add Input Parameter.... *Action Input Parameter* window opens as shown in the Fig. 19.24.
3. Specify name, type, default value and description of the parameter and click on the *OK* button to add the input parameter to the action.

> NOTES: The variable types supported for action parameters include: String, Password, Number, Date, Boolean, Any.

Defining Output Parameter

1. Open *Parameters* tab of the *Properties* pane as shown in the Fig. 19.21.
2. Click on the button Add... and select option Add Output Parameter... . *Action Output Parameter* window opens as shown in the Fig. 19.25.
3. Specify name, type and description of the parameter and click on the *OK* button to add the output parameter to the action.

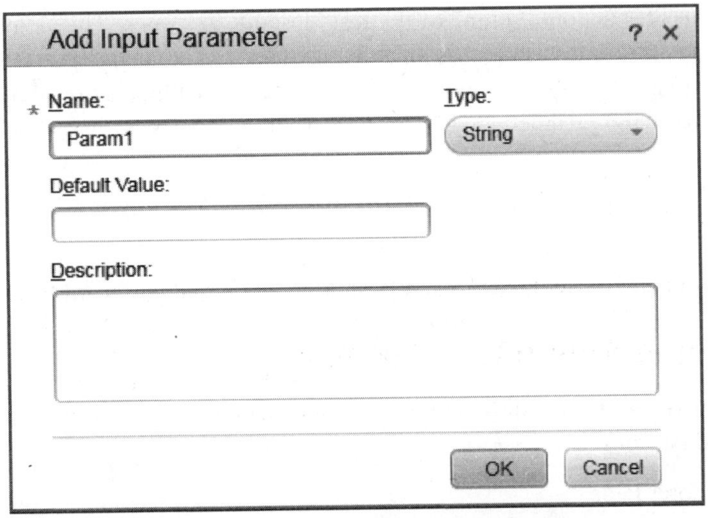

Figure 19.24 *Adding action input parameter*

Assume an action has two input parameters and two output parameters. Shown below is the syntax of this parameterized action call.

```
Syntax : RunAction ActionName[TestScriptName],Iteration,
                         inputParam1, inputParam2, outputParam1, output-
Param2
```

Example 1: `RunAction "Login[LoginPage]", oneIteration,
"TestUser", "testpass", RunStat, ErrMsg`

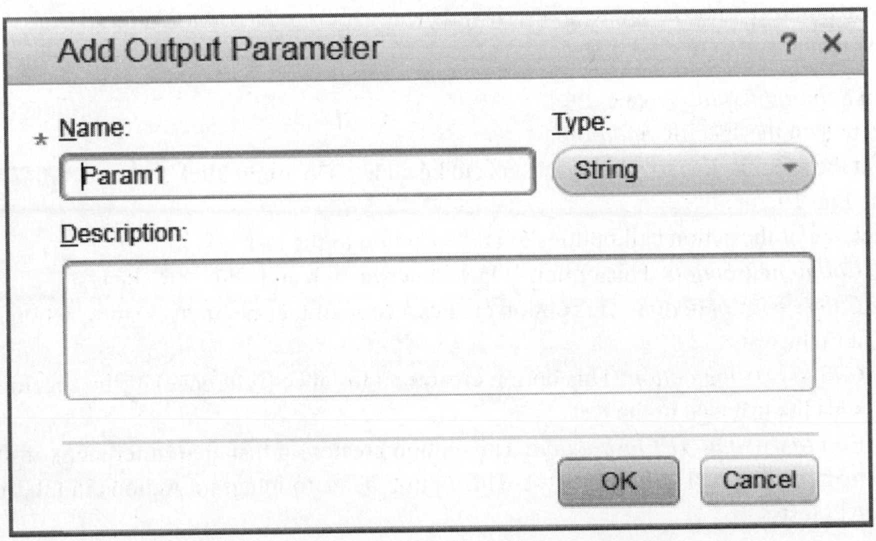

Figure 19.25 *Adding action output parameter*

The above code executes action "Login" of the test "LoginPage" once. The action uses login username 'TestUser' and password 'testpass' as input parameters. The action has two output parameters—"RunStat" and "ErrMsg." "RunStat" provides information to the calling action about the action status whether it has passed ("0") or failed ("–1"). In case of failure, "ErrMsg" variable contains the error message.

Example 2: `RunAction "Login[LoginPage]", oneIteration, , "testpass", RunStat, ErrMsg`

The above code uses default username (as shown in Fig. 19.23) and password 'testpass'.

Creating/Adding Action to a GUI Test

There are various ways to create a new action or add an existing action to a *Test*. Actions can be created or added to a Test from:

- Solution Explorer Pane
- Menu Bar
- Tool Bar
- Keyword View pane
- Editor pane
- Canvas

In this section, we will discuss how to add an action to a test from solution explorer pane.

Creating/Adding an Action to a GUI Test from Solution Explorer Pane

A new 'Action' is created by default whenever a new GUI Test is created as shown in Fig. 19.5. In case, more actions are to be added to a Test, it can be added from *Solution Explorer* pane. Follow the steps below to add action to a GUI test:

1. Open *Solution Explorer* pane.
2. Select/Open the specific *Solution.*
3. Select the specific *Test* to which Action is to be added. Do aright click and select *Add* as shown in the Fig. 19.26.
4. Select one of the action call options to add an action to the test.
   - *Call to new action*: This option creates a new action and adds it to the test.
   - *Call to copy of action*: This option creates a copy of the specified existing action and adds it to the test.
   - *Call to existing action*: This option creates an instance (reference) of the specified action adds the instance to the test.
   - *Call to existing API test/action*: This option creates an instance (reference) of the specified existing API test to the test. This option helps to integrate Actions in GUI tests and API tests.

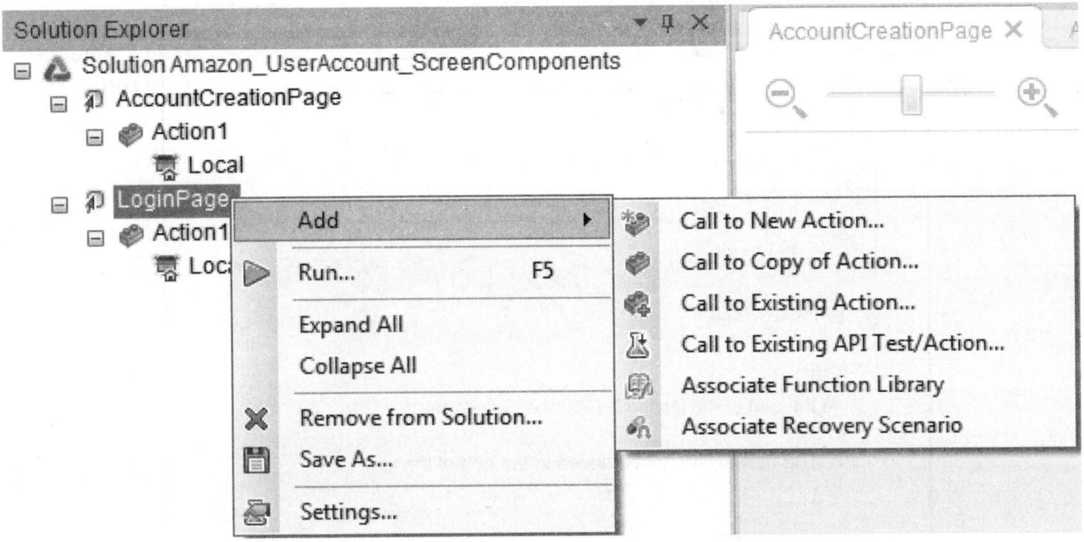

Figure 19.26 *Adding actions from solution explorer pane*

Action Calls

Test automation using QTP/UFT mostly requires calling one action after another in a specified sequence to automate the end user behavior. UFT offers two ways of calling actions – Static action calls and dynamic action calls. Static action calls either creates a new action with all its resources or creates a reference of the existing action in the test. Dynamic action calls dynamically loads the action (with its resources) at run-time to execute the action. In dynamic action calls, no action instance or action resources exist in the test. There exists a line of code that specifies the dynamic action call. During run-time, this code statement is used to load the action from the specified location and execute it. In static action call, all actions (and action resources) exist as *Test* resource and are loaded in memory when the specific test is loaded during run-time. While in dynamic action calls, the called action is only loaded at the point of its call during run-time.

Static Action Calls

There are four ways to make a static call to a GUI action or API test:

- Insert a call to New Action
- Insert a call to Copy of Action
- Insert a call to Existing Action
- Insert a call to Existing API Test/Action

Insert a Call to New Action

Insert call to new action creates a new action in the test. Follow the steps as described below to add a new action to a Test.

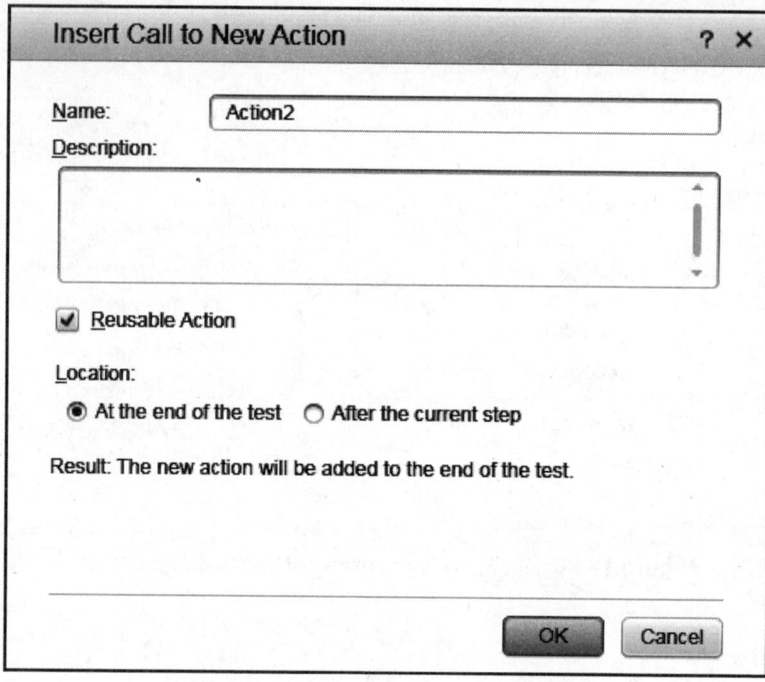

Figure 19.27 *Insert call to new action*

1. Open the test/action to which new action is to be added. Assume test *LoginTest* is selected in Solution Explorer.
2. From Menu bar, select *Design* → *Call to New Action*.
   Insert Call to New Action dialog box opens as shown in the Fig. 19.27.
3. Select *Reusable Action* checkbox to make this action reusable.
4. Specify name of the action, description of action and point at which the new action is to be added. Assume name of the new action is 'InsertNewAction'.
5. Click *OK* button.

   The new action will be created in the test. Figure 19.28 below shows the Solution Explorer pane view with newly created action.

Insert a Call to Copy of Action

Insert a call to copy of action creates a copy of an existing action adds it to the test. In this case, modifications made to the original action does not impacts the copied action or vice versa. Described below are the steps to insert a copy of an existing action to a test (say *LoginTest*).

1. Open the test/action to which new action is to be added. Assume test *LoginTest* is selected in Solution Explorer.
2. From Menu bar, select *Design* → *Call to Copy of Action*.
   SelectAction dialog box opens as shown in the Fig. 19.29.

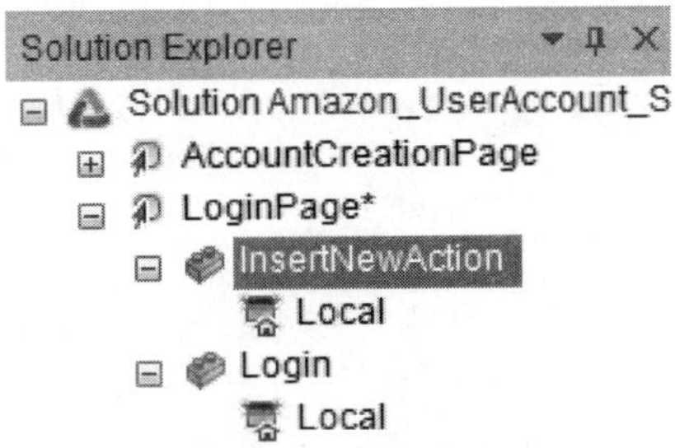

Figure 19.28 *Solution Explorer pane view when new action is inserted to a test*

3. Select the test and the test action whose copy is to be created.
4. Click *OK* button.

   The new action will be created in the test. Figure 19.30 below shows the Solution Explorer pane view with newly created action.

When users insert a call to a copy of an action into a test, the original action is copied in its entirety, including checkpoints, parameterization, data tables, local object repository and associated shared ob-

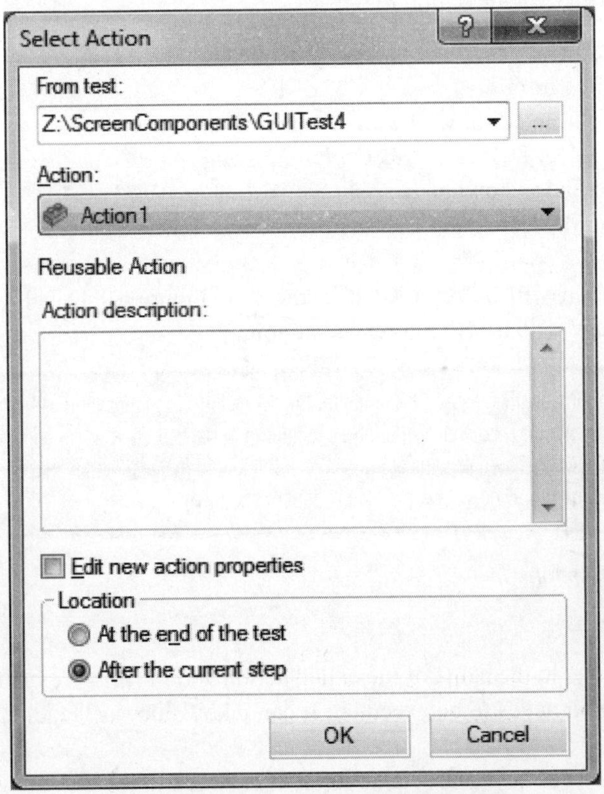

Figure 19.29 *Insert call to copy of action*

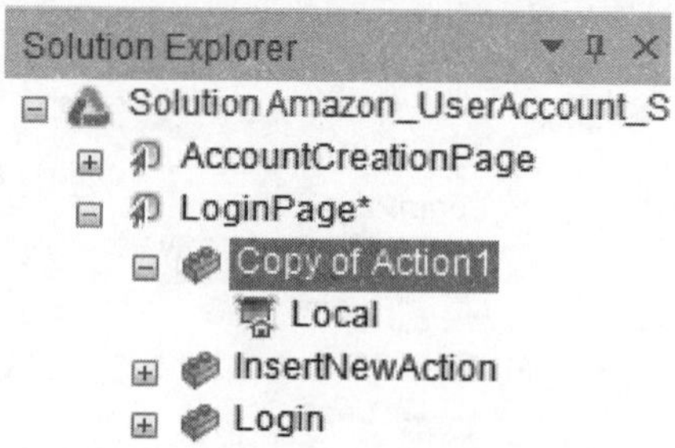

Figure 19.30 *Solution explorer pane view for call to copy of action*

ject repository. The action is inserted into the test as an independent action. If the original action was reusable, the new, copied action is also reusable. After the action is copied into the test, users can add to, delete from, or modify the action just like any other local action. Any changes made to this copied action affect only this action. Also, changes made to the original action do not affect the copied action.

Insert a Call to Existing Action

Insert call to an existing action creates an instance (reference) of the exiting action in the test. In this case, changes made to the original action are reflected automatically in the reference action. Steps below describe how to an existing action to a test.

1. Open the test/action to which new action is to be added. (Assume action *InsertNewAction* is selected and is open in Editor)
2. Place cursor at point in editor where an action call is be inserted.
3. From Menu bar, select *Design* → *Call to Existing Action.*
   Select Action dialog box opens as shown in the Fig. 19.31.
4. Select the test and the test action whose instance (reference) is to be created.
5. Click *OK* button.
   The new action will be referenced in the test. Figure 19.32 below shows the Solution Explorer pane view with newly referenced action.

> NOTES
>
> UFT automatically creates a test code for the action call when an action call is inserted. However, if user wants to call the inserted action at multiple locations in the test, there is no need to insert the action again. Inserting the code that makes the action call is sufficient to make an action call of an already inserted static action. Section below describes the syntax of action call.

Syntax for Calling GUI Action

```
RunAction <Action Name>, <Iteration>
```

Where *Action Name* refers to the name of the called action and *Iteration* refers to the number of iterations for which this action needs to be executed. It can take values as "OneIteration"/"TwoIteration" /"AllIterations"/"1–3," etc.

UFT allows to insert a call to a reusable action that is stored in the current test (local action), or in any other test (external action). Inserting a call to an existing action is similar to linking to it. The test

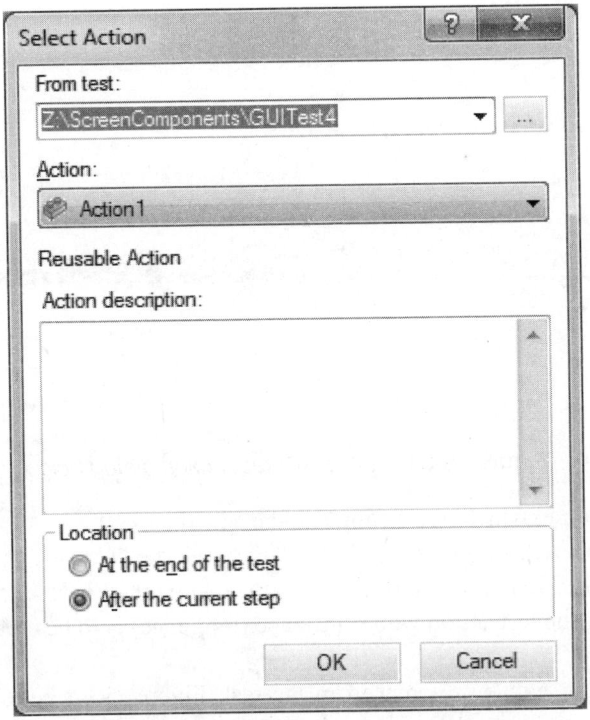

Figure 19.31 *Insert call to existing action*

steps of the inserted action appear read-only and hence cannot be modified. Also, the called action's local object repository (if it has one) is also read-only. For the data in the Data pane, users can choose to import actions' data sheet as a local, editable copy, or to use the (read-only) data from the original action. Data from the called action's global data sheet is always imported into the calling test as a local, editable copy.

Insert a Call to Existing API Test/Action

Insert call an existing API test creates an instance (reference) of the exiting API test in the test. Steps below describe how to an existing action to a test.

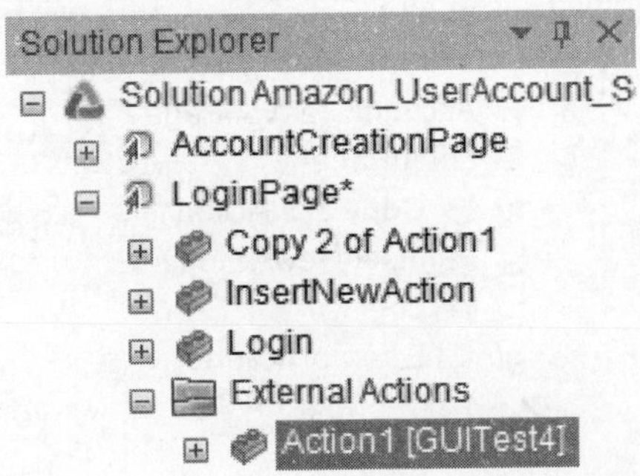

Figure 19.32 *Solution explorer pane view when an existing action is referenced in a test*

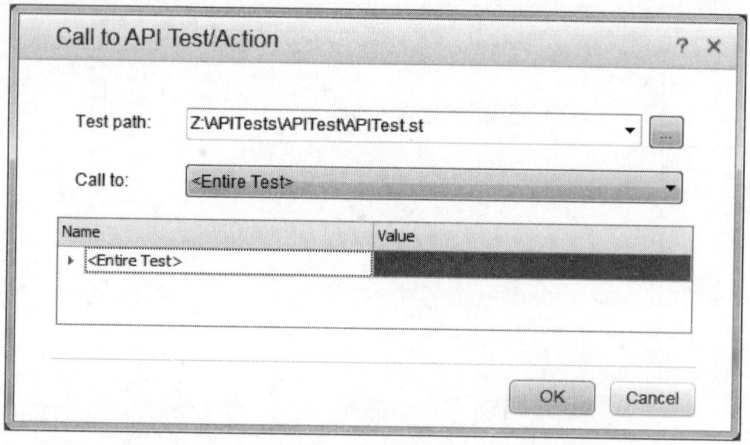

Figure 19.33 *Call to API test/action dialog box*

1. Open the test/action to which new action is to be added.
2. From Menu bar, select *Design* → Call to Existing API Test/Action...
   Call to API Test/Action dialog box opens as shown in the Fig. 19.33.
3. Select the test and the test action whose instance (reference) is to be created.
4. Click *OK* button.
   The new action will be referenced in the test. Figure 19.34 below shows the Solution Explorer pane view with newly referenced action.

Figure 19.35 below shows the canvas view of all the static action calls of test *LoginPage* as shown in the Fig. 19.34.

Dynamic Action Calls

In test automation, there could be scenarios where the action to be executed depends on certain conditions. In this case, we may not want to load actions each time the test is opened, since these actions may not be necessary during the run session. To solve this problem, UFT offers the feature of dynamic action calls for GUI actions. Dynamic action call loads the specified action and then runs the action.

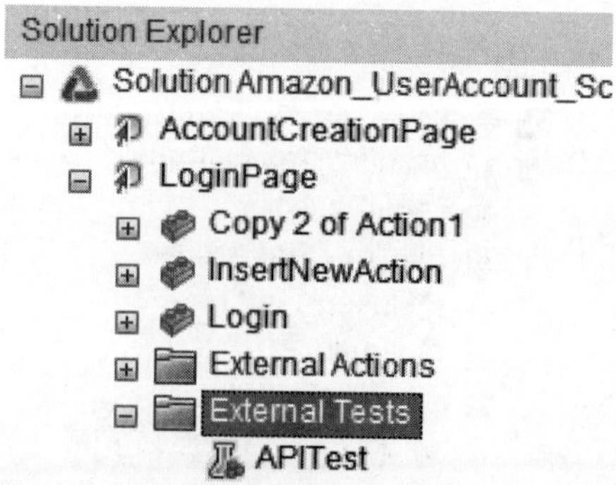

Figure 19.34 *Solution explorer pane view when an existing API test is referenced in a test*

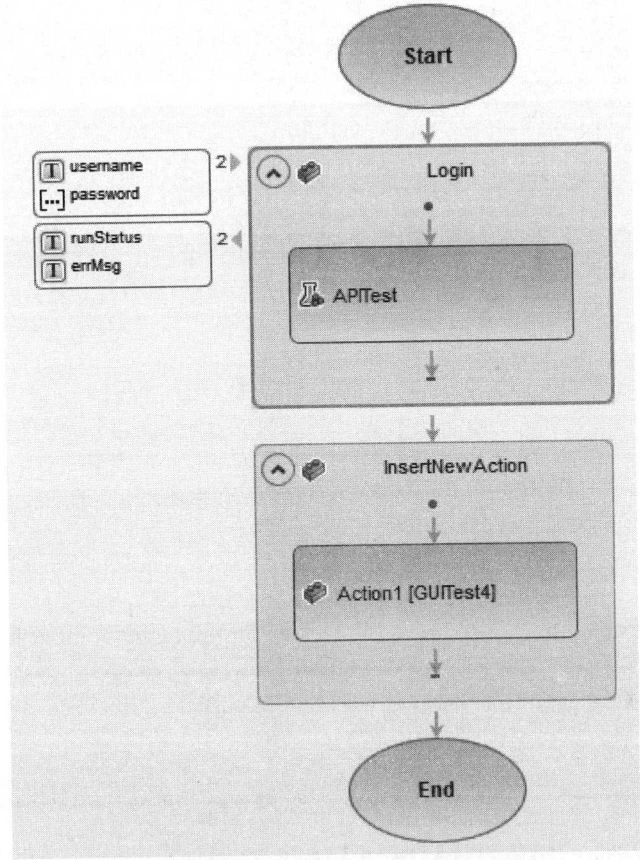

Figure 19.35 *Canvas view of* ***LoginTest***

Syntax for dynamic action call:

```
LoadAndRunAction(TestPath, ActionName, [Iteration], [Parameters])
```

Where,

TestPath is path of the test containing the action. Users can specify the absolute file path, relative path or ALM path.

ActionName is the name of the action.

Iteration is number of times the action is to be executed. This is optional and its default value is **oneiteration** or **0**.

- **oneiteration** or **0** runs the action once, using the row in the action's data sheet that corresponds to the global data sheet iteration counter. If the action's data sheet contains fewer rows than the global sheet, the last row of the action's data sheet will be used for each subsequent iteration.

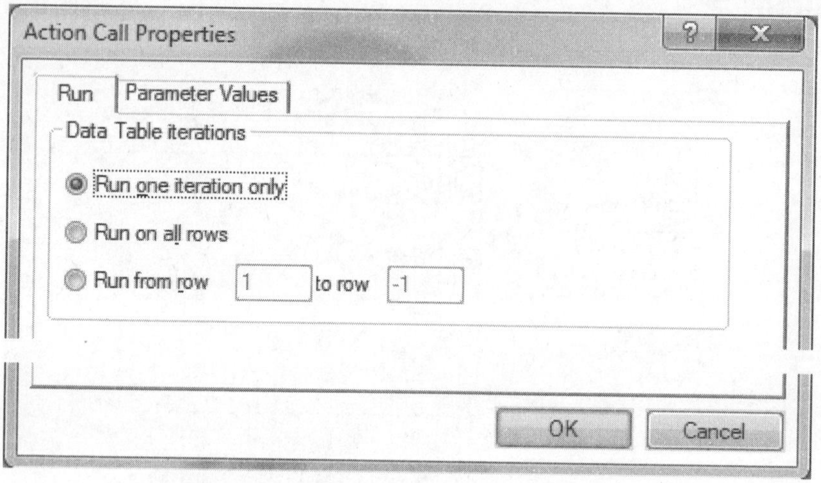

Figure 19.36 *Action call properties dialog box*

- **allIterations** or **1** runs the action for each row data.
- Iteration range (for example "**2-6**") runs the actions for the range of the test data rows.

> **NOTES:** Dynamic action calls are not listed in Solution Explorer pane, Canvas, Errors pane of UFT and Dependencies tab of the ALM Test Resource module.

Action Call Properties (Static Action Calls)

Action Call Properties dialog box controls the way the action behaves in a specific call to the action. It defines run settings such as run iterations and parameters values such as input and output parameters. Figure 19.36 below shows *Action Call Properties* dialog box.

Action Call Properties dialog box can be opened from *Canvas* pane. Users to right click on an action on canvas and select option *Action Call Properties* as shown in the Fig. 19.22.

Types of Actions

There are three four of actions in UFT—Non-reusable action, Local reusable action, External reusable action and nested action.

Non-reusable Action

A non-reusable action is one which cannot be referenced in any other external test or action. A non-reusable action can be called only in the test script it resides and can be called only once. Users can store a copy of a non-reusable action with the test and then insert a call to the copy, but users cannot directly insert a call to a non-reusable action saved with another test.

Local Reusable Action

Local reusable action is an action which can be called multiple times from the test script it resides and also from other test scripts. It is always advisable to make actions as reusable to maximize reusability and reduce code redundancy. New actions are reusable by default. To make an action reusable or non-reusable refer Fig. 19.27.

External Reusable Action

External reusable actions are the reusable actions that reside in another test script. These actions are read only in the calling test or action.

> NOTES: Local reusable action and the external reusable are one and the same action and are generally referred as reusable action. If a reusable action is called in the same test in which it was created then it is called local reusable action. In addition, if a reusable action is called in a different test other than the one in it was created then it is referred as external reusable action.

Nested Action

An action can call another action and so on. This is termed as nesting an action

Renaming Action

UFT creates an action with a default name as Action1, Action2, and so on whenever a new action is created with default values. It is always good to name the action on the basis of business functionality or application screen it automates. To rename an action, select the respective action on Solution Explorer pane → Right click and Select Rename option (or press F2).

Removing a Called Action from a Test or Action

UFT provides the flexibility to remove a called action from the calling action. This can be done in three ways:

- By removing the action call code statement from Editor.
- By removing the action from Keyword View.
- By removing the action from the Solution Explorer pane.

Removing the *RunAction* statement from the action test code in the Editor removes the call to the specified action. However, the action itself exists as it is in the Test (refer Solution Explorer pane). Removing the RunAction code only ensures the action will not be called anymore. Removing the called action from the Keyword View pane or Solution Explorer pane permanently deletes the instance of the called action (including action resources) from the calling action or Test. The implication of removing an action from Keyword View window or Solution Explorer pane depends on the type of the action being removed.

- When a call to non-reusable action is removed, the entire action including its datatables, local object repository, and local environment variables is permanently deleted.
- When a call to a reusable action existing within the test is removed, all action calls and the action itself are removed permanently. This will cause the any test script calling this action to fail.
- When a call to external reusable action is removed, the instance (reference) of the action is removed from the Test. However, the original action still exists inside the test it was created and can be seen in the action list.

Follow the steps below to remove action call from Solution Explorer pane or Keyword View pane:

1. Select the called action which needs to be removed.
2. Press {DELETE} key or right click and select delete option Delete Action .
3. Dialog box opens to confirm delete action. Click OK button to delete action.

> **NOTES** A Test and its associated actions can be removed from a Solution from Solution Explorer pane. To remove a Test from a Solution, select the Test and press F2 or right click and select option Remove from Solution... . This only removes the association of the Test with the Solution. The Test and its Actions exist as it is on storage disk.

Deleting an Action

An action can be deleted from Solution Explorer pane or Keyword View pane by using the 'Delete Action' option. Only locally created actions can be deleted. Deletion of locally created actions removes the action and all its resources from storage disk as well.

Exiting Test/Action

In test automation, there could be many scenarios when an action needs to be exited if the required test condition is not met. One of the uses of exit action feature would be to handle the run-time errors. The pass or fail status of the action remains as it was in the step prior to the UFT exit action/test statements. UFT provides the below method to exit an action or test:

- **ExitAction**: Exits the currently executing action. No further iterations of action are executed. Let us assume that an action is called to execute five iterations with five different test data sets. Suppose that the test condition fails during iteration 2 and the code reaches the "ExitAction" line. In this case, iterations 2, 3, 4, and 5 will be skipped.

  Syntax: **ExitAction**[(*RetVal*)]

Argument	Type	Description
RetVal	Variant	Optional. This is returned to the statement that called the action. The return value can be string or a number (but not name of a variable).

- **ExitActionIteration**: Exits the current iteration of the action. For the scenario mentioned above, the current iteration, iteration 2, will be skipped and the test script will start executing from iteration 3.

  Syntax: **ExitAction**[(*RetVal*)]

- **ExitComponent**: Exits the current business component run.
    - If the business component is not part of a component group, then any remaining component iterations are skipped and the run proceeds to the next component in the test.
    - If the business component is part of a component group, then the entire component group is skipped and the run proceeds to the next component after the component group.

    Syntax: **ExitComponent**[(*RetVal*)]

- **ExitComponentIteration**: Exits the current business component iteration run.
    - If the business component is not part of a component group, then the remaining steps in the component are skipped and the run proceeds to the next component iteration.
    - If the business component is part of a component group, then the remaining steps of the current component and any remaining components in the component group are skipped, and the run proceeds to the next group iteration.

    Syntax: **ExitComponentIteration**[(*RetVal*)]

- **ExitTest**: Exits the UFT test or ALM business process test, regardless of the run-time iteration settings.
- **ExitTestIteration**: Exits the current iteration of the UFT test or ALM business process test and proceeds to the next iteration.

Action Features

- Actions help implement the modularity concept in QTPUFT. Modular test scripts help maximize code reusability, improve script maintainability, and reduce code redundancy.
- Actions help to break the complete test case or test scenario functionality to smaller reusable functionalities. The reusable functionalities are automated as actions. These reusable actions can be called in multiple test scripts to automate a test case.
- When a new test is created, it contains a call to one action.
- Whenever a new action is created, local object repository and local datasheet of the action are created by default.
- Actions help to parameterize the script using data sheets and input/output parameters.
- Actions help to execute specific business functionality multiple times. UFT provides the flexibility to execute actions for the desired number of iterations with the desired data set.
- Actions make it easier to implement changes.
- Each and every action has its own data sheet. The name of the data sheet is the same as the Action name.
- "Global" data sheet is the datasheet available to share data between different actions. All actions can access global datasheet. (UFT also provides methods so that one action can directly access data sheet of another action. For details refer chapter "DataTables.")

Table 19.1 Comparison between an action and function

Action	Function
Action is internal to UFT	Functions are supported both by UFT and VBScript
Actions can optionally pass and receive input and output parameters	All input parameters need to be defined while calling a function
Action can return more than one value	Function can return only one value
Arrays cannot be used as input or output parameter in an Action	Arrays can be used as input or output parameter in function

Difference Between Action and Function

Action is similar to a function with few differences as mentioned in the Table 19.1 above.

Creating Action Template

Action template is created so that whenever a new action is created, it contains some predefined information including specific lines of code. Action template could be the default script development template being followed by the automation team. It helps the complete automation team to follow scripting standards and guidelines as specified in the project documents. To create an action template:

- Open a notepad file.
- Specify the information or lines of code/comments or default script development template as required by the test automation project.
- Save the file with name "ActionTemplate.mst" inside the *dat* folder of UFT installation. For UFT, the location is ... *\HP\Unified Functional Testing \dat*

NOTES

Refer Appendix A for a test script template.

Action Limitations and Its Workaround Solution

- If you make a copy of an existing test, then you cannot insert a call to the same action from both of these tests into the same test.
  Workaround: Instead of creating a copy of the test, use Save As to create a duplicate of the test.
- You should not create a call to a new action whose name is Global, since Global is the name reserved for the Global sheet in the Data table. If you create an action called Global, you will not be able to select the local or global data sheet when parameterizing.
- Calling an external action from a function library using the RunAction statement results in a runtime error.
  Workaround: Call the action dunamically using the LoadAndRunAction Statement.
- You cannot add a new action as a nested action to an external action.
  Workaround: Open the external action and add the call to the nested action directly.

QUICK TIPS

- ✓ Use reusable actions.
- ✓ Values passed to the action input/output parameter must match the type of the parameter.
- ✓ A test can contain "n" number of actions. It is always advisable to keep similar functionality actions in a test.
- ✓ Always a standard template for an action is to be used (refer Appendix A).
- ✓ Always standard and user-friendly naming convention for an action is to be chosen.

PRACTICAL QUESTIONS

1. What is an action?
2. In an action, there are two input parameters (username and password) and two output parameters (runStatus and errMsg). The default value of the input parameters as defined in test parameters window are—user1 and pass1. What would be the value of the input parameter 'username' inside the action when the action is called as:

```
RunAction "Test[Action]", oneIteration,"", "testpass", RunStat, ErrMsg
RunAction "Test[Action]", oneIteration, , "testpass", RunStat, ErrMsg
```

3. What is the difference between an action and function?
4. What is a reusable action?
5. What are the various action calls?
6. How can an action be deleted from test?
7. How can an action be parameterized?
8. How is a default action template created?

Chapter 20

Canvas

The canvas provides a visual representation of the GUI or API test flow. Test flow is displayed as a series of actions for GUI tests and as steps for API tests. Figure 20.1 shows UFT canvas tab of action Login of GUI test LoginPage. Action login has two input parameters—username and password and two output parameters—runStatus and errMsg.

> **NOTES** Business process tests and flows are not shown in canvas. Instead, they are displayed in a grid view. Grid view is discussed in detail in the chapter 'Business Process Testing'

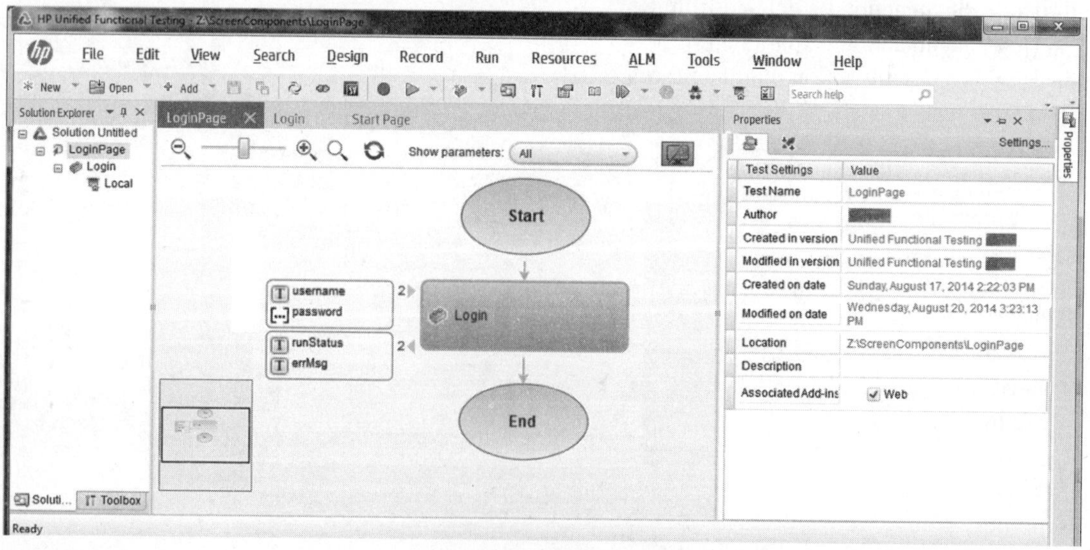

Figure 20.1 *Canvas*

CANVAS FEATURES

Canvas offers various features for creating and managing test flows of GUI and API tests. In this section, we will discuss the various features of canvas for GUI and API tests.

Canvas Features for GUI Tests

Figure 20.2 shows the Canvas tab for a GUI test. In this figure, the test has three local actions—*Login*, *BookTicket* and *CancelTicket*. Here,

- *Login* action login to the application
- *BookTicket* action books the ticket by making calls to existing actions—*PlanTravel* and *DebitCardPayment*.
    - *PlanTravel* action selects the ticket to book by making calls to existing actions—*SearchTicket* and *SelectTicket*.
        - *SearchTicket action searches for the ticket based on the defined search criteria.*
        - *SelectTicket action selects the appropriate ticket to book.*
    - *DebitCardPayment* action makes payment using debit card details to book the ticket.
- *CancelTicket* action cancels the booked ticket.

> **NOTES** Above example is just for illustration and is not the most appropriate test flow for the test scenario.

Canvas opens as a tab in the document pane. Canvas can be used to manage actions (for GUI tests) and test steps (for API tests). Canvas allows users to change order of actions or test steps, run them or debug them from a selected action or up to a selected action, and manage testing parameters. Figure 20.2 shows the actions that can be taken for *BookTicket* action.

Test Flow View (API and GUI Testing)

Canvas provides options to zoom in, zoom out and reset zoom features to view test flow. It also allows users to show or hide details of parameters of actions and test steps (refer Show Parameters drop down options of Fig. 20.1). It also provides option to show or hide mini map ( ) of the test flow (refer Fig. 20.1).

Test Action Management (GUI Testing Only)

Canvas allows users to access Action Properties and as well as Action call Properties of an action. Action Call Properties dialog box allows users to set the run (iteration) settings of an action and view/edit/set the parameters of an action. Action Properties allows users to view/edit/set the general attributes of action say action name, description, reusable or non-reusable action etc. It as well enables users to define the action parameters and associated object repositories. Also, Action Properties dialog box provides information on the tests which are using this action to automate tests.

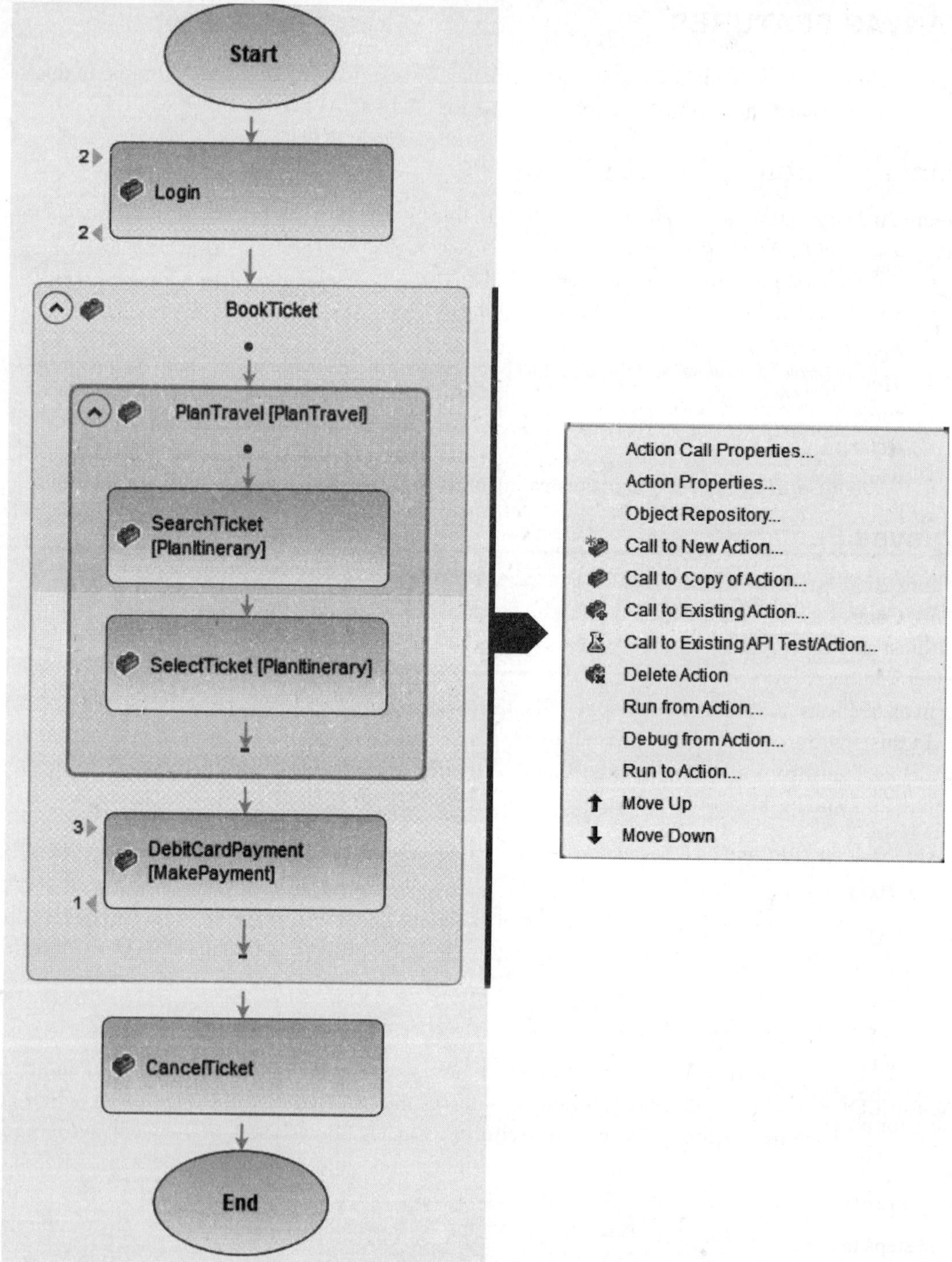

Figure 20.2 *Canvas for a GUI Test*

Action Calls (GUI Testing Only)

Canvas also allows users to make various types of action calls.

Test Runs (GUI Testing Only)

Canvas allows users to run the test from a specific action or debug the test from a specific action. This helps user to debug specific actions of test instead of debugging the complete test which could otherwise be time consuming.

Test Flow Manipulation

Canvas allows users to manipulate the test flow in the many ways. Listed below are few of them:

- ***Reorder***: Drag an action from one location to another in the test flow.
- ***Move up and Move Down***: change the order of actions using the Move Up or Move Down commands as shown in Fig. 20.2.
- ***Delete***: Delete an action from the tests flow. This feature permanently deletes the local action while removes the reference (instance) of the called existing action from the test.

Canvas Features for API Tests

Figure 20.3 shows canvas for a typical API test. This API test shows the use 'if' logical statement of Flow Control tool of Toolbox pane. It also shows use of String Manipulation and Math tools. This API test also makes a call to Java class and a GUI test. Figure 20.4 shows the various tools available under Toolbox pane for creating API tests. These tools can be dragged into canvas to develop the test flow of API test.

In this section, we will discuss the various features of canvas to create and manage API tests.

Test Flow View (API and GUI Testing)

The test flow view features for API tests are same as GUI tests as described above.

Toolbox Pane

For an API test, Toolbox pane provides various tools to create API tests. Figure 20.4 shows the Toolbox pane and the list of tool categories it contains. The tools can be dragged into the canvas to create API tests. The dragged tool appears as a test step in canvas.

For example, 'if' condition appears as a test step in Fig. 20.3. This 'if' tool is available from *Flow Control* tool of the Toolbox pane

Another example is the *Add* tool. The *Add* tool appears as a test step in Fig. 20.3. The input parameters for a test step are defined from *input* tab of the *Properties* pane. Figure 20.4 shows the *input* data and *checkpoints* of *Add* step.

Alerts (API Testing Only)

Test steps that require additional information to completely define the test step such as *HTTP Request/Response* or *SOAP Request*, *Database Connection*, *Custom Code*, and *Wait* post an alert in their top right corner as shown in the Fig. 20.5. Clicking on this alert button displays the missing values for the test step.

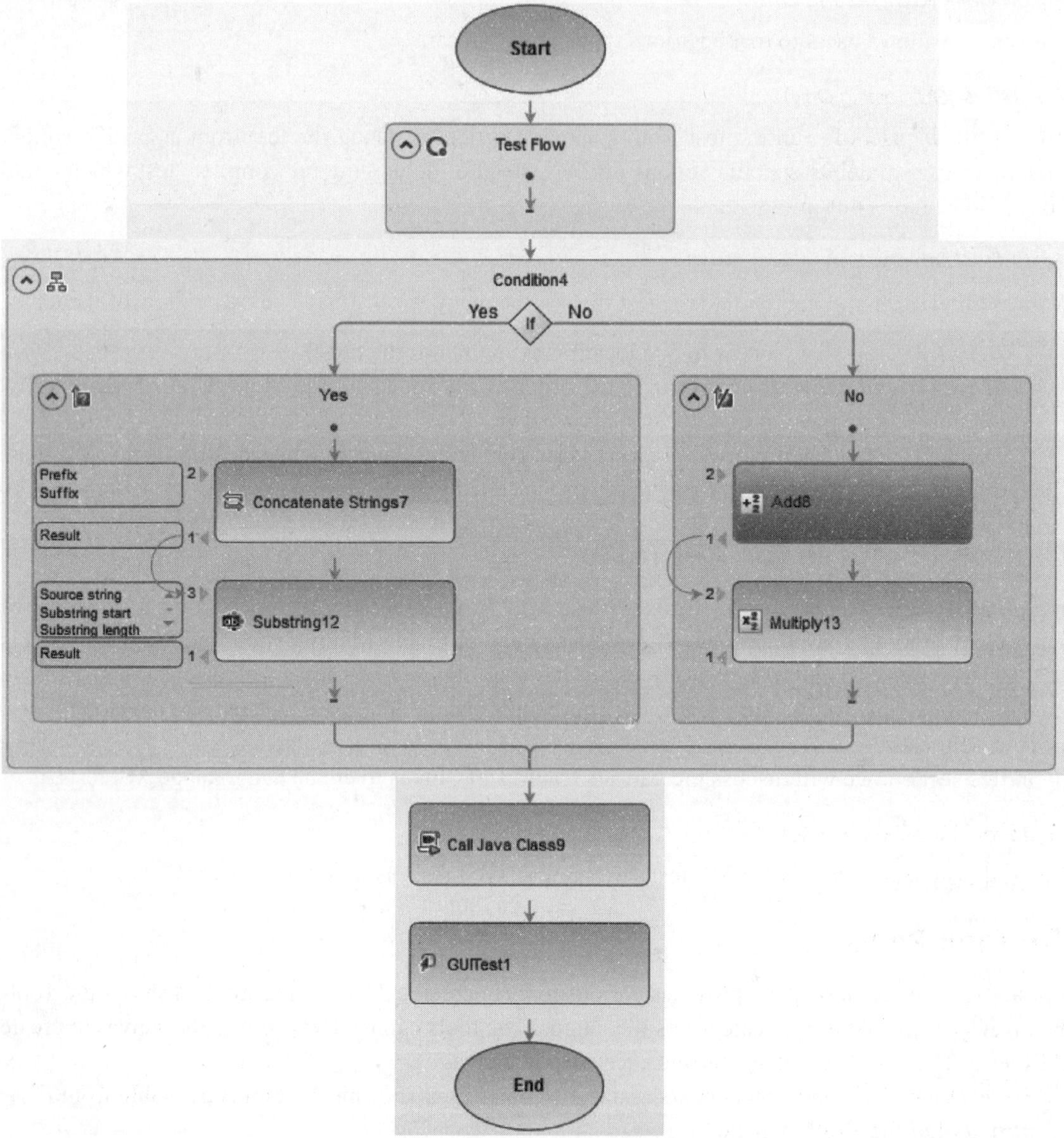

Figure 20.3 *Canvas for an API test*

Figure 20.3 shows *DB Connection* step. This has one input parameter—*DB Connection string* and two output parameters *Result* and *Result message*. The input parameter value of this step is defined *input* tab of the *Properties* pane as shown in the Fig. 20.6. If this parameter is not defined, then the test step displays an alert as shown in the Fig. 20.5. A click on this alert button displays an error message as shown in the Fig. 20.3.

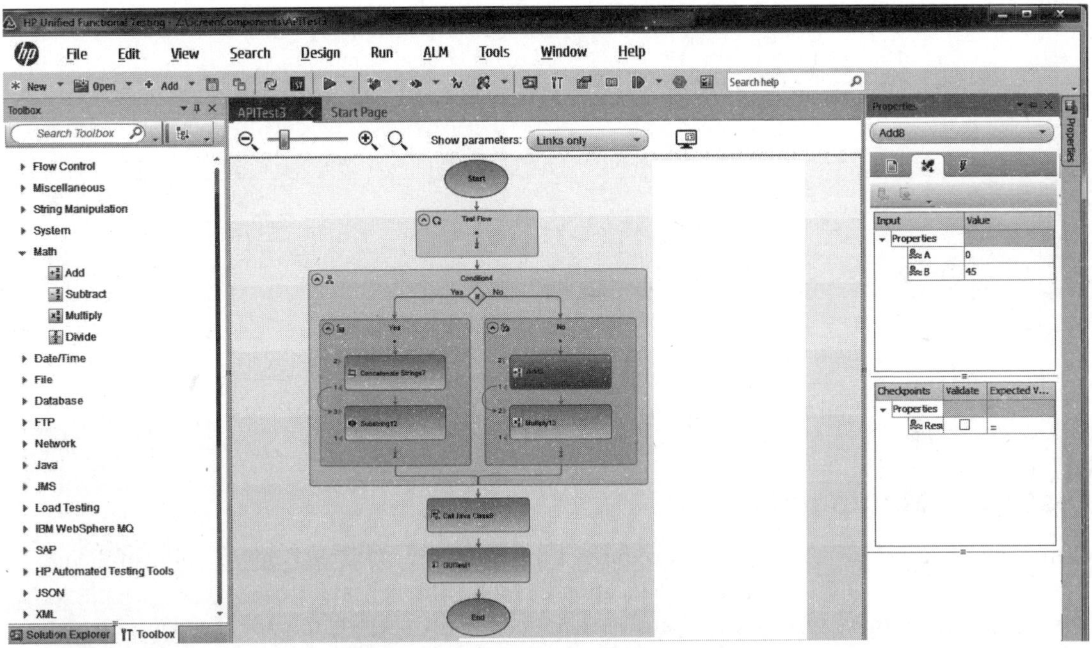

Figure 20.4 *Toolbox pane for API test*

A mouse click on the error message opens *input* tab (*Properties* pane). This tab allows users to define the input parameters of the test step. Figure 20.6 shows the *input* tab for the *Open Connection* step of Fig. 20.5.

These errors are also displayed in the *Error* pane. This error pane can be opened from Menu bar as: *View* → *Errors* or by pressing keys: CTRL+ALT+E. Fig. 20.7 shows the error pane for the *Open Connection* test step of Fig. 20.5.

Step Input/Output Property Connections (API Testing only)

Canvas allows to link output parameters of a test step as input parameter of another test step. This relationship is displayed as an arrow between the test steps. For example, in Fig. 20.3 output parameter of test step 'Concatenate Strings7' is used as input parameter for test step 'Substring12'.

Figure 20.5 *Canvas alerts for API test DB Connection step*

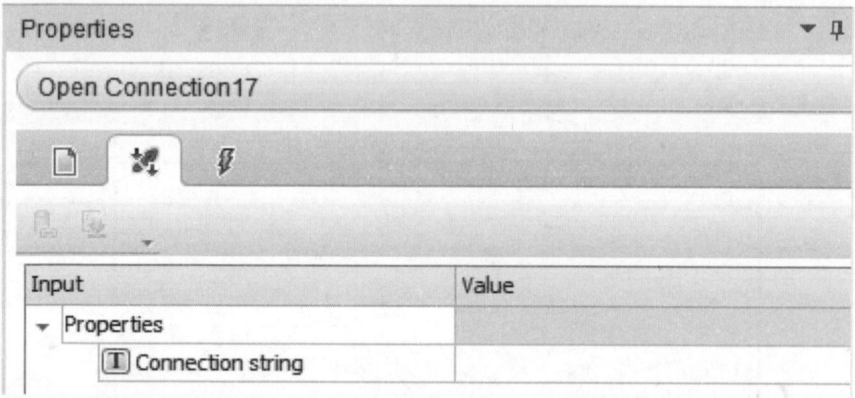

Figure 20.6 Input *tab for DB connection test step of API test*

Test Step Manipulation

Canvas allows users to manipulate the test flow in the many ways. Listed below are few of them:

- ***Reorder***: Drag a test step from one location to another in the test flow.
- ***Copy and Paste***: (API Tests only) Select a step and press CTRL+C to copy the step to the clipboard. Press CTRL+V to paste it into another location within the Test Flow.
- ***Delete***: Select a step and press the keyboard's Delete button to delete the step.

Tests Runs (API Testing only)

The Run Step utility allows users to run a single test step without running the entire test. During the execution, the test step uses the test data defined in the Properties pane. After test step execution is complete, the results are displayed in the Run Step Results pane.

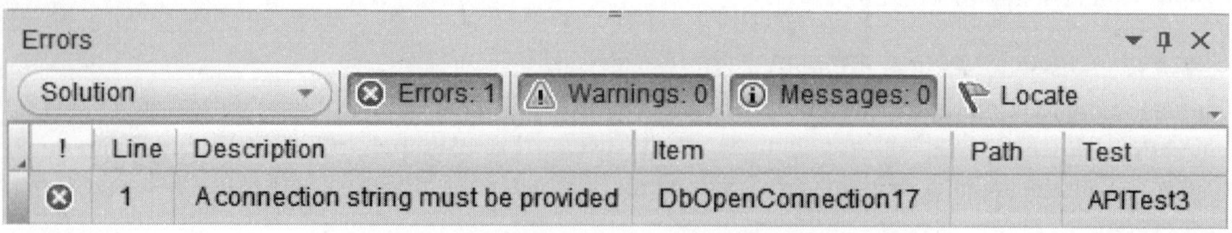

Figure 20.7 *Errors pane for API test step errors*

Chapter 21

Objects

The first step towards developing test code for an action (GUI test) is to identify the GUI objects and the operations to be performed on them. For example, development of login action would involve:

- On username edit box performing set operation to set the user name.
- On password edit box performing set operation to set the password.
- On login button performing a mouse click operation to login to the application.

Once the GUI objects have been identified, next step is to capture the attributes/properties that describe the object and store this description. UFT stores this description in an object storehouse called *Object Repository*. Each GUI object is assigned a unique name in object repository. This is called the *logical name* of the object. This logical name is used to locate a GUI object in object repository and to view/edit its description properties. Once GUI objects description is captured, next step is to write test code to simulate user actions on GUI objects. The test code uses logical name of the object to refer to a GUI object and instruct desired action (operation) on it. When this test code is executed, UFT first looks for an object in GUI that matches the description already stored. If a unique match (only one match) is found, then UFT executes the specified operation on the GUI object. For example, suppose a test code instructs to perform click action on the login button. Assume logical name of the login button is *Login*. UFT looks into the object repository to find the description properties of the object whose logical name is *Login*. Next, UFT looks into the AUT to find the GUI object whose description matches with the description of the *Login* button in object repository. If a unique match (only one match) is found, then UFT takes the action on the object as specified in the test code. In this case, UFT will execute a 'mouse click' action on the login button.

UFT OBJECT CLASS

All text boxes, check boxes, radio buttons, and other GUI objects are referred as an *Object* in UFT. When capturing these GUI objects, UFT maps these objects to a standard UFT object class for recognizing these objects. For example, for a web-based application, text box is recognized as WebEdit and check box as WebCheckBox. If UFT does not find a standard mapping class for an object in GUI, then that object is recognized as WebElement. Table 21.1 describes some of the widely used GUI objects of a web applications and its standard mapping class in UFT.

Table 21.1 Web application GUI objects and its standard mapping class in UFT

GUI Object	UFT Icon	Standard UFT Mapping Class
Browser		Browser
Page		Page
Frame		Frame
Edit box		WebEdit
Image		Image
Link		Link
Button		WebButton
Checkbox		WebCheckBox
List		WebList
Radio button		WebRadioGroup
Table		WebTable
Element		WebElement

OBJECT DESCRIPTIONS

Till now we discussed, UFT uses the description of the GUI object to identify the object during run-time. An important question you may ask here is—What are these object descriptions? Listed below are the various object descriptions which can be used to uniquely describe an object:

- Attributes of the object
- XPath of the object
- CSS path of the object
- Visual relation of the object with other objects in GUI
- Ordinal position of the object
- Image of the object

Attributes of the Object

The attributes of an object such as *name, html id, html tag* etc. can be used to uniquely describe an object. These attributes are defined for an object by the developer when he develops the GUI interface. A developer may choose to define one or more attributes for an object. These attributes are referred as *Description Properties* in UFT.

An important question you may ask is—How to find which attributes have been defined for an object in AUT? There are two ways of finding out the object attributes defined for an object by the developer—by viewing HTML code of the object or by using UFT Object Spy tool.

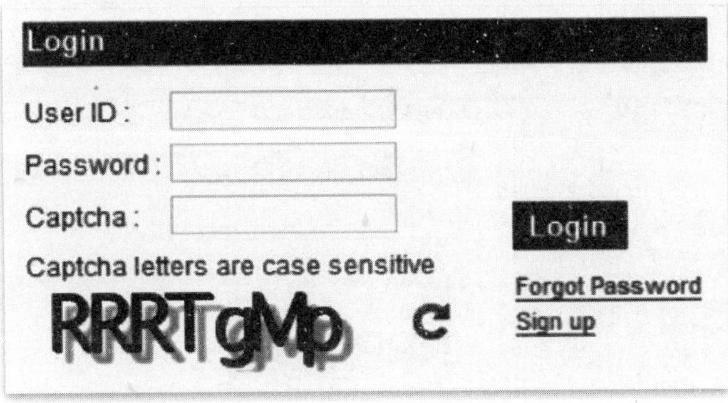

Figure 21.1 *Login page of a sample application*

Viewing Object Attributes in HTML Code

Browser provides various tools to view HTML code of the web page and HTML code of the specific object of the web page.

Consider the login section (page) of a sample application as shown in the Fig. 21.1. In this section, we will discuss how to view HTML code of an object using IE, Firefox and Chrome browser.

Finding Object Attributes Using IE Browser

Follow the steps below to view HTML code of a webpage object in IE Browser:

- Navigate *Tools* → *Developer tools* or press F12 key.
  The developer tools frame opens as shown in the Fig. 21.2.
- Click on the arrow button (Select element by click) and point and click it on the GUI object whose HTML code is to be viewed.
  HTML code of the object will be highlighted in the developer tools frame as shown in the Fig. 21.2. Figure 21.2 shows the HTML code of the *UserID* edit box.

Finding Object Attributes Using Firefox Browser

Follow the steps below to view HTML code of a webpage object in Firefox Browser:

- Install Firefox addin *Firebug* and Firebug addon *Firepath*.
- Launch firebug by clicking on the firebug button .
  Firebug frame opens as shown in the Fig. 21.3.
- Open tab 'Firepath'.
- Click on the arrow button (click an element on the page to inspect) and point and click it on the GUI object whose HTML code is to be viewed.
  HTML code of the object will be highlighted in the developer tools frame as shown in the Fig. 21.3a below. Figure 21.3 shows the HTML code of the *UserID* edit box.
- Alternatively, Firebug HTML tab can also be used to view object attributes. Figure 21.3b below shows the HTML code of the 'UserId' object as viewed in HTML tab.

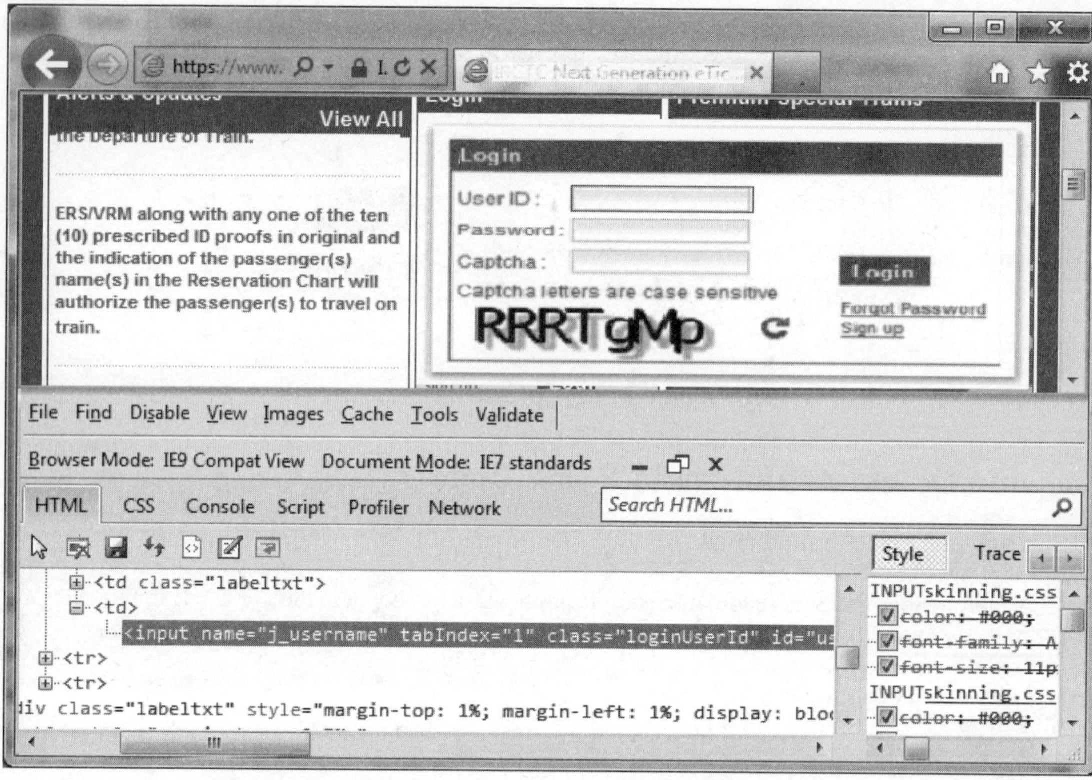

Figure 21.2 *HTML code of the **User ID** edit box (IE Browser)*

As shown in the Fig. 21.3 above HTML code of the *UserID* edit box is:

```
<input id= "usernameId" class= "loginUserId" type= "text" tabi-
ndex= "1" maxlength= "35" size= "15" autocomplete= "off" name=
"j_username">
```

Table 21.2 lists out the attributes that the developer has defined for the *UserID* edit box (as visible in the HTML code).

Table 21.2 Attributes of UserID edit box

Object Attribute	Attribute Value
id	usernameId
class	loginUserId
type	Text
tabindex	1
maxlength	35
size	15
autocomplete	Off
name	j_username

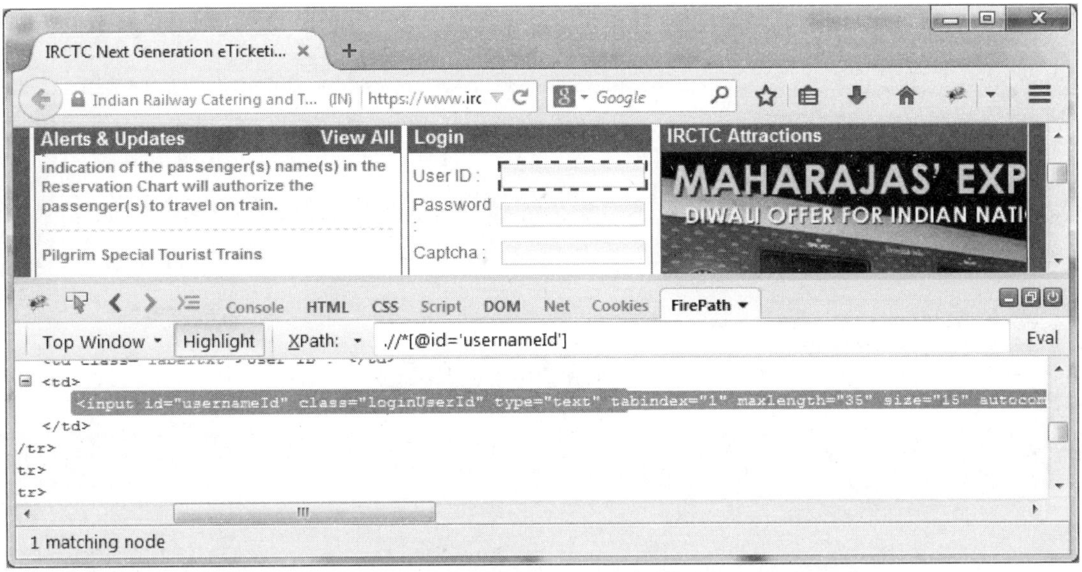

Figure 21.3a *HTML code of the User ID edit box (Firepath tab)*

> **NOTES**
> For the above HTML code, <input> is tag name of the object. Edit boxes, buttons, radio buttons and checkboxes have tag name <input>, link objects have tag name <a> and list boxes have tag name <select>.

> **NOTES**
> A developer may choose to define more attributes (say *href* of an object) or less attributes depending on the object type and GUI object development standards for the project.

In UFT, one or more than one attribute can be used to uniquely describe an object. Unique description of an object implies that the description of the object is sufficient to find one exact object in the GUI (web page) whose description matches to the unique description.

Assume both *UserId* and *Password* edit box have *maxlength* attribute defined as 35. Now consider using this attribute to create a unique description of the *UserID* edit box. However, this description will result in two matches—UserID edit box and Password edit box, this is because the maxlength attribute value of both the objects is 35. Hence, this attribute cannot be used alone to uniquely describe the object.

Now assume *class* attribute value of UserId and Password edit box are *loginUserId* and *loginPasswordId* respectively. Consider using attributes *maxlength=35* and *class=loginUserId* to create a unique description of *UserId* edit box. This description will result in one unique match which is – *UserId* edit box. This is because this is the only object whose description matches with the created description.

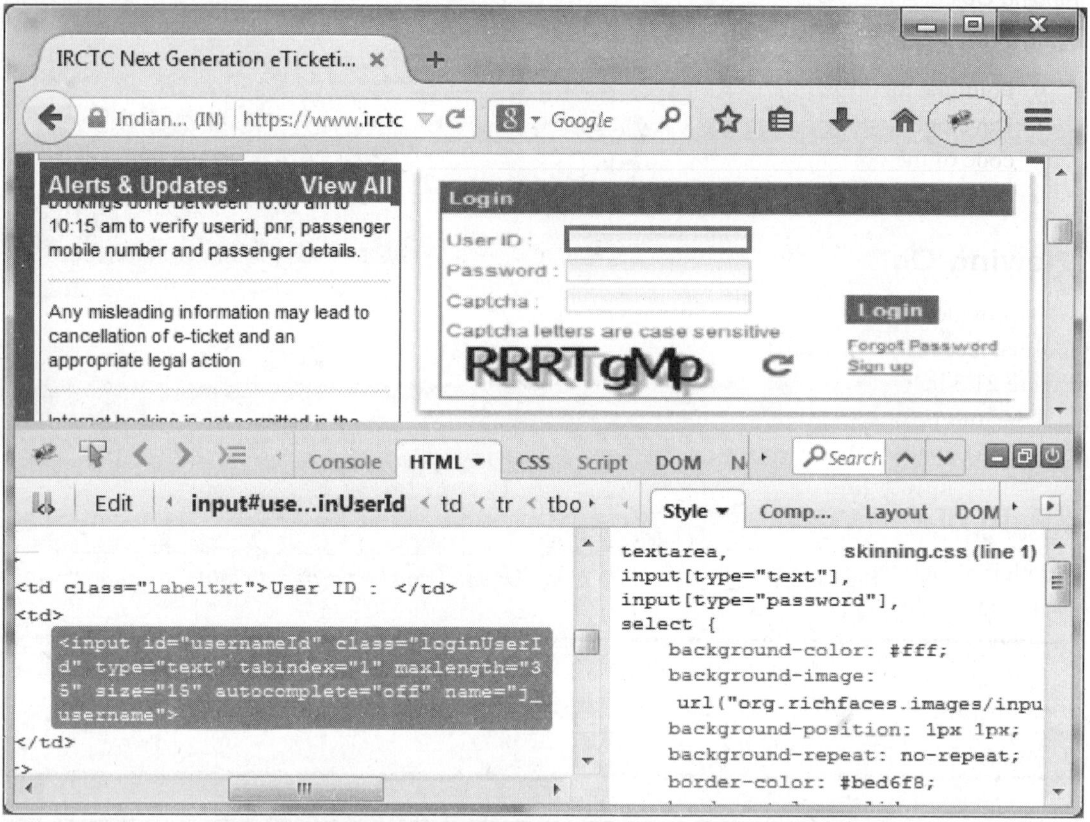

Figure 21.3b *HTML code of the User ID edit box (HTML tab)*

> **NOTES**
> Alternatively, we may also choose one or more combination of attributes *html id, html tag, name* etc. to uniquely describe an object.

> **NOTES**
> Attributes *maxlength, size* etc. are not reliable attributes. Hence, use of these attributes is to be avoided while creating a unique description of the object. This is because developers may create multiple objects with same attributes values for these attributes. Also, developer can change these attributes any time during development cycle as per his liking and without the need of a change requirement. In this case, the test code will fail as it will find no object in GUI which matches the defined description of the object. Reliable object attributes such as *html id, html tag, name, class* etc. are to be used while creating a unique description of the object.

> **NOTES**
> *html id* is the most reliable attribute to describe an object. This is because for any web page, no two GUI objects should have same value for *html id* attribute.

Finding Object Attributes Using Chrome Browser

Follow the steps below to view HTML code of a webpage object in Chrome Browser:

- Point the mouse on the object and right click and select option 'Inspect Element'.
  Developer tools frame opens as shown in the Fig. 21.4 below. This frame highlights the HTML code of the object.
  Figure 21.4 below shows the HTML code of the edit box object 'Select Departure City".

Viewing Object Attributes Using Object Spy Tool

UFT provides *Object Spy* tool to view attributes of an object. Viewing object attributes using this tool has been discussed in detail in Chapter "Solution, Test And Action" and 'Object Repository'. Figure 21.5 below shows the attributes of the *UserID* object as captured by the object spy tool.

UFT offers various ways of capturing GUI objects description to object repository. This is discussed in detail in the chapter 'Object Repository'.

XPath of the Object

XPath is a query language for selecting nodes from XML document. It is a language based on the tree representation of the XML document. Since, HTML document also has a tree structure; XPath can be used to describe objects based on its node position in the tree and the node attributes. Assume the HTML code of the *UserID* edit box object is as shown in Fig. 21.6.

As per the above HTML code, the XPath of the *UserId* editbox is:

```
html/body/div/div/div[3]/form/div/div[2]/input
```

This XPath traverses through all the nodes of the HTML document till the node of the UserId node (object) is reached. Since, this path uses all the nodes to describe the XPath position of the object it is called absolute XPath. An important disadvantage of this XPath expression is - it fails to describe the element even if a small node say <div> node is inserted in the node tree. Any such node insertion causes a change in the absolute position of the node (edit box) in the tree.

A solution to this problem can be to directly look for a specific node type say input, form, etc. That is, look for an object using its tag name. Each web object has a specific tag name. for example, tag name for a edit box object is '*input*', and tag name for a link object is '*a*'. The XPath expression to locate an object whose tag name is input is shown below:

```
//input
```

This expression looks for an object whose node type is *input*. In other words, it tries to search (locate) for an object whose tag name is input.

There are three edit boxes in Fig. 21.1. This implies there are three objects whose tag name is *input*. Hence, this expression is not sufficient to uniquely describe the *UserId* edit box.

A solution to this problem is to use object attributes in XPath expression to describe the object. The XPath expression using *class* attribute of the of the *UserId* edit box is shown below:

```
//input[@class='loginUserId']
```

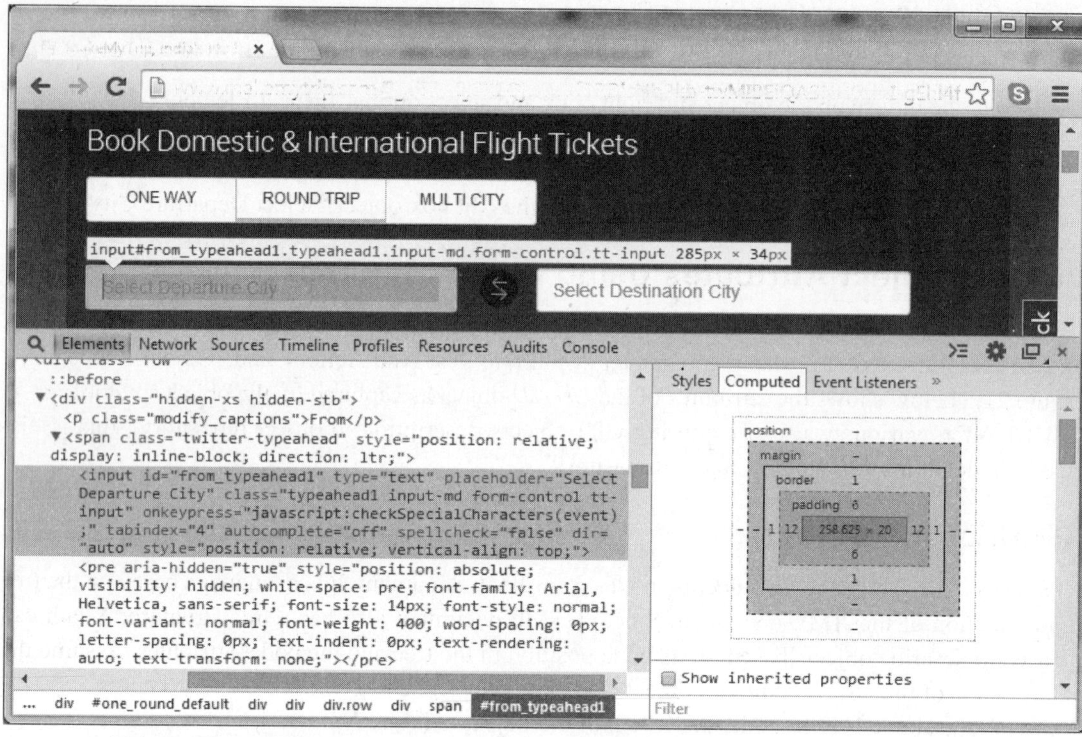

Figure 21.4 *HTML code of the* Select Departure City *edit box (Chrome Browser)*

This XPath expression describes a node (object) whose node type (tag name) is <input> and *class* attribute value is *loginUserId.*

In many scenarios, one attribute is not sufficient to uniquely describe the object. XPath allows using multiple attributes to describe an object. The XPath expression below describes *UserId* edit box object using three of its attributes – *class*, *id* and *name*.

```
//input[@class='loginUserId'][@id='usernameId'][@name='j_username']
```

The above XPath expression describes an <input> object whose *class* attribute value is *loginUserId*, *id* attribute value is *usernameId* and *name* attribute value is *j_username*. This XPath is termed as logical XPath of the object.

Using XPath expression to identify objects is described in detail in chapter "Object Identification using XPath".

CSS Path of the Object

Cascading Style Sheets (CSS) is a style sheet language that defines the presentation semantics (the look and formatting) of a HTML or XML document. For example, CSS describes fonts, colors, margins, height, width, background images, and many other presentation semantics. The purpose of CSS is to separate the presentation information from the markup or content.

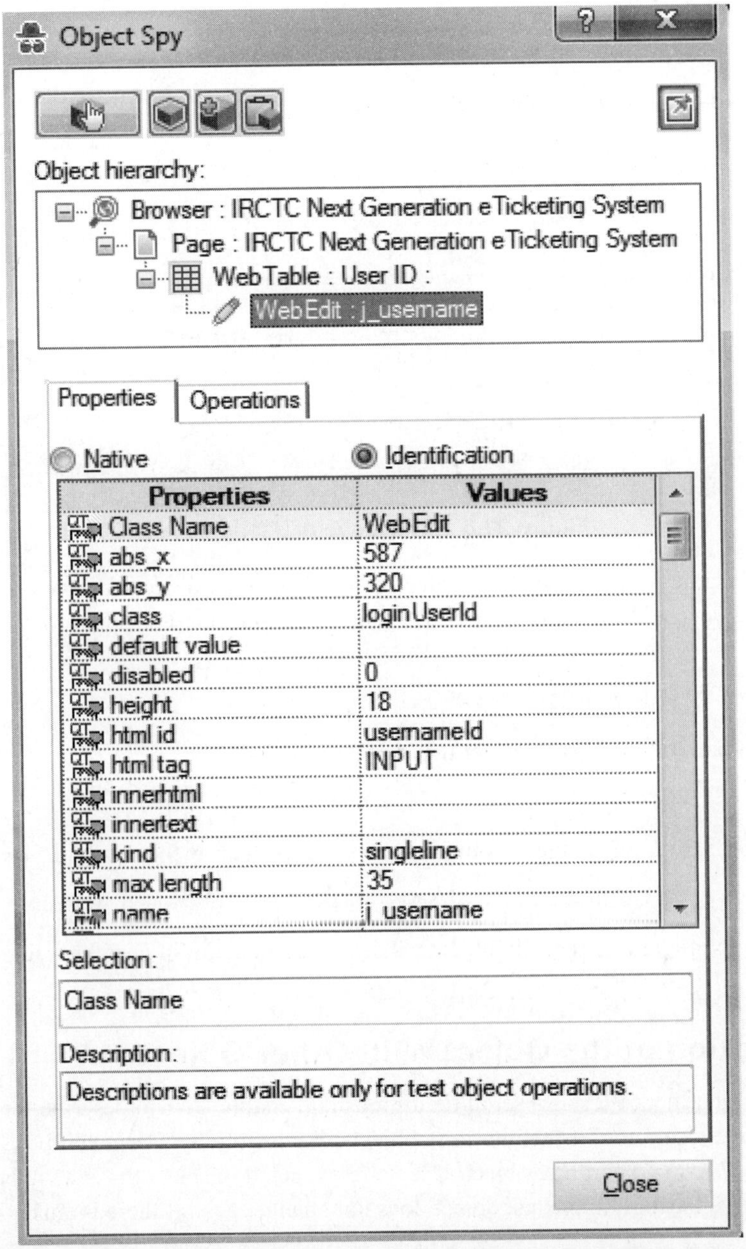

Figure 21.5 *Viewing attributes of **UserId** edit box using Object Spy tool*

CSS defines a list of pattern-matching rules which determine which style is to be applied to elements in the DOM. These patterns are called Selectors. If all rules in the pattern are satisfied for a certain element, then the Selector matches the element. Browser applies the defined style to the matched element.

```
⊟ <html>
   ⊞ <head>
   ⊟ <body>
      ⊟ <div class="container_16">
         ⊟ <div class="container">
            ⊞ <div class="grid_9">
            ⊞ <div class="grid 7">
            ⊟ <div class="grid_4" style="margin-top: 0.2%;">
               ⊞ <script type="text/javascript">
               ⊞ <div id="loginerrorpanel" style="visibility: hidden;">
               ⊟ <form id="loginFormId" method="post" action="home">
                  ⊟ <div class="grid_16 alpha g_box" style="height:250px;position: rela
                     ⊞ <div class="g_head g_padding ">
                     ⊟ <div class="grid_16 alpha" style="margin-top:2%;">
                        ⊟ <input id="usernameId" class="loginUserId" type="text" tab
                          index="1" maxlength="35" size="15" autocomplete="off" name
                          ="j_username">
```

Figure 21.6 *HTML code of* UserId *object*

UFT uses the same principles of CSS Selectors to identify an object in HTML tree. CSS path of an object can be designed in a similar way as XPath. The absolute CSS path for *UserId* edit box is shown below:

```
html>body>div>div>div>div>form>div>div>input
```

The logical CSS path of the *UserId* object using node name is:

```
input
```

The logical CSS of the *UserId* object using node type and node (object) attributes is:

```
//inputclass='loginUserId'][id='usernameId'][name='j_username']
```

Using CSS path expression to identify objects is described in detail in chapter "Object Identification using CSS Path".

Visual Relation of the Object With Other Objects in GUI

Visual Relation Identifier (VRI) is a set of definitions that enable UFT to describe the object in reference to the relative location of its neighboring objects. For example, *UserId* edit box object is always vertically above *Password* edit box object. Users are expected to select those neighboring objects as VRI whose relative location to the test object does not change, even if there is a user interface design modification.

This identification mechanism is to be used when the UI is under continuous changes. Visual relation identification mechanism is discussed in detail in chapter "Virtual Relation Identification".

Ordinal Position of the Object

Ordinal position of the object refers to the order in which the object appears in application UI (location) or application code (index) or the order in which the application is launched (creation time). For example, for the Fig. 21.1, username object is the first edit box in UI and password object is the second edit box in UI. So the ordinal (location) value of username edit box is 0 and ordinal (location) value of password edit box is 1.

Chapter "Ordinal Based Identification" describes in detail about ordinal identifiers and how to use them to describe (or identify) GUI objects.

Image of the Object

Image of the object can be used to describe the object. At run-time, UFT looks for an object whose image description matches with the stored image. Image based identification is useful when all other methods to describe the object uniquely has failed. This generally happens if UFT does not support the technology which has been used to develop the GUI.

Chapter 'Image based Identification (Insight)' discussed in detail on how to identify object using image based identification mechanism.

WHICH DESCRIPTIONS TO CHOOSE TO DESCRIBE AN OBJECT

So far, we discussed various object descriptions that can be used to describe a GUI object. While developing tests, an important question that can come to our mind is which description to use to describe the object. Listed below is prioritized list of description methods to use for creating a unique definition of an object.

- Attributes of the object
- XPath or CSS path of the object
- Visual relation of the object with other objects in GUI
- Ordinal position of the object
- Image of the object

We should first try to uniquely describe the object using its attributes. If object attributes are not sufficient to uniquely describe the object then XPath or CSS Path is to be used. If XPath or CSS path also fails to uniquely describe the object then visual relation of the object with other visible GUI objects is to be used. If this also fails then ordinal position of the object is to be used to create a unique definition of the object. If all the above mechanisms fail, then as a last resort, image of the object is to be used to describe the object.

UFT offers the flexibility to define one or more of the descriptions of an object in object repository. Figure 21.7 below shows the various descriptions (except image and ordinal position) captured in object repository for *UserId* edit box object.

Figure 21.8 below shows the visual relation identification description as specified (described) in OR. The below description instructs UFT to looks for an object which is vertically above the password edit box object.

Figure 21.9 below shows the ordinal description and image description as stored in OR for describing *UserId* object.

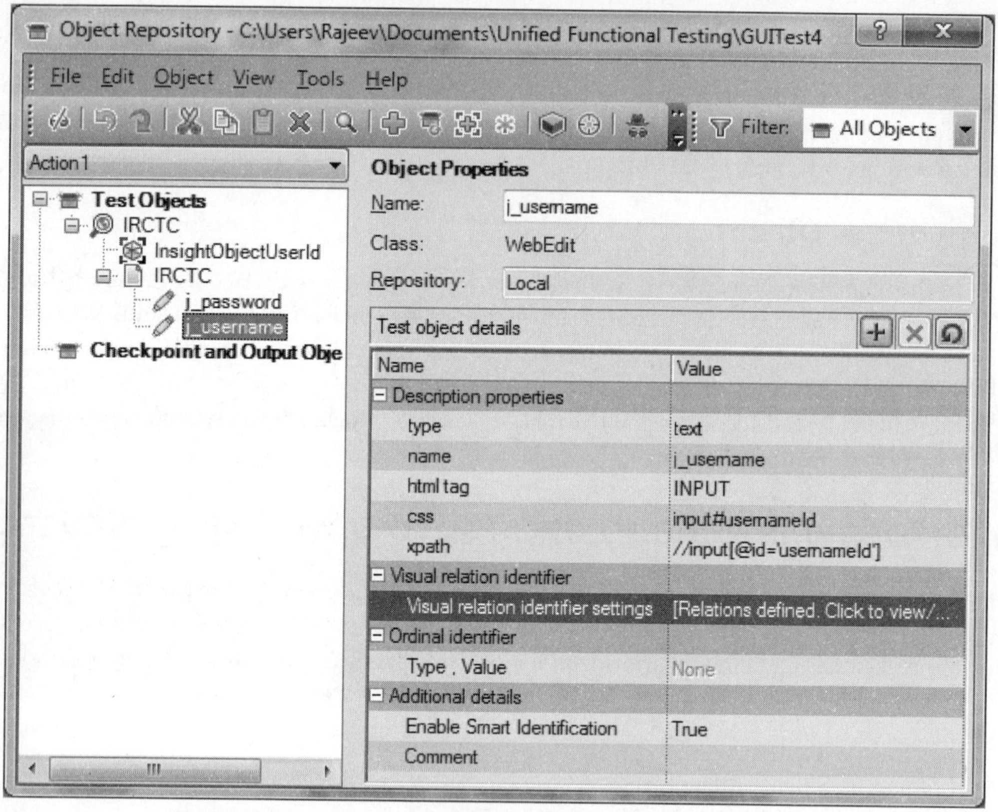

Figure 21.7 *Description of UserId object as captured in OR*

How UFT Identifies Objects During Run Time

UFT uses the description of the object captured in object repository to locate the object in UI. When test code is executed, UFT first looks for an object in GUI that matches the description already stored. If a unique match (only one match) is found, then UFT executes the specified operation on the GUI object. UFT object identification mechanism has been discussed in detail in the chapter 'Object Identification Mechanism'.

How UFT Identifies Objects during run time when Multiple Descriptions of An Object are Defined in OR

UFT allows the flexibility to use one or more than one description methods to describe the object. The definition of the object per description method is saved in object repository as shown in the Fig. 21.7, 8 and 9. UFT creates a sequence of all these description (identification) methods. During test code execution, UFT uses the description methods to locate the object one after another as per the sequence. If a specific description method is able to uniquely identify the object, then the object is declared found and rest of the description methods is ignored. Flow diagram (Fig. 21.10) below describes the object identification mechanism used by UFT.

- XPath or CSS properties are considered as description properties during UFT object identification process (refer Fig. 21.7).
- If Web object identifiers such as XPath or CSS properties are defined for these test objects, then they are used before other description properties. If one or more objects are found, UFT continues to identify the object using the description properties. For details, refer section on 'Object Identification'.

UFT Add-ins for Object Identification

UFT provides various add-ins to automate various types of applications such as Java, SAP, Terminal Emulator etc. Appropriate add-ins are to be loaded in UFT before starting to automate the specific application. If the respective add-in is not loaded, the UFT won't be able to identify the GUI objects of the application. For example, if a Java application is to be automated but Java add-in is not loaded in UFT, then UFT won't be able to recognize Java objects such as buttons, edit boxes, etc. In this case,

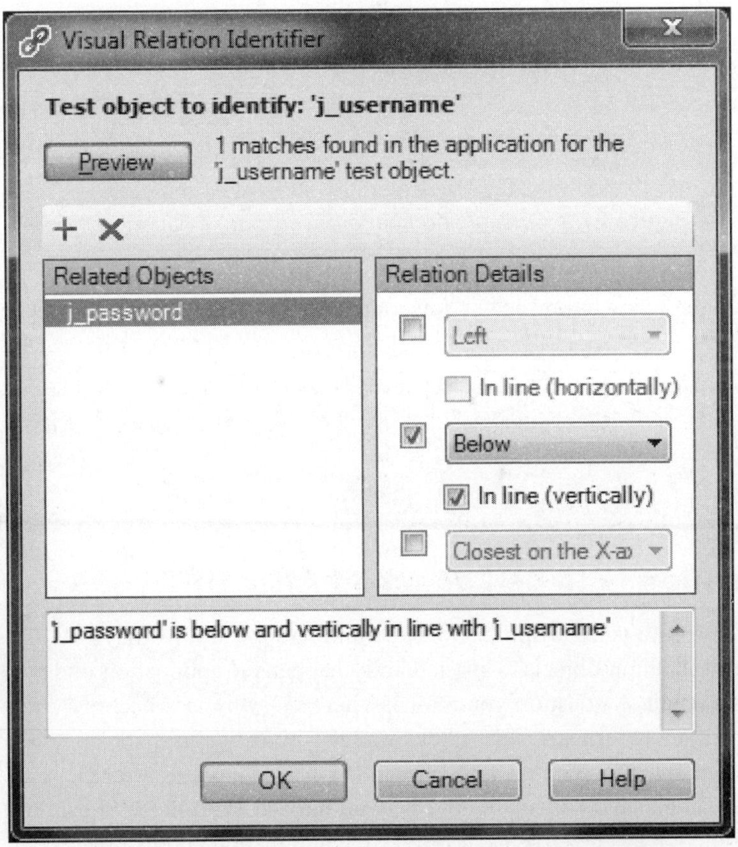

Figure 21.8 *Visual relation description of* UserId *object*

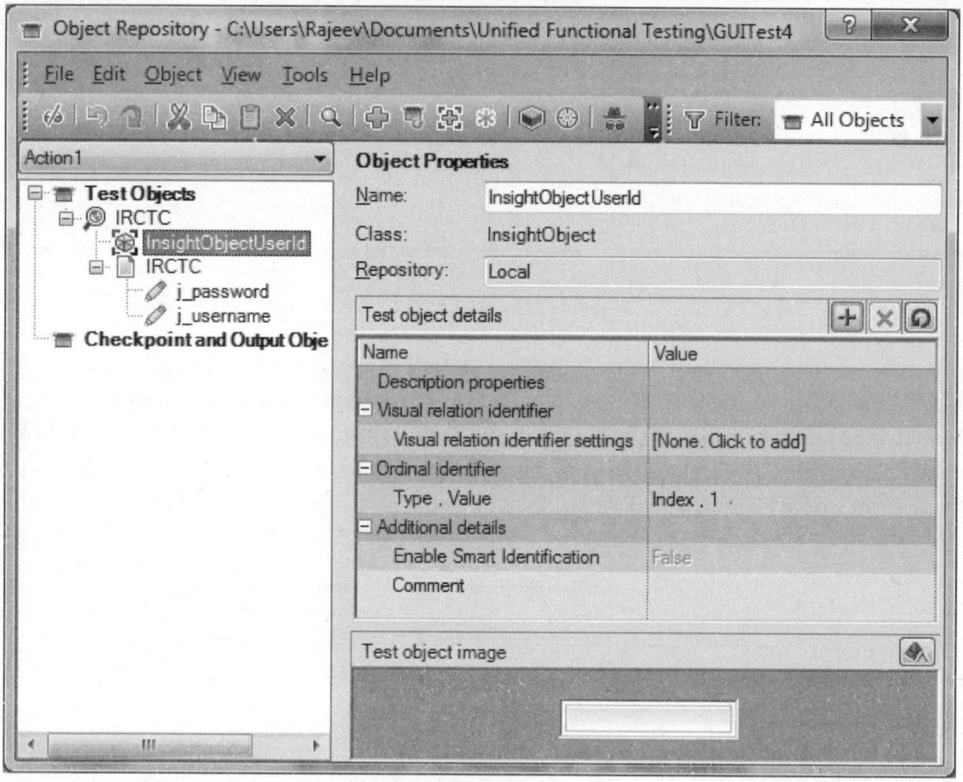

Figure 21.9 *Ordinal and Image description of* UserId *object*

UFT will identify the Java window as window (application) object and no objects inside this window will be identified.

> **NOTES** Standard Windows add-in is loaded by default in UFT. UFT does not provide option to avoid loading this add-in, so this add-in is always loaded.

Why Application is to be Launched After UFT

When trying to automate various applications, certain times you must have observed that UFT fails to recognize the application objects. This generally happens if application under test is opened first and then UFT is opened. A question you may ask here is—why is it necessary to open UFT before starting the application under test? This is because UFT places certain hooks in the operating system environment to communicate with the application. If UFT is launched after the AUT, then UFT is not able to place these hooks and hence not able to communicate with the application. In the absence of this communication, UFT is not able to recognize the application and its objects.

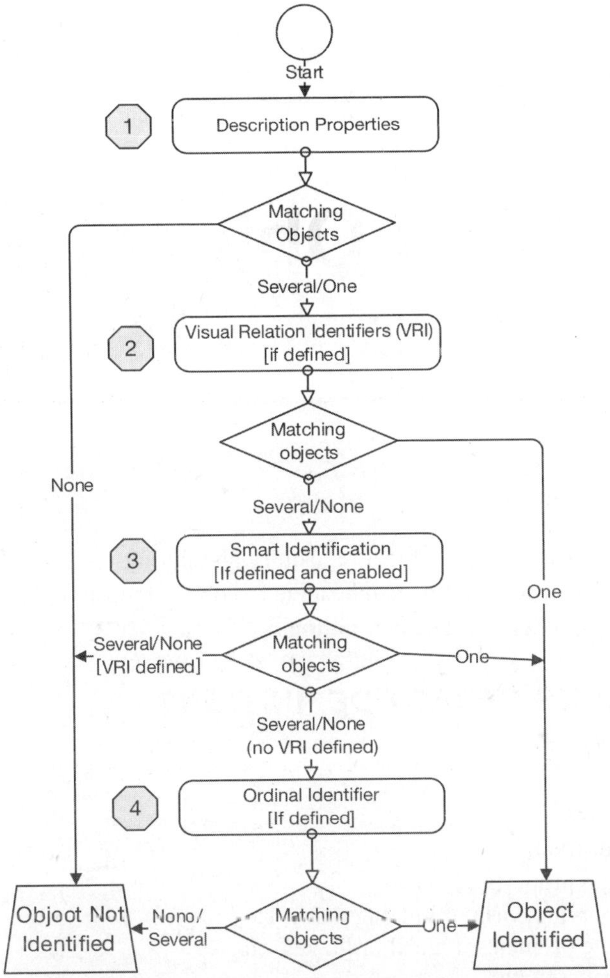

Figure 21.10 *UFT Object Identification Mechanism*

> NOTES
>
> A hook is a point in the system message-handling mechanism where an application (say UFT) can install a subroutine to monitor the message traffic in the system (say AUT) and process certain types of messages before they reach the target window procedure. In other words, a *hook* is a mechanism by which an application can intercept events, such as messages, mouse actions, and keystrokes.

However, there are some exceptions to this behavior. For example, it is not necessary to launch any native window application after UFT. Even if the application is launched before UFT, UFT will be able to recognize the application and its objects (Window, WinButton, Dialog, etc.). This is because UFT uses native window APIs to interact with native window applications. These APIs are available as soon as the Windows system is started. Another example is SAP, wherein UFT (SAP add-in) uses SAP GUI Scripting to communicate with SAP GUI objects. Therefore, it is not necessary to launch UFT before SAP application launch.

Chapter 22

Test Object Learning Mechanism

UFT captures the object definition in object repository and during test execution uses this definition to locate objects in UI. Object definition can be added to object repository by using Objet Spy tool or by using the add objects to object repository button of OR.

HOW UFT LEARNS OBJECT DEFINITION?

Object definitions which help uniquely describe an object can be one of the following:

- Object source index
- Object automatic xpath
- Object description properties such as
  - Object attributes such as html id, tag name, etc.
  - Object absolute ordinates, logical ordinates, etc.
  - Object automatic xpath
  - Object XPath
  - Object CSS path
- Object Visual Relation Identifiers (VRI)
- Object ordinal identifiers
  - Object source index
  - Object index
  - Object location
  - Object creation time
- Object image (insight)
- Object source index is the native source index property of the object.
- Automatic xpath is same as xpath of the object. The difference is xpath property is to be manually specified by the user while UFT automatically learns automatic xpath.
- Automatic xpath and source index definitions are hidden and are not displayed on the object repository window. UFT automatically learns these properties if it is configured to do so. During

run-time, UFT may use these definitions to locate the object, if it is configured to do so. Since, these definitions are hidden; users cannot view or edit these definitions.

- When UFT learns an object, object description properties (except object xpath and object css path) and ordinal identifiers are automatically captured by UFT as object definitions in OR.

WHICH OBJECT DEFINITIONS UFT LEARNS?

UFT classifies the object learnable descriptions in broadly four categories—source index, automatic xpath, description properties and ordinal identifiers.

Out of the various description properties discussed above, UFT automatically captures object attributes, object ordinates, object source index and object automatic xpath while learning object definition. That is while capturing object definition to object repository.

UFT first learns the description properties of the object. Once it has learned all defined description properties, then it learns the ordinal identifier of the object. At a time UFT learns only two ordinal identifiers. One is source index and other can be creationtime, index or location.

Object XPath, CSS path, object VRI and object image needs to be explicitly defined by the user to object descriptions in OR, if required. UFT does not automatically captures these object descriptions to OR, while learning object definition.

WHAT IS SOURCE INDEX?

Source index is the native object property. It refers to position of the object in the HTML DOM. Though source index property of an object is not visible in object repository, it can be viewed in UI using object spy. Figure 22.1 shows the source index property of Google Search page edit box object.

Source index property of test object can be retrieved using UFT code as shown below:

```
Set oPg = Browser("Google").Page("Google")
Print oPg.WebEdit("q").GetTOProperty("source_index") 'Output:: 139
```

Source index property of run-time object can be retrieved using UFT code as shown below:

```
Print                    oPg.WebEdit("q").GetROProperty("attribute/
sourceindex") 'Output::139
Alternatively,
Print oPg.WebEdit("q").Object.sourceIndex    'Output::139
Alternatively,
Print oPg.WebEdit("q"). GetROProperty("source_index")    'Output::139
```

WHAT IS AUTOMATIC XPATH?

Automatic xpath is the xpath of the object automatically learned by UFT. Though this property of the object is not displayed in object repository, it can found using UFT code as shown below:

Example: Find automatic xpath as learned by UFT for Google Search page edit box.

```
Set oPg = Browser("Google").Page("Google")
Print oPg.WebEdit("q").GetTOProperty("_xpath")  'Output:://INPUT[@
id="gbqfq"]
```

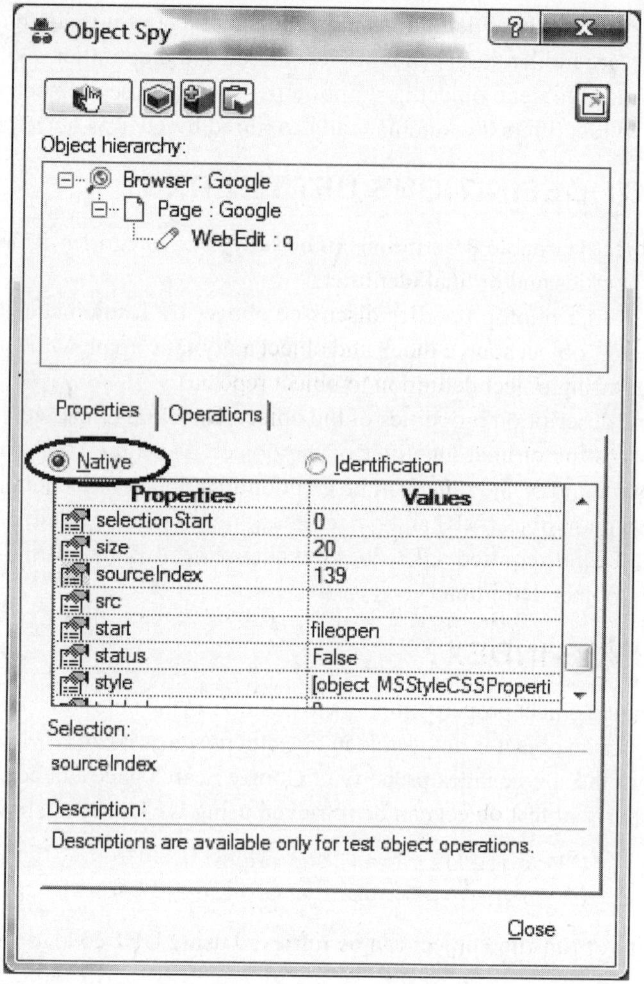

Figure 22.1 *Viewing objects native property 'source index'*

Run-time xpath aproperty of the object can be found using the UFT code as shown below:

```
Print oPg.WebEdit("q").GetROProperty("_xpath") 'Output://INPUT[@
id="gbqfq"]
```

WHAT ARE DESCRIPTION PROPERTIES?

Description properties are the object properties that define an object. It can be object attributes, object ordinates, object xpath or css path.

Object attributes define the type of the object and the features of the object. Example—html tag, html id, name, class, etc.

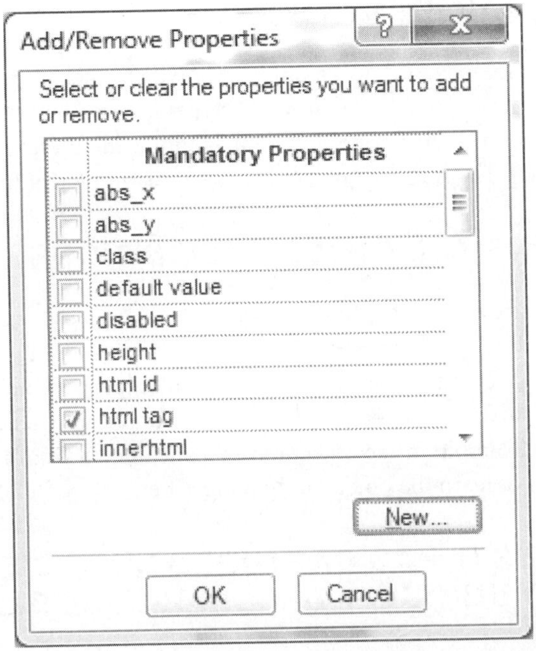

Figure 22.2 *List of UFT supported description properties for WebEdit Object*

Object ordinates describe the location of the object relative to the screen or page. Example—x, y, abs_x,abs_y, etc,

XPath describes the hierarchical position of the object in the HTML document tree. Example—xpath.

CSS refers to look and feel semantics of the object. Example—css.

The complete list of UFT supported description properties for an object can be viewed in Object Identification dialog box. For example, follow the steps below to view the UFT supported description properties of WebEdit object:

1. On Menu bar, navigate *Tools → Object Identification...*

   Object Identification dialog box opens.
2. On Object Identification dialog box, select *Environment = Web* and *Test Object Classes = WebEdit*.
3. Click on the *Add/Remove* button.

   Add/Remove Properties dialog box opens as shown in Fig. 22.2. This dialog box displays all of the UFT supported description properties for the selected object.

At a time, UFT can learn one or more description properties. UFT provides a default set of description properties that UFT will learn for every UFT test object. The description properties that UFT uses learn an object can be configured from Object Identification dialog box.

WHAT ARE ORDINAL IDENTIFIERS?

Ordinal identifiers refer to the position of the object relative to other objects in source code or UI. It is a numerical value and starts with 0. UFT provides three ordinal identifiers to describe an object—index, location and creationtime. At a time, UFT leans only ordinal identifier. The ordinal identifier which UFT should learn for describing an object is configured in Object Identification dialog box.

DOES UFT LEARNS ALL OBJECT DEFINITIONS?

So far we discussed the various object definitions which UFT uses or learns to uniquely describe an object. Now a question which you may ask—Does UFT captures all object definitions to OR when learning an object? The answer is UFT does not captures all object definitions to OR. It only captures those definitions which is sufficient to uniquely describe the object and hence, uniquely locate it in UI during test execution. For example, if the object attributes learned are sufficient to uniquely describe the object, then UFT will not learn the object ordinal identifiers.

HOW UFT DECIDES IT HAS CAPTURED SUFFICIENT INFORMATION TO UNIQUELY DESCRIBE AN OBJECT?

UFT classifies the object learnable descriptions in broadly two categories—description properties and ordinal identifiers. UFT learns the ordinal identifiers only if it is not able to uniquely describe the object using all defined description properties.

UFT first uses the description properties one by one to describe the object. After learning a specific description property, UFT uses this learned description to check if the learned description is sufficient to uniquely locate the object in UI. If UFT is able to uniquely locate the object then it stops learning other remaining description properties and ordinal identifiers of the object. The learned description of the object is then created or updated in object repository. In case, UFT is not able to uniquely locate the object, then it will pick and learn one of the remaining description properties. Then, UFT will use the current learned description property along with the previously learned description properties to check if all these learned descriptions are sufficient to uniquely identify the object in UI. This process goes on till UFT is able create to a unique description of the object or it runs out of the description properties.

If UFT runs out of the description properties but still not able to uniquely describe the object then it learns the ordinal identifier of the object. UFT uses the learned ordinal identifier value of the object along with all the learned description properties to check if it is able to uniquely locate the object in UI. Ordinal identifier helps UFT to uniquely describe the object. This is because at any given time an object in UI always has a unique ordinal identifier.

SOURCE INDEX LEARNING MECHANISM

UFT learns the source index of the object if it is configured to do so. Follow the steps below to activate source index learning mechanism:

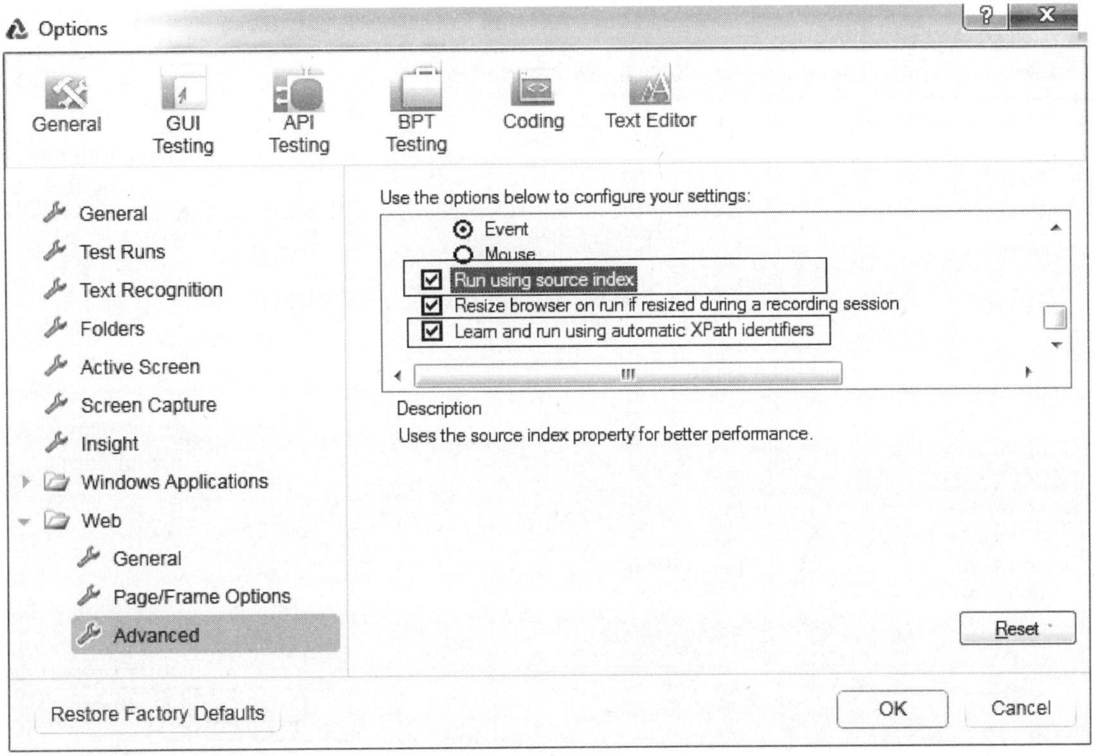

Figure 22.3 *Enabling UFT learning mechanism for source index and automatic xpath*

1. Navigate *Tools → Options*.
   Options dialog box opens.
2. Select tab *GUI Testing*.
   GUI Testing tab opens.
3. Select node *Web → Advanced*.
   Advanced web settings are displayed.
4. Scroll down and enable option '*Run using source index*' as shown in the Fig. 22.3.

AUTOMATIC XPATH LEARNING MECHANISM

UFT automatically learns the xpath of the object if it is configured to do so. Follow the steps as mentioned above and select checkbox '*Learn and Run using XPath identifiers*' to activate automatic xpath learning mechanism.

DESCRIPTION PROPERTIES LEARNING MECHANISM

In the above section, we discussed UFT provides a set of description properties which can be used to describe an object. While learning an object, UFT uses only those description properties which it has been instructed to use to describe an object. Now you may ask—Where UFT defines which descrip-

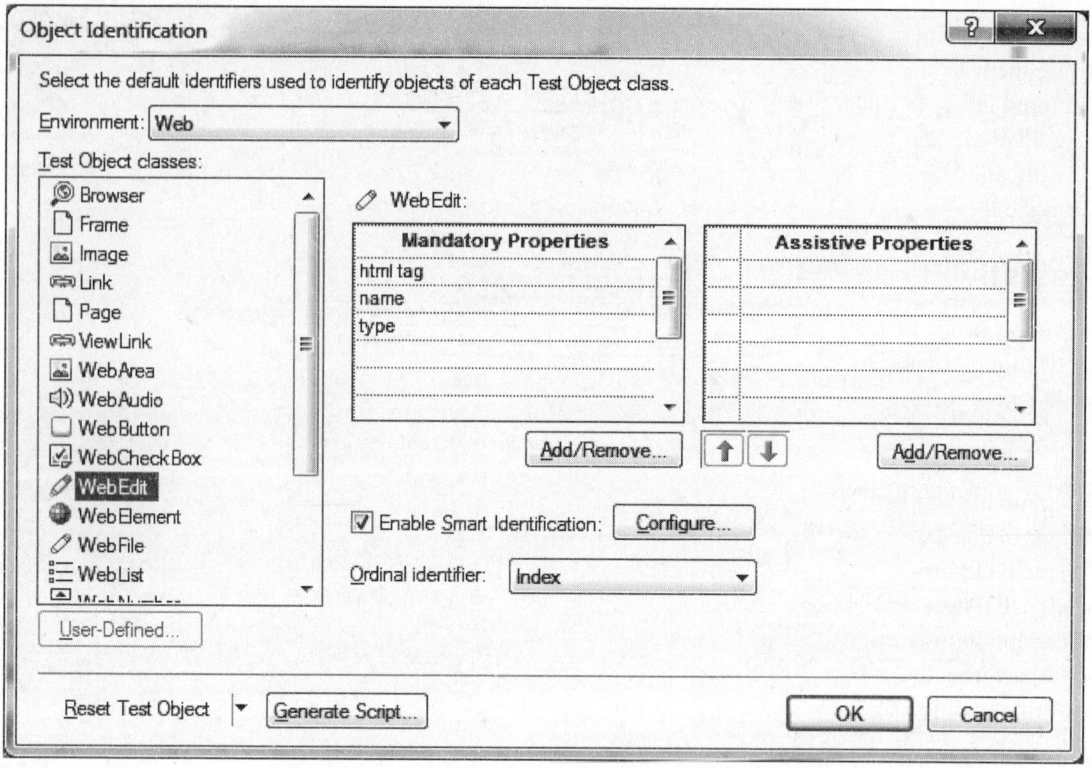

Figure 22.4 *Description properties for WebEdit object*

tion properties to use to describe an object? This information is defined in *Object Identification* dialog box as shown in Fig. 22.4. For every test object class, there exists a default set of properties which UFT uses to describe an object. This set of properties is configurable.

Figure 22.2 shows the default description properties that UFT uses for learning a WebEdit class object. For a specific object, out of all the description properties available, UFT learns only those description properties which are defined in the object identification dialog box for the specific object. To view all the available description properties of an object, click on the 'Add/Remove' button. A 'Add/Remove' property dialog box opens as shown in Figure 22.1. This dialog box displays all the UFT supported description properties for the selected object.

UFT learns all the mandatory properties of the object as specified in the object identification dialog box. Also, UFT may learn one or more assistive properties (if defined and) if mandatory properties are not sufficient to uniquely describe the object.

UFT classifies the description properties in two categories—mandatory properties and assistive properties.

Mandatory Properties

Mandatory properties are the properties that UFT always learns for a particular test object. These are the basic properties of an object. A change in the basic properties of the object would essentially mean that it is a different object. For example, the html tag property value of an WebEdit object is 'input' while the html tag property value of a link object is 'a'. All the mandatory properties are learned and captured in object repository.

As we discussed the set of mandatory properties to be captured for an object is defined in object identification dialog box. This set of properties is to be selected in a way that it is sufficient to uniquely describe the object. For example—html tag, name and html id property of a WebButton.

Assistive Properties

Assistive properties are properties that UFT learns only if the learned mandatory properties descriptions of a particular object in the AUT are not sufficient to create a unique description. If several assistive properties are defined for an object class, then UFT learns one assistive property at a time, and stops as soon as it creates a unique description for the object. Assistive properties are the properties that can be used to uniquely describe an object incase mandatory properties of two objects is same. This can happen when two similar objects exist in UI. For example, existence of two 'Search' buttons in UI. In this case, properties such as innerhtml or outerhtml can be used to differentiate between two 'Search' buttons.

If UFT does learn assistive properties, those properties are added to the test object description (description properties) in object repository.

Apart from these properties UFT also learns UFT first uses all the mandatory properties to uniquely identify an object in AUT. If more than one object with specified mandatory properties is found, then UFT uses the defined assistive properties one by one to describe the object till it uniquely describes the object or the properties get exhausted. If at any point of object learning process, the number of matched objects comes to be zero, then UFT will assume that it cannot learn the object using this mandatory/assistive properties mechanism. In this case, UFT will skip this learning process even if more assistive properties are available. Thereafter, UFT will try to use the defined ordinal identifier to describe the object.

Ordinal Identifier

UFT provides three ordinal identifiers – index, location and creationtime. At a time UFT uses only one ordinal identifier to describe the object. The type of ordinal identifier to use is configured in Object Identification dialog box as shown in Figure 22.3. Here, UFT has been configured to use 'index' ordinal identifier for describing WebEdit class objects. So in this case, UFT will use the index value of the edit box to uniquely describe the object.

NOTES

- UFT provides three ordinal identifiers for Browser class objects, namely, creationtime, index and location.
- UFT provides two ordinal identifiers for rest of the object, namely, index and location.

Example 1: Consider the create account page of a sample application as shown in the Figure 22.5 below.

Assume the HTML code if the ‘First Name’, ‘Last name’ and ‘Email Address’ edit box object are:

```
<input id="create-account-firstname
" type="text" name="firstname" value=""/>
<input id="create-account-last-
name" type="text" name="lastname" value=""/>
<input id="create-account-
email" type="text" name="email" value=""/>
```

As per HTML code, both the *name* attribute and the *id* attribute of the object is unique in the login page. It implies, either *name* or *id* attribute can be used to uniquely describe the object.

Assume the object identification configuration for WebEdit class object is as shown in Figure 22.2.

Now let’s see the description properties that UFT uses to learn this object. Figure 22.6 shows the description properties captured (learned) by UFT for this object.

Assume Smart Identification (SI) is turned off. SI can be turned off from *Run* node of *Test Settings* dialog box.

Here we observe that:

- Though *id (html id)* is also a unique attribute, this property has not been learned by UFT. This is because this property is not defined as either mandatory or assistive property in object identification dialog box.
- Though *name* attribute value is unique and is alone sufficient to uniquely describe the object, but still UFT has learned the *text* property. This is because UFT learns all the mandatory properties.

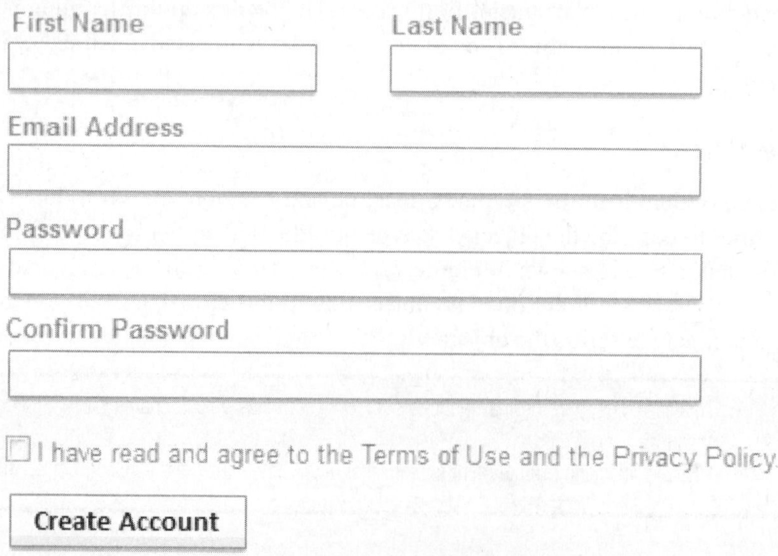

Figure 22.5 *Create account page of a sample application*

- No assistive properties have been learned as none is defined in object identification dialog box. Even if assistive properties were defined, UFT would not have learned it as mandatory properties are sufficient to uniquely describe the object.

Example 2: Assume Mandatory/Assistive property for WebEdit object is configured in object identification dialog box as mentioned below. Also, assume and ordinal identifier configuration is index.

WebEdit:

Mandatory Properties
html tag
type

	Assistive Properties
	visible
	default value
	name
	html id
	class

Now let's see how UFT learns the 'First name' edit box using above configuration. Figure below shows the description properties as learned by UFT.

Test object details

Name	Value
⊟ Description properties	
visible	True
type	text
name	firstname
html tag	INPUT
default value	
⊟ Visual relation identifier	
Visual relation identifier settings	[None. Click to add]
⊟ Ordinal identifier	
Type , Value	None
⊟ Additional details	
Enable Smart Identification	True
Comment	

Here we observe that:

- UFT has learned all the mandatory properties.
- UFT has learned three assistive properties—visible, default value and name. UFT has not learned the fourth and fifth assistive properties—html id and class. This is because the mandatory properties and three assistive properties are sufficient to uniquely describe the object. Hence, UFT has ignored rest of the assistive properties.
- UFT has not learned ordinal identifer. This is because UFT has been able to uniquely describe the object using mandatory/assistive properties.

Here, UFT first learns all the mandatory properties and then checks if the description created is unique. However, it finds that three objects exist with the same description. Hence, it learns the first assistive

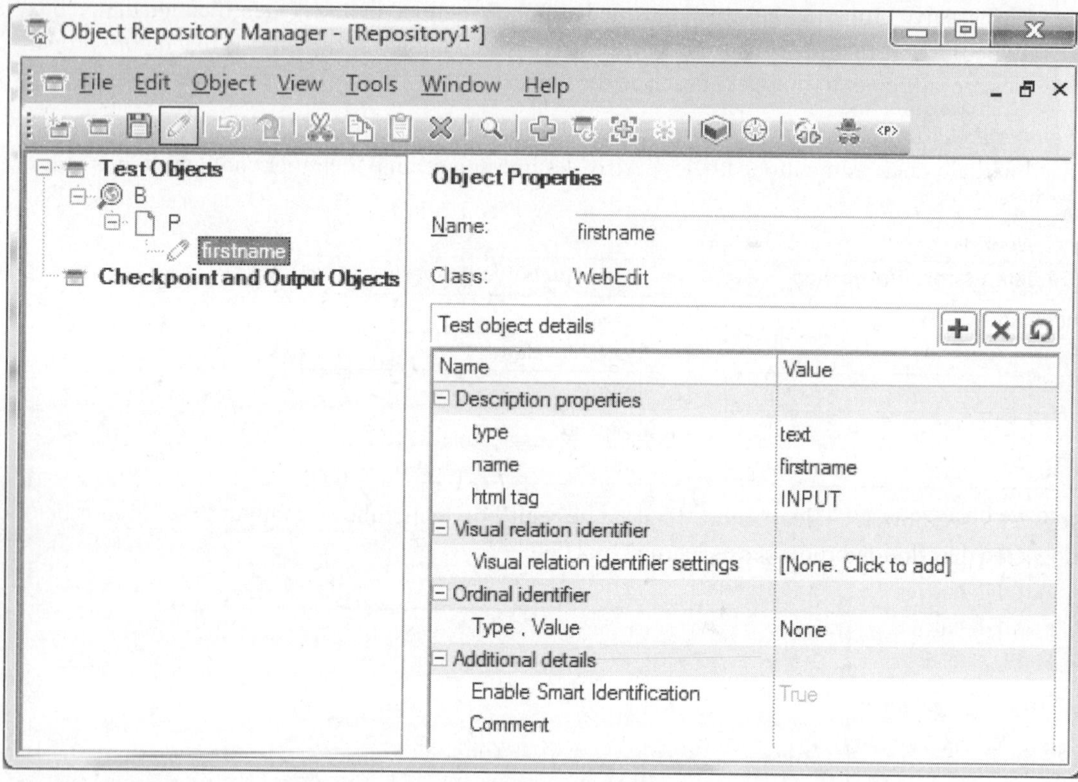

Figure 22.6 *'First Name' Address' WebEdit Object description as learned by UFT*

property 'visible=true' and then again checks if the current set of mandatory and assistive property set uniquely defines the object. However, again it finds three matching objects. So UFT again learns next assistive property 'default value'. UFT checks if the currently learned descriptions creates a unique description of the object. However, again it finds three matching objects. UFT now learns the next available assistive property 'name'. UFT again checks if the current set of learned 'mandatory' and 'assistive' properties uniquely describes the object. UFT finds that it finds one match. Then UFT creates the description of the object with the current learned mandatory and assistive properties. The rest of the assistive properties (html id and class) are ignored since UFT has been able to create a unique description with the currently learned description.

Example 3: Assume Mandatory/Assistive property for WebEdit object is configured in object identification dialog box as mentioned below and ordinal identifier is index.

WebEdit:

Mandatory Properties
html tag
type

	Assistive Properties
	visible
	default value

Now let's see how UFT learns the 'First name' edit box using above configuration. Figure below shows the description properties as learned by UFT.

Test object details

Name	Value
⊟ Description properties	
visible	True
type	text
html tag	INPUT
default value	
⊟ Visual relation identifier	
Visual relation identifier settings	[None. Click to add]
⊟ Ordinal identifier	
Type , Value	Index , 0
⊟ Additional details	
Enable Smart Identification	True
Comment	

Here we observe that:

- UFT has learned all the mandatory properties.
- UFT has learned all assistive properties.
- UFT has learned ordinal identifier—index.

Here, after learning all mandatory and assistive properties UFT finds the learned description still matches to 3 objects. Since, UFT has not been able to create a unique description of the object even after using all assistive properties, hence next, it learns the ordinal identifier of the object. As the configured ordinal identifer here is index, UFT learns the index value of the object,

Example 4: Assume Mandatory/Assistive property for WebEdit object is configured in object identification dialog box as mentioned below and ordinal identifier is location.

WebEdit:

Mandatory Properties
html tag
type

	Assistive Properties

Now let's see how UFT learns the 'First name' edit box using above configuration. Figure below shows the description properties as learned by UFT.

Test object details

Name	Value
⊟ Description properties	
type	text
html tag	INPUT
⊟ Visual relation identifier	
Visual relation identifier settings	[None. Click to add]
⊟ Ordinal identifier	
Type , Value	Location , 0
⊟ Additional details	
Enable Smart Identification	True
Comment	

Here we observe that:

- UFT has learned all the mandatory properties.

- UFT has not learned any of the assistive properties. This is because no assistive property has been defined in the configuration settings.
- UFT has learned ordinal identifier—Location. This is because:
  - Learned mandatory/assistive property description is not sufficient to uniquely describe the object.
  - UFT has been configured to learn 'location' ordinal identifier.

Here, after learning madatory properties UFT finds it has not been able to create a unique description of the object. Next, UFT finds that no assistive property has been configured to be learned for this object. Hence, UFT uses the configured ordinal identifer to learn a unique description of the object.

> NOTES
>
> - UFT uses description properties(mandatory/asssitive properties) learning mechanism only while learning an object when adding an object to OR. An object can be added to OR either manually using 'add objects' tool or automatically using UFT record feature. When capturing objects to OR while recording, UFT uses the same learning mechanism.
> - Description properties learning mechanism is only used for learning objects and not for recognizing object during test run. During test run, UFT uses all description properties that are defined in OR to locate the object in UI.

CONFIGURING MANDATORY/ASSISTIVE PROPERTIES

UFT provides the flexibility to the users to configure mandatory/assistive properties for all test class objects. These properties can be configured from Object Identification dialog box. Follow the steps below to configure these properties:

1. Navigate *Tools → Object Identification.*
   Object Identification dialog box opens up as shown in Figure 22.4.
2. Select the appropriate *Environment*. Suppose, we select Web.
3. Select the Test Object Class whose mandatory/assistive properties need to be configured. Suppose, we select WebEdit.
4. To modify mandatory properties, click on *Add/Remove button* below mandatory properties list.
   Add/Remove Properties dialog box opens up as shown in Figure 22.2.
5. Select the properties to be included in the mandatory properties and deselect the rest.
6. Click OK button. Add/Remove Properties dialog box will close and the modified set of mandatory property list will be displayed in Object Identification dialog box.
7. Repeat steps 4–6 to modify the assistive properties.
8. Use buttons [↑][↓] to set the preferred order of assistive properties.
   UFT uses this order to learn assistive properties.

NOTES: The assistive properties order should be sequenced in a way that UFT needs minimum assistive properties to uniquely describe the object.

NOTES: The same property cannot be included in both mandatory and assistive property list.

CONFIGURE ORDINAL IDENTIFIERS

UFT provides three ordinal identifiers to describe objects, namely, index, location and creationtime. However, at a time only one of the ordinal identifiers can be used to describe the object. UFT provides the flexibility to the users to configure which ordinal identifier UFT should use to create the objects' description. Follow the steps below to configure ordinal identifier for an object:

1. Open object identification dialog box.
2. Select the appropriate environment. Suppose, we select Web.
3. Select the Test Object Class whose mandatory/assistive properties need to be configured. Suppose, we select WebEdit.
4. Select one of the ordinal identifiers.

WHY TO CONFIGURE OBJECT IDENTIFICATION PROPERTIES?

In the previous sections, we discussed how to configure object identification settings. Now you may ask

- Why to configure object identification settings?
- Why not to use the default configuration settings provided by UFT?

Application developers can create UI objects using a variety of object attributes depending upon projects UI development standards. Since, different applications may follow different UI standards; the objects so created may have different object attributes.

Now, let's analyze how defined object attributes can vary from application to application. Assume there are two applications A and B. Consider the HTML code of 'username' edit box of both applications is as mentioned below:

Application A login page 'username' edit box HTML code is:

```
<input class="CreateAcctForm" type="text" val-
ue="" size="23" maxlength="100" name="userName"/>
```

Application B login page 'username' edit box HTML code is:

```
<input id="loginid" type="text" name="loginid" value=""  />
```

Here, we observe that application A defines *class* attribute while application B does not. Similarly, application A does not define *id* attribute while application B does. Since, different applications use different object attributes to create objects, it is very important to configure the object identification settings. Mandatory/Assistive properties are to be configured in a way that minimum properties are required to uniquely describe the object.

Also, UFT provides the flexibility to configure the learned object properties in OR. Configuring learned object description in OR is discussed in detail in the chapter ‘Object Repository’.

POINTS TO CONSIDER FOR CONFIGURING OBJECT IDENTIFICATION SETTINGS

Before starting to capture the objects to the OR, it is very important to configure the object identification settings. Object identification settings define the mandatory and associative properties required to identify a test object during run time. A random study of the application objects has to be done to identify the essential properties required to identify an object. The mandatory and assistive properties are to be chosen in a way that it avoids or limits the need of SI and ordinal identifiers to identify an object. The reason for avoiding SI is that it can behave unpredictably during the run session. Similarly, values of ordinal identifiers such as index and creation time vary during run time. Moreover, the index property of an object can easily be changed by the application developer without requiring any change request. Again, such a change mostly will not have any impact on the look and feel of GUI or application functionality. Therefore, such changes always go unnoticed both by testers and by the management. However, at the same time, such a change will require test scripts to be upgraded and tested again before they can be executed. It becomes very difficult to show a change effort in test scripts to the management without any actual change in the application. In addition, since such type of changes cannot be predicted or monitored, the maintenance changes to the test scripts and OR become cyclic, time consuming, and costly. Hence, it is always advisable to avoid the use of the ordinal identifiers. Object identification properties are to be selected in a way that it supports easy handling of the dynamic objects of the application and as well as minimal changes to the test script and the OR in case of a change. Object identification settings need to be configured in a way that test scripts and the test objects require change only in the cases where change to the application is visible.

QUICK TIPS

- ✓ Object identification settings are to be configured before starting any automation activity.
- ✓ Description properties learning mechanism is used only for learning object descriptions when an object is added to object repository.
- ✓ During test run, UFT does not use description property learning mechanism to identify test objects in UI. Infact, UFT uses all the description properties that are defined in OR to locate the object in UI.
- ✓ Object identification settings are to be configured in a way that minimum object properties are used to create a unique description of the object.
- ✓ UFT provides the flexibility to edit the learned properties in object repository.

PRACTICAL QUESTIONS

1. Why the default object identification settings require configuration?
2. Identify the object identification settings (mandatory and assistive properties) of UFT for www.expedia.com application.
3. Out of the so many object definitions available, how UFT decides which object definitions to learn to uniquely describe the object?
4. How UFT decides it has captured sufficient information to uniquely describe an object?
5. What is the difference between mandatory and assistive properties?
6. Explain how UFT learns objects when recording a test.
7. Does UFT use the test object learning mechanism to locate object in UI during test run?

Chapter 23

Object Repository

All text fields, buttons, checkboxes, etc. are referred as objects in UFT. UFT maps the Graphical User Interface (GUI) objects to its standard object class. For example, for a web application, edit field is mapped to WebEdit class, check box is mapped to WebCheckbox class and so on.

UFT stores the definition of the GUI objects in Object Repository (OR). This definition consists of object properties such as name, class, and html id, visual relation identifiers, and ordinal identifiers. UFT uses these properties to uniquely identify the object at run-time in the AUT. Object Repository can also be used to view or modify the object properties of the objects stored in OR.

TYPES OF OBJECT REPOSITORIES

There are two types of object repositories in UFT:

1. Local OR or per-action OR
2. Shared OR.

Local ORs have their scope within an action, i.e., objects captured in local OR are available to that action only. Shared ORs have a global scope. Any action can be associated to a shared OR. In short, shared OR is reusable and local OR is non-reusable.

For local OR, in case object properties of an object changes, all test scripts (actions) that use the specific object need to be identified and the object properties of respective objects in OR need to be changed. In case of large number of scripts (actions), change identification and modification becomes time consuming and costly. For shared OR, users can open the specific shared object repository file from *Object Repository Manager* and modify the object properties of the specific object. This change will automatically reflect in all the scripts where this object repository is used. Therefore, it is advisable to always use shared object repository. Local object repository can be used only when object repository size is small and no other test script needs to use those objects.

Figure 23.1 shows a flight reservation application In this chapter, we will use this sample application to discuss various UFT object repository features.

Figure 23.2 shows Object Repository Manager window. This window has loaded a shared object repository file 'Expedia.tsr'. This OR file has captured some of the objects of the sample flight reservation application as shown in Fig. 23.1.

Figure 23.1 *Flight reservation application*

Table 23.1 Explains the description of various tools of shared object repository shown in Fig. 23.2.

OR Tool	Description
New	(CTRL+N) Creates new shared object repository.
Open	(CTRL+O) Opens existing shared object repository.
Save	(CTRL+S) Saves existing shared OR.
Enable Editing	Toggle switch to enables/disable object repository for editing.
Undo	(CTRL+Z) Erases the last change done to the object repository.
Redo	(CTRL+Y) Recovers the last erased change from the object repository.
Cut	(CTRL+X) Copies the selected test object and all its child objects from test object pane to memory and removes the test object and all its child objects from object repository.
Copy	(CTRL+C) Copies the selected test object and all its child objects from test object pane to memory.

Paste	(CTRL+V) Pastes the objects from memory to object repository.
Delete	(Del) Deletes the selected object including its child objects from object repository.
Find & Replace	(CTRL+F) Opens Find & Replace dialog box to search objects in object repository using various search criterias such as object logical name, object attribute name, object attribute value, etc.
Add Objects	Adds GUI objects to object repository.
Update from Application	Updates the object attributes captured in OR from application GUI.
Add Insight Object	Adds image of an object to OR for Insight (image based) identification.
Define New Test Object	Opens Define New Test Object dialog box to create a new test object and add it to OR.
Highlight in Application	Locates and highlights the test object in application GUI.
Locate in Repository	Locates and highlights an AUT object in object repository.
ALM Connection	Connects Object Repository Manager to ALM to access Shared ORs stored in ALM.
Object Spy	Enables users to view attributes of a GUI object.
Manage Repository Parameters	Enables users to manage properties that can be used to parameterize object attribute values.

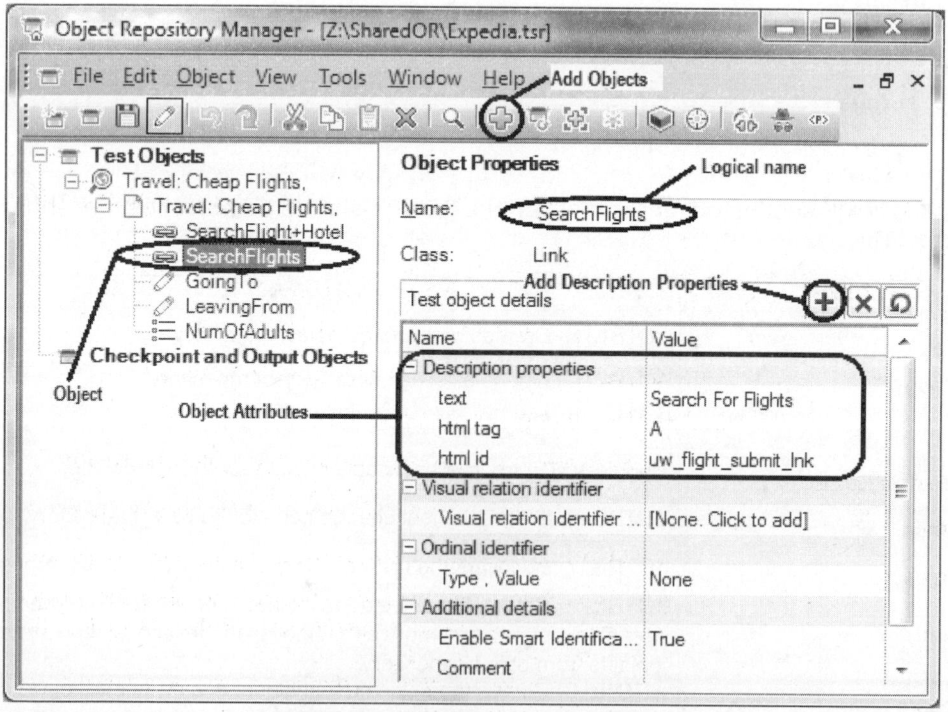

Figure 23.2 *Shared object repository*

ADDING NEW OBJECTS TO SHARED OR

The AUT objects that are added to object repository are called 'Test Objects'. The following steps show how to add test objects (TO) to the shared OR.

1. Navigate *Resources* → *Object Repository Manager*.
   Object Repository Manager window opens.
2. Navigate *File* → *New* to create a new shared OR.
   Alternatively, Navigate *File* → *Open* to open an existing shared OR.
3. Click the *Save* button and specify the location to save the OR.
   (Switch once between application window and OR manager window, so that when ALT+TAB is pressed with OR manager as active window, AUT window becomes active)
4. Click on the *Add Objects* button to add objects to OR.
   A hand tool appears.
5. Point this hand tool to an object in AUT that needs to be added to the OR.
6. Pop-up window *Object Selection – Add to repository* appears as shown in the Fig. 23.3.
7. Select the object to be added to OR and click *OK*.
   The selected object will be added to shared object repository as shown in the Fig. 23.2.
8. If we select browser or page object, then *Define Object Filter* dialog box opens. Figure 23.4 shows this dialog box. This dialog box provides the flexibility to the user to add specific objects or all web page objects to object repository..Listed below are the options provided by this dialog box:
   - *Selected Object Only (no descendants)*
     This option will capture only the object which is selected in previous '*Object Selection – Add to* Repository' window.to OR.
   - *Default Object Types*
     This option adds a predefined set of standard child objects of the selected object to OR.
   - *All Object Types*
     This option adds all the child objects including webelements of the selected object to OR.

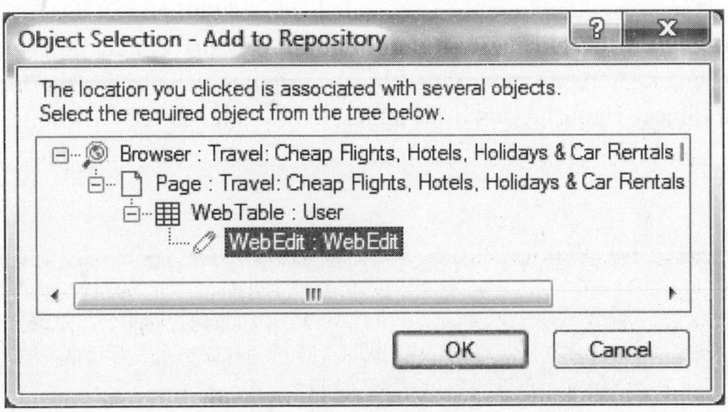

Figure 23.3 *Select object to add to OR*

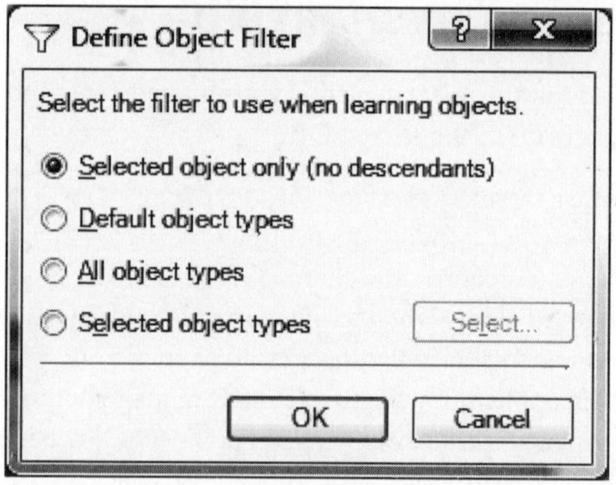

Figure 23.4 *Object selection options*

- *Selected Object Types*
  This option allows users to add all objects of specific object types to OR.
  For example adding all web buttons to OR.
  Click on the button 'Select' opens a 'Select object Types' dialog box as shown in Fig. 23.5. Users can define the object types to add to OR from this window.

> **NOTES** Navigate and Learn options discussed above may add lot unwanted objects to OR. This makes object repository size huge. Hence, it is advised to add the desired objects to OR one by one.

9. Change the logical name of the object, if required. UFT identifies the test objects in OR through its logical name only.
10. Modify the object attributes and attribute values defined in *Description Properties* part of object repository, if required. Section below 'Add/Remove Object Description Properties' describes in detail on how to create a unique and reliable object description using object attributes.11. After modifying object attributes in OR, use the highlight button to ensure the object (with modified attributes) is recognized. If UFT fails to recognize the modified object description, then repeat steps 10 and 11 till the object is recognized by UFT.

> **NOTES** Note that hierarchy of screen objects added to OR is different from the hierarchy that we see in *Object Selection – Add to Repository* dialog box. Hierarchy of GUI objects added to OR is *Browser Object→ Page Object→ Objects present in the web page.* While adding objects to OR, UFT remembers only that hierarchy that is necessary to identify the object during run-time.

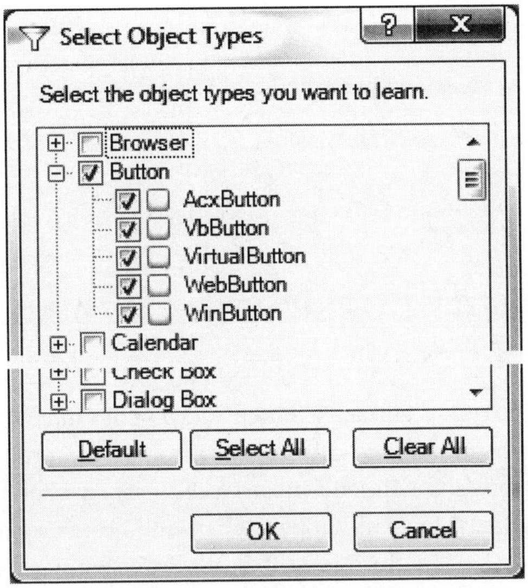

Figure 23.5 *Select object types*

Navigate and Learn

UFT provides option to automatically add multiple GUI objects to shared object repository. Follow the steps below to allow UFT to automatically add GUI objects to shared OR:

1. Navigate *Resources* → *Object Repository Manager* on UFT window, Object Repository Manager window opens.
2. On Object Repository Manager window, navigate *Object*→*Navigate and Learn* or press F6 key. Navigate and Learn window opens as shown in the Fig. 23.6.
3. Click on the *Filer* button to define the objects which is to be automatically captured from AUT web page by UFT.
   Define Object Filter dialog box opens as shown in the Fig. 23.4 Follow steps eight of section 'Add New Objects to Shared OR' to define the specific objects to be captured from AUT to shared OR.

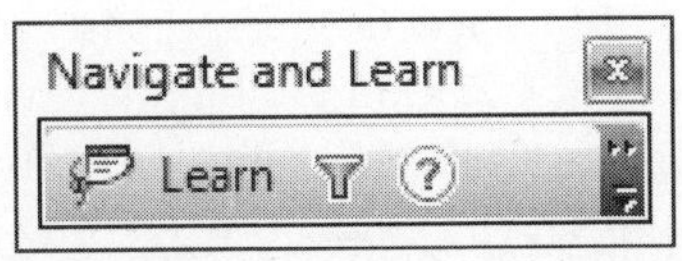

Figure 23.6 *Navigate and learn*

4. Click on *Learn* button to add the active (in focus) parent object and its descendants (child objects) to the shared object repository, according to the defined filter

> NOTES
> This button is disabled if there is no recognized active parent object.

ADDING NEW OBJECTS TO LOCAL OR

The following steps show how to add TOs to the local OR.

1. Navigate *Resources → Object Repository...*
2. Local OR window opens.
3. Follow steps 4–11 of 'Adding New Objects to Shared OR' to add objects to local OR.

HOW TO AVOID OBJECT DUPLICATION IN OBJECT REPOSITORY

When we add objects such as webbuttons and webedit to OR, many times, it happens that QuickTest creates a new browser → page heirachy. Once the objects have been added to OR, we need to see whether properties of browser/page are same or not. If the properties of the two browsers/pages are same, we need to move the added object (webbutton, webedit, etc.) to the previous hierarchy and delete the current one. This can happen when one browser has creation time property as CreationTime=None and other as CreationTime=0. Both browsers/page objects refer the same AUT screen object. However, because of the variation in creation time property value, UFT understands second browser object to be a different object than the first one.

ADD/REMOVE OBJECT PROPERTIES

In Fig. 23.7, object attributes–*text*, *html tag*, and *html id* have been used to identify *SearchFlights* link object. In UFT, object attributes are termed as description properties. UFT classify these properties as *mandatory properties* (as per Object Identification settings) of object and uses these properties to identify this object during run-time.

To remove any property from mandatory property identification list, follow the following steps on OR Manager window:

1. Select desired property row.
2. Click on the button 'Remove Selected Description Properties' ✕ to remove the property from mandatory property identification list.

To add new object property to mandatory property identification list, follow the following steps on OR Manager window:

1. Click on the 'Add description properties' button + to add object properties. *Add Properties* pop-up window opens as shown in the Fig. 23.8
2. Double click on the object property that needs to be added to the object identification list.

NOTES

Object property values can also be modified to a different value or can be modified to a regular expression.

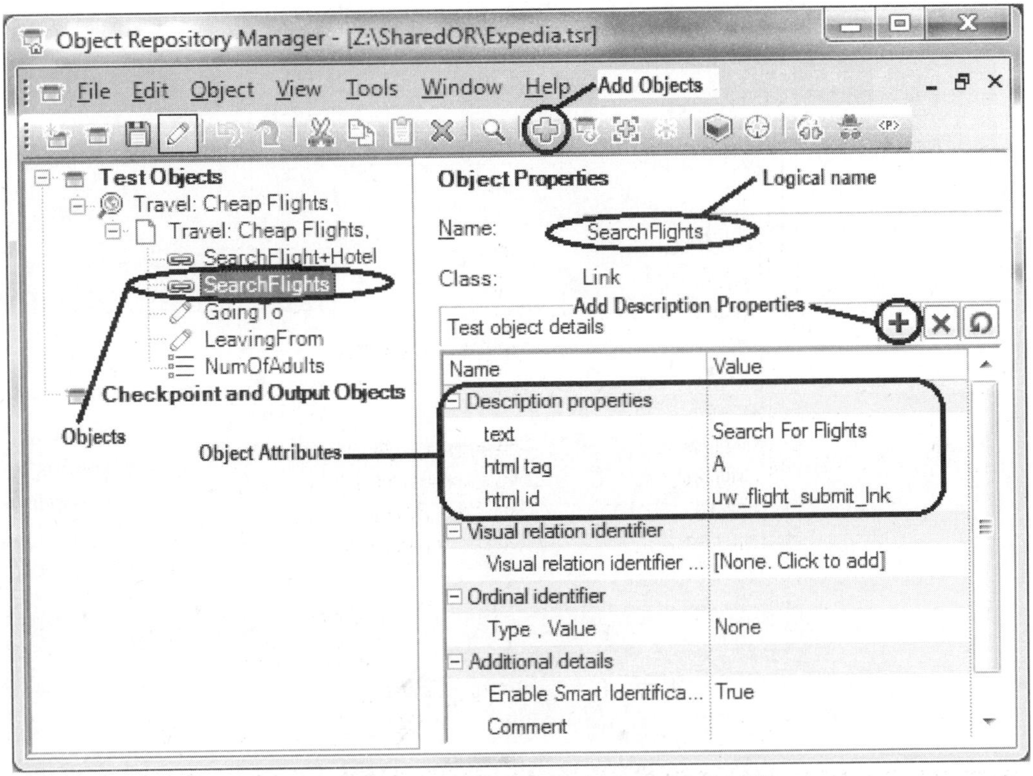

Figure 23.7 *Add/modify objects of shared OR*

Add New Property

UFT 'Add properties' dialog box as shown in the Fig. 23.8 displays the object properties as captured by UFT. In case, we need to add few more object properties which has not been captured by UFT; the 'Add New Property' feature of UFT can be used to achieve the same. To add a new property, follow the steps below:

1. Click on the 'Define New Property' button of the 'Add Properties' dialog box.
   New Property dialog box opens as shown in Fig. 23.9.
2. Specify the property name and the property value and click *OK* button.
   The new property is added to the 'Add Property' dialog box. Then this property can be added from add property dialog box to mandatory 'Description Properties' of shared OR window.

Significance of New Property Feature

UFT recognizes and learns the identification properties only but not the native properties of the object. In certain scenarios, it may require to use native properties to identify objects. UFT 'New Property' dialog box allows users to add native properties of object to UFT object identification mechanism so that they can be learned by UFT. Chapter 'Working with Object Native Properties' discusses in detail the significance and process of configuring UFT to help UFT learn native proeprties of the object.

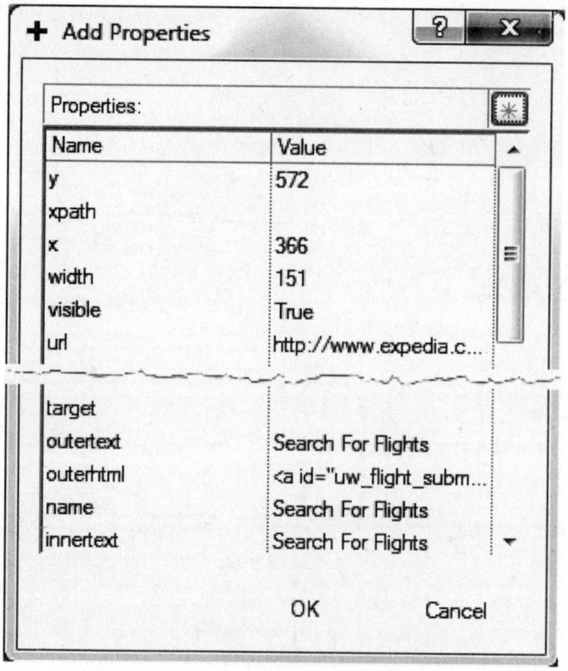

Figure 23.8 *Add properties*

MODIFY OBJECT PROPERTY VALUES–REGULAR EXPRESSION

UFT provides the flexibility to modify object property values and as well replace them with regular expressions. This feature is extensively used to identify dynamic objects. A dynamic object is one whose property values changes with every test run.

Consider the *ListOfTickets* web table shown below.The *column names* property value of this object changes dynamically with every run. Or in other words, this value of this property varies from time to time. Because of this, UFT will not be able to identify this web table object during run-time.

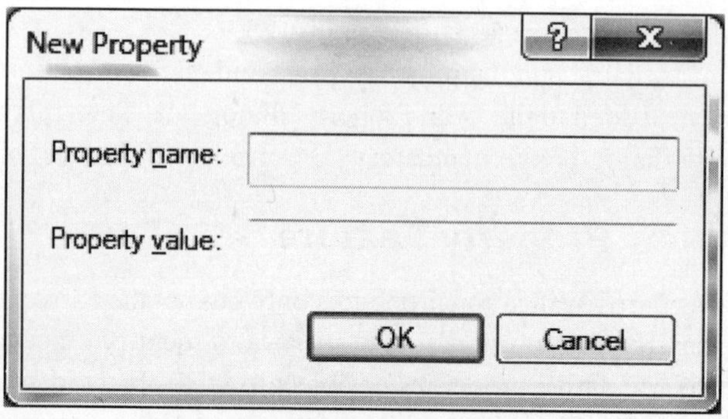

Figure 23.9 *New property dialog box*

S#	Transaction ID	PNR Number	From	To	Total Amount	Refund Amount	Cancelled On	Type of Ticket
1	0156644096	2265959350	NDLS	LKO	242.0	192.0	30-11-2009	eticket
2	0136774911	6131306072	GAYA	NDLS	723.0	314.0	17-9-2009	eticket
3	0130365059	2262414464	NDLS	KQR	997.0	917.0	15-9-2009	eticket

Figure 23.10 *Webtable of list of tickets*

Assume the *column names* property value of WebTable *ListOfTickets* (Figures 23.10 and 23.11) is: *List Of Tickets e-ticket i-ticket S#Transaction ID PNR NumberFrom To Total Amount Refund AmountCancelled OnType of Ticket1 0156644096 2265959350NDLSLKO242.0192.030-11-2009eticket2 0136774911 6131306072GAYANDLS723.0314.017-9-2009eticket3 0130365059 2262414464NDLSKQR997.0917.015-9-2009eticket*

We observe that dynamically changing values such as ticket number, date, and amount are a part of this property value. Therefore, next time, if a new transaction id is populated in WebTable, UFT will not be able to recognize it based on WebTable properties that it has captured (as *column name* property value will change). Therefore, to overcome these situations, we try to identify two things within the property values:

1. Fixed pattern
2. Dynamically changing pattern.

We leave the fixed pattern as it is while replace the dynamically changing pattern with regular expressions.

In the *column names* property value, we observe that column names of table (Figure 23.11) S#, Transaction ID, PNR Number, From, To, etc. form a fixed pattern. These values will always be a part of the *column names* property value. Values such as *0156644096* and *2265959350NDLSLKO242* are dynamically changing values. These values can be replaced with regular expressions.

Therefore, our new column name property value becomes:
S#Transaction ID PNR NumberFrom To Total AmountRefund AmountCancelled OnType of Ticket.
To use regular expression in OR Manager, follow the steps below.

1. Click on the button <#> (Figure 23.11).
2. *Repository Parameter* window opens (Figure 23.12).
3. Delete the existing string and replace it with the newly designed property value.
4. Check *Regular expression* checkbox.
5. A pop-up window appears. Click *No* button of this pop-up window. (*Yes* button can be clicked if special characters used needs to be treated literally. For example, instead of treating '.' as regular expression, it can be treated literally if it is written as '\.').

Figure 23.11 *Properties and property values of WebTable list of tickets*

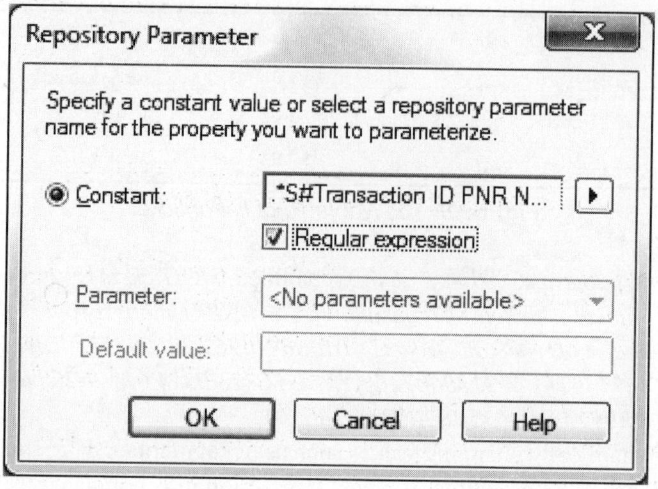

Figure 23.12 *Using regular expressions in property values*

6. Click the *OK* button.
7. The icon will appear against the property whose value now consists of regular expressions.

Let us consider one more example of Calendar object (Figure 23.13).
Here, we observe for *column names* property:
Fixed pattern – None
Dynamic pattern – Month, Year, so regular expression can be - .*
For *text* property:
Fixed pattern – wkSunMonTueWedThuFriSat
Dynamic pattern – March,2010×«‹ … 812345697891011121310141516… So, regular expression can be - .*wkSunMonTueWedThuFriSat.*

Object Properties Parameterization

Apart from allowing use of regular expressions for object property values, UFT also provides the feature to parameterize the object property values. UFT allows use of action Data table or Environment variables to parameterize object description property values.

Object properties parameterization is useful when working with dynamic objects. For example, in an application text property value of various objects such as buttons, labels, text boxes, etc. change in a localized application depending on the language of the user interface. Since, the text value attribute of the object changes depending on the language loaded, use of constant values will result on object identification failures. UFT offers to parameterize the object property values so that specific parameterized value can be used depending upon the language used.

UFT allows to parameterize object property values of both local and shared object repository.

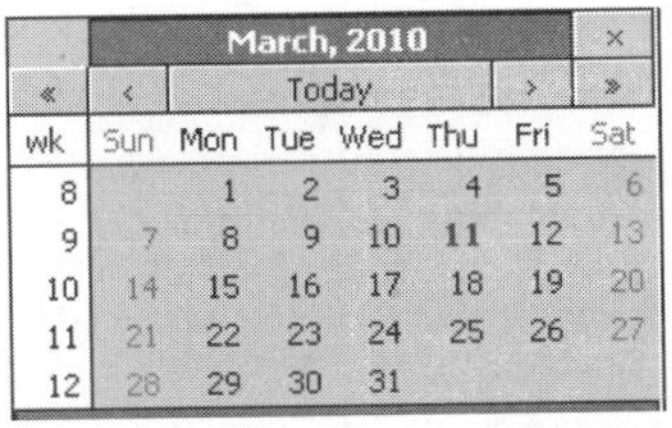

Description properties	
html tag	TABLE
column names	March, 2010
text	March, 2010×«‹Today›»wkSunMonTueWed...
name	WebTable

text:="March,2010×«‹Today›»wkSunMonTueWedThuFriSat81234569 78910111213101415161718192011212223242526271228293031"

Figure 23.13 *Calendar object and its object properties*

Local OR Object Properties Parameterization

UFT provides the feature to parameterize local OR object property values using data table, evvironment variables or using any auto-generated random number. Described below are the steps to parameterize test object properties:

1. On UFT Menu bar, navigate *Resources → Object Repository.*
   Local Object Repository window opens. Figure 23.14 below shows a local object repository window.

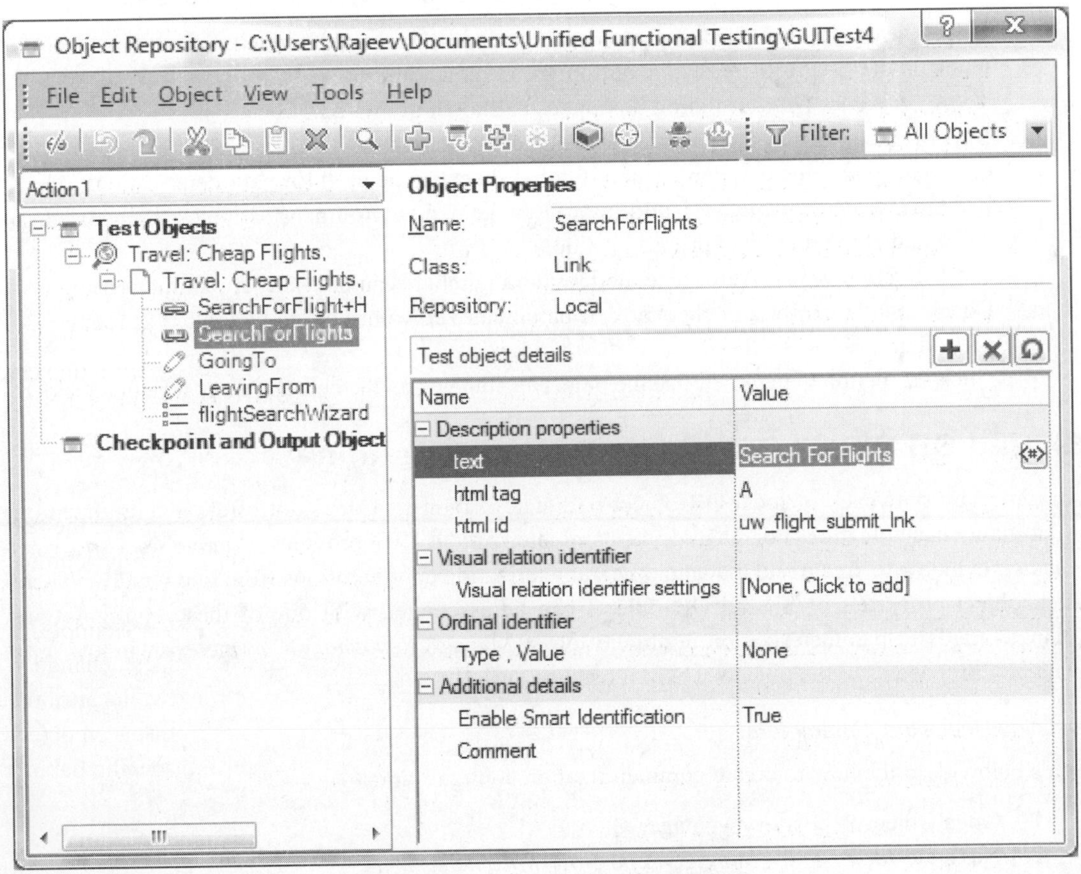

Figure 23.14 *Local object repository*

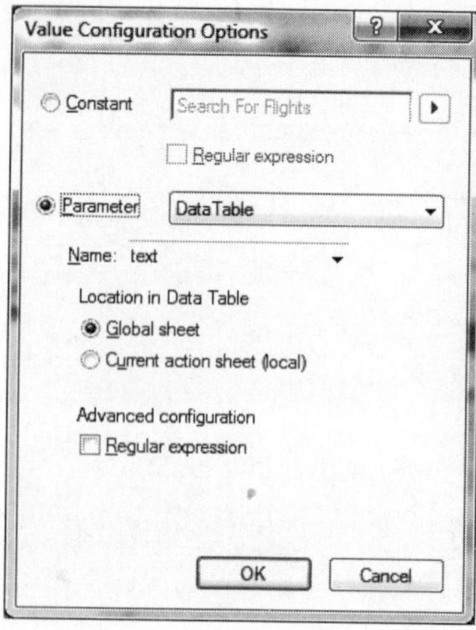

Figure 23.15 *Object properties parameterization using data table*

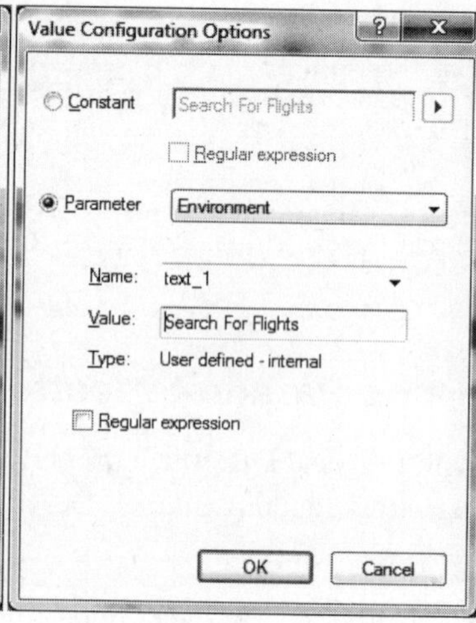

Figure 23.16 *Object properties parameterization using environment variable*

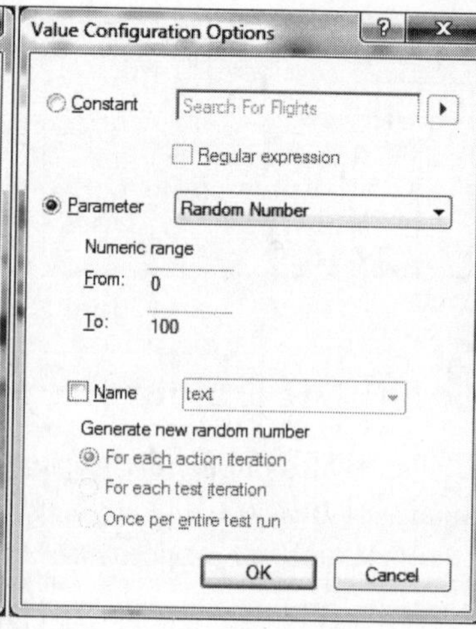

Figure 23.17 *Object properties parameterization using random number*

2. Select the description property whose value needs to be parameterized.
3. Click on the *Configure the value* button as shown in Fig. 23.14.
   Value Configure Options dialog box opens as shown in Fig. 23.15.
4. UFT offers three ways to parameterize object properties:
   a. *Data table:* Local action sheet or Global sheet can be used for parameterization.
   b. *Environment variables:* Build-in or User-defined environment variables can be used for parameterizing object property value.
   c. *Random number:* Auto-generated random numbers can be used for parameterization.
5. Check regular expression checkbox, if parameterized values are to be treated as regular expressions.
6. Click *OK* button to parameterize the object attribute using the configuration as defined above.

Shared OR Object Properties Parameterization

An important drawback of local OR object parameterization is it does not offers a centralized one point maintenance feature. For Shared OR parameterization, UFT provides *Manage Repository Parameters* window to create and manage all parameterization configurations from one window. Thereafter, object properties of Shared OR objects can be associated with one of these configurations. Changes made to parameterization configuration at Manage *Repository Parameters* window automatically propagates to the objects where it has been used.

Defining Repository Parameters

Steps below describe how to create parameterization configuration:

1. Open Object Repository Manager.
2. Navigate *Tools* → *Manage Repository Parameters*.
   Manage Repository Parameters dialog box opens as shown in the Fig. 23.18.

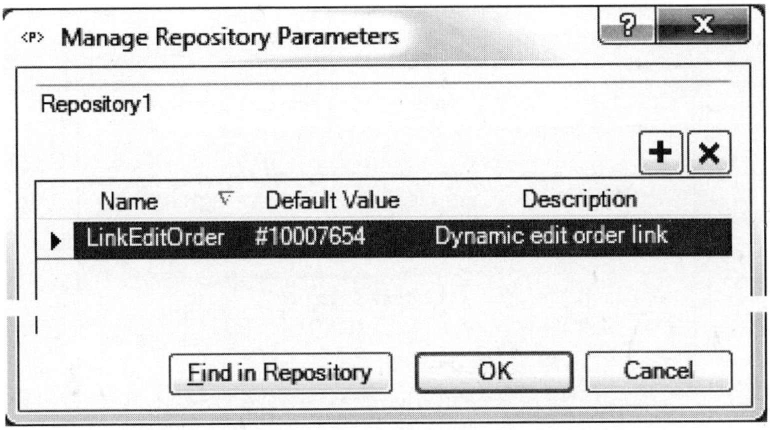

Figure 23.18 *Manage repository parameters*

3. Click on the 'Add Repository Parameter' button to add a repository parameter. *Add Repository Parameter* window opens as shown in the Fig. 23.19.
4. Specify repository parameter name and default value.
5. Click *OK* button to add the repository parameter.

Associating Repository Parameters to Shared OR Object Properties

1. Open object repository manager and load a shared OR.
2. Select the object whose description property is to be parameterized.
3. Select the description property which needs to be parameterized.
4. Click on the *Configure the value* button as shown in the Fig. 23.14. *Repository Parameter* dialog box opens as shown in the Fig. 23.20 below.
5. Select the appropriate repository parameter.
6. Click *OK* button to associate the repository parameter to the object description property. Figure 23.21 below shows the added repository parameter to a shared OR.

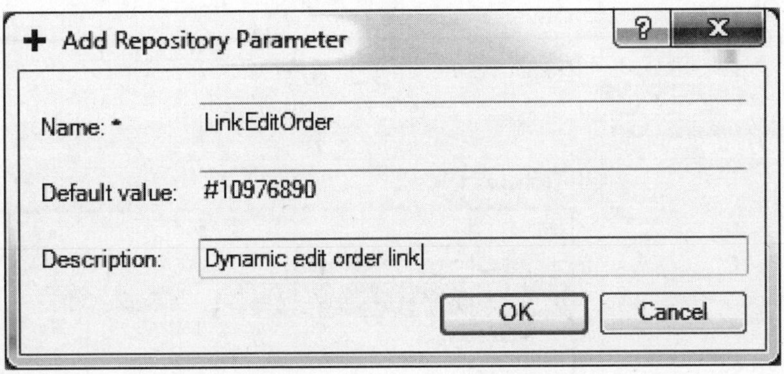

Figure 23.19 *Add repository parameter*

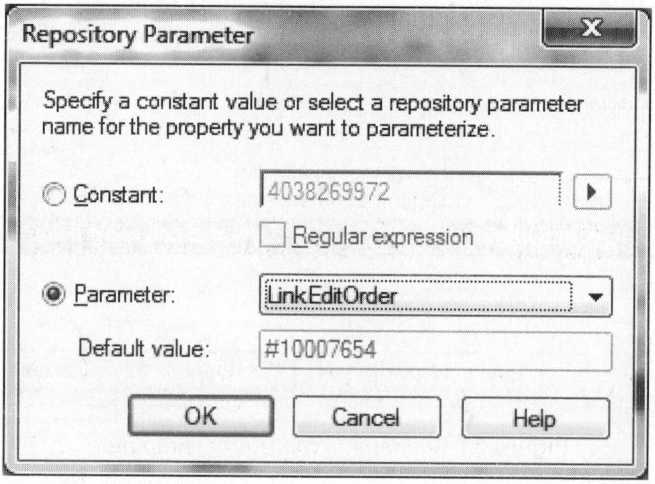

Figure 23.20 *Associating a repository parameter to an object property*

> **NOTES** UFT does not provide the feature to parameterize a shared OR object description property using Data Table or Environment variables.

ASSOCIATING A SHARED OBJECT REPOSITORY TO A TEST SCRIPT

The OR files need to be associated with the test before any actual scripting can start. The following steps show how to associate an OR file to a test.

1. Open the desired test script (action).
2. Navigate *Resources* → *Associate Repositories ... Associate Repositories* dialog box opens (Figure 23.22).

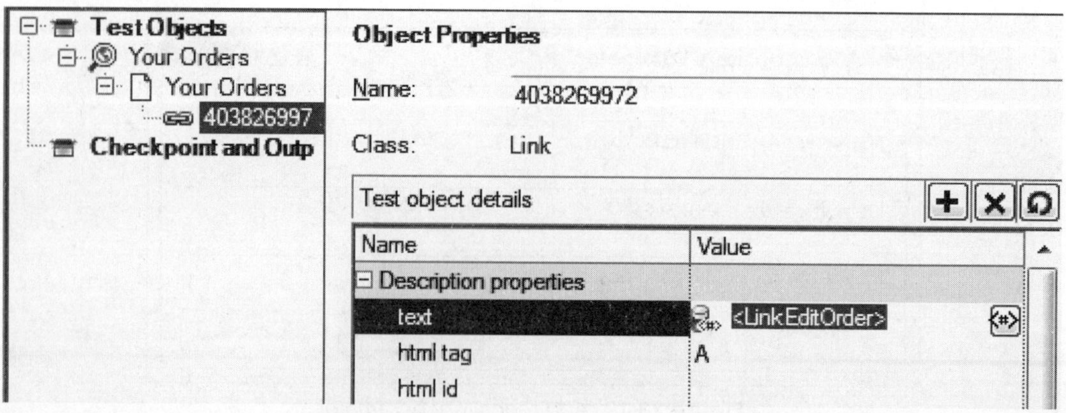

Figure 23.21 *Parameter shared OR object*

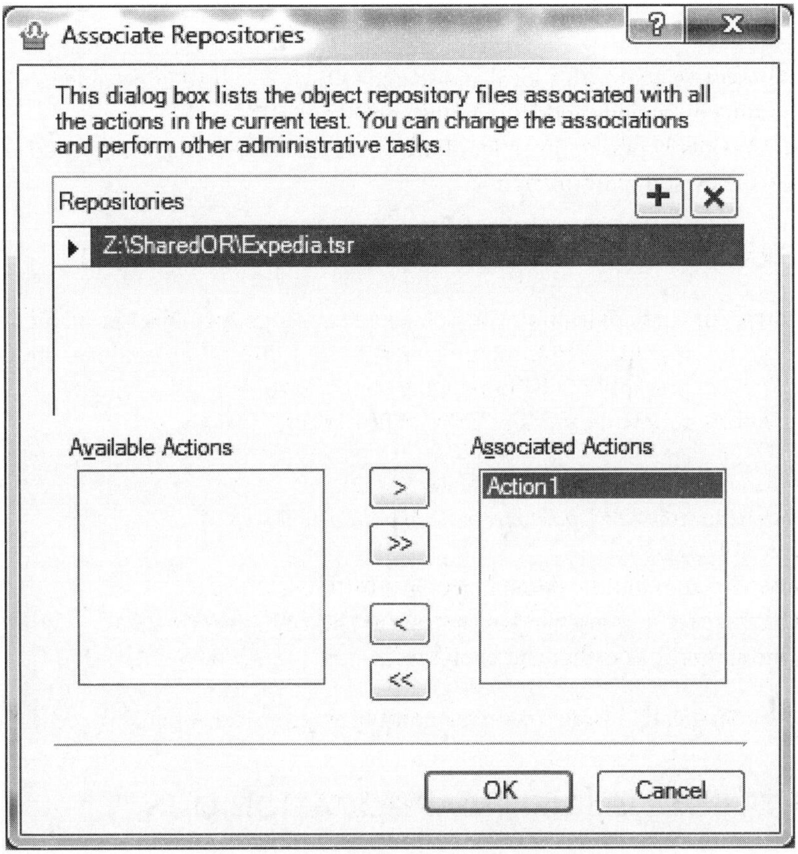

Figure 23.22 *Associate repositories*

3. In *Repositories* block, click on the 'Add Repository' button + and open the desired shared OR.
4. In the *Available Actions* block, select the actions to which this shared OR needs to be associated.
5. Select the desired action and click on the button > to associate the shared OR to the action. Selected actions will show in *Associated Actions* block. Use the button >> to associate all actions of the test script with the selected shared OR.
6. Click on the *OK* button to apply the changed OR association settings

NOTES

Since we can associate an action with one or more repository files, there can be a conflict situation when object with the same logical name is present in two or more ORs. Here are some simple rules that determine which TO will be used for identification:

- If an object with the same name is located in both the local OR and in a shared OR associated with the same action, the action uses the local object definition.
- If an object with the same name is located in more than one shared OR associated with the same action, the object definition is used from the first occurrence of the object, according to the order in which the shared ORs are associated with the action.

In addition,

- If an action is associated with a local and shared OR, UFT will add new objects to the local OR while recording operations and NOT to the shared one.
- If an object is already present in either of the two repositories, UFT will not add any object and instead use the existing information.

UPDATE OBJECT PROPERTIES FROM APPLICATION

Many times, it happens that application code developers change the object properties such as *name* and *html id* of objects as per the change requirements. In UFT, there is an option to directly update the TO properties of object present in OR from application GUI object.

To update an object, follow the steps below on OR Manager window:

1. Select the object that needs to be updated.
2. Click on the button *Update from Application.*
   A hand tool appears.
3. Point the hand tool to the desired object in AUT GUI.
   'Object Selection' pop-up window appears as shown in the Fig. 23.3.
4. Select the appropriate object and click *OK.*

The TO will be automatically updated with the new object properties of GUI object.

HIGHLIGHT TEST OBJECT IN APPLICATION GUI

The highlight button can be used to highlight a TO of OR in application GUI. The highlight button is generally used to check whether UFT identifies the TO in application GUI or not. If UFT is able to identify the object in GUI, then it will highlight it (Figure 23.23).

> NOTES: If UFT identifies the object successfully and Smart Identification is set to true, then it might be possible that UFT is using Smart Identification to locate the object. In this case, the test script may error out during run-time. To avoid this, it is recommended to set the Smart Identification to False for the object before trying to locate these objects.

Figure 23.23 *Highlight test object in application*

HIGHLIGHT APPLICATION OBJECT IN OBJECT REPOSITORY

The repository button can be used to check if an object in application GUI is present in OR or not. This is used to avoid multiple additions of the same object that unnecessarily increases the OR size and makes OR maintenance difficult and costly.

DEFINE NEW TEST OBJECT

In agile automation, automation activities need to be started in parallel to the application development activities. In most scenarios, developing automated tests involve GUI objects and in the absence of these GUI objects it becomes impossible to write the tests. This problem can be solved by finding the object attributes (properties) that the developer is going to assign to the object when he creates the object. Once the object properties are known, a custom object can be created in UFT with these properties. This way we can create test objects (TOs) in the OR that do not yet exist in the application. This enables us to prepare an OR and build test scripts or components for our application even before the application GUI is developed.

To define a new test object:

1. Open Object Repository Manager.
2. Navigate *Object → Define New Test Object…*
3. *Define New Test Object* window opens as shown in the Fig. 23.24 below.
4. Select appropriate environment—Standard Windows, Web, All, etc.
5. Select appropriate class—Browser, WebEdit, WebTable, etc.
6. Input name, for example, WebTableTest.
7. Click on the add button to add more description properties.
8. Input *Value* of description properties.
9. Click the *Add* button to add this object to OR.

> NOTES
>
> This feature of self-defining object properties is extensively used when automation is carried out in agile environment. In agile environment, when the developers are still developing the GUI end, automation developers can find out the object property values that developers are going to code for various objects. Automation developers can define these values for the custom objects created. This helps in carrying out automation task in parallel to the application development.

OBJECT SPY

Object Spy tool is used to view object identification properties, object native properties and object methods that are supported by an application object. Object methods provide an insight on the operations that can be performed on the object such as mouse click, setting text etc.

To launch object spy:

1. Navigate *Tools → Object Spy…*
2. *Object Spy* window will open.
3. Click on the hand tool button .
   Hand tool appears.

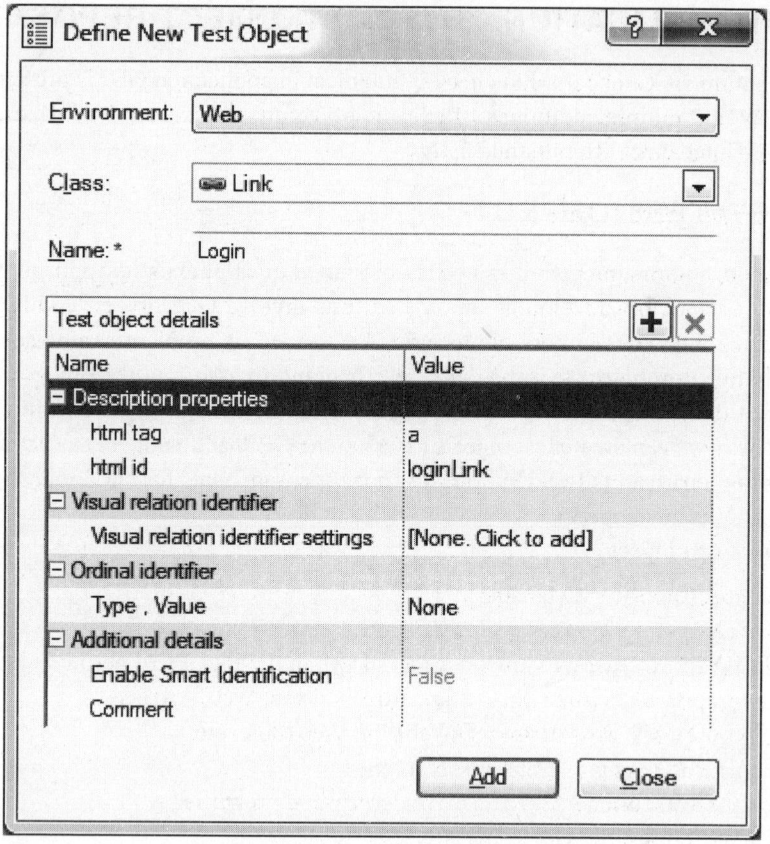

Figure 23.24 *Define new test object*

4. Point the hand tool on the application object whose properties needs to be viewed.
5. Object properties of the application object can be seen on Object Spy window as shown in Fig. 23.25.

Tool	Description
	Allows to view object properties and methods.
	Highlights the selected object application. Users to select the desired object on object hierarchy section of Object Spy window and then click on this button to highlight this object in AUT.
	Adds the selected object to Object Repository. The object to added to local object repository, if object spy is launched from local OR window. The object to added to shared object repository, if object spy is launched from shared OR window. If object spy is launched from UFT window then object is added to local object repository.
	Copies the object properties to clipboard.
	Keeps object spy window on top while spying.

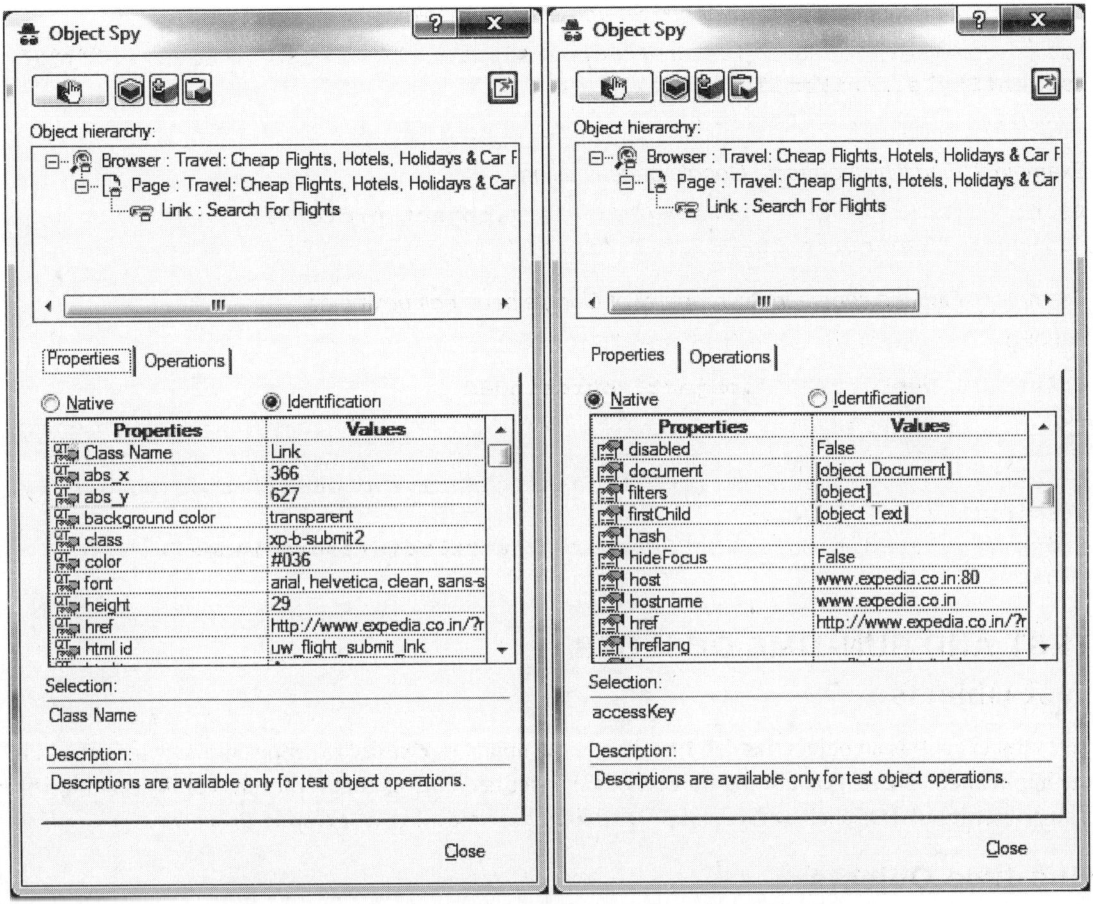

Figure 23.25 *Object spy identification and native properties*

IDENTIFICATION AND NATIVE PROPERTIES

Identification properties are the properties of the object for which UFT has built-in support. This means UFT can automatically learn these properties. While native properties are the object properties defined by the developer for the object while creating the object. For example, there are certain native properties provided by Microsoft to work with Microsoft Internet Explorer objects. Similarly, for every object in AUT such as webbutton and webedit, there exist some native properties as created by the developer.

In UFT automation, native properties are used when identification properties do not provide the functionality we need, viz., finding font family of link text. Figure 23.25 shows how to view native properties of an object using object spy tool. In test code, the native properties of an object can be accessed by using the *Object* property.

Example 1: Find font family of 'Advanced Search' link on Google page

```
Print Browser("Google").Page("Google").Link("Advanced Search").Object.
currentStyle.fontFamily
'Output: "arial, sans-serif"
```

Example 2: Find which protocol Google page is using

```
Print Browser("Google").Page("Google").object.protocol
'Output: "HyperText Transfer Protocol"
```

Example 3: Find the source index property of Google page edit box object.

```
Set oPg = Browser("Google").Page("Google")
Print oPg.WebEdit("q").object.sourceindex
'Output: 139

Alternatively,UFT also allows accessing native properties using syntax:
attribute/*.
Print oPg.WebEdit("q").GetROProperty("attribute/sourceindex")
'Output: 139
```

TEST AND RUN-TIME OBJECTS

Test Objects

Test Object (TO) is an object that UFT creates in the object repository to represent the actual object in the application. These TOs are the objects of UFT-defined classes that represent application objects. The properties of TOs such as *type*, *name*, and *html tag* are called *Test Object Properties*.

Run-time Objects

Run-time objects (ROs) are the actual application objects on which actions are performed during test run. The properties of ROs such as *outertext*, *rows*, and *cols* are called RO properties.

Objects captured in OR are called test objects (TO) while objects present in application are called run-time objects (RO).

Programmatically Reading Test Object Properties of an Object

'GetTOProperty' method is used to retrieve the TO properties during run-time.

```
Syntax : GetTOProperty(propertyName)
```

Example:

```
'Read 'name' property value of object UserName sUsrNm = Browser("IRCTC_
Login").Page("IRCTC_Login").
WebEdit("UserName").GetTOProperty("name") 'Read html tag property value
object UserName
sHtmlTag = Browser("IRCTC_Login").Page("IRCTC_Login").
WebEdit("UserName").GetTOProperty("html tag")
```

Reading all Test Object Properties and Values of an Object

'GetTOProperties' method is used to retrieve all the TO properties of an object during run-time.

```
Syntax : GetTOProperties()
```

Example:

```
'Retrieve all properties of object UserName
Set objUSrNmProps = Browser("IRCTC_Login").Page("IRCTC_Login").
WebEdit("UserName").GetTOProperties()

'Print all properties and property values
Print "Property Name" & vbTab & "Property Value"
For iCnt = 1 To objUSrNmProps.Count-1 Step 1
'Print Property Name and Property Value
Print objUSrNmProps(iCnt).Name & vbTab & objUSrNmProps(iCnt). Value
Next
Set objUSrNmProps = Nothing
```

Changing Test Object Properties at Run Time

'SetTOProperty' method is used to change the value of the TO properties during time. This change is temporary and valid till the run session only.

```
Syntax : SetTOProperty(propertyName, propertyValue)
```

Example: Change the 'column names' property of the test object so that this dynamic object is recognized during run-time.

```
'Set html tag property of object Username during run time Browser("IRCTC_
Login").Page("IRCTC_Login ").
WebEdit("UserName").SetTOProperty("html tag", "INPUT")

'Set column names property of Calendar object sMnthYr=MonthName(Month(Date))
& "," & Year(Date) Browser("IRCTC_Login").Page("IRCTC_Login").
WebTable("Calendar").SetTOProperty("column names", sMnthYr)
```

Retrieving Run-time Object Properties During Script Execution

'GetROProperty' is used to retrieve the run-time property value of an object. This method helps to extract the actual property values of a GUI object during script execution.

```
Syntax : GetROProperty(propertyName)
```

Example: Find the run-time value of

```
'Read text that has been inserted into UserName edit box sUsrNm =
Browser("IRCTC_Login").Page("IRCTC_Login ").
WebEdit("UserName").GetROProperty("value")
```

COMPARING SHARED OBJECT REPOSITORIES

UFT provides the *Object Repository Comparison Tool* to compare two shared ORs. The purpose of this tool is to identify similarity, variations, and changes between two different set of shared ORs or two different versions of the same OR. One possible case for comparing shared OR can be tracking changes in different versions of the same OR. After the comparison process, the comparison tool provides a statistical report. The statistical report contains information such as the objects that are present in both ORs with same logical name but with different object properties, the objects that are common to both and the objects that are unique to their own OR. Object properties and their values can also be viewed and analyzed from the graphic report. The actual shared OR files remains unchanged during the comparison process.

In order to compare two shared ORs, follow the steps as discussed below:

1. Navigate *Resources* → *Object Repository Manager*. *Object Repository Manager* window opens.
2. In *Object Repository Manager* window navigate to *Tools* → *Object Repository Comparison Tool*. *New Comparison* tool opens as shown in Fig. 23.26.
3. Select the shared ORs for comparison and Click the *OK* button.
4. Comparison results window along with comparison summary results pop-window appear as shown in Fig. 23.27.
5. To interpret the results of object comparison, refer the *Color Settings* schema for object comparison results as shown in Fig. 23.28.

ANALYZING COMPARISON RESULTS

The comparison tool automatically compares the objects and identifies them by classifying them into one of the following types:

Unique objects: Objects exist in only one of the shared ORs.
Identical objects: Objects exist in both of the ORs. All the description properties and values of these objects are same in both the repositories including the logical name.

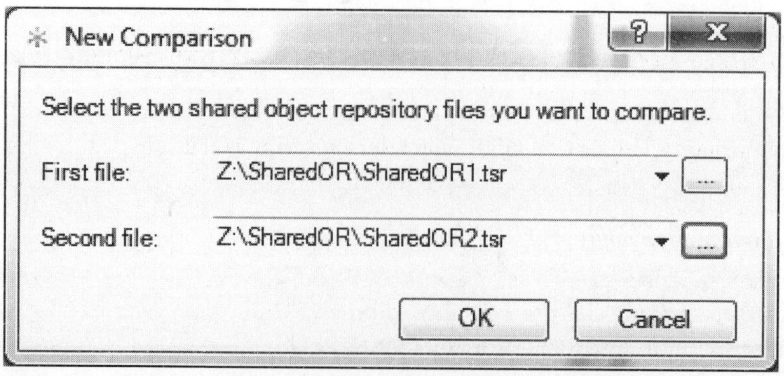

Figure 23.26 *Object repositories comparison*

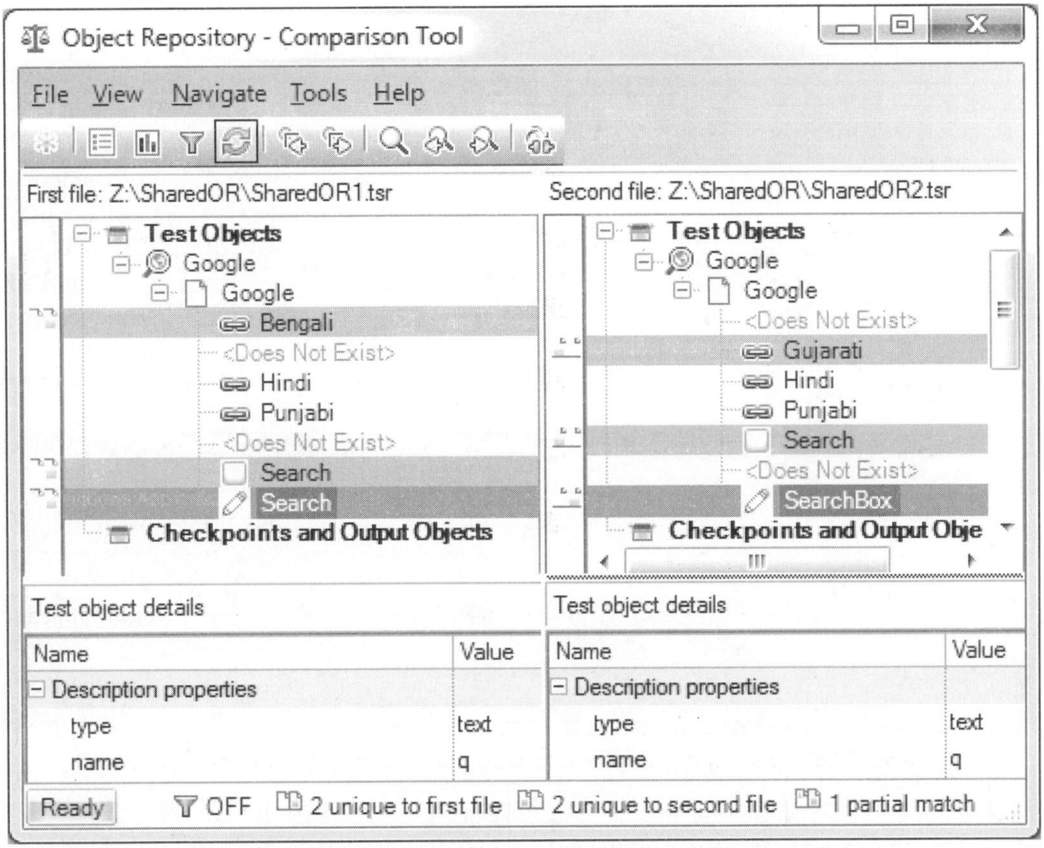

Figure 23.27 *Object repository comparison results*

Identical description, different logical name objects: Objects whose description properties and values are similar in both the ORs but logical names are different.
Similar description objects: Objects whose description properties and values are similar but not identical in both of the objects repositories. One of the objects always has a super set properties over the other object.

Figure 23.28 shows the color schema for interpreting object comparison results. After comparison, UFT provides two sets of reports—comparison statistics report and detailed object comparison report (Figure 23.37). Comparison statistics report as shown in Fig. 23.14 provides the summary report of the comparison. It identifies the number of objects that are similar, identical, unique, or partial match. Comparison results report contains detailed reports with color schema of which object falls in which category. It also contains the complete description properties of all the objects as shown in Fig. 23.27.

Let us assume that there are two ORs 'SharedOR1.tst' and 'SharedOR2.tsr' as shown in Fig. 23.29 and 23.30. These ORs contain objects of Google page as shown in Fig. 23.31.

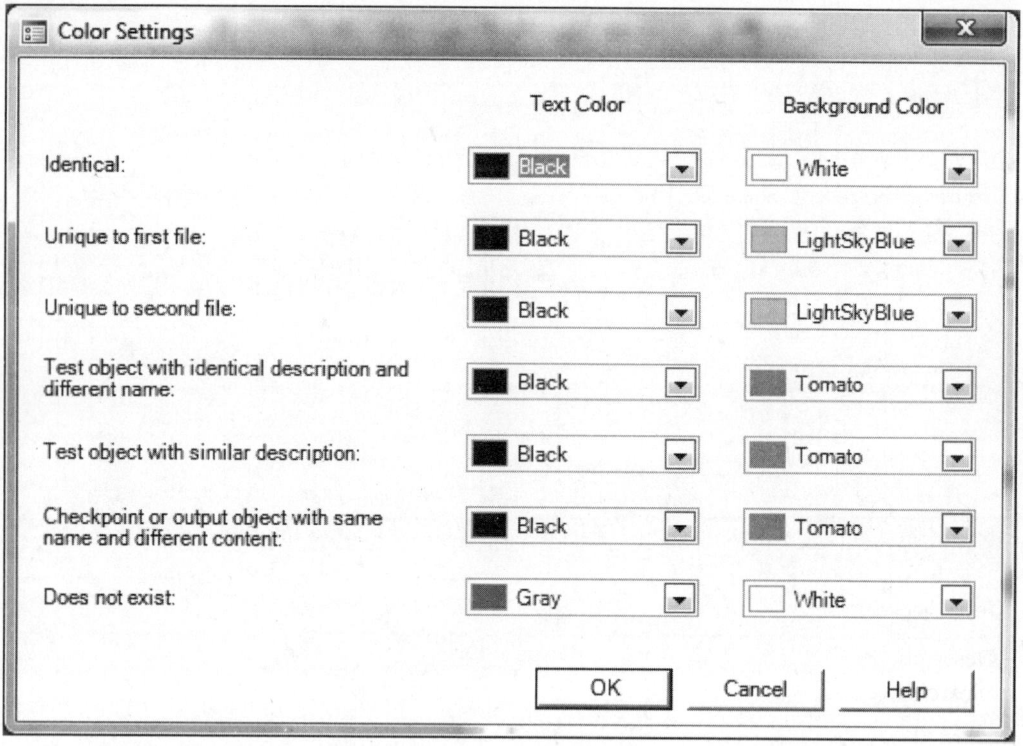

Figure 23.28 *Color scheme for analyzing object repository comparison results*

- Description properties of Bengali' link pf SharedOR1.tsr GUI objects is not present in SharedOR2.tsr. (Figure 23.31). Therefore, this object is classified as *Unique* object. Similarly, the description properties of 'Gujarati link object of Shared2.tsr do not match with the description properties of any object of Shared1.tsr. Therefore, this is also classified as *Unique* object of Shared2.tsr OR.
- GUI objects – Browser object 'Google,' page object 'Google,' link object 'Hindi,' and link object 'Punjabi,' have the same logical name, description property names, and description property values in both the shared ORs. These objects are classified as *Identical* objects.

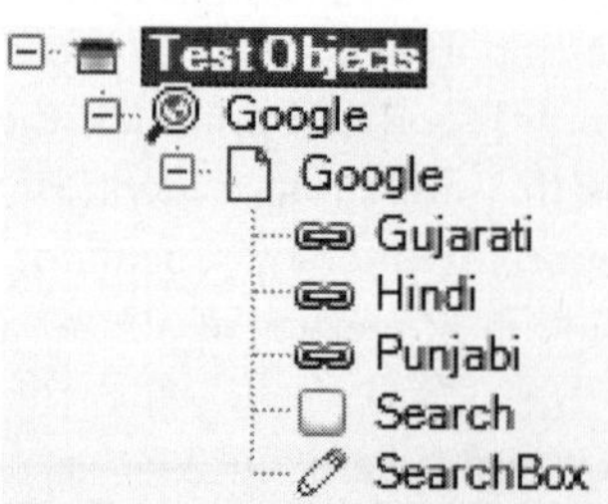

Figure 23.29 *SharedOR1.tsr*

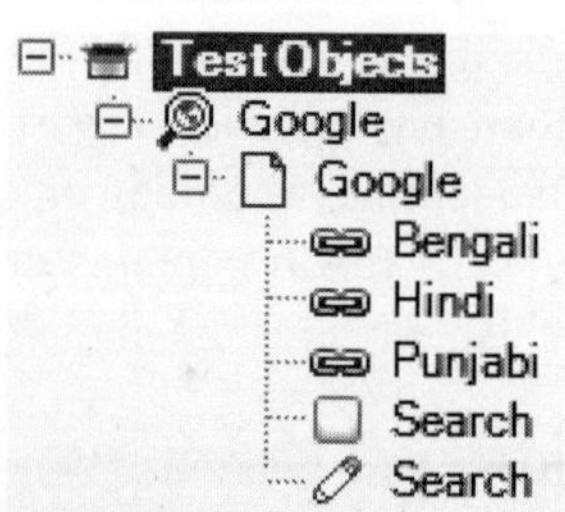

Figure 23.30 *SharedOR2.tsr*

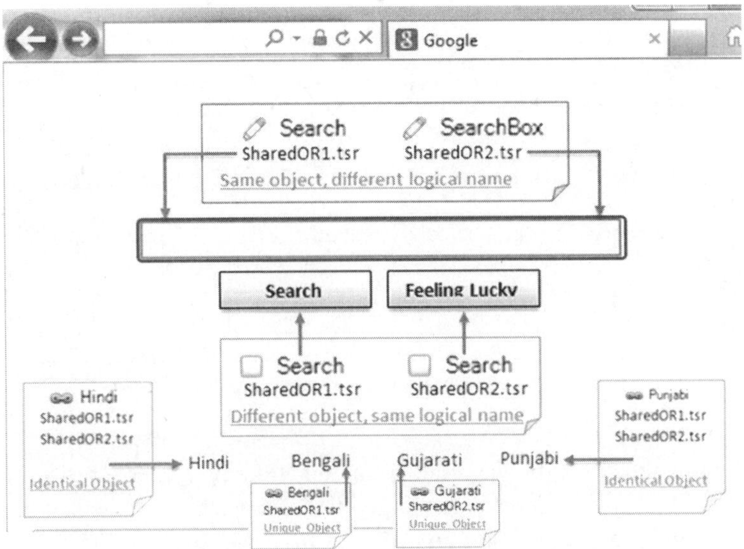

Figure 23.31 *Object classification*

- Description properties of 'Search' edit box object match with the description properties of the 'SearchBox' edit box object but the logical names of these two objects are different. Therefore, these objects are classified as *Partial Match* objects.

MERGING SHARED OBJECT REPOSITORIES

UFT provides the flexibility to merge two ORs into a new third OR using Object Repository Merge Tool. This tool enables us to merge two shared ORs (called *Primary* and *Secondary* ORs) into a new third OR called the target OR. Objects in the primary and secondary ORs are automatically compared and then added to the target OR as per the pre-configured rules. These rules specify how the conflict between the objects is to be resolved. One practical example of the use of Object Re-

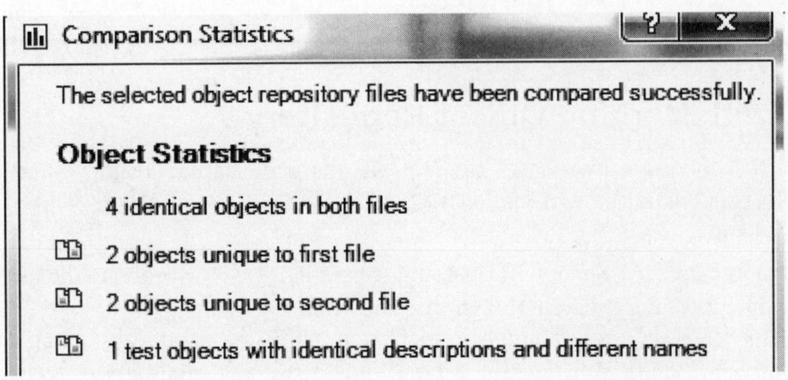

Figure 23.32 *Object repository comparison statistics*

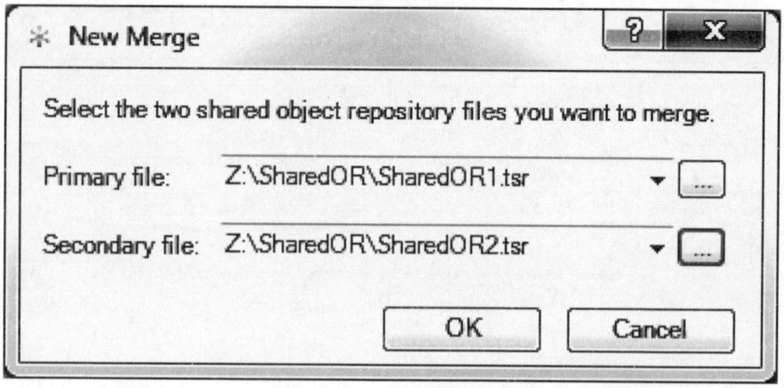

Figure 23.33 *Shared object repositories merge*

pository Merge Tool is the situation where all the automation developers are working on their individual shared ORs and the same needs to be merged to the project OR at the end of the day. Though, this object merge work mechanism may give rise to many object identification issues and is not recommended.

> **NOTES** In order to merge local OR objects with shared OR, first export the local OR and save it as shared OR. Thereafter, two shared ORs can easily be merged.

Follow the following steps to merge two shared ORs:

1. *Resources* → *Object Repository Manager*. *Object Repository Manager* window opens.
2. Navigate *Tools* → *Object Repository Merge Tool*. *New Merge* dialog box opens as shown in Fig. 23.33.
3. Specify the two shared ORs to be merged and click the *OK* button.
4. Merge details and merge statistics summary appears as shown in Fig. 23.34.
5. Analyze the merge results and resolve conflicts as required for *Target* OR.
6. Save the OR as *Shared Target* OR (Figure 23.34).

This shared OR can now be associated with the various tests.

Problems with Merging Object Repository

Let us assume that there are two tests—SharedOR1.mts and Shared2OR.mts—that are associated with shared ORs SharedOR1.tsr and SharedOR2.tsr, respectively. Figures 23.35 and 23.36 show the code written in the two tests.

Now, let us merge the OR 'SharedOR1.tsr' and 'SharedOR2.tsr' to generate the target OR 'SharedOR3.tsr.' The objects of the 'SharedOR3.tsr' are shown in Fig. 23.37.

Let us associate 'SharedOR3.tsr' with the two tests and disassociate the previously associated ORs from them. Now, on execution, it is observed that the second test 'SharedOR2.mts' is failing. The reason is:

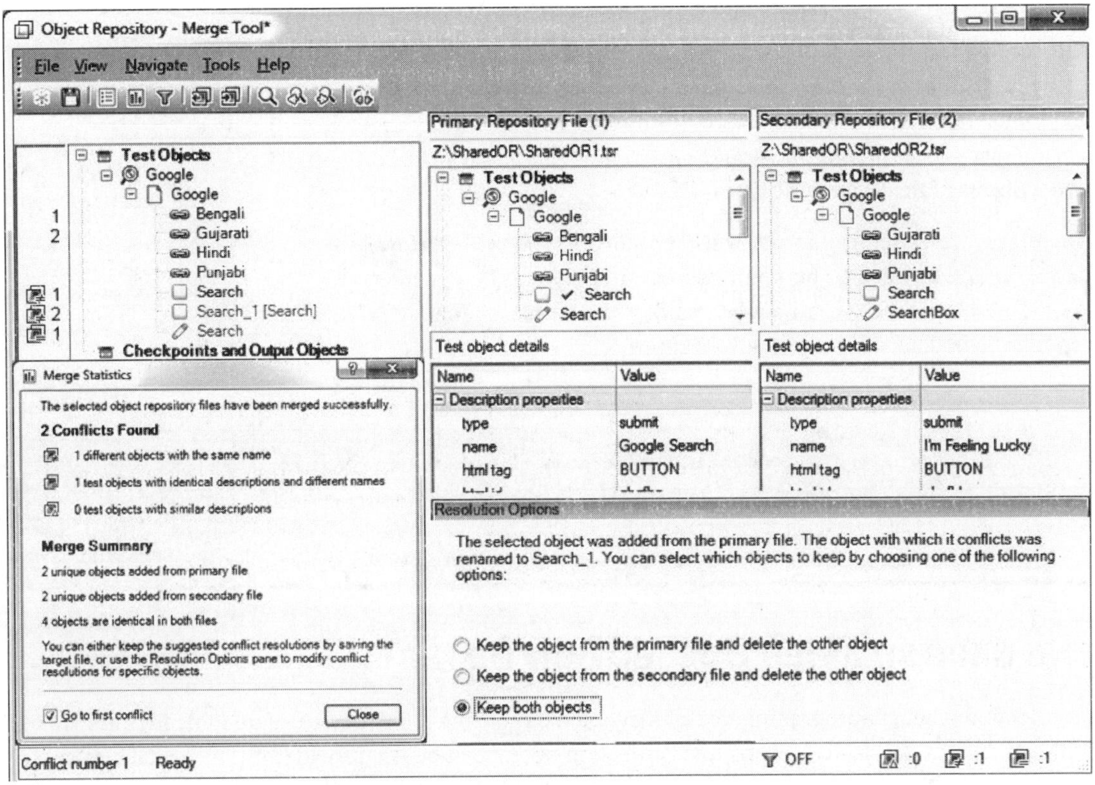

Figure 23.34 *Object repository merge tool*

```
Main
Browser("Google").Page("Google").Link("Hindi").GetROProperty("href")
Browser("Google").Page("Google").Link("Punjabi").GetROProperty("href")
Browser("Google").Page("Google").Link("Bengali").GetROProperty("href")
Browser("Google").Page("Google").WebEdit("Search").Set "Test OR Merge"
Browser("Google").Page("Google").WebButton("Search").Click
```

Figure 23.35 *SharedOR1.mts*

```
Main
Browser("Google").Page("Google").Link("Hindi").GetROProperty("href")
Browser("Google").Page("Google").Link("Punjabi").GetROProperty("href")
Browser("Google").Page("Google").Link("Gujarati").GetROProperty("href")
Browser("Google").Page("Google").WebEdit("SearchBox").Set "Test OR Merge"
Browser("Google").Page("Google").WebButton("Search").Click
```

Figure 23.36 *SharedOR2.mts*

- 'SearchBox' object does not exist in 'SharedOR3.tsr' as coded in the test 'SharedOR2.mts.'
- Also, the "Search' button object to which the 'SharedOR2.mts' is referring now (SharedOR3.mts) is not the correct one. After object merger, it should now refer to 'Search_1' button object of the SharedOR3.tsr OR.

Therefore, we observe that the tests are not in sync with the new target OR. Tests need to be upgraded before they can be executed. As the number of tests and action inside tests increases, the effort required to update scripts will also multiply.

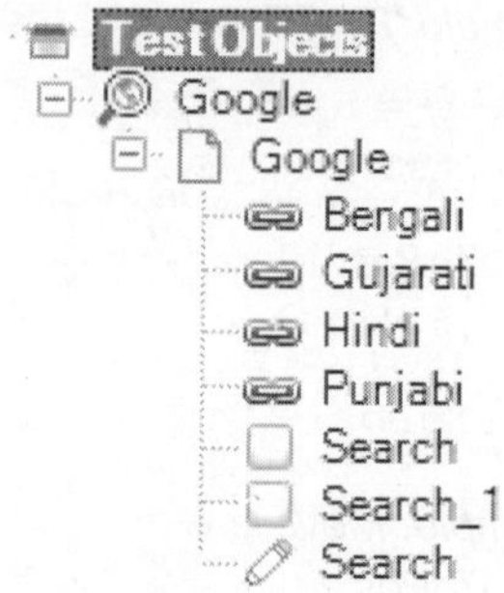

Figure 23.37 *SharedOR3.tsr*

> **NOTES** The use of merge tool to merge ORs may result in many object identification issues. It may result in the loss of synchronization between the shared OR and the test scripts using those ORs. It is always advisable to use project level ORs that are stored in one central location. Read or write access of the OR is to be given to the automation developers as and when required. This avoids duplicity of objects. This saves lot of time and effort. Backup of these ORs need to be taken at periodic intervals to avoid loss of data.

THE REPOSITORIES COLLECTION OBJECT

A collection object to programmatically manage the run-time collection of shared OR files associated with the current action. The repository collection object can be used to add or remove ORs to an action.

> **NOTES** The operations performed on the RepositoriesCollection object affect only the run-time copy of the collection. Once the test execution is over, the action's OR collection is just as it was before starting the test execution.

Methods

The following methods are associated with the RepositoriesCollection object.

Add: Adds an OR to the specified position in the run-time collection object of the shared OR.

```
Syntax : RepositoriesCollection.Add
RepositoryPath [, Position]
```

Example: Add object repository SharedOR1.tsr to the to the run-time RepositoriesCollection object

```
RepositoriesCollection.Add "Z:\Automation\ObjectRepository\SharedOR1.tsr"
```

Find: Finds the index position of the specified OR file.

```
Syntax : nORPos = RepositoriesCollection.Find RepositoryPath
```

Example: Find the position of SharedOR1.tsr in the run-time RepositoriesCollection object

```
nORPos = RepositoriesCollection.Find "Z:\Automation\ObjectRepository\Share-
dOR1.tsr"
```

MoveToPos: Moves the OR file from the current position to the new position.

```
Syntax : RepositoriesCollection.
MoveToPos CurrentPosition, NewPosition
```

Example: Move SharedOR1.tsr from the current position 1 to new position 2. RepositoriesCollection. MoveToPos 1, 2

Remove: Removes the object repository at the specified position from the run-time repository collection object.

```
Syntax : RepositoriesCollection.Remove Position
```

Example: Remove object repository SharedOR1.tsr from the to the run-time RepositoriesCollection object

```
RepositoriesCollection.Add   "Z:\Automation\ObjectRepository\SharedOR1.
tsr"
```

RemoveAll: Removes all object repository files from the run-time repository collection object.

```
Syntax : RepositoriesCollection.RemoveAll
```

Example: Remove all object repository files from the to the run-time RepositoriesCollection object

```
RepositoriesCollection.RemoveAll
```

Properties

The following properties are associated with the RepositoriesCollection object.

Count: Returns the number of OR files in the run-time collection of shared OR files associated with the current action.

```
Syntax : nORCnt = RepositoriesCollection.Count
```

Example: Find the number of object repositories associated with the run-time Repositories Collection object

```
nORCnt = RepositoriesCollection.Count
```

Item: Returns the path of the OR file located in the specified index position.

```
Syntax : sORPath = RepositoriesCollection.Item (Position)
```

Example: Find the object repository path of the first OR file within the run-time collection of shared object repository files associated with the current action.

```
sORPath = RepositoriesCollection (1)
```

QUICK TIPS

- ✓ Shared OR is to be used instead of local OR.
- ✓ It is advisable to keep one shared OR per project application or per project application module depending on the size of the OR.
- ✓ Large OR size can reduce the execution speed of test script.
- ✓ The use of multiple repository files needs to be avoided. The use of multiple ORs may result in object duplication in many OR files leading to maintenance issues.
- ✓ It is always better to avoid using object merger tool. The merging of ORs can result in object identification issues.
- ✓ Instead of creating multiple ORs and merging them later, it is better to give read/write access of the shared OR files to the automation developers as and when required.
- ✓ Periodic backup of shared OR is to be taken.

PRACTICAL QUESTIONS

1. What is OR?
2. What is the difference between local OR and shared OR? Which one is preferable?
3. How to associate a shared OR to a test script?
4. How object property values can be replaced with regular expressions? What is the use of the same?
5. What are the ways to parameterize test object description properties?
6. What is the difference between TO property and RO property?
7. What is object spy? What is its use in test automation?
8. What is the difference between native properties and identification properties?
9. How a user-defined custom object can be created in OR?
10. What are the problems associated with merging two or more repositories?
11. Explain the various OR design techniques. Which OR design technique is best?

Chapter 24

Object Repository Design

The way objects are added and organized in the OR has a huge impact on the test automation maintenance effort. A well-designed OR has good readability, avoids object duplicity, and supports easy change identification and implementation. OR with well-designed hierarchy helps to easily identify whether an object already exists in OR or not. A standard naming convention of objects helps to easily find out the respective GUI object in the object repository.

Before starting to capture the objects to the OR, it is very important to configure the object identification settings. This is discussed in detail in the chapter 'Object Identification.' Object identification settings define the mandatory and associative properties required to identify a TO during run-time. A random study of the application objects has to be done to identify the essential properties that are required to identify an object. The mandatory and associative properties are to be chosen in a way that it avoids or limits the need of Smart Identification (SI) and ordinal identifiers to identify an object. The reason for avoiding SI is that it can behave unpredictably during the run session. Similarly, the values of ordinal identifiers such as index and creation time may vary during run-time. Moreover, the index property of an object can be easily changed by the application developer without requiring any change request. Again, such a change mostly will not have any impact on the look and feel of GUI or application functionality. Therefore, such changes always go unnoticed both by the manual testers and the management. However, at the same time, such a change will require test scripts and OR to be upgraded and tested again before they can be executed. It becomes very difficult to show a change effort in test scripts to the management without any actual change in the application. In addition, since such type of changes cannot be predicted or monitored, the maintenance effort for these changes to the test scripts and OR become cyclic, time consuming, and costly. Hence, it is always advisable to avoid the use of the ordinal identifiers. Object identification properties of the TOs are to be selected in a way that it supports easy handling of the dynamic objects of the application. It as well should support minimal changes to the test script and the OR in case of a change application object properties. Those object properties which developers intend to change frequently should not be used to identify an object. ORs need to be designed in a way that test scripts and the TOs require change only in the cases where change to the application is visible.

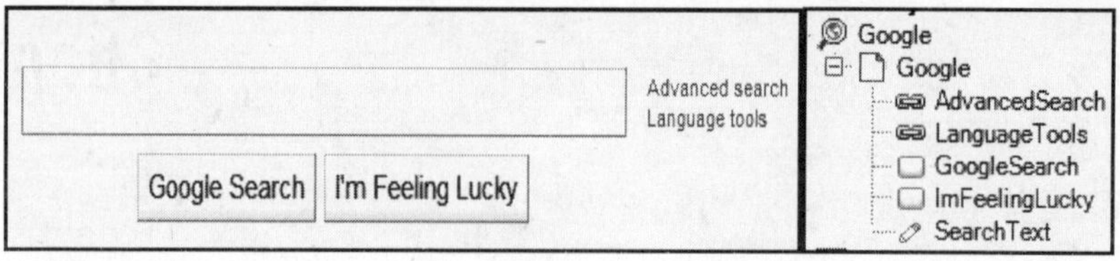

Figure 24.1 *Application objects and their naming convention in the OR*

Naming Convention of Objects in OR

Logical name of the TOs are to be chosen in way that improves its readability. It as well should make it easier for users to logically map the TOs with the GUI objects without using the UFT utilities. Script writing in UFT requires creating instance of the TOs and executing its methods. The use of 'highlight' feature to identify the TOs for each and every line of code will increase the test development effort. If proper naming convention is not used, then during maintenance phase, it becomes time consuming to identify the required object that needs change among the group of hundreds of objects that are present in OR. A proper naming convention of the objects can be to name the objects as per their GUI (label) name. For example, name of the WebEdit object can be chosen as per the name that is mentioned against it in the GUI. Special characters such as 'White Space,' '#,' and '$' are to be avoided. Two words within the name can be separated using a capital character as shown in Fig. 24.1. If more separators are required then, underscore sign ("_") can be used. In case of lengthy names, logically meaningful abbreviations are to be used.

OBJECT REPOSITORY DESIGN

The way by which the objects are organized in OR is referred as OR design. The hierarchy of the objects in OR should be in a way that it supports easy identification of specific objects among the group of objects in the OR. There are five ways of organizing objects in the OR:

1. Default Capture Hierarchy Design
2. Screen-based Hierarchy Design
3. Functionality-based Hierarchy Design
4. Screen Creation Time-based Hierarchy Design
5. Screen Creation Time and URL-based Hierarchy Design

Default Capture Hierarchy Design

In Default Capture Hierarchy Design, object hierarchy is the same as captured by UFT. UFT decides the object hierarchy based on the object properties and the object hierarchy in AUT. If the properties of the object such as ordinal identifier is changed, then UFT starts adding object duplicates in OR. For example, suppose that the 'CreationTime' property of browser is changed from 'None' to '0.' In this case, even when the creation time=0 browser objects are added to OR, a new hierarchy level is created. Object duplicates in OR not only increases the OR size but makes it difficult to

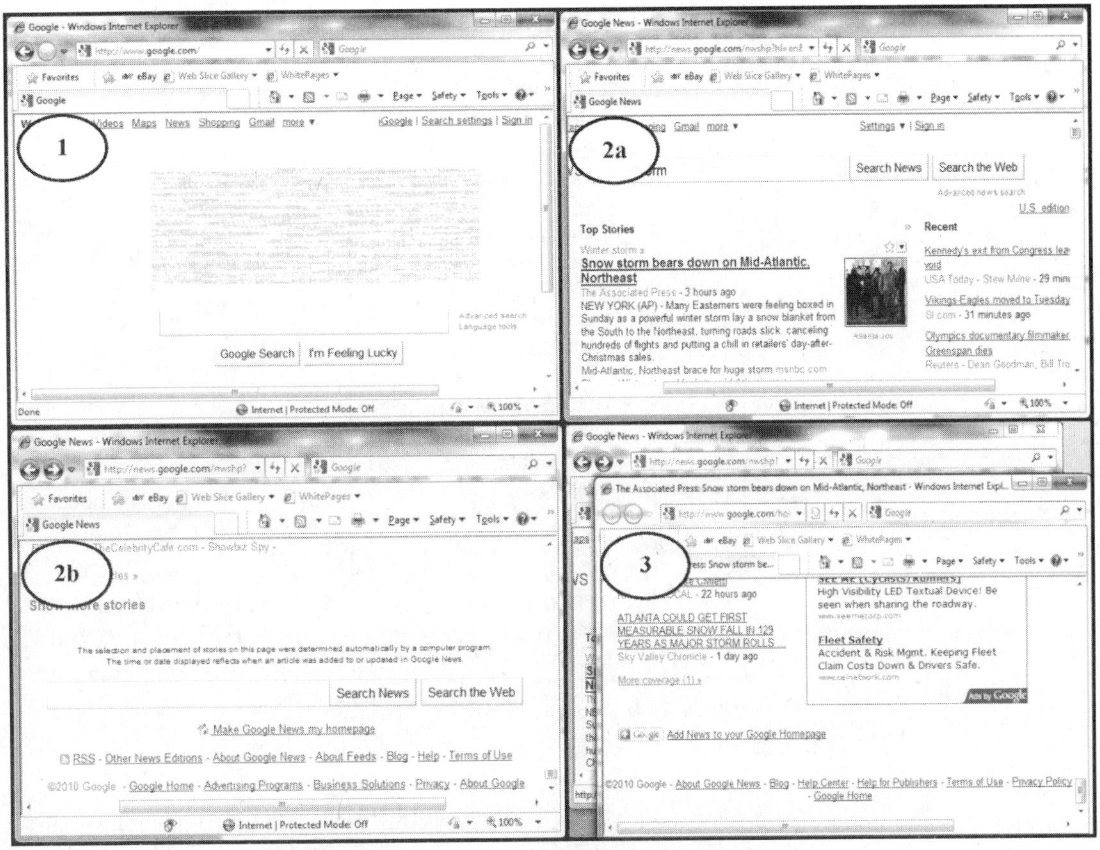

Figure 24.2 *Example test scenario GUI page/object*

implement object changes. It becomes difficult and time consuming to identify an object among multiple objects. This is the most primitive object hierarchy design and is associated with a very high OR maintenance cost.

For explanation purposes, let us consider the test scenario, which is listed as follows:

- Launch Google page.
- Click on link 'News.' 'News' page opens.
- Search specific news.
- Click on the first news link. A new browser opens. Now, at the same time, two browsers are open, which are not synchronized. In addition, there are certain objects such as link object 'Terms of Use' that is present in both the browsers.
- Click on the link 'Terms of Use' of the new browser.

Figure 24.2 shows the various GUI pages and objects as visible of Google site. Figure 24.3 shows the default hierarchy design created by UFT, when these objects are added to OR.

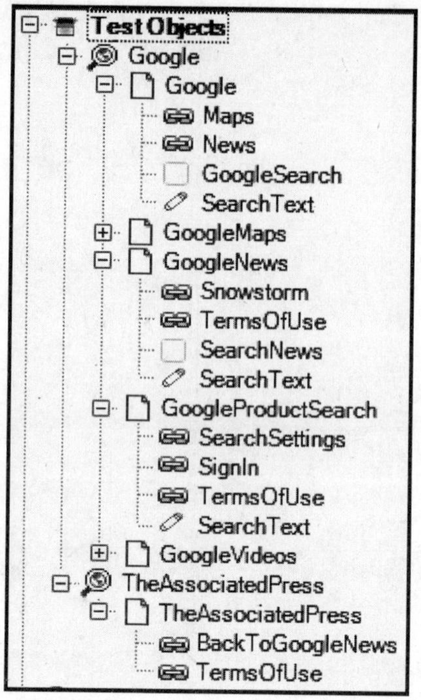

Figure 24.3 *Default hierarchy design*

Disadvantages

- If the creation time property of the browser is changed from '0' to 'none' or otherwise, UFT starts creating a new object hierarchy (example Google_2) leading to duplicate object creation.
- Link object 'TermsOfUse' is one and the same object, but had to be added again and again for each hierarchy.
- If the properties of link object 'TermsOfUse' or 'Maps' object changes at certain point of time, then it will become time consuming to identify all the instances of these objects in OR.
- Object duplicity not only increases OR size but also increases OR maintenance effort and cost.

Screen-based Hierarchy Design

In this design technique, a new page or screen object is created for each new page or screen. It helps to easily map the GUI object to the TO in OR and vice-versa. However, on the opposite side, the number of object duplications is much higher. For example, almost all pages of 'Google' has link object 'TermsOfUse.' If the number of 'page' objects runs into 500, duplicate objects will also be 500. This makes maintenance of OR almost impossible and defeats the very objective of Shared OR concept. For client-server applications where the number of screens is less, this technique can be used. In this technique:

- Browsers or AUT screens are classified based on their ordinal identifier (creation time or index).
- Page objects or sub-screen objects are classified based on page or sub-screen present in AUT.

In this technique, all the objects of a page are added to that respective page object only.

Disadvantages

Huge object duplication makes this technique very difficult to maintain and use.

Functionality-based Hierarchy Design

To overcome the problems associated with the screen-based classification of objects came the concept of functionality-based hierarchy design. In this design, for each business functionality, a new hierarchy is designed. Therefore, even if the functionality spans over multiple pages, all the object of these pages get added to the same 'Page' object in OR. For example, suppose that various functionalities of 'Google' page such as 'Maps,' 'News,' Images,' and 'Videos' need to be automated. Then, first of all, the functionalities of the 'Google' page are categorized into various page objects—SignIn, SearchSettings, Videos, Maps, News, etc. In this technique:

- Browsers or AUT screens are classified based on their ordinal identifier (creation time or index).
- Pages or sub-screens are classified based on AUT functionality they capture. A separate page object is designed for each category—'SignIn,' 'SearchSettings,' 'Videos,' etc. The 'SignIn' page, object will contain all the objects of the sign-in functionality. Here, even if 'SignIn' requires navigating through 2–3 pages, no more 'page' object is created. All the objects of 'SignIn' functionality spanning over multiple pages are added under 'SignIn' page object only in the OR.

Disadvantages

Though this design is better then the default capture design, it is more difficult to maintain this design. The person who has no know-how of OR design cannot update it. In addition, it is difficult to identify a GUI object in OR as direct mapping does not exist as it does in screen-based classification. Moreover, because of the presence of objects such as link object 'TermsOfUse' that forms part of other business functionality as well, it becomes impossible to have a clearly defined boundary line on which 'Page' object hierarchy the GUI object is to be added. Such confusion again leads to object duplication. Though object duplicity is lesser than the screen-based classification, still this method is also not able to reduce object duplication to a maintainable level. The time required to identify a GUI object in OR is also high.

> NOTES: If the logical name of the object in OR is different from what UFT sets during default capture, then 'Locate in Repository' feature may not work. In addition, if the object properties are modified viz. the use of regular expression, then too UFT may not be able to identify a TO in OR using 'Locate in Repository' feature.

Figure 24.4 shows how the OR design, as shown in Fig. 24.3, can be customized and designed as per the functionality-based hierarchy design.

Screen Creation Time-based Hierarchy Design

Screen creation time-based hierarchy design is the most effective organization of objects minimizing object duplication and improving maintainability. This technique of object organization in OR

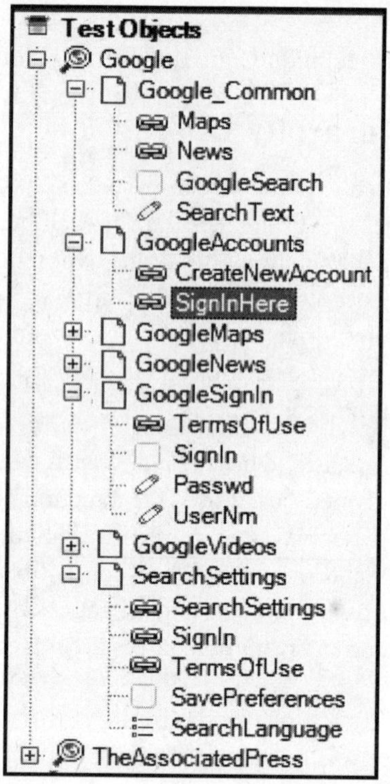

Figure 24.4 *Functionality based hierarchy design*

has been designed by the author, Rajeev Gupta. Browsers are classified based on the creation time and all the objects (including the page object) are placed under the respective browser object. In this technique:

- Browser object is classified based on the creation time of the browser.
- Page object is classified based on the creation time of the browser.
- For every browser object, there is only one page object.
- All the objects are placed under one 'Page' object.
- There exists only one browser object for each browser instance in AUT.

Figure 24.5 shows the organization of objects used this technique. 'Google_0' is the creation time=0 browser. There is only one page object inside this browser object. All the objects associated with browser creation time=0 are added under the 'Google_0' page object. 'Google_1' is the cre- ation time=1 browser. All the objects including page object of the creation time=1 browser are added in this hierarchy. Similarly, for each and every browser instance, there exist a browser object and all the objects of that browser instance are added to its hierarchy.

Advantages

1. There is no object duplication within the same browser object. Duplication of objects is reduced to a great extent.

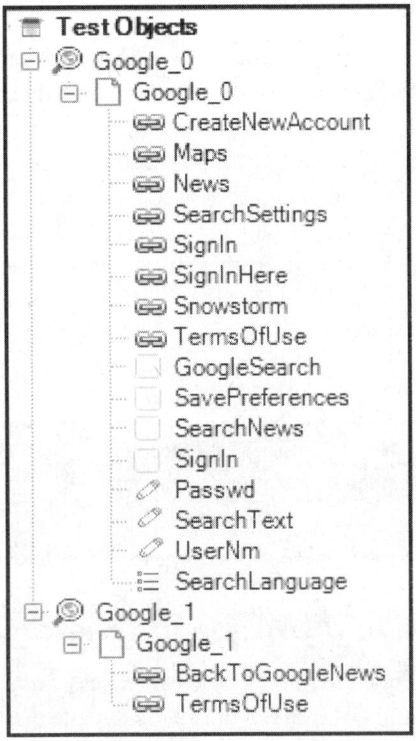

Figure 24.5 *Screen creation time-based hierarchy design*

2. OR becomes more readable and easily maintainable.
3. It is easy to logically map GUI objects to the TOs without using UFT 'Highlight' or 'Locate in Reposi- tory' feature, as only one instance of an object exists in one browser. The naming convention of the object is similar to that of GUI.
4. Script code becomes more readable and easily understandable.
5. It becomes easy to identify a specific TO among a group of hundreds of the objects.

For this technique to work effectively, the object identification settings of browser and page need to be configured properly as shown below:

```
Browser
   name: Google.*
   Creation Time=0
Page
   title: Google.*
```

Regular expressions are to be used in the name property of browser and title property of page object as required.

Disadvantages

In case same object is present in both creation time=0 and creation time=1, browser with no sync between the two browsers, and SI gets activated, then UFT may behave unpredictably. Suppose that at an instant two browsers 'Google_0' and 'Google_1' are active on the screen. Both these browsers contain the link object 'TermsOfUse.' Now, suppose that the code is written to click on link 'TermsOfUse' of the second browser. Assume that UFT is not able to identify the object using normal identification, then in this case SI will get activated. Once SI gets activated, it can behave unpredictably and execute a click method on the link 'TermsOfUse' of the first browser. To solve this problem, 'Screen Creation Time and URL-based Hierarchy Design' OR design technique has been designed. However, this problem may not occur if the AUT browsers are in sync with each other.

NOTES: Sync between AUT browsers ensures that if application browser with creation time=1 is open, then user is not able to activate or work on browser with creation time=0.

Screen Creation Time and URL-based Hierarchy Design

This OR design technique is designed to maximize the chances of object recognition during UFT *Normal Identification* phase only. This technique reduces the dependency on SI and ordinal identifiers to recognize an object. This technique is also designed by the author, Rajeev Gupta. For this technique to work effectively, *Object Identification* settings need to be set as per application objects identification requirements. Appendix A provides the generalized object identification settings for web application objects. In this technique, browsers are classified based on the browser creation time. However, the properties of browser are defined in such a way that the 'creation time' of browsers is not required to identify the browser object. In OR, two properties of browser—'name' and 'openurl'—are also defined in addition to the ordinal identifier 'creation time.' Regular expressions are used in both the 'name' and 'openurl' property in such a way that UFT is easily able to differentiate among the multiple browsers without the need of ordinal identifiers or SI. The 'title' property of the page is used to identify the page object. If required, regular expressions are to be used for this property too. In this technique:

- Browser object is classified based on the 'creation time,' 'name,' and 'openurl' property of the browser.
- Regular expressions are used for 'name' and 'openurl' property of the browser.
- For every browser object, there is only one page object.
- All the objects are placed under one 'Page' object.
- There is only one browser object for browser with creation time=0.
- There can be multiple browser objects for browsers with creation time>0. This is because 'openurl' properties of no two browser instances are same.

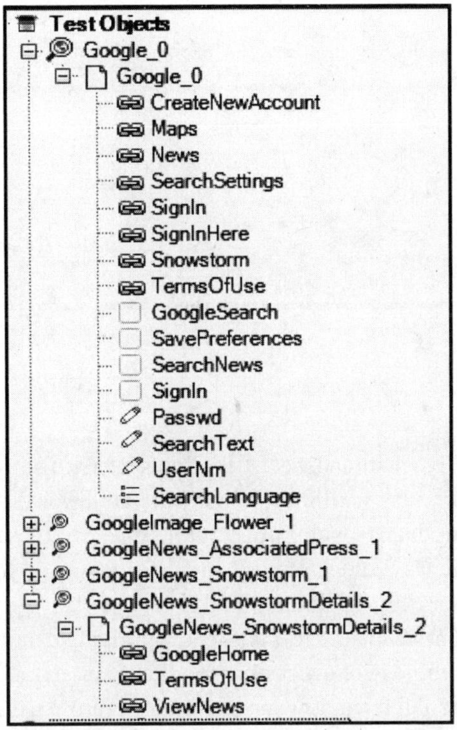

Figure 24.6 *Screen creation time & URL based hierarchy design*

Figure 24.6 shows the object hierarchy using this technique. Only one instance of browser object ‘Google_0’ exists for the creation time=0 browser. Browsers with creation time>0 have multiple instances—‘GoogleImage_Flower_1,’ ‘GoogleNews AssociatedPress 1,’ etc. ‘_0’ refers to the creation time=0 browsers; ‘_1’ refers to the creation time=1 browser; and so on.

Chapter 25

Datatables

Datatables are similar to MS Excel spreadsheets. It allows users to store and use data in its cells and also perform mathematical formulas within the cells. Data tables or data pane provide a way to data drive the test scripts. Test input data as well as test output data can be saved in the datatables. During test execution, test script retrieves the test input data from the datatables and updates the test output data back to the datatable. Every test has one global datatable that is accessible to all actions inside that test, and each action present inside the test has its own private datatable known as local datatable. Both the local and global datatables are accessible to all actions. The values of the datatable or data sheets can be edited within the UFT window as shown in Figure 25.1. It also shows local data table of action *Login*.

WORKING WITH GLOBAL AND ACTION SHEETS

Inserting Parameters in Datatables

Global and local datatable is used to parameterize the test and actions as per test case requirement. The first step is to define the name of the parameter or field in the datatable. This is done by editing the first row of the datatable marked 'A', 'B', 'C' and so on. Below the parameter name, parameter values can be specified as shown in Fig. 25.1. To edit the parameter name, double-click on it. A pop-up window opens. Specify the parameter name or field name and click OK.

Formulas in Data Tables (GUI Testing only)

UFT allows users to use Microsoft Excel formulas in the data tables. This enables users to create contextually relevant data during the run session. These formulas can also be used as part of a checkpoint.

Example 1: Use formula in data table to add data of two cells.

Consider the data table shown in Fig. 25.3. Cell A1 and B1 have integer data and cell C1 has a formula to calculate sum of cells A1 and B1. Formulas can be written in data table cells in the same way as it is written in Excel file.

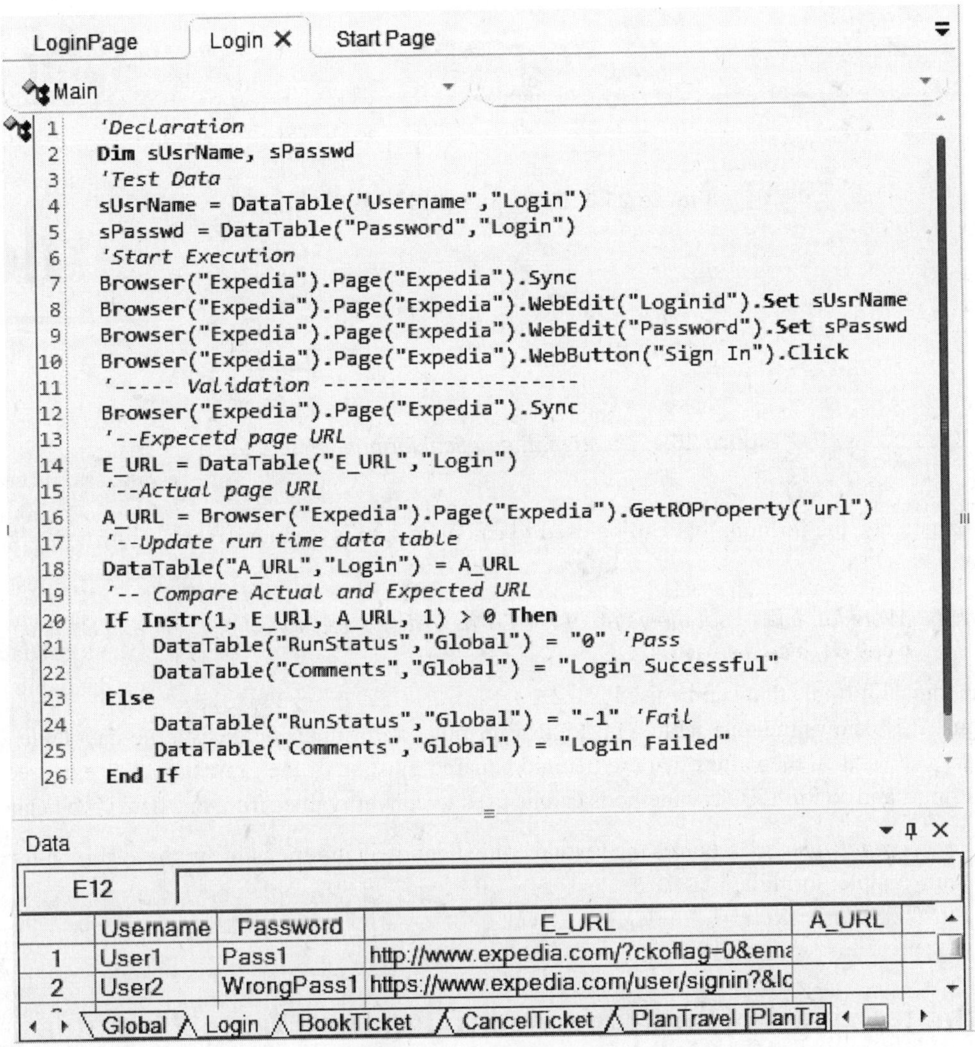

Figure 25.1 *Local datatable*

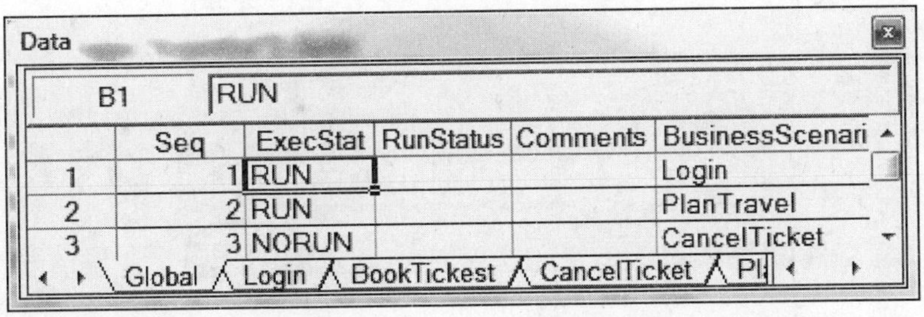

Figure 25.2 *Global datatable*

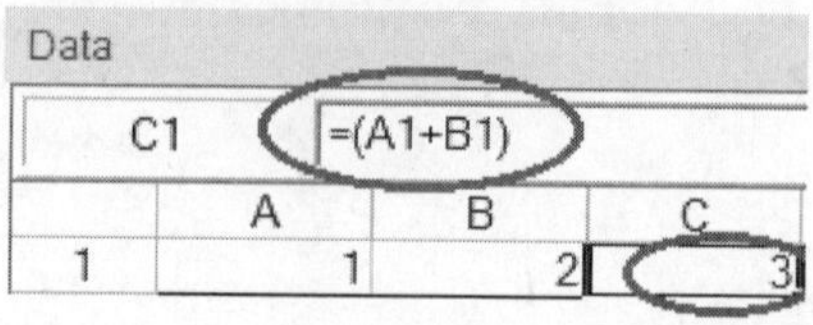

Figure 25.3 *Using formulas in data tables*

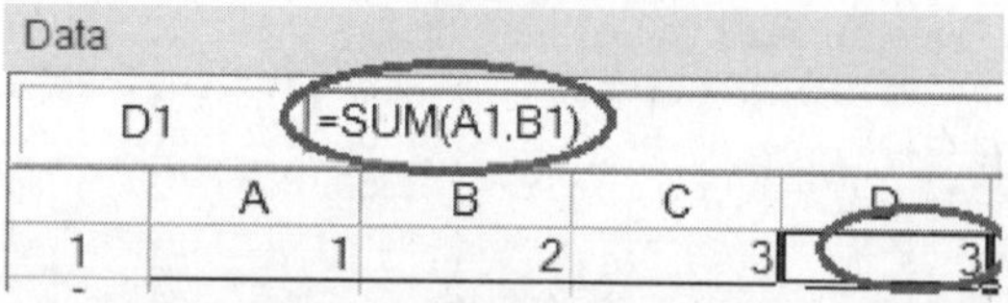

Figure 25.4 *Using mathematical formula in data table*

Alternatively, the formula that can be used to calculate sum is Sum(A1,B1) as shown in Fig. 25.4 below.

Example 2: Write formula to set the value of cell D1 as TRUE if addition of cells A1 and B1 is correctly calculated in cell C1; else display FALSE.

The logical formula that can be used is: `=IF(C1=SUM(A1,B1),TRUE,FALSE)`

Figure 25.5 shows the data table with logical formula. If formulas defined in the data table are to compare values, then the values that are being compared must be of the same type. For example integers, strings, and so forth. Below methods can be used to convert values from one data type to another.

- *TEXT(value, format)*: Returns the textual equivalent of a numeric value in the specified format. For example, formula `=TEXT(9.8,'00.00')` is "09.80".
- *VALUE(string)*: Returns the numeric value of a string. For example, formula `= VALUE("$9.80")` is 9.8.

Parameterizing Object Properties Using Data Table Formulas

As discussed in the chapter 'Object Repository', object properties of an object (in local object repository) can be parameterized using data tables. Now instead of using constant values for parameterization, formulas can be used to specify dynamic values for parameterization.

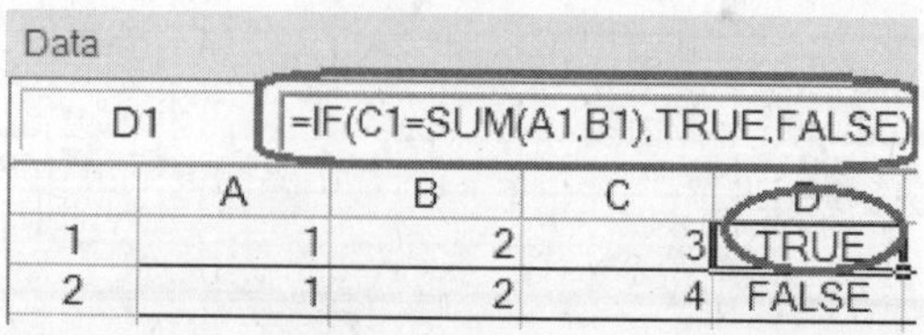

Figure 25.5 *Using logical formula in data table*

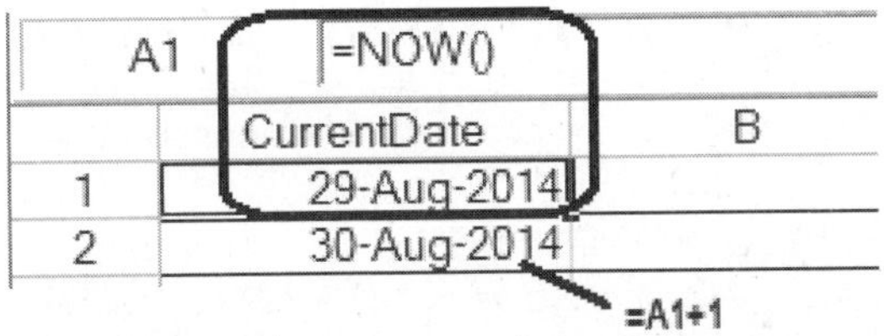

Figure 25.6 *Parameterizing object properties using data table*

For example, consider a scenario where text property value of a calendar object is the current date value. Here we can set the format of a column or cell in data table as date format and use Now() formula in the cell to always dynamically calculate current date. Figure 25.6 shows the data table with this formula.

> **NOTES**
> Data table cells in UFT can have various formats like General, Percent, Date, Scientific, etc. described below are the steps to change data table cells format type.

- Select the cells or columns or rows or range of data table whose format is to be changed.
- Right click and Select option Format. Various data format options will be listed out as shown in the Fig. 25.7.
- Select the appropriate format option to set the specific data type to selected cells.

Parameterizing Test Data Using Data table formulas

The data table cells containing formulas can as well be used to parameterize test data. For example, if current date needs to be set to a text box, then the test code can be parameterized with the formula cell A1 as shown in the Fig. 25.7.

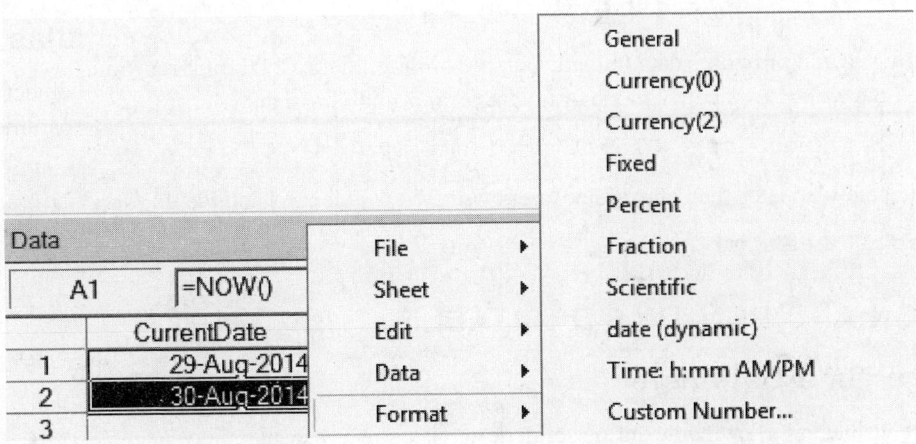

Figure 25.7 *Setting data type of data table cells*

PARAMETERIZE ACTION WITH LOCAL DATATABLE

Parameters defined in local datatable can be accessed in actions using the code mentioned below.

```
Syntax :  DataTable.Value(paramName, dtLocalSheet)
          DataTable.Value(paramName, dataTableName)
          DataTable(paramName, dataTableName)

'Retrieve username from local action Login sUsrNm =
DataTable("UserName", dtLocalSheet)

'Retrieve password from local action Login sPasswd =
DataTable("Password", dtLocalSheet)
```

Alternatively, we can also retrieve parameter values of one action from other action. The code below shows the method to retrieve parameter value "UserName" which is local to action "Login" from action "PlanTravel"

```
sUsrNm = DataTable("UserName", "Login")
```

PARAMETERIZE ACTION WITH GLOBAL DATATABLE

Parameters defined in the global datatable can be accessed in actions using the code mentioned below.

```
Syntax :  DataTable.Value(paramName, dtGlobalSheet)
          DataTable.Value(paramName, dataTableName)
          DataTable(paramName, dataTableName)

'Retrieve SeqNo from Global datatable nSeqNo =
DataTable("SeqNo","Global")
```

ADD/UPDATE DATA TO DATATABLE

UFT allows to add or update data to the Datatable programmatically during run-time.

Code below updates the data value of field *ExecStat* in global datatable.

```
DataTable("ExecStat","Global") = "Complete"
```

The code below updates the data value of field *UserName* in local datatable *Login*

```
DataTable("UserName","Login") = "NewUser"
```

DESIGN AND RUN-TIME DATATABLE

Design Time Datatable

Datatable visible in UFT window during script design is known as design time datatable. (refer Fig 25.2)

Run-time Datatable

During script execution, UFT makes a copy of the design time datatable and makes all changes into this copied datatable. This copied datatable is referred as run-time datatable. The run-time datatable is visible in test results window. To open run-time data table from *Run Results* window, navigate *View → Data*. *Data pane* containing run-time data opens Fig. 25.8 shows run-time datatable of design time datatable shown if Fig. 25.1. We observe that in Fig. 25.8 "*A_URL*" has also been updated.

> **NOTES**
> External spreadsheets can be used as test datatable. External data files can be loaded in test scripts programmatically as discussed in chapter "Working with MS Excel."

DATATABLE METHODS

Following are some of the methods that are supported by the Datatable object.

- ***Import***: Import method is used to import the complete Excel file in test script run-time datatables.

  ```
  Syntax : DataTable.Import(NameofExcelFilewithPath)
  ```

  Example: Import Excel file ".xls" to the current run-time datatable.

  ```
  DataTable.Import     "C:\Temp\.xls"
  ```

> **NOTES**
> Excel sheet name and datatable/action name should match for proper file import.

- ***ImportSheet***: This method is used to import MS Excel sheet into the test run-time datatable.

  ```
  Syntax : DataTable.ImportSheet(NameofExcelFilewithPath, NameoftheSource
  Sheet, NameoftheDestinationSheet)
  ```

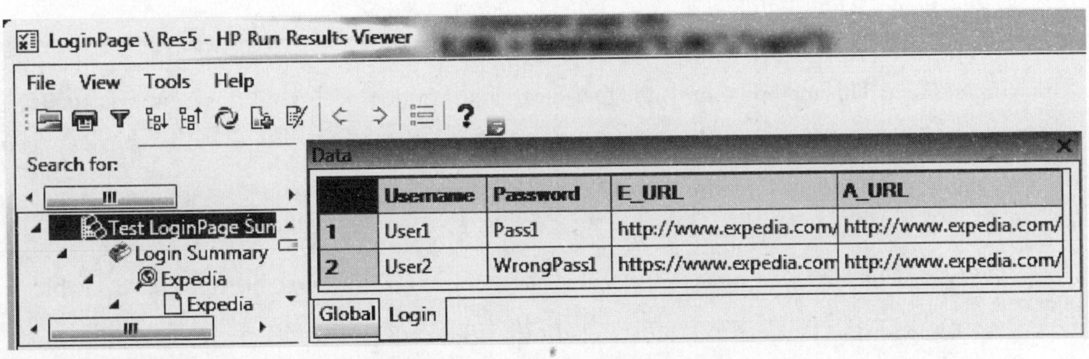

Figure 25.8 *Run-time datatable*

Example: Import "Login" sheet data to "Login" run-time datatable.

```
DataTable.ImportSheet "C:\Temp\.xls", "Login", "Login"
```

- ***Export***: This method saves the global and all the local (action) run-time datatables in an external file at the specified location.

  Syntax : DataTable.Export(*NameofExcelFilewithPath*)

  Example: Save the run-time datatable to the Excel file .xls. (If this file is not present, then it is dynamically created at run-time.)

  ```
  DataTable.Export     "C:\Temp\.xls"
  ```

- ***ExportSheet***: This method saves the specified run-time local or global datatable in an external specified file at specified location.

  Syntax : DataTable.Export(*NameofExcelFilewithPath*, *NameofDataTable*)

  Example: Save the run-time local datatable "Login" to the Excel file .xls. (If this file or sheet is not present, then it is dynamically created at run-time.)

  ```
  DataTable.ExportSheet "C:\Temp\.xls", "Login"
  ```

- ***AddSheet***: This method adds a specified datasheet to the run-time datatable.

  Syntax : DataTable.AddSheet(*SheetName*)

  Example: Add datatable "BankDetails" to the run-time datatable.

  ```
  DataTable.AddSheet "BankDetails"
  ```

- ***DeleteSheet***: This method deletes the specified sheet from the run-time datatable.

  Syntax : DataTable.DeleteSheet *SheetName*

  Example: Delete sheet "BankDetails" from the run-time datatable.

  ```
  DataTable.DeleteSheet "BankDetails"
  ```

- ***LocalSheet***: This method returns the current active local sheet object of the run-time datatable.

  Syntax : DataTable.LocalSheet

  Example: Add a new parameter "LoginTime" to the local sheet

  ```
  DataTable.LocalSheet.AddParameter("LoginTime", "9:00")
  ```

- ***GlobalSheet***: This method returns the first sheet object (global sheet) of the run-time datatable.

  Synatx : DataTable.GlobalSheet

  Example: Add a new parameter "LoginTime" to the global sheet

  ```
  DataTable.GlobalSheet.AddParameter("LoginTime", "9:00")
  ```

- ***GetSheet***: This method returns the specified sheet object (DTSheet) of the run-time datatable.

  Syntax : DataTable.GetSheet (*SheetID*)

> *SheetID* can be either sheet name or sheet index. Sheet index starts from 1.

Example: Add a new parameter "LoginTime" to sheet "Login."

```
DataTable.GetSheet("Login").AddParameter("LoginTime", "9:00" )
Or, DataTable.GetSheet(2).AddParameter("LoginTime", "9:00")
```

- ***GetSheetCount***: This method returns the total number of sheets in the run-time datatable.

  ```
  Syntax : DataTable.GetSheetCount
  ```

  Example: Find the total number of rows of the current accessed sheet.

  ```
  nSheetCount = DataTable.GetSheetCount
  ```

- ***GetRowCount***: This function is used to get the number of rows of data present in a particular sheet.

  ```
  Syntax : Datatable.GetSheet(Sheetname).GetRowCount
  ```

  Example: Find the row count of the datatable "Login".

  ```
  nDTRowCnt = Datatable.Getsheet("Login").GetRowCount
  ```

- ***GetCurrentRow***: This method is used to get the current row of the sheet to which test script currently points to.

  ```
  Syntax : Datatable.GetSheet(Sheetname).GetCurrentRow
  ```

  Example: Find the datatable row to which the action "Login" points to.

  ```
  nDTCurrRow     = Datatable.GetSheet("Login").GetCurrentRow
  ```

> When an action is run by using run setting as "run on all rows," then that action will run as many times as the number of rows in the datasheet (datatable) of the action. We use GetCurrentRow method in order to find the row for which action is currently executing.

- ***SetCurrentRow***: This method sets the row of the datasheet of the action from where data will be read.

  ```
  Syntax : Datatable.GetSheet(Sheetname).SetCurrentRow(RowNum)
  ```

  Example: Set the row from which test data to be picked be 2.

  ```
  Datatable.GetSheet("Login").SetCurrentRow(2) nDTCurrRow =
  DataTable("UserName", "Login") 'Output: User2
  ```

> When an action is run by using run setting as "run one iteration only," that action will execute once for the first row of data specified in the datasheet (datatable) of the action. We use SetCurrentRow method to define the row of the datasheet for which the action should be currently executing.

- ***SetNextRow***: This method sets the current active row to be the next row of the run-time datatable.

```
Syntax : DataTable.SetNextRow
```

Example: Set the current active row to be the next row of the run-time datatable.

```
DataTable.SetNextRow
```

- ***SetPrevRow***: This method sets the current active row to be the previous row of the run-time datatable.

```
Syntax : DataTable.SetPrevRow
```

Example: Set the current active row to be the previous row of the run-time datatable.

```
DataTable.SetPrevRow
```

- ***Value***: This method sets or retrieves the value of the specified cell of the datatable.

```
Syntax : DataTable.Value (ParameterId [,SheetID])
Or,      DataTable      (ParameterId [,SheetID])
           Where,
             ParameterId is the column name or column index. Index
             starts with 1.
             SheetID is the sheet name or sheet index. Index starts
             with 1. This parameter is optional.
```

Example 1: Retrieve the current row value of the "UserName" column of the action "Login."

```
sValue = DataTable("UserName", "Login") Or, sValue = DataTable(1,2)
```

Example 1: Set the row=2 value of the "UserName" column of the action "Login."

```
'Set current row Datatable.GetSheet("Login").SetCurrentRow(2)
'Set value using column and datatable name DataTable("UserName",
"Login") = sValue
'Set value using column and datatable index DataTable(1,2) = sValue
```

- ***ValueByRow***: This method retrieves the value of the specified row for the specified parameter.

```
Syntax : DataTable.GetSheet(Sheetname).GetParameter(ParameterName)
.ValueByRow(RowNum)
```

Example: Retrieves the second row value of the parameter "UserName"

```
DataTable.GetSheet("Login").GetParameter("UserName"). ValueBy-
Row(2)   'Output : User2
```

- ***RawValue***: This method retrieves the raw value of the cell. Raw value is the actual string of the cell such as actual text from a formula.

```
Syntax : DataTable.RawValue ParameterId [, SheetID]
  Where,
    ParameterId is the column name or column index. Index starts with 1.
    SheetID is the sheet name or sheet index. Index starts with
    1. This parameter is optional.
```

Example: Find the cell formula used in the current row of the "Time" column of the action "FillDetails."

```
DataTable.RawValue ("Time", "FillDetails")
```

HOW TO READ ALL DATA OF GLOBAL DATASHEET

The example below shows how to read the complete global datatable value inside an action.

```
'Number of parameters present in global datatable nColCnt = DataTable.
GlobalSheet.GetParameterCount
'Number of rows of data present in the global datatable nRowCnt = DataT-
able.GlobalSheet.GetRowCount
For iCnt = 1 To nRowCnt
   DataTable.SetCurrentRow(iCnt)
   For jCnt = 1 To nColCnt
      'Retrieve data of global sheet
      sCellText =DataTable(jCnt, dtGlobalsheet)
      If sCellText <> "" Then
      Print "Text in Row:" & iCnt & " & Column:" & jCnt & "="
      & sCellText
      End If
   Next
Next
```

LOCAL DATATABLE SETTINGS

Local datatable settings decide how the datatable will be accessed and how the action execution will happen during run-time (Figure 25.9).

- *Run one iteration only* implies the action will execute only one iteration with the data defined in the first row of the datatable.
- *Run on all items* implies the action execution will iterate as many times the number of rows of data in the datatable. For first iteration, data from datatable with row=1 will be used. For the second iteration, data from datatable with row=2 will be used and so on.
- *Run from _ to row _* implies the action execution will iterate as for each row of data defined.

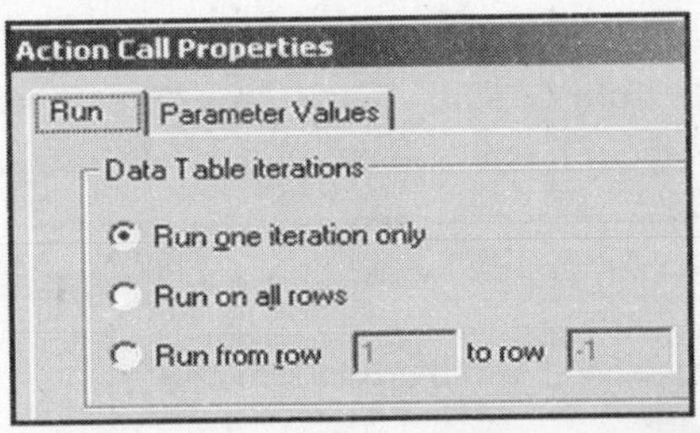

Figure 25.9 *Local datatable settings*

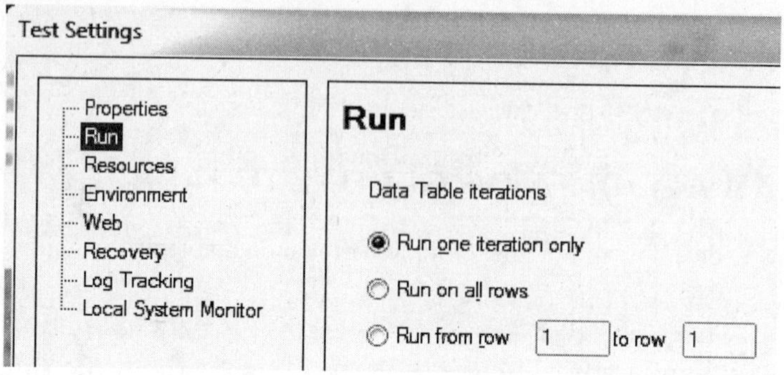

Figure 25.10 *Global datatable settings*

The following are the steps to configure local datatable settings:

1. Open Canvas..
2. Select *Login* action.
3. Right click on the action and Select option *Action Call Properties...*
4. On *Action Call Properties...* window as shown in the Fig. 25.4, select the appropriate data table iteration option.
   - *Run one iteration only*: Execute the action once. By default, UFT executes the action script with the first row data present in the local action datatable.
   - *Run on all rows*: Action is executed once for each row of data present in the local action datatable.
   - *Run from row to row* : Action is executed once for each row selected.
5. Click button OK to save the run-iteration settings.

GLOBAL DATATABLE SETTINGS

Global datatable settings decide how the datatable will be accessed and how the test execution will happen during run-time. Global data table settings window can be accessed from *Test Settings* window *Run* tab. Figure 25.10 below shows the global data table iteration configuration options.

Described below are various iteration configuration options available for a test in UFT.

- *Run one iteration only* implies the test will execute only one iteration with the data defined in the first row of the datatable.
- *Run on all items* implies the test execution will iterate as many times the number of rows of data in the datatable. For the first iteration, the data from datatable with row=1 will be used. For the second iteration, the data from datatable with row=2 will be used and so on.
- *Run from _ to row _* implies the test execution will iterate as for each row of data defined.

NOTES

All the actions inside the test will be executed the same number of iterations as specified in the global datatable settings. For example, if option Run on all items is chosen, then all the actions inside the test will execute as many times the number of rows of data defined in the global datatable (Figure 25.10).

Following are the steps to configure global datatable settings:

1. Navigate *File → Settings...*
2. Click on tab *Run*.
3. Select the appropriate datatable iteration option.
   Run one iteration only: Execute the test script once. By default, UFT executes the action script with the first row data present in the global datatable.
   Run on all rows: Test script is executed once for each row of data present in the global data- table.
   Run from row _ to row _: Test script is executed once for each row selected.
4. Click button OK to save the settings

QUICK TIPS

- ✓ Datatables are used as test data files.
- ✓ Both action and checkpoints can be parameterized with the datatable data.
- ✓ Excel sheets are easier to maintain than datatables.
- ✓ It is easier to define test data and restrict only valid value input in Excel sheets.
- ✓ Excel sheet data can be imported in datatables.
- ✓ If the datatable size is large, it occupies lot of RAM. Therefore, it is advisable to use Excel sheets and access it as database.
- ✓ Accessing Excel sheet as worksheet loads the complete Excel file in RAM during run-time.
- ✓ This consumes RAM and can adversely impact script execution especially only test suite size is large. This happens because of memory leak issues. Therefore, it is advisable to use Excel sheets as database. This loads only the required data in RAM.
- ✓ Accessing Excel sheets as database rather than as worksheets has specific advantages which are discussed in the chapter "Working with MS Excel."

PRACTICAL QUESTIONS

1. What is a datatable?
2. What is the difference between action and global datatables?
3. Write the code to access local and global datatable value in an action.
4. What is the use of datatable in test automation?
5. Explain how datatable can be exported as Excel file.
6. Can Excel data be imported in the datatables? If yes, how?
7. Write the VBScript code for importing Excel data to test global datatable.

Chapter **26**

Working with Web Application Objects

A web application consists of many objects such as text box, buttons, and links. UFT maps these objects to its standard class. If for any GUI object no standard class is found in UFT, then it is mapped to the 'WebElement' class. Fig. 26.1 shows some of the objects of web application and their standard mapping class in UFT.

Web Application Object	UFT Icon	Standard UFT Mapping Class
Browser		Browser
Page		Page
Frame		Frame
Edit box		WebEdit
Image		Image
Link		Link
Button		WebButton
Checkbox		WebCheckBox
List box		WebList
Radio button		WebRadioGroup
Table		WebTable
Element		WebElement

Figure 26.1 *Web application objects*

WORKING WITH BROWSER

UFT support wide range of browsers. UFT 12.01 supports Microsoft Internet Explorer version 8, 9 , 10 and 11 ; Mozilla Firefox till version 31, Chrome till version 36 and Safari version 6 and 7. Note: Refer HP site for latest supported browser versions.

Methods

Following are a few of the methods associated with the 'Browser' object.

- ***Sync***—Waits for the browser to complete the current navigation.

  Example: `Browser("EXPEDIA").Navigate "www.google.com"`

  `Browser("Google").Sync`

- ***Back***—Simulates the 'Back' button click.

  Example: `Browser("EXPEDIA").Back`

- ***Forward***—Simulates 'Forward' button click.

  Example: `Browser("EXPEDIA").Forward`

- ***Home***—Simulates 'Home' button click.

  Example: `Browser("EXPEDIA").Home`

- ***Refresh***—Reloads specified browser. Simulates 'refresh' button click.

  Example: `Browser("EXPEDIA").Refresh`

- ***FullScreen***—Displays the browser in full-screen mode.

  Example: `Browser("EXPEDIA").FullScreen`

- ***CaptureBitmap***—Takes screenshot of the specified browser or object as .png or .bmp file

  Syntax: *Object*.CaptureBitmap(*fullFileName, optional]OverideExisting*)

  Example:

  ```
  Browser("EXPEDIA").CaptureBitMap "C:\Temp\Err.bmp", True
  Browser("EXPEDIA").CaptureBitMap "C:\Temp\Err.png", False
  ```

  Captured screenshot can be saved as either .png or .bmp file. If 'OverrideExisting' flag is set as *True*, then it will overwrite the existing file.

- ***RefreshObject***—Instructs UFT to reidentify the specified object.

  Example: `Browser("EXPEDIA").RefreshObject`

> **NOTES** *RefreshObject* is used when the object referenced by the last step is refreshed or changed in some way in AUT; however, it still matches the test object description. In these scenarios, UFT fails to recognize the changed object unless changed object is identified again using *RefreshObject* method.

- ***OpenNewTab***—Opens a new tab in the browser.

  Example: Browser("EXPEDIA").OpenNewTab

- ***IsSiblingTab***—Indicates whether the specified tab is a sibling tab of the same browser window.

  Example: `Browser("Expedia").Sync`

  ```
  'Open new tab
  Browser("EXPEDIA").OpenNewTab
  'Get name of browser
  Print Browser("CreationTime:=0").GetROProperty("name")
       'Output:Expedia
  ```

```
'Navigate to Google page on newly opened tab
Browser(“CreationTime:=1”).Navigate www.Google.com
'Get name of application opened in the newly opened tab
newTabAppName =  Browser(“CreationTime:=1”).GetROProperty(“name”)
Print newTabAppName        'Output:Google
Print Browser(“name:=” & newTabAppName).IsSiblingTab(Browser(“EXPE
DIA”))
'Output:True
```

- ***Close***—Closes the current browser tab if more than one browser tabs are open. Else closes the browser.
  Example: `Browser(“EXPEDIA”).Close`
- ***CloseAllTabs***—closes all tabs in a browser and closes the browser window.
  Example:

```
Browser(“EXPEDIA”).OpenNewTab
Browser(“CreationTime:=1”).Navigate www.Google.com
Browser(“CreationTime:=1”).CloseAllTabs
' Or
' Browser(“EXPEDIA”).CloseAllTabs
```

- ***ClearCache***–Clears the browser cache.
  Example: `Browser(“EXPEDIA”).ClearCache`

> **NOTES** Above method does not delete browser cookies.

- ***DeleteCookies***–Deletes browser cookies..
  Syntax: *Object*.DeleteCookies ([*Optional*]*FromSource*)
  Example 1: Delete all browser cookies
  `Browser(“EXPEDIA”).DeleteCookies`
  Example 2: Delete all cookies stored for site expedia.com
  `Browser(“EXPEDIA”).DeleteCookies(“expedia.com”)`
  Example 3: Delete all browser cookies for domain expedia
  `Browser(“EXPEDIA”).DeleteCookies(“expedia”)`
- ***ToString***—Returns the logical name of the test object.
  Example:

```
Print Browser(“EXPEDIA”).ToString
'Output:EXPEDIA browser
```

- ***DialogExists***—Checks whether a browser dialog box (such as an alert, confirmation, or prompt) exists. Returns Boolean value.
  Example: Verify if dialog box exists for browser object Expedia.
  `Print Browser(“EXPEDIA”).DialogExists`
- ***GetDialogText***—Retrieves the text displayed in a browser dialog box such as alert, confirmation, or prompt.

Example:

```
Print Browser("EXPEDIA").GetDialogText
```

- ***HandleDialog***—Clicks on a button on the browser dialog box after entering a value if necessary.

```
Syntax: Object.HandleDialog ([button],[value])
 Where,
   Parameter button is optional. Accepts micDialogButton value for
   clicking on specific button of dialog box. Default value is 0
   (zero).
   Parameter variant is optional. Accepts a variant value for enter-
   ing text on dialog box.
```

Example: Check whether a dialog box exists and close it.

```
 If Browser("EXPEDIA").DialogExists Then
   Print Browser("EXPEDIA").GetDialogText
   Browser("EXPEDIA").HandleDialog
 End If
```

- ***EmbedScript***—Runs the specified JavaScript each time a page or frame loads or refreshes in the browser.

```
Syntax: Object.EmbedScript Script
```

- ***EmbedScriptFromFile***—Runs the JavaScript stored in the specified file each time a page or frame loads or refreshes in the browser.

```
Syntax: Object.EmbedScriptFromFile ScriptFileLocation
```

NOTES

The script or script file remains embedded until user closes the browser, or until the run session ends.

NOTES

To be able to embed scripts to browser the security settings in the Web browser must be set to allow active scripting. In IE 9, this setting is under: Tools → Internet Options → Security → Custom Level → Scripting → Active scripting.

- ***GetROProperty***—This method is used to retrieve run-time object properties.

```
'Find type of browser
sVar = Browser("EXPEDIA").GetROProperty("application version")
                                'Output : internet explorer 6

'Find version of browser
sVar = Browser("EXPEDIA").GetROProperty("version")
                                'Output : internet explorer 6
```

- ***ChildObjects***—Returns the collection of child objects contained within the object.

```
Syntax: Object.ChildObjects ([Description])
```

Example: Find all the browser child objects of desktop.

Suppose two Browser instances are open. First browser has three tabs open while second browser has two tabs open. Find the URL of the applications open in all the browser. Assume applications open in the browsers are:

Browser 1: Amazon, Walmart, Flipkart
Browser 2: Expedia, MakeMyTrip

Code below shows how to find all the open browser and browser tabs:

```
Set oBrwDesc = Description.Create
oBrwDesc("micclass").value = "Browser"
Set colBrowsers = Desktop.ChildObjects(oBrwDesc)
For i = 0 To colBrowsers.count-1 Step 1
    Print colBrowsers(i).getroproperty("url")
  Next
  'Output:
  http://www.amazon.com
  http://www.walmart.com
  http://www.flipkart.com
  http://www.expedia.com
  http://www.makemytrip.com
```

- ***ReadyState***—Returns the loading status of the browser.

```
Browser(browserNm).Object.ReadyState
```

- ***Busy***—Returns whether the browser is still busy loading.

```
Browser(browserNm).Object.Busy
```

- ***Resizable***—This method can be used to make browser resizable or non-resizable.

```
'Make browser non-resizable
Browser(browserNm).Object.Resizable = "FALSE"
```

- ***LocationURL***—Retrieves the full URL path of the specified opened browser.

```
Browser("EXPEDIA").Object.LocationURL
```

Example: `Desktop.CaptureBitmap "c:\temp\Err.bmp"`

- RefreshObject is used when the object referenced by the last step is refreshed or changed in some way in AUT; however, it still matches the test object description. In these scenarios, QTP fails to recognize the changed object unless changed object is identified again using *RefreshObject* method.

> **NOTES** Screenshots of application screen can be taken in case of the occurrence of an exception during script execution. *Desktop. CaptureBitmap* could be used to capture desktop screenshot. Example: Desktop.Capture-Bitmap "C:\Temp\Err.bmp"

LAUNCH INTERNET EXPLORER AND WEB APPLICATION

There are various ways to launch internet explorer and open a browser-based application.

Method 1

```
'Launch specified browser
SystemUtil.Run "iexplore.exe"
```

```
'Open website Expedia.co.in
Browser("EXPEDIA").Navigate "www.Expedia.co.in"
```

Method 2

```
'Launch default browser and open website Expedia.co.in
SystemUtil.Run "www.Expedia.co.in"
```

Browser Identification

Multiple Browsers of Same Application

In case multiple browsers (or tabs) of same application with identical properties are opened on desktop, then *creationtime* or index ordinal identifiers can be used to identify and differentiate one browser from the other. For example, if Google.com page is opened in three different browsers or browser tabs, then 'creation time' or 'index' ordinal identifier can be used to identify and differentiate one browser or browser tab from the other during run- time.

Creation time—The browser that is opened first is assigned creationtime value 0, next opened browser is assigned value 1, and so on.

Index—The browser that is opened first is assigned index value 0, next opened browser is assigned value 1, and so on.

Multiple Pop-up Browser Window of Same Application

In case multiple pop-up browser windows of the same application is opened on desktop, then *OpenURL* or *OpenTitle* property of browser can be used to differentiate one pop-up browser from the another. It can also be used to differentiate the pop-up window from the parent window as well. OpenUrl property of browser specifies browser's initial URL when the browser is first launched. In case the current web page is opened by navigating through some previous page, then *openurl* property specifies URL of previous page. Similarly, OpenTitle property of browser specifies browser's initial title when the browser is first launched or the title of the previous browser in case current page is opened by navigating through some previous page.

Example: Write code to set the settings of the browser such as browser size.

```
'Launch new browser
SystemUtil.Run "www.google.com"

Browser("micclass:=Browser").Page("micclass:=Page").Sync

'Resize browser
Browser("micclass:=Browser").Object.Left = 450
Browser("micclass:=Browser").Object.Top = 0
Browser("micclass:=Browser").Object.Height = 450
Browser("micclass:=Browser").Object.Width = 550

'Make browser non resizable
Browser("micclass:=Browser").Object.Resizable = False

'Activate browser
```

```
nHWnd = Browser("micclass:=Browser").GetROProperty("hwnd")
Window("hwnd:=" & nHWnd).Activate
'Disable all internet explorer popup dialog box
Browser("micclass:=Browser").Object.Silent = True
```

> **NOTES** The object model of Internet Explorer can be used to configure the IE settings such as activating/deactivating Java script option and enabling pop-ups. UFT supports configuring IE settings through VBScript code before launching IE browser.

WORKING WITH PAGE

```
'create a wrapper object of Page
Set oPage = Browser("EXPEDIA_BookTckt").Page("EXPEDIA_BookTckt")
```

Methods

Explained below are some of the methods associated with the 'Page' object.

- ***RunScript***—Runs the specified JavaScript.
  Example 1: Write code using Javascript to retrieve the FirstName edit box object of create account page of the application shown in the Fig. 26.2.

  Assume HTML code of the *firstname* edit box object is:

```
<input id="create-account-firstname" type="text" name="create-account-firstname" value="" placeholder="">
```

  Assume *FirstName* edit box native object information as viewed in Object Spy is as shown in the Fig. 26.3:

  Code below shows how to retrieve and modify native properties of *FirstName* editbox through native operations.

```
Set oFirstName = Browser("B").Page("P").RunScript(
      "document.getElementsByName(
                        'create-account-firstname')(0);")
```

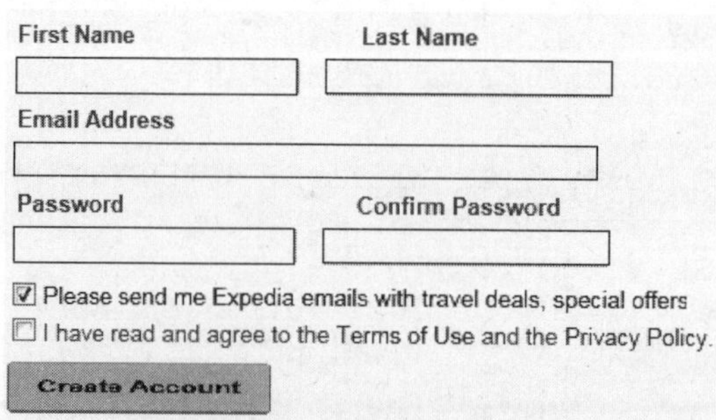

Figure 26.2. *Create accopunt page of a sample web application*

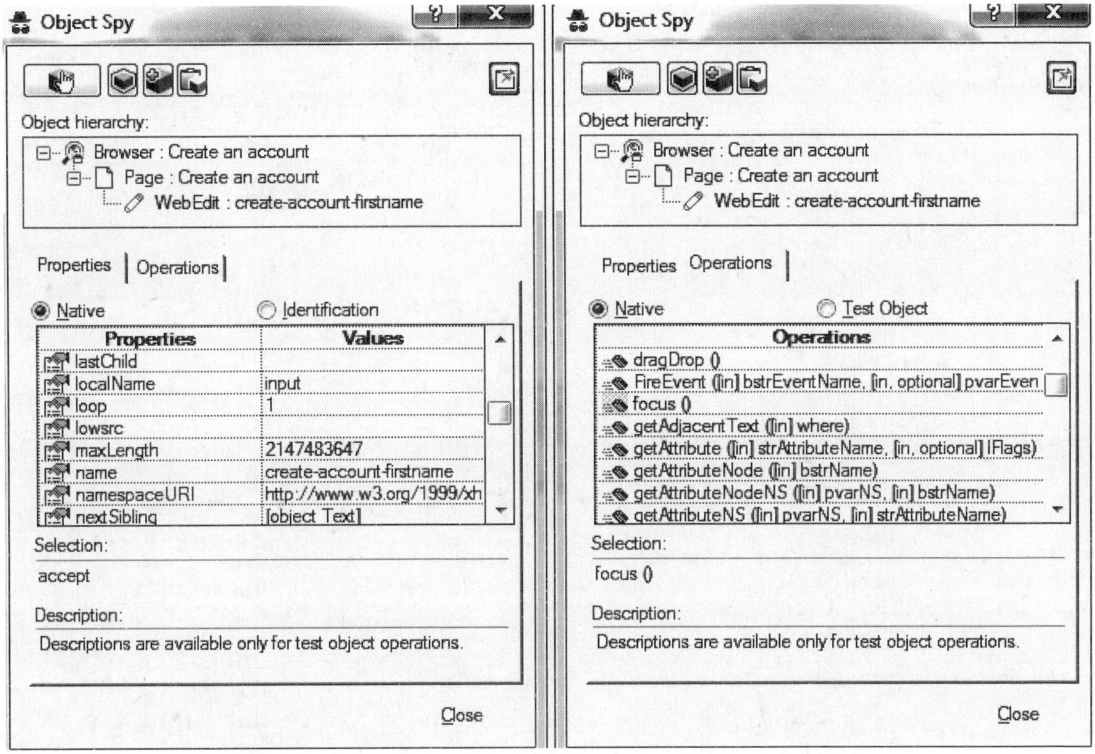

Figure 26.3. *FirstName edit box native properties and operations*

```
'Retrieve id property value
Print oFirstName.id
'Set focus on the edit box using native focus operation
oFirstName.focus
'Enter email address to edit box
oFirstName.value = "EmailAddress@gmail.com"
```

Example 2: Write code using JavaScript to find all the check boxes which are checked in Fig. 26.2.

```
'Get all checkbox objects which are checked
Set colCheckedCheckboxes = Browser("B").Page("P").
                                RunScript("jQuery.find(':checked');")
'Get total count of checked checkboxes
Print colCheckedCheckboxes.length       'Output:1
```

Figure 26.4 shows the UFT debug window view for the check boxes array object returned by JavaScript code.

If the JavaScript returns a JavaScript array as is the case in example 2 above, then standard VBScript syntax cannot be used to access the array index (for example, arr(0)) nor JavaScript syntax can be used (for example arr[0]). However, JavaScript operations such as pop, push,

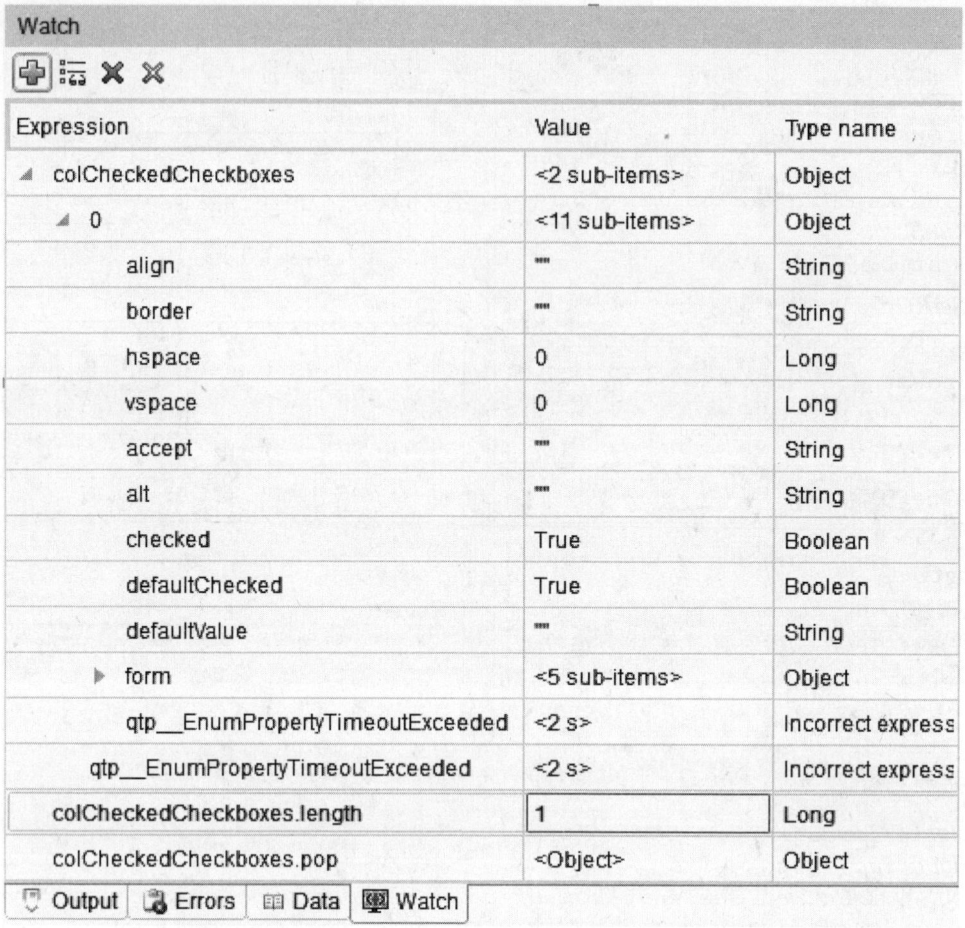

Figure 26.4. *Checkboxes array object as viewed in UFT Watch pane*

shift or length can be used to access JavaScript array items. But such operations may modify the content of the array. Hereе, one option is to clone the array and then use these operations on the cloned array. Alternatively, a JavaScript functioban also be executed that converts the returned array to a safearray. Thereafter, standard VBScript syntax can be used to iterate through the array.

Example 3: Write code that clones the JavaScript array returned in the example 2 above.

JavaScript code for cloning JavaScript array is:

```
function cloneArray(arr) {
        var clonedArr = [];
        for (var i = 0; i < arr.length; ++i)
            clonedArr.push(arr[i]);
        return clonedArr;
    }
```

Assume cloneArray.js is saved at location "c:\temp\coleArray.js".

Now, VBScript code to clone the array is:

```
Browser("B").EmbedScriptFromFile "C:\Temp\cloneArray.js"
Browser("B").Refresh
Set clonedCheckedCheckboxes = Browser("B").Page("P").
RunScript("cloneArray(jQuery.find(':checked'));")
```

- ***RunScriptFromFile***—Runs the JavaScript stored in the specified file.

  Syntax: *Object*.RunScriptFromFile ScriptFileLocation
- ***GetROProperty***—This method is used to retrieve the object run-time properties.

```
'Find URL
Browser("EXPEDIA_BookTckt").Page("EXPEDIA_BookTckt").
                                  GetROProperty("url")

Alternatively, oPage.GetROProperty("url")

Alternatively,Browser("EXPEDIA_BookTckt").Page("EXPEDIA_BookTckt").
Object.url
```

- ***bgColor***—Dynamically find or change back ground color of page.

```
'Find background color of page
Print Browser(browserNm).Page(pageNm).Object.bgcolor
'Change background color of page
Browser(browserNm).Page(pageNm).Object.bgcolor = "RED"

Alternatively,
Browser(browserNm).Page(pageNm).Object.bgcolor = "00ff00"
```

Example: Capture the wintoolbar text from a web page when mouse is hovered on any object in GUI (Figure 26.5).

```
'Set focus on link object
Browser("EXPEDIA").Page("EXPEDIA").Link("SignUp").Object.focus

'Retrieve status bar text
```

Figure 26.5 *Capture wintoolbar text when mouse id hovered on a link object*

```
Print Browser("EXPEDIA").WinStatusBar("msctls_statusbar32").
  GetROProperty("text")
                                        'Output : Shortcut to register.do?click=
                                                  true

'Retrieve status bar content
Print Browser("EXPEDIA").WinStatusBar("msctls_statusbar32").GetContent
                                       'Output : Shortcut to home.do at www.rail-
                                                  tourismindia.com
                                                 Internet
```

WORKING WITH WEBEDIT

All text/edit fields present in a page of browser are referred to as 'WebEdit' objects in UFT.

```
'create a wrapper object of webedit
Set oEdit = Browser("EXPEDIA").Page("EXPEDIA").WebEdit("Passwd")
```

Methods

- ***Set***—Set method is used to input values on edit fields.

  Example:

  ```
  Browser("EXPEDIA").Page("EXPEDIA").WebEdit("Passwd").Set "Pass1"
  Alternatively,
  oEdit.Set "Pass1"
  ```

- ***SetSecure***—This method is used to input an encrypted string to a text field. Generally, this method is used to input encrypted passwords to password text fields. SetSecure method decrypts the string first and then writes the decrypted string to the text field.

  Example:

  ```
  Browser("EXPEDIA").Page("EXPEDIA").WebEdit("Passwd").SetSecure
                                  "4ba9b4ee0510d18cace7e5b9b9e99826"
  Alternatively,
  oEdit.SetSecure "4ba9b4ee0510d18cace7e5b9b9e99826"
  ```

- ***GetROProperty***—This method is used to retrieve the object run-time properties.

  Syntax : *Object*.GetROProperty(*propertyName*)

  Example:

  ```
  'Retrieve latest updated value of WebEdit at run-time
  Msgbox Browser("EXPEDIA").Page("EXPEDIA").WebEdit("Passwd").
                                                GetROProperty("value")

  'Retrieve default updated value of text field at run-time
  Msgbox Browser("EXPEDIA").Page("EXPEDIA").WebEdit("Passwd").
                                        GetROProperty("default value")
  ```

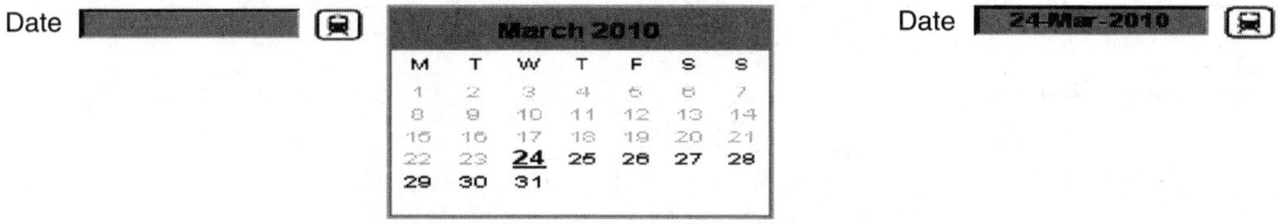

Figure 26.6 *Write text on read only field*

```
'Find whether text field is read only or not at run-time
Msgbox Browser(browserName).Page(pageName).WebEdit("Calendar").
                                          GetROProperty("readonly")
                                          'Output : 0 for editable
                                          'Output : 1 for read only
'Write text on read only edit fields at run-time
```

Figure 26.6 shows an example scenario where text field is disabled; however, its value is automatically written when we select the date in the calendar object. Sometimes, calendar object is not properly recognized by UFT and there is a requirement to set the date field. In these scenarios, we can directly write on disabled field as follows.

```
Browser(browserName).Page(pageName).WebEdit("Calendar").
                                       Object.value = "24-Mar-2010"
```

- ***Focus***—Sets focus on the specified object.

```
Browser("EXPEDIA").Page("EXPEDIA").WebEdit("Passwd").Object.focus
Browser("EXPEDIA").Page("EXPEDIA").WebEdit("UsrNm").SetSecure
                             "4ba9b4ee0510d18cace7e5b9b9e99826"
```

We will observe that value 'Pass1' is written on the username text field.

> NOTES: We can find (decrypt) the QTP encrypted string value by writing the encrypted string using *SetSecure* method in non-password text field.

WORKING WITH WEB BUTTON

All buttons present in a page of browser are referred to as 'WebButton' objects in UFT (Figure 26.7).

```
'create a wrapper object of webbutton
Set oButton = Browser("B").Page("P").WebButton("Login")
```

Methods

- ***Click***—Click method simulates mouse click on a button object.

Example: `Browser("EXPEDIA").Page("EXPEDIA").WebButton("Login").Click`

```
Alternatively, oButton.Click
```

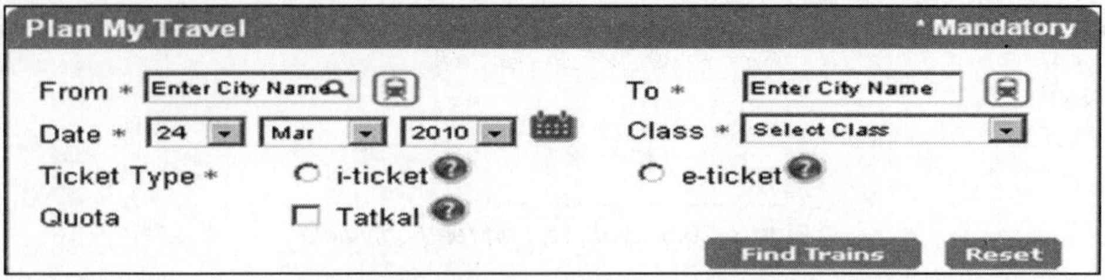

Figure 26.7 *Plan travel screen*

- ***GetROProperty***—This method is used to retrieve run-time properties of an object.

```
'Find whether WebButton is enabled or disabled at run-time
Msgbox Browser("EXPEDIA").Page("EXPEDIA").WebButton("Login").
                                        GetROProperty("disabled")
                                        'Output : 0 for enabled
                                        'Output : 1 for disabled
```

- ***Focus***—Sets focus on the specified object.

```
Browser("EXPEDIA").Page("EXPEDIA").WebEdit("UsrNm").Object.focus
Browser("EXPEDIA").Page("EXPEDIA").WebButton("Login").Object.focus
```

WORKING WITH WEBCHECKBOX

All checkboxes present in web application are referred to as WebCheckBox in UFT.

```
'create a wrapper object of webcheckbox
Set oChkBox = Browser("PlanTrvl").Page("PlanTrvl").WebCheckBox("Tatkal")
```

Methods

- ***Click***—Selects the checkbox, if not selected or deselects the checkbox, if already selected.

```
Browser("PlanTrvl").Page("PlanTrvl").WebCheckBox("Tatkal").Click
Alternatively,
oChkBox.Click
```

- ***Set***—Selects or deselects the checkbox, as specified.

```
Syntax : Object.WebCheckBox(checkbox).Set "ON"
         Object.WebCheckBox(checkbox).Set "OFF"
'Select Checkbox
Browser("PlanTrvl").Page("PlanTrvl").WebCheckBox("Tatkal").Set "ON"
'Deselect Checkbox
Browser("PlanTrvl").Page("PlanTrvl").WebCheckBox("Tatkal").Set "OFF"
```

- ***GetROProperty***—Retrieves run-time properties of an object.

```
'Find whether WebCheckBox is enabled or disabled
Msgbox Browser("PlanTrvl").Page("PlanTrvl").WebCheckBox("Tatkal").
                                        GetROProperty("disabled")
                                        'Output : 0 for enabled
                                        'Output : 1 for disabled
'Find run-time value of WebCheckBox
Msgbox Browser("PlanTrvl").Page("PlanTrvl").WebCheckBox("Tatkal").
                                            GetROProperty("value")
```

WORKING WITH WEBLIST

All list type objects of web application are called 'WebList' in UFT.

```
'create a wrapper object of weblist
Set  oList  =  Browser("PlanTrvl").Page("PlanTrvl").
WebList("ResvClass")
```

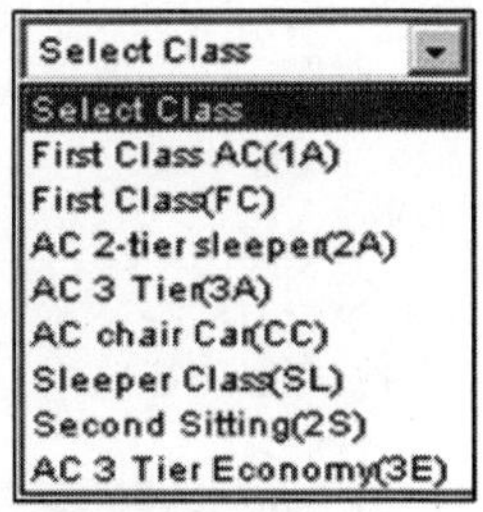

Figure 26.8 *WebList*

Methods

- ***Select***—Selects the specified item from the list.

```
Syntax : Object.Select itemName
         Object.Select itemIndex
```

WebList can be selected by its item name or item index. For Fig. 26.8, item name will be Select Class, First Class AC(1A), etc. Item indexes of the same will be 0, 1, 2, and so on.

```
Browser("PlanTrvl").Page("PlanTrvl").WebList("ResvClass").Select
                                               "First Class AC(1A)"
Alternatively,
oList.Select "First Class AC(1A)"
Alternatively,
Browser("PlanTrvl").Page("PlanTrvl").WebList("ResvClass").Select "#1"
Alternatively,
Browser("PlanTrvl").Page("PlanTrvl").WebList("ResvClass").      Se-
lect(1)
```

- ***ExtendSelect***—Selects multiple items from a list.

```
'Select Item1
Browser(browserNm).Page(pageNm).WebList(listNm).Select "Item1"
'Select Item1, Item2
Browser(browserNm).Page(pageNm).WebList(listNm).ExtendSelect
"Item2"
'Select Item1, Item2, Item3
```

```
Browser(browserNm).Page(pageNm).WebList(listNm).ExtendSelect
"Item3"
```

- ***Deselect***—Deselects an item from the list.

```
'Deselect Item2
Browser(browserNm).Page(pageNm).WebList(listNm).Deselect "Item2"
```

- ***GetItem***—Retrieves the value of the item specified by index.

```
'Retrieve item value corresponding to index 2
Browser("PlanTrvl").Page("PlanTrvl").WebList("ResvClass").Get-
Item(2)              'Output : First Class AC(1A)
```

- ***GetROProperty***—Retrieves run-time properties of an object.

```
'Retrieve all item values from a list at run-time
Msgbox Browser("PlanTrvl").Page("PlanTrvl").WebList("ResvClass").
                                         GetROProperty("all items")
              'Output :
              Select Class;First Class AC(1A);First Class(FC);AC
              2-tier  sleeper(2A);AC  3  Tier(3A);AC  chair
              Car(CC);Sleeper Class(SL);Second Sitting(2S);AC 3
              Tier Economy(3E)

'Retrieve number of items present in a list at run-time
Msgbox     Browser("PlanTrvl").Page("PlanTrvl").
WebList("ResvClass").

GetROProperty("items count")
                                    'Output : 9
```

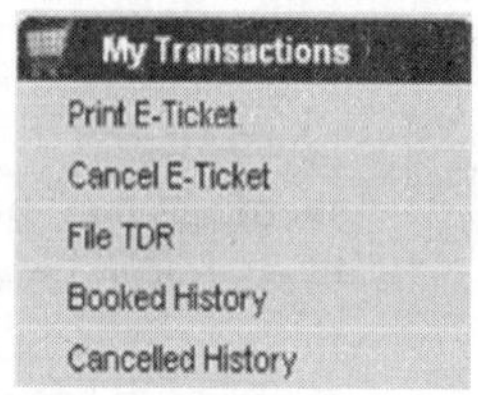

Figure 26.9 *Link*

WORKING WITH LINK

Hyperlinks present in web application are referred to as 'Link' in UFT (Figure 26.9).

```
'create a wrapper object of Link
Set oLink = Browser("PlanTrvl").Page("PlanTrvl").Link("CancelledHistory")
```

Methods

- ***Click***—Click on the specified hyperlink.

```
Browser("PlanTrvl").Page("PlanTrvl").
                Link("CancelledHistory").Click

  Alternatively,
  oLink.Click
```

- ***RightClick***—Right click on the specified object.

```
oLink.RightClick
```

- ***MiddleClick***—Mouse middle button click on the specified object.

```
oLink.MiddleClick
```

- ***GetROProperty***—Retrieves run-time properties of an object.

```
'Find URL to which link object points to
Msgbox Browser("PlanTrvl").Page("PlanTrvl").Link("CancelledHistory").
                                              GetROProperty("href")
Msgbox Browser("PlanTrvl").Page("PlanTrvl").Link("CancelledHistory").
                                               GetROProperty("url")
             'Output : http://www.Expedia.co.in/cgi-
             bin/bv60.dll/Expedia/services/history.do ...
'Find link color
Msgbox Browser("PlanTrvl").Page("PlanTrvl").Link("CancelledHistory").
                                            GetROProperty("color")
                                            'Output : #0000ff
'Find link background color
Msgbox Browser("PlanTrvl").Page("PlanTrvl").Link("CancelledHistory").
                                   GetROProperty("background color")
                                           'Output : #2881bb
```

- ***FireEvent***—This method triggers an event.

  Suppose that there is a web application containing nested menu links as shown in Figure 26.10. Link 'SubItem 1.1' and 'Sub Item 1.2' are visible on the screen when mouse is hovered on link 'Folder 1.' In order to click on link 'Sub Item 1.1,' first it should be made visible on the screen by hovering mouse on the 'Folder 1' link. This can be done by using 'FireEvent' method. FireEvent method simulates an event. The following code shows how to simulate mouse hover event using FireEvent method.

```
Set oPage = Browser("Browser").Page("Page")
'Hover mouse on link 'Folder 1' to make the nested links visible
oPage.Link("Folder1").FireEvent "onmouseover"
'Click on link 'Sub Item 1.2'
oPage.Link("SubItem1.2").Click
```

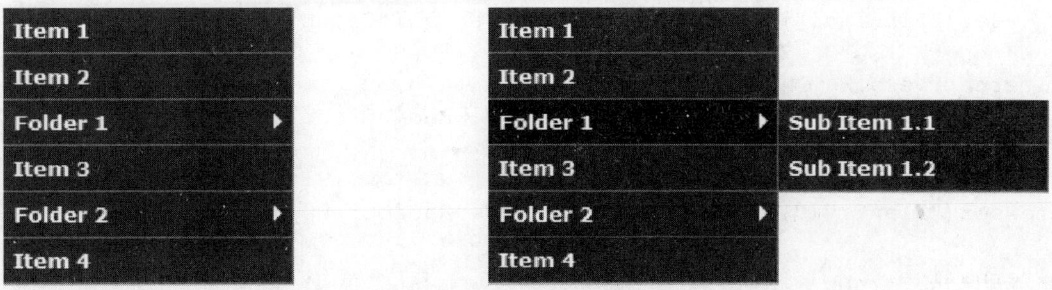

Figure 26.10 *Nested menu links*

WORKING WITH WEB RADIOGROUP

WebRadioGroup refers to the radio buttons present in the web application.

Radio buttons always exist in a group and at a time, only one radio button can be selected in the group. UFT reads the properties of only that radio button that is selected.

```
'create a wrapper object of webtable
Set oRadGrp = Browser("PlanTrvl").Page("PlanTrvl").WebRadioGroup("TcktTyp")
```

Methods

- *Click*—Select the specified radio button. Click method can only be used to when we need to select the first(default) radio button of the group.

```
Browser("PlanTrvl").Page("PlanTrvl").WebRadioGroup("TcktTyp").Click
Alternatively,
oRadGrp.Click
```

> NOTES: Above-mentioned statement always selects 'i-ticket' option if 'Description properties' for each and every radio button is the same as that of the OR window. To select other radio buttons, specify the property of radio button in OR that differentiates it from other radio buttons in the group (one property could be *html id*).

- *Select*—Select the specified radio button.

```
Syntax:  Object.Select itemValue
         Object.Select itemIndex
```

Radio buttons in a radio group can be selected by its item value or item index. Figure 26.7 shows a radio group *TicketType* with two radio buttons—*eticket* and *iticket*. Item values of these radio buttons are *eticket* and *iticket* and item index *0* and item index *1*. The item value of a radio button can be seen in *value* property in object spy window. To find out the *value* property, first select the radio button and then object spy on it.

```
'Select 'iticket' option
Browser("PlanTrvl").Page("PlanTrvl").WebRadioGroup("TcktTyp").
                                                    Select "iticket"
Alternatively,
Browser("PlanTrvl").Page("PlanTrvl").WebRadioGroup("TcktTyp").
                                                    Select "#0"
'Select 'eticket' option
Browser("PlanTrvl").Page("PlanTrvl").WebRadioGroup("TcktTyp").
                                                    Select "eticket"
Alternatively,
Browser("PlanTrvl").Page("PlanTrvl").WebRadioGroup("TcktTyp").Select "#1"
```

> **NOTES** Here, 'Description Properties' of radio button in OR should be defined in a way that it does not uniquely point to a different radio button in the group.

- ***GetROProperty***—Retrieve run-time properties of radio button.

```
'Find total number of radio buttons present in radio group
Msgbox Browser("PlanTrvl").Page("PlanTrvl").WebRadioGroup("TcktTyp").
                                      GetROProperty("items count")
                                      'Output : 2

'Find value of all radio buttons present in radio group
Msgbox Browser("PlanTrvl").Page("PlanTrvl").WebRadioGroup("TcktTyp").
                                      GetROProperty("all items")
                                      'Output : iticket;eticket

'Find which radio button is currently selected
Browser("PlanTrvl").Page("PlanTrvl").WebRadioGroup("TcktTyp").
                                      Select "eticket"
Msgbox Browser("PlanTrvl").Page("PlanTrvl").WebRadioGroup("TcktTyp").
                                    GetROProperty("selected  item
                                    index")
                                         'Output : 2
```

WORKING WITH WEB TABLE

Tables present in web application are referred to as 'WebTable' in UFT. Figure 26.11 shows a WebTable of cancelled railway tickets on IRCTC site.

```
'create a wrapper object of webtable
Set oWebTbl = Browser("IRCTC").Page("IRCTC").WebTable("CncldTckts")
```

S#	Transaction ID	PNR Number	From	To	Total Amount	Refund Amount	Cancelled On	Type of Ticket
1	0156644096	2265959350	NDLS	LKO	242.0	192.0	30-11-2009	eticket
2	0136774911	6131306072	GAYA	NDLS	723.0	314.0	17-9-2009	eticket
3	0130365059	2262414464	NDLS	KQR	997.0	917.0	15-9-2009	eticket
4	0126704277	6229823508	KQR	NDLS	749.0	654.0	21-8-2009	eticket
5	0126453074	2624164458	NDLS	KQR	749.0	327.0	17-9-2009	eticket

Figure 26.11 *WebTable of cancelled tickets*

Methods

- ***RowCount***—Counts the number of rows present in WebTable.

  Syntax: *object*.RowCount

  Example:

```
'find row count of WebTable of Figure 26.11
Print Browser("IRCTC").Page("IRCTC").WebTable('CncldTckts').RowCount
                                                     'Output : 6
Alternatively, we can code
Print oWebTbl.RowCount                               'Output : 6
```

- ***ColumnCount***—Counts the number of columns present in a particular row of WebTable.

  Syntax: *object*.ColumnCount(*RowNumber*)

  Example:

```
'find column count of first row of WebTable of Figure 26.11
Print oWebTbl.CoulumnCount(1)                        'Output : 9
```

- ***GetCellData***—Retrieves data of a particular x,y cell coordinate.

  Syntax: *object*.GetCellData(*Row*, *Column*)

  Example:

```
'find cell data of cell with row=1 and column=2
Print oWebTbl.GetCellData(1,2)              'Output : Transaction ID
```

- ***GetRowWithCellText***—Finds first row whose cell data matches to the specified data.

  Syntax:*object*.GetRowWithCellText (*Text*, [optional]*Column*,
  [optional]*StartFromRow*)

  Example:

```
'find row number containing data 'NDLS'
Print oWebTbl.GetRowWithCellText("NDLS") 'Output : 2
```

- ***ChildItem***—Retrieves specified object present in a particular cell of WebTable.

  Syntax: *Object*.ChildItem(*Row*, *Column*, *MicClass*, *Index*)

  Example:

```
'Click on hyperlink of S#=3
Method 1
Set oLink = oWebTbl.ChildItem(4,2,"Link",0)
oLink.Click
Method 2
oWebTbl.ChildItem(4,2,"Link",0).Click
```

> Here, observe that transaction ids hyperlinks are dynamic objects. These are called dynamic objects because their properties can change dynamically from one run session to another. For example, if user cancels one more ticket, then transaction id 0156644096 will move from row 2 to row 3. It might also happen that with time some older tickets may not be visible at all in this webtable. The properties (name, href, url, etc.) of hyperlinks will change dynamically from one run session to another. Suppose that the requirement is to click on every link present in this webtable and check if it properly works, then even if we capture these link objects to OR; during run session UFT may not be able to recognize it as these objects may not be present in GUI during next run session. To overcome these issues, we use ChildItem method to dynamically identify objects present inside a webtable cell.

- ***ChildItemCount***—Retrieves the number of specified objects in a specified cell of a webtable.

  Syntax: *Object*.ChildItemCount(*Row*, *Column*, *MicClass*)

  Example: find number of link objects present in cell = 2,2

  ```
  Print oWebTbl.ChildItemCount(2,2,"Link")        'Output : 1
  ```

- ***GetROProperty***—Retrieves run-time properties of WebTable.

  Syntax: *Object*. GetROProperty (*Property*, [optional]*Property Data*)

  Example:

  ```
  'find name of link of webtable of cell=2,2
  Print oWebTbl.ChildItem(2,2,"Link").GetROProperty("name")
                                            'Output : 0156644096
  ```

- ***ChildObjects***—Retrieves specified objects present in the WebTable. ChildObject method is similar to ChildItem method with a difference that it finds all specified child objects within an object. For example, ChildObject can be used to find all WebEdit objects inside a page or to find all WebCheckBoxes inside a WebTable.

  Syntax : *Object*.ChildObjects([optional]*Description*)

  Example: find all hyperlink objects inside webtable of Figure 26.11

  ```
  'create a description object
  Set oLink = Description.Create

  'specify properties of object
  oLink("micclass").Value = "Link"

  'find all link objects present in webtable
  Set colLink = oWebTbl.ChildObjets(oLink)

  'find number of link objects present in webtable
  Print colLink.Count                              'Output : 5

  'find printed text of link of row=4
  colLink(2).GetROProperty("outertext")    'Output : 0130365059
  ```

```
'click on link present in row=4
colLink(2).Click
```

Finding Native Properties of the Run-time Objects

GetROProperty method is used to retrieve the run-time identification properties of the object. Similarly, UFT provides the flexibility to the user to retrieve run-time native properties of the object. There are two ways to retrieve the run-time native properties of the object:

- By using *.Object* method
- By using *attribute/** notation

Example 1: Find the maxLength native property value of the Google Search page edit box. (refer Figure 26.3)

```
Set oWebEdit = Browser("Google").Page("Google").WebEdit("q")
Print oWebEdit .Object.maxLength          'Output:: 2147483647
Alternatively,
Print oWebEdit.GetROProperty("attribute/maxlength")          'Output::
2147483647
```

Example 1: Find the sourceindex native property value of the Google Search page edit box.

```
Set oWebEdit = Browser("Google").Page("Google").WebEdit("q")
Print oWebEdit .Object.sourceindex     'Output:: 139
Alternatively,
Print oWebEdit.GetROProperty("attribute/sourceindex")     'Output:: 139
```

NOTES: Index of colLink starts with 0.

FUNCTION TO FIND CELL ORDINATES OF A KEYWORD PRESENT IN WEBTABLE

Function *fnGetWebTableXY* has been designed to find the *x,y* coordinate of any keyword text present in the webtable. It takes webtable object and searches keyword string as input parameters and returns the cell ordinates of the keyword in the webtable in the variable skey in format *x,y*. In case of any failures, the value of function *fnGetWebTableXY* becomes –1 and skey contains the error message.

Input Parameters

```
objWebTable - WebTable wrapper object
sKey - Keyword string whose x,y coordinates need to be found.
```

Output Parameters

sKey - *x,y* coordinate of the searched string. In case, the value of fnGetWebTableXY is non-zero (0), it contains error description.
fnGetWebTableXY - "0" indicates function ran successfully. Any other value indicates function failed to execute properly.

Usage

Let us find out the ordinates of keyword *PNR Number* using this function.

```
Dim sKey
'create webtable wrapper object
Set objWebTable = Browser("EXPEDIA").Page("EXPEDIA").
WebTable("CncldTckts")
sKey = "PNR Number"
'call function
fnStat = fnGetWebTableXY(objWebTable, sKey)
                        'Output : fnStat = "0"
                                   sKey = "1,3"

Function fnGetWebTableXY (objWebTable, sKey)
   ON ERROR RESUME NEXT
   Dim bFoundFlg
   bFoundFlg = "False"
   dicTab=sKey
   nRow = objWebTable.GetROProperty("rows")
   'Find "Key" row
   For rCnt=1 To nRow Step 1
      nCol = objWebTable.ColumnCount(rCnt)
      For cCnt=1 To nCol Step 1
            sKey = Trim(objWebTable.GetCellData(rCnt,cCnt))
            If StrComp(sKey,dicTab,1)=0 Then
                  'Required x,y cordinates
                  sKey = cstr(rCnt) & "," & cstr(cCnt)
                  cCnt = nCol+1
                  rCnt = nRow+1
                  bFoundFlg = "True"
            End If
      Next
   Next
   'Search Keyword not found in WebTable
   If bFoundFlg = "False" Then
      fnGetWebTableXY = "-1"
      sKey = "Search Keyword not found in WebTable"
      Exit Function
   End If
   'Required Operation failed
```

```
    If Err.Number<>0 Then
        fnGetWebTableXY = "-1"
        sKey = "fnGetWebTableXY:" & Err.Description
    End If
    'Required Operation Successfully Performed
    If Err.Number=0 Then
        fnGetWebTableXY = "0"
    End If

End Function
```

EXPORTING WEBTABLE VALUES TO DATATABLE

Function *fnExportWebTbl2DataTbl* exports data values of webtable to a new run-time sheet in data table.

Input Parameters

bHdrRow - Header row exists in webtable or not. (True or False)
sAddSheetNm - Sheet name to which data needs to be exported
objWebTable - WebTable wrapper object

Output Parameters

fnExportWebTbl2DataTbl - "0" indicates function ran successfully. Any other value indicates function failed to execute properly.

Usage

Let us see how we can use this function.

```
Set objWebTable = Browser("EXPEDIA").Page("EXPEDIA").
WebTable("CncldTckts")
fnStat = fnExportWebTbl2DataTbl(True, "CancldTckts", objWebTable)
Function fnExportWebTbl2DataTbl(bHdrRow, sAddSheetNm, objWebTable)
  ON ERROR RESUME NEXT
  ReDim arrTbl(1,1)      'dynamic array
  'add a new data sheet
  Set oNewSheet = DataTable.AddSheet(sAddSheetNm)
  'retrieve number of rows
  nRow = objWebTable.RowCount
  'retrieve number of  columns of first row
  nCol = objWebTable.ColumnCount(1)
  ReDim arrTbl(nRow,nCol) 'redefine array limits
  'retrieve webtable data to an array
  For iCnt=1 To nRow Step 1
     For jCnt=1 To nCol Step 1
         If bHdrRow=True  Then
               nDataRow = iCnt+1
```

```
        Else
              nDataRow = iCnt
        End If
      arrTbl(iCnt,jCnt) = Trim(objWebTable.GetCellData(nDataRow, jCnt))
     Next
  Next
  'add header to data sheet
  For jCnt=1 To nCol Step 1
    If bHdrRow=True Then
       arrTbl(0,jCnt) =
Replace(Trim(objWebTable.GetCellData(1, jCnt))," ","_")
    Else
     arrTbl(0,jCnt)  = "Attrb" & jCnt
    End If
       oNewSheet.AddParameter arrTbl(0,jCnt), ""
  Next
  'add data values to data sheet
  For iCnt=1 To nRow Step 1
   oNewSheet.SetCurrentRow(iCnt)
   For jCnt=1 To nCol Step 1
      oNewSheet.GetParameter(arrTbl(0,jCnt)).Value = arrTbl(iCnt,jCnt)
     Next
  Next
  If Err.Number <>0  Then
        fnExportWebTbl2DataTbl = "-1:" & Err.Description
  Else
   fnExportWebTbl2DataTbl = "0"
  End If
End Function
```

EXPORTING WEB TABLE VALUES TO DICTIONARY OBJECT

Function *fnRetrvWebTblData* is designed to export all the data contents of a webtable to a dictionary object. It takes table type, webtable wrapper object, and dictionary object as input parameters and returns table contents in the specified input dictionary object. Table type value can be 1, 2, or 3 depending on the table format as shown in Tables 26.1a, 26.1b, and 26.2, respectively.

Input Parameters

```
nTblTyp - Type of table. Possible values 1, 2, or 3.
objWebTable - WebTable wrapper object
dicTab - Dictionary object
```

Output Parameters

```
dicTab - Contains data values of webtable in key,value pair form.
  fnRetrvWebTblData - "0" indicates function ran successfully. Any other
  value indicates function failed to execute properly.

   Table Type = "1"
   'Key      Key      Key
```

```
'Value    Value   Value
'Value    Value   Value

Table Type = "2"
'Key  Key              Key              Key
'Key  Value            Value            Value
'Key  Value            Value            Value

Table Type = "3"
'Key      Value ,      Key      Value, Key      Value
'Key      Value ,      Key      Value, Key      Value
```

In Table 26.1a, row 1 consists of the *key* elements such as S# and Transaction ID. Therefore, this table can be treated as table of type 1. In Table 26.1b, both first row (Transaction ID, PNR Number, etc.) and first column (0156644096, 0136774911, etc.) can be treated as *key* elements. Therefore, we can consider this table of type 2. Table 26.2, shows an example of table of type 3. In Table 26.2, *Employee ID*, *Employee Name*, *Sex*, etc. are *key* elements while *10001*, *XYZ*, *Male*, etc. are the *values* of these key elements.

Table 26.1a

S#	Transaction ID
1	2222276878
2	7678979986
3	7797987979
4	7978999989

Table 26.1b WebTable of type 2

Transaction ID	PNR Number	From	To
0156644096	2265959350	NDLS	LKO
0136774911	6131306072	GAYA	NDLS
0130365059	2262414464	NDLS	KQR

> **NOTES**
> There should be no duplication of key values in tables.

Usage

Let us see how we can use this function.

Table Type = 1

```
Set objWebTable = Browser("EXPEDIA").Page("EXPEDIA").
WebTable("CncldTckts")
Set dicTab = CreateObject("Scripting.Dictionary")

fnStat = fnRetrvWebTblData("1", objWebTable, dicTab)
Print dicTab.Keys                    'OutPut (array): "1" "2" "3" "4" "5"
```

Table 26.2 WebTable of type 3

Employee ID	10001	Employee Name	XYZ
Sex	Male	Joining Date	22-Mar-06
Designation	Consultant	Role	Developer

```
Print dicTab.Count                  'OutPut : 5
Print dicTab("1").Keys              'OutPut (array): "S#" "Transation ID" …
Print dicTab("1").Items             'OutPut (array): "1" "0156644096"  …
Print dicTab("1").Item("Refund Amount") 'OutPut : "192.0"
Print dicTab("5").Item("PNR Number")    'OutPut : "2624164458"
```

Table Type = 2

```
Set objWebTable = Browser("EXPEDIA").Page("EXPEDIA").WebTable("Type2")
Set dicTab = CreateObject("Scripting.Dictionary")
fnStat = fnRetrvWebTblData("2", objWebTable, dicTab)
Print dicTab.Keys                   'OutPut (array):"0156644096" "0135774911" …
Print dicTab.Count                  'OutPut : 3
Print dicTab("0156644096").Keys 'OutPut (array): "Transation ID" "PNR …
Print dicTab("0156644096").Items 'OutPut (array): "2265959350" "NDLS" …
Print dicTab("0135774911").Item("To")          'OutPut : "NDLS"
Print dicTab("0130365059").Item("PNR Number")  'OutPut : "2624164464"
```

Table Type = 3

```
Set objWebTable = Browser("").Page("").WebTable("Type3")
Set dicTab = CreateObject("Scripting.Dictionary")
fnStat = fnRetrvWebTblData("3", objWebTable, dicTab)
Print dicTab.Keys         'OutPut (array):"Employee ID" "Employee Name" …
Print dicTab.Items        'OutPut (array):"10001" "XYZ" "Male" …
Print dicTab.Count                  'OutPut : 6
Print dicTab("Employee Name").Item 'OutPut : "XYZ"
Print dicTab("Designation").Item   'OutPut : "Consultant"
```

NOTES: Dictionary of dictionary object has been used for table types 1 and 2 while for table type 3 only single dictionary object has been used.

```
Public Function fnRetrvWebTblData(nTblTyp, objWebTable, dicTab)
ON ERROR RESUME NEXT

'nTblTyp="1"
'Key       Key    Key
'Value     Value  Value

'Value     Value  Value

'nTblTyp="2"
'Key         Key          Key          Key
'Key         Value        Value        Value
'Key         Value        Value        Value

'nTblTyp="3"
'Key      Value,      Key      Value,      Key      Value
'Key      Value,      Key      Value,      Key      Value
```

```
Dim bKeyColFndFlg
Dim nKeyRow

nTblTyp = cstr(nTblTyp)
'Check if webtable exists
If objWebTable.exist(5) = False Then
 fnRetrvWebTblData = "-1:Table does not exist"
 Exit Function
End If

'remove all key, value pairs
dictab.RemoveAll

'---------------------------------------------------------------
If nTblTyp="1" or nTblTyp="2" Then
 'retrieve number of rows
 nRow = objWebTable.GetROProperty("rows")

 'retrieve column count of row 1
 nCol = objWebTable.ColumnCount(1)

 'Find "Key" row
 For rCnt=1 To nRow Step 1
       For cCnt=1 To nCol Step 1
       sKey = Trim(objWebTable.GetCellData(rCnt,cCnt))
       'Key row is the first row with valid data
       If sKey <>"" And len(sKey) >4 Then
     nkeyRow = rCnt     'Key row Position
       cCnt = nCol+1
       rCnt = nRow+1
    End If
    Next
 Next

'Form Key value Pair
 nValRow = nkeyRow+1
 nKeyCol="1"
 For rCnt=nValRow To nRow Step 1
     For cCnt=1 To nCol Step 1
    'retrieve key value
    sKey = Trim(objWebTable.GetCellData(nkeyRow,cCnt))
    'retrieve pair value
    sValue = Trim(objWebTable.GetCellData(rCnt,cCnt))

    'create dictionary of dictionary
    If dicTab.Exists(nKeyCol)="False"  And sKey<>"" Then
```

```
        dicTab.add nKeyCol,CreateObject("Scripting.Dictionary")
      End If

      'add key,value pairs to dictionary
      If sKey <>""  Then
        dicTab(nKeyCol).Add sKey,sValue
      End If
    Next
    nKeyCol = cstr(cint(nKeyCol) + 1)
  Next
End If

'----------------------------------------------------------------------
If nTblTyp="3" Then
      'retrieve number of rows
      nRow = objWebTable.GetROProperty("rows")
      nKeyCntr = 1
      For rCnt=1 To nRow Step 1
    'find column count of specified row
    nCol = objWebTable.ColumnCount(rCnt)
       For cCnt=1 to nCol Step 1
            'retrieve key value
   sKey = Trim(objWebTable.GetCellData(rCnt,cCnt))
            cCnt= cCnt + 1
            'retrieve pair value
            sValue = Trim(objWebTable.GetCellData(rCnt,cCnt))
            If Trim(sKey)<>""  Then
             If dicTab.Exists(sKey) Then
                   'increment key value
                   sKey = sKey & Cstr(nKeyCntr)
                   nKeyCntr = nKeyCntr + 1
           End If
           'add key,value pair to dictionary
           dicTab.Add sKey,sValue
         Else
           cCnt = cCnt-1
         End If
       Next
    Next
    End If
'----------------------------------------------------------------------
   'Required Operation Successfully Performed
   If Err.Number = 0  Then
        fnRetrvWebTblData = "0"
   End If
```

```
  'Required Operation failed
  If Err.Number <>0  Then
   fnRetrvWebTblData = Err.Description
  End If
End Function
```

SOME USEFUL METHODS

Name	Value
colObject.Count	62
colObject(1).getroproperty("micclass")	"Link"
colObject(1).getroproperty("name")	"Images"
colObject(38).getroproperty("micclass")	"WebButton"
colObject(38).getroproperty("name")	"Google Search"

Figure 26.12 *Output*

- ***FireEvent***—This method is used to trigger an event.

  Example: Set focus on link 'Advanced Search' on Google page

  ```
  Browser("Google").Page("Google").
  Link("AdvancedSearch").FireEvent
  "onfocus"
  ```

- ***ChildObjects***—This method is used to find out all the objects present within an object (Figure 26.12).

  Example 1: Find all objects that exist within a Google page

  ```
  Set colObjects = Browser("Google").Page("Google").ChildObjects
  'retrieve total number of objects in page
  Print colObjects.Count
  'retrieve class and name of 2nd object in collection object
  Print colObject(1).GetROProperty("micclass")
  Print colObject(1).GetROProperty("name")
  'retrieve class and name of 38th object in collection object
  Print colObject(38).GetROProperty("micclass")
  Print colObject(38).GetROProperty("name")
  ```

Example 2: Find all webbutton objects within Google page

```
'create a description object
Set oWebBtnDsc = Description.Create
oWebBtnDsc("micclass").Value = "WebButton"

'find all webbuttons that exist within Google page
Set colWebBtn = Browser("Google").Page("Google").
                                  ChildObjects(oWebBtnDsc)
```

Figure 26.13 shows that collection object *colWebBtn* has two webbutton objects one with name 'Google Search' and the other with name 'I'm feeling Lucky.'

- ***Submit***—This method simulates pressing the *Enter* key, while the focus is on the specified object.

  Example: Enter search text on Google page and hit enter key.

  ```
  Browser("Google").Page("Google").WebEdit("SearchText").Set "UFT10"
  Browser("Google").Page("Google").WebEdit("SearchText").Submit
  ```

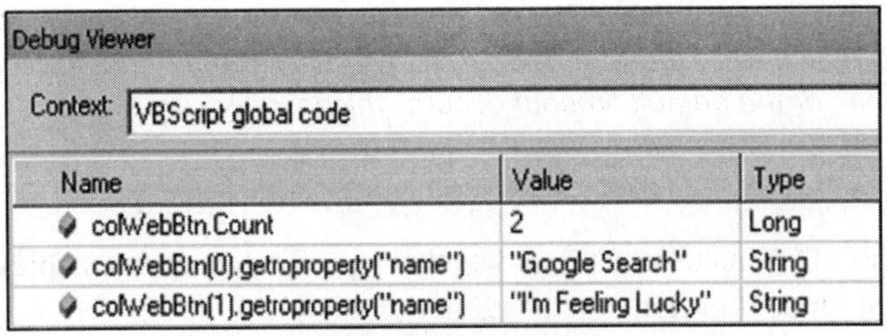

Figure 26.13 *Output*

- ***GetTOProperty***—This method returns the specified property value of test object (stored in OR).

  Example: Find href property of link 'Advanced Search' as present in object repository.

```
Print Browser("Google").Page("Google").Link("AdvancedSearch").
                                        GetTOProperty("href")
```

- ***GetTOProperties***—This method returns collection of properties and values of the specified test object.

  Example: Find collection list of properties and values of 'Advanced Search' link object of Google page.

```
Set colLnkPrpts = Browser("Google").Page("Google").Link("Advanced
Search").GetTOProperties
```

- ***SetTOProperty***—This method is used to redefine certain property values of a test object during run-time. It changes the specified property values that are used to identify an object during a run session. The changes made are valid for the run session only.

  Example: Change default value and add additional identification properties for edit box present on Google page.

```
Set oEdit = Browser("Google").Page("Google").WebEdit("SearchText")
oEdit.SetTOProperty "default value", "UFT10"
oEdit.SetTOProperty "html id ", ""
oEdit.SetTOProperty "html tag", "INPUT"
oEdit.Set "Agile Automation & UFT10"
```

- ***GetROProperty***—This method retrieves run-time property values of an object (as discussed earlier).
- ***WaitProperty***—This method instructs UFT to pause the test script until a particular object property achieves specified value.

  Example 1: Use WaitProperty method to wait for the object webbutton 'Advanced Search' readystate property to be complete or for 5 seconds or 5000 milliseconds to pass, whichever comes first.

```
Browser("Google").Page("Google").Link(AdvancedSearch").Click
Set oGoogleAdvSrch = Browser("AdvSrch").Page("AdvSrch").
                                        WebButton("AdvSrch")
If oGoogleAdvSrch.WaitProperty("attribute/readystate", "complete",
5000)  Then
     MsgBox "Done"
End If
```

Example 2: Write code to pause UFT execution till the 'value' property value of Google 'Advance Search' button matches to the string 'Search.' The UFT pause should timeout after the object property matches or the default timeout occurs whichever occurs first.

```
Set Object = Browser("AdvSrch").Page("AdvSrch").WebButton("AdvSrch")
Print Object.WaitProperty("value", micRegExpMatch(".*Search.*"))
```

- ***CheckProperty***—This method checks whether specified property achieved specified value within specified timeout or not.

Example 1: Verify whether WebList object 'Results per Page' has items count *property value 5 or not.*

```
Set oGoogleAdvSrch = Browser("AdvSrch").Page("AdvSrch").WebList
                                                    ("Results/Page")
Print oGoogleAdvSrch.CheckProperty("items count", 5, 5000)
                                          'Output : True
Print oGoogleAdvSrch.CheckProperty("items count", 4, 5000)
                                          'Output : False
```

Example 2: Verify whether the 'value' property of the 'Google Search' button contains string 'Search' or not.

```
Set Object = Browser("AdvSrch").Page("AdvSrch").WebButton("AdvSrch")
Print Object.CheckProperty("value", micRegExpMatch(".*Search.*"))
```

- ***ToString***—This method returns the logical name of the specified test object.

Example: Write object logical name to test results in case of error

```
sLinkObjNm = Browser("Google").Page("Google").Link("AdvancedSearch").
                                                       ToString
                                        'Output : AdvancedSearch
sBtnObjNm = Browser("Google").Page("Google").ToString
                                        'Output : Google
```

- ***Object***—This method is used to access or modify the internal properties of the run-time object.

Example 1: Change background color of Google page to red

```
'Find current back ground color of Google page
sBgColor = Browser("Google").Page("Google").Object.bgcolor
                                        'Output : "#ffffff"
'change background color to red
Browser("Google").Page("Google").Object.bgcolor = "RED"
sBgColor = Browser("Google").Page("Google").Object.bgcolor
                                   'Output : "#ff0000"
```

Example 2: Find font of link object 'Advanced Search'

```
'find font family
Print Browser("Google").Page("Google").Link("Advanced Search").
Object.currentStyle.fontFamily
                                   'Output : "arial,sans-serif"
```

```
'find font style
Print Browser("Google").Page("Google").Link("Advanced Search").
Object.currentStyle.fontStyle
                                    'Output : "normal"
```

Example 3: Find color of AdvancedSearch *link object on Google page when clicked*

```
'find color of link object
Print Browser("Google").Page("Google").Link("AdvancedSearch").
Object.currentStyle.Color
                                    'Output : "#551a8b"
'Drag link object and drop it on edit box
Browser("Google").Page("Google").Link("AdvancedSearch").Drag
Browser("Google").Page("Google").WebEdit("SearchString").Drop
'find color of link object
Print Browser("Google").Page("Google").Link("AdvancedSearch").
Object. currentStyle.Color
                                    'Output : "#ff0000"
```

Observe change in color of link object when it is clicked.

Example 4: Find color of ForgotPassword *link object on* EXPEDIA *site when on focus*

```
'Find color of link object before focus
Print browser("EXPEDIA").Page("EXPEDIA").Link("ForgotPassword").
                                    Object.currentStyle.color
                                    'Output : "#284f59"
'Set focus on link object
Browser("EXPEDIA").Page("EXPEDIA").Link("ForgotPassword").Object.
focus
'Find color of link object when object is on focus (when mouse is
pointed to that object)
Print browser("EXPEDIA").Page("EXPEDIA").Link("ForgotPassword").
                                      Object.currentStyle.color
                                    'Output : "#504ad5"
```

Observe change in color of link object when it is on focus.

Example 5: Find Google page's cookie

```
'cookie collection object
Set colCookie = Browser("Google").Page("Google").Object.Cookie
```

Use WebUtil.DeleteCookies to delete browser cookies.

Example 6: Find status bar text when focus is on a link object

```
'Highlight AdvancedSearch link on Google page
Browser("Google").Page("Google").Link("AdvancedSearch").HighLight
Wait 2
'Set focus on link object
Browser("Google").Page("Google").Link("Advanced Search").Object.focus
'Find status bar text when focus is on link object
Print Browser("Google").WinStatusBar("msctls_statusbar32").
GetVisibleText
        'Output : "Shortcut to advanced_search?hl=en  Internet"
Alternatively,
Print Browser("Google").WinStatusBar("nativeclass:=msctls_statusbar32").
GetVisibleText
```

SOME USEFUL UTILITY OBJECTS

OptionalStep

An optional step is a step that is not necessarily required to successfully execute. Suppose that while downloading a file from application, sometimes, a download confirmation pop window opens; however, sometimes, it does not. In these situations, we can mark this step optional. Therefore, even if this statement fails, UFT ignores this failure and proceeds execution from next step.

Example:

```
OptionalStep.Browser("Browser").Dialog("Download").WinButton
("Confirm").Click
```

Random Number

This object is used to generate random numbers between two specified values

```
Syntax : RandomNumber(ParameterName Or StartNumber, EndNumber)
```

Example:

```
Print RandomNumber(10,99)
Print RandomNumber(1,9)
```

SystemUtil

This object is used to control application and processes during a run session.

Methods

Run Opens a program, document, Web site, or application

Example:

```
'Open internet explorer
SystemUtil.Run "iexplore.exe"

'Open internet explorer and navigate to google.com
SystemUtil.Run "iexplore.exe",  "www.google.com"

'Open internet explorer, if not already opened
'and navigate to google.com
SystemUtil.Run "www.google.com"
```

CloseProcessByName Closes a process by its name. Returns the number of instances of the application has been closed.

Example:

```
'close notepad
bStat = SystemUtil.CloseProcessByName("notepad.exe")
'close internet explorer
bStat = SystemUtil.CloseProcessByName("iexplore.exe")
```

CloseProcessById Closes a process by its process ID. Returns True or False indicating process successfully closed or not.

Example: Close Excel file

```
nPID = Window("Book1").GetROProperty("process id")
    SystemUtil.CloseProcessById nPID
```

CloseProcessByWndTitle Closes all processes whose window title matches the specified title.

```
Syntax : Object.CloseProcessByWndTitle(WindowTitle, bRegExp)
```

Example: Out of three browsers opened on desktop, two of Google and one of EXPEDIA, close all the Google browsers.

```
'Window title with regular expression
SystemUtil.CloseProcessByWndTitle("Google.*", True)
```

CloseProcessByHwnd Closes a process by its window handle.

Example—Out of two EXPEDIA browser sites opened, close the one opened later.

```
  hWnd = Browser("name:=ΕΞΠΕΔΙΑ.*","creationtime:=1").
GetROProperty("hwnd")
      SystemUtil.CloseProcessByHwnd hWnd
```

CloseDescendentProcesses Closes all processes that are opened by UF

Example: Close all processes opened by UFT

```
SystemUtil.CloseDescendentProcesses
```

PathFinder

UFT saves the path of automated components (actions, library, etc.) in two ways – absolute path and relative path. In case of absolute path, complete path of automated component is specified. While in case of relative path, UFT provides the facility to first define a set of folders in which UFT can look for automated components. These can be defined in *Tools → Options ... → Folders pane*. Now, suppose that at a later stage, when we need to insert a call to copy an action, we will just have to provide name of the test script and not the complete path. UFT will automatically search the specified test script in the given list of folders string from top to bottom. UFT provides *PathFinder.Locate* method to programmatically find complete path of a file.

Example:

```
sPath = PathFinder.Locate(fileName)
```

Setting

This object is used to retrieve or modify the test settings during run-time.

```
Syntax:
'retrieve settings
Value = Setting(keyName)
'modify settings
Setting(keyName) = Value
```

Table 26.3 lists KeyName, their description, and possible values.

Methods

Add Adds a user-defined setting during run-time.

```
Syntax : Setting.Add SettingNm, SettingValue
```

Example: Create a setting for reporting run status

```
Setting.Add "RunStatus", "0"
Print Setting("RunStatus")    'Output : "0"
```

Exists Verifies if setting has been defined or not.

```
Syntax : Setting.Exists(Key)
```

Example: Check if key *RunStatus* exists

```
If Setting.Exists("RunStatus") = True Then
MsgBox "RunStatus key exists"
End If
```

Remove Removes only user-defined added settings during run-time.

```
Syntax : Setting.Remove SettingName
```

Example: Remove setting key RunStatus

```
Setting.Remove "RunStatus"
```

Table 26.3 Test settings key names

KeyName	Description
AutomaticLinkRun	True – Automatic checkpoints are executed. False – Automatic checkpoints are not executed.
DefaultLoadTime	Time to add, in seconds, to the load time recorded during recording test script.
DefaultTimeout	Maximum time (milliseconds) to wait before it is determined that an object cannot be found.
SnapshotReportMode	Indicates the run-time situations in which UFT should capture screenshots: 0 – always captures images. 1 – captures images only if an error occurs. 2 – captures images if an error or warning occurs. 3 – never captures images. Default = 1.
WebTimeout	Maximum time (seconds) to wait before it is determined that a URL address cannot be found.

Properties

Item Retrieves or modifies specified key values

WebPackage Retrieves or modifies specified key values for the Web Add-in

Register User Function

This Object is used to override an existing method or add a new one to a test object.

```
Syntax : RegisterUserFunc TOClass, MethodName, FunctionName, [option-
al]SetAsDefault
```

TOClass refers to the test object class
MethodName refers to the name of the method that is to be registered
FunctionName refers to the user-defined function
SetAsDefault True indicates that the registered function is used as the default operation for the test object. Default = False.

Example 1: Override Select *function for the* WebList *test object. The overridden function should first convert the item value to lower case and then select it in application.*

```
'Create a function which takes weblist
'wrapper object and item value as parameters
'and converts item value to lower case
'before selecting it in GUI
Sub SelectLCase(Object, sItemNm)
Object.Select LCase(sItemNm)
End Sub

'register the newly designed function
RegisterUserFunc "WebList", "Select", "SelectLCase"
```

```
'select 20 results from WebList results/page
Browser("AdvSrch").Page("AdvSrch").WebList("Rslt/Pg").Select
                                                 "20 REsULTs"
```

The above-mentioned statement now calls the function SelectLCase to select an item from WebList, instead of directly calling select method.

Example 2: Create a new function to select items from the WebList *test object. The function should first convert the item value to lower case and then select it in application.*

```
Sub SelectLCase(Object, sItemNm)
   Object.Select LCase(sItemNm)
End Sub

'register the newly designed function with new method name
RegisterUserFunc "WebList", "SelectLCase", "SelectLCase"

'select 20 results from WebList results/page
Browser("AdvSrch").Page("AdvSrch").WebList("Rslt/Pg").SelectLCase
                                                 "20 REsULTs"
```

UFT uses the user-defined function as a method of the specified test object class for the remainder of the run session, or until the method is unregistered.

UnRegister User Function

This object instructs UFT to unregister the currently registered method.

```
Syntax : UnRegisterUserFunc TOClass, MethodName
```

Example: Unregister SelectLCase *method of test object* WebList

```
UnRegisterUserFunc "WebList", "Select"
```

SOME USEFUL EXAMPLES

Example 1: How to use object logical name and output parameter as variable in test scripts.

Suppose that there is an application that has facets as shown in Fig. 26.14. The test case requirement is to verify that the facets can be minimized and maximized on mouse click. The simplest way of doing the same is by executing a click method on the respective object one by one. If the number of facets is huge, then the code lines will also increase proportionally. To reduce the number of code lines, all the facet objects can be stored in an array and then using a 'For' loop all the facets can be verified.

The following code shows the conventional method of verifying whether facets can be minimized/maximized or not.

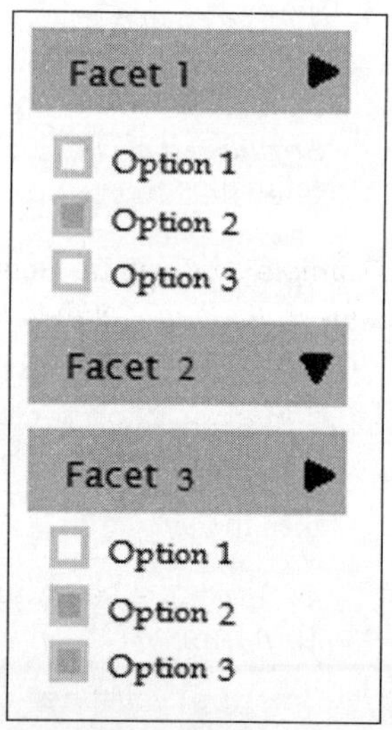

Figure 26.14

```
'minimize facet1
Browser("Browser").Page("Page").
Image("Facet1Minimize").Click
```

```
'Verify facet1 is minimized
bExist = Browser("Browser").Page("Page").
WebElement("Facet1").Exist
'Set output parameter
Parameter("Out1") = bExist
```

The above-mentioned code needs to be repeated for each facet.
The following code shows how to use object names as variables inside test scripts.

```
'Store object logical names in array
arrFacetMinimize  = Array("Facet1Minimize"," Facet2Minimize ",
"Facet3Minimize")
arrFacet = Array("Facet1","Facet2","Facet3")
arrOut = Array("Out1"," Out2"," Out3")
For iCnt=0 To UBound(arrFacet) Step 1
   'Verify facet is minimized
   Browser("Browser").Page("Page").Image(arrFacetMinimize(iCnt)).Click
   bExist = Browser("Browser").Page("Page").WebElement(arrFacet(iCnt)).
                                                              Exist
   Parameter(arrOut(iCnt)) = bExist
Next,
```

If the requirement is to find all the child links inside the facet boxes, then the same can be achieved by using the 'ChildObjects' method as follows.

```
'Create a link description object
Set oLink = Description.Create
oLink("micclass").value = "Link"
'find al link objects inside facet webelements
Set colLink = Browser("Browser").Page("Page").WebElement(arrFacet(iCnt)).
                                                ChildObjects(oLink)
```

Example 2: Write a function to find whether an object is visible on the screen or not.

Many times, it happens that though an object is not visible on the page, still UFT is able to find that object in the page. This happens because the object is present on the page but is hidden by the application developers. The easiest way to find whether the object is visible on the page or not is by funding the *x,y* position of the object. The object that is not visible to a user has its coordinate value as zero. In addition the height and width property value of such objects is zero. Therefore, if any object identified by UFT has these values equal to zero, it implies that though the object is present in the application code, it is not visible to the user.

Function 'fnIsObjVisible' finds out whether an object is visible on the page or not during run-time. It takes the specified object as input parameter and returns a flag specifying whether object is visible on the screen or not.

Input Parameters

```
Object: The object whose visibility on the page is to be found
```

Output Parameters

```
    Returns 'True' if object is visible on the screen.
    Returns 'False' if object is not visible on the screen.
    Returns error message in case a script error occurs
```

Usage

```
    Set oEdit = Browser("Browser").Page("Page").WebEdit("EditBox")
    bVisible = fnIsObjVisible(oEdit)

Function fnIsObjVisible(oGuiObject)
    On Error Resume Next

    'find x-position of the object
    nXPos = oGuiObject.GetROProperty("x")

    'find y-position of the object
    nYPos = oGuiObject.GetROProperty("y")

    'find height of the object
    nHeight = oGuiObject.GetROProperty("height")

    'find width of the object
    nWidth = oGuiObject.GetROProperty("width")

    If nXPos=0 Or nYPos=0 Or nHeight=0 Or nWidth=0 then
        fnIsObjVisible = "False" 'object is not visible on the screen
    Else
        fnIsObjVisible = "True"  'object is visible on the screen
    End If

    If Err.Number <>0 Then
        fnIsObjVisible = "-1:" & Err.Description
    End If
End Function
```

Example 3: Write a function to find whether the specified text is visible on the screen or not.

Most of the times, we observe that the messages that appear on the screen are recognized by UFT as WebElement. The only way to test whether a specified message/text is present on the screen is to check whether the WebElement object exists or not. Therefore, for each and every message, a WebElement needs to be added to the OR. Moreover, it is generally found that both the positive and negative error messages are present the page. However, only one message is visible on the screen at a time. In these scenarios, even UFT is able to recognize a WebElement on the page even though it is present hidden on the screen. Most application developers keep all the positive and negative messages in the JSP code itself. During run-time only that message is made visible for which the test condition is true. Since, UFT is not able to differentiate visible and invisible texts, during run-time, it is able to recognize all the messages (WebElements) on the page. This makes it difficult to validate whether proper message has been displayed on the screen or not and whether the test case has been passed or not.

Function 'fnVerifyTextExistOnPage' finds out whether the specified text/string is visible on the screen or not. It takes page object, string to find on the page, and a variable to store text found on the page as input parameters. If the specified text is found on the page, then that text value is stored in the specified variable. The function returns '0' id the specified text is found on the page. It returns error description in case an error occurs during code execution.

Input Parameters

```
oPage - Page object
sTextToFind - Text/String to find on the page
sTextFnd - Any variable to store the matching text/string found on the page
```

Output Parameters

```
sTextFnd - Returns the matching string found on the page. If no match
is found this variable is left as it is.
```

The function returns '0' if a matching text is found on the screen. In case an error occurs during script execution, then the function returns error reason along with flag '–1.'

Usage

```
Set oPage = Browser("Browser").Page("Page")
sTextToFind = "Specify the text to look for in the page"
sTextFnd = ""
fnStat = fnVerifyTextExistOnPage(oPage , sTextToFind, sTextFnd)
```

```
Function fnVerifyTextExistOnPage(oPage , sTextToFind, sTextFnd )
   'Description - Find if the specified text exists on the page
   'Usage
   'Set oPage = Browser().Page()
   'sText = <Specify Text to find on Page>
   'fnStat = fnVerifyTextExistOnPage(oPage, sText, bTextFnd)
           On Error Resume Next
           Dim oWebElement, sTextVal
           bTextFnd = False
           sTextFnd=""
           'Create description object for webelement
           Set oWebElement = Description.Create()
           oWebElement("micclass").value="WebElement"
           oWebElement("html tag").value=".*[A-Za-z0-9].*"
           oWebElement("outertext").value =".*[A-Za-z0-9].*"
           oWebElement("visible").value = True
           'Find all WebElement objects present on the specified page
           set colWebElements = oPage.ChildObjects(oWebElement)
           'Find if specified text exists on the screen  or not
           For iCnt=0 to colWebElements.count-1
                'Capture text value of the webelement
                sTextVal = Trim(colWebElements(iCnt).
                GetROProperty("outertext"))
               If Instr(1, sTextVal, sTextToFind,1)>0 Then
                        sTextFnd = sTextVal
                        Exit For
```

```
                End If
            Next

            If sTextFnd<>""  And Err.Number=0 Then
                fnVerifyTextExistOnPage = 0  'Search text found on screen
            End If

            'Error occurred during script execution
            If Err.Number<>0  Then
            fnVerifyTextExistOnPage = "-1:" & Err.Description
        End If
End Function
```

QUICK TIPS

- ✓ Creation time and index property to be used to identify and differentiate multiple browsers with similar properties.
- ✓ OpenUrl and OpenTitle properties to be used to identify and differentiate multiple pop-up browser windows of same application.
- ✓ Use 'SET' method to turn on/off a checkbox instead of 'CLICK' method.

? PRACTICAL QUESTIONS

1. Write a code to input value to a disabled edit box.
2. Write a code to delete browser cookies.
3. Write a code to extract all the data from WebTable to a dictionary.
4. Write a code to find whether an object is visible to the user or not.
5. Write a code to find whether a text is visible on the page or not.
6. Explain one real-time use of fireevent method.
7. Explain one real-time use of RegisterUserFunc.
8. Write a code to find all the objects inside WebTable.
9. Write a code to find all the objects inside page.
10. Which method is used to find run-time properties of an object?

Chapter 27

Descriptive Programming

Designing test scripts by explicitly defining object properties within the test script is called Descriptive Programming (DP). In DP code, object repository is not used, which means doing away with all the advantages associated with the Object Repository (OR) mechanism. This chapter examines the situations in which the advantage of object repository is outweighed by the flexibility that descriptive programming offers. One example where DP becomes necessary is clicking on the first 'Transaction Id' link of the WebTable shown in Fig. 27.1. The value of transaction id keeps on changing as more tickets are booked. This makes the link object a dynamic one. Here, the object repository method of automation will fail as during run-time the link object values would have changed. To overcome such problems, DP is used. The link object is retrieved at run-time and then a click method is executed on it. In DP, object recognition occurs in the same way as normal object identification mechanism of OR. The only difference is that instead of defining object properties in the object repository, they are explicitly defined in the test script itself.

```
Syntax : Class ("Property1:=Value1", "Property2:=Value2")
```

For example, the descriptive code for browser synchronization is:

```
Browser ("name:=Expedia", "openurl:= http://www.expedia.co.in").Sync
```

For the code above, during run-time UFT searches for a browser whose *name* property is *Expedia* and *openurl* property is http://www.expedia.co.in. If UFT is able to find this browser, it executes *Sync* method on it, or else returns an error.

> The identification properties and its value for an object can be found using Object Spy tool.

WHEN TO USE DESCRIPTIVE PROGRAMMING

- **Application GUI not ready**—DP can be used to automate test cases even if application graphical user interface (GUI) is not ready/stable.

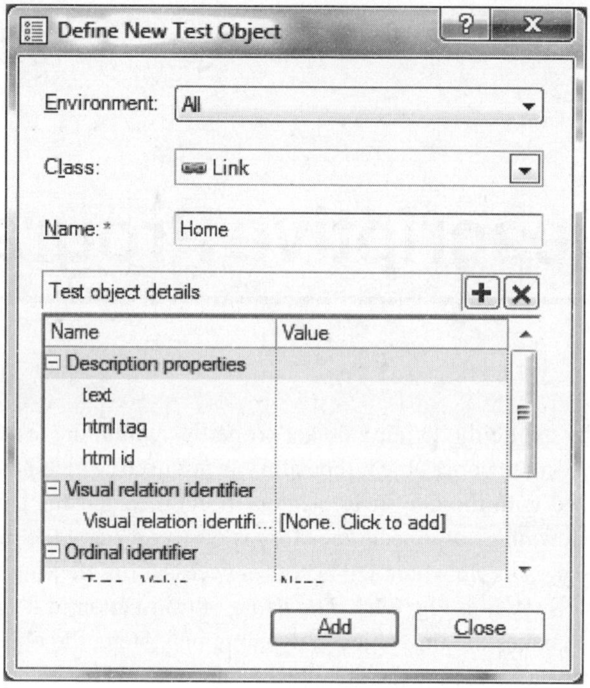

Figure 27.1 *Define new test object*

UFT provides the feature to define new test objects. In case GUI objects are not developed, but the properties of the same are available from the application developers, then instead of using DP it is better to develop new test objects. These test objects can be created in shared object repository. This feature is especially helpful in agile test automation where test automation is carried out in parallel to application development. In agile environment, most of the time objects are still under development while automation scripting is going on. In such scenarios, creation of self-defined test objects help save a lot of time. To create a new test object:

1. Navigate Resources → Object Repository Manager…
2. Object Repository Manager window opens.
3. Click on the *Define New test Object* button . Define New Test Object window opens as shown in Fig. 27.1.
4. Select appropriate environment—Web, Standard, SAP,, Java, ettc..
5. Select appropriate class—browser, page, WebEdit., etc.
6. Specify the logical name of the object.
7. Click on the button . Add Properties dialog box opens.
8. Select appropriate object properties.
9. Click the OK button.
10. Specify the values of the object properties.
11. Click the button 'Add' to add the 'Test Object' to the shared object repository.

- **Dynamic Objects**—DP is a more reliable method to handle the objects whose properties change during run-time.
- **Large Object Repository**—Large size of object repository increases script execution time.

DP could be used in cases to avoid unnecessary addition of objects to OR. For example, if test scenario is to select all checkboxes present in a table, there is no need to add all check boxes to OR, instead using DP code all the checkboxes can easily be selected.

This test object will now be accessible to all the tests that are associated with this OR

DESCRIPTIVE PROGRAMMING SYNTAX

There are two ways of writing DP code:

- Description strings
- Description objects

Description Strings

In this method, the description of the object is defined in a single string. For example, the description string to click on Expedia site login button will be:

```
'Get the page object—objects are accessed using OR mechanism Set oPage
= Browser("Expedia").Page("Expedia")
```

```
'Click on login button using DP approach oPage.WebButton("name:=Login",
"html id:=Button1").Click
```

Alternatively, browser and page object can also be accessed using DP strings. BrwNm = "Expedia "

```
    PgTitle = "Expedia"
sOpenUrl = "http://www.expedia.co.in"
Set oBrw = Browser("name:= " & BrwNm & , "openurl:= " & sOpenUrl)
Set oPage = oBrw.Page("title:= " & PgTitle) oPage.WebButton("name:=Login",
"html id:=Button1").Click
```

> NOTES: For DP, it is better to define minimum number of properties that are required to recognize an object uniquely during run-time. Once DP code is used, only DP can be used down the hierarchy. For example, if browser object is specified with descriptive code, then page and WebButton objects also need to be specified with descriptive codes only.

Description Objects

In description object, an object is created, which defines the properties and values for identifying AUT objects during run-time. Use of description objects makes the code more readable and reduces code redundancy. For example, a user needs to use browser and page objects to access every object inside the page. In case of description strings user needs to define browser and page properties in every line where one needs to work on objects on the page. To avoid this, a description object can be created. Once it is created, it can be used anywhere in the test script.

Example 1: Create a description object for browser.

```
'Create description object
Set oBrwDesc =  Description.Create

'Define descriptive property-value pairs
oBrwDesc("micclass").value =  "Browser"
oBrwDesc("name").value =  "Expedia"
```

Example 2: Find all browsers on which Expedia app is opened on desktop using DP.

```
'Create description object
Set oBrwDesc =  Description.Create

'Define descriptive property-value pairs
oBrwDesc("micclass").value =  "Browser"
oBrwDesc("name").value =  "Expedia"

'Get all opened browsers with Expedia app open
Set colBrowsers =  Desktop.ChildObjects(oBrwDesc)

'Find count of opened Expedia browsers MsgBox
colBrowsers.Count
```

Example 3: Write the DP code to click on the Expedia login page login button.

```
'Create description object
Set oWebBtnDesc =  Description.Create

'Define descriptive property-value pairs
oWebBtnDesc ("micclass").value =  "WebButton"
oWebBtnDesc ("name").value =  "Login"
oWebBtnDesc ("html id").value =  "Button1"

'Click on login button
Browser("Expedia").Page("Expedia").WebButton(oWebBtnDesc).Click
```

Example 4: Capture tool tip text when mouse is hovered on Flights link object on Expedia home page.

```
'Set focus on link object
Browser("Expedia").Page("Expedia").Link("Flights").Object.focus
'Alternatively, if object.focus method does not focus on the
object; then mouse MIddleClick method can be used.
' Browser("Expedia").Page("Expedia").Link("Flights").MiddleClick
'Retrieve tool tip text
Print Window("nativeclass:=tooltips_class32").GetROProperty("text")
      'Output : http://www.expedia.co.in/Flights
```

> **NOTES** In the descriptive code mentioned earlier, UFT assumes that object oWebBtnDesc is of class WebButton as this object is defined for class WebButton in the code above. Therefore, there is no need to specify class of description object.

REGULAR EXPRESSIONS

In situations where the properties of objects are dynamically varying, regular expressions can be used in object property values to identify the object during run-time.

For example, let us analyze the *column names* property of WebTable *ListOfTickets* (see Fig. 27.2). Value of this property is:

List of Tickets e-ticket i-ticket S#Transaction ID PNR NumberFrom to Total AmountRefund Amount-Cancelled OnType of Ticket1 0156644096 2265959350NDLSLKO242.0192.030-11- 2009eticket2 0136774911 6131306072GAYANDLS723.0314.017-9-2009eticket3 0130365059 2262414464NDLSKQR997.0917.015-9-2009eticket

It is observed that dynamically changing values such as ticket number, date, and amount are a part of this property value. Therefore, next time, if a new transaction id is populated in WebTable, UFT will not be able to recognize it based on WebTable properties that it has captured (as *column names* property value will change). To overcome these situations, it is essential to identify two things within the property values:

- Fixed pattern
- Dynamically changing pattern

Fixed pattern is the part of the string that remains static or unchanged during various runs. Dynamically changing pattern is the part of the string whose value keeps on changing with each run. The fixed pattern is left as it is while the dynamically changing pattern is replaced with the regular expressions.

Dynamically changing string can have either a regular or an irregular changing pattern. For example, if the dynamically changing string is of date type, then the pattern is of date type. Alternatively, if the dynamically changing string is always a number, then the pattern is of number type. This implies that if dynamically changing strings are following a regular changing pattern, then a regular expression can be designed to replace the dynamic string. If the dynamic string does not follow any pattern, then that string is replaced by '.*'. This implies that UFT will not take into account the complete dynamic string while identifying the objects. It is always better to identify the dynamically changing pattern and code appropriate regular expressions for it. This increases the chances of object recognition during run-time.

S#	Transaction ID	PNR Number	From	To	Total Amount	Refund Amount	Cancelled On	Type of Ticket
1	0156644096	2265959350	NDLS	LKO	242.0	192.0	30-11-2009	eticket
2	0136774911	6131306072	GAYA	NDLS	723.0	314.0	17-9-2009	eticket
3	0130365059	2262414464	NDLS	KQR	997.0	917.0	15-9-2009	eticket

Figure 27.2 *WebTable of list of tickets*

As shown in Fig. 27.2 the *column names* property value is—S#, Transaction ID, PNR Number, From, To, etc. form a fixed pattern. These values will always be a part of the *column names* property value. Values such as 0156644096 and 2265959350NDLSLKO242 are dynamically changing values. These values can be replaced with regular expressions.

Fixed pattern—*S#Transaction ID PNR NumberFrom To Total Amount Refund Amount Cancelled On Type of Ticket*

Dynamic pattern—This pattern is random with no two occurrences related to each other. Since no dynamic pattern is followed, regular expression '.*' can be used.

Therefore, our new column name property value becomes:

```
.*S#Transaction ID PNR NumberFrom To Total AmountRefund AmountCancelled
OnType of Ticket.*
```

Alternatively, if few column name values are sufficient to recognize the WebTable object, then it can be written as:

```
.*S#Transaction ID PNR NumberFrom.*
```

Code below shows how to access this WebTable object using DP approach with regular expressions.

Regular Expressions in Description Strings

```
Set oPage =  Browser("IRCTC").Page("IRCTC")
Set oWebTbl =  oPage.WebTable("column names:=.*S#Transaction ID PNR Num-
berFrom.* ")
MsgBox oWebTbl.GetCellData(2,2) ' Output : 0156644096
```

Regular Expressions in Description Objects

```
Set oWebTblDesc =  Description.Create
'Define descriptive property-value pairs
oWebTblDesc("column names").value = ".*S#Transaction ID PNR Number-
From.* "
'Access web table cell data
Set oWebTbl =  Browser("IRCTC").Page("IRCTC").WebTable(oWebTblDesc)
MsgBox oWebTbl.GetCellData(2,2) 'Output : 0156644096
```

> **NOTES** The dynamically changing values are said to follow a pattern if they increase numerically, are always alphabets, are always date type, etc. If no dynamic pattern is followed, then regular expression '.*' can be used.

Implicit and Explicit Properties

When object description properties are specified using Descriptive Programming, there are certain properties that UFT assumes the object already has. Automation Developers need not defined these properties in description code. Now a question you may ask—Which object properties are automatically referenced by UFT. Though, UFT documentation does provide any details on this; a detailed analysis suggests that the properties (or object attributes) automatically referenced includes *html tag* of the referenced object. For example, *html tag* of a link object is always 'a'.

Suppose test code to click on the *Flights* link object on Expedia on home page is:

```
Set oPg = Browser("Expedia").Page("Expedia")
  oPg.Link("name:=Flights").click
```

So when we write the below code to click on the 'Flights' link object, UFT assumes the *html tag* of this object is 'a'. If the 'html tag' of this object is not 'a' then UFT will fail to identify this object. (If an objects' html tag is not 'a', then essentially it is not a link object.). Since, here UFT already assumes the *html tag* property; there is no need to define this property again in the descriptive test code.

Listed below are few UFT object classes and properties UFT automatically expects in these objects.

UFT Standard Object Class	Assumed Properties
Link	html tag:=a
WebEdit	html tag:=input
Image	html tag:=img
WebCheckbox	Html tag:=input

An exception to this is *WebElement* class object. For any object which is referenced as WebElement, users are to define the *html tag* property of the object. This is because, UFT classifies an object as WebElement when the assumed properties of the object does not match to the UFT standard object class default assumed properties. For example, consider the below HTML code.

```
<html>
      <head><title>UFT WebElement</title></head>
      <body>
            <div class="div1">
                  <p>WebElement Object</p>
            </div>
      </body>
</html>
```

For above HTML code, objects <div> and <p> are classified by UFT as web elements. As we see here, html tag is different for both the objects. Since, WebElement class does not assumes html tag property, this property needs to be defined while describing the object in descriptive code.

Consider the UFT code below:

```
Set oPg = Browser("name:=UFT WebElement").Page("title:=UFT WebElement")
oPg.WebElement("outertext:=WebElement Object").Highlight
```

The above code when executed will fail with error that there are multiple objects with same description and hence UFT is not able to uniquely locate the object. This problem can be solved by specifying the *html tag* as well in the object description code as shown below:

```
oPg.WebElement("html tag:=P","outertext:=WebElement Object").Highlight
```

CHILD OBJECTS

UFT provides ChildObjects() method to retrieve all the child objects of any parent object. For example, all the objects present inside the page object are called child objects. The page object is called the parent object.

Example 1: Retrieve all the link objects of WebTable shown in Fig. 27.2.

```
'Description object for link object
Set oLnkDesc =  Description.Create
oLnkDesc("micclass").value =  "Link"

'Collection of link objects present in the table
Set colLink =  oWebTbl.ChildObjects(oLnkDesc)

'Total number of link objects
MsgBox colLink.Count      'Output : 3

'Name of the first link object
MsgBox colLink(0).GetRoProperty("name")      'Output : 0156644096
```

Example 2: Select all the checkboxes present in a page with name property value starting with chk.

```
'Description object
Set oChkBoxDesc =  Description.Create
oChkBoxDesc("micclass").value =  "WebCheckBox"
oChkBoxDesc("name").value =  "chk.*"

'Get all checkboxes present in the page
Set colChkBox =  Browser().Page().ChildObjects(oChkBoxDesc)

'Select all checkboxes
For iCnt=0 To colChkBox.Count-1
colChkBox(iCnt).Set "ON"
Next
```

Example 3: Retrieve all child objects of a web page.

```
'Description object
Set oDesc =  Description.Create

'Get all child objects of the page
Set colChildObj =  Browser().Page().ChildObjects(oDesc)

'Print class and name properties of all child objects
For iCnt=0 To colChildObj.Count-1
   Print colChildObj(iCnt).GetROProperty("micclass")
   Print colChildObj(iCnt).GetROProperty("name")
Next
```

CONVERTING AN OR-BASED TEST SCRIPT TO A DP-BASED TEST SCRIPT

DP requires a careful selection of object properties for object identification. Consider the OR-based test script code mentioned below. The code enters username and password on IRCTC login site and clicks the login button.

OR-Based Test Script Code

Object	Object Logical Name	Object Properties
Browser	IRCTC	name:= IRCTC Online Passenger Reservation System openurl:= http://www.irctc.co.in
Page	IRCTC	title:= IRCTC Online Passenger Reservation System
WebEdit	UserName	name:=userName
WebEdit	Password	name:=password
WebButton	Login	name:=Login

```
Browser("IRCTC").Page("IRCTC").WebEdit("UserName").Set        "User1"
Browser("IRCTC").Page("IRCTC").WebEdit("Password").Set        "Pass1"
Browser("IRCTC").Page("IRCTC").WebButton("Login").Click
```

DP-based Test Script Code

```
sBrwNm =  "IRCTC Online Passenger Reservation System"
sOpenUrl =  "http://www.irctc.co.in"
Set oBrw =  Browser("name:=  " & sBrwNm , "openurl:=  " & sOpenUrl)
Set oPage =  oBrw.Page("title:=  " & sBrwNm)

oPage.WebEdit("name:=userName").Set "User1"
oPage.WebEdit("name:=password").Set   "Pass1"
oPage.WebButton("name:=Login", "html id:=Button1").Click
```

USING DP-BASED OBJECT REPOSITORY

As seen from the above code, if some changes in the object properties come up, then change identification and implementation in test scripts not only becomes a difficult task, but also becomes resource intensive and time consuming. To avoid this, we can define object properties in a .vbs file and access all the objects in the test scripts from the .vbs file itself. The .vbs file will emulate the behavior of UFT object repository.

```
ObjectRepository.vbs
   'Declare DP strings
   Const BrwNm =  "name:=IRCTC Online Passenger Reservation System"
   Const PgNm =  "title:=IRCTC Online Passenger Reservation System"
   Const EdtUserNm =  "name:=userName"
```

```
    Const EdtPassWd =   "name:=password"
    Const BtnLgn =   "name:=Login"

Test Script
    'Declare DP objects
    Set oBrw =   Browser(BrwNm)
    Set oPage =   oBrw.Page(PgNm) oPage.Sync
    oPage.WebEdit(EdtUserNm).Set "User1"
    oPage.WebEdit(EdtPassWd).Set "Pass1"
    oPage.WebButton(BtnLgn).Click
```

Working with Multiple Browsers or Browser Tabs

UFT provides *CreationTime* and *Index* ordinal identifiers to identify the desired browser or browser tab from multiple opened browsers or browser tabs at run-time. The value of the ordinal identifiers can be 0, 1, 2… and so on. The browser which is opened first is assigned a creation time and index value of 0; next opened browser is assigned a value of 1, and so on.

Suppose three browser instances are open on desktop. Assume the application open on these three browser is Expedia.co.in. Now since, the attributes of all these browsers are same, it is difficult to differentiate the browsers on the basis of description properties. To resolve this problem UFT offers ordinal identifiers (creationtime and index) to uniquely identify a browser when multiple browsers with same properties are open. This problem is generally observed when a web application opens multiple browsers with same browser and page attributes.

Working with Multiple Browsers

In this section, we will discuss how to use ordinal identifiers to work on multiple open browsers with same attributes. For easier understanding, we would assume that different applications are open on different browsers.

Note: Here, note that if different applications are open on different browsers, then the browser and page description properties would be different. This can be used to uniquely locate a browser. Ordinal identifiers are used only when all the description properties of the various objects or opened browsers are same, In the example below, we are considering different applications for easier understanding of ordinal identifiers concept.

In the code above, we observe that:

- Browser creationtime and index value is not impacted by user activity of various browsers. Even after doing a 2nd browser refresh on line 22, creationtime and index value of all the browsers remains unchanged. (This is in contrast with previous versions of QTP where index value used to change with user activity on various browsers.)
- Browser creationtime and index values are re-initialized if any browser is closed. Line 36 closes the second browser (amazon.in). Once this browser is closed, any reference to the third browser throws an error 'Object not found'. This is because once a browser is closed, the remaining opened browsers are assigned new creationtime and index values depending upon the sequence in which they were opened. After this initialization, no browser object with creationtime=2 (or index=2) exists.

```
1  'Open expedia site
2  SystemUtil.Run "iexplore.exe", "www.expedia.co.in"
3  Wait 2
4  'Open amazon site
5  SystemUtil.Run "iexplore.exe", "www.amazon.co.in"
6  Wait 2
7  'Open flipkart site
8  SystemUtil.Run "iexplore.exe", "www.flipkart.com"
9  wait 5
10
11 'find which creation time refers to which browser
12 Print (Browser("CreationTime:=0").GetROProperty("url"))
13 Print (Browser("CreationTime:=1").GetROProperty("url"))
14 Print (Browser("CreationTime:=2").GetROProperty("url"))
15
16 'find which index refers to which browser
17 Print (Browser("index:=0").GetROProperty("url"))
18 Print (Browser("index:=1").GetROProperty("url"))
19 Print (Browser("index:=2").GetROProperty("url"))
20
21 'Do some activity on 2nd browser
22 Browser("CreationTime:=1").Refresh
23 wait 2
24
25 'find which creation time refers to which browser
26 Print (Browser("CreationTime:=0").GetROProperty("url"))
27 Print (Browser("CreationTime:=1").GetROProperty("url"))
28 Print (Browser("CreationTime:=2").GetROProperty("url"))
29
30 'find which index refers to which browser
31 Print (Browser("index:=0").GetROProperty("url"))
32 Print (Browser("index:=1").GetROProperty("url"))
33 Print (Browser("index:=2").GetROProperty("url"))
34
35 'Close 2nd browser
36 Browser("CreationTime:=1").close
37 wait 2
38
39 'find which creation time refers to which browser
40 Print (Browser("CreationTime:=0").GetROProperty("url"))
41 Print (Browser("CreationTime:=1").GetROProperty("url"))
42 Print (Browser("CreationTime:=2").GetROProperty("url"))
43
44 'find which index refers to which browser
45 Print (Browser("index:=0").GetROProperty("url"))
46 Print (Browser("index:=1").GetROProperty("url"))
47 Print (Browser("index:=2").GetROProperty("url"))
```

Print Log (lines 11–14):

```
http://www.expedia.co.in
http://www.amazon.in
http://www.flipkart.com
```

Print Log (lines 16–19):

```
http://www.expedia.co.in
http://www.amazon.in
http://www.flipkart.com
```

Print Log (lines 25–28):

```
http://www.expedia.co.in
http://www.amazon.in
http://www.flipkart.com
```

Print Log (lines 30–33):

```
http://www.expedia.co.in
http://www.amazon.in
http://www.flipkart.com
```

Print Log (lines 39–42):

```
http://www.expedia.co.in
http://www.flipkart.com
```

This line throws error

Print Log (lines 44–47):

```
http://www.expedia.co.in
http://www.flipkart.com
```

This line throws error

Figure 27.3 *Working with multiple browsers*

Working with Multiple Browser Tabs

UFT recognizes multiple open browser tabs in the way as it recognizes multiple open browsers. To analyze the behavior of multiple open browser tabs replace code lines 1–9 of Fig. 27.3 with the code as shown in Fig. 27.4.

The output of this code is same as shown in Fig. 27.3.

> **NOTES:** Already open browsers for running tests may result in object identification issues. Test Automation framework is to be designed in a way that it closes all open browsers before starting to execute a test.

```
'Open expedia,amazon and flipkart on different tabs
SystemUtil.Run "iexplore.exe", "www.expedia.co.in"
wait 2
Browser("CreationTime:=0").OpenNewTab
Browser("CreationTime:=1").Navigate("www.amazon.co.in")
wait 2
Browser("CreationTime:=1").OpenNewTab
Browser("CreationTime:=2").Navigate("www.flipkart.com")
wait 5
```

Figure 27.4 *Working with multiple browser tabs*

Writing DP Code Using HTML code

So far we learned writing descriptive code using the object properties as visible in UFT Object Spy window. UFT Object Spy tool captures the properties (or attributes) of the object from GUI and displays them in the Object Spy too. However, Object Spy tool may not show all the properties (or attributes) defined for an object in GUI. The complete list of attributes defined for an object can be viewed in the HTML source code of the objectIn order to find the complete list of properties defined for an object.

In HTML, object properties are referred as object attributes and an object is referred as an element,

How to view source code of an object

Chapter 'Objects' describes in detail how to find out the HTML code of an object using IE, Firefox and Chrome browser.

UFT offers three ways of describing objects in DP so that they can be identified during run-time. It includes—object attributes description, object xpath description and object css path description.

- *Object attributes:* Object attributes such as *html id*, *name*, *className*, etc. can be used to create a unique description of the object.
- *Object XPath:* XPath of the object can be used to uniquely locate the object during run-time.
- *Object CSS path:* CSS path of the object including CSS attributes such as *font*, *style* etc. can be used to create a unique description of the object.

DP using Object Attributes

Object attributes such as *html tag*, name, className, etc. can be used to create a unique description of this object. During test execution UFT uses this description to locate the object in UI.

Example 1: Consider the Flight Reservation application shown in the Fig. 27.5. Write DP code to locate the 'Going to' edit box element using the object HTML attributes.

Assume HTML code for page element is:

```
<title>Travel: Cheap Flights, Hotels, Holidays & Car Rentals | Expedia.
co.in</title>
```

Assume HTML code of the edit box 'Going To' element is as shown below:

```
<input id="uw_flight_destination_input" class="xp-b-clear" type="text"
maxlength="100" notequalmessage="notequalmessage" notequal=
```

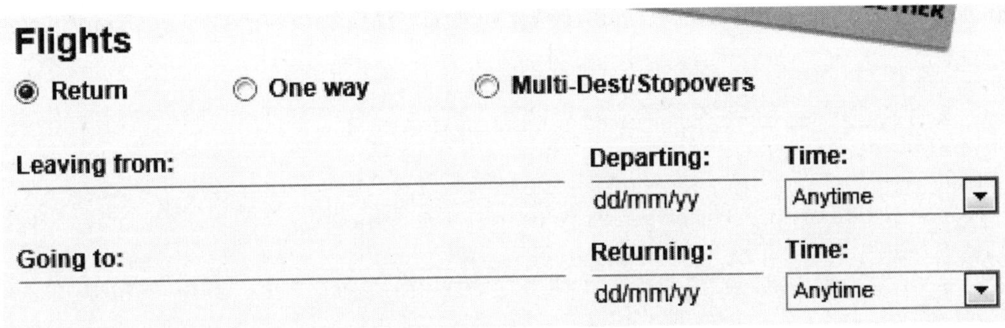

Figure 27.5 *Flight reservation application*

```
"uw_flight_origin_input" requiredmessage="requiredFieldMessa
ge" required="true" value="" autocomplete="off">
```

(a) Let's use attribute *id* to create a unique description of the object. UFT code for entering some text on this edit box is shown below:

```
BrwNm = ".*Expedia\.co\.in"
PgTitle = BrwNm

Set oPg = Browser("name:=" & BrwNm).Page("Title:=" & PgTitle)
oPg.WebEdit("html id:= uw_flight_destination_input").Set "Some
Text"
```

> **NOTES** *id* attribute is referred as 'html id' in UFT. So UFT will be able to recognize the object if DP code is used as `oPg.WebEdit("id:= uw_flight_destination_input").Set` "Some Text"

(b) Let's use attribute *class* to create a unique description of the object. UFT code for entering some text on this edit box is shown below:

```
oPg.WebEdit("class:=xp-b-clear").Set "Some Text2"
```

> **NOTES** 'Class Name' property as displayed in Object Spy is different from the *class* attribute displayed in HTML code. 'Class Name' refers to standard UFT object class name of an object such as WebEdit, Link etc. While *class* is an attribute of an element (or object).

(c) Let's use attributes – *html tag, id, noteequalmessage*, to describe the edit box element. The tag name of an element is represented as node name of the element in HTML code. In the HTML code of the edit box above, the node name is *input*. Hence, *input* is the tag name of this element.

```
oPg.WebEdit("html tag:=input","html id:=uw_flight_destination_inpu
t","notequalmessage:=notequalmessage").Set "Some Text3"
```

Example 2: Consider the HTML code shown below. Write code to locate all the <p> paragraph elements.

```
<html>
   <head>
      <title>Locating Elements</title>
   </head>
   <body>
      <h4>Locating elements of a web page</h4>
      <div class=”parentDivClass”>
            <p class=”p1”>My 1st paragraph.</p>
            <p>My 2nd paragraph.</p>
            <div class=”firstDivChild”>
                  <p>My 3rd paragraph.</p>
            </div>
      </div>
      <p class=”p4”>My 4th paragraph.</p>
   </body>
</html>
```

(a) Write code to access <h4> element.

```
BrwNm = “Locating Elements”
PgTitle = BrwNm

Set oPg = Browser(“name:=” & BrwNm).Page(“Title:=” & PgTitle)
oPg.WebElement(“html tag:=h4”).Highlight
```

(b) Write code to highlight first paragraph element (<p>My 1st paragraph</p>)

```
oPg.WebElement(“html tag:=div”,”class:=parentDivClass”).
WebElement(“html tag:=p”,”index:=0”).Highlight
```

Alternatively,

```
oPg.WebElement(“html tag:=p”,”class:=p1”).Highlight
```

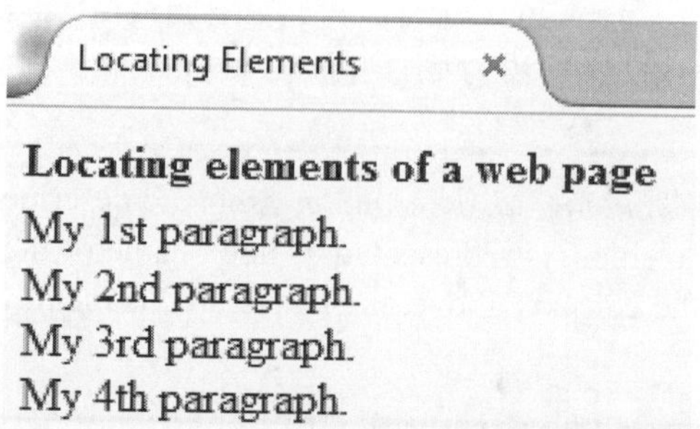

Figure 27.6 *Locating elements HTML page*

Alternatively,

```
oPg.WebElement("html tag:=div","class:=parentDivClass").
WebElement("html tag:=p","class:=p1").Highlight
```

Alternatively,

```
Set oDesc = Description.Create
oDesc("micclass").value = "WebElement"
oDesc("html tag").value = "p"
Set colPElements = oPg.WebElement("html
tag:=div","class:=parentDivClass").ChildObjects(oDesc)
colPElements(0).Highlight
colPElements.Count 'Output:3
```

(c) Write code to highlight second paragraph element

```
oPg.WebElement("html tag:=div","class:=parentDivClass").
WebElement("html tag:=p","index:=1").Highlight
```

Alternatively,

```
colPElements(1).Highlight
```

(d) Write code to highlight third paragraph element

```
oPg.WebElement("html tag:=div","class:=firstDivChild").
WebElement("html tag:=p").Highlight
```

Alternatively,

```
colPElements(2).Highlight
```

(e) Write code to highlight fourth paragraph element

```
oPg.WebElement("html tag:=p","class:=p4").Highlight
```

DP Using XPath

XPath of an element refers to hierarchical position of the element in the node tree. UFT offers the flexibility on identify elements using xpath of an element.

As we observe in the example 2 above, identification of paragraph <p> elements involving nesting of WebElements (finding WebElements of WebElements). This is not a good practice to locate elements. Instead, it is advisable to use XPath of an element to uniquely locate an element. Here, a question you may ask- How to find XPath of an element?

How to Find XPath of An Element

In this section, we will discuss how to use Firefox browser to find XPath of an element. First of all, ensure that Firefox add-on *Firebug* is installed. Once *Firebug* is installed, restart *Firefox* and verify if *Firepath* is installed, If not install *Firepath* as well. *Firepath provides the functionality of Object Spy tool of UFT and Highlight feature of object repository.* Follow the below steps to find the XPath of an element using Firefox browser:

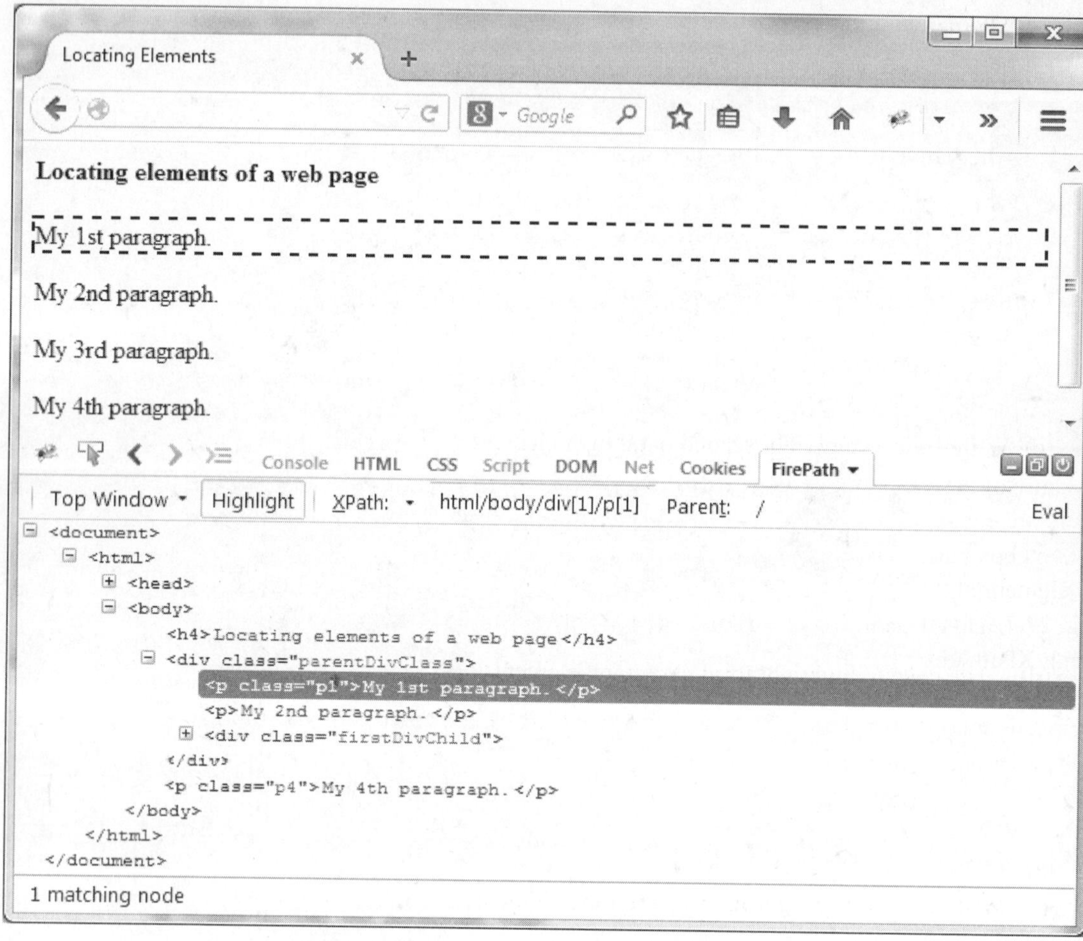

Figure 27.7 *How to find XPath of an element*

1. Open Firefox browser
2. Click on the Firebug button to activate Firebug.
   Firebug frame opens as shown in the Fig. 27.7.
3. On Firebug window, Select tab *Firepath.*
4. Select option XPath XPath: ▾
5. Click on *Highlight* button if it is not already selected. This button highlights the element and elements HTML code whose XPath is calculated in XPath edit box.
6. Click on the inspect button .
7. Point and click the left mouse button on the element whose XPath is to be automatically calculated by *Firepath.*
   Assume the mouse is pointed and clicked on first paragraph element as shown in the Fig. 27.7.
8. Firepath calculates the XPath of the element in the text box as shown in the Fig. 27.7 below.
   XPath: ▾ html/body/div[1]/p[1]

Also, Firepath highlights the element and elements HTML code as shown in the Fig. 27.7 below.

> NOTES
>
> The XPath of an element calculated by *firepath* is not a reliable xPath. This is because:
>
> - Most often *Firepath* maps the entire tree structure while developing XPath as shown in the Fig. 27.7 below. Because of this any insertion or deleting of any element in the tree will change the XPath of the element. Since, we know most of the web pages are under continuous changes; use of this path will require continuous maintenance of this XPath in tests.
> - Most often *Firepath* uses index values of elements to calculate XPath. As we know index values make scripts unstable and prone to failures. Index values should be avoided while creating XPath of an element.
> - Most often *Firepath* uses unnecessary elements for creating element XPath. Unnecessary references to other elements for creating XPath make XPath prone to UI changes.

Because of the above reasons, it is advisable never to use the XPath as calculated by Firepath. Instead users are encouraged to develop a reliable XPath. Users can verify the accuracy of the XPath using the text box where Firepath shows the elements XPath. If the XPath written on the text box matches to an element, then Firepath highlights the element as well as the elements HTML code as shown in the Fig. 27.7. This is similar to the *Highlight* feature of Object repository. Chapter 'Object Identification using XPath' discusses in detail on how to develop reliable and stable XPath.

XPath is a powerful object identification mechanism. If used wisely, it helps create stable test scripts with minimum or no dependency on ordinal identification. Also, if XPath is developed wisely it is less prone to UI changes.

DP Using Object XPath

(a) Write code to access <h4> element using XPath

```
oPg.WebElement("xpath:=//h4").Highlight
```

(b) Write code to highlight first paragraph element (<p>My 1st paragraph</p>)

```
oPg.WebElement("xpath:=//p[@class='p1']").Highlight
```

(c) Write code to highlight second paragraph element

```
oPg.WebElement("xpath:=//p[@class='p1']/following-sibling::p").
Highlight
```

> NOTES
>
> Here note that the above xpath expression avoids any dependency on index values or <div> elements for identifying elements.

(d) Write code to highlight third paragraph element

```
oPg.WebElement("xpath:=//div[@class='firstDivChild']/child::p").
Highlight
```

(e) Write code to highlight fourth paragraph element

```
oPg.WebElement("xpath:=//p[@class='p4']").Highlight
```

DP Using CSS Path

Cascading Style Sheets (CSS) is a style sheet language used for describing the look and formatting of a document.

UFT offers the feature to identify GUI objects using CSS path of an element (object).

How to Find CSS Path of an Element

Firepath can be used to find CSS path of an element as well. In order to find the CSS path of an element, select option CSS CSS: (X) ▾ on *Firepath* window. Repeat the steps as discussed in the section 'How to find XPath of an element' above to find CSS path of element.

For the HTML code discussed above, the CSS path 'My 1st Paragraph.' element as developed by Firepath window is 

,

Note: However, as discusses above for XPath, the CSS path so created by Firepath is not the most reliable CSS Path. So automation developers are advised to develop a custom reliable CSS path which uniquely locates the element and is less prone to UI changes. Chapter 'Object Identification using CSS' discusses in detail how to develop a reliable CSS path.

DP Using Object CSS Path

(a) Write code to access <h4> element using XPath

```
oPg.WebElement("css:=h4").Highlight
```

(b) Write code to highlight first paragraph element (<p>My 1st paragraph</p>)

```
oPg.WebElement("css:=p.p1").Highlight
```

(c) Write code to highlight second paragraph element

```
oPg.WebElement("css:=div.parentDivClass>p:nth-child(2)").High-
light
```

(d) Write code to highlight third paragraph element

```
oPg.WebElement("css:=div.firstDivChild>p").Highlight
```

(e) Write code to highlight fourth paragraph element

```
oPg.WebElement("css:=p.p4").Highlight
```

DP Using Object Native Properties

In rare scenarios, it might be possible that the identification properties (as visible in Object Spy) are not sufficient to uniquely identify the object in UI. In such scenarios, native properties of the object can be used to uniquely locate the object in UI.

UFT provides `attribute/*` notation to access custom native properties of web-based objects or events associated with Web-based objects. UFT allows using these native properties or events to identify objects by adding the notation to the object's description properties using the Object Identification Dialog Box, or by using programmatic descriptions.

Example 1: Consider the HTML code of the 'Going To' edit box of Fig. 27.5. Write code set the value of this edit box.

```
<input id="uw_flight_destination_input" class="xp-b-clear"
type="text" maxlength="100" notequalmessage="notequalmessage"
notequal="uw_flight_origin_input" requiredmessage="requiredFieldMessa
ge" required="true" value="" autocomplete="off"/>
```

The HTML code above contains custom attributes such as *noteuqalmessage*, *requiredFieldMessage*, *notequal*, *requiremessage*, etc. These custom attributes are not supported by UFT by default. This can be verified by viewing the list of description properties supported by UFT for WebEdit class object in Object Identification dialog box. Since, UFT does not support these attributes; UFT does not learn these attributes (object description properties) either in Object Spy or Object repository. UFT provides the flexibility to the automation developers to use these custom attributes to locate objects. Code below shows how to locate object using native attribute *requiredFieldMessage* using descriptive programming.

```
Set oPg = Browser("Google").Page("Travel: Cheap Flights,")
```

oPg.WebEdit("attribute/requiredMessage:=requiredFieldMessage").**Set** "Delhi"

Most often we observe that one property is not sufficient enough to uniquely locate the object. In such scenarios, multiple object custom attributes can be used to locate the object in UI. Code below shows how to locate the 'Going To' edit box object using two custom properties *requiredFieldMessage* and *notequalmessage*.

```
oPg.WebEdit("attribute/requiredMessage:=requiredFieldMessage", "attri-
bute/notequalmessage:=notequalmessage").Set "Delhi"
```

Also, it may happen that the object has limited custom attributes which may not be sufficient to uniquely identify the object in UI. In such cases, object identification attributes can be used along with its native attributes to uniquely locate the object. Code below shows how to locate the 'Going To' edit box object using one identification attribute *html id* and one custom attribute *requiredFieldMessage*

```
oPg.WebEdit("html id:= uw_flight_destination_input", "attribute/required
Message:=requiredFieldMessage" ).Set "Delhi"
```

Example 2: Suppose a web page has an object with an onclick event attached to it as mentioned below:

```
"alert('OnClick event for edit.');"
```

Write code to identify this object.

This object can be identified by adding *attribute/onclick* notation to the objects programmatic description properties as shown below:

```
Browser("B").Page("P").WebEdit("attribute/onclick:=alert\('OnClick
event for edit\.'\);").Set "Text"
```

Object Type Casting

In object type casting one object reference can be type cast into another object reference. Object casting is essentially useful when the UI object is a custom object and UFT fails to map the object to a standard UFT class object. That's is, UFT recognizes the object as WebElement (for web applications), WinObject (for windows apps), etc.UFT does not provides a direct method to maximize or minimize browser window, This can be problematic when the test executions happen in lab machines and there is a requirement is to monitor the execution for debugging some issue.

In this section, we will discuss how to type cast a Browser object to Windows object to maximize a browser window.

```
'Get window handle
hwnd = Browser("B").Object.HWND
Print hwnd           'Output: 264062
window("hwnd:=" & hwnd).Maximize
```

Microsoft Windows operating environment identifies each form in an application by assigning it a handle, or hWnd . The hWnd property is used with Windows API calls. hWnd is a dynamic value. hWnd should be used carefully as its value can change while a program is running.

Stale Object

Certain times it is observed that UFT abruptly stops recognizing the web page objects when test execution is in progress. Though the object exists on the page but UFT still is not able to identify it. This generally happens when the web page gets refreshed for some reason.

Let's consider an example of a web page as shown in the Fig. 27.8. This web page contains refine search options to search the product by specific brands. Baby age render etc. one user select a refine search option say 'Samsung' , the page refreshes to load the new search results, The side bar refine search options as is after page refresh to allow users to select more refine options.

Suppose, a UFT test is written to refine search by 'Samsung' and 'Fisher-Mobile'. While executing the test, we will observe that after selecting refine search option 'Samsung', the page refreshes and thereafter UFT fails to recognize 'Fisher-Mobile' checkbox object. Though this object exists on the page but still UFT throws an object not found error.

Now let's analyze why UFT throws an 'object not found' error though the object exists on the page. When page refresh occurs application re-creates new objects with same attributes of the older objects, For example, here after page refresh, application recreates 'Fisher-Mobile' checkbox object with the identical attributes of 'Fisher-Mobile' object before page refresh. Since the reference of these objects (objects before page refresh) is lost, these objects are called *stale objects*.

Figure 27.8 *Web page with refine search options that refresh the page*

Whenever UFT interacts with a page object for first time, it caches the page objects and maps it to a Run-time object. This caching is done to improve object identification process. But when the application state changes because of page refresh (or page change), these object references are no more valid (as application has already created new objects with identical attributes). Since, UFT uses cache to identify test objects usng the invalid references of cache; it fails to identify the object. UFT has provided *RefreshObject* method to re-identify the stale object,

Listed below are two major reasons because of which an object can become a stale object for UFT:

- Object deletion
- Object is no more attached to the DOM

Object Deletion

The most common cause of UFT referring a stale object are scenarios where a JS library has deleted an object and replaced it with another object with the same ID or attributes. In this case, although the replacement objects may look identical they are different.

Object is no more attached to the DOM

A common technique used for simulating a tabbed UI in a web app is to implement DIVs for each tab, but only attach one at a time and store the rest in variables. In this case, objects of the specific tab are associated with DOM when user selects the specific tab. Suppose automation developer write UFT code to work on Tab 1 , then Tab 2 and then again on Tab 1. In this case, the UFT code may throw 'object not found' error when it interacts again with Tab 1. This is because the objects for Tab 1 which UFT has in cache lost its reference when the objects were removed from DOM because of user navigation to Tab 2. The objects that exist on Tab 1 when user navigates back to this tab are new objects whose reference does not exists in cache.

Tips for Using DP

- **Adhere to DP Syntax:** The syntax for using DP is: `Object(PropertyName:=PropertyValue)`.
  Here, not that there is no space before or after ':='. It is recommended to not use any spaces before or after ':=' as this may result in object identification issues.

```
' sets edit box value to aaa
Browser("P").Page("P").WebEdit("name:=q").Set "aaa"
' throws error
Browser("P").Page("P").WebEdit("name :=q").Set "aaa"
' sets edit box value to aaa
Browser("P").Page("P").WebEdit("name:= q").Set "aaa"
```

- **Appropriate description properties:** The description properties defined for identifying an object should be minimum, relevant and sufficient enough to uniquely describe (or locate) the object. Use of unnecessary description properties is to be avoided. Consider the description property of an edit box as shown below:

```
Set oDesc = Description.Create
oDesc("micclass").Value = "WebEdit"
oDesc("html tag").Value = "input"
oDesc("name").Value = "q"
oDesc("html id").Value = "searchBoxId"
oDesc("readonly").Value = 0
```

  → The above description describes a WebEdit object. Since this is a standard UFT WebEdit class object, UFT assumes the *micclass* value to be WebEdit and *html tag* to be *input*. There is no need to define these properties.

> NOTES: Properties such as *name, defaultvalue, innertext,* etc. to be used only if either *html id* has not been defined or the application developer has violated the HTML standards and created multiple objects with same *html id.*

  → Property *html id* is supposed to be unique for all objects within a page document. This attribute alone is sufficient to uniquely locate the object. Hence, there is no need to use *name* property.
  → Property *readonly* has no significance here in locating this object. So this property should be removed from description object.

- **Use *micclass* instead of *Class Name:*** UFT object displays the standard object class name as I'*Class Name*' in object spy but refers this as ,'*micclass*'. Use of different names in object spy and DP can create confusion. Users are to use term 'micclass' in DP for defining object standard class.

- **Object properties are considered regular expressions by default:** UFT treats the object property values as regular expression by default. If certain property values uses regular expression characters say '*' (as in oDesc("name "),value = "*expedia "), then in order to instruct UFT to treat '*' as string, escape character '\' is to be used before '*'. So actual description definition should look like: oDesc("name ").value= "*expedia ".

> NOTES: Alternatively, use below code to turn off regular expression recognition for a specific description property in a description object:

```
oDesc("name ").RegularExpression = False
```

- **Object properties are case sensitive:** Object property values are considered case sensitive if regular expression is turned off foe the specific decription property.

  For example, when regular expression is turned on, both the code statements below refer to object with property value as 'expedia'.

```
oDesc("name ").value= "Expedia"   Or,
oDesc("name ").value= "EXPEDIA"
```

However, if regular expression is turned off for a description property, then the property value is treated as is. For example, the below code defines an object whose *name* property value is 'Expedia' (case-sensitive).

```
oDesc("name ").RegularExpression = False
oDesc("name ").value= "Expedia"
```

FUNCTION TO CLOSE ALL OPENED BROWSERS EXCEPT THE ONE WHICH WAS OPENED FIRST

During test execution, sometimes it can happen that some scripts have opened new pop-up application browsers but failed thereafter. It results in more than one browser opened on desktop, which can cause run-time object identification issues. If the two browsers are in sync with each other, then UFT will not be able to work on the first browser unless the second browser is closed. Function *fnCloseAllBrowsersE1* closes all browsers except the one which was opened first or except the home page of the application.

Usage

```
Call fnCloseAllBrowsersE1

Public Function fnCloseAllBrowsersE1()
   On Error Resume Next
```

```
    Set oDesc =  Description.Create()
    oDesc("micClass").Value =  "Browser"
    'Retrieve all browser objects
    Set oBrowsers =  Desktop.ChildObjects(oDesc)
    sBrowserCnt =  oBrowsers.Count

    For nCntr =  sBrowserCnt-1 to 1 step -1
       Browser("CreationTime:=" & nCntr).Close
    Next
    If Err.Number =  0     Then
       fnCloseAllBrowsersE1="0"  'All Browsers Closed Successfully
    End If
    If Err.Number <>0     Then
       fnCloseAllBrowsersE1=  Err.Description      'Error description
    End If
End Function
```

ADVANTAGES OF DESCRIPTIVE PROGRAMMING

Following are the advantages of DP:

- **Test scripts can be designed even if GUI is not ready/stable:** Automation developers can code the test case flow based on knowledge (object properties values) shared by application developers.
- **Dynamic objects:** OR-based approach fails to recognize objects whose properties change dynamically during run-time. Such dynamic objects can be easily recognized using DP approach. For example, link objects present in Fig. 27.9.
- **OR size:** Test script execution can go slow if the OR size is huge. Wise use of DP can help keep OR to an acceptable size.

DISADVANTAGES OF DESCRIPTIVE PROGRAMMING

Following are the disadvantages of DP:

- **Code readability:** Since the entire required object properties are coded in the test script itself, it makes the code lengthy and less readable.
- **Development cost:** High development cost as automation developer first needs to identify the minimum properties required to identify an object before coding it in the test script. Test script needs to be executed again and again to test object identification. In case of OR-based approach, using the button *Highlight in Application* one can easily check whether object will be identified during run-time or not.
- **Maintenance cost:** If object property of browser changes, then same needs to be changed in the multiple places wherever it is used in the test script. This increases the change identification and change implementation cost manifold. In case of OR approach, only one change in object repository needs to be done.

Booked Ticket History

S#	Transaction ID	PNR Number	From	To	Resv Amount
1	T15664098	P22659593678	NDLS	HYD	976.0
2	T15664001	P28764988097	SCB	PUNE	889.0
3	T15234578	P75890589095	MUM	CHE	989.0

Cancelled Ticket History

S#	Transaction ID	PNR Number	From	To	Refund Amount
1	T15676589	P22659579878	HYD	MAS	976.0
2	T15664551	P67849880973	HRY	PUNE	889.0
3	T15234898	P75856890954	CHE	NDLS	989.0

Figure 27.9 *Web page with dynamic link objects*

A Myth About DP

A common myth about Descriptive Programming is if a test scenario is not automatable using OR approach then it cannot be automated using DP approach as well. This is a wrong assumption. The actual fact is if UFT is not able to recognize an object (using object spy) inspite of all the add-ins loaded, then neither OR nor DP approach will be able to recognize the objects.

DP offers lot of flexibility to automation developers to help simulate user actions on objects which otherwise is not possible using OR approach. This is especially true in case of dynamic objects. Let's consider the below example to understand how DP can be used to work on dynamic objects which is otherwise not possible using OR approach.

Suppose, in a web application, the booked ticket history page displays details of booked and can celled tickets as shown in the Fig. 27.9. The page displays list of last 10 booked and last 10 cancelled tickets in last 30 days. However, if in last 30 days a user has booked, say, only 3 tickets, then only three ticket details will be displayed. It implies that the number of transaction ids displayed on the page is dynamic in nature and would vary from one run to another. Assume, the requirement is to identify all *transaction id* links displayed on the page for booked tickets.

Below are the two reasons why this scenario is not feasible to automate using OR approach only:

- Number of 'Transaction ID' links displayed on the page varies from time to time. Suppose at test design time only two links exist which were added to OR, But at run-time there are three links. This means the test code (based on OR approach only) will never know that third link exists. In this case, it is never possible to know at test design time how many links will exist at run-time. So, it is not possible to automate this scenario using OR approach only.
- The 'Transaction ID' links refer to the actual booked ticket 'transaction ids'. Suppose at design time there were 15 tickets booked which got added to OR. Assume during the time gap between test design and test run time, 20 more tickets got booked. Now during test run, the application will display last 10 booked tickets transaction ids. Since, these link objects were never added

```
'Open ticket history page
Browser("PlanTravel").Page("PlanTravel").Link("TicketHistory").Click

'Locate transaction ids of all booked tickets
Set oDescTranIds = Description.Create
oDescTranIds("micclass").Value = "Link"
oDescTranIds("name").value = "T.*"

Set oTable = Browser("PlanTravel").Page("PlanTravel").WebTable("BookedTicketHistory")
Set colTranIds = oTable.ChildObjects(oDescTranIds)
For iterator = 0 To colTranIds.count-1 Step 1
    Print colTranIds(iterator).getROProperty("name")
Next
```

Figure 27.10 *DP code to locate dynamic link obejcts*

to OR and the ones added are not displayed on GUI, UFT tests will fail with 'object not found;' error. Since, these links are dynamic objects, it is not possible to automate this scenario by adding these link objects to OR.

Now let's see how this scenario can be automated using DP approach. DP allows locating all the transaction id links during run-time. Using DP, a test code can be written that dynamically looks for all 'transaction id' link objects of booked ticket history table. Figure 27.10 .below shows the DP code to locate these dynamic object.

Fig. 27.11 below.shows the output of the code of Fig. 27.10.

COMPARISON OF OR AND DP APPROACHES

Implementation of a completely descriptive code defeats the benefits gained from the shared object repository. Even a single update in the object property requires multiple changes in the test

Script. The situation becomes worse when it involves multiple changes in multiple test scripts. With shared OR, the same can be done within few minutes. Even implementation of VBScript-based descriptive OR file is difficult to develop and maintain as com- pared to shared OR. In case object is not available in GUI, but its properties are known, then it is better to 'design a new test object' rather than designing a VBS OR file or a keyword OR file. In OR approach, it is easy to find whether the description used for the object uniquely locates the object using *Highlight* feature of UFT. In DP, it's very difficult to find whether the defined description is sufficient to uniquely locate the object unless the test code is executed and UFT throws an error Automation developers have to execute the code

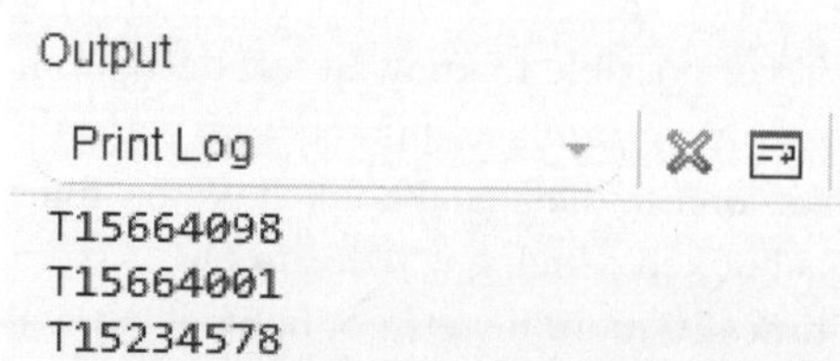

Figure 27.11 *Output of Figure 14.7 code*

Table 27.1 Comparison between OR and DP approaches

	OR Approach	DP Approach
GUI Not Ready	Test script can be written	Test scripts can be written
Dynamic Objects	Difficult or not possible to handle	Can be easily handled
Object Highlight feature	Avaliable	Not Available
Script Development Cost	Low	High
Script Maintenance Cost	Low	High

every time they customize the object description. This unnecessarily consumes a lot of time. Although, shared object repository has lot of benefits, it has its limitations too. OR approach is not able to uniquely locate all dynamic objects. Moreover, there are certain scenarios, where it is more beneficial to use DP approach rather than using OR approach such as selecting all the checkboxes visible on the screen (the count and property values of checkboxes can vary during run-time). In this case, an automation developer is always unsure how many checkboxes will appear on the screen during run-time and which checkboxes will be visible. Using OR approach, the automation developer has to check for the existence of each checkbox before selecting one. The larger the number of checkboxes, the more will be the lines of code. This same scenario can be easily automated by DP approach. Using DP, all the checkboxes (child objects) that exist on the page at run-time can be found and the turned ON. The best way to write a test script is to use a combination of OR and DP approaches. Utilizing the benefits of both the approaches in the test script makes it easier to develop and maintain the test scripts. Moreover, the scripts developed are robust (Table 27.1).

QUICK TIPS

- ✓ Creation time is a more reliable ordinal identifier for browsers than index.
- ✓ Open URL property of the browsers to be used to differentiate between the application and the application pop-up browsers.
- ✓ DP to be used when object cannot be identified using OR approach.
- ✓ A combination of OR and DP approaches to be used to develop robust and easily maintain- able test scripts.

PRACTICAL QUESTIONS

1. What is the use of descriptive programming test automation?
2. What are the advantages and disadvantages of DP?
3. Why a complete descriptive code needs to be avoided?
4. Write the descriptive code to select all the checkboxes present on a page.
5. Write the descriptive code to click on the first link object present on the WebTable shown in Fig. 27.2.

Chapter 28

Synchronization

Synchronization points are used in UFT to keep the code in sync with the application under test. UFT executes the code statements in a fraction of second while it may take more than a second or a minute for the application to respond. Synchronization code is used in these scenarios to pause UFT execution till the application under test (AUT) responds. Synchronization between the code and the application is required because application response time is not always the same. Depending on server load, database volume, network speed, and code performance the application response varies from time to time. Synchronization code helps halt UFT execution only until the object is not loaded into the application. As soon as the object is properly loaded, UFT execution starts.

Let's us assume that IRCTC page needs to be automated. After log on to a user account, the user needs to fill the reservation details such as 'station from' and 'station to' fields. Line 1 code clicks on the login button, and line 2 code sets the 'From Station' edit box value to 'New Delhi.'

```
1.Browser("IRCTC_Login").Page("IRCTC_Login").WebButton("Login").
  Click
2.Browser("BookTckt").Page("BookTckt").WebEdit("FromStn").Set
  "NewDelhi"
```

After multiple execution of the above code, it is observed that code execution fails generally at Step 2. This happens because application takes time to load browser 'BookTckt.' While the application is busy loading AUT objects, UFT starts executing Step 2. Since the browser objects have not loaded successfully yet, UFT is not able to find the object and hence reports an error. To avoid this, 'Sync' method is used to wait till the browser loads properly.

Therefore, the new code becomes:

```
1.Browser("IRCTC_Login").Page("IRCTC_Login").WebButton("Login").
  Click
2.Browser("BookTckt").Page("BookTckt").Sync
3.Browser("BookTckt").Page("BookTckt").WebEdit("FromStn").Set "NewDelhi"
```

> **NOTES:** Sync on page checks whether the page has loaded properly. It may happen sometimes that though the page has loaded properly, the objects present in the page such as radio buttons, list box, and web tables have still not loaded. This is generally observed in pages that have objects whose properties change dynamically.

Synchronization points need to be used in the following cases:

1. Browser navigation path changes
2. Page properties changes

For example, suppose that there are two web lists – WebList 'A' and WebList 'B' – and the items of list 'B' change dynamically depending on the items selected in list 'A.' In this case, properties of the page change on change of the item selected in 'WebList A'. Therefore, a 'Sync' statement is required between the code statements of 'WebList A' and 'WebList B'.

SYNCHRONIZATION METHODS

There are various methods provided by QuickTest to keep the UFT code in sync with the application. While *Sync* method helps to keep the running code in sync with the page object, synchronization methods such as *WaitProperty* or *CheckProperty* help to keep the UFT code in sync with the objects within the page.

Sync

Sync method halts code execution till the browser completes navigation or a default timeout occurs. This method is only applicable to browser or page object. The default object synchronization timeout in UFT is 20 s. If even after 20 s the object is not found, then UFT throws an error. The advantage of Sync method is that it only halts the code execution till the object is not found or the timeout occurs. For example, if an object is found after 10 s during first run, then UFT will start code execution after 10 s. Suppose that the next time if the object is found after 15 s, then UFT will start code execution after 15 s.

```
Syntax : Object.Sync
```

Example:

```
Browser("IRCTC_Login").Sync Browser("BookTckt").Page("BookTckt").Sync
```

> **NOTES:** The default object synchronization timeout is defined in the Run settings. To view or change the object synchronization timeout, navigate File → Test Settings… → Run (tab) → *Object Synchronization timeout*

Object synchronization timeout time can also be specified programmatically. The following code shows how to set or change the default object synchronization timeout time using UFT code.

```
Setting("WebTimeOut") = ValueInMilliSeconds
```

Wait

Wait method halts code execution for the specified period of time. This method is usually used when there is no way of knowing whether the object has loaded successfully or not. This can happen in situations when the object is either not recognized by UFT or the object itself does not exist. For example, suppose that a button on application opens an MS Excel file. Now, before reading data from the Excel file, the Excel application object must be successfully loaded. The load time of the Excel object can vary from time to time depending on the data size of the Excel file. In this situation, the maximum time for excel to load can be analyzed. Thereafter, Wait method can be used to pause UFT code execution for the specified period of time. Another example can be when we are working on the 'PuTTY' window without TE addin. The PuTTY window is a text-based window. Suppose that we need to execute a batch or a job on the PuTTY window and wait till the batch execution is complete before working on the application under test again. Since PuTTY window is a text-based window with no objects, it is difficult to find when will the batch or the job execution be over. In these circumstances, the maximum time required for the batch/job execution is found out. Thereafter, the Wait statement is used to halt UFT code execution till that time interval.

```
Syntax : Wait Seconds,[optional]milli seconds
```

Example: Halt UFT code execution for 5 s.

```
Wait 5
```

WaitProperty

WaitProperty method halts code execution till the object achieves the specified property value or the timeout occurs. Sync method helps synchronize UFT code with the browser and page object while the WaitProperty method helps synchronize UFT code with the objects within the page. This method is generally used in situations when the browser loads successfully but the page objects such as dynamic WebList or WebTable take more time to load. In these circumstances, UFT code fails even if Sync method is used on the page object. This happens because though page object has loaded successfully but the objects within the page are still getting loaded. Therefore, though a Sync method on page executes successfully. When UFT tries to access the object, it is not found as the object has not loaded yet. Therefore, to synchronize UFT directly with the objects within the page WaitProperty method is used. UFT halts the code execution till the specified object achieves the desired value or the timeout occurs.

```
Syntax : object.WaitProperty(PropertyName, PropertyValue, [optional]
TimeOut)
```

Example 1: Write UFT code to halt UFT execution till 'Login' button gets enabled or timeout of 5 s is reached.

```
Browser("IRCTC_Login").Page("IRCTC_Login").WebButton("Login")
    .WaitProperty("Enabled",True,5000)
```

Example 2: Write UFT code to pause UFT execution till 'Login' button gets enabled or default timeout is reached.

```
Browser("IRCTC_Login").Page("IRCTC_Login").WebButton("Login")
    .WaitProperty("Enabled",True)
```

Example 3: Write code to pause UFT execution till the 'value' property of Google 'Advance Search' but- ton matches to the string 'Search.' The UFT pause should timeout after the object is found or the default timeout occurs, whichever occurs first.

```
Set  Object  =  Browser("AdvSrch").Page("AdvSrch").WebButton("AdvSrch")
Print Object.WaitProperty("value", micRegExpMatch(".*Search.*"))
```

Exist

Exist method verifies whether specified object exists in the application under test or not. UFT waits for the object to appear on the screen for the specified period of time. If even after the specified period of time the object is not found, then the timeout occurs and UFT starts executing the next line of code.

```
Syntax : Object.Exist [optional]TimeOut
```

Example:

```
'Verifies whether table List of Tickets is present in AUT or not for
maximum of 5 s
bExist = Browser("BckdTckt").Page("BckdTckt").WebTable("ListOfTckts").
Exist(5)
'Verifies whether table List of Tickets is present in AUT or not till the
default timeout occurs.
bExist = Browser("BckdTckt").Page("BckdTckt").WebTable("ListOfTckts").
Exist
```

> NOTES: In case of Wait code execution halts for the specified period of time while in case of Sync, WaitProperty, and Exist if UFT finds the specified object before the specified timeout, then the code execution resumes before the timeout.

BROWSER NATIVE SYNCHRONIZATION METHODS

Apart from the above synchronization methods provided by UFT, there are also some properties provided by HTML document to identify the loading state of the browser. Described below are some of the native properties to help achieve browser synchronization using UFT code.

ReadyState

This property returns the loading status of the browser. It returns one of the four values – 1,2, 3 or 4

Return Value	Description
1	(uninitialized) HTML document has not started loading yet.
2	(loading) HTML document is busy loading.
3	(interactive) HTML document has loaded enough and user can interact with it.
4	(Fully loaded) HTML document has fully loaded with all the objects of the HTML document.

Note: The above return values for different states hold good, if application developers have adhered to the W3C HTML standards.

Busy

This property returns whether the HTML document is still busy loading document objects. It returns *True*, if browser is busy loading; and returns *False* if browser is not busy.

Example : Write code to find browser state when browser is busy loading.

```
'do a browser refresh
1. Browser("CreationTime:=0").Refresh

'find browser state when browser is busy loading
2. Print Browser("CreationTime:=0").Object.ReadyState      'Output:1
3. Print Browser("CreationTime:=0").Object.Busy            'Output:True
4. wait 5
'find browser state when browser has finished loading
5. Print Browser("CreationTime:=0").Object.ReadyState      'Output:4
6. Print Browser("CreationTime:=0").Object.Busy            'Output:False
```

> **NOTES**
> If Browser("name:=Google").Object.ReadyState or Browser("Google").Object.readyState code is used then UFT blocks the code execution till browser has loaded. In this case, we will observe that code execution halts for a moment while executing code line 2. The output of this code line will be '4' (as browser has loaded). Here it is assumed that OR defines the *name* attribute of the browser. If only creationtime property is defined in OR (no description property or visual identifier); then the output of the above code using OR will be same as discussed in the descriptive code above.

DEFINING DEFAULT TIMEOUT TIME

The following steps show how to view or change default object synchronization timeout time.

1. Navigate *File → Test Setttings...*
2. Click on Run tab.
3. Specify the Object Synchronization timeout as shown in Fig. 28.1 as per requirement.

QUICK TIPS

- ✓ Synchronization points are used in UFT code to keep code execution in sync with the application response time.
- ✓ Sync method halts code execution till the browser completes navigation or a default timeout occurs.
- ✓ Wait method halts code execution for the specified period of time.
- ✓ WaitProperty method halts code execution till the object achieves the specified property value or the timeout occurs.
- ✓ Exist method verifies whether specified object exists in the application under test or not.

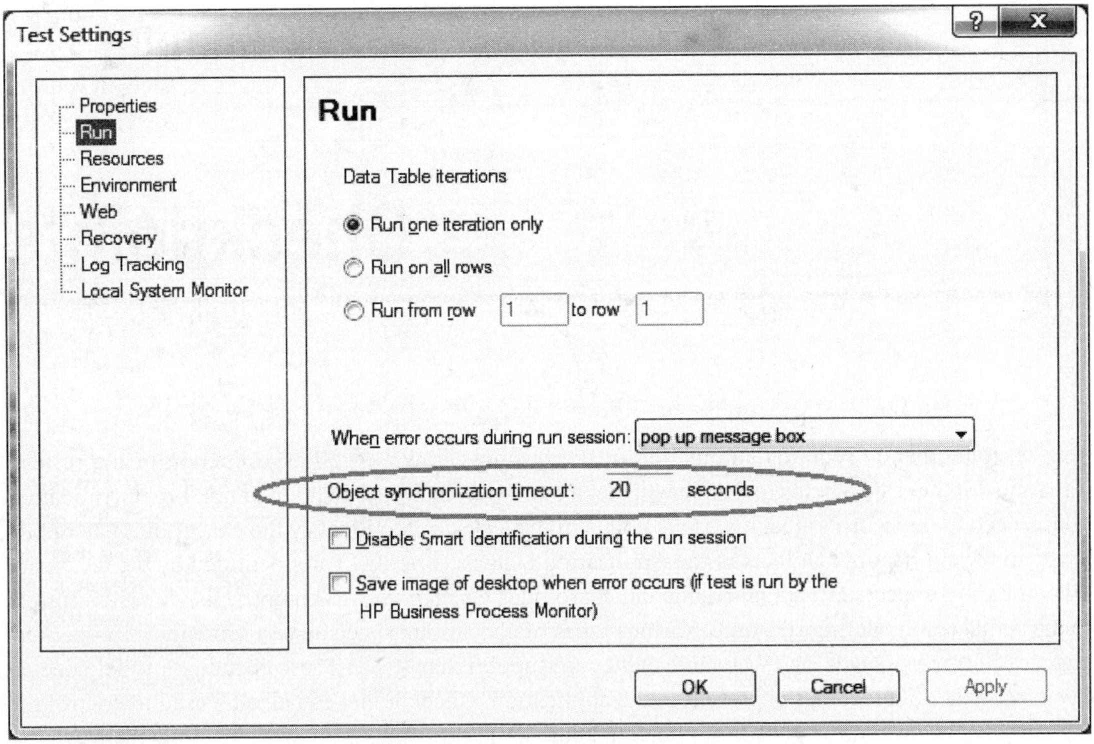

Figure 28.1 *Setting synchronization timeout*

PRACTICAL QUESTIONS

1. What is the use of synchronization points in test automation?
2. What is the difference between 'sync' and 'wait' statements?
3. What is the difference between 'wait' and 'waitproperty' statements?
4. What is the difference between 'sync' and 'waitproperty' statements?
5. Write one real-time scenario where:
   (a) Sync statement is necessary to use.
   (b) Wait statement is necessary to use.
   (c) WaitProperty statement is necessary to use.
   (d) Exist statement is necessary to use.

Chapter 29

Checkpoints

Test case automation requires automation of the business flow as well as validation of the results. Validation of the results helps to decide whether a bug exists in the application or not. Proper validation points need to be incorporated at various points in the test script to identify the exact point where bug exists in the application. Defects in the Application Under Test (AUT) are identified by the test script by comparing expected to actual results. UFT provides *Checkpoints* to compare the expected results to the actual results during run-time. Various types of checkpoints such as verifying object properties, page text, error messages, and web table values are supported by UFT. These check-points help decide the exact type of defect that is present in the application. Checkpoints can also be used to control the logical flow of the code as per the application behavior at run-time.

CHECKPOINT

A checkpoint or verification point is used to verify the actual run-time results against the expected results. It helps decide the pass/fail status of the test case being executed. Checkpoints can also be used as decision points to decide the logical flow of the code. There are two ways to incorporate checkpoints in the test scripts.

- UFT inbuilt checkpoints
- Coded checkpoints

UFT Inbuilt checkpoints are provided by the UFT tool. These checkpoints can easily be inserted into the test scripts. These can be used to find the exact point of deviation in the test script by comparing the actual run-time values with the expected values. The major disadvantage with these checkpoints is that most of the UFT inbuilt checkpoints can be incorporated into the test script using record/ playback technique only. Since record/playback technique is not good for test automation, insertion of even a single line of built-in checkpoints makes the complete test script vulnerable to script failures. To keep the scripts free from the record/playback technique, it is better to use *Coded* Checkpoints. Coded checkpoints are programmatically written and implement the same functionality as inbuilt checkpoints. These also provide more flexibility to the user as compared to the built-in checkpoints. Since coded checkpoints are programmatically written they make the code free from record/playback disadvantages.

Reusable Checkpoints

UFT enables automation developers to reuse the existing checkpoints. For example, a checkpoint created to check whether the *name* property of a checkbox is *input* can be reused to verify whether the edit box *name* attribute value is *input* or not as well. Listed below are some example scenarios where an existing checkpoint can be reused:

- Verifying whether logo is being displayed on all application pages.
- Verifying whether the header and footer links are being displayed on desired multiple pages.
- Verifying whether various checkboxes on different pages are selected when page loads.

Checkpoint Insertion Modes

UFT provides two ways (or modes) to insert checkpoints in tests—*Simple Mode* and *Advanced Mode*.

Simple Mode

Simple Mode enables users to check a basic set of properties and values. This type of checkpoint is visible and editable in both UFT and ALM.

Advanced Mode

Advanced Mode enables users to view basic as well as advanced checkpoint properties. The adanced checkpoint properties are visible in UFT but not in ALM. If a user views a checkpoint containing advanced properties in ALM, a disclaimer opens indicating that some properties are checked but are not shown.

UFT Inbuilt Checkpoints

UFT supports various types of checkpoints to help identify the exact cause and nature of deviation. Table 29.1 shows the various types of checkpoints provided by UFT to verify the test results of a web application.

Limitations of UFT Checkpoints

- All of the checkpoints except XML,database and File checkpoint can only be added in record mode.
- Expected value of checkpoint cannot be changed through code.

NOTES

DataTable can be used to parameterize the hard-coded data of recorded checkpoints.

Coded Checkpoints

Coded checkpoints are an alternative to UFT inbuilt checkpoints. In coded checkpoint, we write VBScript code to compare the expected and the actual results. Coded checkpoints are more flexible in nature and help validate complex test scenarios.

Table 29.1 UFT checkpoints

Checkpoint Type	Description	Example of Use
Standard Checkpoint	Checks properties of objects	Check whether or not the checkbox is selected
Table Checkpoint	Validates data present on the application screen with predefined values (This checkpoint type is inserted by selecting the Standard Checkpoint option and then selecting to check any table object)	Check that the table header has correct names
Page Checkpoint	Validates page properties such as number of links and page load time (This checkpoint type is inserted by selecting the Standard Checkpoint option and then selecting to check a Web Page object)	Check if web page contains broken links
Image Checkpoint	Compares image properties such as source file location, width, and height (This checkpoint type is inserted by selecting the Standard Checkpoint option and then selecting to check a Web Image object)	Check that image source file is always the same on the screen
Bitmap Checkpoint	Compares previous captured bitmap image with run-time bitmap image on the screen pixel by pixel	Check that an image is properly displayed on the screen
Text Checkpoint	Validates that an expected string is placed at the expected place on the screen/page	Check whether or not 'on' is displayed on the screen between text 'Book' and 'UFT'
Text Area Checkpoint	Validates that an expected string is placed at the expected place on the screen within a predefined area of the screen/page	Check particular area of application always displays the specified text
Database Checkpoint	Validates the specified contents of AUT database	Check whether or not the amount has been deducted from the account after the transfer of funds
Accessibility Checkpoint	Checks the web page for World Wide Web Consortium (W3C) Web Content Accessibility Guidelines compliance	Check if image on the web page have ALT properties as required by W3C guidelines
XML Checkpoint (From Application)	Checks the content of XML document in Web pages and frames	Check tag values
XML Checkpoint (From Resource)	Checks the data content of .xml documents in ,xml files	Check tag values
File Checkpoint	Checks the text in a dynamically generated (or accessed) file	Verify correct text is displayed on specific lines in on specific pages in a dynamically generated pdf file

REGULAR EXPRESSIONS IN CODED CHECKPOINTS

Payment Details	
Payment Option	ICICI
Ticket Charge	Rs 587.00
Internet Service Charge	Rs 20.00
Total	Rs 607.00

Figure 29.1 *Plan travel page*

Regular expressions can be used in the coded checkpoints to successfully test a dynamic property value. For example, in order to test whether the text 'Rs' is shown on the page (as shown in Figure 29.1) or not, we can use regular expressions on each of the amount fields. The following Code shows how to use regular expressions to verify whether the 'Total' field contains text 'Rs' or not. Since the amount value changes every time, it is a dynamic value.

```
Set oTotalAmount = Browser("B").Page("P").Webelement("Total") 'verify
text property of the WebElement object contains text 'Rs' or not
Print oTotalAmount.CheckProperty("text", micRegExpMatch(".*Rs.*"))
```

STANDARD CHECKPOINT

Standard checkpoint verifies the value of an object property. For example, it can be used to check if a button is enabled in GUI or not.

Inserting Standard Checkpoint Using Record/Playback Method

Example: Verify whether the button Search as shown in the Figure 29.3 is enabled or not.

The following steps show how to record a standard checkpoint:

1. Open thetest script.
2. Open application under test.
3. Click on the *Record* button .
   Recording toolbar opens as shown in the Fig. 29.2 and recording begins.
4. Either click on the checkpoint insertion tool on recording toolbar or Navigate Design → Checkpoint → Standard Checkpoint… Hand toolbar appears.
5. Point the hand toolbar to the object for which standard checkpoint needs to be created. (Assume, hand tool is pointed and clicked on *the Search* button of the flight booking application as shown in the Fig. 29.3.)
6. *Standard Checkpoint* dialog box opens as shown in the Fig. 29.4. Select the object on which checkpoint needs to be applied and click OK button.
7. *Checkpoint Properties* dialog box opens as shown in the Fig. 29.5.
8. Select the properties which need to be added to checkpoint.
   i. Select option 'Constant' if a constant value is to be specified for the property value.
      a. Click on button *Constant Value Options* , if the constant value specified needs to be replaced with a regular option value.

Figure 29.2 *Recording toolbar*

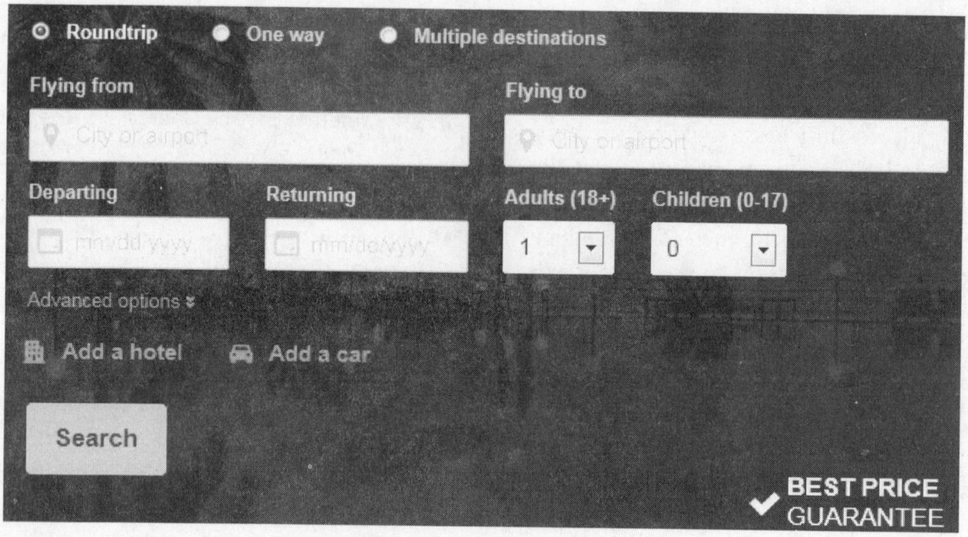

Figure 29.3 *Plan travel page*

On user click on button, *Constant Value Options dialog* box opens as shown in Fig. 29.6.

b. Specify the regular expression value and select the regular expression checkbox, if the specified value is a regular expression.

c. Click *OK* button.

d. *Checkpoint Properties* dialog box is displayed with the updated modifications.

e. Click *OK* button to add the checkpoint.

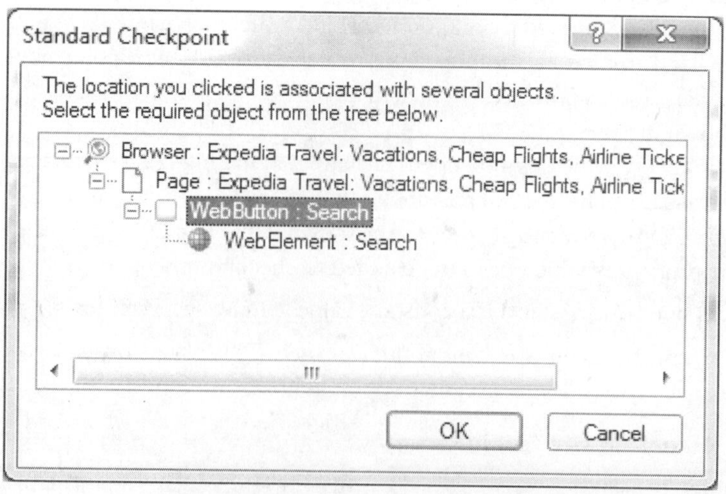

Figure 29.4 *Object selection dialog*

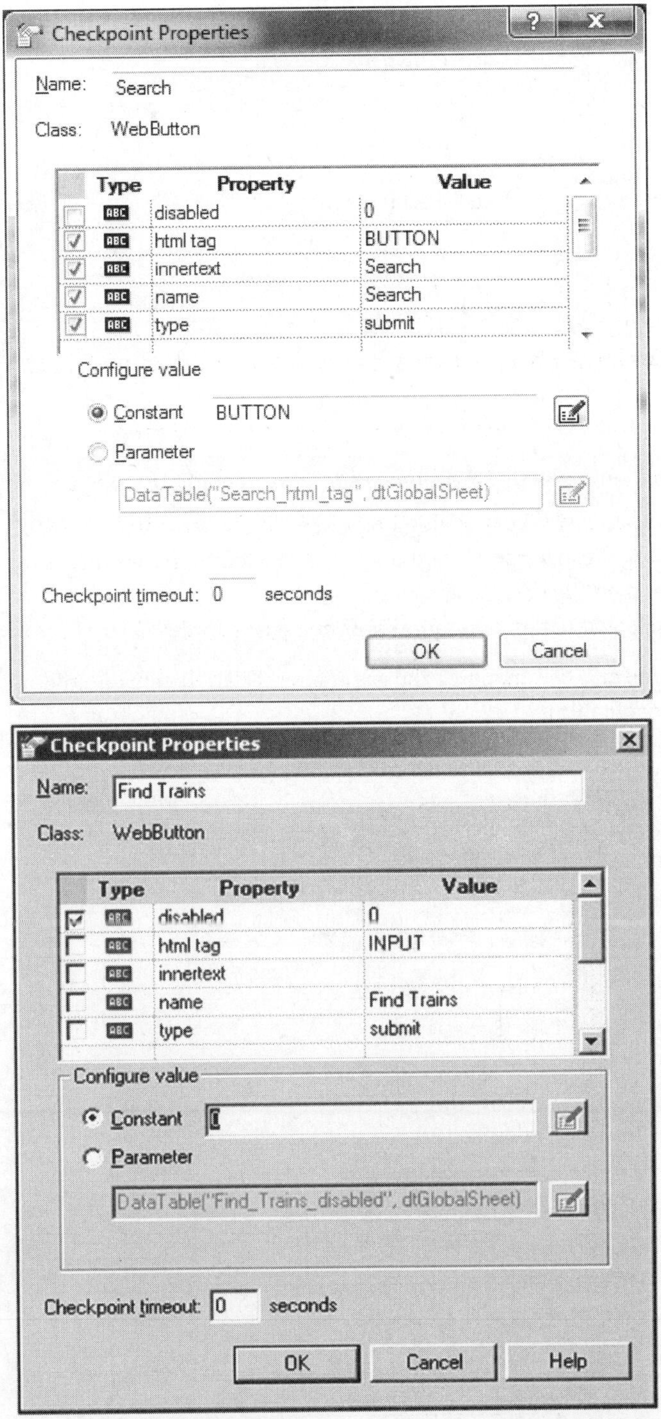

Figure 29.5 *Select properties to verify*

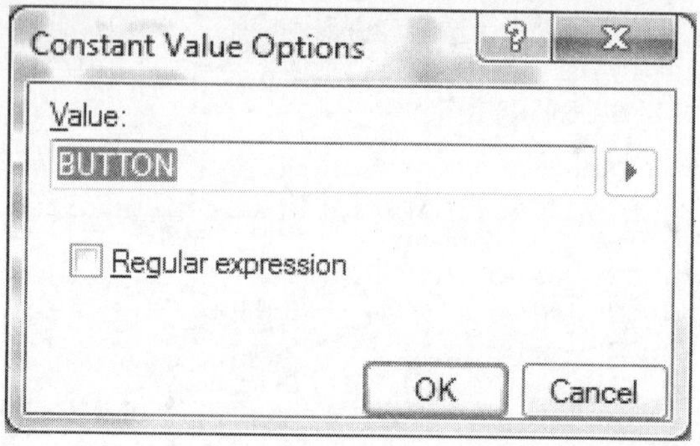

Figure 29.6 *Using regular expressions for standard checkpoint value*

ii. Select option *Parameter* in order to parameterize the property value used for checkpoint.

a. Click on the button *Parameter Options* to configure the parameterization options.

Parameter Options dialog box opens as shown in the Fig. 29.7.

b. Select the parameterization type—data table, environment or random number as shown in Fig. 29.8.

c. If selected parameterization option is Data Table:

- Specify the name of the parameter. (UFT creates a column with same name in data table).

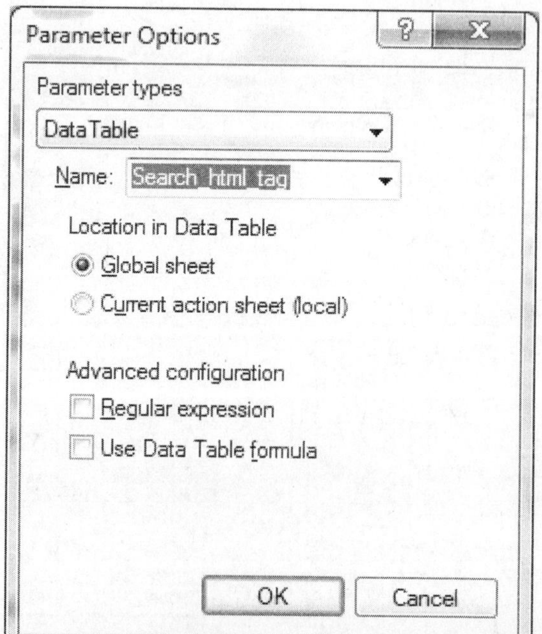

Figure 29.7 *Configuring checkpoint parameterizations options*

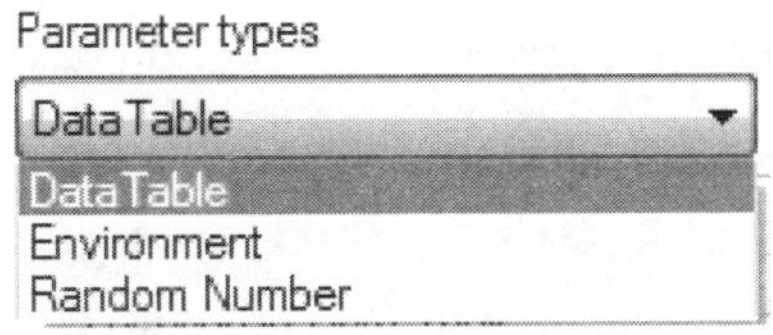

Figure 29.8 *Select parameterization type*

- Select *Global sheet* to create the parameter column in global sheet. Or, else select option *Current action* to create the parameter in the local data table sheet.
  - Select option checkbox *Regular expression* if the value specified in the data table is to be treated as a regular expression. Once user selects this option, *Use Data Table formula* option is disabled.
  - Select option checkbox *use Data Table formula* to use the formula as specified the data table. Once user selects this option, *Regular expression* option is disabled.
- Click *OK* button to create the parameter in the data table.
- *Checkpoint Properties* dialog box is displayed with the updated modifications.
- Click *OK* button to add the checkpoint.
- Parameterized option is created in the data table as shown in Figure 29.9.

d. If selected parameterization option is *Environment*, follow the steps as mentioned below. Figure 29.10 shows the *Parameter Options* dialog box with parameterization type as *Environment*.

- Specify the environment variable *name* and its *value*.
- Select checkbox *Regular Expression*, if the specified value is a regular expression.
- Click *OK* button to create this new environment variable.

e. If selected option is *Random Number*, follow the steps as mentioned below. Figure 29.11 shows the *Parameter Options* dialog box with parameterization type as *Random Number*.

- Specify the numeric range
- (optional) Specify name and action or test iteration to instruct UFT to use a random sequence number for each iteration.
- Click *OK* button to add parametrized option to checkpoint.

9. Specify checkpoint timeout time. If the object property value does not matches the specified value as specified in the checkpoint within this time, then UFT fails the checkpoint.

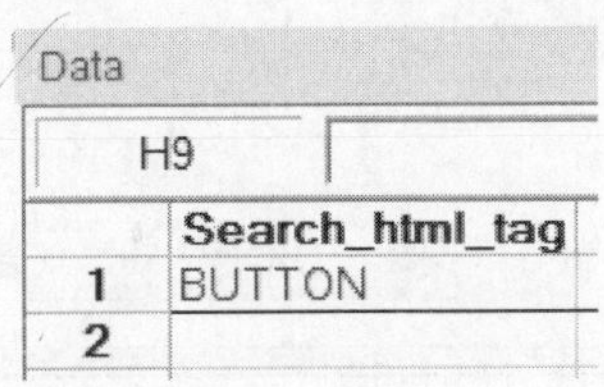

Figure 29.9 *Checkoint parameterized option in data table*

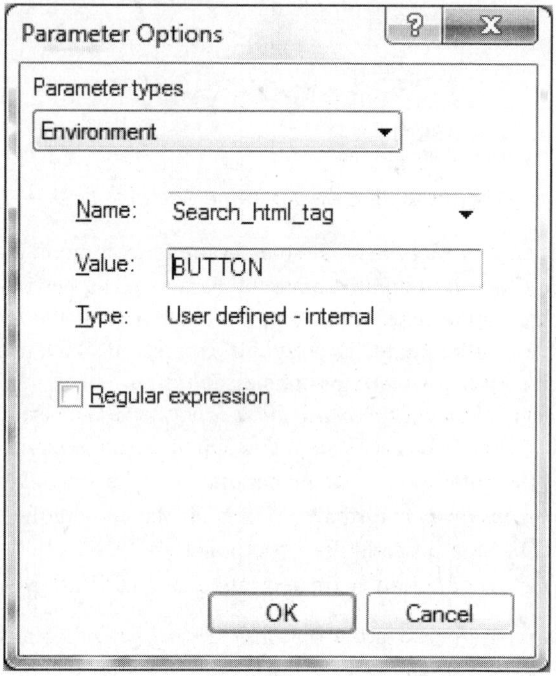

Figure 29.10 *Parametrizing checkpoint using environment variables*

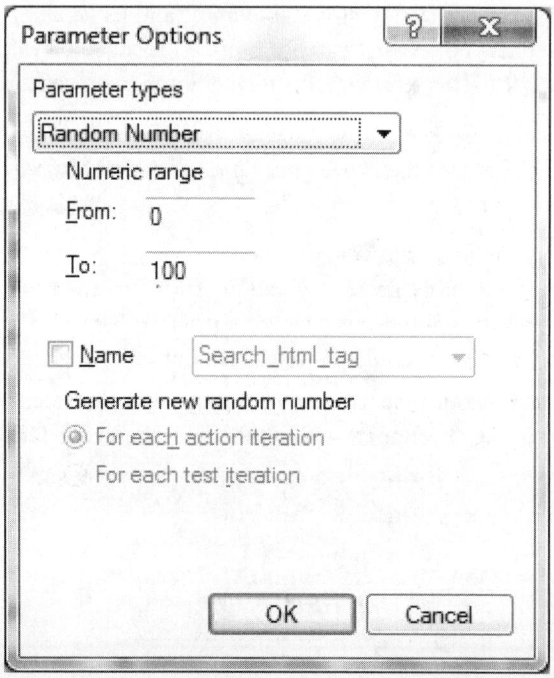

Figure 29.11 *Parameterizing checkpoint using random number*

10. Click the OK button.
11. Click on the *Stop* button to stop recording.
12. The following code will appear on the test script.

> **NOTES** Non-zero checkpoint timeout time may cause unnecessary test execution delays.

The UFT code for the recorded standard checkpoint will be as follows.

```
Browser("B").Page("P").WebButton("Search").Check CheckPoint("Search")
```

To find whether the checkpoint has passed or failed, retrieve the return value of the checkpoint as follows:

```
bCheckpointStatus = Browser("B").Page("P").WebButton("Search").Check
CheckPoint("Search")
```

Scripting Coded Standard Checkpoint

Now, let us see how we can write a coded checkpoint in test scripts to verify whether a button is enabled or disabled in GUI.

```
'Retrieve the run-time value of the disabled property of the button object
bBtnStat = Browser("B").Page("P").WebButton("Search").
GetROProperty("disabled")

If bBtnStat=0 Then 'enabled
   MsgBox "Button is enabled"
ElseIf bBtnStat=1 Then    'disabled
   MsgBox "Button is disable" End If
```

Alternatively,

```
bBtnStat = Browser("B").Page("P").WebButton("Search").
CheckProperty("disabled",1,0)

If bBtnStat=False Then    'enabled
   MsgBox "Button is enabled"
ElseIf bBtnStat=True Then 'disabled
   MsgBox "Button is diabled"
End If
Note: Syntax of method CheckProperty:
   CheckProperty(propertyName, propertyValue, [optional]timeout time)
```

In order to specify a regular expression match, use method micRegExpMatch. Code below shows how to implement regular expressions in coded standard checkpoint. The below code does a regular expression match for name attribute value of Search button.

```
bBtnStat = Browser("B").Page("P").WebButton("Search").CheckProperty("na
me",micRegExpMatch(".*Search.*"),0)
```

TABLE CHECKPOINT

Table checkpoint is used to verify table data. For example, to verify that the ticket charge in the table is correct or not.

Inserting Table Checkpoint Using Record/Playback Method

Example: Verify whether ticket booking charges as displayed in Figure 29.12 is correct or not.

1. Open the test script.
2. Open application under test.
3. Click on the *Record* button . *Recording* toolbar opens as shown in the Figure 29.2 and recording begins.
4. Navigate Design → Checkpoint → Standard Checkpoint… Hand toolbar appears.
5. Point the hand toolbar to the object for which standard checkpoint needs to be created. (Assume, hand tool is pointed and clicked on *the Payment details* web table as shown in the Fig. 29.12).
6. *Standard Checkpoint* dialog box opens as shown in the Fig. 29.4. Select the web table object on which checkpoint needs to be applied and click OK button.
7. *Table Checkpoint Properties* window opens as shown in Fig. 29.13.
8. Select the data for which checkpoint needs to be applied.
9. Follow step 8 of 'Standard Checkpoint' section to configure table checkpoint.
10. Click the OK button to add the checkpoint to the test.
11. Click on the *Stop* button to stop recording.
12. The following code will appear on the test script.

```
Browser("B").Page("P").WebTable("Ticket_Charges").Check
CheckPoint("Ticket_Charges")
```

Payment Details

Payment Option	ICICI
Ticket Charge	Rs 587.00
Internet Service Charge	Rs 20.00
Total	Rs 607.00

Figure 29.12 *Payment details web table*

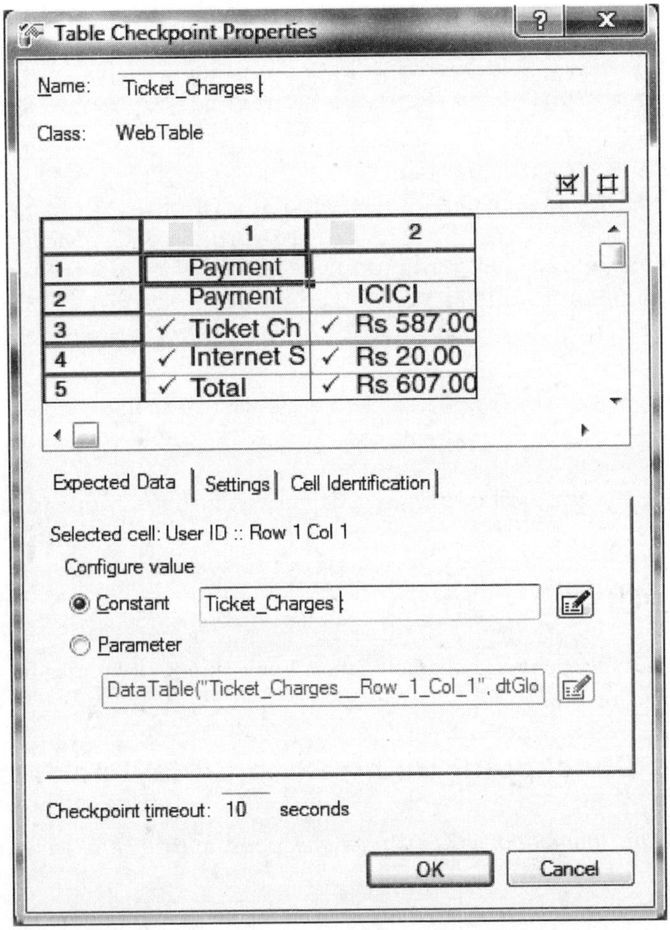

Figure 29.13 *Table checkpoint properties dialog box*

To find whether the checkpoint has passed or failed, retrieve the return value of the checkpoint as follows:

```
bChkpntStat = Browser("B").Page("P").WebTable("Ticket_Charges").Check
CheckPoint("Ticket_Charges")
```

Scripting Coded Table Checkpoint

Now, let us see how we can write a coded checkpoint in test scripts to verify whether the booking charges displayed on the Fig. 29.12 is correct or not.

```
A_TcktChrg = Browser("B").Page("P").WebTable("PaymentDetails").
                                                    GetCellData(3,2)

A_IntrntSrvcChrg = Browser("B").Page("P").WebTable("PaymentDetails")
                                                   .GetCellData(4,2)
```

```
A_Total      =      Browser("B").Page("P").WebTable("PaymentDetails")
                                                      .GetCellData(5,2)
A_TcktChrg = CDbl(Trim(Replace(nTcktChrg, "Rs",""")))
A_IntrntSrvcChrg = CDbl(Trim(Replace(nIntrntSrvcChrg, "Rs","")))
A_Total = CDbl(Trim(Replace(nTotal, "Rs","")))
If A_TcktChrg <> E_TcktChrg Then
   Reporter.ReportEvent micFail, "Mismatch: Ticket Charge. " , "Exp-" &
                                        E_TcktChrg & " , Act-" & A_TcktChrg
ElseIf A_IntrntSrvcChrg <>E_IntrntSrvcChrg Then
   Reporter.ReportEvent micFail, "Mismatch: Internet Service Charge." &
      "Exp-" & E_IntrntSrvcChrg & " , Act-" & A_IntrntSrvcChrg
ElseIf A_Total <> E_Total Then
   Reporter.ReportEvent micFail, "Mismatch: Total Charge." , "Exp-" &
      E_Total & " , Act-" & A_Total
Else
   Reporter.ReportEvent micPass, "Correct Charges applied","Pass"
End If
```

PAGE CHECKPOINT

Page checkpoint verifies the web page characteristics. For example, it verifies broken links of a web page or checks the page load time.

Inserting Page Checkpoint Using Record/Playback Method

Example: Verify load time, number of links, number of images, and any broken links in a web page.

1. Open the test script.
2. Open application under test.
3. Click on the *Record* button .
   Recording toolbar opens as shown in the Fig. 29.2 and recording begins.
4. Navigate Design → Checkpoint → Standard Checkpoint… Hand toolbar appears.
5. Point the hand toolbar to the web page. *Standard Checkpoint* dialog box opens as shown in the Figure 29.4.
   Select the page object on which checkpoint needs to be applied and click OK button.
6. *Page Checkpoint Properties* window opens as shown in the Fig. 29.14.
7. Configure the checkpoint attributes as mentioned in Step 8 of 'Standard Checkpoint' section.
8. Click *OK* button to add the page checkpoint to the test.
9. Click on the *Stop* button to stop recording.
10. The following code will appear in the test script.

```
Browser("B").Page("P").Check CheckPoint("Expedia Travel")
```

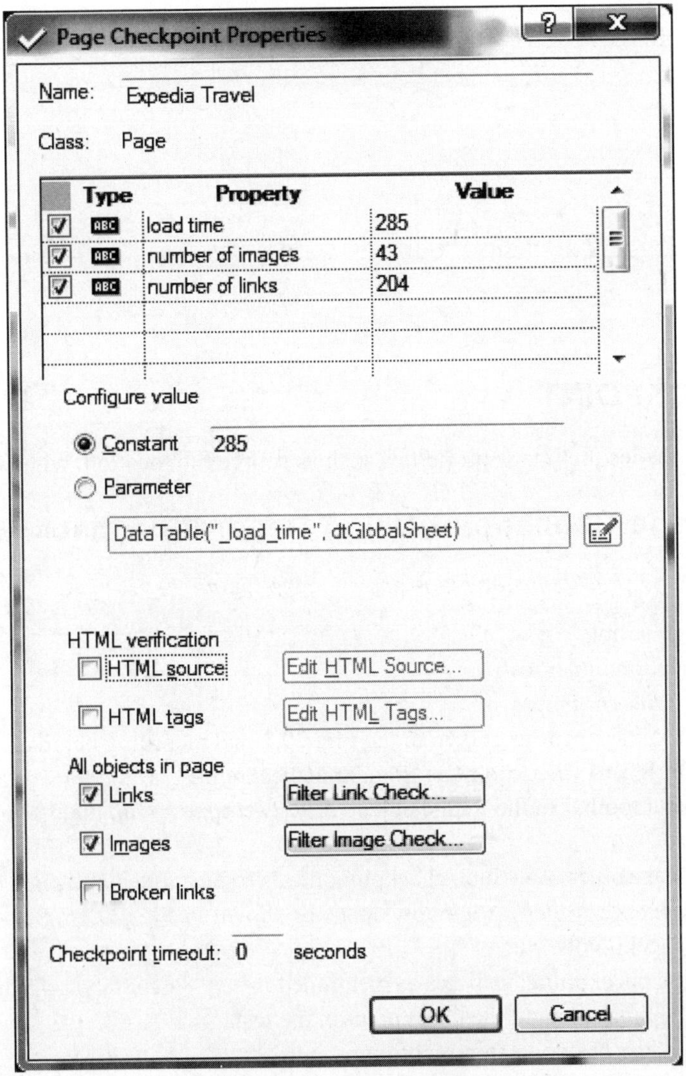

Figure 29.14 *Page checkpoint*

Scripting Coded Page Checkpoint

The following code demonstrates how to check the number of links present in the IRCTC plan travel page.

```
'Create description object
Set oLink = Description.Create()
oLink("micclass").Value = "Link"
oLink("html tag").Value = "A"
```

```
'Get all link objects of page
Set colLink = Browser("IRCTC").Page("IRCTC").ChildObjects(oLink)
'Link count
nLinkCnt = colLink.Count
If nLinkCnt = nExpLinkCnt Then
   MsgBox "Pass"
Else
   MsgBox "Failed: Exp Link Count-" & nExpLinkCnt & "Actual-" & nLinkCnt
End If
Set colLink = Nothing Set oLink = Nothing
```

IMAGE CHECKPOINT

Image checkpoint verifies the image properties such as source file location, width, and height.

Inserting Image Checkpoint Using Record/Playback Method

Example: Insert image checkpoint for image shown in the Figure 29.15.

1. Open the test script.
2. Open application under test.
3. Click on the *Record* button.
   Recording toolbar opens as shown in the Fig. 29.2 and recording begins.
4. Navigate Design → Checkpoint → Standard Checkpoint… Hand toolbar appears.
5. Point the hand toolbar to the image object. *Standard Checkpoint* dialog box opens as shown in the Figure 29.4.
   Select the image object on which checkpoint needs to be applied and click OK button

1. *Image Checkpoint Properties* window opens as shown in Fig. 29.16. Select the appropriate attributes as checkpoints.
2. Configure the checkpoint attributes as mentioned in step 8 of 'Standard Checkpoint' section.
3. Click the OK button to add the checkpoint in the test.
4. Click on the *Stop* button to stop recording.
5. The following code will appear in the test script.

```
Browser("B").Page("P").Image("logo").Check
                                        CheckPoint("logo ")
```

To find whether the checkpoint has passed or failed, retrieve the return value of the checkpoint as follows:

```
bChkPntStat = Browser("B").Page("P").Image("logo").Check
              CheckPoint("logo")
```

Figure 29.15 *Pearson logo image*

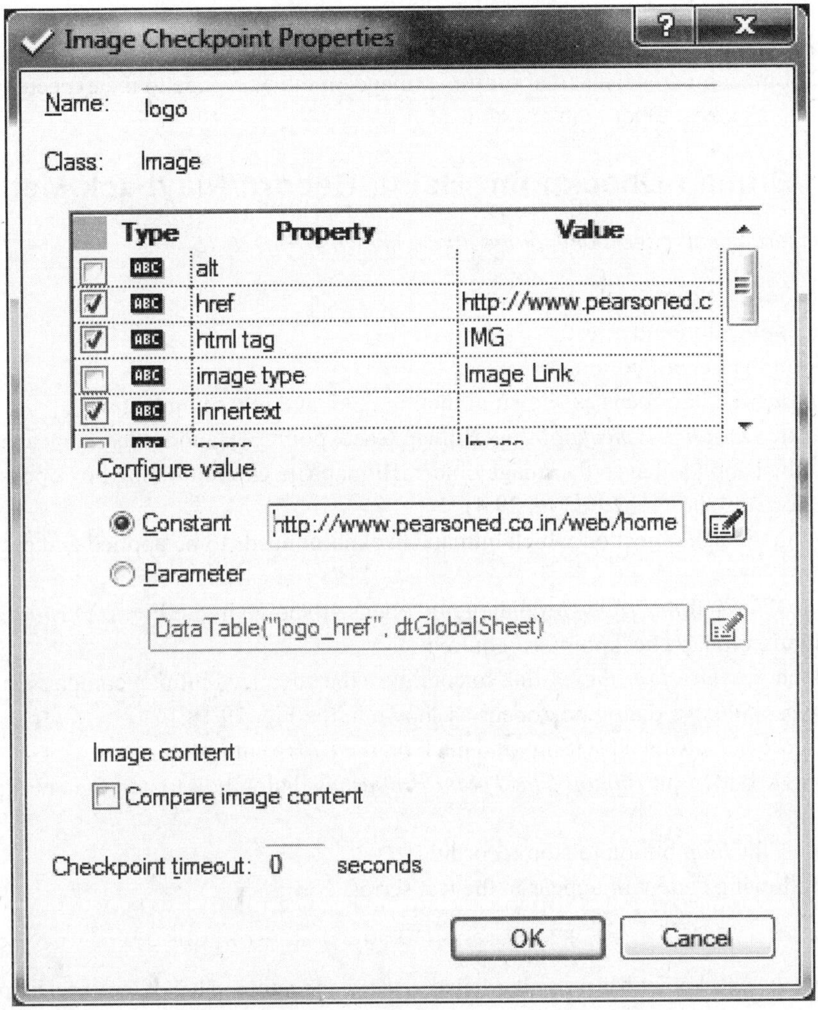

Figure 29.16 *Image checkpoint*

Scripting Coded Image Checkpoint

The following code demonstrates how to check the *href* property of an image.

```
A_Href = Browser("B").Page("P").Image("logo").
                                            GetROProperty("href")
If StrComp(A_Href, E_Href,1) = 0 Then
   MsgBox "Pass"
Else
   MsgBox "Failed: Mismatch Href. Exp-" & E_Href & ", Actual-" & A_Href
End If
```

BITMAP CHECKPOINT

Bitmap checkpoint compares the actual run-time image on the web page to the expected saved image pixel by pixel to check whether both are same or not.

Inserting Bitmap Checkpoint Using Record/Playback Method

Example 1: Insert bitmap checkpoint for the image shown in Fig. 29.15.

1. Open the test script.
2. Open application under test.
3. Click on the *Record* button .
   Recording toolbar opens as shown in the Fig. 29.2 and recording begins.
4. Navigate *Design* → *Checkpoint* → Bitmap Checkpoint... Hand toolbar appears.
5. Point the hand toolbar to the image object. Bitmap Checkpoint dialog box opens (it is same as dialog box shown in the Fig. 29.4).
   Select the image object on which bitmap checkpoint needs to be applied and click OK button
6. *Bitmap Checkpoint Properties* dialog box opens as shown in the Fig. 29.17.
7. Configure bitmap checkpoint as required.
8. Click on *Advanced settings...* link to configure the advanced bitmap comparison settings. *Advanced Settings* dialog box opens as shown in the Fig. 29.18.
9. Configure the advanced settings and click on the *Close* button.
10. Click *OK* button on *Bitmap Checkpoint Properties* dialog box to add the checkpoint to the test.
11. Click on the *Stop* button to stop recording.
12. The following code will appear in the test script.

```
Browser("B").Page("P").Image("logo").Check CheckPoint("logo")
```

To find whether the checkpoint has passed or failed, retrieve the return value of the checkpoint as follows:

```
bChkPntStat = Browser("B").Page("P").Image("logo").Check
CheckPoint("logo")
```

NOTES: Dynamic images can also be compared in UFT by selecting multimedia option in the Add-in manager.

Scripting Coded Bitmap Checkpoint

The following code shows how to compare two images bitmap-wise in UFT using coded checkpoint. The code assumes that expected image file is already present at the specified location. During execution, the actual image is saved in the specified location. Thereafter, an instance of Mercry.

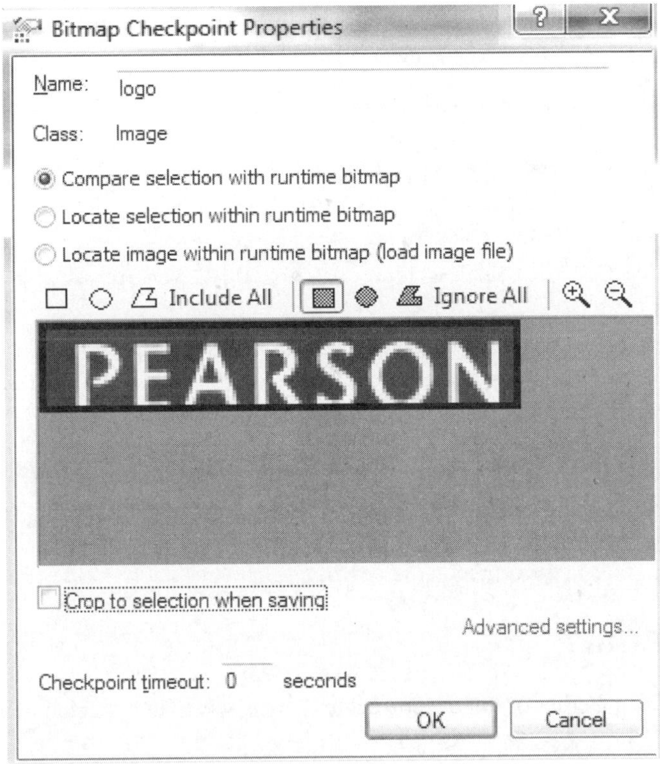

Figure 29.17 *Bitmap checkpoint properties dialog box*

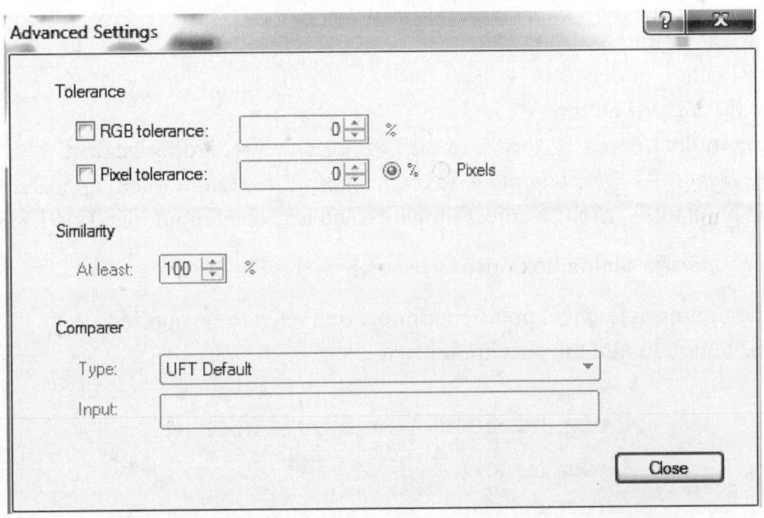

Figure 29.18 *Bitmap checkpoint advanced settings*

FileCompare is created to compare the actual and the expected image files. The comparison returns *True*, if both files match, or else returns *False*.

```
'Path where expected image is saved
E_ImgPath = "Z:\Data\Module1\Images\logo.bmp"
'Path where actual run-time image will be saved
A_ImgPath = "C:\Temp\Temp.bmp"
'Capture actual run-time image
Browser("B").Page("P").Image("logo").CaptureBitmap
A_ImgPath,True
'Or bitmap image of a button object can also be captured using below code:
'Browser("B").Page("P").WebButton ("Search").CaptureBitmap
A_ImgPath, TrueSet oFileCompare = CreateObject("Mercury.FileCompare")
If oFileCompare.IsEqualBin(E_ImgPath, A_ImgPath, 0, 1) Then
   MsgBox "Pass"
Else
   MsgBox "Failed: Expected and actual files are different"
End If
```

TEXT CHECKPOINT

Text checkpoint verifies whether or not the correct text is displayed at expected place on the web page.

Inserting Text Checkpoint Using Record/Playback Method

Example: Insert text checkpoint to check whether or not proper text is displayed on the web application as shown in Fig. 29.19.

1. Open the test script.
2. Open application under test.
3. Click on the *Record* button .
   Recording toolbar opens as shown in the Fig. 29.2 and recording begins.
4. Navigate *Design* → *Checkpoint* → Text Checkpoint… Hand toolbar appears.
5. Point the hand toolbar to the object on which the text checkpoint needs to be created.

Text Checkpoint Properties dialog box opens as shown in the Fig. 29.20.

1. Select the appropriate checkpoint conditions that need to be applied.
2. Click OK button to add the checkpoint to the test.

Congratulations! Your flight is booked.

Order number: 5437856547.

Order details

Figure 29.19 *web application with flight booking details*

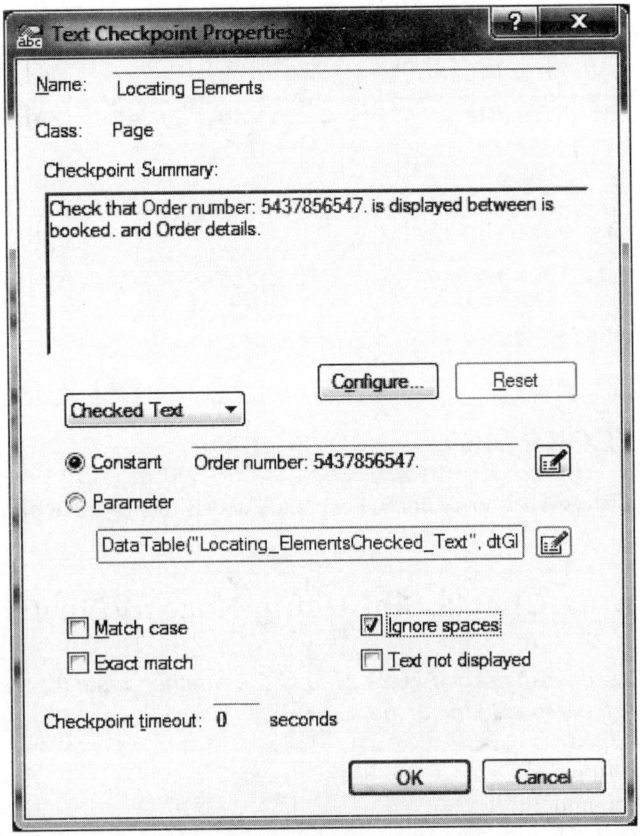

Figure 29.20 *Text checkpoint*

3. Click on the *Stop* button to stop recording.
4. The following code will appear in the test script.

```
Browser("B").Page("P").Check CheckPoint("Msg")
```

To find whether the checkpoint has passed or failed, retrieve the return value of the checkpoint as follows:

```
bChkPntStat =
   Browser("B").Page("P").Check CheckPoint("Msg")
```

Scripting Coded Text Checkpoint

The following code shows how to implement coded checkpoint for above-mentioned scenario. The code demonstrates how to capture screen text during run-time.

```
E_BookTcktMsg = "Congratulations. You have…"
If Browser("B").Page("P").WebTable("Msg").
                                    GetROProperty("text").Exist Then
```

```
    A_BookTcktMsg = Browser(“B”).Page(“P”).WebTable(“Msg”).
                                                          GetROProperty(“text”)
    A_BookTcktMsg = Trim(A_BookTcktMsg)
    If StrComp(E_BookTcktMsg, A_BookTcktMsg, 1) = 0 Then
       MsgBox “Correct Message displayed”
    Else
       MsgBox “Incorrect Message displayed. Exp-” & E_BookTcktMsg & “,
                                                    Actual-” & A_BookTcktMsg
    End If
Else
    MsgBox “Incorrect Message displayed on Screen”
End If
```

TEXT AREA CHECKPOINT

Text area checkpoint verifies whether or not the expected text is displayed at particular area of a windows application.

Inserting Text Area Checkpoint Using Record/Playback Method

Example: Insert text area checkpoint on Fig. 29.21 to check whether or not the text 'Available Software Updates' is displayed at the defined area of the screen.

5. Open the test script.
6. Open application under test.
7. Click on the *Record* button.
   Recording toolbar opens as shown in the Fig. 29.2 and recording begins.

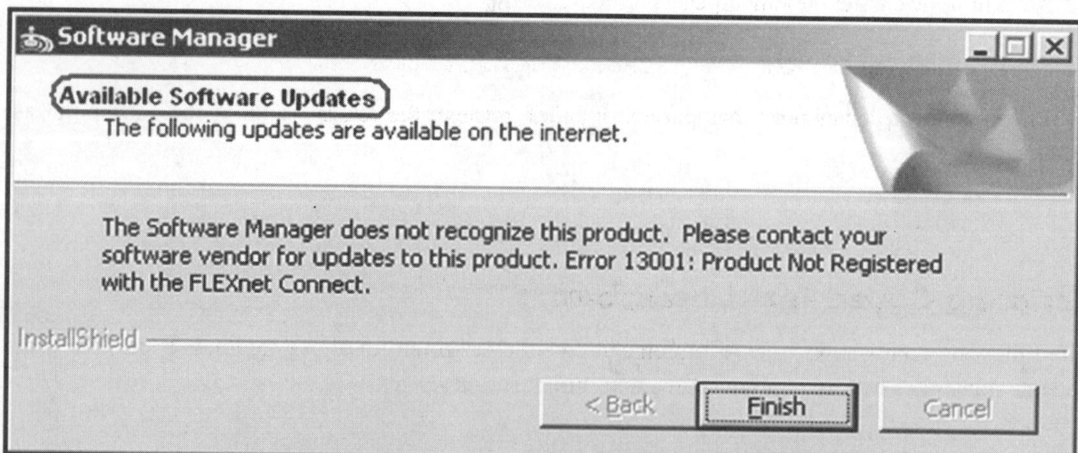

Figure 29.21 *Verify specified text within the specified text area*

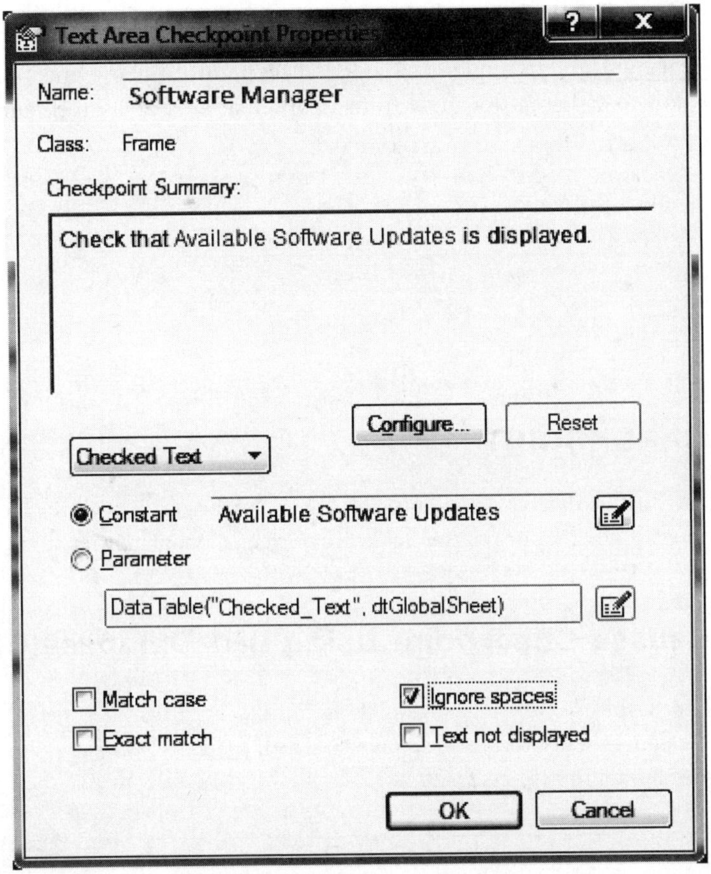

Figure 29.22 *Text area checkpoint*

8. Navigate *Design → Checkpoint → Text Area Checkpoint*… Cross Hair toolbar appears.
9. Use cross-hair toolbar to select GUI area whose text needs to be verified.
10. *Text Area Checkpoint Properties* window opens as shown in the Fig. 29.22.
11. Select the appropriate checkpoint conditions that need to be applied.
12. Click the OK button to add the checkpoint to the test.
13. Click on the *Stop* button to stop recording.
14. The following code will appear in the test script.

```
Dialog("Software Manager").Activate
Dialog("Dialog").Check CheckPoint("Software Manager")
```

To find whether the checkpoint has passed or failed, retrieve the return value of the checkpoint as follows:

```
bChkPntStat =
   Dialog("Dialog").Check CheckPoint("Software Manager")
```

Scripting Coded Text Area Checkpoint

The following code shows how to implement coded checkpoint for above-mentioned scenario. The code demonstrates how to capture screen text from a particular area of a screen during run-time.

```
E_Msg = "Available Software Updates"
A_Msg = Trim(Dialog("Software Manager").Static("AvlSoftUpdt").
                                                    GetROProperty("text"))
If StrComp(E_Msg, A_Msg, 1) = 0 Then
   MsgBox "Pass"
Else
   MsgBox "Fail"
End If
```

DATABASE CHECKPOINT

Database checkpoint verifies database contents of AUT. It can be used to verify the screen data with database data or to verify whether or not the fields are correctly updated after some GUI operation or batch execution.

Inserting Database Checkpoint Using UFT Database Checkpoint

1. Open the test script.
2. Navigate Design → Checkpoint → Database Checkpoint… *Database Query Wizard* dialog box opens as shown in Fig. 29.23-29.24.

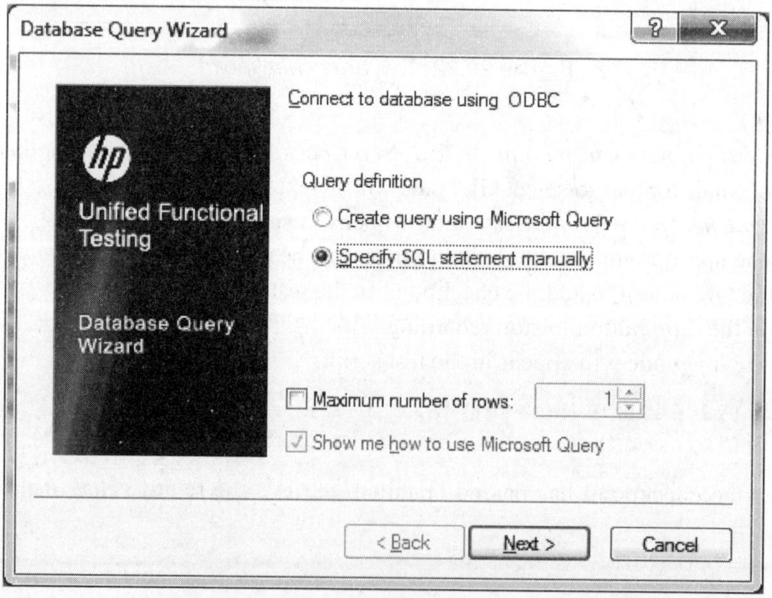

Figure 29.23 *Database Query Wizard—Creating Query*

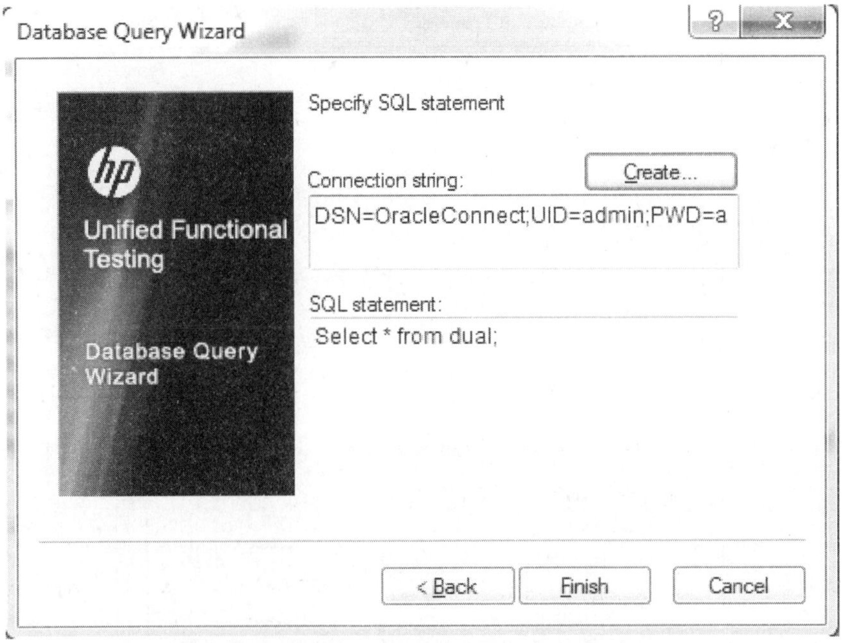

Figure 29.24 *Database query wizard—Specify query*

UFT allows users to create a query using Microsoft Query wizard or manually specify the query, if query is handy. Microsoft Query wizard can be used to develop the query. If query is handy users can select the option *Specify SQL statement manually* option is to be selected.

3. Select option *Specify SQL statements manually* to manually specify connection string and SQL query.
4. Click the *Next* button
5. Specify connection string or create one using the *Create* button.
6. Specify SQL statement.
7. Click the *Finish* button.
   Database Checkpoint Properties window opens as shown in the Fig. 29.25.
8. Select the fields that need to be verified.
9. Configure the checkpoint as required. (Refer Step 8 of Standard Checkpoint section).
10. Click the OK button to add the checkpoint to the test.
    The following code will appear in the test script.
    ```
    DbTable("DbTable").Check CheckPoint("DbTable")
    ```

Scripting Coded Database Checkpoint

Refer chapter 'Working with Database' for scripting coded database checkpoints.

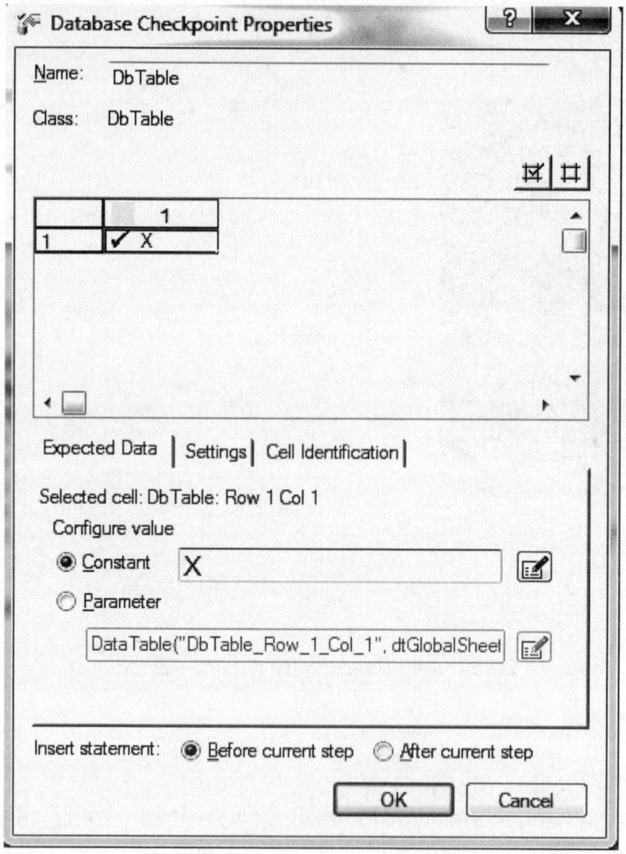

Figure 29.25 *Database checkpoint*

ACCESSIBILITY CHECKPOINT

Accessibility checkpoint is specific to web application. It is used to check whether the web pages are World Wide Web Consortium (W3C) compliant or not.

Inserting Accessibility Checkpoint Using Record/Playback Method

1. Open the test script.
2. Open application under test.
3. Click on the *Record* button .
   Recording toolbar opens as shown in the Fig. 29.2 and recording begins.
4. Navigate *Design* → *Checkpoint* → *Accessibility Checkpoint.*
   Hand tool appears.
5. Point and click the hand tool on the web page. *Accessibility* dialog box opens.
6. Select the page object on the accessibility dialog box and click *OK* button.

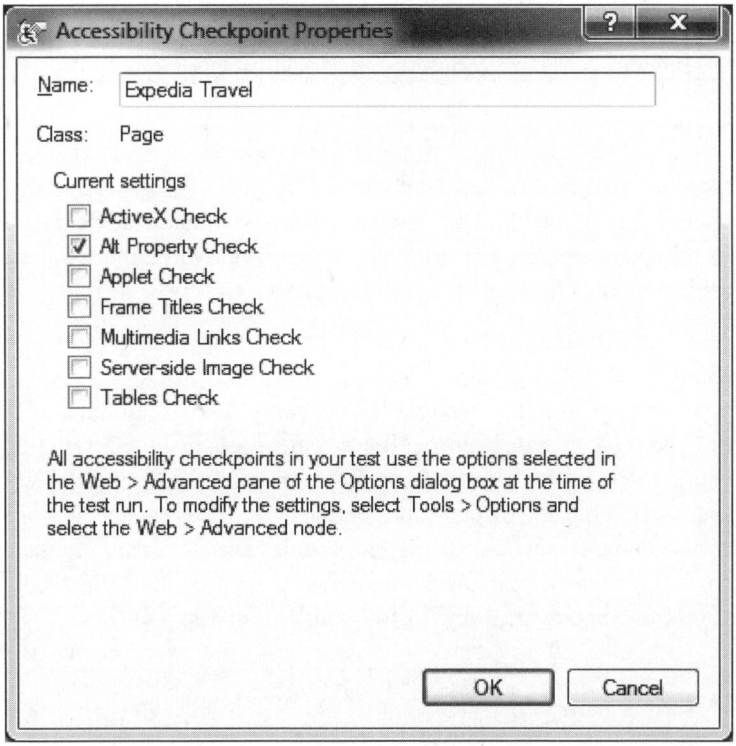

Figure 29.26 *Accessibility Checkpoint Properties dialog box*

7. *Accessibility Checkpoint Properties* dialog opens as shown in Fig. 29.26.
8. Select the required properties to verify.
9. Click *OK* button to add the checkpoint to the test.
10. Click on the *Stop* button to stop recording.

The following code will appear in the test script.

```
Browser("B").Page("P").Check CheckPoint("Expedia Travel")
```

XML CHECKPOINT

XML checkpoint verifies the data content of XML documents in XML files or XML documents in web pages. There are two types of XML checkpoints:

- **XML checkpoint (From Application):** This checkpoint can only be applied in record/playback mode. It checks the data content of XML documents in web pages/frames.
- **XML checkpoint (From Resource):** This checkpoint can be applied without using record/playback mode. It checks the data content of XML documents in XML files.

Scripting Coded XML Checkpoint

Refer chapter 'Working with XML' for scripting coded XML checkpoints.

File Checkpoint

File content checkpoint compares the textual content of a file that is generated during a run session with the textual content of a source file. This enables test automation developers to verify that the generated file contains the expected data. For example, we may want to verify that the account statement PDF report of a banking application contains correct customer address.

- File checkpoint can perform a checkpoint on text in one line, multiple lines, or the entire document, as needed.
- File checkpoint allows users to specify what to ignore. For example, automation developers cap specify the lines (or areas) to ignore. Ignored areas are excluded from the checkpoint.
- When automation developers select a source document to compare, UFT converts a copy of this document to a text file and displays the content in the file content editor area of the "Checkpoint Properties Dialog Box". This dialog box enables users to configure the checkpoint.
- File checkpoint allows use of parameters and regular expressions, as needed.
- File checkpoint can be performed for the following file types:
    - HTML
    - Microsoft Word
    - Text
    - RTF
    - PDF

If File Checkpoint step fails during a run session, then the Data pane of the Run results Viewer displays side-by-side comparison of the generated document and the source document. This enables users to quickly analyze and find the failure reason and the defect, if any.

> NOTES: Maintenance Run Mode does not support complex checkpoint (and Output) types such as XML checkpoints and File checkpoints. During the Maintenance Run, these checkpoints are executed as they would in a regular run session and will fail if there are differences between expected and actual values.

Inserting File Checkpoint Using UFT

In this section, we will discuss how to insert file checkpoint using UFT. Assume the requirement is to verify the contents of the filr shown in Fig. 29.27.

1. Open the test script..
2. Navigate *Design → Checkpoint → File Content Checkpoint…*
   Windows explorer opens to locate and open the source file.
3. Open the source file.
   Assume source file is a ODF file and is kept at location - C:\Temp\File Checkpoint.pdf
   File Content Checkpoint Properties window opens as shown in the Fig. 29.28.

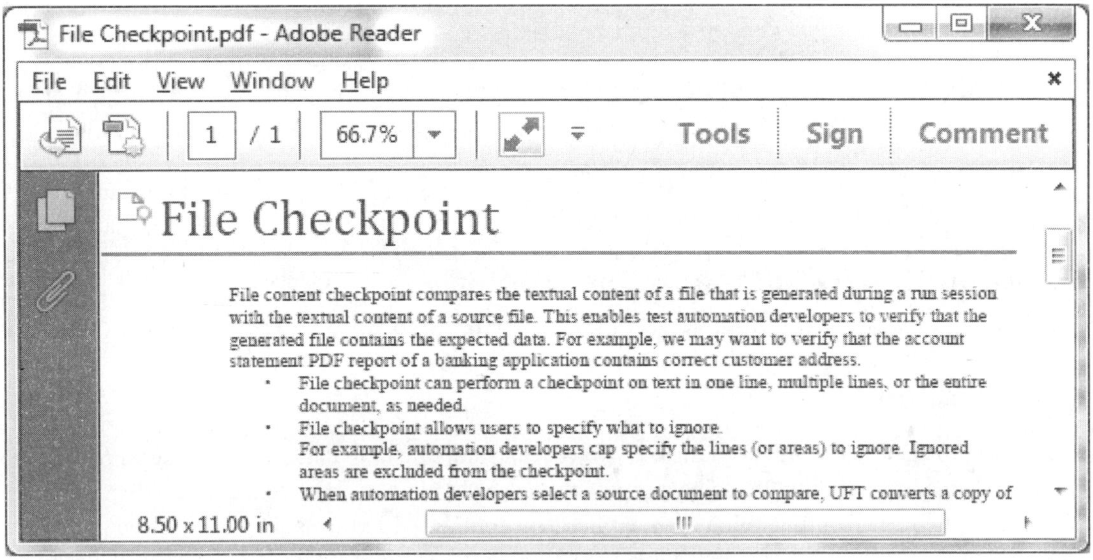

Figure 29.27 *Source PDF file for file checkpoint*

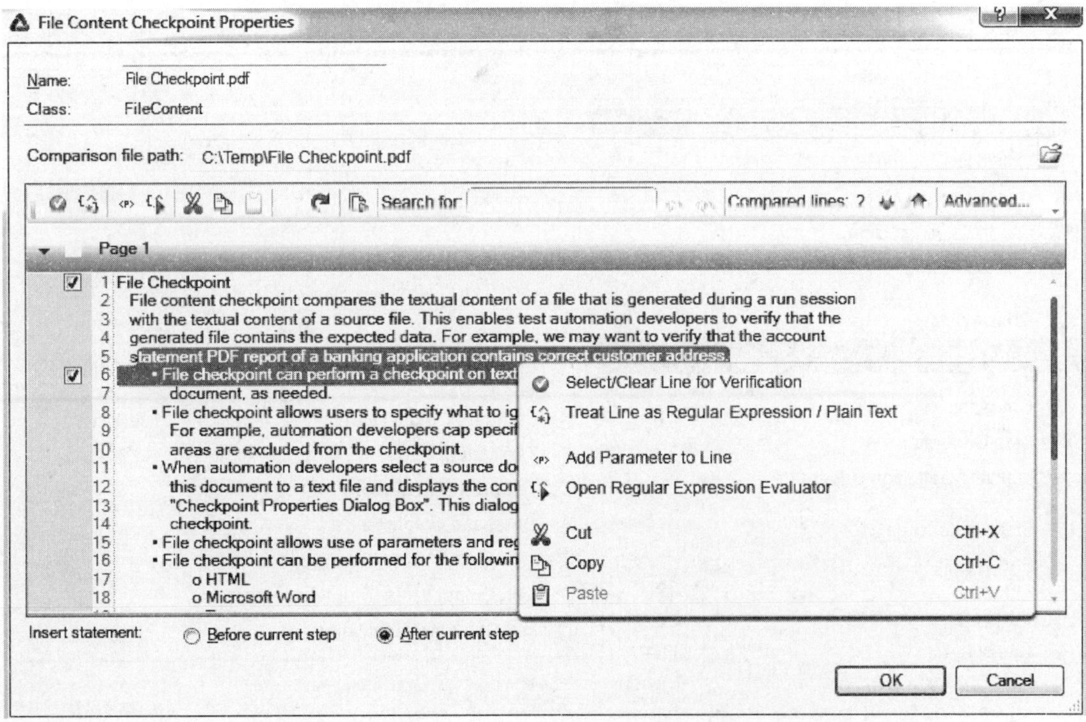

Figure 29.28 *File Content checkpoint properties window*

4. Configure the checkpoint as per requirement.
   (For example, verifying specific text content, parameterizing content such as order amount, using regular expressions for dynamically changing text content such as account balance, etc.)
5. Click on the *OK* button to add the checkpoint to the test.

The following code will appear in the test script.

```
FileContent("File Checkpoint.pdf").Check CheckPoint("File Checkpoint.pdf")
```

Scripting Coded Database Checkpoint

Refer section 'Advanced VBScript' for scripting coded file checkpoint.

Output Value

UFT allows to capture the values of the GUI objects and store them in data tables. These values can be values displayed on a web table, object properties such as html id or value, text displayed on the page, XML content etc. The output values can applied and configured in the same way as checkpoints are applied. Fig. 29.29 shows the various types of output values that can be inserted in a test.

> **NOTES**
> Option 'Existing Output Value' allows users to add an already created (existing) output value to a new step. For example, if a standard output value is created for say login edit box to capture its 'value' property, then:
> - this output value can as well be applied to password edit box
> - this output value can as well be applied to login button.

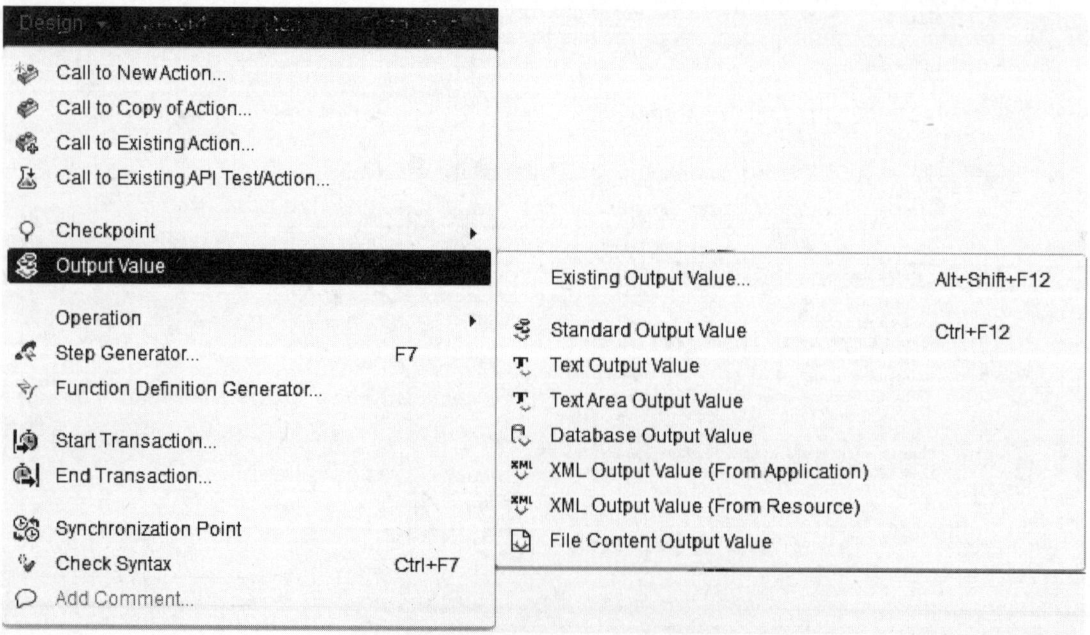

Figure 29.29 *Inserting output value*

This option allows users to reuse already created output values.

Similarly, option 'Existing Checkpoint' allows to reuse an already developed checkpoint.

Inserting Output value in a test

Example: Write code to output the payment details of the web table shown in Fig. 29.12 to local data table.

Described below are the steps to insert a table output value in a test:

1. Open the test script.
2. Open application under test.
3. Click on the *Record* button .
   Recording toolbar opens as shown in the Fig. 29.2 and recording begins.
4. Navigate Design → Output Value → Standard Output Value… Hand toolbar appears.
5. Point the hand toolbar to the table object for which table checkpoint needs to be created. (Assume, hand tool is pointed and clicked on *the Payment details* web table as shown in the Fig. 29.12).
6. *Standard Output Value* dialog box opens. (This dialog box is similar as shown in the Fig. 29.4). Select the web table object on which checkpoint needs to be applied and click OK button.
7. *Table Output Values Properties* window opens as shown in Fig. 29.30.
8. Select the table cells for which output value is to be created. An icon appears for the table cell for which output value is created.
9. Select the table cell whose output configuration is to be modified.
10. Click on the button *Modify* to configure the output value settings. Window *Output Options* opens as shown in the Fig. 29.32.
11. On Output Options dialog box, select the output type—data table or environment.

    a. If selected output type is 'Data Table', then:

    - **i.** Modify the name of the output value, if required. A column will be created in data table using the same name.
    - **ii.** Select data table—Global or Local

    b. If selected output type is 'Environment', then:

    - **i.** Modify the name of the output value, if required. A internal (inbuilt) environment variable will be created using the same name.

12. Click *OK* button to save the configuration options. *Table Output Value Properties* dialog box opens with the updated configurations.
13. Repeat steps 9 to 12 to modify configuration options of various table cells.
14. Click *OK* button to insert the output value in the test
15. Following code is inserted in the test:

```
Browser("B").Page("P").WebTable("Payment Option").Output
CheckPoint("Payment Option")
```

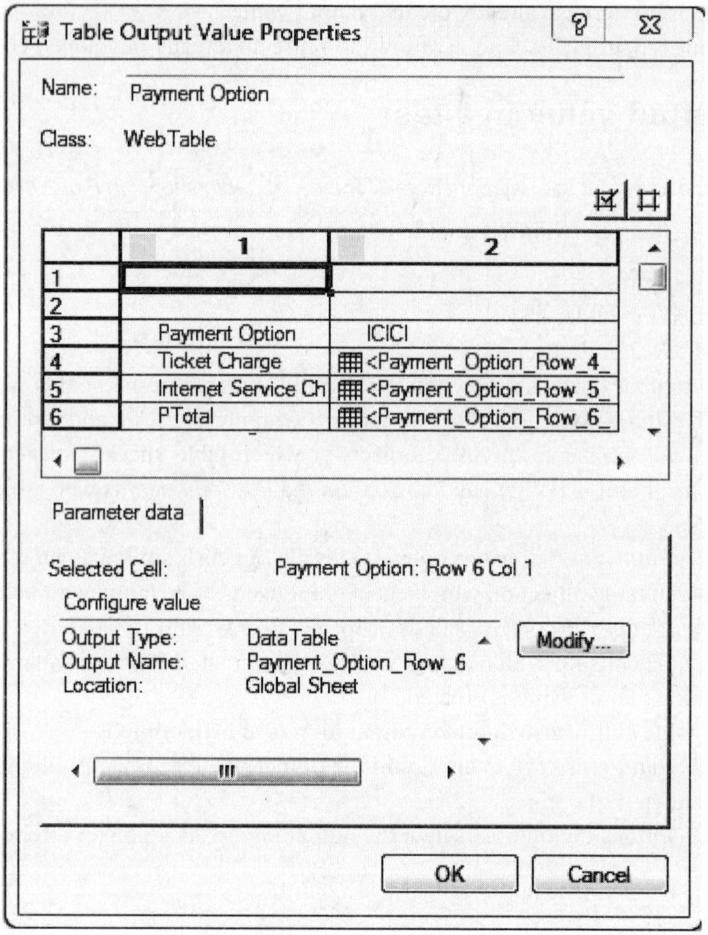

Figure 29.30 *Inserting table output value*

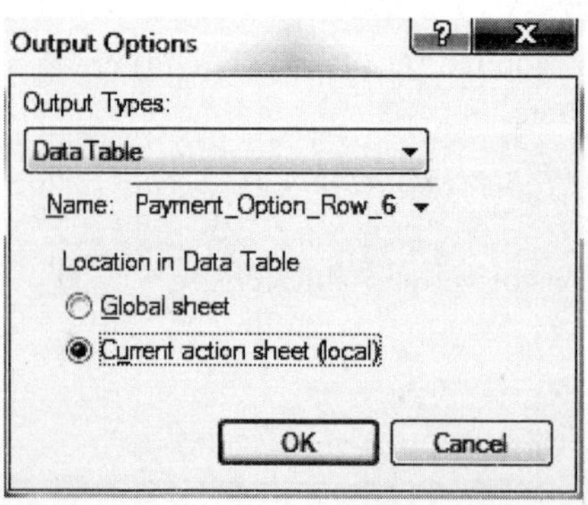

Figure 29.31 *Output value to data table*

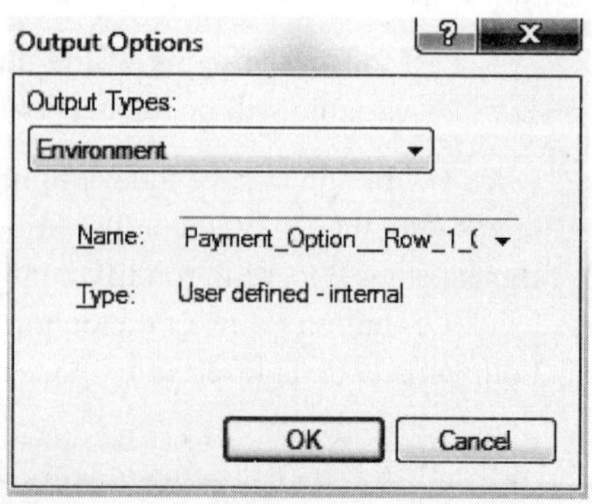

Figure 29.32 *Output value to environment variable*

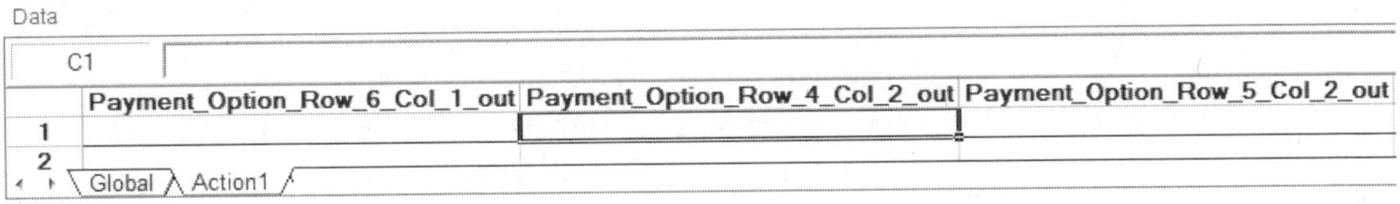

Figure 29.33 *Columns created in local data table for output values*

16. Assume local data table option was chosen as the output option for all the tests. In this case, a new column will be created in the local data table for every selected cell as shown in the Fig. 29.33. During run-time, UFT will update table cell values against these columns.

> **NOTES**
>
> Output value is used to capture test output data values such as purchase order number, flight booking number etc. to data tables or environment variables. These output values can then be used as input parameter for executing a specific step within the test such as 'order tracking using purchase order number' or can be used to track the transaction created by the test once execution is over. This is essentially useful to track the failure reason, in case UFT test fails.

Scripting Output Values

Code can be written to capture values of various objects in the same way as coded checkpoints are implemented. The output values can be updated as environment variables or updated in data table, Excel files, flat files, or databases, as desired.

QUICK TIPS

- ✓ Checkpoints are used to compare the expected results with the actual run-time results. It is used to determine whether a test case has passed or failed.
- ✓ Output value is used to capture test output data such as purchase order number, flight booking number etc. to data tables or environment variables.
- ✓ Most of the UFT inbuilt checkpoints are based on the record/playback technique.
- ✓ It is advisable to use coded checkpoints than record/playback-based UFT inbuilt checkpoints.
- ✓ Image checkpoint checks the properties of the image such as source file location, height, and width.
- ✓ Bitmap checkpoint compares two images pixel by pixel.
- ✓ Text checkpoint checks whether the specified text is displayed on the screen or not.
- ✓ Text area checkpoint checks whether the specified text is displayed at the specified location on the screen or not.

? PRACTICAL QUESTIONS

1. What is the use of checkpoints in test automation?
2. What are the advantages of coded checkpoints over recorded checkpoints?
3. What is the difference between Image checkpoint and Bitmap checkpoint?
4. What is the difference between Text checkpoint and Text-Area checkpoint?
5. Write one real-time scenario where:
   a. Sync statement is necessary to use.
   b. Wait statement is necessary to use.
   c. WaitProperty statement is necessary to use.
   d. Exist statement is necessary to use.

Chapter **30**

Debugging

After a test script or a function has been created, it needs to be tested. In automation, testing of the developed code is done to check if the code is performing the intended operation or not. If any issue is found in the code, then it is fixed. Automation developers should ensure that the developed code is running smoothly without any errors in syntax or logic. HP Unified Functional Testing provides various debugging features to help the automation developers analyze the code behavior during run-time.

UFT also provides the flexibility to modify variable values and executes commands during run-time. For example, breakpoints can be placed at desired points in the test script to pause script execution at that particular point during run-time. Similarly, the 'Pause' button can be used to pause test script execution at any point during script execution. Once the script is in 'Paused' state, 'watch' tab of the Debug Viewer pane can be used to see specific variable values at that particular point during run-time (see Figure 30.1). The 'Variables' tab can be used to watch the values of all the variables in the current scope at that point during run-time. QTP provides 'Command' tab to execute spe- cific commands such as assigning values to variables or checking browser existence during run-time. UFT supports various step commands to execute the test script line by line.

NOTES

UFT allows script debugging only if Microsoft Script Debugger is installed.

Debug Session Speed

UFT offers two test execution modes—*Normal* and *Fast*.

Normal mode displays execution marker. It is generally used to debug tests. UFT allows to add a desired pause time between execution of two steps in Normal mode to make debugging easier. This pause time can be configured from *Runs* node as:

- Navigate *Tools* → *Options* → *GUI Testing tab* → *Test Runs* node.
  Runs node opens.
- Configure the pause time in Runs node as shown in the figure below.

In Fast mode, no execution marker is displayed. UFT execute tests steps quickly in Fast mode. Generally, this mode is used for executing runs.

The various debug features that UFT provides are discussed below.

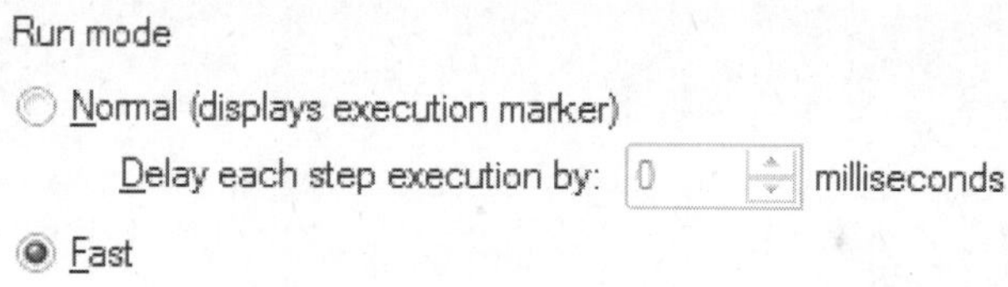

Figure 30.1 *Configuring UFT run mode*

BREAKPOINTS

Breakpoints are inserted in a test to pause script execution at a particular line of the script. UFT enters into debug mode from execution mode at the point where breakpoint is placed. Break- points can be applied by the following ways:

(a) Right click the mouse on the left side of the line where code needs to be debugged,
(b) Pressing F9 key on the line where code needs to be debugged, or
(c) Inserting breakpoints from menu bar as *Run* → *Insert/Remove Breakpoint* on the line where code needs to be debugged.

A red circle appears on the left side of the line where breakpoint is placed. Suppose that breakpoint is applied at line 4 of the following code; then, the code execution will happen till line 3 and thereafter it will pause at line 4.

```
'Debugging UFT Code
 1. Dim nSum, fnStat
 2. Dim nNum1: nNum1=10
 3. Dim nNum2: nNum2=20
 4. ●Msgbox "nNum1:" & nNum1 & vbTab & "nNum2:" & nNum2
 5. fnStat = fnSumNbr(nNum1, nNum2, nSum)
 6. Print fnStat & "::" & nSum
 7. Function fnSumNbr(nNum1, nNum2, nSum)
 8.    On Error Resume Next
 9.    nSum = nNum1 + nNum2
10.    ●If Err.Number <> 0 Then
11.            fnSumNbr = "-1" 'Function execution failed
12.            nSum = "fnSumNbr::" & Err.Description
13.    Else
14.            fnSumNbr = "0"      'Function executed successfully
15.    End If
16. End Function
```

> **NOTES**: Test scripts can also be paused at run-time by clicking on the 'Pause' button located on the *Tool* bar.

STEP COMMANDS

Once the test script is in the paused state, UFT provides various step commands to continue code execution either step by step or after certain steps as desired. The various step commands of UFT are as follows:

- Step Into (F11)—Step Into is used to execute only the current step in the active test script or function library. If the current step is a call to an action or a function, then the test execution pauses at the first line of the called action or function and the same is displayed on the UFT window. For example, if we press F11 at line 5, the code execution will pause at line 8. Step into is used to debug any function or action that are part of the code. To use step into command, press F11 or the Step Into button.
- Step Over (F10)—Step Over is used to execute the current step of the test script. If the current step is an action or a function, then complete action or function is executed in one go and is not displayed in UFT window. After execution of the current step, script execution halts at the next step. However, if breakpoints are defined inside the function or the action, then the script execution will halt at that particular breakpoint. For example, in the above case, if we press F10 at line 5, script execution will halt at line 10. If there would have been no breakpoint at line 10, then script execution would have paused at line 6. Step over is used to execute code step by step. To use step over command, press F10 or click the Step Over button.
- Step Out (Shift + F11)—Step Out is used to come out of any action or function. Step out completely executes the current action or function and thereafter returns to the calling action or function library and then pauses the test script at the next line (if it exists). For example, if we press Shift + F11 at line 11, then code execution will pause at line 6. Step out is used to return to the called action or function library. To use step out command, press Shift + F11 or the Step Out button.

DEBUG VIEWER PANE

UFT provides Debug Viewer pane to change variable values or analyze application behavior during run-time. The various tabs of the Debug Viewer pane are:

1. Output tab
2. Watch tab,
3. Local Variables tab, and
4. Console tab

Output Tab

Output tab displays the output of the *Print* statement. Figure 30.2 shows the output of the *print* statement of line 6.

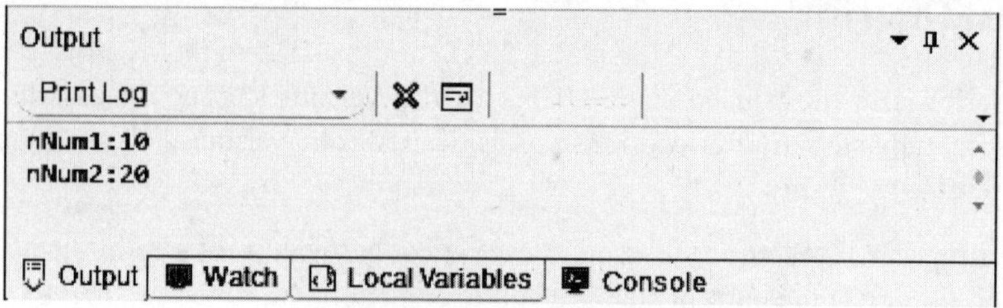

Figure 30.2 *Output tab*

Watch Tab

In watch tab, we can view, add and edit variable values during run-time. To add variables in the watch pane, select the variable → Right Click → select option *Add to Watch*. Alternatively, we can also directly write the variable name in the name field of Watch tab and UFT will automatically populate the variable value and variable type in the *Value* and *Type* field of watch expression pane. To modify any variable value, we can directly click on the Value field and change its value as shown in Fig. 30.3.

We can observe in Fig. 30.3 that the value of variable *sString* has been changed manually in the watch tab. Initially, the value of the variable sString was 'Book on Test Automation & QTP' After modifying the variable value from 'watch' tab, its value is 'Book on Agile Automation & UFT'

UFT also provides the flexibility to execute single-line VBScript or UFT statements in the watch tab. For example, the following code checks whether UFT is able to recognize the page object in GUI at that particular point at run-time or not.

```
Browser().Page().WebTable().Exist
```

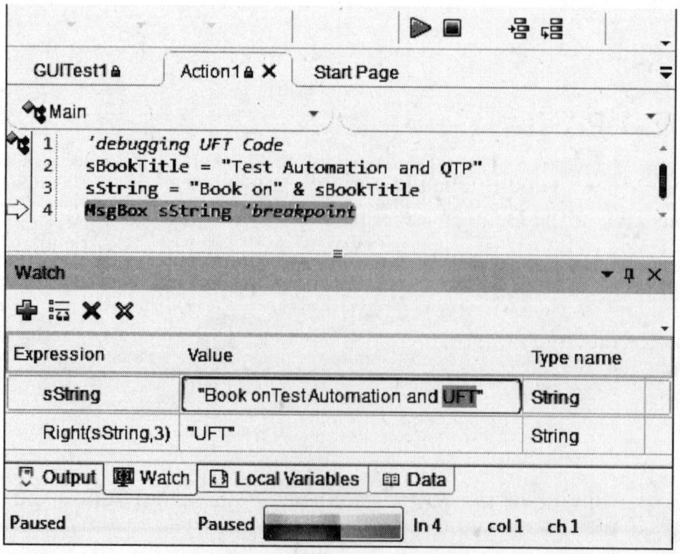

Figure 30.3 *Watch tab*

Similarly, the following code can be executed in 'watch' tab during the time script is in 'pause' state. This code clicks on an image object inside cell (1,2) of a WebTable.

```
Browser().Page().WebTable().ChildItem(1,2,"Image",0).Click
```

VBScript statements can also be executed in 'watch' tab as shown in Fig. 30.3.

```
Right(sString,3)
```

The watch tab can also be used to execute single-line UFT commands. UFT statements such as retrieving run-time object properties, checking object existence, and clicking on a button can be executed in the watch tab. Figure 30.4 shows an example of how to execute single-line UFT statements in the watch tab.

- Line 1 of the watch tab highlights the "FlyingFrom' edit box in the application.
- Line 2 retrieves the 'html id' property value of the 'FlyingFrom' edit box object.
- Line 3 shows even descriptive code can be executed from Watch tab. The third line retrieves the 'value' property of the edit box object whose 'html id' is 'flight-origin'.
- Line 4 clicks on the 'Search' button object.

> **NOTES** The watch tab can also be used to view the values of arrays, objects, and collections.

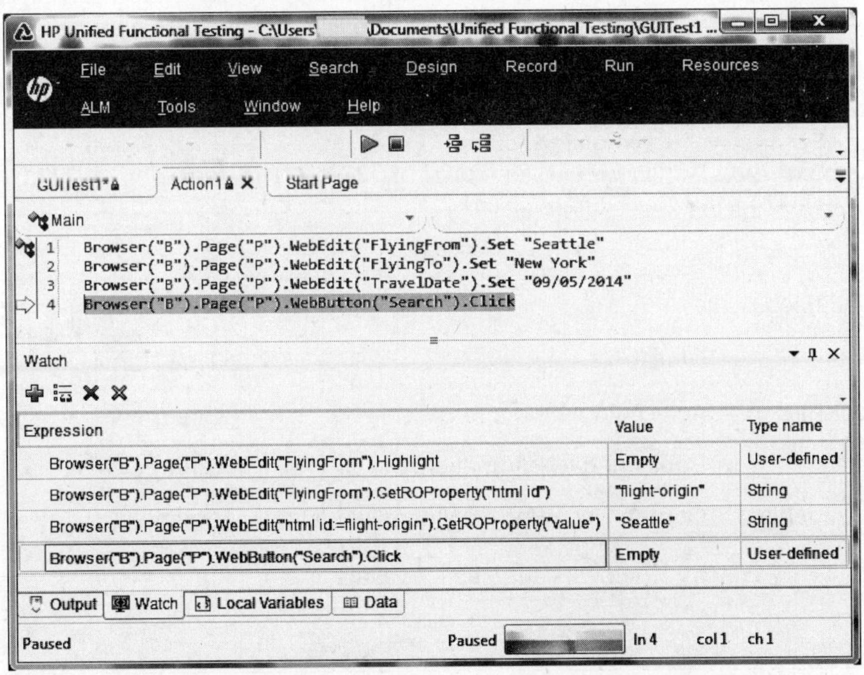

Figure 30.4 *Executing UFT statements in watch tab*

Local Variables Tab

In local variables tab, we can see all the variable names, variable values, and variable types that fall in the local scope of the test script or function library that is currently in execution (see Figure 30.5).

Console Tab

Console tab is used to execute VBScript or UFT statements or code. Console tab can be activated during debug mode from Menu bar as *View* → *Debug* → *Console*. To execute a code statement we can write that statement as it is in the command prompt of the Console tab as shown in Fig. 30.6. New variables created in Console tab can be viewed in variables tab or watch tab.

In Fig. 30.6, values to variables 'sVar' and 'sString' are assigned from Console tab. Fig. 30.7 shows that how these variables can be seen in 'Local Variables' tab.

NOTES

We can also execute single-line QTP statements/code in the Console tab. For example:

```
bExistFlg = Browser().Page().WebTable().Exist
Browser().Page().WebTable().ChildItem(1,2,"Image",0).Click
```

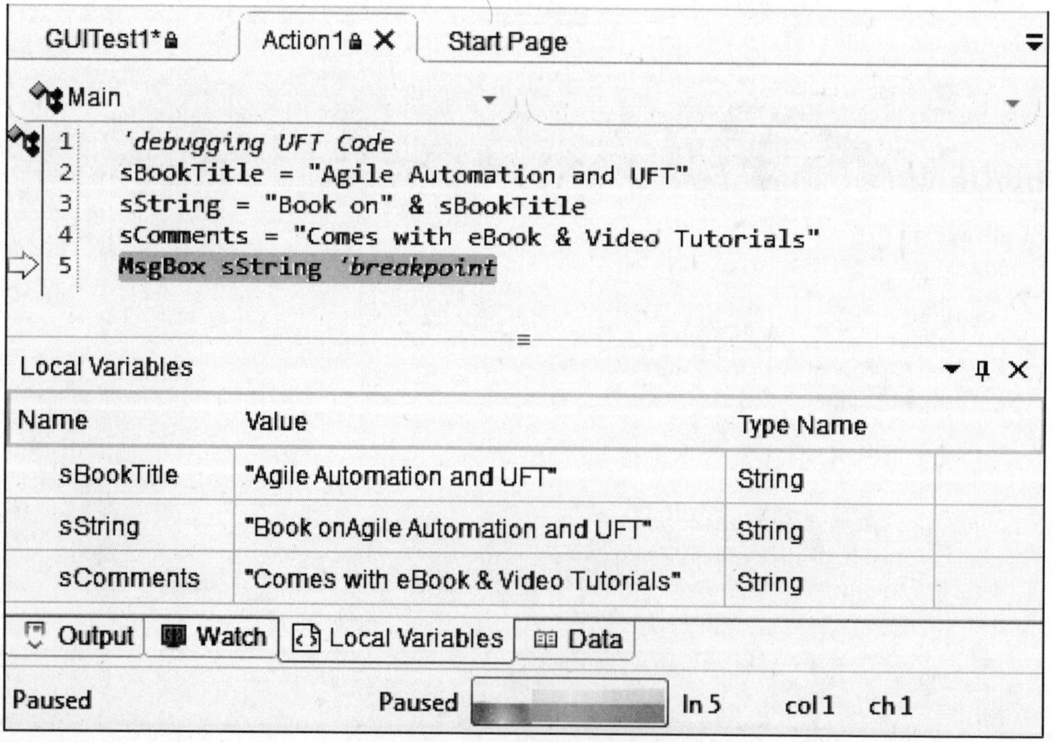

Figure 30.5 Local *variables tab*

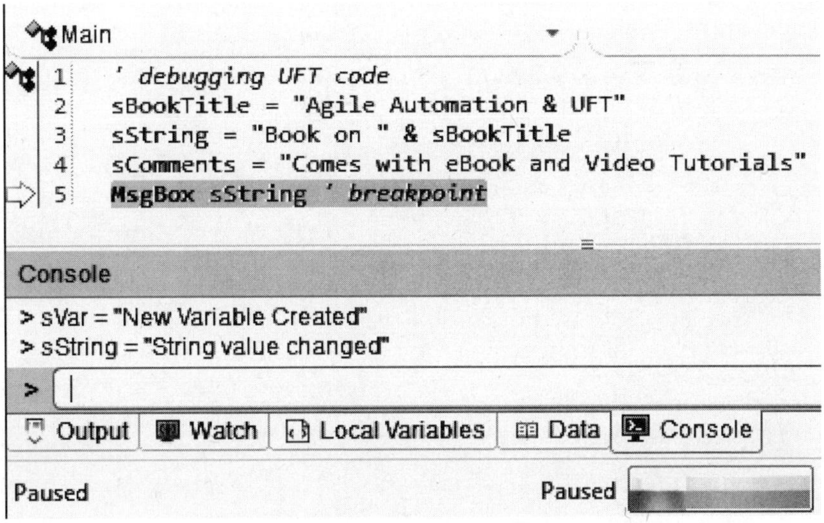

Figure 30.6 *Executing code statements from console tab*

Error Pane

Errors pane provides information on the coding errors in an action. It also provides information on missing resources such as missing library files, OR files, configuration files, or any other file which was previously associated with the action or test but currently cannot be found at the specified location. Figure 30.8 shows the missing resources pane for missing object repository'AppName.tsr'.

Run/Debug Commands

UFT always runs a test or component from the first step, unless specified otherwise. UFT can be instructed to:

- Starts a run session from the selected step.
- Starts a debug session from the selected step.
- Star a run session till the selected step

Local Variables

Name	Value	Type Name
sBookTitle	"Agile Automation & UFT"	String
sString	"String value changed"	String
sComments	"Comes with eBook and Video Tutorials"	String
sVar	"New Variable Created"	String

Figure 30.7 *Local variables tab*

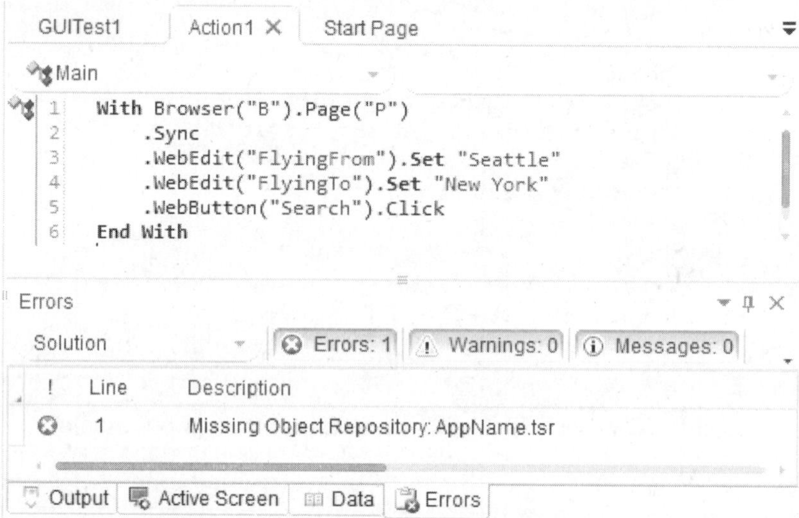

Figure 30.8 *Errors pane showing missing resources*

QUICK TIPS

- ✓ UFT allows script debugging only if Microsoft Script Debugger is installed.
- ✓ Breakpoints are used to automatically pause script execution at run-time.
- ✓ Step Over is used to execute current step of the test script. It could be a one-line UFT code or a function/action call.
- ✓ Step Into is used to execute only the current step in the active test script or function library.
- ✓ Step Out is used to come out of any action or function.
- ✓ Watch tab is used to analyze specific variable/array values at run-time.
- ✓ Watch tab can also be used to execute single-line UFT commands.
- ✓ Variable tab shows the values of all the variables at run-time.
- ✓ Command tab is used to execute single-line UFT statements/commands.
- ✓ Missing resources pane provides information about missing library files, OR files, configuration files, etc.

PRACTICAL QUESTIONS

1. What is breakpoint? What is its significance in script debugging?
2. Explain the difference between step over, step into, and step out.
3. Explain the difference between watch tab and local variables tab?
4. Can 'watch' tab be used to execute commands?

Chapter 31

Recovery Scenario and Error Handler

Automated test scripts are developed to run in batches in an unattended mode. However, when tests are run in unattended mode, many unforeseen run-time issues can occur. These issues can completely stop the execution of the test suite and can disrupt the results. For example, occurrence of an unexpected pop-window during run-time can cause the complete test suite to fail. If these run-time issues are not handled, then they become regular phenomena that greatly impact the regression runs. Continuous failure of the regression runs becomes a showstopper for the automation team and defeat the basic objective of test automation. It is very essential to make sure that run-time errors are properly handled. Automation developers need to develop a code to handle the run-time errors in a way that the complete test suite executes successfully. UFT provides recovery scenarios to handle such run-time exceptions. In addition, VBScript error handlers are to be used in situations where recovery scenarios are not sufficient to handle the exception.

Whenever an unhandled exception occurs during test script execution, UFT pauses the test script execution and throws a pop-up window that contains details of the run-time error as shown in Fig. 31.1.

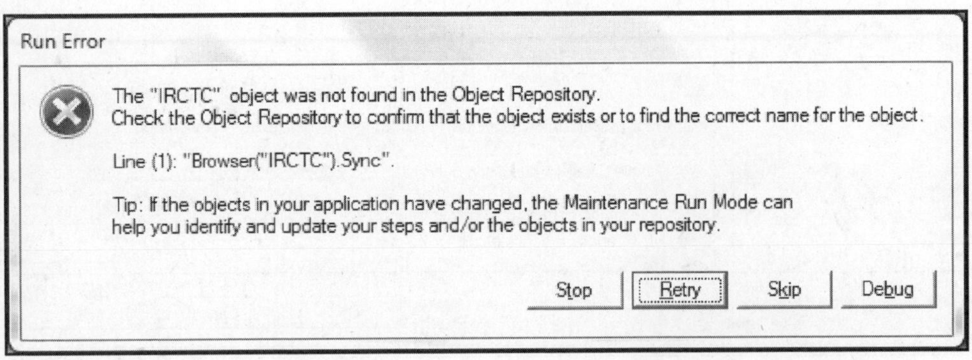

Figure 31.1 *UFT run-time error window*

The execution of the test suite is paused if even once this error occurs during execution. For unattended execution, it becomes a must to suppress this error so that the complete test suite executes successfully. There are three ways of suppressing this error:

- By modifying UFT run-time setting in *Test settings...* tab
- By designing recovery scenarios
- By designing VBScript error handlers

MODIFYING UFT TEST SETTINGS

UFT provides an option to suppress the 'pop message boxes' that occur when an error occurs during script execution. This can be achieved by modifying the run-time settings of UFT in test settings... tab. Follow the steps below to modify run-time settings:

Navigate *File* → *Settings... Test Settings* window opens as shown in the Fig. 31.2.

Click on node *Run*. Run-time settings node shows on the screen.

Select appropriate option from the list box corresponding to label 'When error occurs during run session' as shown in Fig. 31.2.

(i) **Pop-up message box:** If this option is selected, then UFT throws a pop-up error message box whenever an exception occurs during script execution.

(ii) **Proceed to next action iteration:** On occurrence of a run-time error, UFT skips the execu-

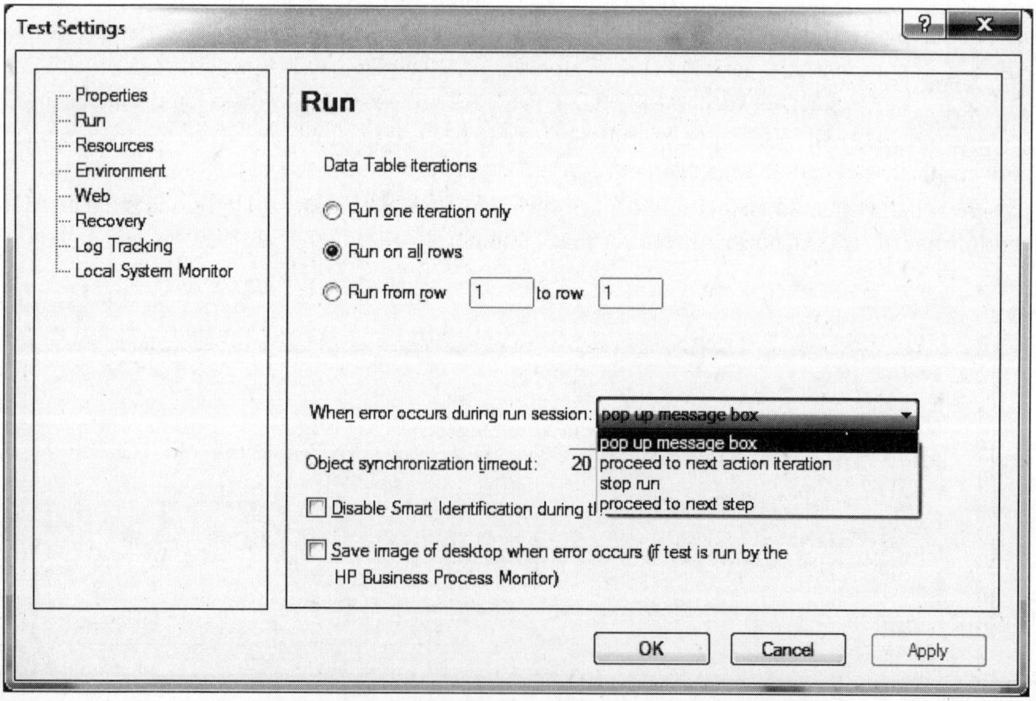

Figure 31.2 *Configuring error-handling condition*

tion of the current action iteration and starts executing the next iteration. No pop-up error message is thrown to the user.

(iii) Stop run: UFT stops the test execution if an exception occurs during run-time. In this case, no pop-up error message is thrown to the user.

(iv) Proceed to next step: UFT skips the execution of the current step and starts executing the next step. In this case also, the error is neglected and no pop-up error message box is thrown to the user.

RECOVERY SCENARIOS

UFT recovery scenario provides a mechanism to handle run-time errors or exceptions that occur during script execution. There are two types of exceptions that can occur during script execution:

- Expected exception
- Unexpected exception

Expected exception includes scenarios where certain pop-up window appears randomly. Here, we know that a window can appear, but we are not certain of it. Such exceptions are called *expected exceptions*. *Unexpected exceptions* include scenarios whose occurrence cannot be predicted, such as 'object not found' error or 'divide by zero' error. Recovery scenario and error handlers provide features to effectively handle expected and unexpected exceptions. Exception handling helps to execute test scripts successfully in an unattended mode.

In UFT, a recovery scenario consists of three events: trigger event, recovery action, and post-recovery action. Trigger event defines when the specified recovery scenario will get activated. Once the recovery scenario has been activated, recovery action decides how to handle the occurred exception. After the exception has been handled properly, post-recovery action decides whether the next step of the test script is to be executed or the test script execution is to be skipped or do something else (as defined in a function). Depending on the run-time errors, one or more recovery scenarios can be designed and associated with the test.

Trigger event: An event that interrupts test script execution. This event acts as trigger event to activate recovery scenario. Trigger events could be one of the following:

Pop-up window: An unexpected pop-up window is opened during script execution.

Object state: Property value of an object matches specified values.

Test run error: A step in the test script does not run successfully.

Application crash: Application crashes during script execution.

Recovery action: This defines how to handle the occurred exception. UFT provides the following recovery options:

Keyboard or Mouse operation: Emulate keyboard or mouse click

Close application process: Close any application process such as iexplore.exe

Function call: Make a call to a function. The function contains code, which defines how to handle the exception

Restart Microsoft Windows: Restart Windows

Post-recovery action: This specifies how UFT should proceed after the recovery action has been taken. The following post-recovery options are available:

Repeat current step and continue proceed to next step
Proceed to next action or component iteration Proceed to next test iteration
Restart current test run Stop the test run

RECOVERY SCENARIO DESIGN

In day-to-day automation, it is observed that application developers most often change the application objects prop- erties without informing the test automation team. As a result of which, when test scripts are executed UFT throws an error 'object not found.' Let us design a recovery scenario that handles this error. Here,

- Trigger event will be 'test run error'.
- Recovery action will be to take a screenshot of application, and
- Post-recovery action will be to stop current test case execution and start executing the next test case. To design a recovery scenario follow the steps below:
    - Navigate Resources → *Recovery Scenario Manager…*
      Recovery Scenario Manager window opens as shown in Fig. 31.3.
    - Click on the button 'New Scenario'
      Recovery Scenario Wizard window opens as shown in Fig. 31.4.
    - Click on the button *Next*
      Select Trigger Event window is displayed as shown in Fig. 31.5.
    - Define *Trigger* event.

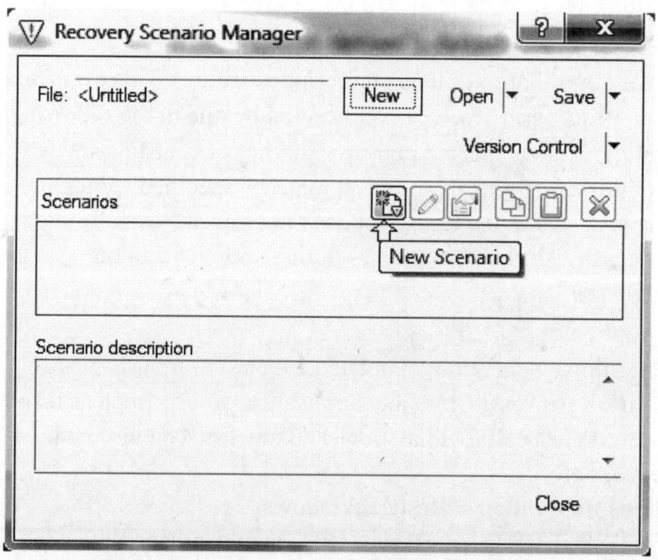

Figure 31.3 *Recovery scenario manager*

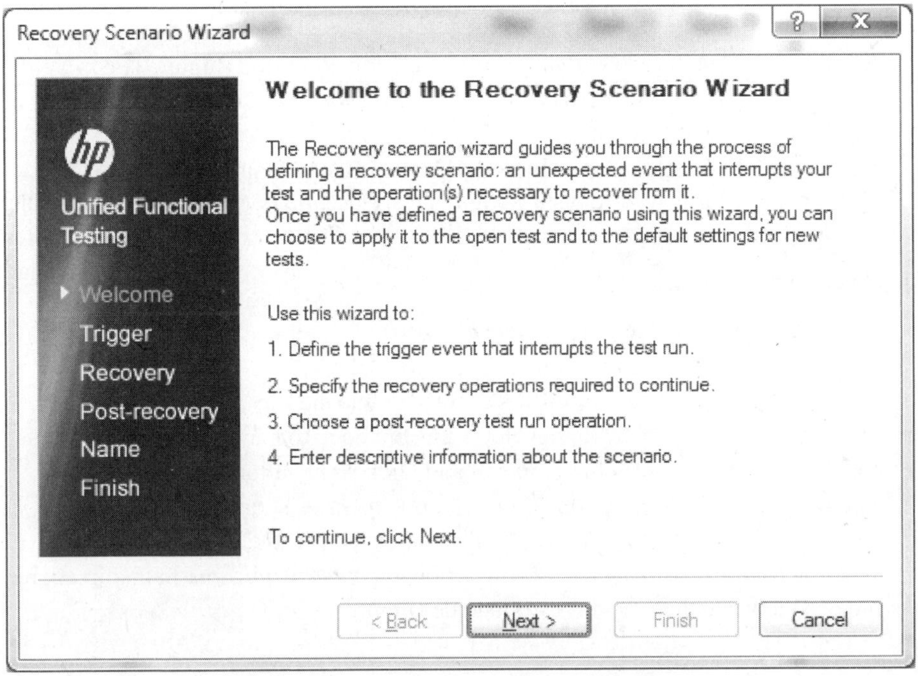

Figure 31.4 *Recovery scenario wizard*

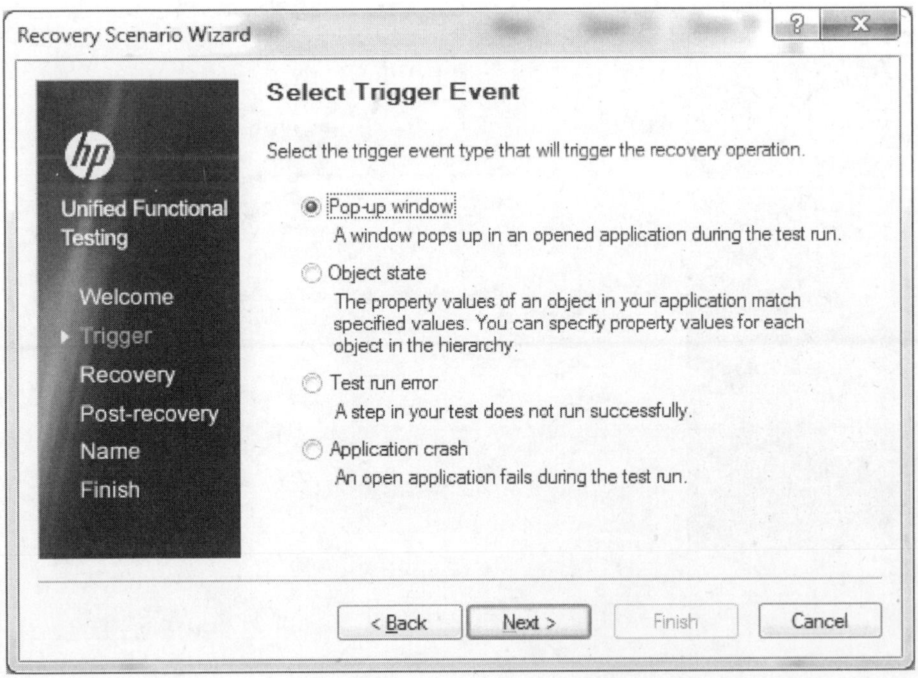

Figure 31.5 *Select trigger event*

Trigger Event

- Select trigger event as *Test Run Error* and click next button (Figure 31.5).
  Recovery Scenario Wizard displays *Select Test Run Error* window as shown in the Fig. 31.6.
- Select error type as *Any Error* and click *Next* button. (Figure 31.6).
  Recovery Scenario Wizard displays *Recovery Operations* window as shown in Fig. 31.7.

Recovery Action

- Click *Next* .button on *Recovery Operations* window shown in Fig. 31.7.
  Recovery Operation window opens as shown in Fig. 31.8.
- *Recovery Operation* window allows users to define the way the exception is to be handled. Here, we will discuss how to develop a custom code to handle exceptions.
- Select recovery action as function call and click *Next* button.
- *Recovery Operation—Function Call* window opens as shown in the Fig. 31.9.
- *Recovery Operation—Function Call* window select the function library where this function needs to be designed. Select option *Define new function.* In the function window, we need to write the recovery action code (Figure 31.9).

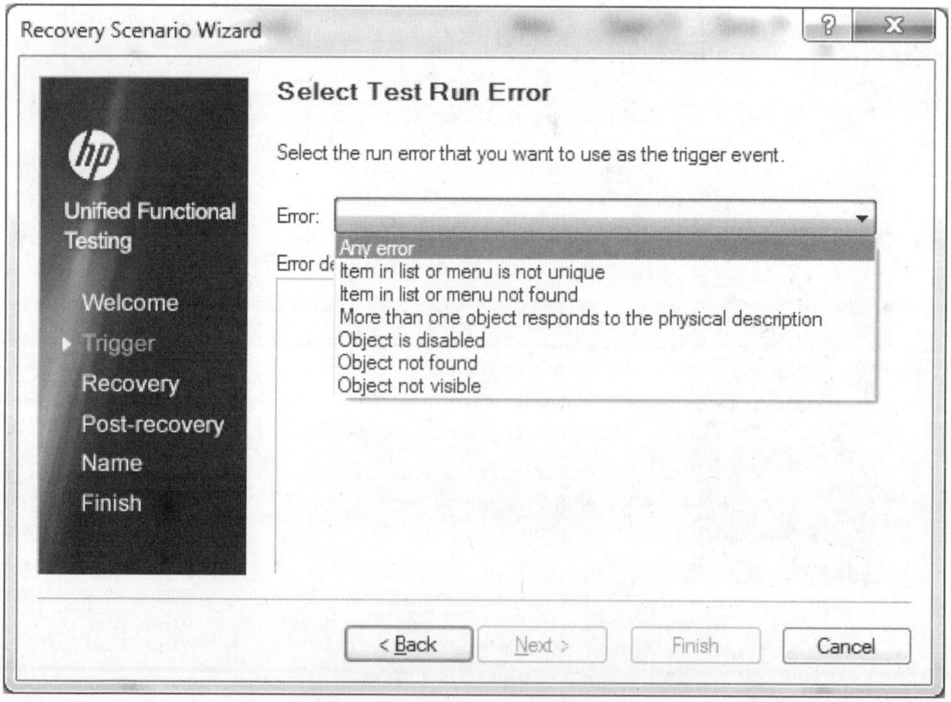

Figure 31.6 *Select error type*

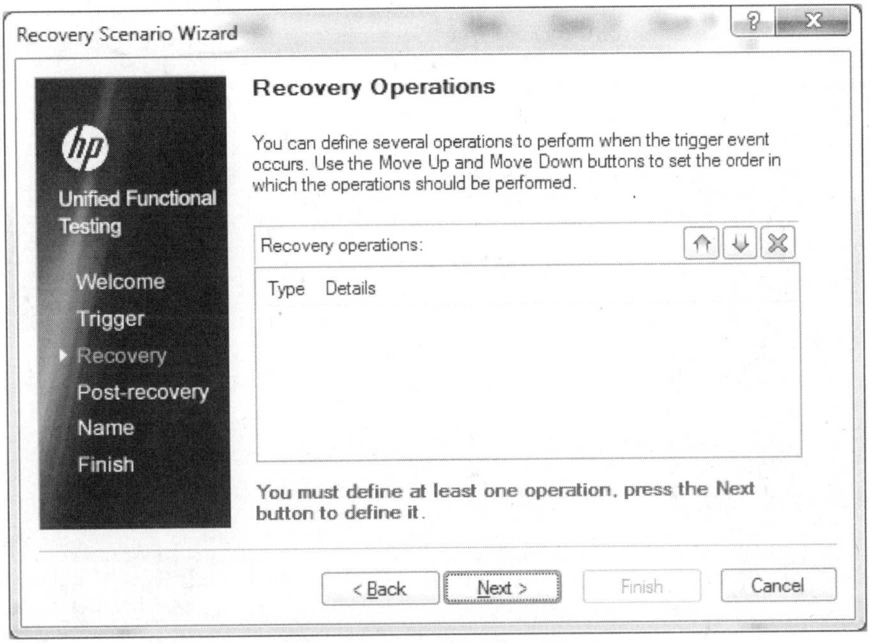

Figure 31.7 *Recovery operations*

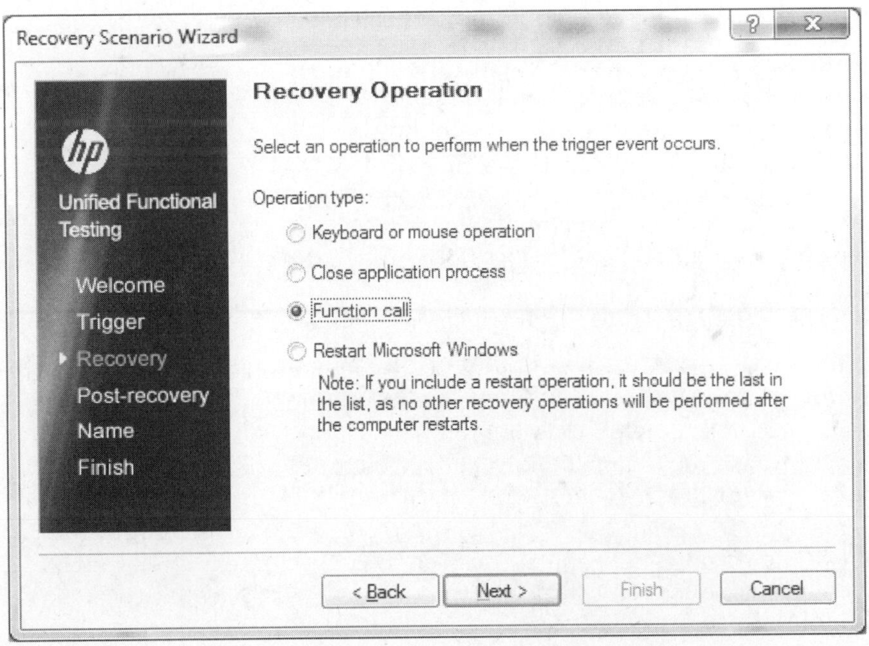

Figure 31.8 *Select recovery operation*

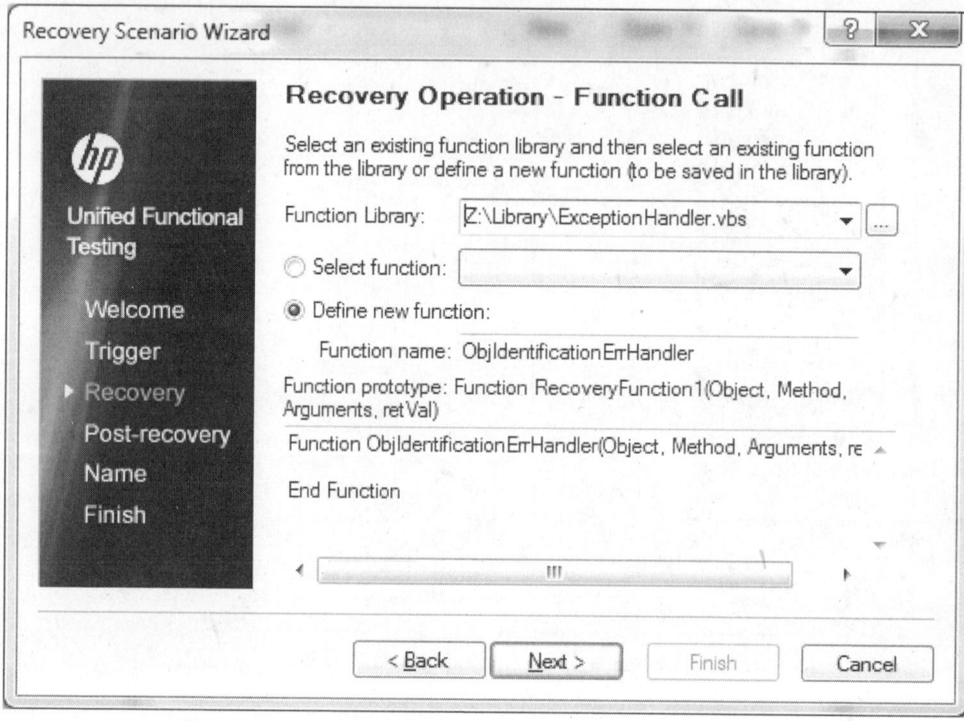

Figure 31.9 *Define function*

```
Function RecvryScnroObjErr(Object, Method, Arguments, retVal)
    'Environment.Value("ErrScrnShotsPath") = "C:\Temp\"
    'mention which object was not found
    Environment.Value("RunStatMsg") = "Error : " &
                                        Object.ToString & " not Found"
    'Create a string of current date and time
    sCurrDtTm = Day(Date) & "-" & MonthName(Month(Date),True) & "-"
                                                & Year(Date) &" " & time
    sCurrDtTm = Replace(sCurrDtTm,":","-")

'Create a string of current date, time, and current action, which
was executing and object, which was not found
Environment.Value("ErrScrnShotsPath") =
    Environment.Value("ErrScrnShots") & sCurrDtTm & "_" &
        Environment.Value("ActionName") & "_" &
                                                Object.ToString & ".bmp"
    'Capture desktop screenshot and save it to the given path.
    Desktop.CaptureBitmap(Environment.Value("ErrScrnShotsPath"))
End Function
```

Output : 29-Mar-2010 10-11-24 AM_Logon [Logon]_[Logout] link.bmp

NOTES

1. For trigger event: Pop-up Window or Object State
   Function template is

```
Function RecoveryFunction1(Object)
        ... ... ...
  End Function
Object—refers to the object that is found in application
```

2. For trigger event: Test run error
   Function template is

```
Function RecoveryFunction2(Object, Method, Arguments, retVal)
        ... ... ...
End Function
Object—refers to the current step object
Method—refers to the current step method
Arguments—refers to the method arguments as array
retVal—return value
```

3 For trigger event: Application crash Function template is

```
Function RecoveryFunction3(ProcessName, ProcessID)
    ... ... ...
End Function
ProcessName—refers to the process that crashed ProcessID—
refers to the process id of the process name.
```

Specify function name and define function as shown (Figure 31.9).

3. Post-Recovery Action

- Click *Next* button on *Recovery Operation—Function call* window. *Recovery Operations* window opens as shoen in the Fig. 31.10. This window displays the summary of the 'recovery actions' created.
- Click *Next* button on *Recovery Operations* window.
  Post-recovery Test Run Options window opens as shown in the Fig. 31.11.
- On *Post-recovery Test Run Options* window, select post-recovery action as *Proceed to next action or component iteration* (Figure 31.11) and click *Next* button.
  Name and Description window opens as shown in the Fig. 31.12.
- Define recovery scenario name and its description (Figure 31.12) and click *Next* button.
  Completing the Recovery Scenarion Wizard Window opens as shown in the Fig. 31.13. Figure 31.13 shows the 'Recovery Scenario Wizard' screen, which shows the summary details of the designed recovery scenario.
- Click *Finish* button.
- Pop-up window opens to save the recovery sceanario. Save the recovery scenario say as RecoveryScenarios.qrs.

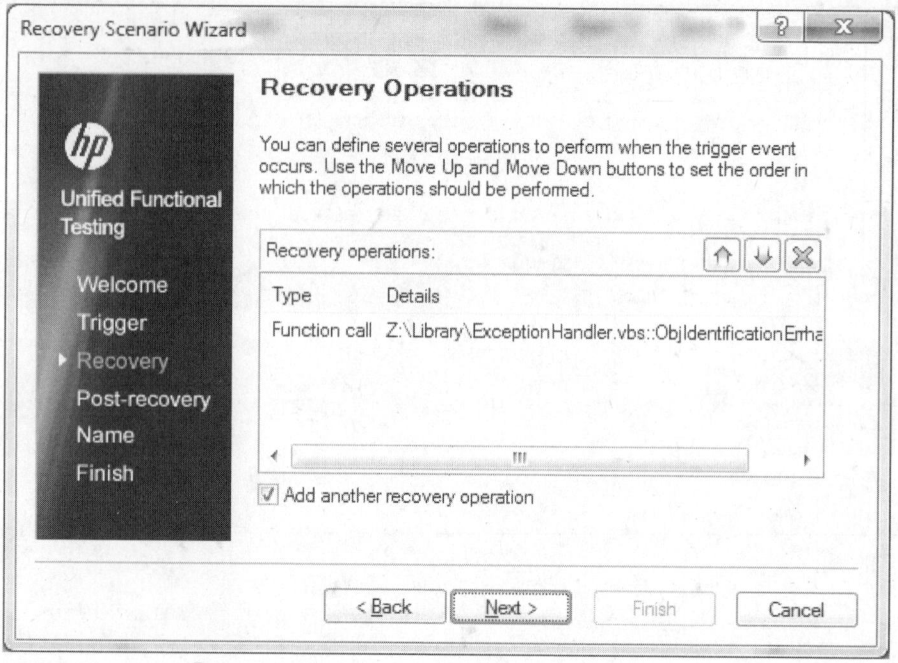

Figure 31.10 *Recovery operations window*

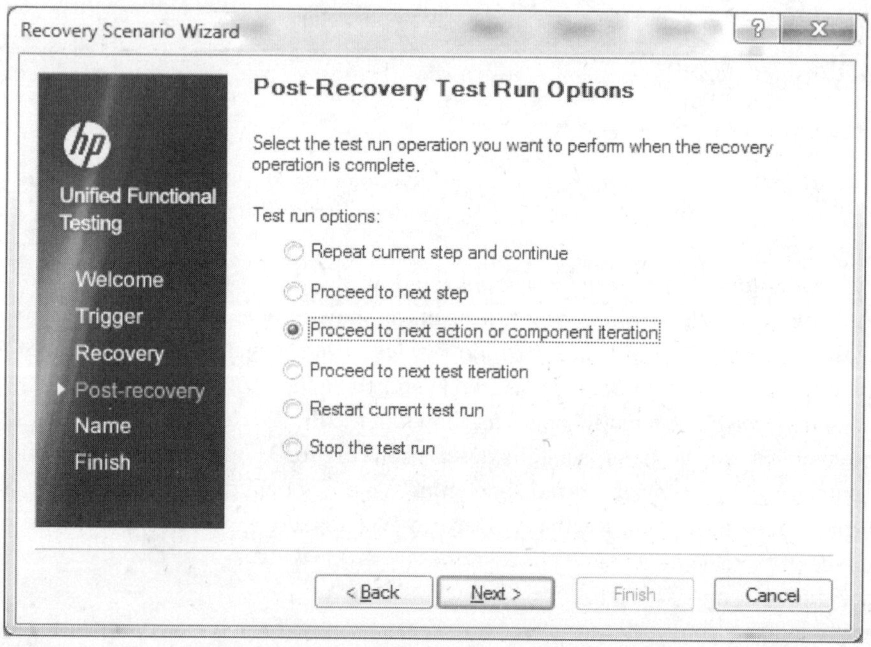

Figure 31.11 *Select post-recovery action*

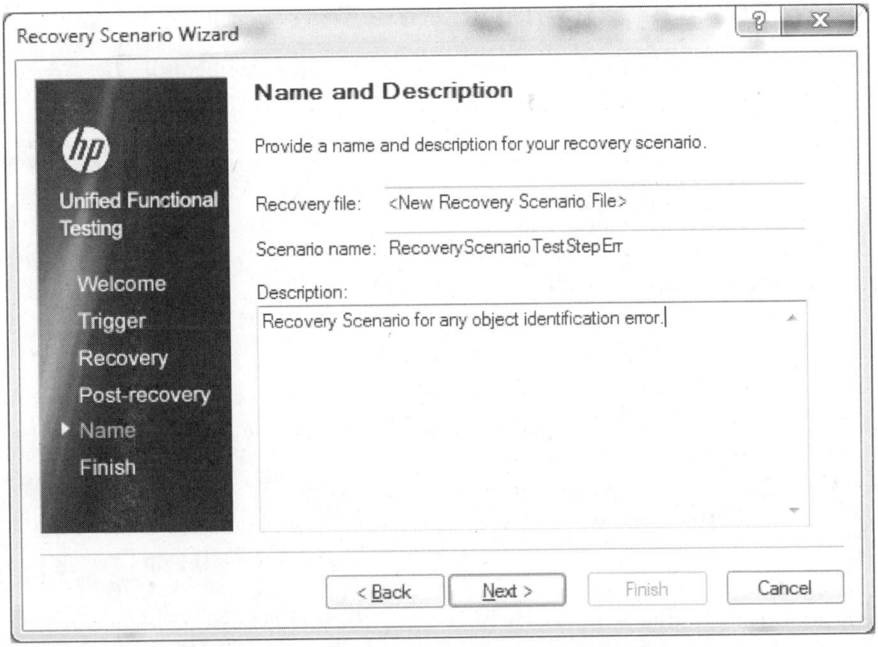

Figure 31.12 *Define recovery scenario name*

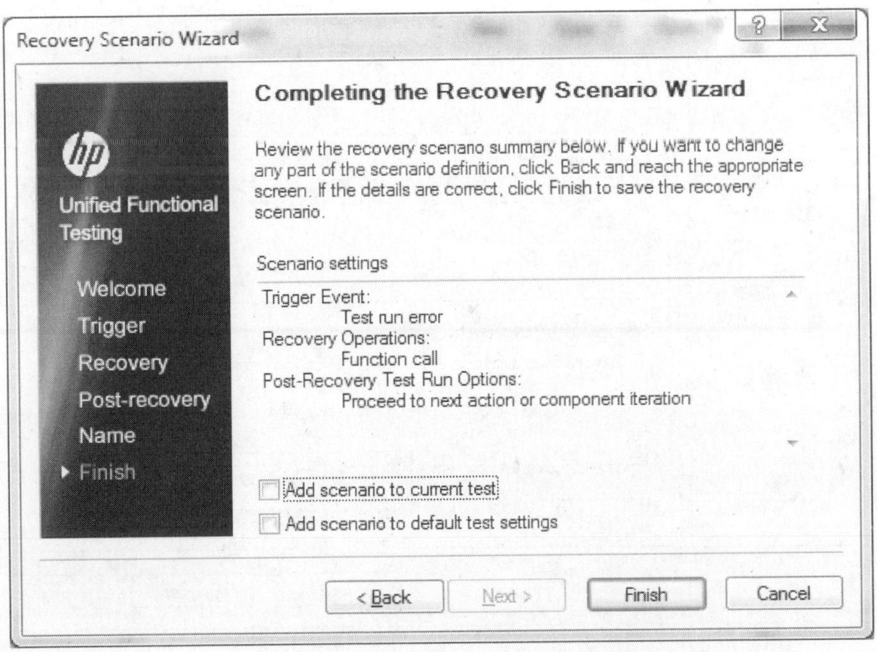

Figure 31.13 *Recovery scenario wizard*

Associating Recovery Scenarios to a Test

Recovery Scenarios can be associated with test from the *Recovery* node of the *Test Settings* window. Follow the steps below to associate a recovery scenario with a test.

Open the test.
Navigate *File* → *Settings*... *Test Settings* window opens.
Click on the *Recovery* node.
Recovery window opens as shown in the Figure 31.14 below.
To associate a recovery scenario, click on the *Add* button.
Add Recovery Scenario dialog box opens.
Locate the recovery scenario say RecoveryScenario.qrs.
Click button '*Add Scenario*' to associate the recovery scenario to the test.
Recovery Scenario node opens with updated associated recovery scenarios as shown in the Fig. 31.14.
Select one of the recovery scenario activation condition:

- **(i)** On every step: The recovery scenario mechanism is activated after every step.
- **(ii)** On error: The recovery scenario mechanism is activated if a test step throws an error.
- **(iii)** Never: The recovery scenario mechanism is disabled.

Click *OK* button to save the settings.

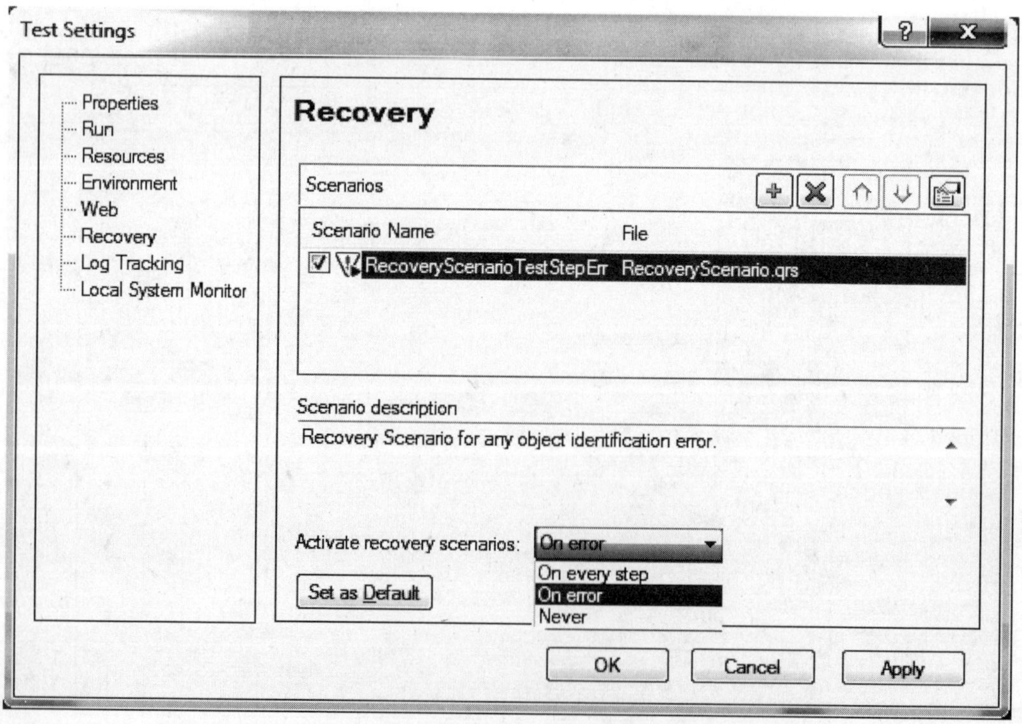

Figure 31.14 *Associating recovery scenarios to a test*

RECOVERY SCENARIO OBJECT

Recovery scenario object provides an interface to control or modify recovery settings during run-time using code.

Methods

The methods supported by the recovery scenario object are as follows:

Add: Adds the specified recovery scenario to a test script.

```
Syntax : Object.Add ScenarioFile, ScenarioName, [optional]Position
```

Find: Finds position of the specified recovery scenario. For example, if three recovery scenarios, recov1, recov2, and recov3, are added with order 1, 2, and 3, then the position of recov2 will be 2.

```
Syntax : Object.Find (ScenarioFile, ScenarioName)
```

MoveToPos: Changes the position of the recovery scenario. Syntax : Object.MoveToPos CurrentPos, NewPos Remove: Removes specified recovery scenario

```
Syntax : Object.Remove RecovScenarioPosition
```

RemoveAll: Removes all recovery scenarios

```
Syntax : Object.RemoveAll
```

SetActivationMode: Sets the activation mode of recovery scenario—OnEveryStep or OnError.

```
Syntax : Object.SetActivationMode "OnError"
                                      Object.SetActivationMode "OnEveryStep"
```

SetAsDefault: Sets current list of recovery scenarios as default list for all new test scripts and business components.

```
Syntax : Object.SetAsDefault
```

Properties

The properties supported by the recovery scenario object are as follow:

Count: Counts number of recovery scenarios associated with the test script or business component.

```
Syntax : Object.Count
```

Enabled: Sets or indicates the status of the recovery mechanism—enabled or disabled (True of False).

```
Syntax : Object.Enabled = True
Object.Enabled = False
```

Item: Returns the recovery scenario item present in the specified position.

```
Syntax : Object.Item(RecovScenarioPosition)
```

ADDING RECOVERY SCENARIO TO SCRIPTS AT RUN-TIME

The following code shows how to add recovery scenarios to the test programmatically during run-time.

```
'Declaration
Dim oUFTApp, oUFTTstRecov

'Create UFT object
Set oUFTApp = CreateObject("QuickTest.Application")

'Return recovery object for current test script Set oUFTTstRecov =
oUFTApp.Test.Settings.Recovery

'Remove all recovery scenarios associated with the test script
oUFTTstRecov.RemoveAll

'Add recovery scenarios
oUFTTstRecov.Add "C:\Temp\RecovScnro.qrs",  "ObjectNotFound", 1
oUFTTstRecov.Add "C:\Temp\RecovScnro.qrs",  "PopUpMessage", 2
oUFTTstRecov.Add "C:\Temp\RecovScnro.qrs",  "ApplicationCrash", 3
'Enable all recovery scenarios
For iCnt=1 To oUFTTstRecov.Count Step 1
   oUFTTstRecov.Item(iCnt).Enabled = True
Next
'Enable recovery mechanism oUFTTstRecov.Enabled = True
'Set recovery activation mode oUFTTstRecov.SetActivationMode "OnError"
'Release objects
Set oUFTTstRecov = Nothing
Set oUFTApp = Nothing
```

SCENARIOS WHERE RECOVERY SCENARIO FAILS

Although recovery scenario is designed to handle the run-time exceptions, there are few situations where recovery scenarios do not work. Recovery scenarios are not able to handle VBScript run-time errors. To handle exceptions that occur while executing a VBScript statement, VBScript error handlers need to be used. A few examples of VBScript run-time errors are:

Arithmetic errors: VBScript errors such as 'divide by zero error' and 'array index out of bounds error' are situations where recovery scenarios do not work.

File Access errors: Errors related to opening a file, and reading or writing data to a file are not caught by recovery scenarios.

Remote Machine errors: Errors related to network errors such as 'remote machine not responding' and 'connection time-out' are not caught by recovery scenarios.

VBSCRIPT ERROR HANDLERS

VBScript error handler is used to handle run-time errors that cannot be handled through recovery scenarios. VBScript provides three error-handling statements:

- **On Error Resume Next:** On occurrence of an error, neglect error and start executing next line.
- This statement disables the error pop-up dialog box.
- **On Error GoTo 0:** Deactivates 'On Error Resume Next' mode. In case of occurrence of an error, script behave as normal, that is, throws error pop-up dialog box.
- **On Error GoTo <ErrorHandler>:** This statement is not supported by UFT.

Methods

The methods of the error handler object are:

- **Err.Number:** Number id of error. Value of Err.Number becomes nonzero if an exception occurs during execution of a VBScript statement. If no exception occurs after executing a VBScript statement, then its value is zero.
- **Err.Description:** Description of the run-time error.

The following code shows how to handle run-time exceptions using VBScript error handlers. Function *fnDivision* divides two numbers and returns the result. The function takes three input parameters. 'nNum1' and 'nNum2' are the two numbers, which needs to be divided. 'nResult' is a null value variable where the results of division are stored. All the input parameters are 'Pass by Reference.' Therefore, the changes made to the 'nResult' value inside the function are accessible to the test script calling that function.

```
nResult=""
fnStat = fnDivison(5, 0, nResult)
If fnStat = "-1" Then
   Print nResult   'Output : "Divide By Zero"
End If

Public Function fnDivison(nNum1, nNum2, nResult)
   On Error Resume Next

   'Divide the two numbers
   nDiv = nNum1/nNum2

   'Check if an exception has occurred
   If Err.Number <> 0 Then
      nResult = Err.Description
      fnDivison = "-1"
      Exit Fuction
   Else
      nResult = nDiv
      fnDivison = "0"
   End If
End Function
```

☞ QUICK TIPS

- ✓ When working with tests, we can click the Generate Script button in the General pane of the Test Settings dialog box to automatically generate an automation script containing the current global testing options, including those represented by the Recovery object.
- ✓ Recovery scenarios are designed to handle run-time UFT exceptions.
- ✓ Recovery scenarios cannot handle run-time VBScript exceptions.
- ✓ Run-time VBScript errors can be handled using VBScript error-handling methods.

? PRACTICAL QUESTIONS

1. What is recovery scenario?
2. What is the difference between recovery and post-recovery actions?
3. In an application, a pop-up window occurs unexpectedly on various pages. The users are required to override the pop-up window to continue working on the application. A recovery scenario needs to be designed for this error, so that the test scripts execute successfully. Specify the trigger condition, recovery action, and post-recovery action of the recovery scenario.
4. Design a recovery scenario for 'object not found' run-time error. The conditions are as follow:
   Trigger condition—Object not found error
   Recovery action—Take screenshot of the application and exit current action iteration
   Post-recovery action—Start executing next action
5. In an automation environment the application under test crashes frequently. The work is on the way to fix the environment, but there is an urgent need to execute the regression run. Design a recovery scenario that meets the following conditions:
   Trigger condition—Application crash
   Recovery action—Exit current action execution, close application, and wait for 2min.
   Post-recovery action—Restart the application and start executing the next action.

Chapter 32

Test Results

UFT 12.5 can generate both UFT 'Run Results Viewer' compatible reports as well as HTML reports. User can define the report type format in the 'Run Sessions' tab of the options window. Figure 32.1 shows the 'Run Sessions' tab. HP UFT run reports provides a step-by-step detailed execution and summary report of a UFT run session. The run results are contained in a set of panes that users can show, hide, dock, move, and otherwise customize as per need. Each pane contains specific type of information. The run results tree pane shows a hierarchical representation of the run results. The remaining pane provide information such as result summary, number of test iterations, test input and output data, optional screen images or videos, and optional system information. The Run Results Viewer also provides the feature to directly jump to a specific step in UFT. The UFT test results are saved in XML format.

By default, the Run Results Viewer opens automatically at the end of the run session. To disable the same, navigate Tools " Options " General " Run Sessions and uncheck the 'View results when run session ends' check box.

Figure 32.2 shows an example test summary report of Expediasite. Figure 32.2a shows the 'Run Report Viewer' compatible report and Figure 32.2b shows UFT HTML report. The *Test Result* report can include following details:

- High-level summary report.
- Pass/fail status of test script.

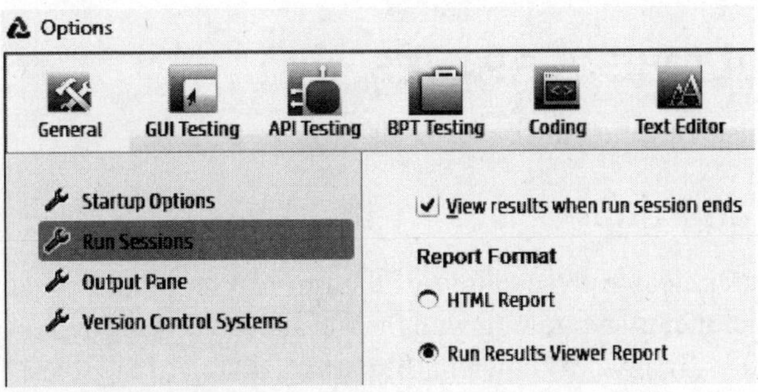

Figure 32.1 *UFT Report format selection*

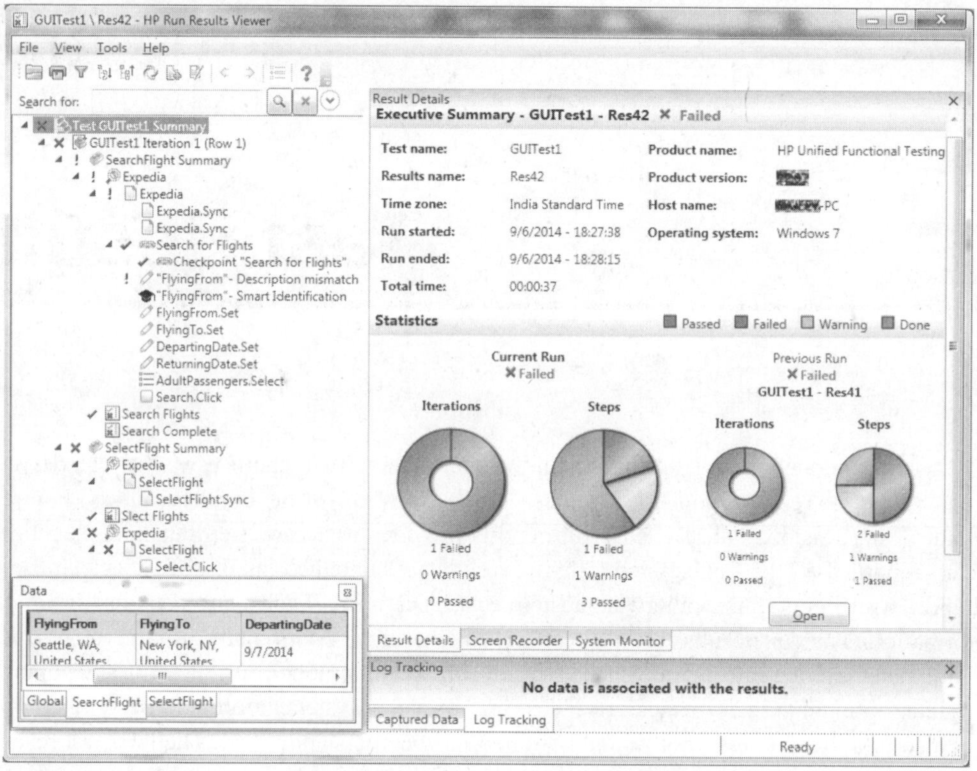

Figure 32.1a *Test results summary*

- Time at which execution started and ended.
- Number of pass/fail/warning steps within results window.
- Expandable tree view of executed steps specifying pass/fail at each step.
- Embedded HTML files.
- Application screenshots, desktop screenshots, or image files.
- Movie clip of entire test script execution.
- Any System Counter that was monitored such as memory usage and page faults.
- Quality Center information for the test script.

UFT RUN RESULT VIEWERPANES

UFT Run Results consists of following panes:

Run Results Tree Pane

This pane shows the graphical representation of the run results in an expandable hierarchy tree. It displays the test or components steps along with the run status for each step (pass, fail, warning, etc.). HTML files or image files, if any are shown in the particular step of the tree.

This pane also has a search box to search for a specific step in the results tree.

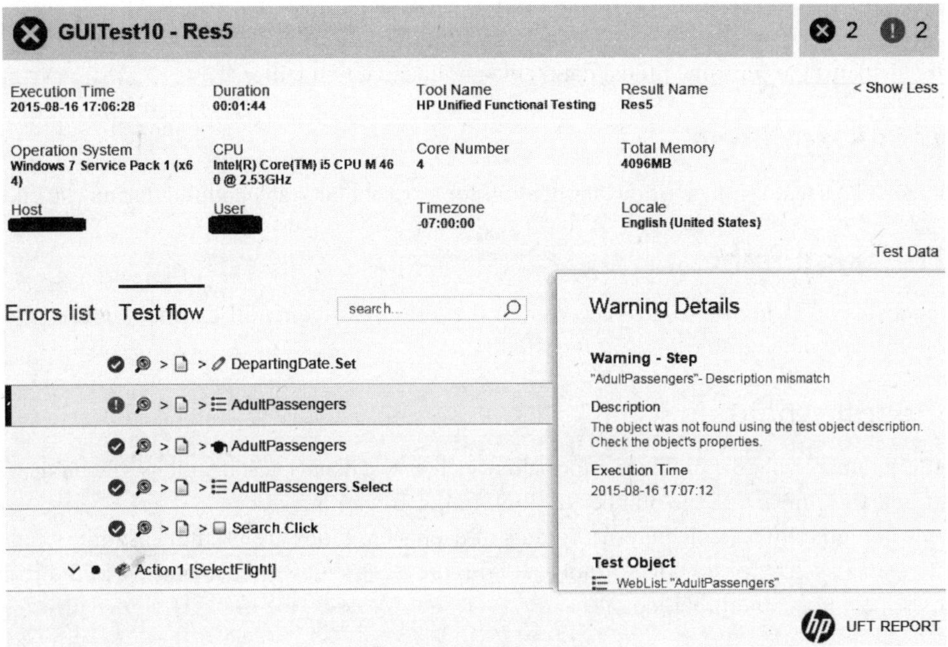

Figure 32.1b *HTML report*

Result Details pane

This pane displays high-level results overview report. It consists of executive summary and statistics of run results.

Executive Summary

This page section displays test pass/fail status, test details and execution OS environment information..

Statistics

This page section displays run result statistics for current run and previous run. This allows users to compare the current results with the previous results.

Run statistics graph displays number of test iterations along with run status of iterations. It also displays the number of test steps passed, failed, or has warnings.

Open button opens the details run results of the previous run.

Screen Recorder Pane

This pane displays recorded movie clip of the step-by-step execution of the test script.

System Monitor Pane

This pane displays line graph of the monitored System Counters such as memory usage and page faults/sec.

Data Pane

Data pane displays the run-time global data table and local action tables.

Captured Data Pane

This pane displays a still image of the application for a particular step captured during run-time.

Log Ttracking Pane

This pane displays the log messages received for the test or component. Log tracking can be enabled from *Log Tracking* node of the *Test Settings* dialog box.

Test Result Analysis

Test Result summary window provides information such as test details, test iterations, the name of result file, start and end times, and the number of pass, fail, and warning steps.

Test result hierarchy pane displays run status of each step. Icons are used to easy interpretation of test result status such as pass, fail, warning, etc. Figure 32.3 shows the icons used in the result tree hierarchy pane and its interpretation.

Icons	Description
✓	This symbol denotes passed step.
✖	This symbol denotes failed step.
ì	(UFT GUI tests only) This symbol denotes an information step. This does not indicate pass/fail status of the step. For example, an optional step failed and ignored.
!	This symbol denotes warning step. It means step did not succeed but did not cause the test script to fail.
! 	This symbol denotes that step failed unexpectedly.
	(UFT GUI tests and Components only) This symbol denotes step was recognized using smart identification.
	(UFT GUI tests and Components only) This symbol denotes recovery scenario was activated at this step.
	This symbol denotes test script execution was forcefully stopped at this step.
 [Password].SetSecure	(UFT GUI tests and Components only). This denotes a dynamically created object which is not saved in the object repository. Square brackets around a test object name indicate that the test object was created dynamically during the test run session. A dynamic test object can be created either using programmatic descriptions or by using an object returned by a ChildObjects method
	(UFT GUI tests and Components only). This denotes updates made during maintenance mode run.

Figure 32.3 *Test results summary*

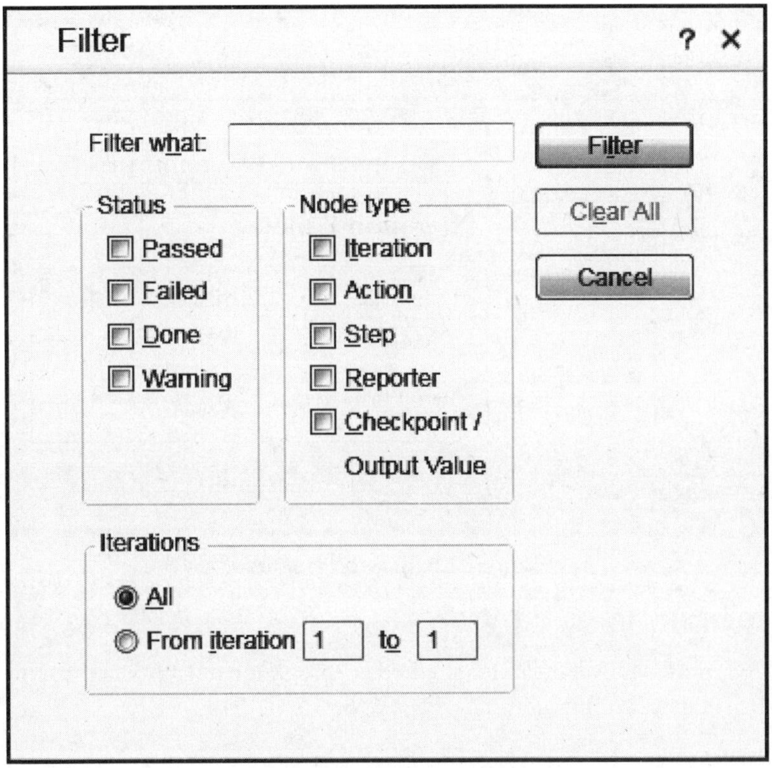

Figure 32.4 *Test filter dialog box*

TEST RESULT FILTERS

Test Result filters are used to customize the view of test results. This is useful when results tree is very long. Customizing results view helps easily analyze the failures and the failure reason.

Filter dialog box can be opened from test result viewer menu bar as –navigate *View → Filters*. Filters dialog box opens as shown in Fig. 32.4.

- ***Filter what***: This filter option allows user to filter the test report using text values as displayed in the report. For example, strings such as 'Set', 'Report', etc. can be used to display only those test steps which contain this string.
- ***Status***: This filter option allows users to filter test steps by their run status – Passed, Failed, Done.and Warning.
- ***Node Type***: This filter option allows users to filter test result tree by the node type of the tree – Iteration, Action, Step, Reporter and Checkpoint/Output value.
- ***Iterations***: This filter option allows users to filter test results for *All* iterations or specified iteration only.

Figure 32.5 displays the test results filtered to view failed and warning steps only.

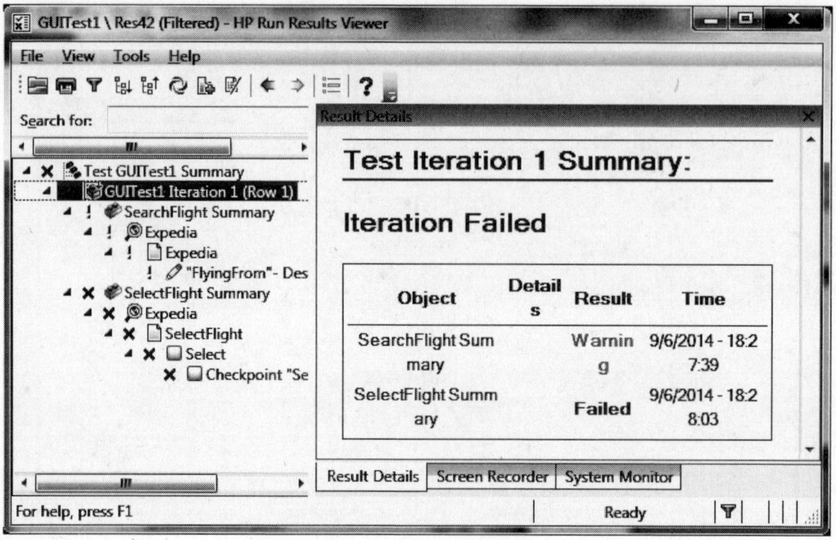

Figure 32.5 *Filtered test result*

Report.Filter

Alternatively, UFT provides Report.Filter method to programmatically suppress test steps results from being published in test result viewer.

```
Syntax : Report.Filter = ReportingMode
```

Following reporting modes are available in UFT:

```
0 or rfEnableAll - Report all test steps. This is default setting of UFT
or rfEnableErrorsAndWarnings - Report only failed steps and warning steps
or rfEnableErrorsOnly - Report only failed steps
or rfDisableAll - Do not report any step
```

Example: The following code shows how to suppress a pass/fail status in test results.

```
'Retrieve the current report mode
sCurrReportMode = Reporter.Filter
'Disable reporting of failed steps
Reporter.Filter = rfDisableAll
If Instr(1, A_SearchFlightsURL, E_SearchFlightsURL, 1) >0 Then
   Reporter.ReportEvent micPass, "Search Flights page opened.",
   "Pass"
Else
   errMsg = "Actual URL-" & A_SearchFlightsURL & vbTab & "Expected URL-"
                                                 &_E_SearchFlightsURL
   Reporter.ReportEvent micFail, "Search Flights page not opened.",
                                                               errMsg
End If
```

```
'Restore previous reporting mode
Reporter.Filter = sCurrReportMode
```

REPORTER OBJECT

UFT provides *Reporter* object to write customized statements to the test results. These statements help make analysis of the test results easier.

UFT *Reporter* object supports following methods:

- **ReportEvent** – This method is used to display custom test line reports in test results. In addition, image files can be inserted in test reports using this method.

```
Syntax : Reporter.ReportEvent EvenStatus, ReportStepName, Details,
[optional]ImageFilePath
```

- **ReportNote** – this method adds a note to the test resuls.

```
Syntax : Reporter.ReportNote(NoteContent)
```

UFT *Reporter* object supports following properties:

- **Filter** – This property is used to suppress pass/fail status from getting published in test results as dis- cussed.
- **ReportPath** – This property retrieves the current path of the test result.
- **RunStatus** – This property retrieves the status of the run at the current point of the run session.

CUSTOMIZING TEST RESULTS

UFT provides options to write custom steps and add files and screenshots in test results. These custom steps can be used to denote pass/fail status of the test scenario or test step or to provide any additional information in test results.

Inserting Custom Statements in Test Results

Reporter method can be used to write custom statements to run results.

```
Syntax : Reporter.Reportevent EvenStatus, ReportStepName, Details,
```

EventStatus should be one of the following variables:

micPass—denotes step passed
micFail—denotes step failed
micDone—denotes step executed successfully
micWarning—denotes step executed with some warning

Example: The following code shows an example of login to a site.

ReportEvent has been used to write custom lines of result steps to test results. 'expected link that should open after clicking login button

```
E_URL = "app-url after login"

'Click on login button Browser("B").Page("P").WebButton("Login").Click

'Wait for Plan Travel page to load
Browser("B").Page("P1").Sync

'find actual URL opened after clicking login button
A_URL = Browser("B").Page("P1").GetROProperty("url")

'compare expected and actual results
If Instr(1, A_URL, E_URL, 1) >0 Then 'write custom
   step result to test results
   Reporter.ReportEvent micPass, "Link Opened", "Pass"
Else
   errMsg = "Actual URL-" & A_URL & vbTab & "Expected URL-" &_ E_URL
   Reporter.ReportEvent micFail, "Link Not Opened", errMsg End If
```

Inserting Image Files in Test Results

UFT provides the option to capture AUT image screenshots and save them in test results. UFT can be configured to capture screenshot for every step executed or for the failed steps only. Apart from this, UFT also offers the flexibility to UFT automation developers to programmatically add AUT screenshot images to the test results. Described below are various ways to save images to test results.

Method 1

In this method, we will use the optional parameter *ImagePath* of *ReportEvent* method to attach image files to test results.

```
Syntax  :  Reporter.Reportevent  EvenStatus,  ReportStepName,  Details,
ImagePath
```

Example:

```
sImgPath = "C:\Temp\errLink.png"
'Capture desktop screenshot and save it at the specified location
Desktop.CaptureBitmap(sImgPath)
If Instr(1, A_URL, E_URL, 1) >0 Then
   'write custom step and attach image file to test result
   Reporter.Reportevent micPass, "Link Opened", "Pass", sImgPath
Else
   errMsg = "Act URL-" & A_URL & ", Exp URL-" & E_URL
   Reporter.Reportevent micFail, "Link Not Opened", "Fail", sImgPath
End If
```

NOTES: Desktop screenshots can also be captured in .bmp format. The size of a .png file is smaller than a .bmp file.

Method 2

Alternatively, by configuring UFT *Run* options, we will be able to save application screenshots (.png file) to test results (Figure 32.6).

- Navigate *Tools* → *Options* → *GUI Testing* tab → *Screen Capture* node.
- Select the checkbox '*Save still image captures to results*'.
- From the list menu, specify when to capture the screenshot:

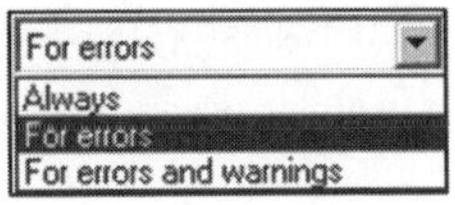

 – *Always* – AUT Screenshot will be captured in test results at every step of test script execution.
 – *For Errors* – AUT Screenshots will be captured in test results only in case any step in test script fails.
 – *For Errors and Warnings* – AUT Screenshots will be captured in test results only in case any step is an error step or warning step.

Capturing application screenshots at every step makes test results file bulky.

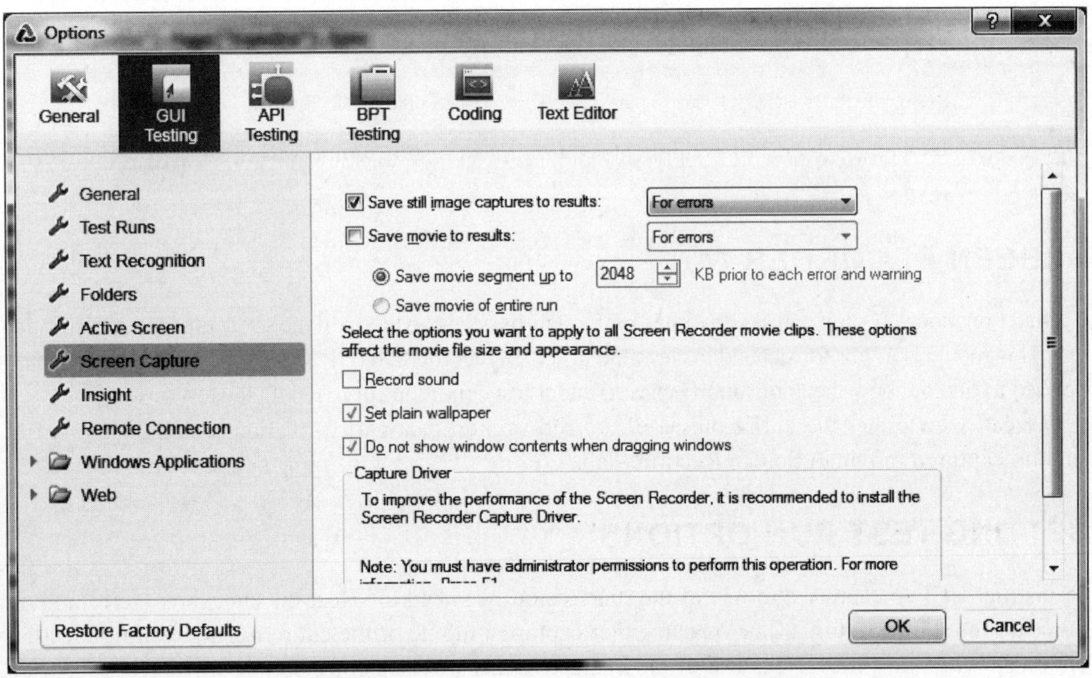

Figure 32.6 *Configure screen capture settings*

Method 3

In this method, we use the *Setting* object provided by UFT to access and modify *Snapshot Report-Mode*. *Setting* object allows us to change screen capture mode at any point of the code.

```
Syntax : Setting("SnapshotReportMode") = nValue
```

nValue	*Meaning*
0	Capture image at every step
1	(default mode) Capture image only if an error occurs on the page. Default setting
2	Capture image only if an error or warning occurs on the page
3	Never capture image

Example: The following code captures screenshot of the application only if test script or test scenario fails.

```
'find previous screen capture mode
nPrevScrnCapMd = Setting("SnapshotReportMode")
'disable screen capture
Setting("SnapshotReportMode") = 3
Browser("B").Page("P").WebButton("Login").Click 'enable
screen capture on error or warning
Setting("SnapshotReportMode") = 2
'capture application screen shot
bExistFlg = Browser("B").Page("P1").Exist(5)
'revert back to previous screen capture mode
Setting("SnapshotReportMode") = nPrevScrnCapMd
```

Figure 32.7 shows the screenshot of application within test results window when the step which veries page sync to page 'P1' fails.

SCREEN RECORDER TAB

Unified Functional Testing can save a movie of the step-by-step execution of the script on application under test. This movie is in .fbr format and is viewable in screen recorder tab (HP Micro Player). This movie can be used to find out how the application behaved under test conditions or to debug the test script.

We can view either the entire movie of the run session or a part of it. Figure 32.8 shows a run session captured movie in Screen Recorder tab.

SETTING TEST RUN OPTIONS

To instruct UFT to capture a movie of the run session, we need to select the checkbox 'select movie to results' as shown in Fig. 32.6. We can either capture a movie of the entire run session by selecting option '*Always*' or a movie capture of only selective steps by selecting option '*For Errors*' or '*For Errors and Warnings*'.

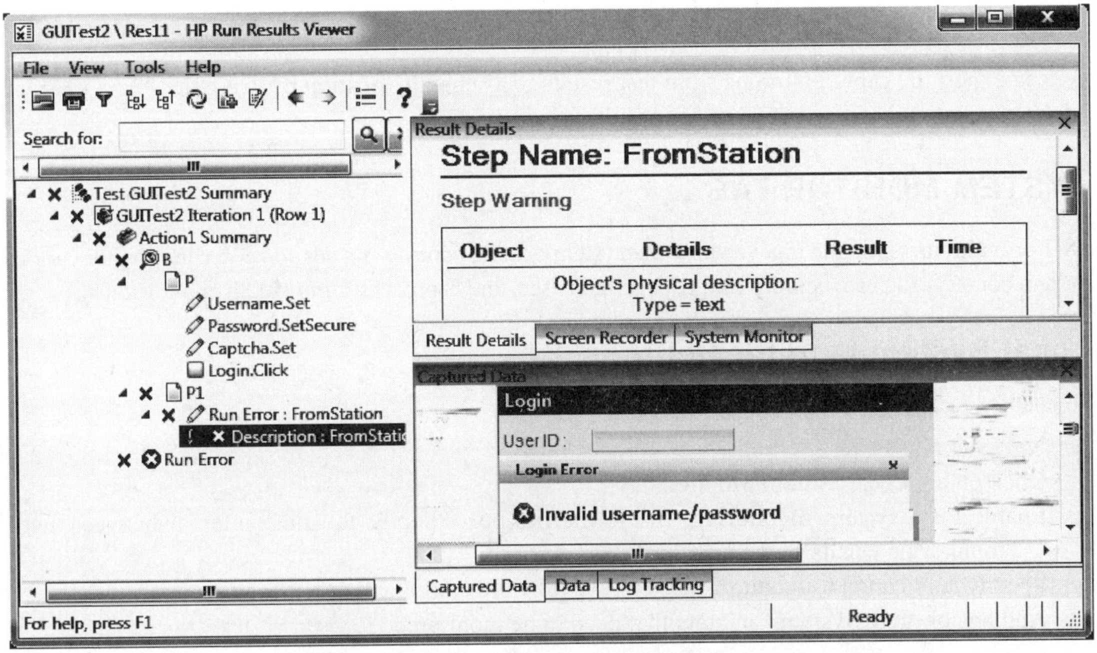

Figure 32.7 *Test results with AUT screenshots*

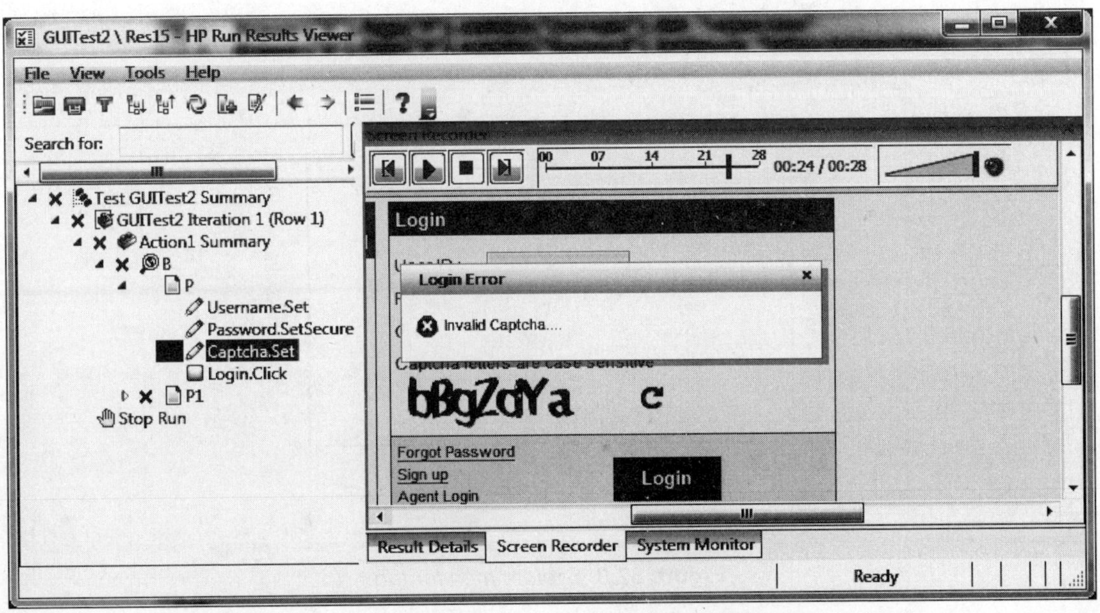

Figure 32.8 *Screen recorder tab—capturing movie of the run session*

EXPORTING CAPTURED MOVIE FILES

We can export the captured movie from test results to a separate location by using the *File → Export Movie to File...* menu bar option of test results window.

SYSTEM MONITOR TAB

UFT provides the option to analyze how the system behaved during run session. We can monitor various system counters such as memory usage, page faults/sec, and %processor time of an application.

Local System Monitor Settings

To enable local system monitoring:

Navigate File → Test Settings.

Click on tab Local System Monitor.

Enable local system monitoring. Inside the list box, specify the time interval between two monitoring events.

Specify application to monitor such as AUT, iexplore, and Excel as per requirement.

Add one or more System Counters that need to be monitored.

Figure 32.9 shows System Monitor tab of test results. The test scenario executed here is login to a demo site and monitored system counters are – memory usageand %processor time.

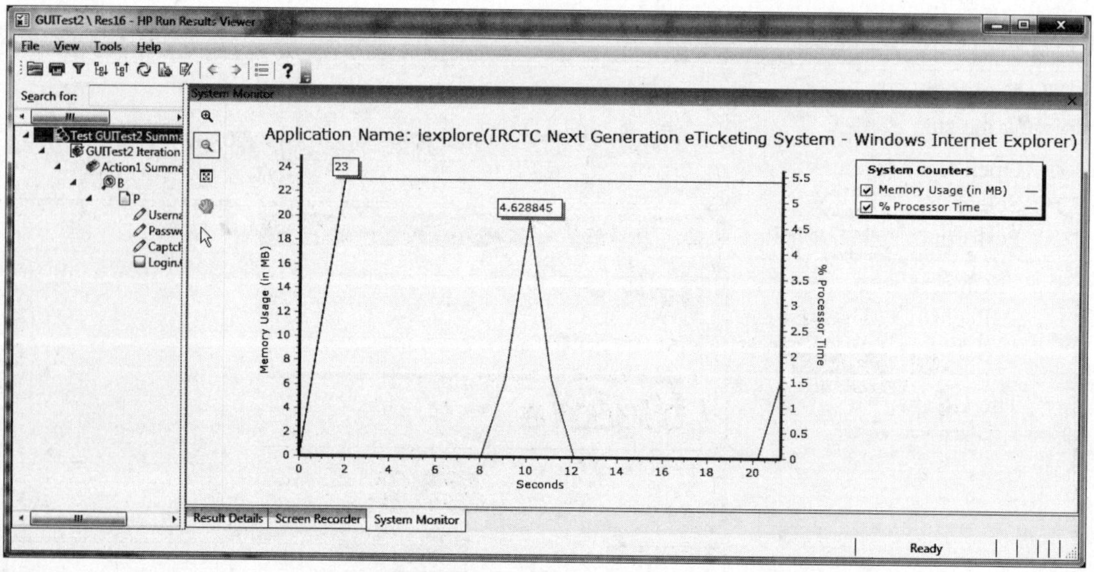

Figure 32.9 *System monitor tab*

EXPORTING SYSTEM MONITOR TAB RESULTS

We can export the System Monitor tab data to an external file. The file types that are supported by this system are .csv, .txt, .xls, .xml, and .html.

To export system monitor tab data select *File → Export System Monitor Data to File*. Table 32.1 shows the various UFT reports and the formats in which they can be saved.

Report Type	Save as Type (Report Format)
Step Details	• HTML (*.htm, *.html) [default] • PDF (*.pdf) • DOC (*.doc)
Data Table	Excel (*.xls)
Log Tracking	XML (*.xml)
Screen	FlashBack (*.fbr)
Recorder System Monitor	• Text (*.csv, *.txt) [default] • Excel (*.xls) • XML (*.xml) • HTML (*.htm, *.html) Note: Only the System Monitor data can be exported and not the graph

HOW TO JUMP TO A STEP IN UFT

UFT provides the flexibility to jump to a step in UFT corresponding to a node in the Run Results tree. To view the step in the test that corresponds to a node:

- Open test in UFT whose test results are displayed in the Run Results Viewer.
- Select the node in the run results tree whose code is to be viewed in UFT.
- Perform of the following:
  - Click the *Jump to Step in UFT* button from the Run Results toolbar. Or,
  - Right-click and select *Jump to Step in UFT*. Or,
  - Select *View → Jump to Step in UFT*.
- The UFT window gets activated and the step is highlighted.

QUICK TIPS

- ✓ Test results provide a summary and detailed report of the test execution.
- ✓ Custom statements and image files can be inserted in the test results through UFT code.
- ✓ Test results settings can be configured to automatically capture application screenshot for each and every step executed in UFT.
- ✓ Test result settings can be configured to automatically capture a movie of the complete run session.
- ✓ 'System Monitor Tab' of the test results can be used to analyze system and application performance.

PRACTICAL QUESTIONS

1. What is test result? What is its use?
2. Explain the meaning of various symbols used in the test results.
3. What is the use of filters in the test results?
4. How is a custom statement written to test results from the test script?
5. How image files can be attached to the test results?
6. Explain the settings required to capture movie of the run session.
7. It is required that UFT captures the application screenshot in the test results only when an error occurs during run-time. Explain the settings that need to be done for the same.
8. Explain the significance of 'System Monitor Tab' in the test results.

Section 6 API Testing

- API Testing—Introduction
- Automated Web Service Testing

Chapter 33

API Testing: Introduction

Application Program Interface (API) is a collection of routines, protocols, and tools for building software applications. APIs makes it possible for different software applications to seamlessly communicate with one another. Examples of some of the most popular APIs include—Google Maps API, You Tube API, Twitter API, etc.

APIs and Web services are completely invisible to software users or end-users. APIs run silently in the background, providing a way for applications to work with each other to get the user the information or functionality he needs. A good API makes it easier to develop a program by providing all the building blocks. Web services can be implemented using SOAP or REST standard. SOAP and REST are protocols, that is, a set of rules for requesting information from a server using a specific technique.

(Simple Access Object Protocol) (SOAP)

SOAP internally uses XML to send data back and forth. SOAP messages have rigid structure and the response XML then needs to be parsed.

(Representational State Transfer) (REST)

REST is not as rigid as SOAP. RESTful web-services use standard URIs and methods to make calls to the webservice. When request to a URI is made, it returns the representation of an object, on which various operations can be performed. In REST, users are not limited to picking XML to represent data. JSON or anything else can be used to represent data. JSON and XML, are functionally equivalent, and either could be chosen. XML is thought of as being too verbose, and harder to parse, so many-a-times, data is more adequately represented using JSON.

WEB SERVICE COMMUNICATION PROCESS

A Web service is a URL-addressable piece of software that can return information in response to client requests. Web services are integrated into their parent applications or Web sites and can be used by external software application which exists on other servers. For example, when a user signs in to his Yahoo email account using Facebook login feature, then in this case Yahoo email login page is making web service calls to Facebook APIs (servers) to authenticate the user.

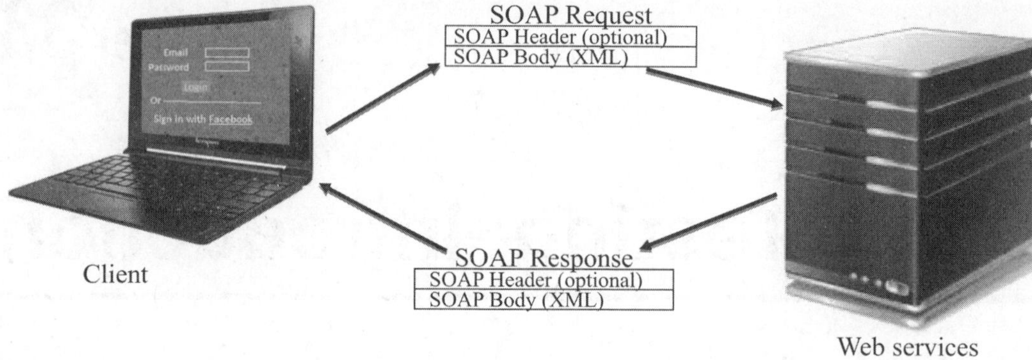

Figure 33.1 *Web services communication process*

Figure 33.1 shows the web services communication process. Here, Web service provides a programmatic interface using the communication protocol SOAP (Simple Object Access Protocol). Web services are called are using HTTP and XML (SOAP) and web services returns the results using HTTP and XML (SOAP). Web service operations or data are described in XML with the Web Service Description Language (WSDL). Web services are located in internet or intranet via the Universal Description, Discovery and Integration (UDDI) based registry of services.

XML Schemas

XML schema describes the structure of an XML document. XML schemas are defined using the same basic XML syntax of tags and end tags. The purpose of an XML Schema is to define the building blocks of an XML document. An XML schema defines:

- elements that can appear in a document
- attributes that can appear in a document
- which elements are child elements
- the order of child elements
- the number of child elements
- whether an element is empty or can include text
- data types for elements and attributes
- default and fixed values for elements and attributes

Consider the 'example.xsd' XML schema file shown below. This schema file defines the XML document 'example.xml'.

```
<?xml version="1.0"?>
<xs:schema xmlns:xs="http://www.w3.org/2001/XMLSchema"
targetNamespace="http://www.abc.com"
xmlns=http://www.abc.com elementFormDefault="qualified">
<xs:element name="note">
  <xs:complexType>
    <xs:sequence>
```

```
      <xs:element name="EmployeeName" type="xs:string"/>
      <xs:element name="EmployeeType" type="xs:string"/>
    </xs:sequence>
  </xs:complexType>
</xs:element>
</xs:schema>
```

The below XML document has reference to above schema file.

```
<?xml version="1.0"?>
<example
xmlns="http://www.abc.com"
xmlns:xsi="http://www.w3.org/2001/XMLSchema-instance"
xsi:schemaLocation="http://www.abc.com example.xsd">
  <EmployeeName>Brett</EmployeeName>
  <EmployeeType>Contractor</EmployeeType>
</example>
```

(Simple Object Access Protocol) (SOAP)

SOAP is a mechanism for exchanging structured and typed information between peers in a decentralized distributed environment using the World Wide Web's Hypertext Transfer Protocol (HTTP) and its Extensible Markup Language (XML) as the mechanisms for information exchange. Its advantages are a light-weight implementation, open-standards origins and platform independence. SOAP specifies how to encode an HTTP header and an XML file so that a program in one computer can call a program in another computer and pass it information. It also specifies how the called web service program can return a response. The protocol consists only of a single HTTP request and a corresponding response between a sender and a receiver. A SOAP request is an HTTP POST request. The SOAP data part consists of:

- envelope
- binding framework
- encoding rules
- body

API TESTING

Just like any other software, APIs need to be tested. API testing is focused on the functionality of the software's business logic and hence, it is entirely different from GUI testing. It mainly concentrates on testing the business logic layer of the software architecture. This testing won't cover the look and feel of an application.

API testing requires construction of a test harness that simulates the use of the API by end-user applications. Test harness is an application that communicates with the APIs and methodically exercises its functionality. Few examples of test harness applications are: Firefox add-ons SOA Client and Rest-Client. In next chapter, we will discuss, how to develop test harness programmatically for API testing.

The problems to target for API testing include:

- Ensure that the test harness varies parameters of the API calls in ways that verify functionality and expose failures. This includes assigning common parameter values as well as exploring boundary conditions.
- Generate parameter value combinations for calls with two or more parameters.
- Determine the content under which an API call is made. This might include setting external environment variables (files, peripheral devices, etc.) and also internal stored data that affect the way API behaves.
- Sequence API calls to vary the order in which the functionality is exercised.

WHY TO AUTOMATE API TESTING

APIs needs to be tested to ensure that they perform the intended function. Automated API testing helps to speed up the testing process. Automated API calls can also be made in automated GUI tests to reduce test execution time and as well increase test flakiness (unintended random test failures). Automated API test runs helps to increase test coverage which thereby reduces risks of application upgrades or deployment of new services. A well-constructed API test helps answer below questions:

- Does the API respond quickly enough for the intended users?
- Does the API respond with the correct values?

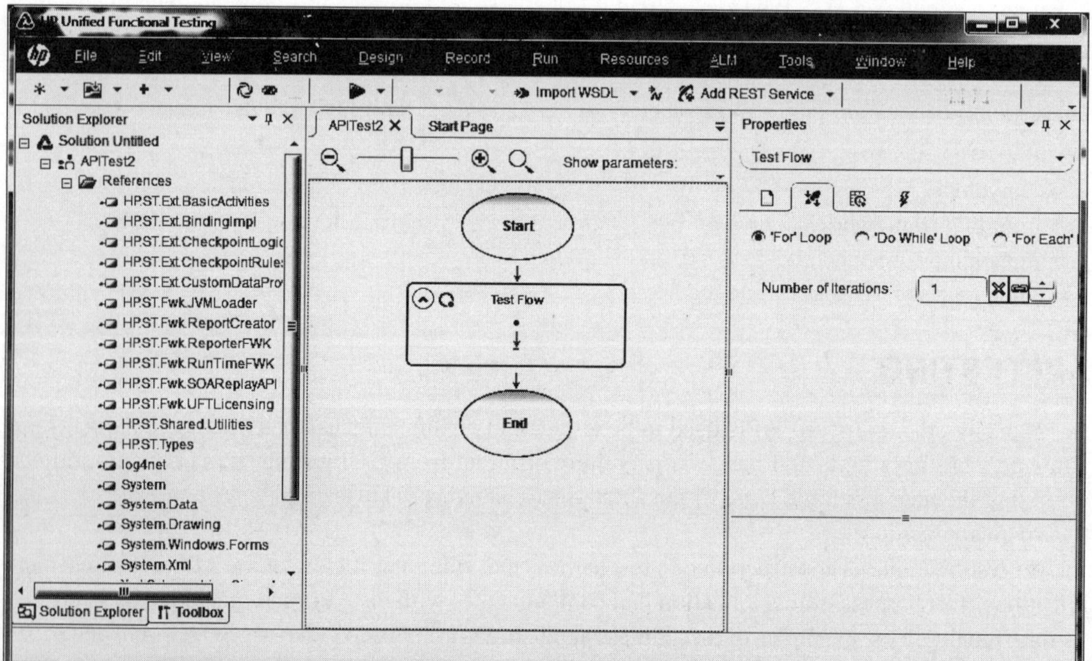

Figure 33.2 *UFT API Test Window*

- Is the API able to handle exceptions and illegal input values?
- Is the API performance stable under expected and unexpected user loads?

UFT API TESTING

UFT contains an extensible framework for the development and execution of functional tests of GUI-less applications or the non-GUI parts of an application. UFT provides API test feature to allow users to create API tests. The API tests can be executed standalone or can be called in any other GUI or API test. Figure 33.2 shows the API test window of UFT.

The specification of an API is defined by WSDL (Web Service Descriptor Language). WSDL is a specification of what requests can be made, with which parameters, and what they will return.

UDDI (Universal Description, Discovery and Integration) is an XML-based directory that allows businesses to list themselves, find each other and communicate using Web services. WDSL is the SOAP of the UDDI. In other words, WDSL is the XML-based language that businesses use to describe the offered services in the UDDI.

Chapter **34**

Automated Web Service Testing

Web services provide seamless connection from one software application to another. The communication between applications happen using SOAP protocol and data is exchanged in the form of XML documents. XML file format needs to follow specific rules as specified in XML Schemas. XML schema describes the structure of an XML document.

Testing of Web services is useful to prevent late detection of errors. Web service testing involves verifying the functionality and performance of the web service under various load conditions. In agile methodology, time to test is always limited. An automated test approach helps to speed up the testing process and as well increase the test coverage. Automated web service testing ensures that the modified web service can be regression and performance tested quickly. Testing of Web services involves three steps:

- The discovery of Web services (from UDDI, URL or file)
- The data format exchanged (i.e. WSDL) and
- Request/response mechanisms (i.e. SOAP)

TESTING WEB SERVICES MANUALLY

Let us consider a temperature conversion web service which needs to be tested. This web service offers the feature of converting temperature value from Celsius to Fahrenheit and vice-versa. Functional testing requirement is to validate that the web service conversion is correct and accurate. In this chapter, first we will discuss how to test this web service manually using Firefox add-ons *SOA Client* and *Poster*. Next we will discuss how to automate the web service testing process.

Consider the 'Temperature Converter' web service has two methods—FahrenheitToCelsius and CelsiusTo Fahrenheit. The former method converts Celsius temperature value to Fahrenheit while the latter methods convert Fahrenheit temperature value to Celsius.

Assume,

- WSDL location of this web service is:
  `http://www.abc.com/webservices/tempconvert.asmx?wsdl`

- SOAP request/response format of 'CelsiusTo Fahrenheit' web service method is:

  Request

```
POST /webservices/tempconvert.asmx HTTP/1.1
Host: www.abc.com
Content-Type: text/xml; charset=utf-8
Content-Length: length
SOAPAction: "http://www.abc.com/webservices/CelsiusToFahrenheit"

<?xml version="1.0" encoding="utf-8"?>
<soap:Envelope xmlns:xsi="http://www.w3.org/2001/XMLSchema-instance"
xmlns:xsd="http://www.w3.org/2001/XMLSchema" xmlns:soap="http://sche-
mas.xmlsoap.org/soap/envelope/">
       <soap:Body>
         <CelsiusToFahrenheit xmlns="http://www.abc.com/webservices/">
            <Celsius>RequestValue</Celsius>
         </CelsiusToFahrenheit>
       </soap:Body>
</soap:Envelope>
```

  Response

```
HTTP/1.1 200 OK
Content-Type: text/xml; charset=utf-8
Content-Length: length

<?xml version="1.0" encoding="utf-8"?>
  <soap:Envelope xmlns:soap="http://schemas.xmlsoap.org/soap/en-
velope/" xmlns:xsi="http://www.w3.org/2001/XMLSchema-instance"
xmlns:xsd="http://www.w3.org/2001/XMLSchema">
  <soap:Body>
   <CelsiusToFahrenheitResponse xmlns="http://www.abc.com/webser-
   vices/">
     <CelsiusToFahrenheitResult>ResponseValue</CelsiusToFahrenhei-
     tResult>
   </CelsiusToFahrenheitResponse>
  </soap:Body>
</soap:Envelope>
```

- HTTP POST request/response format of 'CelsiusTo Fahrenheit' web service method is:

  Request

```
POST /webservices/tempconvert.asmx/CelsiusToFahrenheit HTTP/1.1
Host: www.abc.com
Content-Type: application/ x-www-form-urlencoded
Content-Length: length

Celsius=RequestValue
```

Response

```
HTTP/1.1 200 OK
Content-Type: text/xml; charset=utf-8
Content-Length: length

<?xml version="1.0" encoding="utf-8"?>
<string xmlns="http://www.abc.com/webservices/">ResponseValue</
string>
```

While testing, the ' RequestValue' is to be replaced with the actual numeric value. A working example of 'Temperature Converter' web service can be found at site www.w3schools.com.

Manual Testing Using SOAP Request

Add-on 'SOA Client' can be used to test web service using SOAP requests. This add-on can be installed on both Firefox and Chrome browser. Steps below describe how web service method 'CelsiusToFahrenheit' can be tested manually using SOAP request:

1. Download add-on 'SOA Client' and install it.
2. Open the 'SOA Client' add-on in the browser.
3. Specify URL as WSDL location as discussed above.
4. Specify HTTP Request Method as POST (or refer Figure 34.1).

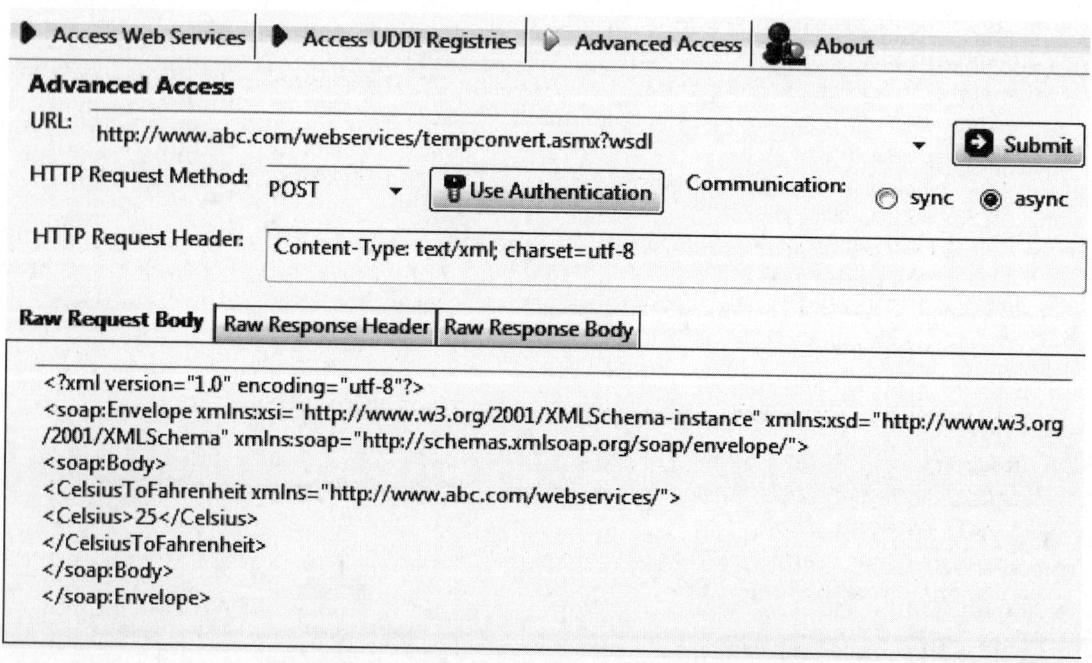

Figure 34.1 *Testing Web serviices using SOA Client*

Raw Request Body | Raw Response Header | **Raw Response Body**


```
<?xml version="1.0" encoding="utf-8"?><soap:Envelope xmlns:soap="http://schemas.xmlsoap.org
/soap/envelope/" xmlns:xsi="http://www.w3.org/2001/XMLSchema-instance"
xmlns:xsd="http://www.w3.org/2001/XMLSchema"><soap:Body><CelsiusToFahrenheitResponse
xmlns="http://www.abc .com/webservices
/"><CelsiusToFahrenheitResult>77</CelsiusToFahrenheitResult></CelsiusToFahrenheitResponse>
</soap:Body></soap:Envelope>
```


Status: 200 OK

Figure 34.2 *Web service Response XML*

5. Specify authentication credentials, if required. Authentication credentials are only required if web service is accessible to specific users only. For this web service, assume no authentication is required.
6. Specify header as discussed above.
7. Specify the 'Request Body' as discussed above (or refer Figure 34.1).
8. Click on the 'Submit' button.
9. The XML request will be submitted and the XML response will be displayed on the tab 'Raw Response Body'. Figure 34.2 below shows the XML response and the response status code.

MANUAL TESTING USING HTTP POST REQUEST

Add-on 'Poster' can be used to test web service using HTTP POST requests. This add-on can be installed on both Firefox and Chrome browser. Steps below describe how web service method 'CelsiusToFahrenheit' can be tested manually using HTTP POST request:

1. Download add-on 'Poster' and install it.
2. Open the 'Poster' add-on in the browser.
3. Specify URL as discussed above (or refer Figure 34.3).
4. Specify 'Content-Type' as discussed above.
5. Specify the request as 'Celsius=25' as shown in Fig. 34.3 for finding the Fahrenheit value of 25°C.
6. Click on POST button to submit the request.
7. Figure 34.4 shows the XML response and the response status code.

TESTING WEB SERVICES USING UFT

Now lets us see how to write an automated test for this web service. In this section, we will discuss how to create a UFT API test to test the 'Temperature Converter' web service. UFT provides two ways to import a WSDL in UFT:

- Import WSDL from URL to UDDI…
  This option imports a WSDL from a web URL or UDDI.
- Import WSDL from File or ALM Application Component

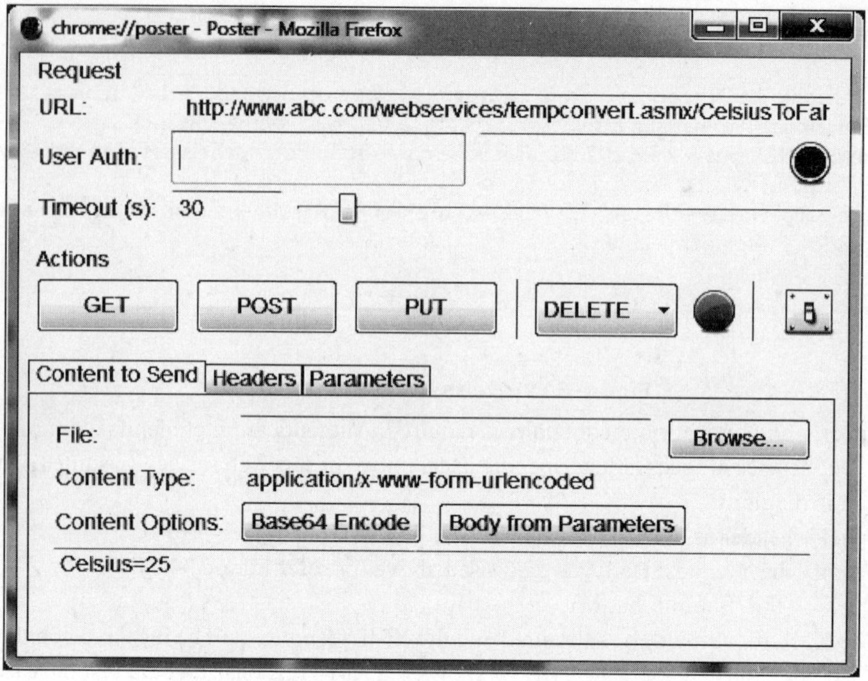

Figure 34.3 *Testing Web services using Poster*

This option imports WSDL from a file stored in local/shared storage device or from ALM. Described are the steps below to create an API test to test 'CelsiusToFahrenheit' method of temperature converter we b service.

Import Web Service in UFT

1. Create a new API test in UFT.
2. Select option 'Import WSDL from URL to UDDI'. Window 'Import WSDL from URL to UDDI' opens as shown in the Fig. 34.5.
   a. Select import location as URL or UDDI, as applicable and specify the WSDL location path.
   b. Specify advanced settings, as required.

Figure 34.4 *Web service Response XML*

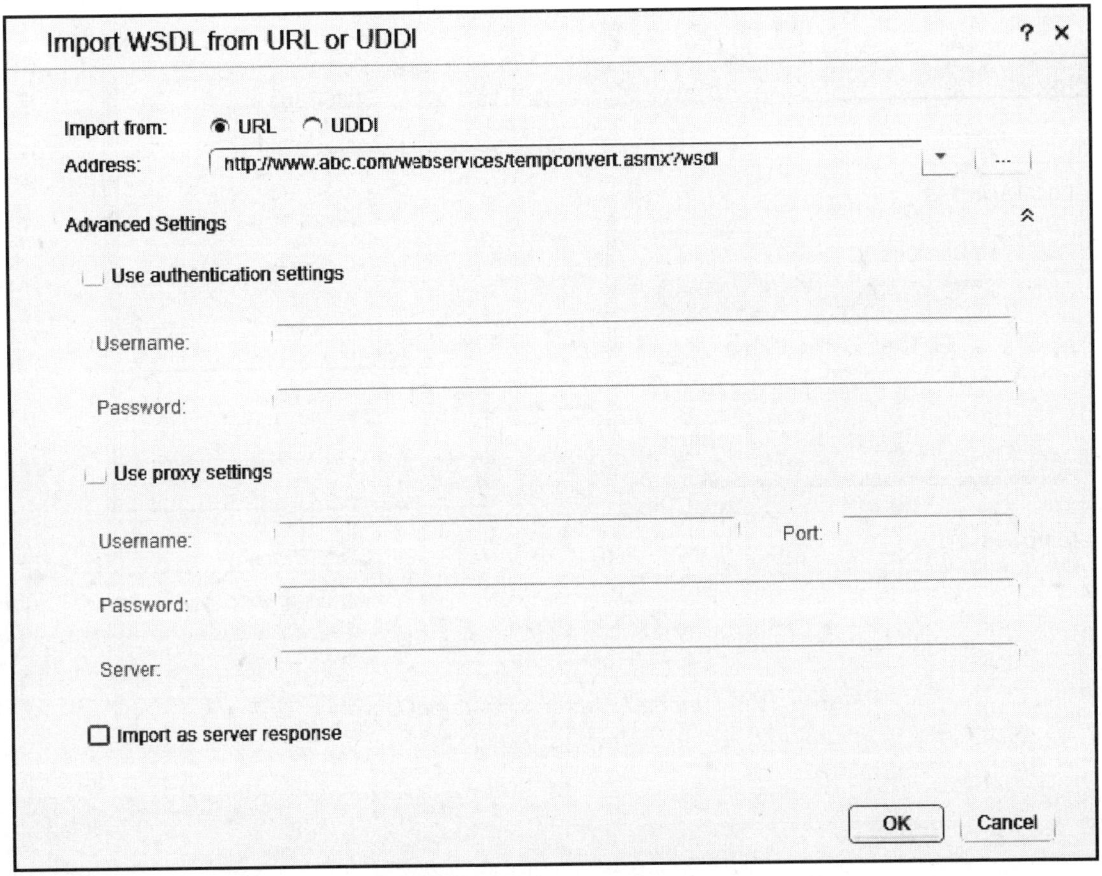

Figure 34.5 *Import WSDL window*

3. Click 'OK' button. UFT imports the web service and displays it in 'Local Activities' pane as shown in the Figure 34.6 below.

Add Web Service Method to API Test

4. Drag the web service method 'CelsiusToFahrenheit' from 'Local Activities' pane to 'Test Flow' block in API Test pane. Figure 34.7 shows the API test pane with web service method 'CelsiusTofahrenheit' added to test flow.
   Once web service method is added to Test Flow, its XML request and expected response layout can be viewed in Properties pane.

Modify SOAP Request XML

5. To modify the XML request, click on 'Grid' tab and modify the XML as required. 'Grid' tab displays the XML as a grid table. In order to view or edit SOAP request as XML, click on the tab 'Text'. Figure 34.8 shows the SOAP request XML. UFT also allows to load SOAP

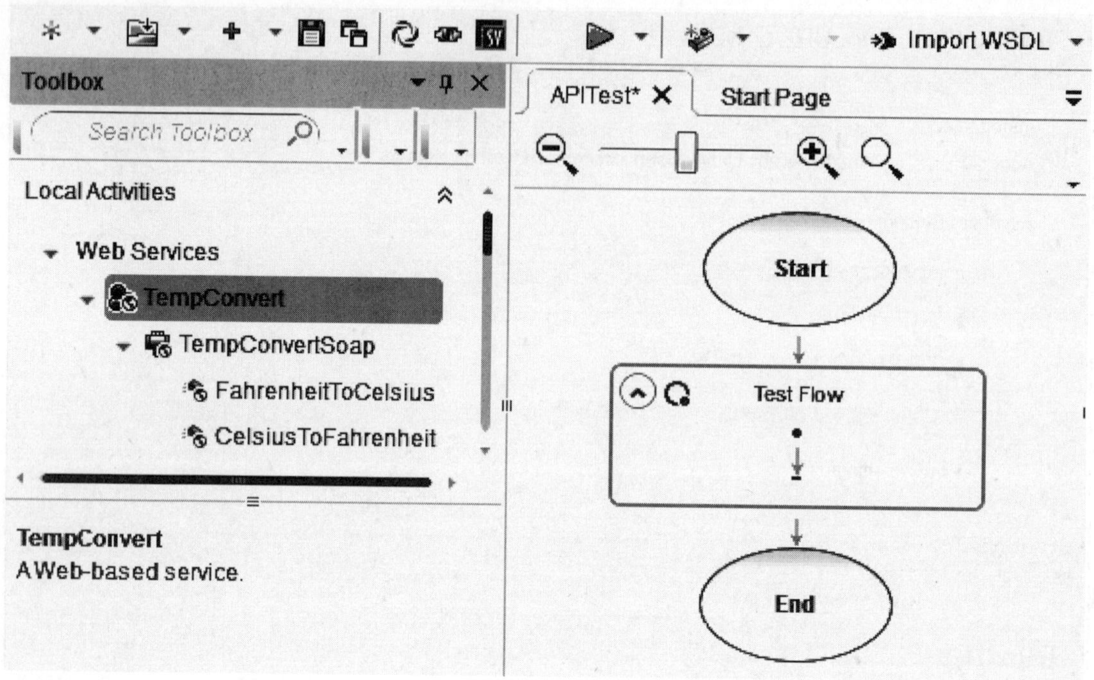

Figure 34.6 *Imported Web service 'TempConvert' in UFT*

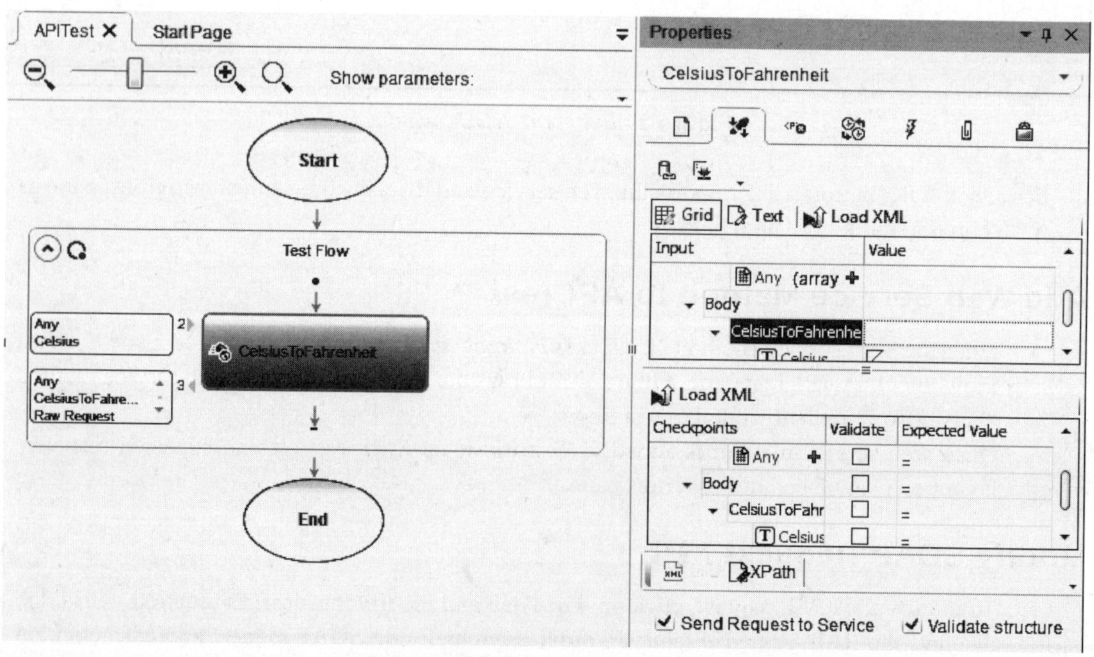

Figure 34.7 *API test with 'CelsiusToFahrenheit' webservice method*

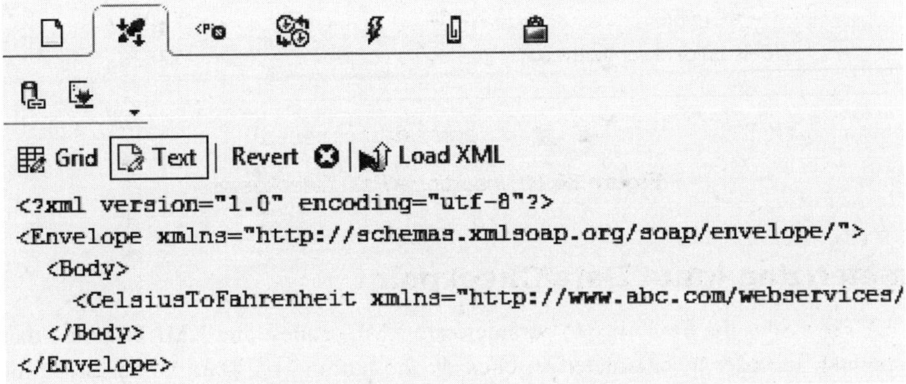

Figure 34.8 *SOAP request XML*

request XML file from local/shared storage system. Click on 'Load XML' button to import request XML to the test from a stored location.

Validating SOAP Response XML (Checkpoints)

UFT provides option to users to insert checkpoints to SOAP Response XML. The checkpoint can either be inserted using 'XML' tab or 'XPath' tab. The 'XML' tab inserts checkpoint in grid view while the 'XPath' tab inserts a checkpoint based on XPath of the XML.

6. Checkpoint can be inserted in 'Grid' view by selecting the specific tag which needs validation. Next comparison type and expected tag value is to be specified. Figure 34.9 inserts a checkpoint which checks whether the SOAP response XML file has a tag 'CelsiusToFahrenheitResult' whose tag value is equal to '25'.
7. The checkpoint as discussed in #6 can also be inserted as XPath checkpoint from XPath tab (refer Figure 34.9). Figure 34.10 shows the XPath checkpoint.

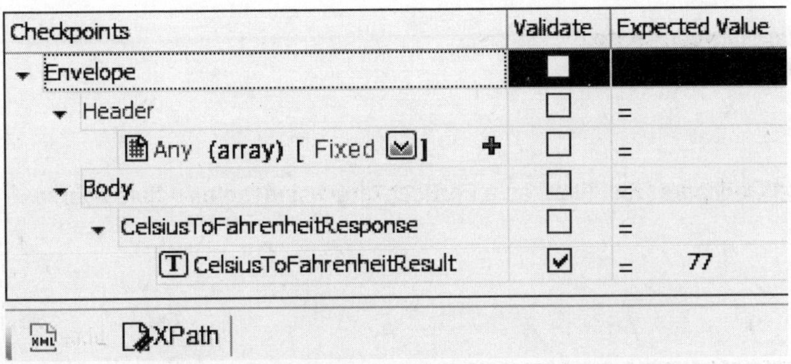

Figure 34.9 *Inserting Checkpoint in Grid view*

Figure 34.10 *Inserting XPath Checkpoint*

Parameterizing Input Data/Checkpoint

8. UFT provides the flexibility to parameterize XML request and XML response data (checkpoints). In order to parameterize, click on the button ' Data Drive Entire Step' (refer Figure 34.7). 'Data Driving' dialog box opens as shown in Fig. 34.11..
9. On 'Data Driving' pane select the option where data resides (Excel or XML) and data driven section.

   UFT allows to parameterize input data and checkpoints of API tests using Excel, XML and Datatable.
10 Click on 'OK' button to data drive API test. Figure 34.12 shows UFT generated Excel data file.

   Code below shows UFT generated data driven SOAP XML request file as visible in ' input/checkpoints' tab of 'Properties' pane.

```
<Celsius>({DataSource.CelsiusToFahrenheit_Input_1!MainDetails.
Celsius}_Link3)</Celsius>
```

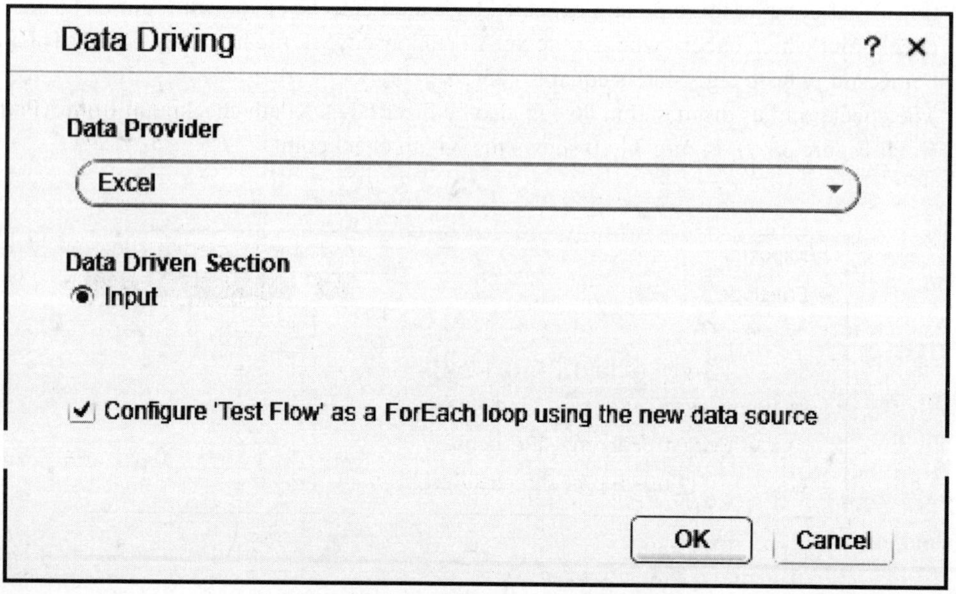

Figure 34.11 *Parameterizing API Tests*

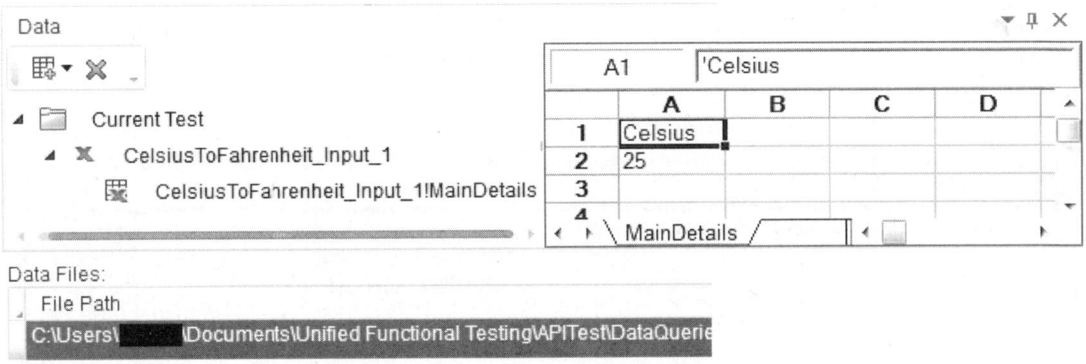

Figure 34.12 *UFT generated Excel data file*

Defining/Modifying Test Flow

11. UFT provides options to define/modify test flow. These options include performing various VBScript operations such as mathematical, logical, etc., defining flow control, conditional statements, calling external Java files etc. All the test operations are listed in 'Standard Activities' pane as shown in Fig. 34.13. Users can define the API test flow by dragging the required test flow operations from 'Standard Activities' pane to Test Flow.

Figure 34.13 *Standard Activities Pane*

Executing Test Steps

Once API test step is defined, it can be executed individually using 'Run Step' option. To run a specific step in the test flow, select the specific step in API test → Right Click → Select Run Step option. Figure 34.14 shows the run results of 'CelsiusToFahrenheit' test step. The test results displays step name, input/output SOAP envelop and checkpoints pass/fail status.

Executing API Test

Once API test is created, it can be executed individually using 'Run' button option. To run an API test either use key 'F5' or click on the 'Run' button on tool bar. Figure 34.15 shows the run results of test 'APITest'. The test results displays execution results of each and every step of API test including checkpoints.

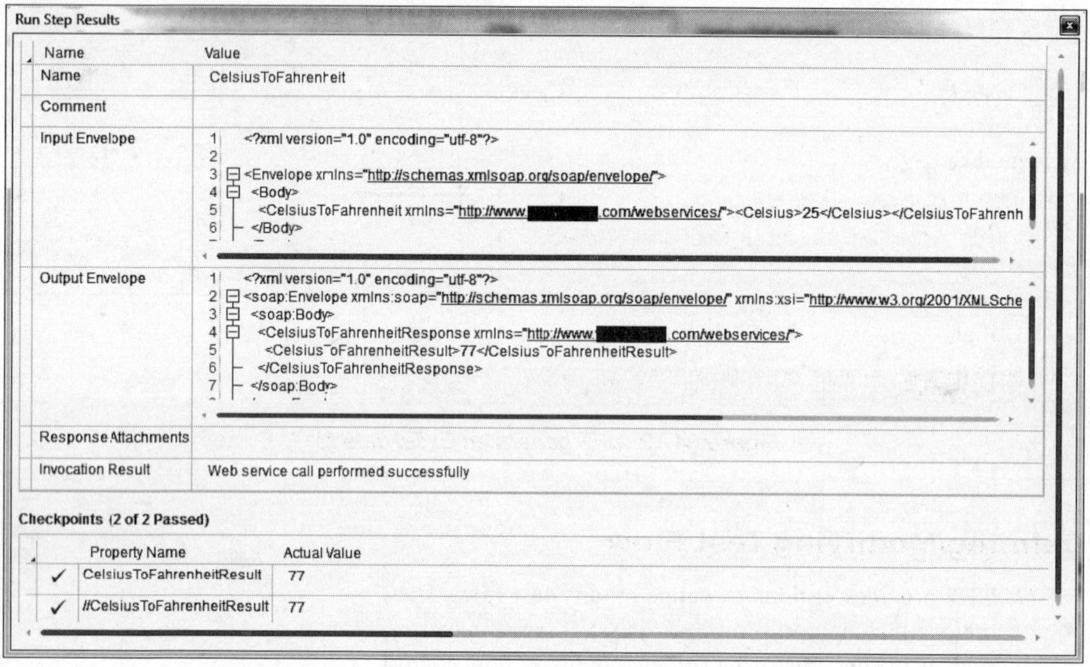

Figure 34.14 *Run Results of 'CelsiusToFahrenheit' test step*

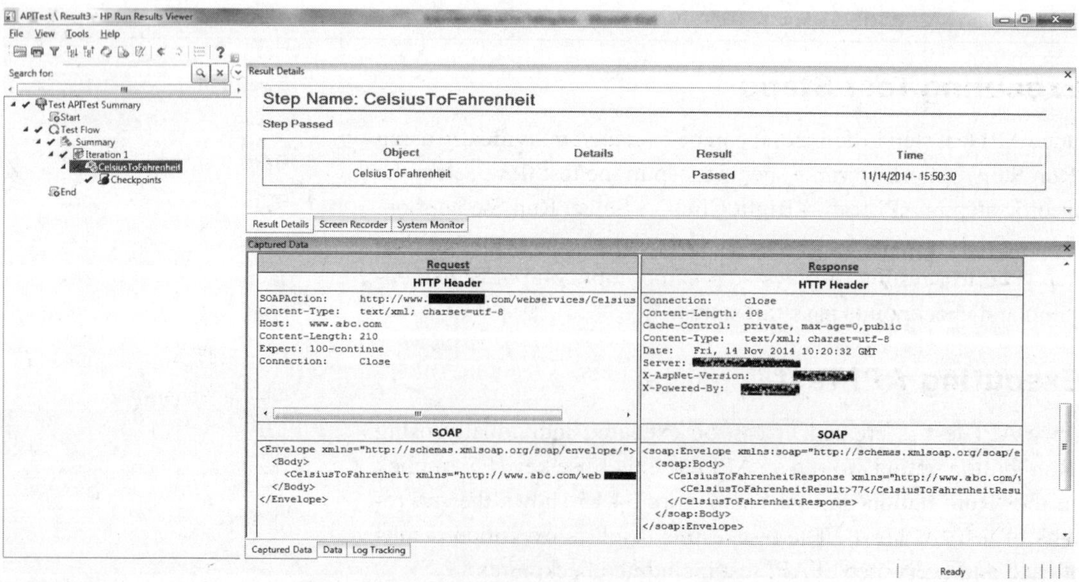

Figure 34.15 *Test Result of API test 'APITest'*

TESTING WEB SERVICES PROGRAMMATICALLY

In the last section, we discussed UFT approach of automating web services. Though this approach is very user-friendly but it is less flexible when it comes to integrating API tests with UI tests. An example would be an order purchase automation scenario where a new account is created using API while order purchase using same account happens using GUI. Programmatic approach of API automation offers a lot more flexibility and reusability. If framework and API test architecture design is proper, programmatic API tests provide considerable performance enhancement.

In this section, we will discuss how to automate web services using APIs XMLHTTPRequest, XMLUtil and XMLDOM. XMLHTTPRequest (XHR) is an API available to send HTTP or HTTPS request to a web server and load the server response data back into the script. XMLUtil and XMLDOM are APIs used to parse XML data and read or extract required information from XML files.

XMLHTTP Request

XMLHTTPRequest is a JavaScript object designed by Microsoft to communicate with HTTP and HTTPS servers. It provides an easy way to retrieve data from a URL without requiring a full page refresh. This helps to carry out asynchronous communication with web servers. XMLHTTPRequest can be used to retrieve any type of data, not just XML. It also supports protocols other than HTTP including file and ftp.

Events

XMLHTTPRequest has events as describes in the table below.

Event	Description
onreadystatechange	Sets or retrieves the event handler for asynchronous requests.
ontimeout	Occurs when there is an error that prevents the completion of the request.

Methods

Table below describes some of the XMLHTTPRequest methods.

Method	Description

open(*method, url, [async], [username], [password]*)	Specifies the arguments and attributes of a request.
	• Following HTTP methods are support for *method* argument:
	  ◦ Get – Request URI
	  ◦ Post – Send data to server
	  ◦ Head – Request URI without body
	  ◦ Put – Store data for URI
	  ◦ Delete – Delete data for URI
	  ◦ Options – Request URI options
	• url – specifies the web service URL.
	• async – [optional] A *true* value specifies asynchronous communication while a *false* value specifies synchronous communication. If not specified, default value is *true.*
	• username – [optional] Specifies username required for authentication.
	• password – [optional] Specifies password required for authentication.

set Request Header (*header, value*)	Adds header to request.
over ride Mime Type (*mime*)	Sets the Content-Type header for the response to the MIME provided.
send(*[content]*)	Sends an HTTP request with or without content to the server and receives the response.
abort()	Cancels the HTTP request.
get Response Header (*header*)	Returns the specified response header.
get All Response Headers()	Returns all response headers.

Properties

Table below describes some of the XMLHTTPRequest properties.

Properties	Description
readyState	Returns the state of the request operation as: • 0 – object created but not initialized. • 1 – request opened but not sent. • 2 – request sent. • 3 – receiving response. Full response is still to be received. • 4 – response received.
response	Returns the response received from the server.
responseBody	Retrieves the response body as an array of unsigned bytes.
responseText	Retrieves the response body as a string.
responseType	Describes the data type of the response.
responseXML	Retrieves the response body as XML.
status	Retrieves the HTTP status code of the request. A successful response status code is 200.
statusText	Retrieves the text value of the status code.
timeout	Gets or Sets the number of milliseconds that the browser is to wait for a server response before timing out.

XMLDOM

The XML Document Object Model (DOM) defines a standard way for accessing and manipulating XML documents. It is discussed in detail in chapter 'Working with XML'. In this chapter, we will discuss parsing XML response data using XMLDOM API.

XMLUtil

XMLUtil is a built-in UFT object to access and manipulate XML documents. It is discussed in detail in chapter 'Working with XML'.

Programmatic Web Service Testing for SOAP Request

In this section, we will discuss how to programmatically test web services for SOAP requests. Assume, the requirement is to test the web service method 'CesiusToFahrenheit'. Below is the code for submitting a SOAP request and reading the XML response.

Submitting SOAP Request

```
' soap request XML
nRequestValue = 25
soapRequest = "<?xml version=""1.0"" encoding=""utf-8""?>" &_
"<soap:Envelope xmlns:xsi=""http://www.w3.org/2001/XMLSche-
ma-instance"" xmlns:xsd=""http://www.w3.org/2001/XMLSchema""
xmlns:soap=""http://schemas.xmlsoap.org/soap/envelope/"">" &_
   "<soap:Body>" &_
     "<CelsiusToFahrenheit xmlns=""http://www.abc.com/webser-
     vices/"">" &_
       "<Celsius>" & nRequestValue & "</Celsius>" &_
     "</CelsiusToFahrenheit>" &_
   "</soap:Body>" &_
"</soap:Envelope>"


' Soap post action url
url = "http://www.abc.com/webservices/tempconvert.
asmx?op=CelsiusToFahrenheit"
' create a XMLHTTP object
Set oSoapRequest = CreateObject("Microsoft.XMLHTTP")
' specify request attributes
oSoapRequest.open "POST", url,  false
' specify request header
oSoapRequest.setRequestHeader "Content-Type", "text/xml;
charset=utf-8"
' submit request
oSoapRequest.send soapRequest

' get response status
Print "Response status code:" & oSoapRequest.status
Print "Response status text:" & oSoapRequest.statusText
' Output::
'     Response status code:200
'     Response status text:OK

' get response
sResponse = oSoapRequest.responseText

' print response
Print sResponse
'     Output::
<?xml version="1.0" encoding="utf-8"?>
<soap:Envelope xmlns:soap="http://schemas.xmlsoap.org/soap/en-
velope/" xmlns:xsi="http://www.w3.org/2001/XMLSchema-instance"
```

```
xmlns:xsd="http://www.w3.org/2001/XMLSchema">
<soap:Body>
   <CelsiusToFahrenheitResponse xmlns="http://www.abc.com/webser-
   vices/">
       <CelsiusToFahrenheitResult>77</CelsiusToFahrenheitResult>
   </CelsiusToFahrenheitResponse>
</soap:Body>
</soap:Envelope>
```

Reading XML Response

In this section, we will discuss how to read XML response using XMLDOM API. Alternatively, UFT API XMLUtil can also be used to read XML files.

```
' create XMLDOM object instance
Set oXMLDOM = CreateObject("Microsoft.XMLDOM")
oXMLDOM.loadXML(sResponse)

' get CelsiusToFahrenheitResult tag value
Set oElement = oXMLDOM.getElementsByTagName("CelsiusToFahrenheitResu
lt")
Print oElement(0).text    'Output::77

Set oXMLDOM = Nothing
```

> NOTES: XML file tags can also be read using XPath. Refer chapter 'Working with XML' for various ways of reading or retrieving data from XML files.

Programmatic Web Service Testing for HTTP Request

In this section, we will discuss how to programmatically test web services for HTTP requests. Assume, the requirement is to test the web service method 'CesiusToFahrenheit'. Below is the code for submitting a SOAP request and reading the XML response.

```
' http request url
url="http://www.abc.com/webservices/tempconvert.asmx/CelsiusToFahren-
heit"
' request content
content="Celsius=25"

' create request object instance
Set oRequest = CreateObject("Microsoft.XMLHTTP")
oRequest.open "POST", url, false
' set http request header
oRequest.setRequestHeader "Content-Type", "application/x-www-form-
```

```
urlencoded"
' submit request
oRequest.send(content)
' get response
sResponse = oRequest.responseText
' print response
Print sResponse
' Output::
'       <?xml version="1.0" encoding="utf-8"?>
'       <string xmlns="http://www.abc.com/webservices/">77</string>
```

Section 7 Object Identification

- Object Identification Mechanism
- Object Identification using Source Index and Automatic Xpath
- Object Identification Using Xpath
- Object Identification Using CSS Selectors
- Object Identification Using Visual Relation Identifiers
- Smart Identification
- Object Identification Using Ordinal Identifiers
- Image-based Identification (Insight)

Chapter 35

Object Identification Mechanism

All text boxes, check boxes, radio buttons, and other GUI objects are referred as an Object in UFT. UFT maps these objects to a standard UFT object class for recognizing these objects. For example, for a web-based application, text box is recognized as WebEdit and check box as WebCheckBox. If UFT does not find a standard mapping class for an object in GUI, then that object is recognized as WebElement. Table 35.1 provides information about GUI objects and its standard mapping class in UFT for some widely used objects for a web-based application.

Table 35.1 Web application objects and its standard mapping class in UFT

Web Application Object	UFT Icon	Standard UFT Mapping Class
Browser		Browser
Page		Page
Frame		Frame
Edit box		WebEdit
Image		Image
Link		Link
Button		WebButton
Checkbox		WebCheckBox
List box		WebList
Radio button		WebRadioGroup
Table		WebTable
Element		WebElement

OBJECT IDENTIFICATION METHODS

UFT stores the information of objects in object repository. These objects in object repository are called Test Objects. During test execution, UFT looks for objects in AUT which matches Test Object's description. If UFT is successful in uniquely identifying the object, then it executes the desired action on the object as mentioned in the test. Else, UFT fails the test and records an object identification failure at the said point. UFT offers five ways of identifying objects in AUT:

- Object description-based object identification
- Visual relation identifier-based object identification
- Smart Identification
- Ordinal identifier based object identification
- Image-based object identification (Insight)

UFT TEST OBJECT IDENTIFICATION MECHANISM

UFT classifies the test objects into two categories—standard UFT object and insight object. Standard UFT object is the standard UFT test class object as such WebEdit, WebElement, WebButton, etc. While Insight object is the image of the GUI object. The complete list of UFT standard test class objects can be viewed in the *Object Identification* dialog box.

UFT uses different identification mechanism for standard test objects and insight objects. Figure 35.1 below shows the identification mechanisms used by UFT to locate standard test class objects and insight objects in GUI.

Standard Object Identification Mechanism

Standard object identification mechanism comprises of four identification mechanisms to help uniquely identify the object in UI. At a time, UFT uses only one identification mechanism. If object

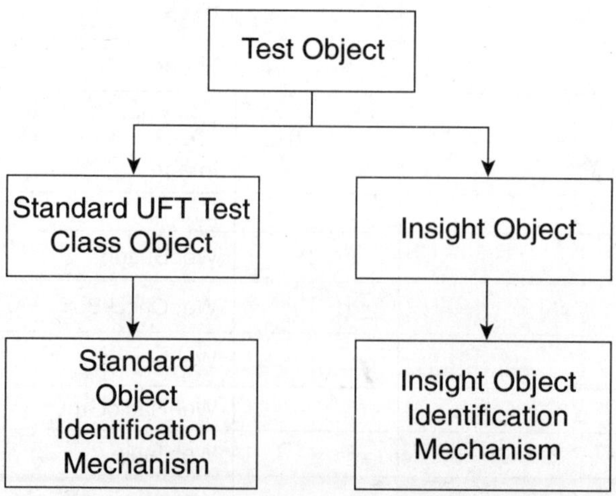

Figure 35.1 *UFT test object identification mechanism*

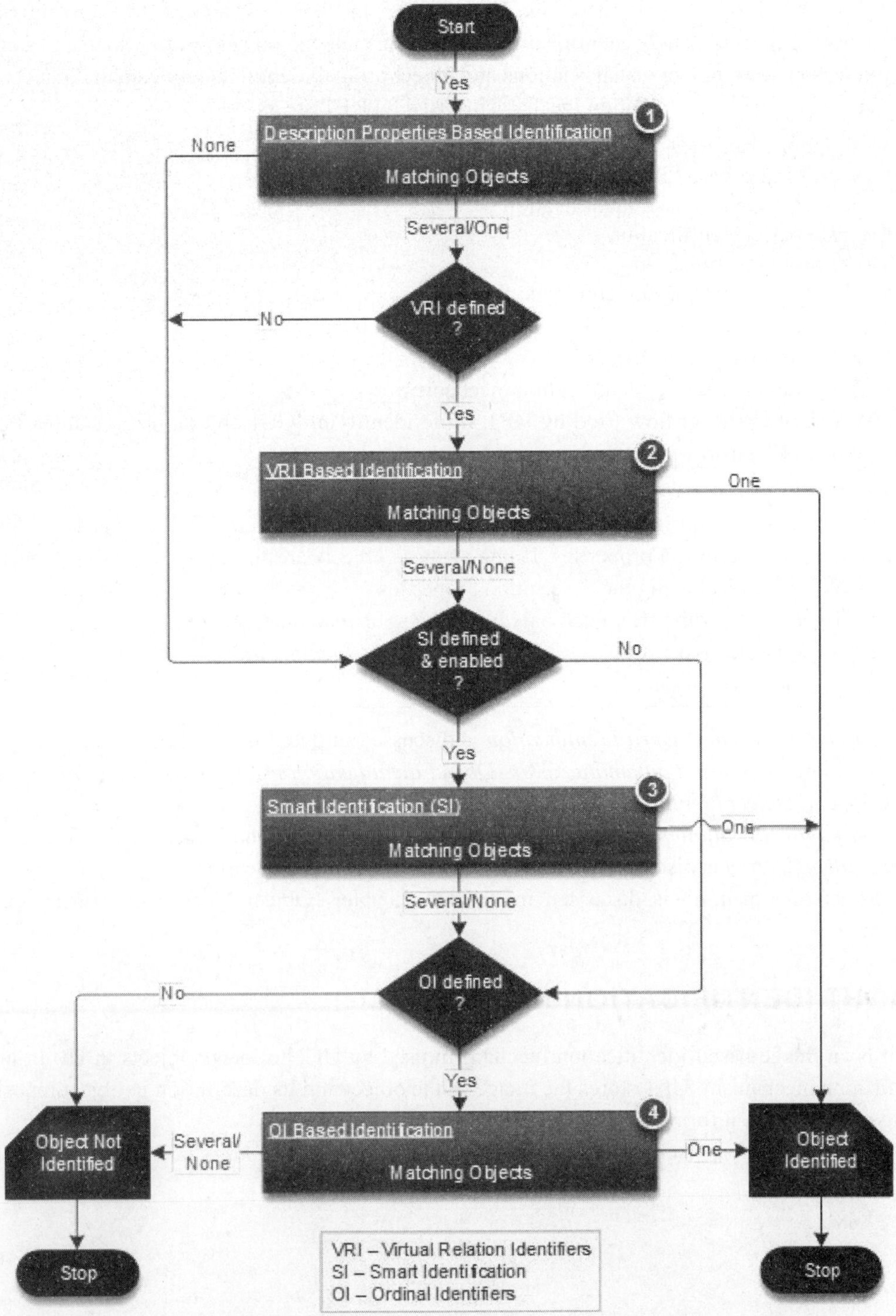

Figure 35.2 *Object identification process flow*

is uniquely located in UI using one of the identification mechanisms, the rest of the identification mechanisms are ignored. These identification mechanisms use the object information such as object description properties, object visual relations and object ordinal identifiers to locate the object.

The standard object identification mechanisms used by UFT are as below:

- Description properties-based identification mechanism
    - source index based identification
    - automatic xpath based identification
    - xpath based identification
    - css based identification
    - object attributes based identification
- Visual Relation Identifier (VRI) based identification mechanism
- Smart identification mechanism
- Ordinal Identifier-based identification mechanism.

Figure 35.2 shows process flow used by UFT while identifying GUI objects using standard object identification mechanism.

> For web-based objects:
>
> - If web object identifiers such as XPath or CSS properties are defined, then they are used before the description properties. If one or more objects are found, then UFT continues to identify the object using the description properties.
> - UFT-generated properties, such as *source index* or *automatic XPath*, may also affect the object identification process. Refer chapter *Object Identification using source index and automatic xpath* for details.

Description Properties based Identification is discussed in detail in chapters—*Object Identification using source index and automatic xpath, Object Identification using xpath, Object Identification using CSS, and Object Identification using Object Attributes.*

VRI based Identification is discussed in detail in chapter 'Object Identification using VRI'.

Smart Identification is discussed in detail in chapter 'Smart Identification'.

OI Based Identification is discussed in detail in chapter 'Object Identification using Ordinal Identifiers'.

INSIGHT IDENTIFICATION MECHANISM

Insight is an image-based identification mechanism used by UFT to locate objects in UI. In insight identification mechanism, UFT stores the image of the object and its description in object repository. During run-time, this information is used to identify the object.

Insight Identification mechanism is discussed in detail in chapter *Image Based Identification (Insight).*

Chapter 36

Object Identification Using Source Index and Automatic Xpath

UFT learns source index and automatic xpath of an object automatically, if configured. These object identification properties are not visible in the object repository; hence users cannot edit or modify them. During test run, UFT uses these properties first to locate the object in UI.

SOURCE INDEX

Source Index is a zero based integer value which represents the position of the element among all elements in HTML document. UFT learns this property automatically when learning the object description. However, this property is hidden in object repository; hence, users cannot edit or modify the value of this description property.

Retrieving Source Index Value of Test and Run-time Object

Though source index property of an object is not visible in object repository, it can be viewed in UI using object spy. Figure 36.1 shows the source index property of Google Search page edit box object.

Source index property of test object can be retrieved using UFT code as shown below:

```
Set oPg = Browser("Google").Page("Google")
Print oPg.WebEdit("q").GetTOProperty("source_index")        'Output:: 139
```

Source index property of run-time object can be retrieved using UFT code as shown below:

```
   Print oPg.WebEdit("q").GetROProperty("attribute/sourceindex")
'Output::139
   Alternatively,
Print oPg.WebEdit("q").Object.sourceIndex    'Output::139
Alternatively,
Print oPg.WebEdit("q"). GetROProperty("source_index")      'Output::139
```

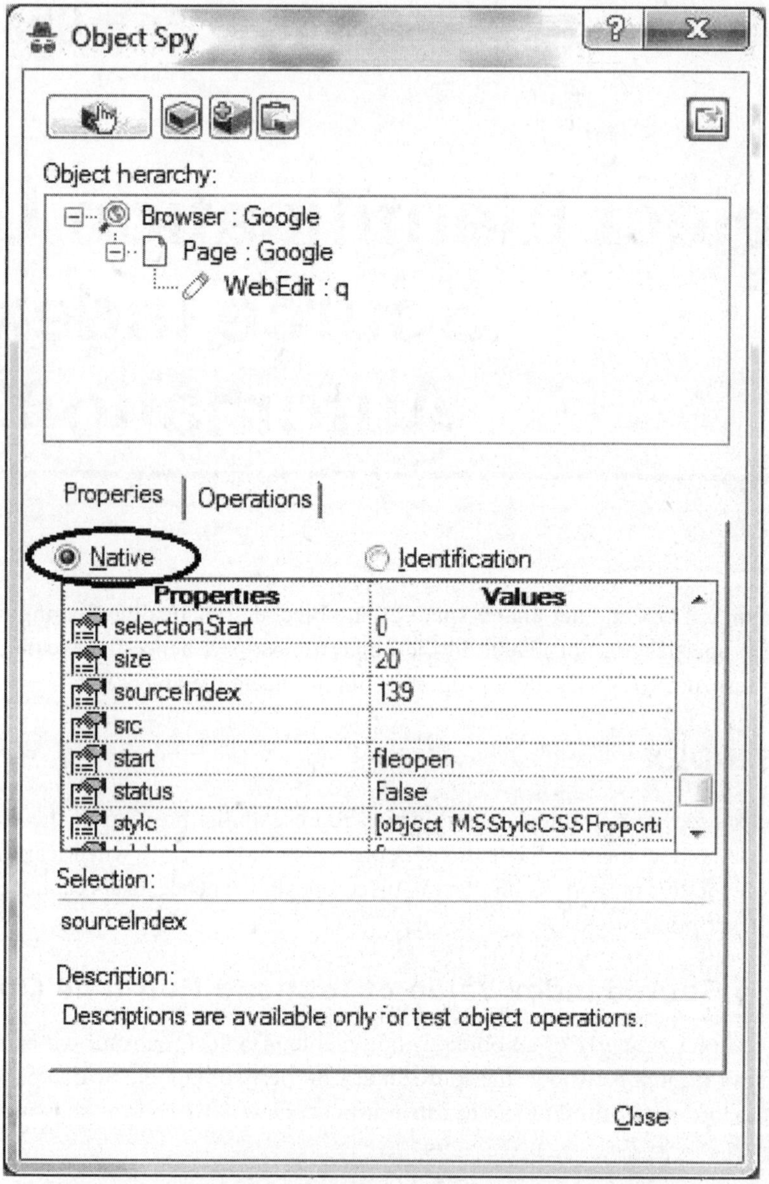

Figure 36.1 *Viewing objects native property 'source index'*

Configuring Source Index Identification Mechanism

UFT provides the flexibility to enable or disable source index identification mechanism. To enable source index identification mechanism, open GUI testing tab of *Options* dialog box and navigate to node *Web* → *Advanced*. Then select checkbox option *Run using source index* as shown in Fig. 36.2..

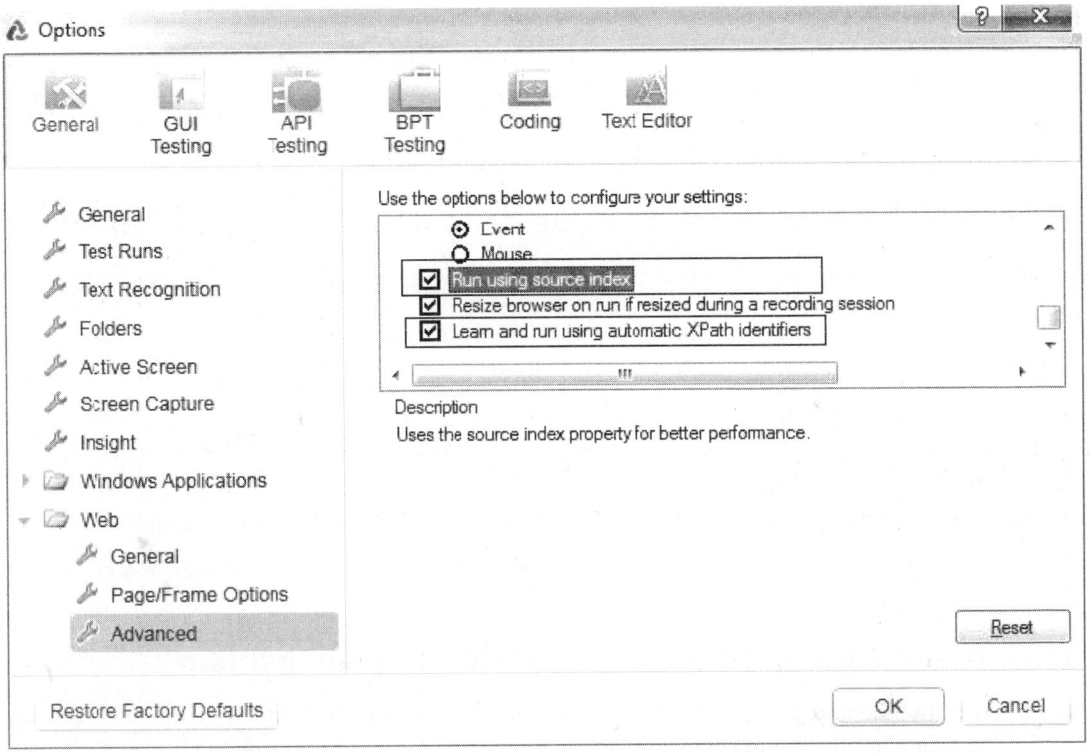

Figure 36.2 *Enabling UFT object identification mechanism for source index and automatic xpath*

Object Identification Mechanism Using Source Index

UFT learns the source index value when learning web test objects. During test run sessions, UFT uses the learned source index value to return the relevant DOM element from the application and then verifies that this object matches the test object description. This operation is faster than searching the entire DOM for objects that match the test object description. If the returned object does not match the object description, the source index is ignored and UFT attempts to identify the object using the standard object identification process.

The source index is also ignored during a run session in the following scenarios:

- If the description for a test object includes the XPath or css identifier. Or,
- If the Index ordinal identifier for the test object has been manually defined. Or,
- If the test run is being performed using a browser other than Internet Explorer.

> **NOTES** If the automated tests are planned to be executed against multiple browsers, then avoid using this mechanism for object identification.

AUTOMATIC XPATH

Automatic xpath is the xpath of the object automatically learned by UFT. UFT learns this property automatically when learning the object description. However, this property is hidden in object repository; hence, users cannot edit or modify the value of this description property.

Retrieving Automatic XPath Value of Test and Run-time Object

Though automatic xpath property of an object is not visible in object repository, it can found using UFT code as shown below:

Example: Find automatic xpath as learned by UFT for Google Search page edit box.

```
Set oPg = Browser("Google").Page("Google")
Print oPg.WebEdit("q").GetTOProperty("_xpath")       'Output::/INPUT[@
id="gbqfq"]
```

Run-time xpath aproperty of the object can be found using the UFT code as shown below:

```
Print oPg.WebEdit("q").GetROProperty("_xpath")       'Output::/INPUT[@
id="gbqfq"]
```

Configuring Automatic XPath Identification Mechanism

UFT provides the flexibility to enable or disable automatic xpath identification mechanism. To enable automatic xpath identification mechanism, open GUI testing tab of *Options* dialog box and navigate to node *Web → Advanced.* Then select checkbox option *Learn and Run using automatic XPath identifiers* as shown in Fig. 36.2.

Object Identification Mechanism Using Automatic XPath

UFT learns the XPath value of the object and stores it in object repository when learning web test objects. The same value is value used during a run session to improve object identification reliability. During test run sessions, UFT uses the learned XPath value to return the respective DOM element from the application and then verifies that this object matches the test object description. If the returned object does not match the object description, the automatic XPath is ignored and UFT attempts to identify the object using the standard object identification process.

The automatic XPath is also ignored during a run session in the following scenarios:

- If the description for a test object includes the XPath or css identifier. Or,
- If the *Run using source index* option is selected

QUICK TIPS

✓ Users cannot edit properties source index and automatic xpath through object repository.

✓ Source index property is only supported for IE browser.

PRACTICAL QUESTIONS

1. What is source index of an object?
2. Explain UFT object identification mechanism when both source index and automatic XPath has been learned by UFT and
   (a) Both identification mechanisms are enabled during test run.
   (b) Source Index identification mechanism is disabled and automatic XPath is enabled during test run.

Chapter 37

Object Identification Using XPath

XPath is XML path language based on a tree representation of the XML document. It is a query language for selecting nodes from XML document. It provides the ability to navigate around the tree by selecting nodes by using a variety of criteria.

With QTP 11, HP has provided the feature to locate GUI objects based on their XPath definition. UFT learns XPath definition automatically while learning an object. It as well provides the flexibility to the user to define custom XPath expressions for identifying objects in UI. As discussed in the chapter *Object Identification using source index and automatic xpath*, UFT automatically learned XPath is called *Automatic XPath*. This expression is used in background as a performance enhancement during test execution. Also, this property is hidden from users and hence, it can neither be viewed nor be edited. Automation developers can use the 'xpath' description property to define custom xpath expressions to locate objects.

Table 37.1 below explains the difference between automatic xpath and xpath identification mechanisms.

Table 37.1 Difference between automatic xpath and user-defined xpath

Scenario	Automatic XPath	User-Defined XPath
Muliple objects match the XPath value	UFT ignores the learned XPath and continues with standard object identification process.	UFT continues to use description properties to identify the matching object.
No objects match the XPath value	UFT ignores the learned XPath and continues with standard object identification process.	Description Properties based Object Identification fails, and UFT continues to identify the object using Smart Identification.

HOW TO FIND XPATH OF A GUI OBJECT?

XPath of an object can be used to uniquely locate the object in a web page. There are various tools available to find XPath of an object. In this section, we will discuss how to find XPath of an object using Firefox browser.

Figure 37.1 *Login page of a 'Sample' application*

Consider the login page of a sample application as shown in Fig. 37.1. Now let's see how to find xpath of 'Email' edit box object using Firefox browser.

Firefox plug-in *Firebug path* can be used to design XPath locators which can identify an element in the DOM tree. Follow the below steps to view the XPath locator path of an object:

- Ensure Firefox addon *Firebug* is installed.
- Ensure Firebug plug-in *Firepath* is installed.
- Open Firefox and then activate Firebug window by clicking on the bookmark . Firebug window opens as shown in Fig. 37.2.
- On Firebug window, click on the FirePath ▾ tab. Firepath window opens (refer Figure 37.2).
- On Firepath tab, select one or more of the options – *Show Parent toolbar*, *Generate absolute XPath* or *Show Entire DOM*.

Avoid selecting 'Generate absolute XPath' option as this generates absolute XPath of the object. For current discussion, assume that this option is selected.

- On Firepath window, select locator as 'XPath' as shown in Fig. 37.3.
- To view XPath of an object, click on the mouse icon and then point and click the arrow on the desired object. Firepath automatically builds the XPath of the object and displays it on the Firepath window as shown in Fig. 37.4.

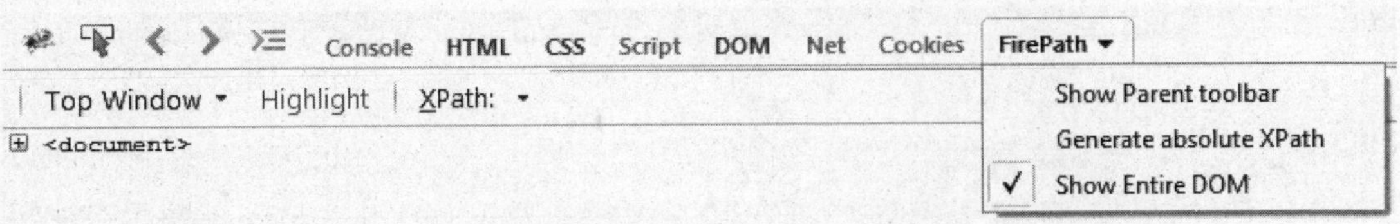

Figure 37.2 *Specifying firepath opttions*

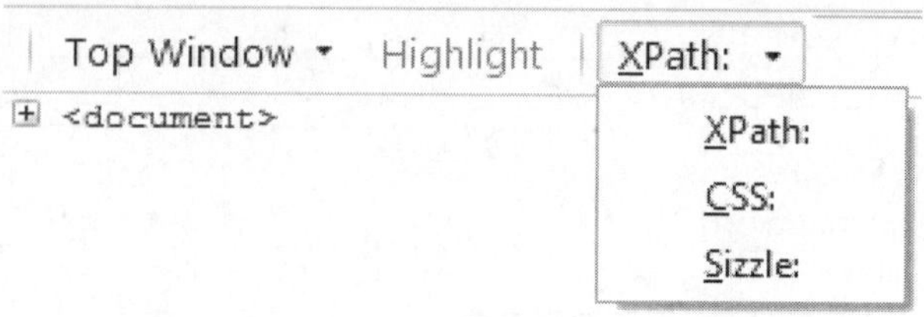

Figure 37.3 *Specifying locator strategy*

In order to find the XPath of 'Email' edit box object, click on the mouse icon and then point and click the arrow on edit box object. The calculated XPath of the edit box object will be displayed as shown in Fig. 37.4.

As shown in Fig. 37.4,

- Firepath displays the calculated XPath in Firepath frame window edit box.
- Firepath highlights all the objects in GUI that matches the XPath expression using dotted line.
- Firepath highlights the HTML code of the matched objects in Firepath frame window.
- Firepath displays the number of matching nodes (matching objects).

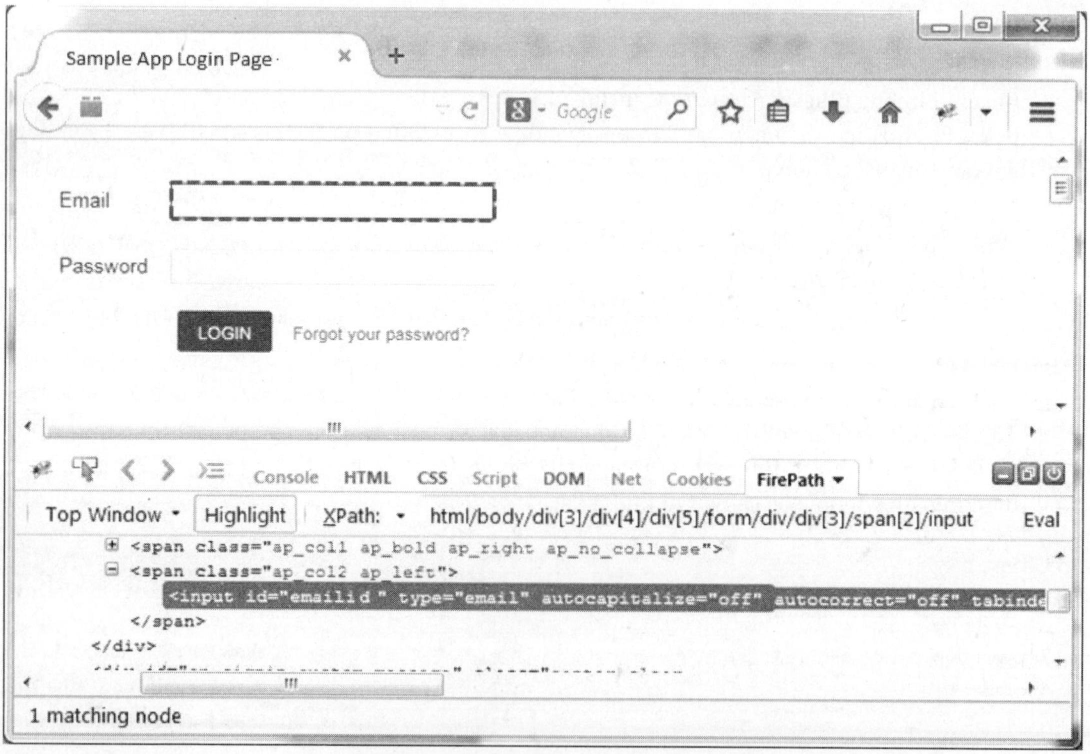

Figure 37.4 *XPath of email edit box object*

The above absolute XPath expression (html/body/div[3]/div[4]/div[5]/form/div/div[3]/span[2]/input) is not a reliable mechanism to locate objects. This is because any addition or deletion of an element (even a label element) may change the absolute XPath of existing objects. Such continuous changes in the web pages will require continuous change in test scripts. This makes automation maintenance difficult. In order to avoid this problem, relative XPath of an element is to be used.

Assume HTML code of the *Email* edit box field is:

```
<input  id="emailid"  type="email"  autocapitalize="off"  autocorrect="
off" tabindex="1" maxlength="128" size="30" value="" name="email"/>
```

The above HTML code describes the various attributes of the object such as its id, name, size, maxlength etc. One or more of these attributes can be used to uniquely identify the edit box object. One of the reliable attributes of the edit box object is its '*id*' attribute. Relative XPath of the *Email* edit box using this 'id' attribute can be designed as:

```
//input[@id='emailid ']
```

The above XPath locates an *input* element whose *id* attribute value equals *emailid*.

> **NOTES** In order to verify whether this locator path uniquely identifies the edit box element or not, write this locator path on Firepath window and hit Enter key. If the object is uniquely identified, then the respective element and its HTML code will be highlighted and the number of matches displayed on the Firepath window will be equal to 1.

OBJECT IDENTIFICATION USING XPATH

UFT allows the flexibility to the automation developers to use xpath of the object to identify it during test execution. Object xpath can be used to locate objects in both descriptive programming as well as object repository approach of UFT automation.

Using XPath in Descriptive Programming

UFT provides the description property 'xpath' to locate objects based on the xpath of the object. Code below shows, how to identify the *email* edit box object using its xpath value:

```
Set oPg = Browser("B").Page("P")
oPg.WebEdit("xpath:=//input[@id='emailid ']").Set "abc@gmail.com"
Alternatively,
Set oDescEditBox = Description.Create
oDescEditBox("micclass").value = "WebEdit"
oDescEditBox("xpath").value = "//input[@id='emailid']"

oPg.WebEdit(oDescEditBox).Set "abc@google.com"
```

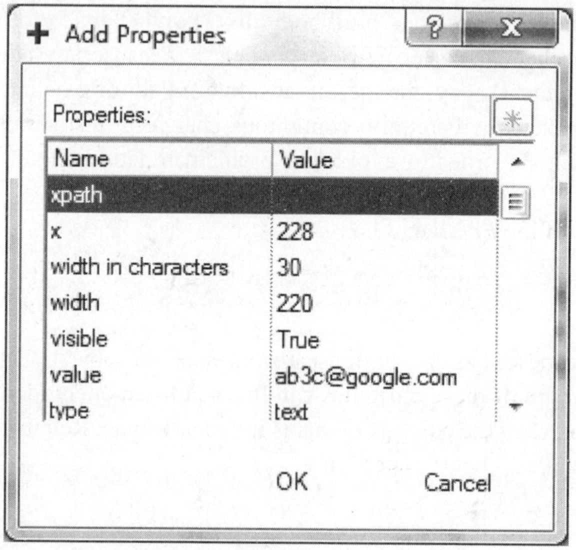

Figure 37.5 *Add properties dialog box*

Using XPath in Object Repository

The XPath so designed can be used to define objects in Object Repository as well. Follow the below steps to specify a user-defined xpath for a test object in OR:

1. Open the specific object repository.
2. On OR window, select the object whose xpath property is to be defined.
3. Click on the add properties button. *Add Properties* dialog box opens as shown in Fig. 37.5.
4. Double click on 'xpath' property to add it to the list of description properties.
5. Specify the custom designed 'xpath' to xpath description property as shown in Fig. 37.6.
6. Use 'Highlight in Application' button to verify that the object is uniquely identified by UFT.

XPATH BASED OBJECT IDENTIFICATION MECHANISM

UFT treats 'xpath' as one of the description properties. During run-time, UFT uses all the defined description properties including XPath to uniquely identify the object. The identification process is same as standard object identification process.

WHY TO BUILD CUSTOM RELATIVE XPATH OF AN OBJECT

So far we discussed about absolute and relative xpaths and how to use them to create a unique description of the object. Firepath can automatically generate both absolute and relative xpath of an object. However, both of these automatically generated xpath expressions are unreliable.

Now you may ask here?—Why to build custom relative xpaths? And Why not to use xpath expression as generated by Firepath?

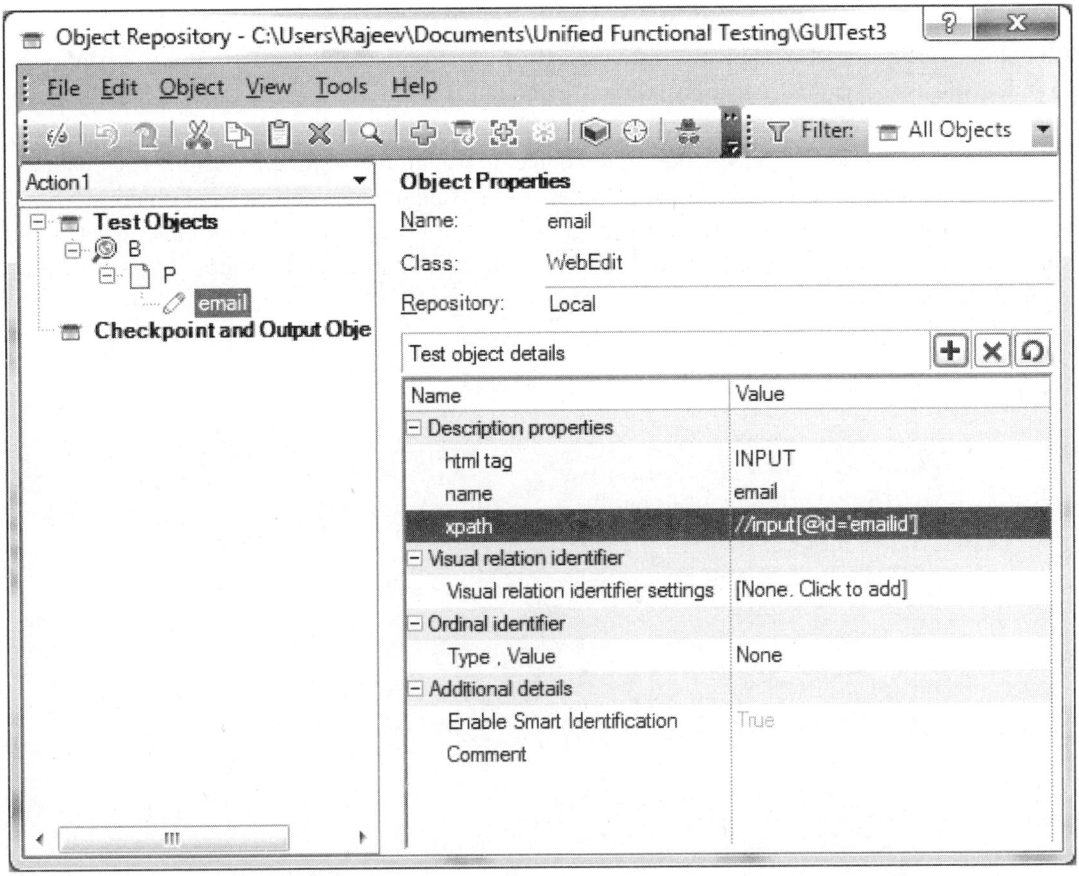

Figure 37.6 *Adding xpath property to object description properties*

This is because the xpath expression generated by Firepath does not always helps to uniquely locate the object. For example, consider the absolute xpath expression generated by Firepath. As we discussed earlier, even a minor change in UI can result in a change in the absolute xpath of the object. Hence, use of absolute xpaths is to be strictly avoided.

Again, consider the relative xpath as built by Firepath for objects. Figure 37.7 shows Firepath generated relative xpath for the '*Forgot your password?*' link object.

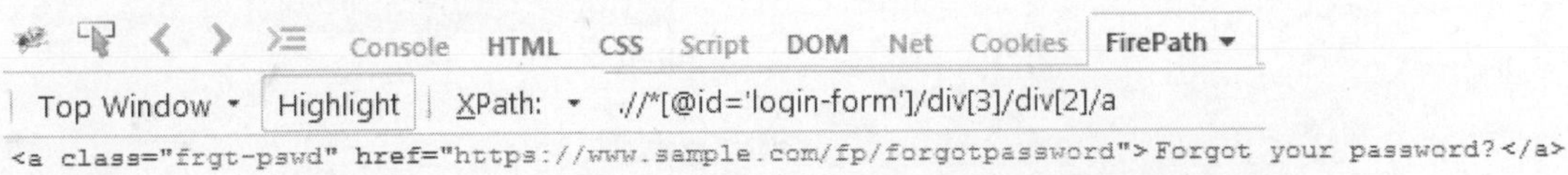

Figure 37.7 *Firepath generated relative xpath of email edit box*

As shown above the relative xpath uses reference of <div> elements and their index values to create a unique description of the object. Unnecessary use of node elements such as <div>, <span>, <p> and index values makes the object description unreliable and prone to UI changes. This ultimately results in high object identification failure rate.

It is advisable to use the HTML code of the object to design the xpath expression. The xpath expression should consist of node name of the object such as input, a, select, etc. and object attributes such as id, class, name etc. The most accurate relative path for the forgot password link object would be an expression that looks for a link (<a>) element whose '*class*' attribute value is '*frgt-pswd*'. So, the xpath expression can be:

```
xpath:= //a[@class='frgt-pswd']
```

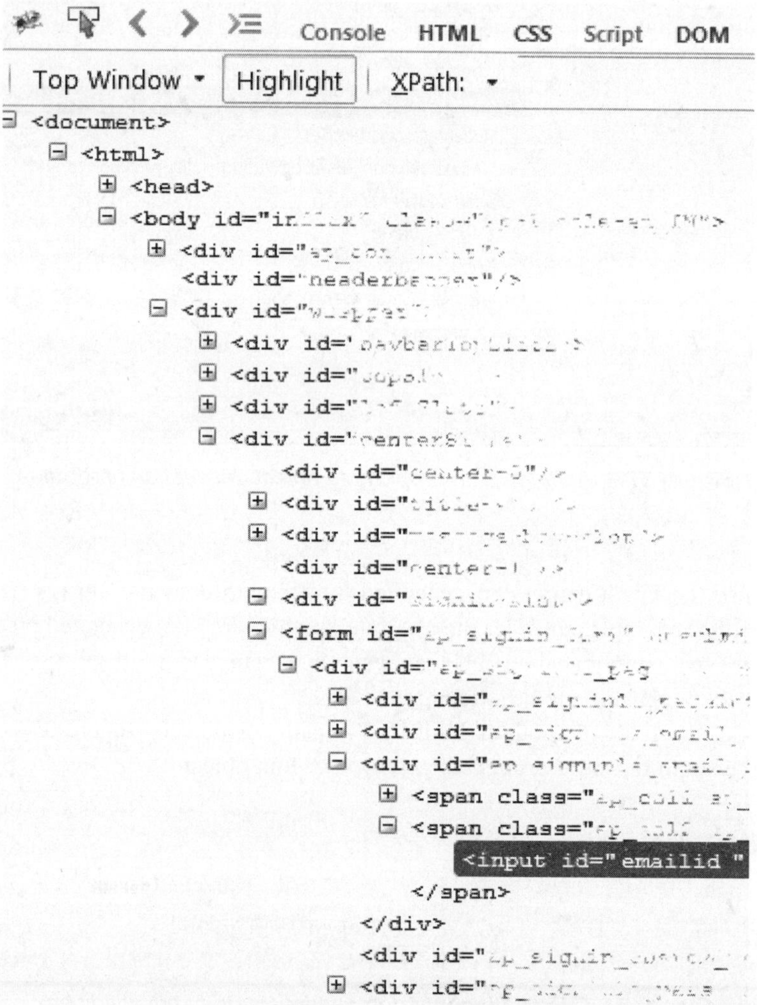

Figure 37.8 *HTML document tree of the login page of the sample application*

XPATH QUERY LANGUAGE FEATURES

XPath query language provides a wide range of wildcards, operators and functions to uniquely locate an element in XML document tree or HTML document tree. These features of XPath query language can be used to create an expression that uniquely describes an element in the HTML node tree.

Expressions

Consider the HTML document tree of the login page of the sample application. Figure 37.8 shows the HTML document tree of the login page.

Assume HTML code of the *Email* and *Password* edit boxes of Fig. 37.4 is as below:

```
HTML code of Email edit box:
<input id="emailid" type="email" autocapitalize="off"
autocorrect="off" tabindex="1" maxlength="128" size="30" val-
ue="" name="email"/>
```

```
HTML code of Password edit box:
<input id="passwordid" class="password" type="password" on
keypress="displayCapsWarning(event
,'ap_caps_warning', this);" tabin-
dex="2" size="20" maxlength="224" name="password"/>
```

Table below describes some of the wild card expressions used to locate specific nodes of HTML document tree as shown in the Fig. 37.8.

Expression	Objective	Example	Description
<node name>	Locates the specific node.	html	Locates the *html* node.
/	Locates the next node from the root node.	html/body	Locates the *body* node.
//	Locates all the named nodes no matter where it exists in the HTML tree.	//input	Locates all elements with node name as *input* (*input* node elements).
.	Locates the current node.	//label[.='Email']	Locates the 'Email' label element.
..	Locates the parent node of the current node.	//label[.='Email']/..	Locates the parent node of the 'Email' label element.
@	Locates node by its attributes.	//input[@id='emailid']	Locates node element whose 'id' attribute value is 'emailid'. Locates 'Email' edit box.

Wildcards

In UFT, many times we use childobjects, childitems etc. to locate child objects of an object to locate an object which is otherwise inaccessible. XPath query language provides wildcards to find specific node element (object) matches. Table below lists out some of the wildcards that can be used to uniquely locate an object which is otherwise inaccessible to UFT.

Wildcards	Objective	Example	Description
*	Matches any element node.	//*[.='Email']	Locates node element whose text value is Email. (here node name could be anything say <p>,<span> or <label>)
@*	Matches a node any of whose attribute values is as specified.	//input[@*='emailid']	Locates node element whose attribute value is 'emailid' for any attribute (say class, name or id).

Operators

XPath query language supports use of operators in xpath expression. This helps to build logical conditions within the xpath expression. These logical conditions can not only be used to build a unique description of a dynamic object but can also be used to return integers, strings or Boolean. The table below lists out the operators supported by XPath query language.

Assume HTML code of the *Email* and *Password* edit boxes of Fig. 37.4 is as below:

```
HTML code of Email edit box:
<input id="emailid" type="email" autocapitalize=
"off" autocorrect="off" tabin-
dex="1" maxlength="128" size="30" value="" name="email"/>
```

```
HTML code of Password edit box:
<input id="passwordid" class="password" type="password" onkey
press="displayCapsWarning(event,'ap_caps_warning', this);"tabi-
ndex="2" size="20" maxlength="224" name="password"/>
```

Operators	Objective	Example	Description
or	Or operation	//input[@id='emailid' or @id='email_id']	Locate an *input* node element whose 'id' attribute value is either 'emailid' or 'email_id'. Locates *email* edit box.
		//input[@id='emailid' or @type='email ']	Locate an *input* node element whose either 'id' attribute value is 'emailid' or 'type' attribute value is 'email'. Locates *email* edit box.
and	And operation	//input[@id='emailid' and @type='email ']	Locate an *input* node element whose 'id' attribute value is 'emailid' and 'type' attribute value is 'email'. Locates *email* edit box.
mod	Modulus (calculates remainder)	13 mod 2	Remainder 1
|	Matches node sets	//input|//a	Locates all *<input>* and *<a>* nodes.
+	Addition	3+2	5
-	Subtraction	3-2	1

Operators	Objective	Example	Description
*	Multiplication	3*2	6
div	Division	4div2	2
=	Equals to	//input[@id='emailid']	Local *input* elements whose 'id' attribute *equals to* 'emailid'. Locates *email* edit box.
		//input[@maxlength=128]	Local *input* elements whose 'maxlength' attribute *equals to* 128. Locates *email* edit box.
!=	Not equals to	//input[@id!='passwordid']	Local *input* elements whose 'id' attribute does *not equals to* 'password'. Locates *email* edit box.
<	Smaller than	//input[@maxlength<129]	Local *input* elements whose 'maxlength' attribute *equals to* 128. Locates *email* edit box.
<=	Smaller than or equal to	//input[@maxlength<=128]	Local *input* elements whose 'maxlength' attribute value is less than or equal to 128. Locates *email* edit box.
>	Greater than	//input[@maxlength>128]	Local *input* elements whose 'maxlength' attribute value is greater than 128. Locates *password* edit box.
>=	Greater than or equal to	//input[@ maxlength>=128]	Local *input* elements whose 'maxlength' attribute value is greater than or equal to 128. Locates *email* and *password* edit boxes.

XPath Functions

XPath query language provides various functions to locate elements whose attribute values are not constant but follow specific dynamic patterns (dynamic objects). It includes *start-with(an,av)*, *endswith(an,av)* and *contains(an,av)*, where an=attribute name and av=attribute value. XPath functions are discussed in detail in section 'Finding Elements using Partial Match of Attribute Values' below.

XPath Axis

XPath query language supports locating an object on the basis of its axis path. This is discussed in detail in the section 'Finding Elements using XPath Axis' below.

HOW TO BUILD CUSTOM XPATH EXPRESSION?

We discussed in the last section the various features provides by XPath query language to help unqwely locate an element in HTML document tree. In this section, we will discuss how to use these features to build an xpath expression that uniquely defined an element.

Finding Elements Using Absolute XPath

Absolute path refers to the absolute hierarchical location of the element with respect to the root node of the DOM. XPath absolute path describes the complete parent-child hierarchy of the element.

Example 1: Find the absolute XPath of the Email Address field of Fig. 37.1
As shown in the Fig. 37.4 the absolute path of the Email Address field is:

```
html/body/div[2]/div[2]/div[5]/form/div/div[3]/span[2]/input
```

UFT code to locate the element is:

```
Set oPg = Browser("B").Page("P")
xpathExprsn = "html/body/div[2]/div[2]/div[5]/form/div/div[3]/
span[2]/input"
oPg.WebEdit("xpath:=" & xpathExprsn).Set "abc@gmail.com"
```

> **NOTE** Two html tags in XPath are separated by a '/' sign. Unlike CSS, index can be used to identify element tags. For example , as visible in fig 4 and fig 8 above, between *form* node and *div* node there is only one *div* node so this has been represented as *.../form/div/...* However, between this *div* node and the next *div* node that contains the *Email Address* <input> there are three div elements, so the next node has been represented as *.../form/div/div[3]...* Similarly, between this *div* node and the next node (*span*) that contains the *Email Address* field, they are two *span* nodes. So, the next node has been located as *.../form/div/div[3]/span[2]...*

Locating elements using its absolute path has one drawback. The element identification is dependent on the node structure of the tree. The tree node structure can be under frequent changes depending upon the development work on the page. Even a small change such as introduction of new *div* element in the tree will result in change in the absolute xpath of the *Email Address* field. In order for the scripts to work, the xpath for the element in the scripts needs to be updated frequently as per the change. Such frequent changes will result in huge automation maintenance cost. Moreover, it will severely impact regression run executions because of high failures due to failed object identification. To solve this problem, we can use relative xpath of the elements.

Finding Elements Using Relative XPath

An element can also be located in the DOM tree with respect to the position of other elements in the DOM tree. Since this path is relative to the position of another element, hence it is called *relative* path. For example, we can locate the *Email Address* field for Fig. 37.1 using code:

```
oPg.WebEdit("xpath:=//input[1]").Set "abc@gmail.com"
```

Above code locates the first <input> element in the web page DOM tree.

Example 1: Assume the sample application login page has many images. Locate all the image elements of this page and click on the first image element ( ).

UFT code to locate all the image elements of the above DOM tree is:

```
Set oDesc = Description.Create
oDesc(“micclass”).value = “Image”
oDesc(“xpath”).value = “//img”

Set colImages = oPg.ChildObjects(oDesc)
colImages(0).Click
```

```
Alternatively,
   oPg.Image(“xpath:=//img[1]”).Click
```

Example 2: Locate all the link elements of the Fig. 37.1.

UFT code to llocate all the link (<a>) elements of the above DOM tree is:

```
Set oDesc = Description.Create
oDesc(“micclass”).value = “Link”
oDesc(“xpath”).value = “//a”

Set colLinks = oPg.ChildObjects(oDesc)
```

Finding Elements Using Index with XPath

As we observer in the Example 2 above, there are multiple links in the DOM tree. In order to locate a specific link element in the DOM tree, position (index) of the element can be specified along with its node name. For example, in the code above, location of link *Forgot your password* is first in the DOM tree. So, XPath expression //a[1] can be used to identify this link.

Example: Locate the Password field in Fig. 37.1.

Password field is the second <input> field in the DOM tree. So, the XPath expression to identify this element will be //input[2].

UFT code to locate this element using its index value is:

```
oPg.WebEdit(“xpath:=//input[2]”).Set “Pass1”
```

> NOTES
>
> Identifying elements using its index value is not a reliable method of locating elements. This is because, in case, one more input element is added between the <input> node of *Email Address* and *Password* field, then the scripts fail as //input[2] no longer points to the Password field.

Finding Elements Using Attribute Values with XPath

XPath query language offers the flexibility to locate elements by using the attribute values of the element. For example, an element can be identified using its *id*, *class*, *type*, *alt*, *value*, *name* etc. attribute values. ‘@’ symbol is used to specify the attribute with the XPath.

Example 1: Locate the Email Address field using its attribute values.

The HTML code for the *email address* field is:

```
<input id="emailid" type="email" autocapitalize="off" autocorrect="off"
tabindex="1" maxlength="128" size="30" value="" name="email"/>
```

The above HTML code defines the attributes *id, type, autocapitalize, autocorrect, tabindex, maxlength, size, value* and *name.* Any of values of these attributes can be used to identify the *email address* element on the webpage.

Code below uses *id* attribute to identify the *Email Address* field.

```
oPg.WebEdit("xpath:=//input[@id='emailid']") .Set "abc@gmail.com"
```

Alternatively, *Email Address* field can also be recognized using *name* attribute value

```
oPg.WebEdit("xpath:=//input[@name='email']") .Set "abc@gmail.com"
```

Alternatively, *Email Address* field can also be recognized using *type* attribute value

```
oPg.WebEdit("xpath:=//input[@type='email']") .Set "abc@gmail.com"
```

Similarly, the *email address* field can also be identified in web page using its other attribute values say *tabindex, size, maxlength,* etc. However, these are not reliable attributes for element identification. The reason being the value of *tabindex* can be changed by the developer anytime. Also, addition or deletion of new elements on the page can change the *tabindex* value. Other attributes are related to GUI look and feel attributes which are susceptible to change.

Example 2: Locate the Forgot your password? link as shown in Fig. 37.1 using XPath locator

Assume the HTML code of the *Forgot your password?* link is:

```
<a class="frgt-pswd" href="https://www.sample.com/fp/
forgotpassword">Forgot your password?</a>
```

The above HTML code defines the *href* attribute of the link element <a>. UFT code to locate this element using its *href* attribute value can be:

```
   xpathValue = "//a[@href='https://www.sample.com/fp/forgotpassword']"
oPg.Link("xpath:=" & xpathValue).Click
```

Example 3: Locate the image as shown in Fig. 37.1 using XPath locator.

The HTML code of the image is:

```
<img width="100" border="0" height="30" alt="logo" src="https://logo-
images.png"/>
```

The above HTML code defines the *alt, width, border, height* and *src* attributes of the image. UFT code to identify this element using its *alt* attribute will be:

```
oPg.Image("xpath:=//img[@alt='logo']").Click
```

> **NOTES**
> Attributes *tabindex, height, size, width* etc. needs to be avoided for element identification. This is because the values of these attributes may vary from browser to browser. Also, these values can be changed by developer even in the absence of any valid change requirement.

Finding Elements Using Multiple Attribute Values with XPath

In real world scenario, one attribute may not be always sufficient enough to uniquely identify an element in a HTML page. In such situations, we can identify an element using multiple attribute values. The locator XPath is defined in such a way that it tries to locate the element by using more than one attribute values of the element. Example below demonstrates how to locate an element using multiple attribute values.

Example 2: Locate the Email Address field element using multiple attribute values.

The HTML code for the Email Address field is:

```
<input id="emailid" type="email" autocapitalize="off" autocorrect="off"
tabindex="1" maxlength="128" size="30" value="" name="email"/>
```

UFT code to identify the element using its *id* and *name* attributes is:

```
xpathValue = "//input[@id='emailid'][@name='email']"
oPg.WebEdit("xpath:=" & xpathValue).Set "abc@gmail.com"
```

Also, UFT code to identify the element using its *id, name* and *type* attributes is:

```
xpathValue = "//input[@id='emailid'][@name='email'][@type='email']"
oPg.WebEdit("xpath:=" & xpathValue).Set "abc@gmail.com"
```

Example 2: Locate the third checkbox of Fig. 37.9.

HTML code of the above checkboxes is:

```
<input id="id0" type="checkbox" value="1" name="country"/>US
<input id="id1" type="checkbox" value="1" name="country"/>CANADA
<input id="id2" type="checkbox" checked="true/" value="1"
name="country"/>INDIA
<input id="id3" type="checkbox" value="1" name="country"/>JAPAN
<input id="id4" type="checkbox" checked="true/" value="1"
name="country"/>UK
```

Figure 37.9 *Checkboxes*

Table 37.2 XPath partial match expressions

Syntax	Objective	Example	Description
starts-with()	Identify element whose attribute value **starts with** <string>	Input[starts-with(@id, 'User')]	Locate <input> element whose *id* attribute value starts with text *User*. For example elements with id value as – Username, UserName, User123, User_Name etc.
ends-with()	Identify element whose attribute value **ends with** <string>	Input[ends-with(@id, 'Name')]	Locate <input> element whose *id* attribute value ends with text *Name*. For example elements with id value as – firstUser, second_User, 1User, _User etc.
contains()	Identify element whose attribute value **contains** <string>	Input [contains (@id, 'User')]	Locate <input> element whose *id* attribute contains string *User*. For example elements with id value as – firstUser, second_UserName, 1User123, _User2 etc.

UFT code to identify the third checkbox using its *id, type* and *name* attribute will be:

```
xpathValue = "//input[@type='checkbox'][@id='id2'][@name='country']"
oPg.WebCheckBox ("xpath:=" & xpathValue).Click
```

Finding Elements Using Partial Match of Attribute Values (Use of Regular Expressions in Attribute Values)

In real life scenario, there are many instances where attribute values of the elements change dynamically. For dynamic elements, every time the web page is opened, elements attribute values changes. Such elements whose attribute values change dynamically during run-time are called *dynamic elements*. One example would be *Order Confirmation Page* which displays order number message 'Order number is: 112345'. The complete string is dynamic as the order number will vary from one run to another. Another example could be a page displaying a list of recent 5 order numbers as link elements. Since the page will get updated with latest order numbers every time; the *linkText* attribute of order number link elements will change dynamically.

XPath, like CSS, provides the flexibility to locate elements matching partial attribute values. The table 37.2 explains the use of XPath partial match expressions:

Example 1: Identify the order number link elements that is displayed on a web page as shown Fig. 37.10.

Assume the HTML code of the link element 112453 is:

```
<a href="reforderID1=112453">112453</a>
<a href="reforderID2=110987">112453</a>
```

For the above link, method *linkText* to identify the link won't work as the text of the link will vary from one run to another. The *href* attribute of the link also cannot be used as it is as it contains the order

Order Number	Date	Status
112453	07-Feb-2013	Shipped
110987	01-Jan-2013	Delivered
110567	31-Dec-2012	Delivered

Figure 37.10 *Web table in a web page*

number. However, a partial match of *href* attribute value can be used to locate the link element. UFT code to identify this element can be:

```
xpathValue = "//a[starts-with(@href,'reforderID1')]"
oPg.Link ("xpath:=" & xpathValue).Click
```

Example 2: Find all the links whose status is shipped in Fig. 37.10.

Assume the HTML code of the shipped link is:

```
<a href="reforderID=112453/Details/Shipped">Shipped</a>
```

For the above HTML code, we observe that the end string of the *href* attribute is always 'shipped'. So this element can be identified using this string. UFT code to locate all *Shipped* links will be:

```
xpathValue = "//a[ends-with(@href,'Shipped')]"
Or,
xpathValue = "//a[contains(@href,'Shipped')]"

Set oDesc = Description.Create
oDesc("micclass").value = "Link"
oDesc("xpath").value = xpathValue

Set colLinks = oPg.ChildObjects(oDesc)
```

Example 3: Find all the Order numbers displayed in Fig. 37.6.

For the HTML code as discussed in example 1, the UFT code to locate all order number link elements can be:

```
Set oDesc = Description.Create
oDesc("micclass").value = "Link"
oDesc("xpath").value = "//a[contains(@href,'reforderID')]"

Set colOrders = oPg.ChildObjects(oDesc)
```

Example 4: Figure 37.11 shows an alert box which is opened on clicking button 'Open Alert Box'. Write code to click on this button.

Assume HTML code of the page with button is as shown below.

```
<!DOCTYPE html>
<html>
```

```
<body>
<p>Click the button to display a JavaScript alert box.</p>
<button onclick="functionShowAlertBox()">Open Alert Box</button>
<p id="alertBox"></p>
<script>
function functionShowAlertBox()
{
var x;
var r=confirm("Press a button!");
if (r==true)
  {
  x="You pressed OK!";
  }
else
  {
  x="You pressed Cancel!";
  }
document.getElementById("alertBox").innerHTML=x;
}
</script>
</body>
</html>
```

As evident from the code above, no 'id' attribute for the button is defined. If there are multiple such button in GUI then it will be difficult to uniquely identify the button element. To resolve this problem, a button element (or other elements say paragraph element <p>) can also be identified by using the text that is displayed for the specific element. Here text 'Open Alert Box' can be used to uniquely locate the button element.

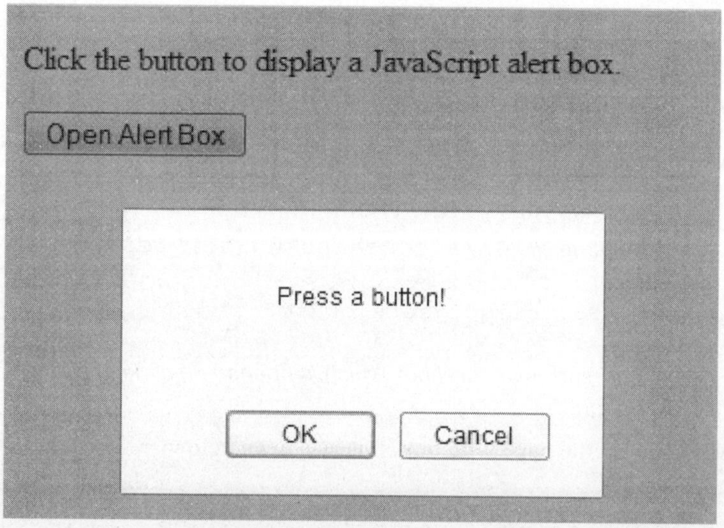

Figure 37.11 *XPath identifier for button*

```
oPg.WebButton("xpath:=//button[contains(.,'Open Alert')] ").Click
Or,
oPg.WebButton("xpath:=//button[contains(text(),'Open Alert')]
").Click
```

Finding Elements Using Attribute Name with XPath

XPath provides the flexibility to locate elements using attribute names. This approach is bit different from the previous approach we just discussed. In previous approach, we were using the attribute values to identify an element. In this approach we would use attribute name to identify an element.

Example 1: Find all the link elements whose href attribute is defined.

Code below shows how to find all <a> link elements whose *href* attribute is defined.

```
Set oDesc = Description.Create
oDesc("micclass").value = "Link"
oDesc("xpath").value = "//a[@href]"

Set colLinks = oPg.ChildObjects(oDesc)
```

Example 2: Find all the <input> elements whose id attribute is defined.

Code below shows how to find all <input> link elements whose *id* attribute is defined.

```
Set oDesc = Description.Create
oDesc("micclass").value = "Link"
oDesc("xpath").value = "//a[@id]"

Set colLinks = oPg.ChildObjects(oDesc)
```

Example 3: Find all the elements whose id attribute is defined.

In order to locate all elements whose *id* attribute is defined, the tag name in the XPath can be replaced with '*' to denote all elements. Code below shows how to find all elements whose *id* attribute is defined.

```
Set oDesc = Description.Create
oDesc("micclass").value = "WebElement"
oDesc("xpath").value = "//*[@id]"

Set colElements = oPg.ChildObjects(oDesc)
```

Finding Elements by Matching any Attribute with a Value

XPath provides the flexibility to identify an element by matching any of the attributes of an element to an attribute value. For example, suppose requirement is to locate an <input> element any of whose attribute values is 'password'. This can be achieved by replacing the attribute name with symbol '*' as shown below.

```
Set oDesc = Description.Create
oDesc("micclass").value = "WebElement"
oDesc("xpath").value = "//input[@*='password']"

Set colElements = oPg.ChildObjects(oDesc)
```

In order to locate all the edit boxes any of whose attribute values is 'password' use object test class 'WebEdit' instead of 'WebElement' as shown below.

```
Set oDesc = Description.Create
oDesc("micclass").value = "WebEdit"
oDesc("xpath").value = "//input[@*='password']"

Set colElements = oPg.ChildObjects(oDesc)
```

Consider1 the HTML code below. The code contains 6 elements—1 image element, 4 input elements and 1 link element.

```
<span id="Logo">
<img width="100" border="0" height="30" alt="app" src="https://img-
app.png"/>
</span>
<input id="emailid" type="email" autocapitalize="off" autocorrect="off"
tabindex="1" maxlength="128" size="30" value="" name="email"/>
<input id="passwordid" class="password" type="password"  tabindex="2"
size="20" maxlength="224" name="password"/>
<input id="checkbox1"  type="checkbox" checked="true/" value="1"
name="country"/>US
<input id="checkbox2"  type="checkbox" checked="true/" value="1"
name="country"/>UK
<a href="https://www.sample.com/fp/forgotpassword">Forgot your pass-
word?</a>
```

Example 1: For the HTML code above, find the <input> element any of whose attribute values is passwordid

The above HTML code has 4 input elements—2 checkboxes and 2 text fields. The *Password* field has its *id* attribute value as *passwordid.* UFT code to locate this element is:

```
xpathValue = "//input[@*='passwordid']"
oPg.WebElement("xpath:=" & xpathValue).Set "pass1"
```

The above code checks all the <input> elements and their attributes for any of their attribute values is *passwordid* and returns the matching element.

Alternatively, a better approach would be to reference 'WebEdit' class:

```
oPg.WebEdit("xpath:=" & xpathValue).Set "pass1"
```

Example 2: For the HTML code above, find an element any of whose attribute values is passwordid

The above HTML code has 6 elements—1 image, 2 checkboxes 2 text fields and 1 link. The code below checks all the elements to see which element attribute value matches with value *ap_password* and then returns the matching element.

```
xpathValue = "//*[@*='passwordid']"
oPg.WebElement("xpath:=" & xpathValue).Set "pass1"
```

Example 3: For the HTML code above, locate all the checkboxes

The above HTML code has two checkboxes. The *type* attribute value of both the checkboxes equals *checkbox*.

```
<input id="checkbox1" type="checkbox" checked="true/" value="1"
name="country"/>US
<input id="checkbox2" type="checkbox" checked="true/" value="1"
name="country"/>UK
```

UFT code to identify all checkboxes for above code can be:

```
Set oDesc = Description.Create
oDesc("micclass").value = "WebCheckBox"
oDesc("xpath").value = "//*[@type='checkbox']"

Set colCheckboxes = oPg.ChildObjects(oDesc)
```

Alternatively,

```
oDesc("xpath").value = "//*[@*='checkbox']"
```

Also, we observe that the *name* attribute value of both the checkboxes equals *country*. This attribute value can also be used to locate these checkboxes.

```
oDesc("xpath").value = "//*[@name='country']"
```

Finding Elements Using XPath Axis

An axis defines a node-set relative to the current node. An axis stores certain information about the context node or other nodes within the document tree. The information stored depends on the axis being used. For example, an axis called 'child' stores information about the children of the context node. Therefore, this axis can be used to select a child from the context node.

Consider the *Employee* table as shown below. This table contains information about employee id, employee name and employee designation.

The HTML code of the above table is as shown below.

```
<html>
<body>
<table>
```

Employee ID	Employee Name	Designation
122768	Charles	Software Developer
122657	Joseph	Automation Developer

Figure 37.12 *Employee web table in a web page*

```
<tr>
<td>Employee ID</td>
<td>Employee Name</td>
<td>Designation</td>
</tr>
<tr>
<td>122768</td>
<td>Charles</td>
<td>
<input id="id1" type="text" name="designation" value="Software Devel-
oper"/>
</td>
</tr>
<tr>
<td>122657</td>
<td>Joseph</td>
<td>
<input id="id2" type="text" name="designation" value="Automation Devel-
oper"/>
</td>
</tr>
</table>
```

Figure 37.13 shows the DOM tree representation of the HTML elements.

List of Axes

Figure 37.4 shows some of the XPath axes. There are many other axes which we can use within XPath expressions. Table 37.3 lists of the axes we can use with XPath:

Example 1: For Fig. 37.1, locate the element that precedes the Password field

XPath axis *preceding* can be used to find the preceding element. To locate all the preceding element wildcard '*' can be with *preceding* axis. Let's suppose the element that precedes the *Password* field is the label element 'Password'. UFT code to locate this label element can be:

```
Set oDesc = Description.Create
oDesc("micclass").value = "WebElement"
oDesc("xpath").value = "//input[@id='passwordid']//preceding::*"

Set colElements = oPg.ChildObjects(oDesc)
```

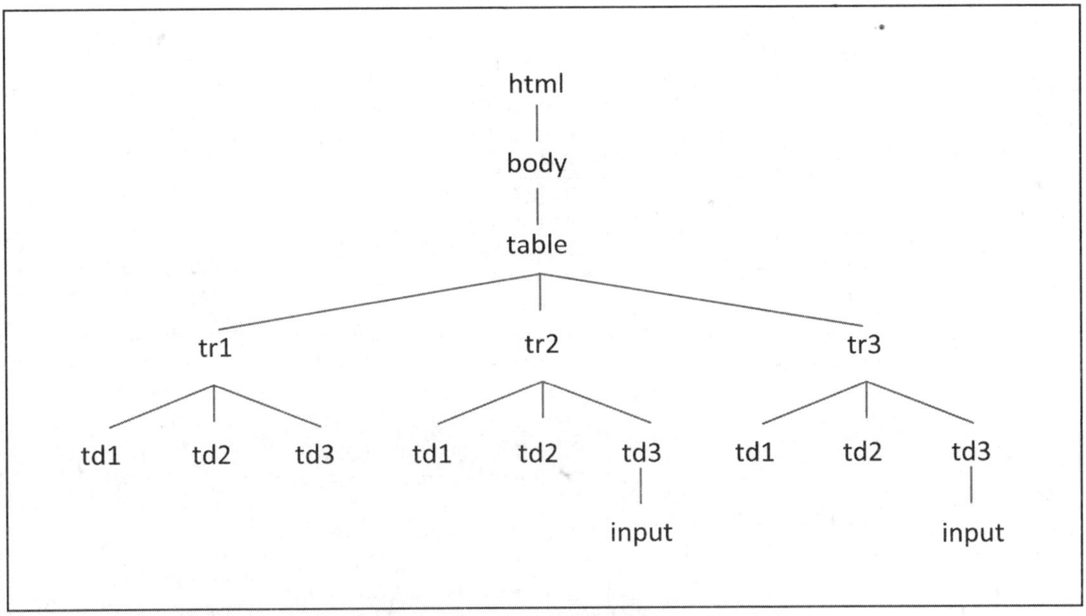

Figure 37.13 *DOM tree of the employee web table*

Table 37.3 XPath axes

Axis Name	Description	Example	XPath Expression
ancestor	Selects all ancestors (parent, grandparent,..) of the current node	Locate the row element which contains employee '122768' details	//td[text()='122768']/ancestor::tr
		Locate the table which contains employee '122768' details	//td[text()='122768']/ancestor::table
ancestor-or-self	Selects all ancestors (parent, grandparent,..) of the current node and current node itself	Locate the row element which contains employee '122768' details	//td[text()='122768']/ancestor-or-self::tr
		Locate the table element which contains employee '122768' details	//td[text()='122768']/ancestor-or-self::table
		Locate the cell element which contains employee '122768' details	//td[text()='122768']/ancestor-or-self::td
attribute	Selects all the attributes of the current node	Locate the *value* attribute of the <input> field *Designation*	//td[text()='122768']/attribute::value
child	Selects all children of the current node	Locate all <input> child elements of the cell row=3, column=3	//table//tr[3]/td[3]/child::input
descendant	Selects all descendants (children, grandchildren,…) of the current node	Locate all the rows of the table	//table/descendant::tr
		Locate the third row of the table	//table/descendant::tr[3]
		Locate all the cells of column 3 of the table	//table/descendant::tr/td[3]
		Locate all the cells of the table	//table/descendant::td
		Locate all <input> child elements of the cell row=3, column=3	//table/descendant::td/input

Axis Name	Description	Example	XPath Expression
descendant-or-self	Selects all descendants (children, grandchildren,..) of the current node and current node itself	Locate all the rows of the table	//table/descendant-or-self::tr
		Locate the cell element which contains employee '122768' details	//td[text()='122768']/ descendant-or-self::td
following	Selects all nodes in the document after the closing tag of the current node	Locate all cells after the cell containing value '122768'	//td[text()='122768']/ following::td
		Locate all the rows after the row containing cell value '122768'	//td[text()='122768']/ following::tr
following-sibling	Selects all siblings of the current node	Locate all the sibling cells of the cell containing value '122768'	//td[text()='122768']/ following-sibling::td
parent	Selects the parent node of the current node	Locate the cell that contains the <input> element with *id* attribute value equal to *id1*	//input[@id='d1']/ parent::td Or, //input[@id='d1']/ parent::*
		Locate the cell that contains the <input> element with '*value'* attribute value equal to '*Automation Developer*'	//input[@ value='Automation Developer']/parent::td
		Locate the row that contains value '122768'	//td[text()='122768']/ parent::tr
preceding	Selects all nodes that appear before the current node	Select the row element that precedes the row containing value '122768'	//td[text()='122768']/ preceding::tr
		Select all the cells of the row element that precedes the row containing value '122768'	//td[text()='122768']/ preceding::td Or, //td[text()='122768']/ preceding::*
preceding-sibling	Selects all the sibling nodes before the current node	Select all the cells of row 2 that precedes the cell 3,3	//table//tr[3]//td[3]/ preceding-sibling::td

```
Print colElements (0).GetROProperty("outertexttext")
'Output::Password
Print colElements (0).GetROProperty("html tag")     'Output::label
```

A more appropriate approach would be to build xpath that directly looks for the label element preceding the 'password' edit box element as shown below:

```
oDesc("xpath").value = "//input[@id='passwordid']//preceding::label"
```

Example 2: For Fig. 37.1, locate all the <input> elements that precede the Password field.

HTML tag name can be specified with the XPath axis *preceding* to locate all the <input> elements that precede an element.

For Fig. 37.1, there is one <input> element (email edit box) that precede the *Password* field.

```
Set oDesc = Description.Create
oDesc("micclass").value = "WebElement"
oDesc("xpath").value = "//input[@id='passwordid']//preceding::input"

Set colElements = oPg.ChildObjects(oDesc)
```

Example 3: For Fig. 37.1, locate all the edit box <input> elements that precede the Password field.

In order to locate all edit boxes that precede the 'password' field, we can specify 'micclass' as 'WebEdit' instead of 'WebElement'.

```
Set oDesc = Description.Create
oDesc("micclass").value = "WebEdit"
oDesc("xpath").value = "//input[@id='passwordid']//preceding::input"

Set colElements = oPg.ChildObjects(oDesc)
```

Example 4: For Fig. 37.1, locate all the radio buttons that succeed the Password field.

The requirement of the above example is to locate all the <input> elements with attribute type=radio that succeed the Password element. This can be done by defining the attributes of the succeeding element in the XPath axis. That is, attribute value "type=radio" is to be defined in the *following* axis definition of the XPath expression.

For Figure 37.1, there are 2 radio buttons that succeed the *Password* field. UFT code to locate all these elements can be:

```
Set oDesc = Description.Create
oDesc("micclass").value = "WebRadioGroup"
oDesc("xpath").value = "//input[@id='passwordid']//following::input[@
type='radio']"

Set colRadioElements = oPg.ChildObjects(oDesc)
```

HOW TO VERIFY THAT CUSTOM XPATH WORKS?

It is advisable to use *Firepath* to build custom reliable xpaths. Once the custom xpath is written in the Firepath edit box, Firepath automatically locates the elements that matches in UI and highlights them. It as well highlights the HTML code of the matched elements and displays the number of matched nodes. The custom XPath is to be enhanced till Firepath shows one unique matched node.

DEFINING DESCRIPTION PROPERTIES INCLUDING XPATH IN OBJECT REPOSITORY

As discussed above, UFT allows automation developers to define xpath as well as one or more description properties such as html id, class, name etc. However, it must be noted that XPath allows us-

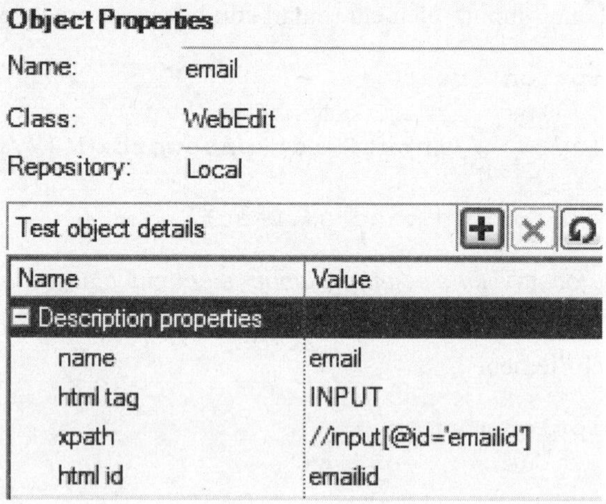

Figure 37.14 *Email edit box OR description with unnecessary description properties*

ers to create a xpath expression using these description properties. It is advisable to use only the xpath description when defining an object in OR. It needs to be ensured that the attributes defined in xpath expression is not duplicated in the description properties.

For example, consider the below description of '*Email*' edit box as used in OR in Fig. 37.14 below. Here, description properties *html id*, and html *tag* are not required as xpath expression already defines these properties. Also, if the defined xpath expression is able to uniquely locate the edit box object, then there is no need to define *name* description property.

Moreover, if *name* attribute is required to uniquely describe the object, then the same should be used in xpath expression as - //input[@id='emailid'][@name='email'].

XPath is a very powerful mechanism to locate objects, hence it needs to be developed and used carefully. Most of the times, no description property is required to create a unique description of the object if xpath or css is defined. Figure 37.15 shows the *Email* edit box description in OR using xpath alone.

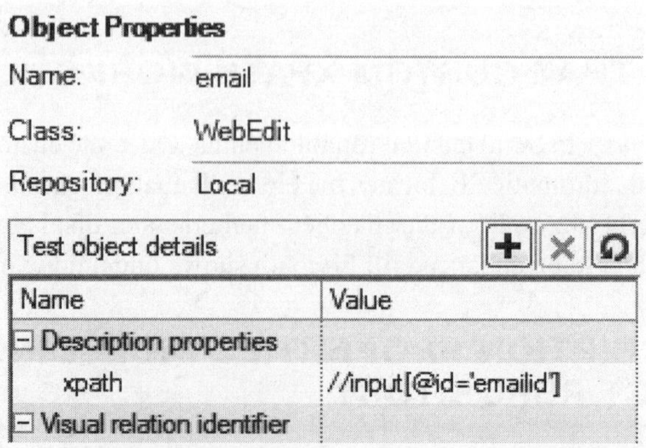

Figure 37.15 *Email edit box OR description with only xpath description property*

QUICK TIPS

- ✓ Avoid using the xpath expression generated by Firepath.
- ✓ Use Firepath to design custom xpath expression based on objects' HTML code.
- ✓ XPath can be effectively used to locate dynamic elements and child elements.
- ✓ Define only 'xpath' description property in object repository as far as possible.
- ✓ UFT may not locate the same objects using an xpath expression as is located by the xpath expression in Firefox.
- ✓ UFT does not support *frame* html tag in xpath expression.
- ✓ XPath is not supported for .Net web forms.
- ✓ UFT in maintenance mode run may replace test objects with XPath property values with new objects from the application. To avoid this, use the *Update from Application* option in the Object Repository Manager to update specific test objects with XPath identifier property values.
- ✓ *Update from Application* option will remove the XPath definition of the object from object repository. The new captured definition will follow the object learning mechanism as discussed in chapter *Test Object Learning Mechanism*.

PRACTICAL QUESTIONS

1. What is XPath? When to use XPath for locating elements?
2. Give an example how you will locate a dynamic element using XPath locator.
3. Build XPath expression for locating 'Login' button of Fig. 37.1.
4. What is XPath axis? When to use XPath axis for locating elements?
5. Why not to rely on Firepath for building reliable xpaths?
6. Why not to use other object description properties when xpath is already defined for an object in object repository?

Chapter 38

Object Identification Using CSS Selectors

Cascading Style Sheets (CSS) is a style sheet language that defines the presentation semantics (the look and formatting) of a HTML or XML document. For example, CSS describes fonts, colors, margins, height, width, background images and many other presentation semantics. The purpose of CSS is to separate the presentation information from the markup or content.

CSS defines a list of pattern-matching rules which determine which style is to be applied to elements in the DOM. These patterns are called selectors. If all rules in the pattern are satisfied for a certain element, then the selector matches the element. Browser applies the defined style to the matched element.

UFT uses the same principles of CSS selectors to identify an element in DOM. UFT provides 'css' description property for identifying elements using style attribute of an element. In this chapter, we will discuss the various ways in which CSS locator path can be used to identify an element in HTML DOM. Figure 38.1 shows the login page of a sample application.

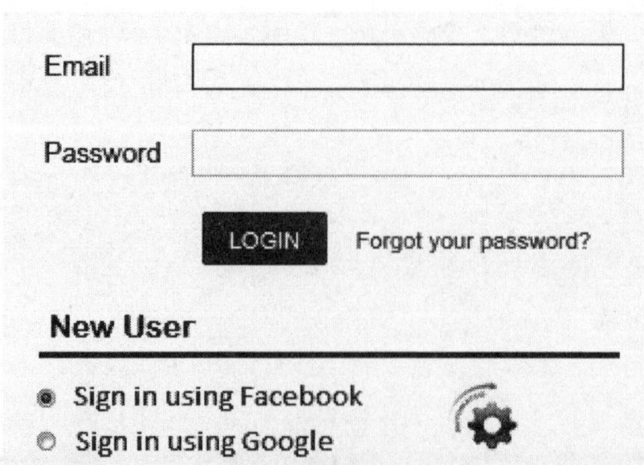

Figure 38.1 *Login page of a sample application*

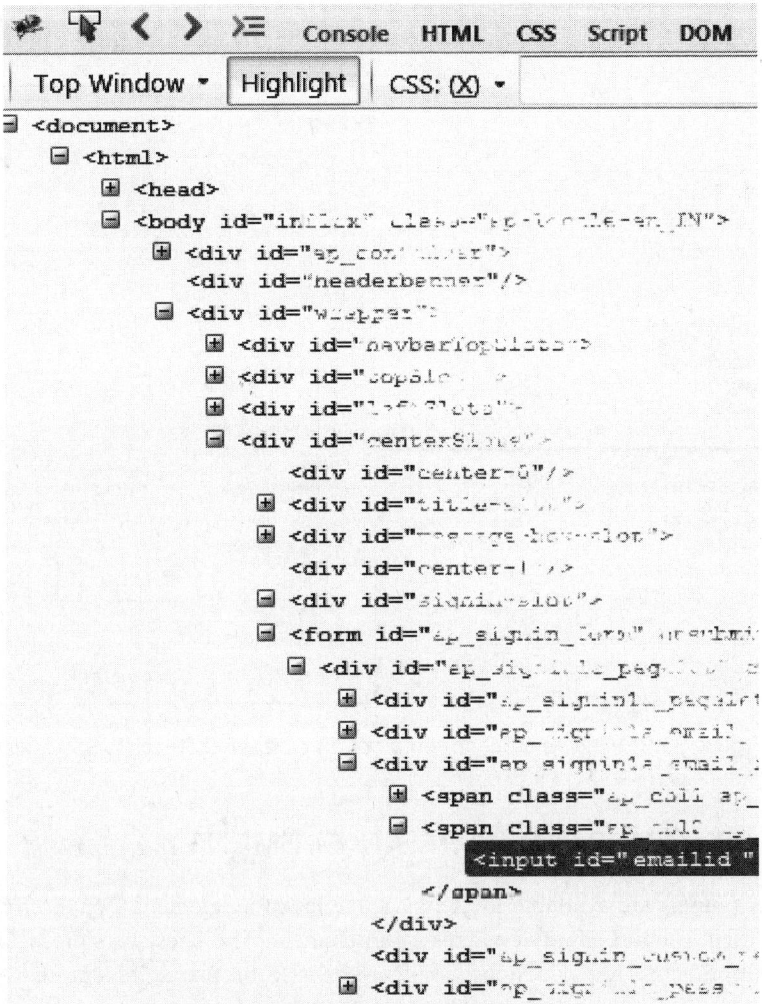

Figure 38.2 *HTML code of the email edit box field*

Assume the HTML code for the *email* address input field is as shown in Fig. 38.2.

Assume HTML code of the *email* and *password* edit boxes of Fig. 38.2 is as below:

<u>HTML code of Email edit box:</u>

```
<input id="emailid" type="email" autocapitalize="
off" autocorrect="off" tabindex="1" maxlength="128" size="30"
value="" name="email"/>
```

<u>HTML code of Password edit box:</u>

```
<input id="passwordid" class="password" type="password" onkey
press="displayCapsWarning(event,'ap_caps_warning', this);
" tabindex="2" size="20" maxlength="224" name="password"/>
```

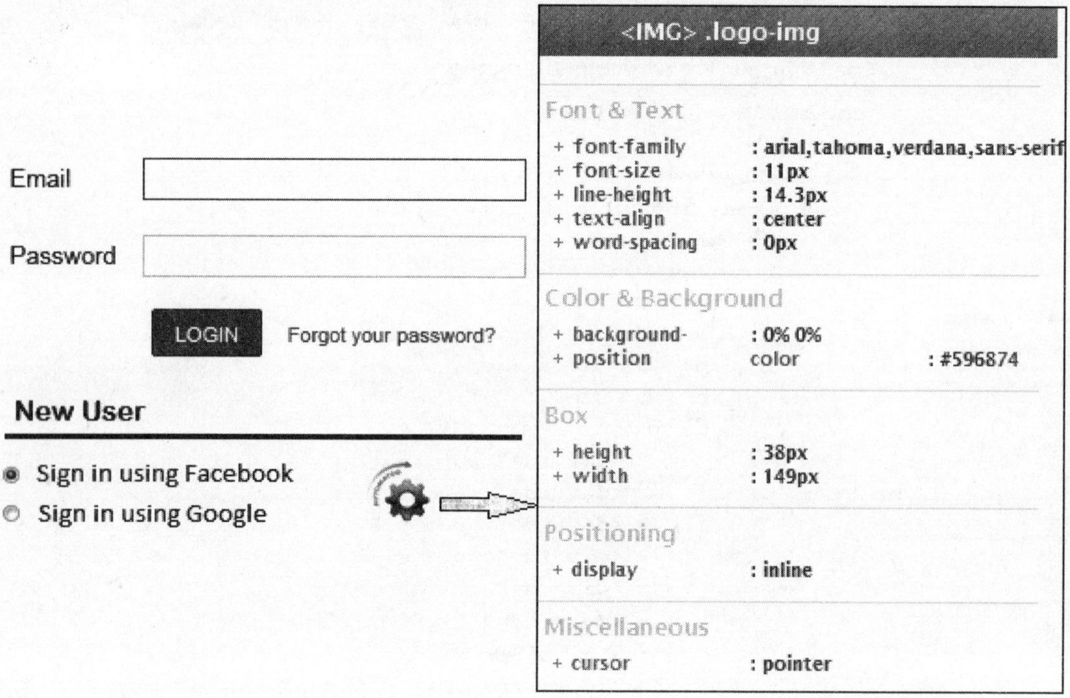

Figure 38.3 *Viewing CSS attributes of an element by using CSS viewer*

HOW TO FIND CSS STYLES OF AN ELEMENT?

Various browser plugins are available to view CSS styles of an element. For Firefox browser, CSS Viewer can be used to find CSS style values of an element. The latest version of CSS Viewer can be downloaded from site—https://addons.mozilla.org/en-US/firefox/addon/css-viewer/. Follow the steps below to view CSS attributes of an element using CSS Viewer:

- Open Firefox browser.
- Navigate to the desired page, say login page of www.sample.com.
- On Firefox browser, navigate Tools → CSS Viewer.
- Hover the mouse arrow over the element whose CSS styles are to be viewed. On mouse hover, CSS Viewer window opens and displays the CSS styles of the element. Figure 38.3 shows the CSS style attributes of the logo image.

HOW TO LOCATE ELEMENTS USING CSS ATTRIBUTES?

CSS Attributes of an element can be used to uniquely locate the element in a web page. Firefox plug-in Firepath can be used to design CSS locators which can identify an element in the DOM tree. FirePath plug-in can be installed from site http://code.google.com/p/firepath/. This plug-in also helps to

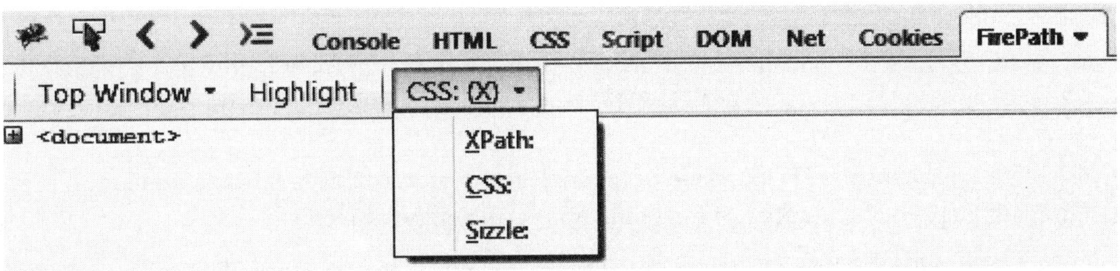

Figure 38.4 *Firepath window*

view/design XPath locator and Sizzle locator of an element. Follow the below steps to view the CSS locator path of an element.

- Open firefox and then activate firebug window by clicking on the bookmark .
- On *firebug* window, click on the tab FirePath. *Firepath* window opens.
- On *firepath* window, select locator as '*CSS*' as shown in Fig. 38.4.
- To view CSS locator path of an element, click on the mouse icon and then point and click the arrow on the desired element. The relative CSS path of the element is displayed on the *firepath* window.

Figure 38.5 shows the CSS locator path of the *email* edit box object as generated by firepath.

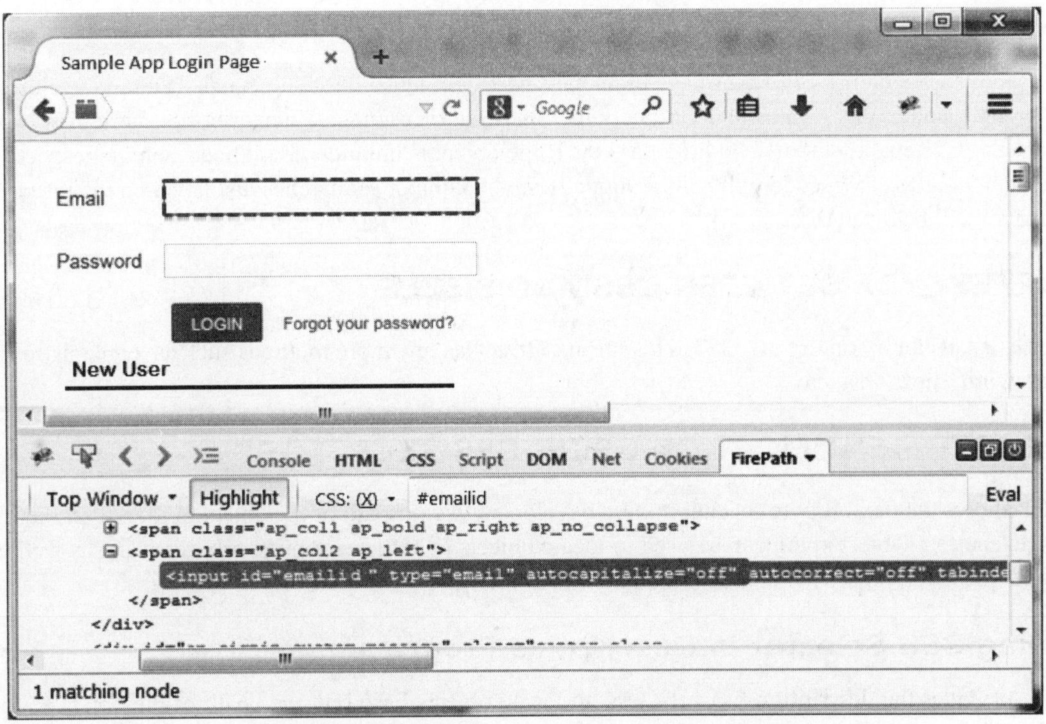

Figure 38.5 *CSS locator path of email edit box object*

As shown in the Fig. 38.5,

- Firepath displays the calculated CSS locator path in firepath frame window edit box.
- Firepath highlights all the objects in GUI that matches the CSS path expression using dotted line.
- Firepath highlights the HTML code of the matched objects in firepath frame window.
- Firepath displays the number of matching nodes (matching objects).

Similar to XPath, the CSS locator path generated by firepath is not the most accurate CSS path and hence is not reliable. For example, the CSS locator path generated by firepath in Fig. 38.5 looks for an element whose 'id' attribute value is 'emailid'. A more appropriate CSS locator path would be an expression that looks for an 'input' element whose 'id' attribute value is 'emailid'. For example, consider the custom developed CSS locater path—*input#emailid*.

The best way to build CSS locator path of an element is by using the HTML attributes of the element. Assume the HTML code of the logo image of Fig. 38.1 to be:

```
<img width="100" border="0" height="30" alt="Sample" src="https://imag-
es-sample.com/logo.png" style=""/>
```

The above HTML code describes the various attributes of the element such as its height, width, alt, src, etc. One or more of these attributes can be used to uniquely identify the logo mage. One of the reliable attributes of the logo image is its 'alt' attribute. CSS locator path of the logo image element using its 'alt' attribute can be built as:

```
img[alt='Sample]
```

The above CSS path locates an image element whose 'alt' attribute value equals 'Sample'. In order to verify whether this locator path uniquely identifies the logo image element or not, write this locator path on Firepath window and hit enter key. If the object is uniquely identified, then the respective element and its HTML code will be highlighted and the number of matches displayed on the Firepath window will be equal to 1.

DIFFERENCE BETWEEN CSS AND SIZZLE

Sizzle is a js library on top of CSS3. This means Sizzle has few more methods such as :contains(text), :password, :first, :last, etc.

OBJECT IDENTIFICATION USING CSS SELECTORS

UFT allows the flexibility to the automation developers to use xpath of the object to identify it during test execution. Object xpath can be used to locate objects in both descriptive programming as well as object repository approach of UFT automation.

Using CSS Selector in Descriptive Programming

UFT provides the description property 'css' to locate objects based on the xpath of the object. Code below shows, how to identify the *email* edit box object using its css selector value:

```
Set oPg = Browser("B").Page("P")
oPg.WebEdit("css:=input#emailid").Set "abc@gmail.com"
```

```
Alternatively,
Set oDescEditBox = Description.Create
oDescEditBox("micclass").value = "WebEdit"
oDescEditBox("xpath").value = "input#emailid"

oPg.WebEdit(oDescEditBox).Set "abc@gmail.com"
```

Using CSS Selector in Object Repository

The CSS locator path so designed can be used to define objects in object repository as well. CSS locator can be defined in Object Repository in the same way as XPath is defined. The only difference is users are to select description property 'css' instead of 'xpath'. After defining the 'css' description property in OR, use *highlight in application* feature to verify that the built css locator path uniquely identifies the object.

CSS SELECTOR METHODS

Table 38.1 shows the list of commonly used CSS selector methods. First column of this table lists the selectors, second column illustrates an example usage of this selector and third column describes the outcome of the example illustrated.

Table 38.1 CSS Selector Methods

Selector	Example	Example description
.class	.ap_col2_ap_left	Selects all elements with class="ap_col2_ap_left"
#id	#firstname	Selects the element with id="firstname"
*	*	Selects all elements
element	p	Selects all <p> elements
element,element	div,p	Selects all <div> elements and all <p> elements
element element	div p	Selects all <p> elements inside <div> elements
element>element	div>p	Selects all <p> elements where the parent is a <div> element
element+element	div+p	Selects all <p> elements that are placed immediately after <div> elements
[attribute]	[attribute name]	Selects all elements with a target attribute
[attribute=value]	[attribute name=attribute value]	Selects all elements with attribute name="attribute value "
[attribute~=value]	[title~=MakeOrder]	Selects all elements with a title attribute containing the word "MakeOrder"
[attribute|=value]	[lang|=en]	Selects all elements with a lang attribute value starting with "en"
:link	a:link	Selects all unvisited links
:visited	a:visited	Selects all visited links
:active	a:active	Selects the active link
:hover	a:hover	Selects links on mouse over

Selector	Example	Example description
:focus	input:focus	Selects the input element which has focus
:first-letter	p:first-letter	Selects the first letter of every <p> element
:first-line	p:first-line	Selects the first line of every <p> element
:first-child	p:first-child	Selects every <p> element that is the first child of its parent
:before	p:before	Insert content before the content of every <p> element
:after	p:after	Insert content after every <p> element
:lang(language)	p:lang(it)	Selects every <p> element with a lang attribute equal to "it" (Italian)
element1~element2	p~ul	Selects every <ul> element that are preceded by a <p> element
[attribute^=value]	a[src^="https"]	Selects every <a> element whose src attribute value begins with "https"
[attribute$=value]	a[src$=".pdf"]	Selects every <a> element whose src attribute value ends with ".pdf"
[attribute*=value]	a[src*="w3schools"]	Selects every <a> element whose src attribute value contains the substring "w3schools"
:first-of-type	p:first-of-type	Selects every <p> element that is the first <p> element of its parent
:last-of-type	p:last-of-type	Selects every <p> element that is the last <p> element of its parent
:only-of-type	p:only-of-type	Selects every <p> element that is the only <p> element of its parent
:only-child	p:only-child	Selects every <p> element that is the only child of its parent
:nth-child(n)	p:nth-child(2)	Selects every <p> element that is the second child of its parent
:nth-last-child(n)	p:nth-last-child(2)	Selects every <p> element that is the second child of its parent, counting from the last child
:nth-of-type(n)	p:nth-of-type(2)	Selects every <p> element that is the second <p> element of its parent
:nth-last-of-type(n)	p:nth-last-of-type(2)	Selects every <p> element that is the second <p> element of its parent, counting from the last child
:last-child	p:last-child	Selects every <p> element that is the last child of its parent
:root	:root	Selects the document's root element
:empty	p:empty	Selects every <p> element that has no children (including text nodes)
:target	#news:target	Selects the current active #news element (clicked on a URL containing that anchor name)
:enabled	input:enabled	Selects every enabled <input> element
:disabled	input:disabled	Selects every disabled <input> element
:checked	input:checked	Selects every checked <input> element
:not(selector)	:not(p)	Selects every element that is not a <p> element
::selection	::selection	Selects the portion of an element that is selected by a user

> **NOTES** One important difference between XPath and CSS is—XPath allows searching elements both backward and forward in the DOM tree whereas CSS allows searching only in forward direction. That is, XPath allows locating a parent element from a child element whereas CSS does not.

BUILDING CSS LOCATOR PATHS

Section below describes in detail on how to build the CSS locator path using various attributes of the HTML element.

Finding Elements Using Absolute Path

CSS absolute path refers to the absolute hierarchical location of the element with respect to the root node of the DOM. CSS absolute path describes the complete parent–child hierarchy of the element.

Example 1: For example, the absolute CSS path for the email address field of Fig. 38.1 will be

```
html body div div div form div div span input#emailid
```

Code below shows how to identify the *email address* field using UFT code:

```
Set oPg = Browser("B").Page("P")
cssValue = "html body div div div form div div span input"));
   oPg.WebEdit("css:=" & cssValue).Set "abc@gmail.com"
```

While creating CSS absolute path, space is provided between parent child elements. Also, the white spaces can be replaced with a greater than (>) separator.

Example 2: Example below shows how to define the absolute CSS path using '>' separator.

```
cssValue = "html>body>div>div>div>form>div>div>span>input"
oPg.WebEdit("css:=" & cssValue).Set "abc@gmail.com"
```

Using absolute CSS path for locating elements is not a good technique of element identification. The reason being it's dependency on the complete tree hierarchy. Any change in the tree hierarchy will result a change in the absolute CSS locator path. Such changes will cause the scripts to fail and will require the element identification definition be changed in tests. Frequent such changes will not only impact regression run but will also result in high maintenance effort. To avoid this problem, we can use the relative CSS locator path of an element for element identification.

Finding Elements Using Relative Path

CSS locator path of an element can also be defined with respect to the position of other elements in the hierarchical tree. Since this path is relative to the position of another element, hence it is called *relative* path. Example below shows how to identify the first <input> element in the HTML DOM. For the sample application login page as shown in Fig. 38.1, the first <input> element is *email address* field.

Example 1: Code below shows how to locate all the 'input' elements of the login page.

```
Set oDesc = Description.Create
oDesc("micclass").value = "WebElement"
oDesc("css").value = "input"

Set colElements = oPg.ChildObjects(oDesc)
```

Example 2: Write code to locate all the edit box elements of the login page.

```
Set oDesc = Description.Create
oDesc("micclass").value = "WebEdit"
oDesc("css").value = "input"

Set colElements = oPg.ChildObjects(oDesc)
```

> **NOTES** Use of 'WebElement' test class to locate objects is to be avoided as far as possible. This is because use 'WebElements' locates all matching nodes such as div, span, p etc. Use of standard test class objects such as WebEdit, WebButton, Link etc. helps to locate standard GUI objects only.

As we observe, above CSS locator path 'input' is not sufficient to locate specific edit box objects such as *Email* field. To solve this problem, we can also define the CSS path of an element using its attributes say Class, Id etc.

> **NOTES** In case multiple elements have the same CSS description, UFT throws an error.

Finding Elements Using ID Selector

The ID attribute of an element can be used to uniquely locate an element in the DOM tree. The id attribute of an element is defined in CSS path by a preceding hash (#) sign.

Example: As shown in Fig. 38.2, the HTML code for the email address field is

```
<input id="emailid" type="email" autocapitalize="off" autocorrect="off"
tabindex="1" maxlength="128" size="30" value="" name="email"/>
```

As evident from the code, the value of attribute 'id' is 'emailid'. UFT code to uniquely identify the element in the DOM tree using its *id* attribute will be:

```
cssValue = "#emailid"
oPg.WebEdit("css:=" & cssValue).Set "abc@gmail.com"
```

Above code will locate all the elements whose *id* attribute value is *emailid.* In situations where two or more elements have the same *id* attribute, the above code may fail to uniquely identify the required element. To resolve this issue, we can specify the HTML tag of the of the element node along with its *id* description. The HTML tag of the *email address* field node is ‘`input`’. So the new CSS path for element identification will be:

```
cssValue = “input#emailid”
oPg.WebEdit(“css:=” & cssValue).Set “abc@gmail.com”
```

> **NOTES:** Ideally, *id* attribute of an element needs to be unique throughout the DOM tree.

Finding Elements Using Class Selector

The *Class* attribute can be used to uniquely locate an element in the HTML DOM tree. The ‘class’ attribute of an element is defined in CSS path by a preceding dot (.) sign.

Example: Consider the HTML code of the Password field as shown in fig

```
<input id=”passwordid” class=”password” type=”password” onkeypress=”dis
playCapsWarning(event,’ap_caps_warning’, this);” tabindex=”2” size=”20”
maxlength=”224” name=”password”/>
```

As evident from the code, the value of attribute class is password. UFT code to uniquely identify the element in the DOM tree using its *class* attribute will be:

```
cssValue = “.password”
oPg.WebEdit(“css:=” & cssValue).Set “password”
```

Above code will locate all the elements whose *class* attribute value is *password.* As we know, the *class* attribute value of two or more elements can be same. In such situations, UFT will fail to locate the required element. To resolve this issue, we can specify the HTML tag of the of the element node along with its *class* description. The HTML tag of the *password* field node is input. So the new CSS path for element identification will be:

```
cssValue = “input.password”
oPg.WebEdit(“css:=” & cssValue).Set “password”
```

Finding Elements Using Other Attributes Selector

Apart from *ID* and *Class* attribute, other element attributes such as *name, alt, tabindex* etc. can also be used to locate the element.

Example 1: Consider the HTML code of the password field. This element can also be located using its name attribute.

```
cssValue = “[name=password]”
oPg.WebEdit(“css:=” & cssValue).Set “password”
```

Above code will locate the element whose *name* attribute value is *password.* Sometimes this description won't be sufficient to uniquely identify an element as *name* attribute value of two or more elements can be same. To help uniquely identify an element, *html tag* of the element can also be used as one of its identification properties as shown below:

```
cssValue = "input[name=password]"
oPg.WebEdit("css:=" & cssValue).Set "password"
```

Above code will locate the <input> element whose *name* attribute value is *password.*

Example 2: Alternatively, the password element can also be identified in DOM tree using its type attribute.

```
cssValue = "input[type=password]"
oPg.WebEdit("css:=" & cssValue).Set "password"
```

Above code will locate the first <input> element whose *type* attribute value is *password.*

Example 3: Alternatively, the password element can also be identified in DOM tree using its tabindex attribute.

```
cssValue = " input[tabindex='2']"
oPg.WebEdit("css:=" & cssValue).Set "password"
```

Above code will locate the <input> element whose *tabindex* attribute value is *2.*

Example 4: Consider the HTML code of the login button 

is

```
<input id="signInSubmit" width="201" type="image" height="22" border="0"
value="Continue" tabindex="5" alt="Continue" onload="if (typeof uet ==
'function') { uet('cf'); }" src="https://images-sample.com/images/.../
V192194766.gif"/>
```

The above element can also be identified using its *alt* attribute as

```
cssValue = input[alt='Continue']"
oPg.WebButton("css:=" & cssValue).Click
```

Finding Elements Using Multiple Attributes Selector

In real world scenario, one attribute may not be always sufficient enough to uniquely identify an element in a HTML page. In such situations, we can locate an element using multiple attributes. Example below demonstrates how to locate an element using multiple attribute values.

Example 1: Let us consider, we need to uniquely identify the login button 

on sample.com login page. Code below shows how to uniquely identify the element using more than one element attributes.

```
cssValue = input[id='signInSubmit'][alt='Continue']"
oPg.WebButton("css:=" & cssValue).Click
```

Above code locates the *Login* button using two attributes *id* and *alt*.

Example 2: Code below shows how to use more than two attributes to locate an element.

```
cssValue = input[id='signInSubmit'][alt='Continue'][value='Continue']"
oPg.WebButton("css:=" & cssValue).Click
```

Above code locates the *Login* button using two attributes *id*, *alt* and *value* attribute.

Example 3: Alternatively, the Login button can also be uniquely located by using other element attributes such as tabindex, size, height etc.

```
cssValue = "input[id='signInSubmit'][type='image'][tabindex='5']
[height='22']"
oPg.WebButton("css:=" & cssValue).Click
```

> **NOTES** Attributes *tabindex, height, size, width* etc. needs to be avoided for element identification. This is because the values of these attributes may vary from browser to browser. Also, these values can be changed by developer even in the absence of any valid change requirement.

Finding Elements Using Attribute Name Selector

CSS provides the flexibility to locate elements using attribute names. This approach is bit different from the previous approach we just discussed. In previous approach, we were using the attribute values to identify an element. In this approach we use attribute name to identify an element.

Example 1: Let's consider a scenario where in the requirement to ensure that all <input> elements on sample.com home page should have attribute id defined. The first step here will be to identify all <input> elements whose id attribute is not defined. This list can then be send to the developers for a code fix.

Code below shows how to find all <input> elements whose *id* attribute is defined.

```
Set oDesc = Description.Create
oDesc("micclass").value = "WebElement"
oDesc("css").value = "input[id]"

Set colElements = oPg.ChildObjects(oDesc)
```

Again suppose the requirement is to locate all <input> elements whose *id* attribute is not defined. This can be achieved by using a Boolean not pseudo-class. The CSS selector for the same will be

```
Set oDesc = Description.Create
oDesc("micclass").value = "WebElement"
oDesc("css").value = "input:not([id])"

Set colElements = oPg.ChildObjects(oDesc)
```

Figure 38.7 *Checkboxes*

Example 2: Let's consider another scenario where there are 5 checkboxes in a web page and we need to identify these checkboxes and select/deselect them (Figure 38.7).

Suppose, the HTML code of these elements is:

```
<input type="checkbox" name="country" value="1"/>US
<input id="id1" type="checkbox" name="country" value="1"/>CANADA
<input id="id2" type="checkbox" name="country" value="1"/>INDIA
<input id="id3" type="checkbox" name="country" value="1"/>JAPAN
<input id="id4" type="checkbox" name="country" value="1"/>UK
```

Suppose, the requirement is to locate all checkboxes which has an *id* attribute. The UFT code for the same will be

```
Set oDesc = Description.Create
oDesc("micclass").value = "WebCheckBox"
oDesc("css").value = " input[type='checkbox'][id]"

Set colCheckboxes = oPg.ChildObjects(oDesc)
```

> **NOTES:** Avoid using 'WebElement' test class if the standard test object class is known.

Again, suppose the requirement is to locate all checkboxes whose *id* attribute is not defined. This can be achieved by using a Boolean not pseudo-class. The CSS locator path for the same will be

```
oDesc)("css").value = "input[type='checkbox']:not([id])"
```

Table 38.2 Finding elements using partial match

Syntax	Objective	Example	Description
^=	Identify element whose attribute value **starts with** <string>	Input[id^= 'User']	Locate <input> element whose *id* attribute starts with *User*. For example elements with id value as—Username, UserName, User123, User_Name etc.
$=	Identify element whose attribute value **ends with** <string>	Input[id$= 'User']	Locate <input> element whose *id* attribute starts with *User*. For example elements with id value as—firstUser, second_User, 1User, _User etc.
*=	Identify element whose attribute value **contains** <string>	Input[id*= 'user']	Locate <input> element whose *id* attribute contains string *User*. For example elements with id value as—firstUser, second_UserName, 1User123, _User2 etc.

Finding Elements Using Partial Match (Regular Expressions)

In real life scenario, there are many instances where attribute values of the elements change dynamically. Every time the web page is opened the specific elements attribute values change. Such elements whose attribute values change dynamically during run-time are called *dynamic elements*. One example would be ASP.NET applications where IDs are generated dynamically. Another example could be a page containing a list of recent 5 order numbers as link elements. Since the page will get updated with latest order numbers every time; the *text* attribute of order number link elements will change dynamically.

CSS selector provides the flexibility to locate elements matching partial attribute values. The Table 38.2 explains the use of CSS partial match expressions:

Example 1: For the Fig. 38.1, write UFT code to identify the link element whose href attribute starts with '/gp/css/'

For Figure 38.1, there is only one link element 'Your Account' whose *href* attribute value starts with '/gp/css/'. The HTML code of this link element is:

```
<a href="/gp/css/homepage.html/ref=ap_frn_ya">Forgot your Pass-
word?</a>
```

Symbol '^' is used along with attribute name to locate elements whose attribute value starts with the specified string. Below is the UFT code to locate an element by looking for an element whose *href* attribute value starts with '/gp/css/'.

```
cssValue = "a[href^='/gp/css/']"
oPg.Link("css:=" & cssValue).Click
```

Example 2: For the example above, write code find the link element whose href attribute value ends with string 'ap_frn_ya'.

Symbol '$' is used along with attribute name to locate elements whose attribute value ends with the specified string. Below is the UFT code to locate an element by looking for an element whose *href* attribute value starts with string `'ap_frn_ya'`.

```
cssValue = "a[href$='ap_frn_ya']"
oPg.Link("css:=" & cssValue).Click
```

Example 3: For the example above, write code find the link element whose href attribute value contains string 'homepage.html'.

Symbol '*' is used along with attribute name to locate elements whose attribute value contains the specified string. Below is the UFT code to locate an element by looking for an element whose *href* attribute value contains string 'homepage.html'.

```
cssValue = "a[href*='homepage.html']"
oPg.Link("css:=" & cssValue).Click
```

Finding Elements Using Pseudo-Class Selectors

Pseudo classes are used to add special effects to some selectors. Pseudo classes classify elements on characteristics other than their name, attributes or content. That is, on characteristics that cannot be deduced from the Document tree. Pseudo-elements create abstractions about the document tree which are beyond those specified by the document language. For example, document languages do not offer mechanisms to access the first letter or first line of an element's content. CSS pseudo elements allow style sheet designers to refer and apply style to this otherwise inaccessible content. Neither pseudo elements nor pseudo classes appear in the document source or DOM tree.

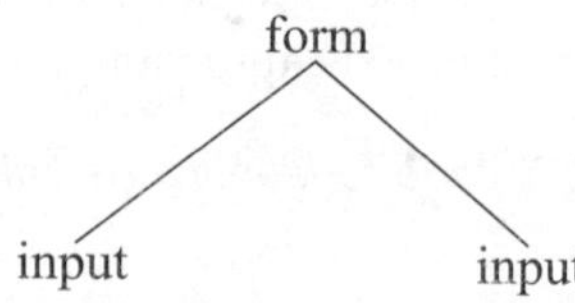

UFT provides the flexibility to access DOM elements using CSS pseudo class.

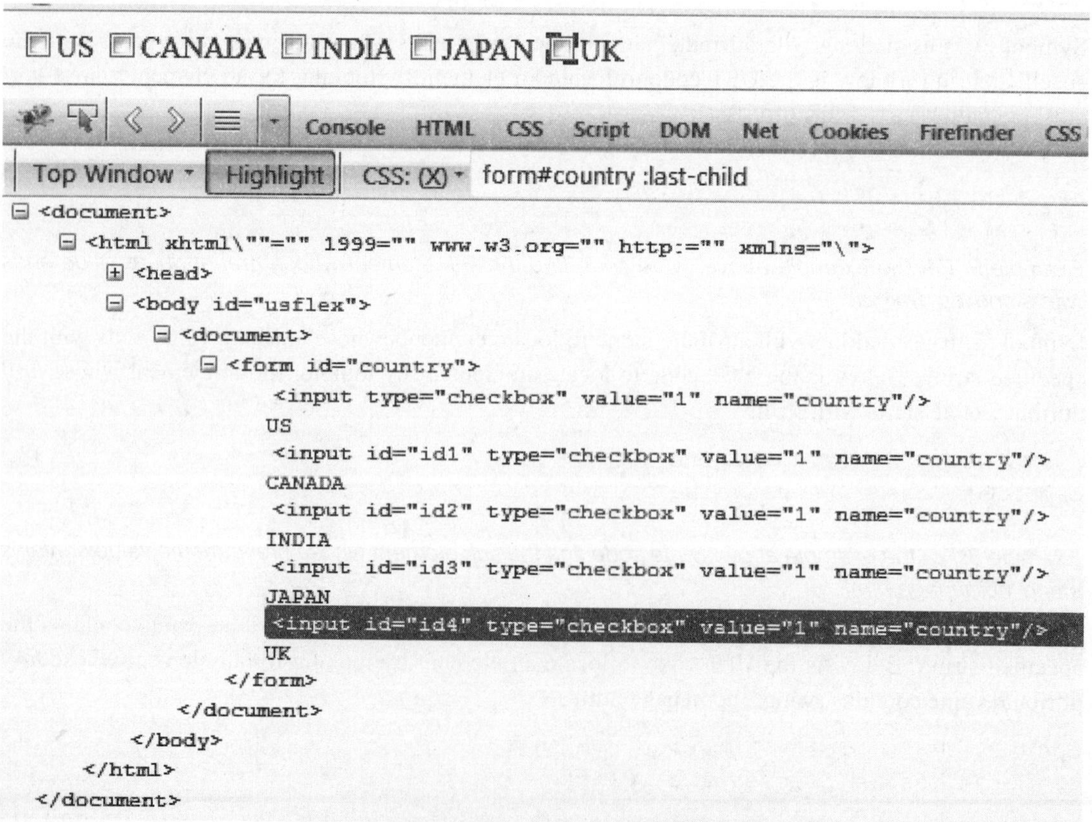

Figure 38.8 *HTML code of checkboxes*

Finding Elements Using Child Elements Psuedo-Class

CSS Selectors provide various ways to locate a child element from parent element. Figure 38.8 is a sample code of sample.com site.

We can locate the first element in this code using pseudo-class: first-child. Let's assume the parent element in the code above is

```
<form id="country">
```

UFT code to identify this element will be

```
cssValue = "form#country"
Set formElement = oPg.WebElement("css:=" & cssValue)
```

Example 1: Write UFT code to locate the first child element (checkbox US) of the above parent element will be

```
cssValue = "form#country :first-child"
oPg.WebCheckBox("css:=" & cssValue).Click
```

> **NOTES:** There is a white space between parent element class description value and symbol ":".

Pesudo-class '*n*th-child(<n>)' is used to find the *n*th child of any parent element.

Example 2: UFT code to find the 4th child element (checkbox JAPAN) of the above parent element will be:

```
cssValue = "form#country :nth-child(4)"
oPg.WebCheckBox("css:=" & cssValue).Click
```

The Table 38.3 shows some of the pseudo classes used to identify child elements.

Finding Elements Using Sibling Elements

CSS Selector also provides the flexibility to locate sibling elements of any element. Operator '+' is used to locate a sibling element.

Example 1: The sibling element—checkbox INDIA can be identified in the document tree using the below code.

```
cssValue = "form#country > input + input + input"
oPg.WebCheckBox("css:=" & cssValue).Click
```

In situations where a *tagname* changes dynamically during run-time, the *tagname* can be specified by '*'. For example, the above CSS locator path can also be written as

```
cssValue = "form#country > input + * + input"
```

Table 38.3 Finding elements using pseudo-class

Pseudo-Class		Example	Description
:first-child	Locates the first child element	form#country:first-child	Locates the checkbox US
:last-child	Locates the last child element	form#country:last-child	Locates the checkbox UK
:*n*th-child(<n>)	Locates the *n*th child element	form# country:nth-child(4)	Locates the checkbox JAPAN

Finding Elements Using User Action Pseudo-Class

CSS Psuedo class can be used to validate the user actions. For instance, CSS provides the flexibility to validate whether the clicked link appears in red color or not. Another example, would be validate the current element has focus or not.

Example 1: Consider the Search Result page as shown in the Fig. 38.9. Suppose the requirement is to find all the links that has been unvisited (link color=blue). The UFT code to find all link unvisited link elements will be

```
Set oDesc = Description.Create
oDesc("micclass").value = "Link"
oDesc("css").value = "a:link"

Set colUnvisitedLinks = oPg.ChildObjects(oDesc)
```

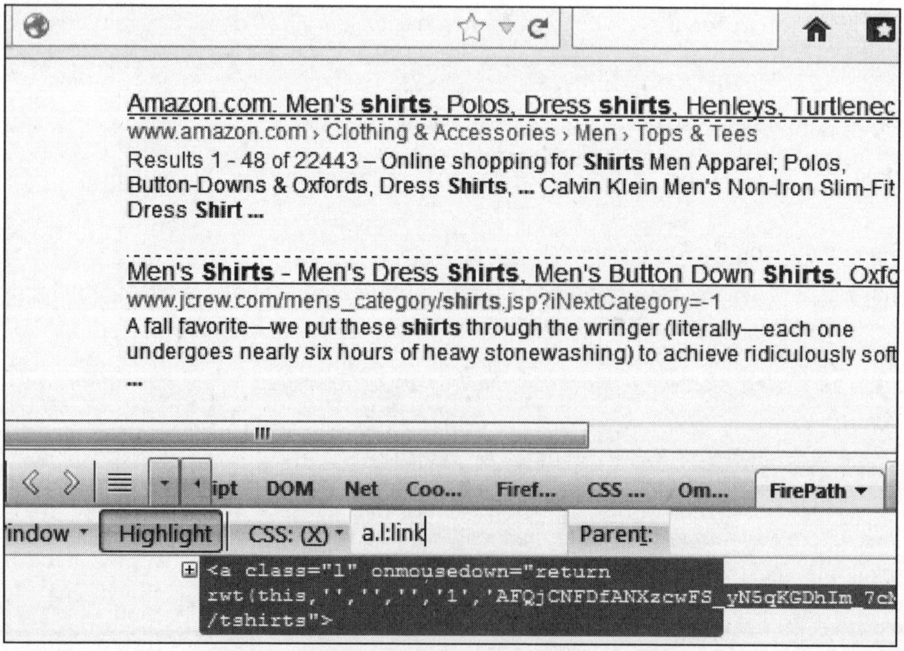

Figure 38.9 *Search page*

Table 38.4 Finding elements using user-action pseudo class

Psuedo-class	Example	Description
:link	a:link	Identify all link elements which has not been visited
	a.l:link	Identify the specific link (with *class* attribute *l)* has been visited or not
:visited	a:visited	Identify all link elements which has not been visited
	a.l:visited	Identify the specific link (with *class* attribute *l)* has been visited or not
:hover	a:hover	Identify the link element that has mouse hover
	a.l:hover	Identify the specific link has mouse hover or not
:active	a:active	Identify the links that are active
	a.l:active	Identify the specific link is active or not
:focus	a:focus	Identify the link element that has focus
	input:focus	Identify the <input> element that has focus
	a.l:focus	Identify the specific link element has focus or not

Example 2: Suppose the requirement is to find whether a specific link has been visited or not. UFT code for the same will be

```
cssValue = "a.l:link"
If Not(oPg.Link("css:=" & cssValue).Exist(0.5)) Then
    Print "Link has not been visited")
End If
```

Table 38.4 shows some of the user action pseudo classes.

Example 3: Suppose the requirement is to find the link that has focus and mouse hover during any given point of run-time. This can be achieved by combining the pseudo-classes. UFT code for the same is:

```
cssValue = "a:focus:hover"
Set LinkwhichHasFocusAndIsActive = oPg.Link("css:=" & cssValue)
```

Finding Elements Using UI State Pseudo-Class

UI state pseudo-classes are used to locate elements for various states such as enabled, disabled or checked. These classes can also be used to validate user action. For instance, validating whether a checkbox appears checked after clicking on it.

Example: Let us suppose the requirement is to find out whether checkbox US shown in Fig. 38.3 is checked or not. This validation can be done using: checked pseudo class.

```
<input id="id1" type="checkbox" value="1" name="country"/>CANADA
```

UFT code for the same will be

```
' select checkbox
cssValue = "input#id1"
oPg.WebCheckBox("css:=" & cssValue).Click
' find selected checkbox element
cssValue = "input#id1:checked"
```

Table 38.5 Finding elements using UI state pseudo-class

Pseudo-class	Example	Description
:enabled	input:enabled	Locate all <input> elements which are enabled
:disabled	input:disabled	Locate all <input> elements which are disabled
:checked	input:checked	Locate all <input> elements which are checked

```
If oPg.WebCheckBox("css:=" & cssValue).Exist(0.5) Then
    Print "Checkbox is selected"
Else
    Print "Checkbox is NOT selected"
End If
```

Table 38.5 describes the UI state pseudo classes.

Verifying CSS Styles of an Element

Various styles are applied on the elements of the web page to make the web page look attractive and user-friendly. Developers add these styles from CSS. Sometimes, we may require to test whether respective styles have been correctly applied or not. For example, it may be required to verify the font-family and font-size of the text on a <input> button. Another example could be to verify the background color of the button. Object native properties can be used retrieve the CSS styles of an object. Chapter *Working with Web Application Objects* describes in detail how to retrieve CSS styles of an object.

QUICK TIPS

- ✓ Avoid using the CSS locator path generated by Firepath.
- ✓ Use Firepath to design custom CSS locator path based on objects' HTML code.
- ✓ CSS can be effectively used to locate dynamic elements and child elements.
- ✓ Define only 'css' description property in object repository as far as possible.
- ✓ UFT may not locate the same objects using css locator path as is located by the css expression in Firefox.
- ✓ CSS property is not supported for .Net web forms.
- ✓ UFT in maintenance mode run may replace test objects with CSS property values with new objects from the application. To avoid this, use the *Update from Application* option in the Object Repository Manager to update specific test objects with CSS identifier property values.
- ✓ *Update from Application* option will remove the CSS definition of the object from object repository. The new captured definition will follow the object learning mechanism as discussed in chapter *Test Object Learning Mechanism*.

PRACTICAL QUESTIONS

1. What is CSS Selector? How it works?
2. How you will find CSS attributes of an element in Firefox and Chrome browser?
3. What is the difference between absolute CSS path and relative CSS path of an element?
4. You see an Automation Developer using the same CSS locator path in UFT code as it is displayed in Firebug/Firepath. What you will advise him and why?
5. What is Pseudo Class CSS Selector?
6. What is the difference between Action class and UI state CSS selector?
7. Develop the CSS path for locating below elements of sample.com login page
   a. Email address edit box
   b. Password edit box
   c. Login button
   d. Forgot password link

Chapter 39

Object Identification Using Visual Relation Identifiers

Visual Relation Identifier (VRI) is a set of definitions that enable UFT to locate the object in AUT according to the relative location of its neighboring objects. Users are expected to select those neighboring objects as VRI whose relative location to the test object does not change, even if there is a user interface design modification.

VRI enables UFT to identify similar objects much as a human tester would, and helps create more stable object repositories that can withstand predictable changes to the application's user interface. Ordinal Identifier mechanism is not used if VRI is defined for a test object.

HOW VISUAL RELATION IDENTIFIERS WORK

Suppose that someone shows you a photograph as shown in Fig. 39.1a. In this photograph, there exist two identical twins—Twin 1st and Twin 2nd and other people. He informs you that identical twins are standing at different positions and then asks you to remember the differences between them so that you can identify each twin successfully when shown different photographs at a later time.

You are told that:

- Twin 1st always wears a grey tie, and that the other twin (twin 2nd) always wears a red tie.
- Each twin has an assigned partner, which means that even if the twins stand at different positions in other photographs, they always stand next to their assigned partners.
    - Twin 1st always stands left to his partner.
    - Twin 2nd always stands in front of his partner.

> **NOTES**
>
> When testing application with multiple identical objects, UFT assigns an ordinal identifier to every object which is not uniquely identifiable using its Mandatory and Assistive properties. However, any change in the location of the object in user interface or change in relative initialization of the object in code results in a change in ordinal identifiers of the test object. This makes ordinal identifiers not so reliable mechanism for locating objects.

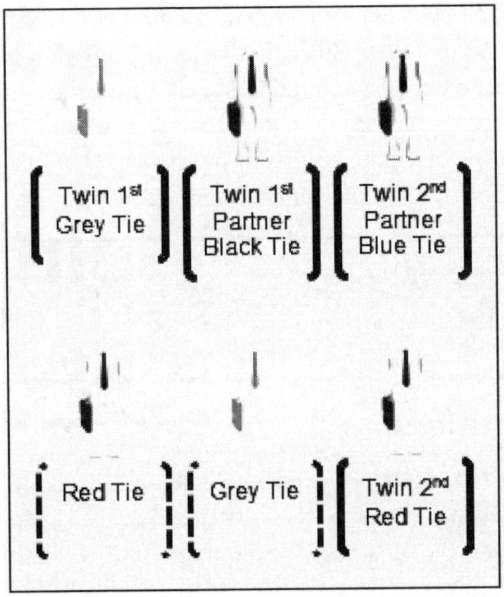

Figure 39.1a *Group photo of twins*

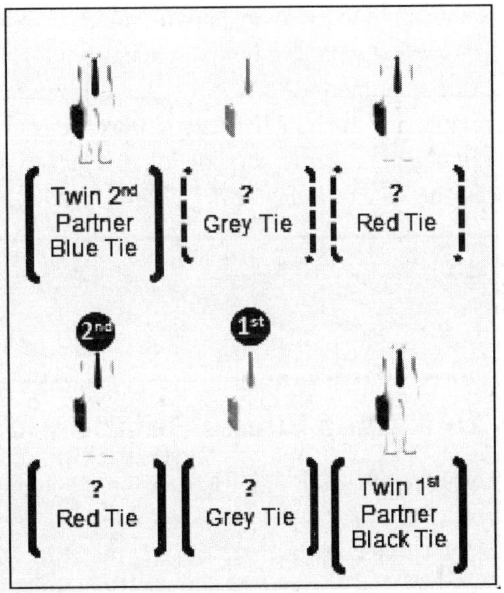

Figure 39.2b *Group photo with positions changed*

- Twin 1st partner always wears a black tie and is the only person in the group to wear a black tie.
- Twin 2nd partner always wears a blue tie and is the only person in the group to wear a blue tie.
- There are two persons in the group wearing red tie.
- There are two persons in the group wearing grey tie.

Now, you are shown a second photograph of the same group as shown in Fig. 39.1b and asked to identify both the twins. One way to locate or identify twin 1st is*: Look for a person with grey tie and is standing left to a person wearing black tie.* Similarly, twin 2nd can be identified as: *Look for a person with red tie and is standing in front of a person wearing blue tie.*

UFT uses visual relation identifiers in a similar way. Here,

- People in photographs can be considered as test objects.
- Tie color of people can be considered as description property of the test object.
- Neighbors can be considered as visual relations.

UFT uses the defined description properties and visual relation of the test object to identify the object during run-time.

VRI BASED OBJECT IDENTIFICATION MECHANISM

For the Fig. 39.1a and Fig. 39.1b discussed above, let's see how UFT can identify the twin 1st object. During identification process, UFT first looks for an object that matches twin 1st description properties. UFT finds two matches as two persons are wearing red tie. [Next, UFT has option to use ordinal identifiers or visual relation identifiers (as defined in test object description in object repository). Here, we will observe that ordinal identifier value (say index) for twin 1st in Fig. 39.1a is zero. However, since people have changed positions, twin 1st position is no more zero in Fig. 39.1b. Moreover, there is no way to predict position value (ordinal identifier value) of twin 1st in Fig. 39.1b. Hence, ordinal identifier mechanism to locate twin 1st will fail here]. Now let's see how visual relation identifier mechanism can be successfully used to uniquely identify twin 1st in Fig. 39.1b. Since, in this case, even after using all description properties of twin 1st, UFT has not been able to locate it uniquely; UFT uses the defined visual relation identifiers. UFT tries to look for a person whose description property is grey tie and whose visual relation identifier is standing left to a person wearing black tie. Using this mechanism, UFT is able to successfully locate twin 1st. Twin 2nd is also identified by UFT in a similar manner.

NOTES

Ordinal Identifier mechanism is not used if VRI is defined for a test object.

How UFT Uses Visual Relation Identifiers

- During a run session, UFT first attempts to identify the test object using the object's description properties.
- If UFT finds one or more objects matching the test object's description, it attempts to identify the object using the defined visual relation identifier.
- If no objects or more than one object is found, the visual relation identifier fails, and UFT continues to Smart Identification (if defined).
- If Smart Identification as well fails to uniquely identify the object, then no ordinal identifiers are used to locate the test object even if it is defined.

Note: For defining visual relation identifiers:

- A test object cannot be used as a related object to itself.
- The following test objects cannot be defined as related objects for another test object's visual relation identifier:
  - A test object that has a visual relation identifier.
  - A child test object for one of its parent objects

HOW TO DEFINE VISUAL RELATION IDENTIFIERS IN OR

Consider an application that allows users to place inventory fulfillment order. Figure 39.3 shows the request inventory page of this application.

Product Category	Product Brand	Product Code	Request Inventory
Shirts	REI	6549878765	Request Inventory
Jackets	Novara	7684543297	Request Inventory
Shoes	ASICS	8795432499	Request Inventory
Shoes	Vibram	3256598745	Request Inventory
Shoes	Adidas	9876453428	Request Inventory

Figure 39.3 *Request inventory demo page*

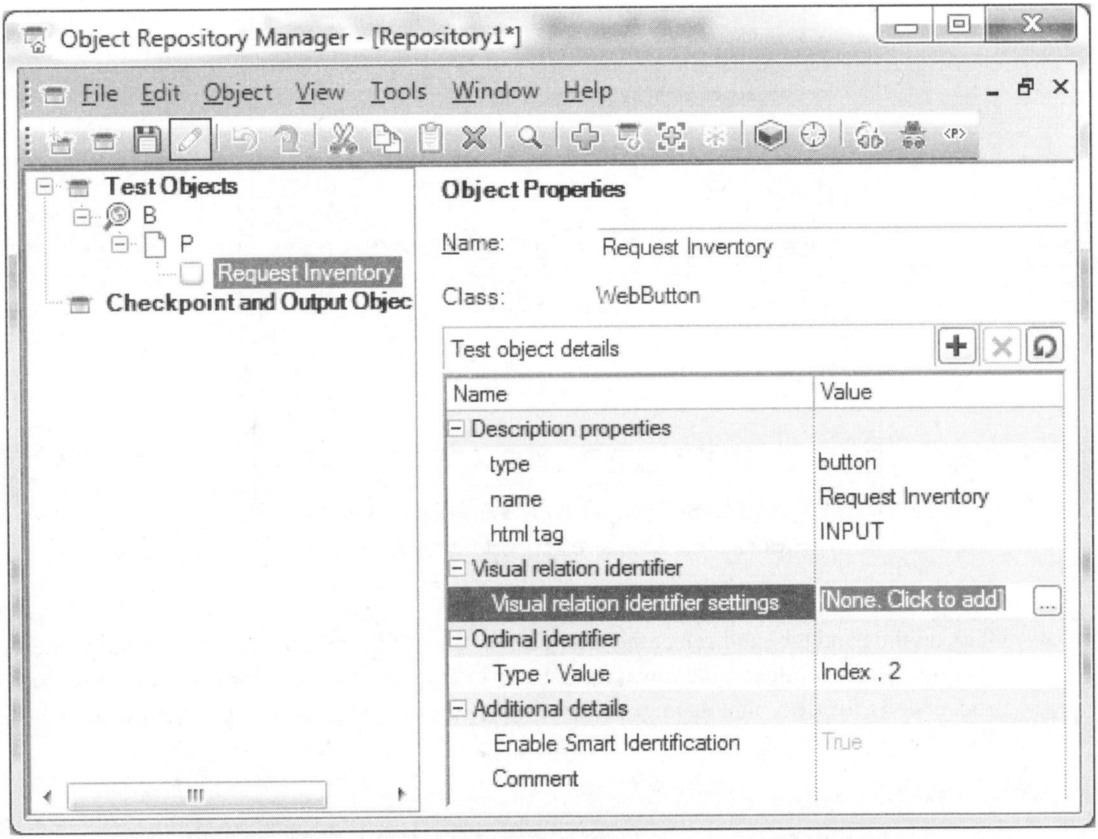

Figure 39.4 *UFT learned description for 3rd 'Request Inventory' button*

Suppose the requirement is to place inventory fulfillment order for product code=8795432499. Assume the description properties of all the web buttons 'Request Inventory' are same.

Now let's see, how UFT learns the 'Request Inventory' button for product code= 8795432499. Figure 39.4 shows the learned description of this object in OR.

As evident from Fig. 39.4, UFT was not able to uniquely describe the 3rd 'Request Inventory' object using description properties, hence it learned the ordinal identifier (index=2).

As we know, ordinal identifiers are not a reliable mechanism to locate objects. So, let's see how we can use visual relation identifiers to create reliable description of the object. To create a VRI, follow the steps as mentioned below:

1. Click on the visual relation identifier settings button [...]. *Visual Relation Identifier* dialog box opens as shown in Fig. 39.5.
2. Click on the button 'Add a related object to the list' +.
   'Select Test Object' dialog box opens ass shown in Fig. 39.6.
3. As per requirement, either select the visual related object from the object tree or click on the hand tool to select the visual related object from the web page. Since, here required visual related object is not available, we will use the hand tool.

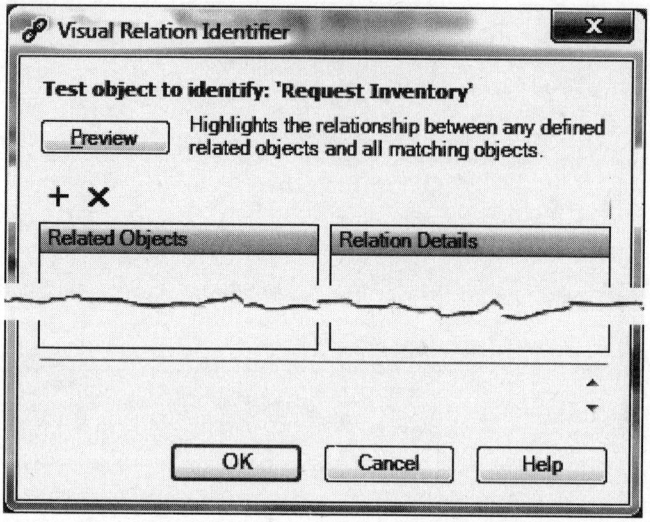

Figure 39.5 *Visual relation identifier dialog box*

4. Click on the hand tool and select the element '8795432499' (product code) as visual related identifier. Here, product code always exist left to the 'request inventory' button and since product code for a product is unique, hence there is no way this code will be duplicated. So product code can be used as a reliable related identifier.

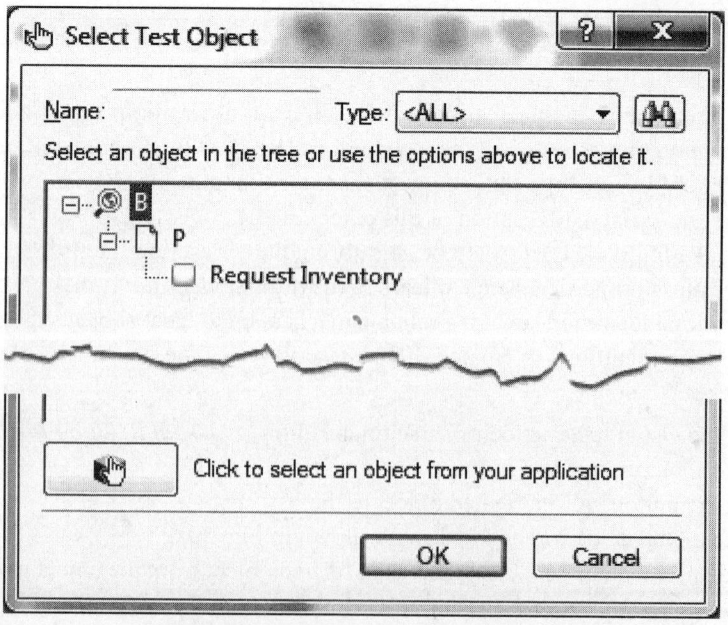

Figure 39.6 *Select test object dialog box*

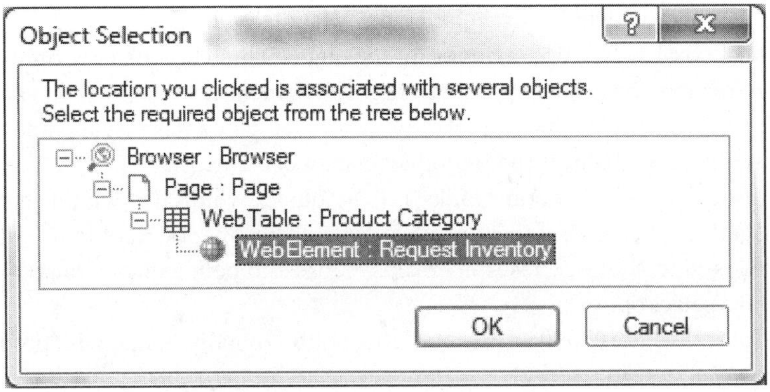

Figure 39.7 *Object selection dialog box*

Once the related object is selected from GUI, 'Object Selection' dialog box appears as shown in Fig. 39.7.

5. Select the required object (here, webelement) and click 'OK' button.
   Visual Relation Identifier dialog box appears with the WebElement object added as shown in Fig. 39.8.

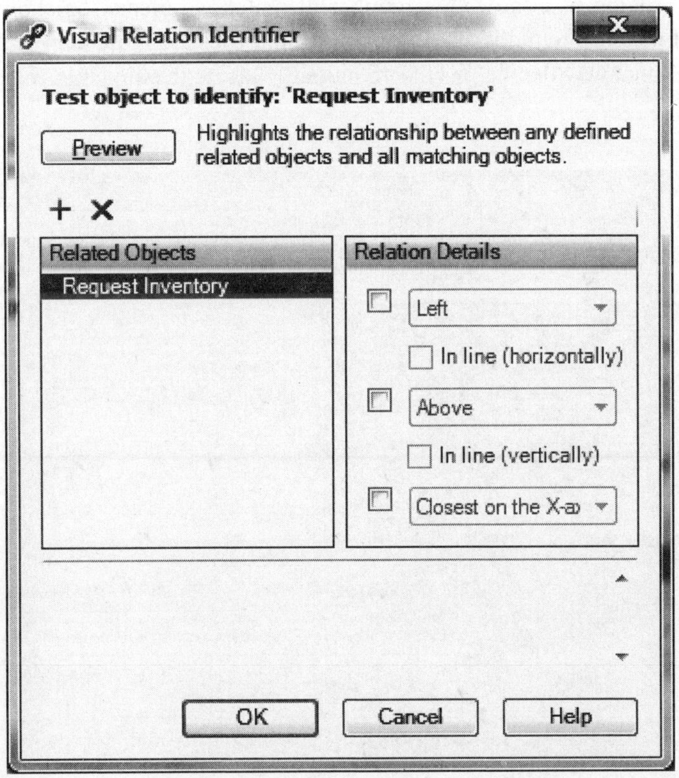

Figure 39.8 *VRI settings dialog box*

6. Select the relation details as required from VRI dialog box.
   a. Checkbox 1—This option looks for the object which lies visually right or left of the visually related object (here product code webelement).
   b. Checkbox 2—This option looks for the object which lies visually above or below of the visually related object (here product code webelement).
   c. Checkbox 2—This option looks for the object which lies within the proximity of the visually related object (here product code webelement). Here four options are available – Closest to X-axis, Closest to Y-axis, Closest to both axis or Contains.

   Suppose we select options:
   – 'Request Inventory' button is to the left and horizontally in line with product code webelement 'Request Inventory'.
   – 'Request Inventory' button is the closest object on the Y-axis to product code webelement 'Request Inventory'.
7. Click on the preview button to verify that the defined VRI configuration uniquely locates the object.
   On clicking 'Preview' button, UFT attempts to locate the objects as defined in VRI settings. UFT highlights the matched object/objects. Figure 39.9 shows the matched object as highlighted by UFT.
8. Also, VRI dialog box shows the number of matched objects. As shown in Fig. 39.9, the number of matches found is '1'. If number of matches are more than 1, then VRI settings to be changed in a way that helps UFT to uniquely locate the object.

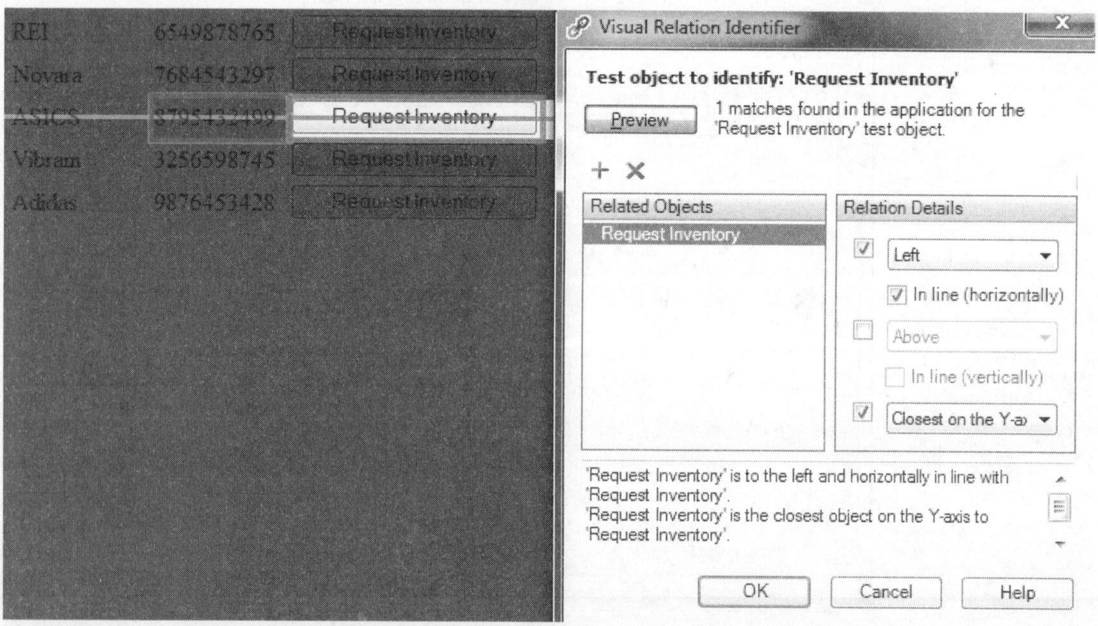

Figure 39.9 *Verifying VRI settings uniquely locates the object*

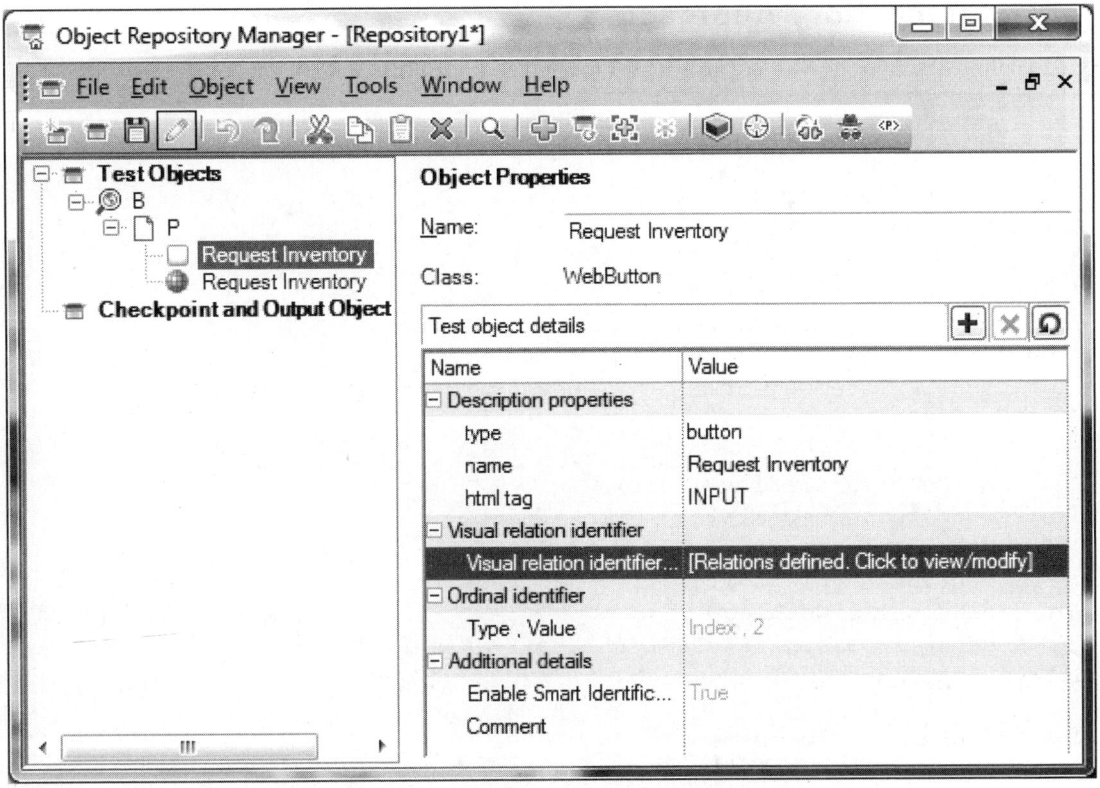

Figure 39.10 *Object repository with VRI defined*

9. Click on the *OK* button to add the VRI information to the test object description information in the object repository. Figure 39.10 shows the OR window with VRI settings defined.

   Here observe that:
   - Newly added product code WebElement 'Request Inventory' is automatically added to the OR.
   - Ordinal Identification mechanism is automatically disabled.
10. Select the WebButton object and Click on the 'Highlight in Application' button to verify that the object is uniquely identified using VRI mechanism.

CREATING VISUAL RELATION IDENTIFIERS USING CODE

UFT also provides the flexibility to create visual relation identifiers using code. UFT supports both OR approach as well as descriptive programming approach for creating coded visual relation identifiers.

Object Repository Approach

Code below describes how to create VRI for the 'inventory fulfillment' example discussed above.

```
' create VRI object
Set oVRI = VisualRelations.Create

' add a new relation object
Set oRelation1 = oVRI.Add

' Define the related object
' This object must be already added to OR
' Here this object will be product code webelement 'Request Inventory'
oRelation1.RelatedObjectPath = "Browser(""B"").Page(""P"").
WebElement(""Request Inventory"")"

' Define the VRI relation (left)
oRelation1.relativeposition = micRelLeft
' Set the argument inline horizontal
oRelation1.setargument micrelinline, True
Set oRelation1 = Nothing
' Define new relation (Closest on the Y-axis)
Set oRelation2 = oVRI.Add

' Define the related object
oRelation2.RelatedObjectPath = "Browser(""B"").Page(""P"").
WebElement(""Request Inventory"")"

' Define the VRI relation (closest to y-axis)
oRelation2.relativeposition = micRelClosestY
Set oRelation2 = Nothing

' Update the defined test object with the new visual relation identifier
Browser("B").Page("P").WebButton("Request Inventory").SetTOProper-
ty "visual relations", oVRI

Browser("B").Page("P").WebButton("Request Inventory").Highlight
```

NOTES: The related identifier object must be added to OR before its reference in code.

Descriptive Programming Approach

UFT provides the flexibility to programmatically set VRI settings to an object. To implement the same, replace the code for code section *'Update the defined test object with the new visual relation identifier'* above with below DP code.

```
' Update the defined test object with the new visual relation identifier
Set oDesc = Description.Create
oDesc("visual relations").value = oVRI
Browser("B").Page("P").WebButton("Request Inventory").Highlight
```

QUICK TIPS

- ✓ VRI mechanism locates object by referring the relation of the related object with this object.
- ✓ If VRI mechanism is enabled, ordinal identifier mechanism is automatically disabled.

PRACTICAL QUESTIONS

1. Explain how visual relation identifier mechanism works.
2. A test object in OR has both visual relation identifier and ordinal identifier defined. Which identification mechanism will be used to identify the object during run-time?
3. How visual relation identifier can be defined using DP code?
4. Give one example where you have used VRI mechanism successfully.

Chapter **40**

Smart Identification

Smart Identification (SI) is used by UFT to identify objects during run time when learned description is not sufficient to uniquely identify an object. The SI mechanism classifies object properties into two categories—base filter properties and optional filter properties.

Base Filter Properties

Base filter properties are the most fundamental properties of a particular test object class. The values of these objects cannot be changed without changing the essence of the original object. For example, if a Web link's tag was changed from <A>to any other value, we can no longer call it the same (link) object.

Optional Filter Properties

Optional filter properties are the properties other than base filter properties that can help identify objects of a particular class. These properties are unlikely to change on a regular basis, but can be ignored if they are no longer applicable.

To configure SI properties of an object use Tools → Object Identification → Configure. Base and optional filter properties can be configured in the same way as mandatory and assistive properties are configured. Figure 40.1 shows *Smart Identification Properties* dialog box.

SI MECHANISM

If UFT activates the SI mechanism during a test, it follows the following process to identify the object:

1. UFT forgets the recorded test object description and creates a new object candidate list containing the objects (within the object's parent object) that match all of the properties defined in the base filter property list. If a unique object is found then the object is declared as identified. If not, then UFT uses the optional filter properties one by one to find a unique object among the new object candidate list.
2. From the new object candidate list, UFT filters out any object that does not match the first property listed in the Optional Filter Properties list. The remaining objects become the new object candidate list.

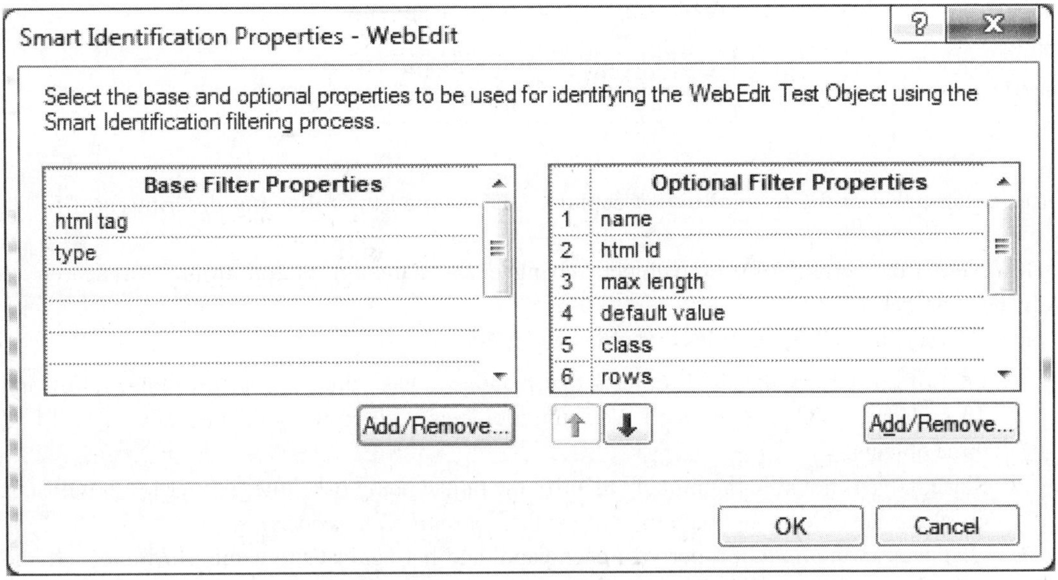

Figure 40.1 *Smart identification properties*

3. If the new object candidate list still has more than one object, then UFT uses the next available optional filter property. The objects that match the property form a new object candidate list. If the new object candidate list is empty, then UFT ignores this optional filter property, returns to the previous object candidate list, and repeats step 2 for the next optional filter property in the list.
   If the object candidate list contains exactly one object, then UFT concludes that it has identified the object and performs the statement containing the object.
4. UFT continues the process described in steps 2 and 3 until it either identifies one object or runs out of optional filter properties to use.
   If, after completing the SI elimination process, UFT still cannot identify the object, then UFT uses learned description and ordinal identifier to uniquely identify the object. Even after this, if UFT cannot uniquely identify an object, then it stops the test run and displays a Run Error message.
   Suppose that we have a web application that has the following objects:
   a. WebButton object with name AdvSearch
   b. WebButton object with name Next
   c. WebButton object with name Previous

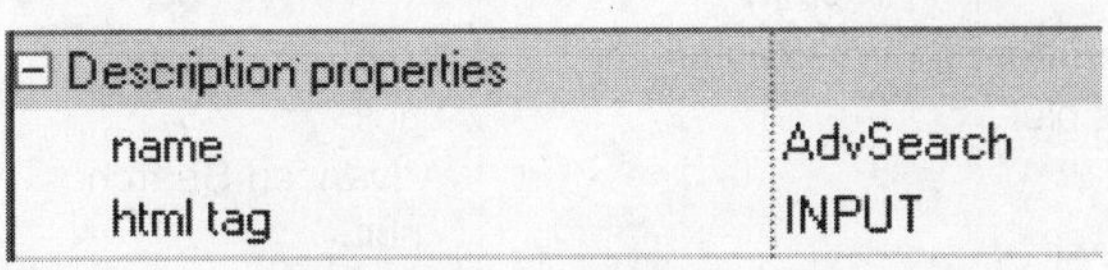

Figure 40.2 *Object properties*

Table 40.1 Base filter properties

Property	Value
html tag	INPUT

Let us assume that at the time of object capture, UFT learned the following description of Search WebButton (Figure 40.2).

However, after certain time, developers changed the name of button from "AdvSearch" to "Advanced Search."

Now let's see how UFT identifies this object using SI.

1. First of all, UFT will list all objects that match the base filter properties (Tables 40.1 and 40.2). Here, it will list down all WebButton objects with html tag = INPUT. UFT will find three objects.
2. Since, UFT is not able to uniquely identify the object using base filter properties; it will start checking the object candidate list against the *optional filter properties*.
3. UFT checks the *name* property of each candidate list against the value: *AdvSearch*. As no object candidate list has name property value as 'AdvSearch', the new candidate list has zero objects. Since, UFT still has more optional properties available, it ignores this (name) property and the new object candidate list (with zero objects). UFT reverts back to the previous object candidate list and uses the next available optional property (type) to identify the object.
4. UFT checks the *type* property of each candidate list against the value: *submit*. UFT finds that all three objects in the object candidate list have the type property value: submit. These three objects now form the new object candidate list.
5. UFT checks the *html id* property of each candidate list against the value: *null*. UFT finds that two objects have html id value as null while one object has some value for html id property. The object with some value for html id is filtered out and the remaining two objects become the new object candidate list.
6. UFT checks the *value* property of each candidate list against the value: *Advanced Search*.

Only one object has this property value as "Advanced Search." UFT understands that it has now uniquely identified the object and executes the particular test step Fig. 40.3 shows the test result report of smart identification mechanism.

Table 40.2 Optional filter properties

Property	Value
name type html id value class visible	AdvSearch submit <null> Advanced Search <null> 1

Step Name: "Advanced Search"- Smart Identification

Step Done

Object	Details	Result	Time
"Advanced Search"- Smart Identification	The smart identification mechanism was invoked. Reason: object not found. **Original description:** name=AdvSearch micclass=WebButton html tag=INPUT **Smart Identification Alternative Description:** <u>Base filter properties (3 objects found)</u> micclass=WebButton html tag=INPUT <u>Optional filter properties</u> name=AdvSearch **(Skipped)** type=submit **(Used**, 3 matches) html id= **(Used**, 2 matches) value=Advanced Search **(Used**, 1 matches) class= **(Ignored)** visible=1 **(Ignored)**	Done	4/28/2014 - 16:51:58

Figure 40.3 *Test results details for smart identification step*

> **NOTES** Smart Identification mechanism slows down test execution as this mechanism is activated only if regular identification fails.

CONFIGURING SI

To configure SI properties of an object use Tools → Object Identification → Configure. Base and optional filter properties can be configured in the same way as mandatory and assistive properties are configured.

WHEN TO USE SMART IDENTIFICATION?

Smart Identification mechanism is to be enabled only for test object classes that have defined Smart Identification configuration. However, even if Smart Identification configuration is defined for a test object class, we may not always want UFT to learn the Smart Identification property values. To prevent UFT from learning the Smart Identification properties, clear the *Enable Smart Identification* check box in Object Identification dialog box.

Even if a captured test object has learned Smart Identification properties, Smart Identification mechanism for the specific object can be disabled by setting *Smart Identification=False* for the object in Object Repository. Smart Identification mechanism for a run session can also be disabled at UFT *Test* level from *Run* pane of the Test Settings dialog box.

However, if Smart Identification properties have not been learnt, we cannot enable the Smart Identification mechanism for an object later during run session. In order to re-learn Smart Identification properties of an object in OR, either update the object using 'Update from Application' feature or re-capture the object in OR.

QUICK TIPS

- ✓ Base filter properties and optional filter properties cannot have a description property in common.
- ✓ SI mechanism can be configured in the same way as mandatory/assistive properties are configured.
- ✓ SI mechanism of object identification slows down test execution.
- ✓ If Smart Identification properties have not been learned by UFT during its object learning process, then SI mechanism cannot be used for that object during run session.

PRACTICAL QUESTIONS

1. Configure the SI settings (base and optional) for raileurope.com application
2. When Smart Identification mechanism is triggered?
3. Explain the mechanism of object identification using SI.
4. Does Smart Identification uses image based identification?

Chapter **41**

Object Identification Using Ordinal Identifiers

Creation time, index, and location of an object in GUI are referred as ordinal identifiers of the object. The ordinal property value is a relative value and its value is decided in relation to other objects present in GUI application during the time of object capture. Therefore, any change in GUI screen layout or composition of application page can change the ordinal identifier value. For this reason, UFT learns ordinal identifier value only in the case where it cannot uniquely identify an object using all mandatory and assistive properties.

Creation time: Creation time identifier is for objects of browser class only. The browser that is opened first is assigned creation time zero, and so on such as 0, 1, 2…

For example, if UFT learns that three browsers were opened at 10:01 am, 10:03 am, and 10:10 am, then UFT will assign Creationtime=0 to browser opened at 10:01 am, Creationtime=1 to browser opened at 10:03 am, Creationtime=2 to browser opened at 10:10 am. The code below will identify the first opened browser.

```
Browser("CreationTime:=0").Sync
```

Index: Indicates the order in which the object appears in the application code relative to other objects with an otherwise identical description.

For example, suppose that the application code created objected in the order as mentioned below.

- WebEdit object with name 'UserName'.
- Image object with name 'Search'.
- WebButton object with name 'Search'.
- Image object with name 'Search'.

The following code statement refers to the third item in the list, as it is the first 'Search' WebButton object in the code.

```
WebButton("name:=Search," "Index:=0")
```

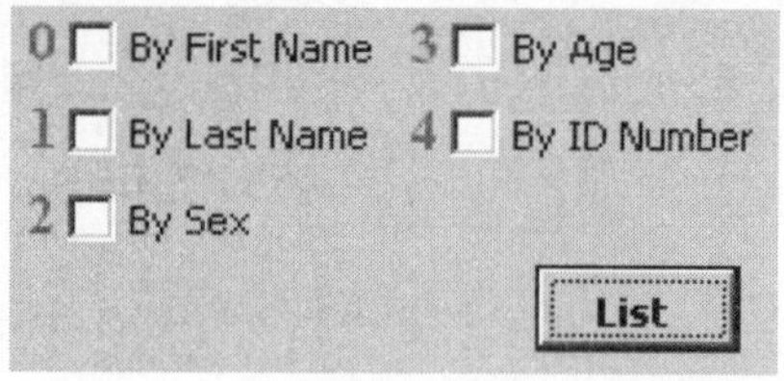

Figure 41.1 *Location ordinal identifier*

While the following code statement refers to the second item in the list, as it is the first object of any type (WebElement) with the name Search.

```
WebElement("name:= Search," "Index:=0")
```

The code statement below refers to the fourth item in the list, as it is the second object of Image type with name Search.

```
Image("name:= Search ," "Index:=1")
```

Location: Indicates the order in which the object appears within the parent window frame or dialog box relative to other objects with an otherwise identical description. Values are assigned in the order of top to bottom and left to right. In Fig. 41.1, check boxes are numbered according to their location property relative to all check boxes present in the screen.

For example, suppose that an application page contains the following objects.

- WebEdit with name 'UserName'
- Image with name Search
- WebButton with name Search
- Image with name Search

The following code statement refers to the third item in the list as it is the first WebButton object with name Search.

```
WebButton ("name:=Search," "Location:=0")
```

While the code statement below refers to the second object as it is the first object of any type (WebElement) with the name Search.

```
WebElement ("name:=Search,"Location:=0")
```

> **NOTES** UFT uses ordinal identifier properties to identify an object during run session only if it is not able to uniquely identify an object using learned description and the SI mechanism.

QuickTips

Before starting to capture the objects to the OR, it is very important to configure the object identification settings. Object identification settings define the mandatory and assistive properties required to identify a test object during run time. A random study of the application objects has to be done to identify the essential properties required to identify an object. The mandatory and assistive properties are to be chosen in a way that it avoids or limits the need SI and ordinal identifiers to identify an object. The reason for avoiding SI is that it can behave unpredictably during the run session. Similarly, values of ordinal identifiers such as index and creation time vary during run time. Moreover, the index property of an object can easily be changed by the application developer without requiring any change request. Again, such a change mostly will not have any impact on the look and feel of GUI or application functionality. Therefore, such changes always go unnoticed both by testers and by the management. However, at the same time, such a change will require test scripts to be upgraded and tested again before they can be executed. It becomes very difficult to show a change effort in test scripts to the management without any actual change in the application. In addition, since such type of changes cannot be predicted or monitored, the maintenance changes to the test scripts and OR become cyclic, time consuming, and costly. Hence, it is always advisable to avoid the use of the ordinal identifiers. Object identification properties are to be selected in a way that it supports easy handling of the dynamic objects of the application and as well as minimal changes to the test script and the OR in case of a change. Object identification settings need to be configured in a way that test scripts and the test objects require change only in the cases where change to the application is visible.

QUICK TIPS

- ✓ Try to uniquely identify an element by using various attributes of mandatory and assistive properties only.
- ✓ Avoid using WebElements as far as possible.
- ✓ WebTables to be used instead of WebElements wherever possible.
- ✓ Avoid the use of ordinal identifiers and SI as far as possible.
- ✓ CreationTime ordinal identifier to be used for browser object.
- ✓ Location ordinal identifier to be preferred over index ordinal identifier.
- ✓ Ordinal Identifier mechanism is not used if VRI is defined for a test object.

PRACTICAL QUESTIONS

1. What is the difference between location and index ordinal identifier?
2. Why WebElements are not considered a reliable object for object identification?

Chapter 42

Image-based Identification (Insight)

UFT provides the feature to identify GUI objects based on what they look like. This is an image based identification technique and is called *Insight*. Insight mode enables users to record or learn any control (object) displayed on AUT screen, whether or not UFT recognizes the object's technology and is able to retrieve its properties or activate its methods. In this mode, UFT recognizes controls based on their appearance, and not their native properties. This can be useful to test controls from an environment that UFT does not support. It can as well be used to test application running on a remote computer with a non-Windows operating system.

INSIGHT IDENTIFICATION MECHANISM

When using Insight, UFT stores an image of the object along with its ordinal identifiers (if required) in object repository. This object is called *Insight Test Object*. UFT learns the ordinal identifier if there exits two objects (objects image) with same look and feel. During run session, UFT uses this image as the main description property to identify the object in the application.

Note: For dual monitor support, Insight is supported only on the primary monitor. Therefore, when working with dual monitors, ensure that the application is visible on the primary monitor.

INSIGHT TEST OBJECT DESCRIPTIONS

When using Insight, UFT learns objects based on their appearance. UFT stores an image of the object, as its description property. This image can be used later to identify the object. If parts of the object do not always look the same, UFT can be instructed to ignore those areas when it uses the image to identify the object. If required, UFT can also learn an ordinal identifier to create a unique description for the object.

UFT also supports VRI identification mechanism for insight test objects. This helps to improve identification of the object and avoid use of ordinal identifiers. After the insight test object is added to OR, visual relation identifiers can be added.

UFT also provides the flexibility to add the **similarity** identification property to the test object description. Similarity property is a percentage match specification. It defines how similar a control in the application has to be to the test object image for it to be considered a match.

Note: Mandatory and assistive properties, and smart identification, are not relevant for Insight test objects.

ADDING INSIGHT OBJECTS TO OR

(INSIGHT TEST OBJECT LEARNING MECHANISM)

Insight test objects can be added to OR during recording session or when adding test objects to an object repository manually. When adding insight test objects to an object repository, users can add an object directly from the application, or even from a picture of the object displayed on the screen. In this section, we will discuss how to add insight test objects to OR manually.

Insight Test Object Hierarchy

The Insight object is always added to the object repository as a child of the test object that represents its containing application, such as a Window or Browser object. The new object's parent object is also added if it does not already exist in the object repository.

UFT provides two modes to add an insight test object to OR—automatic and manual. In *Automatic* mode, UFT automatically defines the boundaries of the object and then captures the image of the object within boundary to the OR. In *Manual* mode, automation developers are required to specify the boundary of the object (as a rectangle). UFT then captures the image within boundary to the OR.

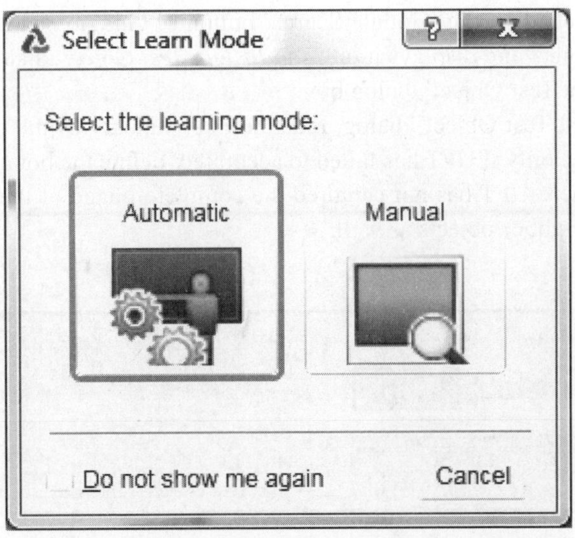

Figure 42.1 *Select learn mode dialog box*

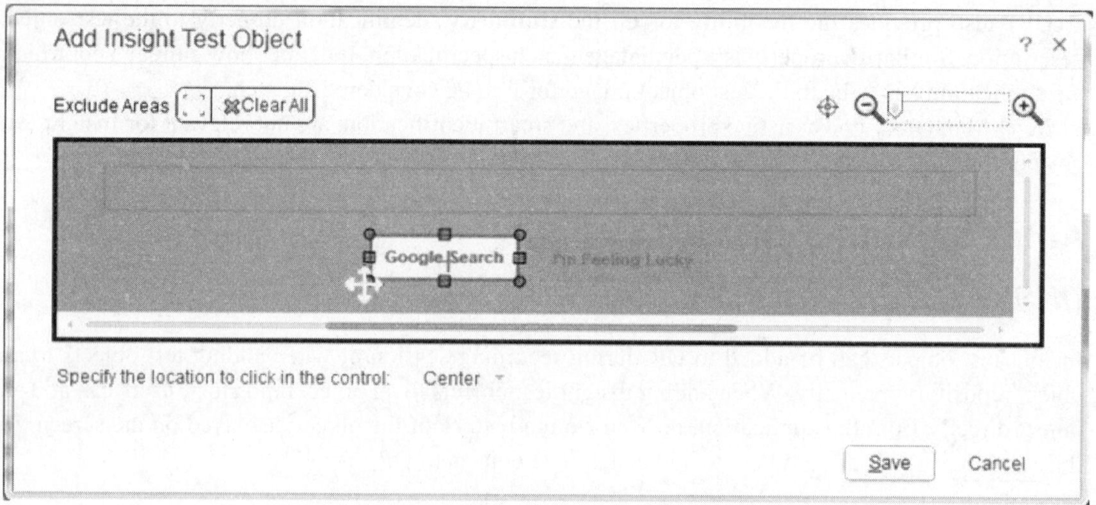

Figure 42.2 *Add insight test object dialog box*

Adding Insight Objects Using Automatic mode

Described below are the steps to add insight test objects to OR using automatic mode:

1. Open object repository.
2. Click on the '*Add Insight Objects*' button.
   '*Select Learn Mode*' dialog box opens as shown in the Fig. 42.1.
3. Select option '*Automatic*'.
   Hand tool appears.
4. Point and click the hand tool on the object whose image is to be captured. Suppose the hand tool is clicked on the 'Google Search' button of Google Search page. UFT learns the image of the object and displays it on '*Add Insight Test Object*' dialog box. Fig. 42.2 shows the 'Add Insight Test Object' dialog box.
6. On 'Add Insight Test Object' dialog, redefine the boundary of the object, if required. This needs to be done only if UFT has failed to accurately define the boundary of the object. That is scenarios where UFT has not captured the complete image of the object or has captured the image of neighbor objects as well.

Figure 42.3 *Defining areas excluded for image identification*

Figure 42.4 *Defining custom click location for insight object*

7. On 'Add Insight Test Object' dialog, specify areas to exclude and the location to click in the control.
   - 'Exclude Areas' (Exclude Areas [ ] Clear All) option enables users to exclude the areas which may change during run session. The idea here is to allow users to select only that part of the image which is static. Figure 42.3 shows, for instance, how exclude areas for image identification. Here, greyed out image area ( ) is excluded for image match.
   - 'Specify the location to click in the control' option enables users to specify objects *Click-Point*, i.e., where to execute a click within the image. The options here are:
     (i) Centre: Click on the centre of the image.
     (ii) Custom: Click on the specified ordinates of the image. Figure 42.4 shows custom ordinates defined for Fig. 42.2 insight object.

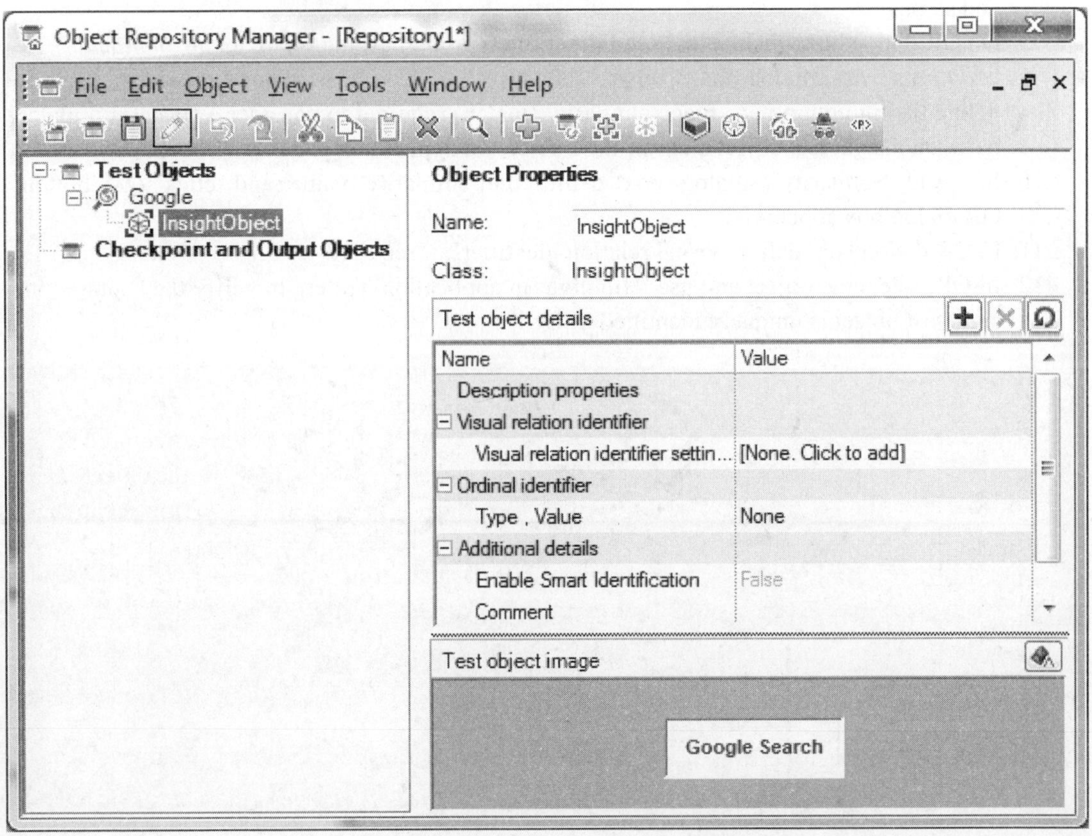

Figure 42.5 *Insight test object in OR*

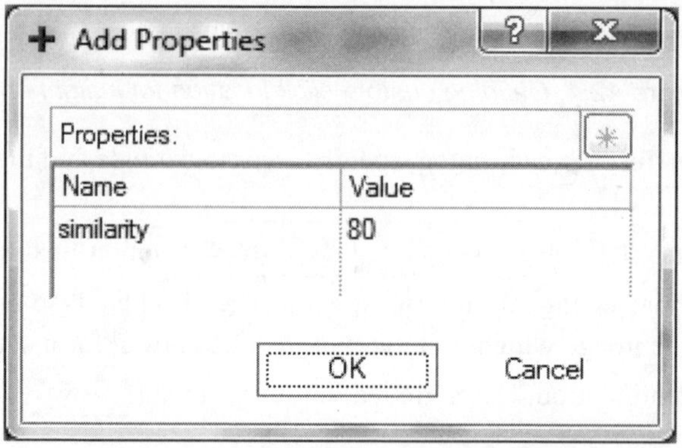

Figure 42.6 *Define percentage similarity*

7. Click on the 'Save' button to the object to OR. Figure 42.5 shows the 'Google Search' insight test object in OR.
8. In OR dialog box, Rename the logical name of the insight object to a meaningful name. UFT, by default, names the insight objects as InsightObject, InsightObject_2, InsightObject_3, and so on.
9. On OR dialog box, click on the 'add description properties' button to define *Similarity*. '*Add properties*' dialog box opens as shown in Fig. 42.6. This dialog box allows users to define the minimum percentage similarity (match) required to consider a successful match between insight test object and run-time object on application page.
10. In 'Add Similarity', dialog box define the similarity value and click *OK* button. OR dialog box appears.
11. In OR dialog box, define 'visual relation identifier', if required.
12 In OR, select the object and use 'Highlight in application' feature to verify the captured insight test object is uniquely identified in GUI.

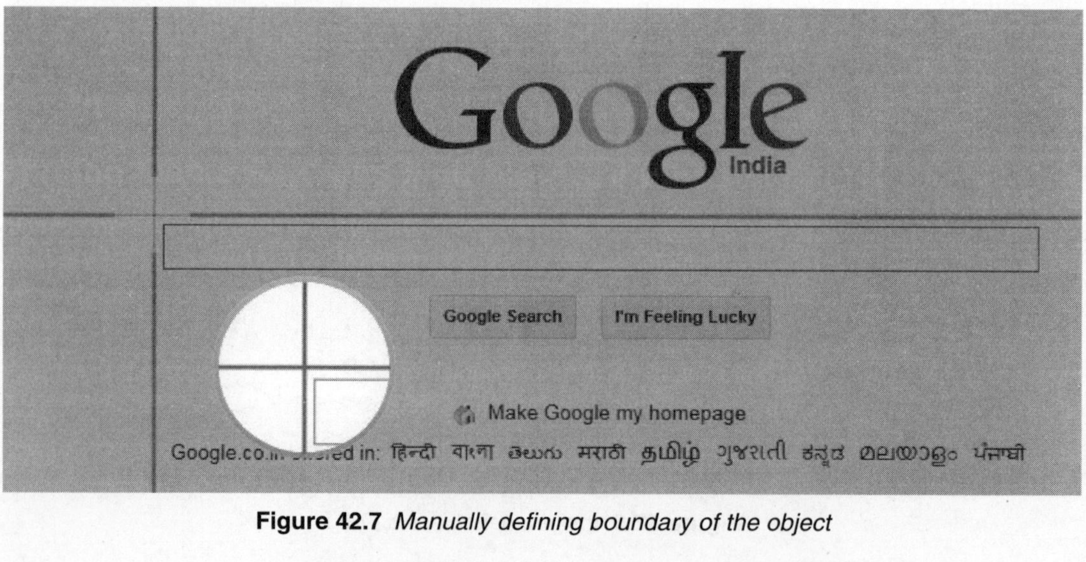

Figure 42.7 *Manually defining boundary of the object*

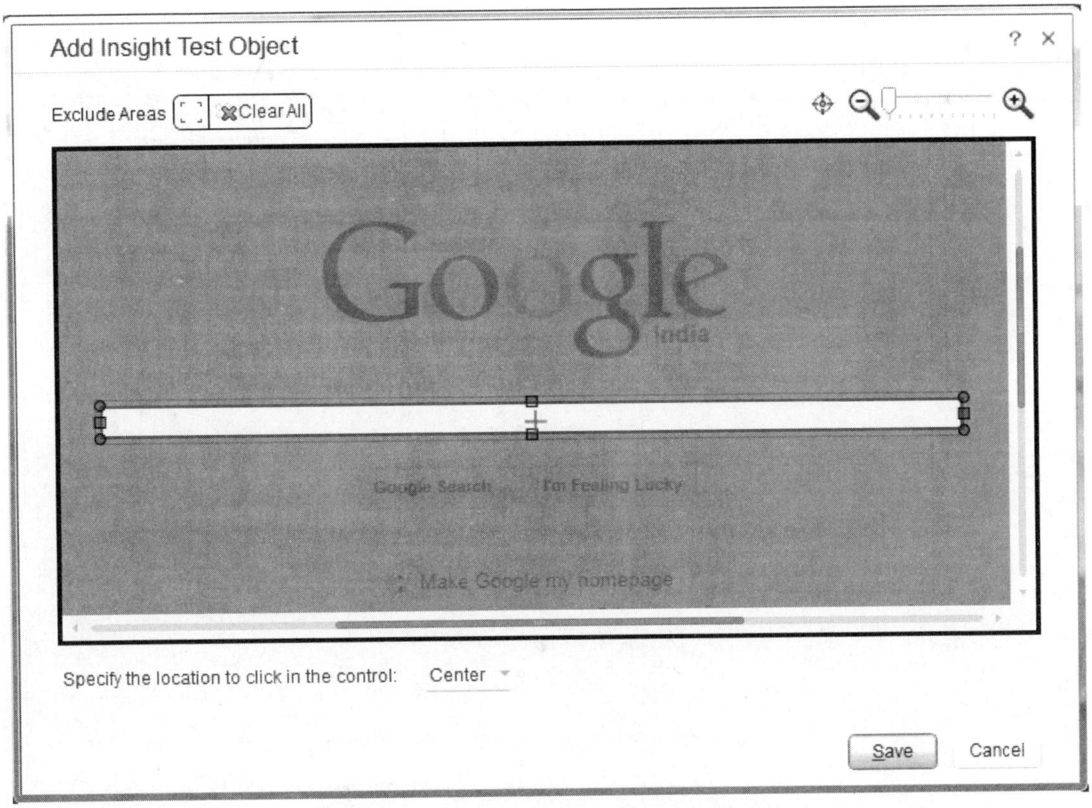

Figure 42.8 *Add insight test object dialog box*

Adding Insight Objects Using Manual mode

Described below are the steps to add insight test objects to OR using manual mode:

1. Open object repository.
2. Click on the '*Add Insight Objects*' button.
   '*Select Learn Mode*' dialog box opens as shown in the Fig. 42.1.
3. Select option '*Manual*'.
   Cross-hair cursor appears as shown in Fig. 42.7.
4. Using cross-hair cursor, define the boundary of the object.
   'Add Insight Test Object' dialog box opens with selected object image as shown in Fig. 42.8.
5. Follow steps 5–12 of section 'Adding Insight Objects using Automatic Mode' to customize the image of the object and add it to object repository.

DEVELOPING CODE USING INSIGHT TEST OBJECTS

In this section, we will discuss how to develop UFT code for insight objects. Suppose the requirement is perform a google search using insight mechanism. Assume the insight test objects have been added to OR as shown in Fig. 42.9.

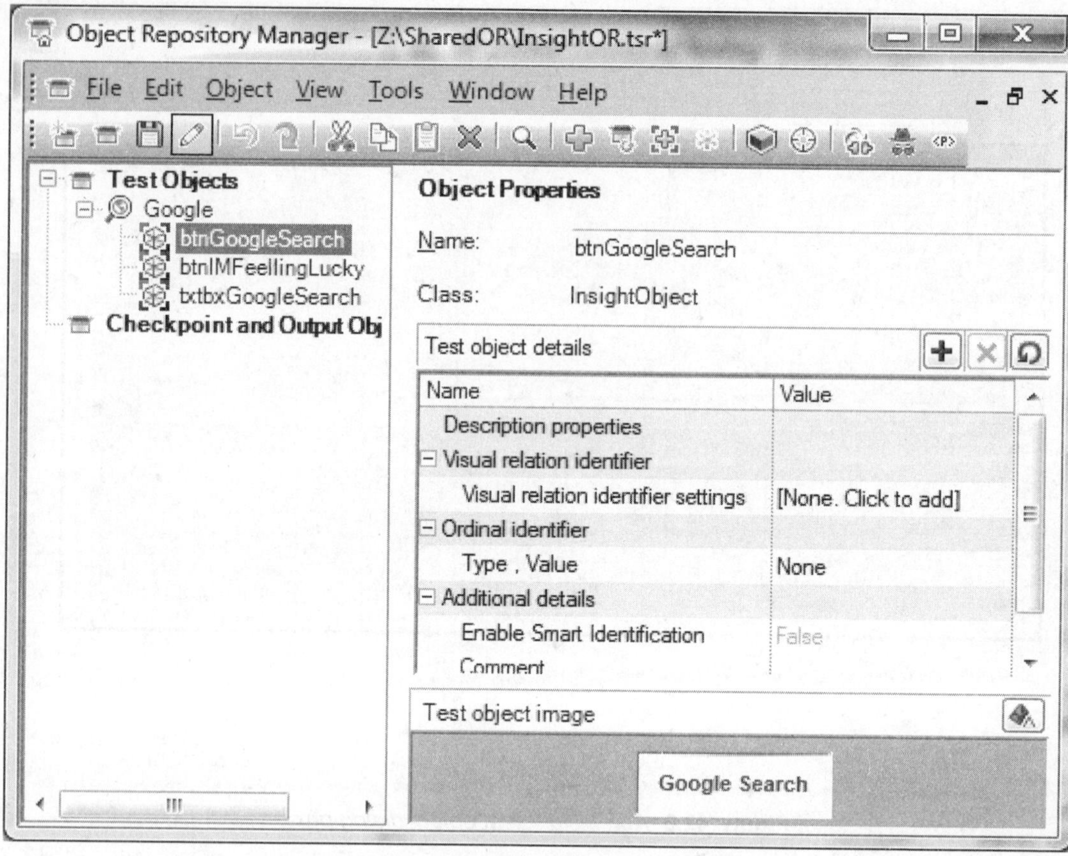

Figure 42.9 *OR with Google page insight objects*

> **NOTES:** Use button 'Change Test Object Image' to edit or replace the captured insight object image in OR. Figure 42.10 shows the UFT code for google search using insight objects.

CONFIGURING INSIGHT LEARNING/IDENTIFICATION MECHANISM

UFT provides the flexibility to configure the insight object learning and identification mechanism. Steps below describe the configuration steps:

```
Browser("Google").Sync
Browser("Google").InsightObject(        ).Type "UFT"

Browser("Google").InsightObject( Google Search ).Click
```

Figure 42.10 *UFT code using insight objects*

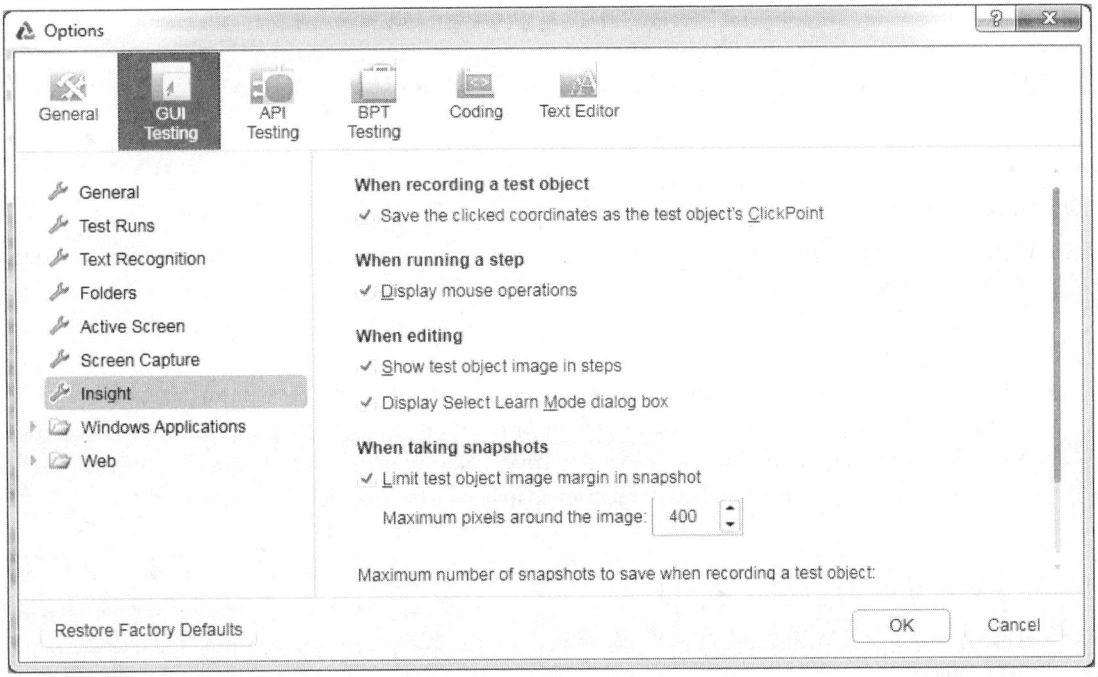

Figure 42.11 *Insight pane*

1. Open *Options* dialog box.
2. Open *GUI Testing* tab and navigate to node *Insight*.
   Insight Pane is displayed as shown in Fig. 42.11.

Recording Settings

Option '*Save the clicked coordinates as the test object's ClickPoint*' - Instructs UFT to use user clicked location as the ClickPoint of each Insight test object added to the OR during a recording session. If this option is deselected, the ClickPoint for objects learned by recording is set to center.

Test Run Configuration

Option '*Display mouse operations*' - Instructs UFT to show mouse clicks and mouse drag operations when running steps on Insight test objects.

Test Editing Configuration

- Option '*Show test object image in steps*'—Instructs UFT to display Insight test object images in steps in the Editor. If cleared, UFT displays the test object names instead as shown in Fig. 42.12.
- Option '*Display select learn mode dialog box*'—Insert UFT to display '*Select Learn Mode*' dialog box as shown in Fig. 42.1. If this option is cleared, UFT no longer displays this dialog box on clicking *Add Insight Objects*' button .

```
Browser("Google").Sync
Browser("Google").InsightObject("txtbxGoogleSearch").Type "UFT"
Browser("Google").InsightObject("btnGoogleSearch").Click
```

Figure 42.12 *UFT code using insight objects*

Snapshots Configuration (When adding Insight objects to OR)

- Option '*Limit test object image margin in snapshot*'—Instructs UFT to limit the snapshot size (area of the screen around the control) when adding a new Insight test object. The margin size can be specified in the Maximum pixels around the image box. If cleared, UFT includes the whole screen in the snapshot.
- Option '*Maximum pixels around the image*'—Instructs UFT the maximum size of the area around the control to include in the snapshot. (maximum value = 1000)
- Option '*Maximum numbers of snapshots to save when recording a test object*'—Instructs UFT not to save more than the specified number of snapshots when recording a test object.

QUICK TIPS

✓ Use Insight mechanism only for applications, environments, or controls that UFT does not recognize.

✓ The Insight recording technology is based on image processing. During a recording session, clicking on control images that contain straight lines may result in the object being recorded incorrectly. Make sure that you click in the center of such objects.

✓ Avoid using insight recording mode as it may result in invalid parent-insight object hierarchy and as well invalid order of steps. This is because UFT does not synchronizes to different windows for Insight recording.

✓ Instead, manually add the insight objects to OR, and then write the UFT code.

✓ Insight mechanism requires more disk space than normal OR approach because of the test object image and the snapshots stored with the test object.

✓ Insight configuration is to be done only once and before starting any automation activity.

INTERVIEW QUESTIONS

1. Explain insight object learning mechanism.
2. Explain insight identification mechanism.
3. Can UFT use the SI mechanism along with insight mechanism to identify objects?
4. Can UFT use the VRI mechanism along with insight mechanism to identify objects?

Section 8 Advanced VBScript

- Windows Scripting
- Working with Notepad
- Working with Microsoft Excel
- Working with Database
- Working with XML
- Working with Microsoft Word
- Working with An E-Mail Client

Chapter 43

Windows Scripting

Microsoft Windows provides a powerful multi-language scripting environment for automating various Windows tasks. For example, *FileSystemObject* provides access to Windows file system, drives, text streams, etc. Again, *Windows Script Host* (WSH) provides access to Windows system admin tasks. This chapter discusses how to access and modify the various Windows system files and administrative tasks.

MANAGING FILES

The *FileSystemObject* provides a number of methods to copy, move, or delete a file.

```
Set oFSO = CreateObject ("Scripting.FileSystemObject")
```

Methods

The followings are the various methods to access and modify various Windows files (Fig. 43.1).

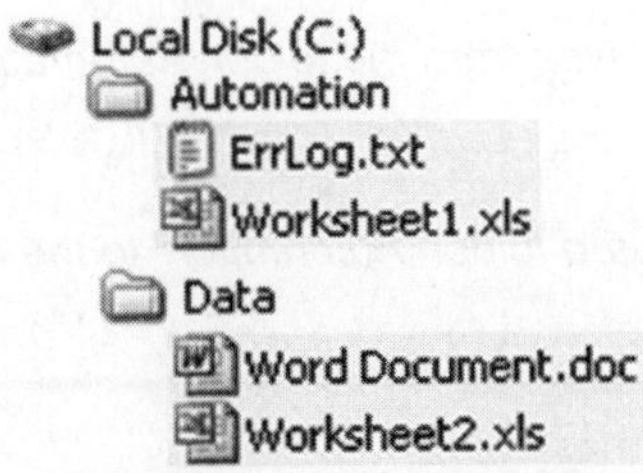

Figure 43.1 *Managing files*

- **GetFile**—This method is used to bind to the specified file.

  Example: Connect to the file ErrLog.txt inside C: \Automation

  ```
  Set oFile = oFSO.GetFile ("C:\Automation\ErrLog.txt")
  ```

- **FileExists**—Check if specified file exists or not.

  Example: Check if the file ErrLog.txt exists inside the folder C:\Automation

  ```
  bExistFlg = oFSO.FileExists ("C:\Automation\ErrLog.txt")
  ```

- **CopyFile**—Copy specified file from source to destination location.

  Syntax : *Object*.CopyFile (*Source*, *Destination*, [optional] Overwrite)

  Example 1: Copy the file ErrLog.txt to location C:\Data

```
oFSO.CopyFile "C:\Automation\ErrLog.txt", "C:\Data\", False
```

  Example 2: Copy and rename the file ErrLog.txt to location C:\Data

```
oFSO.CopyFile "C:\Automation\ErrLog.txt", "C:\Data\LogErr.txt", False
```

> **NOTES** If file with the specified name 'LogErr.txt' already exists, then an error 'File Already Exists' will be thrown. To overwrite the existing file with newly copied file, make overwrite flag 'True.'

  Example 3: Copy all MS Excel files from the folder 'Automation' to the folder 'Data'

```
oFSO.CopyFile "C:\Automation\*.xls", "C:\Data\", True
```

  Example 4: Copy all files from the folder 'Automation' to the folder 'Data'

```
oFSO.CopyFile "C:\Automation\*.*", "C:\Data\", True
```

- **MoveFile**—Move specified file from source to destination location.

  Syntax : *Object*.MoveFile (*Source*, *Destination*)

  Example 1: Move the file ErrLog.txt to the location C:\Data

```
oFSO.MoveFile "C:\Automation\ErrLog.txt", "C:\Data\"
```

  Example 2: Move and rename file ErrLog.txt to location C:\Data

```
oFSO.MoveFile "C:\Automation\ErrLog.txt", "C:\Data\LogErr.txt"
```

  Example 3: Move all MS Excel files from the folder 'Automation' to the folder 'Data'

```
oFSO.MoveFile "C:\Automation\*.xls", "C:\Data\"
```

  Example 4: Move all files from the folder 'Automation' to the folder 'Data'

```
oFSO.MoveFile "C:\Automation\*.* ", "C:\Data\"
```

- **DeleteFile**—Delete specified files.

  Syntax : *Object*.DeleteFile (*FileName*, [optional]*bForceDeleteFlag*)

  Example 1: Delete the file Worksheet1.xls from the folder 'Automation'

```
oFSO.DeleteFile  "C:\Automation\Worksheet1.xls", False
```

> **NOTES** *bForceDeleteFlag* is by default False. If *bForceDeleteFlag* is false and file to be deleted is read only, then an error 'Permission Denied' will be thrown. In order to force delete a file, make this flag True.

Example 2: Delete all files with name substring 'Err' from the folder 'Automation'

```
oFSO.DeleteFile  "C:\Automation\*Err*.*", True
```

Example 3: Delete all .xls files from the folder 'Automation'

```
oFSO.DeleteFile "C:\Automation\*.xls", True
```

Example 4: Delete all files from the folder 'Automation'

```
oFSO.DeleteFile "C:\Automation\*.* ", True
```

ACCESSING FILE PROPERTIES

The following code demonstrates how to read various properties of a file.

```
Set oFSO = CreateObject("Scripting.FileSystemObject")
Set oFile = oFSO.GetFile("C:\Data\Word Document.doc")
Print oFile.DateCreated            'Output : 4/23/2010 12:48:04 PM
Print oFile.DateLastAccessed       'Output : 4/23/2010 12:48:22 PM
Print oFile.DateLastModified       'Output : 4/23/2010 12:48:22 PM
Print oFile.Drive                  'Output : C:
Print oFile.Name                   'Output : Word Document.doc
Print oFile.ParentFolder           'Output : C:\Data
Print oFile.Path                   'Output : C:\Data\Word Document.doc
Print oFile.ShortName              'Output : WORDDO~1.DOC
Print oFile.ShortPath              'Output : C:\Data\WORDDO~1.DOC
Print oFile.Size                   'Output : 52224 (Kb)
Print oFile.Type                   'Output : Microsoft Word Document
Print oFSO.GetAbsolutePathName (oFile)    ' Output : C:\Data\Word Document.
                                          doc
Print oFSO.GetParentFolderName (oFile)  'Output : C:\Data
Print oFSO.GetFileName (oFile)          'Output : Word Document.doc
Print oFSO.GetBaseName (oFile)          'Output : Word Document
Print oFSO.GetExtensionName (oFile)     'Output : doc
Set oFSO = Nothing
```

MANAGING FOLDERS

The *FileSystemObject* can be used to retrieve information about folders present in disk drive. The *FileSystemObject* provides a number of methods to copy, move, or delete a folder. In Windows shell, folders are *Component Object Model* (*COM*) objects. This implies an object reference needs to be created to access folder properties.

```
Set oFSO = CreateObject ("Scripting.FileSystemObject")
```

Methods

The followings are the various methods to access and modify various Windows folders (Fig. 43.2).

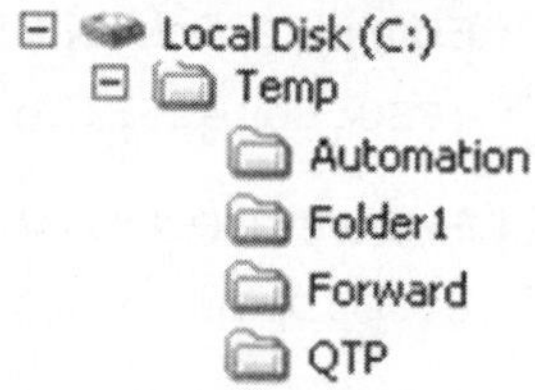

Figure 43.2 *Managing folders*

- **GetFolder**—This method is used to bind to the specified folder

  Example: Bind to the folder 'Temp' in C:\drive

```
Set oFolder = oFSO.GetFolder("C:\Temp")
```

- **FolderExists**—Check if specified folder exists or not.

  Example: Check if the folder 'Temp' exists in C:\drive

```
bFolderExist = oFSO.FolderExists("C:\Temp")
```

- **CreateFolder**—Create a new folder

  Example: Create a new folder 'Automation' inside c:\temp

```
Set oNewFolder = oFSO.CreateFolder("C:\Temp\Automation")
```

- **CopyFolder**—Copy specified folder, its sub folders, and files to destination location.

  Syntax: *Object*.CopyFolder (*Source*, *Destination*, [optional] Overwrite)

  Example 1: Copy the folder C:\Temp\Automation to C:\Log

```
oFSO.CopyFolder "C:\Temp\Automation", "C:\Log", False
```

> NOTES: If the folder 'Log' already exists and overwrite flag is 'False,' then an error 'File Already Exists' will be thrown. If the folder 'Log' does not exist, then a folder 'Log' will be created all source folder and its data will be moved to destination folder. Mark the overwrite flag as 'True,' if the folder 'Log' already exists. The data of the folder 'Log' will remain as it is and the specified folders will be copied to it.

Example 2: Copy all folders with name starting with 'Fo' to the folder C:\Log

```
oFSO.CopyFolder "C:\Temp\Fo*", "C:\Log", True
```

> NOTES: CopyFolder copies all the subfolders and their files of parent folder to destination location. Wild characters can be used to copy specific folders only.

- **MoveFolder**—Move specified folder, its sub folders, and their files to destination location.

  Syntax : *Object*.MoveFolder (*Source*, *Destination*)

  Example: Move all folders from location C:\temp\Automation to the location C:\NewLog

```
oFSO.MoveFolder "C:\Temp\Automation", "C:\NewLog"
```

Example: Rename the folder 'Automation' as 'Test Automation'

```
oFSO.MoveFolder "C:\Temp\Automation", "C:\Temp\Test Automation"
```

- **DeleteFolder**—Delete specified folder.

  Syntax : *Object*.DeleteFile (*FileName*, [optional]*bForceDeleteFlag*)

  Example 1: Delete the folder 'Automation' inside the location C:\temp

  ```
  oFSO.DeleteFolder("C:\Temp\Automation")
  ```

> **NOTES** *bForceDeleteFlag* is by default False. If file to be deleted is read-only, then an error 'Permission Denied' will be thrown. In order to force delete a folder, make this flag True.

Example 2: Delete all folders with name starting with 'Fo' inside the folder 'Temp'

```
oFSO.DeleteFolder "C:\Temp\Fo*", True
```

ACCESSING FOLDER PROPERTIES

The following code demonstrates how to read various properties of a folder.

```
Set oFSO = CreateObject("Scripting.FileSystemObject")
Set oFolder = oFSO.GetFolder("C:\Temp\Test Automation")
Print oFolder.DateCreated          'Output : 4/20/2010 4:28:24 PM
Print oFolder.DateLastAccessed     'Output : 4/20/2010 4:29:51 PM
Print oFolder.DateLastModified     'Output : 4/20/2010 4:28:24 PM
Print oFolder.Drive                'Output : C:
Print oFolder.IsRootFolder         'Output : False
Print oFolder.Name                 'Output : Test Automation
Print oFolder.ParentFolder         'Output : C:\Temp
Print oFolder.Path                 'Output : C:\Temp\Test Automation
Print oFolder.ShortName            'Output : TESTAU~1
Print oFolder.ShortPath            'Output : C:\Temp\TESTAU~1
Print oFolder.Size                 'Output : 10752 (Kb)
Print oFolder.Type                 'Output : File Folder
Set oFSO = Nothing
```

ENUMERATING FILES AND FOLDERS

The *Folder* object has *SubFolders* and *Files* property that returns collection of all the sub folders and files inside a folder, respectively.

Enumerating Folders

Example 1: Find all the folders inside the folder 'Folder' (refer Fig. 43.3).

```
Set oFSO = CreateObject("Scripting.FileSystemObject")
Set oFolder = oFSO.GetFolder("C:\Temp\Folder")
Set colSubfolders = oFolder.Subfolders
For Each oSubfolder in colSubfolders
      Print oSubfolder.Name & vbTab & oSubfolder.Path
Next
```

Enumerating Sub Folders

Example 2: Find all the sub folders inside the folder 'Folder' (Figs. 43.4 and 43.5).

```
Set dicFolder = CreateObject("Scripting.Dictionary")
Set FSO=CreateObject("Scripting.FileSystemObject")
Set oFolder = FSO.GetFolder("C:\Temp\Folder")
Call fnShowSubfolders(oFolder, dicFolder )
Function fnShowSubFolders(oFolder, dicFolder)
```

Figure 43.3 *Enumerating folders*

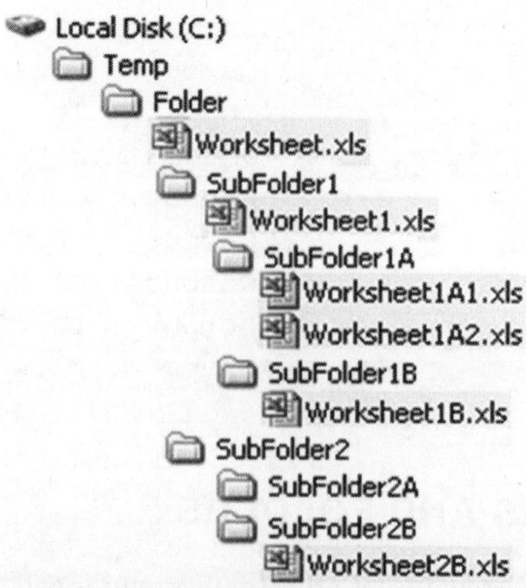

Figure 43.4 *Enumerating folders and files*

dicFolder.keys	<Array>
(0)	"SubFolder1"
(1)	"SubFolder1A"
(2)	"SubFolder1B"
(3)	"SubFolder2"
(4)	"SubFolder2A"
(5)	"SubFolder2B"

dicFolder.items	<Array>
(0)	"C:\Temp\Folder\SubFolder1"
(1)	"C:\Temp\Folder\SubFolder1\SubFolder1A"
(2)	"C:\Temp\Folder\SubFolder1\SubFolder1B"
(3)	"C:\Temp\Folder\SubFolder2"
(4)	"C:\Temp\Folder\SubFolder2\SubFolder2A"
(5)	"C:\Temp\Folder\SubFolder2\SubFolder2B"

Figure 43.5 *Sub folders name and path as viewed in debug tab*

```
  For Each oSubfolder in oFolder.SubFolders
     dicFolder.Add oSubfolder.Name, oSubfolder.Path
     Call fnShowSubfolders(oSubfolder, dicFolder)
  Next
End Function
```

Enumerating Files Inside Sub Folders

Example 3: Find all MS Excel files inside the folder 'Folder' and its sub folders (Fig. 43.6).

```
Set dicFolder = CreateObject("Scripting.Dictionary")
Set oFSO = CreateObject("Scripting.FileSystemObject")
Set oFolder = oFSO.GetFolder("C:\Temp\Folder")
Call fnFindSubfolders (oFSO, oFolder, dicFolder )

Function fnFindSubfolders (oFSO, oFolder, dicFolder)
  For Each oFile in oFolder.Files
       If  oFSO.GetExtensionName (oFile) = "xls"  Then
           dicFolder.Add oFile.Name, oFile.Path
       End If
  Next
  For Each oSubfolder in oFolder.SubFolders
        Call fnFindSubfolders (oFSO, oSubfolder, dicFolder)
  Next
End Function
```

dicFolder.keys	<Array>	dicFolder.items	<Array>
(0)	"Worksheet.xls"	(0)	"C:\Temp\Folder\Worksheet.xls"
(1)	"Worksheet1.xls"	(1)	"C:\Temp\Folder\SubFolder1\Worksheet1.xls"
(2)	"Worksheet1A1.xls"	(2)	"C:\Temp\Folder\SubFolder1\SubFolder1A\Worksheet1A1.xls"
(3)	"Worksheet1A2.xls"	(3)	"C:\Temp\Folder\SubFolder1\SubFolder1A\Worksheet1A2.xls"
(4)	"Worksheet1B.xls"	(4)	"C:\Temp\Folder\SubFolder1\SubFolder1B\Worksheet1B.xls"
(5)	"Worksheet2B.xls"	(5)	"C:\Temp\Folder\SubFolder2\SubFolder2B\Worksheet2B.xls"

Figure 43.6 *Excel sheets name and path as viewed in debug tab*

Enumerating Files Inside a Drive

Example 4: Find all files inside C:\ drive.

```
Set oFSO = CreateObject ("Scripting.FileSystemObject")
Set oFiles = oFSO.Drives ("C:").RootFolder.Files
For each oFile in oFiles
    Print oFile.Name & vbTab & oFile.Path
Next
```

CONNECTING TO NETWORK COMPUTERS

Windows Management Interface (WMI) allows us to connect to remote machine and retrieve information about it. It can also be used to execute commands on remote machine. However, remote machine needs to be configured to service WMI requests.

Enumerating Files Inside a Folder

WMI can be used to enumerate through files and folders on network computers.

Example 1: Connect to remote machine and find all files inside the folder 'Folder.'

```
Dim sComputer

sComputer = "RemoteMachineName"

Set objWMIService = GetObject("winmgmts:" &_
                    "{impersonationLevel=impersonate}!\\" &_
                    sComputer & "\root\cimv2")

Set colFile = objWMIService.ExecQuery ("ASSOCIATORS OF " &_
                    "{Win32_Directory.Name='C:\Temp\Folder'} " &_
                    "Where ResultClass = CIM_DataFile")

For Each oFile In colFile
   Print oFile.Name
Next
```

NOTES: If sComputer value is replaced with '.' then, the code will execute on local machine.

Windows Task Manager

WMI can be used to retrieve information from remote machine's Windows Task Manager, viz., the number of process running, name, memory usage, and the CPU usage of running process, etc.

Example 2: Find whether QTP application is open on local machine or not.

```
'Specify computer name. Dot symbol is used to refer
' local computer. For accessing remote computer, specify computer's name
sComputer = "."
'Access local system
Set oWmi = GetObject("winmgmts:{impersonationLevel=impersonate}!\\" &
sComputer & "\root\cimv2")

'Find QTP application is open or not
Set colProcessList = oWmi.ExecQuery("Select * from Win32_Process Where
Name = 'QTPro.exe'")

If colProcessList.Count >= 1 Then
        MsgBox "QTP application is open."
Else
        MsgBox "QTP application is not open."
End If
```

Example 3: Find memory usage and average CPU usage of QTP application on local machine.

Code below shows how to find out whether a remote or local QTP machine is executing a test script or not. If a QTP machine is idle then its CPU usage is zero. And if a QTP machine is busy executing a script then the CPU usage is a non-zero value.

```
'Specify remote machine to access
sComputer = "RemoteMachineName"'Specify'.'for accessing local machine
Set oWmi = GetObject("winmgmts:{impersonationLevel=impersonate}!\\" &
sComputer & "\root\cimv2")

'Find QTP application is open or not
Set colProcessList = oWmi.ExecQuery("Select * from Win32_Process Where
Name = 'QTPro.exe'")

'If QTP application is Open, find its CPU usage for a period of time
If colProcessList >=1 Then
   For nCntr = 1 To 30 Step 1
      'Find CPU usage by QTP at any given instant
      Set colSettings = oWmi.ExecQuery("Select * from Win32_
      PerfFormattedData_PerfProc_Process Where Name='QTPro'", , 48)
      For Each objItem In colSettings
         If objItem.Name = "QTPro" Then
            'Add all CPU usage value obtained over various instants.
            nAppCpuUsage = nAppCpuUsage + objItem.PercentProcessorTime
         End If
      Next
   Next
End If
nAppCpuUsage = nAppCpuUsage / 30

MsgBox "CPU Usage of QTPro is " & nAppCpuUsage
```

In the code above, it can be observed that CPU usage of QTPro has been calculated for a period of time and not for any single instant. This is because at any given instant the CPU usage of QTPro can be zero though QTP is running. This is because the operating system might be processing another application request at that moment.

Windows Environment Variables

Example 1: Retrieve the value of Windows environment variable TEMP.

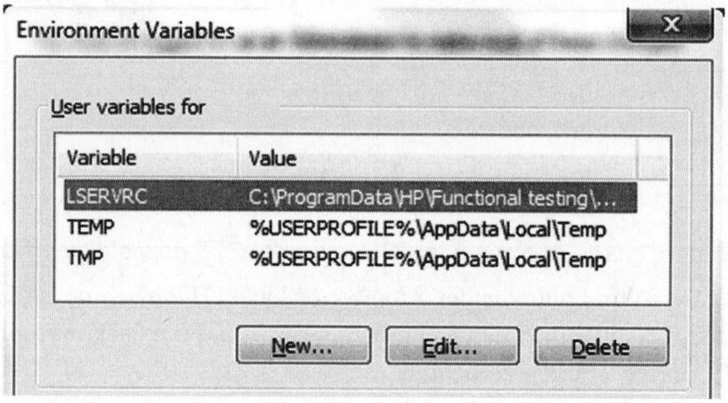


```
Set oShell = CreateObject("WScript.Shell")
Set colEnvironment = oShell.Environment("SYSTEM")
MsgBox colEnvironment("Temp")

' Alternatively,
MsgBox oShell.ExpandEnvironmentStrings("TEMP=%TEMP%")

Set colEnvironment = Nothing
Set oShell = Nothing
```

Example 2: Add QTP bin folder to Windows PATH environment variable.

Code below shows how to add the QTP 'bin' folder path to the system environment variable 'PATH'

```
'QTP folder path
sAppendPath = "C:\QTP\bin"

Set oShell = CreateObject("WScript.Shell")

'Create an object that can access system environment variables
Set oSystemEnv = WshShell.Environment("SYSTEM")

'Append QTP folder path
oSystemEnv("Path") = oSystemEnv("Path") & sAppendPath
```

How to Prevent System from Locking

It is often observed that QTP scripts start failing for certain applications if the QTP machine is locked. In order to prevent auto-locking of the QTP machine, the code shown below can be used. This code can be executed as a .bat or .vbs file.

```
Do While True
    Set oIE = CreateObject("InternetExplorer.Application")
    Wscript.Sleep 1000
    oIE.Quit
    Set oIE = Nothing
    Wscript.Sleep 60000
Loop
```

WINDOWS SCRIPT HOST (WSH)

WSH is a powerful multi-language scripting environment ideal for automating system administration tasks. It is a feature of Microsoft Windows family of operating system. It is a program that provides an environment in which users can execute scripts in a variety of languages, and languages that use a variety of object model to perform tasks. Scripts running in the WSH environment can leverage the power of WSH objects and other COM-based technologies that support automation, such as Windows management instrumentation (WMI) and active directory service interfaces (ADSI), to manage the Windows subsystems that are central to many system administration tasks. WSH provides several objects for direct manipulation of script execution, as well as helper functions for to accomplish various tasks such as printing messages on screen, mapping network drives, connecting to printers, retrieving and modifying environment variables, modifying registry keys, and emulating keyboard events.

The following script creates a new instance of the ADSI System Information object. The code uses this instance to find the domain name and username of the logged on user.

```
Set oSysInfo = CreateObject("ADSystemInfo")
MsgBox "Domain DNS name : " & oSysInfo.DomainDNSName
MsgBox "Domain Username : " & oSysInfo.UserName
```

Scheduling Script Execution

In test automation, it is often required to execute certain tasks (scripts) continuously as per prescribed schedule. The ability to run scripts without the need for any human intervention is one of the major advantages of automation scripting. The following code shows schedule execution of the file StartQTP.vbs at 12:30 PM every Monday, Wednesday, and Friday.

```
Set oService = GetObject("winmgmts:")
Set oJob = oService.Get("Win32_ScheduledJob")
oNewJob.Create _
    ("Wscript Z:\Utility\StartQTP.vbs", "********123000.000000-420", _
                                        True , 1 OR 4 OR 16, , , JobID)
```

Tasks can also be scheduled on remote machines using the following code. The following code schedules Notepad to run at 12:30 PM every Monday, Wednesday, and Friday.

```
strComputer = "RemoteMachine1" '\\158.66.33.258
Set objWMIService = GetObject("winmgmts:" _
   & "{impersonationLevel=impersonate}!\\" & strComputer &
                                          "\root\cimv2")
Set objNewJob = objWMIService.Get("Win32_ScheduledJob")
errJobCreated = objNewJob.Create _
   ("Notepad.exe", "********123000.000000-420", _
       True , 1 OR 4 OR 16, , , JobID)
```

Simulating Keyboard Events

The following code shows how to simulate the keyboard events. This code continuously presses *NumLock* key on/off to prevent the system from locking (auto lock). The continuous on/off of *NumLock* key prevents screen saver from getting activated.

AvoidSysremL3ock.vbs

> **NOTES** WScript object and methods are not supported by QTP. The above-mentioned code can be executed from a VBScript (.vbs) file.

```
Do While True
   Set oShell = CreateObject("WScript.Shell")
   oShell.SendKeys "{NUMLOCK}"
   Set oShell = Nothing
   Wscript.Sleep 60000
Loop
```

Timed Pop-up Window

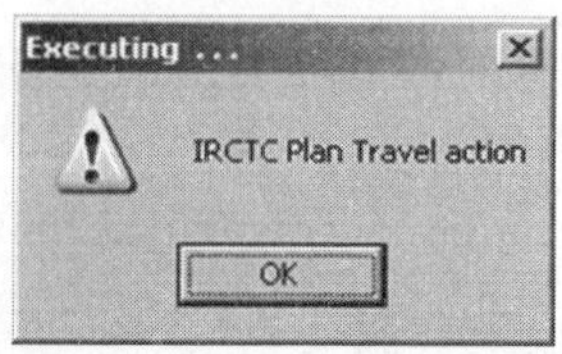

The *Pop-up* method of WScript object displays a timed text in a pop-up message box. Timed pop-up message boxes are used in test automation to convey specific information to user without involving any manual interference. Information such as business/test scenario currently executing, pass/fail status of test case, and percentage execution can be displayed in timed pop-up message boxes. The following function displays a user-defined message in a pop-up message box for 2 s. After 2 s, the pop-up message box automatically closes.

```
Call fnPopupMsg("IRCTC Plan Travel action")
Function fnPopupMsg(sMsg)
```

```
    Set WshShell = CreateObject("WScript.Shell")
    nBtnClkVal = WshShell.popup(sMsg, 2, "Executing ...", 0 + 48)
    Set objWshShell = Nothing
End Function
```

System Computer Name and Username

```
Set oWshNet = CreateObject("Wscript.Network")
'Find local computer name
sLocalCompName = oWshNet.ComputerName
'Find user logged on
sLocalCompUser = oWshNet.UserName
Set oWshNet = Nothing
```

WINDOWS API (APPLICATION PROGRAMMING INTERFACE)

An Application Programming Interface (API) is a code interface that a program library provides in order to support requests for services to be made of it by a computer program. Windows API is Microsoft's core set of APIs available in the Microsoft Windows Operating System. It is set of pre-defined Windows standard functions and procedures used to control the appearance and behavior of every element of Windows such as desktop outlook and memory allocation.

Extern Object

Windows APIs can be used in QuickTest environment using *Extern* object.

```
Syntax : Extern.Declare (RetType, MethodName, LibName, Alias
[, ArgType(s)])
```

RetType—Data type of the value returned by the method
Method Name—Any valid procedure name
LibName—Name of the DLL that contains the declared procedure
Alias—Name of the procedure in the DLL. If Alias name is an empty string, MethodName is used as Alias
ArgType(s)—List of data types of the arguments that are passed to the procedure.

Example 1: Retrieve the value of Windows environment variable TEMP.

```
'Declare windows environment variable
Extern.Declare micLong, "GetEnvVar" , "kernel32.dll", "GetEnvironment Variable", _
                                     micString, micString+micByRef, micLong

'Get TEMP environment variable value
Extern.GetEnvVar "TEMP" , sEnvVal , 255

MsgBox sEnvVal
```

Example 2: Write code to allow QTP to wait till cursor is displayed as hour glass on the screen (or halt QTP script execution till page has properly loaded).

```
Extern.Declare micLong, "GetForegroundWindow", "user32.dll",
"GetForegroundWindow"
```

```
Extern.Declare micLong, "GetCurrentThreadId", "kernel32.dll",
"GetCurrentThreadId"
Extern.Declare micLong, "GetCursor", "user32.dll", "GetCursor"
Extern.Declare   micLong,   "GetWindowThreadProcessId",   "user32.dll",
                          "GetWindowThreadProcessId", micLong, micLong
Extern.Declare micLong, "AttachThreadInput", "user32.dll",
                        "AttachThreadInput", micLong, micLong, micLong

nCursorId = 65575

'Click on link
Browser().Page().Link().Click

'Loop till normal cursor style is displayed on screen
While n CursorId = 65575
   nCursorId  = fnCursor
Wend

Function fnCursor()
   hwnd = Extern.GetForegroundWindow()
   nPID = Extern.GetWindowThreadProcessId(hwnd, NULL)
   nThreadId = Extern.GetCurrentThreadId()
   Extern.AttachThreadInput nPID, nThreadId, True
   fnCursor = Extern.GetCursor()
   Extern.AttachThreadInput nPID, nThreadId, False
End Function
```

QUICK TIPS

- ✓ The 'FileSystemObject' provides a number of methods to copy, move, or delete a file or folder.
- ✓ The 'FileSyatemObject' can be used to access file or folder properties such as file creation date and created by.
- ✓ Windows Script Host (WSH) is a powerful multi-language scripting environment ideal for automating system administration tasks.
- ✓ The 'Pop-up' method of WScript object displays a timed text in a pop-up message box.
- ✓ WMI allows us to connect to remote machine and retrieve information about it.

PRACTICAL QUESTIONS

1. Write a code to find all MS Word files inside a folder.
2. Write a code to find all the VBScript (.vbs) files inside c:\drive. In addition, find out the complete path of each and every file.

3. Write a code to delete a file.
4. Write a code to find out the creation date of an MS Excel file.
5. An unsaved MS Excel file is already open on the screen. Write a code to extract the contents of the file and save it at the location c:\temp.
6. Write a code to schedule QTP test script execution.
7. Write a code to prevent auto machine.
8. Write a code to read 'TEMP' variable value of Windows environment file.
9. Write a code to add QTP bin folder to Windows PATH environment variable.
10. Write a code to allow QTP to wait till cursor is displayed as hour glass on the screen.

Chapter 44

Working with Notepad

Notepad is a basic text editor used to create simple documents. In test automation, Notepad can be used to store script execution status flags, error logs, or any other information relevant to automation. In addition, we can use QuickTest to extract information from the Notepad files created by AUT.

METHODS

The following are the various methods of the Notepad application object.

- **CreateTextFile**—It creates a specified file name and returns a TextStream object that can be used to read from or write to the file.

  ```
  Syntax : Object.CreateTextFile (FileName, bOverwriteFlag)
  FileName specifies the file to create
  bOverwriteFlag If this is set to True, then existing file will be
        overwritten.
  ```

  Example: Write code to create a new Notepad file.

  ```
  Set oFSO = CreateObject("Scripting.FileSystemObject")
  Set oNtpdFile = oFSO.CreateTextFile("C:\Temp\testfile.txt", True)
  ```

- **OpenTextFile**—It opens an existing Notepad file and returns a TextStream object that can be used to read, write, or append data to the file.

  ```
  Syntax:
  Object.OpenTextFile (FileName, [IOMode][,CreateNew][,Format])
  FileName Notepad file to be opened
  IOMode   Optional. Can be ForReading(1), ForWriting(2) or
           ForAppending(8).
  CreateNew Optional. If marked True creates a new file, if the specified
           file does not exist.
  Format   Optional. Indicates format of the opened file—Unicode, ASCII,
           or system default.
  Values can be TristateTrue, TristateFalse, or TristateUseDefault.
  ```

Example: Write code to open Notepad for appending data to it.

```
Set oNtpdFile = oFSO.OpenTextFile("C:\Temp\test.txt", ForAppending,
                                                        False)
```

- **Read**—It retrieves a specified number of characters from a TextStream file and returns the resulting string.

  Syntax : *Object*.Read (*characters*)

Example: Write a code to read the first 7 characters of Notepad file shown in Fig. 44.1.

Figure 44.1 *Notepad file contents*

```
Const nRead = 1
Const nWrite = 2
Const nAppend = 8
Set oNtpdFile = oFSO.OpenTextFile
("C:\Temp\test.txt", nWrite, True)
oNtpdFile.WriteLine "Hello World !!!"
oNtpdFile.WriteLine "Book on Test Automation & QTP"
oNtpdFile.WriteLine "by Rajeev Gupta"
Set oNtpdFile = oFSO.OpenTextFile("C:\Temp\test.txt", nRead)
sData = oNtpdFile.Read(7)                    'Output : "Hello W"
```

- **ReadAll**—It retrieves an entire TextStream file and returns the resulting string.

  Syntax : *Object*.ReadAll

Example: Write a code to read all contents of Notepad file shown in Fig 44.1.

```
Msgbox oNtpdFile.ReadAll
```

- **ReadLine**—It retrieves an entire line (not including the newline character) from a TextStream file and returns the resulting string.

  Syntax : *Object*.ReadLine()

Example: Write a code to read second line of Notepad shown in Fiq 44.1.

```
oNtpdFile.ReadLine
sData  = oNtpdFile.ReadLine 'Output : "Book on Test Automation & QTP"
```

- **Skip**—It skips a specified number of characters when reading a TextStream file.

  Syntax : *Object*.Skip (*characters*)

Example: Write a code to skip the first 6 characters and read rest data of line 1 of notepad file shown in Fig 44.1.

```
oNtpdFile.Skip(6)
sData  = oNtpdFile.ReadLine 'Output : "World !!!"
```

- **SkipLine**—It skips the next line when reading a TextStream file.

  Syntax : *Object*.SkipLine()

Example: Write a code to read lines 1 and 3 of Notepad file shown in Fig 44.1.

```
sDataLine1 = oNtpdFile.ReadLine   'Output : "Hello World !!!"
oNtpdFile.SkipLine
sDataLine3 = oNtpdFile.ReadLine   'Output : "by Rajeev Gupta"
```

- **Write**—It writes the specified string to TextStream file.

  Syntax : *Object*.Write (*string*)

  Example: Write a code to write 'Working with Notepad' text in Notepad file shown in Fig 44.1.

```
Set oNtpdFile = oFSO.OpenTextFile("C:\Temp\test.txt", nWrite, True)
oNtpdFile.Write "Working with Notepad"
```

- **WriteLine**—It writes the specified string and newline character to TextStream file.

  Syntax : *Object*.WriteLine (*string*)

  Example: Write line 'Working with Notepad' text in Notepad file.

```
oNtpdFile.WriteLine "Working with Notepad"
```

- **WriteBlankLines**—It writes a specified number of newline characters to a TextStream file.

  Syntax : *object*.WriteBlankLines(*lines*)

  Example: Write a code to write two blank lines between two lines of text.

```
oNtpdFile.WriteLine "Line1"
oNtpdFile.WriteBlankLines 2
oNtpdFile.WriteLine "Line4"
```

> NOTES: All the existing contents of the Notepad will be lost in case any of the Write methods is used on a file opened in write mode.

- **Close**—It closes an opened TextStream file.

  Syntax : *Object*.Close()

  Example: Write a code to close an already opened Notepad file.

```
oNtpdFile.Close
```

PROPERTIES

The various properties of the Notepad application object are described in the following.

- **AtEndOfLine**—It returns True if file pointer has reached end of line or else returns False.

  Example: Read all characters of the first line of a notepad file.

```
Do While oNtpdFile.AtEndOfLine = False
  Print oNtpdFile.Read(1)
Loop
```

- **AtEndOfStream**—It returns True if file pointer has reached end of file or else returns False.

  Example: Read all contents of Notepad file

```
Do While oNtpdFile.AtEndOfStream = False Then
  Print oNtpdFile.ReadLine
Loop
```

- **Column**—It returns the column number of the current character position in a TextStream file.

  Example: Find column number of character 'l' in 'Hello World!!!' line.

```
Print oNtpdFile.Column                         'Output : 1
oNtpdFile.Skip(9)
Print oNtpdFile.Column                         'Output : 10
```

- **Line**—It returns the current line number in TextStream file.

  Example:

```
Print oNtpdFile.Line                           'Output : 1
oNtpdFile.SkipLine
oNtpdFile.SkipLine
Print oNtpdFile.Line                           'Output : 3
```

CREATING A NEW NOTEPAD FILE

The following code shows how to create a new Notepad file.

```
Set oFSO = CreateObject("Scripting.FileSystemObject")
'Create a new notepad file, if existing overwrite it
Set oNtpdFile = oFSO.CreateTextFile("C:\Temp\testfile.txt", True)
'Write data to notepad file
oNtpdFile.Write "Working with Notepad."
oNtpdFile.Close
```

OPEN AN EXISTING NOTEPAD FILE

The following code shows how to open and read data from an existing Notepad file.

```
Const nRead=1
Set oFSO = CreateObject("Scripting.FileSystemObject")
'Create a new notepad file, if existing overwrite it
Set oNtpdFile = oFSO.OpenTextFile("C:\Temp\test.txt", nRead, False)
'Read data from notepad file
Do While oNtpdFile.AtEndOfLine = False
        Print oNtpdFile.ReadLine
Loop
oNtpdFile.Close
```

APPEND DATA TO AN EXISTING NOTEPAD FILE

The following code shows how to append data to an existing Notepad file.

```
Const nAppend=8
Set oFSO = CreateObject("Scripting.FileSystemObject")
'Create a new notepad file, if existing overwrite it
Set oNtpdFile = oFSO.OpenTextFile("C:\Temp\test.txt", nAppend, False)
```

```
'Append data to notepad file
oNtpdFile.WriteBlankLines 1
oNtpdFile.WriteLine "Data appended to notepad."
oNtpdFile.Close
```

Example: Write a code to take scheduled backup of the automation project.

Like any other development project, automation project code is also susceptible to loss of code because of various reasons such as corruption of files, by mistake deletion of code, or server crash. It is very important to take regular backup of the complete automation project in a backup server to keep the automation tasks alive even in worst conditions. Figure 44.2 shows the utility for taking automatic scheduled backup of the automation project. The utility consists of two batch files – AutomationProjectBackupScript.bat and AutomationProjectBackupDriver.bat. AutomationProjectBackupScript.bat is called by the AutomationProjectBackupDriver.bat to take test automation project backup in a particular server machine. The AutomationProjectBackupScript.bat copies the automation project files to a specific location on the server. The AutomationProjectBackupDriver.bat script triggers the automation backup activity and generates a log file of all the files whose backup is being taken. In case of an error, an error file is generated to help the users analyze the cause of backup failure.

Figure 44.2 shows the two batch files and the project backup log and error log files. 'logThu08052010' is the log file generated for the automation backup taken on May 8, 2010. On May 16, 2010, automation project backup failed, this is the reason why an error log file is generated for this date with name 'errorlogFri16052010.txt.'

Name	Type	Size
AutomationProjectBackupDriver.bat	Windows Batch File	1 KB
AutomationProjectBackupScript.bat	Windows Batch File	1 KB
errorlogFri16052010.txt	Text Document	1 KB
logFri16052010.txt	Text Document	0 KB
logThu08052010.txt	Text Document	94 KB

Figure 44.2 *Automation project backup files*

In order to schedule regular automation project backup, a windows scheduler can be setup to trigger file 'AutomationProjectBackupDriver.bat' at the specified regular intervals. This file when triggered will automatically take the backup of the automation project and will generate the required log files. The log files can be used to identify the success or failure of the automation project backup and also the backup failure reason, if any.

Figure 44.3 shows the code of AutomationProjectBackupScript.bat. This script is triggered by the driver script to take backup of the complete automation project at the specified server location.

Figure 44.4 shows the code of AutomationProjectBackupDriver.bat. This script calls AutomationProjectBackupScript.bat to initiate automation project backup. The script assumes that the server location is \\Server\AutomationBackup\ and the backup utility location is Z:\AutomationBackupUtility\

```
' Current date
Set dt= %DATE%
set newdate=%dt:~1,3%%dt:~5,2%%dt:~8,2%%dt:~11,4%
set newdate=%newdate:~0,12%

' Server path
Set sServerLocation =\\Server\AutomationBackup\Automation%newdate%\

'Copy automation project files to teh server location
xcopy Z:\Automation %sServerLocation% /S /Y
```

Figure 44.3 *Automation project backup script*

```
' server location
CD \\Server\AutomationBackup

' current date
Set dt= %DATE%
set newdate=%dt:~1,3%%dt:~5,2%%dt:~8,2%%dt:~11,4%
set newdate=%newdate:~0,12%

Set LogFile=log%newdate%.txt
set ErrorFile=errorlog%newdate%.txt

' create a log file containg details of the files copied
' in case of an error generate a error log file
' and write to it the backup failure reason
Z:\AutomationBackupUtility\AutomationProjectBackupScript.bat>%LogFile% 2>%ErrorFile%
```

Figure 44.4 *Automation project backup driver script*

AutomationProjectBackupScript.bat. During the backup, this script generates a log file of all the files whose backup has been taken. In case of any error during file copy, a separate error log file is generated.

Figure 44.5 shows the log file generated for the backup taken on May 8, 2010. The log file specifies the date–time and the server location where backup of the automation project has been taken. Next the log file lists all the files which have been copied from the automation project to the backup server.

Figure 44.6 shows the error log file generated for the backup activity executed on May 16, 2010. This file got generated because the automatic project backup failed on that day. The error log file lists down the reason for the failure of the backup task.

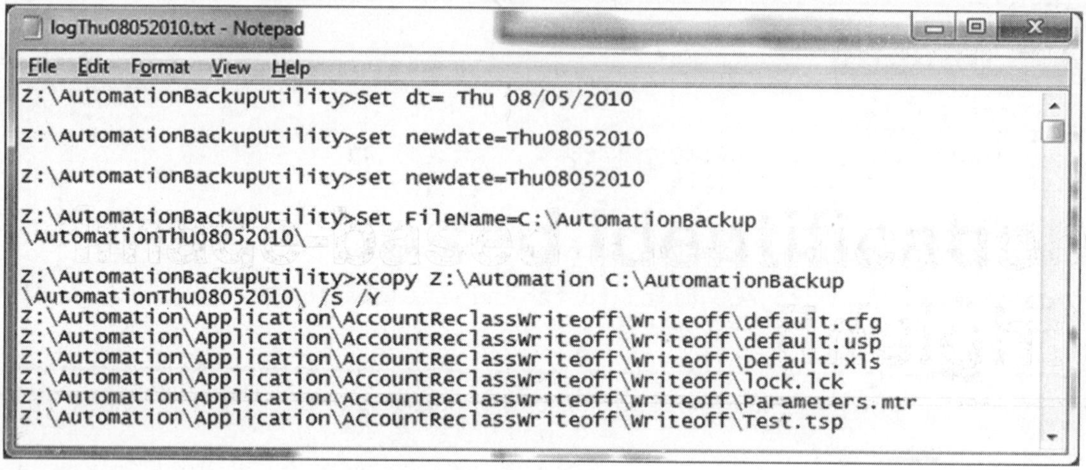

Figure 44.5 *Automation backup report*

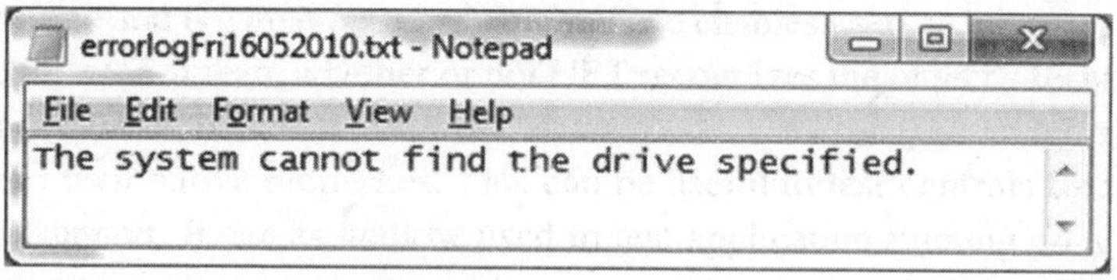

Figure 44.6 *Error log file generated while taking automation project backup*

☞ QUICK TIPS

✓ In test automation, Notepad file can be used for a variety of purposes. For example,

- For maintaining log of test execution
- For defining execution status flags
- For maintaining error logs
- For maintaining logs of automation backup

✓ Notepad file can be accessed in read, write, or append mode.

? PRACTICAL QUESTION

1. Write a code to create a new Notepad file and write to it the test automation project backup details.

Chapter 45

Working with Microsoft Excel

Microsoft Excel is a spreadsheet application developed by Microsoft Corporation for storing, organizing, and manipulating data. It features calculation, graphic tools, pivot tables, and a macro programming language called VBA (Visual Basic for Applications). Generally, in test automation, Excel is used as test data sheets for storing the test input data. There are two ways in which we can access MS Excel file in test automation:

- Excel as workbook
- Excel as database

Excel object model is used to access Excel as workbook. In case of using Excel as database, Excel is treated as any other database such as MS Access and SQL queries are executed on it. In test automation, using MS Excel as database has specific advantages over using Excel as workbook.

EXCEL OBJECT MODEL

The MS Excel object model contains thousands of objects, properties, methods, and predefined, enumerated values. This chapter describes some of the most important items of Excel object model required for test automation. Figure 45.1 shows a part of the MS Excel object model.

The Application object is the root object of the Excel object model. All the other objects in the Excel object model can only be accessed through the Application object.

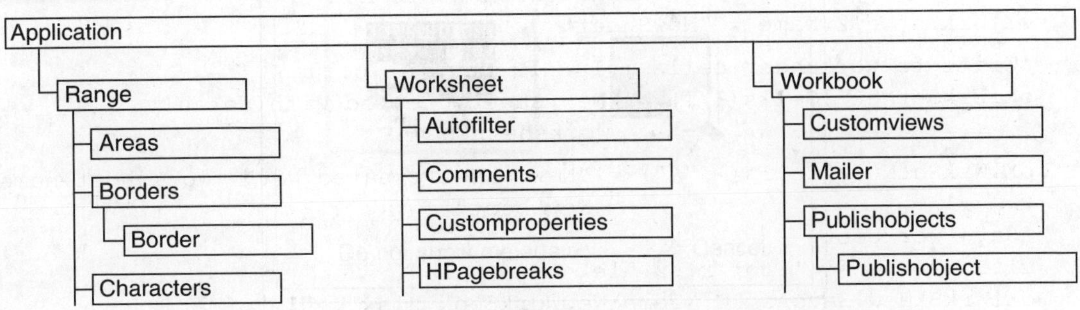

Figure 45.1 *MS Excel object model*

The Workbooks collection represents a collection of currently opened workbooks. Its object represents a single open Excel workbook file containing one or more worksheets. The methods of Workbook allow finding and manipulating the worksheets. The Worksheets collection represents a collection of worksheets in the referenced open workbook. The Worksheet object represents a single worksheet in the referenced open workbook. This object's properties and methods allow manipulating the contents of the worksheet's cells. The Worksheet object's Range property returns a Range object that represents a rectangular block of cells on the worksheet. Range object is used to manipulate groups of data in the Excel sheet.

Creating an Instance of Excel Application

An instance of Excel can be created by creating an object of the Excel application.

```
Set oXlApp = CreateObject("Excel.Application")
'Make excel application visible
oXlApp.Visible = True
MsgBox "Instance of Excel Application created."
'Terminate excel application
oXlApp.Quit
Set oXlApp = Nothing
```

Creating a New Workbook and Worksheet

The Add method of the Excel application object is used to create a new workbook and also to add a new worksheet to a workbook. The following code shows how to create a new workbook and add worksheets to it.

```
Set oXlApp = CreateObject("Excel.Application")
oXlApp.Visible = True
'Create new workbook
Set oXlWrkBkNew = oXlApp.Workbooks.Add
'Add new worksheet to workbook with default name
Set oXlWrkShtNew1 = oXlWrkBkNew.Worksheets.Add
'Add new worksheet to workbook with name 'NewSheet'
Set oXlWrkShtNew2 = oXlWrkBkNew.Worksheets.Add
oXlWrkShtNew2.Name = "NewSheet"
'Write to worksheet cells 1,1 - 1st row, 1st column
oXlWrkShtNew1.Cells(1,1) = "New sheet created with default
                           worksheet name"
oXlWrkShtNew2.Cells(1,"A") = "New sheet created with  worksheet name
                             NewSheet"
'Save workbook
fileFormat = 51 ' for xlsx file
oXlWrkBkNew.SaveAs "C:\Temp\NewWorkBook.xlsx", fileFormat
' To create an excel file use fileFormat=57
```

```
'Close workbook
oXlWrkBkNew.Close
'Terminate excel application
oXlApp.Quit
Set oXlWrkShtNew2 = Nothing
Set oXlWrkShtNew1 = Nothing
Set oXlWrkBkNew = Nothing
Set oXlApp = Nothing
```

> NOTES: SaveAs method will throw error if an Excel file with a specified name already exists at the specified location. Use oXlApp.DisplayAlerts = False to disable Excel overwrite confirmation dialog box. In addition, the SaveAs method is used to save a newly created Excel file while the Save method is used to save an existing Excel file.

Workbook.SaveAs Method

This method allows to save an excel file with a different name of file format.

Syntax

oXlWrkBk.SaveAs(***FileName***, ***FileFormat***, ***Password***, ***WriteResPassword***, ***ReadOnlyRecommended***, ***CreateBackup***, ***AccessMode***, ***ConflictResolution***, ***AddToMru***, ***TextCodepage***, ***TextVisualLayout***, ***Local***)

All the parameters of *SaveAs* method are optional. For example, suppose the requirement is to specify parameter *writerespassword* but not parameter *password*. Code for the same can be written as:

```
oXlWrkBk.SaveAs "C:\Temp\Book.xlsx",51, "passcode"
```

Table 45.1 describes the parameters of the *SaveAs* method.

Open an Existing Workbook

The *Open* method of the Excel application object is used to open an existing workbook. The workbook can be opened in visible or invisible mode. In the visible mode, the workbook is visible on the user screen. The following code first checks whether the specified workbook file exists or not. If the file exists, then it is opened in the visible mode.

```
sFilepath = "C:\Temp\NewWorkBook.xlsx"
Set oXlApp = CreateObject("Excel.Application")
oXlApp.Visible = True
'Check if NewWorkBook.xlsx exists
Set oFSO = CreateObject("Scripting.FileSystemObject")
If oFSO.FileExists(sFilepath) = True Then
    'Open existing  workbook
    Set oXlWrkBk = oXlApp.Workbooks.Open(sFilepath)
Else
```

Table 45.1 Parameters of *SaveAs* method

Name	Description
Filename	A string that indicates the name of the file to be saved.
FileFormat	The file format to use when you save the file. For xlsx file use *XlFileFormat*=51. For a list of valid choices, refer *XlFileFormat* enumeration in Excel Object Browser or refer link - http://msdn.microsoft.com/en-us/library/office/ff198017%28v=office.15%29.aspx.
Password	Case-sensitive protection password for file.
WriteResPassword	If a file is saved with this password and the password isn't supplied when the file is opened, the file is opened as read-only.
ReadOnlyRecommended	**True** to display a message when the file is opened, recommending that the file be opened as read-only.
CreateBackup	**True** to create a backup file.
AccessMode	The access mode for the workbook.
ConflictResolution	An *XlSaveConflictResolution* value that determines how the method resolves a conflict while saving the workbook. If set as *xlUserResolution*, the conflict-resolution dialog box is displayed. If set as *xlLocalSessionChanges*, the local user's changes are automatically accepted. If set as *xlOtherSessionChanges*, the changes from other sessions are automatically accepted instead of the local user's changes. If this argument is omitted, the conflict-resolution dialog box is displayed.
AddToMru	**True** to add the workbook to the list of recently used files. The default value is **False**.
TextCodepage	Ignored for all languages in Microsoft Excel. **Note:** When Excel saves a workbook to one of the CSV or text formats, it uses the code page that corresponds to the language for the system locale in use on the current computer. This system setting is available in the Control Panel, by clicking Region and Language, clicking the Location tab, under Current location.
TextVisualLayout	Ignored for all languages in Microsoft Excel.
Local	**True** saves files against the language of Microsoft Excel (including control panel settings). **False** (default) saves files against the language of Visual Basic for Applications (VBA) (which is typically US English.

```
    'Create new workbook
    Set oXlWrkBk =  oXlApp.Workbooks.Add
    oXlWrkBk.SaveAs sFilepath, 51
End If

'Access worksheet Sheet1
Set oXlWrkSht = oXlApp.ActiveWorkbook.Worksheets("Sheet1")

'write to excel sheet - Sheet1 from cell 1,1 to cell 3,3
Set oRange = oXlWrkSht.Range("A1:C3")
oRange.Formula = "1"
oRange.Font.Bold = True

'Save workbook
```

```
oXlWrkBk.Save
'Close workbook
oXlWrkBk.Close
'Terminate excel application
oXlApp.Quit
```

> **NOTES** Current active worksheet can also be set using sheet occurrence sequence number in workbook. Suppose that there are three sheets Sheet1, Sheet2, and Sheet3, respectively, in a workbook. Then to access Sheet2 without using sheet name, the code will be:
>
> ```
> Set oXlWrkSht = oXlApp.ActiveWorkbook.Worksheets(2)
> ```

Read an Excel Workbook

The Cells method of the workbook/worksheet object is used to read/update data to an Excel file.

The following code opens an existing workbook and reads data from it. Consider the test data sheet of *FillForm* business component as shown in Fig. 45.2. This test data sheet contains test input data such as passenger name, age, sex, berth preference, and senior citizenship eligibility. We can observe that certain parts of the sheet exist as list such as ExecStatus, BusnScnro, Sex, BerthPref, and SeniorCitizen. The purpose of using a list is to avoid any mistakes while entering data in the Excel sheets as the list allows only predefined values to be written to cells. In addition, it makes the test data entry task easier.

```
sFilepath = "Z:\Data\IRCTCBookTicket.xlsx"
Set oXlApp = CreateObject("Excel.Application")
oXlApp.Visible = False
'Open existing workbook
Set oXlWrkBk = oXlApp.Workbooks.Open(sFilepath)
'Access worksheet PassengerDetails
Set oXlWrkSht = oXlApp.ActiveWorkbook.Worksheets("PassengerDetails")
'Read cell 2,7 - 2nd row, 7th column
```

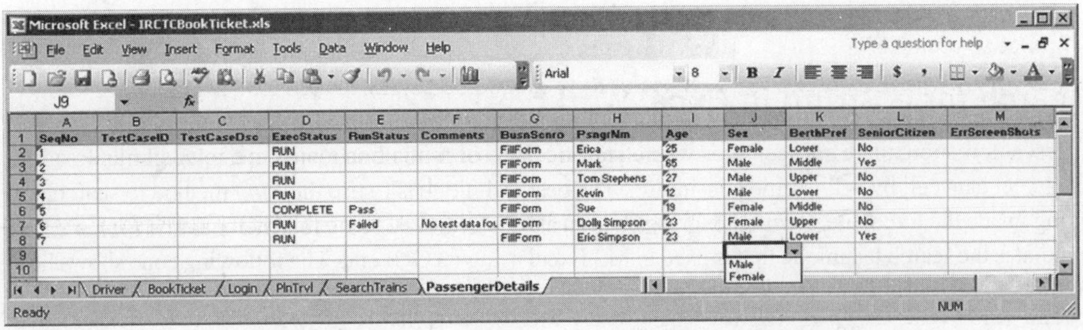

Figure 45.2 *Excel workbook (test cases and test data)*

```
sData = oXlWrkSht.Cells(2,7).Value          'Output : "FillForm"
'Read data from cell 1,1 to 7,12
arrData1 = oXlWrkSht.Range("A1:L7").Value
MsgBox arrData1(6,4)                        'Output : "Complete"
'Read all data of column A to column E
arrData2 = oXlWrkSht.Range("A:E").Value
MsgBox arrData2(6,5)                        'Output : "Pass"
'Close workbook
oXlWrkBk.Close
'Terminate excel application
oXlApp.Quit
```

Write to an Excel Workbook

The Cells method of the workbook/worksheet is used to write to a cell of an Excel file. The following code opens an existing workbook, writes data to it, and saves it.

```
sFilepath = "Z:\Data\IRCTCBookTicket.xlsx"
Set oXlApp = CreateObject("Excel.Application")
oXlApp.Visible = False
'Open existing workbook
Set oXlWrkBk = oXlApp.Workbooks.Open(sFilepath)
'Access worksheet PassengerDetails
Set oXlWrkSht = oXlApp.ActiveWorkbook.Worksheets("PassengerDetails")
'Write text to cell 6,4
oXlWrkSht.Cells(6,4).Value = "RUN"
'Write data from cell 2,2 to 8,3
oXlWrkSht.Range("B2:C8").Value = "TstScenrioFillResvForm"
'Save workbook
oXlWrkBk.Save
'Close workbook
oXlWrkBk.Close
'Terminate excel application
oXlApp.Quit
```

Search for a String in Excel Workbook

In test automation, there are scenarios where specific data needs to be searched in the Excel file. Reading the Excel data cell by cell is time consuming. The best technique is to use the *Find* method to search any string inside the Excel file. Regular expressions can also be searched using this method. The *Find* method simulates the search technique that is used in MS Excel using its GUI end. The following code shows how to find the cell ordinate location of a string in Excel workbook from column A to column C.

```
sFilepath = "Z:\Data\IRCTCBookTicket.xlsx"
Set oXlApp = CreateObject("Excel.Application")
```

```
oXlApp.Visible = False
'Open existing workbook
Set oXlWrkBk = oXlApp.Workbooks.Open(sFilepath)
'Access worksheet PassengerDetails
Set oXlWrkSht = oXlApp.ActiveWorkbook.Worksheets("PassengerDetails ")
'Search for text TstScenrioFillResvForm in excel workbook
Set oFind = oXlWrkSht.Range("A:C").Find("TstScenrioFillResvForm")
If oFind Is Nothing = True Then
            MsgBox "Search string not found"
Else
            nRowNbr = oFind.Row
            nColNbr = oFind.Column
End If
'Find next occurence of text TstScenrioFillResvForm
Set oNextFind = oFind.Next
If oNextFind Is Nothing = True Then
            MsgBox "Search string not found"
Else
            nRowNbr1 = oNextFind.Row
            nColNbr1 = oNextFind.Column
End If
Set oNextFind = oNextFind.Next
Set oNextFind = oNextFind.Next
'Find previous occurence of text TstScenrioFillResvForm
Set oPrevFind = oNextFind.Previous
If oPrevFind Is Nothing = True Then
            MsgBox "Search string not found"
Else
            nRowNbr2 = oPrevFind.Row
            nColNbr2 = oPrevFind.Column
End If
'Close workbook
oXlWrkBk.Close
'Terminate excel application
oXlApp.Quit
```

Replace All Occurrences of a String with Another String in Excel Workbook

The *Replace* method is used to replace a searched string with another string inside the Excel file. The following code replaces all occurrences of string *TstScenrioFillResvForm* with string *FillRevsForm* in the Excel workbook.

```
sFilepath = "Z:\Data\IRCTCBookTicket.xlsx"
Set oXlApp = CreateObject("Excel.Application")
oXlApp.Visible = False
'Open existing workbook
Set oXlWrkBk = oXlApp.Workbooks.Open(sFilepath)
'Access worksheet PassengerDetails (sheet location sequence = 6)
Set oXlWrkSht = oXlApp.ActiveWorkbook.Worksheets(6)
'Find if string TstScenrioFillResvForm exists in workbook
bFind =  oXlWrkSht.Range("A:C").Find("TstScenrioFillResvForm")
'Search for text TstScenrioFillResvForm in excel workbook
If bFind="Some Value" Then
   bReplace = oXlWrkSht.Range("A:C").Replace("TstScenrioFillResvForm",
                                                     "FillRevsForm")
End If
'Save workbook
oXlWrkBk.Save
'Close workbook
oXlWrkBk.Close
'Terminate excel application
oXlApp.Quit
```

Modifying Excel Cell Properties

MS Excel provides methods to modify the cell properties such as font, color, and format programmatically.

Example 1: The following code changes cell text font, text color, and cell background color.

```
'Change text font
oXlWrkSht.Cells(2,5).Font.Size = 12
oXlWrkSht.Cells(2,5).Font.Bold = True
'Change text color
oXlWrkSht.Cells(2,5).Font.ColorIndex = 3
'Change cell background color
oXlWrkSht.Cells(2,5).Interior.ColorIndex =6
```

Example 2: The following code changes the cell format.

```
'Change cell format to General
oXlWrkSht.Range("A:Z").NumberFormat = "General"
'Change cell format to Text
oXlWrkSht.Range("A:Z").NumberFormat = "@"
'Change cell format to Nummeric
oXlWrkSht.Range("A:Z").NumberFormat = "0.00"
```

```
'Hide cell data
oXlWrkSht.Range("A:Z").NumberFormat = ";;;"
```

Example 3: The following code adds formula to a cell.

```
'Add formula to cell to add cell data from cell 1,2 to cell 1,4
oXlWrkSht.Range("A9:A9").Formula = "=Sum(I2:I8)"

'Add formula to find current location of the workbook
oXlWrkSht.Range("A10:A10").NumberFormat = "General"
oXlWrkSht.Range("A10:A10").Formula = "=Cell(""FileName"")"
MsgBox "File Path - " & oXlWrkSht.Cells(10,1).Value
    'Output : "File Path -
    Z:\Data\[IRCTCBookTicket.xlsx]PassengerDetails"
```

Deleting All Blank Rows of a Worksheet

The following code demonstrates how to delete all blank rows of a worksheet. The code first finds used range of rows and columns. Within the used range, if any row is found whose all cells have null value, then that row is deleted.

Syntax : Call fnDelBlankRows(*sFilepath*, *sWorksheet*)

Function input parameters:

sFilepath—Complete path of file
sWorksheet—Worksheet name whose blank rows need to be deleted

Example: Delete blank rows of sheet Login

```
sfnStat = fnDelBlankRows("Z:\Data\IRCTCBookTicket.xlsx", "Login")

Public Function fnDelBlankRows(sFilepath, sWorksheet)
     Dim nLastUsedRow, nLastUsedCol, bFlag
     On Error Resume Next
     Set oXlApp= CreateObject("Excel.Application")
     oXlApp.Visible = False

     Set oXlWrkBk = oXlApp.Workbooks.Open(sFilepath)
     Set oXlWrkSht = oXlApp.ActiveWorkbook.Worksheets(sWorksheet)

     'Find last used row
     nLastUsedRow = oXlWrkSht.UsedRange.Rows.Count

     'Find last column
     nLastUsedCol = oXlWrkSht.UsedRange.Columns.Count

     'Find blank rows
     For iCnt = nLastUsedRow To 1 Step -1
          bFlag = "False"
          For jCnt = nLastUsedCol To 1 Step -1
               If (IsNull(oXlWrkSht.Cells(iCnt, jCnt).value) = "True") or
                    (Trim(oXlWrkSht.Cells(iCnt, jCnt).value) <> "") Then
```

```
            bFlag = "True"
               End If
            Next
          'Delete blank rows
          If bFlag = "False" Then
             oXlWrkSht.Rows(iCnt).EntireRow.Delete
          End If
      Next
      oXlWrkBk.Save
      oXlWrkBk.Close
      oXlApp.Quit
    'Return 0 if function executed successfully, else return error reason
    If Err.Number <> 0 Then
      fnDelBlankRows = Err.description
    Else
      fnDelBlankRows = "0"
    End If
    Set oXlWrkSht = Nothing
    Set oXlWrkBk = Nothing
    Set oXlApp = Nothing
    End Function
```

To Access Data of an Already Opened Excel File

Suppose that an Excel file opens while performing certain task in AUT. Since the Excel file opens dynamically, it does not have path reference in hard disk as it is not yet saved there. In these situations, we can use *GetObject* to get the reference of an already opened file.

```
ReDim arrXlData(2,2)
'Get the reference of opened workbook
Set oXlApp = GetObject(,"Excel.Application")
'Make workbook visible
oXlApp.Visible = True
'Activate workbook
oXlApp.ActiveWorkbook.Activate
'Get the name of opened workbook
sXlFileNm = oXlApp.ActiveWorkbook.FullName
'Get the value of cells(1,1) of currently opened worksheet
Msgbox oXlApp.ActiveWorkbook.ActiveSheet.Cells(1,1)
'Find the total number of worksheets present in workbook
nWrkShtCnt = oXlApp.ActiveWorkbook.WorkSheets.Count
```

```
'Suppose the number of worksheets are 3
'Retrieve the data in Cells(2,2) of 2nd worksheet
MsgBox oXlApp.ActiveWorkbook.WorkSheets(2).Cells(2,2)
'Find second worksheet name
MsgBox oXlApp.ActiveWorkbook.WorkSheets(2).Name
'Retrieve all data  of 3rd worksheet
   'Find used row range
   nUsdRowCnt = oXlApp.ActiveWorkbook.WorkSheets(3).UsedRange.Rows.Count
   'Find used Column range
   nUsdColCnt = oXlApp.ActiveWorkbook.WorkSheets(3).UsedRange.Columns.Count
   'Retrieve data
   ReDim arrXlData(nUsdRowCnt, nUsdColCnt)
   For iCnt=1 To nUsdRowCnt Step 1
      For jCnt=1 To nUsdColCnt Step 1
         sXlData = oXlApp.ActiveWorkbook.WorkSheets(3).Cells(iCnt, jCnt)
         If Trim(sXlData) <> Empty  Then
            arrXlData(iCnt,jCnt) = sXlData
         Else
            arrXlData(iCnt,jCnt) = Cstr(sXlData)
         End If
      Next
   Next
   MsgBox arrXlData(1,3)
```

To Save an Excel File Which Opens Dynamically in Application

In order to save the file that is opened dynamically by the application under test, the *SaveAs* method of the Excel application object is used. The following code shows how to save a dynamically opened Excel file.

```
'Get the reference of opened workbook
Set oXlApp = GetObject(,"Excel.Application")
'Make workbook visible
oXlApp.Visible = True
'Activate workbook
oXlApp.ActiveWorkbook.Activate
'Disable overwrite confirmation u dialog box
oXlApp.DisplayAlerts = False
'Save Workbook
oXlApp.ActiveWorkbook.SaveAs "C:\Temp\ExcelFileNm.xlsx", 51
oXlApp.Quit
```

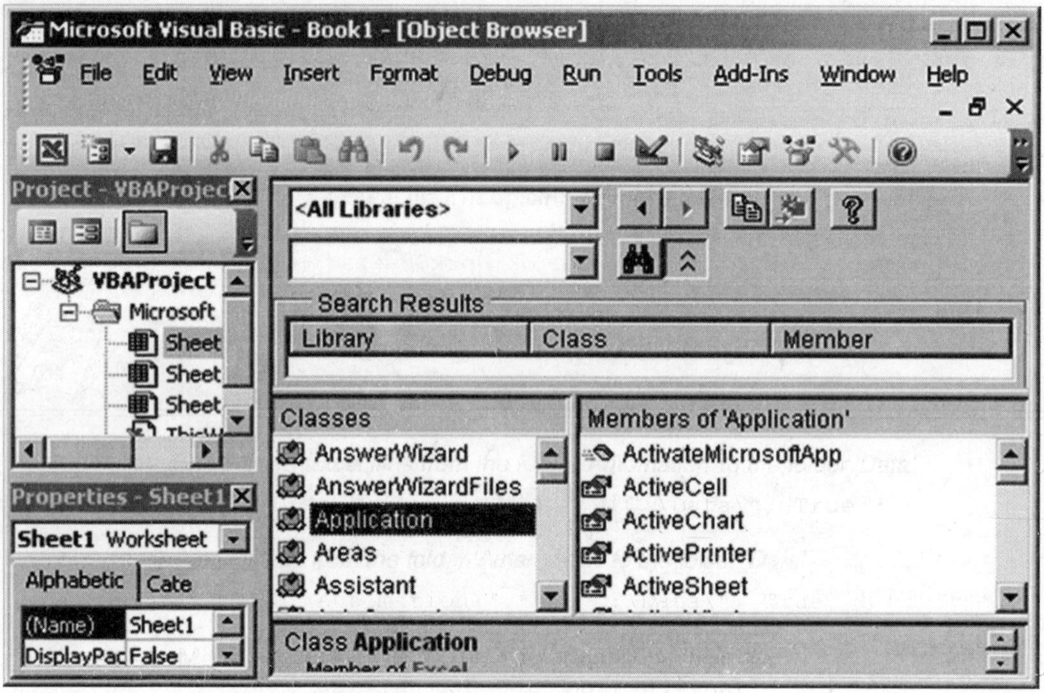

Figure 45.3 *Excel object browser*

EXCEL OBJECT BROWSER

The Excel Object Browser allows browsing through all available objects in the project and seeing their properties, methods, and events. In addition, the users can see the procedures and constants that are available from object libraries in their project (Fig. 45.3).

To navigate the object browser:

1. Open a new/existing Excel file
2. Press ALT+F11. Microsoft Visual Basic script editor will open.
3. Press F2. Object browser window will open.

Excel object browser is helpful in understanding the objects and the methods we can work on in VBScript environment. Knowledge of Excel browser objects helps in converting VBA (Visual Basic for Application) code (Macro code) to VBScript code.

EXCEL AS DATABASE

Access is a good database application but as far as test automation is considered, it is a bit complicated. For test automation, the database should offer the same ease of reading/updating data manually or programmatically. Test automation requires that test input data be defined manually. The features of Excel such as list, sort, and filter come handy and help in easy and fast manual update of the Excel file. In the absence of these features, it becomes a nightmare to update the MS Access database manually.

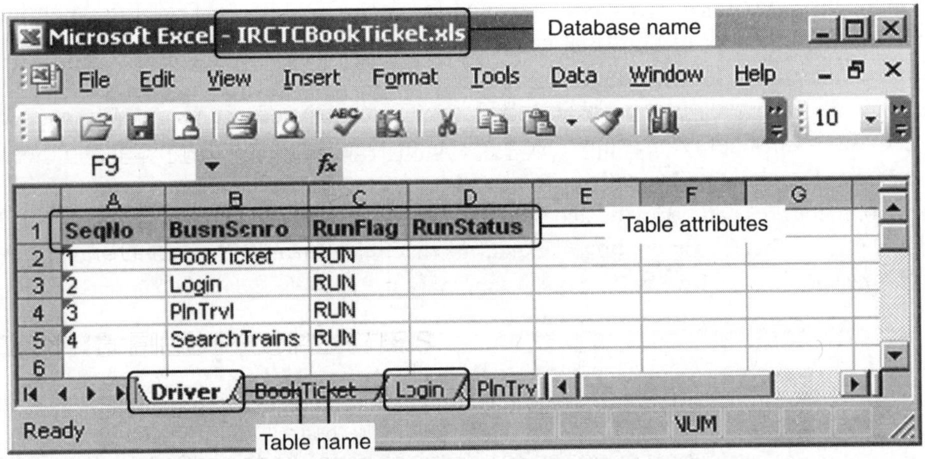

Figure 45.4 *Excel database attributes*

During script execution, the Excel file can easily be updated by executing SQL queries. Moreover, use of Excel as database provides the flexibility to add any number of rows and columns to Excel within the existing columns without impacting the test scripts. Inserting of rows or columns within the existing rows or columns is required to keep the test data file readable and structured. For MS Access, this is not possible and such updates make the Access database complicated and less readable.

Use of Excel as database has specific advantages over use of Excel as workbook. In case of use of Excel as workbook, the addition, deletion or update are all dependent on cell ordinates. So insertion of rows or columns within the existing rows/columns changes the ordinates of the cell. Such ordinate changes require script maintenance. In case of use of Excel as database, these changes have no impact on the script as data access from database is dependent on the database fields and not on the cell ordinates.

In order to use Excel as database, the data inside Excel needs to be structured in the list format. Figure 45.4 shows various database attributes as mapped to Excel sheets.

- Name of the Excel workbook is the Excel database name.
- Sheet name is the table name of the Excel database. Each worksheet represents one table.
- First column of worksheet represents column names.

A database connection needs to be established with the Excel file before data can be read or updated to it. There are two ways to connect to an Excel database:

- ODBC (Open Data Base Connectivity) or DSN (Data Source Name) connection
- DSN-less connection

> **NOTES** It is a good practice to convert Excel sheets into text format, before entering any data to it. After conversion, SQL queries should treat all the fields of Excel database as text format. This helps in avoiding confusion while reading or updating data to Excel database. For defining the table attributes, the restrictions of SQL apply. For example, the attribute name should not contain white spaces and should not start with numeric or special characters.

In DSN connection, a separate DSN is created for each Excel book. Therefore, with increase in Excel database, the number of DSN that needs to be created goes on increasing. Moreover, the DSN needs to be created on all the machines from where the test script is to be executed. This makes maintenance difficult. To overcome this, a DSN-less connection is used to dynamically connect to any Excel database. It does not require any machine-specific setup such ODBC creation. DSN-less connection requires Excel file path and driver name to connect to Excel database. The details once stored in the environment files can easily be accessed by all the test scripts to connect to the Excel database without any prior ODBC setup on the test execution machine. Since, ODBC connection is not recommended for test automation, we will be discussing only the DSN-less database connection technique.

NOTES

- For Excel 2003 or earlier file formats, use the '*Microsoft Jet OLE DB Provider*' for connecting to Excel database.
- For Excel 2007 or later file formats, use the '*Microsoft Office 12.0 Access Database Engine*' for connecting to Excel database. Ensure this program is installed before trying to connect to Excel DB. This program can be downloaded from Microsoft site. Link for MS Excel 2010 DB engine is—http://www.microsoft.com/en-us/download/details.aspx?id=13255. Link for MS Excel 2013 DB engine is—http://www.microsoft.com/en-us/download/details.aspx?id=39358.

DSN-less Connection

In DSN-less connection, ADODB connection can be used to connect to Excel database. Once connection is established, SQL queries can be executed on the Excel database. Results of queries are saved in RecordSet object.

- ADODB connection object is used to create an open connection to a data source
- RecordSet object is used to store SQL query results

Connecting to an Excel file

The following code shows how to open a connection with Excel file.

```
'Create connection object
Set oConn = CreateObject("ADODB.Connection")
'Create recordset  object
Set oRecSet = CreateObject("ADODB.Recordset")
```

XLS File

```
' For Excel 2003 or earlier file formats
With oConn
      .Provider = "Microsoft.Jet.OLEDB.4.0"
      .ConnectionString = "Data Source=Z:\Data\IRCTCBookTicket.
                          xls;" & _
                          "Extended Properties=Excel 8.0;"
      .Open
End With
```

XLSX File

```
' For Excel 2010 or later file formats
 With oConn
     .Provider =  "Microsoft.ACE.OLEDB.12.0"
     .ConnectionString = "Data Source=Z:\Data\IRCTCBookTicket.
                         xlsx;" & _
                         "Extended Properties=Excel 12.0 Xml;"
     .Open End With
 Or,
' For Excel 2010 or later file formats
 With oConn
     .Provider =  "Microsoft.ACE.OLEDB.12.0"
     .ConnectionString =  "Data Source=Z:\Data\IRCTCBookTicket.
                         xlsx;" & _
                       "Extended  Properties=Excel  12.0  Xml;"  &_
                       "HDR=YES"
     .Open End With
 Note: "HDR=YES" indicates that the first column contains column-
 names, not data.  "HDR=NO" indicates the opposite.
```

Treating Excel File data as text

```
 With oConn
     .Provider =  "Microsoft.ACE.OLEDB.12.0"
     .ConnectionString =  "Data Source=Z:\Data\IRCTCBookTicket.
                       xlsx;" & _
                       "Extended  Properties=Excel  12.0  Xml;"  &_
                       "HDR=YES;IMEX=1"
     .Open End With
```

XLSB Files

```
 With oConn
     .Provider =  "Microsoft.ACE.OLEDB.12.0"
     .ConnectionString =  "Data Source=Z:\Data\IRCTCBookTicket.
                       xlsb;" & _
                       "Extended   Properties=Excel   12.0;"   &_
                       "HDR=YES;"
     .Open End With
```

XLSM Files

```
 With oConn
     .Provider =  "Microsoft.ACE.OLEDB.12.0"
     .ConnectionString =  "Data Source=Z:\Data\IRCTCBookTicket.
                       xlsm;" & _
                       "Extended Properties=Excel 12.0 Macro;" &_
                       "HDR=YES;"
     .Open End With
```

Read/Update/Delete Data from Excel (XLSX) File

SQL queries can be used to read/insert/update/delete data from an Excel file. The following code shows how to read, update, and delete data from an Excel database.

Example 1: Read all data corresponding to SeqNo=1 from Driver worksheet as shown in Fig. 45.4.

```
sSql = "Select * from [Driver$] where SeqNo='1'  "
Set oRecSet = oConn.Execute(sSql)
```

Example 2: Insert a New Row of Data Set to Driver Worksheet.

```
sSql = "Insert into [Driver$] (SeqNo, BusnScnro, RunFlag) Values
      ('5','Login', 'RUN' ) "
Set oRecSet = oConn.Execute(sSql)
```

Example 3: Update Field RunFlag with Status COMPLETE for SeqNo=2.

```
sSql = "Update [Driver$] Set RunFlag='COMPLETE' Where SeqNo='2'  "
Set oRecSet = oConn.Execute(sSql)
```

Example 4: Delete Record with SeqNo=2.

```
sSql =  "Delete from [Driver$] where SeqNo='2' "
Set oRecSet = oConn.Execute(sSql)
```

Export Query Result to a Global Array

In test automation, most of the times it is required to access the data returned from the Excel database in multiple test scripts and functions. The best way to make the data returned from SQL queries globally available is to save it in the global arrays and global variables.

The following code shows how to save the query results to global variables and arrays. Function `fnExecuteXlQuery` takes SQL query and Excel file path as input parameters. Excel file path is used to establish an ADODB connection with the specified Excel file. The SQL query is executed on the database through the established Excel database connectivity. The results returned by the database are saved in the global variables and arrays. Let us assume that there are two global variables *nRowCnt* and *nColCnt* and one global two-dimensional array *arrResultSet*. Here,

- *nRowCnt* and *nColCnt* stores the number of rows and columns of data returned by the query, respectively.
- *arrResultSet stores* the results retrieved from the SQL query.

Function `fnExecuteXlQuery` executes a SQL query on Excel database and stores the query results in a global array. The function returns '0,' if the query is successfully executed. Else, it returns error reason.

Input parameters:

```
sSql = SQL query
sFilepath = Complete path of the Excel file
```

Output parameters:

arrResultSet stores the results retrieved from the SQL query.

The function returns '0,' if the query is successfully executed. Else, it returns error reason along with flag '–1.'

```
Syntax : Call fnExecuteXlQuery(sSql, sFilepath)
```

Usage:

Select data from Excel sheet *Driver* where *RunStat* is *RUN*.

```
sSql = "Select SeqNo, BusnScnro from [Driver$] Where RunStat='RUN'
sFilepath = "Z:\Data\IRCTCBookTicket.xlsx"
fnStat = fnExecuteXlQuery(sSql, sFilepath)
MsgBox arrResultSet(2,2)                    'Output : "Login"
```

EnvironmentVariables.vbs

```
Dim arrResultSet(50,30)
Dim nRowCnt, nColCnt
```

Library.vbs

```
Public Function fnExecuteXlQuery(sSql, sFilepath)
    On Error resume next
    Dim nDataCnt, rCnt,cCnt
    nRowCnt = 1
    nColCnt = 1
    rCnt=1
    cCnt=1

    'Clear array
    Erase arrResultSet

    'Create connection object
    Set oConn = CreateObject("ADODB.Connection")
    'Create recordset  object
    Set oRecSet = CreateObject("ADODB.Recordset")

    With oConn
            18. .Provider =  "Microsoft.ACE.OLEDB.12.0"
            .ConnectionString = _
                "Data Source=" & sFilepath & ";" & _
                "Extended Properties=Excel 12.0 Xml;"
            .Open
    End With
    If Err.Number <> 0 Then
        fnExecuteXlQuery=err.description
        Exit Function
    End If

```

```
    'Execute SQL query
    Set oRecSet = oConn.Execute(sSql)
    If Err.Number <> 0 Then
        fnExecuteXlQuery=err.description
        Exit Function
    End If

    'Find returned record count
    nDataCnt = oRecSet.fields.Count

    'Store query result to an array
    If nDataCnt > 0 Then
        Do While Not oRecSet.EOF
            cCnt = 1
            For Each oField In oRecSet.fields
                  'Store column names of table
            arrResultSet(0, cCnt) = oField.Name
            'Store data retrieved from query to an array
            If Trim(oField.Value) <> "" Then
                        arrResultSet(rCnt, cCnt) = oField.Value
            End If
                cCnt = cCnt + 1
            Next
            'Access next record
            oRecSet.moveNext
            rCnt = rCnt + 1
        Loop
    End If

    nRowCnt = rCnt-1
    nColCnt = cCnt-1

    'Close RecordSet object
    If oRecSet.State <> 0 Then
        oRecSet.Close
    End If
    'Close connection
    oConn.Close
    If Err.Number <> 0 Then
         fnExecuteXlQuery = "-1" & err.description
         Exit Function
    End If

    Set oConn = Nothing
    Set oRecSet = Nothing

```

```
75.    'If function executed successfully, return 0 else return error reason
76.    If err.number=0 Then
77.         fnExecuteXlQuery="0"
78.    End If
79. End Function
```

Export Query Results to Dictionary

The code above described how to store the query results to the global variables. Instead of using global variables, Dictionary object can also be used to store query results. The following example shows how to store the data returned by the Excel database in a dictionary.

Function `fnExecXlQueryDic` executes a SQL query on specified Excel database and stores the query result in the specified dictionary object. It has three input parameters—`sSql`, `sFilepath`, and `dicResultSet`.

Input parameters:

`sSql`–`SQL query`
`sFilepath`–`complete path of the Excel file`
`dicResultSet`–`dictionary object`

Output parameters:

dicResultSet stores the results retrieved from the SQL query.
The function returns "0," if the query is successfully executed. Else, it returns error reason along with flag "–1."

Syntax : Call fnExecuteXlQuery(*sSql, sFilepath, dicResultSet*)

```
1. Public Function fnExecXlQueryDic(sSql, sFilepath, dicResultSet)
       Code from line 2 to line 35 will be same as mentioned in function
       fnExecuteXlQuery
36.        'Find returned record count
37.        nDataCnt = oRecSet.fields.Count
38.
39.
40.        dicResultSet.Add 0, CreateObject("Scripting.Dictionary")
41.        dicResultSet(0).Add "ColumnCnt", nDataCnt
42.
43.
44.           'Store query result to an array
45.           If nDataCnt > 0 Then
46.              Do While Not oRecSet.EOF
47.                 'Create dictionary of dictionary object
48.                 dicResultSet.Add rCnt, CreateObject
                    ("Scripting.Dictionary"")
49.                 For Each oField In oRecSet.fields
50.                    'Store data retrieved from query to dictionary
51.                    dicResultSet(rCnt).Add oField.Name, oField.Value
52.                 Next
53.                 oRecSet.moveNext
```

```
54.             rCnt = rCnt + 1
55.         Loop
56.       End If
57.
58.       'Number of rows of data in query result
59.       dicResultSet(0).Add "RowCnt", rCnt-1
60.
61.       'Line 61 to 79 will be same as mentioned in function
          fnExecuteXlQuery
```

Usage:

Extract data from Excel sheet *PassengerDetails* where *ExecStat* is *RUN*.

```
sSql = "Select SeqNo, PsngrNm, Age, Sex, BerthPref, SeniorCitizen from
     [PassengerDetails$] Where ExecStatus='RUN'"
sFilepath = "C:\Automation\Temp\Automation\Data\IRCTCBookTicket.xlsx"
Set dicResultSet = CreateObject("Scripting.Dictionary")
fnStat = fnExecXlQueryDic(sSql, sFilepath,dicResultSet )
nPrimaryRecordCnt = dicResultSet.Count
arrPrimaryKeys = dicResultSet.Keys
nRowCnt = dicResultSet(0).Item("RowCnt")
nColCnt = dicResultSet(0).Item("ColumnCnt")
nSecondaryRecordCnt = dicResultSet(1).Count
arrSecondaryKeys = dicResultSet(1).Keys
arrRow1Items = dicResultSet(1).Items
sRow1PsngrNm = dicResultSet(1).Item("PsngrNm")
```

Figure 45.5 shows values stored in dictionary object and how to retrieve them.

Name	Value
dicResultSet.Count	7
dicResultSet.Keys	<Array>
(0)	0
(1)	1
(2)	2
(3)	3
(4)	4
(5)	5
(6)	6
dicResultSet(0).Item("RowCnt")	6
dicResultSet(0).Item("ColumnCnt")	6

Name	Value
dicResultSet(1).Keys	<Array>
(0)	"SeqNo"
(1)	"PsngrNm"
(2)	"Age"
(3)	"Sex"
(4)	"BerthPref"
(5)	"SeniorCitizen"
dicResultSet(1).Items	<Array>
(0)	"1"
(1)	"Erica"
(2)	"25"
(3)	"Female"
(4)	"Lower"
(5)	"No"
dicResultSet(1).Item("PsngrNm")	"Erica"

Figure 45.5 *dicResultSet values*

Connection to Excel DB Throws Error 'Could not find installable ISAM', How This can be Fixed?

Many times we observe that the code statement *conn,open* throws error 'Could not find installable ISAM'. This could be because of various reasons. Refer the solutions below to resolve this error.

Solution 1

Ensure that MS Excel bit version or Access DB Engine bit version installed is same as the OS bit version. That is, if OS is 64 bit, then MS Excel or Access DB Engine should also be 64-bit. Similarly, if OS is 32-bit, then MS Excel should also be 32-bit.

- OS bit version of Win 7 can be verified as: Open Control Panel and then navigate to System and Security " System.
- Bit version of MS Excel file can be verified as:
    - For Excel 2010, open Excel file and then navigate File → Help. Refer section 'About Microsoft Excel'.
    - For Excel 2013, open Excel file and then navigate File → Account → Office Updates. Refer section 'About Microsoft Excel'.
    - For MS Access DB Engine, refer the installation directory or Add/Remove Programs for bit version installed.

Solution 2

Change the connection string such that 'HDR' is not defined as shown below:

```
With oConn
       .Provider = "Microsoft.ACE.OLEDB.12.0"
       .ConnectionString = _
          "Data Source=" & sFilepath & ";" & _
          "Extended Properties=Excel 12.0 Xml;"
       .Open
End With
```

Above example will also work for 64-bit Win 7 OS and 32-bit MS Excel.

Solution 3

It may happen that the ISAM driver files may be corrupt. In this case, try re-installing the MS Excel or DB Engine after completely removing it from the machine.

Advantages of Using Excel as Database Over Excel as Worksheet/Data Table

	Excel as worksheet	Excel as database
Co-ordinate dependency	Data is retrieved by specifying cell ordinates. Any insertion of row/column in between used rows/columns will change the cell ordinates. Since cell ordinates are hardcoded in test scripts, all the scripts need to be changed to extract the required data.	Data is retrieved using SQL query. Any insertion of row/column in between used rows/columns will not impact data retrieved from SQL query. Because of this, no change in test scripts is required in case of addition/deletion of row/columns of worksheet.

	Excel as worksheet	Excel as database
Memory	Complete worksheet needs to be loaded in memory while reading/writing data from Excel file. If worksheet size is large, test scripts may hang while execution.	A connection is established and data is retrieved using the same connection. Since complete file is not loaded in memory, memory usage is less.
Speed	Data needs to be extracted cell by cell. This slows down the speed of execution. Only one cell can be read/updated at a time.	It generally takes less time to retrieve data using SQL query. Queries can be designed to read/update more then one cell values in one go as per requirement.
Code length	Programming logic needs to be coded to extract specific data from worksheets. For example, to extract *SeqNo* and *BusnScro* from Excel sheet with *ExecStatus=RUN* from excel sheet as shown in Fig. 45.2, extra code logic needs to be written. Most of the times it requires complex and lengthy codes to dynamically filter and sort Excel data as per requirement.	Powerful SQL queries can be designed to retrieve filtered and sorted data from worksheets. Most of the times single line query will be sufficient.
Maintenance	Generally, in test automation data in test data sheets can vary from one regression run to another. For example, in one run, test cases need to be executed with 10 data sets while in another 20. Dynamic handling of these variations is difficult in use of Excel as worksheet, as data retrieval is cell ordinate dependent. The cell ordinate changes with increase or decrease in data sets.	A query to extract all data from worksheets whose *ExecStatus* is *RUN* will not require any dynamic handling. If for one run only 10 data sets are there in Excel sheet for the mentioned condition then all 10 data sets will be retrieved. While for another regression run, if 20 data sets are defined in Excel, then 20 data sets will be retrieved automatically.

Advantages of Using MS Excel vs MS Access as Test Cases and Test Data Set

MS Excel's advantage is its universal usage, comparative ease of use, and quick solutions for simple databases. MS Access needs to be used in case of complex requirements. Test automation requires simple database with good text editing features. Editing features are required in case of manual addition/deletion/updation of test cases and test data in test data set. Excel provides excellent features to make list, sort and filter data, search specific data, etc. These features lower the cost and effort required to maintain test data set. We can create lists in Excel and restrict the data that a user can enter into it. This reduces the chances of manual error and increases efficiency as well (Refer *Sex* column of Fig. 45.2). Multiple data can be easily created using drag features of Excel. In case of Access, each data needs to be entered manually.

☞ QUICK TIPS

- ✓ It is advisable to use MS Excel as data sheet than as compared to MS Access or any other database.
- ✓ Excel object model is used to access Excel as workbook.
- ✓ Accessing MS Excel as database has lot more advantages for test automation than accessing it as workbook.
- ✓ Use DSN-less connection to connect to the Excel database.

? PRACTICAL QUESTIONS

1. Why is it better to use Excel as test data file as compared to any other database?
2. Why is it advisable to access Excel as database than as worksheet in test automation?
3. What is an Excel application object?
4. Write a code to create a new Excel file, write data to it, and save it.
5. Write a code to add worksheet to an existing workbook.
6. Write a code to access data from an already opened MS Excel file.
7. Write a code to retrieve data from an Excel database.

Chapter 46

Working with Database

QTP provides built-in support to databases. Connection to the application database is required to verify the expected results against the actual results. Suppose that we are automating a retail banking Web site, and we need to validate that the transaction amount is equal to the amount debited from the debtor account. In this case, we can directly connect to the AUT database and can match the amount deducted from debtor account to the transaction amount. QTP provides the flexibility to connect to the AUT database using database checkpoint. In this chapter, we will discuss how we can connect to various databases and extract required data from them using Microsoft's ActiveX Data Objects (ADO). ADO is an application programmer's interface (API) that provides developers with an easy way to access and manipulate data of various databases, viz. Oracle, IBM DB2, SQL server, MS Access, MS Excel. etc. In ADO object model there are six objects:

- *ADODB.connection*—The Connection object is used to connect to a database instance.
- *ADODB.recordSet*—The RecordSet object contains query results.
- *ADODB.fields*—The Field object represents individual columns of the RecordSet object.
- *ADODB.error*—The Connection object may have an associated collection of Error objects. ADO utilizes the Error collection objects when the connection returns more than one error at a time. This collection is optional.
- *ADODB.command*—The Command object represents an SQL statement or a stored procedure that is to be executed against a data source. Use of Command object is optional as data can also be extracted directly from the Connection object.
- *ADODB.parameter*—The Parameter collection provides additional information to the data source when executing the command. The Parameter collection is associated with Command object and is optional.

CONNECTION OBJECT

ADODB Connection object is used to create an open connection to a data source. Through this connection, database can be accessed and manipulated.

```
Set oConn = CreateObject("ADODB.Connection")
```

Property

The following are the various properties of the Connection object.

- *ConnectionTimeout*—Set/get the number of seconds to wait while attempting to open a connection to a data source, before cancelling the attempt and generate an error. Default is 15 sec.

  Example: `oConn.ConnectionTimeout = 10`

- ConnectionString—Set/get the details used to connect to a data source

  Example:

  ```
  oConn.ConnectionString = "DataSource=Z:\Data\IRCTCBookTick-
  et.xls; Extended Properties=Excel 8.0; "
  ```

- *Provider*—Set/get the provider name for the specified connection object.

  Example: `oConn.Provider = "Microsoft.Jet.OLEDB.4.0"`

- *Mode*—Set/get the data access permission.

Value	Description
1	Read only access
2	Write only access
3	Read/Write access
4	Prevents others from opening a connection with read permissions
8	Prevents others from opening a connection with write permissions
12	Prevents others from opening a connection
16	Allows others to open a connection with any permissions
3	Read/Write access

  Example: `oConn.Mode = 12`

- *State*—Get the object status, open or closed.

  Example: `sConnStat = oConn.State`

- *CommandTimeout*—Set/get the number of seconds to wait while attempting to execute a command. Default is 30 sec.

  Example: `oConn.CommandTimeout = 10`

Methods

The following are the various methods of the Connection object.

- *Open*—It opens a connection with specified data source.

  ```
  Syntax : ConnectionObject.Open ConnectionString, UserID, Password,
  Options
  ```

Parameter	Description
ConnectionString	Optional. Connection string contains data source connection details separated by semi-colon. Connection Details Provider = Provider name File Name = File path Remote Provider = Name of the provider to open a client-side connection Remote Server = Path name to the server to open a client-side connection URL = Absolute URL address to use for the connection.
UserID	Optional. Data source user name
Password	Optional. Data source password
Options	Optional. Default –1 –1 Opens the connection synchronously 16 Opens the connection asynchronously

Example: `oConn.Open`

- *Execute*—It executes an SQL query or stored procedure. If the query returns any results, then the same will be stored in RecordSet object. If the query returns no results, then a closed RecordSet object will be returned.

  Example: Retrieve all data from worksheet driver

```
'Create RecordSet object
Set oRecSet = CreateObject("ADODB.RecordSet")
Set oRecSet = oConn.Execute("Select * from [Driver$]")
```

- *Close*—It closes an already open connection.

  Example: `oConn.Close`

RECORDSET OBJECT

RecordSet object is used to store the records returned by the database. A RecordSet object consists of records and columns (fields).

```
Set oRecSet = CreateObject("ADODB.RecordSet")
```

Property

The following are the various properties of the RecordSet object.

- *EOF*—It returns True or False depending on whether end of RecordSet object is reached or not.

  Example 1: Print all column names of table present in RecordSet object.

```
Do While Not oRecSet.EOF
        For Each oField in oRecSet.Fields
               Print oField.Name
        Next
        oRecSet.MoveNext
Loop
```

Example 2: Print all data present in RecordSet object.

```
Do While Not oRecSet.EOF
        For Each oField in oRecSet.Fields
               Print oField.Value
        Next
        oRecSet.MoveNext
Loop
```

- *State*—It returns the state of RecordSet object. '1' denotes connection is open. '0' denotes connection is closed.

  Example: `oRecSet.State`

Methods

The following are the various methods of the RecordSet object.

- *Close*—It closes a RecordSet object.

  Example:

```
If oRecSet.State <> 0 Then
      oRecSet.Close
End If
```

Collections

The RecordSet object consists of the following collection objects.

Properties—Collection of provider-specific properties.

Fields—Contains all the field objects in the RecordSet object.

Property

The following are *Fields* collection properties:

- *Count*—It returns the number of items in *Fields* collection. Its index starts at 0.

  Example: `nCnt = oRecSet.Fields.Count`

- *Item*—It returns the specified item from *Fields* collection.
  Syntax : *RecordSetObject*.Fields.Item(*namedItem*)

  Example: `sItemFields = oRecSet.Fields.Item("Name")`

CONNECTION TO A DATABASE

There are two ways to establish connection to a database:

- DSN connection
- DSN-less connection

In DSN connection, Microsoft ODBC wizard is used to create a DSN (Data Source Name) that contains the connection details such as data source name, user name, and password. One DSN can be used to connect to only one database at a time. Therefore, in case we need to work on multiple databases, multiple DSN needs to be created. Moreover, each and every machine which needs to connect to DB server must have a DSN created on them. In DSN-less connection, there is no requirement to create a DSN. Instead, a connection string is designed in VBScript code. This connection string contains details such as data source, user name, and password. This connection string code can be kept in library file and can be parameterized to connect to various databases. DSN-less connection strings is far easier to maintain than DSN connection.

DSN Connection

In DSN connection, ODBC (Open Database Connectivity) wizard can be used to create a DSN (Data Source Name). To create a DSN, perform the following steps:

1. Open the *ODBC Data Source Administrator* dialog box.
2. Click on the button *Add. Create New Data Source* dialog box will opens (refre Fig. 46.1)
3. Select appropriate driver applicable for the database and click the button *Finish*. For example, to connect to Oracle database, select driver the *Microsoft ODBC for Oracle*. Oracle

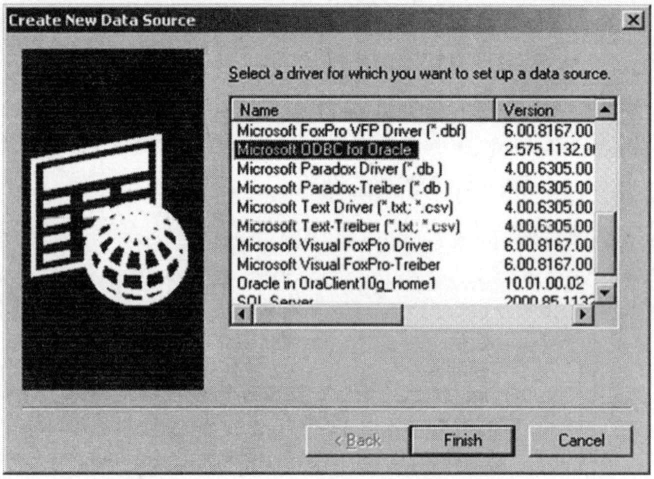

Figure 46.1 *Select driver*

   drivers such as *Oracle in OraClient10g_home1* can also be used.
4. Depending on the driver selected, a driver configuration setup window opens (Fig. 46.2). In this window, we need to provide a data source name, location, user name, password, etc. Various connection settings such as connection timeout can also be set in this window. For Oracle specific driver, the *Oracle ODBC Driver Configuration* window will open.
5. Click on the *Test Connection* button, if available, to test the connection.
6. If connection is successful a connection successful message appears on the screen (as shown in Fig. 46.2) else an error message appears. Click on the 'Ok' button. The newly created DNS appears as shown in Fig. 46.3.

Building Connection Strings

ConnectionString is one of the properties of Connection object that defines connection details as discussed earlier.

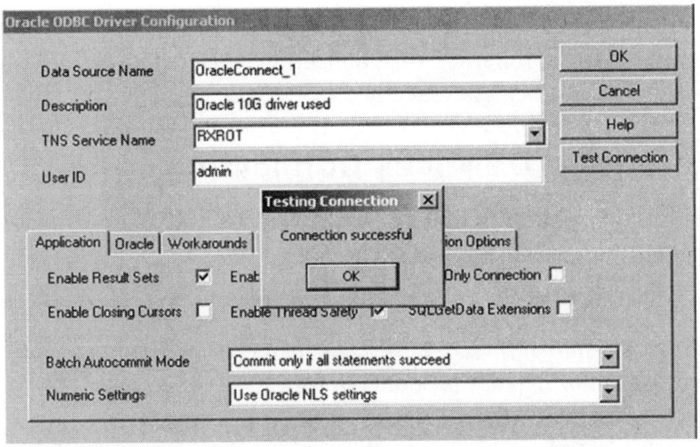

Figure 46.2 *Fill database details and test connection*

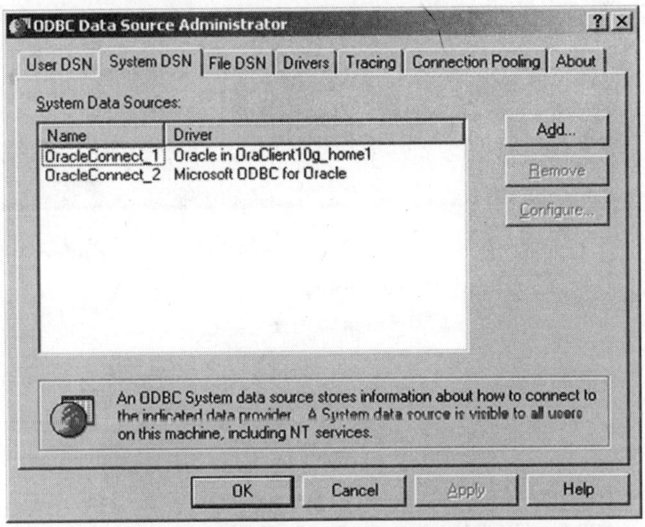

Figure 46.3 *ODBC data source administrator*

Connection String for DSN Connection

Suppose that we need to connect to an Oracle DB server, then the connection string can be created using the following connection string format:

```
"DSN=DSNName;uid=UserNm;pwd=Password"
```

For DSN name *OracleConnect_1*, user name and password *admin*, the connection string will be:

```
sConnString = "DSN=OracleConnect_1;uid=Admin;pwd=Admin"
```

DSN-less Connection

In DSN-less connection, a connection string is created which explicitly defines the driver to use, host IP address, database service name, etc.

Building Connection Strings

ConnectionString is one of the properties of Connection object that defines connection details as discussed above.

Connection String for DSN-less Connection

Suppose that we need to connect to an Oracle DB server, then the connection string can be created using the following connection string format:

```
"Driver={Driver Name};Server=SID;uid=UserName;pwd=Password"
```

Let us assume that driver is *Microsoft ODBC for Oracle*, database SID name is *PROJECT*, user name is *Admin*, and password is *Admin*, then the connection string will be:

```
sConnString = "Driver={Microsoft ODBC for
               Oracle};Server=PROJECT;uid=Admin;pwd=Admin"
```

> **NOTES** We can find the oracle database SID name from tnsnames.ora file of oracle client machine. In case we want to create a connection string without relying on tnsnames.ora file of local (oracle client) machine, then all the connection details such as host IP, port address, and connection protocol need to be defined in the connection string itself. These details can be extracted from the tnsnames.ora file of the Oracle DB server.

Code below shows how to explicitly create a connection string. This string avoids the dependency on the tnsnames.ora file for connecting to oracle database.

```
sConnString = "Driver={DriverNm};" &_
              "CONNECTSTRING=(DESCRIPTION=" & _
              "(ADDRESS=(PROTOCOL=TCP)" & _
              "(HOST=SrvrIP)(PORT=PortNo))" & _
              "(CONNECT_DATA=(SERVICE_NAME=SrvcNm)));
              uid=UsrNm;pwd=Pass;"
```

Suppose that host IP is 172.21.186.21, port address is 7001, and service name is PROJECT, then the connection string will be:

```
sConnString = "Driver={Microsoft ODBC for Oracle};" &_
              "CONNECTSTRING=(DESCRIPTION=" & _
              "(ADDRESS=(PROTOCOL=TCP)" & _
              "(HOST=172.21.186.21)(PORT=7001))" & _
              "(CONNECT_DATA=(SERVICE_NAME=PROJECT)));
              uid=Admin;pwd=Admin;"
```

CONNECTING TO MS EXCEL DATABASE

Let us assume that we need to extract data from IRCTCBookTicket.xls file kept at location Z:\Data.

```
'Create connection object
Set oConn = CreateObject("ADODB.Connection")
```

```
'Create recordset  object
Set oRecSet = CreateObject("ADODB.Recordset")
'Connection details
With oConn
     .Provider = "Microsoft.ACE.OLEDB.12.0"
     .ConnectionString = "DataSource="Z:\Data\IRCTCBookTicket.xls;"
                         & _ "Extended Properties=Excel 12.0; xml;
                         HDR=Yes;"";"
     .Open
End With
'Query
sSql = "Select * from [Sheet1$]"
'Execute query
Set oRecSet = oConn.Execute(sSql)
'Retrieve query results
oRecSet.MoveFirst
Do While Not oRecSet.EOF
   For Each oField in oRecSet.Fields
       MsgBox oField.Name &  "::" & oField.Value
   Next
   oRecSet.MoveNext
Loop
If oRecSet.State <> 0 Then
    oRecSet.Close
End If
oConn.Close
```

CONNECTING TO MS ACCESS DATABASE

Let us assume that we need to extract employee details from Employee table of database EmployeeDetails.mdb

```
'Create connection object
Set oConn = CreateObject("ADODB.Connection")
'Create recordset  object
Set oRecSet = CreateObject("ADODB.Recordset")
'Connection details
With oConn
        .Provider = "Microsoft.ACE.OLEDB.12.0"
        .ConnectionString =  "Data  Source=C:\Temp\EmployeeDetails.
                            mdb;" &_ "User Id =Admin;Password=Admin;"
        .Open
End With
```

```
'Query
sSql = "Select * from Employee"
'Execute query
Set oRecSet = oConn.Execute(sSql)
'Retrieve query results
oRecSet.MoveFirst
Do While Not oRecSet.EOF
      For Each oField in oRecSet.Fields
            MsgBox oField.Name & "::" & oField.Value
      Next
      oRecSet.MoveNext
Loop
If oRecSet.State <> 0 Then
    oRecSet.Close
End If
oConn.Close
```

CONNECTING TO MS SQL SERVER DATABASE

```
'Create connection object
Set oConn = CreateObject("ADODB.Connection")
'Create recordset  object
Set oRecSet = CreateObject("ADODB.Recordset")
'Connection details
With oConn
        .Provider = "sqloledb"
        .ConnectionString = "Data Source=SQLServerName; Initial
                            Catalog=DBName;" &_
                            "User Id=sa;Password=password;"
        .Open
End With
'Query
sSql = "Select * from Table"
'Execute query
Set oRecSet = oConn.Execute(sSql)
'Retrieve query results
oRecSet.MoveFirst
Do While Not oRecSet.EOF
      For Each oField in oRecSet.Fields
            MsgBox oField.Name & "::" & oField.Value
      Next
      oRecSet.MoveNext
```

```
Loop
If oRecSet.State <> 0 Then
     oRecSet.Close
End If
oConn.Close
```

CONNECTING TO ORACLE DATABASE

Method 1

```
'Create connection object
Set oConn = CreateObject("ADODB.Connection")
'Create recordset  object
Set oRecSet = CreateObject("ADODB.Recordset")
'Connection details
sConnString = "Driver={DriverNm};" &_
              "CONNECTSTRING=(DESCRIPTION=" & _
              "(ADDRESS=(PROTOCOL=TCP)" & _
              "(HOST=SrvrIP)(PORT=PortNo))" & _
              "(CONNECT_DATA=(SERVICE_NAME=SrvcNm)));
                uid=UsrNm;pwd=Pass;"
With oConn
        .Provider = "sqloledb"
        .ConnectionString = sConnString
        .Open
End With
'Query
sSql = "Select * from Table"
'Execute query
Set oRecSet = oConn.Execute(sSql)
'Retrieve query results
oRecSet.MoveFirst
Do While Not oRecSet.EOF
    For Each oField in oRecSet.Fields
           MsgBox oField.Name &  "::" & oField.Value
    Next
    oRecSet.MoveNext
Loop
If oRecSet.State <> 0 Then
   oRecSet.Close
End If
oConn.Close
```

Method 2

```
sConnString = "driver=Oracle in ORA92; DBQ=DB_Name ;DBA=R"
sDBuserName = "Admin"
sDBuserPass = "Admin"
'SQL or procedure
sSQL_or_ProcedureName = "Select * from Table"
'Create connection object
Set oConn = CreateObject("ADODB.Connection")
'Create recordser object
Set oRecSet = CreateObject("ADODB.Recordset")
'Open connection to DB
oConn.Open sConnString , sDBUID, sDBPWD
'Create the Command Object reference to the database
Set oCommand = CreateObject("ADODB.Command")
'Set connection string
oCommand.ActiveConnection = oConn
'Build SQL Query
oCommand.CommandText = sSQL_or_ProcedureName
'Execute the SQL
Set oRecSet = oCommand.Execute
'Retrieve query results
oRecSet.MoveFirst
'Retrieve
Do While Not oRecSet.EOF
   For Each oField in oRecSet.Fields
       MsgBox oField.Name & "::" & oField.Value
   Next
   oRecSet.MoveNext
Loop
If oRecSet.State <> 0 Then
   oRecSet.Close
End If
'Close the connection
oConn.Close
```

FUNCTION TO EXECUTE QUERY ON ORACLE DB

Function `fnExecQuery` executes an SQL query on a specified Oracle database and stores the query result in the specified dictionary object.

Syntax: Call fnExecQuery (*sSql*, *dicResultSet*)

Input parameters:

sSql—SQL query to be executed

dicResultSet—dictionary object

Return type:

```
String. Returns "0," if function executes successfully.
Returns error reason of failure, if function execution fails.
```

Usage: Extract data from table dual.

```
sSql = "Select * from dual"

'Create dictionary object
Set dicResultSet = CreateObject("Scripting.Dictionary")
fnStat = fnExecXlQueryDic(sSql, dicResultSet )

nPrimaryRecordCnt = dicResultSet.Count
arrPrimaryKeys =  dicResultSet.Keys
nRowCnt = dicResultSet(0).Item("RowCnt")
nColCnt = dicResultSet(0).Item("ColumnCnt")
nSecondaryRecordCnt = dicResultSet(1).Count
arrSecondaryKeys = dicResultSet(1).Keys
arrRow1Items = dicResultSet(1).Items
sRow1Data = dicResultSet(1).Item("FieldName")
```

Config.vbs

```
Environment("HostIPAddr") = "172.21.187.76"
Environment("PortNo") = "1523"
Environment("SrvcNm") = "PROJECT"
Environment("DBUsrNm") = "Admin"
Environment("DBPassword") = "admin"
```

Library.vbs

```
Public Function fnExecuteQuery(sSql, dicResultSet)
    On Error resume next

    Dim rCnt
    Dim sHostIPAddr, nPortNo, sSrvcNm, sDBUsrNm, sDBPassword

    rCnt = 1
    sHostIPAddr = Environment("HostIPAddr")
    nPortNo = Environment("PortNo")
    sSrvcNm = Environment("SrvcNm")
    sDBUsrNm = Environment("DBUsrNm")
    sDBPassword = Environment("DBPassword")

    'Clear dictionary
    dicResultSet.RemoveAll

    'Create connection object
    Set oConn = CreateObject("ADODB.Connection")

    'Create recordset  object
    Set oRecSet = CreateObject("ADODB.Recordset")

    sConnString = "Driver={ Microsoft ODBC for Oracle};" &_
                  "CONNECTSTRING=(DESCRIPTION=" & _
                  "(ADDRESS=(PROTOCOL=TCP)" & _
```

```
                  "(HOST=" & sHostIPAddr & ")(PORT=" & nPortNo & "))" & _
                  "(CONNECT_DATA=(SERVICE_NAME=" & sSrvcNm & "))); " &_
                  "uid=" & sDBUsrNm;pwd=" & sDBPassword & ";"
    With oConn
         .Provider = "Microsoft.Jet.OLEDB.4.0"
         .ConnectionString = sConnString
         .Open
    End With
    If Err.Number <> 0 Then
        fnExecuteQuery = "-1" & err.description
        Exit Function
    End If
    'Execute SQL query
    Set oRecSet = oConn.Execute(sSql)
    If Err.Number <> 0 Then
        fnExecuteQuery = "-1" & err.description
        Exit Function
    End If
      'Find returned record count
      nDataCnt = oRecSet.fields.Count
      dicResultSet.Add 0, CreateObject("Scripting.Dictionary")
      dicResultSet(0).Add "ColumnCnt", nDataCnt
      'Store query result to an array
         If nDataCnt > 0 Then
            Do While Not oRecSet.EOF
                 'Create dictionary of dictionary object
                 dicResultSet.Add rCnt, CreateObject("Scripting.Dictionary")
                 For Each oField In oRecSet.fields
                     'Store data retrived from query to dictionary
                     dicResultSet(rCnt).Add oField.Name, oField.Value
                 Next
                 oRecSet.moveNext
                 rCnt = rCnt + 1
      Loop
     End If
   'Number of rows of data in query result
   dicResultSet(0).Add "RowCnt", rCnt-1
   'Close RecordSet object
   If oRecSet.State <> 0 Then
       oRecSet.Close
End If
   'Close connection
   oConn.Close
```

```
  If Err.Number <> 0 Then
       fnExecuteQuery = "-1" & err.description
       Exit Function
    End If
    Set oConn = Nothing
    Set oRecSet = Nothing
    'If function executed successfully, return 0 else return error reason
    If err.number=0 Then
         fnExecuteQuery ="0"
    End If
End Function
```

QUICK TIPS

- ✓ It is always advisable to use DSN-less connection for accessing database in test automation. This helps prevent dependency on local machine ODBC for accessing database. With DSN-less connection, any machine can connect to the database without any pre-setups such as ODBC connection setup.
- ✓ ADODB connection object is used to create an open connection to a data source. Through this connection, database can be accessed and manipulated.
- ✓ RecordSet object is used to store the records returned by the database. A RecordSet object consists of records and columns (fields).
- ✓ ADODB fields object represents individual columns of the RecordSet object.
- ✓ ADODB Command object represents an SQL statement or a stored procedure that is to be executed against a data source. Use of Command object is optional as data can also be extracted directly from Connection object.

PRACTICAL QUESTIONS

1. Write a code to read data from Oracle database.
2. Write a code to update data to MS Access database.

Chapter 47

Working with XML

XML stands for eXtensible Markup Language. XML is a universal file format for storing and exchanging structured information. Some common uses of XML on the web are web development, documentation, database development, etc. A number of new internet languages have been created with XML. Some of them are as follows:

- XHTML
- WSDL for describing available web services
- WAP and WML as markup languages for handheld devices
- RSS languages for news feeds
- RDF and OWL for describing resources and ontology
- SMIL for describing multimedia for the web

QTP provides a built-in utility object to allow parsing and manipulating XML files. This chapter discusses how to access, manipulate, and create an XML file.

XML STRUCTURE

The elements in an XML document form a document tree. The tree starts at the root and branches to the lowest level of the tree. The first node in an XML file is called the *root* node. In the following example, node *<Bookstore>* is the root node. Node <Book> has four *child* nodes—<title>, <author>, <year>, and <price>. Child nodes are the children of an enclosing parent node. Node *<Book>* is called the *parent* node of these child nodes. The value assigned to any particular node is called *node value*. Node <title> has node value Harry Potter. A node can have *attributes*. For example, third node of book has two attributes—*category* and *cover* with attribute values *technical* and *paperback*, respectively.

```
<?xml version="1.0" ?>
<Bookstore>
      <Book category="children">
            <title lang="en">Harry Potter</title>
            <author>J K. Rowling</author>
            <year>2005</year>
            <price>29.99</price>
```

```
    </Book>
    <Book category="children">
          <title lang="en">Alice in Wonderland </title>
          <author>Lewis Carroll</author>
          <year>1865</year>
          <price>39.95</price>
    </Book>
    <Book category="technical" cover="paperback">
          <title lang="en">Learning XML</title>
          <author>Eric Thomson </author>
          <author>James Lyod </author>
          <year>2010</year>
          <price>49.95</price>
    </Book>
</Bookstore>
```

XML DOM

The XML Document Object Model (DOM) defines a standard way for accessing and manipulating XML documents. The DOM models XML as a set of node objects. XML file can be loaded by creating an instance of *Microsoft.XMLDOM.* XML DOM provides an application programming interface for working with XML data. As an XML representation, it conforms to the W3C DOM specification. As a set of API, XML DOM objects are COM objects that implement interfaces and can be used in XML applications written in programming languages such as C/C++, Visual Basic, VBScript, and JScript.

```
'Create XML object
Set oXMLDoc = CreateObject("Microsoft.XMLDOM")

'Load XML file
bFlag = oXMLDoc.Load("C:\ Temp\Book.xml")
```

Methods

Some of the methods of the XML DOM are described below:

- getElementsByTagName(name)—It retrieves all elements with a specified tag name.

Example: Write code to retrieve all values associated with tag author in the XML document.

```
'Get all tag values with tag author
Set oElements = oXMLDoc.getElementsByTagName("author")
'Print all tag values with tag name <author>
For iCnt =0 to oElements.Length-1 Step 1
          Print oElements.Item(iCnt).nodeName & "::" & oElements.
          Item(iCnt).text
```

```
Next
        'Output :
              author::J K. Rowling
              author::Lewis Carroll
              author::Eric Thomson
              author::James Lyod
```

- **appendChild(node)**—It inserts a child node
- **removeChild(node)**—It removes a child node

Properties

Some of the methods of the XML DOM are described below.

- **nodeName**—It retrieves tag name of the node
- **nodeValue**—It retrieves tag value of the node
- **attributes**—It retrieves attributes of the specified node

Example 1: Retrieve all attribute values associated with tag Book in the XML document.

```
'Get all tag values with tag Book
Set oElements = oXMLDoc.getElementsByTagName("Book")
'Print all attribute name and values associated with tag name
<Book >
For iCnt=0 To oElements.Length-1 Step 1
        For jCnt=0 To oElements(iCnt).attributes.Length-1  Step 1
        Print oElements(iCnt).attributes.Item(jCnt).nodeName & "::" &_
        oElements(iCnt).attributes.Item(jCnt).nodeValue
        Print vbCrLF
        Next
        Print "------------------------"
Next
        'Output :
             category::children
             ------------------------
             category::children
             ------------------------
             category::technical
             cover::paperback
```

- **parentNode**—It retrieves parent node of the specified node
- **childNodes**—It retrieves all child nodes of the specified node

Example 2: Retrieve all child node and values of XML document

```
For each oElement in oXMLDoc.documentElement.childNodes
       Print oElement.nodeName & "::" & oElement.text
Next
```

```
        'Output :
            Book::Harry Potter J K. Rowling 2005 29.99
            Book::Alice in Wonderland  Lewis Carroll 1865 39.95
            Book::Learning XML Eric Thomson  James Lyod  2010 49.95
```

Example 23 Retrieve all child node names and values of first Book node.

```
For each oElement in oXMLDoc.documentElement.childNodes(0).child-
Nodes
    Print oElement.nodeName & "::" & oElement.text
Next
       'Output :
              title::Harry Potter
              author::J K. Rowling
              year::2005
              price::29.99
```

QTP XML OBJECTS

QTP provides in-built objects to access and manipulate XML documents. Some of the useful objects are described below:

- **XMLUtil**—It is used to create a new XML file or read an existing XML file.
- **XMLAttribute**—It is used to retrieve name and values of attributes of the specified node.
- **XMLAttributeColl**—It is used to retrieve attributes collection.
- **XMLElement**—It is used to retrieve an XML element. An XML element can have one more attributes, child nodes, nodes, and node values.
- **XMLElemetsColl**—It is used to retrieve a collection of XML elements.
- checkxpath

Loading XML File

QTP provides XMLUtil object to create/access an XML file.

```
'Create an XML object
Set oXMLDoc = XMLUtil.CreateXML

'Load XML file
oXMLDoc.LoadFile "C:\Temp\Book.xml"

Alternatively,
'Load XML file in .txt format
'oXMLDoc.LoadFile "C:\Temp\Book.txt"

Alternatively,
'Load XML document in single step
Set oXMLDoc = XMLUtil.CreateXMLFromFile ("C:\Temp\Book.txt")
```

Saving XML File

The SaveFile method is used to save an XML file. The following example shows how to save an XML file.

```
'Load XML document
Set oXMLDoc = XMLUtil.CreateXMLFromFile ("C:\Temp\Book.xml")

'Save XML file
oXMLDoc.SaveFile "C:\Temp\Book1.xml"
```

Retrieving XML File Data in a Single String

The following example shows how to read the complete XML file.

```
'Load XML document
Set oXMLDoc = XMLUtil.CreateXMLFromFile ("C:\Temp\Book.xml")

'XML data string
sXMLData = oXMLDoc.ToString

'Create new XML file
Set oXMLDocNew = CreateObject("Microsoft.XMLDOM")
oXMLDocNew.LoadXML(sXMLData)

'Save XML file
oXMLDocNew.Save "C:\Temp\Book2.xml"
```

Reading XML File

The following example shows how to read specific data from an XML file.

```
'Load XML document
Set oXMLDoc = XMLUtil.CreateXMLFromFile ("C:\Temp\Book.xml")

'Get root element
Set oXMLRoot = oXMLDoc.GetRootElement

'Get all nodes with tagname Book
Set oElements = oXMLRoot.ChildElementsByPath("Book")

For iCnt=1 To oElements.Count Step 1
     Set oChildElements = oElements.Item(iCnt)
     For jCnt=1 To oChildElements.ChildElementsByPath("author").Count
          sTagValue = oChildElements.ChildElementsByPath("author").
          Item(jCnt).Value
Next
Next
```

```
'Output :
     author::J K. Rowling
     author::Lewis Carroll
     author::Eric Thomson
     author::James Lyod
```

Reading XML from Web Browser

XML files opened by performing an action on the application are loaded in memory. Since these files are not saved to a location in hard disk, the LoadXML method cannot be used to open the file. Moreover, the file is already open. Therefore, the need is to access the instance of the opened file. The opened XML file can be referred by calling the GetData method on the instance of the opened file. The following example shows how to retrieve an XML document which is dynamically opened in a web browser by the application under test.

```
'Get data of already opened XML document
Set oXMLDoc = Browser("creationtime:=0").WebXML("micclass:=WebXML").
                                         GetData

'Save File
oXMLDoc.SaveFile "C:\Temp\XMLFile.xml"
```

LOCATING XML ELEMENTS XPATH QUERY

XPath is XML path language based on a tree representation of the XML document. It is a query language for selecting nodes from XML document. It provides the ability to navigate around the tree by selecting nodes by using a variety of criteria. XPath is very useful in locating dynamic elements of an XML file. A dynamic XML element can be one whose tag name is not fixed and keeps on changing from one run session to another. In such situations the explicit path (position in xml tree) can be used to locate the element using XPath.

Developing XPath Expression for XML

XPath for an element in XML file can be developed by developing the node navigation path of the XML DOM. Two nodes in XPath expression are separated by symbol slash '\'. All the axis of the XPath such as child, parent, ancestor, following-sibling, etc. can be used to develop a XPath expression.

Firefox *Firebug* add-on FirePath can be used to verify whether the developed XPath expression locates the specified element in XML DOM tree or not. The identified element is highlighted in the FirePath window. In order to develop XPath for locating an XML element steps below is to be followed.

1. Open the XML file in Firefox browser.
2. Activate the Firebug *Firepath* tab.
3. Write down the XPath expression in *Firepath* XPath text box.

Figure 47.1 shows how to locate all the <title> elements of the Bookstore XML file.

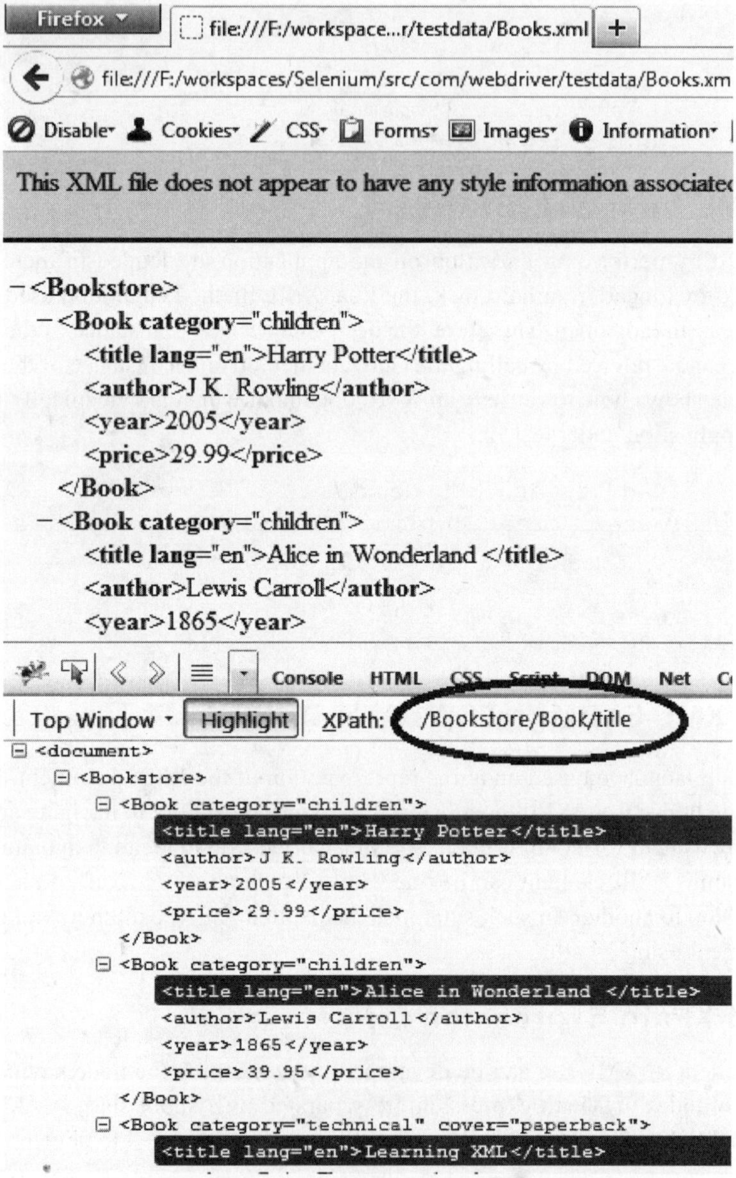

Figure 47.1 *Locating XML elements using XPath*

Example 1: Develop XPath expression for locating all <title> elements.

```
XPath Expression= /Bookstore/Book/title
```

Or,

```
XPath Expression= /Bookstore//title
```

```
⊟ <Bookstore>
    ⊞ <Book category="children">
    ⊞ <Book category="children">
    ⊞ <Book category="technical" cover="paperback">
```

Figure 47.2 *XML Elements located of XPath expression of Example 2*

Or,

```
XPath Expression= //title
```

Example 2: Develop XPath expression to locate the <Book> node that has title element 'Alice in Wonderland'.

```
XPath Expression= /Bookstore/Book[contains(title,'Alice in Wonderland')]
```

Or,

```
XPath Expression= //Book[contains(title,'Alice in Wonderland')]
```

Figure 47.2 shows the elements as located by Firefox using above XPath expression.

Example 3: Develop XPath expression to locate the <title> node that has title element 'Alice in Wonderland'.

```
XPath Expression= //Book[contains(title,'Alice in Wonderland')]/title
```

Figure 47.3 shows the elements as located by Firefox using above XPath expression.

Example 4: Develop XPath expression to locate the <price> node that has title element 'Alice in Wonderland'.

```
XPath Expression= //Book[contains(title,'Alice in Wonderland')]/price
```

Example 5: Develop XPath expression to locate all <Book> node whose <price> element value ends in .95.

```
XPath Expression= //Book[contains(price,'.95')]
```

```
⊟ <Bookstore>
    ⊞ <Book category="children">
    ⊟ <Book category="children">
          <title lang="en">Alice in Wonderland </title>
          <author>Lewis Carroll</author>
          <year>1865</year>
          <price>39.95</price>
      </Book>
    ⊞ <Book category="technical" cover="paperback">
```

Figure 47.3 *XML element located of XPath expression of Example 3*

```
⊟ <Bookstore>
    ⊞ <Book category="children">
    ⊞ <Book category="children">
    ⊞ <Book category="technical" cover="paperback">
```

Figure 47.4 *XML Elements located of XPath expression of Example 5*

Figure 47.4 shows the elements as located by Firefox using above XPath expression.

Example 6: Find all the books (title) which has been published in year 2005.

```
XPath Expression= //Book[contains(year,’2005’)]/title
```

Or,

```
XPath Expression= //year[contains(.,’2005’)]/parent::Book/title
```

Example 7: Find all the nodes next to the node <author> for all books whose author is J.K. Rowling.

```
XPath Expression= //Book[contains(author,’Rowling’)]/author/following-
sibling::*
```

Figure 47.5 shows the elements as located by Firefox using above XPath expression.

Example 8: Find the node next to the node <author> for all books whose author is J. K. Rowling.

```
XPath Expression= //Book[contains(author,’Rowling’)]/author/following-
sibling::*[1]
```

Figure 47.6 shows the elements as located by Firefox using above XPath expression.

Example 9: Find all the attributes (child nodes) of book whose author is J. K. Rowling.

```
XPath Expression= //Book[contains(author,’Rowling’)]/child::*
```

```
⊟ <Bookstore>
    ⊟ <Book category="children">
          <title lang="en">Harry Potter</title>
          <author>J K. Rowling</author>
          <year>2005</year>
          <price>29.99</price>
```

Figure 47.5 *XML elements located of XPath expression of Example 7*

```
⊟ <Bookstore>
    ⊟ <Book category="children">
          <title lang="en">Harry Potter</title>
          <author>J K. Rowling</author>
          <year>2005</year>
          <price>29.99</price>
       </Book>
```

Figure 47.6 *XML elements located of XPath expression of Example 8*

```
⊟ <Bookstore>
   ⊟ <Book category="children">
         <title lang="en">Harry Potter</title>
         <author>J K. Rowling</author>
         <year>2005</year>
         <price>29.99</price>
      </Book>
   ⊞ <Book category="children">
   ⊞ <Book category="technical" cover="paperback">
```

Figure 47.7 *XML elements located of XPath expression of Example 9*

Figure 47.7 shows the elements as located by Firefox using above XPath expression.

Example 10: Find all the books (title) whose price ends in either .95 or is published in year 2010.

```
XPath Expression= //Book[contains(price,'.95') or contains(year,'2010')]/
title
```

Example 11: Find all the books (title) whose price ends in .95 and is published in year 2010

```
XPath Expression= //Book[contains(.,'.95')][contains(.,'2010')]/title
```

Example 12: Find all Books (<Book> nodes) whose category is 'children.

```
XPath Expression: //Book[@category=children]
```

Figure 47.8 shows the elements as located by Firefox using above XPath expression.

Example 13: Find all Books (<Book> nodes) whose category is 'technical' and cover is 'paperback'.

```
XPath Expression: //Book[@category='technical'][@cover='paperback']
```

Reading XML File Using XPath Query

XML DOM provides *setProperty* method to set the SelectionLanguage property of the DOM document to "XPath". If this property is not set, then the results can be odd.

Code below shows how to locate XML elements and read XML nodes using XPath Query.

```
'Create XML object
Set oXMLDoc =  CreateObject("Microsoft.XMLDOM")
oXMLDoc.async = False
'Set selectionlanguage as XPATH
oXMLDoc.setProperty "SelectionLanguage", "XPath"
```

```
⊟ <Bookstore>
   ⊞ <Book category="children">
   ⊞ <Book category="children">
   ⊞ <Book category="technical" cover="paperback">
```

Figure 47.8 *XML elements located of XPath expression of Example 12*

```
'Load XML file
bFlag =  oXMLDoc.Load("C:\Temp\Book.xml")

'select a single node
```

'Example 2: XPath expression to locate the <Book> node that has title element 'Alice in Wonderland'

```
sXPathQuery = "/Bookstore/Book[contains(title,'Alice in Wonderland')]"
Set bookNode= oXMLDoc.selectSingleNode(sXPathQuery)
```

'This test checks whether bookNode was found or not

```
If bookNode Is Nothing Then
  'error not found!
Else
  Print bookNode.NodeName 'Output:Book
End If

'select multiple nodes
```

'Example 5: XPath expression to locate all <Book> node whose <price> element value ends in .95

```
sXPathQuery = "//Book[contains(price,'.95')]"
Set bookNodes= oXMLDoc.selectNodes(sXPathQuery)
```

'This test checks whether book nodes were found or not

```
If bookNodes.Length = 0 Then
  'error not found!
Else
  For Each bookNode In bookNodes
     Print bookNode.nodeName &_
         ":" & bookNode.attributes.Item(0).nodeName  &_
         ":" & bookNode.attributes.Item(0).nodevalue
  Next
End If
'Output:
'Book:category:children
'Book:category:technical
Set oXMLDoc =  Nothing
```

Comparing XML Files

In certain applications, requirements are there to compare the XML file created during script execution with a base line file. QuickTest provides methods to compare two XML files for their equality. The following code shows the method to compare two XML documents for their equality.

```
'Load actual XMLfile generated during script execution
Set oXMLDoc1 = XMLUtil.CreateXMLFromFile ("C:\Temp\A_Book.xml")
'Load baseline/expected XMLfile
Set oXMLDoc2 = XMLUtil.CreateXMLFromFile ("C:\Temp\E_Book.xml")
```

```
'Compare XML files.
'Returns 1, if the specified files are equal
bFlag = oXMLDoc1.Compare(oXMLDoc2, oRsltXMLFile)
If bFlag=1 Then
      Print "Pass : Documents matched"
Else
      Print "Failed : Documents do not match"
End If
```

Converting XML to Excel File

Exporting XML file data to Excel file makes it easier to identify and differentiate one XML data from another. Excel file can be used either as worksheet or database to access XML data. In the exported Excel file, first row of Excel sheet contains all tag values and attribute values of an XML file. The Excel rows following first row contains tag and attribute values. Figure 47.9 shows Excel file obtained after importing XML file data to Excel file. Here, we observe that the first row of Excel file contains tag and attribute values such as category, cover, title, and author. Rows following first row contains the values of respective tags or attributes. Thus, importing XML file data in Excel makes the XML file data more readable for automation. By executing customized SQL queries on this Excel file, required XML data can be extracted. For example, extracting the book details of all books with book category as *children*.

Function `fnConvertXML2XLS` mentioned in the following converts imports XML file data to Excel file in the specified format.

Input parameters:

`sXMLLoc`–File path of XML file

`sXSLLoc`–Path to save Excel file containing data imported from XML file

Usage:

```
sXMLLoc =  "C:\Temp\Book.xml"
sXSLLoc = "C:\Temp\Book.xls"
Call fnConvertXML2XLS(sXMLLoc, sXSLLoc)
```

```
Function fnConvertXML2XLS (sXMLLoc, sXSLLoc)
   Set oExcel = CreateObject("Excel.Application")
   oExcel.Visible = False

   'Import XML file data into excel file
   oExcel.Workbooks.OpenXML sXMLLoc, 1,2
```

category	cover	title	lang	author	year	price
children		Harry Potter	en	J K. Rowling	2005	29.99
children		Alice in Wonderland	en	Lewis Carroll	1865	39.95
technical	paperback	Learning XML	en	Eric Thomson	2010	49.95
technical	paperback	Learning XML	en	James Lyod	2010	49.95
*						

Figure 47.9 *Converting XML file to XLS file*

```
    'Save excel file
    oExcel.ActiveWorkbook.SaveAs "" & sXSLLoc
    oExcel.ActiveWorkbook.Close
    Set oExcel = Nothing
End Function
```

Exporting XML Data to Array

XML data can be exported in an array by sequentially accessing XML file data and storing them in an array.

Example: Export all tag name and tag values to an array.

Function `fnExtractXMLData` extracts XML tag-value pairs in an array.

Input parameters:

`sXMLFile`–XML file path
`arrXMLData`–Two-dimensional array

Output:

`arrXMLData`–Array contains XML tags and its values
Returns 0, if function executes successfully, else returns –1

Usage:

```
      Dim arrXMLData(50,1)

      'Load XML document
      Set oXMLDoc = XMLUtil.CreateXMLFromFile ("C:\Temp\Book.xml")

      'Get root element
      Set oXMLRoot = oXMLDoc.GetRootElement

      'Get all nodes with tagname Book
      Set oElements = oXMLRoot.ChildElementsByPath("Book")
      sXMLFile = "C:\Temp\Book.xml"

Call fnExtractXMLData (sXMLFile, arrXMLData)
            'Output :
                  arrXMLData(1,0) = "ti6le"
                  arrXMLData(1,1) = "Harry Potter"
                  arrXMLData(2,0) = "author"
                  arrXMLData(2,1) = "J K. Rowling"
                  …

Function fnExtractXMLData(sXMLFile, arrXMLData)
      On Error Resume Next
      Dim iCnt: iCnt = 1

      'Get a file scripting object
      Set oFSO = CreateObject("Scripting.FileSystemObject")
```

```
    'Open notepad file in read only mode
    Set oNtpdFile = oFSO.OpenTextFile(sXMLFile, 1, False)

    'Read data from notepad file
    Do While oNtpdFile.AtEndOfStream = False
       sText = Trim(oNtpdFile.ReadLine)

       'Find start and end position of tag names
       nTagNmStartPos = Instr(1, sText, "</", 1)
       nTagNmEndPos = Instr(nTagNmStartPos+1, sText, ">", 1)
       If nTagNmStartPos<>0 And IsNumeric(nTagNmStartPos) Then

         'find tag name
         sTagNm = Mid(sText, nTagNmStartPos+2, nTagNmEndPos-nTag-
                 NmStartPos-2)

         'Store tag name value in array
         arrXMLData(iCnt,0) = sTagNm
      End If
      'Find start and end position of tag values
      nTagValStartPos = Instr(1, sText, ">", 1)
      nTagValEndPos = Instr(1, sText, "</", 1)
      If nTagValStartPos<>0 And IsNumeric(nTagValStartPos)
                                 And nTagValEndPos>nTagValStartPos Then
         'find tag name
         sTagval = Mid(sText, nTagValStartPos+1, nTagValEndPos-
                  nTagValStartPos-1)

         'Store tag value in array
         arrXMLData(iCnt,1) = sTagVal
         iCnt = iCnt + 1
      End If
   Loop

   oNtpdFile.Close
   If err.Number <> 0 Then
      fnExtractXMLData = "-1"
   Else
      fnExtractXMLData = "0"
   End If
End Function
```

QUICK TIPS

- ✓ XML is a universal file format for storing and exchanging structured information.
- ✓ The XML Document Object Model (DOM) defines a standard way for accessing and manipulating XML documents.

PRACTICAL QUESTIONS

1. Explain the methods and properties of the XML DOM.
2. Write a code to load an XML file, write data to it, and save it.
3. Write a code to read XML file from web browser.
4. Write a code to convert XML file to Excel file. Read data from the saved Excel file.
5. Write a code to retrieve XML data in a dictionary object.

Chapter 48

Working with Microsoft Word

Microsoft Word is a word processor designed by Microsoft Corporation. It is widely used to create documents for books, brochures, reports, etc. In automation, MS Word COM interface is used to access Word file data. This Word file could be the reports generated by the AUT. In addition, Word COM interface can be used to dynamically generate test automation regression-run reports.

WORD AUTOMATION OBJECT MODEL

Figure 48.1 shows an abstract word object model.

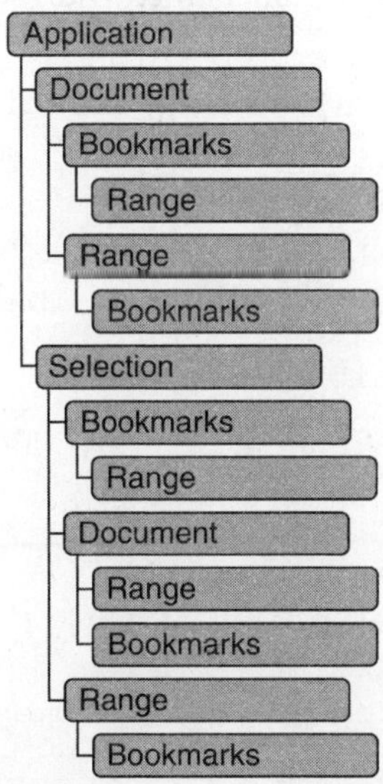

Figure 48.1 *Abstract word object model*

MS Word provides hundreds of objects to interact with a Word file. The top-level word objects are briefly described in the following list:

- **Application object:** The application object represents the Word application. It is the parent of all other objects.
- **Documents object:** The documents object represents a collection of all open Word documents.

- **Selection object:** The selection object represents the area currently selected in a Word document.
- **Range object:** The range object represents a contiguous area in a document. It is defined by a starting character position and an ending character position.
- **Bookmark object:** The bookmark object is used to mark a location in a Word document.

Creating an Instance of Word Application

An instance of the Word application is used to access or create a Word file. The following code shows how to create a new instance of MS Word.

```
'Create an instance of word application
Set oWordApp = CreateObject("Word.Application")

'Make word application visible
oWordApp.Visible = True

Msgbox "Word Instance Created"

'Close word application
oWordApp.Quit

Set oWordApp = Nothing
```

Creating a New Document

The following code creates a new Word document file, writes some text to it, and then saves it.

```
'Create an instance of word application
Set oWordApp = CreateObject("Word.Application")

'Make word application visible
oWordApp.Visible = False

'Add word document
Set oWordDoc = oWordApp.Documents.Add

'Turn-off text overtype option
If oWordApp.Options.Overtype = True Then
      oWordApp.Options.Overtype = False
End If

'Write text to word document
Set oWordSel = oWordApp.Selection
oWordSel.Style = "Heading 2"
oWordSel.TypeText "Writing Text to Word Document" & VbCrLf & "WordDoc.docx"

'Save word file
oWordDoc.SaveAs "C:\Temp\WordDoc.docx"

'Close word document
oWordDoc.Close

'Close word application
oWordApp.Quit

Set oWordApp = Nothing
```

Opening an Existing Document

The following code shows how to open an existing Word document and copy all of its data to clipboard.

```
'Create an instance of mercury clipboard
Set oMerClipboard = CreateObject("Mercury.Clipboard")

'Clear clipboard
oMerClipboard.Clear

'Create an instance of word application
Set oWordApp = CreateObject("Word.Application")

'Make word application visible
oWordApp.Visible = False

'Open existing word file
Set oWordDoc = oWordApp.Documents.Open("C:\Temp\WordDoc.docx",,True)

'Copy whole document data to clipboard
oWordApp.Selection.WholeStory
oWordApp.Selection.Copy

'Copy clipboard data
sWordData = oMerClipboard.GetText
Print sWordData

'Close word document
oWordDoc.Close

'Exit word application
oWordApp.Quit

Set oWordApp = Nothing
```

Adding Picture to Documents

The following code shows how to insert pictures in a Word documents programmatically. This is essentially required while preparing custom test-run reports through code.

From now on, we will assume that a Word file is already open and the object *oWordApp* is an instance of it.

```
'Get the selection object
Set oWordSel = oWordApp.Selection

With oWordSel
     'Set cursor to the end of the document
     .EndKey 6,0

     'Insert picture
     Set oInsertedImg = .InLineShapes.AddPicture("C:\Temp\Image.
                                              jpg", False, True)

     'Scale the image to 30% of the original size
```

```
        oInsertedImg.Width = oInsertedImg.Width * .30
        oInsertedImg.Height = oInsertedImg.Height * .30
        'Centre alignment of image
        oInsertedImg.Range.ParagraphFormat.Alignment = 1
        'write caption
        .TypeParagraph
        .TypeText "Image Inserted"
        .TypeParagraph
    End With
```

Printing Documents

In certain scenarios, it is required to print a Word documents. The 'PrintOut' method can be used to print all the pages of a Word file.

```
oWordDoc.PrintOut
```

Formatting Text in Documents

While preparing the custom-run reports, it is also important to make it readable by selecting different fonts and styles in a Word document. MS Word provides many methods to define the font and style of the Word document. The following example shows how to set the font and styles programmatically for text in a Word document.

```
Set oWordSelect = oWordApp.Selection
With oWordSelect
        'Select font Times New Roman
           .Style = "Heading 1"
           .Font.Name = "Times New Roman"
           .Font.Size = 10
           .Font.Bold = True
           .Font.ColorIndex = 1
           .TypeText "Font style - Times New Roman. Font
            Size - 10"
           .TypeParagraph
        'Select font Arial Narrow
           .Font.Name = "Arial Narrow"
           .Font.Size = 10
           .Font.Bold = False
           .Font.Italic = True
           .Font.ColorIndex = 2
           .TypeText "Font style - Arial Narrow. Font
            Size - 10"
           .TypeParagraph
End With
```

Counting Words and Characters in Documents

The following code shows how to count the number of words and characters in a Word document.

```
'Select whole word document
oWordDoc.Range.Select
Set oWordSelect = oWordApp.Selection

'Word count
MsgBox oWordSelect.Words.Count

'Character count
MsgBox oWordSelect.Characters.Count
```

Searching for Text in Documents

The 'Find' method is used to search for specific strings inside a Word document.

Example: To find the count of matching expressions in a Word document.

```
Dim nMchCnt : nMchCnt = 0
'Create an instance of word application
Set oWordApp = CreateObject("Word.Application")

'Make word application visible
oWordApp.Visible = False

'Open existing word file
Set oWordDoc = oWordApp.Documents.Open("C:\Temp\WordDoc.docx")

Set oWordSelect = oWordApp.Selection

With oWordSelect.Find
          .Text = "Search Strinq"
          .Forward = True
          .Wrap = wdFindContinue
          .Format = False
          .MatchCase = False
          .MatchWholeWord = False
          .MatchWildcards = False
          .MatchSoundsLike = False
          .MatchAllWordForms = False
End With

Do While True
      oWordSelect.Find.Execute
      If oWordSelect.Find.Found Then
           nMchCnt = nMchCnt + 1
      Else
           Exit Do
      End If
Loop
```

```
'Count of matched expressions
MsgBox nMchCnt

'Close word document
oWordDoc.Close

'Exit word application
oWordApp.Quit

Set oWordApp = Nothing
```

Replacing Texts in Documents

The ‘Replace’ method is used to replace one string with another inside a Word document.

```
Dim nMchCnt : nMchCnt = 0
Const wdReplaceNone = 0
Const wdReplaceOne = 1
Const wdReplaceAll = 2

'Create an instance of word application
Set oWordApp = CreateObject("Word.Application")

'Make word application visible
oWordApp.Visible = False

'Open existing word file
Set oWordDoc = oWordApp.Documents.Open("C:\Temp\WordDoc.docx")

Set oWordSelect = oWordApp.Selection

With oWordSelect.Find
          .Text = "Actual Text"
          .Replacement.Text = "Replaced Text"
          .Forward = True
          .Wrap = wdFindContinue
          .Format = False
          .MatchCase = False
          .MatchWholeWord = False
          .MatchWildcards = False
          .MatchSoundsLike = False
          .MatchAllWordForms = False
End With

'Replace expressions
oWordSelect.Find.Execute ,,,,,,,,,,wdReplaceAll

'Save document
oWordDoc.Save

'Close word document
oWordDoc.Close
```

```
'Exit word application
oWordApp.Quit
Set oWordApp = Nothing
```

Creating Tables in Documents

For custom test-run word reports, tables can be created to make the reports more readable. The following code shows how to create a table inside a Word document.

Example: Create a table of (5, 3) and add data to its cells.

```
'Create an instance of word application
Set oWordApp = CreateObject("Word.Application")
'Make word application visible
oWordApp.Visible = False
'Open existing word file
Set oWordDoc = oWordApp.Documents.Open ("C:\Temp\WordDoc.docx")
Set oWordSelect = oWordApp.Selection
'Add table of 5, 3
Set oNewTbl = oWordSelect.Tables.Add (oWordSelect.Range, 5, 3)
'Add header row data
'Set the font and style of table
oNewTbl.Range.Style = "Table Grid"
oNewTbl.Range.Font.Size = 10
oNewTbl.Range.Font.Bold = True
For iCnt = 1 to 3 Step 1
      oNewTbl.Cell(1,iCnt).Range.Text = "Col" & iCnt
Next
'Add data to table
oNewTbl.Range.Font.Size = 10
oNewTbl.Range.Font.Bold = False
For iCnt=2 to 5 Step 1
      For jCnt = 1 to 3 Step 1
            oNewTbl.Cell(iCnt,jCnt).Range.Text = iCnt & "," & jCnt
      Next
Next
'Save document
oWordDoc.Save
'Close word document
oWordDoc.Close
Exit word application
oWordApp.Quit
Set oWordApp = Nothing
```

QUICK TIPS

✓ The Application object represents the Word application. It is the parent of all other objects.

✓ The Documents object represents a collection of all open Word documents.

PRACTICAL QUESTIONS

1. Write a code to create a new Word file, write data to it, and save it.
2. Write a code to open an already created file in invisible mode.
3. Write a code to read an already opened file on the screen.
4. Write a code to create a table inside a Word file and write data to it.
5. Write a code to change the text style and the color of the text of the Word file.

Chapter 49

Working with An E-Mail Client

E-mail client is an application that runs on a personal computer or workstation and enables the user to send, receive, and organize an e-mail. It is called a client, as the e-mail systems are based on the client–server architecture. E-mail is sent from many clients to a central server, which re-routes the e-mail to its intended destination. Microsoft Office Outlook, IBM Lotus Notes, and Windows Live e-mail are a few examples. In this chapter, we discuss how to automate the e-mail clients and send and receive e-mails using codes.

MICROSOFT OUTLOOK

Microsoft Outlook is the e-mail client included with the Microsoft Office suite. It is designed to operate as an independent personal information manager, as an Internet e-mail client, or in conjunction with the Microsoft Exchange Server for group scheduling, e-mail, and task management. It manages e-mails, calendars, contacts, tasks, to-do lists, and documents or files on the hard drive. Figure 49.1 shows a part of the object model of Outllok. Figure 49.2 shows the *Object Browser* window of the Outlook application.

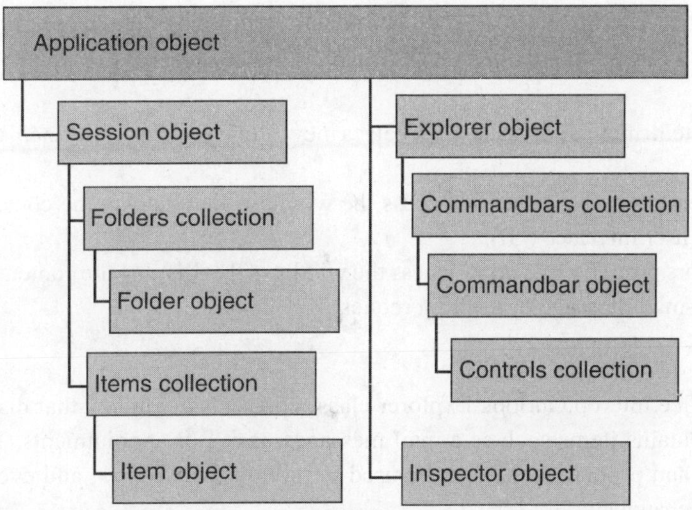

Figure 49.1 *Outlook object model diagram*

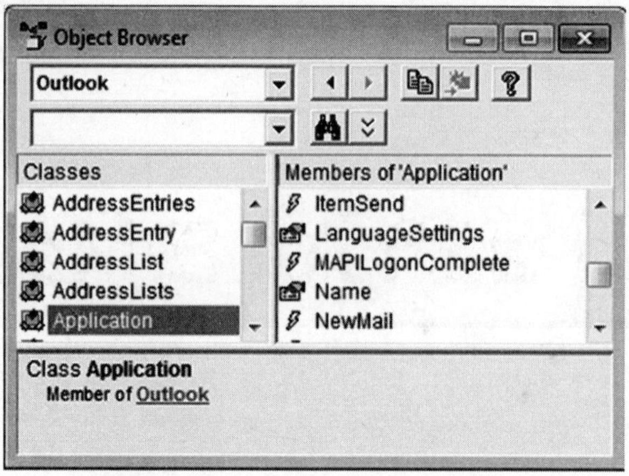

Figure 49.2 *Outlook object browser*

Object Model

Outlook provides many classes with which we can interact. The following sections briefly describe some of the top-level classes and their interaction with each other. These classes include the following:

- Microsoft.Office.Interop.Outlook.Application
- Microsoft.Office.Interop.Outlook.Explorer
- Microsoft.Office.Interop.Outlook.Inspector
- Microsoft.Office.Interop.Outlook.MAPIFolder
- Microsoft.Office.Interop.Outlook.MailItem
- Microsoft.Office.Interop.Outlook.AppointmentItem
- Microsoft.Office.Interop.Outlook.TaskItem
- Microsoft.Office.Interop.Outlook.ContactItem

Application Class

The Microsoft.Office.Interop.Outlook.Application class represents the Outlook application. It is the highest-level class in the Outlook object model. The following are some of the most important members of this class:

- The CreateItem method is used to create a new item such as an e-mail message, task, or appointment.
- The Explorers property is used to access the windows that display the contents of a folder in the Outlook user interface (UI).
- The Inspectors property is used to access the windows that display the contents of a single item, such as an e-mail message or meeting request.

Explorer Class

The Microsoft.Office.Interop.Outlook.Explorer class represents a window that displays the contents of a folder that contains items such as e-mail messages, tasks, or appointments. The Explorer class includes methods and properties that can be used to modify the window, and events that are raised when the window changes.

Inspector Class

The Microsoft.Office.Interop.Outlook.Inspector class represents a window that displays a single item such as an e-mail message, task, or appointment in the Outlook UI. The Inspector class includes methods and properties that can be used to modify the window, and events that are raised when the window changes.

MAPIFolder Class

The Microsoft.Office.Interop.Outlook.MAPIFolder class represents a folder that contains e-mail messages, contacts, tasks, and other items. Outlook provides 16 default MAPIFolder objects. The default MAPIFolder objects are defined by the Microsoft.Office.Interop.Outlook.OlDefaultFolders enumeration values. For example, OlDefaultFolders.olFolderInbox corresponds to the Inbox folder in the Outlook.

MailItem Class

The Microsoft.Office.Interop.Outlook.MailItem class represents an e-mail message. MailItem objects are usually in folders such as Inbox, Sent Items, and Outbox. The MailItem class exposes properties and methods that can be used to create and send e-mail messages.

AppointmentItem Class

The Microsoft.Office.Interop.Outlook.AppointmentItem class represents a meeting, a one-time appointment, or a recurring appointment or meeting in the Calendar folder. The AppointmentItem class includes methods that perform actions such as responding to or forwarding meeting requests, and properties that specify meeting details such as the location and time.

TaskItem Class

The Microsoft.Office.Interop.Outlook.TaskItem class represents a task to be performed within a specified time frame. The TaskItem objects are located in the Tasks folder. To create a task, use the CreateItem method of the Microsoft.Office.Tools.Outlook.Application class, and pass in the value Microsoft.Office.Interop.Outlook.OlItemType.olTaskItem for the parameter.

ContactItem Class

The Microsoft.Office.Interop.Outlook.ContactItemclass represents a contact in the Contacts folder. The ContactItem objects contain a variety of contact information for the people they represent, such as street addresses, e-mail addresses, and telephone numbers.

Launching Microsoft Outlook

```
'Create an instance of outlook application
Set oOutlookApp = CreateObject("Outlook.Application")

'Get reference of namespace object
Set oMAPI = oOutlookApp.GetNamespace("MAPI")
```

Login to Outlook

The Logon method of Namespace object is used to login to Outlook.

```
Syntax : Object.Logon(Profile, Password, ShowDialog, NewSession)
```

However, the Profile and Password fields can be left blank if Microsoft Outlook is already configured to login to default profile.

```
'Login
oMAPI.Logon    ,False, True

'Logoff
oMAPI.Logoff
```

Sending An E-mail

The following code sends an e-mail by creating an instance of Outlook.

```
Dim nMailItem : nMailItem = 0

'Create an instance of outlook application
Set oOutlookApp = CreateObject("Outlook.Application")

'Create a new e-mail item
Set oMailItem = oOutlookApp.CreateItem(nMailItem)

'Define TO field of e-mail
oMailItem.To = "abc@gmail.com;xyz@yahoo.com"

'Define CC field of e-mail
oMailItem.Cc = "def@gmail.com;pqr@yahoo.com"

'Define subject field of e-mail
oMailItem.Subject = "Subject of E-mail"

'Turn-off read receipt request
oMailItem.ReadReceiptRequested = False

'Define body of e-mail
oMailItem.Body = "Body Text of E-mail"

'Add attachments to e-mail
oMailItem.Attachments.Add ("C:\Temp\Attachment.doc")

'Send e-mail
oMailItem.Send
```

Generally, in test automation, e-mail client automation is done to automatically send the test-run results to the concerned people. The e-mail client automation becomes helpful when the QTP machines are kept in a separate server room or if a user needs to track the test-run results from his home. In these circumstances, there is a requirement to e-mail multiple test-run results to the user. One way to achieve this is to zip all the requisite files first and then send them as a single file. Function `fnZipFile` shows the code to zip all the contents of a folder using application Winzip32.

Input parameters:

```
sSrcLoc—Source folder to zip
sDestLoc—Destination location of zipped file
```

Output parameter:

```
sZipFileNm—Zipped file name and path
```

Usage:

```
sSrcLoc = "Z:\Results\Mod1\TestResults_12Jul2010_105858AM"
sDestLoc = "C:\Temp"

Call fnZipFile(sSrcLoc, sDestLoc, sZipFileNm)
MsgBox  sZipFileNm        ' Output : "C:\Temp\ResultLog.zip"
```

```
Public Function fnZipFile(sSrcLoc, sDestLoc, sZipFileNm)
    On Error Resume Next
    '-------  Copy Result data Files to C:\Temp ---------------------
    sDestFile = sDestLoc & "\ResultLog"
    Set filesys = CreateObject("Scripting.FileSystemObject")
    filesys.CopyFolder sSrcLoc, sDestFile, True
    Set filesys = Nothing

    sZipFileNm = sDestFile & ".zip"

    'Zip file using Winzip32
    Set oShell = CreateObject("WScript.Shell")
    iRC = oShell.Run("winzip32 -a " & sDestFile & " " & sDestFile, 2, True)
    Set oShell = Nothing
End Function
```

Outlook Security Dialog Box

Outlook Express throws a security modal dialog box (see Fig. 49.3) when an attempt is made to send e-mails using the codes. The user is required to click 'yes' to send the e-mail. There are various ways to deal with this pop-up dialog box.

Method 1

Design a VBScript code that can click 'yes' on this dialog box. This code needs to be activated before sending the e-mail or it should be run on the e-mail client machine all the time.

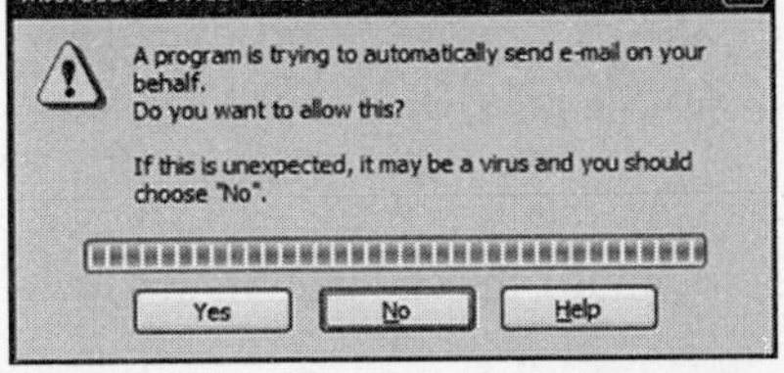

Figure 49.3 *Outlook security pop-up*

```
OutlookPopupClick.vbs
      Set oFSO = CreateObject("WScript.Shell")
      While oFSO.AppActivate("Microsoft Office Outlook") = FALSE
            wscript.sleep 1000
      Wend
      wscript.sleep 10000
      oFSO.SendKeys "a", True
      oFSO.SendKeys "y", True
      Set oFSO = Nothing
```

In Windows 7 environment, this code may not work. The following code could be used to click on the 'yes' button in Windows 7 operating system.

```
OutlookPopupClick.vbs
      Set oFSO = CreateObject("WScript.Shell")
      While oFSO.AppActivate("Microsoft Office Outlook") = FALSE
            wscript.sleep 1000
      Wend
      fso.AppActivate("Microsoft Office Outlook")
      wscript.sleep 10000
      fso.AppActivate("Microsoft Office Outlook")
      fso.SendKeys "{LEFT}"
      fso.AppActivate("Microsoft Office Outlook")
      fso.SendKeys "{LEFT}"
      wscript.sleep 2000
      fso.SendKeys "{LEFT}"
      wscript.sleep 2000
      fso.SendKeys "{RIGHT}"
      fso.SendKeys "{ENTER}"
```

Method 2

After sending the e-mail through .vbs code file, use QTP test script to click on the 'yes' button on this dialog box.

Method 3

Automate Microsoft Outlook and send e-mail using its GUI end. The e-mail sent through Outlook GUI end does not throw any security warning dialog box.

Method 4

Use utility `ClickYes` to click on the 'yes' button.

The following code shows how to suppress the 'Security Window' dialog box to send e-mail programmatically.

Function `fnSendMail_OE` uses Method 1 to send an e-mail to the desired recipients.

Input parameters:

```
      sEmailTo = "abc@gmail.com; pqr@yahoo.co.in"
      sEmailCc= "xyz@gmail.com"
```

```
    sSubject= "Regression Run on Release " & Now
    sBodyText = " Test cases executed , Test cases passed, Test cases
    failed "
    sAttachment = "C:\Temp\ResultLog.zip"
```

Usage:

```
    Call fnSendMail_OE(sEmailTo, sEmailCc, sSubject, sBodyText, sAttachment)

Public Function fnSendMail_OE(sEmailTo, sEmailCc, sSubject, sBodyText,
sAttachment)
    Dim oOutlookApp
    Dim oShell

    'Execute a vbs file to click 'yes' on outlook security popup
    Set oShell = CreateObject("WScript.Shell")
    oShell.Run "Z:\Utility\OutlookPopupClick.vbs"
    Set oShell = Nothing

    Set oOutlookApp = CreateObject("Outlook.Application")

    Set oMailItem = oOutlookApp.CreateItem(0)
    With oMailItem
        .To = sEmailTo
        .CC =sEmailCc
        .Subject = sSubject
        .Body = sBodyText
        .Attachments.Add (sAttachment)
    End With

    oMailItem.Send

End Function
```

Enumerating Mailbox Folders

The Namespace object provides Folders Collection for the top-level folders in the mailbox. The Folders Collection object is used to enumerate all the e-mails available in the mailbox.

```
'Create an instance of outlook application
Set oOutlookApp = CreateObject("Outlook.Application")

'Get reference of namespace object
Set oMAPI = oOutlookApp.GetNamespace("MAPI")

'Enumerate top level folders
For Each oFolder In oMAPI.Folders
    MsgBox oFolder.Name                 'Output : "Public Folders"
Next
```

Mailbox folders can also be accessed by their index or name. The following are the various ways of accessing mailbox top-level folders:

```
Set oTopLvlFolder = oMAPI.Folders.GetFirst
Set oTopLvlFolder = oMAPI.Folders.Item(1)
Set oTopLvlFolder = oMAPI.Folders.Item("Public Folders")
```

Reading an E-mail Messages

The Outlook Item Collection object can be used to access e-mail messages inside a folder. The following code shows how to retrieve the count of unread e-mail messages in the Inbox folder.

```
nUnreadCnt = 0

'Create an instance of outlook application
Set oOutlookApp = CreateObject("Outlook.Application")

'Get reference of namespace object
Set oMAPI = oOutlookApp.GetNamespace("MAPI")

'Define inbox constant folder value
Const nInboxFolder = 6

'Get reference of inbox folder
Set oInbox = oMAPI.GetDefaultFolder(nInboxFolder)

'Get mailbox items
Set oMailItems = oInbox.Items

'Count number of unread e-mails
For Each oMailItem in oInbox.Items
	If oMailItem.Unread = True Then
		nUnreadCnt = nUnreadCnt + 1
	End If
Next

'Display count of unread e-mails
Print nUnreadCnt
```

This code iterates through all e-mail items to find the unread e-mails. If the count of e-mails in the mailbox is large, the code execution will take time. The solution to this is to use the *Restrict* method of Items Collection. This method can be used to filter out the desired e-mails.

Example 1: Write a code to retrieve all unread e-mails from the Inbox.

```
'Get mailbox items
Set oMailItems = oInbox.Items

'Retrieve all unread e-mails from inbox
Set colUnreadMailItems = oMailItems.Restrict("[Unread] = True")
Print colUnreadMailItems.Count
```

Example 2: Write a Code to Retrieve all e-Mails from a Particular Sender.

```
Set colUnreadMailItems = oMailItems.Restrict("[Unread] = True And [From] =
                        'Penny Wilson' ")
Print colUnreadMailItems.Count
```

Example 3: Write a Code to Retrieve all E-Mails not Sent from a Particular Sender.

```
Set colUnreadMailItems = oMailItems.Restrict("[Unread] = True And Not
                         [From] = 'Penny Wilson' ")
Print colUnreadMailItems.Count
```

Example 4: Write a Code to Retrieve all E-Mails with a Specific Subject Name.

```
Set colUnreadMailItems = oMailItems.Restrict("[Unread] = True And
                        [Subject] = 'Test Run Results' ")
Print colUnreadMailItems.Count
```

> **NOTES** The restrict method supports AND, OR, and NOT operations. However, it does not support the LIKE operator.

Reading Subject, Body, and Addresses of E-mail Messages

Example 5: Write a Code to Read the Subject, Body, and Addresses of E-mail Messages.

```
'Create an instance of outlook application
Set oOutlookApp = CreateObject("Outlook.Application")

'Get reference of namespace object
Set oMAPI = oOutlookApp.GetNamespace("MAPI")

'Define inbox constant folder value
Const nInboxFolder = 6

'Get reference of inbox folder
Set oInbox = oMAPI. GetDefaultFolder (nInboxFolder)

'Get mailbox items
Set oMailItems = oInbox.Items

Set colUnreadMailItems = oMailItems.Restrict("[Unread] = True")

iCnt=1
For Each oUnreadMailItem In colUnreadMailItems
      'Get senders name
      arrEmailSenderNm(iCnt) = oUnreadMailItem.SenderName

      'Get senders e-mail address
      arrEmailSenderEmailAddr(iCnt) = oUnreadMailItem.SenderEmailAddress
```

```
        'Get the e-mail addresses of the To field
        arrTo(iCnt) = oUnreadMailItem.To

        'Get the e-mail addresses of the Cc field
        arrCc(iCnt) = oUnreadMailItem.Cc

        'Get the e-mail subject
        arrEmailSubject(iCnt) = oUnreadMailItem.Subject

        'Get the e-mail body
        arrEmailBody(iCnt) = oUnreadMailItem.Body

        iCnt = iCnt + 1
Next
```

Downloading Attachments

The attachment property of Items Collection can be used to download attachments of an e-mail.

```
'Set oEmailItem = oMailItems (1)
'Or,
Set oEmailItem = colUnreadMailItems(1)

'Download attachments
For Each oAttachment In oEmailItem.Attachments
        oAttachment.SaveAsFile("C:\Temp\" & oAttachment.FileName)
Next
```

IBM LOTUS NOTES

Lotus Notes is the client side of a client–server, collaborative application developed and sold by IBM Software Group. IBM describes the software as an 'integrated desktop client option for accessing business e-mail, calendars and applications on [an] IBM Lotus Domino server.'

Launching Lotus Notes

The following code shows how to programmatically open Lotus Notes.

```
'Start a session to notes
Set oSession = CreateObject("Notes.NotesSession")

'Get the sessions username and then calculate the e-mail file name
'It may or may not be needed as for e-mail db name with some systems, one
'can pass an empty string
sUserName = oSession.UserName

sMailDbName = Left(sUserName, 1) & Right(sUserName, (Len(sUserName) -
InStr(1, sUserName, " "))) & ".nsf"
```

```
'Open the e-mail database in notes
Set oMaildb = oSession.GETDATABASE("", sMailDbName)

'Use code below instead of above if db file name is not required
'Set oMaildb = oSession.GETDATABASE("", "e-mail.box")

If oMaildb.IsOpen = True Then
      'Already open
Else
      oMaildb.OPENMAIL
End If
```

Sending An E-mail

The following code shows how to send an e-mail programmatically using Lotus Notes.

```
'Create new e-mail
Set oMailDoc = oMaildb.CREATEDOCUMENT
oMailDoc.Form = "Memo"

'Define e-mail receipients
oMailDoc.sendto = "abc@yahoo.com, pqr@gmail.com"
oMailDoc.copyto = "xyz@yahoo.com"

'Define subject of e-mail
oMailDoc.Subject = "Subject Line"

'Write e-mail body text
oMailDoc.Body = "Body test of the e-mail"

'Save e-mail copy
oMailDoc.SAVEMESSAGEONSEND = SaveIt

'Send the document
oMailDoc.Send 0, sEmailTo
```

Sending An E-mail with Attachments

The following code shows how to send an e-mail with attachments using Lotus Notes.

```
sAttachment = "C:\Temp\ResultLog.zip"
Set oAttachME = oMailDoc.CREATERICHTEXTITEM("Attachment")
Set oEmbedObj = oAttachME.EMBEDOBJECT(1454, "", sAttachment,
              "Attachment")
oMailDoc.CREATERICHTEXTITEM ("Attachment")

'Send the document
oMailDoc.Send 0, sEmailTo
```

Function `fnSendMail_LotusNotes` sends an e-mail to recipients using Lotus Notes e-mail client. It first launches Lotus Notes and if it is not opened, then sends an e-mail with attachments to recipients.

Input parameters:

```
    sEmailTo = "abc@gmail.com, pqr@yahoo.co.in"
    sEmailCc = "xyz@gmail.com"
    sSubject = "Regression Run on Release" & Now
    sBodyText = " Test cases executed, Test cases passed, Test cases
             failed"
sAttachment = "C:\Temp\ResultLog.zip"
```

Usage:

```
Call fnSendMail_LotusNotes(sEmailTo, sEmailCc, sSubject, sBodyText,
   sAttachment)

Function fnSendMail_LotusNotes(sEmailTo, sEmailCc, sSubject,
   sBodyText, sAttachment)
  On Error Resume Next
    Dim oMaildb           'e-mail database
    Dim sUserName         'current users notes name
    Dim sMailDbName       'current users notes e-mail database name
    Dim oMailDoc          'e-mail document itself
    Dim oAttachME         'attachment richtextfile object
    Dim oSession          'notes session
    Dim oEmbedObj         'embedded object (Attachment)

    'Save e-mail recepients to array
    arrEmailTo = Split(sEmailTo, ",", -1, vbTextCompare)
    arrEmailCc = Split(sEmailCc, ",", -1, vbTextCompare)


    ' Start a session to notes
    Set oSession = CreateObject("Notes.NotesSession")

    ' Get the sessions username and then calculate the e-mail file name
    sUserName = oSession.UserName

sMailDbName = Left(sUserName, 1) & Right(sUserName, (Len(sUserName) -
InStr(1, sUserName, " "))) & ".nsf"

    ' Open the e-mail database in notes
    Set oMaildb = oSession.GETDATABASE("", sMailDbName)
    ' Set oMaildb = oSession.GETDATABASE("", "e-mail.box")
    If oMaildb.IsOpen = True Then
        'Already open for e-mail
    Else
        oMaildb.OPENMAIL
    End If
```

```
    'Set up the new e-mail document
    Set oMailDoc = oMaildb.CREATEDOCUMENT
    oMailDoc.Form = "Memo"
    oMailDoc.sendto = arrEmailTo
    oMailDoc.copyto = arrEmailCc
    oMailDoc.Subject = sSubject
    oMailDoc.Body = sBodyText
    oMailDoc.SAVEMESSAGEONSEND = SaveIt

    'Set up the embedded object and attachment and attach it
    If sAttachment <>"" Then
        Set oAttachME = oMailDoc.CREATERICHTEXTITEM("Attachment")
        Set oEmbedObj = oAttachME.EMBEDOBJECT(1454, "", sAttachment,
                                              "Attachment")
        oMailDoc.CREATERICHTEXTITEM ("Attachment")
    End If
    ' Send the document
    oMailDoc.Send 0, arrEmailTo

    ' Destroy variables
    Set oMaildb = Nothing
    Set oMailDoc = Nothing
    Set oAttachME = Nothing
    Set oSession = Nothing
    Set oEmbedObj = Nothing

End Function
```

Sending An E-mails using Telnet via Gmail

Telnet is a network protocol used on the Internet or local area networks to provide a bidirectional interactive text-oriented communications facility via a virtual terminal connection. It enables one computer to communicate with another via the Internet. The program is used to make a connection with the server. Such connection acts as the client in this situation. The term Telnet may also refer to the software that implements the client part of the protocol. Gmail is a free, advertising-supported webmail, POP3, and IMAP service provided by Google. In this section, we discuss how to send e-mails using Telnet protocol via Gmail. To send e-mails using the Telnet protocol, the Telnet client must first be enabled on the system from which the e-mail needs to be sent. Type the following code in command prompt to send e-mail using Telnet client via Gmail.

```
telnet gmail-smtp-in.l.google.com 25
HELO gmail-smtp-in.l.google.com
EHLO [10.0.0.1]\0D\0A
MAIL FROM: <zone@gmail.com>
RCPT TO: <zones@gmail.com>
'data
From:<zone@gmail.com>
```

```
To:<zones@gmail.com>
Cc:<zone1@yahoo.co.in>
Date:Mon, 07 July 2008
Subject: Test Message

Hello Anyone
This is a Test message
.
Quit
#End data with <CR><LF>.<CR><LF>
.
Quit
```

The following code shows how to send an e-mail using Gmail.

Function `fnSendMail_GMail` shows how to send e-mails using Telnet protocol via Gmail.

Input parameters:

```
sFrom = "pqr@gmail.com"
dtMailDate = "Mon, 07 July 2008"
sEmailTo = "abc@gmail.com"
sEmailCc= "xyz@yahoo.co.in"
sSubject= "Regression Run on Release" & Now
sBodyText = " Test cases executed, Test cases passed, Test cases
             failed"
```

Usage:

```
    Call fnSendMail_GMail(sFrom, dtMailDate, sEmailTo, sEmailCc,
sSubject, sBodyText)


Public Function fnSendMail_GMail(sFrom, dtMailDate. sEmailTo, sE-
mailCc, sSubject, sBodyText)
  'ENABLE TELNET CLIENT AND
  'TYPE THE LINES BELOW IN COMMAND PROMPT TO SEND E-MAIL
  SystemUtil.Run "C:\Windows\system32\cmd.exe"
  Wait(2)
  Window("regexpwndclass:=ConsoleWindowClass").Type "telnet gmail-
                                       smtp-in.l.google.com 25"
  Window("regexpwndclass:=ConsoleWindowClass").Type micReturn
  Wait(15)
  Window("regexpwndclass:=ConsoleWindowClass").Type "HELO gmail-
                                       smtp-in.l.google.com"
  Window("regexpwndclass:=ConsoleWindowClass").Type micReturn
  Wait(2)
  Window("regexpwndclass:=ConsoleWindowClass").Type "EHLO
                                       [10.0.0.1]\0D\0A"
  Window("regexpwndclass:=ConsoleWindowClass").Type micReturn
```

```
    Wait(2)
    Window("regexpwndclass:=ConsoleWindowClass").Type "E-MAIL FROM: " & sFrom
    Window("regexpwndclass:=ConsoleWindowClass").Type micReturn
    Wait(2)
    Window("regexpwndclass:=ConsoleWindowClass").Type "RCPT TO: " & sEmailTo
    Window("regexpwndclass:=ConsoleWindowClass").Type micReturn
    Wait(2)
    Window("regexpwndclass:=ConsoleWindowClass").Type "data"
    Window("regexpwndclass:=ConsoleWindowClass").Type micReturn
    Wait(2)
    Window("regexpwndclass:=ConsoleWindowClass").Type "From:" & sFrom
    Window("regexpwndclass:=ConsoleWindowClass").Type micReturn
    Wait(2)
    Window("regexpwndclass:=ConsoleWindowClass").Type "To:" & sEmailTo
    Window("regexpwndclass:=ConsoleWindowClass").Type micReturn
    Wait(2)
    Window("regexpwndclass:=ConsoleWindowClass").Type "Cc:" & sEmailCc
    Window("regexpwndclass:=ConsoleWindowClass").Type micReturn
    Wait(2)
    Window("regexpwndclass:=ConsoleWindowClass").Type "Date:" & dtMailDate
    Window("regexpwndclass:=ConsoleWindowClass").Type micReturn
    Wait(2)
    Window("regexpwndclass:=ConsoleWindowClass").Type "Subject:" & sSubject
    Window("regexpwndclass:=ConsoleWindowClass").Type micReturn
    Wait(2)
    Window("regexpwndclass:=ConsoleWindowClass").Type ""
    Window("regexpwndclass:=ConsoleWindowClass").Type micReturn
    Wait(2)
    Window("regexpwndclass:=ConsoleWindowClass").Type sBodyText
    Window("regexpwndclass:=ConsoleWindowClass").Type micReturn
    Wait(2)
    Window("regexpwndclass:=ConsoleWindowClass").Type "."
    Window("regexpwndclass:=ConsoleWindowClass").Type micReturn
    Wait(2)
    Window("regexpwndclass:=ConsoleWindowClass").Type "Quit"
    Window("regexpwndclass:=ConsoleWindowClass").Type micReturn
    Wait(2)
    Window("regexpwndclass:=ConsoleWindowClass").Type "."
    Window("regexpwndclass:=ConsoleWindowClass").Type micReturn
    Wait(2)
    Window("regexpwndclass:=ConsoleWindowClass").Type "Quit"
    Window("regexpwndclass:=ConsoleWindowClass").Type micReturn
    Wait(2)
    Window("regexpwndclass:=ConsoleWindowClass").Close

End Function
```

Launching QTP Using An E-mail Trigger

Method 1

Macros can be written in Outlook environment to execute QTP script execution on trigger of an e-mail. Rules can be set using *Rules Wizard* that monitors every new e-mail received, and depending on the rule set, it can execute an Outlook macro code.

```
  'Rule script to be executed when an e-mail with subject line RunQTP-
Script_MasterDriver is called
   Public Sub RunQTPScript_MasterDriver(Item As Outlook.MailItem)
          Set oShell = CreateObject("WScript.Shell")
          oShell.Run "Z:\Utility\RunQTP.vbs " & sParameters , , False
          Set oShell = Nothing
   End Sub
```

To write the macro code in Outlook, perform the following steps:

1. Open Outlook
2. Press Alt+F11
3. Create a new module
4. Inside the module, write a subroutine that can execute QTP scripts

> **NOTES** It is advisable to launch and execute QTP from external .vbs file than from Outlook. If QTP is launched and executed from Outlook environment, Outlook will get blocked till QTP script execution.

5. Go to *Tools Rules & Alerts*.
6. Click *New Rule* button. *Rules Wizard* window opens. Now configure the rule as desired.

Check the checkbox *Run a script* and select the function rule RunQTPScript_MasterDriver.

Method 2

An external .vbs file can be written that continuously monitors the Microsoft Outlook for new e-mails received. A predefined rule specifying the QTP execution condition can be coded like launch of QTP and execution of a particular test script, if an e-mail is received with subject line `RunQTPScript_MasterDriver`.

> **NOTES** For how to launch QTP and execute test scripts in QTP using VBScript code (.vbs file), refer chapter QTP Automation Object Model.

☞ QUICK TIPS

✓ In test automation, automation of an e-mail clients is done to automatically send test-run reports or updates to the concerned users.

✓ Automation of e-mail clients can also be used to automatically trigger regression suite execution on receipt of a e-mail. For example, to automatically trigger regression execution on receipt of a e-mail suggesting successful deployment of the build.

? PRACTICAL QUESTIONS

1. Write a code to send a e-mail using Microsoft Outlook.
2. Write a code to read the subject of all unread Outlook e-mails.
3. Write a code to find the count of all e-mails received within a specific time range, e.g., between 10:00 am and 11:00 am.
4. Write a code to send a e-mail using Lotus Notes.
5. Write a code to send an attachment using Lotus Notes.

Section 9 Advanced UFT

- Working with Object Native Properties
- HTML DOM
- Object Repository Automation
- UFT Automation Object Model

Chapter 50

Working with Object Native Properties

Native properties are the attributes of the object defined by the application developer while creating the object. UFT has built-in support for most of the standard HTML object attributes. The UFT supported attributes are termed as Identification Properties. UFT can automatically learn the identification properties of the object. Most often identification properties are sufficient to uniquely describe and identify the object. However, in rare scenarios the identification properties may not be sufficient enough to uniquely describe or locate the object. In such situations, automation developers can explore the native properties of the object and can use them to uniquely identify the object in UI.

In this chapter, we will discuss how to identify and retrieve native properties of the object. We will also discuss how to use native properties of the object to identify object using descriptive programming and object repository approach.

FINDING OBJECT NATIVE PROPERTIES

The first step towards working on object native properties is to find what native properties have been defined by the developer for the object. There are two ways to view the native properties of the object:

- Using object spy tool
- Using HTML code of the object

Consider a flight reservation site as shown in the Fig. 50.1.

Using Object Spy to View Object Native Properties

UFT Object Spy tool provides the flexibility to the automation developers to view the native properties and native methods of the object.

Consider a flight reservation site as shown in Figure 50.1 below.

Let's see how Object Spy tool can help us view and analyze the native properties of the objects in this application. To view native properties of the object using object spy tool select the 'Native' radio button on the object spy tool. Figure 50.2 below shows the native properties of the 'Going to' edit box object.

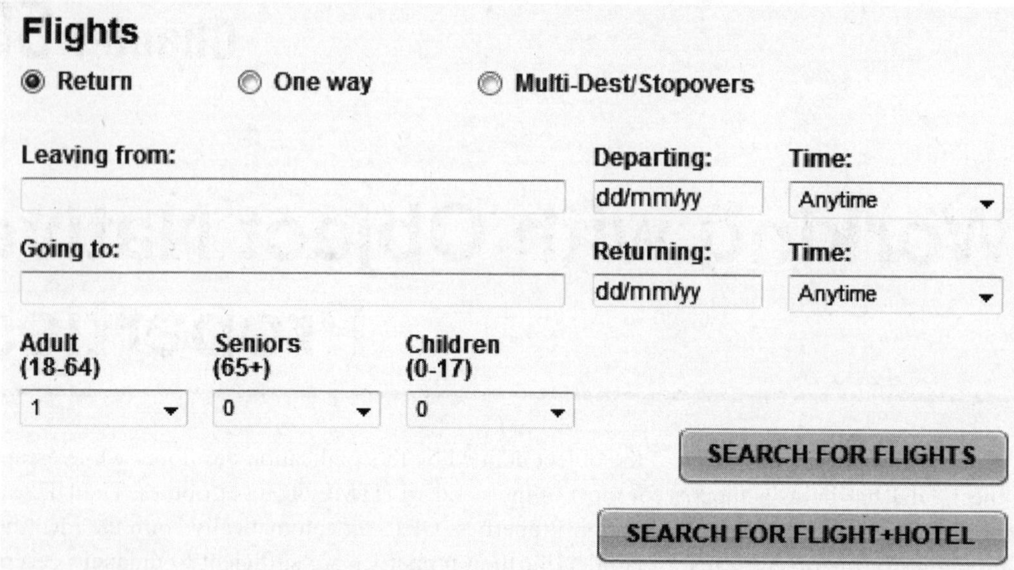

Figure 50.1 *Sample flight reservation application*

Using HTML Code of the Object to View Object Native Properties

The HTML code of the object contains all the attributes defined for the object. Refer chapter 'Objects' for how to view HTML code of an object in various browsers. Figure 50.3 below shows the HTML code of the 'Going To' edit box as viewed in Firefox browser.

Alternatively, HTML code of the object can also be viewed in the '*outerHTML*' property of object spy window (refer Figure 50.2).

RETRIEVING OBJECT NATIVE PROPERTIES

UFT provides the flexibility to the automation developers to read or retrieve the native properties of the object using UFT test code. There are two ways to retrieve the run-time native properties of the object:

- By using .Object method
- By using attribute/* notation

Using .Object Method to Read Native Properties

Example 1: Retrieve the maxLength attribute of the 'Going To' edit box.

Consider the HTML code of the 'Going To' edit box as shown in Figure 50.2 is as mentioned below.

```
<input id="uw_flight_destination_input" class="xp-b-
clear" type="text" maxlength="100" notequalmessage="notequalmessage
" notequal="uw_flight_origin_input" requiredmessage="requiredFieldMe
ssage" required="true" value="" autocomplete="off"/>
```

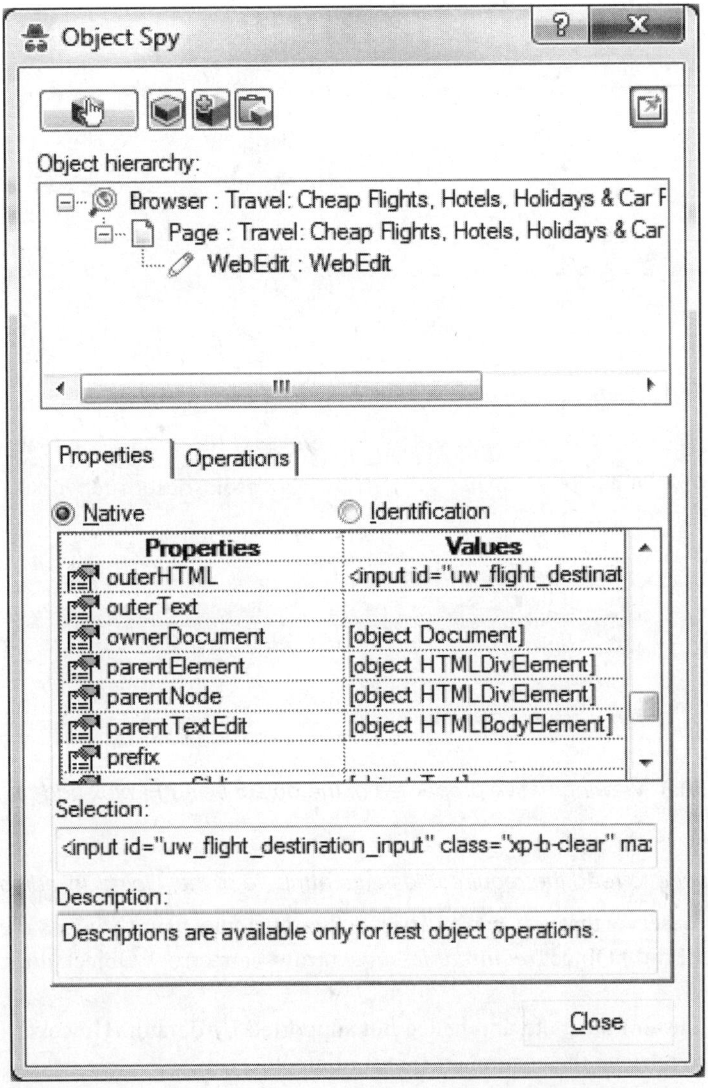

Figure 50.2 *Viewing native properties of the object using object spy*

Code below shows how to retrieve *maxLength* attribute value using .*Object* method:

```
Set oPg = Browser("B").Page("P")
Print oPg.WebEdit("WebEdit").Object.maxLength    'Output::100
```

Example 2: Write code to read the 'id' attribute of the 'Going To' edit box object.

Code below shows how to retrieve *id* attribute value using .*Object* method:

```
Print oPg.WebEdit("WebEdit").Object.id
'Output:: uw_flight_destination_input
```

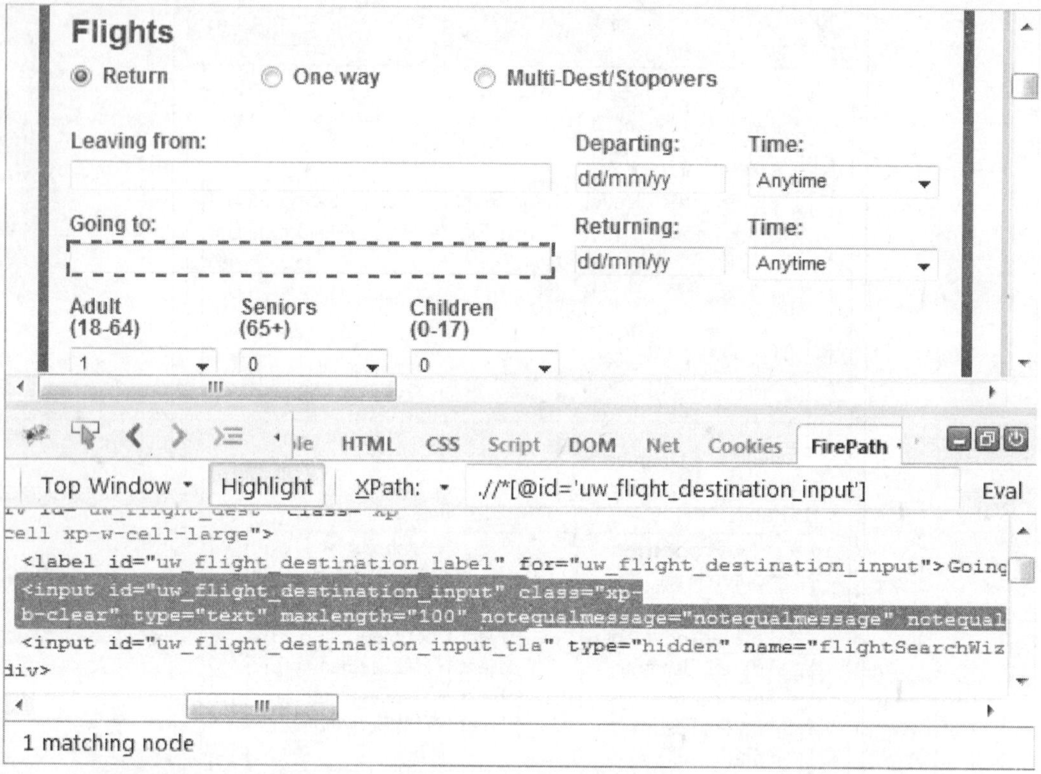

Figure 50.3 *Viewing native properties of the object using Firefox add-on Firebug*

Example 3: Write code to read the requiredMessage attribute of the 'Going To' edit box.

Here, we will observe that we can't retrieve this attribute using *.object* method. Code Print oPg.WebEdit("WebEdit").Object.*requiredMessage* throws an error' Object does not support this property or method'.

Since, this is a custom attribute and hence not supported by default. However, UFT provides *attribute/** notation to retrieve the custom attributes of an object.

> Custom attributes are not visible in object spy identification properties as well unless UFT is configured to learn these attributes,

USING ATTRIBUTE/* NOTATION TO READ NATIVE PROPERTIES

Example 1: Retrieve the 'maxLength' attribute of the 'Going To' edit box.

```
Print oPg.WebEdit("WebEdit").GetROProperty("attribute/maxlength")
'Output::100
```

Example 2: Write code to read the 'id' attribute of the 'Going To' edit box object.

```
Print oPg.WebEdit("WebEdit").GetROProperty("attribute/maxlength")
Output:: uw_flight_destination_input
```

Example 3: Write code to read the 'requiredMessage' attribute of the 'Going To' edit box.

```
Print oPg.WebEdit("WebEdit").GetROProperty("attribute/requiredmes-
sage")
'Output:: requiredFieldMessage
```

Example 4: Write code to read the 'notequal' attribute of the 'Going To' edit box.

```
Print oPg.WebEdit("WebEdit").GetROProperty("attribute/notqeual")
'Output:: uw_flight_origin_input
```

OBJECT IDENTIFICATION USING OBJECT NATIVE PROPERTIES

In this section, we will discuss how to identify objects in UI during test run. UFT supports both descriptive programming and object repository approach for identifying objects using native properties.

Descriptive Programming Code Using Object Native Properties

Notation '*attribute/**' is used to locate object in UI using native properties of the object.

Example 1: Use native property 'requiredMessage' to locate 'Going To' edit box.

```
oPg.WebEdit("attribute/requiredmessage:=requiredFieldMessage).
Set "Text"
```

Example 2: Most often we observe that one property is not sufficient enough to uniquely locate the object. In such scenarios, multiple object custom attributes can be used to locate the object in UI. Write code to locate the 'Going To' edit box object using two custom properties requiredFieldMessage and notequalmessage.

```
oPg.WebEdit("attribute/requiredmessage:=requiredFieldMessage",
"attribute/notequalmessage:=notequalmessage").Set "Text"
```

Example 3: It may happen that the object has limited custom attributes which may not be sufficient to uniquely identify the object in UI. In such cases, object identification attributes can be used along with its native attributes to uniquely locate the object. Write code to locate the 'Going To' edit box object using one identification attribute html id and one custom attribute requiredFieldMessage.

```
oPg.WebEdit("html id:= uw_flight_destination_input", "attribute/requi
redmessage:=requiredFieldMessage").Set "Text"
```

Object Repository based Code Using Object Native Properties

As we discussed, earlier UFT does not recognizes the custom attributes by default. Custom attributes are neither visible in Object Spy tool nor in Object Repository (for default UFT identification settings). However, UFT provides the flexibility to the automation developers to configure UFT to recognize custom attributes and treat them as identification properties.

Configuring UFT to Recognize Custom Attributes (Native Properties) of an Object

Steps below describe how to configure UFT object identification mechanism to recognize native properties 'requiredMessage' and 'notequal' of a webedit object:

1. Open *Object Identification* dialog box.
2. Select the appropriate *Environment* and test class object.
   Here, select Environment=*Web* and test class object as *WebEdit*.
3. Click on the '*Add/Remove*' button.'Add/Remove Properties' dialog box opens as shown in Fig. 50.4.
4. Click on the button 'New' (refer Fig. 50.4).
   'New Property' dialog box opens as shown in the Fig. 50.5.
5. Specify the custom attribute (native property) as attribute/*CustomAttributeName*. For example – *attribute/requiredMessage* or *attribute/notequal*.

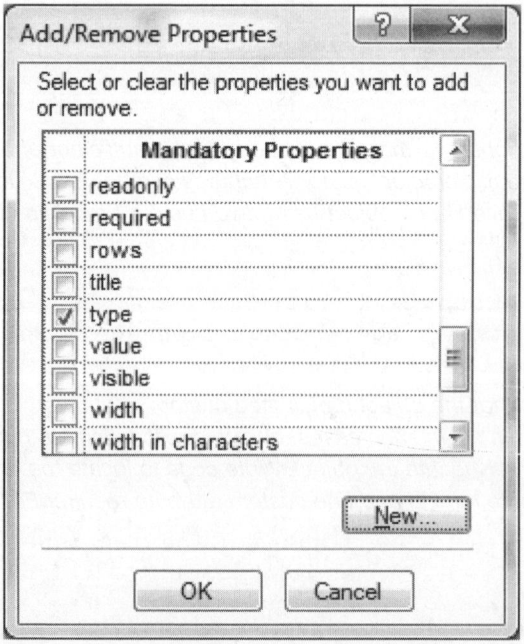

Figure 50.4 *Add/Removefi properties dialog box*

Figure 50.5 *New Property dialog box*

6. Click *OK* button to add the custom attribute to the UFT supported list of object properties. 'Add/Remove Properties' dialog box opens as shown in the Fig. 50.6.
7. Click *OK* button to save the current settings to UFT object identification settings.
8. The newly created properties can be added as mandatory or assistive property. Figure 50.7 below shows custom attributes added as mandatory properties.
6. Click on *OK* button to save the settings.

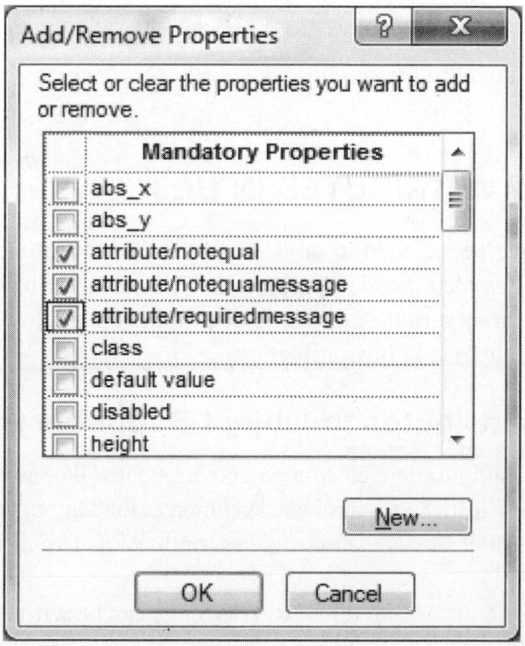

Figure 50.6 *Add/Remove properties dialog box with newly added custom attributes*

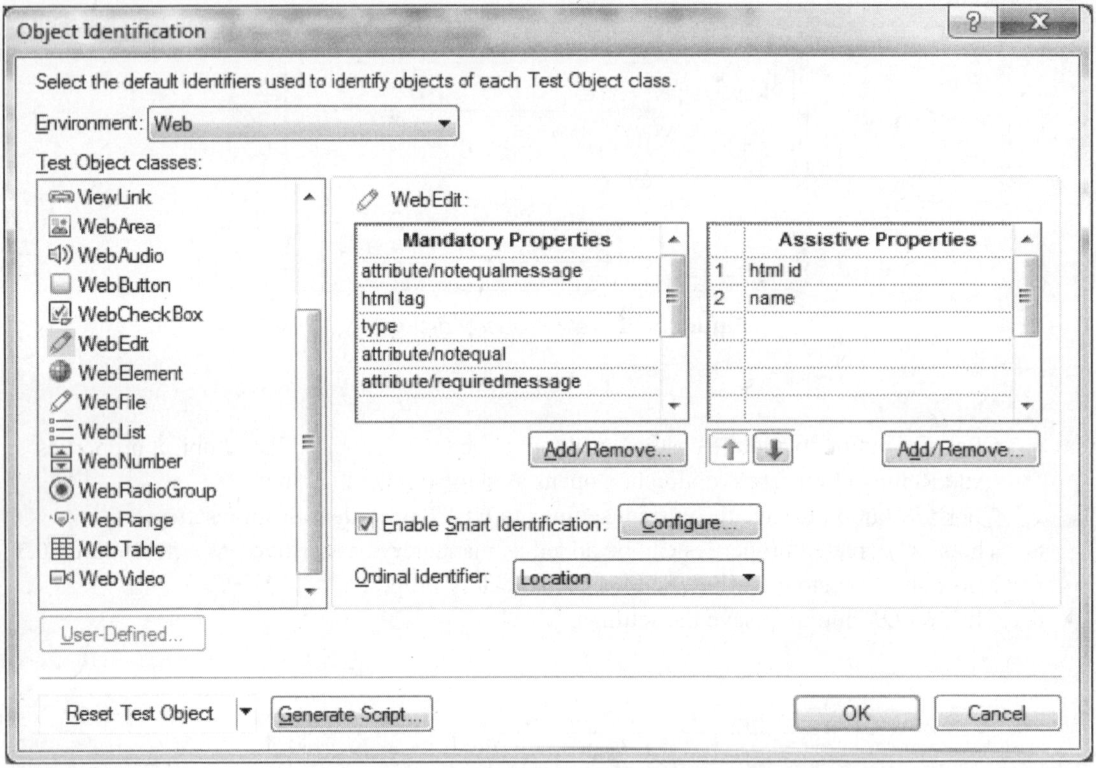

Figure 50.7 *Object Identification settings with custom attributes as mandatory properties*

VIEWING CUSTOM ATTRIBUTES IN OBJECT SPY TOOL

Once custom attributes have been added to the UFT object identification settings; UFT starts treating these custom attributes as identification properties. Thereafter, UFT object spy tool can be used to view and analyze the custom attributes of the object. Figure 50.8 below shows the object spy tool which has learned the 'Going To' edit box properties.

Viewing Custom Attributes in Object Repository

After object identification configuration, custom objects are treated the same way as any other identification properties. If the custom attributes has been specified as mandatory property, then it will always get captured to OR. Figure 50.9 shows the objects descriptions of 'Going To' edit box as captured in object repository.

Once the unique description is captured in OR, UFT code can be written for automating the test.

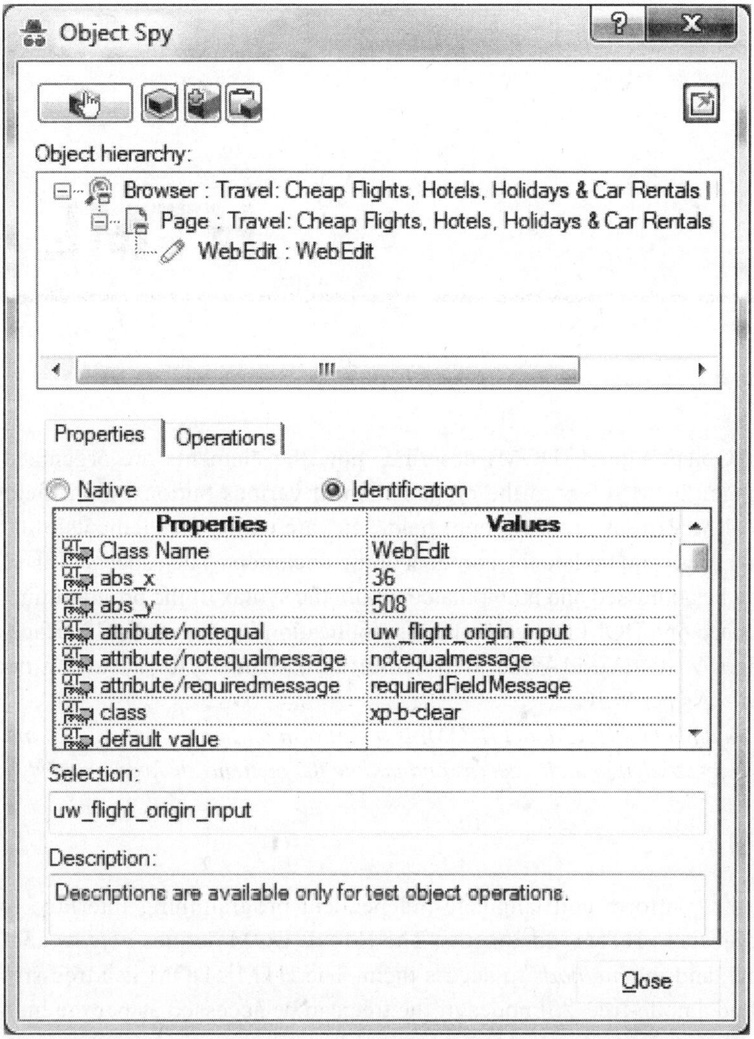

Figure 50.8 *Object spy tool showing custom attributes*

Name	Value
⊟ Description properties	
type	text
html tag	INPUT
html id	uw_flight_destination_input
attribute/requiredmessage	requiredFieldMessage
attribute/notequalmessage	notequalmessage
attribute/notequal	uw_flight_origin_input

Figure 50.9 *'Going To' edit box description properties*

Chapter 51

HTML DOM

The Document Object Model (DOM) describes how the elements are organized in a document. In an HTML page, DOM refers to the organization of various buttons, input fields, etc. inside the page document. The various buttons, input fields, etc. are called the elements of the document. The DOM is used to access and update the contents of the document. The aspects of the DOM (such as its 'Elements') may be addressed and manipulated within the syntax of the programming language in use. The public interface of a DOM is specified in its Application Programming Interface (API).

The DOM is a W3C (World Wide Web consortium) standard for accessing documents such as HTML and XML. As per W3C,

"*The W3C Document Object Model (DOM) is a platform and language-neutral interface that allows programs and scripts to dynamically access and update the content, structure, and style of a document.*"

HTML DOM

HTML DOM is a platform and language-independent programming interface for accessing and manipulating objects in HTML documents. The HTML DOM defines *objects* and *properties* of all HTML elements, and the *methods* to access them. The HTML DOM is a tree-structure. This tree-structure is called a node-tree. All nodes of the tree can be accessed as per the hierarchical order of the tree. The nodes in the node tree have a hierarchical relationship to each other:

- The top node is called the root.
- Every node, except the root, has exactly one parent node.
- A node can have any number of children.
- A leaf is a node with no children.
- Siblings are node with same children.

Consider the following HTML source code:

```
<html>
        <head>
                <title>HTML DOM</title>
        </head>
```

```
    <body>
        </h1>HTML DOM Basics</h1>
        <p>Hello world!!!</p>
    </body>
</html>
```

For the above-mentioned HTML code:

- <html>has no parent node; therefore, it is the root node.
- The <html>node has two child nodes <head> and <body>.
- The <head>node has one child node <title>.
- The <body>node has two child nodes and.
- Nodes <h1> and <p> are sibling nodes, as they have the same parent node <body>.
- Parent node of <html> and <body> nodes is <html> node.

HTML DOM OBJECTS

Document Object

Document object is the HTML document loaded into the browser window. It provides access to all HTML elements within a page.

The following code shows the ways to create a document object of an HTML document:

```
Set oDocument = Browser("").Page("").Object
Alternatively,
Set oDocument = Browser("").Page("").Object.documentElement
Alternatively,
Set oDocument = Browser("").Page("").Object.documentElement.document
```

HTML Element Object

HTML Element object represents an element in an HTML document such as buttons and input fields. It refers to a node in the DOM. Each element provides methods and properties depending on the type of the element.

HTML Element Object Properties

Property	Description
accessKey	Sets or returns an access key for an element
className	Sets or returns the class attribute of an element
disabled	Sets or returns the disabled attribute of an element
firstChild	Returns the first child of an element
height	Sets or returns the height attribute of an element
id	Sets or returns the id of an element
innerHTML	Sets or returns the HTML contents (text) of an element
lang	Sets or returns the language code for an element

lastChild	Returns the last child of an element
length	Returns the length of HTML element collection
nextSibling	Returns the element immediately following an element
nodeName	Returns the tag name of an element (in uppercase)
nodeType	Returns the type of the element
nodeValue	Returns the value of the element
ownerDocument	Returns the root element (document object) for an element
parentNode	Returns the parent node of an element
previousSibling	Returns the element immediately before an element
style	Sets or returns the style attribute of an element
tabIndex	Sets or returns the tab order of an element
tagName	Returns the tag name of an element as a string (in uppercase)
title	Sets or returns the title attribute of an element
width	Sets or returns the width attribute of an element

Document Object Properties

The properties of Document Object are discussed in Table 51.1.

Table 51.1 Document object properties

Property	Description	Example	Output
title	Sets or returns the title of the document	`Browser ("PlnTrvl"). Page ("PlnTrvl").Object. title`	`:: IRCTC :: - Plan My Travel`
URL	Returns the full URL of the document	`Browser ("PlnTrvl"). Page ("PlnTrvl").Object. url`	`https://www.irctc.co.in/cgi-bin/bv60.dll/irctc/booking/planner.do...`
referrer	Returns the URL of the document that loaded the current document	`Browser ("PlnTrvl"). Page ("PlnTrvl"). Object. referrer`	`http://www.irctc.co.in/`
domain	Returns the domain name of the server that loaded the document	`Browser ("PlnTrvl"). Page ("PlnTrvl"). Object. domain`	`www.irctc.co.in`
readyState	Returns the (loading) status of the document	`Browser ("PlnTrvl"). Page ("PlnTrvl"). Object. readyState`	`complete`
cookie	Returns all name/value pairs of cookies in the document	`Browser ("PlnTrvl"). Page ("PlnTrvl"). Object. cookie`	`__utma= 168397 561. 1228735899...`

Document Object Methods

Document object provides methods to access document elements.

- **getElementById**—Returns the first element with the specified id
- **getElementsByName**—Returns all elements with a specified name
- **getElementsByTagName**—Returns all elements with a specified tag name

Figure 51.1 *Plan my travel*

getElementById—Returns the first element with the specified id

Suppose that in 'IRCTC Plan My Travel' page (Fig. 51.1), the calendar image has the following html code:

```
<a href="#" class="cal_control" onclick="$('JDate').select();showCalendarControl($('JDate'),'1');return false"><img class="cal_control" src="/images/img_1.gif" id="calendar_icon1" title="Click to open calendar" alt="Calendar" tabindex="3"/></a>
```

The calendar object can be accessed using the following code:

```
Set oCal = Browser("PlnTrvl").Page("Plntrvl").Object.getElementById
                                            ("calendar_icon1")

'Retrieve object native property values
Print oCal.nodeName                         'Output : "IMG"
Print oCal.id                               'Output : "calendar_icon1"
Print oCal.src                              'Output : "https://www.irctc.
                                                       co.in/images/img_1.gif"
Print oCal.href                             'Output : "https://www.irctc.
                                                       co.in/images/img_1.gif"
Print oCal.title                            'Output : "Click to open
                                                       calendar"
Print oCal.alt                              'Output : "Calendar"
Print oCal.tabIndex                         'Output : 3
Print oCal.fileName                         'Output : "cal_control"
Print oCal.fileSize                         'Output : 1162
'Find font family
Set oCalStyle = oCal.currentStyle          'Get currentStyle object
Print oCalStyle.fontFamily                 'Output : "Arial"
Print oCal.currentStyle.fontFamily         'Output : "Arial"
'Click on calendar object
oCal.click
```

> **NOTES:** The property names viz. nodeName, id, title, etc. should be exactly similar (case insensitive) to the property names as seen in native operations *Properties* tab of object spy. Only those operations, viz. click, focus, and blur, can be performed on the object that are seen in object spy native *Operations* tab.

getElementsByName—Returns all elements with a specified name

Suppose that in 'IRCTC Plan My Travel' page, the *From* edit box has the following html code:

```
<input type="text" name="stationFrom" size="16" value=""
onkeyup="XMLhttpPost(document.BookTicketForm.stationFrom);"
onblur="defaultText3();return pressSubmit();" onfocus="defaultText4();"
class="formText135">
function defaultText3()
{
       if(document.BookTicketForm.stationFrom.value=="")
      {
       document.BookTicketForm.stationFrom.value="Enter City Name";
      }
}
function defaultText4()
{
       if(document.BookTicketForm.stationFrom.value=="Enter City Name")
          {
              document.BookTicketForm.stationFrom.value="";
          }
}
```

The specified edit box can be accessed using the following code:

```
Set colObjects = Browser("PlnTrvl").Page("Plntrvl").Object.getElements
ByName("stationFrom")
'Retrieve object native property values
Print colObjects.length                'Output : 1
Print colObjects(0).nodeName           'Output : "INPUT"
Print colObjects(0).className          'Output : "formText135"
Print colObjects(0).isContentEditable 'Output : True
Print colObjects(0).isTextEdit         'Output : True
Print colObjects(0).maxLength          'Output : 2147483647
Print colObjects(0).value              'Output : "Enter City Name"
Print colObjects(0).outerHTML          'Output : <INPUT class=formText135
                                          onblur="defaultText3();return
                                          pressSubmit();
                                       "onkeyup=XMLhttpPost(document.
                                          BookTicketForm.stationFrom);
                                       onfocus=defaultText4(); size=16
                                          value="Enter City Name"
                                          name=stationFrom>
```

```
'Set some value in edit box
colObjects(0).value = "NDLS"
'Or,
'colObjects(0).innertext = "MUMBAI"
```

> **NOTES:** If more than one object is found with the specified name, then colObjects will have collection of all those objects. In this case, we can use other properties of the object, to uniquely identify the desired object.

getElementsByTagName—Returns all elements with a specified tag name.

Suppose that there is a test case that checks whether all the hyperlinks of the IRCTC Plan Travel page are working fine or not. The following code checks whether all the links of IRCTC site Plan Travel page are working properly or not.

```
'Get all objects with html tag 'A'
Set colLinks = Browser("PlnTrvl").Page("PlnTrvl").Object.getElementsBy
                                                            TagName("A")
Print "Link Name" & vbTab & "Case Status"
'Check if the links are working or not
For iCnt = 0 to colLinks.length-1
     Set colLinks = Browser("PlnTrvl").Page("PlnTrvl").Object.getEle-
     ments ByTagName("A")
     If Trim(colLinks(i).innertext)<>"" And Trim(colLinks(i).innertext)<>
                                                        "Log Out" Then
       'Get the link to which the link object points to
       E_url = colLinks(i).href
       'Click on the link object
       colLinks(i).Click
       Browser("creationtime:=0").Page("micclass:=Page").Sync
       'Get the address of currently opened page
       A_url = Browser("creationtime:=0").Page("micclass:=Page").
       GetROProperty("url")
       'Compare expected page to be opened and actual page opened to
       identify page crash
       If Strcomp(E_url,A_url,1) <> 0 Then
         sStatus = "Fail"
       Else
         sStatus = "Pass"
       End If
       Print colLinks(i).innertext & vbTab & sStatus
       'Click back to return to previous page
       Browser("creationtime:=0").back
       Wait 5
       Browser("creationtime:=0").Page("micclass:=Page").Sync
     End If
Next
```

Edit Box

Suppose that HTML source code of an edit box is:

```
<input type="text" name="stnFrom_nm" id="stnFrom_nm" size="16"
value="Enter City" class="StnFrm1">
```

The various ways to write text on this edit box are:

```
Set oDocument = Browser("Browser").Page("Page").Object.documentElement.
                                                            document
Browser("Browser").Page("Page").WebEdit("stnFrom").Object.value =
                                                        "New York"
or, Browser("Browser").Page("Page").WebEdit("stnFrom").Object.innertext=
                                                            "New York"
or, oDocument.getElementById("stnFrom_id").value = "New York"
or, oDocument.getElementById("stnFrom_id").innertext = "New York"
or, oDocument.getElementById("stnFrom_id").outertext = "New York"
or, oDocument.getElementsByName("stnFrom_nm")(0).value = "New York"
or, Set colElements = oDocument.getElementsByTagName("INPUT")
For Each oElemnt in colElements
   If oElemnt.className = "StnFrm1" Then
      oElemnt.value = "New York"
   End If
Next
```

Button

Suppose that HTML source code of a button is:

```
<input type="submit" id=submit_id name="Submit_nm" value="Find Trains" >
```

The various ways to click on this button are:

```
Set oDocument = Browser("Browser").Page("Page").Object.documentElement.
                                                            document
oDocument.all("submit_id").click
or, oDocument.all("Submit_nm").click
or, oDocument.getElementById("submit_id").Click
or, oDocument.getElementsByName("Submit_nm")(0).Click
or, Set colBtn = oDocument.getElementsByName("Submit_nm")
colBtn(0).Click
```

Link

Suppose that HTML source code of a link is:

```
<A href="http://www.irctc.co.in" id=booktckt_id name=rsrvtckt_nm>Book
Ticket</A>
```

The various ways to click on this link are:

```
Set oDocument = Browser("Browser").Page("Page").Object.documentElement.
                                                            document
```

```
oDocument.links("booktckt_id").Click
or, oDocument.links("rsrvtckt_nm").Click
or, oDocument.all("booktckt_id").click
or, oDocument.all("rsrvtckt_nm").click
or, oDocument.getElementById("booktckt_id").Click
or, oDocument.getElementsByName("rsrvtckt_nm")(0).Click
or, Set colLink = oDocument.getElementsByName("rsrvtckt_nm")
colLink(0).Click
```

> **NOTES** oDocument.all will throw error 'Object doesn't support this property or method' if two or more elements have the same name or id property.

Image

Suppose that HTML source code of an image is:

```
<a href="http:\\www.google.com" class="cal_control" onclick="http:\\
www.google.com">
<img class="cal_control" src="C:\Temp\cal.gif" id="calendar_icon1"
title="Click to open calendar" alt="Calendar" /></a>
```

The various ways to click on image are:

```
Set oDocument = Browser("Browser").Page("Page").Object.documentElement.
                                                            document
Set oImage = oDocument.getElementbyId("calendar_icon1")

'Click on image
oImage.Click
```

Combo or List Box

Suppose that HTML source code of a list box is:

```
<Select option size=1 name="SelectClass_nm">
   <option value="AC(1A)">First Class</option>
   <option value="AC(2A)">AC 2 Tier</option>
   <option value="AC(3A)">AC 3 Tier</option>
</Select>
```

The various ways to select a value from list box are:

```
Set oDocument = Browser("Browser").Page("Page").Object.documentElement.
                                                            document
Set oListBox = oDocument.getElementsByName("SelectClass_nm").Item(0)

'Find length
Print oListBox.Options.length
```

```
'Find list options
Print oListBox.Options.innertext

'Select options using index
oListBox.Options(1).Selected = True

'Select options using list value
oListBox.value = "AC(3A)"

'Alternatively,
'Select options using index
Browser("Browser").Page("Page").WebList("Select Class").Object.select-
                                                              ed Index = 1

'Select options using list value
Browser("Browser").Page("Page").WebList("Select Class").Object.value  =
                                                              "AC(3A)"
```

Check Box

Suppose that HTML source code of a check box is:

```
<input type="checkbox" name="tatkalnew">
```

The various ways to select a checkbox box are:

```
Set oDocument = Browser("Browser").Page("Page").Object.documentElement.
                                                         document
Set oChkBox = oDocument.getElementsByName("tatkalnew").item(0)

'Select a checkbox if not selected or deselect it if selected
oChkBox.Click

'Select a checkbox
oChkBox.Checked = True

'Deselect a checkbox
oChkBox.Checked = True

'Alternatively, check box can also be selected using following code
Browser("Browser").Page("Page").WebList("Select Class").Object.
Checked = True
```

Radio Button

QuickTest recognizes radio buttons as radio group. Only one radio button from radio group can be selected at a time. Radio buttons with same name form a radio group.

Suppose that HTML source code of a radio group is:

```
<input type="radio" name="TcktTyp" value="i-Ticket" checked="checked"/>
<input type="radio" name="TcktTyp" value="e-Ticket" />
```

The various ways to select a radio button are:

```
Set oDocument = Browser("Browser").Page("Page").Object.documentElement.
                                                         document

'Find number of radio buttons in radio group
Print oDocument.getElementsByName("TcktTyp").length

'Select e-Ticket option
oDocument.getElementsByName("TcktTyp").item(1).Click

'Or,
oDocument.getElementsByName("TcktTyp").item(1).Checked = True

'Select i-Ticket option
oDocument.getElementsByName("TcktTyp").item(0).Checked = True

'Alternatively,
Browser("Browser").Page("Page").WebCheckBox("tatkalnew").Object.
                                               checked = True
```

Table

Suppose that HTML source code of a table with first column of table containing link object and second column data.

```
<table id="Table_id" class="refer" cellspacing="0" cellpadding="0" bor-
der="1" width="100%">
   <tr>
      <th width="20%" align="left" >Collection Object </th>
      <th width="73%" align="left">Description</th>
   </tr>
   <tr>
      <td>cells[]</td>
      <td>Returns an array containing each cell in a table</td>
   </tr>
   <tr>
      <td>rows[]</td>
      <td>Returns an array containing each row in a table</td>
   </tr>
</table>
```

The table object returns two collection objects:

- **Cells**—Returns an array containing each cell in the specified table.
- **Rows**—Returns an array containing each row in the specified table.

The various ways to access table cell data are:

```
Set oDocument = Browser("Browser").Page("Page").Object.documentElement.
document
Set oTable = oDocument.getElementById("Table_id")

'Find number of rows
Print oTable.rows.length                                    'Output : 3

'Find number of cells
Print oTable.cells.length                                   'Output : 6

'Find number of cells in row 1
Print oTable.rows(0).cells.length                           'Output : 2

'Find data in cell (1,0) - second row , first column
Print oTable.rows(1).cells(0).outerText                     'Output : cells[]

'Find data in cell (1,1)
Print oTable.rows(1).cells(1).outerText                     'Output : rows[]

'Find data of 4th cell
Print oTable.cells(4).outerText                             'Output : cells[]
```

QUICK TIPS

- ✓ HTML DOM is a platform and language-independent programming interface for accessing and manipulating objects in HTML documents.
- ✓ The HTML DOM defines *objects* and *properties* of all HTML elements and the *methods* to access them.
- ✓ The Document object provides access to all HTML elements within a page.
- ✓ The HTML Element object represents an element in an HTML document such as buttons and input fields..
- ✓ 'getElementById'returns the first element with a specified id.
- ✓ 'getElementByName' returns all elements with a specified name.
- ✓ 'getElementByTagName' returns all elements with a specified tag name.

PRACTICAL QUESTIONS

1. What is HTML DOM?
2. What is the use of HTML DOM in test automation?
3. Explain in detail Document object methods used to access document elements.
4. Write a code to find out whether a text box is enabled or disabled.
5. Write a code to find:
   a. The number of cells in a table.
   b. The number of cells in a row of table.
   c. The number of rows in a table.

Chapter 52

Object Repository Automation

UFT object repository automation model enables users to manipulate object repositories and their contents from outside of UFT. Any language and development environment that supports automation can be used to write OR automation programs. For example VBScript, JavaScript, Visual Basic, Visual C++ or Visual Studio.NET. All object repository manipulation activities like add, remove, rename etc. can be performed using code.

Automating object repository proves to be useful when requirement is to perform the same tasks multiple times or on multiple shared object repositories.

UFT provides two APIs to automate object repository:

- ObjectRepositoryUtil object
- TOCollection object

> **NOTES** Object Repository automation object model can be used to manipulate shared object repositories saved in the file system. Hence, this API cannot be used to add/modify objects dynamically to a OR which is already loaded in a test and is running.

ObjectRepositoriesUtil Object

ObjectRepositoryUtil API enables users to manipulate object repository files.

Methods

Listed below are the methods of this API.

AddObject	Adds the specified object to the object repository under the specified parent object.Adds the specified object to the object repository under the specified parent object.
Convert	Converts the specified object repository file (version 8.2.1 or earlier) to the current format.Converts the specified object repository file (version 8.2.1 or earlier) to the current format.

CopyObject	Creates a copy of the specified object in the object repository.Creates a copy of the specified object in the object repository.
ExportToXML	Exports the specified object repository to the specified XML file.
GetAllObjects	Retrieves all objects under the specified parent object.
GetAllObjectsByClass	Retrieves all objects of the specified class under the specified parent object.
GetChildren	Retrieves all direct children of the specified parent object.
GetChildrenByClass	Retrieves all direct children of the specified class under a specified parent.
GetLogicalName	Retrieves the name of the specified object.
GetObject	Retrieves the object according to the specified path.
GetObjectByParent	Retrieves the object according to the specified parent object and object name.
ImportFromXML	Imports the specified XML file to the specified object repository.
Load	Loads the specified object repository file.
RemoveObject	Removes the specified object from the object repository.
RenameObject	Renames the specified object in the object repository.
Save	Saves any changes made while running an object repository automation script.
UpdateObject	Updates the object repository with any changes made to the specified object.

In the section below, we will discuss some example usage of this API.

Converting OR Files to Latest Format

Method ‘Convert’ can be used to convert OR files from previous QTP versions to latest file format of UFT version.

```
Set oORUtil = CreateObject("Mercury.ObjectRepositoryUtil")
oORUtil.Convert "C:\Temp\OldTSRFile.tsr", "C:\Temp\NewTSRFile.tsr"
```

Converting OR File to XML File

Method ‘ExportToXML’ can be used to convert a test script repository ‘.tsr’ file to ‘xml’ file.

```
oORUtil.ExportToXML "C:\Temp\NewTSRFile.tsr", "C:\Temp\NewTSRFile.xml"
```

NOTES

This method cannot export BDB files

Similarly, method ‘ImportFromXML’ can be used to create a TSR file from XML file.

TOCOLLECTION OBJECT

TOCollection object is a collection of object repository objects, returned by methods of the ObjectRepositoryUtil object.

Methods

Listed below are the methods of this API.

Count	Returns the number of items in the object collection.Returns the number of items in the object collection.Adds the specified object to the object repository under the specified parent object.
Item	Returns the object with the specified index from the object collection.Converts the specified object repository file (version 8.2.1 or earlier) to the current format.

In the example below, we will discuss some example usage of this API.

```
Set oORUtil = CreateObject("Mercury.ObjectRepositoryUtil")
'load tsr file
oORUtil.Load "C:\Temp\NewTSRFile.tsr"
'get all test objects
Set oTOCollection = oORUtil.GetChildren(Root)
'get count of test objects
Print oTOCollection.Count
'get first test object
Set oTestObject = oTOCollection.Item(0)
'get the class type of test object
Print oTestObject.GetTOProperty("micclass")
```

Chapter 53

UFT Automation Object Model

An object model is a collection of classes and interfaces provided by the application software to control the application operations from outside the application environment. Object models are essentially used to write scripts that essentially automates the application software itself.

HP Unified Functional Testing Automation Object Model (AOM) provides an interface to automate UFT tool. UFT AOM provides objects, methods, and properties to write programs that can automatically launch UFT tool, configure UFT options, and run desired test scripts (Fig. 53.1). Automation scripts are especially useful for performing the same tasks multiple times or on multiple tests or components, or for quickly configuring UFT according to test run needs for a particular environment or application.

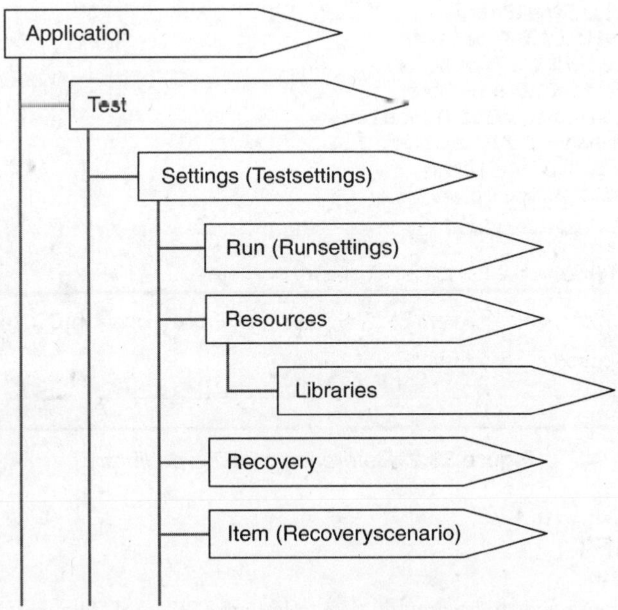

Figure 53.1 *UFT automation object model diagram*

AUTOMATING UFT

HP UFT AOM is used to automate UFT. UFT automation scripts can be written in any language and development environment that supports automation; for example, VBScript, JavaScript, Visual Basic, Visual C++, or Visual Studio.Net. Some of the development environments support referencing a type library. A *type library* is a binary file containing complete description of the object model viz. its objects, methods, interfaces, etc. Developments environments that support referencing a type library have the advantages of IntelliSense, automatic statement completion, and help tips. For UFT, the type library is *QTObjectModel.dll*. This file is saved in <UFT Installation folder>/bin. Suppose that we are using Microsoft Visual Basic as development environment, then follow following steps to refer UFT type library (Fig. 53.2):

1. Select *Project → References*. References dialog box opens.
2. Select *Unified Functional Testing 10.00 Object Library.*
3. Click *OK.*

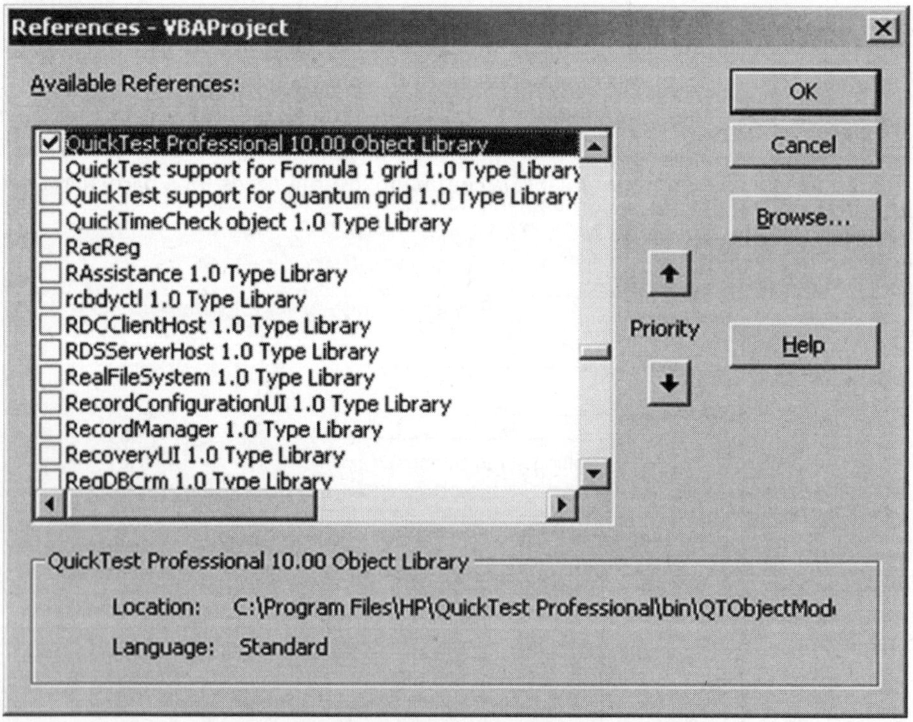

Figure 53.2 *Referencing UFT type library*

LAUNCHING UFT

A UFT application object needs to be created first to launch UFT tool. The code statement for creating an application object varies from language to language.

VBScript

```
Dim oQtpApp
Set oQtpApp = CreateObject("UFT.Application")       'Create application
                                                            object
oQtpApp.Launch                                       'Launch UFT tool
oQtpApp.Visible = True                               'Make UFT visible
```

Visual Basic

```
Dim oQtpApp As UFT.Application         'Declare application object
Set oQtpApp = New UFT.Application      'Create application object
oQtpApp.Launch                                 'Launch UFT tool
oQtpApp.Visible = True                         'Make UFT visible
```

JavaScript

```
var oQtpApp = new ActiveXObject
            ("UFT.Application"); // Create application object
oQtpApp.Launch();                         // Launch UFT tool
oQtpApp.Visible = true                    // Make UFT visible
```

Visual C++

```
#import "QTObjectModel.dll"               // Import UFT type library
UFT::_ApplicationPtr ptrQtpApp;  // Declare application pointer
ptrQtpApp.CreateInstance
          ("UFT.Application");   // Create the application object
ptrQtpApp->Launch();                      // Launch UFT tool
ptrQtpApp->Visible = VARIANT_TRUE;        // Make UFT visible
```

LAUNCHING UFT ON REMOTE MACHINE

UFT AOM provides the flexibility to launch UFT and run desired automation scripts on remote machine. However, to achieve this:

1. UFT needs to be installed on remote machine.
2. Distributed COM (DCOM) configuration properties of the remote machine are to be configured to allow executing UFT from other machine in network.

Setting DCOM Configuration Settings

1. Select Start → Run.
2. Enter dcomcnfg and press Enter. Depending on the operating system, the DCOM Configuration Properties dialog box or the Component Services window will open.
3. Select Unified Functional Testing Automation from the list of COM application available on the computer. Right click and select Properties. The Unified Functional Testing Automation Properties dialog box opens up.

4. Select the Security tab.
5. In the Launch and Activation Permissions, select Customize and click on the Edit button.
6. Use the Add and Remove buttons to select network users or groups who are allowed to launch UFT remotely. Click OK to save settings.
7. In the Unified Functional Testing Automation Properties dialog box, click on the Identity tab and select option Interactive User.
8. Click OK to save settings.
9. Click OK to close the DCOM Configuration Properties dialog box or the Component Services window.

Setting UFT Run Options

UFT *Tools* options need to be configured to allow remotely executing test scripts on UFT machine. To configure *Tools* options settings, follow the following steps:

1. Navigate *Tools* → *Options…*.
2. Click on the *Run* tab.
3. Select option *Allow other HP products to run tests and components*.

Creating a UFT Application Object on Remote Machine

The following code shows how to launch UFT on a desired remote UFT machine.

```
Dim oQtpApp
'Create UFT application object on remote machine
Set oQtpApp = CreateObject("UFT.Application", "RemoteMcCompNm")
oQtpApp.Launch                                          'Launch UFT tool
oQtpApp.Visible = True                                  'Make UFT visible
```

Alternatively, instead of using remote machine computer name, remote machine IP address can also be used to create a UFT application object on remote UFT machine.

```
Set oQtpApp = CreateObject("UFT.Application", "176.34.555.999")
```

> NOTES: If *RemoteMcNm* is replaced with '.', then application object will be created on local machine. No DCOM settings need to be changed to create application object on local machine. However, UFT need to be installed on local machine.

Executing Desired Test Script on Remote UFT Machine

UFT AOM provides the flexibility to execute UFT test scripts from outside UFT environment. This is achieved by calling the *Run* method of the UFT instance object.

```
Dim oQtpApp, sComputer
sComputer = "ComputerName" 'remote UFT machine name
```

```
'Create UFT application object on remote machine
Set oQtpApp = CreateObject("UFT.Application", "sComputer")
oQtpApp.Launch                                    'Launch UFT tool
oQtpApp.Visible = True                            'Make UFT visible
oQtpApp.Open "Z:\Driver\IRCTC_Login", False       'Open test script
oQtpApp.Test.Run                                  'Execute test script
'When execution is complete, close the test script and terminate UFT
                                                   application
oQtpApp.Quit
Set oQtpApp = Nothing
```

UFT OBJECT MODEL

HP Unified Functional Testing provides a set of objects, methods, and properties to control essentially all the configuration and run functionality provided by the UFT interface. The object model of UFT is used to automate UFT operations. Figure 53.1 shows some of the objects exposed by UFT AOM to automate UFT tool.

Application Object

Application object is used to create instance of UFT application. Only one instance of UFT can be created on a UFT machine. Application object returns other objects that can be used to perform application-level operations such as loading add-ins, launching UFT, and creating or opening test scripts.

```
Set oQtpApp = CreateObject("UFT.Application", ".")
```

Methods

The various methods of the UFT application object are as follows.

- ***GetAssociatedAddinsForTest***—It returns the collection of add-ins associated with the specified test script. Launching UFT is not required to retrieve add-ins name associated with a test script.

  `Syntax : Object.GetAssociatedAddinsForTest (TestScriptPath)`

  Return Type: An array of add-in objects

Example: Find add-ins associated with the test script Z:\BusinessComponents\Login.

```
Dim arrAsctdAddins
'Get associated add-ins
arrAsctdAddins = oQtpApp.GetAssociatedAddinsForTest
                                   ("Z:\BusinessComponents\Login")
For iCnt=0 To UBound(arrAsctdAddins) Step 1
      Print arrAsctdAddins(iCnt)  'Print names of associated
                                                  add-ins
Next
```

- ***SetActiveAddins***—It loads specified UFT add-ins when UFT opens.

  Syntax : Object.SetActiveAddins (arrAddinNames, [optional] ErrDesc)

  Syntax Details:

Argument	Description
arrAddinNames	An array containing names of add-ins to load. To find add-ins name navigate *Help → About Unified Functional Testing.*
LibraryFilePath	Full path of library file containing the baseline
Baseline	Name or ID of the baseline. If baseline ID is specified, then enter empty string for *LibraryFilePath* argument
ErrDesc	If any error occurs while loading add-ins, then error description of error is stored in argument *ErrDesc*

  Return Type:

  True—The add-ins loaded successfully

  False—UFT failed to load specified add-ins

Example: Write a code to load 'Web' and 'ActiveX' add-ins when UFT opens.

```
Dim arrAddins(1)
arrAddins(0) = "ActiveX"
arrAddins(1) = "Web"
oQtpApp.SetActiveAddins arrAddins, ErrDesc
oQtpApp.Launch
```

- ***ActivateView***—It activates the specified view—Keyword View or Expert View.

```
Syntax : Object.ActivateView View
         Object is an object of type Application.
         Value of View can be either "KeywordView" or "ExpertView"
```

  Return Type: None

Example: Write a code using UFT AOM to open UFT in Keyword view.

```
oQtpApp.ActivateView "KeywordView"
oQtpApp.Launch
```

- ***Launch***—It opens the UFT application.

  Syntax : Object.Launch

  Return Type: None

Example: Write a code to open UFT application, if it is not open.

```
If Not oQtpApp.Launched Then
      oQtpApp.Launch
End If
```

- ***Open***—It opens an existing test script.

  Syntax : Object.Open TestScriptPath, [optional]OpenMode, [optional]Save

Syntax Details:

Argument	Description
TestScriptPath	Complete path of the test script
OpenMode	**True**—It opens the test script in read-only mode. **False**—It opens the test script in editable mode (Default).
Save	**True**—It saves the current open document. **False**—It closes the current open document without saving (Default).

Return Type: None

Example: Write a code to open test script Login at path Z:\BusinessComponents\Login in read-only mode.

```
oQtpApp.Open "Z:\BusinessComponents\Login", True
```

- ***OpenTestFromBaseline***—It opens an existing test script from the specified Quality Centre baseline.

  `Syntax : Object.OpenTestFromBaseline TestScriptPath, LibraryFile-Path, Baseline, [optional]Save`

  Syntax Details:

Argument	Description
TestScriptPath	Full path of the test script in QC.
LibraryFilePath	Full path of library file containing the baseline.
Baseline	Name or ID of the baseline. If baseline ID is specified, then enter empty string for LibraryFilePath argument.
Save	**True**—It saves the current open document. **False**—It closes the current open document without saving (Default).

Return Type: None

- ***GetStatus***—It returns the current status of UFT application.

  `Syntax : Object.GetStatus`

  Return Type: Not launched, Ready, Busy, Running, Recording, Waiting, Paused

Example: Write a code to find status of UFT when test script is executing.<>

```
Msgbox oQtpApp.GetStatus        'Output : Running
```

- ***Quit***—It closes UFT application. The *Quit* statement fails, if opened test script is not saved.

  `Syntax : Object.Quit`

  Return Type: None

Example: Write a code to close UFT.

```
oQtpApp.Quit
```

Example: Write a code to open UFT in expert view with add-ins associated with IRCTC login script.

```
Dim oQtpApp, arrAsctdAddins, bAddAddins, bAddAddinStat
Set oQtpApp = CreateObject("UFT.Application")
                                        'Create application object
'Find add-ins associated with Login test script
arrAsctdAddins = qtApp.GetAssociatedAddinsForTest("Z:\Business
                                        Components\Login")
bAddAddins = False                          'Make flag false
'Find all add-ins associated with test script are loaded or not. If not,
make a note that add-ins need to be loaded
For Each Addin In arrAsctdAddins
       If oQtpApp.Addins (Addin).Status <> "Active" Then
             bAddAddins = True
             Exit For
       End If
   Next
   'Load all the add-ins associated with the test script
   If bAddAddins = True Then
       bAddAddinStat = oQtpApp.SetActiveAddins(arrAsctdAddins, ErrDesc)
       If  bAddAddins = False Then
                  Msgbox ErrDesc
                  WScript.Quit
       End If
   End If
   oQtpApp.ActivateView "KeywordView"        'Display UFT keyword view
   'If Quicktest is not open, then open it
   If Not  oQtpApp.Launched Then
           oQtpApp.Launch
   End If
   oQtpApp.Visible = True                    'Make UFT visible on screen
   oQtpApp.Open "Z:\BusinessComponents\Login", True
                                             'Open specified test script
   oQtpApp.Quit                              'Close UFT
```

OBJECTREPOSITORIES COLLECTION OBJECT

ObjectRepositories Collection object represents the object repository files associated with an action. This object provides methods to add/remove specified object repository files to an action. It represents the Associated Repositories tab of the Action Properties dialog box.

```
Set oQtpApp = CreateObject("UFT.Application")
oQtpApp.Launch
oQtpApp.Visible = True
```

```
'Open test script PlanTravel
oQtpApp.Open "Z:\BusinessComponents\PlanTravel", False
'Get object repository collection object of action FillForm
Set colQtpOR = oQtpApp.Test.Actions("FillForm").ObjectRepositories
```

Methods

The various methods of the *ObjectRepositories* Collection object are as follows.

- ***Add***—It associates specified object repository file to an action in the desired position in OR collection.
  `Syntax :` *Object*.Add *ObjectRepositoryFilePath,* [optional]*Position*
  Syntax Details:

Argument	Description
Object	An Object of type ObjectRepositories
ObjectRepositoryFilePath	Complete or relative path of the shared object repository file
Position	Position where file needs to be added. By default, file is added at last position in the collection. Position value begins with 1.

  Return Type: None

Example: Write a code to associate action FillForm with the OR file PlanTravel.tsr in third position of OR collection object.

```
colQtpOR.Add "Z:\Object Repository\PlanTravel.tsr", 3
```

- ***Find***—It returns position of specified object repository file in OR collection.
  `Syntax : Object.Find ObjectRepositoryFilePath`

  Syntax Details: *ObjectRepositoryFilePath* refers to complete or relative path of the object repository file.
  Return Type: Position of the OR file. Returns -1 if OR file is not found in OR collection object.

Example: Write a code to find position of the OR file PlanTravel.tsr.

```
nORFilePos = colQtpOR.Find("Z:\Object Repository\Plan
                                    Travel.tsr")
```

- ***MoveToPos***—It changes the position of shared OR file from current position to the specified position.
  `Syntax : Object.MoveToPos CurrPos, NewPos`

  Syntax Details: *CurrPos* refers to the current position of OR file in OR Collection object
  NewPos refers to the new position of OR file in OR Collection object

  Return Type: None.

Example: Write a code to move position of the OR file PlanTravel.tsr from third to second position.

```
colQtpOR.MoveToPos 3, 2
```

- ***Remove***—It disassociates an OR file from an action.

  `Syntax : Object.Remove Pos`

  Syntax Details: *Pos* refer to the current position of OR file in OR Collection object

  Return Type: None.

Example: Write a code to remove PlanTravel.tsr at position second in OR Collection object in action FillForm.

```
colQtpOR.Remove 2
```

- ***RemoveAll***—It disassociates all OR files from an action.

  `Syntax : Object.RemoveAll`

  Return Type: None.

Example: Write a code to remove all OR files from OR Collection in action FillForm.

```
colQtpOR.RemoveAll
```

- ***SetAsDefault***—It sets the list of OR files associated with the current action as the default associated OR files for all new actions.

  `Syntax : Object.SetAsDefault`

  Return Type: None.

Example: Write a code to set the OR files associated with action FillForm as the default associated OR files for all new actions.

```
colQtpOR.SetAsDefault
```

Properties

The various properties of the *ObjectRepositories* Collection object are as follows.

- ***Count***—It returns the number of OR files associated with the current action.

  `Syntax : Object.Count`

  Return Type: Number of OR files

Example: Write a code to find the number of OR files associated with action FillForm.

```
nORCount = colQtpOR.Count
```

- ***Item***—It returns the path of the OR file located in the specified position.

  `Syntax : Object.Item(Pos)`

  Syntax Details: *Pos* refer to the current position of OR file in OR Collection object

  Return Type: Path of OR files

Example: Write a code to find the Path of the OR file PlanTravel.tsr at position second in the OR Collection associated with the action FillForm.

```
sPlnTrvlORPath = colQtpOR.Item(2)
```

Example: Write a code to open a test script; configure object repository files of one of its actions and save test script.

```
Set oQtpApp = CreateObject("UFT.Application")
    oQtpApp.Launch
    oQtpApp.Visible = True

'Open test script PlanTravel
oQtpApp.Open "Z:\BusinessComponents\PlanTravel", False, False

'Get object repository collection object of action FillForm
Set colQtpOR = oQtpApp.Test.Actions("FillForm").ObjectRepositories

'Associate Login.tsr if it's not already in the collection
If colQtpOR.Find("Z:\OR\Login.tsr") = -1 Then
     colQtpOR.Add "Z:\OR\Login.tsr", 1 'Add the repository file to the
                                                             collection
End If

'If PlanTravel.tsr is at 2nd position, then move it to position 1
If colQtpOR.Count > 1 And colQtpOR.Item(2) = "C:\InnerWnd.tsr" Then
   colQtpOR.MoveToPos 1, 2 'Switch between the first two object repositories
End If

'Set the new object repository configuration as the default for all new
actions
colQtpOR.SetAsDefault

'Save the test and close UFT
oQtpApp.Test.Save '
oQtpApp.Quit

Set oQtpOR = Nothing
Set oQtpApp = Nothing
```

TESTLIBRARIES COLLECTION OBJECT

Resources object provides methods to associate external files (resources) to an existing test script. It represents the Library window of Resources pane of the Test Settings dialog box.

```
Set oQtpApp = CreateObject("UFT.Application")
oQtpApp.Launch
oQtpApp.Visible = True

'Open test script PlanTravel
oQtpApp.Open "C:\Temp\Test2", False, False

'Get libraries collection object
colQtpLib = oQtpApp.Test.Settings.Resources.Libraries
```

Methods

The various methods of the *TestLibraries* Collection object are as follows.

- ***Add***—It associates the specified library or environment configuration file (.vbs, .txt, or .qfl) to a test script in the desired position in Resources collection.

  Syntax : Object.Add FilePath, [optional]Position

Syntax Details:

Argument	Description
Object	An Object of type Libraries
FilePath	Complete or relative path of the file
Position	Position where file needs to be added. By default, file is added at last position in the collection. Position value begins with 1.

Return Type: None

Example: Write a code to associate the library file Library.vbs with test script PlanTravel.

```
colQtpLib.Add("Z:\Library\Library.vbs")
```

- ***Find***—It returns position of the specified library or environment configuration file.

  ```
  Syntax : Object.Find FilePath
  ```

  Syntax Details: *FilePath* refers to complete or relative path of the +library file.

  Return Type: Position of the library file. Returns -1 if library file is not found in the specified path.

Example: Write a code to find the position of Library.vbs.

```
nLibFilePos = colQtpLib.Find("Z:\Library\Library.vbs")
```

- ***MoveToPos***—It changes the position of library or environment configuration file from current position to the specified position.

  ```
  Syntax : Object.MoveToPos CurrPos, NewPos
  ```

  Syntax Details: *CurrPos* refers to the current position of the specified file in library Collection object

  NewPos refers to the new position of the specified file in library Collection object

  Return Type: None.

Example: Write a code to move position of environment configuration file from second to first position.

```
colQtpLib.MoveToPos 2, 1
```

- ***Remove***—It disassociates a library file from the current test script.

  ```
  Syntax : Object.Remove PathOrPos
  ```

  Syntax Details: *PathOrPos* refer to the path or position of the file.

  Return Type: None.

Example 1: Write a code to remove library file present at second position.

```
colQtpLib.Remove 2
```

Example 2: Write a code to remove the library file library.vbs.

```
colQtpLib.Remove("Z:\Library\Library.vbs")
```

- ***RemoveAll***—It disassociates all library files from the current test script.

  ```
  Syntax : Object.RemoveAll
  ```

  Return Type: None.

Example: Write a code to remove all OR files from OR Collection in action FillForm.

```
colQtpLib.RemoveAll
```

- ***SetAsDefault***—It sets the list of current environment and library files associated with the current test script as the default associated files for all new test scripts.

  `Syntax : Object.SetAsDefault`

  Return Type: None.

Example: Write a code to set the OR files associated with the action FillForm as the default associated OR files for all new actions.

```
colQtpLib.SetAsDefault
```

Properties

The various properties of the *TestLibraries* Collection object are as follows.

- ***Count***—It returns the number of files associated with the current test script.

  `Syntax : Object.Count`

  Return Type: Number of associated files

Example: Write a code to find the number of files associated with the test script PlanTravel.

```
nLibCount = colQtpLib.Count
```

- ***Item***—It returns the relative or full path of the .vbs, .txt, or .qfl file located in the specified position in Library Collection object.

  `Syntax : Object.Item(Pos)`

  Syntax Details: *Pos* refer to the current position of OR file in OR Collection object

  Return Type: Path of OR files

Example: Write a code to find the path of the library file Library.vbs at second position in Library Collection object associated with the test script PlanTravel.

```
sPlnTrvlLibPath = colQtpLib.Item(2)
```

> NOTES: Environment configuration files should be positioned before the library files in the Library Collection object. This is because library files might be accessing certain global variables, arrays, or environment variables that have been defined or initialized in configuration file.

Example: Write a code to open a test script, configure test script's library collection object, and save the test script.

```
Set oQtpApp = CreateObject("UFT.Application")
oQtpApp.Launch
oQtpApp.Visible = True
```

```
'Open test script PlanTravel
oQtpApp.Open "Z:\BusinessComponents\PlanTravel", False, False
'Get libraries collection object
colQtpLib = oQtpApp.Test.Settings.Resources.Libraries
'Add EnvVariables.vbs if it is not in the library collection
If colQtpLib.Find("Z:\Library\Library.vbs") = -1 Then
      colQtpLib.Add("Z:\Library\Library.vbs")
End If
'Move EnvVariables.vbs to top position in the library collection
                                                              object
colQtpLib.MoveToPos colQtpLib.Count, 1
'Remove EnvVariablesTemp.vbs from collection
nLibPos = colQtpLib.Find("Z:\Library\ EnvVariablesTemp.vbs")
If nLibPos <> -1 Then
             colQtpLib.Remove("Z:\Library\ EnvVariablesTemp.vbs")
End If
'Set the new library files configuration as default for new test scripts
colQtpLib.SetAsDefault
'Save the test and close UFT
qtApp.Test.Save
qtApp.Quit
Set qtLibraries = Nothing
Set qtApp = Nothing
```

RECOVERY OBJECT

Recovery object provides methods to add/remove recovery scenarios to a test script. It represents the Recovery pane of the Test Settings dialog box.

```
Set oQtpApp = CreateObject("UFT.Application")
oQtpApp.Launch
oQtpApp.Visible = True
'Open test script BookTcktDriver
oQtpApp.Open "Z:\Driver\BookTcktDriver", False, False
'Get the Recovery object
Set colQtpRecovScnro = oQtpApp.Test.Settings.Recovery
```

Methods

The various methods of the *Recovery* object are as follows.

- ***Add***—It associates specified recovery scenario (.qrs file) to current test script at the specified position.

  ```
  Syntax : Object.Add RecovScnroFilePath, RecovScnroNm, [optional]
                                                         Position
  ```

Syntax Details:

Argument	Description
Object	An object of type Recovery object
RecovScnroFilePath	Complete or relative path of the recovery scenario file
RecovScnroNm	The name of the recovery scenario to be added
Position	The Position where file needs to be added. By default, file is added at last position in the collection (position = −1)

Return Type: None

Example: Write a code to add the recovery scenario ObjectNotFndErr from RecovScnro.qrs to the driver script BookTcktDriver.

```
colQtpRecovScnro.Add "Z:\Recovery Scenario\Recovery.qrs",
                       "ObjectNotFndErr", 1
```

- ***Find***—It returns the position of the specified recovery scenario.
  `Syntax : Object.Find RecovScnroFilePath, RecovScnroNm`
  Syntax Details:

Argument	Description
RecovScnroFilePath	Complete or relative path of the recovery scenario file
RecovScnroNm	Name of the recovery scenario to be added

Return Type: The position of recovery scenario. Returns -1, if the specified recovery scenario is not found.

Example: Write a code to find if the recovery scenario AppCrash is associated with script BookTckt-Driver or not.

```
nPos = colQtpRecovScnro.Find "Z:\Recovery Scenario\Recovery.
                                                    qrs", "AppCrash"
```

- ***MoveToPos***—It changes the position of recovery scenario as specified.

  `Syntax : Object.MoveToPos CurrPos, NewPos`

  Syntax Details: *CurrPos* refers to the current position of the specified recovery scenario
  NewPos refers to the new position of the specified recovery scenario
  Return Type: None.

Example: Write a code to move the position of the recovery scenario ObjectNotFndErr from second to first position.

```
colQtpRecovScnro.MoveToPos 2, 1
```

- ***Remove***—It removes the recovery scenario at the specified position from the current test script.
  `Syntax : Object.Remove Pos`

  Syntax Details: *Pos* refer to the position of the recovery scenario.

  Return Type: None.

Example: Write a code to remove recovery scenario present at second position.

```
colQtpRecovScnro.Remove 2
```

- ***RemoveAll***—It removes all recovery scenarios from the current test script.

  `Syntax : Object.RemoveAll`

  Return Type: None.

Example: Write a code to remove all recovery scenarios from test script BookTcktDriver.

```
colQtpRecovScnro.RemoveAll
```

- ***SetActivationMode***—It sets the activation settings of all recovery scenarios within the current test script.

  `Syntax : Object.SetActivationMode ActivationModeSetting`

  Syntax Details:

Argument	Description
ActivationModeSetting	It can take two values: **OnEveryStep**—This recovery mechanism is activated after every step. **OnError**—This recovery mechanism is activated in case an error occurs while executing a step.

Example: Write a code to set the recovery scenario activation mode OnError for current test script execution.

```
colQtpRecovScnro.SetActivationMode "OnError"
```

- ***SetAsDefault***—It sets the current list of recovery scenarios associated with the current test script as the default associated recovery scenarios for all new test scripts.

  `Syntax : Object.SetAsDefault`

  Return Type: None.

Example: Write a code to set the recovery scenarios associated with the test script BookTcktDriver as the default associated recovery scenarios for all new test scripts.

```
colQtpRecovScnro.SetAsDefault
```

Properties

The various properties of the *Recovery* object are as follows.

- ***Count***—It returns the number of recovery scenarios associated with the current test script.

  `Syntax : Object.Count`

  Return Type: The number of associated recovery scenarios. Returns 0, if no recovery scenario is associated with the current test script.

Example: Write a code to find the number of recovery scenarios associated with the test script bookTcktDriver.

```
nRecovScnroCount = colQtpRecovScnro.Count
```

- ***Enabled***—It indicates whether recovery mechanism is enabled or not. This method can also be used to enable or disable recovery mechanism.

```
Syntax : Object.Enabled
         Object.Enabled = value
```

  Syntax Details: *Value* can be True or False. The value True enables recovery mechanism while the value False disables it.

  Return Type: The value True or False depends on whether the recovery mechanism is enabled or not.

Example: Write a code to enable the recovery mechanism, if the recovery mechanism is not enabled.

```
If colQtpRecovScnro.Enabled = False Then
   colQtpRecovScnro.Enabled = True
End If
```

- ***Item*** – It returns the recovery scenario object located in the specified position.

```
Syntax : Object.Item(Pos)
```

  Syntax Details: *Pos* refer to the position of recovery scenario

  Return Type: Recovery Scenario object

Example 1: Write a code to find the recovery scenario object located at second position of the current test script.

```
Set oRecovScnro2 = colQtpRecovScnro.Item(2)
```

Example 2: Write a code to disable recovery scenario at second position of the current test script.

```
colQtpRecovScnro.Item(2).Enabled = False
```

RECOVERY SCENARIO OBJECT

Recovery Scenario object provides methods to find name and path of recovery scenarios. It can also be used to enable or disable the recovery scenarios.

```
'Get recovery scenario object at position 1
Set oRecovScnro = colQtpRecovScnro.Item(1)
```

Properties

The various properties of the *RecoveryScenario* object are as follows.

- ***Enabled***—It indicates whether recovery mechanism is enabled or not. This method can also be used to enable or disable the recovery mechanism.

```
Syntax : Object.Enabled
         Object.Enabled = value
```

  Syntax Details: *Value* can be True or False. The value True enables the recovery mechanism while the value False disables it.

  Return Type: The value True or False depends on whether the recovery mechanism is enabled or not.

Example: Write a code to enable the recovery scenario, if the recovery scenario is not enabled.

```
If oRecovScnro.Enabled = False Then
    oRecovScnro.Enabled = True
End If
```

- ***File***—It returns the name and path of the recovery scenario file (.qrs) in which the recovery scenario is saved.

  `Syntax : Object.File`

  Return Type: Recovery scenario file path

Example: Write a code to find the name of the file where recovery scenario is saved.

```
sRecovFileNm = oRecovScnro.File
```

- ***Name***—It returns the name of the recovery scenario

  `Syntax : Object.Name`

  Return Type: Recovery scenario name

Example: Write a code to find the name of the file where recovery scenario is saved.

```
sRecovFileNm = oRecovScnro.Name
```

Example: Write a code to open an existing test script, associate recovery scenarios to it, and enable recovery scenarios and recovery mechanism.

```
Set oQtpApp = CreateObject("UFT.Application")
oQtpApp.Launch
oQtpApp.Visible = True
'Open test script BookTcktDriver
oQtpApp.Open "Z:\Driver\BookTcktDriver", False, False
'Get the Recovery object
Set colQtpRecovScnro = oQtpApp.Test.Settings.Recovery
'Remove all recovery scenarios associated with the test script
If colQtpRecovScnro.Count> 0 Then
   colQtpRecovScnro.RemoveAll
End If
'Add recovery scenarios
colQtpRecovScnro.Add "Z:\RecoveryScenarios\ObjectNotFndErr"
colQtpRecovScnro.Add "Z:\RecoveryScenarios\PopUpErr"
colQtpRecovScnro.Add "Z:\RecoveryScenarios\AppCrashErr"
'Enable all recovery scenarios
For iCnt=1 To colQtpRecovScnro.Count Step 1
colQtpRecovScnro.Item(iCnt).Enabled = True
Next
'Enable recovery mechanism
If colQtpRecovScnro.Enabled= False Then
colQtpRecovScnro.Enabled = True
End If
```

```
'Set Activation mode OnError
colQtpRecovScnro.SetActivationMode "OnError"

'Find path of recovery scenario file of the recovery scenario at position 1
sRecovScnroFilePath1 = colQtpRecovScnro.Item(1).File

'Find name of the recovery scenario at position 1
sRecovScnroNm1 = colQtpRecovScnro.Item(1).Name

Set oQtpApp = Nothing
Set colQtpRecovScnro = Nothing
```

RUNSETTINGS OBJECT

Run Settings object provides methods to configure the test run execution settings. It represents the Run pane of the Test Settings dialog box.

```
Set oQtpApp = CreateObject("UFT.Application")
oQtpApp.Launch
oQtpApp.Visible = True

'Open test script BookTcktDriver
oQtpApp.Open "Z:\Driver\BookTcktDriver", False, False

'Get RunSettings object
Set oQtpRunSet = oQtpApp.Test.Run
```

Properties

The various properties of the *RunSettings* object are as follows.

- ***IterationMode***—It finds or sets the Data Table iteration mode.

  ```
  Syntax : Object.IterationMode
           Object.IterationMode = value
  ```

  Syntax Details:

Argument	Description
Object	An Object of type Run Settings object
value	Possible values: **oneIteration**—It executes the test script only once, using only first row data in that global Data Table **rngAll**—It executes the test script for all rows of data present in global Data Table. The number of iterations is same as the number of rows of data. **rngIterations**—It executes the test script with iterations using data values in the global Data Table for the specified range. The range is specified by the *StartIteration* and *EndIteration* properties.

  Return Type: Iteration type

- ***StartIteration***—It finds or sets the Data Table row number from where data will be accessed for the test script execution.

  ```
  Syntax : Object.StartIteration
           Object.StartIteration = value
  ```

Syntax Details: *Value* can be any valid Data Table row number

Return Type: Start iteration value

- ***EndIteration***—It finds or sets the Data Table row number till where data will be accessed for the test script execution.

```
Syntax : Object.EndIteration
         Object.EndIteration = value
```

Syntax Details: *Value* can be any valid Data Table row number

Return Type: End iteration value

Example: Write a code to set test execution settings of the current test script to start execution from row=2 till row=5 of global data table.

```
oQtpRunSet.IterationMode = "rngIterations"
oQtpRunSet.StartIteration = 2
oQtpRunSet.Endration = 5
```

- ***ObjectSyncTimeOut***—It finds or sets the maximum time (milliseconds) UFT waits for an object to load before executing a test script step.

```
Syntax : Object.ObjectSyncTimeOut
         Object.ObjectSyncTimeOut = value
```

Return Type: Object synchronization time out time

Example 1: Write a code to find synchronization time-out time of the current test script.

```
nSyncTmOutTm = oQtpRunSet.ObjectSyncTimeOut
```

Example 2: Write a code to set synchronization time-out time of the current test script to be 10 ms.

```
oQtpRunSet.ObjectSyncTimeOut = 10
```

- ***DisableSmartIdentification***—It finds or sets the status (enable/disable) of the smart identification mechanism.

```
Syntax : Object.DisableSmartIdentification
         Object.DisableSmartIdentification = value
```

Return Type: The value True or False depends on whether the smart identification is disabled or enabled.

Example 1: Write a code to find whether the smart identification mechanism is enabled or disabled.

```
bSIFlg = oQtpRunSet.DisableSmartIdentification
```

Example 2: Write a code to disable smart identification mechanism.

```
oQtpRunSet.DisableSmartIdentification = True
```

- ***OnError***—It finds or sets how to handle run-time errors during script execution.

```
Syntax : Object.OnError
         Object.OnError = value
```

Syntax Details: *Value* can take following possible values:

Dialog UFT—It displays the error message dialog box when an error occurs.

NextIteration UFT—It ignores the current step error and starts executing next iteration of the test script when an error occurs.
Stop UFT—It stops script execution when an error occurs.
NextStep UFT—It ignores current step error and proceeds execution with the next step when an error occurs.

Return Type: Error method selected.

Example 1: Write a code to find the current error handling method defined for the test script.

```
sErrHndlngMethd = oQtpRunSet.OnError
```

Example 2: Write a code to configure settings, so that script execution stops on occurrence of run-time error.

```
oQtpRunSet.OnError = "Stop"
```

RUNOPTIONS OBJECT

RunOptions object provides methods to configure test run options for all test scripts. It represents the Run pane of the Options dialog box.

```
Set oQtpApp = CreateObject("UFT.Application")
   oQtpApp.Launch
   oQtpApp.Visible = True
   'Get RunOptions object
   Set oQtpRunOpt = oQtpApp.Options.Run
```

Properties

The various properties of the *RunOptions* object are as follows.

- ***RunMode***—It finds or sets the test script execution mode – normal or fast.

```
Syntax : Object.RunMode
         Object.RunMode = value
```

Syntax Details:

Argument	Description
Object	An Object of type RunOptions object
value	Possible values: **Normal**—It executes test script with an arrow pointer pointing to the current step of execution in the left margin of the keyword view. **Fast**—It executes test script without any arrow pointer pointing to the current step of execution in the left margin of the keyword view. The execution speed is better in the *Fast* mode than as compared to the *Normal* mode. In addition, more system resources are required for the *Normal* mode.

NOTES

Microsoft Script Debugger needs to be installed to execute test scripts in the Normal mode.

Return Type: *Normal* or *Fast*

Example: Write a code to configure **TestOptions** *to execute test script in the* **Fast mode***.*

```
oQtpRunOpt.RunMode = "Fast"
```

- ***StepExecutionDelay*** – It finds or sets wait time (milliseconds) before executing each step.

```
Syntax : Object.StepExecutionDelay
         Object.StepExecutionDelay = value
```

  Syntax Details: *Value* can be any numeric value

  Return Type: Numeric value representing delay time in milliseconds

Example 1: Write code to find the currently specified delay time between executions of two steps.

```
nStepExecDelayTm = oQtpRunOpt.StepExecutionDelay
```

Example 2: Write code to set the delay time between executions of two steps to 10 ms.

```
oQtpRunOpt.StepExecutionDelay = 10
```

- ***ViewResults***—It configures settings to display or not to display test results after test script execution.

```
Syntax : Object.ViewResults
         Object.ViewResults = value
```

  Syntax Details: *Value* variable can accept two values—True or False. True indicates test results window will be displayed on screen after test execution. False indicates test results window will not be displayed on the screen after test execution.

  Return Type: The value *True* or *False* depends on whether the test results window appears after test script execution or not.

Example 1: Write a code to find the currently configured setting for view results.

```
bVwRsltFlg = oQtpRunOpt.ViewResults
```

Example 2: Write a code to configure options to avoid automatic test results display after test script execution.

```
oQtpRunOpt.ViewResults = False
```

- ***ImageCaptureForTestResults***—It finds the existing setting or configures setting when to capture still images of AUT in Test Results.

```
Syntax : Object.ImageCaptureForTestResults
       Object.ImageCaptureForTestResults = value
```

  Syntax Details: *Value* can be any of the following:

  Always—The images are captured in Test Results for all steps in the run.

  OnError—The images are captured only for steps that return error.

  OnWarning—The images are captured only for steps that return error or warning.

  Never—The images are never captured.

  Return Type: Currently configured option – Always, OnError, OnWarning, or Never.

Example 1: Write a code to find the currently configured setting for image capture to test results.

```
sImgCaptureSet = oQtpRunOpt.ImageCaptureForTestResults
```

Example 2: Write a code to configure options to avoid automatic test results display after test script execution.

```
oQtpRunOpt.ImageCaptureForTestResults = "OnWarning"
```

- ***MovieCaptureForTestResults*** – It finds the existing setting or configures setting when to capture movies in Test Results.

```
Syntax : Object.MovieCaptureForTestResults
         Object.MovieCaptureForTestResults = value
```

Syntax Details: *Value* can be any of the following:

Always—The images are captured in Test Results for all steps in the run.

OnError—The images are captured only for steps that return error.

OnWarning—The images are captured only for steps that return error or warning.

Never—The images are never captured.

Return Type: Currently configured option—Always, OnError, OnWarning, or Never.

Example 1: Find the currently configured setting for movie capture to test results.

```
sMovieCaptureSet = oQtpRunOpt.MovieCaptureForTestResults
```

Example 2: Configure options to capture movie only for failed or warning steps.

```
oQtpRunOpt.MovieCaptureForTestResults = "OnWarning"
```

- ***SaveMovieOfEntireRun***—It finds or configures settings whether the movie clip includes the entire test script or not.

```
Syntax : Object.SaveMovieOfEntireRun
         Object.SaveMovieOfEntireRun = value
```

Syntax Details: *Value* can be True or False.

True—It saves entire movie if one or more errors or warning occur.

False—It saves only movie segments as defined for the *MovieSegmentSize*.

Return Type: True or False

> NOTES: This property can be used only when *MovieCaptureForTestResults* is set to *OnError* or *OnWarning.*

Example 1: Find the currently configured setting for movie clip capture.

```
bMovieClipSet = oQtpRunOpt.SaveMovieOfEntireRun
```

Example 2: Configure options to save entire movie to test results, if an error or warning occurs.

```
oQtpRunOpt.SaveMovieOfEntireRun = True
```

- ***MovieSegmentSize***—It finds or configures settings to set the maximum movie file size to store for each error or warning.

```
Syntax : Object.MovieSegmentSize
        Object.MovieSegmentSize = value
```

Syntax Details: *Value* can be between 400 and 2097152. It denotes the maximum number of kilobytes of movie clip that can be stored on occurrence of error or warning.

Return Type: Numeric value denoting maximum kilobytes of movie clip that can be saved.

Example 1: Find the currently configured movie segment size.

```
bMovieClipSet = oQtpRunOpt.MovieSegmentSize
```

Example 2: Configure options to set maximum movie clip size to be 500 KB.

```
oQtpRunOpt.MovieSegmentSize = 500
```

Example: Write a code to open a test script and configure run settings and options. Next, execute the test script and print the test result status and path.

> **NOTES** This property is used only when *MovieCaptureForTestResults* is set to *OnError* or *OnWarning* and *SaveMovieOfEntireRun* is False or not defined.

```
Set oQtpApp = CreateObject("UFT.Application")
oQtpApp.Launch
oQtpApp.Visible = True

'Get RunOptions object
Set oQtpRunOpt = oQtpApp.Options.Run

'Get RunSettings object
Set oQtpRunSet = oQtpApp.Test.Run

'Configure RunOptions
oQtpRunOpt.RunMode = "Fast"             'Fast run mode
oQtpRunOpt.ViewResults = False          'Do not display test results
                                                after test execution
    'Capture images to test results only when error or warning occurs
oQtpRunOpt.ImageCaptureForTestResults = "OnWarning"
    'Capture movie for every step executed
oQtpRunOpt.MovieCaptureForTestResults = "Always"

'Open the test script in read only mode
oQtpApp.Open "Z:\Driver\BookTcktDriver", True
'Configure RunSettings
oQtpRunSet.DisableSmartIdentification = True     'Disable smart iden-
                                                   tification mechanism
oQtpRunSet.ObjectSyncTimeOut = 10       'Object synchronization time
                                        out=10ms
```

```
oQtpRunSet.OnError = "NextIteration"     'Start executing next
iteration in case of error
oQtpRunSet.IterationMode = "rngIterations"'Execute specified range
'Execution 3 iterations fusing global Data Table data from row=2  to
                                                              row=5
oQtpRunSet.StartIteration = 2
oQtpRunSet.Endration = 5
'Create RunResultsOption object
Set oQtpRsltOpt = CreateObject("UFT.RunResultsOptions")
'Set the location where result to be saved
oQtpRsltOpt.ResultsLocation = "Z:\Results\BookTckt\" & Replace(Time-
                                                          (Now) ,":","")
'Execute test script; Wait till execution of test script is complete
oQtpApp.Test.Run oQtpRsltOpt
'Print result location
Print oQtpApp.Test.LastRunResults.Path
'Print test run status
Print oQtpApp.Test.LastRunResults.Status
'Close the test script
oQtpApp.Test.Close
Set oQtpRsltOpt = Nothing
Set oQtpRunSet = Nothing
Set oQtpRunOpt = Nothing
Set oQtpApp = Nothing
```

TEST OBJECT

Test Object provides methods and properties to access test script details such as author and the date of script creation and to execute or save attest script. It represents opened test script or business component.

```
Set oQtpApp = CreateObject("UFT.Application")
oQtpApp.Launch
oQtpApp.Visible = True
oQtpApp.Open "Z:\Driver\BookTcktDriver", False, False
'Get Test object
oQtpTest = oQtpApp.Test
```

Methods

The various methods of the *Test* object are as follows.

- ***Save*** – It saves the open test script or business component (new or existing).
  `Syntax : Object.Save`

Syntax Details:

Argument	Description
Object	An object of type Test object

Return Type: None

Example: Write a code to save an opened test script.

```
oQtpApp.Test.Save
```

- ***SaveAs***—It saves the open test script or business component with a new name.
  `Syntax :` *Object*.SaveAs *TestScriptPath*, [optional]*CopyActiveScreen*, [optional]*CopyTestResults*
  Syntax Details:

> NOTES: If UFT is in minimized mode (visible=False) or opened test script is untitled, the above-mentioned statement fails.

Argument	Description
TestScriptPath	Full path with test script name where test script needs to be saved
CopyActiveScreen	Possible values:True or False (Default = True).True implies all Active Screen images will be copied to the new test script.
CopyTestResults	Possible Values:True or False (Default = False).True implied all test results of the test script will be copied to the new test script.

Return Type: None

Example: Write a code to save an open test script with new name.

```
oQtpApp.Test.SaveAs "C:\Temp\CopyOfBookTcktDriver"
```

- ***ValidateAddins***—It validates whether all the add-ins associated with test script are currently loaded or not and whether there are any conflicts between loaded add-ins or not.
  `Syntax : Object.ValidateAddins ([optional]ErrDesc)`
  Syntax Details: *ErrDesc* contains error description. *ErrDesc* argument receives values only if Test.ValidateAddins statement returns False.

  Return Type: True or False.
  Returns True, if all the add-ins are properly loaded without any error.
  Returns False, if one or more add-ins associated with the test script are not loaded or returned error. Error can occur because of conflicting add-ins in the specified add-ins list.

Example: Write a code to validate whether add-ins are properly loaded or not.

```
bValidateAddins = oQtpApp.Test.ValidateAddins(ErrDesc)
```

- ***GetAssociatedAddins***—It returns the list of add-ins associated with the test script or business component.
  `Syntax : Object.GetAssociatedAddins`
  Return Type: It returns an array of *Add-in* objects. These objects represent the add-ins present in the currently open test script's *Associated Add-ins* list.

Example: Write a code to find the list of add-ins associated with the test script.

```
arrAddins = oQtpApp.Test.GetAssociatedAddins()
```

- ***SetAssociatedAddins***—It sets the list of add-ins associated with the test script or business component.

  `Syntax : Object.SetAssociatedAddins (arrAddinNames, [optional]ErrDesc)`

  Syntax Details:

Argument	Description
arrAddinNames	An array consisting of the name of the add-ins to be associated with the test script
ErrDesc	The description of the error that occurred while associating add-ins to test script. Argument *ErrDesc* will contain value only if Test.SetAssociatedAddins statement returns False

  Return Type: True or False.

  Returns True, if specified list of add-ins returned no error.

  Returns False, if error was returned for the specified list of add-ins. Error can occur due to conflicting add-ins present in the specified add-in list or certain add-in was not in the list. Some add-ins require other add-ins to be loaded with it.

Example: Write a code to associate Web, Web Services, and Java add-ins with the current open test script.

```
Dim arrAddins(2)
arrAddins(0) = "Web"
arrAddins(1) = "Web Services"
arrAddins(2) = "Java"
bSetAddinFlg = oQtpApp.Test.SetAssociatedAddins(arrAddins, ErrDesc)
```

- ***Run***—It executes an open test script or business component and saves test results in the specified file or Quality Centre path.

  ```
  Syntax : Object.Run  [optional]ResultsOption,  [optional]WaitOnReturn, [optional]Parameters
  ```

  Syntax Details:

Argument	Description
ResultOptions	Path where test results are to be saved. If undefined, the default value for the RunResultsOptions is used. By default, test results are saved in a unique folder with the test script or business component folder.
WaitOnReturn	Possible values: True or False (Default = True). Specify True, if automation script execution should halt and wait till test script execution is complete. Specify False, if automation script needs to be executed while test script execution is in progress. Select this option only if statements following *Test.Run* can be performed even while test script or business component is executing.
Parameters	The *Parameters* collection containing the parameters to be passed to the test script or business component.

  Return Type: None

Example: Write a code to execute a test script with specified parameter values.

Suppose that Login action has two input parameters *UsrNm* and *Passwd* and one output parameter *RunStat* to find out whether the login was successful or failed.

```
Set oQtpApp = CreateObject("UFT.Application")
   oQtpApp.Launch
oQtpApp.Visible = True
oQtpApp.Open "Z:\BusinessComponents\Login", False, False
'Get the parameters collection defined for the test script
Set colParamList = oQtpApp.Test.ParameterDefinitions
'Print parameter names and their values
For iCnt=1 To colParamList.Count Step 1
     Set oParamDetails = colParamList.Item(iCnt)
MsgBox "ParamName-" & oParamDetails.Name & ";ParamTyp-" & oParam
                                                    Details.Type &_
";InOut-" & oParamDetails.InOut & ";Description-" & oParamDetails.
                                                        Description &_
";DefaultValue-" & oParamDetails.DefaultValue
Next
'Get the input and output parameters of the test script
         Set oParamInOut = colParamList.GetParameters()
'Get input parameter UsrNm
Set oParamInUsrNm = oParamInOut.Item("UsrNm")
'Get input parameter Passwd
Set oParamInPasswd = oParamInOut.Item("Passwd")
'Change Input parameter values
oParamInUsrNm.Value = "TestUser"
oParamInPasswd.Value = "Password"
'Execute test script with new parameter values
oQtpApp.Test.Run  "Z:\TestResults\Login", True, oParamInOut
'Display output parameter value after test script execution is complete
MsgBox oParamInOut.Item("RunStat").Value
'Close the test script
oQtpApp.Test.Close
Set oParamInUsrNm = Nothing
Set oParamInPasswd = Nothing
Set oParamInOut = Nothing
Set colParamList = Nothing
Set oQtpApp = Nothing
```

- ***Pause***—It pauses the test script run session
  `Syntax : Object.Pause`
  Return Type: None

  Example: `oQtpApp.Test.Pause`

- ***Continue***—It continues the run session. This method is used to continue executing the paused test script.
  `Syntax : Object.Continue`

  Return Type: None

  Example: `oQtpApp.Test.Continue`

- ***Stop***—It stops the test script run session
  `Syntax : Object.Stop`

  Return Type: None

  Example: `oQtpApp.Test.Stop`

> **NOTES** To be able to Pause, Continue, or Stop execution of a test script from the automation script, the WaitOnReturn argument of Test.Run method must be set to False.

- ***Close***—It closes the current open test script and opens a blank test script.
  `Syntax : Object.Close`

  Return Type: None

  Example:

  ```
  oQtpApp.Test.Close
  ```

Properties

The various properties of the *Test* object are as follows.

- ***Actions***—It returns a collection of all actions of the test script.
  `Syntax : Object.Actions`

  Return Type: *Action* object

  Example:

  ```
  colAction = oQtpApp.Test.Actions
  ```

- ***Environment***—It returns an *Environment* object that can be used to define environment variables.
  `Syntax` : *Object*.Environment

  Return Type: *Environment* object

Example:

```
oEnv = oQtpApp.Test.Environment
```

- ***Name***—It returns the name of the open test script or business component.
  `Syntax : Object.Actions`

  Return Type: Test script name

Example:

```
sTestScriptNm = oQtpApp.Test.Name
```

- ***Location***—It returns the location of the open test script or business component.
  `Syntax :` *Object*.Location

  Return Type: Full path where test script is saved

Example:

```
sTestScriptNm = oQtpApp.Test.Name
```

- ***IsRunning***—It finds out whether the open test script or business component is currently executing.
  `Syntax : Object.IsRunning`

  Return Type: True or False

  ```
  True, if test script is currently executing
  False, if test script is not executing
  ```

Example:

```
sTestScriptNm = oQtpApp.Test.IsRunning
```

- ***LastRunResults***—It returns the *LastRunResults* object, which contains the latest run results for the test script or business component.
  `Syntax : Object.LastRunResults`

  Return Type: *LastRunResults* object

Example:

```
sTestScriptNm = oQtpApp.Test.LastRunResults
```

Example: Write a code to execute a test script with specified environment settings after validating add-ins.

```
Set oQtpApp = CreateObject("UFT.Application")
oQtpApp.Launch
oQtpApp.Visible = True
oQtpApp.Open "Z:\BusinessComponents\Login", False, False

'Set AUT database environment variables
oQtpApp.Test.Environment.Value("DBSID") = "Oracle10g"  'Set database SID
oQtpApp.Test.Environment.Value("DBUsrNm") = "Admin" 'Set database
                                            user name
oQtpApp.Test.Environment.Value("DBPasswd") = "Admin" 'Set database
                                                    password
```

```
'Set run options
Set oQtpRunOptions = CreateObject("UFT.RunResultsOptions")
                                        'Get RunOptions object
'Set location where test run results are to be saved
oQtpRunOptions.ResultsLocation "Z:\TestResults\Login\"
'Start test script execution and as well execute next line of the
                                         automation script
oQtpApp.Test.Run oQtpRunOptions,False
'Wait till execution is complete
Do While oQtpApp.Test.IsRunning= True
Loop
'Find test script execution environment
sOS = oQtpApp.Test.Environment.Value("OS")
'Find execution result status
sRunStat = oQtpApp.Test.LastRunResults.Status
'Save test script
oQtpApp.Test.Save
'Exit UFT
oQtpApp.Quit
Set oQtpRunOptions = Nothing
Set oQtpApp = Nothing
```

Example: Write a code to convert the test scripts from the older version of UFT to UFT 10.

Let us assume that we have four test scripts PlanTravel, FillForm, BookTckt, and GetAvailability, are inside the folder BookTckt.

```
'Get folder path
sFolderPath = InputBox(" Enter the location where all test scripts
      are kept")
'sFolderPath = "Z:\BusinessComponents\BookTckt"
'Find all test scripts inside specified location
Set oFSO = CreateObject("Scripting.FileSystemObject")
Set oFolder = oFSO.GetFolder(sFolderPath)
Set colSubfolders = oFolder.Subfolders
'Open UFT
Set oQtpApp = CreateObject("UFT.Application")
oQtpApp.Launch
oQtpApp.Visible = True
'Covert test  script to UFT 10 version
For Each oSubfolder in colSubfolders
oQtpApp.Open oSubfolder.Path,False, False
oQtpApp.Test.Save
Next
Set oQtpApp = Nothing
```

QUICK TIPS

- ✓ UFT AOM provides objects, methods, and properties to write programs that can automatically launch UFT tool, configure UFT options, and run desired test scripts.
- ✓ 'Application' object is used to create an instance of the UFT application.
- ✓ 'ObjectRepositories' collection object is used to add, remove, or find object repositories associated with an action.
- ✓ 'TestLibraries' collection object is used to associate a library file to a test.
- ✓ 'Recovery' object provides methods to add or remove recovery scenarios to a test script.
- ✓ 'Recovery Scenario' object provides methods find name and path of recovery scenarios.
- ✓ 'RunOptions' object provides methods to configure test run options for the current run session.
- ✓ 'Test Object' provides methods and properties to access test script details such as author and the date of script creation and as well to execute or save attest script. It represents opened test script or business component.

PRACTICAL QUESTIONS

1. What is UFT AOM?
2. Write a code to launch UFT from a VBScript file.
3. Write a code to remove JAVA add-ins and add SAP add-ins to UFT add-ins group.
4. Write a code to define the run settings of UFT.
5. Which object is used to find the library files associated with a test?
6. Which object is used to add object repositories to an action?
7. Write a code to associate specific environment, library, and recovery scenario files to a test during run-time.

Section 10 Business Process Testing

- Integrating UFT with ALM
- Business Process Testing

Chapter 54

Integrating UFT with ALM

HP Quality Center (QC) is a web-based test management tool from HP. HP QC offers software quality assurance, including requirements management, test management, defect tracking, traceability matrix, and business process testing for IT and application environments. HP QC can also be used to store QTP scripts. Integration of QTP with QC helps in managing and executing the automated tests from QC itself. Test results are automatically marked pass or fail after the text script execution.

HP QC has four primary tabs:

- Requirements—To store business requirements in a structured form
- Test Plan—To store the tests
- Test Lab—To execute the tests
- Defects—To log defects and track them

INTEGRATING QTP WITH QC

In order to execute the automated test scripts from QC environment, QC needs to be integrated with QTP. To integrate QTP with QC, perform the following steps:

1. Navigate *File → Quality Center Connection.*
2. *Quality Center Connection - Server Connection* dialog box opens. (see Fig. 54.1). Enter the QC server URL.

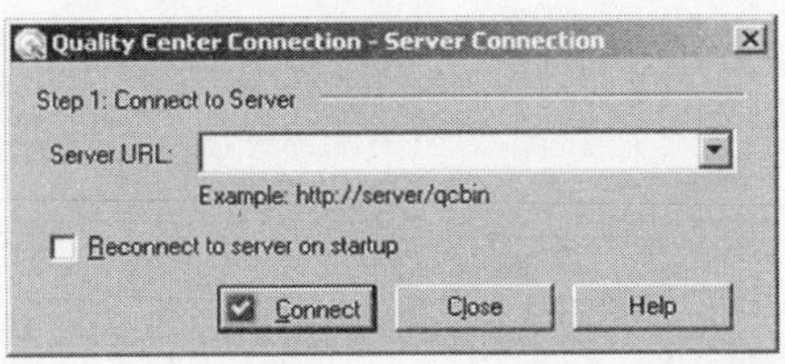

Figure 54.1 *Quality center connection—server connection*

3. Click the *Connect* button
4. *Quality Center Connection* dialog window will open (see Fig. 54.2)
5. Input username and password

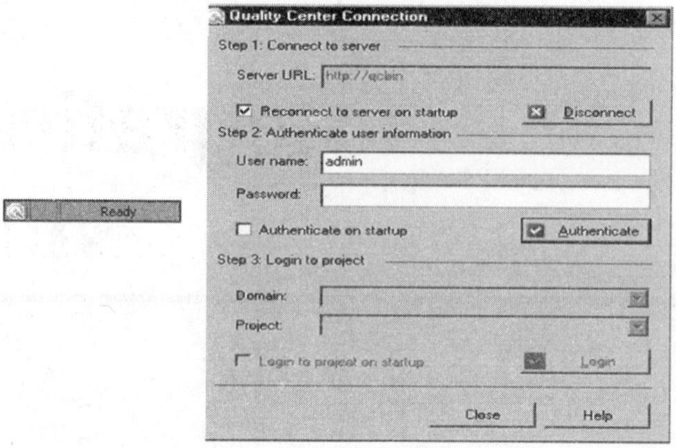

Figure 54.2 *Quality center connection—Project details*

6. Click the *Authenticate* button
7. Select appropriate domain
8. Select appropriate project
9. Click Login
10. Click the *Close* button to close the QC Connection dialog box. The QC icon is displayed on the status bar to indicate that QuickTest is currently connected to a QC project.

> **NOTES** QC Connectivity Add-in is required to integrate QC with QTP. This add-in is automatically installed on QTP machine when QTP is connected to QC using QC dialog box. It can also be installed manually from the QC add-ins page by choosing Help Add-ins Page HP Quality Center Connectivity in QC.

Alternatively, QTP can also be connected to QC using the QTP Automation Object Model (AOM).

```
' Create QuickTest instance
Set oQtpApp = CreateObject("QuickTest.Application")

' Launch QTP
oQtpApp.Launch
oQtpApp.Visible = True

' Connection details
Set oQCConn = oQtpApp.TDConnection
sServerURL = "http://10.666.44.001:8007/qcbin"
sDomain = "DEFAULT"
sPrjctNm = "SystemTest"
```

```
sUser = "defaultuser"
sPasswd = "password"

' Check if connection is already open,  close it
If oQCConn.IsConnected=True Then
    ' Disconnect the connection
    oQCConn.Disconnect
End If

' Connect to QC
oQCConn.Connect sServerURL, sDomain, sPrjctNm, sUser, sPasswd,False

' Get the TDConnection object reference
Set oTDConn = oQCConn.TDOTA

' Disconnect the connection
oQCConn.Disconnect
```

> **NOTES** In order to use encrypted passwords, first encrypt the password using QTP Password Encoder tool. This encrypted password can then be passed as a parameter to the connection string as follows.

```
sEncryptPasswd = "876ghgh9890hj00jo78987ht76586yihh"
' Connect to QC
oQCConn.Connect  sServerURL,  sDomain,  sPrjctNm,  sUser,  sEncryptPasswd,
True
```

QC Database

The QC project database stores system information, user information, and information produced while using QC modules.

Requirement Module

Requirement data is stored primarily in table REQ.

Test Plan Module

Users design and define tests in test plan module. The main table is TEST.

Test Lab Module

Users organize designed tests in a specific test groups (test set) as per requirement in test lab module. The test set thereafter can be executed as a single testing unit. The main table is CYCLE.

Business Components Module

In business components module, subject matter experts or business analysts create a high-level business component that represents steps in the business process. The main table is COMPONENT.

Defect Module

Users use defect module to update test results and to log and track defects. The main table is BUG.

History

Any change to data is tracked in the tables AUDIT_LOG and AUDIT_PROPERTIES.

Alerts and Reminders

Data of alerts and reminders are maintained in ALERT and RULES table.

> Refer *Database Reference* document in QC help to get the complete details and list of QC database tables. To download this file, perform the following steps:
> 1. Login to QC
> 2. Navigate *Help* → *Documentation Library*
> 3. Click on link Mercury Quality Center Database Reference to download database reference (.chm) document

Connecting QTP with QC Database

QC Open Test Architecture (OTA) provides methods and properties to connect to QC database and extract or update QC data. The following code connects to QC database using a connection object between QTP and QC.

```
' Create QuickTest instance
Set oQtpApp = CreateObject("QuickTest.Application")

' Launch QTP
oQtpApp.Launch
oQtpApp.Visible = True

' Connection details
Set oQCConn = oQtpApp.TDConnection
sServerURL = "http://10.444.68.900:8009/qcbin"
sDomain = "DEFAULT"
sPrjctNm = "SystemTest"
sUser = "default"
sPasswd = "password"

' Check if connection is already open, close it
If oQCConn.IsConnected=True Then
   ' Disconnect the other connection
   oQCConn.Disconnect
End If

' Connect to QC
oQCConn.Connect sServerURL, sDomain, sPrjctNm, sUser,
sPasswd, False
```

```
' Get the TDConnection object reference
Set oTDConn = QCUtil.TDConnection

Set oTDCmd = oTDConn.Command

' Query - find the count of total test cases present in test plan
module
sSql = "Select Count(*) As TestCasesCnt  from TESTCYCL "
oTDCmd.CommandText = sSql

' Execute Query
Set oRecordSet = oTDCmd.Execute

' Retrieve query results from record set
While Not oRecordSet.EOR
    Print " Test Case Count : " &
oRecordSet.FieldValue("TestCasesCnt")
    oRecordSet.Next
Wend

' Query - find  defect details which has been reopened
sSql = "Select BG_BUG_ID, BG_RESPONSIBLE, BG_SUMMARY from BUG
                                            Where
                                      BG_STATUS='Reopen'"
' Execute Query
Set oRecordSet = oTDCmd.Execute

' Retrieve query results from record set
While Not oRecordSet.EOR
       Print oRecordSet.FieldValue("BG_BUG_ID") & vbTab &_

oRecordSet.FieldValue("BG_RESPONSIBLE")  &_
                      vbTab & oRecordSet.FieldValue("BG_SUMMARY")
       oRecordSet.Next
Wend

' Close Connection
oQCConn.Disconnect
```

Connecting with QC Database Without Using QTP Object Reference

Database connectivity to QC can also be achieved without an instance of QTP application. This can be done by directly creating an instance of `TDAPIole80.TDConnection` using QTP AOM.

```
' Create an instance of TDConnection
oQCConn = CreateObject("TDAPIole80.TDConnection")

' Connection details
sServerURL = "http://10.444.68.900:8009/qcbin"
sDomain = "DEFAULT"
sPrjctNm = "SystemTest"
sUser = "default"
sPasswd = "password"

' Close connection, if already open
If oQCConn.Connected=True Then
    oQCConn.Disconnect
End If

' Connect to QC server
' Connect to QC server
oQCConn.InitConnectionEx sServerURL

' Connect to the specified QC project
oQCConn.ConnectProjectEx  sDomain, sPrjctNm, sUser, sPasswd

MsgBox oQCConn.Connected

oQCConn.Disconnect
oQCConn.Logout
oQCConn.ReleaseConnection
```

Export QC Test Cases to Excel Via QTP

Database connectivity with QC can be used to retrieve or update QC database details. Updating the QC database fields, by directly using query, can save a lot of effort and time. For example, suppose that *Short Description* field of more than 100 test cases needs to be updated in QC. The manual effort required to do this is huge. However, if we use query to directly update the database-specific fields, then the same task can be done in minutes. Another potential usage of QC database connectivity in test automation can be to update test cases status in QC after executing the test script from QTP. This will prevent the need to connect QTP to QC. Presently, it is required to execute test scripts from QC to automatically mark the QC test cases as pass or fail as per the script execution status. Updating QC test case status using update query from QTP environment is very useful in cases where test automation frameworks do not support easy integration with QC. QC database connectivity can also be used to extract details of all test cases present in QC and then export this data to the Excel workbook. The following code shows how to export QC test cases to Excel sheet.

```
' Create QuickTest instance
Set oQtpApp = CreateObject("QuickTest.Application")

' Launch QTP
oQtpApp.Launch
oQtpApp.Visible = True

' Connection details
Set oQCConn = oQtpApp.TDConnection
sServerURL = "http://10.444.68.900:8009/qcbin"
sDomain = "DEFAULT"
sPrjctNm = "SystemTest"
sUser = "default"
sPasswd = "password"

' Check if connection is already open,  close it
If oQCConn.IsConnected=True Then
    ' Disconnect the other connection
    oQCConn.Disconnect
End If

' Connect to QC
oQCConn.Connect sServerURL, sDomain, sPrjctNm, sUser, sPasswd,False

' Get the TDConnection object reference
Set oTDConn = QCUtil.TDConnection

Set oTDCmd = oTDConn.Command

' Query -  get details of a specific test case
sSql = "SELECT TS_TEST_ID,TS_NAME,DS_STEP_ORDER, DS_DESCRIPTION, "
      " DS_EXPECTED, DS_STEP_NAME" &_
      " FROM TEST, DESSTEPS Where TS_TEST_ID = DS_TEST_ID and " &_
      " TS_Name='TestCaseName' ORDER BY TS_TEST_ID, DS_STEP_ORDER"

' Query -  get details of all test cases
' sSql = "SELECT TS_TEST_ID,TS_NAME,DS_STEP_ORDER, DS_DESCRIPTION, "
      ' " DS_EXPECTED, DS_STEP_NAME" &_
      ' " FROM TEST, DESSTEPS Where TS_TEST_ID = DS_TEST_ID and " &_
      ' " ORDER BY TS_TEST_ID, DS_STEP_ORDER"

oTDCmd.CommandText = sSql

' Execute Query
Set oRecordSet = oTDCmd.Execute
```

```
' Export test cases to excel
Set oXlApp = CreateObject("Excel.Application")
oXlApp.Visible = False

' Create new workbook
iCnt = 1
jCnt = 1
Set oXlWrkBkNew = oXlApp.Workbooks.Add
Set oXlWrkShtNew = oXlWrkBkNew.Worksheets.Add
oXlWrkShtNew.Name = "QC_TEST_CASES"
oXlWrkShtNew.Cells(iCnt,jCnt)  = "TS_TEST_ID"
oXlWrkShtNew.Cells(iCnt,jCnt+1)  = "TS_NAME"
oXlWrkShtNew.Cells(iCnt,jCnt+2)  = "DS_STEP_ORDER"
oXlWrkShtNew.Cells(iCnt,jCnt+3)  = "DS_DESCRIPTION"
oXlWrkShtNew.Cells(iCnt,jCnt+4)  = "DS_EXPECTED"
oXlWrkShtNew.Cells(iCnt,jCnt+5)  = "DS_STEP_NAME"

' Retrieve query results from record set
While Not oRecordSet.EOR
      iCnt = iCnt + 1
      oXlWrkShtNew.Cells(iCnt,jCnt)  =
oRecordSet.FieldValue("TS_TEST_ID")
      oXlWrkShtNew.Cells(iCnt,jCnt+1)  =
oRecordSet.FieldValue("TS_NAME")
      oXlWrkShtNew.Cells(iCnt,jCnt+2)  =
oRecordSet.FieldValue("DS_STEP_ORDER")
      oXlWrkShtNew.Cells(iCnt,jCnt+3)  =
oRecordSet.FieldValue("DS_DESCRIPTION")
      oXlWrkShtNew.Cells(iCnt,jCnt+4)  =
oRecordSet.FieldValue("DS_EXPECTED")
      oXlWrkShtNew.Cells(iCnt,jCnt+5)  =
oRecordSet.FieldValue("DS_STEP_NAME")

      oRecordSet.Next
Wend

' Save workbook
oXlWrkBkNew.SaveAs "C:\Temp\QC_TEST_CASES.xls", True

' Close workbook
oXlWrkBkNew.Close

' Terminate excel application
oXlApp.Quit

' Close Connection
oQCConn.Disconnect
```

Export QC Test Cases to Excel Without QTP

The above-mentioned code will work only if QTP is installed on the system. In order to extract QC test cases without using QTP, an instance of TDApiOle80.TDConnection needs to be created. Moreover, the above-mentioned example exports specific or all test cases of QC to Excel. However, if there is a requirement to export test cases of a specific folder of QC, the above code will not work. To achieve this requirement, we need to design a query that extracts test case details only from the specific folder path. Function `fnExportQCTest2Xl` exports all test cases of a specified QC folder to Excel.

Input parameters:

```
oQCConn = QC Connection object
sFolderPath = QC folder path
sDestLoc = Destination to save excel file
```

Usage:

```
Set oQCConn = CreateObject("TDApiOle80.TDConnection")
sServerURL = "http://10.555.77.999:9899/qcbin"
sDomain = "DEFAULT"
sPrjctNm = "SystemTest"
sUser = "default"
sPasswd = "password"
```

Code:

```
' Close connection, if already open
If oQCConn.Connected=True Then
    oQCConn.Disconnect
End If

' Connect to QC server
oQCConn.InitConnectionEx sServerURL

' Connect to the specified QC project
oQCConn.ConnectProjectEx  sDomain, sPrjctNm, sUser, sPasswd

sFolderPath = "Subject\RegTestSuite\ModuleM1\"
sDestLoc = "C:\Temp\QC_TEST_CASES.xls"
Call fnExportQCTest2Xl(oQCConn, sFolderPath, sDestLoc)

oQCConn.Disconnect
oQCConn.Logout
oQCConn.ReleaseConnection
```

```
Function fnExportQCTest2Xl(oQCConn, sFolderPath, sDestLoc)
    Dim oXl, oXlWrkSht
    Dim oTreeMgr, oTestTree, oTestFactory, oTestList
    Dim arrNodesList()
    Dim nRow, oNode, oTestCase
    Dim oDesignStepFactory, oDesignStep, oDesignStepList
    ' Open Excel
    Set oXl = CreateObject("Excel.Application")
    ' Add a new workbook
    oXl.WorkBooks.Add()
    ' Get the first workoXlWrkSht.
    Set oXlWrkSht = oXl.ActiveSheet
    oXlWrkSht.Name = "QC_TEST_CASES"

    With oXlWrkSht.Range("A1:I1")
        .Font.Name = "Arial"
        .Font.FontStyle = "Bold"
        .Font.Size = 10
        .Font.Bold = True
        .HorizontalAlignment = -4108      'xlCenter
        .VerticalAlignment = -4108  'xlCenter
        .Interior.ColorIndex = 15   'Light Grey
    End With

    oXlWrkSht.Cells(1, 1) = "Scenario (Folder Name)"
    oXlWrkSht.Cells(1, 2) = "Test ID"
    oXlWrkSht.Cells(1, 3) = "Test Name"
    oXlWrkSht.Cells(1, 4) = "Description"
    oXlWrkSht.Cells(1, 5) = "Designer"
    oXlWrkSht.Cells(1, 6) = "Status"
    oXlWrkSht.Cells(1, 7) = "Step Name"
    oXlWrkSht.Cells(1, 8) = "Step Description"
    oXlWrkSht.Cells(1, 9) = "Expected Result"


    Set oTreeMgr = oQCConn.TreeManager

    'Specify the folder path in TestPlan, all the tests under that
folder will be exported.
    Set oTestTree = oTreeMgr.NodeByPath(sFolderPath)
    Set oTestFactory = oTestTree.TestFactory
   Set oTestList = oTestFactory.NewList("") 'Get a list of all from node.


    ReDim Preserve arrNodesList(0)
    'Assign root node of subject tree as NodeByPath node.
    arrNodesList(0) = oTestTree.Path
```

```
    'Gets subnodes and return list in array NodesList
    Call fnGetNodesList(oTestTree, arrNodesList)

    nRow = 2
    For Each oNode In arrNodesList
        Set oTestTree = oTreeMgr.NodeByPath(oNode)
        Set oTestFactory = oTestTree.TestFactory
        Set oTestList = oTestFactory.NewList("")

        ' Iterate through all the tests.
        For Each oTestCase In oTestList

            Set oDesignStepFactory = oTestCase.DesignStepFactory
            Set oDesignStepList = oDesignStepFactory.NewList("")

            If oDesignStepList.Count = 0 Then
                ' Save specified fields.
                oXlWrkSht.Cells(nRow, 1).Value =
oTestCase.Field("TS_SUBJECT").Path
                oXlWrkSht.Cells(nRow, 2).Value =
oTestCase.Field("TS_TEST_ID")
                oXlWrkSht.Cells(nRow, 3).Value =
oTestCase.Field("TS_NAME")
                oXlWrkSht.Cells(nRow, 4).Value =
oTestCase.Field("TS_DESCRIPTION")
                oXlWrkSht.Cells(nRow, 5).Value =
oTestCase.Field("TS_RESPONSIBLE")
                oXlWrkSht.Cells(nRow, 6).Value =
oTestCase.Field("TS_STATUS")
                nRow = nRow + 1
            Else
                For Each oDesignStep In oDesignStepList
                    'Save specified fields.
                    oXlWrkSht.Cells(nRow, 1).Value =
oTestCase.Field("TS_SUBJECT").Path
            oXlWrkSht.Cells(nRow, 2).Value =
oTestCase.Field("TS_TEST_ID")
                    oXlWrkSht.Cells(nRow, 3).Value =
oTestCase.Field("TS_NAME")
                    oXlWrkSht.Cells(nRow, 4).Value =
                        fnRmvHTMLTags(oTestCase.Field("TS_DESCRIPTION")
                   )
                    oXlWrkSht.Cells(nRow, 5).Value =
oTestCase.Field("TS_RESPONSIBLE")
                    oXlWrkSht.Cells(nRow, 6).Value =
oTestCase.Field("TS_STATUS")
```

```
                    'Save design steps.
                    oXlWrkSht.Cells(nRow, 7).Value =
oDesignStep.StepName
                    oXlWrkSht.Cells(nRow, 8).Value =
fnRmvHTMLTags(oDesignStep.StepDescription)
                    oXlWrkSht.Cells(nRow, 9).Value =
fnRmvHTMLTags(oDesignStep.StepExpectedResult)
                    nRow = nRow + 1
                Next
            End If
        Next
    Next

    oXl.Columns("A:I").ColumnWidth = 15

    'Set Auto Filter mode.
    If Not oXlWrkSht.AutoFilterMode Then
        oXlWrkSht.Range("A1").AutoFilter
    End If

    'Freeze first row.
    oXlWrkSht.Range("A2").Select
    oXl.ActiveWindow.FreezePanes = True

    'Save the newly created workbook and close Excel.
    oXl.ActiveWorkbook.SaveAs(sDestLoc)
    oXl.Quit

    Set oXl = Nothing
    Set oDesignStepList = Nothing
    Set oDesignStepFactory = Nothing
    Set oTestList = Nothing
    Set oTestFactory = Nothing
    Set oTestTree = Nothing
    Set oTreeMgr = Nothing
End Function


Function fnGetNodesList(ByVal oNode, ByRef arrNodesList)
    Dim nNewUpper
    'Run on all children nodes
    For iCnt = 1 To oNode.Count
        'Add more space to dynamic array
        nNewUpper = UBound(arrNodesList) + 1
        ReDim Preserve arrNodesList(nNewUpper)
```

```
        'Add node path to array
        arrNodesList(nNewUpper) = Node.Child(iCnt).Path

        'If current node has a child then get path of child nodes too.
        If oNode.Child(iCnt).Count >= 1 Then
            Call fnGetNodesList(oNode.Child(i), arrNodesList)
        End If
    Next
End Function


Function fnRmvHTMLTags(sHTMLString)
      sHTMLString = Replace(Replace(sHTMLString,"<HTML>","",1,-
1,1),"</HTML>","",1,-1,1)
      sHTMLString = Replace(Replace(sHTMLString,"<BODY>","",1,-
1,1),"</BODY>","",1,-1,1)
      sHTMLString = Replace(Replace(sHTMLString,"<BR>","",1,-
1,1),"</BR>","",1,-1,1)
      sHTMLString = Replace(sHTMLString,"&quot;", Chr(34),1,-1,1)
      sHTMLString = Replace(sHTMLString,"&lt;", "<",1,-1,1)
      sHTMLString = Replace(sHTMLString,"&gt;", ">",1,-1,1)
      fnRmvHTMLTags = sHTMLString
End Function
```

> **NOTES** The root folder for the Test Plan tab is Subject. In order to access a folder, suppose that 'SystemTest-Suite,' inside the Test Plan tab of QC from outside the QC environment, the path will be 'Subject\System-TestSuite\.' The explicit path of this is '[QualityCenter] Subject\SystemTestSuite\.

This code can also be executed from a .vbs file. The requirement is to copy the entire code in a new .vbs file and replace the hard-coded QC login details, QC test cases source details, and Excel destination details with parameters. Thereafter, the .vbs file can be executed with required parameters from the command prompt.

Executing QC Test Suite Using an E-mail Trigger

It is often required to automatically execute the QC smoke test suite (or build verification test suite) and/or QC regression suite once the build has been successfully deployed. The following code shows how to automatically execute a specific QC test suite from any mail client. A specific received mail can be used as a trigger to execute a specific QC test suite. Mail clients such as MS Outlook and Lotus Notes provide the flexibility to develop customized mail rules. Customized mail rules can be developed to execute a specific macro on receipt of a specific mail type. An example is executing macro 'ExecuteBVT' whenever a mail with the subject 'BVT Deployment Successful' is received. Inside the macro, the code can be written that automatically executes the QC test suite. Else, the macro can be coded to execute a VBScript file kept at the central shared location for the automation project. Inside the VBScript file, the code can be written to execute a specific QC test suite whenever the VBScript file is executed. Code can also be written to execute the QC suite on specific QTP lab machines.

`fnRunQCTestSet` is a subroutine that takes QC test folder path, test set name, and the QTP machine name where the run is to be executed as input parameters. The subroutine searches for the test set inside the QC folders. If the test set is found, it is executed on the specified QTP machine; else, an error is thrown at run-time.

Input parameters:

`sTestFolderNe`—Test set folder path
`sTestSetNm`—Name of the test set to be executed
`sRunOnMachine`—The machine on which test set needs to be executed
It can take following values:
0—Execute test run on local machine
1—Execute run on the machine as specified in the input parameter `sHostMachine`
2—Execute run on the machines as specified in the tests in QC
`sHostMachine`—The QTP machine where test needs to be executed
It needs to be specified only when value of sRunOnMachine is 1.

Macro code:

```
' Load system DLL files
Private Declare Sub Sleep Lib "Kernel32.dll" (ByVal dwMilliseconds As
Long)
Private Declare Function timeGetTime Lib "WinMM.dll" () As Long

Sub main()
    Call RunTestSet("Test Suite\TestFolder", "TestSet", 2, "")
End Sub

Public Sub fnRunQCTestSet(sTestSetFolderNm, sTestSetNm, sRunOnMachine,
sHostName)

    On Error GoTo RunTestSetErr

    sErrMsg = "RunTestSet: " & sTestSetNm

    ' Create QC connection object
    Set oQCConn = CreateObject("TDApiOle80.TDConnection.1")
```

```
    ' Open QC connection
    oQCConn.InitConnectionEx "http://linkname01:8080/qcbin/"
    oQCConn.ConnectProjectEx "QCProjectName", "QCBuildName",
"QCUserNm", "QCUserPswrd"

    Set oTestSetFact = oQCConn.TestSetFactory
    Set oTestTreeMgr = oQCConn.TestSetTreeManager

    Dim nPath$
    nPath = "Root\" & Trim(sTestSetFolderNm)

    ' Find test set folder in QC
    Set oTestFolderNm = oTestTreeMgr.NodeByPath(nPath)
    If oTestFolderNm Is Nothing Then
        Err.Raise vbObjectError + 1, sErrMsg , "Could not find folder "
& nPath
        GoTo RunTestSetErr
    End If

   'Find test set in QC
    Set oTestSetList = oTestFolderNm.FindTestSets(sTestSetNm)
    If oTestSetList.Count > 1 Then
        sErrMsg  = sErrMsg  & "FindTestSets found more than one test
set: refine search"
        GoTo RunTestSetErr
    ElseIf oTestSetList.Count < 1 Then
        sErrMsg  = sErrMsg  & "FindTestSets: test set not found"
        GoTo RunTestSetErr
    End If

    Set oRunTestSet = oTestSetList.Item(1)
    Debug.Print oRunTestSet.ID

    Set oScheduler = oRunTestSet.StartExecution("")

    Select Case sRunOnMachine
        Case 0
            ' Run test on local QTP machine
            oScheduler.RunAllLocally = True

        Case 1
            ' Run test on the specified QTP machine
            oScheduler.TdHostName = sHostName

       Case 2
          ' Run test on the QTP machines as specified in the test set
```

```
in QC
          Set oTSTestFact = oRunTestSet.TSTestFactory
          Set oTestFilter = oTSTestFact.Filter
          oTestFilter.Filter("TC_CYCLE_ID") = oRunTestSet.ID
          Set oTestList = oTSTestFact.NewList(oTestFilter.Text)
          Debug.Print "Test instances and planned hosts:"
          For Each oTest In oTestList
                 Debug.Print "Name: " & oTest.Name & " ID: " &
oTest.ID &_
                            " Planned Host: " & oTest.HostName
                 oScheduler.RunOnHost(oTest.ID) = oTest.HostName
          Next oTest
          oScheduler.RunAllLocally = False
    End Select

    ' Start execution
    oScheduler.Run

    ' Find execution status
    Set oExecStatus = oScheduler.ExecutionStatus

    While ((bRunFinished = False))
        nIter = nIter + 1
        oExecStatus.RefreshExecStatusInfo "all", True
        bRunFinished = oExecStatus.Finished
        Set oEventsList = oExecStatus.EventsList

        For Each oExecEventInfo In oEventsList
            Debug.Print "Event: " & oExecEventInfo.EventDate & " " & _
                    oExecEventInfo.EventTime & " " & _
            "Event Type: " & oExecEventInfo.EventType & "

     ' Event types: 1-fail, 2-finished, 3-env fail, 4-timeout, 5-
     manual
       Next

       Debug.Print oExecStatus.Count & " exec status"
       For iCnt = 1 To oExecStatus.Count
           Set oTestExecStatus = oExecStatus.Item(i)
           Debug.Print "Iteration " & nIter & " Status: " & _
                       " Test " & oTestExecStatus.TestId & _
                       " ,Test instance " &
oTestExecStatus.TestInstance & _
                        " ,order " & oTestExecStatus.TSTestId & " " & _
                        oTestExecStatus.Message & ", status=" & _
                        oTestExecStatus.Status
```

```
            fnWat (5 * 1000)
        Next iCnt

        fnWat (5000)
    Wend

    If oQCConn.Connected Then
        oQCConn.Disconnect
        oQCConn.ReleaseConnection
        Set oQCConn = Nothing
    End If
    Debug.Print "Scheduler finished around " & CStr(Now)

Exit Sub
RunTestSetErr:
    If oQCConn.Connected Then
        oQCConn.Disconnect
        oQCConn.ReleaseConnection
        Set oQCConn = Nothing
    End If
    MsgBox Err.Description

End Sub

Function fnWait(nMilliseconds)
    Dim nSleepTime As Long, tmTimeNow As Long
    Dim tmSleepTo As Long, tmSleepEnd As Long

    Const nMaxSleep As Long = 100

    tmTimeNow = timeGetTime()
    nSleepTime = nMilliseconds \ 10
    If (nSleepTime > nMaxSleep) Then nSleepTime = nMaxSleep
    tmSleepTo = tmTimeNow + nMilliseconds

    Do
        DoEvents
        tmTimeNow = timeGetTime()
        tmSleepEnd = tmSleepTo - tmTimeNow
        If (tmSleepEnd <= nSleepTime) Then Exit Do
        Call Sleep(nSleepTime)
    Loop

    If (tmSleepEnd >0) Then Call Sleep(tmSleepEnd)
End Function
```

Connecting to ALM Using Java Program

So far we discussed how to connect to ALM using UFT code or VBScript/VB code. It is also possible to connect to ALM using Java code. Connecting to ALM using Java code is essentially required when the test platform is also Java (Selenium WebDriver) and the requirement is to continuous interact with ALM using code. One such example would be to write code that extracts the defects from ALM and JIRA on daily basis. It might happen that in an organization one team (say online team) is using JIRA while another team (say SAP team) uses ALM. In rder to track the progress of the project as a whole, it becomes imperative to analyze the defects logged on both JIRA and ALM. While manually extracting the information is time consuming, using different snippets of code creates additional manual tasks of merging the defect data of both test management systems. In such cases, if a single snipped of code is used to extract information from multiple systems then not only it saves time but helps to create a meaningful and user-friendly report.

In this section, we will discuss how we can connect to ALM using OTAClient.dll library. First step is to find the OTAClient.dll file and then create a wrapper that translates requests to a native language. This is because OtaClient.dll is not a Java library and hence, cannot be used directly by Java program.

Find OTAClient.dll

Depending on version of the ALM or QC, OTAClient.dll may be located at different locations. It can either be located at:

```
C:\Program Files (x86)\Common Files\MercuryInteractive\Quality Center\
```

Or,

```
C:\Users\{username}\AppData\Local\HP\ALM-Client\
```

> **NOTES** The system should have ALM or QC client installed. One way to install this is connecting to ALM or QC server from the machine. On first login, ALM server automatically installs the required library files on the system. Also, ALM can also be installed by installing the UFT add-in for ALM.

Create a Wrapper for OTAClient.dll

OTAClient.dll is not a Java library and hence cannot be used by Java. Java library *COM4J* can be used to create a wrapper for OTAClient that translates requests to a native language. Follow the steps below to create a wrapper for dll:

Download com4j

COM4J can be downloaded from—https://github.com/kohsuke/com4j/downloads or http://qctools4j.sourceforge.net/ or http://java.net/projects/com4j/downloads. If it is a zipped file and unzip it. Save com4j.jar file at location c:\temp\com4j. COM4J folder contains jar files—args4j.jar, com4j.jar and tlbimp.jar.

Generate Java library with the wrapped classes

- Open command prompt
- Navigate to the directory where com4j.jar file is kept as shown in the Fig. 54.3.
- Assume the wrapper files are to be created inside folder 'C:\temp\otaclientjar'. Execute the below command as shown in the figure 1 below.

```
java -jar tlbimp.jar -o "C:\Temp\OTAClientJar" -p com.alm "C:\Temp\
OTAClient.dll"
```

Here,

-o is for the destination directory
-p is for the Java package of the destination

Above code may throws error on 64-bit OS. This is because com4j is compatible with only 32-bit JRE. Use the 32-bit JRE as shown in the Fig. 54.3:

- Once the command is executed successfully, sources are ready at location—c:\temp\otaclient-jar\com\alm.

Write Java Code to Connect to ALM

- Open a Java IDE say Eclipse.
- Create a new Java project and import the Java libraries created above.
- Create new Java class and write Java code as below.

```
import com4j.*;
import com.alm.*;

public class ALMConnect{
    public static void main(String[] args) {
        //ALM url
        String url = "http://alm server/qcbin";
        //username for login
        String username = "username";
        //password for login
        String password = "password";
        //alm domain
        String domain = "domian name";
        //alm project
        String project = "project name";
```

Figure 54.3 *Generating Java wrapper classes for OTAClient.dll*

```
            ITDConnection itdc = ClassFactory.createTDConnection();
            itdc.initConnectionEx(url);
            itdc.connectProjectEx(domain, project, username,
    password);
        }
  }
```

QUICK TIPS

- ✓ HP QC is a web-based test management tool from HP.
- ✓ QC provides the flexibility to execute or schedule execution of automation scripts from QC environment.

PRACTICAL QUESTIONS

1. Write a code to connect QTP with QC.
2. Write a code to export specific QC test cases to Excel file.

Chapter 55

Business Process Testing

HP Business Process Testing (BPT) is a complete package for functional test case design for both automated and manual testings. It helps in structured testing of an application by enabling non-technical subject-matter experts to collaborate effectively with automation engineers and by automating the creation of test-plan documentation. BPT is not dependent on the completion of detailed test scripts for test execution. Application can be tested manually till the time automated scripts are not ready.

BPT enables nontechnical subject-matter experts to become an integral part of the quality optimization process by allowing them to automate scripts in a script-free environment. For automation of complex scenarios that involve logical conditions scripting environment is also provided. Subject matter experts define and document business processes, business components, and business process tests, while automation developers create the required resources and settings, such as test scripts, object repositories, function libraries, and recovery scenario. Either of them or both can create, data-drive, document, and execute business process tests without requiring programming knowledge on the part of the subject matter experts.

BPT model is a role-based testing model. In BPT testing model, subject matter experts create components and define manual steps in the *Design Steps* tab of each component. Then, the required components are integrated to form a business process tests. These business process tests resemble manual test scenarios and can be executed manually till the time components are not automated.

During the development phase, automation developers' work with the subject matter experts to define the resources and the settings required for the business components. On the basis of the knowledge gathered, automation developers create the required *Application Area*. An *application area* defines the resources and the settings such library files, environment files, and object repositories

NOTES

The automated business component needs to be associated with one of the application areas.

required to execute a business component. After the application area is created, the required resources are associated with the application area.

BPT is based on the creation, implementation, and execution of business components tests. Three modules of quality centre (QC) are used to execute the life cycle of BPT, namely, *Business Components*, *Test Plan*, and *Test Lab*.

- The business components module is used to create, manage, and automate reusable business components. Each business component comprises of test steps that perform a specific business task in a business process.
- The test plan module is used to create and debug business process tests. Business process tests are created by dragging and dropping business components to a business process test in a specific order.
- The test lab module is used to create and execute test sets and view the run results. A test set is comprised of one or many business process tests.

Business components are reusable units that perform a specific business task. They form the building blocks of business process tests. Each business component is comprised of several steps that are executed together in a specific sequence. For example, consider a simple web application of railway ticket booking. Here, the various components can be *login*, *search ticket*, *fill passenger details*, and *make payment*. Each component tests a specific functionality of the application. Each component comprises of various steps to test the specific functionality of the application. For example, for *login* component, there are four steps. First step is to enter the username. Second step is to enter password. Third step is to click on the login button. And, fourth step is to verify whether login is successful or not. Business components are designed in a way to test the specific part of the application. These business components are then integrated to test a specific business task (business scenario). The components are designed to be modular and reusable, so that they can be used in multiple business process tests. For example, *login* component can be used in multiple business process tests to automate various business scenarios.

QuickTest provides two types of components—QuickTest keyword-driven components and scripted components. QuickTest keyword-driven components are developed using keyword-driven method. These components are fully integrated with both QuickTest and QC enabling both automation developers and subject matter experts (or testers) to create, modify, and execute them. Scripted components are more complex and are developed using programming logic code. Due to the programming complexity involved, scripted components can be created and modified only in QuickTest. Specialized automation developers are required to create or modify a scripted component. Subject matter experts (or testers) can use these scripted components in the business process tests but they cannot modify them. However, they can view the scripted components.

LIFE CYCLE OF BPT

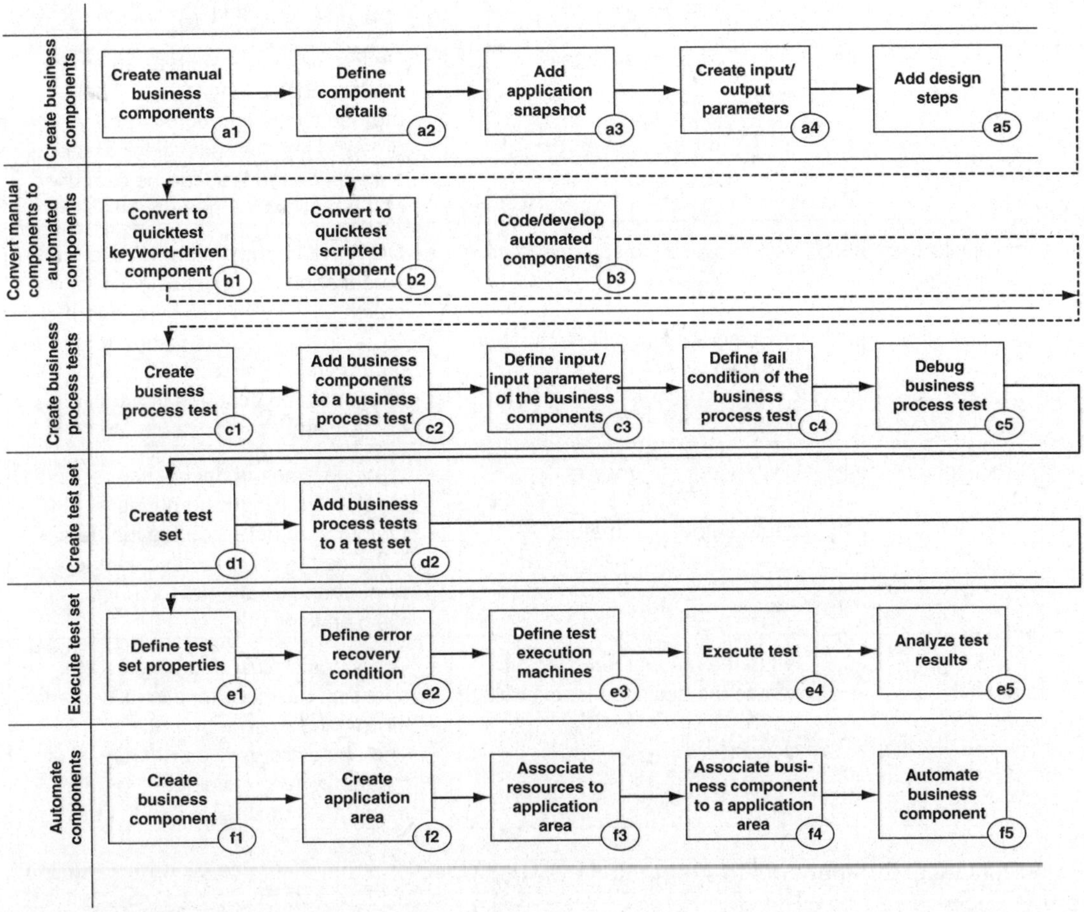

Create Business Components			
No	**Activity**	**Sub-Activity**	**Description**
a1	Create manual business components	a1.1 Click on the business component module a1.2 Create new folder a1.3 Create new business component	• Opens business component module • Creates a new folder where business components can be stored • Creates a new manual component
a2	Define component details	a2.1 Select the Details tab a2.2 Define *general* details	• The Details tab is displayed on the screen • Define the details such as automation developer name and status of component

(*Continued*)

Create Business Components (*Continued*)			
No	Activity	Sub-Activity	Description
		a2.3 Specify *Description* details	• Define the details such as summary of the business scenario to be implemented by the component and the pre- and the post-conditions of the application required for the execution of the business component
a3	Add application screenshot	a3.1 Taking application screenshot from QC a3.2 Attaching an image file to the business component	• QC provides the feature to take the screenshot of an application and attach it to a business component • QC also provides the flexibility to attach an image file to QC. Only one image can be attached to a business component
a4	Create input/ output parameters	a4.1 Create input parameters a4.2 Create output parameters	• Input parameters define the test data input to a business component • Output parameters define the data outputted by the business component after execution of the business functionality
a5	Add design steps	a5.1 Define the manual test steps to execute the business functionality	• The steps are used to execute the specified business functionality manually as and when required • The steps are used as reference by the automation developers to automate the component

Convert Manual Components to Automated Components			
No	Activity	Sub-Activity	Description
b1	Convert to QuickTest keyword-driven component	b1.1 Convert the manual business component to keyword-driven component	• The business component is automated as a keyword-driven component. • This business component opens and needs to be developed in the QuickTest *Keyword View*. • This component can be developed by even the subject matter experts.
b2	Convert to QuickTest-scripted component	b2.1 Convert the manual business component to scripted component	• The business component is automated as a scripted component. • This business component opens and needs to be developed in the QuickTest *Expert View*. • Experienced automation developers are required to code this component.

(*Continued*)

Convert Manual Components to Automated Components (*Continued*)			
No	Activity	Sub-Activity	Description
b3	Code automated component in QuickTest	b3.1 Open automated component in QuickTest	• The automated component can be opened in QuickTest by either from QC or from QuickTest. • In order to open an automated component from QuickTest, QuickTest Professional (QTP) tool must be integrated with QC tool.
		b3.2 Associate the business component to an application area	• The newly created business component must be associated with one of the *application areas.*
		b3.3 Code/develop the business component	• Develop the code to automate the business functionality. • For keyword-driven component, appropriate keywords need to be selected and their value defined in the Keyword View of the QuickTest tool. • For scripted component, code needs to be written in the Expert View of the QuickTest tool.

Create Business Process Tests			
No	Activity	Sub-Activity	Description
c1	Create business process test	c1.1 Click on the test plan module	• Opens QC *Test Plan* module.
		c1.2 Create new folder	• Creates a new folder where business process tests can be stored.
		c1.3 Create new business process test	• Creates a new business process test.
		c1.4 Define description of the business process test	• Description specifies priority, severity, creator, business functionality, etc. of the business process test.
c2	Add business components to the business process test	c2.1 Click on the *Select Components* button	• Displays the list of business components.
		c2.2 Add business components to the business process test	• Drag and drop the business components from the business components display list to the business process test. • Re-arrange the business components in the desired sequence to automate a business scenario.

(*Continued*)

Create Business Process Tests (*Continued*)			
No	**Activity**	**Sub-Activity**	**Description**
c3	Define input parameters of each business component	c3.1 Define input parameters of each business component	• Actual data can directly be specified for the business component in a business process data. • Alternatively, output parameter of one business component can be used as the input parameter of the other business component as and when required. • Alternatively, input parameters can be parameterized to receive values from data table or Excel data sheets. • Alternatively, run-time input parameters can be used as per the requirement. • QC also provides the flexibility to attach an image file to QC. Only one image can be attached to a business component.
c4	Define fail condition of the business process test	c4.1 Specify fail/exit condition of the business process test	• This specifies the action to be taken when a business component in the business process test fails. It allows two values – Exit and Continue. • 'Exit' condition implies the business process test must stop executing if the respective business component fails. • 'Continue' condition implies the business process test must keep on continuing execution of the business process test (next business component in sequence) even if the current business component fails.
c5	Debug business process test	c5.1 Debug in *Normal* mode	• In *Normal* mode, QC executes the business components one after another in QuickTest unless and otherwise user pauses the execution using the 'Pause' button of QTP. • A summary of the test result is displayed on the screen as soon as execution is complete.
		c5.2 Debug in *Debug* mode	• In *Debug* mode, QC pauses the execution of the business process test on the first line of every business component. • Users are required to manually trigger the run for each business component by clicking on the 'Run' button of the QTP. • A summary of the test result is displayed on the screen as soon as execution is complete.

Create Test Set

No	Activity	Sub-Activity	Description
d1	Create test set	d1.1 Click on the *Test Lab* module d1.2 Create a new test set d1.3 Define test set description	• Opens *Test Lab* module of the QC. • Creates a new *Test Set* with a specific name inside a specified folder. • Specify the details such as regression run version, environment details, and application version.
d2	Add business process tests to a test set	d2.1 Click on the *Select Tests* button d2.2 Add business process test to the test set	• Displays the list of the business process tests. • Use filter option to selectively filter out specific business process tests. • Drag and drop the business process test from the display list to the test set.

Execute Test Set

No	Activity	Sub-Activity	Description
e1	Define test set properties	e1.1 Click on the *Test Set Properties* tab of the *Test Set* e1.2 Specify e-mail notification conditions.	• Opens the test set properties tab of the test set. • Defines the situations when an e-mail notification is to be sent to a group of users while test set is execution is in progress or when test execution is over.
e2	Define error recovery condition	e2.1 Define error recovery steps	• Specifies how a test should behave in case an error occurs during the execution of one of the business process tests. • The *Test Set* may choose to re-execute or skip the failed business process test depending on the options defined.
e3	Define test execution machines	e3.1 Define the QuickTest machines where tests can be executed.	• QC provides the flexibility to execute the test set on the local machine or on remote machines. • Execution machines need to be specified for each and every business process test in the test set.
e4	Execute test set	e4.1 Click on the *Run* button	• Executes the business process tests one by one on the execution machines as specified. • The test results get automatically updated with the current pass/fail/continuing execution progress of the business process tests of the test set. • Users can view the current execution process of the test set.

(*Continued*)

Execute Test Set *(Continued)*			
No	Activity	Sub-Activity	Description
e5	Analyze test results	e5.1 View and analyze test results	• Test set provides both the pass/fail status of the each business process test as well as details test report of the each business process test. • Moreover, test reports of the past runs are stored in QC for reference.

Automate Components			
No	Activity	Sub-Activity	Description
f1	Create business component	a1.1 Create a new business component	• Business components can be created either from QuickTest or from QC. • If a business component is already created then the business component can be opened either from QC or from QuickTest.
f2	Create application area	a2.1 Open QuickTest a2.2 Create a new application area	• Launches QTP application. • Creates a new application area
f3	Associate resources to application area	a3.1 Associate resources to application area	• Associate resources such as object repository files, environment files, and library files to an application area
f4	Associate business components to a application area	a4.1 Open business component a4.2 Associate business component to a specific application area	• Opens the specific business component. • All the resources of the application area become available to the business component for use.
f5	Automate business component	a5.1 Develop code to automate the business functionality	• For keyword-driven component, appropriate keywords need to be selected and their value defined in the Keyword View of the QuickTest tool. • For scripted component, code needs to be written in the Expert View of the QuickTest tool.

CREATING BUSINESS COMPONENTS

Business components are reusable scripts that perform a specific task in business process. These components can be either manual or automated. Automated business components can be keyword-driven or scripted components.

Creating Manual Business Components

The following steps describe how to create a new business component in QC.

1. **Open Business Component module**
   Click on the *Business Components* module. The *Business Components* module opens (refer Fig. 55.1).

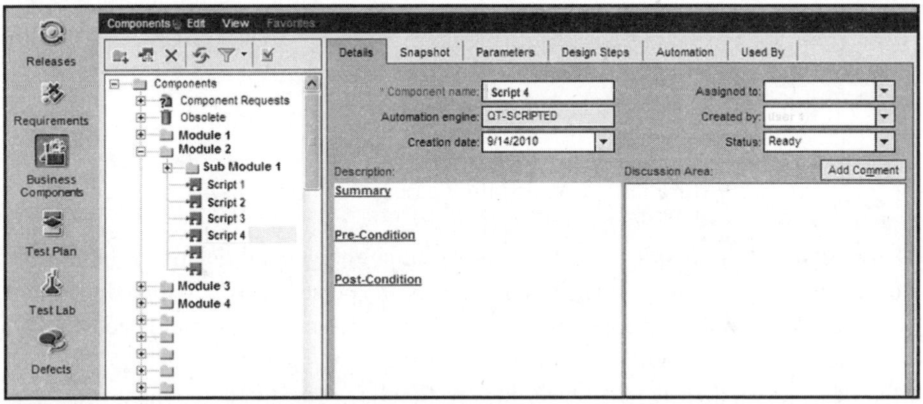

Figure 55.1 *Business components tab*

2. **Create new folder where business components need to be stored**
   Click on the 'New Folder' button to create a new folder. The *New Folder* dialog box opens (refer Fig. 55.2). Enter the desired folder name (application module or sub-module name) and click on the 'OK' button. The new folder gets added to the folder tree.
3. **Create a new business component**
   Click on the 'New Component' button. The *New Component* dialog box opens (refer Fig. 55.3) specify the name of the business component and click on the 'OK' button. The new business component gets added to the selected hierarchy tree.

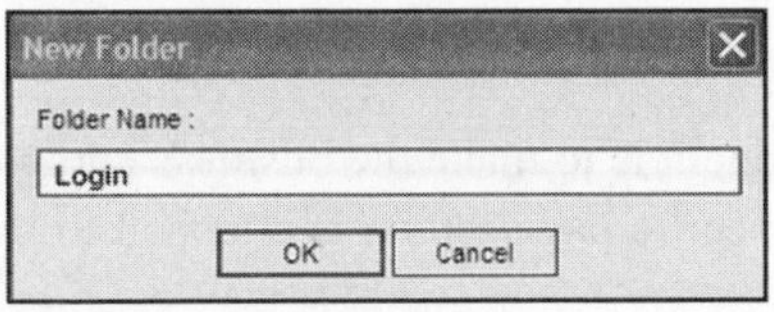

Figure 55.2 *Create new folder in QC*

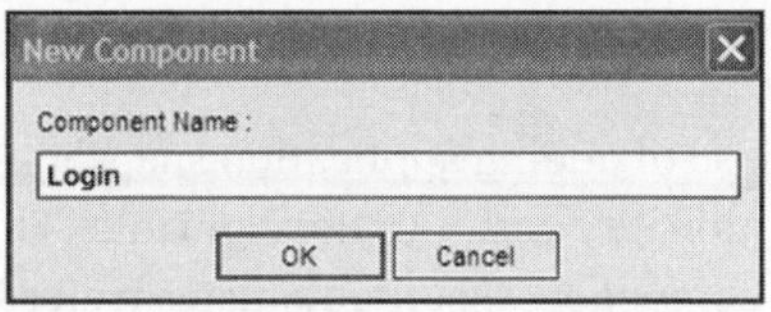

Figure 55.3 *Create new business component in QC*

DEFINING COMPONENT DETAILS

The following steps describe how to define the details of a business component in QC.

1. **Select the details tab:** Click on the *Details* tab (if the existing business component details need to be changed, then first select that business component and then click on the Details tab). The *Details* tab appears on the screen as shown in Fig. 55.4.

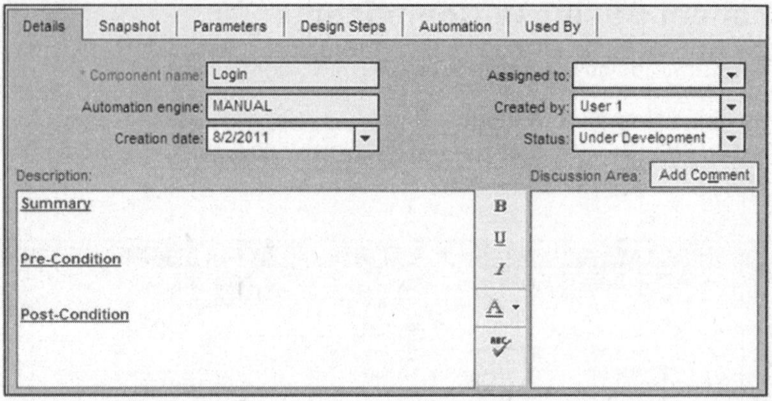

Figure 55.4 *Details tab of a business component*

2. **Define general details:** The next step is to define the general details of the business component such as purpose of business component, the person who is assigned to automate this component, and business component creation date. 'Assigned To' field needs to be updated with the name of the specific automation developer who needs to develop this component. This field is specified when subject matter experts create the components and automation developers build them.
3. **Define component description:** The *Description* area describes a short description of the intended business functionality and the pre-condition and post-condition of the application under test.

> NOTES: The 'Status' field value needs to be changed to 'Ready' when the component has been built by the automation developers.

ADDING SNAPSHOT

The purpose of adding application snapshot to a business component is to make the business component functionality easily understandable. The snapshot of the specific page/screen is attached to the business component that it automates (refer Fig. 55.5).

There are two ways to add application snapshot to a business component – directly taking a snapshot of the application using the 'Snapshot' button or by loading an image file.

Snapshot.. Taking application snapshot from QC

1. Click on the *Snapshot* button Snapshot... *Snapshot* dialog box opens as shown in Fig. 55.6.
2. Click on the *Drag Me* button and point it to the screen whose snapshot needs to be taken (drag and drop this button to the screen whose snapshot is to be taken). The *Snapshot* window opens with the snapshot of the application.

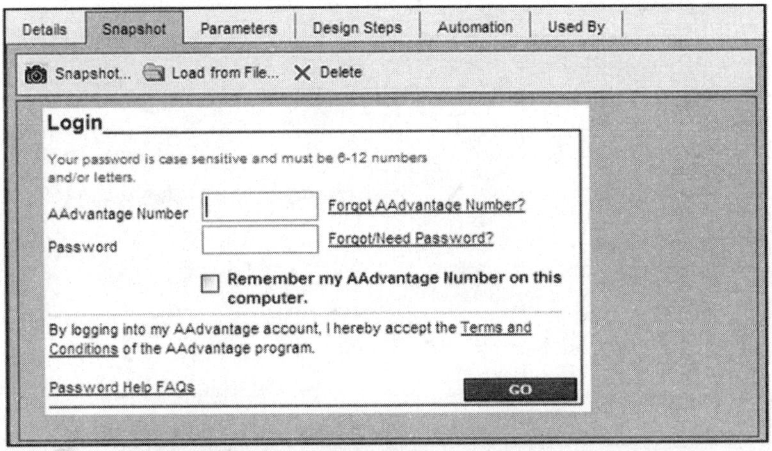

Figure 55.5 *Snapshot tab of a business component*

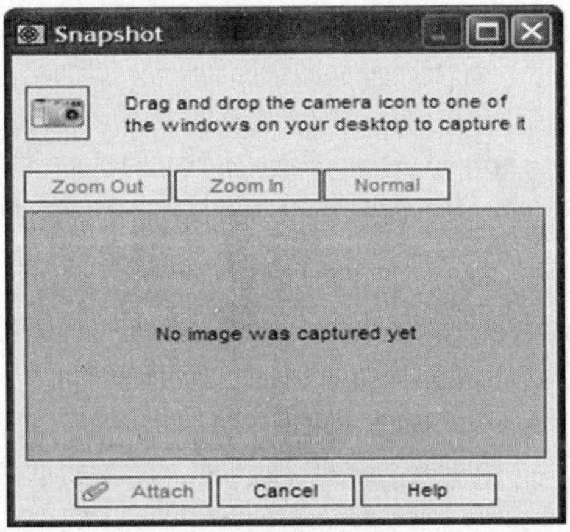

Figure 55.6 *Add snapshot to a business component*

3. Click on the *Attach* button to attach the snapshot to the business component. The 'Snapshot' tab is displayed on the screen as shown in Fig. 55.6.

Load from File... **Attaching application snapshot to a business component** The other way of attaching an application snapshot to a business component is by directly loading the image file of the application using the 'Load From File' button.

DEFINING BUSINESS COMPONENT PARAMETERS

Parameterization helps to execute the same business component against a variety of data set. The business components can be parameterized for both input and output parameters. Figure 55.7 shows the *Parameters* tab of the *Login* business component.

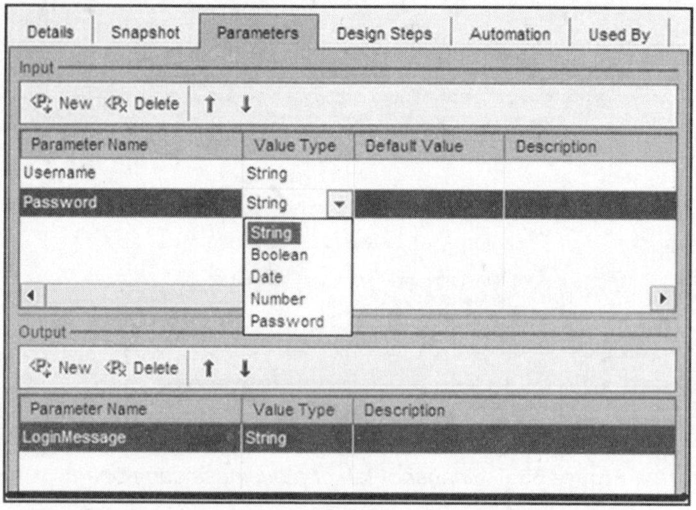

Figure 55.7 *Defining business component parameters*

Defining Input Parameters

1. Click on the 'New Parameter' button New of the 'Input' section as shown in Fig. 55.8. The 'New Parameter' dialog box opens as shown in Fig. 55.8
2. Specify the parameter name say 'Username' and click on the 'OK' button.
3. The *Parameters* tab of the business component is displayed on the screen with the updated parameter name.
4. Choose the 'ValueType' of the parameter. It can be—String, Boolean, Date, Number, or Password.
5. Specify the 'DefaultValue' of the parameter, if applicable.
6. Specify the 'Description' of the parameter.

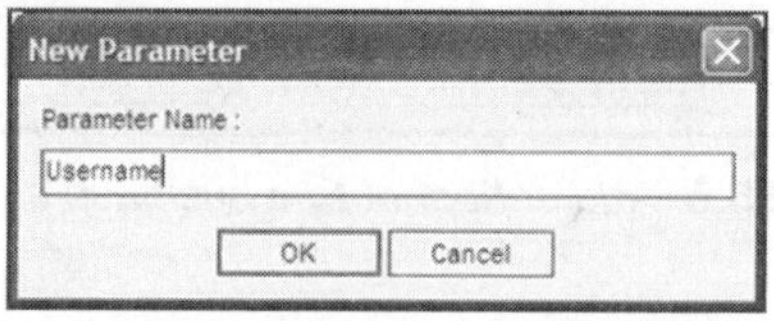

Figure 55.8 *Defining a new input parameter for business component*

Defining Output Parameters

For defining output parameters click on the 'New Parameter' button of the 'Output' section of the 'Parameters' tab of the business component. Repeat the steps specified for 'Defining Input Parameters' to define output parameters.

NOTES

Use the delete button Delete to delete a parameter.
Use the 'Move up' or 'Move down' button to change the order of the parameters.

ADDING DESIGN STEPS

Design steps are the manual steps of the business task. These manual steps can be used as test steps for manually testing the application or they can be used as guidelines for automation. Figure 55.9 shows the *Design Steps* tab with the defined manual steps.

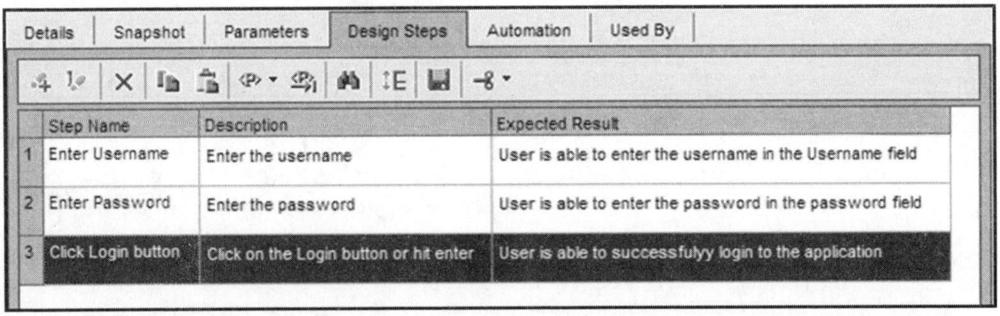

Figure 55.9 *Defining design steps of a business component*

The following steps describe how to define the design steps of a business component in QC.

1. Click on the tab *Design Steps*. The *Design Steps* tab opens.
2. Click on the 'Add New Step' button. *Component Step Editor* dialog box opens as shown in Fig. 55.10.
3. Specify the *Step Name*, *Description*, and *Expected Result* of the step in the *Component Step Editor*.
4. Click on the 'OK' button. The *Design Steps* tab is displayed with the step added as shown in Fig. 55.10.
5. Click on the 'Save' button to save the test steps.
6. Repeat steps 2–5 to add more test steps.

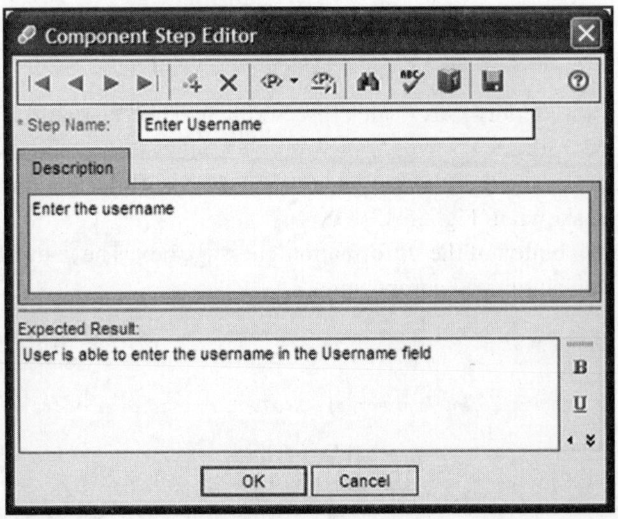

Figure 55.10 *Adding design steps to a business component*

CONVERTING MANUAL COMPONENT TO AUTOMATED COMPONENT

The next step is to convert the manual component to the automated component, so that the automation developers can build (code) the component. To convert a manual component to an automated component, refers the steps as follows (Fig. 55.11).

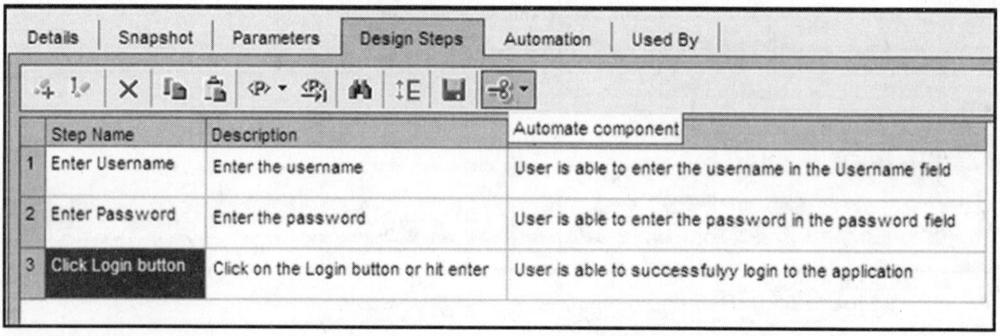

Figure 55.11 *Converting manual component to automated component*

1. Click on the tab *Design Steps*. The *Design Steps* tab opens.
2. Click on the 'Automate Component' button. Automate component options are listed on the screen as shown in Fig. 55.12.
   There are two ways to automate a manual component—QuickTest Keyword-Driven and QuickTest Scripted.

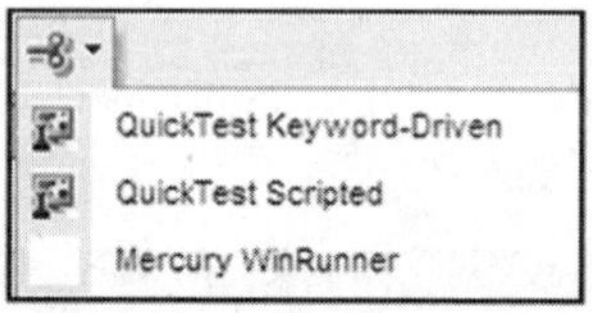

Figure 55.12 *Automated component types*

3. Choose one of the options, say QuickTest Scripted. The 'Warning' message box opens as shown in Fig. 55.13(a).
4. Click the 'Yes' button of the 'Warning' message box. The 'Information' message box appears on the screen as shown in Fig. 55.13(b).
5. Click on the 'OK' button of the 'Information' message box. The manual business component is converted to an automated component.

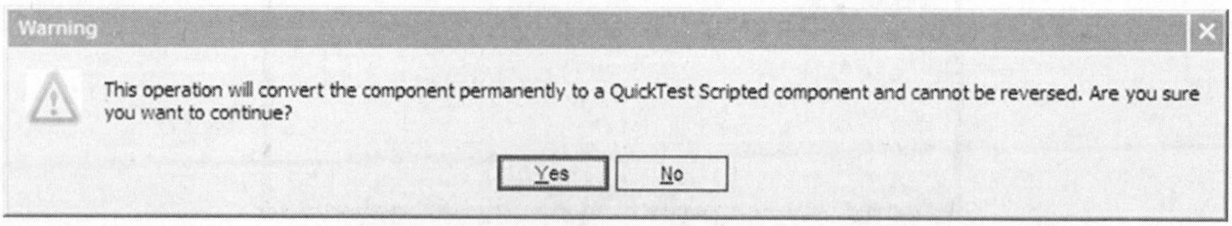

Figure 55.13(a) *Conversion confirmation dialog box*

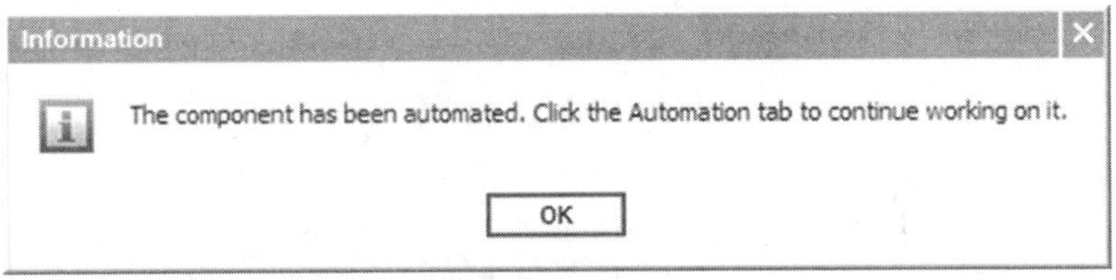

Figure 55.13(b) *Conversion Information message box*

> **NOTES**
>
> Once the component has been automated, the next task is to write code or build the component. The business component can be developed in QuickTest application. Keyword-driven approach is used for automating 'QuickTest Keyword-Driven' automated component while code can be explicitly written in the 'Expert View' tab of QuickTest for 'QuickTest Scripted' automated component.

OPENING AUTOMATED COMPONENT IN QUICKTEST

There are two ways to open the automated business components in QuickTest. One is directly opening the specific business component from QTP using 'Open' option on QuickTest window. Second is to click on the 'Launch' button of the business component in QC. In order to open a business component in QuickTest from QC, refer the following steps:

1. Select the business component (automated) in QC which needs to be opened in QTP.
2. Click on the tab 'Automation.' The 'Automation' tab is displayed as shown in Fig. 55.14.
3. Click on the 'Launch' button ▶ Launch as shown in Fig. 55.14. The automated component is opened in QuickTest. The automation developers are thereafter required to develop/modify this component in QuickTest, as required.

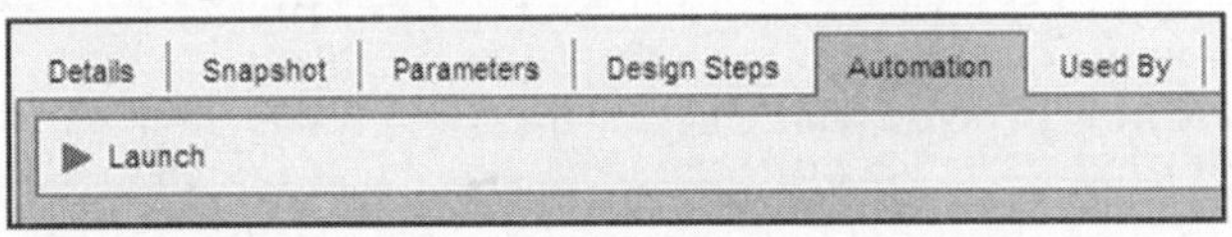

Figure 55.14 *Opening business component in QTP from QC*

CREATING BUSINESS PROCESS TESTS

Business Process Tests are the test scenarios. Test scenarios are formed in BPT testing by creating a serial flow of the business components. Business process tests are created in QC in the 'Test Plan' module. A business process test is successfully created by executing the following four steps:

1. Creating a new business process test.
2. Adding business components to the business process test in a specific sequence.
3. Defining business process test failure/exit condition.
4. Debugging the business process test.

Creating Business Process Test

The following steps describe how to create a business process test.

1. **Open test plan module:** Click on the *Test Plan* module. The *Test Plan* module opens as shown in Fig. 55.15.
2. **Create new folder:** Click on the button 'New Folder' to create a new folder where business process test is to be stored. The 'New Folder' dialog box opens. Specify the name of the folder, say 'Sales Tax' and click on the 'OK' button. The *Test Lab* tab is displayed as shown in Fig. 55.15.

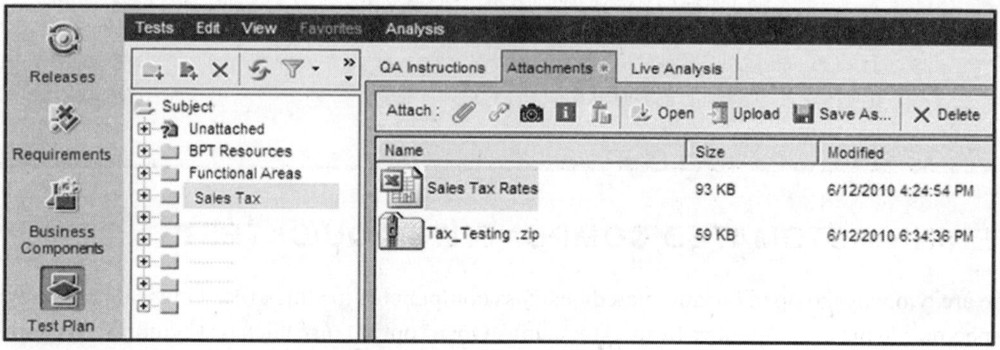

Figure 55.15 *Test Plan module.*

The *QA Instructions* tab of the selected folder can contain any information about the components that are placed inside the folder. The *Attachments* tab can contain functional documents, application screenshots, test data files, or any other relevant data. The Live Analysis tab is used for analyzing the test development progress. It contains three types of graphs – Summary, Progress, and Trend.

3. **Create new business process test:** Click on the 'New Test' button to create a new business process test. The 'Create New Test' dialog box opens as shown in Fig. 55.16. Select 'Test Type' as 'Business Process' Specify the name of the test scenario (business process test) (say *BookTicket*) and click on the 'OK' button.
   The *Test Plan* tab is displayed with the new business process test created as shown in Fig. 55.17.

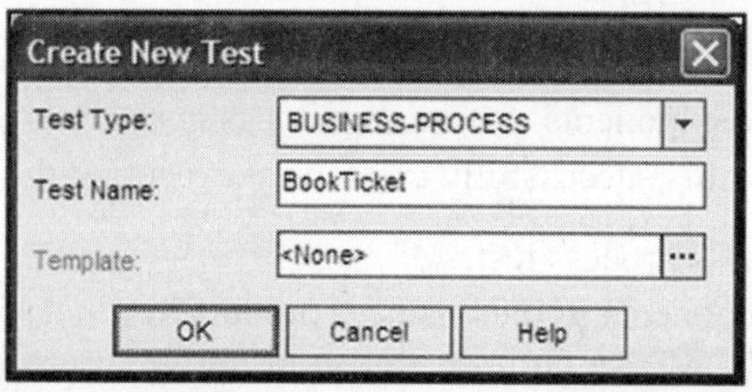

Figure 55.16 *Create new business process test*

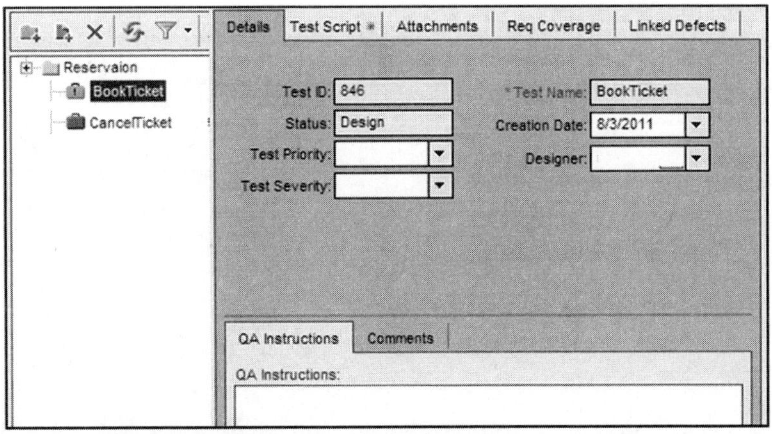

Figure 55.17 *Details tab of a business process test*

4. **Add test description:** The *Details* tab has both mandatory and optional fields. Users can fill the fields as mandated by the project.

Adding Components to a Business Process Test

The business components created in the Business Component module are integrated in the Test Plan module to automate a test scenario. This automated test scenario is termed as business process test.

The following steps describe how to add business components to a business process test.

1. **Display list of business components:** Click on the *Test Script* tab. The *Test Script* tab is displayed. Click on the 'Select Component' button to display the hierarchy tree of the business components as shown in Fig. 55.18.
2. **Add components to the business process test:** Drag and drop the business components from the *Components* tab to the *Test Script* tab (refer Fig. 55.19). Once all the required components are in the *Test Script* tab, use the 'Move up' ↑ and 'Move down' ↓ buttons to rearrange the sequence of business components. Then, click on the 'Save' button to save the business process test.

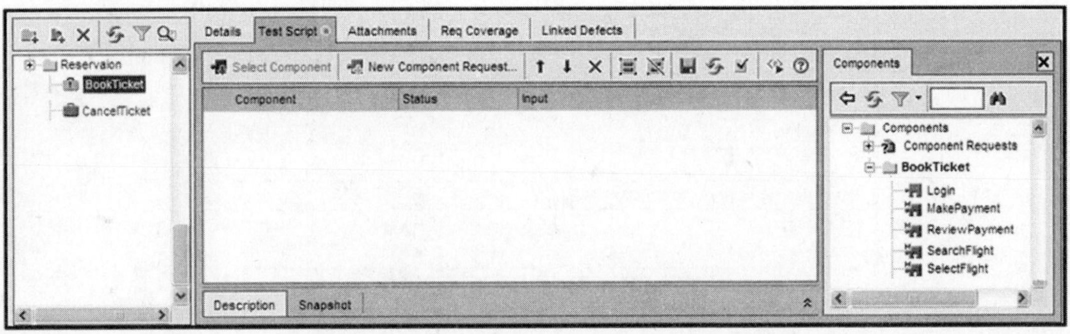

Figure 55.18 *Display list of business components*

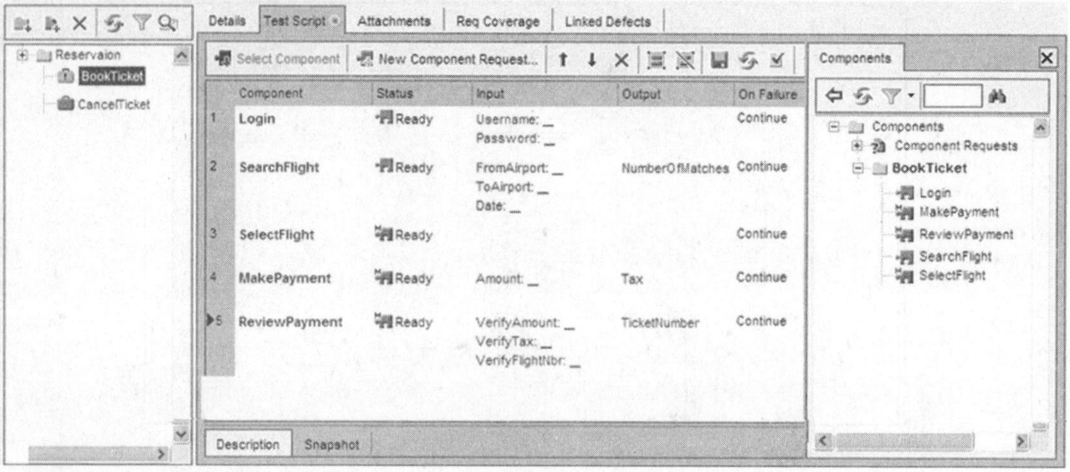

Figure 55.19 *Test Script tab of a business process test after addition of business components*

> **NOTES**
>
> A manual business component is marked with symbol while the automated component is marked with symbol . Only those business process tests that have fully automated components can be executed in QuickTest environment, else they need to be executed manually.

Defining Input Parameters of the Business Components

In order to define the input parameters of the business component, click on the input parameter value of the business component whose input parameter is to be defined. Suppose that user clicks on the parameter 'Username,' then the 'Component <Login> Iterations' window opens as shown in Fig. 55.20. Users

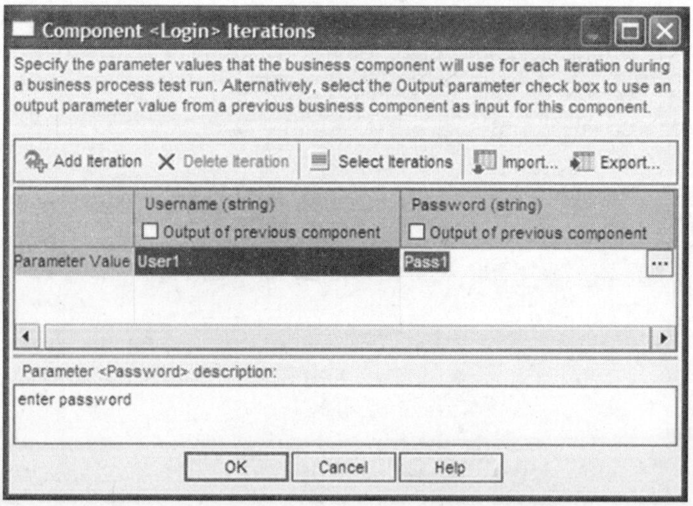

Figure 55.20 *Defining input parameters to Login business component*

can define the value of input parameters as shown in Fig. 55.20. Alternatively, user can also choose to import a CSV formatted datasheet. If the business component needs to execute more than once, then click on the 'Add Iteration' button to create a new row and then define the test data of the row. Once done, click on the 'OK' button to save the test data.

The data so defined above is called fixed data. QC also offers the flexibility to define the run-time data.

In addition, the output data of one business component can be used as the input data other business component. Suppose that we need to verify whether or not the tax amount displayed on the 'MakePayment' screen (business component) matches with the tax amount displayed on the 'ReviewPayment' screen (business component). In order t achieve this, we need to use the value of output parameter 'Tax' of the business component 'MakePayment' as the input parameter (Verify Tax) of the 'ReviewPayment' business component. To implement the same, follow the following steps:

1. Click on the 'VerifyTax' input parameter of business component 'ReviewPayment' as shown in Fig. 55.21(a). The 'Component <ReviewPayment> Iterations' opens as shown in Fig. 55.21(a).

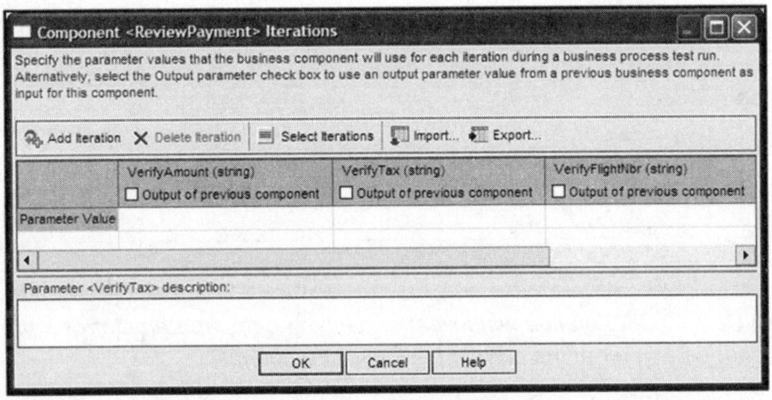

Figure 55.21(a) *Defining output parameter of a previous business component as input parameter to the current business component in the business process test*

2. Click on the checkbox 'Output of the previous component' of parameter 'VerifyTax'. Then, the *Select Output Parameter* window opens as shown in Fig. 55.21(b). This window contains all the output parameters of the previous business components. Select the appropriate output parameter. In this, select the parameter 'Tax' of the business component 'MakePayment' as shown in Fig. 55.21(b) and then click on the 'OK' button. The 'Component <ReviewPayment> Iterations' is displayed on the screen with updated data as shown in Fig. 55.21(c).
3. Define the other parameters of this component as required and click on the 'OK' button.
4. After all the input parameters have been defined the *Test Script* tab will look as shown in Fig. 55.22.

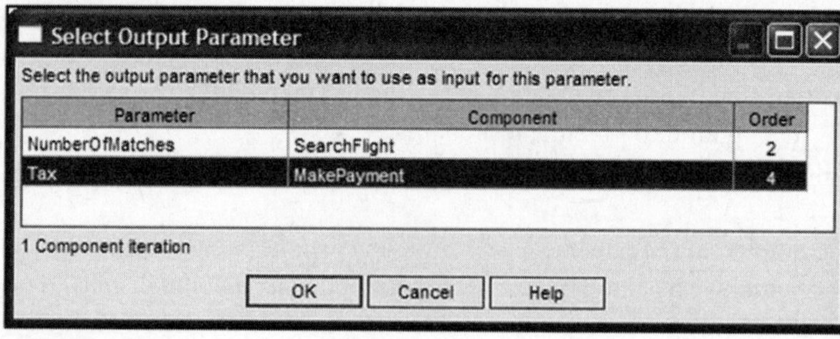

Figure 55.21(b) *Selecting output parameter of a previous business component as the input parameter of the current business component*

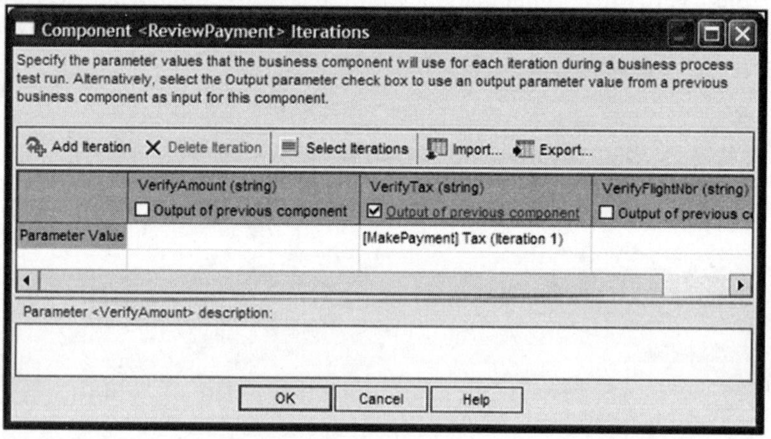

Figure 55.21(c) *Component iteration window after defining output parameter of a previous business component as input parameter of the current business component*

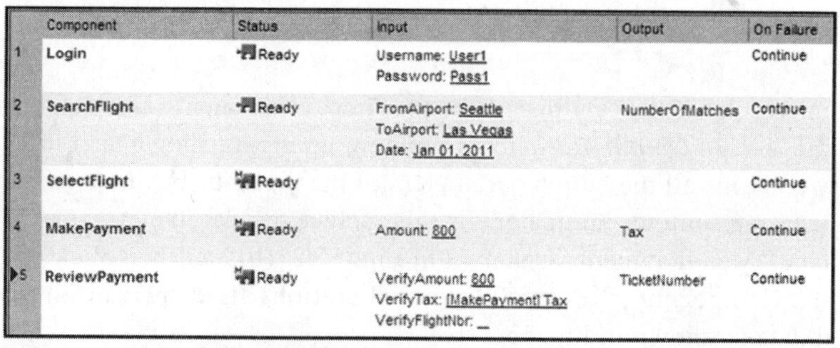

Figure 55.22 *Test Script tab of a business process test after all the input parameters has been defined*

Defining Fail Condition of a Business Process Test

Most of the time, it holds no meaning to continue execution of the remaining business components if one of the business components fails. QuickTest provides the flexibility to define the failure condition of every business component in a business process test. In order to exit the business process test if a business component fails the 'On Failure' condition should be selected as 'Exit' for the specific business component (refer Fig. 55.23). In case, the execution needs to continue even if the business component fails, then the 'On Failure' condition should be selected as 'Continue.'

In order to change the failure condition of a business component, click on the 'Continue' text as shown in Fig. 55.23. A dropdown list will appear as shown in Fig. 55.23. Select the option 'Exit'. Now, during execution, if business component 'SearchTicket' (or 'Login') fails then, the execution of this business process test (Book Ticket) will be stopped at that time only.

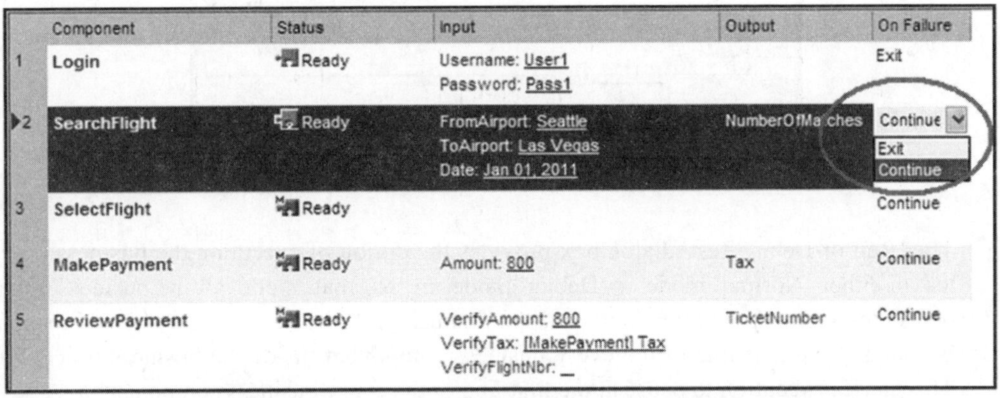

Figure 55.23 *Defining exit condition of a business process test*

DEBUGGING BUSINESS PROCESS TESTS

Debugging helps to check whether the business process test executes properly and locates any possible errors that could have occurred during building of the test or not. For example, it is used to check whether the logic serial arrangement of the business component is correct or not. Another example can be to check whether the input and output parameters of the business components are being correctly applied or not.

In the debug mode, QC opens QuickTest directly from the *Test Plan* module. For QTP 9.2 and QC 9.2, the business components are loaded one by one for execution. For QTP10.0 and QC 10.0 and above all the business components of a business process test are loaded at the start of execution and then executed one by one. During execution, QuickTest executes the steps as coded for the business component. Once execution of the business process test is over a summary of the test results is generated and displayed on the screen.

In order to debug a business process test, follow the following steps:

1. Open QC and click on the *Test Plan* module and select the required business component that needs to be debugged. For example, 'BookTicket.

2. Select the tab *Test Script* and click on the button 'Run or Debug Test' ▶. The 'Run or Debug Test' dialog box opens as shown in Fig. 55.24.

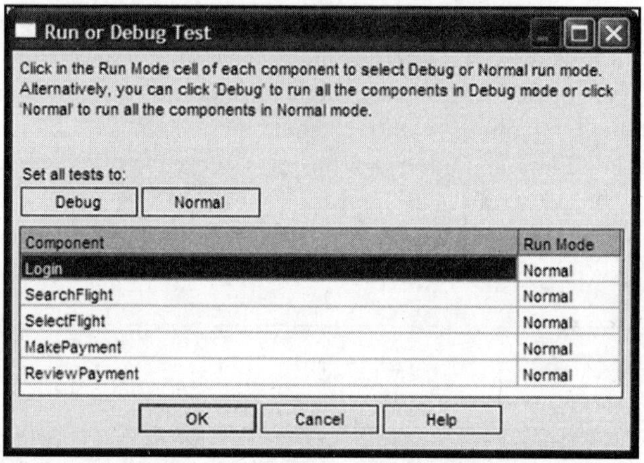

Figure 55.24 *Debugging a business process test*

3. The 'Run or Debug Test' dialog box provides the option of executing the business process test in either 'Normal' mode or 'Debug' mode. In 'Normal' mode, all the business components are executed one after another without pausing. While in 'Debug' mode, a breakpoint is added at the first line of the every business component inside the business process test. This causes execution to pause at the first line of the every business component.
After selecting one of the modes, click on the 'OK' button.
4. After clicking of the 'OK' button, the run starts with the execution of the very first business component of the business process test. In addition, the 'Stop' button is also displayed on the *Test Script* tab. This 'Stop' button can be used to stop the test execution while execution is in progress.
5. Once execution of all the components is over, a summary of the test result is displayed on the screen as shown in Fig. 55.25.

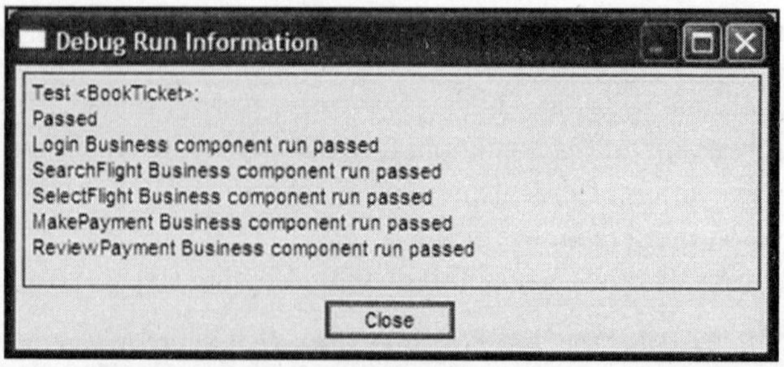

Figure 55.25 *Debug mode run result window*

CREATING TEST SET

A *Test Set* is a group of business process tests, which needs to be executed for a run. A *Test Set* is created in *Test Lab* module of the QC. The following steps describe how to create a *Test Set* (refer Fig. 55.26).

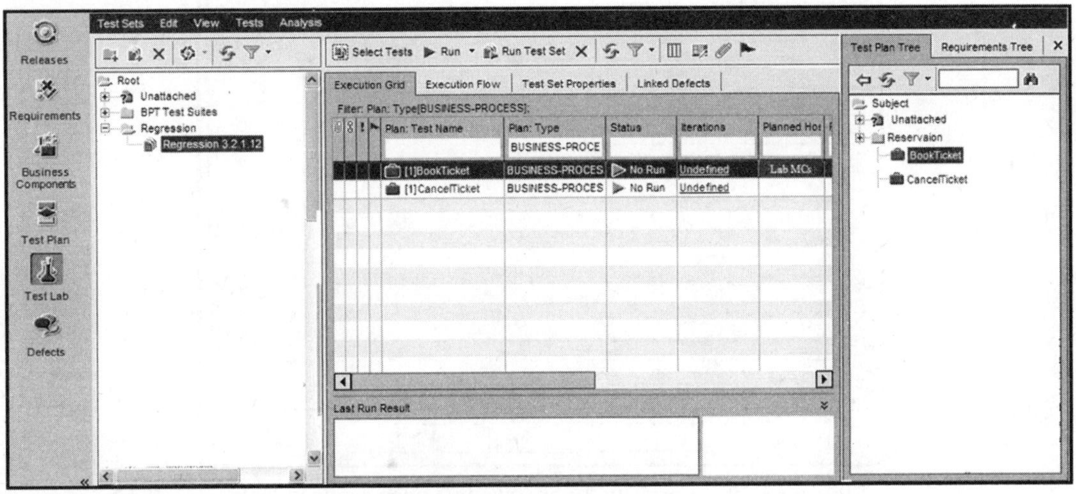

Figure 55.26 *Test Lab tab*

1. **Create new *Test Set***
   Select the folder inside which a new *Test Set* needs to be created. Thereafter, click on the 'New Test Set' button . *New Test Set* dialog box opens as shown in Fig. 55.27. Enter the test set name and description and click on the 'OK' button. A new test set will be created with the specified name as shown in Fig. 55.27.
2. **Adding business process tests to a *Test Set***
   Click on the button 'Select Tests' Select Tests. The 'Test Plan Tree' tab is displayed on the screen as shown in Fig. 55.28. Navigate to the various folders and drag and drop the required business process tests to the 'Execution Grid' tab.

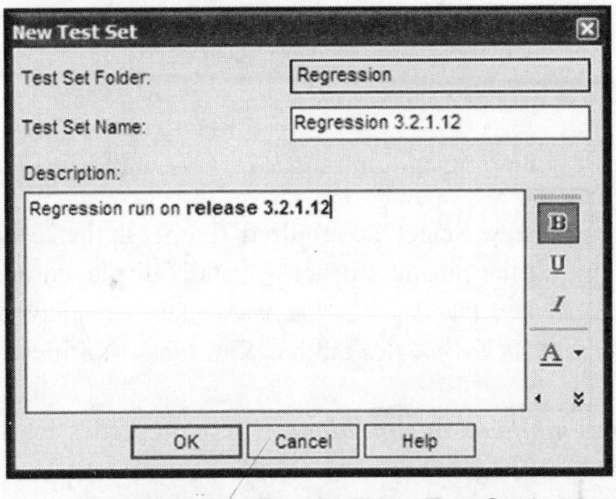

Figure 55.27 *Creating New Test Set*

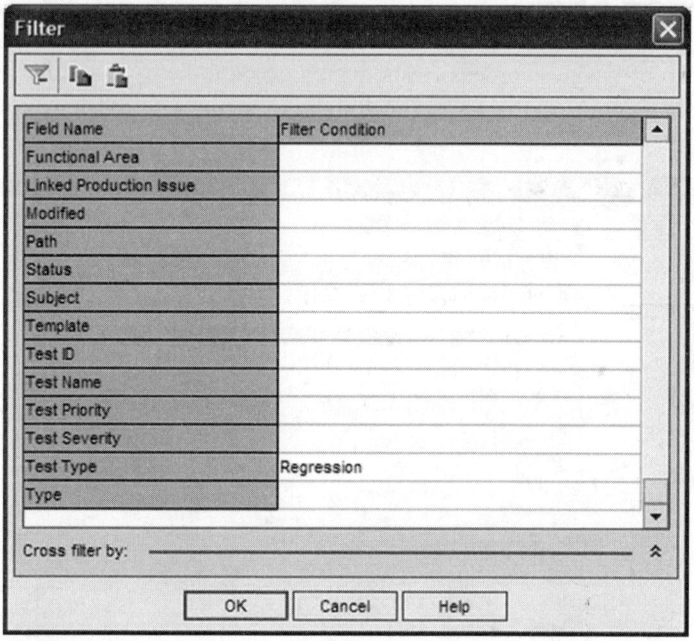

Figure 55.28 *Searching for specific business process tests*

Alternatively, users can also execute a search on a specific folder to search for specific business process tests. Suppose that the scenarios is use to execute a test run of all the business process tests, which has 'Test Type' field marked as 'Regression' in *Test Plan* module. In order to search for all the business process tests marked for regression, first of all click on the 'Set Filter/Sort' button . The 'Filter' dialog box opens as shown in Fig. 55.28.

Select 'Test Type' as 'Regression' in the 'Filter' dialog box and click on the 'OK' button. All the business process tests will automatically get filtered out in the *Test Plan Tree* tab. Thereafter, drag and drop the filtered business process tests from the *Test Plan Tree* tab to the *Execution Grid* tab.

EXECUTING TEST SET

The following steps describe setting up and running a *Test Set* in the *Test Lab* module.

1. **Defining *test set properties:*** Select the required *Test Set* in the *Test Lab* module. The *Execution Grid* containing all the business process tests is displayed on the screen. Next, select the tab *Test Set Properties*. The *Test Set Properties* tab is displayed on the screen as shown in Fig. 55.29. The *Test Set Properties* tab has four tabs—Notifications, On Failure, Attachments, and Details.
   - **(a) Defining e-mail *notification conditions:*** These properties are defined to send a notification mail to the specific group of users as soon as the run finishes or if a test in the *Test Set* fails. Figure 55.29 shows the *Notification* tab.

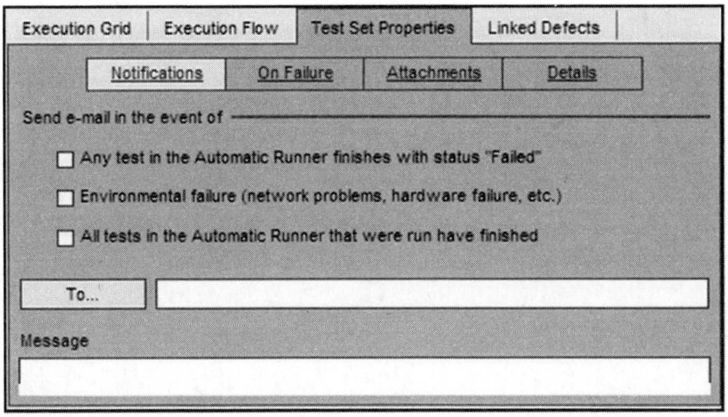

Figure 55.29 *Defining run status e-mail notification conditions for a test set*

(b) Defining error recovery steps: The *On Failure* tab defines the action to be taken in case a test fails. Figure 55.30 shows the various actions that can be taken in case a test script or business process test fails.

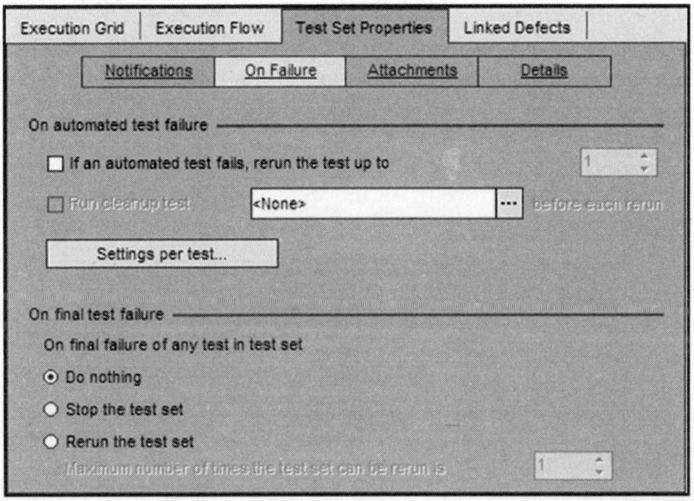

Figure 55.30 *Defining recovery action for failures during Test Set run*

(c) Attaching documents to a: *Test Set* QuickTest provides the flexibility to attach documents to a *Test Set*. This document can contain any relevant information such as bug fixes for the release, impacted business areas, and new developed business functionalities.

(d) Defining run-time variables: QuickTest provides the flexibility to define run-time variables for a *test set* as shown in Fig. 55.31. For example, the same test set needs to be executed in various environments say development and test environments. In this case, the URL of the application varies. This URL can easily be changed from the *Details* tab and the complete test run will execute as per the new environment settings (refer Fig. 55.31).

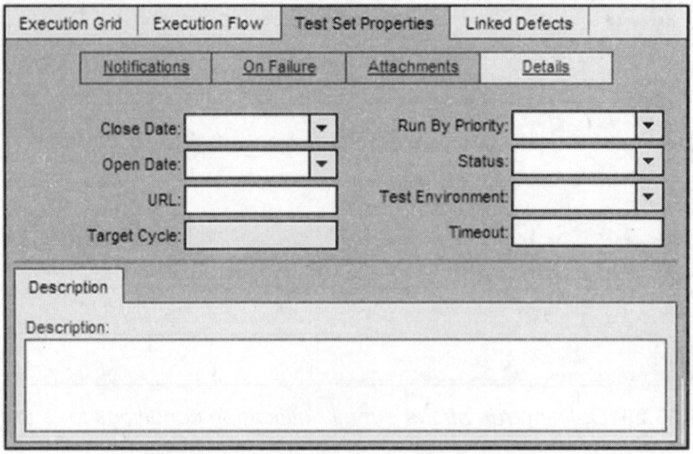

Figure 55.31 *Defining details of a test set*

2. **Executing *Test Set***

   (a) **Identifying tests for run:** QuickTest provides the flexibility to execute specific tests from the *Test Set* or the complete test set. In order to execute specific tests from the *Test Set*, select the tests and then click on the *Run* button ▶ Run. In case complete test set is to be executed, then users need to click on the *Run Test Set* button Run Test Set. Once the 'Run' or 'Run Test Set' button is clicked, *Automatic Runner* dialog box opens as shown in Fig. 55.32.

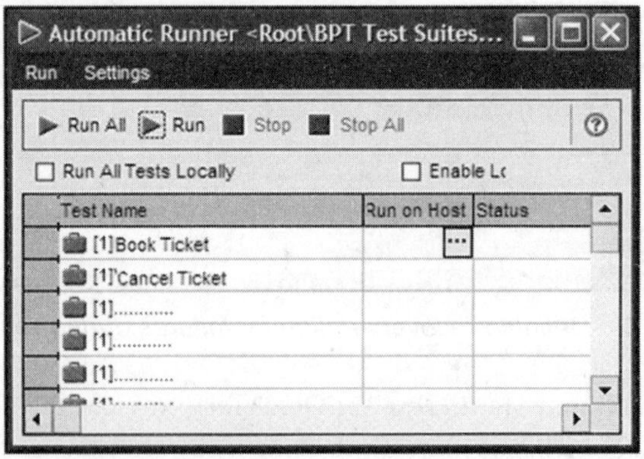

Figure 55.32 *Automatic Runner window*

   (b) **Specifying QTP machine for execution:** QuickTest provides the option to execute the *Test Set* on the local machine or in a specific set of remote lab machines. To run the test set on local machines, the checkbox *Run All Tests Locally* needs to be selected. In order to run the test set of the lab machines, 'Run on Host' for the every test needs to be defined (refer Fig. 55.32).

(c) **Selecting tests for execution:** The *Automatic Runner . . .* window provides the option to execute specific tests or all the tests listed in the window (refer Fig. 55.32).

(d) **Executing *Test Set:*** Click on the button *Run* or *Run All* to start the test run. Fig. 55.33(a) shows the *Automatic Runner . . .* window once test run has been started.

The status of the execution of the tests are updated *Passes/Failed/Not Completed* in the 'Status' field of the respective test (refer Fig. 55.33(b)).

Once the execution is over, users can close the *Automatic Runner...* window. The *Execution Grid* with the actual status of the test run is displayed on the screen. Figure 55.34 shows the results as displayed after test execution on the 'Execution Grid' tab.

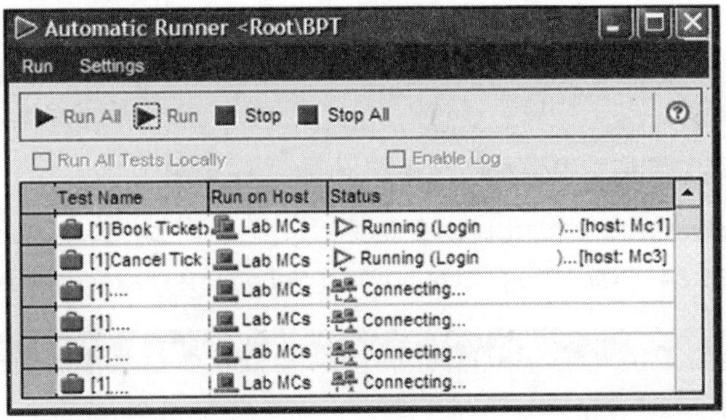

Figure 55.33(a) *Automatic Runner window after initiating the test run*

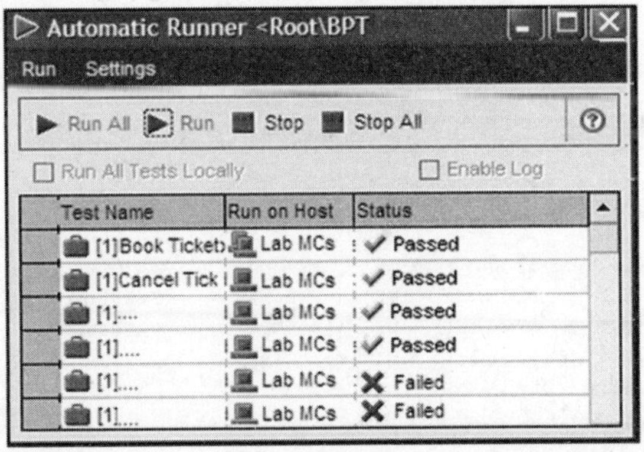

Figure 55.33(b) *Automatic Runner window after test execution is complete*

3. **Analyzing *Test Results:*** Once test execution is over, the result gets updated in the *Execution Grid* of the *Test Plan* module as shown in Fig. 55.34. In order to view the detailed test results of a test, select the test and click on the 'Passed' link of the test that is displayed in the *Last Run Result* section. It may happen that the same test has been executed multiple times in a test set.

In order to view the test results of the previous runs, double-click on the respective test. *Test Instance Properties* window opens. This window (refer Fig. 55.35) shows the test results of all the test runs of the specific test.

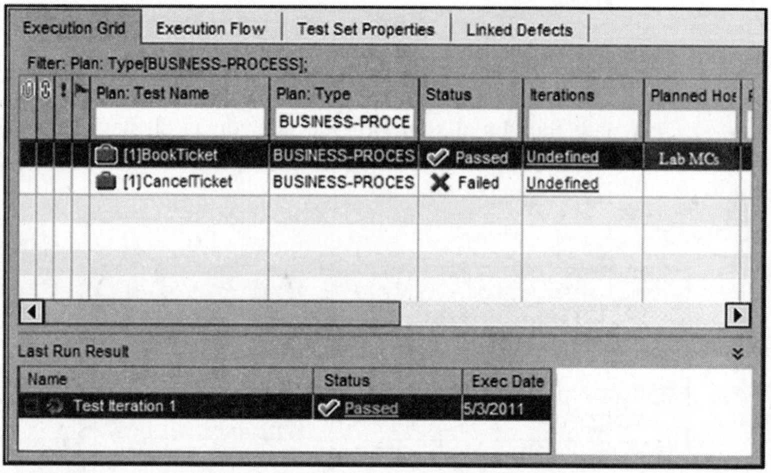

Figure 55.34 *Execution Grid tab of Test Set after test execution is over*

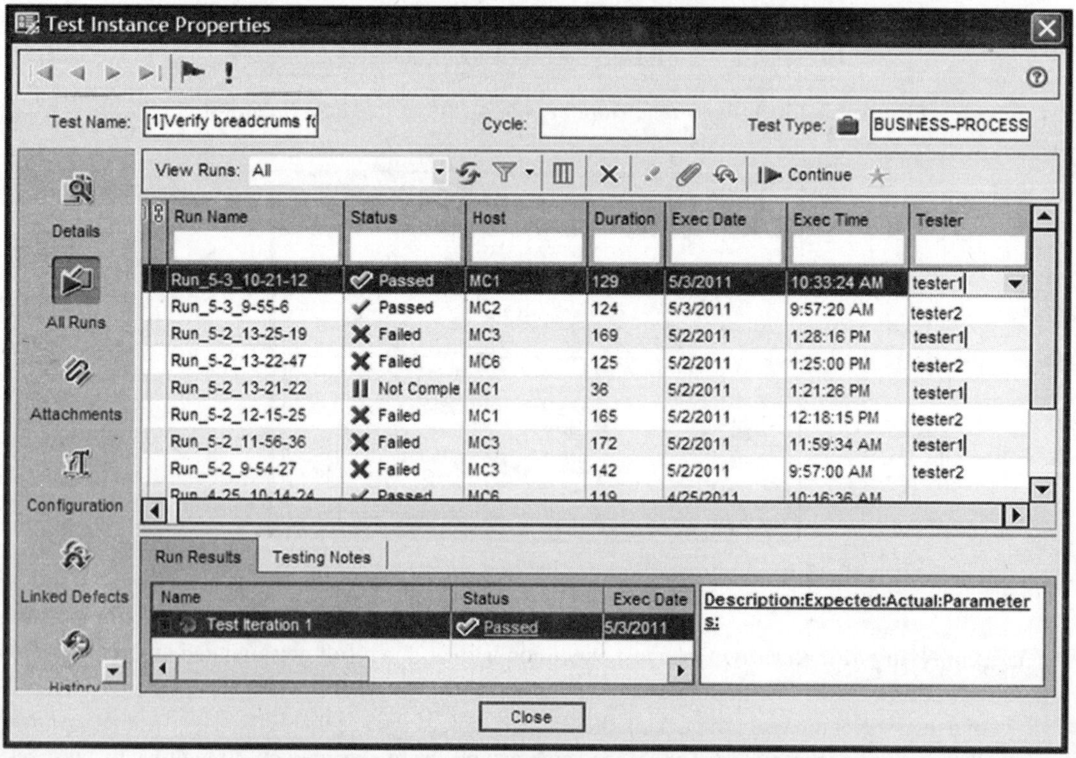

Figure 55.35 *Test results of a business process test*

DEVELOPING BUSINESS COMPONENTS

The business component can be created either from QC or from QuickTest Professional (QTP). To create a keyword-driven business component from QuickTest integrate QTP with QC and then select from the menu bar *New → Business Component. New Business Component* dialog box opens. Select appropriate *application area* and click on the 'OK' button. The newly created Business Component script opens. Use the *Save As* option to save the script at the desired location. In order to create a *Scripted Component*, select menu bar *New → Scripted Component* and then repeat the steps as mentioned above. Once the component is created, the automation developers can automate the component similar to the automation of a normal script.

CREATING APPLICATION AREA

Application Area defines the resources and the settings required for an automated component. These include environment files, library files, recovery scenario files, object repository files, etc. In order to create a new *Application Area* from QuickTest, follow the following steps:

1. Select *New → Application Area. Application Area* opens as shown in Fig. 55.36.
2. Click on the tab *General* and define the description of the application area and the required QuickTest add-ins.
3. Click on the tab *Function Libraries* and associate the required library files with the application area.
4. Click on the tab *Object Repositories* and associate the required library files with the application area as shown in Fig. 55.37.

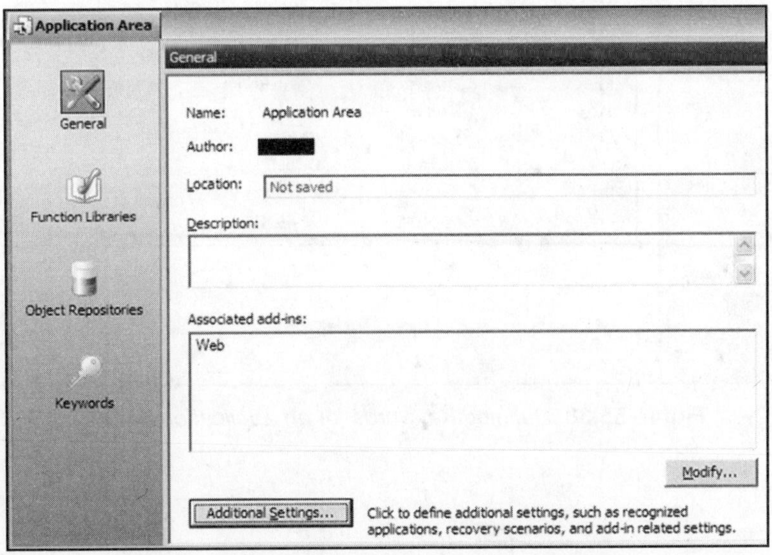

Figure 55.36 *Creating a new Application Area*

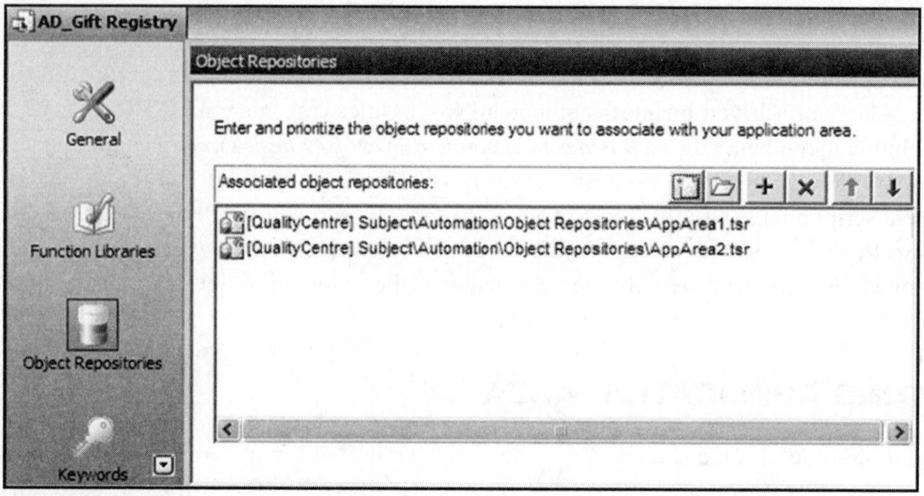

Figure 55.37 *Associating object repositories to an application area*

5. Click on the tab *Keywords* and select the required keywords to make them available in the *application area* as shown in Fig. 55.38.

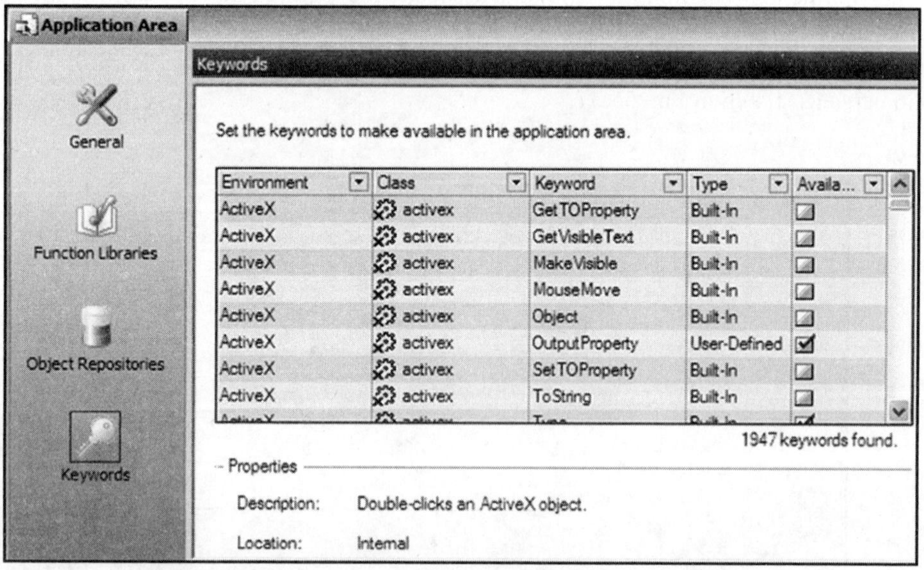

Figure 55.38 *Defining Keywords for an application area*

Appendices

- Appendix A : Test Script Template
- Appendix B : Scripting Guidelines
- Appendix C : VBScript Naming Conventions
- Appendix D : Script Review Checklist
- Appendix E : Test Tool Evaluation CHART
- Appendix F : Object Identification Standards for a Typical Web Application

APPENDIX A—TEST SCRIPT TEMPLATE

```
'###################################################################
  '#  Script Name        :     <Name of the Script>
  '#  Script Type        :     <Type Application/Driver/Utility>
  '#  Creation Date      :     <Creation Date>
  '#  Author             :     <Name of Associate>
  '#  Input Parameters   :     <All the Input Parameters>
  '#  Output Parameters  :     <All the Output Parameters>
  '#  Object Repository  :     <Object Repository Location>
  '#  Functions          :     <Functions Used in the Script>
  '#  External Actions   :     <External actions called>
  '#
  '#  Description :     <Specify functionality covered >
  '#
  '#  Modifications___________________________
  '#
  '#  ModifiedBy   BlockofCode        Date         Comments
  '#  1.
  '#  2.
  '#
  '#
  '#     ----------------------------------------------------------
  '#  Revision History:
  '#  Version      Date               User         Comments
  '#  1.0          15/04/2009         ABC          Initial version
  '#
  '#
  '################################################################
  'Declarations
  'Assignment
  'Test Env Settings
      'Load Configuration file
      'Load Library file
  'Test Data
  'Start Execution
  '############################# END ##############################
```

APPENDIX B—SCRIPTING GUIDELINES

Points to be taken care of in scripts are:

1. Script should not contain the message boxes, input boxes, etc. or anything that requires manual intervention from the user.
2. Proper error handling should be used in all scripts.
3. All test case prerequisites should be taken care of in the script.
4. Script command failure should be eliminated.
5. Only one child window should be opened at a time while playing back the script.
6. Very clear status messages should be used, which tell the user whether a particular step in the test cases has passed or failed.
7. All requisite transaction ids, statuses, etc. should be provided in the Excel/log, which makes debugging easier in case of script failure.
8. Checking of status is required at the appropriate places and the inclusion of appropriate exit conditions is also required.
9. Unnecessary verification points should be removed (to minimize the playback time). However, verification points should be included when required for a business scenario.
10. While picking up clipboard values from putty, we should ensure putty is maximized and the screen is cleared before picking up any value.
11. There should not be any hard coding in the scripts. For example, while selecting values from a list box, combo box.
12. Functions should be made use of wherever possible.
13. Ensure that unique search criteria are specified as far as possible.
14. Ensure that minimal or no use of WebElements in scripts.
15. Sync should be used whenever there is a change in page properties.
16. Appropriate delays should be built into the script to provide for differences in response times across environments.
17. All transaction flow status should be verified and handled appropriately.
18. Focused window should always be maximized.
19. Entry and exit points of a script should be the same.
20. Turn off SI while scripting.
21. Object identification settings must not be changed for any object.
22. Indentation and comments in scripts should be there.
23. Particular script layout should be followed.

APPENDIX C—VBSCRIPT NAMING CONVENTIONS

Variable Naming Conventions

Variable Type	Prefix	Example
Array	arr	arrData
Collection	col	colButtons
Dictionary	dic	dicTableData
Boolean	b	bFound
Date (time)	dtm	dtmStart
Double	dbl	dblTolerance
Error	err	errOrderNum
Numeric	n	nQuantity
Object	o	oCurrent
	obj	objCurrent
String	s	sFirstName
Global variables	g_	g_GlobalVar
Counters/loops	iCnt, jCnt, kCnt, iCntr	
Functions	fn	

Naming Conventions of Objects in OR

Object Type	Prefix	Example
Browser	Name of Object as seen in GUI	Google
Frame		Frame
Image		Submit
Link		Billing
Page		Google
WebButton		Search
WebCheckBox		(innertext Name)
WebEdit		Standard
WebElement		(innertext Name)
WebList		(innertext Name)
WebRadioGroup		(innertext Name)
WebTable		(innertext Name)

Action Naming Convention

Actions to be named as per business scenario it is executing.

APPENDIX D—SCRIPT REVIEW CHECKLIST

Test Automation Checklist					
Project					
Author					
Creation date					
	Check Points	**Yes**	**No**	**N/A**	**Remarks**
	General Checklist				
1	Is test execution being controlled by driver script?	☐			
2	Is driver script directly interacting with the GUI?		☐		
3	Is any 'ExitAction' code present in driver script?		☐		
4	Is a distinction between day 1 cycle and day 2 cycle executions is made?	☐			
5	Are there separate drivers for day1 and day2 cycles?	☐			
6	Are test scripts flexible enough to support unattended execution?	☐			
7	Does MasterDriver support scheduling of test run?	☐			
8	Does driver updates pass/fail condition in data sheet?	☐			
9	Does driver updates screenshot path in data sheet?	☐			
10	Does driver script updates unique transaction identifier in data sheet?	☐			
11	Is the EnvVariables.vbs file associated with the driver script?	☐			
12	Is library file associated with driver script?	☐			
13	Has risk mitigation plans been drafted for non-automatable scenarios?	☐			
14	Are all prerequisites of test script execution properly documented?	☐			
	Functional Checklist				
1	Is sufficient business knowledge gathered before starting automation?	☐			
2	Has test script business flow been verified by the functional team?	☐			
3	Has test script test results been verified by the functional team?	☐			
4	Has scope of test automation been verified and accepted?	☐			
5	Has risk analysis been done for non-automatable scenarios?	☐			
	Data Sheet Design Checklist				
1	Does data sheet layout adhere to the framework?	☐			
2	Does data sheet contain the necessary fields as mandated by framework—SeqNo, TestCaseId, TestCaseDesc, ExecStat, Result, Comments, BusnScnro, and ErrScrnShotsPath?	☐			
3	Does data sheet design support selective as well as exhaustive test executions?	☐			
4	Does data sheet design support positive as well as negative testings?	☐			
5	Is a list created of static fields of data in data sheet?	☐			
6	Does data sheet support dynamic creation of test cases?	☐			
7	Does data sheet support automatic test input data selection from AUT database?	☐			

	Check Points	Yes	No	N/A	Remarks
8	Does data sheet allow to explicitly define test input data?	☐			
9	Does data sheet design supports easy test execution by manual testers?	☐			
10	Does datasheet allow reexecution of failed test cases?	☐			
	Scripting Checklist				
1	Does script layout adhere to the standard scripting layouts?	☐			
	Are test scripts reusable?	☐			
2	Does script require any manual intervention during test execution?		☐		
3	Does script contains any message boxes?		☐		
4	Are proper error-handling techniques used in the scripts?	☐			
5	Does script contain code to analyze pass/fail status of execution?	☐			
	Does script adhere to the standard VBScript naming conventions?	☐			
6	Are recovery scenarios designed to handle expected/unexpected execution errors?	☐			
7	Is unnecessary opening of multiple instances of AUT avoided?	☐			
8	Do scripts pass exact pass/fail status to driver script?	☐			
9	Have sufficient checkpoints been coded in the test scripts?	☐			
10	Have coded checkpoints been placed at appropriated points in the test script?	☐			
11	Are error messages short and clear?	☐			
12	Are exit conditions of the test script properly placed and coded?	☐			
13	Are synchronization points coded in the test script whenever page properties changes?	☐			
14	Is test script free of hard coding?	☐			
15	Are functions been used wherever required?	☐			
16	Is unnecessary use of webelements avoided?	☐			
17	Have appropriate delays been built into the script to provide for differences in response times across environments?	☐			
18	Has all business/screen flow been verified and handled properly?	☐			
19	Has a focus been set on the window before actually working on it?	☐			
20	Are entry and exit points of a test script/action same?	☐			
21	Is SI turned off while scripting?	☐			
22	Do scripts contain proper comments and indentation?	☐			
23	Is duplication of functions/function libraries avoided?	☐			
24	Is duplication of environment variables/files avoided?	☐			
	Object Repository Checklist				
1	Does object naming convention adhere to the project naming conventions?	☐			
	Has shared object repository been created?	☐			
	Has unnecessary use of local OR has been avoided?	☐			
2	Are regular expressions properly used in the object properties of the object in OR?	☐			
3	Are objects in OR being recognized in AUT?	☐			
4	Are objects been placed in proper object hierarchy in OR?	☐			
5	Has duplication of objects in OR been avoided?	☐			

APPENDIX E—TEST TOOL EVALUATION CHART

Test Tools		QTP		RFT	
Test Tool Characteristic	Weight (1–10)	Score (1–5)	Value (1–50)	Score (1–5)	Value (1–50)
Ease of Use					
Learning curve	7				
Easy to maintain the tool	5				
Easy to install	2				
Platform Support					
Platforms supported are WinNT, Win XP, Windows 7, etc.	6				
Multiuser Access					
Can multiple users access the automated scripts?	10				
Network-based test repository	10				
Defect Tracking					
Does the tool come with an integrated defect-tracking feature?	2				
Tool Functionality					
Scripting language	9				
Complexity of scripting language	9				
Avilability of features such as parameters passing and setting environment variables	7				
Debugging features	7				
Support for unattended script execution	8				
Supports AUT GUI	10				
Supports the creation reusable functions, action, and test scripts	9				
Error recovery features	9				
Reporting					
Availability of high-level and low-level reports	6				
Ability to provide graphical results (charts and graphs)	5				
Ability to provide test-run reports with exact pass/fail status	7				
Can reports be customized?	8				
Management Aspects					
Significant achievement from ROI perspective	10				
License cost	9				
Type of License—seat, floating, etc.	5				
Competitiveness of price offered	8				
Maturity of product	8				
Market share of product	7				
Vendor qualifications, such as financial stability and length of existence. What is the vendor's track record?	7				

Value = Weight * Score

APPENDIX F—OBJECT IDENTIFICATION STANDARDS FOR A TYPICAL WEB APPLICATION

Web Object	Mandatory Property	Associative Property
Browser	title	
Image	html id	html tag
	alt	
	filename	
	name	
Link	html id	html tag
	name	text
Page	title	
WebButton	html id	html tag
	name	
WebCheckBox	html id	html tag
	name	type
WebEdit	html id	html tag
	name	type
WebList	html id	html tag
	name	select tag
WebRadioGroup	html id	type
	name	
WebTable	html id	outertext
	Text	html tag
	name	
WebElement	class	outerhtml
	html id	
	innertext	

Note: For 'Browser' object, use 'Creation Time' ordinal identifier.

Index

A

Accessibility checkpoint, 486, 508–509
Accessing file, 667
Accessing folder properties, 669
Action Call Properties, 314, 321, 408
Action calls, 307, 312, 314
Action parameterization, 302
Action template, 318–319
Action, 294, 319–320
  features, 317
  types of, 314
  views, 294
Active X data objects, 710
Adding design steps, 857
Adding insight objects to or, 655, 662
Adding picture to documents, 741
Adding snapshot, 854
Ad-hoc automation, 7
Agile automation framework, 28, 31, 45, 61, 113, 118, 121–123, 125, 127
  business components, 124
  framework components, 122
  framework structure, 137–138
  screen components, 123
Agile automation team composition, 116–117
  automation developers, 116
  toolsmiths, 116
Agile automation values, 114
Agile automation, 111, 127–129, 130
  agile automation principles, 114–115
  challanges, 115
  practices, 118
Agile development model, 23, 26
Agile methodologies and practices, 86–87, 88
Agile methodology, 87–89, 91, 93, 95, 97
  benefits of, 87
Agile principles, 86
Agile team dynamics, 89–90, 93
Agile test automation, 26, 94, 96, 98, 100, 102, 104, 106, 108, 110
Agile values, 85
Analyzing comparison results, 380
API testing tab, 242
API testing, 211–212, 225, 227, 232, 559
Application area, 246, 249, 289
Application lifecycle management, 221
Application object, 340, 356, 375, 378, 389–390, 795
Application program interface, 557
Application programmer's interface, 710
Application programming interface, 258, 677, 725, 776
Application programming interfaces, 211, 258
Application stability, 15–16
  business changes, 15–16
  object changes, 16
Application under test, 17, 37, 41, 46, 50, 62, 478, 484
  objective, 62
Architected solution, 22
Assistive properties, 254–255, 349, 351, 353
Automatability analysis, 8, 24, 51
Automatability criteria, 22, 141
Automated business components, 19, 69, 852, 859
Automatic xpath learning mechanism, 347–348
Automatic xpath, 343, 584–585, 588–589
Automating uft, 792

Automation architects, 6, 18, 23, 35–36, 64, 114, 117
Automation complexity, 9, 66, 68
Automation consultants, 6, 15
Automation deliverables, 7, 15, 23, 47, 59–60
Automation developers, 4, 35, 66, 68–70, 72, 114–117
Automation environment, 25, 60, 119, 142, 540
Automation execution initiation machines, 33
Automation implementation cost, 6, 17
Automation object model, 222, 739, 762, 788, 791, 793, 795, 797, 799, 801, 805
Automation project effort, 6
Automation project server, 33–34
Automation project, 6, 14–15, 33, 36, 40, 47
Automation team lead, 35
Automation test development cost, 17
Automation tool cost, 6
Automation tools, 12, 63–64, 116, 211
AutomationProjectBackupDriver.bat, 684

B

Batch execution, 17–18, 480, 506
BCT, 124–125, 128
benefits of test automation, 9
  comprehensive, 9
  cost reduction, 9
  fast, 9
  programmable, 9
  reliable, 9
  repeatable, 9
  reusable, 9
Bitmap checkpoint, 223, 486, 500, 516
Book ticket, 29–30, 782, 865
Bottle-neck, 4, 76
Break-even point, 16, 21
Breakpoints, 213, 216, 229, 259, 518–519
Browser Identification, 415
Browser native synchronization methods, 481–482
Bug fixtures, 5
Building css locator paths, 623
Building one-point maintenance, 76–77
Burndown chart, 91, 93, 95, 99
Business complexity, 9
Business component table, 124, 128–129, 140, 143
Business components, 122, 144, 153, 158
Business context analysis, 7
Business criticality analysis, 8
Business knowledge gathering, 14, 19, 69, 81, 258, 260
Business knowledge transition phase, 66
Business knowledge–gathering phase, 14
Business owner, 87, 89–90, 92, 94, 101, 108
Business process test, 212, 214, 222, 226, 230, 241, 292, 317, 320, 825, 865
Business process testing, 34, 212, 222, 826, 828, 830, 832, 834, 836, 845, 848, 869
Business process tests, 859
  adding components, 861
  creating, 860
Business scenario identification, 70, 258, 260
Business scenario-driven approach, 29–30, 35, 122, 152

C

Canvas, 214, 219, 223, 292, 320
  features, 321
Cascading style sheets, 334, 468, 616
Case execution cost, 5
Cells method, 691–692
Checkpoint insertion modes, 485
Checkpoint, 148, 67, 484
Child objects, 359, 361, 413, 429, 458
CI cycle, 107
Client–server architecture, 747
Code fix, 24, 228, 627
Coded checkpoints, 485–486, 515
Coding language, 17, 63, 211, 296
Coding tab, 241, 245
Collaboration, 26, 85–86, 103, 109, 117
Co-location, 86, 91
Communication model for regression run, 79
Communication model, 78, 141
Completeness analysis, 8
Component Object Model, 667
Conceptual model, 14, 58
Configuration management, 48, 57, 78
Configuring mandatory, 354

Configuring Object Identification Mechanism, 252
Connecting to alm using Java Program, 842
Connecting to ms excel database, 716–717
Connecting to network computers, 672
Connection object, 710, 717–718
Connection to database, 713
  dsn connection, 713
  dsn-less connection, 713
Continuous Integration, 88, 107, 110
Continuously changing requirements, 112, 115
Control tests, 12
Converting manual component to automated component, 858
Coverage, 10, 23, 50
Creating business components, 852–853
Creating tables in documents, 745
Creating visual relation identifiers using code, 643–644
Creating/adding action to a GUI test, 306
Creation time, 336, 651
creators of scrum, 85
Credit card payment, 29, 147
CSS selectors methods, 621
CSV formatted datasheet, 863
Customer collaboration, 86
Customizing test results, 547

D

Data source name, 698, 713
Data table formulas, 400–401
Database checkpoint, 486, 506
Data-driven testing, 4, 220
Datatable methods, 403
Datatables, 220, 301, 398
DB connection string, 324
Debug session speed, 517
Debug viewer pane, 519
  console tab, 522
  errors pane, 523
  local variables tab, 522
  output tab, 519
  watch tab, 520
Debugging business process tests, 865–866
Debugging, 517, 519, 521, 523–524, 865
Default capture hierarchy design, 390–391
Defect accumulation, 5
Defect-free deployment build, 88
Defining business component parameters, 855–856
Defining default timeout time, 482–483
Defining input parameters, 856, 862
Defining output parameters, 856
Description properties, 248, 252, 328, 344, 613
Descriptive programming Code, 771
Descriptive programming syntax, 453
  advantages of, 474
  description objects, 453
  description strings, 453
  disadvantages of, 474
Descriptive programming, 451, 453, 455, 457, 459
Designing business scenario driver, 259–260
Designing custom library, 282–283
Developer, 89, 328–329, 331
Developing business components, 69, 873
Developing code, 114, 245, 659
Deviations, 5, 20, 35, 42
DevOps, 109–110
Dictionary object, 190–191, 197
Dictionary, 190–192, 195
Difference between action and function, 318
Difference between css and sizzle, 620–621
Difference between LoadFunctionLibrary and ExecuteFile Statement, 282–283
disadvantages of automation testing, 13
  initial cost, 13
  maintenance cost, 13
  no human insight, 13
  no usability testing, 13
Document object methods, 778–779
Document object model, 737, 776
Driver, 20, 795, 804, 806
DSN connection, 700, 713–714, 716
DSN-less connection, 699–700, 715
Dynamic action calls, 307, 312
Dynamic framework, 45, 121, 125, 128, 140
Dynamic system development method, 86
Dynamic variable initialization, 19, 64

E

E-mail client, 747, 749, 751
E-mail matching, 205–206
E-mail trigger, 762, 837
Enter itinerary, 126–127, 149
Enumerating files and folders, 669–670
Enumerating files inside sub folders, 671–672
Enumerating folders, 670
Enumerating mailbox folders, 753
Enumerating sub folders, 670
Environment variables, 268, 803, 819
Error handlers, 18, 525–526
ErrScreenshotsPath, 129–130, 155
Excel as database, 687, 698
Excel data cell, 692
Excel object browser, 698–699
Excel object model, 687, 799
Exchanging structured information, 725, 737
Executing test set, 868–869
Exist method, 191, 481
Exist statement, 483
Extensible markup language, 559, 724
External file support, 17–18
Extreme programming, 85, 88, 105

F

Facilitation analysis, 8
Feasibility analysis phase, 14
Feasibility analysis, 6, 21, 58
Feature driven development, 86, 88, 104
  activities of , 104
File checkpoint, 485, 510
FileSystemObject, 665, 678
Find method, 692, 743
Firefox browser, 329, 618, 768
Flow diagram, 338
Framework design and development phase, 14
Framework design process flow, 64–65
Framework design, 6, 18, 80, 115
Framework setup, 121, 141
Frequent code deployments to test/automation environment, 112
function libraries, 17, 214
Functional experts, 12, 26, 28, 35, 51, 57
Functionality-based hierarchy design, 390, 393

G

Global datatable settings, 408–409
graphical user interface, 4, 16, 211, 451
GUI test flow view, 292
GUI test properties pane, 293
GUI test settings, 294–295
GUI test, 290–291, 294, 296
GUI testing tab, 241, 318, 328
GUI testing, 9, 347, 350, 352, 354, 356, 358, 360, 362, 364
GUI validation, 19, 66

H

Hard-coded data, 4, 38, 302, 485
Hardware configuration, 22, 33
HP quality center, 825–826
HTML code, 328, 330, 767
HTML DOM, 343, 616, 623, 625, 776
  objects, 777
Html id, 16, 41, 252, 648, 771
Human error, 4, 8–9
Hybrid framework, 4, 37, 42, 44–45
Hypertext Transfer Protocol, 378, 559

I

IBM lotus domino server, 756
IBM lotus notes, 747, 756
Identification mechanism, 660
Identification properties, 377
IInputParam, 126
Image checkpoint, 498
Image-based identification, 654
Implicit and explicit properties, 456
Increased test automation scope, 113
Input Parameters, 862
Insight identification mechanism, 584, 654, 662
Insight test object descriptions, 654
Insight test object hierarchy, 655
Integrated GUI and API testing, 220–221
Internal inspections, 48
International federation of information processing societies, 3
Iteration cycles, 91

J

Java, 12, 17, 119, 212, 221, 247, 255
JavaScript, 413, 416, 573, 606, 788
Jenkins, 108

K

Kanban, 88, 93, 102–103
  principles of , 103
key factors of test automation, 5
  budgeted process, 6
  dedicated resources, 6
  process, 6
  realistic expectations, 7
  committed management, 5–6
Keyword-driven framework, 4, 122, 233, 846, 848
Kick-start, 24, 57

L

Launching microsoft outlook, 749–750
Launching uft, 792–793
Library, 279, 793, 796
  creating new, 279
Life cycle of bpt, 847
Limited time for test execution, 113
Local object repository, 220, 224, 291, 296
Login component table, 148
Login to outlook, 749–750

M

Maintenance phase, 14, 20, 31, 75, 128, 390
Maintenance process flow, 75–76
  objectives, 76
Maintenance, 20, 76, 81, 112, 116, 118
Managing files, 665
Mandatory properties, 348–349, 773–774
Manual test cases, 12, 28
Manual test maintenance cost, 17
Manual testers, 4, 33–34
Manual testing problems, 15, 59–60
Master driver script, 71, 76–77, 134, 136, 161
Master driver, 134, 161
MasterDriverTable, 134–135
Meta characters, 200
Methodology, 12, 214, 563
Microsoft corporation, 687, 739
Microsoft excel, 166, 220, 398, 687
Microsoft outlook, 747–748
Microsoft windows operating system, 677
Modifying excel cell properties, 694–695
Modifying uft test settings, 526
MS access database, 698, 723
MS excel sheet, 122, 125
MS Word files, 678
Multiple test execution cycles, 5, 7, 16
Mundane tasks, 9, 11

N

Native properties, 219, 365, 375, 377, 767
Navigate and learn, 363
Need analysis process flow, 59
Need analysis, 15, 59–60
Negative return on investment, 9
New features and enhancements of UFT 11.5, 222–223
New workbook and worksheet, 688
Nonagile application development models, 26
Nonrole-driven framework, 35
Non-windows operating system, 233, 654
Norun, 129, 134
Notepad file, 206,, 208
Notepad, 208, 680
  creating, 683
  open, 683
  properties of, 680

O

Object browser, 419, 421, 747
Object deletion, 471
Object identification dialog box, 254, 582, 649
Object identification mechanism, 240, 252, 257, 594, 637, 772
Object identification, 257, 267, 389, 396
Object identification mechanism, 338, 365, 451, 467, 581
Object model, 667, 675, 748
Object native properties, 767–768
Object properties parameterization, 368
Object repository design, 389–390

Object repository, 220, 327, 358, 390, 393, 613
Object source index, 342, 585
Object spy, 298, 375–376
Object type casting, 470
objective of test automation, 4
ObjectRepositories Collection object, 798–799
ObjectRepositoryUtil API, 788
Odbc creation, 700
Oneiteration, 301, 313, 809
Open data base connectivity, 699, 714
Open method, 573, 689
Opening automated component, 859
Option explicit, 181, 285
  error handing, 181
OR design techniques, 388
Oracle ODBC driver configuration, 714
Ordinal identifiers, 256, 337, 346, 349, 355
OTAclient.dll, 842
Outlook security dialog box, 751–752

P

Page checkpoint, 18, 486, 496
Parameterization, 39, 302, 309, 368, 855
Parameters to automate a test case, 8
  business criticality, 8
  execution time, 8
  repeatability, 8
  reusability, 8
  robust, 8
Parsing dates, 205
Patches, 5
PathFinder, 444
Payment Component Table, 152
Percentage automatability, 50
Performance engineer, 90
Performance engineers, 89
Playback automation tools, 4
Pop-up method, 676, 678
Post-recovery actions, 540
Primary and Secondary Ors, 383
Printing documents, 742
Prioritization analysis, 7
Process, 56–57
Product backlog, 90, 93–94
Product quality, 5, 9
Profitability, 6
Progress, 33, 49, 52
Project budget sheet, 6
Project budget, 6, 18
Project plans, 5
Proof of concept, 14
  objective, 63
Proof of concept, 14, 18, 63
Properties pane, 215, 223, 324
Pseudo-class selectors, 630

Q

QC database, 827–828
QC open test architecture, 828
QC test Suite, 837–838
QTP bin folder, 674, 679
QTP data tables, 123
QTP, 124, 132, 134, 137, 165
Quality centre, 28, 797, 817, 846
Quality control, 6
Quality, 17, 47, 50, 53–54
QuickTest pro, 3, 211, 276, 734, 846, 849, 865
QuickTest recovery scenario, 133–134
QuickTest, 211, 276, 279, 479, 846
QuickTips, 652–653
  components of, 846

R

rail ticket, 141, 144, 151
raileurope.com application, 650
Rajeev Gupta, 28, 178, 394
random numbers, 370, 442
Rational functional tester, 3
Rational Robot, 3
Read an excel workbook, 691
Real-time payment, 28, 30
Record and run settings, 249–250
RecordSet object, 700, 703, 710, 712
Recovery object, 804–805
Recovery scenario design, 528
Recovery scenario fails, 538
Recovery scenario object, 537, 805, 807

Recovery scenario, 527, 540, 806
Regression cycle, 10, 15, 17, 26, 54
Regression run, 55, 57, 72, 108
Regression runs, 24, 76, 78, 111, 525
Regression status tracker, 137, 142
Regression suite, 72, 142, 763, 837
Regular expression, 168, 206, 366, 455, 629
Reporter object, 547
Repositories collection object, 386, 798–799, 800, 822
Representational state transfer, 557
Requirement analysis, 26, 80
Return on investment, 9, 14, 62
Reusable checkpoints, 485
Review itinerary, 147, 150
Review payment, 29–30, 863
Risk analysis, 48, 55, 69
Risk factor, 49
Risk mitigation strategies, 48–49
ROI analysis process flow, 60
ROI analysis, 16, 62, 80
Root, 234, 600, 776
Run results viewer, 222, 226, 511, 541
Run settings object, 809
Runoptions object, 811

S

Schedule and cost tracking, 49, 57
Schedule sorter, 150
Scheduling script execution, 675
Screen component table, 123–124, 139
Screen recorder tab, 550
Screen-based hierarchy design, 390, 392–393
Script debugging, 69, 228, 238, 517, 524
Script design process flow, 69–70
Script design, 14, 19–20, 40
Script development cost, 17, 477
Script development, 26, 45, 52, 64, 66, 68, 70, 81
Script execution cost, 17, 60
Script execution process flow, 71
Script maintenance cost, 17, 477
Script modularization, 17
Scripting and guidelines, 142
Scripting coded bitmap checkpoint, 500
Scripting coded image checkpoint, 499
Scripting coded page checkpoint, 497–498
Scripting coded standard checkpoint, 490
Scripting guidelines, 137, 266
Scripting methods, 122, 261
  descriptive programming (DP) method, 264
  hybrid method, 265–266
  object repository (OR) method, 263
  record & playback method, 261
Scripting output values, 515
Scrum master, 89, 91
Scrum of scrums, 101
Scrum task board, 95, 97
Scrum, 91, 98, 100
Select output parameter, 863
Selectschedules component table, 150
Selenium webdriver, 842
Selenium, 3, 10, 119, 842
Self-explanatory code, 86
Separate data sheets, 4
Sequential flow of keywords, 4
SI mechanism, 646, 650
SilkTest, 3
Simple access object protocol, 557, 559
Simulating keyboard events, 676
Sizzle, 620
Smart identification, 349, 638, 646, 649
  base filter properties, 646
  optional filter properties, 646
Smart Identification, 389, 646, 649
Software developer engineer in test, 90, 116
Software development life cycle, 3, 16, 25
Software systems, 3
Software testing, 3
Solution explorer pane, 214, 315
Solution, 214, 223, 276, 289
  creating, 289
Source index learning mechanism, 346
Source index, 343, 347, 378, 585
Specific keyword, 4
Spring backlog, 92, 95, 99
Sprint demo, 97
Sprint meetings, 92

backlog grooming meeting, 92
daily scrum meeting, 92
sprint demo meeting, 93
sprint planning meeting, 92
sprint review-and-retrospective meeting, 93
Sprint, 91, 98, 100
Spy tool, 328, 333, 342, 774
Stale object, 470–471
Standard checkpoint, 486–487
Standard frameworks, 17, 36
Standardized process, 6
Static action calls, 307, 314
Step tables, 4, 41–42
Swot analysis, 9
Sync method, 451, 478
Synchronization methods, 478, 481
Synchronization, 478, 482–483

T

Table checkpoint, 486, 494
TALC, 49, 59, 81
Telnet client, 759
Test automation approach, 11, 22, 25, 27, 29, 31
Test automation basis, 22, 28
Test automation development model, 23
Test automation development, 33, 142
Test automation documents, 65, 79–80, 141
Test automation framework, 19, 36
components of, 36–37
types of, 37
agile automation framework, 45–46
business model driven framework, 45
data-driven framework, 38–39
hybrid framework, 42
keyword-driven framework, 39–40
modular-driven framework, 37–38
Test automation life cycle, 6, 14, 17, 19, 21, 47, 58
Test automation metrics, 6, 47, 49, 142, 775
technical/functional interchanges, 47
Test automation process, 25, 58
Test automation progress, 52–53
Test automation project backup, 77, 684, 686
Test automation project infrastructure, 22, 33–34
Test automation resources, 24
Test automation scope, 22, 111, 113
Test automation team, 6, 24, 34, 47, 52, 57, 75, 111, 121, 528
Test automation, 3, 28, 522, 544, 548, 550, 552, 554, 669
guidelines, 11
myths and realities, 11–12
opportunities, 10
strength, 10
ensure product quality, 10
fast, 10
increases test coverage, 10
programmable, 10
reduces testing cost and effort, 10
reliable, 10
threats, 10
weakness, 10
Test automation—team dynamics, 22, 34
Test automation—testing types to be covered, 22, 31
Test driven development, 86, 88, 105
steps for, 106–107
Test environment support, 18
Test execution coverage, 51
Test execution, 3, 5, 7, 12, 16, 18, 20
Test input data, 4, 36, 38, 42
Test object, 130, 213, 219, 815–816
Test objects, 224, 242, 252, 361
Test plans, 5, 22, 28, 69
Test result analysis phase, 14
Test result analysis, 14, 17, 20, 58, 60, 74–75, 153, 155, 544
Test result filters, 545
Test results analysis process flow, 72
test result analysis, 74
test results, 73
Test results analysis, 20, 72, 74
Test results, 18, 33, 61, 72
Test script calls, 17
Test script development process, 28, 267
Test script development, 6, 69, 121, 258–259
Test script, 260–261, 263, 267, 388

Test scripts, 5, 265
Test set, 827, 867
Test sub-scenario, 125–126
Test-driven development, 105–106
Testing life span, 15–16
Testing web services using uft, 565–566
Testlibaries collection object, 801
TestSubScnro, 125–126, 149
Text area checkpoint, 486, 504
Text checkpoint, 18, 486, 502, 515–516
Timed pop-up window, 676–677
TOCollection object, 788, 790
Tool analysis, 14, 17
Tool stability, 17, 81
Toolbars and menus, 213
 menu bar, 213
 title bar, 213
 uft Toolbar, 213
Toolbox pane, 213–214, 323
Total automation cost, 17, 61
Total manual cost, 17, 61
Trip details, 144, 146, 150
TstScenrioFillResvForm, 692–693

U

UFT AOM, 792, 822
UFT api testing, 212, 561
UFT automation testing workflow, 227–228
UFT configuration, 228, 237, 240, 243, 245, 247, 249, 251, 253
UFT installation, 222, 233, 235, 237, 239, 792
 access permissions, 233
UFT main window overview, 212–213
 features, 218
 panes, 213–214
 bookmarks pane, 218
 data pane, 215
 debug pane, 216
 document pane, 214
 errors pane, 216
 output pane, 216
 properties pane, 215
 search results pane, 217
 solution explorer pane, 214
 tasks Pane, 217
 toolbox Pane, 214
UFT object model, 795
UFT object, 788
UFT provides regular expression evaluator, 207
UFT provides, 339, 546–547
UFT run result viewerpanes, 542
 captured data pane, 544
 data pane, 544
 log ttracking pane, 544
 result details pane, 542
 result details pane, 543
 run results tree pane, 542
 screen recorder pane, 542
 screen recorder pane, 543
 system monitor pane, 542
 system monitor pane, 543
UFT test automation process, 227
UI state CSS selector, 635
Unattended execution, 10, 18, 526
unRegister user function, 446
Use-case diagrams, 18, 22, 28
User interface, 4, 16, 211, 223, 225, 258, 336, 748

V

VBScript conditional statements, 169–170
VBScript error handler, 525–526, 539
VBScript looping statements, 170
VBScript operators, 168–169
VBScript regular expression, 201–202
VBScript, 165, 202, 204, 206, 208, 211, 214, 219, 227, 793
 data types, 166
 editors, 165
 functions, 172–173
 Scope and Lifetime, 168
 variables, 166–167
Velocity chart, 100
Verification code, 30
Verify credit card payment, 30
Version control tools, 77–78
Virtual relation identification, 336
Visual basic for applications, 687, 690

Visual C++, 788, 793
Visual relation identifier, 336, 636, 638

W

Wait method, 480, 482
WaitProperty method, 439, 480, 482
WaitProperty statement, 483
Waterfall development model, 23–24
W-development model, 25–26
Web event recording configuration, 250
Wildcards, 597–598
Windows api, 677
Windows environment variables, 285, 674
Windows management instrumentation, 675
Windows management interface, 672
Windows script host, 665, 675, 678
Windows scripting, 665, 675, 679
Windows task manager, 672–673
W-model, 23, 25
Word automation object model, 739–740
Work flow of scrum framework, 94
Workbook.SaveAs method, 689
Working with browser, 410–411
Working with database, 507, 710
World Wide Web Consortium, 508, 776, 786
World Wide Web consortium, 486, 776
Wrapper for OTAClient.dll, 842–843
Writing action code, 296–297

X

XML checkpoint, 486, 509–510
XML DOM, 725–726
XML environment file, 132, 271, 275, 277
XML schema, 558
XML structure, 724
XML, 724
XMLDOM, 573, 728, 733,
  qtp xml objects, 727
XMLHTTP request, 573
XMLUtil, 734, 736, 573
XPath Axis, 599, 609
XPath expression, 599, 610, 612
XPath functions, 599
XPath query language features, 597
XPath, 333, 590, 600, 729